UNIVERSITY CASEBOOK SERIES®

CRIMINAL PROCEDURE

RIGHTS AND REMEDIES IN POLICE INVESTIGATIONS

DONALD A. DRIPPS

Warren Distinguished Professor
University of San Diego School of Law

FOUNDATION
PRESS

University Casebook Series is a trademark registered in the U.S. Patent and Trademark Office.

© 2020 LEG, Inc. d/b/a West Academic
    444 Cedar Street, Suite 700
    St. Paul, MN 55101
    1-877-888-1330

Printed in the United States of America

ISBN: 978-1-68467-553-1

SUMMARY OF CONTENTS

TABLE OF CONTENTS

TABLE OF CASES

The principal cases are in bold type.

CRIMINAL PROCEDURE

RIGHTS AND REMEDIES IN POLICE INVESTIGATIONS

INTRODUCTION

The Fourth Amendment provides:

The right of the people to be secure in their persons, houses, papers, and effects, against unreasonable searches and seizures, shall not be violated, and no Warrants shall issue, but upon probable cause, supported by Oath or affirmation, and particularly describing the place to be searched, and the persons or things to be seized.

This single sentence raises four issues that have divided judges and scholars (law students included!) for generations.

The first issue is *scope*. Just what practices does the phrase "searches and seizures" include? When there is no "search" or "seizure," the Amendment does not apply. Whatever limits the Constitution imposes must come from other provisions, such as the Fourteenth Amendment's due process and equal protection clauses.

The second issue is *content*. Just what makes a "search" or "seizure" "unreasonable"? Related to this second issue is a third. What is the relationship between the Fourth Amendment's two clauses, the first declaring a general right against all "unreasonable searches and seizures" and the second a specific prohibition on general warrants? What is the relationship between *warrants and reasonableness*?

The fourth issue arises not from what the Amendment says, but from what it does not say. What government officers commit an unreasonable search or seizure, what legal consequences follow? What is the *remedy or sanction* for violations?

Chapters 2, 3, 4 and 5 address how the law today answers (and sometimes fails to answer) these questions. Those following an originalist approach to constitutional interpretation, including many justices of the Supreme Court, look to history for answers. All concerned, however, do well to know where the Fourth Amendment came from, and how it got to where it is today. Understanding that story is the surest way to understand the modern doctrine built upon it. In the struggle to keep up with the latest developments, we can lose sight of constitutional commitments that don't change, over decades and even centuries. Those who know the headnotes for the latest Supreme Court search-and-seizure decision, and nothing more, will be in no position to argue—or even to understand—the next one. Those who know the Amendment's history will have principles to reason from as long as the Republic stands.

The founders had clear, and hostile, memories of two infamous abuses, general warrants and writs of assistance. State constitutions typically included provisions condemning general warrants, sometimes but not always linked to a general repudiation of "unreasonable searches and seizures." Anti-federalists feared that the new federal government would try to raise revenue, and/or to suppress dissent, by similar means.

Under Article I, Section 8, Congress had power to raise revenue by "imposts" and "excises." Article I, Section 8's grant of power to make all laws "necessary and proper for carrying into execution the foregoing powers" logically included the power to provide for the enforcement of import duties and sales taxes against inevitable smuggling. Absent a Bill of Rights, there was nothing in the Constitution to prevent the new government from resorting to writs or assistance or general warrants. In the Bill of Rights, Congress proposed, and the people ratified, a two-clause provision, like the one John Adams had written for Massachusetts, rather than a one-clause ban on general warrants, like the one George Mason had written for Virginia.

The modern law begins in 1961 with the Supreme Court's decision in *Mapp v. Ohio,* holding that the Fourteenth Amendment's due process clause imposes on the states not just the prohibition of unreasonable searches and seizures, but the obligation to exclude evidence so obtained from proof at trial. Section 1 deals with the abuses that inspired the Fourth Amendment and how the founders responded. Section 2 briefly summarizes one of the central problems for any historical approach to the Fourth Amendment. Today we think of the Fourth Amendment primarily as a regulation of arrests, searches and street detentions by the police. But "the police" did not exist in 1791 and were still a fledgling institution when the Fourteenth Amendment was adopted after the Civil War. Analogies may be attempted, but if we ask quite specifically "how did the founders expect the Fourth Amendment to apply to the police?" we are asking a question with no answer.

Section 3 takes up how the Supreme Court interpreted the Fourth Amendment in federal cases before *Mapp.* The famous *Olmstead* case not only reviews how the federal law developed after *Boyd* and *Weeks,* but introduces the problem of how to apply the Fourth Amendment to police practices that exploit new technology—technology undreamed of in 1791. Section 4 considers search-and-seizure in the states, prior to *Mapp,* and concludes with *Mapp* itself.

After *Mapp* the same constitutional doctrine applied in both federal and state cases. Rules made by the Supreme Court for agents of the Treasury or the Justice department became applicable to big city police departments and rural sheriff's offices. The Supreme Court soon heard cases coming out of the much larger, and more heterogenous, state systems. The Court responded by recognizing categories of police behavior—arrests, street detention, traffic stops, and "searches" defined by reference to reasonable expectations of privacy. For each category, the cases fleshed out rules and standards to determine when the police action is "unreasonable." Those categories and the rules attached to them constitute the modern law. But they are stories to be told in subsequent chapters; first things first.

CHAPTER 1

THE FOURTH AMENDMENT: ORIGINS AND THE FOUNDATIONS OF MODERN DOCTRINE

1. ORIGINS OF THE FOURTH AMENDMENT

The Writs of Assistance Case (Paxton's Case)
Superior Court of Judicature, Massachusetts Bay Colony, 1761–1762*

Writ of Assistance, December 2, 1762

In 1755 a writ of assistance, granting authority to search for and seize uncustomed goods, was issued by the Superior Court of Massachusetts to Charles Paxton, surveyor of the port of Boston. Similar writs were issued in 1758 to the collectors at Salem and Falmouth, in 1759 to the surveyor-general, and the collectors at Boston and Newburyport, and in 1760 to the collectors at Boston and Salem. By law the writs continued until the demise of the Crown and for six months thereafter. In 1761 the former writs, by reason of the death of George II., being about to expire, the surveyor-general, Thomas Lechmere, made application to the court for the grant of such writs to himself and his officers "as usual." On this application a number of merchants of Boston, and others, petitioned to be heard. The application was argued at Boston at the February term, Jeremiah Gridley appearing for Lechmere, and James Otis and Oxenbridge Thacher for the petitioners and against the writ. Judgment was suspended in order that the court might examine the practice in England. November 18, at the second term, the case was again argued by the same counsel, with the addition of Robert Auchmuty in favor of the writ. The judges were unanimous in their opinion that the writ should be granted, as prayed for, and December 2 a writ was issued to Paxton in the form following. March 6, 1762, a bill "authorizing any judge or justice of the peace, upon information on oath by any officer of the customs, to issue a special writ or warrant of assistance, and prohibiting all others," passed the General Court; but the governor, on the advice of the members of the Superior Court, withheld his approval. Writs of assistance do not appear to have been granted elsewhere in the

---

* Source: William MacDonald, Documentary Sourcebook of American History 1606–1898, 105–109 (1908).

colonies, except in New Hampshire; they were, however, legalized by the Townshend Revenue Act of 1767. . . .

In the manuscript from which the writ following is printed, the words in brackets are interlined, and those in italics erased. The writ was drawn by Thomas Hutchinson, the chief justice. . . .

George the third by the grace of God of Great Britain France & Ireland King

Defender of the faith &c.

To All & singular our Justices of the peace Sheriffs Constables and to all other our

Officers and Subjects within our said Province and to each of you Greeting. . . .

And Whereas in & by an Act of Parliament made in the seventh & eighth year of [the reign of the late] King William the third there is granted to the Officers for collecting and managing our revenue and inspecting the plantation trade in any of our plantations [the same powers & authority for visiting & searching of Ships & also] to enter houses or warehouses to search for and seize any prohibited or uncustomed goods as are provided for the Officers of our Customs in England by the said last mentioned Act made in the fourteenth year of [the reign of] King Charles the Second, and the like assistance is required to be given to the said Officers in the execution of their office as by the said last mentioned Act is provided for the Officers in England.

And Whereas in and by an Act of our said Province of Massachusetts bay made in the eleventh year of [the reign of] the late King William the third it is enacted & declared that our Superior Court of Judicature Court of Assize and General Goal delivery for our said Province shall have cognizance of all matters and things within our said Province as fully & amply to all intents & purposes as our Courts of King's Bench Common Pleas & Exchequer within our Kingdom of England have or ought to have.

And Whereas our Commissioners for managing and causing to be levied & collected our customs subsidies and other duties have [by Commission or Deputation under their hands & seal dated at London the 22nd day of May in the first year of our Reign] deputed and impowered Charles Paxton Esquire to be Surveyor & Searcher of all the rates and duties arising and growing due to us at Boston in our Province aforesaid and [in & by said Commission or Deputation] have given him power to enter into [any Ship Bottom Boat or other Vessel & also into] any Shop House Warehouse Hosiery or other place whatsoever to make diligent search into any trunk chest pack case truss or any other parcell or package whatsoever for any goods wares or merchandize prohibited to be imported or exported or whereof the Customs or other Duties have not been duly paid and the same to seize to our use In all things proceeding as the Law directs.

Therefore we strictly Injoin & Command you & every one of you that, all excuses apart, you & every one of you permit the said Charles Paxton according to the true intent & form of the said commission or deputation and the laws & statutes in that behalf made & provided, [as well by night as by day from time to time to enter & go on board any Ship Boat or other Vessel riding lying or being within or coming to the said port of Boston or any Places or Creeks thereunto appertaining such Ship Boat or Vessel then & there found to search & oversee and the persons therein being strictly to examine touching the premises aforesaid & also *according to the form effect and true intent of the said commission or deputation*] in the day time to enter & go into the vaults cellars warehouses shops & other places where any prohibited goods wares or merchandizes or any goods wares or merchandizes for which the customs or other duties shall not have been duly & truly satisfied and paid lye concealed or are suspected to be concealed, according to the true intent of the law to inspect & oversee & search for the said goods wares & merchandize, And further to do and execute all things which of right and according to the laws & statutes in this behalf shall be to be done. And we further strictly Injoin & Command, you and every one of you that to the said Charles Paxton Esqr you & every one of you from time to time be aiding assisting & helping in the execution of the premises as is meet. And this you or any of [you] in no wise omit at your perils. Witness Thomas Hutchinson Esq at Boston the ___ day of December in the Second year of our Reign Annoque Dom 1761.

Argument by James Otis Against the Writs, as Recalled by John Adams
II The Works of John Adams 519–520 (1865)

May it please your honors,

"I was desired by one of the Court to look into the books, and consider the question now before them concerning writs of assistance. I have accordingly considered it, and now appear, not only in obedience to your order, but likewise in behalf of the inhabitants of this town, who have presented another petition, and out of regard to the liberties of the subject. And I take this opportunity to declare, that whether under a fee or not (for in such a cause as this I despise a fee) I will to my dying day oppose with all the powers and faculties God has given me, all such instruments of slavery on the one hand, and villainy on the other, as this writ of assistance is.

It appears to me the worst instrument of arbitrary power, the most destructive of English liberty and the fundamental principles of law, that ever was found in an English law-book. I must, therefore, beg your Honors' patience and attention to the whole range of an argument, that may perhaps appear uncommon in many things, as well as to points of learning that are more remote and unusual; that the whole tendency of my design may the more easily be perceived, the conclusions better discerned, and the force of them be better felt. I shall not think much of my pains in this cause, as I engaged in it from principle. I was solicited to argue this cause as Advocate-General; and because I would not, I have been charged with desertion from my office. To this charge I can give a very sufficient answer. I renounced that office, and I argue this cause, from the same principle; and I argue it with the greater pleasure, as it is in favor of British liberty, at a time when we hear the greatest monarch upon earth declaring from his throne that he glories in the name of Briton, and that the privileges of his people are dearer to him than the most valuable prerogatives of his crown; and as it is in opposition to a kind of power, the exercise of which, in former periods of English history, cost one King of England his head, and another his throne. I have taken more pains in this cause, than I ever will take again, although my engaging in this and another popular cause has raised much resentment. But I think I can sincerely declare, that I cheerfully submit myself to every odious name for conscience' sake; and from my soul I despise all those, whose guilt, malice, or folly has made them my foes. Let the consequences be what they will, I am determined to proceed. The only principles of public conduct, that are worthy of a gentleman or a man, are to sacrifice estate, ease, health, and applause, and even life, to the sacred calls of his country. These manly sentiments, in private life, make the good citizen; in public life, the patriot and the hero. I do not say, that when brought to the test, I shall be invincible. I pray God I may never be brought to the melancholy trial; but if ever I should, it will be then known how far I can reduce to practice principles, which I know to be founded in truth. In the mean time I will proceed to the subject of this writ.

"In the first place, may it please your Honors, I will admit that writs of one kind may be legal; that is, special writs, directed to special officers, and to search certain houses, &c. specially set forth in the writ, may be granted by the Court of Exchequer at home, upon oath made before the Lord Treasurer by the person who asks it, that he suspects such goods to be concealed in those very places he desires to search. The act of 14 Charles II. which Mr. Gridley mentions, proves this. And in this light the writ appears like a warrant from a Justice of the Peace to search for stolen goods. Your Honors will find in the old books concerning the office of a Justice of the Peace, precedents of general warrants to search suspected houses. But in more modern books you will find only special warrants to search such and such houses specially named, in which the complainant has before sworn that he suspects his goods are concealed; and you will find it adjudged that special warrants only are legal. In the same manner I rely on it, that the writ prayed for in this petition, being general, is illegal. It is a power, that places the liberty of every man in the hands of every petty officer. I say I admit that special writs of assistance, to search special places, may be granted to certain persons on oath; but I deny that the writ now prayed for can be granted, for I beg leave to make some observations on the writ itself, before I proceed to other acts of Parliament. In the first place, the writ is universal, being directed 'to all and singular Justices, Sheriffs, Constables, and all other officers and subjects;' so, that, in short, it is directed to every subject in the King's dominions. Every one with this writ may be a tyrant; if this commission be legal, a tyrant in a legal manner also may control, imprison, or murder any one within the realm. In the next place, it is perpetual; there is no return. A man is accountable to no person for his doings. Every man may reign secure in his petty tyranny, and spread terror and desolation around him. In the third place, a person with this writ, in the daytime, may enter all houses, shops, &c. at will, and command all to assist him. Fourthly, by this writ not only deputies, &c., but even their menial servants, are allowed to lord it over us. Now one of the most essential branches of English liberty is the freedom of one's house. A man's house is his castle; and whilst he is quiet, he is as well guarded as a prince in his castle. This writ, if it should be declared legal, would totally annihilate this privilege. Custom-house officers may enter our houses, when they please; we are commanded to permit their entry. Their menial servants may enter, may break locks, bars, and every thing in their way; and whether they break through malice or revenge, no man, no court, can inquire. Bare suspicion without oath is sufficient. This wanton exercise of this power is not a chimerical suggestion of a heated brain. I will mention some facts. Mr. Pew had one of these writs, and when Mr. Ware succeeded him, he endorsed this writ over to Mr. Ware; so that these writs are negotiable from one officer to another; and so your Honors have no opportunity of judging the persons to whom this vast power is delegated. Another instance is this: Mr. Justice Walley had called this same Mr. Ware before him, by a constable, to answer for a breach of Sabbath-day acts, or that of profane swearing. As soon as he had finished, Mr. Ware asked him if he had done. He replied, Yes. Well then, said Mr. Ware, I will show you a little of my power. I command you to permit me to search your house for uncustomed goods. And went on to search his house from the garret to the cellar; and then served the constable in the same manner. But to show another absurdity in this writ; if it should be established, I insist upon it, every person by the 14 Charles II. has this power as well as custom-house officers. The words are, 'It shall be lawful for any person or persons authorized,' &c. What a scene does this open! Every man, prompted by revenge, ill humor, or wantonness, to inspect the inside of his neighbor's house, may get a writ of assistance. Others will ask it from self-defence; one arbitrary exertion will provoke another, until society be involved in tumult and in blood.

"Again, these writs are not returned. Writs in their nature are temporary things. When the purposes for which they are issued are answered, they exist no more; but these live forever; no one can be called to account. Thus reason and the constitution are both against this writ. Let us see what authority there is for it. Not more than one instance can be found of it in all our law-books; and that was in the zenith of arbitrary power, namely, in the reign of Charles II., when star-chamber powers were pushed to extremity by some ignorant clerk of the exchequer. But had this writ been in any book whatever, it would have been illegal. All precedents are under the control of the principles of law. Lord Talbot says it is better to observe these than any precedents, though in the House of Lords, the last resort of the subject. No Acts of Parliament can establish such a writ; though it should be made in the very words of the petition, it would be void. An act against the constitution is void. (*vid.* Viner.) But these prove no more than what I before observed, that special writs may be granted *on oath and probable suspicion*. The act of 7 & 8 William III. that the officers of the plantations shall have the same powers, &c. is confined to this sense; that an officer should show probable ground; should take his oath of it; should do this before a magistrate; and that such magistrate, if he think proper, should issue a special warrant to a constable to search the places. That of 6 Anne can prove no more."

M.H. Smith, The Writs of Assistance Case
391–392 (1978)

The justices of the court withheld their opinion after the initial argument. The Chief Justice of the Massachusetts court, Thomas Hutchinson, wrote to the colony's agent in England, William Bollan, about the English practice with the writs. Bollan replied as follows:

> The writ is directed to the officers of the admiralty, justices of peace, mayors, sheriffs, constables, and all other his majesty's officers, ministers and subjects in England, requiring them to permit the commissioners of the customs and their officers by night or day to enter on board any vessel, to each etc., and in the day time to enter the vaults, cellars, warehouses, hops and other places, where any goods etc. lye concealed, or are suspect to lie concealed, for which the customs are not paid, to inspect and search for the said goods etc. and to do all things which according to the laws should be done, and commanding them to be aiding and assisting to the said commissioners and their officers in the execution of the premises.

[Editor's Note: Based on the English practice the Massachusetts court refused to declare the writs illegal. Writs of assistance were apparently not issued in any of the colonies except Massachusetts, and none appears to have been issued there after 1766, even though the Townshend Acts in 1767 authorized their use.]

Entick v. Carrington
19 Howell's State Trials 1029 (1765) (Ct. Cm. Pleas UK)

This cause was tried at Westminster Hall before the lord chief justice, [Lord Camden] when the jury found a Special Verdict to the following purport.

"The jurors upon their oath say, as to the issue first joined (to the plea not guilty to the whole trespass in the declaration) that as to the coming with force and arms, and also the first trespass in declaration, except the breaking and entering the dwelling-house of the plaintiff, and continuing therein for the space of four hours, and all that time disturbing him in his possession thereof, and searching several rooms, and in one bureau one writing desk, and several drawers of the plaintiff in his house, and reading over and examining several of his papers there, and seizing, taking and carrying away some of his books and papers there found, in the declaration complained of, the said defendants are not guilty. As to the breaking and entering the dwelling-house (alone excepted) the jurors on their oath say, that at the time of making the following information, and before and until and at the time of granting the warrant hereafter mentioned, and from hence hitherto, the earl of Halifax was, and still is one of the lords of the king's privy council, and one of his principled secretaries of state, and that before the time in the declaration, viz. on the 11th of October 1762, at St. Jones's Westminster, one Jonathan Scott of London, bookseller, and publisher, came before Edward Weston, esq. an assistant to the said earl, and a justice of peace for the city and liberty of Westminster, and there made and gave information in writing to and before said Edward Weston against the said John Entick and others, the tenor of which information now produced and given in evidence to the jurors followeth in these words and figures, to wit:

> The voluntary information of J. Scott. "In the year 1755, I proposed setting up a paper, and mentioned it to Dr. Shebbeare, and in a few days one Arthur Beardmore an attorney at law sent for me, hearing of my intention, and desired I would mention it to Dr. Shebbeare, that he Beardmore and some others of his friends had an intention of setting up a paper in this city. Shebbeare met Beardmore, and myself and Entick (the plaintiff) at the Horn Tavern and agreed upon the setting up the paper by the name of the Monitor, and that Dr. Shebbeare and Mr. Entick should have 200*l* a year each. Dr. Shebbeare put into Beardmore's and Entick's hands some papers, but before the papers appeared Beardmore sent them back to me (Scott). Shebbeare insisted on having the proportion of his salary paid to him; he had 50*l*. Which I (Scott) fetched from Vere and Asgill's by their note, which Beardmore gave him; Dr. Shebbeare upon this was quite left out, and the monies have been continued to Beardmore and Entick ever since, by subscription, as I supposed, I know not by whom: it has been continued in these hands ever since. Shebbeare, Beardmore and Entick all told me that the alderman Beckford countenanced the paper: they agreed with me that the profits of the paper, paying all charges belonging to it, should be allowed me. In the paper of the 22d May, called Sejanus, I apprehend the character of Sejanus

meant lord Bute: the original manuscript was in the handwriting of David Meredith, Mr. Beardmore's clerk. I before received the manuscript for several years till very lately from the said hands, and do believe that they continue still to write it. Jona Scott, St. James's 11th October 1762."

The above information was given voluntarily before me, and signed in my presence by Jonathon Scott. Signed/ J. Weston

The jurors further say, that on the 6th of November 1762, the said information was shown to the earl of H and thereupon the earl did then make and issue his warrant directed to the defendants, then and still being the king's messengers, and duly sworn to that office, for apprehending the plaintiff, etc. the tenor of which warrant produced in evidence to the jurors, follows in these words and figures:

George Montagu Dunk, earl of Halifax, viscount Sunbury, and baron Halifax one of the lords of his majesty's honourable privy council, lieutenant general of his majesty's forces, lord lieutenant general and general governor of the kingdom of Ireland, and principal secretary of state, etc. these are in his majesty's name to authorize and require you, taking a constable to your assistance, to make strict and diligent search for John Entick, the author, or one concerned in writing of several weekly very seditious papers, entitled the Monitor, or British Freeholder, No 357, 358, 360, 373, 376, 378, 379, and 380, London, printed for J. Wilson and J. Fell in Pater Noster Row, which contains gross and scandalous reflections and invectives upon his majesty's government, and upon both houses of parliament; and him, having found you are to seize and apprehend, and to bring, together with his books and papers, in safe custody before me to be examined concerning the premisses, and further dealt with according to law; in the due execution whereof all mayors, sheriffs, justices of the peace, constables, and other majesty's officers and military, and all loving subjects whom it may concern, are to be aiding and assisting to you as there shall be occasion; and for so doing this shall be your warrant. Given at St. James's the 6th day of November 1762, in the third year of his majesty's reign, Dunk Halifax. To Nathan Carrington, James Watson, Thomas Ardran, and Robert Blackmore, four of the majesty's 'messengers in ordinary.'

And the jurors further say, the earl caused this warrant to be delivered to the defendants to be executed. And that the defendants afterwards on the 11th of November 1762, at 11 o'clock in the day time, by virtue and for execution of the warrant, but without any constable taken by them to their assistance, entered the house of the plaintiff, the outer door thereof being open, and the plaintiff being therein, to search for and seize the plaintiff and his books and papers, in order to bring him and them before the earl, according to the warrant; and the defendants did then find the plaintiff there, and did seize and apprehend him, and did there search for his books and papers in several rooms and in the house, and in one bureau, one writing desk, and several drawers of the plaintiff there in order to find and seize the same, and bring them along within the plaintiff before the earl according to the warrant, and did then find and seize there some of the books and papers of the plaintiff, and perused and read over several other of his papers which they found in the house, and chose to read and that they necessarily continued there in the execution of the warrant four hours, and disturbed the plaintiff in his house, and then took him and his books and papers from thence, and forthwith gave notice at the office of the said secretary of state in Westminster unto Lovel Stanhope, esq. then before, and still being an assistant to the earl in the examination of persons, books, and papers seized by virtue of warrants issued by secretaries of state, and also then and still being a justice of peace for the city and liberty of Westminster and county of Middlesex, of their having seized the plaintiff, his books and papers, and of their having them ready to be examined, and they then and there at the instance of Lovel Stanhope delivered the said books and papers to him. And the jurors further say, on the 13th of April in the first year of the king, his majesty, by his letters patent under the great seal, gave and granted to the said Lovel Stanhope the office of law-clerk to the secretaries of state. And the king did thereby ordain, constitute, and appoint the law-clerk to attend the offices of his secretaries of state, in order to take the depositions of all such person whom it may be necessary to examine upon affairs which might concern the public, etc. (and then the verdict sets out the letters patent to the law-clerk in *hæc verba*) as by the letters patent produced in evidence to the jurors appears. And the jurors further say, that Lovel Stanhope, by virtue of the said letters patent long before the time when, etc. on the 13th of April in the first year of the king was, and ever since hath been and still is law-clerk to the king's secretaries of state, and hath executed that office all the time. And the jurors further say, that at different times from the time of the Revolution to this present time, the like warrants with that issued against the plaintiff, have been frequently granted by the secretaries of state, and executed by the messengers in ordinary for the time being, and that each of the defendants did respectively take at the time of being appointed messengers, the usual oath, that he would be a true servant to the king, etc. in the place of a messenger in ordinary, etc. And the jurors further say that no demand was ever made or left at the usual place of abode of the defendants, or any of them, by the plaintiff, or his attorney or agent in writing of the perusal and copy of the said warrant, so issued against the plaintiff as aforesaid, neither did the plaintiff commence or bring his action against the defendants, or any of them, within six calendar months next after the several acts aforesaid, and each of them were and was done and committed by them as aforesaid; but whether, upon the whole matter by the jurors found, the defendants are guilty of the trespass here in before particularly specified in breaking and entering the house of the plaintiff in declaration mentioned, and continuing for four hours, and all that time disturbing the plaintiff in the possession thereof, and searching several rooms therein, and one bureau, one writing desk, and several drawers of the plaintiff in his house, and reading over and examining several of his papers there, and seizing and taking and carrying away some of his books and papers there found; or the said plaintiff ought to maintain his said action against them; the jurors are altogether ignorant, and pray the advice of the Court thereupon. And, if upon the whole matter aforesaid by the jurors found, it shall seem to the Court that the defendants are guilty of the said trespass, and that the plaintiff ought to maintain his action against them, the jurors say upon their oath, that the defendants are guilty of the trespass in manner and form as the plaintiff hath therefore complained against them; They assess the damages of the plaintiff of occasion thereof, besides his costs and charges by him about his suit in this behalf laid out to 300*l.* and for those costs and charges, to 40 shillings. But if upon the whole matter by the jurors found, it shall seem to the Court that the defendants are not guilty of the trespass; or that the plaintiff ought not to maintain his action against them; then the jurors do say upon their oath that the defendants are not guilty of the trespass in manner and form as the plaintiff hath therefore complained against them.

"And as to the last issue on the second special justification, the jury found for the plaintiff, that the defendants in their own wrong broke and entered and did the trespass, as the plaintiff in his declaration has alleged."

Lord Chief Judge Camden's Judgment

This record hath set up two defenses to the action, on both of which the defendants have relied.

The first arises from the facts disclosed in the special verdict; whereby the defendants put their case upon the statute of 24 Geo. 2, insisting that they have nothing to do with the legality of the warrants, but that they ought to have been acquitted as officers within the meaning of that act. [The court rejects this statutory-immunity defense in an omitted portion of the judgment.]

The second defense stands upon the legality of the warrants; for this being a justification at common law, the officer is answerable if the magistrate had no jurisdiction. . . .

The question that arises upon the special verdict being now dispatched, I come in my past place to the point, which is made by the justification; for the defendants, having failed in the attempt made to protect themselves by the statute of the 24th of Geo. 2, are under a necessity to maintain the legality of the warrants, under which they have acted, and to shew that the secretary of state in the instance now before us, had a jurisdiction to seize the defendants' papers. If he had no such jurisdiction, the law is clear, that the officers are as much responsible for the trespass as their superior.

This, though it is not the most difficult, is the most interesting question in the cause; because if this point should be determined in favor of the jurisdiction, the secret cabinets and bureaus of every subject in this kingdom will be thrown open to the search and inspection of a messenger, whenever the secretary of state shall think fit to charge, or even to suspect, a person to be the author, printer, or publisher of a seditious libel.

The messenger, under this warrant, is commanded to seize the person described, and to bring him with his papers to be examined before the secretary of state. In consequence of this, the house must be searched; the lock and doors of every room, box, or trunk must be broken open; all the papers and books without exception, if the warrant be executed according to its tenor, must be seized and carried away; for it is observable, that nothing is left either to the discretion or to the humanity of the officer.

This power, so assumed by the secretary of state, is an execution upon all the party's papers, in the first instance. His house is rifled; his most valuable secrets are taken out of his possession, before the paper for which he is charged is found to be criminal by any competent jurisdiction, and before he is convicted either of writing, publishing, or being concerned in the paper.

This power, so claimed by the secretary of state, is not supported by one single citation from any law book extant. It is claimed by no other magistrate in this kingdom but himself: the great executive hand of criminal justice, the lord chief justice of the court of King's-Bench, chief justice Scroggs* excepted, never having assumed this authority.

The arguments, which the defendants' counsel have thought fit to urge in support of this practice, are of this kind.

That such warrants have issued frequently since the Revolution, which practice has been found by the special verdict; though I must observe, that the defendants have no right to avail themselves of that finding, because no such practice is averred in their justifications.

That the case of the warrants bears a resemblance to the case of search for stolen goods.

They say, too, that they have been executed without resistance upon many printers, booksellers, and authors, who have quietly submitted to the authority; that no action hath hitherto been brought to try the right;

---

* [Editor's Note: Lord Camden refers to the infamous Sir William Scroggs, 1623–1683, who earned his reputation as a political stooge and a rabid anti-Catholic, who ridiculed and vilified prisoners on trial, and took sadistic relish in pronouncing sentence.]

and that although they have been often read upon the returns of Habeas Corpus, yet no court of justice has ever declared them illegal.

And it is further insisted, that this power is essential to government, and the only means of quieting clamors and sedition.

These arguments, if they can be called arguments, shall be all taken notice of; because upon this question I am desirous of removing every color of plausibility.

Before I state the question, it will be necessary to describe the power claimed by this warrant in its full extent.

If honestly exerted, it is a power to seize that man's papers, who is charged upon oath to be the author or publisher of a seditious libel; if oppressively, it acts against every man, who is so described in the warrant, though he be innocent.

It is executed against the party, before he is heard or even summoned; and the information, as well as the informers, is unknown.

It is executed by messengers with or without a constable (for it can never be pretended, that such is necessary in point of law) in the presence or the absence of the party, as the messenger shall think fit, and without a witness to testify what passes at the time of the transaction; so that when the papers are gone, as the only witnesses are the trespassers, the party injured is left without proof.

If this injury falls upon an innocent person, he is as destitute of remedy as the guilty: and the whole transaction is so guarded against discovery, that if the officer should be disposed to carry off a bank bill he may do it with impunity, since there is no man capable of proving either the taker or the thing taken.

It must not be here forgot that no subject whatsoever is privileged from this search; because both Houses of Parliament have resolved, that there is no privilege in the case of a seditious libel.

Nor is there pretense to say, that the word "papers" here mentioned ought in point of law to be restrained to the libellous papers only. The word is general, and there is nothing in the warrant to confine it; nay, I am able to affirm, that it has been upon a late occasion executed in its utmost latitude; for in the case of Wilkes against Wood, when the messengers hesitated about taking all the manuscripts, and sent to the secretary of state for more express orders for that purpose, the answer was, "that all must be taken, manuscripts and all." Accordingly, all was taken, and Mr. Wilkes's private pocket book filled up the mouth of the sack.

I was likewise told in the same cause by one of the most experienced messengers, that he held himself bound by his oath to pay an implicit obedience to the commands of the secretary of state; that in common cases he was contented to seize the printed impressions of the papers mentioned in the warrants; but when he received directions to search further, or to make a more general seizure, his rule was to sweep all. The practice has been correspondent to the warrant.

Such is the power, and therefore one should naturally expect that the law to warrant it should be clear in proportion as the power is exorbitant.

If it is law, it will be found in our books. If it is not to be found there, it is not law.

The great end, for which men entered into society, was to secure their property. That right is preserved sacred and incommunicable in all instances, where it has not been taken away or abridged by some public law for the good of the whole. The cases where this right of property is set aside by private law, are various. Distresses, executions, forfeitures, taxes etc are all of this description; wherein every man by common consent gives up that right, for the sake of justice and the general good. By the laws of England, every invasion of private property, be it ever so minute, is a trespass. No man can set his foot upon my ground without my license, but he is liable to an action, though the damage be nothing; which is proved by every declaration in trespass, where the defendant is called upon to answer for bruising the grass and even treading upon the soil. If he admits the fact, he is bound to show by way of justification, that some positive law has empowered or excused him. The justification is submitted to the judges, who are to look into the books; and if such a justification can be maintained by the text of the statute law, or by the principles of common law. If no excuse can be found or produced, the silence of the books is an authority against the defendant, and the plaintiff must have judgment.

According to this reasoning, it is now incumbent upon the defendants to show the law by which this seizure is warranted. If that cannot be done, it is a trespass.

Papers are the owner's goods and chattels: they are his dearest property; and are so far from enduring a seizure, that they will hardly bear an inspection; and though the eye cannot by the laws of England be guilty of a trespass, yet where private papers are removed and carried away, the secret nature of those goods will be an aggravation of the trespass, and demand more considerable damages in that respect. Where is the written law that gives any magistrate such a power? I can safely answer, there is none; and therefore it is too much for us without such authority to pronounce a practice legal, which would be subversive of all the comforts of society.

But though it cannot be maintained by any direct law, yet it bears a resemblance, as was urged, to the known case of search and seizure for stolen goods.

I answer that the difference is apparent. In the one, I am permitted to seize my own goods, which are placed in the hands of a public officer, till the felon's conviction shall entitle me to restitution. In the other, the party's own property is seized before and without conviction, and he has no power to reclaim his goods, even after his innocence is cleared by acquittal.

The case of searching for stolen goods crept into the law by imperceptible practice. It is the only case of the kind that is to be met with. No less a person than my lord Coke (4 Inst.176,) denied its legality; and therefore if the two cases resembled each other more than they do, we have no right, without an act of parliament to adopt a new practice in the criminal law, which was never yet allowed from all antiquity.

Observe too the caution with which the law proceeds in this singular case. There must be a full charge upon oath of a theft committed. The owner must swear that the goods are lodged in such place. He must attend at the execution of the warrant to shew them to the officer, who must see that they answer the description. And, lastly, the owner must abide the event at his peril; for if the goods are not found, he is a trespasser; and the officer being an innocent person, will be always a ready an convenient witness against him.

[Note also:] "If a private person suspect another of felony, and lay such ground of suspicion before a constable, and required his assistance to take him, the constable may justify killing the party if he fly, though in truth he were innocent. But in such case, where no hue and cry is levied, certain precautions must be observed. 1. The party suspecting ought to be present; for the justification is, that the constable did aid him in taking then party suspected. 2. The constable ought to be informed of the grounds of suspicion, that he may judge of the reasonableness of it. From whence it should seem that there ought to a reasonable ground shown for it: otherwise it would be immaterial whether such information were given to the constable or not, as to the point of his justification. And it was formerly supposed to be necessary that there should have been a felony committed in fact, of which the constable must have been ascertained at his peril." East's Pleas of the Crown, ch 5 s. 69

On the contrary, in the case before us nothing is described, no distinguished. No charge is requisite to prove that the party has any criminal papers in his custody; no person present to separate or select; no person to prove in the owner's behalf the officer's misbehavior. To say the truth, he cannot easily misbehave, unless his pilfers; for he cannot take more than all.

If it should be said that the same law which has with so much circumspection guarded the case of stolen goods from mischief, would likewise in this case protect the subject by adding proper checks; would require proofs beforehand; would call up the servant to stand by and overlook; would require him to take an exact inventory, and deliver a copy; nay answer is, that all these precautions would have been long since established by law, if the power itself had been legal; and that the want of them is an undeniable argument against the legality of the thing.

What would the parliament say, if the judges should take upon themselves to mould an unlawful power into a convenient authority, by new restrictions? That would be, not judgment, but legislation.

I come now to the practice since the Revolution, which has been strongly urged, with this emphatical addition, that an usage tolerated from the era of liberty, and continued downwards to this time through the best ages of the constitution, must necessarily have a legal commencement. Now, though that pretense can have no place in the question made by this plea, because no such practice is there alleged; yet I will permit the defendant for the present to borrow a fact from the special verdict, for the sake of giving it an answer.

If the practice began then, it began too late to be law now. If it was more ancient, the Revolution is not to answer for it; and I could have wished, that upon this occasion the Revolution had not been considered as the only basis of our liberty.

The Revolution restored this constitution to its first principles. It did no more. It did not enlarge the liberty of the subject; but gave it a better security. It neither widened nor contracted the foundation, but repaired, and perhaps added a buttress or two to the fabric; and if any minister of state has since deviated from the principles at that time recognized, all that I can say is, that, so far from being sanctified, they are condemned by the Revolution.

With respect to the practice itself, if it goes no higher, every lawyer will tell you, it is much too modern to be evidence of the common law; and if it should be added, that these warrants ought to acquire some strength by the silence of these courts, which have heard them read so often upon returns without censure or animadversion, I am able to borrow my answer to that pretense from the Court of King's Bench which lately declared with great unanimity in the Case of General Warrants, that as no objection was taken to them upon the return, and the matter passed *sub silentio*, the precedents were of no weight. I most heartily concur in that opinion; and the reason is more pertinent here, because the Court had no authority in the present case to determine against the seizure of the papers, which was not before them; whereas in the other they might, if they had thought fit, have declared the warrant void, and discharged the prisoner *ex officio*.

This is the first instance I have met with, where the ancient immemorable law of the land, in a public matter, was attempted to be proved by the practice of a private office.

The names and rights of public magistrates, their power and forms of proceeding as they are settled by law, have been long since written, and are to be found in books and records. Private customs indeed are still to be sought from private tradition. But whoever conceived a notion, that any part of the public law could be buried in the obscure practice of a particular person?

To search, seize, and carry away all the papers of the subject upon the first warrant; that such a right should have existed from the time whereof the memory of man runneth not to the contrary, and never yet have found a place in any book of law is incredible. But if so strange a thing could be supposed, I do not see, how we could declare the law upon such evidence.

But still it is insisted, that there has been a general submission, and no action brought to try the right.

I answer, there has been a submission of guilt and poverty to power and the terror of punishment. But it would be strange doctrine to assert that all the people of this land are bound to acknowledge that to be universal law, which a few criminal booksellers have been afraid to dispute.

The defendants upon this occasion have stopped short at the Revolution. But I think it would be material to go further back, in order to see, how far the search and seizure of papers have been countenanced in the antecedent reigns.

First, I find no trace of such a warrant as the present before that period, except a very few that were produced the other day in the reign of king Charles 2.

But there did exist a search warrant, which took its rise from a decree of the Star Chamber. The decree is found at the end of the 3d volume of Rushworth's Collections. It was made in the year 1636, and recites an older decree upon the subject in the 28th of Elizabeth, by which probably the same power of search was given.

By this decree the messenger of the press was empowered to search in all places, where books were printing, in order to see if the printer had a license; and if upon such search he found any books which he suspected to be libellous against the church or state, he was to seize them, and carry them before the proper magistrate.

It was evident, that the Star-chamber, how soon after the invention of printing I know not, took to itself the jurisdiction over public libels, which soon grew to be the peculiar business of that court.** Not that the courts of Westminster-hall wanted the power of holding pleas in those

---

** [Editor's Note: The court of Star Chamber was the judicial branch of the privy council. *See, e.g.,* James Fitzjames Stephen, I History of the Criminal Law of England 166–180 (1883). Originally concerned mostly with private disputes about property, it came to be the favored forum for prosecution of political offenses, including criminal libel as discussed in *Entick*. Star Chamber procedure differed from common-law procedure in almost every respect. The charge was made by information, rather than indictment; failure to plead a defense was deemed a confession; no defense could be submitted without endorsement by defense counsel, but counsel who tendered defenses found without merit were personally liable; there was no jury. Persons might be summoned to the Star Chamber without any information about the subject of the investigation and obliged to swear the oath *ex officio*, by which they pledged their souls to answer truthfully any question that might be asked about any subject. The Star Chamber had no jurisdiction to impose capital punishment, but it could sentence offenders to tortuous corporal punishments. *See* Lilburne's Case, *infra*, Chapter 8.] In 1640, Charles I assented to a statute abolishing the Star Chamber. 16 Car. 1 c. 10.

cases; but the attorney-general for good reasons chose rather to proceed there; which is the reason, why we have no cases of libels in the King's-bench before the Restoration.

The Star-Chamber from this jurisdiction presently usurped a general superintendance over the press, and exercised a legislative power in all matters relating to the subject. They appointed licensers; they prohibited books; they inflicted penalties; and they dignified one of their officers with the name of the messenger of the press, and among other things enacted this warrant of search.

After that court was abolished, the press became free, but enjoyed its liberty not above two or three years, for the Long Parliament thought fit to restrain it again by ordinance. Whilst the press is free, I am afraid it will always be licentious, and all governments have an aversion to libels. This parliament, therefore, did by ordinance restore the Star-Chamber practice; they recalled the licences, and sent forth again the messenger. It was against the ordinance, that Milton wrote that famous pamphlet called Areopagitica. Upon the Restoration, the press was free once more, till the 13th and 14th of Charles 2, when the Licensing Act passed, which for the first time gave the secretary of state power to issue search warrants; but these warrants were neither so oppressive, nor so inconvenient as the present. The right to enquire into the licence was the pretence of making the searches; and if during the search any suspected libels were found, they and they only could be seized.

This act expired the 32d year of that reign or thereabouts. It was revived again in the 1st year of King James 2, and remained in force till the 5th of king William, after one of his parliaments had continued it for a year beyond its expiration.

I do very much suspect, that the present warrant took its rise from these search-warrants, that I have been describing; nothing being easier to account for than this engraftment; the difference between them being no more than this, that the apprehension of the person in the first was to follow the seizure of papers, but the seizure of papers in the latter was to follow the apprehension of the person. The same evidence would serve equally for both purposes. If it was charged for printing or publishing, that was sufficient for either of the warrants. Only this material difference must always be observed between them, that the search warrant only carried off the criminal papers, whereas this seizes all.

When the Licensing Act expired at the close of king Charles 2's reign, the twelve judges were assembled at the king's command, to discover whether the press might not be as effectually restrained by the common law, as it had been by that statute.

I cannot help observing in this place, that if the secretary of state was still invested with a power of issuing this warrant, there was no occasion for the application to the judges; for though he could not issue the general search warrant, yet upon the least rumor of a libel he might have done more, and seized every thing. But that was not thought of, and therefore the judges met and resolved:

First, that it was criminal at common law, not only to write public seditious papers and false news; but likewise to publish any news without a license from the king, though it was true and innocent.

Secondly, that libels were seizable. This is to be found in the State Trials; and because it is a curiosity, I will recite the passages at large.

The Trial of Harris for a libel. Scroggs Chief Justice.

Because my brethren shall be satisfied with the opinion of all the judges of England what this offence is, which they would insinuate, as if the mere selling of books was no offence; it is not long since that all the judges met by the king's commandment, as they did some time before: and they both times declared unanimously, that all persons, that do write, or print, or sell any pamphlet that is either scandalous to public or private persons, such books may be seized, and the persons punished by law; that all books which are scandalous to the government may be seized, and all persons so expounding may be punished: and further, that all writers of news, though not scandalous, seditious, nor reflective upon the government or state; yet if they are writers, as they are few others, of false news, they are indictable and punishable upon that account [citation omitted].

It seems the chief justice was a little incorrect in his report; for it should seem as if he meant to punish only the writer of false news. But he is more accurate afterwards in the trial of Carre for a libel.

Sir *G Jefferies*, Recorder. All the judges of England having met together to know, whether and person whatsoever may expose to the public knowledge any matter of intelligence, or any matter whatsoever that concerns the public, they give it in as their resolution, that no person whatsoever could expose to the public knowledge any thing that concerned the affairs of the public, without licence from the king, or from such persons as he thought fit to intrust with that power.

Then Scroggs takes up the subject, and says, The words I remember are these. When by the king's command we were to give in our opinion, what was to be done in point of regulation of the press, we did all subscribe, that to print or publish any news-books or pamphlets, or any news whatsoever, is illegal; that it is a manifest intent to the breach of the peace, and they may be proceeded against by law for an illegal thing. Suppose now that this thing is not scandalous, what then? If there had been no reflection in this book at all, yet it is *illicte* done, and the author ought to be convicted for it. [citation omitted].

These are the opinions of all the twelve judges of England; a great and reverend authority.***

Can the twelve judges extrajudicially make a thing law to bind the kingdom by a declaration, that such is their opinion? I say no. It is a matter of impeachment for any judge to affirm it. There must be an antecedent principle or authority, from whence this opinion may be fairly collected; otherwise the opinion is null, and nothing but ignorance can excuse the judge that subscribed it. . . .

I can find no other authority to justify the seizure of a libel, than that of Scroggs and his brethren.

If the power of search is to follow the right of seizure, every body sees the consequence. He that has it or has had it in his custody; he that has published, copied or maliciously reported it, may fairly be under a reasonable suspicion of having the thing in his custody, and consequently become the object of the search warrant. If libels may be seized it ought to be laid down with precision, when, where, upon what charge, against whom, by what magistrate, and in what stage of the prosecution. All these particulars must be explained and proved to be law, before this general proposition can be established.

As therefore no authority in our book can be produced to support such a doctrine, and so many Star Chamber decrees, ordinances, and acts have been thought necessary to establish a power of search, I cannot be persuaded that such a power can be justified by the common law.

I have done now with the argument, which has endeavored to support this warrant by the practice since the Revolution.

It is then said, that it is necessary for the ends of government to lodge such a power with a state officer; and that it is better to prevent the publication before than to punish the offender afterwards. I answer, if the legislature be of that opinion, they will revive the Licensing Act. But if they have not done that I conceive they are not of that opinion. And with respect to the argument of state necessity, or a distinction that has been aimed at between state offenses and others, the common law does not understand that kind of reasoning, nor do our books take notice of any such distinctions.

Serjeant Ashley was committed to the Tower in the 3d of Charles 1st, by the House of Lords only for asserting in argument, that there was a 'law of state' different from the common law; and the Ship-Money judges were impeached for holding, first, that state-necessity would justify the raising money without consent of parliament; and secondly, that the king was judge of that necessity.

***

*** [Editor's Note: As *Entick* indicates, in the *Harris* case Scroggs relied on an advisory opinion solicited from the judges by the Crown. *See* Phillip Hamburger, *The Development of the Law of Seditious Libel and the Control of the Press,* 37 Stan. L. Rev. 661, 686 (1985). George Jeffries, the "hanging judge" who presided over the "Bloody Assizes" in 1685, may be the only English judge with a blacker reputation than that of Scroggs.]

If the king himself has no power to declare when the law ought to be violated for reason of state, I am sure we his judges have no such prerogative.

Lastly, its urged as an argument of utility, that such a search is a means of detecting offenders by discovering evidence. I wish some cases had been shown where the law forceth evidence out of the owner's custody by process. There is no process against papers in civil causes. It has been often tried, but never prevailed. Nay, where the adversary has by force or fraud got possession of your own proper evidence, there is no way to get it back but by action.

In the criminal law such a proceeding was never heard of; and yet there are some crimes, such for instance as murder, rape, robbery, and housebreaking to say nothing of forgery and perjury, that are more atrocious that libelling. But our law has provided no paper search in these cases to help forward the convictions.

Whether this proceedeth from the gentleness of the law towards criminals, or from a consideration that such a power would be more pernicious to the innocent than useful to the public I will not say.

It is very certain that the law obligeth no man to accuse himself; because the necessary means of compelling self-accusation, falling upon the innocent as well as the guilty, would be both cruel and unjust; and it should seem, that search for evidence is disallowed upon the same principle. There too the innocent would be confounded with the guilty.

Observe the wisdom as well as mercy of the law. The strongest evidence before a trial, being only *ex parte*, is but suspicion; it is not proof. Weak evidence is a ground of suspicion, though in a lower degree; and if suspicion at large should be a ground of search, especially in the case of libels, whose hose would be safe?

If, however, a right of search for the sake of discovering evidence ought in any case to be allowed, this crime above all others ought to be excepted, as a wanting such a discovery less than any other. It is committed in open daylight and in the face of the world; every act of publication makes new proof; and the solicitor of the treasury, if pleases, may be the witness himself.

The messenger of the press, by the very constitution of his office, is directed to purchase every libel that comes forth, in order to be a witness.

Nay, if the vengeance of government requires a production of the author, it is hardly possible for him to escape the impeachment of the printer, who is sure to seal his own pardon by his discovery. But suppose he should happen to be obstinate, yet the publication is stopped, and the offense punished. By this means the law is satisfied, and the public secured.

I have now taken notice of every thing that has been urged upon the present point; and upon the whole we are all of opinion, that the warrant to seize and carry away the party's papers in the case of a seditious, is illegal and void.

Before I conclude, I desire not to be understood as an advocate for libels. All civilized governments have punished calumny with severity; and with reason; for these compositions debauch the manners of the people; they excite a spirit of disobedience, and enervate the authority of government; they provoke and excite the passions of the people against their rulers, and the rulers oftentimes against his people.

After this description, I shall hardly be considered a favorer of these pernicious productions. I will always set my face against them, when they come before me; and shall recommend it most warmly to the jury always to convict when the proof is clear. They will do well to consider, that unjust acquittals bring an odium upon the press itself, the consequences whereof may be fatal to liberty; for if kings and great men cannot obtain justice at their hands by the ordinary course of law, they may at last be provoked to restrain that press, which the juries of their country refuse to regulate. When licentiousness is tolerated, liberty is in the utmost danger; because tyranny, bad as it is, is better than anarchy, and the worst of governments is more tolerable than no government at all.

[A great change of the king's ministers happened in the July before the judgement in the preceding case; particularly the marquis of Rockingham was placed at the head of the treasury. The judgment was soon followed with a resolution of the House of Commons, declaring the seizure of papers in the case of a libel to be illegal. Journ. Com. 22 April, 1766. At the same time the Commons passed a resolution condemning general warrants in the case of libels. The latter resolution was afterwards extended by a further vote, which included a declaration, that general warrants were universally illegal, except in cases provided for by act of parliament. Journ. Com. 25th April 1766. All these resolution were in consequence of Mr. Wilkes's complaint of a breach of privilege above two years before. Journ. Com. 15th November,1763. Two prior attempts were made to obtain a vote in condemnation of general warrants and the seizure of papers, one in 1764, the other in 1765. Journ. Com. 14th and 17th February, 1761; 29th January, 1765. {See, too, New Parl. Hist.} But both had miscarried, and one of the reasons assigned for so long resisting such interposition of the House was the pendency of suits in the courts of law. This objection was in part removed by the solemn judgment of the Common Pleas against the seizure of papers, and the acquiescence in it. Whether the question of general warrants ever received the same full and pointed decision in any of the courts, it is not in our power at present to inform the reader. The point arose on the trial of an action by Mr. Wilkes against Mr. Wood; and lord Camden in his charge to the jury appears to have explicitly avowed his own opinion of the illegality of general warrants; but what was done afterwards is not stated. How a regular judgment of the point was avoided, in the case of error in the King's-bench between Money and Leach, by conceding that the warrant was not pursued, we have observed in a former Note [citation omitted]. As to the action, in which Mr. Wilkes finally recovered large damages from the earl of Halifax, it was not tried till after the declaratory vote of the Commons, which most probably prevented all argument on the subject. *Hargrave*]

Virginia Declaration of Rights
1776

Art. X: That general warrants, whereby any officer or messenger may be commanded to search suspected places without evidence of a fact committed, or to seize any person or persons not named, or whose offense is not particularly described and supported by evidence, are grievous and oppressive and ought not to be granted.

Massachusetts Constitution
1780

Art. I, § 14: xiv.—every subject has a right to be secure from all unreasonable searches, and seizures of his person, his houses, his papers, and all his possessions. All warrants, therefore, are contrary to this right, if the cause or foundation of them be not previously supported by oath or affirmation; and if the order in the warrant to a civil officer, to make search in suspected places, or to arrest one or more suspected persons, or to seize their property, be not accompanied with a special designation of the persons or objects of search, arrest, or seizure: and no warrant ought to be issued but in cases, and with the formalities, prescribed by the laws.

Constitution of the United States, am. IV

The right of the people to be secure in their persons, houses, papers, and effects, against unreasonable searches and seizures, shall not be violated, and no Warrants shall issue, but upon probable cause, supported by Oath or affirmation, and particularly describing the place to be searched, and the persons or things to be seized.

Act for the Collection of Revenues
1 Stat. 29, 43 (1st Cong., 1st sess. 1789)

'That every collector, naval officer and surveyor, or other person specially appointed by either of them for that purpose, shall have full power and authority, to enter any ship or vessel, in which they shall have reason to suspect any goods, wares or merchandise subject to duty shall be concealed; and therein to search for, seize, and secure any such goods, wares or merchandise; and if they shall have cause to suspect a concealment thereof, in any particular dwelling house, store, building, or other place, they or either of them shall, upon application on oath or affirmation to any justice of the peace, be entitled to a warrant to enter such house, store, or other place (in the daytime only) and there to search for such goods, and if any shall be found, to seize and secure the same for trial; and all such goods, wares and merchandise, on which the duties shall not have been paid or secured, shall be forfeited.'

Wrexford v. Smith

2 Root 171, 1795 WL 262 (Conn. Super. 1795)

Action for an assault and battery and false imprisonment.

Plea-not guilty. Issue to the court.

This case was, the plaintiff in company with two others, were traveling through Worthington and he went into a store, got some tobacco and carried it off without paying for it. The defendant pursued him for the theft by an advertisement from the owner of the store, took the plaintiff, brought him back, and he was prosecuted and convicted of the theft before Justice Dunham, and punished.

By the Court. When a theft is committed, the owner of the goods stolen, may pursue and take the goods and the thief; and so may any other person with authority from the owner; or even without, and tender the thief to justice, and he will be excusable provided the person taken is found guilty. Stealing is a crime so odious in itself and so destructive to the well being of society, that every good citizen ought to assist in arresting the thief in his flight.

Judgment-Defendants not guilty.

The King v. Dr. Purnell

1 Blackstone W. 37, 96 E.R. 20 (1748) (footnotes omitted)

On an information against a magistrate of a corporation for a misdemesnor, the Court will not grant a rule to inspect the books of the corporation to furnish evidence.

The defendant was vice chancellor of Oxford; and the Attorney-General had ex officio exhibited against him an information, for not taking the deposition of Blacow the evidence, and for neglect of his duty both as vice chancellor and justice of the peace, in not punishing Whitmore and Dawes, who had spoken treasonable words in the streets of Oxford. The defendant appeared to the first information, upon which a noli prosequi was entered, and a second filed, to which also the defendant appeared and pleaded; and a trial at Bar was appointed November 21, but it was countermanded, and a new day, viz. February 6th was afterwards appointed. And now, the last day of the term, the attorney, without any affidavit, moved for a rule directed to the proper officers of the university to permit their books, records and archives to be inspected, in order to furnish evidence against the vice chancellor. This was moved as a motion of course for a peremptory rule, on a suggestion that the King, being visitor of the university, had a right to inspect their books whenever he thought proper. Notice of motion was however given the night before at nine o'clock, and it was opposed by Henley and Evans. And the Court, being of opinion it was not a peremptory motion, only granted a rule to shew cause.

In the next term, Mr. Wilbraham, standing counsel for the university, shewed cause. That the rule was made on no affidavit: that it was drawn in very general terms, (to inspect books, records, and archives).—Records, if any, may be seen elsewhere. Archives cannot be inspected but by a figure, continens pro contenta. But this is a case of too much concern, to stand upon form. The principal case is, whether on a prosecution of a public officer for a supposed misdemesnor, the Court ought to grant inspection of the public books of a corporation. The rule is on Dr. Purnell himself. Nemo tenetur seipsum accusare. The law will not tempt a man to make shipwreck of his conscience, in order to disculpate himself. In Chancery, a man may demur, if on the face of the bill it appears, that the matter to be discovered will affect the defendant in a criminal way. It will be said, the Court usually grants rules to inspect public books. True, but then it is usually when franchises are contested, and the like; when inspection of those books are the only evidence, and the corporation are considered only as trustees, just as lords of manors are, of the public evidences belonging to the manor. But in no case has the Court ever interposed in a criminal prosecution to grant such a rule, and force such inspection. Many indeed have been granted to inspect poor's rates; but those are public evidences which every body has a right to. Was there never any prosecution carried on with the same spirit as this? Why then are no examples produced? By the same reason every person indicted might be obliged to shew, whether he had any evidence against himself. In *Bradshaw qui tam* v. *Philips*, A. D. 1735, in an action for bribery, motion was, to inspect the books of a corporation, to prove the defendant a freeman. Hardwicke, C.J., denied the rule, because the plaintiff was a stranger. This case is much stronger. It is a precedent of the first impression. There seems to be a general want of evidence; but it is to be hoped, there is no other view than for evidence in this particular case. A hundred cases may be shewn where such rules have been granted in quo warranto's, &c. but none in criminal cases. [The Attorney "mentioned *K. and Burkins*, 7 Geo. 1, which was an indictment at a borough sessions, removed into B. R. by certiorari. Court said, the defendant might have a rule on the clerk of the peace, to have a copy of the names on the back of the indictment."] This is by no means a case. The indictment is a public record; he might have had it without a rule.

Mr. Henley on the same side.—This is a rule of the greatest importance to the most respectable body in the nation. It gives authority to the lowest agent of the Crown to rummage the MSS. of the university. One rule, in applications of this kind, is, that the person applying has an interest in the books and papers, so that in justice he is at all times entitled to have recourse to them. Another, that the person in possession is a trustee for the person applying (as a lord of a manor, &c.), and then the trust must be the subject in dispute; the suit must be about land in the manor, and averred by affidavit so to be. So corporations are the trustees and repository of the common franchises, and there is no instance of such a rule against a corporation, but where the franchise has been disputed, as on mandamus or quo warranto. The present rule is on an information against a vice chancellor and justice of peace. The Crown commences a prosecution against an individual of the university, and therefore desires to inspect the records of the university. By parity of reason, on an indictment against a citizen of London, they might inspect the records of the city. But it is suggested, that the King is visitor, and therefore entitled to a rule. I question the fact. The Court will require to be well satisfied of that. But, if so, 'tis a strong reason against granting the rule, for then the Crown may enforce its demands in a visitatorial way. Suppose the Crown has a general interest in the books of a corporation; that will not entitle them to an inspection, except the books are the subject of the dispute. *Crew qui tam and Blackburn*, H. 8 G. 2, an action for interfering in elections of members of Parliament, being a clerk of the post-office: the Court would not grant a rule to inspect the post-office books (though public books), because the cause did not concern them. *Benson and Cole*, M. 22 G. 2; motion to inspect Custom-House books, to prove the plaintiff in an insurance cause had no interest: urged that they were public books: refused, because they were not the subject of dispute. These were civil actions; the present otherwise. The avowed design of this motion being to furnish evidence, some precedent will be necessary; especially as a very bad use may be made of such a rule, when the university is much out of favour with some people.

. . .

[Hereupon Mr. Henley suggested, that the vice-chancellor had the custody of the original statutes.]

Sir John Strange for the Crown.—Affidavits are not usual in such cases. In the case of *The Skinners' Company*, the clerk refused to grant inspection, and an attachment was granted; but it was argued, whether the papers required were proper to be seen, and the Court held that they were. So here, if any thing improper be demanded, the inspection may be refused. Strange, that the university should conceal their statutes; since they are of so public a nature, that all the youth there entered, take oaths to observe them, and yet they are secreted from them. The Crown is the founder and lawgiver of the university, and as such has a right to inspect those laws.

[Lee, C.J.—I apprehend this case is argued to differ from all others (as qui tam actions, &c.) because in those the party applying is a stranger; but that in the present case the King is no stranger, because he is the founder. But how does that appear? Another question; is there any instance of an information against an officer of a corporation for breach of by-laws, and a rule granted to inspect those by-laws?]

Murray, Solicitor-General for the Crown.—Four necessary requisites for inspections of this kind. First, that they be public books. Second, that the party applying has an interest in them. Third, that they be material in a suit in this Court. Fourth, that the person in possession be forced to discover nothing to charge himself criminally.—First, these are of a public nature, given by the King, and open to all members of the university. The very youngest have a copy given them at their matriculation. Second, the King has an interest; he gave them, and has an interest in seeing them obeyed; and may enforce that obedience two ways; as visitor, and as King, where an offence at common law is mixed with the breach of them. Third, there is a suit in this Court, and the statutes may be material; and, if it is suggested that they will be so, the Court will grant the rule. Fourth, the objection is, that in criminal suits no one is bound to furnish evidence against himself. Agreed, but a distinction may be made. When a man is a magistrate, and as such has books in his custody; his having the office shall not secrete those books, which another vice-chancellor must have produced. Besides, the statutes are not in the vice-chancellor's custody only, but also in the hands of the custos archivorum.

Sir R. Lloyd, on the same side.—The university is not accused; the university may therefore very safely produce their books. The King is as much related to the Corporation of the University of Oxford, as to that of the City of York, and no.more a stranger to one than the other. It is to be hoped, that the King is no stranger to either university. If a man were to be indicted for burning the records of a corporation; no doubt but such a rule would then be granted, and why not now? Per Lee, C.J.—This is quite a new case. There is no precedent to warrant it, I therefore chuse to consider of it.

Afterwards, Lee C.J., delivered the opinion of the Court. This rule has been much narrowed, since it was first moved by Mr. Attorney. But still we are all of opinion, that we cannot, consistently with the rules of this Court, make such a rule. We ground ourselves on what has been done in similar cases, though none so strong as this. No case has been cited to support this application, but *The K. and Burkin*, which is not apposite. The clerk of the peace ought ex officio to have given a copy of the indictment, and the Court would have granted a rule on him to do it. The cases which we apprehend to be close to this are, 1st. *Qu. and Mead*, 2 Ann. Ld. Raym. 927. The reasons for denying the motion were, because, 1. The books were of a private nature. 2. Granting such rule would be to make a man produce evidence against himself, in a criminal prosecution. The second case is *The K. and Cornelius and Others, Justices of Ipswich*, T. 17 & 18 Geo. 2, an information for exacting money from persons for licensing ale-houses: a motion to inspect the corporation-books; cause was shewn against it by Sir J. Strange and Sir R. Lloyd. The Court on consideration were of opinion, that the rule could not be granted; as it was in a criminal proceeding, and it tended to make the defendants furnish evidence against themselves. These cases are very similar, only the present is rather stronger; because the information here is for a breach of and crime against the laws of the land, and this is an application to search books, which relate to the defendant's behaviour, as a member of a particular corporation. This case differs much from informations in nature of quo warranto; because these concern franchises, whereof the corporation books are the proper and only evidence, and they concern the Crown and the defendants equally. We know no instance, wherein this Court has granted a rule to inspect books in a criminal prosecution nakedly considered.

The rule was discharged per totam Curiam.

[Note by the reporter, William Blackstone] "N.B. As the university statute-book really contains nothing which could affect the merits of this case in any degree; and as (if it had) printed copies of it are very numerous and easy to be met with; and the custos archivorum, in whose keeping the original is, might have been compelled to have attended with it at the trial: this extraordinary motion seemed only to have been intended, as an excuse for dropping a prosecution, which could not be maintained: and it was accordingly dropped immediately after, having cost the defendant to the amount of several hundred pounds."

2. HISTORICAL NOTE: ORIGINS OF THE POLICE

When the Bill of Rights was ratified in 1791, police departments featuring round-the-clock, paramilitary full-time employees did not exist in the United States. The coroner investigated suspected homicides, and revenue agents patrolled for smugglers. These, however, were the exceptions. Sheriffs and constables executed warrants to arrest or search for stolen goods, but investigation of offenses was largely left to private persons. Public order was left to an ineffectual night watch, or, in cases of all-out riots, the military.

The principal public official in the early criminal process was the Justice of the Peace, an officer with a variety of duties (and, typically, a full-time job in the private sector). When a suspect was arrested, either by private citizens or by a sheriff or constable executing an arrest warrant, the captors brought their prisoner before the JP. The JP would then question the witnesses (under oath) and the prisoner (unsworn). The JP would then bail or commit the prisoner until the grand jury could consider the case.

If indicted by the grand jury, the defendant would stand trial (usually immediately after indictment). The prosecution would be conducted either by the victim personally or by a lawyer paid by the victim or by the government. Even when the government paid the prosecuting attorney, the prosecutor typically had a private practice. The

English rule disallowing counsel for defendants was generally disregarded in America, even before independence.

The modern system evolved during the course of the nineteenth century. Police departments employing uniformed, full-time officers around the clock began to appear in ante-Bellum America. After the war they became standard in all major cities. "Full-time" should not be interpreted as "professional." Police jobs were political plums. Brutality, corruption, and racism were common.

The police assumed the function of investigating unsolved crimes as well as keeping order. Defense lawyers, who would counsel suspects to claim their privilege against self-incrimination, were common in courthouses but excluded from police stations. Interrogation at the stationhouse replaced questioning by a judicial officer. Detective bureaus, vice squads, and undercover officers enabled at least partial enforcement of laws against liquor, prostitution, homosexuality, gambling and obscenity.

Prosecuting Attorney became not just a full-time post but a career path. As police and public prosecutors took over the management of investigations and prosecutions, private prosecutions became unnecessary as well as costly and potentially risky. Grand juries had no sources of information or legal advice other than what was given them by prosecutors or police officers. The trial jury became exceptional too. Early in the twentieth century convictions by guilty plea outnumbered those by trial verdict by factors of three or four to one.

The Fourth, Fifth and Sixth amendments were written in an institutional context that had vanished completely a hundred years after those amendments were adopted. Applying those amendments in a very different world—our world—is the subject of this course.

On the criminal justice system in the eighteenth century, see, e.g., James Fitzjames Stephen, 1 History of the Criminal Law of England (1883); Bruce P. Smith, *English Criminal Justice Administration, 1650–1850: A Historiographic Essay,* 25 Law & Hist. Rev. 593 (2007); Eben Moglen, *Taking the Fifth: Reconsidering the Origins of the Constitutional Privilege Against Self-Incrimination,* 92 Mich. L. Rev. 1086 (1994). On the origins of the police, *see, e.g.,* Wilbur R. Miller, Cops and Bobbies: Police Authority in New York and London, 1830–1870 (1977); Robert C. Wadman & William Thomas Allison, To Protect and Serve: A History of Police in America (2004); Samuel Walker, A Critical History of Police Reform: The Emergence of Professionalism (1977); James F. Richardson, The New York Police: Colonial Times to 1901 (1970); Roger Lane, Policing the City—Boston 1822–1885 (1967). On the replacement of trials by guilty pleas, *see, e.g.,* Raymond Moley, *The Vanishing Jury,* 2 S. Cal. L. Rev. 97 (1928); George Fisher, Plea Bargaining's Triumph: A History of Plea Bargaining in America (2003); Mary E. Vogel, Coercion to Compromise: Plea Bargaining, the Courts, and the Making of Political Authority (2007).

3. THE FEDERAL REGIME BASED ON *BOYD V. UNITED STATES*

Boyd v. United States
116 U.S. 616 (1886)

■ BRADLEY, J.

This was an information filed by the district attorney of the United States in the district court for the Southern district of New York, in July, 1884, in a cause of seizure and forfeiture of property, against 35 cases of plate glass, seized by the collector as forfeited to the United States, under the twelfth section of the 'Act to amend the customs revenue laws,' etc., passed June 22, 1874, (18 St. 186.) It is declared by that section that any owner, importer, consignee, etc., who shall, with intent to defraud the revenue, make, or attempt to make, any entry of imported merchandise, by means of any fraudulent or false invoice, affidavit, letter, or paper, or by means of any false statement, written or verbal, or who shall be guilty of any willful act or omission, by means whereof the United States shall be deprived of the lawful duties, or any portion thereof, accruing upon the merchandise, or any portion thereof, embraced or referred to in such invoice, affidavit, letter, paper, or statement, or affected by such act or omission, shall for each offense be fined in any sum not exceeding $5,000 nor less than $50, or be imprisoned for any time not exceeding two years, or both; and, in addition to such fine, such merchandise shall be forfeited.

The charge was that the goods in question were imported into the United States to the port of New York, subject to the payment of duties; and that the owners or agents of said merchandise, or other person unknown, committed the alleged fraud, which was described in the words of the statute. The plaintiffs in error entered a claim for the goods, and pleaded that they did not become forfeited in manner and form as alleged. On the trial of the cause it became important to show the quantity and value of the glass contained in 29 cases previously imported. To do this the district attorney offered in evidence an order made by the district judge under the fifth section of the same act of June 22, 1874, directing notice under seal of the court to be given to the claimants, requiring them to produce the invoice of the 29 cases. The claimants, in obedience to the notice, but objecting to its validity and to the constitutionality of the law, produced the invoice; and when it was offered in evidence by the district attorney they objected to its reception on the ground that, in a suit for forfeiture, no evidence can be compelled from the claimants themselves, and also that the statute, so far as it compels production of evidence to be used against the claimants, is unconstitutional and void. The evidence being received, and the trial closed, the jury found a verdict for the United States, condemning the 35 cases of glass which were seized, and judgment of forfeiture was given. This judgment was affirmed by the circuit court, and the decision of that court is now here for review. . . .

The fifth section of the act of June 22, 1874, under which this order was made, is in the following words, to-wit:

'In all suits and proceedings other than criminal, arising under any of the revenue laws of the United States, the attorney representing the government, whenever in his belief any business book, invoice, or paper belonging to, or under the control of, the defendant or claimant, will tend to prove any allegation made by the United States, may make a written motion, particularly describing such book, invoice, or paper, and setting forth the allegation which he expects to prove; and thereupon the court in which suit or proceeding is pending may, at its discretion issue a notice to the defendant or claimant to produce such book, invoice, or paper in court, at a day and hour to be specified in said notice, which, together with a copy of said motion, shall be served formally on the defendant or claimant by the United States marshal by delivering to him a certified copy thereof, or otherwise serving the same as original notices of suit in the same court are served; and if the defendant or claimants shall fail or refuse to produce such book, invoice, or paper in obedience to such notice, the allegations stated in the said motion shall be taken as confessed, unless his failure or refusal to produce the same shall be explained to the satisfaction of the court. And if produced the said attorney shall be permitted, under the direction of the court, to make examination (at which examination the defendant or claimant, or his agent, may be present) of such entries in said book, invoice, or paper as relate to or tend to prove the allegation aforesaid, and may offer the same in evidence on behalf of the United States. But the owner of said books and papers, his agent or attorney, shall have, subject to the order of the court, the custody of them, except pending their examination in court as aforesaid.' 18 St. 187.

This section was passed in lieu of the second section of the act of March 2, 1867, entitled 'An act to regulate the disposition of the proceeds of fines, penalties, and forfeitures incurred under the laws relating to the customs, and for other purposes,' (14 St. 547,) which section of said last-mentioned statute authorized the district judge, on complaint and affidavit that any fraud on the revenue had been committed by any person interested or engaged in the importation of merchandise, to issue his warrant to the marshal to enter any premises where any invoices, books, or papers were deposited relating to such merchandise, and take possession of such books and papers and produce them before said judge, to be subject to his order, and allowed to be examined by the collector, and to be subject to his order, and allowed deem necessary. This law being in force at the time of the revision, was incorporated into sections 3091, 3092, 3093, of the Revised Statutes.

. . . . it is contended that, whatever might have been alleged against the constitutionality of the acts of 1863 and 1867, that of 1874, under which the order in the present case was made, is free from constitutional objection, because it does not authorize the search and seizure of books and papers, but only requires the defendant or claimant to produce them. That is so; but it declares that if he does not produce them, the allegations which it is affirmed they will prove shall be taken as confessed. This is tantamount to compelling their production, for the prosecuting attorney will always be sure to state the evidence expected to be derived from them as strongly as the case will admit of. It is true that certain aggravating incidents of actual search and seizure, such as forcible entry into a man's house and searching among his papers, are wanting, and to this extent the proceeding under the act of 1874 is a mitigation of that which was authorized by the former acts; but it accomplishes the substantial object of those acts in forcing from a party evidence against himself. It is our opinion, therefore, that a compulsory production of a man's private papers to establish a criminal charge against him, or to forfeit his property, is within the scope of the fourth amendment to the constitution, in all cases in which a search and seizure would be, because it is a material ingredient, and effects the sole object and purpose of search and seizure.

The principal question, however, remains to be considered. Is a search and seizure, or, what is equivalent thereto, a compulsory production of a man's private papers, to be used in evidence against him in a proceeding to forfeit his property for alleged fraud against the revenue laws-is such a proceeding for such a purpose an 'unreasonable search and seizure' within the meaning of the fourth amendment of the constitution? or is it a legitimate proceeding? It is contended by the counsel for the government, that it is a legitimate proceeding, sanctioned by long usage, and the authority of judicial decision. No doubt long usage, acquiesced in by the courts, goes a long way to prove that there is some plausible ground or reason for it in the law, or in the historical facts which have imposed a particular construction of the law favorable to such usage. It is a maxim that, consuetudo est optimus interpres legum; and another maxim that, contemporanea expositio est optima et fortissima in lege. But we do not find any long usage or any contemporary construction of the constitution, which would justify any of the acts of congress now under consideration. . . . [T]he act of 1863 was the first act in this country, and we might say, either in this country or in England, so far as we have been able to ascertain, which authorized the search and seizure of a man's private papers, or the compulsory production of them, for the purpose of using them in evidence against him in a criminal case, or in a proceeding to enforce the forfeiture of his property. Even the act under which the obnoxious writs of assistance were issued did not go as far as this, but only authorized the examination of ships and vessels, and persons found therein, for the purpose of finding goods prohibited to be imported or exported, or on which the duties were not paid, and to enter into and search any suspected vaults, cellars, or warehouses for such goods. The search for and seizure of stolen or forfeited goods, or goods liable to duties and concealed to avoid the payment thereof, are totally different things from a search for and seizure of a man's private books and papers for the purpose of obtaining information therein contained, or of using them as evidence against him. The two things differ *toto coelo*. In the one case, the government is entitled to the possession of the property; in the other it is not. The seizure of stolen goods is authorized by the common law; and the seizure of goods forfeited for a breach of the revenue laws, or concealed to avoid the duties payable on them, has been authorized by English statutes for at least two centuries past; and the like seizures have been authorized by our own revenue acts from the commencement of the government.

The first statute passed by congress to regulate the collection of duties, the act of July 31, 1789, (1 St. 43,) contains provisions to this effect. As this act was passed by the same congress which proposed for adoption the original amendments to the constitution, it is clear that the members of that body did not regard searches and seizures of this kind as 'unreasonable,' and they are not embraced within the prohibition of the amendment. So, also, the supervision authorized to be exercised by officers of the revenue over the manufacture or custody of excisable articles, and the entries thereof in books required by las to be kept for their inspection, are necessarily excepted out of the category of unreasonable searches and seizures. So, also, the laws which provide for the search and seizure of articles and things which it is unlawful for a person to have in his possession for the purpose of issue or disposition, such as counterfeit coin, lottery tickets, implements of gambling, etc., are not within this category. Com. v. Dana, 2 Metc. 329. Many other things of this character might be enumerated. The entry upon premises, made by a sheriff or other officer of the law, for the purpose of seizing goods and chattels by virtue of a judicial writ, such as an attachment, a sequestration, or an execution, is not within the prohibition of the fourth or fifth amendment, or any other clause of the constitution; nor is the examination of a defendant under oath after an ineffectual execution, for the purpose of discovering secreted property or credits, to be applied to the payment of a judgment against him, obnoxious to those amendments. But, when examined with care, it is manifest that there is a total unlikeness of these official acts and proceedings to that which is now under consideration. In the case of stolen goods, the owner from whom they were stolen is entitled to their possession, and in the case of excisable or dutiable articles, the government has an interest in them for the payment of the duties thereon, and until such duties are paid has a right to keep them under observation, or to pursue and drag them from concealment; and in the case of goods seized on attachment or execution, the creditor is entitled to their seizure in satisfaction of his debt; and the examination of a defendant under oath to obtain a discovery of concealed property or credits is a proceeding merely civil to effect the ends of justice, and is no more than what the court of chancery would direct on a bill for discovery. Whereas, by the proceeding now under consideration, the court attempts to extort from the party his private books and papers to make him liable for a penalty or to forfeit his property.

In order to ascertain the nature of the proceedings intended by the fourth amendment to the constitution under the terms 'unreasonable searches and seizures,' it is only necessary to recall the contemporary or then recent history of the controversies on the subject, both in this country and in England. The practice had obtained in the colonies of issuing writs of assistance to the revenue officers, empowering them, in their discretion, to search suspected places for smuggled goods, which James Otis pronounced 'the worst instrument of arbitrary power, the most destructive of English liberty and the fundamental principles of law, that ever was found in an English law book;' since they placed 'the liberty of every man in the hands of every petty officer.' This was in February, 1761, in Boston, and the famous debate in which it occurred was perhaps the most prominent event which inaugurated the resistance of the colonies to the oppressions of the mother country.

'Then and there,' said John Adams, 'then and there was the first scene of the first act of opposition to the arbitrary claims of Great Britain. Then and there the child Independence was born.' These things, and the events which took place in England immediately following the argument about writs of assistance in Boston, were fresh in the memories of those who achieved our independence and established our form of government. In the period from 1762, when the North Briton was started by John Wilkes, to April, 1766, when the house of commons passed resolutions condemnatory of general warrants, whether for the seizure of persons or papers, occurred the bitter controversy between the English government and Wilkes, in which the latter appeared as the champion of popular rights, and was, indeed, the pioneer in the contest which resulted in the abolition of some grievous abuses which had gradually crept into the administration of public affairs. Prominent and principal among these was the practice of issuing general warrants by the secretary of state, for searching private houses for the discovery and seizure of books and papers that might be used to convict their owner of the charge of libel. Certain numbers of the North Briton, particularly No. 45, had been very bold in denunciation of the government, and were esteemed heinously libelous. By authority of the secretary's warrant Wilkes' house was searched, and his papers were indiscriminately seized. For this outrage he sued the perpetrators and obtained a verdict of £1,000 against Wood, one of the party who made the search, and £4,000 against Lord Halifax, the secretary of state, who issued the warrant. The case, however, which will always be celebrated as being the occasion of Lord CAMDEN'S memorable discussion of the subject, was that of Entick v. Carrington and Three Other King's Messengers, reported at length in 19 How. St. Tr. 1029 .... The action was trespass for entering the plaintiff's dwelling-house in November, 1762, and breaking open his desks, boxes, etc., and searching and examining his papers. The jury rendered a special verdict, and the case was twice solemnly argued at the bar. Lord CAMDEN pronounced the judgment of the court in Michaelmas term, 1765, and the law, as expounded by him, has been regarded as settled from that time to this, and his great judgment on that occasion is considered as on of the landmarks of English liberty. It was welcomed and applauded by the lovers of liberty in the colonies as well as in the mother country. It is regarded as one of the permanent monuments of the British constitution, and is quoted as such by the English authorities on that subject down to the present time.

As every American statesman, during our revolutionary and formative period as a nation, was undoubtedly familiar with this monument of English freedom, and considered it as the true and ultimate expression of constitutional law, it may be confidently asserted that its propositions were in the minds of those who framed the fourth amendment to the constitution, and were considered as sufficiently explanatory of what was meant by unreasonable searches and seizures. The principles laid down in this opinion affect the very essence of constitutional liberty and security. They reach further than the concrete form of the case then before the court, with its adventitious circumstances; they apply to all invasions on the part of the government and its employes of the sanctity of a man's home and the privacies of life. It is not the breaking of his doors, and the rummaging of his drawers, that constitutes the essence of the offense; but it is the invasion of his indefeasible right of personal security, personal liberty. and private property, where that right has never been forfeited by his conviction of some public offense,-it is the invasion of this sacred right which underlies and constitutes the essence of Lord CAMDEN's judgment. Breaking into a house and opening boxes and drawers are circumstances of aggravation; but any forcible and compulsory extortion of a man's own testimony, or of his private papers to be used as evidence to convict him of crime, or to forfeit his goods, is within the condemnation of that judgment. In this regard the fourth and fifth amendments run almost into each other. Can we doubt that when the fourth and fifth amendments to the constitution of the United States were penned and adopted, the language of Lord CAMDEN was relied on as expressing the true doctrine on the subject of searches and seizures, and as furnishing the true criteria of the reasonable and 'unreasonable' character of such seizures? Could the men who proposed those amendments, in the light of Lord CAMDEN's opinion, have put their hands to a law like those of March 3, 1863, and March 2, 1867, before recited? If they could not, would they have approved the fifth section of the act of June 22, 1874, which was adopted as a substitute for the previous laws? It seems to us that the question cannot admit of a doubt. They never would have approved of them. The struggles against arbitrary power in which they had been engaged for more than 20 years would have been too deeply engraved in their memories to have allowed them to approve of such insidious disguises of the old grievance which they had so deeply abhorred. . . .

The views of the first congress on the question of compelling a man to produce evidence against himself may be inferred from a remarkable section of the judiciary act of 1789. The fifteenth section of that act introduced a great improvement in the law of procedure. The substance of it is found in section 724 of the Revised Statutes, and the section as originally enacted is as follows, to-wit:

> 'All the said courts of the United States shall have power in the trial of actions at law, on motion and due notice thereof being given, to require the parties to produce books or writings in their possession or power, which contain evidence pertinent to the issue, in cases and under circumstances where they might be compelled to produce the same by the ordinary rules of proceeding in chancery; and if a plaintiff shall fail to comply with such order to produce books or writings it shall be lawful for the courts respectively, on motion, to give the like judgment for the defendant as in cases of nonsuit, and if a defendant shall fail to comply with such order to produce books or writings, it shall be lawful for the courts respectively, on motion as aforesaid, to give judgment against him or her by default.'

The restriction of this proceeding to 'cases and under circumstances where they [the parties] might be compelled to produce the same [books or writings] by the ordinary rules of proceeding in chancery,' shows the wisdom of the congress of 1789. The court of chancery had for generations been weighing and balancing the rules to be observed in granting discovery on bills filed for that purpose, in the endeavor to fix upon such as would best secure the ends of justice. To go beyond the point to which that court had gone may well have been thought hazardous. Now it is elementary knowledge that one cardinal rule of the court of chancery is never to decree a discovery which might tend to convict the party of a crime, or to forfeit his property. And any compulsory discovery by extorting the party's oath, or compelling the production of his private books and papers, to convict him of crime, or to forfeit his property, is contrary to the principles of a free government. It is abhorrent to the instincts of an Englishman; it is abhorrent to the instincts of an American. It may suit the purposes of despotic power, but it cannot abide the pure atmosphere of political liberty and personal freedom. . . .

We have already noticed the intimate relation between the two amendments. They throw great light on each other. For the 'unreasonable searches and seizures' condemned in the fourth amendment are almost always made for the purpose of compelling a man to give evidence against himself, which in criminal cases is condemned in the fifth amendment; and compelling a man 'in a criminal case to be a witness against himself,' which is condemned in the fifth amendment, throws light on the question as to what is an 'unreasonable search and seizure' within the meaning of the fourth amendment. And we have been unable to perceive that the seizure of a man's private books and papers to be used in evidence against him is substantially different from compelling him to be a witness against himself. We think it is within the clear intent and meaning of those terms. We are also clearly of opinion that proceedings instituted for the purpose of declaring the forfeiture of a man's property by reason of offenses committed by him, though they may be civil in form, are in their nature criminal. In this very case the ground of forfeiture, as declared in the twelfth section of the act of 1874, on which the information is based, consists of certain acts of fraud committed against the public revenue in relation to imported merchandise, which are made criminal by the statute; and it is declared, that the offender shall be fined not exceeding $5,000, nor less than $50, or be imprisoned not exceeding two years, or both; and in addition to such fine such merchandise shall be forfeited. These are the penalties affixed to the criminal acts, the forfeiture sought by this suit being one of them. If an indictment had been presented against the claimants, upon conviction the forfeiture of the goods could have been included in the judgment. If the government prosecutor elects to waive an indictment, and to file a civil information against the claimants,-that is, civil in form,-can he by this device take from the proceeding its criminal aspect and deprive the claimants of their immunities as citizens, and extort from them a production of their private papers, or, as an alternative, a confession of guilt? This cannot be. The information, though technically a civil proceeding, is in substance and effect a criminal one. As showing the close relation between the civil and criminal proceedings on the same statute in such cases we may refer to the recent case of Coffey v. U. S., 116 U. S., S. C. ante, 432, in which we decided that an acquittal on a criminal information was a good plea in bar to a civil information for the forfeiture of goods, arising upon the same acts. As, therefore, suits for penalties and forfeitures, incurred by the commission of offenses against the law, are of this quasi criminal nature, we think that they are within the reason of criminal proceedings for all the purposes of the fourth amendment of the constitution, and of that portion of the fifth amendment which declares that no person shall be compelled in any criminal case to be a witness against himself; and we are further of opinion that a compulsory production of the private books and papers of the owner of goods sought to be forfeited in such a suit is compelling him to be a witness against himself, within the meaning of the fifth amendment to the constitution, and is the equivalent of a search and seizure-and an unreasonable search and seizure-within the meaning of the fourth amendment. Though the proceeding in question is divested of many of the aggravating incidents of actual search and seizure, yet, as before said, it contains their substance and essence, and effects their substantial purpose. It may be that it is the obnoxious thing in its mildest and least repulsive form; but illegitimate and unconstitutional practices get their first footing in that way, namely, by silent approaches and slight deviations from legal modes of procedure. This can only be obviated by adhering to the rule that constitutional provisions for the security of person and property should be liberally construed. A close and literal construction deprives them of half their efficacy, and leads to gradual depreciation of the right, as if it consisted more in sound than in substance. It is the duty of courts to be watchful for the constitutional rights of the citizen, and against any stealthy encroachments thereon. Their motto should be obsta principiis. We have no doubt that the legislative body is actuated by the same motives; but the vast accumulation of public business brought before it sometimes prevents it, on a first presentation, from noticing objections which become developed by time and the practical application of the objectionable law. . . .

We think that the notice to produce the invoice in this case, the order by virtue of which it was issued, and the law which authorized the order, were unconstitutional and void, and that the inspection by the district attorney of said invoice, when produced in obedience to said notice, and its admission in evidence by the court, were erroneous and unconstitutional proceedings. We are of opinion, therefore, that the judgment of the circuit court should be reversed, and the cause remanded, with directions to award a new trial; and it is so ordered.

■ MILLER, J.

I concur in the judgment of the court, reversing that of the circuit court, and in so much of the opinion of this court as holds the fifth section of the act of 1874 void as applicable to the present case. I am of opinion that this is a criminal case within the meaning of that clause of the fifth amendment to the constitution of the United States which declares that no person 'shall be compelled in any criminal case to be a witness against himself.' And I am quite satisfied that the effect of the act of congress is to compel the party on whom the order of the court is served to be a witness against himself. The order of the court under the statute is in effect a subpoena duces tecum, and, though the penalty for the witness' failure to appear in court with the criminating papers is not fine and imprisonment, it is one which may be made more severe, namely, to have charges against him of a criminal nature, taken for confessed, and made the foundation of the judgment of the court. That this is within the protection which the constitution intended against compelling a person to be a witness against himself, is, I think, quite clear. But this being so, there is no reason why this court should assume that the action of the court below, in requiring a party to produce certain papers as evidence on the trial, authorizes an unreasonable search or seizure of the house, papers, or effects of that party. There is in fact no search and no seizure authorized by the statute. No order can be made by the court under it which requires or permits anything more than service of notice on a party to the suit. . . .

Weeks v. United States
232 U.S. 383 (1914)

■ MR. JUSTICE DAY delivered the opinion of the court:

An indictment was returned against the plaintiff in error, defendant below, and herein so designated, in the district court of the United States for the western district of Missouri, containing nine counts. The seventh count, upon which a conviction was had, charged the use of the mails for the purpose of transporting certain coupons or tickets representing chances or shares in a lottery or gift enterprise, in violation of § 213 of the Criminal Code [35 Stat. at L. 1129, chap. 321, U. S. Comp. Stat. Supp. 1911, p. 1652]. Sentence of fine and imprisonment was imposed. This writ of error is to review that judgment.

The defendant was arrested by a police officer, so far as the record shows, without warrant, at the Union Station in Kansas City, Missouri, where he was employed by an express company. Other police officers had gone to the house of the defendant, and being told by a neighbor where the key was kept, found it and entered the house. They searched the defendant's room and took possession of various papers and articles found there, which were afterwards turned over to the United States marshal. Later in the same day police officers returned with the marshal, who thought he might find additional evidence, and, being admitted by someone in the house, probably a boarder, in response to a rap, the marshal searched the defendant's room and carried away certain letters and envelopes found in the drawer of a chiffonier. Neither the marshal nor the police officer had a search warrant.

The defendant filed in the cause before the time for trial the following petition:

Petition to Return Private Papers, Books, and Other Property.

Now comes defendant and states that he is a citizen and resident of Kansas City, Missouri, and that he resides, owns, and occupies a home at 1834 Penn street in said city:

That on the 21st day of December, 1911, while plaintiff was absent at his daily vocation, certain officers of the government whose names are to plaintiff unknown, unlawfully and without warrant or authority so to do, broke open the door to plaintiff's said home and seized all of his books, letters, money, papers, notes, evidences of indebtedness, stock, certificates, insurance policies, deeds, abstracts, and other muniments of title, bonds, candies, clothes, and other property in said home, and this in violation of §§ 11 and 23 to the Constitution of Missouri, and of the 4th and 5th Amendments to the Constitution of the United States;

That the district attorney, marshal, and clerk of the United States court for the western district of Missouri took the above-described property so seized into their possession, and have failed and refused to return to defendant portion of same, to wit:

One (1) leather grip, value about $7; one (1) tin box valued at $3; one (1) Pettis county, Missouri, bond, value $500; three (3) mining stock certificates which defendant is unable to more particularly describe, valued at $12,000; and certain stock certificates in addition thereto, issued by the San Domingo Mining, Loan, & Investment Company; about $75 in currency; one (1) newspaper published about 1790, an heirloom; and certain other property which plaintiff is now unable to describe.

That said property is being unlawfully and improperly held by said district attorney, marshal, and clerk, in violation of defendant's rights under the Constitution of the United States and the state of Missouri.

That said district attorney purposes to use said books, letters, papers, certificates of stock, etc., at the trial of the above-entitled cause, and that by reason thereof and of the facts above set forth defendant's rights under the amendments aforesaid to the Constitution of Missouri and the United States have been and will be violated unless the court order the return prayed for;

Wherefore, defendant prays that said district attorney, marshal, and clerk be notified, and that the court direct and order said district attorney, marshal, and clerk, to return said property to said defendant.

Upon consideration of the petition the court entered in the cause an order directing the return of such property as was not pertinent to the charge against the defendant, but denied the petition as to pertinent matter, reserving the right to pass upon the pertinency at a later time. In obedience to the order the district attorney returned part of the property taken, and retained the remainder, concluding a list of the latter with the statement that, 'all of which last above described property is to be used in evidence in the trial of the above-entitled cause, and pertains to the alleged sale of lottery tickets of the company above named.'

After the jury had been sworn and before any evidence had been given, the defendant again urged his petition for the return of his property, which was denied by the court. Upon the introduction of such papers during the trial, the defendant objected on the ground that the papers had been obtained without a search warrant, and by breaking open his home, in violation of the 4th and 5th Amendments to the Constitution of the United States, which objection was overruled by the court. Among the papers retained and put in evidence were a number of lottery tickets and statements with reference to the lottery, taken at the first visit of the police to the defendant's room, and a number of letters written to the defendant in respect to the lottery, taken by the marshal upon his search of defendant's room.

The defendant assigns error, among other things, in the court's refusal to grant his petition for the return of his property, and in permitting the papers to be used at the trial.

It is thus apparent that the question presented involves the determination of the duty of the court with reference to the motion made by the defendant for the return of certain letters, as well as other papers, taken from his room by the United States marshal, who, without authority of process, if any such could have been legally issued, visited the room of the defendant for the declared purpose of obtaining additional testimony to support the charge against the accused, and, having gained admission to the house, took from the drawer of a chiffonier there found certain letters written to the defendant, tending to show his guilt. These letters were placed in the control of the district attorney, and were subsequently produced by him and offered in evidence against the accused at the trial. The defendant contends that such appropriation of his private correspondence was in violation of rights secured to him by the 4th and 5th Amendments to the Constitution of the United States. We shall deal with the 4th Amendment, which provides:

'The right of the people to be secure in their persons, houses, papers, and effects, against unreasonable searches and seizures, shall not be violated, and no warrants shall issue but upon probable cause, supported by oath or affirmation, and particularly describing the place to be searched, and the persons or things to be seized.'

The history of this Amendment is given with particularity in the opinion of Mr. Justice Bradley, speaking for the court in Boyd v. United States, 116 U. S. 616, 29 L. ed. 746, 6 Sup. Ct. Rep. 524. . . .

In Bram v. United States, 168 U. S. 532, this court, in speaking by the present Chief Justice of *Boyd's Case,* dealing with the 4th and 5th Amendments, said (544):

'It was in that case demonstrated that both of these Amendments contemplated perpetuating, in their full efficacy, by means of a constitutional provision, principles of humanity and civil liberty which had been secured in the mother country only after years of struggle, so as to implant them in our institutions in the fullness of their integrity, free from the possibilities of future legislative change.'

The effect of the 4th Amendment is to put the courts of the United States and Federal officials, in the exercise of their power and authority, under limitations and restraints as to the exercise of such power and authority, and to forever secure the people, their persons, houses, papers, and effects, against all unreasonable searches and seizures under the guise of law. This protection reaches all alike, whether accused of crime or not, and the duty of giving to it force and effect is obligatory upon all entrusted under our Federal system with the enforcement of the laws. The tendency of those who execute the criminal laws of the country to obtain conviction by means of unlawful seizures and enforced confessions, the latter often obtained after subjecting accused persons to unwarranted practices destructive of rights secured by the Federal Constitution, should find no sanction in the judgments of the courts, which are charged at all times with the support of the Constitution, and to which people of all conditions have a right to appeal for the maintenance of such fundamental rights.

What, then, is the present case? Before answering that inquiry specifically, it may be well by a process of exclusion to state what it is not. It is not an assertion of the right on the part of the government always recognized under English and American law, to search the person of the accused when legally arrested, to discover and seize the fruits or evidences of crime. This right has been uniformly maintained in many cases. 1 Bishop. Crim. Proc. § 211; Wharton, Crim. Pl. & Pr. 8th ed. § 60; Dillon v. O'Brien, 16 Cox, C. C. 245, I. R. L. R. 20 C. L. 300, 7 Am. Crim. Rep. 66. Nor is it the case of testimony offered at a trial where the court is asked to stop and consider the illegal means by which proofs, otherwise competent, were obtained,—of which we shall have occasion to treat later in this opinion. Nor is it the case of burglar's tools or other proofs of guilt found upon his arrest within his control.

The case in the aspect in which we are dealing with it involves the right of the court in a criminal prosecution to retain for the purposes of evidence the letters and correspondence of the accused, seized in his house in his absence and without his authority, by a United States marshal holding no warrant for his arrest and none for the search of his premises. The accused, without awaiting his trial, made timely application to the court for an order for the return of these letters, as well or other property. This application was denied, the letters retained and put in evidence, after a further application at the beginning of the trial, both applications asserting the rights of the accused under the 4th and 5th Amendments to the Constitution. If letters and private documents can thus be seized and held and used in evidence against a citizen accused of an offense, the protection of the 4th Amendment, declaring his right to be secure against such searches and seizures, is of no value, and, so far as those thus placed are concerned, might as well be stricken from the Constitution. The efforts of the courts and their officials to bring the guilty to punishment, praiseworthy as they are, are not to be aided by the sacrifice of those great principles established be years of endeavor and suffering which have resulted in their embodiment in the fundamental law of the land. The United States marshal could only have invaded the house of the accused when armed with a warrant issued as required by the Constitution, upon sworn information, and describing with reasonable particularity the thing for which the search was to be made. Instead, he acted without sanction of law, doubtless prompted by the desire to bring further proof to the aid of the government, and under color of his office undertook to make a seizure of private papers in direct violation of the constitutional prohibition against such action. Under such circumstances, without sworn information and particular description, not even an order of court would have justified such procedure; much less was it within the authority of the United States marshal to thus invade the house and privacy of the accused. In Adams v. New York, 192 U. S. 585, this court said that the 4th Amendment was intended to secure the citizen in person and property against unlawful invasion of the sanctity of his home by officers of the law, acting under legislative or judicial sanction. This protection is equally extended to the action of the government and officers of the law acting under it. *Boyd Case*, 116 U. S. 616. To sanction such proceedings would be to affirm by judicial decision a manifest neglect, if not an open defiance, of the prohibitions of the Constitution, intended for the protection of the people against such unauthorized action.

The court before which the application was made in this case recognized the illegal character of the seizure, and ordered the return of property not in its judgment competent to be offered at the trial, but refused the application of the accused to turn over the letters, which were afterwards put in evidence on behalf of the government. While there is no opinion in the case, the court in this proceeding doubtless relied upon what is now contended by the government to be the correct rule of law under such circumstances, that the letters having come into the control of the court, it would not inquire into the manner in which they were obtained, but, if competent, would keep them and permit their use in evidence. Such proposition, the government asserts, is conclusively established by certain decisions of this court, the first of which is Adams v. New York, *supra*. In that case the plaintiff in error had been convicted in the supreme court of the state of New York for having in his possession certain gambling paraphernalia used in the game known as policy, in violation of the Penal Code of New York. At the trial certain papers, which had been seized by police officers executing a search warrant for the discovery and seizure of policy slips, and which had been found in addition to the policy slips, were offered in evidence over his objection. The conviction was affirmed by the court of appeals of New York (68 N. E. 636), and the case was brought here for alleged violation of the 4th and 5th Amendments to the Constitution of the United States. Pretermitting the question whether these Amendments applied to the action of the states, this court proceeded to examine the alleged violations of the 4th and 5th Amendments, and put its decision upon the ground that the papers found in the execution of the search warrant, which warrant had a legal purpose in the attempt to find gambling paraphernalia, was competent evidence against the accused, and their offer in testimony did not violate his constitutional privilege against unlawful search or seizure, for is was held that such incriminatory documents thus discovered were not the subject of an unreasonable search and seizure, and in effect that the same were incidentally seized in the lawful execution of a warrant, and not in the wrongful invasion of the home of a citizen, and the unwarranted seizure of his papers and property. It was further held, approving in that respect the doctrine laid down in 1 Greenleaf, Ev. § 254a, that it was no valid objection to the use of the papers that they had been thus seized, and that the courts in the course of a trial would not make an issue to determine that question, and many state cases were cited supporting that doctrine.

The same point had been ruled in People v. Adams, 68 N. E. 636, from which decision the case was brought to this court, where it was held that if the papers seized in addition to the policy slips were competent evidence in the case, as the court held they were, they were admissible in evidence at the trial, the court saying (p. 358): 'The underlying principle obviously is that the court, when engaged in trying a criminal cause, will not take notice of the manner in which witnesses have possessed themselves of papers, or other articles of personal property, which are material and properly offered in evidence.' This doctrine thus laid down by the New York court of appeals and approved by this court, that a court will not, in trying a criminal cause, permit a collateral issue to be raised as to the source of competent testimony, has the sanction of so many state cases that it would be impracticable to cite or refer to them in detail. Many of them are collected in the note to State v. Turner, 136 Am. St. Rep. 129, 135 et seq. After citing numerous cases the editor says: 'The underlying principle of all these decisions obviously is, that the court, when engaged in the trial of a criminal action, will not take notice of the manner in which a witness has possessed himself of papers or other chattels, subjects of evidence, which are material and properly offered in evidence. People v. Adams, *supra*. Such an investigation is not involved necessarily in the litigation in chief, and to pursue it would be to halt in the orderly progress of a cause, and consider incidentally a question which has happened to cross the path of such litigation, and which is wholly independent thereof.'

It is therefore evident that the Adams Case affords no authority for the action of the court in this case, when applied to in due season for the return of papers seized in violation of the Constitutional Amendment. The decision in that case rests upon incidental seizure made in the execution of a legal warrant, and in the application of the doctrine that a collateral issue will not be raised to ascertain the source from which testimony, competent in a criminal case, comes.

The government also relies upon Hale v. Henkel, 201 U. S. 43, 50 L. ed. 652, 26 Sup. Ct. Rep. 370, in which the previous cases *of Boyd v. United States*, and *Adams v. New York, supra*; Interstate Commerce Commission v. Brimson, 154 U. S. 447, 38 L. ed. 1047, 4 Inters. Com. Rep. 545, 14 Sup. Ct. Rep. 1125, and Interstate Commerce Commission v. Baird, 194 U. S. 25, 48 L. ed. 860, 24 Sup. Ct. Rep. 563, are reviewed, and wherein it was held that a subpoena duces tecum requiring a corporation to produce all its contracts and correspondence with no less than six other companies, as well as all letters received by the corporation from thirteen other companies, located in different parts of the United States, was an unreasonable search and seizure within the 4th Amendment, and it was there stated that (p. 76) 'an order for the production of books and papers may constitute an unreasonable search and seizure within the 4th Amendment. While a search ordinarily implies a quest by an officer of the law, and a seizure contemplates a forcible dispossession of the owner, still, as was held in the Boyd Case, the substance of the offense is the compulsory production of private papers, whether under a search warrant or a subpoena duces tecum, against which the person, be he individual or corporation, is entitled to protection.' If such a seizure under the authority of a warrant supposed to be legal, constitutes a violation of the constitutional protection, *a fortiori* does the attempt of an officer of the United States, the United States marshal, acting under color of his office, without even the sanction of a warrant, constitute an invasion of the rights within the protection afforded by the 4th Amendment. . . .

We therefore reach the conclusion that the letters in question were taken from the house of the accused by an official of the United States, acting under color of his office, in direct violation of the constitutional rights of the defendant; that having made a seasonable application for their return, which was heard and passed upon by the court, there was involved in the order refusing the application a denial of the constitutional rights of the accused, and that the court should have restored these letters to the accused. In holding them and permitting their use upon the trial, we think prejudicial error was committed. As to the papers and property seized by the policemen, it does not appear that they acted under any claim of Federal authority such as would make the amendment applicable to such unauthorized seizures. The record shows that what they did by way of arrest and search and seizure was done before the finding of the indictment in the Federal court; under what supposed right or authority does not appear. What remedies the defendant may have against them we need not inquire, as the 4th Amendment is not directed to individual misconduct of such officials. Its limitations reach the Federal government and its agencies. *Boyd Case,* 116 U. S. 616, and *see* Twining v. New Jersey, 211 U. S. 78, 53 L. ed. 97, 29 Sup. Ct. Rep. 14.

It results that the judgment of the court below must be reversed, and the case remanded for further proceedings in accordance with this opinion.

Reversed.

Olmstead v. United States

277 U.S. 438 (1928)

■ MR. CHIEF JUSTICE TAFT delivered the opinion of the Court.

These cases are here by certiorari from the Circuit Court of Appeals for the Ninth Circuit. 19 F.(2d) 842, 53 A. L. R. 1472, and 19 F.(2d) 850. . . . . They were [brought here with] the distinct limitation that the hearing should be confined to the single question whether the use of evidence of private telephone conversations between the defendants and others, intercepted by means of wire tapping, amounted to a violation of the Fourth and Fifth Amendments.

The petitioners were convicted in the District Court for the Western District of Washington of a conspiracy to violate the National Prohibition Act (27 USCA) by unlawfully possessing, transporting and importing intoxicating liquors and maintaining nuisances, and by selling intoxicating liquors. Seventy-two others, in addition to the petitioners, were indicted. Some were not apprehended, some were acquitted, and others pleaded guilty.

The evidence in the records discloses a conspiracy of amazing magnitude to import, possess, and sell liquor unlawfully. It involved the employment of not less than 50 persons, of two sea-going vessels for the transportation of liquor to British Columbia, of smaller vessels for coastwise transportation to the state of Washington, the purchase and use of a branch beyond the suburban limits of Seattle, with a large underground cache for storage and a number of smaller caches in that city, the maintenance of a central office manned with operators, and the employment of executives, salesmen, deliverymen dispatchers, scouts, bookkeepers, collectors, and an attorney. In a bad month sales amounted to $176,000; the aggregate for a year must have exceeded $2,000,000.

Olmstead was the leading conspirator and the general manager of the business. He made a contribution of $10,000 to the capital; 11 others contributed $1,000 each. The profits were divided, one-half to Olmstead and the remainder to the other 11. Of the several offices in Seattle, the chief one was in a large office building. In this there were three telephones on three different lines. There were telephones in an office of the manager in his own home, at the homes of his associates, and at other places in the city. Communication was had frequently with Vancouver, British Columbia. Times were fixed for the deliveries of the 'stuff' to places along Puget Sound near Seattle, and from there the liquor was removed and deposited in the caches already referred to. One of the chief men was always on duty at the main office to receive orders by the telephones and to direct their filling by a corps of men stationed in another room-the 'bull pen.' The call numbers of the telephones were given to those known to be likely customers. At times the sales amounted to 200 cases of liquor per day.

The information which led to the discovery of the conspiracy and its nature and extent was largely obtained by intercepting messages on the telephones of the conspirators by four federal prohibition officers. Small wires were inserted along the ordinary telephone wires from the residences of four of the petitioners and those leading from the chief office. The insertions were made without trespass upon any property of the defendants. They were made in the basement of the large office building. The taps from house lines were made in the streets near the houses.

The gathering of evidence continued for many months. Conversations of the conspirators, of which refreshing stenographic notes were currently made, were testified to by the government witnesses.

They revealed the large business transactions of the partners and their subordinates. Men at the wires heard the orders given for liquor by customers and the acceptances; they became auditors of the conversations between the partners. All this disclosed the conspiracy charged in the indictment. Many of the intercepted conversations were not merely reports, but parts of the criminal acts. The evidence also disclosed the difficulties to which the conspirators were subjected, the reported news of the capture of vessels, the arrest of their men, and the seizure of cases of liquor in garages and other places. It showed the dealing by Olmstead, the chief conspirator, with members of the Seattle police, the messages to them which secured the release of arrested members of the conspiracy, and also direct promises to officers of payments as soon as opportunity offered.

The Fourth Amendment provides:

'The right of the people to be secure in their persons, houses, papers, and effects, against unreasonable searches and seizures, shall not be violated, and no warrants shall issue, but upon probable cause, supported by oath or affirmation, and particularly describing the place to be searched, and the persons or things to be seized.'

And the Fifth:

'No person * * * shall be compelled in any criminal case to be a witness against himself.'

It will be helpful to consider the chief cases in this court which bear upon the construction of these amendments. [The Court discusses *Boyd* and *Weeks*.]

In Silverthorne Lumber Co. v. United States, 251 U. S. 385, the defendants were arrested at their homes and detained in custody. While so detained, representatives of the government without authority went to the office of their company and seized all the books, papers, and documents found there. An application for return of the things was opposed by the district attorney, who produced a subpoena for certain documents relating to the charge in the indictment then on file. The court said:

'Thus the case is not that of knowledge acquired through the wrongful act of a stranger, but it must be assumed that the government planned or at all events ratified the whole performance.'

And it held that the illegal character of the original seizure characterized the entire proceeding and under the Weeks Case the seized papers must be restored.

In Amos v. United States, 255 U. S. 313, the defendant was convicted of concealing whisky on which the tax had not been paid. At the trial he presented a petition asking that private property seized in a search of his house and store 'within his curtilage' without warrant should be returned. This was denied. A woman, who claimed to be his wife, was told by the revenue officers that they had come to search the premises for violation of the revenue law. She opened the door; they entered and found whisky. Further searches in the house disclosed more. It was held that this action constituted a violation of the Fourth Amendment, and that the denial of the motion to restore the whisky and to exclude the testimony was error.

In Gouled v. United States, 255 U. S. 298, the facts were these: Gouled and two others were charged with conspiracy to defraud the United States. One pleaded guilty and another was acquitted. Gouled prosecuted error. The matter was presented here on questions propounded by the lower court. The first related to the admission in evidence of a paper surreptitiously taken from the office of the defendant by one acting under the direction of an officer of the Intelligence Department of the Army of the United States. Gouled was suspected of the crime. A private in the United States Army, pretending to make a friendly call on him, gained admission to his office, and in his absence, without warrant of any character, seized and carried away several documents. One of these, belonging to Gouled, was delivered to the United States attorney and by him introduced in evidence. When produced it was a surprise to the defendant. He had had no opportunity to make a previous motion to secure a return of it. The paper had no pecuniary value, but was relevant to the issue made on the trial. Admission of the paper was considered a violation of the Fourth Amendment.

Agnello v. United States, 269 U. S. 20, held that the Fourth and Fifth Amendments were violated by admission in evidence of contraband narcotics found in defendant's house, several blocks distant from the place of arrest, after his arrest and seized there without a warrant. Under such circumstances the seizure could not be justified as incidental to the arrest.

There is no room in the present case for applying the Fifth Amendment, unless the Fourth Amendment was first violated. There was no evidence of compulsion to induce the defendants to talk over their many telephones. They were continually and voluntarily transacting business without knowledge of the interception. Our consideration must be confined to the Fourth Amendment.

The striking outcome of the Weeks Case and those which followed it was the sweeping declaration that the Fourth Amendment, although not referring to or limiting the use of evidence in court, really forbade its introduction, if obtained by government officers through a violation of the amendment. Theretofore many had supposed that under the ordinary common-law rules, if the tendered evidence was pertinent, the method of obtaining it was unimportant. This was held by the Supreme Judicial Court of Massachusetts in Commonwealth v. Dana, 2 Metc. 329, 337. There it was ruled that the only remedy open to a defendant whose rights under a state constitutional equivalent of the Fourth Amendment had been invaded was by suit and judgment for damages, as Lord Camden held in Entick v. Carrington, 19 Howell, State Trials, 1029. Mr. Justice Bradley made effective use of this case in *Boyd v. United States*. But in the Weeks Case, and those which followed, this court decided with great emphasis and established as the law for the federal courts that the protection of the Fourth Amendment would be much impaired, unless it was held that not only was the official violator of the rights under the amendment subject to action at the suit of the injured defendant, but also that the evidence thereby obtained could not be received.

The well-known historical purpose of the Fourth Amendment, directed against general warrants and writs of assistance, was to prevent the use of governmental force to search a man's house, his person, his papers, and his effects, and to prevent their seizure against his will. This phase of the misuse of governmental power of compulsion is the emphasis of the opinion of the court in the Boyd Case. This appears, too, in the Weeks Case, in the Silverthorne Case, and in the Amos Case.

Gouled v. United States carried the inhibition against unreasonable searches and seizures to the extreme limit. Its authority is not to be enlarged by implication, and must be confined to the precise state of facts disclosed by the record. A representative of the Intelligence Department of the Army, having by stealth obtained admission to the defendant's office, seized and carried away certain private papers valuable for evidential purposes. This was held an unreasonable search and seizure within the Fourth Amendment. A stealthy entrance in such circumstances became the equivalent to an entry by force. There was actual entrance into the private quarters of defendant and the taking away of something tangible. Here we have testimony only of voluntary conversations secretly overheard.

The amendment itself shows that the search is to be of material things-the person, the house, his papers, or his effects. The description of the warrant necessary to make the proceeding lawful is that it must specify the place to be searched and the person or things to be seized.

It is urged that the language of Mr. Justice Field in *Ex parte Jackson*, already quoted, offers an analogy to the interpretation of the Fourth Amendment in respect of wire tapping. But the analogy fails. The Fourth Amendment may have proper application to a sealed letter in the mail, because of the constitutional provision for the Post Office Department and the relations between the government and those who pay to secure protection of their sealed letters. *See* Revised Statutes, ss 3978 to 3988, whereby Congress monopolizes the carriage of letters and excludes from that business everyone else, and section 3929 (39 USCA s 259), which forbids any postmaster or other person to open any letter not addressed to himself. It is plainly within the words of the amendment to say that the unlawful rifling by a government agent of a sealed letter is a search and seizure of the sender's papers or effects. The letter is a paper, an effect, and in the custody of a government that forbids carriage, except under its protection.

The United States takes no such care of telegraph or telephone messages as of mailed sealed letters. The amendment does not forbid what was done here. There was no searching. There was no seizure. The evidence was secured by the use of the sense of hearing and that only. There was no entry of the houses or offices of the defendants.

By the invention of the telephone 50 years ago, and its application for the purpose of extending communications, one can talk with another at a far distant place.

The language of the amendment cannot be extended and expanded to include telephone wires, reaching to the whole world from the defendant's house or office. The intervening wires are not part of his house or office, any more than are the highways along which they are stretched. . . .

Justice Bradley, in the Boyd Case, and Justice Clarke, in the Gouled Case, said that the Fifth Amendment and the Fourth Amendment were to be liberally construed to effect the purpose of the framers of the Constitution in the interest of liberty. But that cannot justify enlargement of the language employed beyond the possible practical meaning of houses, persons, papers, and effects, or so to apply the words search and seizure as to forbid hearing or sight.

Hester v. United States, 265 U. S. 57, held that the testimony of two officers of the law who trespassed on the defendant's land, concealed themselves 100 yards away from his house, and saw him come out and hand a bottle of whisky to another, was not inadmissible. While there was a trespass, there was no search of person, house, papers, or effects.

Congress may, of course, protect the secrecy of telephone messages by making them, when intercepted, inadmissible in evidence in federal criminal trials, by direct legislation, and thus depart from the common law of evidence. But the courts may not adopt such a policy by attributing an enlarged and unusual meaning to the Fourth Amendment. The reasonable view is that one who installs in his house a telephone instrument with connecting wires intends to project his voice to those quite outside, and that the wires beyond his house, and messages while passing over them, are not within the protection of the Fourth Amendment. Here those who intercepted the projected voices were not in the house of either party to the conversation.

Neither the cases we have cited nor any of the many federal decisions brought to our attention hold the Fourth Amendment to have been violated as against a defendant, unless there has been an official search and seizure of his person or such a seizure of his papers or his tangible material effects or an actual physical invasion of his house 'or curtilage' for the purpose of making a seizure.

We think, therefore, that the wire tapping here disclosed did not amount to a search or seizure within the meaning of the Fourth Amendment.

What has been said disposes of the only question that comes within the terms of our order granting certiorari in these cases. But some of our number, departing from that order, have concluded that there is merit in the twofold objection, overruled in both courts below, that evidence obtained through intercepting of telephone messages by a government agents was inadmissible, because the mode of obtaining it was unethical and a misdemeanor under the law of Washington. To avoid any misapprehension of our views of that objection we shall deal with it in both of its phases. . . .

The common-law rule is that the admissibility of evidence is not affected by the illegality of the means by which it was obtained. Professor Greenleaf, in his work on Evidence (volume 1 (12th Ed., by Redfield) s 254(a)), says:

'It may be mentioned in this place, that though papers and other subjects of evidence may have been illegally taken from the possession of the party against whom they are offered, or otherwise unlawfully obtained, this is no valid objection to their admissibility, if they are pertinent to the issue. The court will not take notice how they were obtained, whether lawfully or unlawfully, nor will it form an issue, to determine that question.'

Mr. Jones, in his work on the same subject, refers to Mr. Greenleaf's statement, and says:

'Where there is no violation of a constitutional guaranty, the verity of the above statement is absolute.' Section 2075, note 3, vol. 5.

The rule is supported by many English and American cases cited by Jones in section 2075, note 3, and section 2076, note 6, vol. 5; and by Wigmore, vol. 4, s 2183. It is recognized by this court in Adams v. New York, 192 U. S. 585. The Weeks Case announced an exception to the common law rule by excluding all evidence in the procuring of which government officials took part by methods forbidden by the Fourth and Fifth Amendments. Many state courts do not follow the Weeks Case. People v. Defore, 242 N. Y. 13, 150 N. E. 585. But those who do treat it as an exception to the general common-law rule and required by constitutional limitations. Hughes v. State, 145 Tenn. 544, 551, 566, 238 S. W. 588, 20 A. L. R. 639; State v. Wills, 91 W. Va. 659, 677, 114 S. E. 261, 24 A. L. R. 1398; State v. Slamon, 73 Vt. 212, 214, 215, 50 A. 1097, 87 Am. St. Rep. 711; Gindrat v. People, 138 Ill. 103, 111, 27 N. E. 1085; People v. Castree, 311 Ill. 392, 396, 397, 143 N. E. 112, 32 A. L. R. 357; State v. Gardner, 77 Mont. 8, 21, 249 P. 574, 52 A. L. R. 454; State v. Fahn, 53 N. D. 203, 210, 205 N. W. 67. The common-law rule must apply in the case at bar.

Nor can we, without the sanction of congressional enactment, subscribe to the suggestion that the courts have a discretion to exclude evidence, the admission of which is not unconstitutional, because unethically secured. This would be at variance with the common-law doctrine generally supported by authority. There is no case that sustains, nor any recognized text-book that gives color to, such a view. Our general experience shows that much evidence has always been receivable, although not obtained by conformity to the highest ethics. The history of criminal trials shows numerous cases of prosecutions of oathbound conspiracies for murder, robbery, and other crimes, where officers of the law have disguised themselves and joined the organizations, taken the oaths, and given themselves every appearance of active members engaged in the promotion of crime for the purpose of securing evidence. Evidence secured by such means has always been received.

A standard which would forbid the reception of evidence, if obtained by other than nice ethical conduct by government officials, would make society suffer and give criminals greater immunity than has been known heretofore. In the absence of controlling legislation by Congress, those who realize the difficulties in bringing offenders to justice may well deem it wise that the exclusion of evidence should be confined to cases where rights under the Constitution would be violated by admitting it.

The statute of Washington, adopted in 1909, provides (Remington Compiled Statutes 1922, s 2656(18) that:

'Every person * * * who shall intercept, read or in any manner interrupt or delay the sending of a message over any telegraph or telephone line * * * shall be guilty of a misdemeanor.'

This statute does not declare that evidence obtained by such interception shall be inadmissible, and by the common law, already referred to, it would not be. People v. McDonald, 177 App. Div. 806, 165 N. Y. S. 41. Whether the state of Washington may prosecute and punish federal officers violating this law, and those whose messages were intercepted may sue them civilly, is not before us. But clearly a statute, passed 20 years after the admission of the state into the Union, cannot affect the rules of evidence applicable in courts of the United States. Chief Justice Taney, in United States v. Reid, 12 How. 361, 363 (13 L. Ed. 1023), construing the thirty-fourth section of the Judiciary Act (now 28 USCA s 77), said:

'But it could not be supposed, without very plain words to show it, that Congress intended to give to the states the power of prescribing the rules of evidence in trials for offenses against the United States. For this construction would in effect place the criminal jurisprudence of one sovereignty under the control of another.'

The judgments of the Circuit Court of Appeals are affirmed. The mandates will go down forthwith under rule 31.

Affirmed.

■ MR. JUSTICE BRANDEIS (dissenting).

. . . 'We must never forget,' said Mr. Chief Justice Marshall in McCulloch v. Maryland, 4 Wheat. 316, 407 4 L. Ed. 579, 'that it is a Constitution we are expounding.' Since then this court has repeatedly sustained the exercise of power by Congress, under various clauses of that instrument, over objects of which the fathers could not have dreamed. We have likewise held that general limitations on the powers of government, like those embodied in the due process clauses of the Fifth and Fourteenth Amendments, do not forbid the United States or the states from meeting modern conditions by regulations which 'a century ago, or even half a century ago, probably would have been rejected as arbitrary and oppressive.' Village of Euclid v. Ambler Realty Co., 272 U. S. 365, 387; Buck v. Bell, 274 U. S. 200. Clauses guaranteeing to the individual protection against specific abuses of power, must have a similar capacity of adaptation to a changing world. . . .

When the Fourth and Fifth Amendments were adopted, 'the form that evil had theretofore taken' had been necessarily simple. Force and violence were then the only means known to man by which a government could directly effect self-incrimination. It could compel the individual to testify-a compulsion effected, if need be, by torture. It could secure possession of his papers and other articles incident to his private life-a seizure effected, if need be, by breaking and entry. Protection against such invasion of 'the sanctities of a man's home and the privacies of life' was provided in the Fourth and Fifth Amendments by specific language. Boyd v. United States, 116 U. S. 616, 630. But 'time works changes, brings into existence new conditions and purposes.' Subtler and more far-reaching means of invading privacy have become available to the government. Discovery and invention have made it possible for the government, by means far more effective than stretching upon the rack, to obtain disclosure in court of what is whispered in the closet.

Moreover, 'in the application of a Constitution, our contemplation cannot be only of what has been, but of what may be.' The progress of science in furnishing the government with means of espionage is not likely to stop with wire tapping. Ways may some day be developed by which the government, without removing papers from secret drawers, can reproduce them in court, and by which it will be enabled to expose to a jury the most intimate occurrences of the home. Advances in the psychic and related sciences may bring means of exploring unexpressed beliefs, thoughts and emotions. 'That places the liberty of every man in the hands of every petty officer' was said by James Otis of much lesser intrusions than these. To Lord Camden a far slighter intrusion seemed 'subversive of all the comforts of society.' Can it be that the Constitution affords no protection against such invasions of individual security?

A sufficient answer is found in Boyd v. United States, 116 U. S. 616, 627–630, a case that will be remembered as long as civil liberty lives in the United States. . . .

In Ex parte Jackson, 96 U. S. 727, 24 L. Ed. 877, it was held that a sealed letter intrusted to the mail is protected by the amendments. The mail is a public service furnished by the government. The telephone is a public service furnished by its authority. There is, in essence, no difference between the sealed letter and the private telephone message. . . . .

The evil incident to invasion of the privacy of the telephone is far greater than that involved in tampering with the mails. Whenever a telephone line is tapped, the privacy of the persons at both ends of the line is invaded, and all conversations between them upon any subject, and although proper, confidential, and privileged, may be overheard. Moreover, the tapping of one man's telephone line involves the tapping of the telephone of every other person whom he may call, or who may call him. As a means of espionage, writs of assistance and general warrants are but puny instruments of tyranny and oppression when compared with wire tapping.

Time and again this court, in giving effect to the principle underlying the Fourth Amendment, has refused to place an unduly literal construction upon it. This was notably illustrated in the Boyd Case itself. Taking language in its ordinary meaning, there is no 'search' or 'seizure' when a defendant is required to produce a document in the orderly process of a court's procedure. 'The right of the people to be secure in their persons, houses, papers, and effects, against unreasonable searches and seizures,' would not be violated, under any ordinary construction of language, by compelling obedience to a subpoena. But this court holds the evidence inadmissible simply because the information leading to the issue of the subpoena has been unlawfully secured. . . .

The provision against self-incrimination in the Fifth Amendment has been given an equally broad construction. The language is:

'No person * * * shall be compelled in any criminal case to be a witness against himself.'

Yet we have held not only that the protection of the amendment extends to a witness before a grand jury, although he has not been charged with crime (Counselman v. Hitchcock, 142 U. S. 547, 562), but that:

'It applies alike to civil and criminal proceedings, wherever the answer might tend to subject to criminal responsibility him who gives it. The privilege protects a mere witness as fully as it does one who is also a party defendant.' McCarthy v. Arndstein, 266 U. S. 34, 40.

The narrow language of the Amendment has been consistently construed in the light of its object, 'to insure that a person should not be compelled, when acting as a witness in any investigation, to give testimony which might tend to show that he himself had committed a crime. The privilege is limited to criminal matters, but it is as broad as the mischief against which it seeks to guard.' Counselman v. Hitchcock, supra, page 562.

Decisions of this court applying the principle of the Boyd Case have settled these things. Unjustified search and seizure violates the Fourth Amendment, whatever the character of the paper; whether the paper when taken by the federal officers was in the home, in an office, or elsewhere; whether the taking was effected by force, by fraud, or in the orderly process of a court's procedure. From these decisions, it follows necessarily that the amendment is violated by the officer's reading the paper without a physical seizure, without his even touching it, and that use, in any criminal proceeding, of the contents of the paper so examined-as where they are testified to by a federal officer who thus saw the document or where, through knowledge so obtained, a copy has been procured. . . .

The makers of our Constitution undertook to secure conditions favorable to the pursuit of happiness. They recognized the significance of man's spiritual nature, of his feelings and of his intellect. They knew that only a part of the pain, pleasure and satisfactions of life are to be found in material things. They sought to protect Americans in their beliefs, their thoughts, their emotions and their sensations. They conferred, as against the government, the right to be let alone-the most comprehensive of rights and the right most valued by civilized men. To protect, that right, every unjustifiable intrusion by the government upon the privacy of the individual, whatever the means employed, must be deemed a violation of the Fourth Amendment. And the use, as evidence in a criminal proceeding, of facts ascertained by such intrusion must be deemed a violation of the Fifth.

Applying to the Fourth and Fifth Amendments the established rule of construction, the defendants' objections to the evidence obtained by wire tapping must, in my opinion, be sustained. It is, of course, immaterial where the physical connection with the telephone wires leading into the defendants' premises was made. And it is also immaterial that the intrusion was in aid of law enforcement. Experience should teach us to be most on our guard to protect liberty when the government's purposes are beneficent. Men born to freedom are naturally alert to repel invasion of their liberty by evil-minded rulers. The greatest dangers to liberty lurk in insidious encroachment by men of zeal, well-meaning but without understanding.

The Eighteenth Amendment has not in terms empowered Congress to authorize any one to violate the criminal laws of a state. And Congress has never purported to do so. Compare Maryland v. Soper, 270 U. S. 9. The terms of appointment of federal prohibition agents do not purport to confer upon them authority to violate any criminal law. Their superior officer, the Secretary of the Treasury, has not instructed them to commit crime on behalf of the United States. It may be assumed that the Attorney General of the United States did not give any such instruction.

Will this court, by sustaining the judgment below, sanction such conduct on the part of the executive? The governing principle has long been settled. It is that a court will not redress a wrong when he who invokes its aid has unclean hands. The maxim of unclean hands comes from courts of equity. But the principle prevails also in courts of law. Its common application is in civil actions between private parties. Where the government is the actor, the reasons for applying it are even more persuasive. Where the remedies invoked are those of the criminal law, the reasons are compelling.

The door of a court is not barred because the plaintiff has committed a crime. The confirmed criminal is as much entitled to redress as his most virtuous fellow citizen; no record of crime, however long, makes one an outlaw. The court's aid is denied only when he who seeks it has violated the law in connection with the very transaction as to which he seeks legal redress. Then aid is denied despite the defendant's wrong. It is denied in order to maintain respect for law; in order to promote confidence in the administration of justice; in order to preserve the judicial process from contamination. The rule is one, not of action, but of inaction. It is sometimes spoken of as a rule of substantive law. But it extends to matters of procedure as well. A defense may be waived. It is waived when not pleaded. But the objection that the plaintiff comes with unclean hands will be taken by the court itself. It will be taken despite the wish to the contrary of all the parties to the litigation. The court protects itself.

Decency, security, and liberty alike demand that government officials shall be subjected to the same rules of conduct that are commands to the citizen. In a government of laws, existence of the government will be imperiled if it fails to observe the law scrupulously. Our government is the potent, the omnipresent teacher. For good or for ill, it teaches the whole people by its example. Crime is contagious. If the government becomes a lawbreaker, it breeds contempt for law; it invites every man to become a law unto himself; it invites anarchy. To declare that in the administration of the criminal law the end justifies the means-to declare that the government may commit crimes in order to secure the conviction of a private criminal-would bring terrible retribution. Against that pernicious doctrine this court should resolutely set its face.

■ MR. JUSTICE HOLMES.

My brother BRANDEIS has given this case so exhaustive an examination that I desire to add but a few words. While I do not deny it I am not prepared to say that the penumbra of the Fourth and Fifth Amendments covers the defendant, although I fully agree that courts are apt to err by sticking too closely to the words of a law where those words import a policy that goes beyond them. But I think, as Mr. Justice BRANDEIS says, that apart from the Constitution the government ought not to use evidence obtained and only obtainable by a criminal act. There is no body of precedents by which we are bound, and which confines us to logical deduction from established rules. Therefore we must consider the two objects of desire both of which we cannot have and make up our minds which to choose. It is desirable that criminals should be detected, and to that end that all available evidence should be used. It also is desirable that the government should not itself foster and pay for other crimes, when they are the means by which the evidence is to be obtained. If it pays its officers for having got evidence by crime I do not see why it may not as well pay them for getting it in the same way, and I can attach no importance to protestations of disapproval if it knowingly accepts and pays and announces that in future it will pay for the fruits. We have to choose, and for my part I think it a less evil that some criminals should escape than that the government should play an ignoble part.

For those who agree with me no distinction can be taken between the government as prosecutor and the government as judge. If the existing code does not permit district attorneys to have a hand in such dirty business it does not permit the judge to allow such iniquities to succeed. *See* Silverthorne Lumber Co. v. United States, 251 U. S. 385. And if all that I have said so far be accepted it makes no difference that in this case wire tapping is made a crime by the law of the state, not by the law of the United States. It is true that a state cannot make rules of evidence for courts of the United States, but the state has authority over the conduct in question, and I hardly think that the United States would appear to greater advantage when paying for an odious crime against state law than when inciting to the disregard of its own. I am aware of the often-repeated statement that in a criminal proceeding the court will not take notice of the manner in which papers offered in evidence have been obtained. But that somewhat rudimentary mode of disposing of the question has been overthrown by *Weeks v. United States* and the cases that have followed it. I have said that we are free to choose between two principles of policy. But if we are to confine ourselves to precedent and logic the reason for excluding evidence obtained by violating the Constitution seems to me logically to lead to excluding evidence obtained by a crime of the officers of the law.

4. SEARCH AND SEIZURE IN THE STATES

People v. Defore
242 N.Y. 13 (1926)

■ CARDOZO, J.

A police officer arrested the defendant on a charge that he had stolen an overcoat. The crime, if committed, was petit larceny, a misdemeanor, for the value of the coat was not over $50. Penal Law, §§ 1296, 1298; Cons. Laws, c. 40. The defendant, when taken into custody, was in the hall of his boarding house. The officer, after making the arrest, entered the defendant's room and searched it. The search produced a bag, and in the bag was a blackjack. The defendant, after trial at Special Sessions, was acquitted of the larceny. In the meantime he had been indicted as a second offender for the possession of the weapon. Penal Law, § 1897. He made a motion before trial to suppress the evidence obtained through search without a warrant. The motion was denied. He made objection again upon the trial when the bag and the contents, i.e., the blackjack and a hat, were offered in evidence by the people. The objection was overruled. He contends that through these rulings he has suffered a denial of his rights under the statute against unreasonable search and seizure (Civil Rights Law, § 8; Cons. Laws, c. 6); a denial of his rights under the provision of the state Constitution which gives immunity against compulsory self-incrimination (Const. art. 1, § 6); and a denial of his rights under the due process clause of the Fourteenth Amendment to the Constitution of the United States.

(1) The search was unreasonable 'in the light of common-law traditions.' People v. Chiagles, 142 N. E. 583, 237 N. Y. 193, 32 A. L. R. 676. A different conclusion might be necessary if the defendant had been lawfully arrested. As an incident to such an arrest, his person might have been searched for the fruits or evidences of crime. *People v. Chiagles, supra*; Carroll v. U. S., 267 U. S. 132, 158. So, it seems, might the place where the arrest was made. Agnello v. U. S., decided October 12, 1925, 46 S. Ct. 4; People v. Cona, 147 N. W. 525, 180 Mich. 641. But the arrest was not lawful. One who, acting without a warrant, arrests for a misdemeanor exceeds the bounds of privilege, whether he be a private person or an officer, unless the crime has been committed or attempted in his presence. Code Cr. Proc. §§ 177, 183. The defendant had neither committed the crime of petit larceny in the presence of the officer nor there attempted to commit it. He had not committed nor attempted it anywhere. There was no lawful arrest to which the search could be an incident.

The people stress the fact that the weapon was contraband, a nuisance subject to destruction. Penal Law, §§ 1899. This might have justified the seizure, the abatement of the nuisance, if the weapon had been exposed to view. It might even have justified the refusal to return the weapon, though discovered by unlawful means. It did not justify the search. There is no rule that homes may be ransacked without process to discover the fruits or the implements of crime. To make such inquisitions lawful, there must be the support of a search warrant issued upon probable cause. Search even then is 'confined under our statute [Code Cr. Proc. § 792] to property stolen or embezzled, or used as the means of committing a felony, or held with the intent to use it as an instrument of crime.' *People v. Chiagles, supra*, at page 196 (142 N. E. 584); People ex rel. Robert Simpson Co. v. Kempner, 101 N. E. 794, 208 N. Y. 16, 46 L. R. A. (N. S.) 970, Ann. Cas. 1914D, 169. The warrant does not issue for things of evidential value merely. *People v. Chiagles, supra*; cf. Gouled v. U. S., 255 U. S. 298; Matter of No. 191 Front Street, Borough of Manhattan, City of New York (C. C. A.) 5 F.(2d) 282; Veeder v. U. S., 252 F. 414, 164 C. C. A. 338. What would be a wrong with a warrant is not innocent without one. To dispense with process in the pursuit of contraband is to dispense with it in the one case in which it may ever issue in the pursuit of anything. Means unlawful in their inception do not become lawful by relation when suspicion ripens into discovery.

We hold, then, with the defendant that the evidence against him was the outcome of a trespass. The officer might have been resisted, or sued for damages, or even prosecuted for oppression. Penal Law, §§ 1846, 1847. He was subject to removal or other discipline at the hands of his superiors. These consequences are undisputed. The defendant would add another. We must determine whether evidence of criminality, procured by an act of trespass, is to be rejected as incompetent for the misconduct of the trespasser.

The question is not a new one. It was put to us more than 20 years ago in People v. Adams, 68 N. E. 636, 176 N. Y. 351, 63 L. R. A. 406, 98 Am. St. Rep. 675, and there deliberately answered. A search warrant had been issued against the proprietor of a gambling house for the seizure of gambling implements. The police did not confine themselves to the things stated in the warrant. Without authority of law, they seized the defendant's books and papers. We held that the documents did not cease to be competent evidence against him though the seizure was unlawful.

In support of that holding, we cited many authorities, and notably a series of decisions by the courts of Massachusetts.

'A trespasser may testify to pertinent facts observed by him, or may put in evidence pertinent articles or papers found by him while trespassing. For the trespass he may be held responsible civilly, and perhaps criminally; but his testimony is not thereby rendered incompetent.' Commonwealth v. Tibbetts, 32 N. E. 910, 157 Mass. 519.

On appeal to the Supreme Court, the judgment was affirmed. Adams v. People of State of New York, 192 U. S. 585.

The ruling thus broadly made is decisive, while it stands, of the case before us now. It is at variance, however, with later judgments of the Supreme Court of the United States. Those judgments do not bind us, for they construe provisions of the federal Constitution, the Fourth and Fifth Amendments, not applicable to the states. Even though not binding, they merit our attentive scrutiny. Weeks v. United States, 232 U. S. 383, held that articles wrongfully seized by agents of the federal government should have been returned to the defendant or excluded as evidence, if a timely motion to compel return had been made before the trial. Silverthorne Lumber Co. v. United States, 251 U. S. 385, held that copies of the things so seized, in that case books and papers, must share the fate of the originals. Gouled v. United States, 255 U. S. 298, and Amos v. United States, 255 U. S. 313, held that a motion before trial was unnecessary if the defendant had no knowledge until the trial that an illegal seizure had been made. Burdeau v. McDowell, 256 U. S. 465, held that a federal prosecutor might make such use as he pleased of documents or other information acquired from a trespasser, if persons other than federal officers were guilty of the trespass. Hester v. United States, 265 U. S. 57, and Carroll v. United States, 267 U. S. 132, drew a distinction between search and seizure in a house and search and seizure in the fields or in automobiles or other vehicles. Finally Agnello v. United States, 267 U.S. 132, held that the evidence must be excluded, though the things seized were contraband, and though there had been no motion before trial if the facts were undisputed. This means that the Supreme Court has overruled its own judgment in *Adams v. People of State of New York,* for the facts were undisputed there. The procedural condition of a preliminary motion has been substantially abandoned, or, if now enforced at all, is an exceptional requirement. There has been no blinking the consequences. The criminal is to go free because the constable has blundered.

The new doctrine has already met the scrutiny of courts of sister states. The decisions have been brought together for our guidance through the industry of counsel. In 45 states (exclusive of our own) the subject has been considered. Fourteen states have adopted the rule of the Weeks Case either as there laid down or as subsequently broadened. Thirty-one have rejected it. Typical among these are Massachusetts (Commonwealth v. Wilkins, 138 N. E. 11, 243 Mass. 356; Commonwealth v. Donnelly, 141 N. E. 500, 246 Mass. 507); California (People v. Mayen, 205 P. 435, 188 Cal. 237, 24 A. L. R. 1383); Connecticut (State v. Reynolds, 125 A. 636, 101 Conn. 224); Ohio (Rosanski v. State, 140 N. E. 370, 106 Ohio St. 442); Kansas (State v. Johnson, 226 P. 245, 116 Kan. 58; *Id.,* 226 P. 251, 116 Kan. 179); Iowa (State v. Rowley, 195 N. W. 881, 197 Iowa, 977, 979); and Virginia (Hall v. Commonwealth, 121 S. E. 154, 138 Va. 727). To what is there written, little of value can be added. The controversy, starting with the courts, has been taken up by the commentators, and with them has been the theme of animated argument. For the most part, there has been adherence to the older doctrine. 4 Wigmore on Evidence (2d Ed.) §§ 2183, 2184; Harno, *Evidence Obtained by Illegal Search and Seizure,* 19 Ill. Law Rev. 303; Knox, *Selfincrimination,* 74 Penn. Law Rev. 139; Fraenkel, *Concerning Searches and Seizures,* 34 Harv. L. R. 361, 386; *contra,* Chafee, *The Progress of the Law,* 35 Harv. Law Rev. 673, 694; Atkinson, *Unreasonable Searches & Seizures,* 25 Col. Law. Rev. 11. With authority thus divided, it is only some overmastering consideration of principle or of policy that should move us to a change. The balance is not swayed until something more persuasive than uncertainty is added to the scales.

We find nothing in the statute (Civil Rights Law, § 8) whereby official trespasses and private are differentiated in respect of the legal consequences to follow them. All that the statute does is to place the two on an equality. In times gone by, officialdom had arrogated to itself a privilege of indiscriminate inquisition. The statute declares that the privilege shall not exist. Thereafter, all alike, whenever search is unreasonable, must answer to the law. For the high intruder and the low, the consequences become the same. Evidence is not excluded because the private litigant who offers it has gathered it by lawless force. By the same token, the state, when prosecuting an offender against the peace and order of society, incurs no heavier liability.

The federal rule as it stands is either too strict or too lax. A federal prosecutor may take no benefit from evidence collected through the trespass of a federal officer. The thought is that, in appropriating the results, he ratifies the means. Essgee Co. of China v. United States, 262 U. S. 151, 156. He does not have to be so scrupulous about evidence brought to him by others. How finely the line is drawn is seen when we recall that marshals in the service of the nation are on one side of it, and police in the service of the states on the other. The nation may keep what the servants of the states supply. *Weeks v. United States, supra*, at page 398; Schroeder v. United States (C. C. A.) 7 F. (2d) 60; U. S. v. One Ford Coupé (D. C.) 3 F.(2d) 64. We must go farther or not so far. The professed object of the trespass rather than the official character of the trespasser should test the rights of government. Dempsey v. Chambers, 28 N. E. 279, 154 Mass. 330, 13 L. R. A. 219, 26 Am. St. Rep. 249. The incongruity of other tests gains emphasis from the facts of the case before us. The complainant, the owner of the overcoat, co-operated with the officer in the arrest and the attendant search. Their powers were equal, since the charge was petit larceny, a misdemeanor. Code Cr. Proc. §§ 177, 183. If one spoke or acted for the state, so also did the other. A government would be disingenuous, if, in determining the use that should be made of evidence drawn from such a source, it drew a line between them. This would be true whether they had acted in concert or apart. We exalt form above substance when we hold that the use is made lawful because the intruder is without a badge of office. We break with precedent altogether when we press the prohibition farther.

The truth, indeed, is that the statute says nothing about consequences. It does no more than deny a privilege. Denying this, it stops. Intrusion without privilege has certain liabilities and penalties. The statute does not assume to alter or increase them. . . .

We are confirmed in this conclusion when we reflect how far-reaching in its effect upon society the new consequences would be. The pettiest peace officer would have it in his power, through overzeal or indiscretion, to confer immunity upon an offender for crimes the most flagitious. A room is searched against the law, and the body of a murdered man is found. If the place of discovery may not be proved, the other circumstances may be insufficient to connect the defendant with the crime. The privacy of the home has been infringed, and the murderer goes free. Another search, once more against the law, discloses counterfeit money or the implements of forgery. The absence of a warrant means the freedom of the forger. Like instances can be multiplied. We may not subject society to these dangers until the Legislature has spoken with a clearer voice. In so holding, we are not unmindful of the argument that, unless the evidence is excluded, the statute becomes a form and its protection an illusion. This has a strange sound when the immunity is viewed in the light of its origin and history. The rule now embodied in the statute was received into English law as the outcome of the prosecution of Wilkes and Entick. *People v. Chiagles, supra.* Wilkes sued the messengers who had ransacked his papers, and recovered a verdict of £ 4,000 against one and £1,000 against the other. Entick, too, had a substantial verdict. Boyd v. United States, 116 U. S. 616, at p. 626; Entick v. Carrington, 19 Howell, State Trials, 1030; Fraenkel, *Concerning Searches and Seizures,* 34 Harv. Law Rev. 363, 364, and cases cited. We do not know whether the public, represented by its juries, is to-day more indifferent to its liberties than it was when the immunity was born. If so, the change of sentiment without more does not work a change of remedy. Other sanctions, penal and disciplinary, supplementing the right to damages, have already been enumerated. No doubt the protection of the statute would be greater from the point of view of the individual whose privacy had been invaded if the government were required to ignore what it had learned through the invasion. The question is whether protection for the individual would not be gained at a disproportionate loss of protection for society. On the one side is the social need that crime shall be repressed. On the other, the social need that law shall not be flouted by the insolence of office. There are dangers in any choice. The rule of the Adams Case strikes a balance between opposing interests. We must hold it to be the law until those organs of government by which a change of public policy is normally effected shall give notice to the courts that the change has come to pass.

(2) There remains a second claim of privilege. 'No person shall be * * * compelled in any criminal case to be a witness against himself.' New York Constitution, art. 1, § 6. This immunity, like the statutory one against unreasonable search and seizure, was considered in the Adams Case, 68 N. E. 636, 176 N. Y. 351, 359, 63 L. R. A. 406, 98 Am. St. Rep. 675. We limited it to cases where incriminatory disclosure had been extorted by the constraint of legal process directed against a witness. The Supreme Court agreed with us. Adams v. People of State of New York, 192 U. S. 585, 597, 598. Other courts (e. g., State v. Flynn, 36 N. H. 64; *Commonwealth v. Wilkins, supra*) and learned commentators (4 Wigmore, Evidence, §§ 2263, 2264) have taken the same ground. Unless that ruling is to be changed, the conclusion is not doubtful.

We put the question aside whether in some other situation differing from the one before us there may be need to qualify or soften a ruling so comprehensive. In putting it aside, we would not be understood as expressing, even by indirection, a belief that change is called for. Enough for present purposes to decide the case at hand. The weapon discovered through this search was an implement of crime. It was not the kind of thing to be protected against prying inquisition. It was a thing to be ferreted out and brought to light and, when found, wrested from the holder. Code Cr. Proc. § 792. There is no relation in such circumstances between the absence of a search warrant and the constitutional immunity against involuntary disclosure. The production of the weapon would have been just as incriminatory and just as involuntary if a warrant had been issued. The law, in providing for the warrant, does not proceed upon the theory that the defendant will thereby be protected against disclosing his own crime. On the contrary, the very object of the warrant is to compel him to disclose it. Things outlawed or contraband, possessed without right, and subject upon seizure to forfeiture or destruction, may be offered in evidence without trenching upon the privilege in respect of self-incrimination whether seizure has been made with warrant or without.

Federal decisions until *Agnello v. United* States (*supra*) kept the two immunities (those of the Fourth and Fifth Amendments) distinct, even though sometimes overlapping. The distinction was of diminishing importance, for evidence was excluded for violation of the one almost as much as for violation of the other. None the less, the seizure of things contraband as the outcome of an unlawful search was classified for many years as a violation of the Fourth Amendment only. The Fifth was not infringed, unless the seizure had relation to things innocent in themselves, but supplying evidence of guilt, such as a defendant's books and papers. *Boyd v. United States, supra*; *Gouled v. United States, supra*; cf. United States v. Welsh (D. C.) 247 F. 239. We are uncertain whether *Agnello v. United States* (*supra*), has abandoned this distinction. What was said as to the Fifth Amendment was not essential to the decision. The result would have been the same though the Fourth only had been applied. We must follow our own rule.

The defendant makes the point that, though the blackjack was contraband, the bag and hat were not. Error in admitting these in evidence, even if error were found, might be disregarded as harmless. But in truth the question is not here. All three articles were offered in evidence together. The objection did not discriminate between them. It was a general one to all alike. If any were admissible, the objection fails.

In this state of the record, we are not required to determine the application of the constitutional privilege to things lawfully possessed. We know that there are times when such things, not contraband at all, may be seized and placed in evidence. In this very case, if the overcoat had been worth $51, instead of $50 only, the arrest (for all that appears) would have been lawful, since the officer might arrest the defendant if a felony had been committed, and there was reasonable cause to believe that the defendant was the perpetrator. In that event, there might have been search of the place where the arrest was made to discover the fruits or even the evidences of larceny. *Agnello v. United States, supra*; People v. Cona, 147 N. W. 525, 180 Mich. 641. The use of things thus seized would be lawful in any ensuing prosecution (*People v. Chiagles, supra*), either for that crime or for another (Gouled v. U. S., *supra*, at page 311

[41 S. Ct. 261]), yet it would none the less be use against the will of the accused (*cf. Carroll v. United States, supra*). Seizure, whether legitimate or a trespass, is not voluntary surrender. There is strong support in this for the ruling of the Adams Case that force is not the test, but rather force accompanied by process aimed against a witness and compelling action on his part. *Cf.* 35 Harv. Law Rev. at page 698. In the words of Baker, J., writing for the Circuit Court of Appeals (Haywood v. United States, 268 F. 795, 802): "'Witness' is the keyword.' A defendant is 'protected from producing his documents in response to a subpoena duces tecum, for his production of them in court would be his voucher of their genuineness.' There would then be 'testimonial compulsion.' *Haywood v. U. S., supra.* The keyword is disregarded, however, when compulsion not testimonial is brought within the orbit of the privilege. People ex rel. Ferguson v. Reardon, 90 N. E. 829, 197 N. Y. 236, 27 L. R. A. (N. S.) 141, 134 Am. St. Rep. 871, went upon the theory that the inspection there permitted by a statute was in effect a proceeding for a discovery or an examination before trial. The distinctions are indeed close. But the line of division will not be drawn with finality till there is before us a record which requires us to trace it.

(3) As a last resort, the defendant invokes the Fourteenth Amendment and the requirement of 'due process.'

The Fourteenth Amendment would not be violated, though the privilege against self-incrimination were abolished altogether. Twining v. New Jersey, 211 U. S. 78; Banks v. State, 93 So. 293, 207 Ala. 179, 24 A. L. R. 1359; certiorari denied, 260 U. S. 736. The like must be true of the immunity against search and seizure without warrant in so far as that immunity has relation to the use of evidence thereafter. Comm. v. Donnelly 141 N. E. 550, 246 Mass, 507; *Banks v. State, supra.*

The judgment of conviction should be affirmed.

■ HISCOCK, C. J., and POUND, MCLAUGHLIN, CRANE, ANDREWS, and LEHMAN, JJ., concur.

Judgment affirmed.

Irvine v. California

347 U.S. 128 (1954)

■ MR. JUSTICE JACKSON announced the judgment of the Court and an opinion in which THE CHIEF JUSTICE, MR. JUSTICE REED and MR. JUSTICE MINTON join.

This case involves constitutional questions growing out of methods employed to convict petitioner on charges of horserace bookmaking and related offenses against the antigambling laws of California. Petitioner exhausted all avenues to relief under state procedures and then sought review here of duly raised federal issues.

We granted certiorari on a petition which tendered four questions. However, petitioner's counsel has now presented two additional questions, one concerning the application of an immunity statute of California and another attacking certain instructions given to the jury by the trial court. Neither of these was mentioned in the petition. We disapprove the practice of smuggling additional questions into a case after we grant certiorari. The issues here are fixed by the petition unless we limit the grant, as frequently we do to avoid settled, frivolous or state law questions. We do not take up the questions numbered 3 and 6 of petitioner's brief because they are improperly presented. . . .

But the questions raised by the officers' conduct while investigating this case are serious. The police strongly suspected petitioner of illegal bookmaking but were without proof of it. On December 1, 1951, while Irvine and his wife were absent from their home, an officer arranged to have a locksmith go there and make a door key. Two days later, again in the absence of occupants, officers and a technician made entry into the home by the use of this key and installed a concealed microphone in the hall. A hole was bored in the roof of the house and wires were strung to transmit to a neighboring garage whatever sounds the microphone might pick up. Officers were posted in the garage to listen. On December 8, police again made surreptitious entry and moved the microphone, this time hiding it in the bedroom. Twenty days later they again entered and placed the microphone in a closet, where the device remained until its purpose of enabling the officers to overhear incriminating statements was accomplished.

We should note that this is not a conventional instance of 'wire tapping.' Here the apparatus of the officers was not in any way connected with the telephone facilities, there was no interference with the communications system, there was no interception of any message. All that was heard through the microphone was what an eavesdropper, hidden in the hall, the bedroom, or the closet, might have heard. We do not suppose it is illegal to testify to what another person is heard to say merely because he is saying it into a telephone. We cannot sustain the contention that the conduct or reception of the evidence violated the Federal Communications Act. 48 Stat. 1103, 47 U.S.C. s 605, 47 U.S.C.A. s 605. Cf. Nardone v. United States, 308 U.S. 338; Schwartz v. State of Texas, 344 U.S. 199.

At the trial, officers were allowed to testify to conversations heard through their listening installations. The snatches of conversation which the prosecution thought useful were received in evidence. They were in the lingo of the race track and need not be recited, but the jury might well have regarded them as incriminating. The testimony was received under objection, properly raising the question that it was constitutionally inadmissible since obtained by methods which violate the Fourteenth Amendment.

Each of these repeated entries of petitioner's home without a search warrant or other process was a trespass, and probably a burglary, for which any unofficial person should be, and probably would be, severely punished. Science has perfected amplifying and recording devices to become frightening instruments of surveillance and invasion of privacy, whether by the policeman, the blackmailer, or the busy-body. That officers of the law would break and enter a home, secrete such a device, even in a bedroom, and listen to the conversation of the occupants for over a month would be almost incredible if it were not admitted. Few police measures have come to our attention that more flagrantly, deliberately, and persistently violated the fundamental principle declared by the Fourth Amendment as a restriction on the Federal Government that 'The right of the people to be secure in their persons, houses, papers, and effects, against unreasonable searches and seizures, shall not be violated, and no Warrants shall issue, but upon probable cause, supported by Oath or affirmation, and particularly describing the place to be searched, and the persons or things to be seized.' The decision in Wolf v. Colorado, 338 U.S. 25, for the first time established that '(t)he security of one's privacy against arbitrary intrusion by the police' is embodied in the concept of due process found in the Fourteenth Amendment.

But *Wolf*, for reasons set forth therein, declined to make the subsidiary procedural and evidentiary doctrines developed by the federal courts limitations on the states. On the contrary, it declared, 'We, hold, therefore, that in a prosecution in a State court for a State crime the Fourteenth Amendment does not forbid the admission of evidence obtained by an unreasonable search and seizure.' 338 U.S. 25, 33. *See* Stefanelli v. Minard, 342 U.S. 117, 119, 122. That holding would seem to control here.

An effort is made, however, to bring this case under the sway of Rochin v. People of California, 342 U.S. 165. That case involved, among other things, an illegal search of the defendant's person. But it also presented an element totally lacking here—coercion (as the Court noted, 342 U.S. at page 173), applied by a physical assault upon his person to compel submission to the use of a stomach pump. This was the feature which led to a result in *Rochin* contrary to that in *Wolf*. Although Rochin raised the search-and-seizure question, this Court studiously avoided it and never once mentioned the *Wolf* case. Obviously, it thought that illegal search and seizure alone did not call for reversal. However obnoxious are the facts in the case before us, they do not involve coercion, violence or brutality to the person, but rather a trespass to property, plus eavesdropping.

It is suggested, however, that although we affirmed the conviction in *Wolf*, we should reverse here because this invasion of privacy is more shocking, more offensive, than the one involved there. The opinions in *Wolf* were written entirely in the abstract and did not disclose the details of the constitutional violation. Actually, the search was offensive to the law in the same respect, if not the same degree, as here. A deputy sheriff and others went to a doctor's office without a warrant and seized his appointment book, searched through it to learn the names of all his patients, looked up and interrogated certain of them, and filed an information against the doctor on the information that the District Attorney had obtained from the books. The books also were introduced in evidence against the doctor at his trial.

We are urged to make inroads upon *Wolf* by holding that it applies only to searches and seizures which produce on our minds a mild shock, while if the shock is more serious, the states must exclude the evidence or we will reverse the conviction. We think that the *Wolf* decision should not be overruled, for the reasons so persuasively stated therein. We think, too, that a distinction of the kind urged would leave the rule so indefinite that no state court could know what it should rule in order to keep its processes on solid constitutional ground.

Even as to the substantive rule governing federal searches in violation of the Fourth Amendment, both the Court and individual Justices have wavered considerably. Compare Harris v. United States, 331 U.S. 145; Trupiano v. United States, 334 U.S. 699; United States v. Rabinowitz, 339 U.S. 56; Brinegar v. United States, 338 U.S. 160; Goldman v. United States, 316 U.S. 129; On Lee v. United States, 343 U.S. 747. Never until June of 1949 did this Court hold the basic search-and-seizure prohibition in any way applicable to the states under the Fourteenth Amendment. At that time, as we pointed out, thirty-one states were not following the federal rule excluding illegally obtained evidence, while sixteen were in agreement with it. Now that the *Wolf* doctrine is known to them, state courts may wish further to reconsider their evidentiary rules. But to upset state convictions even before the states have had adequate opportunity to adopt or reject the rule would be an unwarranted use of federal power. The chief burden of administering criminal justice rests upon state courts. To impose upon them the hazard of federal reversal for noncompliance with standards as to which this Court and its members have been so inconstant and inconsistent would not be justified. We adhere to *Wolf* as stating the law of search-and-seizure cases and decline to introduce vague and subjective distinctions.

Whether to exclude illegally obtained evidence in federal trials is left largely to our discretion, for admissibility of evidence is governed 'by the principles of the common law as they may be interpreted by the courts of the United States in the light of reason and experience.' Fed.Rules Crim.Proc. rule 26, 18 U.S.C.A. As we have pointed out, reason has led state courts to differing conclusions, but about two-thirds of them to acceptance of the illegally obtained evidence. What actual experience teaches we really do not know. Our cases evidence the fact that the federal rule of exclusion and our reversal of conviction for its violation are not sanctions which put an end to illegal search and seizure by federal officers. The rule was announced in 1914 in Weeks v. United States, 232 U.S. 383. The extent to which the practice was curtailed, if at all, is doubtful. The lower federal courts, and even this Court, have repeatedly been constrained to enforce the rule after its violation. There is no reliable evidence known to us that inhabitants of those states which exclude the evidence suffer less from lawless searches and seizures than those of states that admit it. Even this Court has not seen fit to exclude illegally seized evidence in federal cases unless a federal officer perpetrated the wrong. Private detectives may use methods to obtain evidence not open to officers of the law. Burdeau v. McDowell, 256 U.S. 465; *See* McGuire v. United States, 273 U.S. 95, 99; *cf.* Feldman v. United States, 322 U.S. 487; Lustig v. United States, 338 U.S. 74. And the lower federal courts, treating the Fourth Amendment right as personal to the one asserting it, have held that he who objects must claim some proprietary or possessory interest in that which was unlawfully searched or seized. *E.g.,* Connolly v. Medalie, 2 Cir., 58 F.2d 629; Steeber v. United States, 10 Cir., 198 F.2d 615, 617. *See* Goldstein v. United States, 316 U.S. 114, 121; *Wolf v. Colorado, supra,* 338 U.S. at pages 30–31. Cf. United States v. Jeffers, 342 U.S. 48.

It must be remembered that petitioner is not invoking the Constitution to prevent or punish a violation of his federal right recognized in *Wolf* or to recover reparations for the violation. He is invoking it only to set aside his own conviction of crime. That the rule of exclusion and reversal results in the escape of guilty persons is more capable of demonstration than that it deters invasions of right by the police. The case is made, so far as the police are concerned, when they announce that they have arrested their man. Rejection of the evidence does nothing to punish the wrong-doing official, while it may, and likely will, release the wrong-doing defendant. It deprives society of its remedy against one lawbreaker because he has been pursued by another. It protects one against whom incriminating evidence is discovered, but does nothing to protect innocent persons who are the victims of illegal but fruitless searches. The disciplinary or educational effect of the court's releasing the defendant for police misbehavior is so indirect as to be no more than a mild deterrent at best. Some discretion is still left to the states in criminal cases, for which they are largely responsible, and we think it is for them to determine which rule best serves them.

But admission of the evidence does not exonerate the officers and their aides if they have violated defendant's constitutional rights. It was pointed out in *Wolf v. Colorado, supra,* that other remedies are available for official lawlessness, although too often those remedies are of no practical avail. The difficulty with them is in part due to the failure of interested parties to inform of the offense. No matter what an illegal raid turns up, police are unlikely to inform on themselves or each other. If it turns up nothing incriminating, the innocent victim usually does not care to take steps which will air the fact that he has been under suspicion. And the prospect that the guilty may capitalize on the official wrongdoing in his defense, or to obtain reversal from a higher court, removes any motive he might have to inform.

It appears to the writer, in which view he is supported by THE CHIEF JUSTICE, that there is no lack of remedy if an unconstitutional wrong has been done in this instance without upsetting a justifiable conviction of this common gambler. If the officials have willfully deprived a citizen of the United States of a right or privilege secured to him by the Fourteenth Amendment, that being the right to be secure in his home against unreasonable searches, as defined in *Wolf v. Colorado, supra,* their conduct may constitute a federal crime under 62 Stat. 696, 18 U.S.C. (Supp. III) s 242. This section provides that whoever, under color of any law, statute, ordinance, regulation or custom, willfully subjects any inhabitant of any state to the deprivation of any rights, privileges or immunities secured or protected by the Constitution of the United States shall be fined or imprisoned. *See* Williams v. United States, 341 U.S. 97; Screws v. United States, 325 U.S. 91. It does not appear that the statute of limitations yet bars prosecutions. 45 Stat. 51, 18 U.S.C. s 582. We believe the Clerk of this Court should be directed to forward a copy of the record in this case, together with a copy of this opinion, for attention of the Attorney General of the United States. However, Mr. Justice REED and Mr. Justice MINTON do not join in this paragraph.

Judgment affirmed.

■ MR. JUSTICE CLARK, concurring.

Had I been here in 1949 when *Wolf* was decided I would have applied the doctrine of Weeks v. United States, 1914, 232 U.S. 383, to the states. But the Court refused to do so then, and it still refuses today. Thus *Wolf* remains the law and, as such, is entitled to the respect of this Court's membership.

Of course, we could sterilize the rule announced in *Wolf* by adopting a case-by-case approach to due process in which inchoate notions of propriety concerning local police conduct guide our decisions. But this makes for such uncertainty and unpredictability that it would be impossible to foretell—other than by guess-work—just how brazen the invasion of the intimate privacies of one's home must be in order to shock itself into the protective arms of the Constitution. In truth, the practical result of this ad hoc approach is simply that when five Justices are sufficiently revolted by local police action a conviction is overturned and a guilty man may go free. *Rochin* bears witness to this. We may thus vindicate the abstract principle of due process, but we do not shape the conduct of local police one whit; unpredictable reversals on dissimilar fact situations are not likely to curb the zeal of those police and prosecutors who may be intent on racking up a high percentage of successful prosecutions. I do not believe that the extension of such a vacillating course beyond the clear cases of physical coercion and brutality, such as *Rochin*, would serve a useful purpose.

In light of the 'incredible' activity of the police here it is with great reluctance that I follow *Wolf*. Perhaps strict adherence to the tenor of that decision may produce needed converts for its extinction. Thus I merely concur in the judgment of affirmance.

[Justice Black's dissenting opinion, joined by Justice Douglas, is omitted]

■ MR. JUSTICE FRANKFURTER, whom MR. JUSTICE BURTON joins, dissenting.

Mere failure to have an appropriate warrant for arrest or search, without aggravating circumstances of misconduct in obtaining evidence, invalidates a federal conviction helped by such an unreasonable search and seizure. Such was the construction placed upon the Fourth Amendment by Weeks v. United States, 232 U.S. 383. But Wolf v. People of State of Colorado, 338 U.S. 25, held that the rule of the *Weeks* case was not to be deemed part of the Due Process Clause of the Fourteenth Amendment and hence was not binding upon the States. Still more recently, however, in, the Court held that 'stomach pumping' to obtain morphine capsules, later used as evidence in a trial, was offensive to prevailing notions of fairness in the conduct of a prosecution and therefore invalidated a resulting conviction as contrary to the Due Process Clause.

The comprehending principle of these two cases is at the heart of 'due process.' The judicial enforcement of the Due Process Clause is the very antithesis of a Procrustean rule. In its first full-dress discussion of the Due Process Clause of the Fourteenth Amendment, the Court defined the nature of the problem as a 'gradual process of judicial inclusion and exclusion, as the cases presented for decision shall require, with the reasoning on which such decisions may be founded.' Davidson v. New Orleans, 96 U.S. 97, 104. The series of cases whereby, in the light of this attitude, the scope of the Due Process Clause has been unfolded is the most striking, because the liveliest, manifestation of the wide and deep areas of law in which adjudication 'depends upon differences of degree. The whole law does so as soon as it is civilized.' Holmes, J., concurring in LeRoy Fibre Co. v. Chicago, M. & St. P.R. Co., 232 U.S. 340, 354. It is especially true of the concept of due process that between the differences of degree which that inherently undefinable concept entails 'and the simple universality of the rules in the Twelve Tables, or the Leges Barbarorum, there lies the culture of two thousand years.' Ibid.

In the *Wolf* case, the Court rejected one absolute. In *Rochin,* it rejected another.

In holding that not all conduct which by federal law is an unreasonable search and seizure vitiates a conviction in connection with which it transpires, *Wolf* did not and could not decide that as long as relevant evidence adequately supports a conviction, it is immaterial how such evidence was acquired. For the exact holding of that case is defined by the question to which the opinion addressed itself: 'Does a conviction by a State court for a State offense deny the 'due process of law' required by the Fourteenth Amendment, solely because evidence that was admitted at the trial was obtained under circumstances which would have rendered it inadmissible in a prosecution for violation of a federal law in a court of the United States because there deemed to be an infraction of the Fourth Amendment as applied in Weeks v. United States, 232 U.S. 383?' (338 U.S. 25) Thus, *Wolf* did not change prior applications of the requirements of due process, whereby this Court considered the whole course of events by which a conviction was obtained and was not restricted to consideration of the trustworthiness of the evidence.

Rochin decided that the Due Process Clause of the Fourteenth Amendment does not leave States free in their prosecutions for crime. The Clause puts limits on the wide discretion of a State in the process of enforcing its criminal law. The holding of the case is that a State cannot resort to methods that offend civilized standards of decency and fairness. The conviction in the Rochin case was found to offend due process not because evidence had been obtained through an unauthorized search and seizure or was the fruit of compulsory self-incrimination. Neither of these concepts, relevant to federal prosecutions, was invoked by the Court in *Rochin*, so of course the *Wolf* case was not mentioned. While there is in the case before us, as there was in *Rochin*, an element of unreasonable search and seizure, what is decisive here, as in *Rochin*, is additional aggravating conduct which the Court finds repulsive.

Thus, the basis on which this case should be adjudicated is laid down in *Rochin*: 'Regard for the requirements of the Due Process Clause 'inescapably imposes upon this Court an exercise of judgment upon the whole course of the proceedings (resulting in a conviction) in order to ascertain whether they offend those canons of decency and fairness which express the notions of justice of English-speaking peoples even toward those charged with the most heinous offenses." 342 U.S., at page 169, quoting from Malinski v. People of State of New York, 324 U.S. 401, at pages 416–417.

This brings us to the specific circumstances of this case. . . .

There was lacking here physical violence, even to the restricted extent employed in *Rochin*. We have here, however, a more powerful and offensive control over the Irvines' life than a single, limited physical trespass. Certainly the conduct of the police here went far beyond a bare search and seizure. The police devised means to hear every word that was said in the Irvine household for more than a month. Those affirming the conviction find that this conduct, in its entirety, is 'almost incredible if it were not admitted.' Surely the Court does not propose to announce a new absolute, namely, that even the most reprehensible means for securing a conviction will not taint a verdict so long as the body of the accused was not touched by State officials. Considering the progress that scientific devices are making in extracting evidence without violence or bodily harm, satisfaction of due process would depend on the astuteness and subtlety with which the police engage in offensive practices and drastically invade privacy without authority of law. In words that seem too prophetic of this case, it has been said that '(d)iscovery and invention have made it possible for the government, by means far more effective than stretching upon the rack, to obtain disclosure in court of what is whispered in the closet.' Brandeis, J., dissenting in Olmstead v. United States, 277 U.S. 438, 473.

The underlying reasoning of *Rochin* rejected the notion that States may secure a conviction by any form of skulduggery so long as it does not involve physical violence. The cases in which coercive or physical infringements of the dignity and privacy of the individual were involved were not deemed 'sports in our constitutional law but applications of a general principle. They are only instances of the general requirement that States in their prosecutions respect certain decencies of civilized conduct. Due process of law, as a historic and generative principle, precludes defining, and thereby confining, these standards of conduct more precisely than to say that convictions cannot be brought about by methods that offend 'a sense of justice." 342 U.S., at page 173.

Since due process is not a mechanical yardstick, it does not afford mechanical answers. In applying the Due Process Clause judicial judgment is involved in an empiric process in the sense that results are not predetermined or mechanically ascertainable. But that is a very different thing from conceiving the results as ad hoc decisions in the opprobrious sense of ad hoc. Empiricism implies judgment upon variant situations by the wisdom of experience. Ad hocness in adjudication means treating a particular case by itself and not in relation to the meaning of a course of decisions and the guides they serve for the future. There is all the difference in the world between disposing of a case as though it were a discrete instance and recognizing it as part of the process of judgment, taking its place in relation to what went before and further cutting a channel for what is to come.

The effort to imprison due process within tidy categories misconceives its nature and is a futile endeavor to save the judicial function from the pains of judicial judgment. It is pertinent to recall how the Court dealt with this craving for unattainable certainty in the *Rochin* case:

> 'The vague contours of the Due Process Clause do not leave judges at large. We may not draw on our merely personal and private notions and disregard the limits that bind judges in their judicial function. Even though the concept of due process of law is not final and fixed, these limits are derived from considerations that are fused in the whole nature of our judicial process. *See* Cardozo, The Nature of the Judicial Process; The

> Growth of the Law; The Paradoxes of Legal Science. These are considerations deeply rooted in reason and in the compelling traditions of the legal profession. The Due Process Clause places upon this Court the duty of exercising a judgment, within the narrow confines of judicial power in reviewing State convictions, upon interests of society pushing in opposite directions.' 342 U.S., at pages 170–171.

Nor can we dispose of this case by satisfying ourselves that the defendant's guilt was proven by trustworthy evidence and then finding, or devising, other means whereby the police may be discouraged from using illegal methods to acquire such evidence.

This Court has rejected the notion that because a conviction is established on incontestable proof of guilt it may stand, no matter how the proof was secured. Observance of due process has to do not with questions of guilt or innocence but the mode by which guilt is ascertained. Mere errors of law in the conduct of State trials afford no basis for relief under the Fourteenth Amendment, and a wide swath of discretion must be left to the State Courts in such matters. But when a conviction is secured by methods which offend elementary standards of justice, the victim of such methods may invoke the protection of the Fourteenth Amendment because that Amendment guarantees him a trial fundamentally fair in the sense in which that idea is incorporated in due process. If, as in *Rochin,* '(o)n the facts of this case the conviction of the petitioner has been obtained by methods that offend the Due Process Clause', 342 U.S., at page 174, it is no answer to say that the offending policemen and prosecutors who utilize outrageous methods should be punished for their misconduct.

Of course it is a loss to the community when a conviction is overturned because the indefensible means by which it was obtained cannot be squared with the commands of due process. A new trial is necessitated, and by reason of the exclusion of evidence derived from the unfair aspects of the prior prosecution a guilty defendant may escape. But the people can avoid such miscarriages of justice. A sturdy, self-respecting democratic community should not put up with lawless police and prosecutors. 'Our people may tolerate many mistakes of both intent and performance, but, with unerring instinct, they know that when any person is intentionally deprived of his constitutional rights those responsible have committed no ordinary offense. A crime of this nature, if subtly encouraged by failure to condemn and punish, certainly leads down the road to totalitarianism.'[2]

■ MR. JUSTICE DOUGLAS, dissenting.

The search and seizure conducted in this case smack of the police state, not the free America the Bill of Rights envisaged.

---

[2] Statement by Director J. Edgar Hoover of the Federal Bureau of Investigation in FBI Law Enforcement Bulletin, September 1952, p. 1.

The police and their agents first made a key to the home of a suspect. Then they bored a hole in the roof of his house. Using the key they entered the house, installed a microphone, and attached it to a wire which ran through the hole in the roof to a nearby garage where officers listened in relays. Twice more they used the key to enter the house in order to adjust the microphone. First they moved it into the bedroom where the suspect and his wife slept. Next, they put the microphone into the bedroom closet. Then they used the key to enter the house to arrest the suspect. They had no search warrant; but they ransacked the house. Moreover, they examined the suspect's hands under an ultraviolet lamp to see if he had handled betting slips which they had earlier impregnated with fluorescent powder.

The evidence so obtained was used by California to send the suspect, petitioner here, to prison.

What transpired here was as revolting as the abuses arising out of the writs of assistance against which James Otis complained.[3] Otis in his speech against the writs had this to say:

'Now one of the most essential branches of English liberty is the freedom of one's house. A man's house is his castle; and whilst he is quiet, he is as well guarded as a prince in his castle. This writ, if it should be declared legal, would totally annihilate this privilege. Custom-house officers may enter our houses when they please; we are commanded to permit their entry. Their menial servants may enter, may break locks, bars, and every thing in their way: and whether they break through malice or revenge, no man, no court, can inquire. Bare suspicion without oath is sufficient.'

In those days courts put their sanction behind the unlawful invasion of privacy by issuing the general warrant that permitted unlimited searches. There is no essential difference between that and the action we take today. Today we throw the weight of the Government on the side of the lawless search by affirming a conviction based on evidence obtained by it. Today we compound the grievance against which Otis complained. Not only is privacy invaded. The lawless invasion is officially approved as the means of sending a man to prison.

I protest against this use of unconstitutional evidence. It is no answer that the man is doubtless guilty. The Bill of Rights was designed to protect every accused against practices of the police which history showed were oppressive of liberty. The guarantee against unreasonable searches and seizures contained in the Fourth Amendment was one of those safeguards. In 1914 a unanimous Court decided that officers who obtained evidence in violation of that guarantee could not use it in prosecutions in the federal courts. Weeks v. United States, 232 U.S. 383.

---

[3]   Tudor, Life of James Otis (1823), pp. 66–67.

Lawless action of the federal police, it said, 'should find no sanction in the judgments of the courts * * *.' *Id.*, 232 U.S. at page 392.

The departure from that principle which the Court made in 1949 in Wolf v. People of State of Colorado, 338 U.S. 25, is part of the deterioration which civil liberties have suffered in recent years. In that case the Court held that evidence obtained in violation of the Fourth Amendment, though inadmissible in federal prosecutions, could be used in prosecutions in the state courts. Mr. Justice Murphy, dissenting, pointed out the peril of that step, *Id.*, 338 U.S. at page 44.

> 'The conclusion is inescapable that but one remedy exists to deter violations of the search and seizure clause. That is the rule which excludes illegally obtained evidence. Only by exclusion can we impress upon the zealous prosecutor that violation of the Constitution will do him no good. And only when that point is driven home can the prosecutor be expected to emphasize the importance of observing constitutional demands in his instructions to the police.'

Exclusion of evidence is indeed the only effective sanction. If the evidence can be used, no matter how lawless the search, the protection of the Fourth Amendment, to use the words of the Court in the *Weeks* case, 'might as well be stricken from the Constitution.' 232 U.S., at page 393.

The suggestion that the remedy for lawless conduct by the local police is through federal prosecution under the civil rights laws relegates constitutional rights under the Fourth Amendment to a lowly status. An already overburdened Department of Justice, busily engaged in law enforcement, cannot be expected to devote its energies to supervising local police activities and prosecuting police officers, except in rare and occasional instances. And the hostility which such prosecutions have received here (*see* Screws v. United States, 325 U.S. 91, especially pages 138 et seq), hardly encourages putting the federal prosecutor on the track of state officials who take unconstitutional short cuts in enforcing state laws.

If unreasonable searches and seizures that violate the privacy which the Fourth Amendment protects are to be outlawed, this is the time and the occasion to do it. If police officers know that evidence obtained by their unlawful acts cannot be used in the courts, they will clean their own houses and put an end to this kind of action. But as long as courts will receive the evidence, the police will act lawlessly and the rights of the individual will suffer. We should throw our weight on the side of the citizen and against the lawless police. We should be alert to see that no unconstitutional evidence is used to convict any person in America.

Appendix.

Mr. Justice Murphy, when Attorney General, was responsible for the creation of the Civil Rights Section in the Department of Justice. That was on February 3, 1939. In 1947 Mr. Justice Clark, then Attorney

General, reported that the Section had in the eight years of its existence investigated nearly 850 complaints, instituted prosecutions in 178 cases, and obtained the conviction of more than 130 defendants. Clark, *A Federal Prosecutor Looks at the Civil Rights Statutes*, 47 Col.L.Rev. 175, 181. *See also* Report of the President's Committee on Civil Rights: To Secure These Rights (1947), pp. 114 et seq.

A more recent account of the work of the Civil Rights Section will be found in Putzel, *Federal Civil Rights Enforcement: A Current Appraisal*, 99 U. of Pa.L.Rev. 439 (1951). It is there stated that on the average 20 civil rights cases are prosecuted a year, acquittals and convictions being about equally divided. *Id.*, p. 449, n. 43. These figures are confirmed by the Administrative Office of the United States Courts. . . .

People v. Gonzalez
356 Mich. 247 (1959)

In 1914, in Weeks v. United States, 232 U.S. 383, the United States supreme court not only held that the search and seizure there dealt with was unreasonable in a constitutional sense, but also held that the 4th amendment forbade the introduction of evidence in Federal courts seized in such a search by Federal officers.

Michigan (contrary to a majority of the other States) followed this exclusionary rule in interpreting its own constitutional safeguard against unreasonable searches and seizures. People v. Marxhausen, 204 Mich. 559, 171 N.W. 557, 3 A.L.R. 1505; People v. Roache, *supra*; People v. Stein, *supra*.

This last case involved the introduction of a concealed weapon seized in the search of a person arrested on general suspicion. This Court held the arrest and search illegal and excluded the introduction of the weapon thus illegally seized.

Hard on the heels of this case a successful effort was made to amend the Michigan Constitution so as to allow that which the Stein Case forbade. In 1936 the people adopted the following amendment to article 2, § 10:

'Provided, however, That the provisions of this section shall not be construed to bar from evidence in any court of criminal jurisdiction, or in any criminal proceeding held before any magistrate or justice of the peace,* any firearm, rifle, pistol, revolver, automatic pistol, machine gun, bomb, bomb shell, explosive, blackjack, slungshot, billy, metallic knuckles, gas-ejecting device, or any other dangerous weapon or thing, seized by any peace officer outside the curtilage of any dwelling house in this state.'

---

*   In 1952 an amendment added here 'any narcotic or drugs.'

The supreme law of this State, its Constitution, thus directs the admission of evidence of the character with which we are concerned in this case *even if the evidence was produced* by an unconstitutional search and seizure.

Our remaining question is whether or not such State constitutional sanction of the admission of illegally-seized evidence is barred by the Federal Constitution. . . . [The court, relying on *Wolf v. Colorado,* held the Michigan constitutional amendments were not offensive to the Federal constitution.]

Mapp v. Ohio
367 U.S. 643 (1961)

■ MR. JUSTICE CLARK delivered the opinion of the Court.

Appellant stands convicted of knowingly having had in her possession and under her control certain lewd and lascivious books, pictures, and photographs in violation of § 2905.34 of Ohio's Revised Code. As officially stated in the syllabus to its opinion, the Supreme Court of Ohio found that her conviction was valid though 'based primarily upon the introduction in evidence of lewd and lascivious books and pictures unlawfully seized during an unlawful search of defendant's home * * *.' 170 Ohio St. 427–428, 166 N.E.2d 387, 388.

On May 23, 1957, three Cleveland police officers arrived at appellant's residence in that city pursuant to information that 'a person (was) hiding out in the home, who was wanted for questioning in connection with a recent bombing, and that there was a large amount of policy paraphernalia being hidden in the home.' Miss Mapp and her daughter by a former marriage lived on the top floor of the two-family dwelling. Upon their arrival at that house, the officers knocked on the door and demanded entrance but appellant, after telephoning her attorney, refused to admit them without a search warrant. They advised their headquarters of the situation and undertook a surveillance of the house.

The officers again sought entrance some three hours later when four or more additional officers arrived on the scene. When Miss Mapp did not come to the door immediately, at least one of the several doors to the house was forcibly opened[2] and the policemen gained admittance. Meanwhile Miss Mapp's attorney arrived, but the officers, having secured their own entry, and continuing in their definance of the law, would permit him neither to see Miss Mapp nor to enter the house. It appears that Miss Mapp was halfway down the stairs from the upper floor to the front door when the officers, in this highhanded manner,

---

[2] A police officer testified that 'we did pry the screen door to gain entrance'; the attorney on the scene testified that a policeman 'tried * * * to kick in the door' and then 'broke the glass in the door and somebody reached in and opened the door and let them in'; the appellant testified that 'The back door was broken.'

broke into the hall. She demanded to see the search warrant. A paper, claimed to be a warrant, was held up by one of the officers. She grabbed the 'warrant' and placed it in her bosom. A struggle ensued in which the officers recovered the piece of paper and as a result of which they handcuffed appellant because she had been 'belligerent' in resisting their official rescue of the 'warrant' from her person. Running roughshod over appellant, a policeman 'grabbed' her, 'twisted (her) hand,' and she 'yelled (and) pleaded with him' because 'it was hurting.' Appellant, in handcuffs, was then forcibly taken upstairs to her bedroom where the officers searched a dresser, a chest of drawers, a closet and some suitcases. They also looked into a photo album and through personal papers belonging to the appellant. The search spread to the rest of the second floor including the child's bedroom, the living room, the kitchen and a dinette. The basement of the building and a trunk found therein were also searched. The obscene materials for possession of which she was ultimately convicted were discovered in the course of that widespread search.

At the trial no search warrant was produced by the prosecution, nor was the failure to produce one explained or accounted for. At best, 'There is, in the record, considerable doubt as to whether there ever was any warrant for the search of defendant's home.' 170 Ohio St. at page 430, 166 N.E.2d at page 389. The Ohio Supreme Court believed a 'reasonable argument' could be made that the conviction should be reversed 'because the 'methods' employed to obtain the (evidence) were such as to 'offend 'a sense of justice,' '' but the court found determinative the fact that the evidence had not been taken 'from defendant's person by the use of brutal or offensive physical force against defendant.' 170 Ohio St. at page 431, 166 N.E.2d at pages 389–390.

The State says that even if the search were made without authority, or otherwise unreasonably, it is not prevented from using the unconstitutionally seized evidence at trial, citing Wolf v. People of State of Colorado, 1949, 338 U.S. 25, at page 33, in which this Court did indeed hold 'that in a prosecution in a State court for a State crime the Fourteenth Amendment does not forbid the admission of evidence obtained by an unreasonable search and seizure.' On this appeal, of which we have noted probable jurisdiction, 364 U.S. 868, it is urged once again that we review that holding.[3]

I.

Seventy-five years ago, in Boyd v. United States, 1886, 116 U.S. 616, 630, considering the Fourth and Fifth Amendments as running 'almost into each other'[5] on the facts before it, this Court held that the doctrines

---

[3]　Other issues have been raised on this appeal but, in the view we have taken of the case, they need not be decided. Although appellant chose to urge what may have appeared to be the surer ground for favorable disposition and did not insist that *Wolf* be overruled, the amicus curiae, who was also permitted to participate in the oral argument, did urge the Court to overrule *Wolf*.

[5]　The close connection between the concepts later embodied in these two Amendments had been noted at least as early as 1765 by Lord Camden, on whose opinion in Entick v.

of those Amendments 'apply to all invasions on the part of the government and its employes of the sanctity of a man's home and the privacies of life. It is not the breaking of his doors, and the rummaging of his drawers, that constitutes the essence of the offence; but it is the invasion of his indefeasible right of personal security, personal liberty and private property * * *. Breaking into a house and opening boxes and drawers are circumstances of aggravation; but any forcible and compulsory extortion of a man's own testimony or of his private papers to be used as evidence to convict him of crime or to forfeit his goods, is within the condemnation * * * (of those Amendments).'

The Court noted that 'constitutional provisions for the security of person and property should be liberally construed. * * * It is the duty of courts to be watchful for the constitutional rights of the citizen, and against any stealthy encroachments thereon.' In this jealous regard for maintaining the integrity of individual rights, the Court gave life to Madison's prediction that 'independent tribunals of justice * * * will be naturally led to resist every encroachment upon rights expressly stipulated for in the Constitution by the declaration of rights.' I Annals of Cong. 439 (1789). Concluding, the Court specifically referred to the use of the evidence there seized as 'unconstitutional.' At page 638 of 116 U.S., at page 536.

Less than 30 years after *Boyd*, this Court, in Weeks v. United States, 1914, 232 U.S. 383, at pages 391–392, stated that

'the 4th Amendment * * * put the courts of the United States and Federal officials, in the exercise of their power and authority, under limitations and restraints (and) * * * forever secure(d) the people, their persons, houses, papers, and effects, against all unreasonable searches and seizures under the guise of law * * * and the duty of giving to it force and effect is obligatory upon all entrusted under our Federal system with the enforcement of the laws.'

Specifically dealing with the use of the evidence unconstitutionally seized, the Court concluded:

> 'If letters and private documents can thus be seized and held and used in evidence against a citizen accused of an offense, the protection of the Fourth Amendment declaring his right to be secure against such searches and seizures is of no value, and, so far as those thus placed are concerned, might as well be stricken from the Constitution. The efforts of the courts and their officials to bring the guilty to punishment, praiseworthy as they are, are not to be aided by the sacrifice of those great principles

---

Carrington, 19 Howell's State Trials 1029, the *Boyd* court drew heavily. Lord Camden had noted, at 1073:

'It is very certain, that the law obligeth no man to accuse himself; because the necessary means of compelling self-accusation, falling upon the innocent as well as the guilty, would be both cruel and unjust; and it should seem, that search for evidence is disallowed upon the same principle. There too the innocent would be confounded with the guilty.'

established by years of endeavor and suffering which have resulted in their embodiment in the fundamental law of the land.' At page 393 of 232 U.S.

Finally, the Court in that case clearly stated that use of the seized evidence involved 'a denial of the constitutional rights of the accused.' At page 398 of 232 U.S. Thus, in the year 1914, in the *Weeks* case, this Court 'for the first time' held that 'in a federal prosecution the Fourth Amendment barred the use of evidence secured through an illegal search and seizure.' *Wolf v. People of State of Colorado, supra*, 338 U.S. at page 28. This Court has ever since required of federal law officers a strict adherence to that command which this Court has held to be a clear, specific, and constitutionally required—even if judically implied— deterrent safeguard without insistence upon which the Fourth Amendment would have been reduced to 'a form of words.' Holmes J., Silverthorne Lumber Co. v. United States, 1920, 251 U.S. 385, 392, It meant, quite simply, that 'conviction by means of unlawful seizures and enforced confessions * * * should find no sanction in the judgments of the courts * * *,' *Weeks v. United States, supra*, 232 U.S. at page 392, and that such evidence 'shall not be used at all.' *Silverthorne Lumber Co. v. United States, supra*, 251 U.S. at page 392. . . .

II.

In 1949, 35 years after *Weeks* was announced, this Court, in *Wolf v. People of State of Colorado, supra*, again for the first time, discussed the effect of the Fourth Amendment upon the States through the operation of the Due Process Clause of the Fourteenth Amendment. [T]the Court decided that the *Weeks* exclusionary rule would not then be imposed upon the States as 'an essential ingredient of the right.'

. . . While in 1949, prior to the *Wolf* case, almost two-thirds of the States were opposed to the use of the exclusionary rule, now, despite the *Wolf* case, more than half of those since passing upon it, by their own legislative or judicial decision, have wholly or partly adopted or adhered to the *Weeks* rule. *See* Elkins v. United States, 1960, 364 U.S. 206, Appendix, at pages 224–232. Significantly, among those now following the rule is California, which, according to its highest court, was 'compelled to reach that conclusion because other remedies have completely failed to secure compliance with the constitutional provisions * * *.' People v. Cahan, 1955, 44 Cal.2d 434, 445, 282 P.2d 905, 911, 50 A.L.R.2d 513. In connection with this California case, we note that the second basis elaborated in *Wolf* in support of its failure to enforce the exclusionary doctrine against the States was that 'other means of protection' have been afforded 'the right to privacy.'[7] The experience of California that such other remedies have been worthless and futile is buttressed by the experience of other States. The obvious futility of

---

[7] Less than half of the States have any criminal provisions relating directly to unreasonable searches and seizures. [The Court reviews the statutes of the 23 other states.]

relegating the Fourth Amendment of the protection of other remedies has, moreover, been recognized by this Court since *Wolf*. *See* Irvine v. People of State of California, 1954, 347 U.S. 128, 137 . . . .

It, therefore, plainly appears that the factual considerations supporting the failure of the *Wolf* Court to include the *Weeks* exclusionary rule when it recognized the enforceability of the right to privacy against the States in 1949, while not basically relevant to the constitutional consideration, could not, in any analysis, now be deemed controlling.

III.

. . . Today we once again examine *Wolf*'s constitutional documentation of the right to privacy free from unreasonable state intrusion, and, after its dozen years on our books, are led by it to close the only courtroom door remaining open to evidence secured by official lawlessness in flagrant abuse of that basic right, reserved to all persons as a specific guarantee against that very same unlawful conduct. We hold that all evidence obtained by searches and seizures in violation of the Constitution is, by that same authority, inadmissible in a state court.

IV.

Since the Fourth Amendment's right of privacy has been declared enforceable against the States through the Due Process Clause of the Fourteenth, it is enforceable against them by the same sanction of exclusion as is used against the Federal Government. Were it otherwise, then just as without the *Weeks* rule the assurance against unreasonable federal searches and seizures would be 'a form of words', valueless and undeserving of mention in a perpetual charter of inestimable human liberties, so too, without that rule the freedom from state invasions of privacy would be so ephemeral and so neatly severed from its conceptual nexus with the freedom from all brutish means of coercing evidence as not to merit this Court's high regard as a freedom 'implicit in 'the concept of ordered liberty." At the time that the Court held in *Wolf* that the Amendment was applicable to the States through the Due Process Clause, the cases of this Court, as we have seen, had steadfastly held that as to federal officers the Fourth Amendment included the exclusion of the evidence seized in violation of its provisions. Even *Wolf* 'stoutly adhered' to that proposition. The right to privacy, when conceded operatively enforceable against the States, was not susceptible of destruction by avulsion of the sanction upon which its protection and enjoyment had always been deemed dependent under the *Boyd, Weeks* and *Silverthorne* cases. Therefore, in extending the substantive protections of due process to all constitutionally unreasonable searches—state or federal—it was logically and constitutionally necessary that the exclusion doctrine—an essential part of the right to privacy—be also insisted upon as an essential ingredient of the right newly recognized by the *Wolf* case. In short, the admission of the new constitutional right by *Wolf* could not consistently tolerate denial of its most important constitutional privilege, namely, the exclusion of the evidence which an accused had been forced to give by reason of the unlawful seizure. To hold otherwise is to grant the right but in reality to withhold its privilege and enjoyment. Only last year the Court itself recognized that the purpose of the exclusionary rule 'is to deter—to compel respect for the constitutional guaranty in the only effectively available way—by removing the incentive to disregard it.' *Elkins v. United States, supra*, 364 U.S. at page 217.

Indeed, we are aware of no restraint, similar to that rejected today, conditioning the enforcement of any other basic constitutional right. The right to privacy, no less important than any other right carefully and particularly reserved to the people, would stand in marked contrast to all other rights declared as 'basic to a free society.' Wolf v. People of State of Colorado, *supra*, 338 U.S. at page 27. This Court has not hesitated to enforce as strictly against the States as it does against the Federal Government the rights of free speech and of a free press, the rights to notice and to a fair, public trial, including, as it does, the right not to be convicted by use of a coerced confession, however logically relevant it be, and without regard to its reliability. Rogers v. Richmond, 1961, 365 U.S. 534. And nothing could be more certain that that when a coerced confession is involved, 'the relevant rules of evidence' are overridden without regard to 'the incidence of such conduct by the police,' slight or frequent. Why should not the same rule apply to what is tantamount to coerced testimony by way of unconstitutional seizure of goods, papers, effect, documents, etc.? We find that, as to the Federal Government, the Fourth and Fifth Amendments and, as to the States, the freedom from unconscionable invasions of privacy and the freedom from convictions based upon coerced confessions do enjoy an 'intimate relation' in their perpetuation of 'principles of humanity and civil liberty (secured) * * * only after years of struggle.' Bram v. United States, 1897, 168 U.S. 532, 543—544. They express 'supplementing phases of the same constitutional purpose—to maintain inviolate large areas of personal privacy.' Feldman v. United States, 1944, 322 U.S. 487, 489–490. The philosophy of each Amendment and of each freedom is complementary to, although not dependent upon, that of the other in its sphere of influence—the very least that together they assure in either sphere is that no man is to be convicted on unconstitutional evidence.

V.

... There are those who say, as did Justice (then Judge) Cardozo, that under our constitutional exclusionary doctrine '(t)he criminal is to go free because the constable has blundered.' People v. Defore, 242 N.Y. at page 21, 150 N.E. at page 587. In some cases this will undoubtedly be the result. But ... 'there is another consideration—the imperative of judicial integrity.' 364 U.S. at page 222. The criminal goes free, if he must, but it is the law that sets him free. Nothing can destroy a government more quickly than its failure to observe its own laws, or worse, its disregard of the charter of its own existence. As Mr. Justice Brandeis, dissenting, said in Olmstead v. United States, 1928, 277 U.S. 438, 485: 'Our government is the potent, the omnipresent teacher. For good or for ill, it teaches the whole people by its example. * * * If the government becomes a lawbreaker, it breeds contempt for law; it invites every man to become a law unto himself; it invites anarchy.' Nor can it lightly be assumed that, as a practical matter, adoption of the exclusionary rule fetters law enforcement. Only last year this Court expressly considered that contention and found that 'pragmatic evidence of a sort' to the contrary was not wanting. *Elkins v. United States, supra,* 364 U.S. at page 218. The Court noted that

> 'The federal courts themselves have operated under the exclusionary rule of *Weeks* for almost half a century; yet it has not been suggested either that the Federal Bureau of Investigation has thereby been rendered ineffective, or that the administration of criminal justice in the federal courts has thereby been disrupted. Moreover, the experience of the states is impressive * * *. The movement towards the rule of exclusion has been halting but seemingly inexorable.' *Id.,* 364 U.S. at pages 218–219.

. . . Our decision, founded on reason and truth, gives to the individual no more than that which the Constitution guarantees him, to the police officer no less than that to which honest law enforcement is entitled, and, to the courts, that judicial integrity so necessary in the true administration of justice.

The judgment of the Supreme Court of Ohio is reversed and the cause remanded for further proceedings not inconsistent with this opinion.

Reversed and remanded.

■ MR. JUSTICE BLACK, concurring.

. . . I am still not persuaded that the Fourth Amendment, standing alone, would be enough to bar the introduction into evidence against an accused of papers and effects seized from him in violation of its commands. For the Fourth Amendment does not itself contain any provision expressly precluding the use of such evidence, and I am extremely doubtful that such a provision could properly be inferred from nothing more than the basic command against unreasonable searches and seizures. Reflection on the problem, however, in the light of cases coming before the Court since *Wolf,* has led me to conclude that when the Fourth Amendment's ban against unreasonable searches and seizures is considered together with the Fifth Amendment's ban against compelled self-incrimination, a constitutional basis emerges which not only justifies but actually requires the exclusionary rule.

The close interrelationship between the Fourth and Fifth Amendments, as they apply to this problem, has long been recognized and, indeed, was expressly made the ground for this Court's holding in *Boyd v. United States.* There the Court fully discussed this relationship and declared itself 'unable to perceive that the seizure of a man's private books and papers to be used in evidence against him is substantially different from compelling him to be a witness against himself.' . . .

■ MR. JUSTICE HARLAN, whom MR. JUSTICE FRANKFURTER and MR. JUSTICE WHITTAKER join, dissenting.

In overruling the *Wolf* case the Court, in my opinion, has forgotten the sense of judicial restraint which, with due regard for stare decisis, is one element that should enter into deciding whether a past decision of this Court should be overruled. Apart from that I also believe that the *Wolf* rule represents sounder Constitutional doctrine than the new rule which now replaces it. . . .

At the heart of the majority's opinion in this case is the following syllogism: (1) the rule excluding in federal criminal trials evidence which is the product of all illegal search and seizure is a 'part and parcel' of the Fourth Amendment; (2) *Wolf* held that the 'privacy' assured against federal action by the Fourth Amendment is also protected against state action by the Fourteenth Amendment; and (3) it is therefore 'logically and constitutionally necessary' that the *Weeks* exclusionary rule should also be enforced against the States.[10]

This reasoning ultimately rests on the unsound premise that because *Wolf* carried into the States, as part of 'the concept of ordered liberty' embodied in the Fourteenth Amendment, the principle of 'privacy' underlying the Fourth Amendment (338 U.S. at page 27), it must follow that whatever configurations of the Fourth Amendment have been developed in the particularizing federal precedents are likewise to be deemed a part of "ordered liberty," and as such are enforceable against the States. For me, this does not follow at all. . . .

[The concurring opinion of Justice Douglas is omitted.]

---

[10] Actually, only four members of the majority support this reasoning.

CHAPTER 2

BRIEF "SEIZURES" OF THE PERSON FOR PURPOSES OF INVESTIGATION OR CITATION

1. INTRODUCTION: THE DOCTRINAL ARCHITECTURE OF MODERN FOURTH AMENDMENT LAW

As we have seen already, the Fourth Amendment's text poses four questions the text itself does not resolve. The first question concerns the Fourth Amendment's *scope.* Just what are "searches" and "seizures"? If government agents injure private persons without committing any "search" or "seizure," individuals must look to other provisions of the Constitution, or to statutes or the common law, for redress. In *Olmstead,* for example, the Washington police tapped the telephone lines running to Olmstead's house, and the Court held that this was not a search of Olmstead. Second, when government agents commit a search or seizure, the first clause declares a general right against searches or seizures that are "unreasonable." The first clause is often referred to as the declaratory clause. The declaratory clause does not say what features of a search or seizure make the search or seizure reasonable or "unreasonable".

The second clause—the warrant clause—sets out the constitutional requirements of a valid warrant. The warrant clause, however, does not say when—if indeed ever—warrants are necessary to make a search "reasonable" under the declaratory clause. We might look to the warrant clause's condemnation of warrants absent "probable cause" as a guide to the meaning of "unreasonable" searches under the first clause. The warrant clause, however, does not direct us to do that, and in any event leaves open the question of whether "probable cause" must be determined by a judge before the "search" or "seizure" rather than by law-enforcement officers *ex ante* and judicial review of the officers' decisions *ex post.* In *Weeks,* for example, the Court held that the marshall needed a search warrant to enter the suspect's home. Yet the Court did not say that the arrest of Weeks—arguably a greater intrusion than the search— was illegal because the arresting officers had no arrest warrant. The third question, then, is: What is the relationship between the declaratory clause and the warrant clause?

Fourth and finally, if government agents violate the amendment by engaging in "unreasonable searches and seizures", just what remedy or sanction follows the violation? We saw in Chapter 1 that the Fourth Amendment was inspired by writs of assistance and general warrants. In effect, the writs and the general warrants gave officers immunity from common-law tort liability for trespass and false arrest. The text, however, does not say that the legislatures may not modify (or even abolish) officers' tort liability. Nor does it say that the courts are without power to recognize alternative remedies. We will return to this question of constitutional remedies in Chapter 5.

In the U.S. legal system, the courts—and ultimately the Supreme Court—have the last word on constitutional questions. It follows that Fourth Amendment law has features characteristic of both constitutional law and traditional common law. Like common law doctrines of tort or contract, Fourth Amendment law is made by judges who generally observe the principle of *stare decisis*. Unlike the law made by common law courts deciding tort and contract cases, however, Fourth Amendment cases announce constitutional law that legislatures do not have the power to overrule.

So the highest legal authority on Fourth Amendment questions is a precedent from the U.S. Supreme Court. Lawyers arguing Fourth Amendment cases look to the precedents for those that favor their side, and try to distinguish precedents that favor the other side. As with any system of judge-made law, there are likely to be both gaps (where there is no precedent on the precise question) and tensions (where different precedents are relevant but point in opposing directions).

After *Mapp* the Supreme Court's ruling applied to state and local police as well as to federal agents. State and local authorities always have been responsible for most criminal law enforcement. Violations required excluding evidence, often attended by the escape of the guilty. Distinguished commentators pointed out that in these circumstances, case-by-case adjudication gave police officers and lower court judges insufficient guidance about the Fourth Amendment's scope, the criteria of reasonableness, and the role of warrants. *See* Wayne R. LaFave, *"Case by Case Adjudication" Versus "Standardized Procedures": The* Robinson *Dilemma,* 1974 Sup. Ct. Rev. 127; Anthony G. Amsterdam, *Perspectives on the Fourth Amendment,* 58 Minn. L. Rev. 349, 393 (1974). To quote Professor Amsterdam, a case-by-case approach would be "splendid in its flexibility, awful in its unintelligibility, unadministrability, unenforceability, and general ooziness." *Id.* at 415.

In the years since *Mapp* the Supreme Court responded to the challenge of issuing constitutional doctrine applicable to hundreds of thousands of cases each year. The Court responded by recognizing discrete categories of police practices to which the Fourth Amendment applies. For each category, cases over time established general rules about what makes searches or seizures of that type reasonable or unreasonable (including whether a warrant is required before police execute that type of search or seizure).

There are four principal categories, three types of seizures and "searches." A seizure may be classified as an arrest, a brief detention for investigation, or a routine traffic stop. Each type of seizure requires some degree of antecedent suspicion, and (when justified) authorizes some incidental powers to permit the police to carry out the seizure safely and effectively. Just as police authority to detain includes the power to detain safely and effectively, police power to detain is limited by the reasons that justify the power, limited both in time and in the degree of force that may be used incident to the detention. In this chapter we study the lesser intrusions of the "brief detention for investigation" and the "routine traffic stop." We will turn to arrests in Chapter 3, and to "searches" in Chapter 4.

2. HISTORICAL NOTE: STREET PATROL BEFORE *TERRY*

Proactive street patrol was a hallmark of the early police forces. They conducted street patrols under the authority of statutes that made suspicious behavior, as such, a crime. From 1845 to 1850, for example, the New York police reported 144,364 arrests. The great majority of these arrests were for public order offenses (20,252 for "Disorderly conduct," 29,190 for "Intoxication and disorderly conduct," 36,675 for "intoxication," 11,347 for "vagrancy"). *See* Augustine E. Costello, Our Police Protectors 116 (1885). As Caleb Foote showed in a classic article, *Vagrancy-Type Law and its Administration,* 104 U. Pa. L. Rev. 603 (1956), arresting for public order offenses such as "vagrancy" remained a common practice more than a hundred years later. Immediately after *Terry,* the Court held sweeping definitions of "vagrancy" void for vagueness. Papachristou v. City of Jacksonville, 405 U.S. 156 (1972). The Court has repeatedly struck down public-order offenses defined so broadly that the police have practically plenary power to arrest. Coates v. Cincinnati, 402 U.S. 611 (1971) (invalidating ordinance prohibiting three or more persons in public from "annoying" others); City of Chicago v. Morales, 527 U.S. 41 (1999) (plurality opinion) (invalidating ordinance prohibiting any group that includes an apparent gang member from remaining in public with no apparent purpose).

Practically speaking, even today a misdemeanor arrest for a public order offense is often a supplement to police power under *Terry.* Some broad public-order crimes have survived constitutional challenge, and— just as in Caleb Foote's day—many misdemeanor defendants are poor people relying on overstretched public defenders. They often face indefinite pretrial detention if they refuse to plead guilty. Few of them challenge the legality of the arrest, the sufficiency of the evidence of guilt, or the constitutionality of the statute allegedly violated. *See, e.g.,* Alexandra Natapoff, *Misdemeanors,* 85 S. Cal. L. Rev. 1313, 1331–1337 (2012).

3. *TERRY*

Terry v. Ohio
392 U.S. 1 (1968)

■ MR. CHIEF JUSTICE WARREN delivered the opinion of the Court.

This case presents serious questions concerning the role of the Fourth Amendment in the confrontation on the street between the citizen and the policeman investigating suspicious circumstances.

Petitioner Terry was convicted of carrying a concealed weapon and sentenced to the statutorily prescribed term of one to three years in the penitentiary. Following the denial of a pretrial motion to suppress, the prosecution introduced in evidence two revolvers and a number of bullets seized from Terry and a codefendant, Richard Chilton,[2] by Cleveland Police Detective Martin McFadden. At the hearing on the motion to suppress this evidence, Officer McFadden testified that while he was patrolling in plain clothes in downtown Cleveland at approximately 2:30 in the afternoon of October 31, 1963, his attention was attracted by two men, Chilton and Terry, standing on the corner of Huron Road and Euclid Avenue. He had never seen the two men before, and he was unable to say precisely what first drew his eye to them. However, he testified that he had been a policeman for 39 years and a detective for 35 and that he had been assigned to patrol this vicinity of downtown Cleveland for shoplifters and pickpockets for 30 years. He explained that he had developed routine habits of observation over the years and that he would 'stand and watch people or walk and watch people at many intervals of the day.' He added: 'Now, in this case when I looked over they didn't look right to me at the time.'.

His interest aroused, Officer McFadden took up a post of observation in the entrance to a store 300 to 400 feet away from the two men. 'I get more purpose to watch them when I seen their movements,' he testified. He saw one of the men leave the other one and walk southwest on Huron Road, past some stores. The man paused for a moment and looked in a store window, then walked on a short distance, turned around and walked back toward the corner, pausing once again to look in the same store window. He rejoined his companion at the corner, and the two conferred briefly. Then the second man went through the same series of motions, strolling down Huron Road, looking in the same window,

---

[2] Terry and Chilton were arrested, indicted, tried and convicted together. They were represented by the same attorney, and they made a joint motion to suppress the guns. After the motion was denied, evidence was taken in the case against Chilton. This evidence consisted of the testimony of the arresting officer and of Chilton. It was then stipulated that this testimony would be applied to the case against Terry, and no further evidence was introduced in that case. The trial judge considered the two cases together, rendered the decisions at the same time and sentenced the two men at the same time. They prosecuted their state court appeals together through the same attorney, and they petitioned this Court for certiorari together. Following the grant of the writ upon this joint petition, Chilton died. Thus, only Terry's conviction is here for review.

walking on a short distance, turning back, peering in the store window again, and returning to confer with the first man at the corner. The two men repeated this ritual alternately between five and six times apiece—in all, roughly a dozen trips. At one point, while the two were standing together on the corner, a third man approached them and engaged them briefly in conversation. This man then left the two others and walked west on Euclid Avenue. Chilton and Terry resumed their measured pacing, peering and conferring. After this had gone on for 10 to 12 minutes, the two men walked off together, heading west on Euclid Avenue, following the path taken earlier by the third man.

By this time Officer McFadden had become thoroughly suspicious. He testified that after observing their elaborately casual and oft-repeated reconnaissance of the store window on Huron Road, he suspected the two men of 'casing a job, a stick-up,' and that he considered it his duty as a police officer to investigate further. He added that he feared 'they may have a gun.' Thus, Officer McFadden followed Chilton and Terry and saw them stop in front of Zucker's store to talk to the same man who had conferred with them earlier on the street corner. Deciding that the situation was ripe for direct action, Officer McFadden approached the three men, identified himself as a police officer and asked for their names. At this point his knowledge was confined to what he had observed. He was not acquainted with any of the three men by name or by sight, and he had received no information concerning them from any other source. When the men 'mumbled something' in response to his inquiries, Officer McFadden grabbed petitioner Terry, spun him around so that they were facing the other two, with Terry between McFadden and the others, and patted down the outside of his clothing. In the left breast pocket of Terry's overcoat Officer McFadden felt a pistol. He reached inside the overcoat pocket, but was unable to remove the gun. At this point, keeping Terry between himself and the others, the officer ordered all three men to enter Zucker's store. As they went in, he removed Terry's overcoat completely, removed a .38-caliber revolver from the pocket and ordered all three men to face the wall with their hands raised. Officer McFadden proceeded to pat down the outer clothing of Chilton and the third man, Katz. He discovered another revolver in the outer pocket of Chilton's overcoat, but no weapons were found on Katz. The officer testified that he only patted the men down to see whether they had weapons, and that he did not put his hands beneath the outer garments of either Terry or Chilton until he felt their guns. So far as appears from the record, he never placed his hands beneath Katz' outer garments. Officer McFadden seized Chilton's gun, asked the proprietor of the store to call a police wagon, and took all three men to the station, where Chilton and Terry were formally charged with carrying concealed weapons.

On the motion to suppress the guns the prosecution took the position that they had been seized following a search incident to a lawful arrest.

The trial court rejected this theory, stating that it 'would be stretching the facts beyond reasonable comprehension' to find that Officer McFadden had had probable cause to arrest the men before he patted them down for weapons. However, the court denied the defendants' motion on the ground that Officer McFadden, on the basis of his experience, 'had reasonable cause to believe * * * that the defendants were conducting themselves suspiciously, and some interrogation should be made of their action.' Purely for his own protection, the court held, the officer had the right to pat down the outer clothing of these men, who he had reasonable cause to believe might be armed. The court distinguished between an investigatory 'stop' and an arrest, and between a 'frisk' of the outer clothing for weapons and a full-blown search for evidence of crime. The frisk, it held, was essential to the proper performance of the officer's investigatory duties, for without it 'the answer to the police officer may be a bullet, and a loaded pistol discovered during the frisk is admissible.'

After the court denied their motion to suppress, Chilton and Terry waived jury trial and pleaded not guilty. The court adjudged them guilty, and the Court of Appeals for the Eighth Judicial District, Cuyahoga County, affirmed. State v. Terry, 5 Ohio App.2d 122, 214 N.E.2d 114 (1966). The Supreme Court of Ohio dismissed their appeal on the ground that no 'substantial constitutional question' was involved. We granted certiorari, 387 U.S. 929 (1967), to determine whether the admission of the revolvers in evidence violated petitioner's rights under the Fourth Amendment, made applicable to the States by the Fourteenth (1961). We affirm the conviction.

I.

The Fourth Amendment provides that 'the right of the people to be secure in their persons, houses, papers, and effects, against unreasonable searches and seizures, shall not be violated * * *.' This inestimable right of personal security belongs as much to the citizen on the streets of our cities as to the homeowner closeted in his study to dispose of his secret affairs. For, as this Court has always recognized,

'No right is held more sacred, or is more carefully guarded, by the common law, than the right of every individual to the possession and control of his own person, free from all restraint or interference of others, unless by clear and unquestionable authority of law.' Union Pac. R. Co. v. Botsford, 141 U.S. 250, 251 (1891).

We have recently held that 'the Fourth Amendment protects people, not places,' Katz v. United States, 389 U.S. 347, 351 (1967), and wherever an individual may harbor a reasonable 'expectation of privacy,' id., at 361, (Mr. Justice Harlan, concurring), he is entitled to be free from unreasonable governmental intrusion. Of course, the specific content and incidents of this right must be shaped by the context in which it is asserted. For 'what the Constitution forbids is not all searches and seizures, but unreasonable searches and seizures.' Elkins v. United States, 364 U.S. 206, 222 (1960). Unquestionably petitioner was entitled to the protection of the Fourth Amendment as he walked down the street in Cleveland. Beck v. State of Ohio, 379 U.S. 89 (1964); Rios v. United States, 364 U.S. 253 (1960); Henry v. United States, 361 U.S. 98 (1959); United States v. Di Re, 332 U.S. 581(1948); Carroll v. United States, 267 U.S. 132 (1925). The question is whether in all the circumstances of this on-the-street encounter, his right to personal security was violated by an unreasonable search and seizure.

We would be less than candid if we did not acknowledge that this question thrusts to the fore difficult and troublesome issues regarding a sensitive area of police activity—issues which have never before been squarely presented to this Court. Reflective of the tensions involved are the practical and constitutional arguments pressed with great vigor on both sides of the public debate over the power of the police to 'stop and frisk'—as it is sometimes euphemistically termed—suspicious persons.

On the one hand, it is frequently argued that in dealing with the rapidly unfolding and often dangerous situations on city streets the police are in need of an escalating set of flexible responses, graduated in relation to the amount of information they possess. For this purpose it is urged that distinctions should be made between a 'stop' and an 'arrest' (or a 'seizure' of a person), and between a 'frisk' and a 'search.'[3] Thus, it is argued, the police should be allowed to 'stop' a person and detain him briefly for questioning upon suspicion that he may be connected with criminal activity. Upon suspicion that the person may be armed, the police should have the power to 'frisk' him for weapons. If the 'stop' and the 'frisk' give rise to probable cause to believe that the suspect has committed a crime, then the police should be empowered to make a formal 'arrest,' and a full incident 'search' of the person. This scheme is justified in part upon the notion that a 'stop' and a 'frisk' amount to a mere 'minor inconvenience and petty indignity,' which can properly be imposed upon the citizen in the interest of effective law enforcement on the basis of a police officer's suspicion.[5]

On the other side the argument is made that the authority of the police must be strictly circumscribed by the law of arrest and search as

---

[3] Both the trial court and the Ohio Court of Appeals in this case relied upon such a distinction. State v. Terry, 5 Ohio App.2d 122, 125–130, 214 N.E.2d 114, 117–120 (1966). See also, e.g., People v. Rivera, 14 N.Y.2d 441, 252 N.Y.S.2d 458, 201 N.E.2d 32 (1964), cert. denied, 379 U.S. 978 (1965) . . .

[5] The theory is well laid out in the *Rivera* opinion: '(T)he evidence needed to make the inquiry is not of the same degree of conclusiveness as that required for an arrest. The stopping of the individual to inquire is not an arrest and the ground upon which the police may make the inquiry may be less incriminating than the ground for an arrest for a crime known to have been committed. * * *'And as the right to stop and inquire is to be justified for a cause less conclusive then that which would sustain an arrest, so the right to frisk may be justified as an incident to inquiry upon grounds of elemental safety and precaution which might not initially sustain a search. Ultimately the validity of the frisk narrows down to whether there is or is not a right by the police to touch the person questioned. The sense of exterior touch here involved is not very far different from the sense of sight or hearing-senses upon which police customarily act.' People v. Rivera, 14 N.Y.2d 441, 445, 447, 252 N.Y.S.2d 458, 461, 463, 201 N.E.2d 32, 34, 35 (1964), cert. denied, 379 U.S. 978 (1965).

it has developed to date in the traditional jurisprudence of the Fourth Amendment.[6] It is contended with some force that there is not—and cannot be—a variety of police activity which does not depend solely upon the voluntary cooperation of the citizen and yet which stops short of an arrest based upon probable cause to make such an arrest. The heart of the Fourth Amendment, the argument runs, is a severe requirement of specific justification for any intrusion upon protected personal security, coupled with a highly developed system of judicial controls to enforce upon the agents of the State the commands of the Constitution. Acquiescence by the courts in the compulsion inherent in the field interrogation practices at issue here, it is urged, would constitute an abdication of judicial control over, and indeed an encouragement of, substantial interference with liberty and personal security by police officers whose judgment is necessarily colored by their primary involvement in 'the often competitive enterprise of ferreting out crime.' This, it is argued, can only serve to exacerbate police-community tensions in the crowded centers of our Nation's cities.

In this context we approach the issues in this case mindful of the limitations of the judicial function in controlling the myriad daily situations in which policemen and citizens confront each other on the street. The State has characterized the issue here as 'the right of a police officer * * * to make an on-the-street stop, interrogate and pat down for weapons (known in street vernacular as 'stop and frisk').' But this is only partly accurate. For the issue is not the abstract propriety of the police conduct, but the admissibility against petitioner of the evidence uncovered by the search and seizure. Ever since its inception, the rule excluding evidence seized in violation of the Fourth Amendment has been recognized as a principal mode of discouraging lawless police conduct. *See* Weeks v. United States, 232 U.S. 383, 391–393 (1914). Thus its major thrust is a deterrent one, s*ee* Linkletter v. Walker, 381 U.S. 618, 629–635 (1965), and experience has taught that it is the only effective deterrent to police misconduct in the criminal context, and that without it the constitutional guarantee against unreasonable searches and seizures would be a mere 'form of words.' Mapp v. Ohio, 367 U.S. 643, 655 (1961). The rule also serves another vital function—'the imperative of judicial integrity.' Elkins v. United States, 364 U.S. 206, 222 (1960). Courts which sit under our Constitution cannot and will not be made party to lawless invasions of the constitutional rights of citizens by permitting unhindered governmental use of the fruits of such invasions. Thus in our system evidentiary rulings provide the context in which the judicial process of inclusion and exclusion approves some conduct as comporting with constitutional guarantees and disapproves other actions by state agents. A ruling admitting evidence in a criminal trial, we recognize, has the necessary effect of legitimizing the conduct which produced the

---

[6]   See, e.g., Foote, *The Fourth Amendment: Obstacle or Necessity in the Law of Arrest?*, 51 J.Crim.L.C. & P.S. 402 (1960).

evidence, while an application of the exclusionary rule withholds the constitutional imprimatur.

The exclusionary rule has its limitations, however, as a tool of judicial control. It cannot properly be invoked to exclude the products of legitimate police investigative techniques on the ground that much conduct which is closely similar involves unwarranted intrusions upon constitutional protections. Moreover, in some contexts the rule is ineffective as a deterrent. Street encounters between citizens and police officers are incredibly rich in diversity. They range from wholly friendly exchanges of pleasantries or mutually useful information to hostile confrontations of armed men involving arrests, or injuries, or loss of life. Moreover, hostile confrontations are not all of a piece. Some of them begin in a friendly enough manner, only to take a different turn upon the injection of some unexpected element into the conversation. Encounters are initiated by the police for a wide variety of purposes, some of which are wholly unrelated to a desire to prosecute for crime. Doubtless some police 'field interrogation' conduct violates the Fourth Amendment. But a stern refusal by this Court to condone such activity does not necessarily render it responsive to the exclusionary rule. Regardless of how effective the rule may be where obtaining convictions is an important objective of the police, it is powerless to deter invasions of constitutionally guaranteed rights where the police either have no interest in prosecuting or are willing to forgo successful prosecution in the interest of serving some other goal.

Proper adjudication of cases in which the exclusionary rule is invoked demands a constant awareness of these limitations. The wholesale harassment by certain elements of the police community, of which minority groups, particularly Negroes, frequently complain,[11] will not be stopped by the exclusion of any evidence from any criminal trial. Yet a rigid and unthinking application of the exclusionary rule, in futile protest against practices which it can never be used effectively to control, may exact a high toll in human injury and frustration of efforts to prevent crime. No judicial opinion can comprehend the protean variety of the street encounter, and we can only judge the facts of the case before us. Nothing we say today is to be taken as indicating approval of police

---

[11] The President's Commission on Law Enforcement and Administration of Justice found that '(i)n many communities, field interrogations are a major source of friction between the police and minority groups.' President's Commission on Law Enforcement and Administration of Justice, Task Force Report: The Police 183 (1967). It was reported that the friction caused by '(m)isuse of field interrogations' increases 'as more police departments adopt 'aggressive patrol' in which officers are encouraged routinely to stop and question persons on the street who are unknown to them, who are suspicious, or whose purpose for being abroad is not readily evident.' *Id.*, at 184. While the frequency with which 'frisking' forms a part of field interrogation practice varies tremendously with the locale, the objective of the interrogation, and the particular officer, it cannot help but be a severely exacerbating factor in police-community tensions. This is particularly true in situations where the 'stop and frisk' of youths or minority group members is 'motivated by the officers' perceived need to maintain the power image of the beat officer, an aim sometimes accomplished by humiliating anyone who attempts to undermine police control of the streets' [citation omitted].

conduct outside the legitimate investigative sphere. Under our decision, courts still retain their traditional responsibility to guard against police conduct which is over-bearing or harassing, or which trenches upon personal security without the objective evidentiary justification which the Constitution requires. When such conduct is identified, it must be condemned by the judiciary and its fruits must be excluded from evidence in criminal trials. And, of course, our approval of legitimate and restrained investigative conduct undertaken on the basis of ample factual justification should in no way discourage the employment of other remedies than the exclusionary rule to curtail abuses for which that sanction may prove inappropriate.

Having thus roughly sketched the perimeters of the constitutional debate over the limits on police investigative conduct in general and the background against which this case presents itself, we turn our attention to the quite narrow question posed by the facts before us: whether it is always unreasonable for a policeman to seize a person and subject him to a limited search for weapons unless there is probable cause for an arrest. Given the narrowness of this question, we have no occasion to canvass in detail the constitutional limitations upon the scope of a policeman's power when he confronts a citizen without probable cause to arrest him.

II.

Our first task is to establish at what point in this encounter the Fourth Amendment becomes relevant. That is, we must decide whether and when Officer McFadden 'seized' Terry and whether and when he conducted a 'search.' There is some suggestion in the use of such terms as 'stop' and 'frisk' that such police conduct is outside the purview of the Fourth Amendment because neither action rises to the level of a 'search' or 'seizure' within the meaning of the Constitution.[12] We emphatically reject this notion. It is quite plain that the Fourth Amendment governs 'seizures' of the person which do not eventuate in a trip to the station house and prosecution for crime—'arrests' in traditional terminology. It must be recognized that whenever a police officer accosts an individual and restrains his freedom to walk away, he has 'seized' that person. And it is nothing less than sheer torture of the English language to suggest that a careful exploration of the outer surfaces of a person's clothing all over his or her body in an attempt to find weapons is not a 'search,' Moreover, it is simply fantastic to urge that such a procedure performed in public by a policeman while the citizen stands helpless, perhaps facing a wall with his hands raised, is a 'petty indignity.'[13] It is a serious

---

[12] In this case, for example, the Ohio Court of Appeals stated that 'we must be careful to distinguish that the 'frisk' authorized herein includes only a 'frisk' for a dangerous weapon. It by no means authorizes a search for contraband, evidentiary material, or anything else in the absence of reasonable grounds to arrest. Such a search is controlled by the requirements of the Fourth Amendment, and probable cause is essential.' State v. Terry, 5 Ohio App.2d 122, 130, 214 N.E.2d 114, 120 (1966). *See also*, e.g., Ellis v. United States, 105 U.S.App.D.C. 86, 88, 264 F.2d 372, 374 (1959); Comment, 65 Col.L.Rev. 848, 860 and n. 81 (1965).

[13] Consider the following apt description: '(T)he officer must feel with sensitive fingers every portion of the prisoner's body. A through search must be made of the prisoner's arms and

intrusion upon the sanctity of the person, which may inflict great indignity and arouse strong resentment, and it is not to be undertaken lightly.

The danger in the logic which proceeds upon distinctions between a 'stop' and an 'arrest,' or 'seizure' of the person, and between a 'frisk' and a 'search' is twofold. It seeks to isolate from constitutional scrutiny the initial stages of the contact between the policeman and the citizen. And by suggesting a rigid all-or-nothing model of justification and regulation under the Amendment, it obscures the utility of limitations upon the scope, as well as the initiation, of police action as a means of constitutional regulation.[15] This Court has held in the past that a search which is reasonable at its inception may violate the Fourth Amendment by virtue of its intolerable intensity and scope. Kremen v. United States, 353 U.S. 346; Go-Bart Importing Co. v. United States, 282 U.S. 344, 356–358 (1931); see United States v. Di Re, 332 U.S. 581, 586–587 (1948). The scope of the search must be 'strictly tied to and justified by' the circumstances which rendered its initiation permissible. Warden v. Hayden, 387 U.S. 294, 310 (1967) (Mr. Justice Fortas, concurring); see, e.g., Preston v. United States, 376 U.S. 364 (1964); Agnello v. United States, 269 U.S. 20, 30–31 (1925).

---

armpits, waistline and back, the groin and area about the testicles, and entire surface of the legs down to the feet.' Priar & Martin, Searching and Disarming Criminals, 45 J.Crim.L.C. & P.S. 481 (1954).

[15] These dangers are illustrated in part by the course of adjudication in the Court of Appeals of New York. Although its first decision in this area, People v. Rivera, 14 N.Y.2d 441, 252 N.Y.S.2d 458, 201 N.E.2d 32 (1964), cert. denied, 379 U.S. 978 (1965), rested squarely on the notion that a 'frisk' was not a 'search,' see nn. 3–5, supra, it was compelled to recognize in People v. Taggart, 20 N.Y.2d 335, 342, 283 N.Y.S.2d 1, 8, 229 N.E.2d 581, 586, (1967), that what it had actually authorized in Rivera, and subsequent decisions, see, e.g., People v. Pugach, 15 N.Y.2d 65, 255 N.Y.S.2d 833, 204 N.E.2d 176 (1964), cert. denied, 380 U.S. 936 (1965), was a 'search' upon less than probable cause. However, in acknowledging that no valid distinction could be maintained on the basis of its cases, the Court of Appeals continued to distinguish between the two in theory. It still defined 'search' as it had in Rivera—as an essentially unlimited examination of the person for any and all seizable items—and merely noted that the cases had upheld police intrusions which went far beyond the original limited conception of a 'frisk.' Thus, principally because it failed to consider limitations upon the scope of searches in individual cases as a potential mode of regulation, the Court of Appeals in three short years arrived at the position that the Constitution must, in the name of necessity, be held to permit unrestrained rummaging about a person and his effects upon mere suspicion. It did apparently limit its holding to 'cases involving serious personal injury or grave irreparable property damage,' thus excluding those involving 'the enforcement of sumptuary laws, such as gambling, and laws of limited public consequence, such as narcotics violations, prostitution, larcenies of the ordinary kind, and the like.' People v. Taggart, supra, at 340, 283 N.Y.S.2d at 6, 229 N.E.2d at 584. In our view the sounder course is to recognize that the Fourth Amendment governs all intrusions by agents of the public upon personal security, and to make the scope of the particular intrusion, in light of all the exigencies of the case, a central element in the analysis of reasonableness. Cf. Brinegar v. United States, 338 U.S. 160, 183 (1949) (Mr. Justice Jackson, dissenting). Compare Camara v. Muncipal Court, 387 U.S. 523, 537 (1967). This seems preferable to an approach which attributes too much significance to an overly technical definition of 'search,' and which turns in part upon a judge-made hierarchy of legislative enactments in the criminal sphere. Focusing the inquiry squarely on the dangers and demands of the particular situation also seems more likely to produce rules which are intelligible to the police and the public alike than requiring the officer in the heat of an unfolding encounter on the street to make a judgment as to which laws are 'of limited public consequence.'

The distinctions of classical 'stop-and-frisk' theory thus serve to divert attention from the central inquiry under the Fourth Amendment—the reasonableness in all the circumstances of the particular governmental invasion of a citizen's personal security. 'Search' and 'seizure' are not talismans. We therefore reject the notions that the Fourth Amendment does not come into play at all as a limitation upon police conduct if the officers stop short of something called a 'technical arrest' or a 'full-blown search.'

In this case there can be no question, then, that Officer McFadden 'seized' petitioner and subjected him to a 'search' when he took hold of him and patted down the outer surfaces of his clothing. We must decide whether at that point it was reasonable for Officer McFadden to have interfered with petitioner's personal security as he did.[16] And in determining whether the seizure and search were 'unreasonable' our inquiry is a dual one-whether the officer's action was justified at its inception, and whether it was reasonably related in scope to the circumstances which justified the interference in the first place.

III.

If this case involved police conduct subject to the Warrant Clause of the Fourth Amendment, we would have to ascertain whether 'probable cause' existed to justify the search and seizure which took place. However, that is not the case. We do not retreat from our holdings that the police must, whenever practicable, obtain advance judicial approval of searches and seizures through the warrant procedure, *See e.g.,* Katz v. United States, 389 U.S. 347 (1967); Beck v. State of Ohio, 379 U.S. 89 (1964); Chapman v. United States, 365 U.S. 610 (1961), or that in most instances failure to comply with the warrant requirement can only be excused by exigent circumstances, *see, e.g.,* Warden v. Hayden, 387 U.S. 294 (1967) (hot pursuit); *cf.* Preston v. United States, 376 U.S. 364, 367–368 (1964). But we deal here with an entire rubric of police conduct—necessarily swift action predicated upon the on-the-spot observations of the officer on the beat—which historically has not been, and as a practical matter could not be, subjected to the warrant procedure. Instead, the conduct involved in this case must be tested by the Fourth Amendment's general proscription against unreasonable searches and seizures.

Nonetheless, the notions which underlie both the warrant procedure and the requirement of probable cause remain fully relevant in this context. In order to assess the reasonableness of Officer McFadden's

---

[16] We thus decide nothing today concerning the constitutional propriety of an investigative 'seizure' upon less than probable cause for purposes of 'detention' and/or interrogation. Obviously, not all personal intercourse between policemen and citizens involves 'seizures' of persons. Only when the officer, by means of physical force or show of authority, has in some way restrained the liberty of a citizen may we conclude that a 'seizure' has occurred. We cannot tell with any certainty upon this record whether any such 'seizure' took place here prior to Officer McFadden's initiation of physical contact for purposes of searching Terry for weapons, and we thus may assume that up to that point no intrusion upon constitutionally protected rights had occurred.

conduct as a general proposition, it is necessary 'first to focus upon the governmental interest which allegedly justifies official intrusion upon the constitutionally protected interests of the private citizen,' for there is 'no ready test for determining reasonableness other than by balancing the need to search (or seize) against the invasion which the search (or seizure) entails.' Camara v. Municipal Court, 387 U.S. 523, 534–535, 536–537 (1967). And in justifying the particular intrusion the police officer must be able to point to specific and articulable facts which, taken together with rational inferences from those facts, reasonably warrant that intrusion. The scheme of the Fourth Amendment becomes meaningful only when it is assured that at some point the conduct of those charged with enforcing the laws can be subjected to the more detached, neutral scrutiny of a judge who must evaluate the reasonableness of a particular search or seizure in light of the particular circumstances. And in making that assessment it is imperative that the facts be judged against an objective standard: would the facts available to the officer at the moment of the seizure or the search 'warrant a man of reasonable caution in the belief' that the action taken was appropriate? *Cf.* Carroll v. United States, 267 U.S. 132 (1925); Beck v. State of Ohio, 379 U.S. 89, 96–97 (1964). Anything less would invite intrusions upon constitutionally guaranteed rights based on nothing more substantial than inarticulate hunches, a result this Court has consistently refused to sanction. *See, e.g., Beck v. Ohio, supra*; Rios v. United States, 364 U.S. 253 (1960); Henry v. United States, 361 U.S. 98 (1959). And simple "good faith on the part of the arresting officer is not enough.' * * * If subjective good faith alone were the test, the protections of the Fourth Amendment would evaporate, and the people would be 'secure in their persons, houses, papers and effects,' only in the discretion of the police.' *Beck v. Ohio, supra*, at 97.

Applying these principles to this case, we consider first the nature and extent of the governmental interests involved. One general interest is of course that of effective crime prevention and detection; it is this interest which underlies the recognition that a police officer may in appropriate circumstances and in an appropriate manner approach a person for purposes of investigating possibly criminal behavior even though there is no probable cause to make an arrest. It was this legitimate investigative function Officer McFadden was discharging when he decided to approach petitioner and his companions He had observed Terry, Chilton, and Katz go through a series of acts, each of them perhaps innocent in itself, but which taken together warranted further investigation. There is nothing unusual in two men standing together on a street corner, perhaps waiting for someone. Nor is there anything suspicious about people in such circumstances strolling up and down the street, singly or in pairs. Store windows, moreover, are made to be looked in. But the story is quite different where, as here, two men hover about a street corner for an extended period of time, at the end of which it becomes apparent that they are not waiting for anyone or anything; where these men pace alternately along an identical route, pausing to stare in the same store window roughly 24 times; where each completion of this route is followed immediately by a conference between the two men on the corner; where they are joined in one of these conferences by a third man who leaves swiftly; and where the two men finally follow the third and rejoin him a couple of blocks away. It would have been poor police work indeed for an officer of 30 years' experience in the detection of thievery from stores in this same neighborhood to have failed to investigate this behavior further.

The crux of this case, however, is not the propriety of Officer McFadden's taking steps to investigate petitioner's suspicious behavior, but rather, whether there was justification for McFadden's invasion of Terry's personal security by searching him for weapons in the course of that investigation. We are now concerned with more than the governmental interest in investigating crime; in addition, there is the more immediate interest of the police officer in taking steps to assure himself that the person with whom he is dealing is not armed with a weapon that could unexpectedly and fatally be used against him. Certainly it would be unreasonable to require that police officers take unnecessary risks in the performance of their duties. American criminals have a long tradition of armed violence, and every year in this country many law enforcement officers are killed in the line of duty, and thousands more are wounded. Virtually all of these deaths and a substantial portion of the injuries are inflicted with guns and knives.[21]

In view of these facts, we cannot blind ourselves to the need for law enforcement officers to protect themselves and other prospective victims of violence in situations where they may lack probable cause for an arrest. When an officer is justified in believing that the individual whose suspicious behavior he is investigating at close range is armed and presently dangerous to the officer or to others, it would appear to be clearly unreasonable to deny the officer the power to take necessary measures to determine whether the person is in fact carrying a weapon and to neutralize the threat of physical harm.

We must still consider, however, the nature and quality of the intrusion on individual rights which must be accepted if police officers are to be conceded the right to search for weapons in situations where probable cause to arrest for crime is lacking. Even a limited search of the

---

[21] Fifty-seven law enforcement officers were killed in the line of duty in this country in 1966, bringing the total to 335 for the seven-year period beginning with 1960. Also in 1966, there were 23,851 assaults on police officers, 9,113 of which resulted in injuries to the policeman. Fifty-five of the 57 officers killed in 1966 died from gunshot wounds, 41 of them inflicted by handguns easily secreted about the person. The remaining two murders were perpetrated by knives. *See* Federal Bureau of Investigation, Uniform Crime Reports for the United States—1966, at 45–48, 152 and Table 51.The easy availability of firearms to potential criminals in this country is well known and has provoked much debate. See, e.g., President's Commission on Law Enforcement and Administration of Justice, The Challenge of Crime in a Free Society 239–243 (1967). Whatever the merits of gun-control proposals, this fact is relevant to an assessment of the need for some form of self-protective search power.

outer clothing for weapons constitutes a severe, though brief, intrusion upon cherished personal security, and it must surely be an annoying, frightening, and perhaps humiliating experience. Petitioner contends that such an intrusion is permissible only incident to a lawful arrest, either for a crime involving the possession of weapons or for a crime the commission of which led the officer to investigate in the first place. However, this argument must be closely examined.

Petitioner does not argue that a police officer should refrain from making any investigation of suspicious circumstances until such time as he has probable cause to make an arrest; nor does he deny that police officers in properly discharging their investigative function may find themselves confronting persons who might well be armed and dangerous. Moreover, he does not say that an officer is always unjustified in searching a suspect to discover weapons. Rather, he says it is unreasonable for the policeman to take that step until such time as the situation evolves to a point where there is probable cause to make an arrest. When that point has been reached, petitioner would concede the officer's right to conduct a search of the suspect for weapons, fruits or instrumentalities of the crime, or 'mere' evidence, incident to the arrest.

There are two weaknesses in this line of reasoning however. First, it fails to take account of traditional limitations upon the scope of searches, and thus recognizes no distinction in purpose, character, and extent between a search incident to an arrest and a limited search for weapons. The former, although justified in part by the acknowledged necessity to protect the arresting officer from assault with a concealed weapon, Preston v. United States, 376 U.S. 364, 367 (1964), is also justified on other grounds, *ibid.,* and can therefore involve a relatively extensive exploration of the person. A search for weapons in the absence of probable cause to arrest, however, must, like any other search, be strictly circumscribed by the exigencies which justify its initiation. Warden v. Hayden, 387 U.S. 294, 310 (1967) (Mr. Justice Fortas, concurring). Thus it must be limited to that which is necessary for the discovery of weapons which might be used to harm the officer or others nearby, and may realistically be characterized as something less than a 'full' search, even though it remains a serious intrusion.

A second, and related, objection to petitioner's argument is that it assumes that the law of arrest has already worked out the balance between the particular interests involved here—the neutralization of danger to the policeman in the investigative circumstance and the sanctity of the individual. But this is not so. An arrest is a wholly different kind of intrusion upon individual freedom from a limited search for weapons, and the interests each is designed to serve are likewise quite different. An arrest is the initial stage of a criminal prosecution. It is intended to vindicate society's interest in having its laws obeyed, and it is inevitably accompanied by future interference with the individual's freedom of movement, whether or not trial or conviction ultimately follows. The protective search for weapons, on the other hand, constitutes a brief, though far from inconsiderable, intrusion upon the sanctity of the person. It does not follow that because an officer may lawfully arrest a person only when he is apprised of facts sufficient to warrant a belief that the person has committed or is committing a crime, the officer is equally unjustified, absent that kind of evidence, in making any intrusions short of an arrest. Moreover, a perfectly reasonable apprehension of danger may arise long before the officer is possessed of adequate information to justify taking a person into custody for the purpose of prosecuting him for a crime. Petitioner's reliance on cases which have worked out standards of reasonableness with regard to 'seizures' constituting arrests and searches incident thereto is thus misplaced. It assumes that the interests sought to be vindicated and the invasions of personal security may be equated in the two cases, and thereby ignores a vital aspect of the analysis of the reasonableness of particular types of conduct under the Fourth Amendment. *See Camara v. Municipal Court, supra.*

Our evaluation of the proper balance that has to be struck in this type of case leads us to conclude that there must be a narrowly drawn authority to permit a reasonable search for weapons for the protection of the police officer, where he has reason to believe that he is dealing with an armed and dangerous individual, regardless of whether he has probable cause to arrest the individual for a crime. The officer need not be absolutely certain that the individual is armed; the issue is whether a reasonably prudent man in the circumstances would be warranted in the belief that his safety or that of others was in danger. And in determining whether the officer acted reasonably in such circumstances, due weight must be given, not to his inchoate and unparticularized suspicion or 'hunch,' but to the specific reasonable inferences which he is entitled to draw from the facts in light of his experience.

IV.

We must now examine the conduct of Officer McFadden in this case to determine whether his search and seizure of petitioner were reasonable, both at their inception and as conducted. He had observed Terry, together with Chilton and another man, acting in a manner he took to be preface to a 'stick-up.' We think on the facts and circumstances Officer McFadden detailed before the trial judge a reasonably prudent man would have been warranted in believing petitioner was armed and thus presented a threat to the officer's safety while he was investigating his suspicious behavior. The actions of Terry and Chilton were consistent with McFadden's hypothesis that these men were contemplating a daylight robbery—which, it is reasonable to assume, would be likely to involve the use of weapons—and nothing in their conduct from the time he first noticed them until the time he confronted them and identified himself as a police officer gave him sufficient reason to negate that hypothesis. Although the trio had departed the original scene, there was nothing to indicate abandonment of an intent to commit a robbery at some point. Thus, when Officer McFadden approached the three men gathered before the display window at Zucker's store he had observed enough to make it quite reasonable to fear that they were armed; and nothing in their response to his hailing them, identifying himself as a police officer, and asking their names served to dispel that reasonable belief. We cannot say his decision at that point to seize Terry and pat his clothing for weapons was the product of a volatile or inventive imagination, or was undertaken simply as an act of harassment; the record evidences the tempered act of a policeman who in the course of an investigation had to make a quick decision as to how to protect himself and others from possible danger, and took limited steps to do so.

The manner in which the seizure and search were conducted is, of course, as vital a part of the inquiry as whether they were warranted at all. The Fourth Amendment proceeds as much by limitations upon the scope of governmental action as by imposing preconditions upon its initiation. *Compare* Katz v. United States, 389 U.S. 347, 354–356 (1967). The entire deterrent purpose of the rule excluding evidence seized in violation of the Fourth Amendment rests on the assumption that 'limitations upon the fruit to be gathered tend to limit the quest itself.' Thus, evidence may not be introduced if it was discovered by means of a seizure and search which were not reasonably related in scope to the justification for their initiation Warden v. Hayden, 387 U.S. 294, 310 (1967) (Mr. Justice Fortas, concurring).

We need not develop at length in this case, however, the limitations which the Fourth Amendment places upon a protective seizure and search for weapons. These limitations will have to be developed in the concrete factual circumstances of individual cases. *See* Sibron v. New York, 392 U.S. 408, decided today. Suffice it to note that such a search, unlike a search without a warrant incident to a lawful arrest, is not justified by any need to prevent the disappearance or destruction of evidence of crime. *See* Preston v. United States, 376 U.S. 364, 367 (1964). The sole justification of the search in the present situation is the protection of the police officer and others nearby, and it must therefore be confined in scope to an intrusion reasonably designed to discover guns, knives, clubs, or other hidden instruments for the assault of the police officer.

The scope of the search in this case presents no serious problem in light of these standards. Officer McFadden patted down the outer clothing of petitioner and his two companions. He did not place his hands in their pockets or under the outer surface of their garments until he had felt weapons, and then he merely reached for and removed the guns. He never did invade Katz' person beyond the outer surfaces of his clothes, since he discovered nothing in his patdown which might have been a weapon. Officer McFadden confined his search strictly to what was minimally necessary to learn whether the men were armed and to disarm them once he discovered the weapons. He did not conduct a general exploratory search for whatever evidence of criminal activity he might find.

V.

We conclude that the revolver seized from Terry was properly admitted in evidence against him. At the time he seized petitioner and searched him for weapons, Officer McFadden had reasonable grounds to believe that petitioner was armed and dangerous, and it was necessary for the protection of himself and others to take swift measures to discover the true facts and neutralize the threat of harm if it materialized. The policeman carefully restricted his search to what was appropriate to the discovery of the particular items which he sought. Each case of this sort will, of course, have to be decided on its own facts. We merely hold today that where a police officer observes unusual conduct which leads him reasonably to conclude in light of his experience that criminal activity may be afoot and that the persons with whom he is dealing may be armed and presently dangerous, where in the course of investigating this behavior he identifies himself as a policeman and makes reasonable inquiries, and where nothing in the initial stages of the encounter serves to dispel his reasonable fear for his own or others' safety, he is entitled for the protection of himself and others in the area to conduct a carefully limited search of the outer clothing of such persons in an attempt to discover weapons which might be used to assault him. Such a search is a reasonable search under the Fourth Amendment, and any weapons seized may properly be introduced in evidence against the person from whom they were taken.

Affirmed.

■ MR. JUSTICE HARLAN, concurring.

While I unreservedly agree with the Court's ultimate holding in this case, I am constrained to fill in a few gaps, as I see them, in its opinion. I do this because what is said by this Court today will serve as initial guidelines for law enforcement authorities and courts throughout the land as this important new field of law develops.

A police officer's right to make an on-the-street 'stop' and an accompanying 'frisk' for weapons is of course bounded by the protections afforded by the Fourth and Fourteenth Amendments. The Court holds, and I agree, that while the right does not depend upon possession by the officer of a valid warrant, nor upon the existence of probable cause, such activities must be reasonable under the circumstances as the officer credibly relates them in court. Since the question in this and most cases is whether evidence produced by a frisk is admissible, the problem is to determine what makes a frisk reasonable.

If the State of Ohio were to provide that police officers could, on articulable suspicion less than probable cause, forcibly frisk and disarm persons thought to be carrying concealed weapons, I would have little doubt that action taken pursuant to such authority could be constitutionally reasonable. Concealed weapons create an immediate and severe danger to the public, and though that danger might not warrant routine general weapons checks, it could well warrant action on less than a 'probability.' I mention this line of analysis because I think it vital to point out that it cannot be applied in this case. On the record before us Ohio has not clothed its policemen with routine authority to frisk and disarm on suspicion; in the absence of state authority, policemen have no more right to 'pat down' the outer clothing of passers-by, or of persons to whom they address casual questions, than does any other citizen. Consequently, the Ohio courts did not rest the constitutionality of this frisk upon any general authority in Officer McFadden to take reasonable steps to protect the citizenry, including himself, from dangerous weapons.

The state courts held, instead, that when an officer is lawfully confronting a possibly hostile person in the line of duty he has a right, springing only from the necessity of the situation and not from any broader right to disarm, to frisk for his own protection. This holding, with which I agree and with which I think the Court agrees, offers the only satisfactory basis I can think of for affirming this conviction. The holding has, however, two logical corollaries that I do not think the Court has fully expressed.

In the first place, if the frisk is justified in order to protect the officer during an encounter with a citizen, the officer must first have constitutional grounds to insist on an encounter, to make a forcible stop. Any person, including a policeman, is at liberty to avoid a person he considers dangerous. If and when a policeman has a right instead to disarm such a person for his own protection, he must first have a right not to avoid him but to be in his presence. That right must be more than the liberty (again, possessed by every citizen) to address questions to other persons, for ordinarily the person addressed has an equal right to ignore his interrogator and walk away; he certainly need not submit to a frisk for the questioner's protection. I would make it perfectly clear that the right to frisk in this case depends upon the reasonableness of a forcible stop to investigate a suspected crime.

Where such a stop is reasonable, however, the right to frisk must be immediate and automatic if the reason for the stop is, as here, an articulable suspicion of a crime of violence. Just as a full search incident to a lawful arrest requires no additional justification, a limited frisk incident to a lawful stop must often be rapid and routine. There is no reason why an officer, rightfully but forcibly confronting a person suspected of a serious crime, should have to ask one question and take the risk that the answer might be a bullet.

The facts of this case are illustrative of a proper stop and an incident frisk. Officer McFadden had no probable cause to arrest Terry for anything, but he had observed circumstances that would reasonably lead an experienced, prudent policeman to suspect that Terry was about to engage in burglary or robbery. His justifiable suspicion afforded a proper constitutional basis for accosting Terry, restraining his liberty of movement briefly, and addressing questions to him, and Officer McFadden did so. When he did, he had no reason whatever to suppose that Terry might be armed, apart from the fact that he suspected him of planning a violent crime. McFadden asked Terry his name, to which Terry 'mumbled something.' Whereupon McFadden, without asking Terry to speak louder and without giving him any chance to explain his presence or his actions, forcibly frisked him.

I would affirm this conviction for what I believe to be the same reasons the Court relies on. I would, however, make explicit what I think is implicit in affirmance on the present facts. Officer McFadden's right to interrupt Terry's freedom of movement and invade his privacy arose only because circumstances warranted forcing an encounter with Terry in an effort to prevent or investigate a crime. Once that forced encounter was justified, however, the officer's right to take suitable measures for his own safely followed automatically.

Upon the foregoing premises, I join the opinion of the Court.

■ MR. JUSTICE DOUGLAS, dissenting.

I agree that petitioner was 'seized' within the meaning of the Fourth Amendment. I also agree that frisking petitioner and his companions for guns was a 'search.' But it is a mystery how that 'search' and that 'seizure' can be constitutional by Fourth Amendment standards, unless there was 'probable cause' to believe that (1) a crime had been committed or (2) a crime was in the process of being committed or (3) a crime was about to be committed. Police officers need not wait until they see a person actually commit a crime before they are able to 'seize' that person. Respect for our constitutional system and personal liberty demands in return, however, that such a 'seizure' be made only upon 'probable cause.'

The opinion of the Court disclaims the existence of 'probable cause.' If loitering were in issue and that was the offense charged, there would be 'probable cause' shown. But the crime here is carrying concealed weapons; and there is no basis for concluding that the officer had 'probable cause' for believing that that crime was being committed. Had a warrant been sought, a magistrate would, therefore, have been unauthorized to issue one, for he can act only if there is a showing of 'probable cause.' We hold today that the police have greater authority to make a 'seizure' and conduct a 'search' than a judge has to authorize such action. We have said precisely the opposite over and over again.

In other words, police officers up to today have been permitted to effect arrests or searches without warrants only when the facts within their personal knowledge would satisfy the constitutional standard of probable cause. At the time of their 'seizure' without a warrant they must possess facts concerning the person arrested that would have satisfied a magistrate that 'probable cause' was indeed present. . . .

SECTION 4

WHEN HAS A CITIZEN BEEN "SEIZED" FOR FOURTH
AMENDMENT PURPOSES?

107

To give the police greater power than a magistrate is to take a long step down the totalitarian path. Perhaps such a step is desirable to cope with modern forms of lawlessness. But if it is taken, it should be the deliberate choice of the people through a constitutional amendment. Until the Fourth Amendment, which is closely allied with the Fifth,[4] is rewritten, the person and the effects of the individual are beyond the reach of all government agencies until there are reasonable grounds to believe (probable cause) that a criminal venture has been launched or is about to be launched.

There have been powerful hydraulic pressures throughout our history that bear heavily on the Court to water down constitutional guarantees and give the police the upper hand. That hydraulic pressure has probably never been greater than it is today.

Yet if the individual is no longer to be sovereign, if the police can pick him up whenever they do not like the cut of his jib, if they can 'seize' and 'search' him in their discretion, we enter a new regime. The decision to enter it should be made only after a full debate by the people of this country.

4. WHEN HAS A CITIZEN BEEN "SEIZED" FOR FOURTH AMENDMENT PURPOSES?

United States v. Ford

548 F.3d 1 (1st Cir. 2008)

■ STAHL, CIRCUIT JUDGE.

Defendant-Appellant Tyson Ford appeals his conviction under the felon-in-possession statute, 18 U.S.C. § 922(g)(1). His main complaint is that the district court erred in denying his motion to suppress a firearm found on his person because it was obtained during an unconstitutional search and seizure. Finding no error, we affirm the conviction.

I.   Background

On September 8, 2005, Officers Daran Edwards and Daniel Griffin ("the Officers") of the Boston Police Department ("BPD") were on a routine patrol in a high-crime area of Dorchester, Massachusetts. The Officers were in uniform and in a marked police cruiser. They regularly patrolled the Dorchester area and were familiar with many of the area's residents. At approximately 3:00 p.m., the Officers observed Ford, who they did not recognize, walking alone down Harvard Street. Ford looked over his shoulder, observed the cruiser and then lowered his head, began

---

[4]   *See* Boyd v. United States, 116 U.S. 616, 633 'For the 'unreasonable searches and seizures' condemned in the fourth amendment are almost always made for the purpose of compelling a man to give evidence against himself, which in criminal cases is condemned in the fifth amendment; and compelling a man 'in a criminal case to be a witness against himself,' which is condemned in the fifth amendment, throws light on the question as to what is an 'unreasonable search and seizure' within the meaning of the fourth amendment.'

walking rapidly, and turned right onto Gleason Street. The Officers followed Ford the wrong way up Gleason Street for a short distance, ostensibly to conduct a Field Intelligence and Observation Report (FIO), used by BPD police officers for intelligence collection.

Upon coming abreast of Ford, Officer Griffin leaned out of the passenger side window and asked him, "Can I speak to you for a minute?" Ford stopped walking, took his identification out of his front pocket, and voluntarily handed it to Officer Griffin. He told the Officers he had no outstanding warrants and was not on probation. While Officer Edwards ran a search for warrants using the BPD database, Officer Griffin continued to ask Ford questions like "where do you live?" and "where are you headed?" Officer Griffin observed that Ford appeared annoyed, nervous, and hostile at times and that he was breathing rapidly, stuttered his words, and his hands shook. Officer Griffin asked Ford whether he had anything on him that the Officers needed to know about. Ford answered in the negative.

Roughly 45 seconds after taking Ford's driver's license, Officer Griffin exited the cruiser to complete the FIO. Following BPD protocol, Officer Edwards also exited, walked behind the cruiser, and approached Ford from the same direction as Officer Griffin. Neither Officer unholstered his weapon. Ford raised his hands into the air and said, "Come on man, what's this all about?" Officer Griffin asked whether Ford had any weapons on his person. Ford responded, "Yeah, I got a gun in my pocket, but it don't fire." The Officers then placed Ford in handcuffs, and Officer Griffin frisked him, discovering and seizing a Grendel, Inc., P-12 .380 semi-automatic handgun from the pocket of Ford's pants. The Officers arrested Ford, the entire encounter lasting approximately two to three minutes from interception to arrest. Before placing Ford in handcuffs, neither Officer had touched Ford, drawn his weapon, or told Ford he was not free to leave nor had the Officers activated the police cruiser's siren or flashing lights.

On November 1, 2005, a single-count complaint charged Ford as a felon-in-possession of a handgun in violation of 18 U.S.C. § 922(g)(1). On March 3, 2006, Ford moved to suppress the evidence seized in the warrantless search of his person, contending he was seized at the time the Officers exited the vehicle in violation of his Fourth Amendment rights. On July 20, 2006, the district court denied the motion and issued a well-reasoned rescript, finding that the Officers had not seized Ford prior to his incriminating statement.

On October 4, 2006, Ford entered a conditional plea of guilty, *see* Fed.R.Crim.P. 11(a)(2), reserving his right to appeal the denial of his suppression motion. On October 11, 2006, the district court sentenced Ford to a term of imprisonment of 15 years under the Armed Career Criminal Act, 18 U.S.C. § 924(e)(1). Ford now appeals the denial to suppress the handgun and his conviction.

The Motion to Suppress

This appeal primarily concerns the boundary delineating casual encounters with police, as when officers question persons in public places, from seizures requiring probable cause or articulable suspicion. *See* United States v. Young, 105 F.3d 1, 5–6 (1st Cir.1997). Ford challenges the lower court's denial of his motion to suppress in which he argued the Officers seized him before possessing the requisite reasonable suspicion. The Government concedes, and we accept for the purposes of this review, that the Officers lacked the reasonable suspicion required for a seizure and that, if a seizure occurred, the handgun found on Ford's person "must be suppressed as tainted fruit." *See* Florida v. Bostick, 501 U.S. 429, 433–34 (1991).

. . . Not every interaction between a police officer and a citizen constitutes a seizure triggering Fourth Amendment protections. *Bostick,* 501 U.S. at 434; *Cardoza,* 129 F.3d at 14; *Young,* 105 F.3d at 5. While per se rules are inappropriate in determining when a seizure occurs for Fourth Amendment purposes, United States v. Drayton, 536 U.S. 194, 201 (2002) (citing *Bostick,* 501 U.S. at 439), we have observed that encounters "between law enforcement officials and citizens generally fall[ ] within three tiers of Fourth Amendment analysis, depending on the level of police intrusion into a person's privacy." *Young,* 105 F.3d at 5. Because there are no bright-line distinctions between the tiers, we look to the totality of the circumstances to determine where a police encounter falls. *Drayton,* 536 U.S. at 207; Michigan v. Chesternut, 486 U.S. 567, 572 (1988); United States v. Smith, 423 F.3d 25, 29–30 (1st Cir.2005); *Cardoza,* 129 F.3d at 15. *See also Bostick,* 501 U.S. at 439–40 (rejecting per se rule for seizure in favor of totality inquiry).

The lowest tier, which does not implicate the Fourth Amendment, involves minimally intrusive interactions such as when police officers approach individuals on the street or in public places to ask questions. *Young,* 105 F.3d at 5–6; *Bostick,* 501 U.S. at 434. *See Drayton,* 536 U.S. at 201, (observing that law enforcement agents may question and ask a citizen for identification even when they have no basis to suspect the individual so long as they "do not induce cooperation by coercive means"). If the encounter amounts to more than a minimally intrusive interaction, a seizure occurs, either a de facto arrest requiring probable cause or an investigative (or *Terry*) stop necessitating reasonable suspicion. *Young,* 105 F.3d at 6.

The Supreme Court has adopted the standard set forth by Justice Stewart's plurality opinion in United States v. Mendenhall, 446 U.S. 544, 554 (1980), that "a person has been 'seized' within the meaning of the Fourth Amendment only if, in view of all the circumstances surrounding the incident, a reasonable person would have believed that he was not free to leave."[2] *See Drayton,* 536 U.S. at 202; California v. Hodari D., 499 U.S. 621, 627–28 (1991) (compiling cases). To constitute seizure, this Circuit requires one's liberty be restrained by either physical force or an assertion of authority. *Id.* at 626; United States v. Sealey, 30 F.3d 7, 9 (1st Cir.1994); *see Smith,* 423 F.3d at 28 (finding seizure can occur without physical restraint if compliance is coerced and not voluntary). The Court has explained the reasonable person test presumes an innocent person. *Bostick,* 501 U.S. at 438; *Smith,* 423 F.3d at 31, n. 5.

Under the objective totality of the circumstances standard, we look not to "whether the citizen perceived that he was being ordered to restrict his movement, but whether the officer's words and actions would have conveyed that to a reasonable person." *Hodari D.,* 499 U.S. at 628; *Chesternut,* 486 U.S. at 574 (noting objective standard does not vary with mind of each individual). Thus, there is less reason to inquire into a defendant's subjective mindset when considering whether there is a submission to authority, *see Cardoza,* 129 F.3d at 14 n. 4, particularly as all persons feel "some degree of compulsion" and "discomfort" when approached by police officers. *Smith,* 423 F.3d at 28.[3]

Employing this objective test, the inquiry before us today is not whether the Officers could approach and question Ford, but, instead "whether they did so in a manner that would have communicated to a reasonable person that he was not free to refuse to answer and walk away." *Smith,* 423 F.3d at 29. To elucidate this test, the Supreme Court has provided circumstances that may indicate a seizure including "the threatening presence of several officers, the display of a weapon by an officer, some physical touching of the person of the citizen, or the use of language or tone of voice indicating that compliance with the officer's request might be compelled." *Mendenhall,* 446 U.S. at 554. [T]his list of factors is not exhaustive and no single factor is dispositive in any case." *Smith,* 423 F.3d at 29. *See Chesternut,* 486 U.S. at 575 (considering also non-use of patrol car's siren or flashers); United States v. McKoy, 428 F.3d 38, 40 (1st Cir.2005) (adding neighborhood as "only one factor that must be looked at alongside all the other circumstances").

To evaluate the circumstances leading to Ford's arrest, our case law provides guidance for discerning the Fourth Amendment's parameters. In *Cardoza,* police officers drove the wrong way on a one-way street to ask the defendant pointed questions including "Why are you out at this time of night?" 129 F.3d at 15. We found no seizure, noting the police had

---

[2] The Court has explained the reasonable person test presumes an innocent person. *Bostick,* 501 U.S. at 438, 111 S.Ct. 2382; *Smith,* 423 F.3d at 31, n. 5.

[3] Both the Supreme Court and this Circuit have observed that exchanges do not lose their consensual nature simply because people generally answer police officers' questions. *Drayton,* 536 U.S. at 205 (citing *Delgado,* 466 U.S. at 216); *Cardoza,* 129 F.3d at 16 (agreeing with defendant that "few people . . . would ever feel free to walk away from any police question"). *See id.* ("The 'free to walk away' test . . . must be read in conjunction with the Court's frequent admonitions that 'a seizure does not occur simply because a police officer approaches an individual and asks a few questions' ") (quoting *Bostick,* 501 U.S. at 434, and Terry v. Ohio, 392 U.S. 1, 19 n. 16 (1968)).

not used the cruiser's siren or lights, had stopped at the curb before calling out to the defendant, and did not exit the car until they observed the defendant's ammunition round. *Id.* at 16. *Cf. Chesternut,* 486 U.S. at 575 (no seizure where police did not activate siren or lights, did not order defendant to halt, drew no weapons, and did not block defendant's course).

In *Smith,* the police officers framed general, non-threatening questions to ask why the defendant was sitting on the wall of a stranger's house and did not command the defendant to remain on his walled perch. 423 F.3d at 30. Even after the officers exited their vehicle to conduct an FIO and approached the defendant from both sides, we found no seizure because the officers never summoned Smith to the cruiser, did not employ the car's siren or lights, and did not expose their weapons or touch Smith. *Id.* Additionally, because Smith attempted to flee from the officers after he disclosed that he had an outstanding warrant, we noted his action indicated he had not submitted to an assertion of authority. *Id.* at 31.

Applying this precedent to the instant case, we decline to hold that the Officers seized Ford before he disclosed that he was in possession of a firearm. *See Mendenhall,* 446 U.S. at 555 (rejecting proposition that making statements contrary to one's self-interest necessarily indicates involuntary submission). The Officers, like those in *Cardoza,* drove a short distance the wrong way on Gleason Street for the purpose of asking Ford questions but activated neither the cruiser's siren or flashing lights. Their questions were largely general and non-threatening, like those in *Smith.* Throughout the brief encounter, until Ford's incriminating statement, the Officers did not draw their guns or touch Ford.

At the onset of the interaction, Ford approached the cruiser and provided his driver's license voluntarily. While the Officers retained the license during the two- to three-minute exchange, they did not otherwise restrict Ford's movement. Contrast *Smith,* 423 F.3d at 27, 30 (finding no seizure where officers approached the defendant from both sides, telephone pole was directly in front of defendant, and wall directly behind). As in *Smith,* where we found no seizure, the Officers exited the cruiser to complete the FIO.

Ford relies on the Supreme Court's *Florida v. Royer* decision where two detectives retained the defendant's driver's license and airplane ticket while commanding him to accompany them to a private room because they believed he fit the drug courier profile. 460 U.S. 491, 493–94 (1983). The Court held these actions constituted an illegal seizure, *id.* at 501–02, and distinguished Mendenhall in part because the government agents there immediately returned the driver's license and airplane ticket before continuing the encounter. *Id.* at 503 n. 9.

Ford argues *Royer* indicates that the retention of his driver's license during the encounter is compelling evidence of a seizure. We think the concerns of the airport cases, where citizens need documentation to move from place to place, differ from the instant case where Ford was on foot on a public street. *See Drayton*, 536 U.S. at 204 (noting that if the encounter had occurred on the street rather than on a bus, "[i]t is beyond question that . . . it would be constitutional"). Moreover, Ford produced his license voluntarily, not at the request of one of the Officers, and was not removed from the street to a confined space while the Officers ran the background check.

While the retention of Ford's license is an important factor in our analysis, we decline to elevate it above other considerations. *See* United States v. Weaver, 282 F.3d 302, 313 (4th Cir.2002) (refusing to adopt D.C. Circuit's per se rule regarding license retention).

Ford also asserts that a seizure can be evidenced by his raising his hands into the air after the Officers exited the cruiser. But one can draw different inferences from this gesture; while it could reflect submission, raised hands also can be a symbol of protest. On the cold record before us, we cannot recreate the actual gesture demonstrated to the district court. Instead, this type of inquiry recommends our deferential review of the lower court's factual findings.[5]

Evaluating the totality of circumstances, we hold that Ford was not seized for purposes of the Fourth Amendment protections when he told the Officers he possessed a handgun. Assessments of this type "are highly fact-specific and must be performed on a case-by-case basis." United States v. Taylor, 511 F.3d 87, 92 (1st Cir.2007). We acknowledge this method of analysis does not produce a crystalline landscape in our Fourth Amendment jurisprudence. But it reflects most realistically the contextual nature of these encounters. *See Chesternut*, 486 U.S. at 573 ("The test is necessarily imprecise, because it is designed to assess the coercive effect of police conduct, taken as a whole, rather than to focus on particular details of that conduct in isolation.").

5. REASONABLE SUSPICION

United States v. Valentine

232 F.3d 350 (3d Cir. 2000)

■ COWEN, CIRCUIT JUDGE:

After receiving a tip from an informant, two officers stopped Larry Valentine on a city street late at night and discovered a gun. The gun was subsequently suppressed, however, when the government

---

[5] Ford also suggests that the Officer's failure to inform him of his right to refuse to answer questions and to leave rendered the encounter nonconsensual. While it is true that such statements generally make an encounter consensual, *Mendenhall*, 446 U.S. at 558–59, the Supreme Court has explained that a seizure determination "is not affected by the fact that the respondent was not expressly told by the agents that she was free to decline to cooperate with their inquiry, for the voluntariness of her responses does not depend upon her having been so informed." *Id.* at 555. *See also Drayton*, 536 U.S. at 206 ("The [Supreme] Court has rejected in specific terms the suggestion that police officers must always inform citizens of their right to refuse when seeking permission to conduct a warrantless consent search.").

prosecuted Valentine for being a felon in possession of a firearm in violation of 18 U.S.C. § 922(g)(1) and (2).

In suppressing the gun, the District Court reasoned that under Florida v. J.L., 529 U.S. 266 (2000) the informant's tip about Valentine and the surrounding circumstances did not provide reasonable suspicion that Valentine was engaged in crime. The District Court also concluded that Valentine's actions after the officers ordered him to stop should not be considered, notwithstanding the Supreme Court's analysis of seizures under the Fourth Amendment in California v. Hodari D., 499 U.S. 621 (1991).

We will reverse. We hold that the officers had reasonable suspicion before ordering Valentine to stop. This case is distinguishable from *J.L.* and our recent decision in United States v. Ubiles, 224 F.3d 213 (3d Cir.2000). We also conclude that the District Court erred in interpreting *Hodari D.* Valentine's acts after the officers ordered him to stop should have been considered.

I

Around 1:00 a.m. on May 8, 1999, Officers Woodard and Contreras were patrolling near the intersection of Columbia and 18th Avenues in Irvington, New Jersey, an area that the officers described in uncontradicted testimony as "very bad" with "[a] lot of shootings." As the officers approached the intersection, a young black man in his early twenties flagged them down and explained that he had just seen a man with a gun.

The informant said that the gunman was wearing a blue sweat top, blue pants, and a gold chain around his neck. He added that the suspect was dark skinned, had a beard, and was accompanied by a young man. When asked to identify himself, the informant refused, a response that Officer Woodard testified is common, and one that is understandable if the informant feared retribution from the armed man or entanglement with the police. The officers did not question the informant further and immediately went in search of the gunman.

About 50 to 100 feet north of the intersection where the officers had met the informant, Woodard and Contreras saw three men standing in a well-lit parking lot near a chicken restaurant. One of the men matched the informant's description of the armed suspect given moments ago, and another was a young male in his twenties, also as the informant described. The third was an older man who appeared to be in his sixties.

The officers, who were in uniform and in a marked car, stopped and stepped out of their vehicle. The three men in the parking lot reacted by walking away, northwards. Contreras ordered the young male with Valentine to stop, and he obeyed, putting his hands up and walking toward the squad car. But when Woodard told Valentine, who was about ten feet away, to come over and place his hands on the car, Valentine responded, "Who, me?" and charged southwards toward Woodard. As

Valentine ran, trying to push aside Woodard's outstretched arms, the officer grabbed his shirt and wrestled him to the ground. During the scuffle, Woodard heard a ting as Valentine's silver, fully-loaded handgun hit the ground. Neither officer had seen the gun before that moment. . . .

II

Under Terry v. Ohio, 392 U.S. 1 (1968) and subsequent cases, "an officer may, consistent with the Fourth Amendment, conduct a brief, investigatory stop when the officer has a reasonable, articulable suspicion that criminal activity is afoot." Illinois v. Wardlow, 528 U.S. 119 (2000). Reasonable suspicion is "a less demanding standard than probable cause and requires a showing considerably less than preponderance of the evidence." 528 U.S. at ___. Elaborating on this point, the Supreme Court has said, "Reasonable suspicion is a less demanding standard than probable cause not only in the sense that reasonable suspicion can be established with information that is different in quantity or content than that required to establish probable cause, but also in the sense that reasonable suspicion can arise from information that is less reliable than that required to show probable cause." Alabama v. White, 496 U.S. 325, 330 (1990). The question we must address is whether Officers Woodard and Contreras had the "minimal level of objective justification" necessary for a *Terry* stop. United States v. Sokolow, 490 U.S. 1, 7 (1989). And in evaluating reasonable suspicion, "we must consider 'the totality of the circumstances—the whole picture.'" *Sokolow,* 490 U.S. at 8 (quoting United States v. Cortez, 449 U.S. 411, 417 (1981)).

We begin our analysis with the Supreme Court's recent opinion, *J.L.,* the case that prompted the District Court to reconsider its initial denial of Valentine's suppression motion. In *J.L.* the Supreme Court held that police officers lacked reasonable suspicion to make a *Terry* stop when an anonymous caller reported that "a young black male standing at a particular bus stop and wearing a plaid shirt was carrying a gun." *Florida v. J.L.,* 529 U.S. at ___. The Supreme Court explained that the precise issue before the Court was "whether the tip pointing to J.L. had [sufficient] indicia of reliability." 529 U.S. at ___. Finding the tip unreliable, the Court did not consider under what circumstances a reliable tip that someone was carrying a gun would provide the police with reasonable suspicion. Instead, the Court concluded, "All the police had to go on in this case was the bare report of an unknown, unaccountable informant who neither explained how he knew about the gun nor supplied any basis for believing he had inside information about J.L." 529 U.S. at ___.

Discussing the reliability of anonymous tips, the Court explained, "Unlike a tip from a known informant whose reputation can be assessed and who can be held responsible if her allegations turn out to be fabricated, *see* Adams v. Williams, 407 U.S. 143, 146–147 (1972), 'an anonymous tip alone seldom demonstrates the informant's basis of knowledge or veracity.' " *J.L.,* 529 U.S. at ___, (quoting *Alabama v. White,* 496 U.S. at 329). Nevertheless, even in the context of probable cause, the Court has rejected its earlier, inflexible two-prong test for tips set forth in Aguilar v. Texas, 378 U.S. 108 (1964) and Spinelli v. United States, 393 U.S. 410 (1969). Under *Aguilar* and *Spinelli,* the government could not rely on a tip unless the government could demonstrate both the basis of the informant's knowledge and the informant's reliability or veracity. The Court now uses a flexible standard that assesses the relative value and reliability of an informant's tip in light of the totality of the circumstances. See, e.g., Illinois v. Gates, 462 U.S. 213, 230–35 (1983); *Alabama v. White,* 496 U.S. at 329.

The informant's tip in our case is different from the telephone call in *J.L.* First, unlike *J.L.,* the officers in our case knew that the informant was reporting what he had observed moments ago, not what he learned from stale or second-hand sources. At the suppression hearing, Officer Woodard was asked, "Did [the informant] say how long ago that he saw the individual carrying a gun?" Woodard replied, "About—maybe a second ago, two seconds ago." So the officers could expect that the informant had a reasonable basis for his beliefs. The Supreme Court has recognized the greater weight carried by a witness's recent report, such as when "the victim of a street crime seeks immediate police aid and gives a description of the assailant." *Adams v. Williams,* 407 U.S. at 147.

Second, the officers had more reason to believe that the informant was credible than the officers did in *J.L.,* for a tip given face to face is more reliable than an anonymous telephone call. As the Fourth Circuit recently explained, when an informant relates information to the police face to face, the officer has an opportunity to assess the informant's credibility and demeanor. United States v. Christmas, 222 F.3d 141, 144 (4th Cir.2000). And when an informant gives the police information about a neighbor (as in *Christmas*) or someone nearby (as in our case), the informant is exposed to a risk of retaliation from the person named, making it less likely that the informant will lie. *Id.* Similarly, as the Fourth Circuit noted, "citizens who personally report crimes to the police thereby make themselves accountable for lodging false complaints." *Id.* (citing *Illinois v. Gates,* 462 U.S. at 233–34 (1983); *Adams v. Williams,* 407 U.S. at 146–47).

Many cases have recognized the difference between in-person informants and anonymous telephone calls. *See, e.g., Florida v. J.L.,* 529 U.S. at ___ (Kennedy, J., concurring) ("If an informant places his anonymity at risk, a court can consider this factor in weighing the reliability of the tip. An instance where a tip might be considered anonymous but nevertheless sufficiently reliable to justify a proportionate police response may be when an unnamed person driving a car the police officer later describes stops for a moment and, face to face, informs the police that criminal activity is occurring."); Davis v. United States, 759 A.2d 665 (D.C.App.2000) (An officer had probable cause for a

search after an informant who declined to give his name flagged down
the officer and told him that a man nearby in a wheelchair was selling
crack out of his right shoe.); United States v. Salazar, 945 F.2d 47, 50–51
(2d Cir.1991) ("[A] face-to-face informant must, as a general matter, be
thought more reliable than an anonymous telephone tipster, for the
former runs the greater risk that he may be held accountable if his
information proves false."); United States v. Sierra-Hernandez, 581 F.2d
760, 763 (9th Cir.1978) ("[A]lthough the informant did not identify
himself by name, he would have been available for further questioning if
the agent had judged the procedure appropriate. Unlike a person who
makes an anonymous telephone call, this informant confronted the agent
directly."); United States v. Gorin, 564 F.2d 159, 161 (4th Cir.1977) (per
curiam) ("[S]tandards of reliability should not prevent appropriate action
when a victim of a crime immediately has contacted the police. That same
analysis applies [when a witness informs the police in person about a
crime].").

Valentine contends that the District Court made a finding that the
informant left the area after giving the officers the tip, and therefore this
informant could not have been easily held accountable. He also complains
that the officers could have questioned the informant further. In response
to the latter objection, we are not going to second-guess the officers'
decision to pursue the suspect immediately. The officers knew the
suspect was still in the vicinity, and had they stalled for more lengthy
questioning of the informant, the armed suspect could have escaped
detection.

In response to the former objection, we have reviewed the record
carefully and conclude that the District Court made no factual finding
about what the informant did. Indeed, because no evidence was
presented either way on the issue, any factual finding that the informant
did leave the area would have been clearly erroneous. We simply do not
know what the informant did after the officers left.

What matters for our purposes is not that the officers could
guarantee that they could track down the informant again. As the
Supreme Court has said in cases like *Gates,* the question is whether the
tip should be deemed sufficiently trustworthy in light of the total
circumstances. And in this case the circumstances support the reliability
of the tip: the informant was exposed to retaliation from Valentine and
knew that the officers could quickly confirm or disconfirm the tip; and
the officers could assess the informant's credibility as he spoke, knew
what the informant looked like, and had some opportunity to find the
informant if the tip did not pan out. From the fact that the officers acted,
and acted quickly, after receiving the tip, a court may deduce that the
officers thought the tipster's demeanor, voice, and perhaps a host of other
factors supported the reliability of the tip. *Cf. Ornelas,* 517 U.S. at 699
("[A] police officer views the facts through the lens of his police experience

and expertise. The background facts provide a context for the historical facts, and when seen together yield inferences that deserve deference.").

The reliability of a tip, of course, is not all that we must consider in evaluating reasonable suspicion; the content of the tip must also be taken into account, as well as other surrounding circumstances. If we focus on the content of the tip, Valentine can invoke our recent holding that, in some contexts, even if police officers have a reliable tip saying that someone is carrying a gun, that information alone will not provide enough evidence to support a *Terry* stop. *See* United States v. Ubiles, 224 F.3d 213 (3d Cir.2000).

In *Ubiles* several officers were overseeing a festival in the Virgin Islands when an elderly man approached them and pointed out a man he had seen in the crowd with a gun. We suppressed the gun recovered from the officers' frisk of the suspect, and explained, "For all the officers knew, even assuming the reliability of the tip that Ubiles possessed a gun, Ubiles was another celebrant lawfully exercising his right under Virgin Island law to possess a gun in public." *Id*. at 218.

We also acknowledged, however, that reasonable suspicion does not require that the suspect's acts must always be themselves criminal. In many cases the Supreme Court has found reasonable suspicion based on acts capable of innocent explanation. Most recently, in *Wardlow* the Court held that headlong flight from the police in a high-crime area provides reasonable suspicion, despite the fact that flight is not by itself illegal and could have completely lawful and rational explanations. The Court explained:

> Even in *Terry*, the conduct justifying the stop was ambiguous and susceptible of an innocent explanation. The officer observed two individuals pacing back and forth in front of a store, peering into the window and periodically conferring. *Terry*, 392 U.S. at 5–6. All of this conduct was by itself lawful, but it also suggested that the individuals were casing the store for a planned robbery. *Terry* recognized that the officers could detain the individuals to resolve the ambiguity. *Id*. at 30.

Wardlow, 528 U.S. at 125–26.

Despite the obvious danger posed by an armed man in a crowd, we concluded in *Ubiles* that the tip, standing alone, did not provide reasonable suspicion because nothing in "the defendant's behavior pointed to the presence of illegal activity." 224 F.3d at 217. In particular, we said that under the laws of the Virgin Islands, a citizen could lawfully possess a gun during a festival, and there was no reason to think Ubiles's gun was unregistered or had an altered serial number, the two ways we mentioned that the gun possession could have been illegal.

Our case is distinguishable from *Ubiles*. First, there is the broader context. Valentine was walking around at 1:00 a.m. in a high-crime area known for shootings. While an individual's presence in a high-crime area is not by itself sufficient to warrant a *Terry* stop, *Wardlow,* 528 U.S. at 124 (citing Brown v. Texas, 443 U.S. 47 (1979)), "the fact that the stop occurred in a 'high crime area' [is] among the relevant contextual considerations in a *Terry* analysis." *Id.* (citing *Adams v. Williams*, 407 U.S. at 144 and 147–48). The constellation of likely criminal acts in a high-crime area at 1:00 a.m. goes well beyond simply carrying a gun without registration or with altered serial numbers. Indeed, given the large number of potential crimes and the danger posed by an armed criminal, we think that if the police officers had done nothing and continued on their way after receiving the informant's tip, the officers would have been remiss. People who live in communities torn by gunfire and violence are entitled to be free from fear of victimization and have police investigate before shootings occur. As the Supreme Court said in *Wardlow*, when the police learn of potentially suspicious conduct, officers can stop and question the suspects to resolve ambiguity about the suspects' conduct.

Moreover, it is well established that officers are allowed to ask questions of anyone—and gun owners are no exception—without having any evidence creating suspicion. Florida v. Bostick, 501 U.S. 429, 434 (1991) ("Since *Terry* we have held repeatedly that mere police questioning does not constitute a seizure."). Given that the original rationale in *Terry* for permitting frisks was to safeguard officers while they ask questions, *see Terry*, 392 U.S. at 23–24, a ruling in Valentine's favor would produce inexplicable results. We would be holding that while diligent officers would have questioned Valentine after receiving the tip, the officers were not permitted to frisk him, even though they encountered him late at night in a high-crime area known for shootings, and even though, unlike *Terry*, the officers had specific, reliable reasons for believing that he was armed. We do not think the Supreme Court's jurisprudence supports such a result.

As the Supreme Court noted in a case much like ours, an officer has "ample reason to fear for his safety" while investigating a person reported to have a concealed weapon at 2:15 in the morning in a high-crime area. *Adams v. Williams*, 407 U.S. at 147–48. . . . .

In evaluating the totality of the circumstances, we must also take into account that Valentine and the two men with him immediately began walking away from the patrol car when it arrived. Walking away from the police hardly amounts to the headlong flight considered in *Wardlow* and of course would not give rise to reasonable suspicion by itself, even in a high-crime area, but it is a factor that can be considered in the totality of the circumstances. As the Supreme Court recently said, "nervous, evasive behavior is a pertinent factor in determining reasonable suspicion." *Wardlow*, 528 U.S. at 124. *See also United States v. Sokolow,* 490 U.S. at 8–9; United States v. Brignoni-Ponce, 422 U.S. 873, 885 (1975); Florida v. Rodriguez, 469 U.S. 1, 6 (1984) (per curiam). As the First Circuit recently stated in the context of a search of a taxi, "slouching, crouching, or any other arguably evasive movement, when combined with other factors particular to the defendant or his vehicle, can add up to reasonable suspicion." United States v. Woodrum, 202 F.3d 1, 7 (1st Cir.2000) (citing United States v. Sharpe, 470 U.S. 675, 682 n. 3 (1985); United States v. Aldaco, 168 F.3d 148, 152 (5th Cir.1999)). *See also* United States v. Brown, 159 F.3d 147 (3d Cir.1998).

In summary, we conclude that the officers had reasonable suspicion after they received the face-to-face tip, were in a high-crime area at 1:00 a.m., and saw Valentine and his two companions walk away as soon as they noticed the police car.

The government offers another grounds for distinguishing this case from *Ubiles*. Unlike the Virgin Islands, New Jersey not only makes it a crime when a person "knowingly has in his possession any handgun, including any antique handgun, without first having obtained a permit to carry the same," N.J.S.A. § 2C:39–5(b), but also New Jersey presumes that someone carrying a handgun does not have a permit to possess it until the person establishes otherwise. *See* N.J.S.A. § 2C:39–2(b). New Jersey also has strict permit requirements and a rigid investigation and approval process that buttress the statutory presumption. *See* N.J.S.A. § 2C:58–4.

Given the evidence supporting the informant's tip in this case, we need not consider New Jersey's regulatory scheme or determine under what circumstances New Jersey's presumption would provide reasonable suspicion for a *Terry* stop.

III

The District Court expressly held that inquiry about reasonable suspicion in this case should be confined to events before Woodard ordered Valentine to stop. Because the District Court reached this issue, we think it is important to explain why that holding was erroneous.

While it is true that the "reasonableness of official suspicion must be measured by what the officers knew before they conducted their search," *J.L.,* 529 U.S. at ___, the District Court's analysis did not take into account that there can be no Fourth Amendment violation until a seizure occurs. In *Hodari D.* the Supreme Court held that for there to be a seizure, the police must apply physical force to the person being seized or, where force is absent, have the person seized submit to a show of police authority. *Hodari D.,* 499 U.S. at 626–28; Abraham v. Raso, 183 F.3d 279, 291 (3d Cir.1999); United States v. Bradley, 196 F.3d 762, 768 (7th Cir.1999). Thus, if the police make a show of authority and the suspect does not submit, there is no seizure. *Hodari D.,* 499 U.S. at 626; United States v. $32,400 in United States Currency, 82 F.3d 135, 139 (7th Cir.1996). As the Supreme Court recently explained, "Attempted seizures of a person are beyond the scope of the Fourth Amendment." County of Sacramento v. Lewis, 523 U.S. 833, 845 n. 7 (1998). *Cf.* Brower v. Inyo County, 489 U.S. 593, 596–97 (1989) (A seizure did not occur during the 20 miles in which a police car, with flashing lights, chased a suspect, and instead only occurred when the suspect's car crashed into a police blockade.).

The facts of *Hodari D.* illustrate how the concept of a seizure should be applied. When two police officers approached a group of four or five youths gathered around a car, the group immediately dispersed, prompting one officer to pursue Hodari, the respondent. By taking a side street, the officer was able to overtake Hodari. Surprised, Hodari tossed away what appeared to be a small rock, moments before the officer tackled him. The central question before the Supreme Court was whether the small rock, which turned out to be crack, should be suppressed.

The Court held that even assuming that the officers did not have reasonable suspicion to stop Hodari when the pursuit began, the crack should not have been suppressed, for Hodari never complied with the police officers' original show of authority and therefore was not seized when he threw the crack aside.

Other courts have applied *Hodari D.* and considered a suspect's conduct after he failed to comply with an officer's show of authority. *See, e.g.,* United States v. Johnson, 212 F.3d 1313 (D.C.Cir.2000); United States v. Smith, 217 F.3d 746 (9th Cir.2000); United States v. Santamaria-Hernandez, 968 F.2d 980 (9th Cir.1992).

In *Johnson,* for example, two officers in an unmarked car were patrolling a high-crime area and pulled into a parking lot where two people were sitting in a parked car with a young woman standing nearby. As the officers approached, they saw the woman lean into the passenger's window and hand the defendant, Johnson, an object. As the officers drew closer, the woman walked away, and Johnson made what the officers described as a "shoving down" motion. Thinking Johnson might be armed, one officer drew his gun, advised his partner to do the same, and shouted, "Let me see your hands." 212 F.3d at 1315. But Johnson did not comply and continued to shove down with his arms several more times. In response, the officer quickly strode up to the car, reached in, and discovered crack.

The D.C. Circuit reasoned that if the seizure had taken place when the officers drew their guns and ordered Johnson to show his hands, the court "doubt[ed] very much" whether the officers would have had reasonable suspicion to make a stop. *Id.* at 1316. Johnson did not comply, however, with the officers' show of authority. "On the contrary, he continued to make 'shoving down' motions, gestures that were the very opposite of complying with Fulton's order, and which a reasonable officer could have thought were actually suggestive of hiding (or retrieving) a gun." *Id.* at 1316–17. Those actions, the court held, gave the officers reasonable suspicion for the search that revealed the crack. *Cf.* Watkins v. City of Southfield, 221 F.3d 883 (6th Cir.2000) (A suspect's refusal to comply with an officer's order to stop contributed to the officer's suspicion.); United States v. Moorefield, 111 F.3d 10, 14 (3d Cir.1997)

(When officers stopped the defendant's car, his "furtive hand movements and refusal to obey the officers' orders" helped provide the officers with reasonable suspicion.).

We conclude that as in *Johnson* and *Moorefield,* what Valentine did after he failed to comply with the police officers' orders can be considered in evaluating reasonable suspicion. Valentine hopes to distinguish cases like *Johnson* and *Smith* by claiming that in fact he had already been seized before he charged toward Officer Woodard. He says that when Woodard ordered him to come over and place his hands on the car, he momentarily "complied" with the order, stopped, and gave his name. This "compliance," he protests, was enough to trigger a seizure.

We have reviewed the record carefully and find no evidence in support of Valentine's theory that he even momentarily complied, and some evidence, such as Woodard's police report, appears to rebut the theory. But regardless, no factual determination is necessary, for even if we accept Valentine's version, it would not show that he was seized before he charged Woodard.

Under some circumstances we have held that a defendant was seized despite his subsequent flight. In United States v. Coggins, 986 F.2d 651, 653–54 (3d Cir.1993) police officers stopped the defendant in a stairwell at an airport and asked him a number of questions, which he answered. After the defendant later asked permission to go to the bathroom and was allowed to leave, he fled. On appeal we rejected the government's argument that the defendant had not been seized.

But Valentine's case is easily distinguishable, for his momentary "compliance" is a far cry from the lengthy detention in *Coggins.* Cf. United States v. Hernandez, 27 F.3d 1403, 1407 (9th Cir.1994) (The defendant's momentary hesitation and direct eye contact with officer prior to his flight did not constitute a seizure.); United States v. Sealey, 30 F.3d 7, 10 (1st Cir.1994) (A defendant was not seized when an officer approached him and called out, "Hey Stephen, what's up?"); United States v. Washington, 12 F.3d 1128, 1132 (D.C.Cir.1994) (The defendant was not seized when he stopped his car at the curb in response to police commands, but then sped away when the officer approached on foot.). Even if Valentine paused for a few moments and gave his name, he did not submit in any realistic sense to the officers' show of authority, and therefore there was no seizure until Officer Woodard grabbed him.

And once we consider Valentine's actions after Woodard's order, it is clear that we have an independent ground for finding that the officers had reasonable suspicion. For if headlong flight in a high-crime area provides reasonable suspicion under Wardlow, then charging toward a police officer in a high-crime area also by itself provides reasonable suspicion.

For the foregoing reasons, the District Court's order of April 27, 2000, will be reversed. The case will be remanded to the District Court for further proceedings consistent with this opinion.

Illustrative Cases

Carefully consider the facts of the following four cases. In each, is there, or is there not, "reasonable suspicion"?

(1) United States v. Dupree, 2009 WL 1475276 (E.D.Pa. 2009)

I.   FINDINGS OF FACT

1.   On the evening of January 16, 2008, Philadelphia Police Officers Brian Mabry ("Mabry") and Steven Shippen ("Shippen") (collectively, "the officers") were on patrol duty in the 23rd Police District of Philadelphia in the area of the intersection of 18th Street and Cecil B. Moore Avenue. The officers were in uniform, with Shippen driving, and Mabry riding in, a marked radio patrol car.

2.   At approximately 7:00 p.m., the officers received a radio report, or "flash information" ("flash"), that a black male ("suspect"), approximately five feet, eight inches in height, wearing blue jeans and a black hooded sweatshirt, or "hoody," had fired gunshots in the area of 10th and Oxford Streets.

3.   The flash included no further description of the suspect. The officers never received additional information as to the suspect's physical appearance.

4.   The officers knew from the flash that it had been issued at the direction of the commanding officer of Philadelphia's 19th Police District. However, the officers did not know the source of the tip or report underlying the flash. Further, no evidence was received as to when, relative to the time at which the flash was issued, the shots were reported to have been fired.

5.   Soon after the flash issued, the officers received an additional radio report that the suspect had fled eastbound on Oxford Avenue. The report did not state the suspect's manner of flight, i.e., whether the suspect had fled on foot, in a vehicle, on a bicycle or by some other means.

6.   Upon hearing the flash, the officers rapidly drove the approximately ten blocks south and east to 10th and Oxford Streets. At the intersection of 12th and Oxford Streets, Shippen slowed the vehicle to a patrolling speed. The officers crossed 10th Street heading eastbound on Oxford, looking for the suspect. They observed little vehicular or pedestrian traffic, and found the area well-lit by streetlights and residential properties. The officers continued driving east on Oxford until they crossed Marshall Street, which is situated between 7th and 6th Streets as one proceeds east.[8]

---

[8]   The record evidence (and any City map) shows that Marshall crosses Oxford seven blocks east of 10th Street; from 10th Street running east, the intervening cross-streets are: Hutchinson, 9th, Darien, 8th, Perth, Franklin, 7th, and Marshall.

7. On Marshall Street north of Oxford, Mabry saw an individual who he believed matched the description of the suspect. The individual was wearing a dark hooded sweatshirt and jeans, and was riding a bicycle slowly in a southerly direction, toward Oxford. The individual on the bicycle was in fact Defendant Dupree.

8. Shippen had noticed Dupree on Marshall Street as well, but had not "pa[id] attention" because Dupree was riding a bicycle, and the flash and additional reports had included no mention of a bicycle. Shippen continued past Marshall on Oxford.

9. Mabry then told Shippen he had seen an individual on Marshall Street matching the suspect's description. Shippen, who had driven a few feet past Marshall, stopped the patrol car, shifted into reverse, backed up and then turned north onto Marshall, driving approximately five miles an hour.

10. The officers drove north on Marshall Street toward Dupree, who continued to ride slowly on the bicycle south toward the officers' approaching vehicle.

11. Shippen stopped the patrol car diagonally on Marshall Street, several feet north of Oxford Street, and just past Dupree.

12. Mabry immediately exited the patrol car and approached Dupree, who was still riding the bicycle. Quickly drawing alongside Dupree, and without first speaking, Mabry grabbed Dupree with both hands, one hand holding Dupree's right elbow, the other gripping Dupree's right upper arm. While gripping Dupree's arm, Mabry said "Can I talk to you for a minute?" Dupree was still astride the bicycle. Shippen had emerged from the patrol car and approached Dupree as well.

13. By grabbing him, Mabry stopped Dupree's movement. Mabry testified that, "at that point he was stopped for investigation."

14. To that point in time, the officers had not observed Dupree with a weapon, and they had not observed him engaging in any sort of criminal activity.

(2) United States v. Jones, 2009 WL 455661 (D.Neb. 2009)

On September 9, 2008, at 4:41 p.m., Officers Paul Hasiak and Torrey Gully of the Omaha Police Department spotted defendant walking near 32nd and Lake Streets. Defendant was wearing a black hoodie and walking in a manner such that it appeared he was holding something in this pocket or close to his body. The officers testified the defendant watched the patrol car as he walked down the street. Evidence indicates that on that time the temperature was 68 degrees Fahrenheit, but had been as cool as 50 degrees Fahrenheit earlier that morning.

Due to training that Officer Hasiak had previously received, he believed defendant exhibited behavior typical of someone trying to conceal a handgun. At the hearing, Officer Hasiak testified that he has stopped and searched ten other individuals exhibiting this same behavior, and all ten were found to be carrying weapons. The government also presented evidence to show that this area, the "northeast precinct," is known as a high-crime area in Omaha.

As the officers' car turned the corner around 33rd Street, they lost sight of the defendant. When they regained sight of the defendant, he had crossed Lake Street but had not changed the position of his right hand near the hoodie pocket. The officers stopped their patrol car and the defendant stopped walking. They told him to remove his hands from the pocket of his hoodie, and the officers proceeded to conduct a pat-down search of the defendant's outer clothing. The officers located a loaded 9-millimeter pistol in the hoodie pocket and a loaded magazine in the right rear pocket.

(3) United States v. Fuller, 2009 WL 482234 (S.D.Ga. 2009)

FINDINGS OF FACT

The credible testimony at the evidentiary hearing established the following:

[Officer] Wilson participated in a "street sweep" conducted by the Brunswick Police Department on May 30, 2008. Wilson was wearing civilian clothing and a ballistic raid vest that clearly identified him as a police officer. Defendant was riding a bicycle directly toward Wilson when he noticed Wilson and abruptly make a u-turn. Wilson began paralleling Defendant after this maneuver raised his suspicions. Wilson observed Defendant repeatedly check behind him and then return to his previous course. This behavior prompted Wilson to approach Defendant and ask to speak with him.

After agreeing to speak with Wilson, Defendant indicated that he was visiting someone in a nearby public housing complex. However, Defendant was unable to give Wilson the name of the person or the apartment number he visited. Defendant's demeanor was nervous, and Wilson noted that his left hand shook nervously. Wilson asked Defendant several times to keep his hand away from his pocket. Defendant informed Wilson that he was not on probation, out on parole, or barred from visiting the housing complex. Wilson ran a background check on Defendant and as he waited for a response, Defendant stared at Wilson's radio and repeatedly asked if they were talking about him. Wilson's suspicions increased after the police dispatch informed Wilson that the identification number given by Defendant came back as belonging to another person. Wilson felt at that time that Defendant was being evasive and had given him false information.

Wilson became concerned for his personal safety when Defendant asked him if he was wearing a bulletproof vest. Wilson felt it necessary at that point to frisk Defendant for weapons. Wilson took hold of the back of Defendant's shirt. Defendant started to get off his bicycle before abruptly attempting to run. Wilson tried to bring Defendant to the ground with a leg sweep. Wilson noticed Defendant raising a handgun with his right hand as he was executing the leg sweep. Wilson struck Defendant's right arm in a downward motion and heard the gun discharge as the two fell to the ground. Wilson testified that he saw the handgun on the ground near Defendant's right hand and what appeared to be crack cocaine in Defendant's left hand. Defendant then informed Wilson that he had been shot.

(4) United States v. Gonzalez, 2009 WL 613201 (S.D.N.Y. 2009)

On or around March 25, 2008, Detective John Badyna received a tip, from a confidential informant (the "CI") who had provided reliable information in the past, relating to a potential armed robbery in the Bronx, New York. Specifically, over the course of several conversations, the CI informed Detective Badyna that a "couple guys" were going to rob an electronics store located at 20 Bruckner Boulevard in the Bronx, New York on the evening of March 25, 2008, shortly before the store closed;[2] that the robbers would be armed with guns; and that they would arrive in a dark-colored car. On that evening, several officers, including Detectives Badyna and Marinez and Sergeant Rosario, stationed themselves in unmarked vehicles in front of Media Plaza, an electronics store located at that address. From their respective vehicles, Detectives Badyna and Marinez observed a dark gray Honda Accord (the "Accord") drive slowly past Media Plaza and park on the opposite side of the street from the store, a few spaces past its entrance.

Within minutes, Detectives Badyna and Marinez watched defendant Gonzalez exit the Accord from one of its rear doors and walk around the area, initially away from and then towards the direction of Media Plaza. Gonzalez appeared to be talking on his cell phone, looking all around him, and peering towards the store before getting back into the Accord. At this point, once traffic had cleared from the street, Detectives Badyna and Marinez saw the Accord slowly back up and re-park directly across the street from Media Plaza. Within moments, Gonzalez got out of the Accord again, and, while talking on his cell phone, walked across the street toward both Media Plaza and Detective Badyna's car.

As Gonzalez crossed the street toward Media Plaza, Detective Badyna saw Gonzalez suddenly change direction, walk around the front of Detective Badyna's car, and look inside the front window, where Detective Badyna was crouched down in the driver's seat. Detective Badyna noticed that Gonzalez's hands "looked funny" or "rubber-like." Gonzalez made eye contact with Detective Badyna, turned and swiftly moved away from both the Accord and Media Plaza. At that point, Sergeant Rosario broadcast a command on his radio for the surveillance units to "move in," which Detective Badyna understood as a command to block off the Accord. Sergeant Rosario, then Detective Badyna jumped out of their vehicle to pursue Gonzalez; when they reached him, they saw

---

[2] Detective Badyna testified that, according to his tip, "if they don't do it that night they were going to do it the next day."

that he was wearing latex gloves on his hands. Sergeant Rosario and Detective Badyna apprehended and handcuffed Gonzalez.

Detective Marinez also watched Gonzalez exit the Accord for the second time and, while talking on his cell phone, walk across the street towards Media Plaza. Detective Marinez did not see Gonzalez look into Detective Badyna's car, but he noticed that Gonzalez was wearing white gloves; at that point, Detective Marinez thought "this is very real," as "it's common practice [to wear gloves during robberies] so you don't leave fingerprints behind." He saw Gonzalez reach the sidewalk just before he heard Sergeant Rosario's call to "move in" on the Accord.

While Detective Badyna and Sergeant Rosario apprehended Gonzalez, Detective Marinez and additional officers ran to the Accord. Detective Marinez was the first officer to reach the Accord, and he approached with his firearm drawn, "because it was supposed to be an armed robbery so I had my weapon for my safety." He opened the driver's door, ordered the driver, Defendant Franco, to shut off the vehicle, removed Franco from the car, and placed him in handcuffs—"again, for my safety." Five minutes later, Detective Marinez looked inside the Accord, where he observed white latex gloves and duct tape.

Approximately one minute after he left his vehicle to arrest Gonzalez, Detective Badyna crossed the street to approach the Accord, where he found Defendants Franco, Williams and Richardson in handcuffs on the sidewalk. Detective Badyna "went into the car and looked real quick" and saw "a lot of latex gloves sprawled out all over the front of the middle console. I saw duct tape. I seen some hats, some gloves just laying around, very messy car." After their arrests for attempted robbery, all Defendants were taken to the 40th Precinct in the Bronx. To ensure their safety, Detective Badyna and other officers conducted a "quick pat-down," or field search, of Gonzalez before his transport to the precinct; Detective Badyna recovered two cell phones and a set of keys from Gonzalez's person.

6. INCIDENTAL PROTECTIVE SEARCH POWER

United States v. Askew

529 F.3d 1119 (D.C. Cir. 2008) (en banc)

■ EDWARDS, SENIOR CIRCUIT JUDGE:

On the evening of December 19, 2003, police officers received a broadcast "lookout" for an armed robber. Appellant Paul Askew, who wore clothing similar, but not identical to that described in the lookout, was stopped. The police then conducted a *Terry* "frisk" which produced nothing. Some time after the frisk was completed, the police moved appellant to a place where he could be seen by the complaining witness. The officers' purpose was to determine whether the complainant could identify appellant as her assailant. The District Court's findings of fact indicate that appellant complied during the stop and was not handcuffed during the identification show-up. Preparatory to the show-up, but without appellant's consent, one of the officers attempted to unzip appellant's outer jacket to reveal to the complainant what appellant had on under the jacket. The officer's unfastening of the jacket was interrupted when the zipper hit a hard object at appellant's waist. Appellant then pushed the officer's hand away from his jacket. These latter events aroused the officer's suspicion, but the officer did nothing and the show-up continued. Although appellant was not implicated by the complaining witness, the police officers continued to detain him, walked him backwards towards a police vehicle, placed him on the hood of the car, and then fully unzipped his jacket. The officers found a gun in an open waist pouch and arrested appellant.

In April 2004, after the District Court denied his Fourth Amendment motion to suppress the Government's evidence, appellant entered a conditional guilty plea to a one-count indictment charging him with possession of a firearm by a convicted felon in violation of 18 U.S.C. § 922(g)(1). Appellant reserved his right to appeal the District Court's denial of his motion to suppress. *See* Fed.R.Crim.P. 11(a)(2). On June 29, 2004, the District Court sentenced appellant to 36 months' imprisonment, followed by three years' supervised release.

On April 6, 2007, a divided panel of the court affirmed the District Court's denial of appellant's motion to suppress. On July 12, 2007, the panel's judgment was vacated and an order was issued granting appellant's petition for rehearing en banc. The order granting en banc review instructed the parties to address the following issue:

> [W]hether during a *Terry* stop police officers may unzip a suspect's jacket solely to facilitate a show-up. In addressing this question, the parties should consider whether the officers' action was a lawful search under Terry v. Ohio, 392 U.S. 1 (1968), and its progeny.

United States v. Askew, No. 04-3092, Order Granting En Banc Review (D.C.Cir. July 12, 2007). The order made clear that the only issue before the en banc court was whether the first, partial unzipping was unlawful. There is no dispute that if the partial unzipping was unlawful, the discovery of the hard object at appellant's waist during that unzipping cannot justify the second full unzipping that yielded the gun.

On April 10, 2008, after oral arguments were heard by the en banc court, an order was issued instructing the parties to submit supplemental briefs addressing the following questions:

> 1. Assuming, arguendo, that it is not dispositive that the unzipping was a search, was the gun evidence nonetheless inadmissible as the product of steps taken to facilitate a show-up witness' identification, on a theory that there were not reasonable grounds for believing that unzipping the jacket

would establish or negate the suspect's connection with the crime under investigation?

2.   Was the gun evidence admissible as the product of a valid protective search, on a theory that regardless of the officer's subjective intent the initial unzipping was an objectively reasonable response to the suspect's conduct during the pat-down?

3.   Was the gun evidence admissible under the doctrine of inevitable discovery, on a theory that the officers had not completed the pat-down but would have done so after the show-up?

United States v. Askew, No. 04-3092, Order (directing supplemental briefing) (D.C.Cir. Apr. 10, 2008).

As described in its opening brief, the Government submits that the principal question for this court is whether the police "violate[d] appellant's Fourth Amendment rights by partially unzipping [his] outer jacket during a show-up identification procedure, so that a robbery victim could see whether appellant's sweatshirt matched that of the robbery perpetrator." Gov't En Banc Br. at 13; *see also id.* at 22, 24. Applying Minnesota v. Dickerson, 508 U.S. 366 (1993), and the precedent on which it rests, to the District Court's uncontested findings of fact, a five-judge plurality of this court concludes that the answer to this question is yes. Because the police officer's unzipping of appellant's jacket went beyond what was necessary to protect the investigating officers or others nearby, it amounted to precisely the sort of evidentiary search that is impermissible in the context of a *Terry* stop.

Even assuming, arguendo, that an unzipping to facilitate a show-up is permissible under some circumstances, a majority of the court is nonetheless satisfied that the police officer's actions cannot be justified here since there were no reasonable grounds for believing that the unzipping would establish or negate appellant's identification as the robber in question. A majority of the court is also satisfied that the Government's alternative argument, that the search of appellant can be justified as an objectively reasonable continuation of the protective frisk, is both contrary to the District Court's factual findings and unsupportable on any plausible reading of the record.

Finally, the Government concedes that "[t]he gun is not admissible under a theory of 'inevitable discovery.'" Gov't Supplemental Br. at 12. As the Government explains, it "did not make an inevitable-discovery argument before the district court, and thus failed to elicit" the testimony necessary to support such a theory under Nix v. Williams, 467 U.S. 431 (1984). Gov't Supplemental Br. at 14. Moreover, the Government acknowledges that "[b]ecause the inevitable-discovery theory raises factual issues that could have been addressed at the suppression hearing but were not, [it does] not believe that [it is] in a position to request a remand for further development of the record." *Id.* at 15 n. 7.

I. The District Court's Factual Findings

Following completion of the hearing on appellant's suppression motion, the District Court set forth its factual findings in a published opinion. *See* United States v. Askew, 313 F.Supp.2d 1 (D.D.C.2004). "[A]ppellate courts must constantly have in mind that their function is not to decide factual issues *de novo.*" Anderson v. City of Bessemer City, 470 U.S. 564, 573 (1985) (quotation marks omitted). Thus, as the Government rightly points out, "[t]his court must accept the district court's findings of fact unless clearly erroneous." Gov't En Banc Br. at 15. This rule is firmly entrenched in Supreme Court precedent, *see* Ornelas v. United States, 517 U.S. 690, 699 (1996), and in applying it we "overstep[ ] the bounds of [our] duty . . . if [we] undertake[ ] to duplicate the role of the lower court," Bessemer City, 470 U.S. at 573. This is especially so when, as here, the trial court is required to reconcile differences in testimony in order to make factual findings. *See* Mar. 26 Tr. at 29–31; s*ee generally* Bessemer City, 470 U.S. at 573–76.

Notably, neither party challenged the District Court's findings in this case. In fact, in its brief filed with the panel, the Government characterized the District Court's factual findings as "consistent with the government's evidence at the suppression hearing." Gov't Panel Br. at 9. Even if those findings had been challenged, we could not overturn them unless we were "definitely and firmly convinced that a mistake [had] been committed." Bessemer City, 470 U.S. at 573. Because there are no grounds for such a conclusion, the District Court's factual findings constitute the record by which appellate review is bound. Consequently, they are, in pertinent part, reproduced below.

On the night of December 19, 2003, around 11:00 p.m., a radio run alerted Officer Anthony Bowman of the Metropolitan Police Department to a report of an armed robbery in the 700 block of 9th Street, S.E., in Washington, D.C. Officer Bowman canvassed the area in his patrol car, looking for individuals matching the description of the perpetrator: a black male, approximately six-feet tall, wearing a blue sweatshirt and blue jeans. The radio report reflected that the perpetrator had been last seen moving on 9th Street, S.E., in an unknown direction.

Within two minutes of the radio report, and within approximately ten minutes of the robbery, Officer Bowman spotted defendant Paul Askew walking in the 200 block of 9th Street, S.E., five blocks from the scene of the robbery. Upon seeing Officer Bowman, the defendant turned and walked in a different direction, but Officer Bowman continued to follow the defendant in the patrol car. Defendant is a black male, six-feet, three-inches tall, and at the time was wearing clothing quite similar—but not identical—to the description broadcast over the police radio. While the description of the perpetrator mentioned a blue sweatshirt and blue jeans, Officer Bowman testified that the defendant was wearing blue sweatpants, "a navy blue jacket[, and] a darker blue fleece type jacket underneath. He had on two jackets." Officer Bowman reported to the dispatcher that Askew "vaguely match[ed] th[e] description." After noticing that the defendant had a moustache, Officer Bowman checked with the dispatcher to determine whether the robber also had a moustache. When the dispatcher responded affirmatively, Officer Bowman stopped the defendant.

Officer Bowman asked the defendant to come to the patrol car, and he complied. The defendant also complied with Officer Bowman's further requests that he produce some identification, take his hands out of his pockets, and place his hands on the top of his head. Officer Bowman then told the defendant that he was being stopped because of his physical similarity to the description of a robber. When back-up units arrived, Officer Bowman returned to the interior of his car to check whether the police department computer returned any information on the defendant. Officer Bowman's back was turned for the next couple of minutes and he did not see the pat-down of the defendant that followed.

Officer James Koenig conducted a pat-down of the defendant and found nothing. Shortly afterwards, another officer, Officer Benton, drove the robbery victim to the place where the defendant was being detained, for the purpose of conducting a show-up. The victim remained in the car while Officer Koenig and Officer Anthony Willis brought the defendant to a place where he could be seen by the victim. The defendant was not in handcuffs at that time. Preparatory to the show-up, Officer Willis attempted to unzip the defendant's outer jacket to reveal the sweatshirt underneath so the victim could better determine if the defendant was the robber. Officer Willis testified that he remembered the "blue hooded sweatshirt" described in the radio run and "wanted the complainant to see what [the defendant] had on to make sure that he wasn't zipping nothing up to cover up. So I went to unzip it down so that . . . they could see what he had on." Officer Willis had difficulty, however, in unzipping the jacket when the zipper hit what he described as a "hard" or "solid" object and "didn't go past [the object]. It stopped there. And at that time, that's when [the defendant] knocked my hand down," away from the zipper.

After the show-up, Officer Willis and Officer Edward Snead walked the defendant backwards toward the car, placed him on the hood of the car, and unzipped his jacket. Visible once the jacket was unzipped was an open black waist pouch, or "fanny pack," with a silver object sticking out. On further inspection, the silver object was identified as a gun, and the defendant was handcuffed and arrested.

Askew, 313 F.Supp.2d at 2–3 (alterations in original) (footnotes and transcript citations omitted).

In the course of its legal analysis, the District Court concluded that the disputed unzipping was undertaken to facilitate the show-up. *Id.* at 4. This conclusion is consistent with its factual findings that Officer Koenig found "nothing" during the frisk and that the complainant was brought to where appellant was detained "shortly afterwards." *Id.* at 3; *See also id.* at 4. In a footnote, the District Court notes that Officer Koenig did not testify at the suppression hearing. Rather, the testimony regarding the pat down was provided by Officer Willis. *Id.* at 3 n. 2. (In fact, the motions hearing transcript reveals that the Government, as part of its trial strategy, chose not to put on Officer Koenig. *See* Mar. 26 Tr. at 21, 24, 38.) In this same footnote, the Court describes Officer Willis's "suggest[ion] that Officer Koenig had not completed the pat-down . . . when Officer Benton arrived with the robbery victim for a show-up." *Askew*, 313 F.Supp.2d at 3 n. 2 (emphasis added). The Court also notes Officer Willis's testimony that "perhaps" the pat down had not been completed "because of some resistance by the defendant." *Id.* (emphasis added). The Court then points to "[t]he government acknowledge[ment] that when Officer Koenig patted the defendant down, he did not find anything" and reiterates its own finding that "[t]he subsequent discovery of the gun at issue was not the result of this pat-down." *Id.*; *see also id.* at 4 ("[t]he initial pat-down by Officer Koenig did not reveal the presence of any weapon"). In other words, the District Court does not credit Officer Willis's suggestion that the pat down may have been incomplete or Officer Willis's speculation regarding why that may have been the case.

II. Overview

"Time and again" the Supreme Court "has observed that searches and seizures conducted outside the judicial process, without prior approval by judge or magistrate, are per se unreasonable under the Fourth Amendment—subject only to a few specifically established and well delineated exceptions." *Dickerson*, 508 U.S. at 372 (quotation marks omitted) (collecting cases). And the Court has made it clear that the "inestimable right of personal security" embodied in the Fourth Amendment "belongs as much to the citizen on the streets . . . as to the homeowner closeted in his study. . . . For, as [the Supreme] Court has always recognized, 'No right is held more sacred, or is more carefully guarded, by the common law, than the right of every individual to the possession and control of his own person, free from all restraint or interference of others, unless by clear and unquestionable authority of law.'" Terry v. Ohio, 392 U.S. 1, 8–9 (1968) (quoting Union Pac. Ry. Co. v. Botsford, 141 U.S. 250, 251 (1891)).

In *Terry v. Ohio*, the Supreme Court defined one of the few exceptions to the prohibition against warrantless searches of a person. The Court held that in the context of a properly justified on-the-street stop, if a police officer has a reasonable articulable suspicion "that the individual whose suspicious behavior he is investigating at close range is armed and presently dangerous to the officer or to others," that officer may conduct a limited protective search "to determine whether the person is in fact carrying a weapon." 392 U.S. at 24; *see also id.* at 30–31. In Sibron v. New York, 392 U.S. 40 (1968), an opinion issued on the same day as *Terry*, the Court confirmed the limited nature of the *Terry* search exception, explicitly stating that the "only goal which might conceivably" justify a search in the context of a *Terry* stop is a search for weapons. *Id.* at 65.

In subsequent cases, the Court has been unequivocal in explaining that "[t]he purpose of this limited search is not to discover evidence of crime, but to allow the officer to pursue his investigation without fear of violence." Adams v. Williams, 407 U.S. 143, 146 (1972) (emphasis added). Thus, the fruit of a search that "goes beyond what is necessary to determine if [a] suspect is armed . . . will be suppressed." Dickerson, 508 U.S. at 373 (citing *Sibron*, 392 U.S. at 65–66). This is so, the Court explained in *Minnesota v. Dickerson*, because searches that exceed what is necessary to determine if an individual is armed "amount[ ] to the sort of evidentiary search that *Terry* expressly refused to authorize" and that the Court "condemned" in Sibron v. New York, 392 U.S. 40, and Michigan v. Long, 463 U.S. 1032 (1983). *Dickerson*, 508 U.S. at 378.

Appellant argues that pursuant to this well-established body of law, the unzipping of his jacket was unlawful, because it was not undertaken for protective purposes, but rather amounted to an impermissible evidentiary search unsupported by probable cause or a warrant. The Government, in contrast, asserts that this question is not controlled by *Dickerson* and the precedent on which *Dickerson* rests, but rather should be decided through application of the reasonableness balancing test. Under this test, the permissibility of a Government action is determined by "balancing the [governmental] need to search [or seize] against the invasion which the search [or seizure] entails." *Terry*, 392 U.S. at 21 (second and third alteration in original) (quotation marks omitted). Pursuant to this test, the Government argues that because the unzipping of appellant's jacket "was a reasonable, de minimis investigative measure that appropriately facilitated the show-up procedure," it need not have been supported by a warrant or probable cause. Gov't En Banc Br. at 13.

When the Supreme Court has weighed the interests relevant to determining whether a certain type of official conduct is reasonable under the Fourth Amendment, lower courts are not free to strike a new and different balance. With respect to searches of individuals detained during on-the-street encounters on less than probable cause, the balance was struck in *Terry*, 392 U.S. 1, and *Sibron,* 392 U.S. 40. Employing the reasonableness test to which the Government refers, the Court in *Terry* authorized a strictly circumscribed search for weapons when an officer has reasonable articulable suspicion to believe that a properly stopped individual is armed and dangerous to the officers or others nearby. 392 U.S. at 30–31; *see also* New York v. Class, 475 U.S. 106, 117 (1986) ("When a search or seizure has as its immediate object a search for a weapon, . . . we have struck the balance to allow the weighty interest in the safety of police officers to justify warrantless searches based only on a reasonable suspicion of criminal activity."). The *Sibron* Court, applying *Terry*'s holding, made clear that *Terry* did not permit police officers to undertake searches not justified on a safety rationale. *See* 392 U.S. at 63–64. It also established that protective searches that extend beyond the strictly circumscribed bounds of *Terry* are impermissible evidentiary searches. *Id.* at 65–66. Most important, for our purposes, the Court's opinion in *Minnesota v. Dickerson*, 508 U.S. 366, confirms that when an on-the-street search of an individual who has been stopped on reasonable articulable suspicion extends beyond what is authorized in *Terry*, there is no reweighing to be undertaken on the grounds that the search might be described as minimally intrusive or that the evidence sought might provide probable cause to believe that the suspect committed the crime in question.

Because there is no principled way to distinguish the initial unzipping in this case from the search in *Dickerson*, this court is not free to reweigh the interests at issue to create the new and wholly unprecedented identification exception to the warrant and probable cause requirements that the Government urges upon us. Rather, applying the balance that the Supreme Court struck in *Terry* and *Sibron* to the uncontested factual findings of the District Court, we are convinced that the unzipping of appellant's jacket was a non-protective evidentiary search that violated the Fourth Amendment.

III. Analysis of the Legal Issues

A. The Partial Unzipping and Opening of
Appellant's Jacket Was a Search

Before turning to the issues before the en banc court, we must determine whether the unzipping of appellant's jacket was, in fact, a search. Clearly it was. By zipping up his jacket, appellant unquestionably evidenced an intent to keep private whatever lay under it. The only question, then, is whether society is prepared to recognize such an expectation as reasonable. *See* Katz v. United States, 389 U.S. 347, 361 (1967) (Harlan, J., concurring).

This question was unequivocally answered by the Supreme Court in *Terry*. At issue there was the touching of the outer surface of the defendant's overcoat. *Terry*, 392 U.S. at 7. As the Court explained, even that limited action rose to the level of a "search" within the purview of the Fourth Amendment. *Id.* at 16. Because the opening of a fastened coat, like the opening of most other clothing, renders visible whatever lies underneath, such an action involves an even greater intrusion in precisely the same socially recognized expectation of privacy. And such an intrusion is particularly great when, as here, the opening takes place on a public street. In describing the level of personal intrusion occasioned by a public frisk, the *Terry* Court stated:

> [I]t is simply fantastic to urge that such a procedure performed in public by a policeman while the citizen stands helpless, perhaps facing a wall with his hands raised, is a "petty indignity." It is a serious intrusion upon the sanctity of the person, which may inflict great indignity and arouse strong resentment.

Id. at 16–17. The undoing of clothing to reveal whatever is underneath to whomever happens to be on the street necessarily involves an even more serious intrusion upon the sanctity of the person. The involuntary opening of someone's clothing reveals to the world at large (not just to the searching police officer) what an individual obviously intends to keep private.

As noted above, the Government did not dispute the characterization of the unzipping as a search during arguments before the panel. Before the en banc court, however, the Government refused to concede the point. Stating that it was only "assum[ing], arguendo, that the unzipping of appellant's jacket was a 'search,'" Gov't En Banc Br. at 23 n. 11, the Government maintained that the police action did not actually amount to a search because the sweatshirt that the police expected to reveal "presumably was widely visible when appellant was in indoor settings." *Id.* This argument is flawed in both its legal and factual premises.

Relying primarily on United States v. Dionisio, 410 U.S. 1 (1973), the Government likens appellant's sweatshirt to a "physical characteristic . . . constantly exposed to the public." Gov't En Banc Br. at 23 n. 11 (omissions in original). This analogy is inapt. In *Dionisio*, the Supreme Court held that production of a voice exemplar pursuant to a grand jury subpoena did not constitute a search, because "[t]he physical characteristics of a person's voice, its tone and manner, as opposed to the content of a specific conversation, are constantly exposed to the public. Like a man's facial characteristics, or handwriting, his voice is repeatedly produced for others to hear." 410 U.S. at 14. As the Court explained, "while the content of a communication is entitled to Fourth Amendment protection . . . the underlying identifying characteristics—the constant factor throughout both public and private communications—are open for all to see or hear." *Id.* (quotation marks omitted) (omission in original). Consequently, "[n]o person can have a reasonable expectation that others will not know the sound of his voice, any more than he can reasonably expect that his face will be a mystery to the world." *Id.*

The same cannot be said of a piece of clothing when the only information that the police have about that clothing is that the wearer has chosen to shield most of it from public view. Contrary to the

Government's assertion, there is nothing about a sweatshirt that—like the characteristics of an individual's voice, handwriting, or face—must necessarily be revealed to the public in the course of daily life. An individual may choose to expose all or part of an article of clothing to the public or he may choose to keep all or part of that clothing covered.

The only evidence presented by the Government regarding appellant's sweatshirt was that appellant had demonstrated an intent to shield most of it from public view. When a government agent unfastens, lifts, pulls down, pats, or otherwise manipulates clothing to reveal or determine what lies underneath, that manipulation necessarily involves the sort of " 'probing into an individual's private life' " that the Court in Davis v. Mississippi, 394 U.S. 721 (1969), characterized as the mark of a search or interrogation. *Dionisio*, 410 U.S. at 15 (quoting *Davis v. Mississippi*). Citing *Terry*, the *Dionisio* Court reiterated that even the minimal intrusion involved in a *Terry* frisk of outer clothing necessarily amounts to a Fourth Amendment search. Contrasting the seizure of voice exemplars to permissible *Terry* pat downs, the Court explained that the former "does not involve the severe, though brief, intrusion upon cherished personal security, effected by" the latter. *Dionisio*, 410 U.S. at 15 (quotation marks omitted).

The Government's argument that the unzipping of appellant's jacket was not a search is also based on fundamentally flawed factual premises. First, the Government assumes that the unzipping of appellant's jacket would reveal only appellant's already partially visible sweatshirt. One need only consider the special medical needs of certain individuals, including those who are forced to use colostomy bags and heart monitors (to name a few) to recognize the fallacy of this assumption. Such devices frequently are attached to an individual's abdominal area and often require those wearing them to hike up the clothing around their midsection to accommodate the device. Second, many individuals wear clothing that is comfortable to them but would appear unseemly to others. In such circumstances, the individual who does not want the unseemly portions of his clothing publicly exposed will cover or partially cover that clothing with another garment. Appellant's fastening of his jacket effectively expressed a recognized and reasonable expectation of privacy. And its unfastening cannot be characterized as a non-search given the inability of the police to know what other information pertaining to appellant's private life that unfastening would reveal.

B.   *Minnesota v. Dickerson* Dictates the Conclusion That
the Unzipping of Appellant's Jacket Was an
Impermissible Search for Evidence

The legal principles controlling the disposition of this case were largely established in three post-*Terry* Supreme Court cases, all of which were relied on by the Court in *Minnesota v. Dickerson*. Those cases are *Sibron*, 392 U.S. 40; *Ybarra v. Illinois*, 444 U.S. 85 (1979); and *Long*, 463 U.S. 1032. Discussing and applying *Terry*, each makes clear that in the context of an on-the-street seizure based on less than probable cause, there is no balancing of interests to be undertaken in determining whether a particular search of a stopped suspect is reasonable and therefore permissible under the Fourth Amendment. Rather, applying the balance struck in *Terry*, courts are constrained to suppress evidence obtained during such a stop if it is the fruit of a search that was not necessary to protect the investigating officers or others nearby. Put another way, these decisions establish that individuals stopped on no more than reasonable articulable suspicion may not, consonant with the protections of the Fourth Amendment, be searched for the purpose of revealing and gathering evidence pertaining to the illegal behavior of which they are suspected.

Sibron, a companion case to *Terry*, clarified the limits of the search exception authorized in *Terry*, holding that a non-protective evidentiary search of an individual detained on less than probable cause, would not pass Fourth Amendment muster. In that case, a police officer stopped Sibron on suspicion that he was selling narcotics. *See* 392 U.S. at 45. When the officer said to Sibron, "You know what I am after," Sibron "mumbled something and reached into his pocket. Simultaneously, [the officer] thrust his hand into the same pocket" discovering several envelopes of heroin. *Id.* (quotation marks omitted). After first concluding that the officer lacked probable cause to arrest Sibron when he stopped him, *id.* at 62–63, the Court held that the search of Sibron's pocket for evidence of narcotics was unconstitutional. Relying on its decision in *Terry*, the Court concluded that the officer's action was not predicated on any concern that Sibron was armed, but rather constituted a search for evidence of the crime that the officer suspected Sibron of committing. *See id.* at 63–64. As the Court described it, the officer's "opening statement to Sibron . . . made it abundantly clear that he sought narcotics, and his testimony at the hearing left no doubt that he thought there were narcotics in Sibron's pocket." *Id.* at 64. Moreover, as the Court explained, even if the search had been predicated on a reasonable articulable suspicion that Sibron was armed, the search would have been impermissible because it "was not reasonably limited in scope to the accomplishment of the only goal which might conceivably have justified its inception—the protection of the officer by disarming a potentially dangerous man." *Id.* at 65 (emphasis added).

In *Ybarra*, the Court reiterated the limits of its *Terry* search rationale. The search at issue there took place in the Aurora Tap Tavern. 444 U.S. at 88. The police had obtained a warrant authorizing the search of the tavern and an individual named Greg. *Id.* Upon entering the tavern, the officers frisked each of its patrons for weapons. *Id.* During the frisk of Ybarra, an "officer felt what he described as a cigarette pack with objects in it." *Id.* at 88 (quotation marks omitted). After completing the pat down of a number of other patrons, the officer returned to Ybarra, frisked him again, and removed from his shirt pocket a cigarette pack containing what turned out to be packets of heroin. *Id.* at 89. The State argued, inter alia, that the first pat down of Ybarra was a permissible frisk for weapons under *Terry*. *Id.* at 92. The Court rejected the State's argument, concluding that because "[t]he initial frisk of Ybarra was simply not supported by a reasonable belief that he was armed and presently dangerous," *id.* at 92–93, the evidence must be suppressed. As the Court explained, "[t]he *Terry* case created an exception to the requirement of probable cause, an exception whose narrow scope this Court has been careful to maintain. Under that doctrine a law enforcement officer, for his own protection and safety, may conduct a patdown to find weapons that he reasonably believes or suspects are then in the possession of the person he has accosted." *Id.* at 93 (emphasis added) (quotation marks omitted). However, the Court was careful to point out that "[n]othing in *Terry* can be understood to allow a generalized 'cursory search for weapons' or, indeed, any search whatever for anything but weapons." *Id.* at 93–94 (emphasis added).

In *Long,* which extended *Terry*'s protective search doctrine to the interior of cars, the Court confirmed and explained its unwillingness to allow non-protective evidentiary searches based on less than probable cause during run-of-the-mill investigatory stops. The Court there addressed the constitutionality of the search of the interior compartment of an automobile during a lawful investigatory stop of its occupant. 463 U.S. at 1037. Quoting *Terry*, the Court concluded "that the search of the passenger compartment of an automobile, limited to those areas in which a weapon may be placed or hidden, is permissible if the police officer possesses a reasonable belief based on 'specific and articulable facts which, taken together with the rational inferences from those facts, reasonably warrant' the officer in believing that the suspect is dangerous and the suspect may gain immediate control of weapons." *Id.* at 1049. The Court "stress[ed]," however, that its decision did "not mean that the police may conduct automobile searches whenever they conduct an investigative stop." *Id.* at n. 14 (emphasis in original). As the Court explained, this is because the justification for allowing automatic warrantless searches for evidence incident to an arrest does not support an automatic warrantless evidentiary search during a *Terry* stop. *See id.*

> An additional interest exists in the arrest context, i.e., preservation of evidence, and this justifies an "automatic" search. However, that additional interest does not exist in the *Terry* context. A *Terry* search, "unlike a search without a warrant incident to a lawful arrest, is not justified by any need to prevent the disappearance or destruction of evidence of crime. . . . The sole justification of the search . . . is the protection of police officers and others nearby."

Id. (quoting *Terry*, 392 U.S. at 21) (alterations in original).

Relying on the rationale of these cases, the Court in *Minnesota v. Dickerson* again confirmed that non-protective evidentiary searches are not permissible during *Terry* stops. There, on facts essentially indistinguishable from those presented here, the Supreme Court held that a police officer violated the Fourth Amendment proscription against unreasonable searches when, following a protective frisk that produced no evidence of a weapon, he manipulated the outside of a suspect's jacket pocket in an effort to identify as crack cocaine a small lump detected during the frisk. 508 U.S. at 378–79. Dickerson first came to the attention of the searching officer and his partner when he left what was a well-known crack house. *Id.* at 368. "According to testimony credited by the trial court, [Dickerson] began walking toward the police but, upon spotting the squad car and making eye contact with one of the officers, abruptly halted and began walking in the opposite direction." *Id.* at 368–69. Based on these "evasive actions and the fact that he had just left a building known for cocaine traffic, the officers decided to . . . investigate further." *Id.* at 369. They stopped Dickerson and patted him down for weapons. *Id.* Although the pat down revealed no weapons, "the officer conducting the search did take an interest in a small lump in respondent's nylon jacket." *Id.* The officer, who did not immediately recognize the lump as crack cocaine, determined what it was only after "squeezing, sliding and otherwise manipulating the contents of the defendant's pocket." *Id.* at 378 (quotation marks omitted).

The Supreme Court granted certiorari in Dickerson "to resolve a conflict among the state and federal courts over whether contraband detected through the sense of touch during a patdown search may be admitted into evidence." *Id.* at 371. 2130. In essence, the issue before the Court was whether and when the plain view doctrine of Arizona v. Hicks, 480 U.S. 321 (1987), could justify a plain feel exception for nonthreatening evidence detected during a *Terry* pat down.

Citing and discussing *Sibron, Ybarra,* and *Long,* the Court first reviewed the limits on searches conducted during *Terry* stops, *Dickerson,* 508 U.S. at 372–73, concluding with the long "settled" principle that if a "protective search goes beyond what is necessary to determine if the suspect is armed, it is no longer valid under *Terry* and its fruits will be suppressed," *id.* at 373. Turning to the plain view doctrine, the Court explained that "if police are lawfully in a position from which they view an object, if its incriminating character is immediately apparent, and if the officers have a lawful right of access to the object, they may seize it without a warrant." *Id.* at 375. However, the Court continued, if "the police lack probable cause to believe that an object in plain view is contraband without conducting some further search of the object— i.e., if 'its incriminating character [is not] immediately apparent,' the plain-view doctrine cannot justify its seizure." *Id.* (alteration in original) (citations omitted).

Applying these principles to nonthreatening contraband discovered during *Terry* pat downs, the Court concluded that a warrantless seizure would be permissible "so long as the officers' search stays within the bounds marked by *Terry*," *id.* at 373 (emphasis added), and the object's "contour or mass makes its identity immediately apparent," *id.* at 375 (emphasis added).

In addressing the facts before it, the *Dickerson* Court described the "dispositive question" as "whether the officer who conducted the search was acting within the lawful bounds marked by *Terry* at the time he gained probable cause to believe that the lump in respondent's jacket was contraband." *Id.* at 377. Answering that question in the negative, the Court concluded that the "officer's continued exploration of respondent's pocket after having concluded that it contained no weapon was unrelated to '[t]he sole justification of the search [under *Terry*:] . . . the protection of the police officer and others nearby.'" *Id.* at 378 (quoting *Terry*, 392 U.S. at 29) (alterations in original). Thus, the Court found that the manipulation of appellant's pocket "amounted to the sort of evidentiary search that *Terry* expressly refused to authorize, *see* [392 U.S.] at 26, and that we have condemned in" *Sibron*, 392 U.S. at 65–66, and *Long*, 463 U.S. at 1049 n. 14. *Dickerson*, 508 U.S. at 378.

"Once again," the Court explained, "analogy to the plain-view doctrine is apt." *Id.*

> In Arizona v. Hicks, 480 U.S. 321 (1987), this Court held invalid the seizure of stolen stereo equipment found by police while executing a valid search for other evidence. Although the police were lawfully on the premises, they obtained probable cause to believe that the stereo equipment was contraband only after moving the equipment to permit officers to read its serial numbers. The subsequent seizure of the equipment could not be justified by the plain-view doctrine, this Court explained, because the incriminating character of the stereo equipment was not immediately apparent; rather, probable cause to believe that the equipment was stolen arose only as a result of a further search— the moving of the equipment—that was not authorized by a search warrant or by any exception to the warrant requirement.

Dickerson, 508 U.S. at 378–79. Concluding that the search of Dickerson was "very similar" to the search of the stereo equipment, *id.* at 379, the Court held that the disputed search of Dickerson's pocket was unconstitutional.

> Although the officer was lawfully in a position to feel the lump in respondent's pocket, because *Terry* entitled him to place his hands upon respondent's jacket, the court below determined that the incriminating character of the object was not immediately apparent to him. Rather, the officer determined that the item was contraband only after conducting a further search, one not authorized by *Terry* or by any other exception to the warrant requirement. Because this further search of respondent's pocket was constitutionally invalid, the seizure of the cocaine that followed is likewise unconstitutional.

Id.

The disputed search of appellant in this case cannot be distinguished in any meaningful way from the impermissible search in *Dickerson.* Here, as in *Dickerson,* neither the constitutionality of the initial stop nor the protective frisk was at issue. In addition, neither the frisk of Dickerson nor the frisk of appellant produced any evidence of a weapon. Nevertheless, in each case, the police undertook a further search aimed at determining whether certain physical evidence would identify the stopped individual as the perpetrator of the crime in question. In Dickerson, the police officer manipulated the outside of the suspect's jacket pocket to determine whether the small lump in that pocket felt like crack cocaine. Here, the police manipulated appellant's jacket, partially unzipping and opening it, so that the complainant could see the sweatshirt underneath appellant's jacket. In each case, the goal of the officer was to obtain information about a physical object in the suspect's possession that the officer believed might identify the suspect as having committed the crime in question. In other words, the officer's goal in each case was to determine whether the object of the search, the lump in *Dickerson* and the sweatshirt here, had particular incriminating characteristics that would contribute to a probable cause determination. And in each case, the officer sought to accomplish this goal pursuant to a search that exceeded the bounds of *Terry.*

The Government's attempt to distinguish Dickerson is entirely unavailing. The sum and total of the Government's argument consists of a single sentence:

> This case is critically different from Dickerson, because this case does not involve an intrusive search of the person for evidence, but rather involves the very minimal intrusion of partially unzipping a coat to reveal a sweatshirt, not as part of a general search for evidence, but rather as a reasonable incident of an entirely permissible show-up identification procedure.

Gov't En Banc Br. at 38–39. This bald assertion is unsupported by any further explanation and is quite wrong in what it suggests.

The assertion that the impermissible search of Dickerson was more intrusive than the search of appellant is specious. If anything, the search of appellant was more intrusive. First, as the Supreme Court pointed out, when the officer in *Dickerson* undertook the impermissible search, he was at least "lawfully in a position to feel the lump in [Dickerson's] pocket," having just finished a pat down. 508 U.S. at 379. Moreover, throughout the search in *Dickerson,* the officer never strayed from the outside surface of the suspect's jacket pocket. He did not open the pocket. He did not look into it. And he did not reach inside the jacket to feel the pocket's contents. Thus, while the officer in Dickerson felt the lump through the jacket pocket, he did not physically penetrate the outer surface of the jacket. Rather, he simply "squeez[ed], slid[ ], and otherwise manipulat[ed] the contents of the defendant's pocket." *Id.* at 378 (quotation marks omitted).

And, significantly, his actions did not reveal the contents of the pocket to the public at large.

Here, when Officer Willis unzipped to the waist appellant's fastened jacket so that the complainant could see what was underneath, he not only penetrated the outer layer of appellant's clothing, he actually physically peeled a portion of it back. In contrast to the officer in Dickerson, Officer Willis also exposed what lay under that outer layer to the public at large. Consequently, in addition to exposing the sweatshirt to the complainant, the search of appellant's jacket necessarily exposed whatever else appellant had under that portion of his jacket to whomever was present on or looking at the street when his jacket was unzipped. The search here thus involved a greater invasion of the person than the manipulation of the outer surface of Dickerson's jacket pocket.

The Government's second distinction, that the search of Dickerson was a "general search for evidence," while the unzipping of appellant's jacket was "a reasonable incident of an entirely permissible show-up identification procedure," Gov't En Banc Br. at 39, is, at best, puzzling. When pressed at oral argument regarding this alleged distinction between what the police were searching for in *Dickerson* and what they were searching for here, Government counsel asserted that the search of appellant was different from the search of Dickerson, because the search of Dickerson was a "full-blown evidentiary search," Tr. of En Banc Argument (Oct. 11, 2007) at 44, "a pure evidentiary search for contraband," *id.* at 43. In contrast, according to counsel, the officers here "weren't trying to recover physical evidence." *Id.* at 43; *see also id.* at 45.

The Government's argument is unpersuasive. Certainly if the complainant had identified the appellant as her assailant on the basis of his sweatshirt, that sweatshirt would have been seized as physical evidence of appellant's guilt. Moreover, it is clear that the search here was intended to reveal evidence—both physical evidence (the sweatshirt) and testimonial evidence (the complaint's identification of it)—that would either support the probable cause necessary to arrest appellant or dispel the officer's reasonable suspicion that appellant was the robber. It is simply impossible for us to ascertain how that differs from the *Dickerson* officer's attempt to uncover tactile evidence regarding the lump in the suspect's pocket that would support the probable cause necessary to effectuate an arrest or dispel the officer's suspicion that Dickerson was committing a narcotics offense.

C.   The Government's Arguments for an Investigative Identification Search Exception Are Not Supported by Precedent

There is no Supreme Court or federal appellate case law supporting the search of an individual stopped only on reasonable articulable suspicion after a pat down of that individual has produced no evidence of a weapon. At oral argument, Government counsel conceded that there is no such precedent. Tr. of En Banc Argument at 51–52. . . . .

IV. Conclusion

On the record of this case, the police officers violated appellant's Fourth Amendment rights by unzipping his jacket without his permission and without probable cause or a warrant. The judgment of the District Court must therefore be reversed and the case remanded.

So ordered.

▪ GRIFFITH, CIRCUIT JUDGE, with whom CIRCUIT JUDGES ROGERS and TATEL join except as to footnote 2, concurring:

I agree that police officers violated Paul Askew's Fourth Amendment rights and so join the majority opinion in almost every respect. Given the importance of this appeal, I write separately to clarify my rationale for rejecting the government's principal argument before the en banc court. *Hayes v. Florida* noted in dicta that a brief detention for the purpose of fingerprinting a suspect is not necessarily an unconstitutional seizure. 470 U.S. 811, 816–17 (1985). The government argues that this dicta created a new exception to the probable cause requirement for evidentiary searches. Nothing the Supreme Court said in *Hayes* or its progeny supports this argument, and it is not our prerogative to create a new exception to the probable cause requirement of the Fourth Amendment. We are bound by Supreme Court precedent to subject the unzipping of Askew's jacket to "the textual and traditional standard of probable cause." Arizona v. Hicks, 480 U.S. 321, 329 (1987). Because the unzipping cannot satisfy that standard, I agree that we should reverse the judgment of the district court. . . .

▪ KAVANAUGH, CIRCUIT JUDGE, with whom CHIEF JUDGE SENTELLE and CIRCUIT JUDGES HENDERSON and RANDOLPH join, dissenting:

On a December night in 2003, a D.C. police officer stopped Paul Askew on a Washington street based on reasonable suspicion that Askew had just committed an armed robbery. Consistent with Terry v. Ohio, 392 U.S. 1 (1968), the police attempted to frisk Askew to ensure he was not carrying a weapon. After Askew resisted the frisk and the robbery victim arrived for a show-up procedure, the police partially unzipped Askew's outer jacket and discovered he was carrying a loaded .38 caliber gun. Because Askew was already a convicted felon, he was prosecuted in U.S. District Court for being a felon in possession of a firearm. After the District Court denied Askew's motion to suppress and ruled the gun evidence admissible, Askew pled guilty, reserving his right to appeal the Fourth Amendment issue.

In this Court, Askew accepts that the initial stop was lawful under the Fourth Amendment. Askew also acknowledges that the police could frisk him for purposes of officer safety. But Askew contends that the police exceeded the scope of a permissible *Terry* frisk by partially unzipping his outer jacket, which in turn revealed his gun. He argues that the gun evidence therefore must be excluded.

We would uphold the search and affirm Askew's conviction for either of two alternative reasons. First, after Askew actively resisted and impeded the police's initial frisk attempt, unzipping Askew's outer jacket to search for a weapon around his waist area was an objectively reasonable protective step to ensure officer safety. Second, the police may reasonably maneuver a suspect's outer clothing—such as unzipping a suspect's outer jacket—when, as here, doing so could help facilitate a witness's identification at a show-up during a *Terry* stop.

Before explaining why we would affirm Askew's conviction, we point out that the legal import of today's long-pending and badly splintered en banc decision turns out to be zero.

On the protective search question, all 11 members of the en banc Court agree on the settled legal principle that "a protective search may be lawful when a suspect prevents the police from performing a *Terry* frisk." Maj. Op. at 1144. But Part III(E) of Judge Edwards's opinion, which on this point is for a majority, concludes as a factual matter that the police here did not have an objective basis to unzip Askew's jacket as a protective step. Our difference with Part III(E) of the majority opinion is entirely fact-bound and depends solely on our different reading of the suppression hearing testimony and the District Court's opinion. . . .

United States v. King

332 Fed. Appx. 334 (7th Cir. 2009)

Michael King, Jr. pleaded guilty to possessing a firearm as a felon. See 18 U.S.C. § 922(g)(1). Under the plea agreement King reserved his right to appeal the district court's denial of his motion to suppress the gun, which was found when the police opened his car door during a traffic stop. The court sentenced King to 21 months' imprisonment, and he now appeals. Because the officers had the requisite reasonable suspicion to open the door, we affirm the district court's judgment.

In November 2007, officers Nicholas Lichtsinn and Chris Hoffman, assigned to the gang unit of the Fort Wayne, Indiana police department, observed a Buick idling outside a "known gang member hangout." While watching the car Officer Lichtsinn saw two people get into the vehicle and drive off. The officers began following the car, intending to pull it over if the driver committed a traffic violation.

The violation occurred at approximately 10:30 p.m. as the car came to a stop sign and the driver began turning eastbound. He did not signal the turn until the car "was in the process of turning at the intersection," which violated state law, *see* Indiana Code § 9–21–8–25. The officers then initiated the traffic stop with their emergency lights and siren, and the car pulled over a half-block later. As Officer Lichtsinn approached the passenger's side, he noticed the passenger, King, moving his shoulders up and down, possibly placing something in between the seat and door.

The officers agreed that both occupants were gesturing and shifting more than is typical during a traffic stop.

Officer Hoffman, approaching the driver's side, observed the driver with his hand under his right leg. With the driver's window open, he repeatedly ordered both occupants to show him their hands. Neither King nor the driver complied. At that point, fearing for his safety, Officer Lichtsinn opened the passenger door to check for accessible weapons and saw King's hand resting on top of a gun nestled between the seat and car door. Officer Lichtsinn immediately yelled "gun," securing King's hands and forcing him out of the car, while Officer Hoffman put the driver in handcuffs. After determining that King was a convicted felon, the officers placed him under arrest for unlawfully possessing the gun. *See* 18 U.S.C. § 922(g)(1).

King responded to the charge with a motion to suppress the firearm. He conceded that the officers had probable cause to stop the car, but argued that by opening the passenger door Officer Lichtsinn engaged in an unlawful search of the vehicle. Following a suppression hearing, the district court found that the totality of the circumstances-travel from a known gang house, delay before pulling over, the occupants' unusual movements after pulling over, and an apparent refusal to obey Officer Hoffman's commands-justified the protective search. Soon thereafter King reached a plea agreement with the government, and the district court sentenced him to 21 months' imprisonment.

King makes only one argument on appeal. He contends that the court should have suppressed the gun because the officers had no reasonable basis to conclude that he posed a threat to their safety when Officer Lichtsinn opened the passenger door. We review a district court's legal conclusions on a motion to suppress de novo and its factual findings for clear error. United States v. Thomas, 512 F.3d 383, 385 (7th Cir.2008).

At the outset, King rightly does not dispute the constitutionality of the traffic stop. The officers pulled the car over because, in violation of Indiana state law, the driver failed to signal his turn at least 200 feet before the intersection. *See* Indiana Code § 9–21–8–25. Because an officer's subjective motive for a traffic stop is irrelevant to its validity, *see* Whren v. United States, 517 U.S. 806, 810–13 (1996); United States v. Figueroa-Espana, 511 F.3d 696, 701 (7th Cir.2007), the only issue remaining is whether Officer Lichtsinn was justified under the Fourth Amendment in opening the passenger door to conduct a protective search for accessible weapons.

The Fourth Amendment's protection against "unreasonable searches and seizures" extends to "brief investigatory stops of persons or vehicles." United States v. Arvizu, 534 U.S. 266, 273 (2002). At the same time, though, we respect "the need for law enforcement officers to protect themselves and other prospective victims of violence in situations where they may lack probable cause for an arrest." Terry v. Ohio, 392 U.S. 1, 24

(1968). Because of these dangers, an officer may order a vehicle's occupants out of the car during a routine traffic stop. See Maryland v. Wilson, 519 U.S. 408, 410 (1997); United States v. Muriel, 418 F.3d 720, 726 (7th Cir.2005). Alternatively, if the officer has a reasonable suspicion that the driver or passenger is armed or may be able to gain immediate control of a weapon, he may conduct a protective search of the passenger compartment for accessible weapons. See, e.g., Arizona v. Gant, 129 S.Ct. 1710, 1719–20 (2009); Michigan v. Long, 463 U.S. 1032, 1049–50 (1983); United States v. Arnold, 388 F.3d 237, 239 (7th Cir.2004). In doing so, the officer must have "specific, articulable facts which, in combination with inferences to be drawn from those facts, reasonably warrant the intrusion." United States v. Fryer, 974 F.2d 813, 819 (7th Cir.1992); Long, 463 U.S. at 1049. In assessing the reasonableness of any search, we balance the degree of the intrusion against the government's justification for the search. See United States v. Knights, 534 U.S. 112, 118–19 (2001).

Here, the occupants' behavior gave Officer Lichtsinn reason to fear for his safety and authority to open the passenger door to determine if King had a weapon. See United States v. Whitaker, 546 F.3d 902, 911 (7th Cir.2008). Before pulling the car over, the officers saw it leave a "known gang member hangout." Then, after the stop, both occupants made furtive gestures and unusual movements consistent with weapons concealment, followed by multiple refusals to show their hands. All of these factors, combined in their totality, support the reasonableness of Officer Lichtsinn's decision to open the car door to conduct a limited, protective search for an accessible weapon. See Whitaker, 546 F.3d at 911; Arnold, 388 F.3d at 240–41; United States v. Brown, 188 F.3d 860, 865 (7th Cir.1999); Fryer, 974 F.2d at 819; see also United States v. Washington, 559 F.3d 573, 576–77 (D.C.Cir.2009). And once he opened the door, the gun appeared in plain view, entitling him to seize it under the plain-view doctrine. See United States v. Bruce, 109 F.3d 323, 328 (7th Cir.1997).

King responds by arguing that each individual factor does not by itself justify the intrusion. The proper standard, however, is not whether Officer Lichtsinn's decision to open the passenger door to search for an accessible weapon is justified by every single factor offered in support of the search. Rather, it is whether all of the specific, articulable bases, taken together, justified his suspicion that King was armed and dangerous, even if each and every individual factor did not by themselves justify the search. See Long, 463 U.S. at 1049; Brown, 188 F.3d at 865. Furtive movements consistent with weapons concealment and disobedience of an officer's repeated command to show one's hands justifies a limited, minimally intrusive search to see if a weapon is evident.

Accordingly, we **AFFIRM** the judgment of the district court.

7. LIMITS

Rodriguez v. United States

575 U.S. 348 (2015)

■ GINSBURG, J., delivered the opinion of the Court, in which ROBERTS, C.J., and SCALIA, BREYER, SOTOMAYOR, and KAGAN, JJ., joined. KENNEDY, J., filed a dissenting opinion. THOMAS, J., filed a dissenting opinion, in which ALITO, J., joined, and in which KENNEDY, J., joined as to all but Part III. ALITO, J., filed a dissenting opinion.

Opinion

■ JUSTICE GINSBURG delivered the opinion of the Court.

In Illinois v. Caballes, 543 U.S. 405 (2005), this Court held that a dog sniff conducted during a lawful traffic stop does not violate the Fourth Amendment's proscription of unreasonable seizures. This case presents the question whether the Fourth Amendment tolerates a dog sniff conducted after completion of a traffic stop. We hold that a police stop exceeding the time needed to handle the matter for which the stop was made violates the Constitution's shield against unreasonable seizures. A seizure justified only by a police-observed traffic violation, therefore, "become[s] unlawful if it is prolonged beyond the time reasonably required to complete th[e] mission" of issuing a ticket for the violation. *Id.*, at 407. The Court so recognized in *Caballes,* and we adhere to the line drawn in that decision.

I

Just after midnight on March 27, 2012, police officer Morgan Struble observed a Mercury Mountaineer veer slowly onto the shoulder of Nebraska State Highway 275 for one or two seconds and then jerk back onto the road. Nebraska law prohibits driving on highway shoulders, *See* Neb.Rev.Stat. § 60–6,142 (2010), and on that basis, Struble pulled the Mountaineer over at 12:06 a.m. Struble is a K–9 officer with the Valley Police Department in Nebraska, and his dog Floyd was in his patrol car that night. Two men were in the Mountaineer: the driver, Dennys Rodriguez, and a front-seat passenger, Scott Pollman.

Struble approached the Mountaineer on the passenger's side. After Rodriguez identified himself, Struble asked him why he had driven onto the shoulder. Rodriguez replied that he had swerved to avoid a pothole. Struble then gathered Rodriguez's license, registration, and proof of insurance, and asked Rodriguez to accompany him to the patrol car. Rodriguez asked if he was required to do so, and Struble answered that he was not. Rodriguez decided to wait in his own vehicle.

After running a records check on Rodriguez, Struble returned to the Mountaineer. Struble asked passenger Pollman for his driver's license and began to question him about where the two men were coming from and where they were going. Pollman replied that they had traveled to

Omaha, Nebraska, to look at a Ford Mustang that was for sale and that they were returning to Norfolk, Nebraska. Struble returned again to his patrol car, where he completed a records check on Pollman, and called for a second officer. Struble then began writing a warning ticket for Rodriguez for driving on the shoulder of the road.

Struble returned to Rodriguez's vehicle a third time to issue the written warning. By 12:27 or 12:28 a.m., Struble had finished explaining the warning to Rodriguez, and had given back to Rodriguez and Pollman the documents obtained from them. As Struble later testified, at that point, Rodriguez and Pollman "had all their documents back and a copy of the written warning. I got all the reason[s] for the stop out of the way[,] . . . took care of all the business." App. 70.

Nevertheless, Struble did not consider Rodriguez "free to leave." *Id.*, at 69–70. Although justification for the traffic stop was "out of the way," *id.*, at 70, Struble asked for permission to walk his dog around Rodriguez's vehicle. Rodriguez said no. Struble then instructed Rodriguez to turn off the ignition, exit the vehicle, and stand in front of the patrol car to wait for the second officer. Rodriguez complied. At 12:33 a.m., a deputy sheriff arrived. Struble retrieved his dog and led him twice around the Mountaineer. The dog alerted to the presence of drugs halfway through Struble's second pass. All told, seven or eight minutes had elapsed from the time Struble issued the written warning until the dog indicated the presence of drugs. A search of the vehicle revealed a large bag of methamphetamine.

Rodriguez was indicted in the United States District Court for the District of Nebraska on one count of possession with intent to distribute 50 grams or more of methamphetamine, in violation of 21 U.S.C. §§ 841(a)(1) and (b)(1). He moved to suppress the evidence seized from his car on the ground, among others, that Struble had prolonged the traffic stop without reasonable suspicion in order to conduct the dog sniff.

After receiving evidence, a Magistrate Judge recommended that the motion be denied. The Magistrate Judge found no probable cause to search the vehicle independent of the dog alert. App. 100 (apart from "information given by the dog," "Officer Struble had [no]thing other than a rather large hunch"). He further found that no reasonable suspicion supported the detention once Struble issued the written warning. He concluded, however, that under Eighth Circuit precedent, extension of the stop by "seven to eight minutes" for the dog sniff was only a *de minimis* intrusion on Rodriguez's Fourth Amendment rights and was therefore permissible.

The District Court adopted the Magistrate Judge's factual findings and legal conclusions and denied Rodriguez's motion to suppress. The court noted that, in the Eighth Circuit, "dog sniffs that occur within a short time following the completion of a traffic stop are not constitutionally prohibited if they constitute only *de minimis* intrusions." App. 114 (quoting *United States v. Alexander*, 448 F.3d 1014, 1016 (C.A.8

2006)). The court thus agreed with the Magistrate Judge that the "7 to 10 minutes" added to the stop by the dog sniff "was not of constitutional significance." App. 114. Impelled by that decision, Rodriguez entered a conditional guilty plea and was sentenced to five years in prison.

The Eighth Circuit affirmed. The "seven- or eight-minute delay" in this case, the opinion noted, resembled delays that the court had previously ranked as permissible. 741 F.3d 905, 907 (2014). The Court of Appeals thus ruled that the delay here constituted an acceptable "*de minimis* intrusion on Rodriguez's personal liberty." *Id.,* at 908. Given that ruling, the court declined to reach the question whether Struble had reasonable suspicion to continue Rodriguez's detention after issuing the written warning.

We granted certiorari to resolve a division among lower courts on the question whether police routinely may extend an otherwise-completed traffic stop, absent reasonable suspicion, in order to conduct a dog sniff. 573 U.S. ___ (2014). Compare, *e.g.,* United States v. Morgan, 270 F.3d 625, 632 (C.A.8 2001) (postcompletion delay of "well under ten minutes" permissible), with, *e.g.,* State v. Baker, 2010 UT 18, ¶ 13, 229 P.3d 650, 658 (2010) ("[W]ithout additional reasonable suspicion, the officer must allow the seized person to depart once the purpose of the stop has concluded.").

II

A seizure for a traffic violation justifies a police investigation of that violation. "[A] relatively brief encounter," a routine traffic stop is "more analogous to a so-called '*Terry* stop' . . . than to a formal arrest." Knowles v. Iowa, 525 U.S. 113, 117 (1998) (quoting Berkemer v. McCarty, 468 U.S. 420, 439 (1984), in turn citing Terry v. Ohio, 392 U.S. 1 (1968)). *See also* Arizona v. Johnson, 555 U.S. 323, 330 (2009). Like a *Terry* stop, the tolerable duration of police inquiries in the traffic-stop context is determined by the seizure's "mission"—to address the traffic violation that warranted the stop, *Caballes,* 543 U.S., at 407, and attend to related safety concerns, *infra,* at 1619–1620. *See also* United States v. Sharpe, 470 U.S. 675, 685 (1985); Florida v. Royer, 460 U.S. 491, 500 (1983) (plurality opinion) ("The scope of the detention must be carefully tailored to its underlying justification."). Because addressing the infraction is the purpose of the stop, it may "last no longer than is necessary to effectuate th[at] purpose." *Ibid. See also Caballes,* 543 U.S., at 407. Authority for the seizure thus ends when tasks tied to the traffic infraction are—or reasonably should have been—completed. *See Sharpe,* 470 U.S., at 686 (in determining the reasonable duration of a stop, "it [is] appropriate to examine whether the police diligently pursued [the] investigation").

Our decisions in *Caballes* and *Johnson* heed these constraints. In both cases, we concluded that the Fourth Amendment tolerated certain unrelated investigations that did not lengthen the roadside detention. *Johnson,* 555 U.S., at 327–328 (questioning); *Caballes,* 543 U.S., at 406, 408 (dog sniff). In *Caballes,* however, we cautioned that a traffic stop "can become unlawful it is prolonged beyond the time reasonably required to complete th[e] mission" of issuing a warning ticket. 543 U.S., at 407. And we repeated that admonition in *Johnson*: The seizure remains lawful only "so long as [unrelated] inquiries do not measurably extend the duration of the stop." 555 U.S., at 333. *See also* Muehler v. Mena, 544 U.S. 93, 101 (2005) (because unrelated inquiries did not "exten[d] the time [petitioner] was detained[,] . . . no additional Fourth Amendment justification . . . was required"). An officer, in other words, may conduct certain unrelated checks during an otherwise lawful traffic stop. But contrary to Justice ALITO's suggestion, *post,* at 1625, n. 2, he may not do so in a way that prolongs the stop, absent the reasonable suspicion ordinarily demanded to justify detaining an individual. *But see post,* at 1623–1624 (ALITO, J., dissenting) (premising opinion on the dissent's own finding of "reasonable suspicion," although the District Court reached the opposite conclusion, and the Court of Appeals declined to consider the issue).

Beyond determining whether to issue a traffic ticket, an officer's mission includes "ordinary inquiries incident to [the traffic] stop." *Caballes,* 543 U.S., at 408. Typically such inquiries involve checking the driver's license, determining whether there are outstanding warrants against the driver, and inspecting the automobile's registration and proof of insurance. *See* Delaware v. Prouse, 440 U.S. 648, 658–660 (1979). *See also* 4 W. LaFave, Search and Seizure § 9.3(c), pp. 507–517 (5th ed. 2012). These checks serve the same objective as enforcement of the traffic code: ensuring that vehicles on the road are operated safely and responsibly. *See Prouse,* 440 U.S., at 658–659; LaFave, Search and Seizure § 9.3(c), at 516 (A "warrant check makes it possible to determine whether the apparent traffic violator is wanted for one or more previous traffic offenses.").

A dog sniff, by contrast, is a measure aimed at "detect[ing] evidence of ordinary criminal wrongdoing." Indianapolis v. Edmond, 531 U.S. 32, 40–41 (2000). *See also* Florida v. Jardines, 569 U.S. 1, ___–___ (2013). Candidly, the Government acknowledged at oral argument that a dog sniff, unlike the routine measures just mentioned, is not an ordinary incident of a traffic stop. *See* Tr. of Oral Arg. 33. Lacking the same close connection to roadway safety as the ordinary inquiries, a dog sniff is not fairly characterized as part of the officer's traffic mission.

In advancing its *de minimis* rule, the Eighth Circuit relied heavily on our decision in Pennsylvania v. Mimms, 434 U.S. 106 (1977) (*per curiam*). *See* United States v. $404,905.00 in U.S. Currency, 182 F.3d 643, 649 (C.A.8 1999). In *Mimms,* we reasoned that the government's "legitimate and weighty" interest in officer safety outweighs the "*de minimis*" additional intrusion of requiring a driver, already lawfully stopped, to exit the vehicle. 434 U.S., at 110–111. *See also* Maryland v. Wilson, 519 U.S. 408, 413–415 (1997) (passengers may be required to exit vehicle stopped for traffic violation). The Eighth Circuit, echoed in

Justice THOMAS's dissent, believed that the imposition here similarly could be offset by the Government's "strong interest in interdicting the flow of illegal drugs along the nation's highways." *$404,905.00 in U.S. Currency,* 182 F.3d, at 649; *See post,* at 1621.

Unlike a general interest in criminal enforcement, however, the government's officer safety interest stems from the mission of the stop itself. Traffic stops are "especially fraught with danger to police officers," *Johnson,* 555 U.S., at 330 (internal quotation marks omitted), so an officer may need to take certain negligibly burdensome precautions in order to complete his mission safely. *Cf.* United States v. Holt, 264 F.3d 1215, 1221–1222 (C.A.10 2001) (en banc) (recognizing officer safety justification for criminal record and outstanding warrant checks), abrogated on other grounds as recognized in United States v. Stewart, 473 F.3d 1265, 1269 (C.A.10 2007). On-scene investigation into other crimes, however, detours from that mission. *See supra,* at 1615. So too do safety precautions taken in order to facilitate such detours. *But cf. post,* at 1624–1625 (ALITO, J., dissenting). Thus, even assuming that the imposition here was no more intrusive than the exit order in *Mimms,* the dog sniff could not be justified on the same basis. Highway and officer safety are interests different in kind from the Government's endeavor to detect crime in general or drug trafficking in particular.

The Government argues that an officer may "incremental[ly]" prolong a stop to conduct a dog sniff so long as the officer is reasonably diligent in pursuing the traffic-related purpose of the stop, and the overall duration of the stop remains reasonable in relation to the duration of other traffic stops involving similar circumstances. Brief for United States 36–39. The Government's argument, in effect, is that by completing all traffic-related tasks expeditiously, an officer can earn bonus time to pursue an unrelated criminal investigation. *See also post,* at 1617–1619 (THOMAS, J., dissenting) (embracing the Government's argument). The reasonableness of a seizure, however, depends on what the police in fact do. *See Knowles,* 525 U.S., at 115–117. In this regard, the Government acknowledges that "an officer always has to be reasonably diligent." Tr. of Oral Arg. 49. How could diligence be gauged other than by noting what the officer actually did and how he did it? If an officer can complete traffic-based inquiries expeditiously, then that is the amount of "time reasonably required to complete [the stop's] mission." *Caballes,* 543 U.S., at 407. As we said in *Caballes* and reiterate today, a traffic stop "prolonged beyond" that point is "unlawful." *Ibid.* The critical question, then, is not whether the dog sniff occurs before or after the officer issues a ticket, as Justice ALITO supposes, *post,* at 1624–1625, but whether conducting the sniff "prolongs"—*i.e.,* adds time to—"the stop," *supra,* at 1615.

III

The Magistrate Judge found that detention for the dog sniff in this case was not independently supported by individualized suspicion, *see*

App. 100, and the District Court adopted the Magistrate Judge's findings, *see id.*, at 112–113. The Court of Appeals, however, did not review that determination. *But see post,* at 1617, 1622–1623 (THOMAS, J., dissenting) (resolving the issue, nevermind that the Court of Appeals left it unaddressed); *post,* at 1623–1624 (ALITO, J., dissenting) (upbraiding the Court for addressing the sole issue decided by the Court of Appeals and characterizing the Court's answer as "unnecessary" because the Court, instead, should have decided an issue the Court of Appeals did not decide). The question whether reasonable suspicion of criminal activity justified detaining Rodriguez beyond completion of the traffic infraction investigation, therefore, remains open for Eighth Circuit consideration on remand.

* * *

For the reasons stated, the judgment of the United States Court of Appeals for the Eighth Circuit is vacated, and the case is remanded for further proceedings consistent with this opinion.

It is so ordered.

■ JUSTICE KENNEDY, dissenting.

My join in Justice THOMAS' dissenting opinion does not extend to Part III. Although the issue discussed in that Part was argued here, the Court of Appeals has not addressed that aspect of the case in any detail. In my view the better course would be to allow that court to do so in the first instance.

■ JUSTICE THOMAS, with whom JUSTICE ALITO joins, and with whom JUSTICE KENNEDY joins as to all but Part III, dissenting.

Ten years ago, we explained that "conducting a dog sniff [does] not change the character of a traffic stop that is lawful at its inception and otherwise executed in a reasonable manner." Illinois v. Caballes, 543 U.S. 405, 408 (2005). The only question here is whether an officer executed a stop in a reasonable manner when he waited to conduct a dog sniff until after he had given the driver a written warning and a backup unit had arrived, bringing the overall duration of the stop to 29 minutes. Because the stop was reasonably executed, no Fourth Amendment violation occurred. The Court's holding to the contrary cannot be reconciled with our decision in *Caballes* or a number of common police practices. It was also unnecessary, as the officer possessed reasonable suspicion to continue to hold the driver to conduct the dog sniff. I respectfully dissent.

I

. . . Although a traffic stop "constitutes a 'seizure' of 'persons' within the meaning of [the Fourth Amendment]," such a seizure is constitutionally "reasonable where the police have probable cause to believe that a traffic violation has occurred." Whren v. United States, 517 U.S. 806, 809–810 (1996). But "a seizure that is lawful at its inception can violate the Fourth Amendment if its manner of execution

unreasonably infringes interests protected by the Constitution."
Caballes, supra, at 407.

Because Rodriguez does not dispute that Officer Struble had
probable cause to stop him, the only question is whether the stop was
otherwise executed in a reasonable manner. *See* Brief for Appellant in
No. 13–1176 (CA8), p. 4, n. 2. I easily conclude that it was. Approximately
29 minutes passed from the time Officer Struble stopped Rodriguez until
his narcotics-detection dog alerted to the presence of drugs. That amount
of time is hardly out of the ordinary for a traffic stop by a single officer of
a vehicle containing multiple occupants even when no dog sniff is
involved. See, *e.g.,* United States v. Ellis, 497 F.3d 606 (C.A.6 2007) (22
minutes); United States v. Barragan, 379 F.3d 524 (C.A.8 2004)
(approximately 30 minutes). During that time, Officer Struble conducted
the ordinary activities of a traffic stop—he approached the vehicle,
questioned Rodriguez about the observed violation, asked Pollman about
their travel plans, ran serial warrant checks on Rodriguez and Pollman,
and issued a written warning to Rodriguez. And when he decided to
conduct a dog sniff, he took the precaution of calling for backup out of
concern for his safety. *See* 741 F.3d 905, 907 (C.A.8 2014); *see also*
Pennsylvania v. Mimms, 434 U.S. 106, 110 (1977) (per curiam) (officer
safety is a "legitimate and weighty" concern relevant to reasonableness).

As *Caballes* makes clear, the fact that Officer Struble waited until
after he gave Rodriguez the warning to conduct the dog sniff does not
alter this analysis. Because "the use of a well-trained narcotics-detection
dog . . . generally does not implicate legitimate privacy interests," 543
U.S., at 409 "conducting a dog sniff would not change the character of a
traffic stop that is lawful at its inception and otherwise executed in a
reasonable manner," *id.,* at 408. The stop here was "lawful at its inception
and otherwise executed in a reasonable manner." *Ibid.* As in *Caballes,*
"conducting a dog sniff [did] not change the character of [the] traffic stop,"
ibid., and thus no Fourth Amendment violation occurred.

II

Rather than adhere to the reasonableness requirement that we have
repeatedly characterized as the "touchstone of the Fourth Amendment,"
the majority constructed a test of its own that is inconsistent with our
precedents.

A

The majority's rule requires a traffic stop to "en[d] when tasks tied
to the traffic infraction are—or reasonably should have been—
completed." *Ante,* at 1614. "If an officer can complete traffic-based
inquiries expeditiously, then that is the amount of time reasonably
required to complete the stop's mission" and he may hold the individual
no longer. *Ante,* at 1616 (internal quotation marks and alterations
omitted). The majority's rule thus imposes a one-way ratchet for
constitutional protection linked to the characteristics of the individual

officer conducting the stop: If a driver is stopped by a particularly efficient officer, then he will be entitled to be released from the traffic stop after a shorter period of time than a driver stopped by a less efficient officer. Similarly, if a driver is stopped by an officer with access to technology that can shorten a records check, then he will be entitled to be released from the stop after a shorter period of time than an individual stopped by an officer without access to such technology. . . .

The majority's logic would produce similarly arbitrary results. Under its reasoning, a traffic stop made by a rookie could be executed in a reasonable manner, whereas the same traffic stop made by a knowledgeable, veteran officer *in precisely the same circumstances* might not, if in fact his knowledge and experience made him capable of completing the stop faster. We have long rejected interpretations of the Fourth Amendment that would produce such haphazard results, and I see no reason to depart from our consistent practice today.

B

As if that were not enough, the majority also limits the duration of the stop to the time it takes the officer to complete a narrow category of "traffic-based inquiries." *Ante,* at 1616. According to the majority, these inquiries include those that "serve the same objective as enforcement of the traffic code: ensuring that vehicles on the road are operated safely and responsibly." *Ante,* at 1615. Inquiries directed to "detecting evidence of ordinary criminal wrongdoing" are not traffic-related inquiries and thus cannot count toward the overall duration of the stop. *Ibid.* (internal quotation marks and alteration omitted).

The combination of that definition of traffic-related inquiries with the majority's officer-specific durational limit produces a result demonstrably at odds with our decision in *Caballes. Caballes* expressly anticipated that a traffic stop could be *reasonably* prolonged for officers to engage in a dog sniff. We explained that no Fourth Amendment violation had occurred in *Caballes,* where the "duration of the stop . . . was entirely justified by the traffic offense and the ordinary inquiries incident to such a stop," but suggested a different result might attend a case "involving a dog sniff that occurred during an *unreasonably* prolonged traffic stop." 543 U.S., at 407–408 (emphasis added). The dividing line was whether the overall duration of the stop exceeded "the time reasonably required to complete th[e] mission," *id.,* at 407 not, as the majority suggests, whether the duration of the stop "in fact" exceeded the time necessary to complete the traffic-related inquiries, *ante,* at 1616.

C

On a more fundamental level, the majority's inquiry elides the distinction between traffic stops based on probable cause and those based on reasonable suspicion. Probable cause is *the* "traditional justification" for the seizure of a person. *Whren,* 517 U.S., at 817 (emphasis deleted); *See also* Dunaway v. New York, 442 U.S. 200, 207–208 (1979). This Court created an exception to that rule in Terry v. Ohio, 392 U.S. 1 (1968), permitting "police officers who suspect criminal activity to make limited intrusions on an individual's personal security based on less than probable cause," Michigan v. Summers, 452 U.S. 692, 698 (1981). Reasonable suspicion is the justification for such seizures. Prado Navarette v. California, 572 U.S. ___, ___ (2014).

Traffic stops can be initiated based on probable cause or reasonable suspicion. Although the Court has commented that a routine traffic stop is "more analogous to a so-called '*Terry* stop' than to a formal arrest," it has rejected the notion "that a traffic stop supported by probable cause may not exceed the bounds set by the Fourth Amendment on the scope of a *Terry* stop." Berkemer v. McCarty, 468 U.S. 420, 439, and n. 29 (1984) (citation omitted).

Although all traffic stops must be executed reasonably, our precedents make clear that traffic stops justified by reasonable suspicion are subject to additional limitations that those justified by probable cause are not. A traffic stop based on reasonable suspicion, like all *Terry* stops, must be "justified at its inception" and "reasonably related in scope to the circumstances which justified the interference in the first place." *Hiibel,* 542 U.S., at 185 (internal quotation marks omitted). It also "cannot continue for an excessive period of time or resemble a traditional arrest." *Id.,* at 185–186 (citation omitted). By contrast, a stop based on probable cause affords an officer considerably more leeway. In such seizures, an officer may engage in a warrantless arrest of the driver, *Atwater,* 532 U.S., at 354 a warrantless search incident to arrest of the driver, Riley v. California, 573 U.S. ___, ___ (2014), and a warrantless search incident to arrest of the vehicle if it is reasonable to believe evidence relevant to the crime of arrest might be found there, Arizona v. Gant, 556 U.S. 332, 335 (2009). . . .

By strictly limiting the tasks that define the durational scope of the traffic stop, the majority accomplishes today what the *Caballes* dissent could not: strictly limiting the scope of an officer's activities during a traffic stop justified by probable cause. In doing so, it renders the difference between probable cause and reasonable suspicion virtually meaningless in this context. That shift is supported neither by the Fourth Amendment nor by our precedents interpreting it. And, it results in a constitutional framework that lacks predictability. Had Officer Struble arrested, handcuffed, and taken Rodriguez to the police station for his traffic violation, he would have complied with the Fourth Amendment. *See Atwater, supra,* at 354–355. But because he made Rodriguez wait for seven or eight extra minutes until a dog arrived, he evidently committed a constitutional violation. Such a view of the Fourth Amendment makes little sense.

III

Today's revision of our Fourth Amendment jurisprudence was also entirely unnecessary. Rodriguez suffered no Fourth Amendment violation here for an entirely independent reason: Officer Struble had reasonable suspicion to continue to hold him for investigative purposes. Our precedents make clear that the Fourth Amendment permits an officer to conduct an investigative traffic stop when that officer has "a particularized and objective basis for suspecting the particular person stopped of criminal activity." *Prado Navarette,* 572 U.S., at ___ (internal quotation marks omitted). Reasonable suspicion is determined by looking at "the whole picture," *ibid.,* taking into account "the factual and practical considerations of everyday life on which reasonable and prudent men, not legal technicians, act," Ornelas v. United States, 517 U.S. 690, 695, (1996) (internal quotation marks omitted).

■ JUSTICE ALITO, dissenting.

This is an unnecessary, impractical, and arbitrary decision. It addresses a purely hypothetical question: whether the traffic stop in this case *would be* unreasonable if the police officer, prior to leading a drug-sniffing dog around the exterior of petitioner's car, did not already have reasonable suspicion that the car contained drugs. In fact, however, the police officer *did have* reasonable suspicion, and, as a result, the officer was justified in detaining the occupants for the short period of time (seven or eight minutes) that is at issue. . . .

Not only does the Court reach out to decide a question not really presented by the facts in this case, but the Court's answer to that question is arbitrary. The Court refuses to address the real Fourth Amendment question: whether the stop was unreasonably prolonged. Instead, the Court latches onto the fact that Officer Struble delivered the warning prior to the dog sniff and proclaims that the authority to detain based on a traffic stop ends when a citation or warning is handed over to the driver. The Court thus holds that the Fourth Amendment was violated, not because of the length of the stop, but simply because of the sequence in which Officer Struble chose to perform his tasks.

This holding is not only arbitrary; it is perverse since Officer Struble chose that sequence for the purpose of protecting his own safety and possibly the safety of others. *See* App. 71–72. Without prolonging the stop, Officer Struble could have conducted the dog sniff while one of the tasks that the Court regards as properly part of the traffic stop was still in progress, but that sequence would have entailed unnecessary risk. At approximately 12:19 a.m., after collecting Pollman's driver's license, Officer Struble did two things. He called in the information needed to do a records check on Pollman (a step that the Court recognizes was properly part of the traffic stop), and he requested that another officer report to the scene. Officer Struble had decided to perform a dog sniff but did not want to do that without another officer present. When occupants of a vehicle who know that their vehicle contains a large amount of illegal drugs see that a drug-sniffing dog has alerted for the presence of drugs, they will almost certainly realize that the police will then proceed to search the vehicle, discover the drugs, and make arrests. Thus, it is reasonable for an officer to believe that an alert will increase the risk that the occupants of the vehicle will attempt to flee or perhaps even attack the officer. See, *e.g.,* United States v. Dawdy, 46 F.3d 1427, 1429 (C.A.8 1995) (recounting scuffle between officer and defendant after drugs were discovered).

In this case, Officer Struble was concerned that he was outnumbered at the scene, and he therefore called for backup and waited for the arrival of another officer before conducting the sniff. As a result, the sniff was not completed until seven or eight minutes after he delivered the warning. But Officer Struble could have proceeded with the dog sniff while he was waiting for the results of the records check on Pollman and before the arrival of the second officer. The drug-sniffing dog was present in Officer Struble's car. If he had chosen that riskier sequence of events, the dog sniff would have been completed before the point in time when, according to the Court's analysis, the authority to detain for the traffic stop ended. Thus, an action that would have been lawful had the officer made the *unreasonable* decision to risk his life became unlawful when the officer made the *reasonable* decision to wait a few minutes for backup. Officer Struble's error—apparently—was following prudent procedures motivated by legitimate safety concerns. The Court's holding therefore makes no practical sense. And nothing in the Fourth Amendment, which speaks of *reasonableness,* compels this arbitrary line. . . .

United States v. Leal

235 Fed.Appx. 937 (3d Cir. 2007)

■ MCKEE, CIRCUIT JUDGE.

Robert Valdez Leal asks us to review the district court's denial of the motion to suppress he filed following his arrest for possession of a controlled substance with the intent to distribute. For the reasons that follow, we will affirm the District Court's denial of Leal's suppression motion.

I.A. Initial Stop

Leal's first argument that Trooper Volk did not have probable cause to stop his vehicle is frivolous. Volk testified credibly that he stopped Leal because the windows on Leal's car were heavily tinted and appeared to be in violation of a provision of the Pennsylvania Vehicle Code that prohibits excessive window tint. *See* 75 Pa.C.S. § 4524(e)(1). A law enforcement officer's good faith decision to stop a car is "reasonable where the police have probable cause to believe that a traffic violation has occurred." Whren v. United States, 517 U.S. 806, 810 (1996). *See, e.g.,* Holeman v. City of New London, 425 F.3d 184, 190 (2d Cir.2005) (holding that tinted windows alone would justify a police officer's stop if the window tint was so dark that an officer, acting reasonably, would have suspected there was a traffic violation).

Leal argues that his car was exempt from the prohibition against tinted windows because the tint was applied by the manufacturer and therefore his car fit within the statutory exception to the prohibition. We need not respond to that argument. Law enforcement officers have broad leeway to conduct searches and seizures regardless of whether their subjective intent corresponds to the legal justifications for their actions if the legal justification is objectively grounded. *See* United States v. Lopez-Soto, 205 F.3d 1101, 1105 (9th Cir.2000) (citing United States v. Miller, 146 F.3d 274, 279 (5th Cir.1998); *see also* United States v. Sanders, 196 F.3d 910, 913 (8th Cir.1999)) (holding that an officer's mistaken, but objectively reasonable, belief that a traffic violation occurred supported a traffic stop). Whether or not Leal's car was technically in violation of the statute, Officer Volk could have reasonably believed that Leal was in violation of the statute because the windows were heavily tinted. *See* Sanders, 196 F.3d at 913.

Leal attempts to establish that Trooper Volk's testimony was not credible because of discrepancies in Volk's testimony. He argues that Volk's reliance on the window tint violation was mere pretext for the stop and that Volk actually stopped him as part of a "fishing expedition," based only on the fact that Leal was driving an "older vehicle with Texas plates . . . through Western Pennsylvania."

Here again, we need not respond. Trooper Volk's subjective motivation for initiating the traffic stop is irrelevant. In *Whren,* the Court stated: "the fact that the officer does not have the state of mind which is hypothecated by the reasons which provide the legal justification for the officer's action does not invalidate the action taken as long as the circumstances, viewed objectively, justify that action." 517 U.S. at 813 (quoting Scott v. United States, 436 U.S. 128, 136 (1978) (internal quotation marks omitted)). Accordingly, Trooper Volk clearly had probable cause to stop Leal's car.

B.   Investigative Stop

The real issue here is not the initial stop, but the detention that ensued. Leal argues that his continued detention was beyond the parameters of a brief investigatory stop that the Court established in Terry v. Ohio, 392 U.S. 1 (1968). Specifically, he contends that Trooper Volk's decision to detain him pending the arrival of "Zeus" (the drug sniffing dog), was unlawful because it was caused by Leal's refusal to consent to a car search.

The District Court found that Trooper Volk's decision to detain Leal was not based upon Leal's refusal to consent, but instead, in part, upon Leal's statement that he had consulted a lawyer before driving from Texas, which Trooper Volk found to be very unusual. Leal argues that Volk could only continue the stop after Leal refused to consent if there were additional grounds to support what Leal characterizes as a "second stop."

It is well established that a refusal to consent to a search cannot be the basis for a finding of reasonable suspicion. Karnes v. Skrutski, 62 F.3d 485, 495–96 (3d Cir.1995). In *United States v. Williams*, the court recognized that an officer's consideration of a defendant's refusal to consent to a search would violate the Fourth Amendment. 271 F.3d 1262, 1268 (10th Cir.2001), cert. denied, 535 U.S. 1019 (2002). Accordingly, the court ignored that refusal but still upheld the search. The totality of the circumstances there rose to the level of probable cause without factoring in the defendant's refusal to consent to a search. The court explained:

> Williams fails to cite any case, nor can we find any, suggesting that the return of such documentation negates an officer's objectively reasonable suspicions developed during a traffic stop. Although the record indicates that the [trooper] subjectively intended that Mr. Williams was free to go, the relevant inquiry in this case is based on the objective facts known to the [trooper], not upon the [trooper's] subjective state of mind. [citations omitted] . . . Whether the [trooper] never intended to release Mr. Williams or whether he simply changed his mind after the consensual questioning does not alter our analysis if the [trooper] already had sufficient reasonable suspicion to detain [the defendant] for the purpose of the canine drug search. We therefore conclude that the [trooper's] indication to Mr. Williams that he was free to leave bears no significance in our determination of whether the [trooper] had reasonable suspicion to detain Mr. Williams.

Other courts have followed the reasoning of *Williams*. *See, e.g.,* United States v. Foreman, 369 F.3d 776, 784 (4th Cir.2004); United States v. Fuse, 391 F.3d 924, 929 (8th Cir.2004).

Leal is obviously correct in arguing that his refusal to consent cannot contribute to a finding of reasonable suspicion. *See Karnes*, 62 F.3d at 495–96. However, Leal cites no case law, and we have found none, that would require Volk to ignore all that he had observed and all that he knew up to the moment he asked for consent. We need not recite each of the fourteen factors that Volk relied upon in deciding to detain Leal until Zeus could arrive to sniff Leal's car. Although the totality of those circumstances do not rise to the level of probable cause to arrest, they certainly approach that threshold and certainly support a finding of articulable suspicion. Although Volk's information does not rise to the level of probable cause, we can not ignore either the strength or quality of Trooper Volk's suspicion in evaluating his decision to continue to detain Leal for the sole purpose of further investigation under *Terry*.

The more troubling questions are whether the length of the delay between the time Volk radioed for the dog and the time Zeus arrived was so great that it either constituted a de facto arrest, or was inconsistent with the limited intrusion allowed under *Terry*.

C. The Length of the Detention

Leal's strongest argument is that his detention for at least one hour and twenty minutes following the traffic stop was actually a de facto arrest that was unlawful under the Fourth Amendment because it was not supported by probable cause. Leal makes a related but different argument that the length of the delay was simply unreasonable given the limits of *Terry*, whether or not Trooper Volk was justified in "briefly" detaining him.

Leal's argument is not without substantial force. It is clear that *Terry* does not allow police to arrest a suspect only to hold him/her until police can determine if there was probable cause to make an arrest in the first place. Similarly, the intrusion the Court authorized in *Terry* is limited to a brief detention to determine if criminal activity is afoot. *See Terry*, 392 U.S. at 33. A *Terry* stop was never intended to authorize a lengthy detention to complete an investigation that is prompted by the articulable suspicion that is the condition precedent of the intrusion allowed under *Terry*.

The line between a proper *Terry* stop and an improper de facto arrest is elusive and not easily drawn. *See* United States v. Sharpe, 470 U.S. 675, 685 (1985). In considering whether a stop is "so minimally intrusive as to be justifiable on reasonable suspicion," *id.* (quoting United States v. Place, 462 U.S. 696, 709 (1983)), courts consider the duration of the stop, the law enforcement purposes justifying the stop, whether the police diligently sought to carry out those purposes given the circumstances, and alternative means by which the police could have served their purposes. *Id.* at 684–87.

The Supreme Court has set forth an objective standard for determining whether a person has been "seized" for the purposes of the Fourth Amendment: "We conclude that a person has been 'seized' within the meaning of the Fourth Amendment only if, in view of all the circumstances surrounding the incident, a reasonable person would have believed that he was not free to leave." United States v. Mendenhall, 446 U.S. 544, 554 (1980). *See also* Florida v. Bostick, 501 U.S. 429, 435(1991) ("When police attempt to question a person who is walking down the street or through an airport lobby, it makes sense to inquire whether a reasonable person would feel free to continue walking."). Here, Trooper Volk did not intend to let Leal leave before Zeus arrived. In addition, we think it fair to conclude that a reasonable person in Leal's situation would not have felt free to leave. However, that does not necessarily negate a conclusion that Leal was being detained pursuant to *Terry* as opposed to being arrested. A suspect is not free to leave during a *Terry* stop, and Volk did nothing to suggest that Leal could not leave immediately upon the conclusion of the dog sniff if the dog failed to find any additional evidence of drugs in Leal's car. Accordingly, we conclude that Leal was not under arrest before the dog arrived and that his detention was an investigatory stop to determine if Volk's very reasonable suspicion was justified.

However, the foregoing analysis does not end our inquiry. Leal argues persuasively that even a purely investigatory stop initiated under the circumstances here can offend the Fourth Amendment if it is more than the brief intrusion allowed under *Terry*. Thus, we must determine whether Leal's detention went beyond that which is allowed for a *Terry* stop.

In *Dunaway v. New York,* the court explained that a *Terry* stop must be limited in duration, and that a more lengthy detention "must be based on consent or probable cause." 442 U.S. 200, 212 (1979). However, there is "no rigid time limitation on *Terry* stops." *Sharpe,* 470 U.S. at 685. A stop may be too long if it involves "delay unnecessary to the legitimate investigation of the law enforcement officers." *Id.* at 687.

The Supreme Court has refused to impose a stringent time limit on the duration of an investigative stop under *Terry*. Rather, the inquiry considers the nature of the investigatory actions of the police, i.e., "whether the police diligently pursued a means of investigation that was likely to confirm or dispel their suspicions quickly, during which time it was necessary to detain the defendant." *Id.* at 676; *see also* Michigan v. Summers, 452 U.S. 692, 702 n. 14 (1981).

Leal relies heavily on United States v. Place, 462 U.S. 696 (1983). There, the Supreme Court held that a ninety-minute delay before federal agents used a narcotics detection dog to sniff Place's luggage was sufficient "alone [to preclude] the conclusion that the seizure was reasonable in the absence of probable cause." *Id.* at 709. The Court therefore ordered the suppression of the evidence produced in the search. *Id.* In recognizing an individual's "liberty interest in proceeding with his itinerary," 462 U.S. at 708, the Court observed:

> [a] person whose luggage is detained is technically still free to continue his travels or carry out other personal activities pending release of the luggage. Moreover, he is not subjected to the coercive atmosphere of a custodial confinement or to the public indignity of being personally detained. Nevertheless, such a seizure can effectively restrain the person since he is subjected to the possible disruption of his travel plans in order to remain with his luggage or to arrange for its return.

Id. at 708–709 (footnote omitted).

We distinguished *Place* in *United States v. Frost* to hold that an eighty-minute delay under the circumstances of that case was acceptable under *Terry*. 999 F.2d 737, 740–42 (3d Cir.1993), cert. denied, 510 U.S. 1001 (1993). Thus, if we focus only on the length of the delay here, it is a very close case indeed. However, we can not say, given all the facts known to Trooper Volk when he radioed for the canine unit, that the limitations of *Terry* were per se violated based on the length of time it took the unit to arrive at the scene.

In deciding if the delay was nevertheless unreasonable or otherwise so intrusive as to violate *Terry*'s parameters, we begin by stressing that nothing on this record suggests that Trooper Volk knew that it was going to take the canine unit 80 minutes to arrive when Volk radioed for the dog. It is uncontested that Trooper Johnson, the officer bringing Zeus, was delayed en route because of construction. Trooper Volk was diligent in his attempts to further investigate Leal's vehicle, and his efforts to expeditiously resolve his suspicions were frustrated by circumstances beyond his control. Given that, along with the quantity and quality of the factors that gave rise to Trooper Volk's suspicion, we conclude that Leal's detention may have bumped up against the outer limit of a *Terry* stop, but it did not cross it. Accordingly, we hold that the District Court did not err in denying Leal's motion to suppress the physical evidence.[1]

III. CONCLUSION

For the reasons set forth above, we will affirm the order of the District Court denying Leal's motion to suppress physical evidence.

8. EMPIRICAL NOTE: STUDYING POLICE PATROL PRACTICES

One consequence of the Supreme Court's preference for bright-line rules is that the choice of one rule over another typically turns not on the facts in the record of the instant case, but on what happens in thousands of similar cases not before the Court. Fourth Amendment rules aim to guide police actions in *future* cases. Courts fashion such rules with an eye on history and precedent, but with another eye on striking a reasonable balance between liberty and security. Making a good decision depends on having some knowledge about how the police behave in general, and on the probable effect of one rule or another on the police in future cases.

These are questions traditionally asked by legislators. So to the extent legislatures regulate the police, answers to these empirical questions are even more central than they are to courts. Moreover, when trial-level judges prepare institutional reform injunctions, detailed knowledge about the local department's past policies, and likely responses to court-ordered reforms, is essential.

---

[1]   Although we are affirming the denial of the suppression motion here, our holding should not be interpreted as condoning a practice of requesting additional investigation without any concern for the length of the detention. Rather, law enforcement officers in the position that Volk was in here should make appropriate inquiries to ensure that the delay attendant to any additional investigation is not so lengthy or restrictive that it runs afoul of the parameters prescribed by *Terry*. Moreover, the detention allowed under *Terry* is limited even when officers take such precautions. At some point, the detention required for additional investigation can become so restrictive or prolonged that it is tantamount to an arrest and must therefore be supported by probable cause if it is to withstand constitutional scrutiny. We are simply holding that, under the circumstances here, Leal's detention did not reach that point.

But how can judges, legislators, and voters actually know what happens during typical *Terry* stops and typical traffic stops? How can we know whether legal rules actually change police behavior? And if the rules change police behavior, what benefits (if any) are there for civil liberties, at what cost (if any) to public safety?

One approach is direct observation. Researchers can accompany the police on patrol (so-called "ride alongs") and record what they see. *See, e.g.,* Jon B. Gould & Stephen D. Mastrofski, *Suspect Searches: Assessing Police Behavior under the U.S. Constitution,* 3 Criminology & Pub. Pol'y 315 (2004). The Gould & Mastrofski research team observed 115 searches by police in a "medium sized city." They coded these searches as legal or illegal, submitting borderline cases for review by a committee of one former judge and two former prosecutors.

They found that thirty-four of the 115 searches were illegal, and in thirty one of the cases of illegal searches the suspect was not arrested or cited. Those cases never went far enough to be recorded in official statistics. Of the 115 total searches observed, forty-four were frisks during *Terry* stops. The researchers concluded that twenty of these (45.5%) were illegal.

During the latter years of the twentieth century, many police department undertook to document *Terry* stops or traffic stops. These record-keeping policies were often undertaken in response to legislation or court decisions. Whatever their genesis, the data generated by police record-keeping is now a rich source of information.

For example, a RAND Corporation study analyzed NYPD reports of 500,000 *Terry* stops. *See* Greg Ridgeway, Analysis of Racial Disparities in the New York Police Department's Stop, Question, and Frisk Practices (2007). Ninety percent of the reported stops did not result in either an arrest or a citation. *Id.* at xi, xv. The police reported frisking only one third of those stopped. *Id.* at 37 (Table 5.2). Contraband was recovered in 6.4% of the frisks of white suspects, 5.7% of frisks of black suspects, and 5.4% of frisks of Hispanic suspects. *Id.* at 41–42. Most contraband recoveries were for recreational quantities of marijuana. "For every 1,000 frisks of black suspects, officers recovered seven weapons; for every 1,000 frisks of similarly situated white suspects, they recovered eight weapons, a difference that is not statistically significant." *Id.* at 42.

In 2014, newly-elected Mayor de Blasio agreed to settle a class-action law suit, and terminated the aggressive use of stop-and-frisk. Stops, which had become less frequent even before the settlement, dropped from hundreds of thousands per year to tens of thousands per year. Crime in New York generally decline over this period. *See, e.g.,* James Cullen, *Ending New York's Stop-and-Frisk Did Not Increase Crime,* (Apr. 11, 2016) at https://www.brennancenter.org/our-work/analysis-opinion/ ending-new-yorks-stop-and-frisk-did-not-increase-crime It is possible, however, that crime would have fallen even faster had the police continued aggressive use of stop-and-frisk. On this hypothesis, see the

Empirical Note: Studying Institutional Reform Injunctions in Chapter 5, Section 7.

The New York data unquestionably showed that the percentage of blacks and Hispanics in the population of suspects stopped by the police was much higher than the percentage of blacks and Hispanics in the city's population. Whether or not this disparate impact was the result of invidious racial profiling or an unfortunate consequence of concentrating on likely criminals is a question considered in the following excerpt from one of the rulings in the lawsuit that ended in injunctive relief Mayor de Blasio decided not to appeal.

Floyd v. City of New York
959 F.Supp.2d 540 (S.D.N.Y. 2013)

3.   The Fourteenth Amendment Claim

a.   Overview of Key Issues

The crux of plaintiffs' Fourteenth Amendment claim is that blacks and Hispanics are stopped more frequently than they would be if police officers did not discriminate based on race when deciding whom to stop. Assessing this claim required comparing statistics about rates of stops of blacks and Hispanics to "[a] standard, or point of reference, against which [those statistics] can be compared, assessed, measured or judged"—what is known in statistics as a "benchmark." In this case, the benchmark was meant to capture "what the racial distribution of the stopped pedestrians would have been if officers' stop decisions had been racially unbiased."

Conclusions regarding racial bias drawn from statistics "may vary drastically based on which benchmark is used." As such, a central dispute between the experts regarding the Fourteenth Amendment claim was the appropriate benchmark for measuring racial bias in stops.

b.   Competing Benchmarks

Each expert submitted voluminous reports and testified at trial in support of his choice of benchmark. Of necessity, I must simplify their very detailed and complex submissions and testimony to focus on the question at the heart of the parties' dispute: is there statistical evidence of racial discrimination in the NYPD's stop practices? With that caveat, I endeavor to summarize their differing benchmarks.

Dr. Fagan explained his choice of benchmark as follows:

[A] valid benchmark requires estimates of the supply of individuals of each racial or ethnic group who are engaged in the targeted behaviors and who are available to the police as potential targets for the exercise of their stop authority. Since police often target resources to the places where crime rates and risks are highest, and where populations are highest, some measure of population that is conditioned on crime rates is an optimal candidate for inclusion as a benchmark.

Accordingly, Dr. Fagan's "analyses use both population and reported crime as benchmarks for understanding the racial distribution of police-citizen contacts." While there is scholarly disagreement regarding the best benchmark to use in such measurements, none of the sources Drs. Smith and Purtell cited criticized the benchmark used by Dr. Fagan. In addition, at least one other study of a police department's stop patterns—a study of stop patterns in Los Angeles by Dr. Ian Ayres, the William K. Townsend Professor of Law at Yale Law School—used an "[a]lmost identical" benchmark to Dr. Fagan's.

The City's experts, by contrast, used a benchmark consisting of the rates at which various races appear in suspect descriptions from crime victims—in other words, "suspect race description data." The City's experts assumed that if officers' stop decisions were racially unbiased, then the racial distribution of stopped pedestrians would be the same as the racial distribution of the criminal suspects in the area. I conclude that Dr. Fagan's benchmark is the better choice. The reason is simple and reveals a serious flaw in the logic applied by the City's experts: there is no basis for assuming that the racial distribution of stopped pedestrians will resemble the racial distribution of the local criminal population *if the people stopped are not criminals*. The City defends the fact that blacks and Hispanics represent 87% of the persons stopped in 2011 and 2012 by noting that "approximately 83% of all known crime suspects and approximately 90% of all violent crime suspects were Black and Hispanic." This might be a valid comparison if the people stopped were criminals, or if they were stopped based on fitting a specific suspect description. But there was insufficient evidence to support either conclusion. To the contrary, nearly 90% of the people stopped are released without the officer finding any basis for a summons or arrest, and only 13% of stops are based on fitting a specific suspect description. There is no reason to believe that the nearly 90% of people who are stopped and then subject to no further enforcement action are criminals. As a result, there is no reason to believe that their racial distribution should resemble that of the local criminal population, as opposed to that of the local population in general. If the police are stopping people in a race-neutral way, then the racial composition of innocent people stopped should more or less mirror the racial composition of the areas where they are stopped, all other things being equal. Dr. Fagan's benchmark captures what the NYPD's stops would look like in the absence of racial discrimination: his use of local population data reflects who is available to be stopped in an area (assuming, as the evidence shows, that the overwhelming majority of stops are not of criminals), and his use of local crime rates reflects the fact that stops are more likely to take place in areas with higher crime rates.

By contrast, Dr. Smith rejected the assumption that 88% of those stopped were innocent. "[H]ow do we know . . . [i]f they were utterly innocent [?]" Dr. Smith asked at trial. He then proposed a "hypothetical" in which "the stop prevents a crime." If one assumes that those stopped with no further enforcement action are nevertheless criminals, then it is natural to conclude, as Dr. Smith did, that a valid benchmark for measuring racial disparities in stops must "enable us to know who is committing the crime in [an] area." Thus, he concludes that the best benchmark for the population of people who will be stopped in the absence of racial discrimination is the local criminal population. As Dr. Smith testified, "the best proxy for the share of the population by race engaged in the targeted behaviors that lead officers to make *Terry* stops" is the percentage of each racial category that appears in crime suspect data, or more precisely a combination of crime suspect data and arrestee data, because "[t]hat's what we know about who is committing crime."

Based on this analysis, Dr. Smith concludes that the disproportionate stopping of black people can be explained by the disproportionately black composition of the pool of criminals. But even if all stops by the NYPD were based on reasonable suspicion—which is highly unlikely for reasons already stated—the low hit rate would undermine the assumption that the stopped people were *in fact* engaged in criminal activity, and thus members of the criminal population. The City failed to establish that a significant number of the approximately 3.9 million stops that resulted in no further enforcement action were stops of people who were about to commit, but were prevented from committing, a crime. Dr. Smith's theory that a significant number of these stops resulted in the prevention of the suspected crime is pure speculation and not reliable.

Crime suspect data may serve as a reliable proxy for the pool of *criminals* exhibiting suspicious behavior. But there is no reason to believe that crime suspect data provides a reliable proxy for the pool of *non-criminals* exhibiting suspicious behavior. Because the overwhelming majority of people stopped fell into the latter category, there is no support for the City's position that crime suspect data provides a reliable proxy for the pool of people exhibiting suspicious behavior. Moreover, given my finding that a significant number of stops were *not* based on reasonable suspicion—and thus were stops drawn from the pool of *non* criminals *not* exhibiting suspicious behavior—the use of crime suspect data as a benchmark for the pool of people that would have been stopped in the absence of racial bias is even less appropriate. When confronted by plaintiffs' counsel with similar reasoning, Dr. Smith ultimately appeared willing to entertain the possibility that black people, even when they are law-abiding, might simply be more likely to engage in suspicious behavior than white people:

> Q.   So is it your testimony that law-abiding black people in New York City are more likely to engage in suspicious behavior than law-abiding white people?

A. I'm only saying that that's the evidence from the stop
patterns, which we have said, according to Professor Fagan, are
ninety percent apparently justified.

Dr. Smith's position, while surprising, is not illogical once his premises
are accepted. Dr. Smith apparently does not find it plausible that officers'
decisions regarding whether to stop a person may be swayed by conscious
or unconscious racial bias. If a researcher begins with this premise, he
will attempt to find a credible, race-neutral explanation for the NYPD's
stopping of blacks and Hispanics out of proportion to their share of the
population. For example, the researcher may seek to explain the
disproportionate stopping of minorities as the result of the
characteristics of the criminal population. However, as already
explained, there is no evidence that 88% of the people stopped are, in fact,
members of the criminal population. Next, the researcher may analyze
the deployment of police to high crime areas or "hot spots." If these areas
happen to be disproportionately minority, then heavy deployment to
these areas will provide a race-neutral basis for the disproportionate
stopping of minorities. But Dr. Fagan's "Table 5" analysis showed that
blacks and Hispanics are overstopped even after controlling for police
deployment to high crime areas. In the end, if the researcher cannot
think of any relevant race-neutral factors for which Dr. Fagan did not
control, the only remaining race-neutral explanation for the NYPD's stop
patterns may be that members of the overstopped racial groups have a
greater tendency to appear suspicious than members of other racial
groups, even when they are not breaking the law.

Rather than being a defense *against* the charge of racial profiling,
however, this reasoning is a defense *of* racial profiling. To say that black
people in general are somehow more suspicious-looking, or criminal in
appearance, than white people is not a race-neutral explanation for racial
disparities in NYPD stops: it is itself a *racially biased explanation*. This
explanation is especially troubling because it echoes the stereotype that
black men are more likely to engage in criminal conduct than others. In
a recent speech responding to the public controversy surrounding the
shooting of a black teenager, President Obama noted his personal
experience with this stereotype:

There are very few African-American men in this country who
haven't had the experience of being followed when they were
shopping in a department store. That includes me. There are
very few African-American men who haven't had the experience
of walking across the street and hearing the locks click on the
doors of cars. That happens to me, at least before I was a
senator. There are very few African-Americans who haven't had
the experience of getting on an elevator and a woman clutching
her purse nervously and holding her breath until she had a
chance to get off. That happens often.

Another commentator observed in even starker terms:

> What is reasonable to do, especially in the dark of night, is defined by preconceived social roles that paint young black men as potential criminals and predators. Black men, the narrative dictates, are dangerous, to be watched and put down at the first false move. This pain is one all black men know; putting away the tie you wear to the office means peeling off the assumption that you are owed equal respect. Mr. Martin's hoodie struck the deepest chord because we know that daring to wear jeans and a hooded sweatshirt too often means that the police or other citizens are judged to be reasonable in fearing you.

No doubt many people have heard similar fears and stereotypes expressed, whether intentionally or unintentionally. But race alone is not an objective basis for suspicion by the police. Because there is no evidence that law-abiding blacks or Hispanics are more likely to behave *objectively* more suspiciously than law-abiding whites, Dr. Smith's—and the City's—refuge in this unsupported notion is no refuge at all. It is effectively an admission that there is no explanation for the NYPD's disproportionate stopping of blacks and Hispanics other than the NYPD's stop practices having become infected, somewhere along the chain of command, by racial bias.

Why would the people stopped by the NYPD, both criminal and law-abiding, so closely resemble the criminal population—or, more precisely, the NYPD's understanding of the criminal population, based on its limited suspect data? A simple explanation exists: the racial composition of the people stopped by the NYPD resembles what the NYPD perceives to be the racial composition of the criminal population *because that is why they were stopped.* Evidence discussed later in this Opinion shows that the NYPD has an unwritten policy of targeting racially defined groups for stops, based on the appearance of members of those groups in crime suspect data. A strong correlation between the races of people stopped and the known races of criminal suspects is the natural result.

In short, the correlation highlighted by the City and its experts in their attempt to refute the allegation of racial profiling in fact provides evidence of racial profiling. Rather than revealing a valid race-neutral variable that explains the NYPD's disproportionate stopping of blacks and Hispanics, the correlation highlighted by the City's experts suggests how the racial disparities identified by Dr. Fagan might have come about—namely, through a widespread practice of racial profiling based on local criminal suspect data.

———

Researchers have also studied police records on traffic stops. *See, e.g.,* Samuel R. Gross & Katherine Y. Barnes, *Road Work: Racial Profiling and Drug Interdiction on the Highway,* 101 Mich. L. Rev. 651 (2002) (analyzing data from the Maryland State Police). A recent contribution, notable for its massive data set and ingenious research design, is Emma Pierson et al., *A large-scale analysis of racial disparities in police stops across the United States* (Stanford Computation Policy Lab, March 13, 2019) at https://5harad.com/papers/100M-stops.pdf

The Stanford team prepared a database including records of one hundred million traffic stops from dozens of different jurisdictions. They compared the percentage of stops of white and black motorists before and after dark. At night it is more difficult to detect the race of the driver. They found that the percentage of stopped drivers who are black fell (depending on the statistical model used) from between 12% and 24% after dark. To put those numbers in context, if 25% of stopped drivers were black during daylight, and 20% of stopped drivers were black after dark, the percentage of blacks among stopped drivers would have fallen 25% after dark. The study says that these "findings are broadly suggestive of racial discrimination against black drivers in stop decisions." *Id.* at 5.

9. THE ROLE OF FEDERALISM

Cases like *Mapp v. Ohio* and *Sibron v. New York* reflect the Supremacy Clause in Article VI of the Constitution ("This Constitution, and the laws of the United States which shall be made in pursuance thereof; and all treaties made, or which shall be made, under the authority of the United States, shall be the supreme law of the land; and the judges in every state shall be bound thereby, anything in the Constitution or laws of any State to the contrary notwithstanding.") If the U.S. Supreme Court rules that state officers violated the Fourth Amendment, applicable to the states via the Fourteenth Amendment, state law yields to the Constitution.

When, however, state legislation, or state court decisions based on the state constitution, impose limits on the police that are *more,* rather than *less* protective of the suspect's liberty or privacy, the federal constitution does not prohibit the states from adopting rules that are more pro-defendant and less pro-law-enforcement than the rule adopted by the U.S. Supreme Court under the Constitution of the United States. A recent decision by the Oregon Supreme Court illustrates this principle that the U.S. Supreme Court's Fourth Amendment decisions set the national floor, not a national ceiling, on the legal regulation of police practices.

State v. Arreola-Botello

Petitioner on Review, 365 Or. 695 (2019) (en banc)

Opinion

■ NELSON, J.

In this criminal case, we consider the constitutionally permissible scope of a traffic stop under Article I, section 9, of the Oregon Constitution. Defendant was lawfully stopped for failing to signal a turn and a lane change. During the stop, while defendant was searching for his registration and proof of insurance, the officer asked him about the presence of guns and drugs in the vehicle, and requested consent to search the vehicle. Defendant consented, and during the search, the officer located a controlled substance. Defendant contends that the officer expanded the permissible scope of the traffic stop when he asked about the contents of the vehicle and requested permission to search it because those inquiries were not related to the purpose of the stop. For the reasons that follow, we agree with defendant that the trial court erred in denying defendant's motion to suppress, and we reverse the decision of the Court of Appeals.

In reviewing the denial of a motion to suppress evidence, we are bound by the trial court's factual findings to the extent that those findings are supported by evidence in the record. *State v. Stevens*, 311 Or. 119, 126, 806 P.2d 92 (1991). Additionally, "if the trial court does not make findings on all pertinent historical facts and there is evidence from which those facts could be decided more than one way, we will presume that the trial court found facts in a manner consistent with its ultimate conclusion." *Id.* at 127, 806 P.2d 92. We state the following facts in accordance with that standard.

Officer Faulkner of the Beaverton Police Department observed defendant's vehicle change lanes and turn without signaling. Faulkner initiated his patrol car's overhead lights, and defendant pulled over. Faulkner approached defendant's vehicle and requested his driver's license, registration, and proof of insurance. Defendant was able to immediately produce his license but spent about three to four additional minutes searching for his registration and proof of insurance.

While defendant was searching, Faulkner asked him questions. Defendant, who primarily speaks Spanish, was having difficulty understanding the questions in English. At the beginning of the traffic stop, a passenger in the vehicle helped interpret Faulkner's questions, but she left after Faulkner told her that she was free to do so. Faulkner asked defendant about the presence of weapons, drugs, or other illegal items in the vehicle and requested consent to search the vehicle. Defendant responded, "Sure, okay," and consented to the search. During the search, Faulkner located a small package on the floor between the driver's seat and the door. Faulkner examined the package, found it to be consistent with drug packaging, and observed a substance in the package that he believed was methamphetamine. Faulkner placed defendant under arrest.

The state charged defendant with possession of methamphetamine, ORS 475.894. Before trial, defendant moved to suppress the evidence obtained during the traffic stop, arguing that Faulkner had violated his constitutional rights by unlawfully expanding the scope of the lawful traffic stop into matters unrelated to the purpose of the stop, such as whether defendant possessed drugs. Faulkner testified that his questioning had been a routine inquiry, "[a]ll the same spiel every time." He stated, "Every time I walk up, I ask him, I [say], 'hey, Officer Faulkner, Beaverton Police Department,' do my contact with them. 'Do you have anything illegal in the car? Would you consent to a search for guns, drugs, knives, bombs, illegal documents, or anything else that you're not allowed to possess?' " Defendant maintained that Faulkner's questioning went beyond the lawful the scope of the traffic stop. The trial court disagreed and concluded that Faulkner had asked the unrelated questions during an "unavoidable lull,"[2] and that defendant had voluntarily consented to the search of the vehicle. Thus, the trial court denied defendant's motion to suppress. Defendant waived his right to a jury trial, and the trial court convicted defendant of unlawful possession of methamphetamine.

Defendant appealed, assigning error to the denial of his motion to suppress. At the Court of Appeals, defendant argued that Faulkner had unlawfully expanded the scope of the traffic stop by asking investigatory questions that were unrelated to the purpose of the stop without independent constitutional justification. The state responded that Court of Appeals case law authorizes an officer to request consent to search a vehicle during an "unavoidable lull" in an investigation, such as when a person is searching for requested documents. The Court of Appeals agreed with the state and affirmed defendant's conviction in a per curiam decision. *See State v. Arreola-Botello*, 292 Or. App. 214, 418 P.3d 785 (2018) (per curiam) (citing *State v. Hampton*, 247 Or. App. 147, 268 P.3d 711 (2011), which held that questioning about consent to search a vehicle while the driver was searching for registration occurred during an "unavoidable lull" and, thus, did not extend the traffic stop in violation of Article I, section 9, protections against unreasonable seizure).

Defendant petitioned for, and we allowed, review. In this court, defendant renews his argument that Faulkner violated his Article I, section 9, rights when Faulkner asked him questions about drugs and weapons, and requested consent to search his vehicle, because those

---

[2]   As explained below, the Court of Appeals has held that, during an "unavoidable lull," an officer may ask unrelated questions during a traffic stop if those questions do not extend the duration of the stop. *See State v. Nims*, 248 Or. App. 708, 713, 274 P.3d 235 (2012) (so stating); *see also State v. Gomes*, 236 Or. App. 364, 372, 236 P.3d 841 (2010) (concluding that an officer's unrelated inquiries did not violate constitutional protections because they occurred simultaneously with activities related to the traffic stop and did not extend its duration). This court has not previously addressed that line of reasoning.

inquiries were unrelated to the purpose of the stop. Defendant proposes that officer questions or requests for consent to search that expand either the duration or the subject-matter scope of the traffic stop are not reasonably related to the purpose of the stop, and are thus impermissible under Article I, section 9, unless the officer has independent constitutional justification for making such inquiries. Accordingly, defendant argues that, in this case, Faulkner's questions exceeded the scope limitations inherent within Article I, section 9—that is, the questions were not reasonably related to the investigation of defendant's failure to signal—and also were not supported by any independent constitutional justification. According to defendant, when that questioning exceeded the lawful scope of the stop, the stop became an unlawful seizure.

In response, the state contends that questions that are unrelated to the purpose of a stop do not implicate Article I, section 9, unless the questioning extends the duration of the stop. The state maintains that defendant's proposed rule is too rigid and prohibits an officer from making any unrelated inquiry without constitutional justification. The state argues that, as the Court of Appeals has held, additional questioning is permissible during an "unavoidable lull" in an investigation of the traffic violation, such as when the driver is searching for requested documents. Further, the state argues that, when an officer asks questions and requests consent to search a vehicle, it does not amount to a constitutional violation because neither action imposes any additional restraint on a motorist's liberty or freedom of movement beyond what is already in place by virtue of the traffic stop itself.

In addressing the party's arguments, we first reiterate that there are both statutory and constitutional limitations on an officer's authority to investigate unrelated crimes during a traffic stop. For example, ORS 810.410 governs an officer's ability to conduct an investigation during a traffic stop for a traffic violation, and, under that statute, officers are permitted to make additional, unrelated inquiries only in specific circumstances. *See* ORS 810.410(3)(c) (An officer "[m]ay make an inquiry into circumstances arising during the course of a detention and investigation that give rise to a reasonable suspicion of criminal activity."); ORS 810.410(3)(e) (When circumstances give rise to reasonable suspicion of criminal activity, an officer "[m]ay request consent to search in relation to [those] circumstances.").

Notwithstanding that statute, however, any evidence obtained when an officer exceeds that authority cannot be suppressed unless the exclusion of the evidence is required by the state or federal constitutions. *See* ORS 136.432(1) (so stating); *State v. Rodgers/Kirkeby*, 347 Or. 610, 620–21, 227 P.3d 695 (2010) (discussing ORS 136.432(1)). Since ORS 136.432 was enacted, defendants seeking to exclude evidence have, as defendant does here, asserted constitutional arguments in support of their motions to suppress. *See State v. Watson*, 353 Or. 768, 778, 305 P.3d

94 (2013) (so stating). Thus, we turn now to the parties' constitutional arguments.

Article I, section 9, establishes "the right of the people to be secure in their persons, houses, papers, and effects, against unreasonable search, or seizure." For purposes of Article I, section 9, a seizure occurs when (1) a police officer intentionally and significantly interferes with an individual's liberty or freedom of movement; or (2) a reasonable person, under the totality of the circumstances, would believe that his or her liberty or freedom of movement has been significantly restricted. *State v. Ashbaugh*, 349 Or. 297, 316, 244 P.3d 360 (2010). In those circumstances, Article I, section 9, protects a person's liberty or freedom of movement by defining the authority of law enforcement officers in their encounters with citizens.

However, not all encounters between law enforcement officers and citizens implicate Article I, section 9. This court has previously identified three general types of police-citizen encounters and has categorized them according to the requirements for their initiation by law enforcement. *See, e.g.*, *Watson*, 353 Or. at 774, 305 P.3d 94 (setting out three categories of police-citizen encounters); *State v. Holmes*, 311 Or. 400, 407, 813 P.2d 28 (1991) (same). One type of encounter is a "mere conversation," or a "non-coercive encounter," and it does not involve any restraint on the liberty of an individual or his or her freedom of movement, and is not a seizure under Article I, section 9. *Rodgers/Kirkeby*, 347 Or. at 621, 227 P.3d 695. On the other end of the spectrum, an arrest is recognized as a "seizure" under Article I, section 9, and requires probable cause. *Id*. This case involves a traffic stop, which falls somewhere in between: This court has recognized that, when a motorist is stopped for a traffic infraction, that stop implicates Article I, section 9, because:

"[I]n contrast to a person on the street, who may unilaterally end an officer-citizen encounter at any time, the reality is that a motorist stopped for a traffic infraction is legally obligated to stop at an officer's direction * * * and to interact with the officer, * * * and therefore is not free unilaterally to end the encounter and leave whenever he or she chooses."

Id. at 622–23, 227 P.3d 695.

This court has explained, in various circumstances, the limits that Article I, section 9, places on investigatory activities during a traffic stop. For example, in *Rodgers/Kirkeby*, we considered what constitutional limitations, if any, applied to an officer's ability to ask questions unrelated to the purpose of the traffic stop at the end of that stop, rather than issuing a citation or releasing the individual being questioned. In that case, the state argued that this court had already rejected the notion that an officer may never ask questions unrelated to the stop itself. *Id*. at 618, 227 P.3d 695. The state proposed that, as a rule, police questioning that is unrelated to a traffic stop, or a request for consent to search during a lawful traffic stop, does not constitute an unconstitutional seizure if that questioning creates only a *de minimis* delay during an otherwise lawful stop. *Id.* We disagreed, and we held that "police authority to detain that motorist dissipates when the investigation reasonably related to that traffic infraction, the identification of persons, and the issuance of a citation (if any) is completed or reasonably should have been completed." *Id.* at 623, 227 P.3d 695.

In reaching that conclusion, this court agreed with the state that an officer's verbal inquiries are not searches or seizures in and of themselves. *Id.* at 622, 227 P.3d 695. We determined, however, that the show of authority that is inherent in a traffic stop, combined with an officer's verbal inquiries, resulted in a restriction of a personal freedom that, absent reasonable suspicion, violated Article I, section 9. *Id.* at 627–28, 227 P.3d 695. Although we limited our analysis to the facts present in that case, we noted that "[p]olice conduct *during* a noncriminal traffic stop does not further implicate Article I, section 9, so long as the detention is limited and the police conduct is *reasonably related* to the investigation of the noncriminal traffic violation." *Id.* at 624, 227 P.3d 695 (emphases added).

In *Watson*, this court considered the authority of an officer to perform unrelated investigatory activities during a traffic stop. 353 Or. at 769, 305 P.3d 94. In that case, the defendant was stopped for failing to maintain a lane of traffic, and the officer requested his driver's license to verify his driving privileges and to run a warrants check. *Id.* at 769–70, 305 P.3d 94. While waiting for the results of the records check, the officer asked the defendant about community rumors that the defendant was dealing small amounts of marijuana and requested consent to search his vehicle. *Id.* at 770, 305 P.3d 94. The defendant denied the allegations and refused to consent to a search. *Id.* At that point, another officer arrived and reported a "strong odor" of what he believed to be marijuana emanating from the defendant's vehicle. *Id.* at 770–71, 305 P.3d 94. Ultimately, the officers searched the vehicle based on probable cause, located drugs, and arrested the defendant. The defendant moved to suppress the evidence, the trial court denied his motion, and he was convicted. *Id.* at 771–72, 305 P.3d 94.

On review, the defendant argued that an officer's authority to search should be strictly limited to the investigation of the initial traffic violation. 353 Or. at 772, 305 P.3d 94. This court analyzed each individual police action—the initial stop, the records check, the warrants check, the questioning, and the ultimate search of the vehicle—to determine whether the officers' actions had exceeded the scope of their constitutional authority. *Id.* at 783–84, 305 P.3d 94. Considering each action individually, we concluded that each action had been reasonably related to the investigation of the traffic stop itself, had not led to the discovery of suppressible evidence, had not extended the stop, or had been justified by an independent constitutional justification (in that case, probable cause). *Id.* at 783–85, 305 P.3d 94. In reaching that conclusion, we held that, under Article I, section 9, investigatory activities must be reasonably related to the purpose of the traffic stop:

"Thus, both Oregon statutes and this court's Article I, section 9, case law require that law enforcement officers have a justification for temporarily seizing or stopping a person to conduct an investigation, and that the officer's activities be reasonably related to that investigation and reasonably necessary to effectuate it. If the officer's activities exceed those limits, then there must be an independent constitutional justification for those activities."

Id. at 781, 305 P.3d 94.

The holding in *Watson* was subsequently applied in this court's next case that considered the limits on police authority during a traffic investigation, *State v. Jimenez*, 357 Or. 417, 353 P.3d 1227 (2015). In *Jimenez*, we considered whether Article I, section 9, permits a routine weapons inquiry during every traffic stop. *Id.* at 419, 353 P.3d 1227. We concluded that a routine weapons inquiry, absent a showing of reasonable, circumstance-specific concerns for officer safety, fell outside the permissible scope of Article I, section 9. *Id.* In that case, the record did not support a finding that the officer had reasonable, circumstance-specific safety concerns because the officer had waited until he had completed his investigation of the traffic offense before inquiring about weapons. *Id.* at 430, 353 P.3d 1227.

We again considered the permissible scope of Article I, section 9, in relation to a weapons inquiry, in *State v. Miller*, 363 Or. 374, 376, 422 P.3d 240 (2018). Although in *Miller* we ultimately concluded that the officer had a reasonable safety concern under the specific circumstances (and, thus, that the weapons inquiry had been justified), we specifically discussed the constitutional significance of additional verbal inquiries during the course of a traffic stop:

"Although an officer's verbal inquiries 'are not searches and seizures and thus by themselves ordinarily do not implicate Article I, section 9,' when a person is already stopped, the person 'is not free unilaterally to end the encounter and leave whenever he or she chooses,' so questions that are not reasonably related to the purpose of the stop extend the stop in a way that requires some independent justification under Article I, section 9."

363 Or. at 380 n. 4, 422 P.3d 240 (quoting *Rodgers/Kirkeby*, 347 Or. at 622–23, 227 P.3d 695).

The foregoing cases significantly inform the nature of the question before us. As the state recognizes, those cases stand for the proposition there are temporal limitations on an officer's authority in making a stop; therefore, inquiries that unreasonably extend the duration of a stop violate Article I, section 9. However, as we will explain, those cases also stand for the proposition that an officer's investigative *activities* during a stop must be reasonably related to the purpose of the stop or have independent constitutional justification. Accordingly, the narrow question that those cases leave open is whether an officer's investigative *inquiries* during a traffic stop also must be reasonably related to the purpose of that stop. Before further discussing those cases and turning to that question, we briefly address the Court of Appeals' "unavoidable lull" doctrine.

The Court of Appeals first articulated its "unavoidable lull" doctrine in its own consideration of *State v. Rodgers*, 219 Or. App. 366, 182 P.3d 209 (2008), *aff'd*, 347 Or. 610, 227 P.3d 695 (2010) (*Rodgers/Kirkeby*). As previously discussed, that case considered the constitutional question whether, at the end of a stop after the defendant was free to leave, an officer may extend the duration of the stop by asking additional questions that were unrelated to the purpose of the stop. The Court of Appeals concluded that "an officer is free to question a motorist about matters unrelated to the traffic infraction during an unavoidable lull in the investigation, such as while awaiting the results of a records check." *Id.* at 372, 182 P.3d 209. Stated another way, under the unavoidable-lull doctrine, so long as the officer does not delay the processing of a citation or extend the duration of the traffic stop, the officer is permitted to ask unrelated investigatory questions without constitutional justification. Ultimately, the Court of Appeals concluded that the doctrine did not apply in *Rodgers* because the officer had extended the duration of the stop when he began making additional inquiries. *Id.* at 373, 182 P.3d 209. When this court considered *Rodgers* on review, we affirmed the Court of Appeals' disposition, but we did not address the propriety of the unavoidable-lull doctrine because we also concluded that the officer had unlawfully extended the duration of the traffic stop. *Rodgers/Kirkeby*, 347 Or. at 627, 227 P.3d 695.

In a later case, the Court of Appeals concluded that the unavoidable-lull doctrine did apply, holding that the officer's inquiries in that case did not implicate Article I, section 9, because the questioning had not unreasonably extended the duration of the traffic stop. *State v. Gomes*, 236 Or. App. 364, 372, 236 P.3d 841 (2010). In *Gomes*, the Court of Appeals read our decision in *Rodgers/Kirkeby* as holding that the Oregon Constitution recognized only a temporal limitation on an officer's ability to ask questions unrelated to the purpose of the stop. *Id.* at 371, 236 P.3d 841 ("We take that language to confirm our *Rodgers* opinion and our opinion in *State v. Amaya*, 176 Or. App. 35, 29 P.3d 1177 (2001), *aff'd on other grounds*, 336 Or. 616, 89 P.3d 1163 (2004), that there are no Article I, section 9, implications if an inquiry unrelated to the traffic stop occurs during a routine stop but does not delay it.").

We agree with the Court of Appeals that, when an officer's questioning extends the reasonable duration of a traffic stop, Article I, section 9, requires independent constitutional justification. We disagree, however, with the suggestion in *Gomes* that *Rodgers/Kirkeby* confirmed that there is no subject-matter limitation on the permissible scope of police inquiries during a traffic stop under Article I, section 9. Rather, this court in *Rodgers/Kirkeby* expressly chose not to address that issue: "We express no opinion about the effect of unrelated police inquires that occur during the course of the traffic violation investigation and that do not result in any further restriction of movement of the individual." 347 Or. at 627 n. 5, 227 P.3d 695.

Here, the state argues that our decision in *Watson*, decided after *Rodgers/Kirkeby*, confirms that Article I, section 9, imposes only temporal limitations on when an officer who makes a lawful stop may ask unrelated investigatory questions. In support, the state focuses on two conclusions that we reached in *Watson*: First, that the records check in *Watson*, which had been conducted with the purpose of verifying the defendant's driving privileges, was constitutional, and, second, that the warrants check in *Watson*, which had been run simultaneously with the records check, did not render the defendant's detention unconstitutional. The state acknowledges that, in evaluating the constitutionality of the records check in *Watson*, this court expressly considered whether it had been reasonably related to the officer's investigation of the traffic infraction. That is, we considered whether the records check had been reasonably related to the officer's investigation of the traffic infraction before turning to the independent and separate question whether the records check unreasonably extended the duration of the stop. *See Watson*, 353 Or. at 782, 305 P.3d 94 ("Because [the officer] conducted the records check with the purpose of verifying defendant's driving privileges, [the officer]'s detention of defendant to conduct that check did not violate Article I, section 9, unless the detention was unreasonably lengthy."). The state contends, however, that the holding of *Watson* is captured in how this court addressed the warrants check: declining to address whether the warrants check had been reasonably related to the traffic stop because, in part, that check did not extend the length of the stop. The state argues that, when this court did not address whether the warrants check had been reasonably related to the traffic stop, we necessarily concluded that unrelated investigatory activities do not implicate Article I, section 9, if they are conducted during activities related to the stop and do not extend the stop.

We disagree. Contrary to the state's argument, in *Watson*, this court determined that it had no need to resolve the question whether the warrants check had been reasonably related to the stop because that check had not produced suppressible evidence *and* had not extended the stop. *Watson*, 353 Or. at 784, 305 P.3d 94. If, in *Watson*, the warrants check—which had been run simultaneously with the records check and therefore did not extend the duration of the stop—had led to evidence that the defendant sought to suppress, we would have been required to decide whether the warrants check had been reasonably related to the stop. And, if the warrants check had extended the stop, that alone would have required a determination that the check exceeded the permissible scope of the stop. But, as noted, we determined that the warrants check had not produced suppressible evidence *and* had not extended the stop. We therefore declined to reach the question whether the warrants check was reasonably related to the stop.[3] As we stated in *Watson*: When conducting an investigation during a lawful stop, "*activities*" of law enforcement must "be reasonably related to that investigation and reasonably necessary to effectuate it." *Id.* at 781, 305 P.3d 94 (emphasis added).

We did, however, leave open in *Watson* the issue that this case presents—whether the principle that we announced in *Watson* "extends to *inquiries* during the course of a stop." *Id.* at 779 n. 13, 305 P.3d 94 (emphasis added). In other words, *Watson* held that Article I, section 9, imposes both subject-matter and durational limits on an officer's ability to conduct unrelated investigative *activities* during a traffic stop; the question expressly left open was whether an officer's investigative *inquiries* also are subject to subject-matter as well as durational limitations.[4] The facts here require us to address that question, and it is to that question that we now turn.

As stated, Article I, section 9, governs a broad spectrum of law enforcement conduct, and, as this court has recognized, the degree to which law enforcement conduct intrudes on an individual's interest in personal security varies depending on the circumstances. *See State v. Fair*, 353 Or. 588, 600, 302 P.3d 417 (2013) ("The degree to which law enforcement conduct intrudes on a citizen's protected interest in privacy and liberty is significantly affected by where the conduct occurs, such as in the home, in an auto-mobile, or on a public street."). Not every intrusion on an individual's interest in personal security is unconstitutional; Article I, section 9, prohibits only "arbitrary, oppressive, or otherwise 'unreasonable' " intrusions on those interests. *State v. Barnthouse*, 360 Or. 403, 413, 380 P.3d 952 (2016). Thus, some law enforcement conduct constitutes such minimal intrusion on an individual's interests that the conduct is not unreasonable under Article I, section 9. *See Holmes*, 311 Or. at 407, 813 P.2d 28 (a police-citizen encounter involving "mere conversation, a non-coercive encounter" does

---

[3] Here, Faulkner did not perform a warrants check. Therefore, the question whether a warrants check is, or can be, reasonably related to the purpose of a traffic stop, is not before us.

[4] The dissent views our cases differently, understanding them to hold only that police activity that is reasonably related to the purpose of a traffic stop and reasonably necessary to effectuate it "does not result in an extension of the stop beyond the time reasonably necessary to conclude it." 365 Or. at 718, 451 P.3d at 952 (Garrett, J., dissenting). That view of our cases is incorrect. First, that is not what we said in those cases. Second, in *Watson*, we independently considered two different questions when determining whether the officer's activities exceeded the scope of the stop—first considering the subject matter of the records check and then considering its duration. *See Watson*, 353 Or. at 782–83, 305 P.3d 94. We did so because even an investigative activity that is reasonably related to the purpose of a stop may violate Article I, section 9, if it is unreasonably lengthy. Third, in *Watson*, the warrants check did not extend the stop beyond the time necessary to conduct the records check. We did not uphold the warrants check on that basis; we upheld it on the basis that the check had not produced suppressible evidence. *Id.* at 784, 305 P.3d 94.

not require constitutional justification). On the other hand, some law enforcement activity rises to the level of a search or a seizure, which constitutes a more substantial intrusion on an individual's personal security interest.

Generally, an officer cannot seize an individual without probable cause to believe that that individual has engaged or is engaging in criminal activity, and obtaining a warrant permitting the seizure. There are exceptions, however, to both the warrant requirement and the probable cause requirement for seizures that are limited in scope and duration. *See State v. Cloman*, 254 Or. 1, 6, 456 P.2d 67 (1969) (police can stop a car to determine identity of vehicle and its occupants based on reasonable suspicion, and reasonable suspicion is "of less quantum" than probable cause to arrest). In *Cloman*, this court stated that "there is nothing *ipso facto* unconstitutional in the brief detention of citizens under circumstances not justifying an arrest, for purposes of limited inquiry in the course of routine police investigations." 254 Or. at 7, 456 P.2d 67. The Oregon Legislative Assembly codified that decision in statutes regulating the authority of law enforcement to stop individuals. *See* ORS 131.605 to 131.625. Relevant to this case, as part of the enactment intended to codify *Cloman*, the legislature specified in ORS 131.615 that an officer "who reasonably suspects that a person has committed or is about to commit a crime may stop the person and * * * make a reasonable inquiry." *See also State v. Valdez*, 277 Or. 621, 624, 561 P.2d 1006 (1977) (discussing statute). Additionally, ORS 131.615(2) specifies that such a stop shall last no longer than a reasonable time, and ORS 131.615(3)(a) further provides that "[t]he inquiry shall be considered reasonable only if limited to * * * [t]he immediate circumstances that aroused the officer's suspicion." Brief stops to investigate whether an individual has committed a traffic infraction are of that nature. *See* ORS 810.410 (2)(a)–(b) (so stating). Article I, section 9, permits brief traffic stops to investigate unlawful, noncriminal activity when the stops are of limited scope. *See Rodgers/Kirkeby*, 347 Or. at 623, 227 P.3d 695 ("Police authority to perform a traffic stop arises out of the facts that created probable cause to believe that there has been unlawful, noncriminal activity, *viz.*, a traffic infraction.").

Whether an officer is investigating criminal or unlawful noncriminal activity, the officer's authority to stop an individual—based on reasonable suspicion of criminal activity or on probable cause of unlawful noncriminal activity—is founded on the assumption that temporary, investigative stops to investigate particular conduct are permitted for that particular purpose only.[6] It therefore follows that limits apply to an officer's ability, during such a stop, to use that stop for other purposes. As we explained in *Watson*, it is "the justification for the stop" that

---

[6] When an officer stops an individual based on probable cause of a traffic violation, an officer may issue a citation for that traffic violation but may not arrest an individual for the violation. ORS 810.410(2)–(3)(a).

"delineates the lawful bounds of the traffic stop." 353 Or. at 778–79, 305 P.3d 94.

Here, the state argues that we should conclude that defendant's Article I, section 9, rights were not violated because Faulkner's request for consent to search defendant's vehicle did not impose any restraint beyond the stop itself. To support that argument, the state makes two points. First, the state contends that the right to be free from unlawful seizure is a right that protects only the freedom of movement. Article I, section 9, protects at least the right to move freely, and we agree that our test to determine when a seizure has occurred is based on the degree to which an officer has interfered with an individual's freedom of movement. For example, in *Rodgers/Kirkeby*, we stated that a person is seized when an officer "intentionally and significantly interferes with the person's freedom of movement." 347 Or. at 621, 227 P.3d 695. However, the question here is not whether defendant was seized—he was. The question, rather, is whether the officer who seized defendant was limited by Article I, section 9, in the inquiries he could make during that seizure.

Second, the state contends that, because an officer's request for consent to search during a consensual police-citizen encounter does not restrict a defendant's liberty and constitute a search or seizure, a request for consent to search *during* a seizure has no significance under Article I, section 9. We agree that a request for consent to search is not, by itself, a search or a seizure. *See State v. Highley*, 354 Or. 459, 461, 313 P.3d 1068 (2013) (so stating). However, we disagree that, when a request for consent to search is made during a lawful seizure, that request is not of constitutional significance. In *Watson*, the question whether the warrants check was reasonably related to the traffic investigation was of constitutional significance even though that check itself did not impose an independent restraint on the defendant's liberty. 353 Or. at 788–84, 305 P.3d 94. And we explained the reason for the significance of an officer's verbal inquiries in *Miller*:

"Although an officer's verbal inquiries 'are not searches and seizures and thus by themselves ordinarily do not implicate Article I, section 9,' when a person is already stopped, the person 'is not free unilaterally to end the encounter and leave whenever he or she chooses,' so questions that are not reasonably related to the purpose of the stop extend the stop in a way that requires some independent justification under Article I, section 9."

363 Or. at 380 n. 4, 422 P.3d 240 (quoting *Rodgers/Kirkeby*, 347 Or. at 622–23, 227 P.3d 695).

As our cases demonstrate, Article I, section 9, limits not only when a stop may be made, but also the purpose for which it is conducted. A stop that is reasonable for a limited investigatory purpose is not necessarily reasonable for all purposes, and we see no reason to distinguish between the activities that law enforcement officers conduct during such a stop and the questions that they ask; both must be reasonably related to the purpose that permits the officer to stop an individual in the first place. If we were to hold otherwise, then an officer who lacks a warrant, probable cause, or even reasonable suspicion of criminal activity, could stop an individual for a minor traffic offense, and, during that stop, conduct a criminal investigation anyway, making meaningless the rule which requires an officer to have reasonable suspicion before stopping an individual to conduct a criminal investigation. Thus, when determining whether a stop that was reasonable at the outset has become unreasonable, we must consider the totality of its circumstances, not only its duration.

In sum, we conclude that, for the purposes of Article I, section 9, all investigative activities, including investigative inquiries, conducted during a traffic stop are part of an ongoing seizure and are subject to both subject-matter and durational limitations.[7] Accordingly, an officer is limited to investigatory inquiries that are reasonably related to the purpose of the traffic stop or that have an independent constitutional justification. Put simply, an "unavoidable lull" does not create an opportunity for an officer to ask unrelated questions, unless the officer can justify the inquiry on other grounds.

We realize that our decision precludes officers from asking certain investigative questions during investigatory stops—those unrelated to the purpose of the investigation and without independent constitutional justification. But that is as the constitution requires and, for statutory purposes, what the legislature intends.[8] *See* ORS 131.615(3)(a) (officer's inquiries during traffic stop reasonable only if limited to the "immediate circumstances that arouse the officer's suspicion"). Given the near necessity of driving today, it is certainly not uncommon for a citizen to be lawfully stopped for a minor traffic violation. *See* Wayne R. LaFave, *The "Routine Traffic Stop" From Start to Finish: Too Much "Routine," Not Enough Fourth Amendment*, 102 Mich L. Rev. 1843, 1852–53 (2004) (describing the ease of unintentionally committing a minor traffic violation while driving); David A. Harris, Essay, *Car Wars: The Fourth*

---

[7] The dissent criticizes us for failing to expressly justify a rule that police activities and inquiries during a traffic stop must be reasonably related to the purpose of the stop and reasonably necessary to effectuate it. 365 Or. at 719, 451 P.3d at 953 (Garrett, J., dissenting). The dissent may not accept the reasons for those rules, but we have stated them both in *Watson* and here: Police have authority to interfere with an individual's liberty interest and to stop that individual on reasonable suspicion and without probable cause of criminal activity for only a limited purpose—to investigate the matter that gives rise to the reasonable suspicion. It is the justification for the stop that delineates its lawful bounds. Article I, section 9, does not permit a stop that is authorized for a *limited* purpose to be used for *all* purposes. If it did, then in many cases there would be no need for an officer to develop the reasonable suspicion necessary to stop an individual to conduct a criminal investigation, and that protection would be meaningless.

[8] The dissent is concerned about what an officer can do during a ten-minute wait other than conduct activities and make inquiries reasonably related to the purpose of the stop and reasonably necessary to effectuate it. 365 Or. at 720, 451 P.3d at 953 (Garrett, J., dissenting). We do not share that concern. If an officer develops reasonable suspicion that the stopped individual has engaged in illegal activity in addition to that for which the individual was stopped, then the officer may investigate that activity. Without such suspicion, an officer should limit investigative activities and inquires to matters that are, as statute requires, limited to the "immediate circumstances that arouse the officer's suspicion" or that will not result in the discovery of suppressible evidence. ORS 131.615(3)(a).

Amendment's Death on the Highway, 66 Geo Wash. L. Rev. 556, 567–68 (1998) (describing how an officer can easily develop constitutional justification to stop a driver by simply following a vehicle for a short period of time until they observe a traffic infraction). If, after stopping an individual based on probable cause that the individual committed a traffic offense, an officer may inquire into criminal activity without reasonable suspicion of a specific crime, an officer will have less of an incentive to develop the requisite reasonable suspicion of that crime which ordinarily would be required to stop the individual for a temporary criminal investigation. By applying subject-matter limitations to investigative activities and questioning, Article I, section 9, ensures that officers do not turn minor traffic violations into criminal investigations without a constitutional basis for doing so.[9]

With that understanding of Article I, section 9, we conclude, in this case, that Faulkner's questioning and request to search defendant's vehicle violated Article I, section 9. Although Faulkner had probable cause to believe that defendant had committed a traffic infraction when he failed to signal a turn and, therefore, was permitted to stop defendant to investigate that infraction, Faulkner then asked questions that were not reasonably related to that investigation and exceeded its lawful scope. Faulkner stopped defendant for failing to use a turn signal, but then inquired about the possession of guns or controlled substances. The record does not demonstrate that the latter questioning was reasonably related to the investigation of the former investigation. The investigation of defendant's failure to signal a turn may have warranted questions about whether or why defendant acted or failed to take that action, other questions or actions reasonably related to that inquiry, or other questions or actions reasonably necessary to the issuance of a warning or a citation, such as questions to address reasonable officer-safety concerns. But, here, the state does not claim any such connections or concerns, and the record does not support the notion that any exist.

In addition, if there were evidence that, during the stop, Faulkner had learned facts giving rise to reasonable suspicion that defendant had engaged or was about to engage in criminal conduct, an expanded investigation could have been justified. But here, Faulkner did not testify to any particularized suspicion that defendant had weapons, controlled substances, or any other contraband in his vehicle. To the contrary,

---

[9] A subject-matter limitation requires that all additional questioning be based on constitutionally sufficient grounds and not on implicit or explicit biases. The *amicus* brief submitted by the Oregon Criminal Defense Lawyers Association and the Oregon Justice Resource Center presents significant statistical data to illustrate the disparate treatment of black and Hispanic motorists during the course of traffic stops, showing specifically that nationwide, and in Oregon, people of color are statistically more likely to be searched during traffic stops than their white counterparts. *See* Frank R. Baumgartner *et al, Racial Disparities in Traffic Stop Outcomes*, Duke Forum for Law and Social Change Vol 9:21 at 33 (2017). Furthermore, there may be additional biases that motivate an officer to ask unrelated investigatory questions without independent constitutional justification. Our conclusion today—that all questioning must be reasonably related to the purpose for the traffic stop—will ensure that an officer's questions are not based on such biases.

Faulkner testified that he asks such questions every time he makes a stop. Accordingly, Faulkner's questioning and request to search the vehicle were impermissible and a violation of Article I, section 9, protections against unreasonable seizure.

Having concluded that defendant was unlawfully seized in violation of Article I, section 9, we must now determine the effect of that constitutional violation on the admissibility of the evidence obtained during the consensual search of defendant's vehicle. Generally, evidence will be suppressed if the evidence was the product of an unconstitutional act. *State v. Juarez-Godinez*, 326 Or. 1, 9, 942 P.2d 772 (1997) (so stating). Here, defendant's voluntary consent to search the vehicle was granted in response to Faulkner's unlawful line of questioning and request for consent. In some cases, "a defendant's voluntary consent itself may be sufficient to demonstrate that the unlawful conduct did not affect or had only a tenuous connection to the evidence produced." *State v. Unger*, 356 Or. 59, 77–78, 333 P.3d 1009 (2014). It is the state's burden to prove that the consent was "independent of, or only tenuously related to, the illegal police conduct." *Id.* at 84, 333 P.3d 1009. Here, the state reasonably does not argue in this court, and did not argue in the Court of Appeals, that defendant's consent was only tenuously related to Faulkner's illegal inquiries. Accordingly, the trial court erred in denying defendant's motion to suppress the evidence.

The decision of the Court of Appeals is reversed. The judgment of the circuit court is reversed, and the case is remanded to the circuit court for further proceedings consistent with this opinion.

■ GARRETT, J., dissented and filed an opinion, in which BALMER, J., joined.

■ GARRETT, J., dissenting.

This court has held that, in ordinary police-citizen encounters (that is, encounters that are not seizures), police may engage citizens in "mere conversation" and generally ask questions of them without implicating Article I, section 9. *State v. Warner*, 284 Or. 147, 161, 585 P.2d 681 (1978); *see also State v. Holmes*, 311 Or. 400, 407, 813 P.2d 28 (1991) (comparing ordinary "noncoercive" encounters with stops and arrests, which are both seizures requiring constitutional justification). We have also held that, because a traffic stop is a seizure, police may continue the traffic stop for only so long as the basis for that seizure exists; thus, police may not extend the stop with questioning, "mere conversation," or other activities unrelated to the original basis for the stop, unless they have an independent and constitutionally sufficient basis to continue the detention for such activities. *See State v. Rodgers/Kirkeby*, 347 Or. 610, 623–24, 227 P.3d 695 (2010) (so stating).

The question left unanswered until today is what subject matter restrictions, if any, apply to police activity that is not related to the original basis for the traffic stop but that also does *not* cause any prolongation of the stop. The Court of Appeals has addressed the issue and concluded that, so long as unrelated activity occurs during an "unavoidable lull" in the traffic stop, then such activity effects no greater restriction on liberty than was already in place. *See State v. Gomes*, 236 Or. App. 364, 370–71, 236 P.3d 841 (2010). Therefore, it is of no constitutional import. *See id.* ("there are no Article I, section 9, implications if an inquiry unrelated to the traffic stop occurs during a routine stop but does not delay it").

That "unavoidable lull" rule is consistent with the decisions of this court that have defined a "seizure" for purposes of Article I, section 9, to occur "when either (1) a police officer intentionally and significantly interferes with the person's freedom of movement; or (2) the person believes, in an objectively reasonable manner, that his or her liberty of movement has been so restricted." *Rodgers/Kirkeby*, 347 Or. at 621, 227 P.3d 695 (internal quotation marks omitted). Simply put, when an officer's question unnecessarily extends a traffic stop, that question represents an additional interference with that liberty interest and may therefore require an additional justification. But if a person has already been seized as a result of a lawful traffic stop, and the length of the stop is *not* extended, then questioning on unrelated matters does not cause any additional interference with the person's freedom of movement. . . .

CHAPTER 3

"SEIZURES" OF THE PERSON: ARRESTS

1. CLASSIFICATION AS ARREST AND THE PROBABLE CAUSE STANDARD

Cortez v. McCauley

478 F.3d 1108 (10th Cir. 2007)

■ Before TACHA, CHIEF JUDGE, EBEL, KELLY, HENRY, BRISCOE, LUCERO, MURPHY, HARTZ, O'BRIEN, McCONNELL, TYMKOVICH, GORSUCH, and HOLMES, CIRCUIT JUDGES.

ON REHEARING EN BANC

■ KELLY, CIRCUIT JUDGE, joined by TACHA, CHIEF JUDGE, EBEL, HENRY, BRISCOE, LUCERO, and MURPHY, CIRCUIT JUDGES, and joined in part by HARTZ, O'BRIEN, McCONNELL, TYMKOVICH, GORSUCH, and HOLMES, CIRCUIT JUDGES.

We granted rehearing en banc primarily to consider under what circumstances, if any, an excessive force claim is subsumed in an unlawful arrest claim. The panel opinion upheld the district court's denial of qualified immunity except for one excessive force claim, which the panel determined warranted qualified immunity. Cortez v. McCauley, 438 F.3d 980, 1002 (10th Cir.2006). We reject the notion that an excessive force claim is subsumed in an unlawful arrest claim in the facts presented by this case. Because our conclusion necessitates a change in some of the analysis, we vacate the panel opinion. Our jurisdiction to hear this appeal from the denial of partial summary judgment on qualified immunity grounds arises under 28 U.S.C. § 1291. *See* Mitchell v. Forsyth, 472 U.S. 511, 530 (1985). We affirm in part and reverse in part.

Plaintiffs-Appellees, Rick Cortez and Tina Cortez, filed suit alleging claims pursuant to 42 U.S.C. § 1983 as well as claims under New Mexico law, seeking damages from employees of the Bernalillo County Sheriff's Department and the Board of County Commissioners of the County of Bernalillo, New Mexico ("Board"). The Plaintiffs alleged, inter alia, that the Defendants violated the Plaintiffs' Fourth Amendment rights by (1) unlawfully arresting and interrogating the Plaintiffs; (2) using excessive force on the Plaintiffs; and (3) unreasonably searching the Plaintiffs' home. The district court denied the Defendants' motion for partial summary judgment as to Defendants McCauley, Gonzales, Sanchez, and Covington. With respect to the other Defendants, Bowdich and the Board, the court concluded that the Plaintiffs had made a meritorious showing under Fed.R.Civ.P. 56(f). Consequently, these Defendants' motions for partial summary judgment were denied without prejudice pending further discovery.

Background

On May 26, 2001, at 12:24 a.m., the Bernalillo County Sheriff's Department received a telephone call from a nurse at Saint Joseph's Hospital alerting that Raquel Villegas ("Ms. Villegas"), had brought her two-year-old daughter to the hospital alleging that the child had complained that her babysitter's "boyfriend"[1] had "hurt her pee pee." In response to this allegation, the Defendants McCauley, Gonzales, Sanchez, and Covington were dispatched to Plaintiffs' residence. The officers did not wait to receive the results of the medical examination of the child, did not interview the child or her mother, and did not seek to obtain a warrant.

At approximately 1:00 a.m., the deputies made contact with the Plaintiffs. Rick Cortez was asleep when he was suddenly awakened by noises and lights in his fenced back yard. He heard a knock on the front door. Wearing only a pair of shorts, Rick Cortez opened the front door and saw two police officers through the closed screen door. He repeatedly inquired what was going on. The officers did not answer but instead ordered him to exit his house. As he opened the screen door and began to leave the house, the officers seized him, handcuffed him, read him his *Miranda*[2] rights, and placed him in the back of a patrol car where he was subjected to questioning.

Tina Cortez was awakened by her husband as he got out of bed. Shortly after Rick Cortez left the bedroom, she followed him. She reached the front door just in time to watch the Defendants handcuff her husband and place him in the back of the patrol car. Tina Cortez headed toward the bedroom in order to make a telephone call, but before she could complete the call, Defendant McCauley entered the home, seized her by the arm, and physically escorted her from her home. The officer placed her in a separate patrol car where she was subjected to questioning. Defendant McCauley did allow Tina Cortez to use his cell phone. Both Rick and Tina Cortez indicate that an officer seized the keys to their house, locked the door, and would not let them return for approximately an hour. They allege that when they returned, the Defendants informed them that their dog had been maced and his eyes needed to be washed out.

Defendants performed a warrantless search of the home, purportedly to find additional children that might be present and to

---

[1]   Plaintiff Rick Cortez is actually the husband of the babysitter Tina Cortez.

[2]   Miranda v. Arizona, 384 U.S. 436 (1966). Miranda warnings are required for custodial interrogation occasioned by an arrest, but not for questioning during an ordinary investigative detention. Berkemer v. McCarty, 468 U.S. 420, 440 (1984); California v. Beheler, 463 U.S. 1121, 1125 (1983) (per curiam).

eliminate the possibility of any unknown threat to officer safety. During the subsequent interrogations of the Plaintiffs, the Defendants learned that Tina Cortez managed a small day care facility in which she took care of several children. The Defendants further learned that Ms. Villegas had a verbal altercation with the Plaintiffs after the Plaintiffs informed her that they would no longer take care of her child. Additionally, while providing his statement, Rick Cortez also informed the officers that his handcuffs were too tight and caused excessive pain. Despite his declaration and the fact that Rick Cortez supposedly was not under arrest, the officers never loosened the handcuffs.

As these events unfolded at the Cortez residence, Officer Zuniga and Detective Foster made contact with Ms. Villegas at the hospital. Ms. Villegas provided an unsworn written statement in which she described the events that led to her accusation. She also recounted a verbal dispute she had with the Plaintiffs. Additionally, Detective Foster was informed by the nurse who conducted the examination that "no evidence of penile penetration was present." Further, the nurse identified two potential sources of the child's vaginal irritation.[3]

Because the hospital did not find any evidence of molestation, the Plaintiffs were released from detention and permitted to reenter their home. The dispatch report for the incident indicated that they were released sometime between 1:49 a.m. and 2:16 a.m. on May 26, 2001. Rick Cortez was never charged with a crime associated with the allegations of Ms. Villegas.[4]

Based on this early morning encounter with law enforcement officers, the Plaintiffs filed suit. Appellants McCauley, Gonzales, Sanchez, Covington, and Bowdich moved for summary judgment on grounds of qualified immunity as to the § 1983 claims against them in their individual capacities. Defendants McCauley, Gonzales, Sanchez and Covington asserted they did not commit an unreasonable search and seizure against either Plaintiff and that excessive force was not used against either Plaintiff. Defendant Bowdich argued he could not be held liable in his supervisory capacity. Shortly after filing the motion, the Defendants above joined with the Board and moved that discovery be stayed pending the outcome of their motion for summary judgment. On March 17, 2004, the district court denied the Defendants' motion for summary judgment. This appeal followed.

Standard of Review

. . . If . . . a violation has been shown, the plaintiff must then show that the constitutional right was clearly established. . . . Summary judgment based on qualified immunity is appropriate if the law did not

---

[3]   The nurse noted that the child had "urine stained underwear on, which could irritate her vagina." The nurse also noted bubble bath as a potential irritant.

[4]   The Defendants state in their appellate brief and supplemental brief on rehearing en banc that Rick Cortez "may" have violated the child digitally. Aplt. Br. at 5; Aplt. Supp. Br. at 4–5. No evidence in the record supports this completely speculative assertion.

put the officer on notice that his conduct would be clearly unlawful. (Malley v. Briggs, 475 U.S. 335, 341 (1986)).

We have held that, for a right to be clearly established, "there must be a Supreme Court or Tenth Circuit decision on point, or the clearly established weight of authority from other courts must have found the law to be as the plaintiff maintains." Medina v. City of Denver, 960 F.2d 1493, 1498 (10th Cir.1992). The Supreme Court has explained that "officials can still be on notice that their conduct violates established law even in novel factual circumstances." Hope v. Pelzer, 536 U.S. 730, 741 (2002).

The district court's denial of qualified immunity is a question of law which we review de novo. Bisbee v. Bey, 39 F.3d 1096, 1099 (10th Cir.1994). We review the evidence in the light most favorable to the nonmoving party. *Id.* at 1100. Summary judgment is appropriate only "if the pleadings, depositions, answers to interrogatories, and admissions on file, together with the affidavits, if any, show that there is no genuine issue as to any material fact and . . . the moving party is entitled to a judgment as a matter of law." Fed.R.Civ.P. 56(c).

Analysis

The district court held that both Plaintiffs were arrested and searched and that genuine issues of material fact existed as to the presence of probable cause. It also rejected an investigative detention rationale for the Defendants' conduct, noting that the Defendants had "not articulated any specific facts that led them to believe Plaintiffs presented a threat to anyone's safety at the time of the arrest or were about to destroy evidence of a crime." Aplt.App. 178. In a qualified immunity appeal, we are required to consider those facts which the district court found were sufficient to support the denial of the motion for summary judgment. *See* Behrens v. Pelletier, 516 U.S. 299, 313 (1996). Our interlocutory jurisdiction is limited to legal questions drawn from facts that are deemed undisputed for appellate purposes. Johnson v. Jones, 515 U.S. 304, 313 (1995); *Mitchell,* 472 U.S. at 528. We believe our discussion will be clearer if each Plaintiff is discussed separately, along with the actions taken against that Plaintiff.

I.   Plaintiffs' Fourth Amendment Claim Against Unreasonable Seizure

A.   Legal Framework

In Oliver v. Woods, 209 F.3d 1179, 1186 (10th Cir.2000), we stated "[t]he Supreme Court has identified three types of police/citizen encounters: consensual encounters, investigative stops, and arrests." "Consensual encounters are not seizures within the meaning of the Fourth Amendment and need not be supported by suspicion of criminal wrongdoing." *Id.*

An investigative detention is "a seizure within the meaning of the Fourth Amendment but, unlike an arrest, it need not be supported by probable cause." *Id.* An officer "can stop and briefly detain a person for investigative purposes if the officer has a reasonable suspicion supported by articulable facts that criminal activity may be afoot, even if the officer lacks probable cause." *Id.* For an officer to have reasonable suspicion to seize an individual, the officer "must have a particularized and objective basis for suspecting the particular person stopped of criminal activity." *Id.*

A warrantless arrest is permissible when an officer "has probable cause to believe that a person committed a crime." Romero v. Fay, 45 F.3d 1472, 1476 (10th Cir.1995). An arrest is distinguished by the involuntary, "highly intrusive" nature of the encounter. *Oliver,* 209 F.3d at 1186. "[T]he use of firearms, handcuffs, and other forceful techniques" generally exceed the scope of an investigative detention and enter the realm of an arrest. *See* United States v. Melendez-Garcia, 28 F.3d 1046, 1052 (10th Cir.1994). "Probable cause to arrest exists only when the facts and circumstances within the officers' knowledge, and of which they have reasonably trustworthy information, are sufficient in themselves to warrant a man of reasonable caution in the belief that an offense has been or is being committed." United States v. Valenzuela, 365 F.3d 892, 896 (10th Cir.2004) (internal quotation marks omitted).

B.   Seizure of Rick Cortez

Viewing the facts in the light most favorable to the Plaintiffs, the district court determined that "the scope and duration of a lawful investigative detention was quickly exceeded in this case, and the situation became a full custodial arrest." We agree with this characterization as to Plaintiff Rick Cortez. Against this backdrop, we have no difficulty in finding that Rick Cortez has presented facts or allegations showing the Defendants violated a constitutional right, namely the Fourth Amendment right to be free of unreasonable seizure. It appears that the officers: (1) grabbed Rick Cortez, barefoot and wearing only shorts, and pulled him from the doorway of his home; (2) handcuffed him; (3) advised him of his *Miranda* rights; (4) placed him in the back seat of the locked patrol car; and (5) questioned him while he was in the back seat of the locked patrol car. We also note that the encounter took place after midnight.

In evaluating whether the events leading up to this arrest amount to probable cause, we ask whether an objectively reasonable officer could conclude that the historical facts at the time of the arrest amount to probable cause. Maryland v. Pringle, 540 U.S. 366, 371 (2003); Gardenhire v. Schubert, 205 F.3d 303, 318 (6th Cir.2000). Probable cause is based on the totality of the circumstances, and requires reasonably trustworthy information that would lead a reasonable officer to believe that the person about to be arrested has committed or is about to commit a crime. *Pringle,* 540 U.S. at 371 n. 2. As noted, the only information which arguably implicated Rick Cortez was a statement attributed to a barely-verbal two-year old child that her babysitter's "boyfriend" had "hurt her pee pee." The statement was relayed by telephone to the officers, from the nurse, who heard it from the mother who ostensibly heard it from the two-year old. Rather than waiting to receive the results of the medical examination of the child, interview the child or her mother to better understand the circumstances, or seek to obtain a warrant, the officers responded to the statement with an immediate arrest of the babysitter's husband, Rick Cortez.

Plainly, whether we view it as a need for more pre-arrest investigation because of insufficient information,[7] or inadequate corroboration, what the officers had fell short of reasonably trustworthy information indicating that a crime had been committed by Rick Cortez. *See* BeVier v. Hucal, 806 F.2d 123, 128 (7th Cir.1986) ("A police officer may not close her or his eyes to facts that would help clarify the circumstances of an arrest. Reasonable avenues of investigation must be pursued especially when, as here, it is unclear whether a crime had even taken place."). Based on the facts above, Rick Cortez was arrested without probable cause.[8] This warrantless arrest constitutes a constitutional violation.[9]

Under the second sequential question, we must also find that the right was clearly established when the alleged violation occurred. The law was and is unambiguous: a government official must have probable cause to arrest an individual. *See* Tennessee v. Garner, 471 U.S. 1, 7 (1985); United States v. Watson, 423 U.S. 411, 417–22 (1976); *Olsen*, 312 F.3d at 1312 (warrantless arrest without probable cause violates an

---

[7] A concurring and dissenting opinion "do[es] not doubt for a moment that additional investigation would have been a good idea," but then suggests that considering that possibility is "second-guessing" the officers. C & D Op. at 1139–40 (Gorsuch, J. concurring in part, and dissenting in part). The reason for the lack of doubt surely is because of the absence of probable cause in this case; merely because officers are not required to do a more thorough investigation once they have probable cause "does not suggest that an officer has no duty to investigate an alleged crime before making an arrest." *Gardenhire*, 205 F.3d at 318.

[8] When the officers seized Rick Cortez, one of the officers apparently told him that he was not being arrested but that he had merely been placed in investigative detention. Aplt.App. 56. Therefore, the officers may have believed that they were not effecting an arrest but rather an investigative detention. The officers' subjective beliefs are irrelevant. *See* United States v. Charley, 396 F.3d 1074, 1080 (9th Cir.2005). *See also* Graham v. Connor, 490 U.S. 386, 397 (1989) (applying the same principle to the issue of excessive force). Defendants characterize the encounter between the Defendants and both Plaintiffs as an investigative detention but regardless contend that they had probable cause to arrest Rick Cortez. Aplt. Br. at 13. Essentially, their argument is that they had probable cause to arrest Rick Cortez and place him in investigative detention. Aplt. Reply Br. at 6; but see Florida v. Royer, 460 U.S. 491, 499 (1983) (plurality op.) (an investigative detention may be violative of the Fourth Amendment absent probable cause where it approaches the conditions of an arrest). Before the district court, the Defendants argued:

> The County Defendants could have arrested Plaintiff Rick Cortez and taken him to the Detention Center that very night. Law enforcement officers do not need to wait for the convenience of an alleged child molester before they effectuate their duties. On the contrary, there exists an inherent exigency when law enforcement receives a report of child molestation.

Aplt.App. at 110. As did the district court and the panel, we reject this sweeping argument, untethered to basic Fourth Amendment principles.

[9] The en banc court is unanimous that probable cause was lacking to effect a warrantless arrest of Rick Cortez.

arrestee's clearly established Fourth Amendment rights). Furthermore, it was established law that "the probable cause standard of the Fourth Amendment requires officers to reasonably interview witnesses readily available at the scene, investigate basic evidence, or otherwise inquire if a crime has been committed at all before invoking the power of warrantless arrest and detention." *Romero*, 45 F.3d at 1476–77 (footnote omitted); *see also* Baptiste v. J.C. Penney, Co., 147 F.3d 1252, 1259 (10th Cir.1998) ("[P]olice officers may not ignore easily accessible evidence and thereby delegate their duty to investigate and make an independent probable cause determination based on that investigation."). In the present case, witnesses were readily available for interviews, physical evidence was available, and a medical diagnosis was forthcoming. Defendants, however, did not: (1) interview the girl, her mother, the nurse, or the doctor; (2) inspect the girl's clothing for possible signs of sexual assault; or (3) wait for a preliminary report from the doctor. In other words, Defendants conducted no investigation. Instead, the Defendants relied on the flimsiest of information conveyed by a telephone call.

Defendants rely upon the alleged statement of a two-year-old child which was relayed to them by a nurse, who heard it from the girl's mother. The fact that hearsay evidence would not be admissible at trial to prove guilt does not make it unusable as a source of probable cause for a warrantless arrest. *See* United States v. Swingler, 758 F.2d 477, 487 (10th Cir.1985). Defendants have cited the "excited utterance" exception to the hearsay rule contained in Fed.R.Evid. 803(2). Arguably, the statement might also fall within the "medical diagnosis" exception of Fed.R.Evid. 803(4), but there is no need to engage in such analysis. The statement is not being presented for the truth of the matter asserted therein; the issue is whether the officers were justified in relying upon it alone.[10]

---

[10] A concurring and dissenting opinion reminds us that hearsay may be relied upon in establishing probable cause. C & D Op. at 1140 (Gorsuch, J., concurring and dissenting). No one disputes that hearsay (with sufficient indicia of reliability) may be considered as part of the totality of the circumstances in making a probable cause determination. *See* Illinois v. Gates, 462 U.S. 213, 233 (1983). The double-hearsay statement in this case could be considered; but it was insufficient, in and of itself, to support probable cause.

That concurring and dissenting opinion suggests that the officers had other facts corroborating the statement. C & D Op. at 1140–41 (Gorsuch, J., concurring and dissenting). It relies on the fact that the mother (whom that concurring and dissenting opinion assumes knew the child best) believed a crime occurred given that she took the child to the hospital, hospital authorities (presumably, the nurse) reported the allegation to law enforcement, and the child's statement could be consistent with how a child might report being molested. The record does not contain any express evidence that the officers were aware of the nature of the mother's relationship with the child, her opinion concerning the complaint or that the nurse made some sort of decision concerning the allegations. The fact that New Mexico state law requires prompt reporting and action on complaints of child abuse, see N.M. Stat. Ann. § 32A–4–3, does not suggest, let alone require, non-compliance with the requirements of the Fourth Amendment, see Roska ex rel. Roska v. Peterson, 328 F.3d 1230, 1249, 1252 (10th Cir.2003). Merely because the officers claimed that they were investigating a serious felony and sought to separate the accused from any other children that might be in the home does nothing to provide a factual basis for such a claim as we discuss below. *See also supra*, n. 8. The concurring and dissenting opinion of

That unsubstantiated double-hearsay originating from a two-year-old, standing alone, does not give rise to probable cause should have been patently obvious to any reasonable law enforcement official. . . .

In Easton v. City of Boulder, 776 F.2d 1441 (10th Cir.1985), we declined to discount the statements to police of a three-year-old and a five-year-old regarding child abuse based solely on their age, despite some apparent inconsistencies and even though such testimony might not be admissible in court. *Id.* at 1449. We specifically found, however, that the five-year-old's statement had "corroborated all the facts given by [the three-year-old] . . . with respect to the assault [the five-year-old] witnessed." *Id.* at 1443. Here, no such corroboration was present. Additionally in *Easton,* we found that details in both childrens' statements regarding the plaintiff's residence and the site of the assault were independently corroborated by police investigation. *Id.* at 1450.

United States v. Shaw, 464 F.3d 615 (6th Cir.2006), is a case virtually on all-fours with the instant case with respect to the probable cause inquiry. The panel majority found probable cause wanting for an arrest of the defendant based upon a mother's hearsay statements to medical personnel later reported to military police. *Id.* at 626. According to the mother, her three-year-old son claimed that the defendant "had 'touched his pee-pee'" and that the defendant's "'pee-pee had touched his butt.'" *Id.* at 618. The examining physician found no evidence of trauma or penetration. The child was not interviewed and no effort was made to corroborate the allegations as reported by the mother. The Shaw panel majority stated:

> We are not aware . . . of any situation in which the uncorroborated hearsay statement of a child as young as three, standing alone, has been considered sufficient to establish probable cause. . . .

> [W]e *See* no way to affirm the district court's finding of probable cause in this case without carving out what would amount to an exception to the probable-cause requirement in child-molestation cases. We decline to adopt such an exception. . . .

> We hold only that the mother's bare-bones hearsay accusation in this case, with no corroborating evidence, did not suffice to establish probable cause, and that the ensuing arrest was therefore unlawful.

Id. at 624, 626. . . .

In sum, we find that viewing the undisputed facts in the light most favorable to the Plaintiffs, an arrest without probable cause occurred. As we discuss below, no exigent circumstances would justify a warrantless arrest either. This conclusion does not, however, end our analysis. Even law enforcement officials who reasonably but mistakenly conclude that

---

Judge Gorsuch comes very close to saying that, because the allegation was made, repeated by others, and acted on by law enforcement personnel, this particular statement was trustworthy.

probable cause is present are entitled to immunity. *Romero*, 45 F.3d at 1476. Therefore, when a warrantless arrest or seizure is the subject of a § 1983 action, the defendant is entitled to qualified immunity if a reasonable officer could have believed that probable cause existed to arrest or detain the plaintiff. [The court concludes that clearly established law indicated the absence of probable cause and rejects the claim for qualified immunity.]

C.   Seizure of Tina Cortez

We now turn to the seizure of Tina Cortez. Taking the Plaintiffs' allegations as true, and viewing the evidence in the light most favorable to the Plaintiffs, it appears that Tina Cortez (1) was ordered out of her house by the officers; (2) returned to her bedroom (though it is unclear whether she did so after exiting the house in response to the officers' orders, or without exiting the house); (3) was physically separated from her telephone by an officer illuminating the bedroom with a flashlight; (4) was taken by the arm and escorted from her home, (5) was placed in the back seat of a locked patrol car; and (6) was questioned by an officer while in the back seat of the locked patrol car. While in the back seat of the locked patrol car, Tina Cortez was allowed to use an officer's cell phone. The officers seized the keys to the home and locked it. Again we note that all this occurred after midnight.

The seizure of Tina Cortez was less intrusive than that of Rick Cortez to be sure. She was not advised of her *Miranda* rights, was not handcuffed, was allowed to use the officer's cell phone, generally seemed to be subjected to less force than Rick Cortez, and did not seem to be the object of the officers' primary suspicions. Taking the undisputed facts in the light most favorable to the Plaintiffs, these facts establish an investigative detention. *Cf.* Muehler v. Mena, 544 U.S. 93, 100 (2005) (making clear that detaining individuals under intrusive conditions does not automatically convert the detention to an arrest).

We again examine the officers' factual basis. As previously stated, an investigative detention must be based upon reasonable suspicion. The court views the totality of the circumstances to see whether the detaining officer had a "particularized and objective basis" for suspecting legal wrongdoing. United States v. Arvizu, 534 U.S. 266, 273 (2002). Just like her husband's seizure and detention, the seizure and detention of Tina Cortez was based solely on the allegations of a two-year-old girl. The girl's alleged statement, however, asserted no wrongdoing whatsoever as to Tina Cortez. No facts suggest that any evidence was about to be destroyed or that the Defendants or anyone else was somehow endangered by Tina Cortez. *See* Walker v. City of Orem, 451 F.3d 1139, 1149–1150 (10th Cir.2006) (90-minute detention of non-suspects with no exigencies could not be justified on an investigative detention rationale and violated the Fourth Amendment).

An investigative detention must be supported by reasonable suspicion. Hiibel v. Sixth Judicial Dist. Court of Nevada, 542 U.S. 177,

185 (2004). Here there was none. Likewise, the law is clearly established that warrantless entry into the home by law enforcement is not permitted absent exigent circumstances. Brigham City v. Stuart, 547 U.S. 398 (2006); Payton v. New York, 445 U.S. 573, 590 (1980). As we discuss below, there were no exigent circumstances. Therefore, we find that Tina Cortez has demonstrated that a clearly established constitutional right has been violated. Consequently, the Defendants are not entitled to qualified immunity as to her wrongful seizure claim, as the existence of neither reasonable suspicion nor "arguable reasonable suspicion" has been shown.

II.   Exigent Circumstances

A.   Legal Framework

The Defendants contend that they had probable cause to arrest Rick Cortez and that exigent circumstances were present in this case that allowed them to enter the Cortez home, seize Rick and Tina Cortez, and conduct a search of the house. Aplt. Br. at 14. Exigent circumstances may exist when there is a "plausible claim of specially pressing or urgent law enforcement need," Illinois v. McArthur, 531 U.S. 326, 331 (2001), for example the imminent destruction of evidence, *see* Georgia v. Randoph, 547 U.S. 103 n.6 (2006). Obviously, officers may not simply recite urgent needs without factual support. Otherwise, the exception swallows the rule.[20] Exigent circumstances in an emergency situation exist when: (1) the law enforcement officers have objectively reasonable grounds to believe that there is an immediate need to protect their lives or others, and (2) "the manner and scope of the search is reasonable." United States v. Najar, 451 F.3d 710, 718 (10th Cir.2006); *see also* United States v. Huffman, 461 F.3d 777, 783 (6th Cir.2006) (in relying upon the "risk-of-danger" exception to the warrant requirement, the government "must show that there was a risk of serious physical injury posed to the officers or others that required swift action.").

B.   Application

The Defendants have offered nothing, beyond innuendo and speculation, to establish objectively reasonable grounds of an emergency, i.e., an immediate need to protect their lives or others from serious injury or threatened injury. They have failed to articulate any specific facts that led them to believe the Plaintiffs posed a threat to the officers or others. In fact, the record indicates the opposite conclusion is appropriate. The record establishes that the Plaintiffs were asleep at the time the Defendants arrived at the home. The interior, as well as exterior lights, were off. Rick Cortez answered the door wearing only a pair of shorts. He cooperated with the officers as they voiced their commands. No evidence in the record suggests the presence of other people in the home. Additionally, no evidence in the record establishes actual or threatened

---

[20] For similar reasons, we reject Defendants' argument that New Mexico law requiring prompt investigation of child abuse allegations necessarily creates an "inherent exigency."

injury to any person or imminent violence. The only basis for the search was the unsubstantiated allegation of the nurse regarding a child at another location. We do not believe this evidence establishes the existence of emergency conditions at the Cortez home. Therefore, we agree with the district court that a finding of exigency was inappropriate. . . . .

Additionally, we have held that warrantless entry into homes is allowed if: (1) clear evidence of probable cause exists of, (2) a serious crime where destruction of evidence is likely, (3) any such search is limited in scope, and (4) it is supported by clearly defined indicators of exigency that are not subject to police manipulation. United States v. Scroger, 98 F.3d 1256, 1259 (10th Cir.1996). In spite of the fact that the Defendants failed to establish factors one, two, or four, they argue that the warrantless entry into the home was constitutional. We affirm the ruling of the district court denying qualified immunity in this regard.

III. Excessive Force Claims

Plaintiffs also allege a violation of their rights under the Fourth and Fourteenth Amendments to be free from the use of excessive force. Specifically, Plaintiffs claim that Defendants used excessive force in seizing them.

A.   Legal Framework

"[T]he right to make an arrest or investigatory stop necessarily carries with it the right to use some degree of physical coercion or threat thereof to effect it." Graham v. Connor, 490 U.S. 386, 396 (1989). The degree of physical coercion that law enforcement officers may use is not unlimited, however, and "all claims that law enforcement officers have used excessive force . . . in the course of an arrest, investigatory stop, or other 'seizure' of a free citizen should be analyzed under the Fourth Amendment and its 'reasonableness' standard. . . ." Id. at 395. In defining the parameters of this reasonableness standard, the Graham Court stated:

> Determining whether the force used to effect a particular seizure is reasonable under the Fourth Amendment requires a careful balancing of the nature and quality of the intrusion on the individual's Fourth Amendment interests against the countervailing governmental interests at stake. . . . Because the test of reasonableness under the Fourth Amendment is not capable of precise definition or mechanical application . . . its proper application requires careful attention to the facts and circumstances of each particular case, including the severity of the crime at issue, whether the suspect poses an immediate threat to the safety of the officers or others, and whether he is actively resisting arrest or attempting to evade arrest by flight.

490 U.S. at 396 (internal citations and quotations omitted); *see also Garner,* 471 U.S. at 8–9 ("[T]he question [is] whether the totality of the circumstances justifie[s] a particular sort of . . . seizure.").

The *Graham* Court continued:

> The reasonableness of a particular use of force must be judged from the perspective of a reasonable officer on the scene, rather than with the 20/20 vision of hindsight. . . . With respect to a claim of excessive force, the same standard of reasonableness at the moment applies: Not every push or shove, even if it may later seem unnecessary in the peace of a judge's chambers, violates the Fourth Amendment. The calculus of reasonableness must embody allowance for the fact that police officers are often forced to make split-second judgments—in circumstances that are tense, uncertain, and rapidly evolving—about the amount of force that is necessary in a particular situation.

> As in other Fourth Amendment contexts, however, the reasonableness inquiry in an excessive force case is an objective one: the question is whether the officers' actions are objectively reasonable in light of the facts and circumstances confronting them, without regard to their underlying intent or motivation. An officer's evil intentions will not make a Fourth Amendment violation out of an objectively reasonable use of force; nor will an officer's good intentions make an objectively unreasonable use of force constitutional.

Graham, 490 U.S. at 396–97 (internal citations and quotations omitted). Furthermore, we have previously held that "the interests protected by the Fourth Amendment are not confined to the right to be secure against physical harm; they include liberty, property, and privacy interests—a person's sense of security and individual dignity." Holland ex rel. Overdorff v. Harrington, 268 F.3d 1179, 1196 (10th Cir.2001) (internal quotation omitted).

We analyze the force applied in this case in the context of an arrest (Rick Cortez) and an investigative detention (Tina Cortez). While the nature of the inquiry under either alternative does not differ, *see* Graham, 490 U.S. at 396, the benchmark for what is reasonable does differ, *see* United States v. Merritt, 695 F.2d 1263, 1274 (10th Cir.1982). This is in part because police have historically been able to use more force in making an arrest than in effecting an investigative detention. *Cf.* United States v. Perdue, 8 F.3d 1455, 1464 (10th Cir.1993) ("[H]istorically, the maximum level of force permissible in a standard *Terry* stop fell short of placing the suspect in 'custody' for purposes of triggering *Miranda*.").

Thus, the excessive force inquiry evaluates the force used in a given arrest or detention against the force reasonably necessary to effect a lawful arrest or detention under the circumstances of the case. Thus, in a case where police effect an arrest without probable cause or a detention without reasonable suspicion, but use no more force than would have been reasonably necessary if the arrest or the detention were warranted, the plaintiff has a claim for unlawful arrest or detention but not an additional claim for excessive force.

We first consider Defendants' use of force against Rick Cortez, then Defendants' use of force against Tina Cortez. For the reasons stated below, we reverse the district court's denial of qualified immunity to Defendants on the claim that Defendants used excessive force in their dealings with Rick Cortez but affirm with respect to the claim that Defendants used excessive force in their dealings with Tina Cortez.

B.   Defendants' Use of Force Against Rick Cortez

It appears that Defendants (1) grabbed Rick Cortez by the arm and pulled him from the doorway of his home; (2) handcuffed him; (3) placed him in the back seat of a locked patrol car—all in the middle of the night, and (4) ignored his pleas that the handcuffs were too tight and hurting him.

As discussed above, if Plaintiffs' allegations are taken as true, Rick Cortez was arrested. *See* Kaupp v. Texas, 538 U.S. 626, 631 (2003) ("A . . . boy was awakened . . . at three in the morning by at least three police officers. . . . He was taken out in handcuffs, without shoes, dressed only in his underwear in January, placed in a patrol car, driven to the scene of a crime and then to the sheriff's offices, where he was taken into an interrogation room and questioned. This evidence points to arrest. . . ."). Because it also appears, when the evidence is construed in the light most favorable to Plaintiffs, that Defendants lacked probable cause for this arrest, we held above that Defendants are not entitled to qualified immunity on Plaintiffs' claim that Rick Cortez was seized unreasonably. Because the properly supported summary judgment facts suggest an arrest, we analyze the seizure of Rick Cortez as an arrest. We hold that the officers are entitled to qualified immunity on this claim.

Initially, we reject the idea contained in the panel opinion that a plaintiff's right to recover on an excessive force claim is dependent upon the outcome of an unlawful seizure claim. *See Cortez*, 438 F.3d at 995–96. Relying on Eleventh Circuit cases, the panel opinion held that "a plaintiff may not recover on an independent excessive force claim merely because force was applied during an unlawful seizure." *Id.* at 996. *See* Jackson v. Sauls, 206 F.3d 1156, 1171 (11th Cir.2000); Williamson v. Mills, 65 F.3d 155, 158–59 (11th Cir.1995) (per curiam). Thus, were a plaintiff to prevail on an unlawful arrest claim, the plaintiff would not be allowed to recover on an excessive force claim arising out of the arrest. Properly applied, such a rule might control where a plaintiff's excessive force claim is dependent solely on the absence of the power to arrest or detain. *See* Bashir v. Rockdale County, Ga., 445 F.3d 1323, 1332 (11th Cir.2006). We need not decide that issue, however, because Rick and Tina Cortez have made broader allegations concerning the circumstances of their seizures that might suggest excessive force. *See Cortez*, 438 F.3d at 1003–04 (Henry, J., concurring in part and dissenting in part).

Even under the Eleventh Circuit's rule, "[w]hen properly stated, an excessive force claim presents a discrete constitutional violation relating to the manner in which an arrest was carried out, and is independent of whether law enforcement had the power to arrest." *Bashir*, 445 F.3d at 1332. A contrary interpretation would conflict with the Supreme Court's direction that courts engage in careful balancing and examine excessive force claims under a Fourth Amendment reasonableness standard as discussed above. *See Graham*, 490 U.S. at 396. Moreover, a contrary interpretation risks imposing artificial limits on constitutional claims without any basis other than a fear that such a distinction might be too fine for a jury (a fear we do not agree with).

We hold that in cases involving claims of both unlawful arrest and excessive force arising from a single encounter, it is necessary to consider both the justification the officers had for the arrest and the degree of force they used to effect it. If the plaintiff can prove that the officers lacked probable cause, he is entitled to damages for the unlawful arrest, which includes damages resulting from any force reasonably employed in effecting the arrest. If the plaintiff can prove that the officers used greater force than would have been reasonably necessary to effect a lawful arrest, he is entitled to damages resulting from that excessive force. These two inquiries are separate and independent, though the evidence may overlap. The plaintiff might succeed in proving the unlawful arrest claim, the excessive force claim, both, or neither.

Should the officers move for qualified immunity on an excessive force claim, a plaintiff is required to show that the force used was impermissible (a constitutional violation) and that objectively reasonable officers could not have not thought the force constitutionally permissible (violates clearly established law).

We now consider Plaintiffs' claim that Defendants used excessive force against Rick Cortez in arresting him. In his affidavit, Rick Cortez contends that he was "grabbed and pulled out of the house" by one of the officers, and, after being handcuffed and put into the back seat of a patrol car, he complained that the handcuffs were too tight.

> I told the officer in the car with me that the handcuffs were too tight and hurting me. No action was taken to loosen the handcuffs. The handcuffs left red marks on both of my wrists for several days. My wrists were so marked that they were visible to casual observers.

Aplt.App. 88. Defendants argue that because Rick Cortez was accused of committing a violent felony, the Defendants' actions toward him, including ignoring his plea concerning the handcuffs, were appropriate under the circumstances. Aplt. Br. at 19. The Defendants also argue that because no proof of injury was provided either from health care providers or photographs, the self-serving contentions of the Plaintiffs will not suffice. Aplt. Br. at 19. Although the severity of the alleged offense is a factor in evaluating an excessive force claim, a court must also consider officer safety concerns and whether the suspect cooperates or resists. *Graham,* 490 U.S. at 396. There is no indication in the record that Rick Cortez actively resisted seizure or attempted to evade seizure by flight. Rick Cortez opened the door of his residence to police voluntarily. Aplt.App. 88, 96. Although Rick Cortez briefly asked Defendants what was going on before he complied with their commands to exit the residence, Aplt.App. 87, this does not amount to resistance. Likewise, there is no indication in the record that Rick Cortez posed an immediate threat to the safety of Defendants or others. He came to his front door wearing only shorts and cooperated fully. Nothing suggests that the Plaintiffs were armed or that other persons besides the Plaintiffs were present.

We have little difficulty concluding that a small amount of force, like grabbing Rick Cortez and placing him in the patrol car, is permissible in effecting an arrest under the Fourth Amendment. *See* Atwater v. City of Lago Vista, 532 U.S. 318, 354–55 (2001) (noting that a normal lawful custodial arrest where one is handcuffed, placed in a patrol car, and taken to the police station may be inconvenient and embarrassing, but not violative of the Fourth Amendment); *Graham,* 490 U.S. at 396 ("Our Fourth Amendment jurisprudence has long recognized that the right to make an arrest or investigatory stop necessarily carries with it the right to use some degree of physical coercion or threat thereof to effect it."). Although the dignity aspects of this arrest are troubling, specifically hauling Rick Cortez (clad only in his shorts) into the patrol car in the middle of the night without any explanation, the police were investigating a serious felony and claimed a need for quick action to separate the accused from any other children that might be in the home.

The closer issue is whether the failure to adjust Rick Cortez's handcuffs during an arrest constitutes excessive force. In some circumstances, unduly tight handcuffing can constitute excessive force where a plaintiff alleges some actual injury from the handcuffing and alleges that an officer ignored a plaintiff's timely complaints (or was otherwise made aware) that the handcuffs were too tight. See, e.g., Lyons v. Xenia, 417 F.3d 565, 575–76 (6th Cir.2005); Herzog v. Village of Winnetka, 309 F.3d 1041, 1043 (7th Cir.2002); Palmer v. Sanderson, 9 F.3d 1433, 1436 (9th Cir.1993). Although Rick Cortez complained to the officer that the handcuffs were too tight, the summary judgment record presents too little evidence of any actual injury. We believe that a claim of excessive force requires some actual injury that is not de minimis, be it physical or emotional. The only evidence in the record is his affidavit that the handcuffs left red marks that were visible for days afterward. Aplt.App. at 88. This is insufficient, as a matter of law, to support an excessive force claim if the use of handcuffs is otherwise justified.

We hold that the force established does not exceed what would have been reasonable to effectuate a lawful arrest under these circumstances. Therefore, whether or not the arrest itself was lawful, Plaintiffs' claim that Defendants used excessive force against Rick Cortez should not survive summary judgment. Even taking Plaintiffs' allegations as true and viewing the evidence in the light most favorable to Plaintiffs, Plaintiffs have not established that Defendants' use of force against Rick Cortez violated his Fourth and Fourteenth Amendment right to be free from the use of excessive force. In other words, the Defendants are entitled to qualified immunity on Rick Cortez's excessive force claim because no constitutional violation occurred. We therefore reverse the district court's denial of summary judgment to Defendants as to Plaintiffs' claim that Defendants used excessive force against Rick Cortez in connection with an arrest.

C.   Defendants' Use of Force Against Tina Cortez

Taking Plaintiffs' allegations as true, and viewing the evidence in the light most favorable to Plaintiffs, it appears that Defendants (1) entered Tina Cortez's home in the middle of the night without consent, a warrant or exigent circumstances; (2) physically separated Tina Cortez from her telephone; (3) took her by the arm; (4) escorted her from her home; (5) took the keys to her home and locked the door, and (6) placed her in the locked back seat of a patrol car. Tina Cortez has alleged no physical injury based on Defendants' use of force against her. Like her husband Rick, she has provided an affidavit that she was intimidated by the circumstances and the officers' show of force. Aplt.App. at 90.

As we discussed above, when Plaintiffs' allegations are taken as true, Tina Cortez was subjected to an investigative detention. Because Plaintiff's allegations suggest the investigative detention was not justified, we held that Defendants are not entitled to qualified immunity on Plaintiffs' claim that Tina Cortez was seized unreasonably.

For purposes of qualified immunity, we have little doubt that Tina Cortez has alleged a constitutional violation concerning excessive force that survives summary judgment. When Plaintiffs' allegations are taken as true, Plaintiffs have demonstrated that Defendants' use of force against Tina Cortez violated her Fourth and Fourteenth Amendment right to be free from the use of excessive force in the context of an investigative detention. This right was clearly established at the time of Defendants' actions.

We have recognized that, given evidence of officer safety concerns, officers may in appropriate circumstances take steps to protect their personal safety and maintain the status quo during a *Terry* stop. Gallegos v. City of Colorado Springs, 114 F.3d 1024, 1030–31 (10th Cir.1997); *Perdue,* 8 F.3d at 1463. Although *Terry* stops are normally non-intrusive, we have indicated that law enforcement may (1) display some force, (2) place suspects on the ground, (3) use handcuffs, or (4) detain suspects in law enforcement vehicles, even in the absence of probable cause. Perdue,

8 F.3d at 1463. At the same time, "an unreasonable level of force transforms a *Terry* detention into an arrest requiring probable cause." United States v. Shareef, 100 F.3d 1491, 1507 (10th Cir.1996); *see also* Florida v. Royer, 460 U.S. 491, 499 (1983) (plurality op.).

Keeping in mind that Tina Cortez was never the target of the investigation, no evidence suggests that a reasonable law enforcement officer would suspect that she posed a threat. *See* Melendez-Garcia, 28 F.3d at 1052–53. She was unarmed and gave no indication of flight. Though she was attempting to make a telephone call when an officer physically separated her from her telephone, she did not resist and was escorted to the locked patrol car where interrogation commenced. Again, no evidence suggests that this level of intrusiveness was warranted for officer safety concerns.

Defendants assert that if they had left Tina Cortez in her home alone, she could have destroyed evidence, but again they have provided no particularized facts to support this allegation. *See* United States v. Acosta-Colon, 157 F.3d 9, 17 (1st Cir.1998). This is not a situation where officers needed to neutralize certain persons while conducting an investigation. Simply because Tina Cortez was seized does not mean that the force used in effecting the seizure was excessive. Rather, viewing the facts in the light most favorable to Tina Cortez, the level of force the defendants used against her was unreasonable in relation to the threat that she presented and the surrounding circumstances. Although it is generally permissible to hold a person by the arm during an investigative detention, the Defendants have not articulated any reasonable safety concerns or flight concerns that would justify the extra force that they used against Tina Cortez—escorting her from her bedroom in the middle of the night and keeping her in a locked patrol car for nearly an hour.

We also hold that the law was clearly established. With respect to Mrs. Cortez, the officers involved should have known that they were permitted to use only as much force as was necessary to secure their own safety and maintain the status quo. *See* United States v. Hensley, 469 U.S. 221, 235 (1985) (officer is authorized to take such steps as necessary to protect personal safety and maintain status quo). The force used in this case bears no relationship to those purposes. Under prior case law in the Tenth Circuit, officers are required to articulate specific justifications for uses of force during an investigative detention, such as locking a person in a police car. *See, e.g., Melendez-Garcia*, 28 F.3d at 1052–53; *Perdue,* 8 F.3d at 1464. Moreover, we recently made it clear that personal security and individual dignity interests, particularly of non-suspects, should also be considered. *Holland,* 268 F.3d at 1195. . . .

V.   Conclusion

For the foregoing reasons, we AFFIRM the district court's denial of the motion for partial summary judgment on based on qualified immunity as to Plaintiff Rick Cortez's claim of an unlawful seizure (arrest), but REVERSE as to his claim of excessive force in connection with such an arrest. We AFFIRM the district court's denial of qualified immunity as to Tina Cortez as set forth above. The case is remanded for further proceedings consistent with this Opinion.

Maryland v. Pringle
540 U.S. 366 (2003)

■ REHNQUIST, C.J., delivered the opinion for a unanimous Court.

In the early morning hours a passenger car occupied by three men was stopped for speeding by a police officer. The officer, upon searching the car, seized $763 of rolled-up cash from the glove compartment and five glassine baggies of cocaine from between the back-seat armrest and the back seat. After all three men denied ownership of the cocaine and money, the officer arrested each of them. We hold that the officer had probable cause to arrest Pringle—one of the three men.

At 3:16 a.m. on August 7, 1999, a Baltimore County Police officer stopped a Nissan Maxima for speeding. There were three occupants in the car: Donte Partlow, the driver and owner, respondent Pringle, the front-seat passenger, and Otis Smith, the back-seat passenger. The officer asked Partlow for his license and registration. When Partlow opened the glove compartment to retrieve the vehicle registration, the officer observed a large amount of rolled-up money in the glove compartment. The officer returned to his patrol car with Partlow's license and registration to check the computer system for outstanding violations. The computer check did not reveal any violations. The officer returned to the stopped car, had Partlow get out, and issued him an oral warning.

After a second patrol car arrived, the officer asked Partlow if he had any weapons or narcotics in the vehicle. Partlow indicated that he did not. Partlow then consented to a search of the vehicle. The search yielded $763 from the glove compartment and five plastic glassine baggies containing cocaine from behind the back-seat armrest. When the officer began the search the armrest was in the upright position flat against the rear seat. The officer pulled down the armrest and found the drugs, which had been placed between the armrest and the back seat of the car.

The officer questioned all three men about the ownership of the drugs and money, and told them that if no one admitted to ownership of the drugs he was going to arrest them all. The men offered no information regarding the ownership of the drugs or money. All three were placed under arrest and transported to the police station.

Later that morning, Pringle waived his rights under Miranda v. Arizona, 384 U.S. 436 (1966), and gave an oral and written confession in which he acknowledged that the cocaine belonged to him, that he and his friends were going to a party, and that he intended to sell the cocaine or "[u]se it for sex." App. 26. Pringle maintained that the other occupants of the car did not know about the drugs, and they were released.

The trial court denied Pringle's motion to suppress his confession as the fruit of an illegal arrest, holding that the officer had probable cause to arrest Pringle. A jury convicted Pringle of possession with intent to distribute cocaine and possession of cocaine. He was sentenced to 10 years' incarceration without the possibility of parole. The Court of Special Appeals of Maryland affirmed. 141 Md.App. 292, 785 A.2d 790 (2001).

The Court of Appeals of Maryland, by divided vote, reversed, holding that, absent specific facts tending to show Pringle's knowledge and dominion or control over the drugs, "the mere finding of cocaine in the back armrest when [Pringle] was a front seat passenger in a car being driven by its owner is insufficient to establish probable cause for an arrest for possession." 370 Md. 525, 545, 805 A.2d 1016, 1027 (2002). We granted certiorari, 538 U.S. 921 (2003), and now reverse.

Under the Fourth Amendment, made applicable to the States by the Fourteenth Amendment, Mapp v. Ohio, 367 U.S. 643 (1961), the people are "to be secure in their persons, houses, papers, and effects, against unreasonable searches and seizures, . . . and no Warrants shall issue, but upon probable cause . . . ." U.S. Const., Amdt. 4. Maryland law authorizes police officers to execute warrantless arrests, inter alia, for felonies committed in an officer's presence or where an officer has probable cause to believe that a felony has been committed or is being committed in the officer's presence. Md. Ann.Code, Art. 27, § 594B (1996) (repealed 2001). A warrantless arrest of an individual in a public place for a felony, or a misdemeanor committed in the officer's presence, is consistent with the Fourth Amendment if the arrest is supported by probable cause. United States v. Watson, 423 U.S. 411, 424 (1976); *see* Atwater v. Lago Vista, 532 U.S. 318, 354 (2001) (stating that "[i]f an officer has probable cause to believe that an individual has committed even a very minor criminal offense in his presence, he may, without violating the Fourth Amendment, arrest the offender").

It is uncontested in the present case that the officer, upon recovering the five plastic glassine baggies containing suspected cocaine, had probable cause to believe a felony had been committed. Md. Ann.Code, Art. 27, § 287 (1996) (repealed 2002) (prohibiting possession of controlled dangerous substances). The sole question is whether the officer had probable cause to believe that Pringle committed that crime.[1]

The long-prevailing standard of probable cause protects "citizens from rash and unreasonable interferences with privacy and from unfounded charges of crime," while giving "fair leeway for enforcing the law in the community's protection." Brinegar v. United States, 338 U.S. 160, 176 (1949). On many occasions, we have reiterated that the probable-cause standard is a " 'practical, nontechnical conception' " that deals with " 'the factual and practical considerations of everyday life on

---

[1]   Maryland law defines "possession" as "the exercise of actual or constructive dominion or control over a thing by one or more persons." Md. Ann.Code, Art. 27, § 277(s) (1996) (repealed 2002).

which reasonable and prudent men, not legal technicians, act.' " Illinois v. Gates, 462 U.S. 213, 231 (1983) (quoting *Brinegar, supra,* at 175–176); *see, e.g.,* Ornelas v. United States, 517 U.S. 690, 695 (1996); United States v. Sokolow, 490 U.S. 1, 7–8 (1989). "[P]robable cause is a fluid concept—turning on the assessment of probabilities in particular factual contexts—not readily, or even usefully, reduced to a neat set of legal rules." *Gates,* 462 U.S., at 232.

The probable-cause standard is incapable of precise definition or quantification into percentages because it deals with probabilities and depends on the totality of the circumstances. *See ibid.; Brinegar,* 338 U.S., at 175. We have stated, however, that "[t]he substance of all the definitions of probable cause is a reasonable ground for belief of guilt," ibid. (internal quotation marks and citations omitted), and that the belief of guilt must be particularized with respect to the person to be searched or seized, Ybarra v. Illinois, 444 U.S. 85, 91 (1979). In *Illinois v. Gates,* we noted:

> "As early as Locke v. United States, 7 Cranch 339, 348 (1813), Chief Justice Marshall observed, in a closely related context: '[T]he term "probable cause," according to its usual acceptation, means less than evidence which would justify condemnation . . . . It imports a seizure made under circumstances which warrant suspicion.' More recently, we said that 'the quanta . . . of proof' appropriate in ordinary judicial proceedings are inapplicable to the decision to issue a warrant. *Brinegar,* 338 U.S., at 173. Finely tuned standards such as proof beyond a reasonable doubt or by a preponderance of the evidence, useful in formal trials, have no place in the [probable-cause] decision." 462 U.S., at 235.

To determine whether an officer had probable cause to arrest an individual, we examine the events leading up to the arrest, and then decide "whether these historical facts, viewed from the standpoint of an objectively reasonable police officer, amount to" probable cause, *Ornelas, supra,* at 696.

In this case, Pringle was one of three men riding in a Nissan Maxima at 3:16 a.m. There was $763 of rolled-up cash in the glove compartment directly in front of Pringle.[2] Five plastic glassine baggies of cocaine were behind the back-seat armrest and accessible to all three men. Upon

---

[2] The Court of Appeals of Maryland dismissed the $763 seized from the glove compartment as a factor in the probable-cause determination, stating that "[m]oney, without more, is innocuous." 370 Md. 525, 546, 805 A.2d 1016, 1028 (2002). The court's consideration of the money in isolation, rather than as a factor in the totality of the circumstances, is mistaken in light of our precedents. See, e.g., Illinois v. Gates, 462 U.S. 213, 230–231 (1983) (opining that the totality of the circumstances approach is consistent with our prior treatment of probable cause); Brinegar v. United States, 338 U.S. 160, 175–176 (1949) ("Probable cause exists where 'the facts and circumstances within their [the officers'] knowledge and of which they had reasonably trustworthy information [are] sufficient in themselves to warrant a man of reasonable caution in the belief that' an offense has been or is being committed"). We think it is abundantly clear from the facts that this case involves more than money alone.

questioning, the three men failed to offer any information with respect to the ownership of the cocaine or the money.

We think it an entirely reasonable inference from these facts that any or all three of the occupants had knowledge of, and exercised dominion and control over, the cocaine. Thus, a reasonable officer could conclude that there was probable cause to believe Pringle committed the crime of possession of cocaine, either solely or jointly.

Pringle's attempt to characterize this case as a guilt-by-association case is unavailing. His reliance on *Ybarra v. Illinois, supra*, and United States v. Di Re, 332 U.S. 581(1948), is misplaced. In *Ybarra*, police officers obtained a warrant to search a tavern and its bartender for evidence of possession of a controlled substance. Upon entering the tavern, the officers conducted patdown searches of the customers present in the tavern, including Ybarra. Inside a cigarette pack retrieved from Ybarra's pocket, an officer found six tinfoil packets containing heroin. We stated:

> "[A] person's mere propinquity to others independently suspected of criminal activity does not, without more, give rise to probable cause to search that person. Sibron v. New York, 392 U.S. 40, 62–63 (1968). Where the standard is probable cause, a search or seizure of a person must be supported by probable cause particularized with respect to that person. This requirement cannot be undercut or avoided by simply pointing to the fact that coincidentally there exists probable cause to search or seize another or to search the premises where the person may happen to be." 444 U.S., at 91.

We held that the search warrant did not permit body searches of all of the tavern's patrons and that the police could not pat down the patrons for weapons, absent individualized suspicion. *Id.*, at 92.

This case is quite different from *Ybarra*. Pringle and his two companions were in a relatively small automobile, not a public tavern. In Wyoming v. Houghton, 526 U.S. 295 (1999), we noted that "a car passenger—unlike the unwitting tavern patron in Ybarra—will often be engaged in a common enterprise with the driver, and have the same interest in concealing the fruits or the evidence of their wrongdoing." *Id.*, at 304–305. Here we think it was reasonable for the officer to infer a common enterprise among the three men. The quantity of drugs and cash in the car indicated the likelihood of drug dealing, an enterprise to which a dealer would be unlikely to admit an innocent person with the potential to furnish evidence against him.

In *Di Re*, a federal investigator had been told by an informant, Reed, that he was to receive counterfeit gasoline ration coupons from a certain Buttitta at a particular place. The investigator went to the appointed place and saw Reed, the sole occupant of the rear seat of the car, holding gasoline ration coupons. There were two other occupants in the car:

Buttitta in the driver's seat and Di Re in the front passenger's seat. Reed informed the investigator that Buttitta had given him counterfeit coupons. Thereupon, all three men were arrested and searched. After noting that the officers had no information implicating Di Re and no information pointing to Di Re's possession of coupons, unless presence in the car warranted that inference, we concluded that the officer lacked probable cause to believe that Di Re was involved in the crime. 332 U.S., at 592–594. We said "[a]ny inference that everyone on the scene of a crime is a party to it must disappear if the Government informer singles out the guilty person." *Id.*, at 594. No such singling out occurred in this case; none of the three men provided information with respect to the ownership of the cocaine or money.

We hold that the officer had probable cause to believe that Pringle had committed the crime of possession of a controlled substance. Pringle's arrest therefore did not contravene the Fourth and Fourteenth Amendments. Accordingly, the judgment of the Court of Appeals of Maryland is reversed, and the case is remanded for further proceedings not inconsistent with this opinion.

Hill v. California

401 U.S. 797 (1971)

■ MR. JUSTICE WHITE delivered the opinion of Court.

On June 4, 1966, four armed men robbed a resident in Studio City, California. On June 5, Alfred Baum and Richard Bader were arrested for possession of narcotics; at the time of their arrest, they were driving petitioner Hill's car, and a search of the car produced property stolen in the Studio City robbery the day before. Bader and Baum both admitted taking part in the June 4 robbery, and both implicated Hill. Bader told the police that he was sharing an apartment with Hill at 9311 Sepulveda Boulevard. He also stated that the guns used in the robbery and other stolen property were in the apartment. On June 6, Baum and Bader again told the police that Hill had been involved in the June 4 robbery.

One of the investigating officers then checked official records on Hill, verifying his prior association with Bader, his age and physical description, his address, and the make of his car. The information the officer uncovered corresponded with the general descriptions by the robbery victims and the statements made by Baum and Bader.

Hill concedes that this information gave the police probable cause to arrest and the police undertook to do so on June 6. Four officers went to the Sepulveda Boulevard apartment, verified the address, and knocked. One of the officers testified: 'The door was open and a person who fit the description exactly of Archie Hill, as I had received it from both the cards and from Baum and Bader, answered the door. * * * We placed him under arrest for robbery.'

The police had neither an arrest nor a search warrant. After arresting the man who answered the door, they asked him whether he was Hill and where the guns and stolen goods were. The arrestee replied that he was not Hill, that his name was Miller, that it was Hill's apartment and that he was waiting for Hill. He also claimed that he knew nothing about any stolen property or guns, although the police testified that an automatic pistol and a clip of ammunition were lying in plain view on a coffee table in the living room where the arrest took place. The arrestee then produced identification indicating that he was in fact Miller, but the police were unimpressed and proceeded to search the apartment [incident to the arrest. Hill later moved to suppress the evidence found in his apartment incident to the arrest of Miller.]

Based on our own examination of the record, we find no reason to disturb either the findings of the California courts that the police had probable cause to arrest Hill and that the arresting officers had a reasonable, good faith belief that the arrestee Miller was in fact Hill, or the conclusion that '(w) hen the police have probable cause to arrest one party, and when they reasonably mistake a second party for the first party, then the arrest of the second party is a valid arrest.' 69 Cal.2d, at 553, 72 Cal.Rptr. at 643, 446 P.2d, at 523. The police unquestionably had probable cause to arrest Hill; they also had his address and a verified description. The mailbox at the indicated address listed Hill as the occupant of the apartment. Upon gaining entry to the apartment, they were confronted with one who fit the description of Hill received from various sources.[6] That person claimed he was Miller, not Hill. But aliases and false identifications are not uncommon. Moreover, there was a lock on the door and Miller's explanation for his mode of entry was not convincing.[8] He also denied knowledge of firearms in the apartment although a pistol and loaded ammunition clip were in plain view in the room. The upshot was that the officers in good faith believed Miller was Hill and arrested him. They were quite wrong as it turned out, and subjective good-faith belief would not in itself justify either the arrest or the subsequent search. But sufficient probability, not certainty, is the touchstone of reasonableness under the Fourth Amendment and on the record before us the officers' mistake was understandable and the arrest a reasonable response to the situation facing them at the time.[9]

---

[6]   At the preliminary hearing and trial, the only disparities in description established were that Miller was two inches taller and 10 pounds heavier than Hill.

[8]   Petitioner points out that the officers had no idea how Miller gained access to the Hill apartment, and asserts that it was improper for them to assume that he was lawfully there. It is undisputed that Miller was the only occupant of the apartment. One of the officers testified that there was a lock on the door and that he had asked Miller how he had gotten into the apartment; Miller made no specific reply, except to reiterate that he had come in and was waiting for Hill, the tenant.

[9]   Petitioner also claims that it was unreasonable for the officers to disregard Miller's proffered identification. However, Miller's answer to the question about firearms could reasonably be regarded as evasive, and his subsequent production of identification as therefore entitled to little weight. Petitioner stresses that Miller was subsequently booked in his own name when taken to the station house, arguing that this demonstrates that the officers' belief

Nor can we agree with petitioner that however valid the arrest of Miller, the subsequent search violated the Fourth Amendment. It is true that Miller was not Hill; nor did Miller have authority or control over the premises, although at the very least he was Hill's guest. But the question is not what evidence would have been admissible against Hill (or against Miller for that matter) if the police, with probable cause to arrest Miller, had arrested him in Hill's apartment and then carried out the search at issue. Here there was probable cause to arrest Hill and the police arrested Miller in Hill's apartment, reasonably believing him to be Hill. In these circumstances the police were entitled to do what the law would have allowed them to do if Miller had in fact been Hill, that is, to search incident to arrest and to seize evidence of the crime the police had probable cause to believe Hill had committed. When judged in accordance with 'the factual and practical considerations of everyday life on which reasonable and prudent men, not legal technicians, act,' Brinegar v. United States, 338 U.S. 160, 175 (1949), the arrest and subsequent search were reasonable and valid under the Fourth Amendment.

2.   REQUIRED JUDICIAL AUTHORIZATION

United States v. Watson
423 U.S. 411 (1976)

■ MR. JUSTICE WHITE delivered the opinion of the Court.

This case presents questions under the Fourth Amendment as to the legality of a warrantless arrest and of an ensuing search of the arrestee's automobile carried out with his purported consent.

I

The relevant events began on August 17, 1972, when an informant, one Khoury, telephoned a postal inspector informing him that respondent Watson was in possession of a stolen credit card and had asked Khoury to cooperate in using the card to their mutual advantage. On five to 10 previous occasions Khoury had provided the inspector with reliable information on postal inspection matters, some involving Watson. Later that day Khoury delivered the card to the inspector. On learning that Watson had agreed to furnish additional cards, the inspector asked Khoury to arrange to meet with Watson. Khoury did so, a meeting being scheduled for August 22.[1] Watson canceled that engagement, but at noon on August 23, Khoury met with Watson at a restaurant designated by the latter. Khoury had been instructed that if Watson had additional

---

that Miller was Hill was unreasonable. However, the trial judge found that the arresting officer was not responsible for the booking procedures under which Miller would be booked under whatever name he gave at the station house. This conclusion is buttressed by the fact that Miller was not released from custody for a day and a half, after a thorough check of his identification revealed that he had in fact told the truth about his identity, despite his evasiveness in dealing with the officers at the apartment.

[1]   In the meantime the inspector had verified that the card was stolen.

stolen credit cards, Khoury was to give a designated signal. The signal was given, the officers closed in, and Watson was forthwith arrested. He was removed from the restaurant to the street where he was given the warnings required by Miranda v. Arizona, 384 U.S. 436 (1966). A search having revealed that Watson had no credit cards on his person, the inspector asked if he could look inside Watson's car, which was standing within view. Watson said, "Go ahead," and repeated these words when the inspector cautioned that "(i)f I find anything, it is going to go against you." Using keys furnished by Watson, the inspector entered the car and found under the floor mat an envelop containing two credit cards in the names of other persons. These cards were the basis for two counts of a four-count indictment charging Watson with possessing stolen mail in violation of 18 U.S.C. s 1708.

Prior to trial, Watson moved to suppress the cards, claiming that his arrest was illegal for want of probable cause and an arrest warrant and that his consent to search the car was involuntary and ineffective because he had not been told that he could withhold consent. The motion was denied, and Watson was convicted of illegally possessing the two cards seized from his car.

A divided panel of the Court of Appeals for the Ninth Circuit reversed, 504 F.2d 849 (1974), ruling that the admission in evidence of the two credit cards found in the car was prohibited by the Fourth Amendment. In reaching this judgment, the court decided two issues in Watson's favor. First, notwithstanding its agreement with the District Court that Khoury was reliable and that there was probable cause for arresting Watson, the court held the arrest unconstitutional because the postal inspector had failed to secure an arrest warrant although he concededly had time to do so. Second, based on the totality of the circumstances, one of which was the illegality of the arrest, the court held Watson's consent to search had been coerced and hence was not a valid ground for the warrantless search of the automobile. We granted certiorari. 420 U.S. 924 (1975).

II

A major part of the Court of Appeals' opinion was its holding that Watson's warrantless arrest violated the Fourth Amendment. Although it did not expressly do so, it may have intended to overturn the conviction on the independent ground that the two credit cards were the inadmissible fruits of an unconstitutional arrest. *Cf.* Brown v. Illinois, 422 U.S. 590 (1975). However that may be, the Court of Appeals treated the illegality of Watson's arrest as an important factor in determining the voluntariness of his consent to search his car. We therefore deal first with the arrest issue.

Contrary to the Court of Appeals' view, Watson's arrest was not invalid because executed without a warrant. Title 18 U.S.C. § 3061(a)(3) expressly empowers the Board of Governors of the Postal Service to authorize Postal Service officers and employees "performing duties related to the inspection of postal matters" to

> "make arrests without warrant for felonies cognizable under the laws of the United States if they have reasonable grounds to believe that the person to be arrested has committed or is committing such a felony."

By regulation, 39 CFR § 232.5(a)(3) (1975), and in identical language, the Board of Governors has exercised that power and authorized warrantless arrests. Because there was probable cause in this case to believe that Watson had violated § 1708, the inspector and his subordinates, in arresting Watson, were acting strictly in accordance with the governing statute and regulations. The effect of the judgment of the Court of Appeals was to invalidate the statute as applied in this case and as applied to all the situations where a court fails to find exigent circumstances justifying a warrantless arrest. We reverse that judgment.

Under the Fourth Amendment, the people are to be "secure in their persons, houses, papers, and effects, against unreasonable searches and seizures, . . . and no Warrants shall issue, but upon probable cause . . . ." Section 3061 represents a judgment by Congress that it is not unreasonable under the Fourth Amendment for postal inspectors to arrest without a warrant provided they have probable cause to do so. This was not an isolated or quixotic judgment of the legislative branch. Other federal law enforcement officers have been expressly authorized by statute for many years to make felony arrests on probable cause but without a warrant. This is true of United States marshals, 18 U.S.C. § 3053, and of agents of the Federal Bureau of Investigation, 18 U.S.C. § 3052; the Drug Enforcement Administration, 84 Stat. 1273, 21 U.S.C. § 878; the Secret Service, 18 U.S.C. § 3056(a); and the Customs Service, 26 U.S.C. § 7607. . . .

Because there is a "strong presumption of constitutionality due to an Act of Congress, especially when it turns on what is 'reasonable,'" "(o)bviously the Court should be reluctant to decide that a search thus authorized by Congress was unreasonable and that the Act was therefore unconstitutional." United States v. Di Re, 332 U.S. 581, 585 (1948). Moreover, there is nothing in the Court's prior cases indicating that under the Fourth Amendment a warrant is required to make a valid arrest for a felony. Indeed, the relevant prior decisions are uniformly to the contrary.

"The usual rule is that a police officer may arrest without warrant one believed by the officer upon reasonable cause to have been guilty of a felony . . . ." Carroll v. United States, 267 U.S. 132, 156 (1925). In Henry v. United States, 361 U.S. 98 (1959), the Court dealt with an FBI agent's warrantless arrest under 18 U.S.C. § 3052, which authorizes a warrantless arrest where there are reasonable grounds to believe that the person to be arrested has committed a felony. The Court declared that "(t)he statute states the constitutional standard . . . ." Id., at 100.

The necessary inquiry, therefore, was not whether there was a warrant or whether there was time to get one, but whether there was probable cause for the arrest. In Abel v. United States, 362 U.S. 217, 232 (1960), the Court sustained an administrative arrest made without "a judicial warrant within the scope of the Fourth Amendment." The crucial question in Draper v. United States, 358 U.S. 307 (1959), was whether there was probable cause for the warrantless arrest. If there was, the Court said, "the arrest, though without a warrant, was lawful . . . ." *Id.*, at 310. Ker v. California, 374 U.S. 23, 34–35 (1963) (opinion of Clark, J.), reiterated the rule that "(t)he lawfulness of the arrest without warrant, in turn, must be based upon probable cause . . ." and went on to sustain the warrantless arrest over other claims going to the mode of entry. Just last Term, while recognizing that maximum protection of individual rights could be assured by requiring a magistrate's review of the factual justification prior to any arrest, we stated that "such a requirement would constitute an intolerable handicap for legitimate law enforcement" and noted that the Court "has never invalidated an arrest supported by probable cause solely because the officers failed to secure a warrant." Gerstein v. Pugh, 420 U.S. 103, 113 (1975). . . .

The cases construing the Fourth Amendment thus reflect the ancient common-law rule that a peace officer was permitted to arrest without a warrant for a misdemeanor or felony committed in his presence as well as for a felony not committed in his presence if there was reasonable ground for making the arrest. 10 Halsbury's Laws of England 344–345 (3d ed. 1955); 4 W. Blackstone, Commentaries; 1 J. Stephen, A History of the Criminal Law of England 193 (1883); 2 M. Hale, Pleas of the Crown; Wilgus, Arrest Without a Warrant, 22 Mich.L.Rev. 541, 547–550, 686–688 (1924); Samuel v. Payne, 1 Doug. 359, 99 Eng.Rep. 230 (K.B.1780); Beckwith v. Philby, 6 Barn. & Cress. 635, 108 Eng.Rep. 585 (K.B.1827). This has also been the prevailing rule under state constitutions and statutes. "The rule of the common law, that a peace officer or a private citizen may arrest a felon without a warrant, has been generally held by the courts of the several States to be in force in cases of felony punishable by the civil tribunals." Kurtz v. Moffitt, 115 U.S. 487, 504 (1885). . . .

Because the common-law rule authorizing arrests without a warrant generally prevailed in the States, it is important for present purposes to note that in 1792 Congress invested United States marshals and their deputies with "the same powers in executing the laws of the United States, as sheriffs and their deputies in the several states have by law, in executing the laws of their respective states." Act of May 2, 1792, c. 28, § 9, 1 Stat. 265. The Second Congress thus saw no inconsistency between the Fourth Amendment and legislation giving United States marshals the same power as local peace officers to arrest for a felony without a warrant.[8] This provision equating the power of federal marshals with

---

[8]   Of equal import is the rule recognized by this Court that even in the absence of a federal statute granting or restricting the authority of federal law enforcement officers, "the law of the

those of local sheriffs was several times re-enacted and is today § 570 of Title 28 of the United States Code. That provision, however, was supplemented in 1935 by § 504a of the Judicial Code, which in its essential elements is now 18 U.S.C. § 3053 and which expressly empowered marshals to make felony arrests without warrant and on probable cause. It was enacted to furnish a federal standard independent of the vagaries of state laws, the Committee Report remarking that under existing law a "marshal or deputy marshal may make an arrest without a warrant within his district in all cases where the sheriff might do so under the State statutes." H.R.Rep.No.283, 74th Cong., 1st Sess., 1 (1935). *See* United States v. Riggs, 474 F.2d 699, 702–703, n. 2 (CA2), cert. denied, 414 U.S. 820 (1973).

The balance struck by the common law in generally authorizing felony arrests on probable cause, but without a warrant, has survived substantially intact. It appears in almost all of the States in the form of express statutory authorization. In 1963, the American Law Institute undertook the task of formulating a model statute governing police powers and practice in criminal law enforcement and related aspects of pretrial procedure. In 1975, after years of discussion, A Model Code of Pre-arraignment Procedure was proposed. Among its provisions was § 120.1 which authorizes an officer to take a person into custody if the officer has reasonable cause to believe that the person to be arrested has committed a felony, or has committed a misdemeanor or petty misdemeanor in his presence.[11] The commentary to this section said: "The Code thus adopts the traditional and almost universal standard for arrest without a warrant."

This is the rule Congress has long directed its principal law enforcement officers to follow. Congress has plainly decided against conditioning warrantless arrest power on proof of exigent circumstances.[13] Law enforcement officers may find it wise to seek arrest

---

state where an arrest without warrant takes place determines its validity." United States v. Di Re, 332 U.S. 581, 589 (1948). Accord, Miller v. United States, 357 U.S. 301, 305 (1958); Johnson v. United States, 333 U.S. 10, 15 n.5 (1948); Bad Elk v. United States, 177 U.S. 529, 535 (1900). This rule is consistent with the express statutory authority of United States marshals discussed in the text, as well as with the Act of Sept. 24, 1789, c. 20, § 33, 1 Stat. 91, providing that for any offense against the United States the offender may be arrested by any judge or justice of the United States "agreeably to the usual mode of process against offenders in such state" as he might be found. *See* United States v. Di Re, supra, 332 U.S., at 589 n. 8.

[11] Section 120.1 of the Model Code provides, in pertinent part: "(1) Authority to Arrest Without a Warrant. A law enforcement officer may arrest a person without a warrant if the officer has reasonable cause to believe that such person has committed "(a) a felony; "(b) a misdemeanor, and the officer has reasonable cause to believe that such person "(i) will not be apprehended unless immediately arrested; or "(ii) may cause injury to himself or others or damage to property unless immediately arrested; or "(c) a misdemeanor or petty misdemeanor in the officer's presence."

[13] Until 1951, 18 U.S.C. s 3052 conditioned the warrantless arrest powers of the agents of the Federal Bureau of Investigation on there being reasonable grounds to believe that the person would escape before a warrant could be obtained. The Act of Jan. 10, 1951, c. 1221, s 1, 64 Stat. 1239, eliminated this condition. The House Report explained the purpose of the amendment, H.R.Rep.No.3228, 81st Cong., 2d Sess., 1–2 (1950), U.S.Code Cong. Service 1950, p. 4322, and the amendment was given effect by the courts in accordance with its terms.

warrants where practicable to do so, and their judgments about probable cause may be more readily accepted where backed by a warrant issued by a magistrate. *See* United States v. Ventresca, 380 U.S. 102, 106 (1965); Aguilar v. Texas, 378 U.S. 108, 111 (1964); Wong Sun v. United States, 371 U.S. 471, 479–480 (1963). But we decline to transform this judicial preference into a constitutional rule when the judgment of the Nation and Congress has for so long been to authorize warrantless public arrests on probable cause rather than to encumber criminal prosecutions with endless litigation with respect to the existence of exigent circumstances, whether it was practicable to get a warrant, whether the suspect was about to flee, and the like.

Watson's arrest did not violate the Fourth Amendment, and the Court of Appeals erred in holding to the contrary.

III

Because our judgment is that Watson's arrest comported with the Fourth Amendment, Watson's consent to the search of his car was not the product of an illegal arrest. To the extent that the issue of the voluntariness of Watson's consent was resolved on the premise that his arrest was illegal, the Court of Appeals was also in error.

We are satisfied in addition that the remaining factors relied upon by the Court of Appeals to invalidate Watson's consent are inadequate to demonstrate that, in the totality of the circumstances, Watson's consent was not his own "essentially free and unconstrained choice" because his "will ha(d) been overborne and his capacity for self-determination critically impaired." Schneckloth v. Bustamonte, 412 U.S. 218, 225 (1973). . . .

In consequence, we reverse the judgment of the Court of Appeals.

So ordered.

Reversed.

■ MR. JUSTICE STEWART, concurring in the result.

The arrest in this case was made upon probable cause in a public place in broad daylight. The Court holds that this arrest did not violate the Fourth Amendment, and I agree. The Court does not decide, nor could it decide in this case, whether or under what circumstances an officer must obtain a warrant before he may lawfully enter a private place to effect an arrest. *See* Gerstein v. Pugh, 420 U.S. 103, 113 n. 13; Coolidge v. New Hampshire, 403 U.S. 443, 474–481; Jones v. United States, 357 U.S. 493, 499–500.

Compare United States v. Coplon, 185 F.2d 629, 633–636 (CA2 1950), cert. denied, 342 U.S. 920 (1952), with Coplon v. United States, 89 U.S.App.D.C. 103, 108–109, 191 F.2d 749, 753–754 (1951), cert. denied, 342 U.S. 926 (1952).

County of Riverside v. McLaughlin

500 U.S. 44 (1991)

■ O'CONNOR, J., delivered the opinion of the Court, in which REHNQUIST, C.J., and WHITE, KENNEDY, and SOUTER, JJ., joined.

In Gerstein v. Pugh, 420 U.S. 103 (1975), this Court held that the Fourth Amendment requires a prompt judicial determination of probable cause as a prerequisite to an extended pretrial detention following a warrantless arrest. This case requires us to define what is "prompt" under Gerstein.

I

This is a class action brought under 42 U.S.C. § 1983 challenging the manner in which the County of Riverside, California (County), provides probable cause determinations to persons arrested without a warrant. At issue is the County's policy of combining probable cause determinations with its arraignment procedures. Under County policy, which tracks closely the provisions of Cal.Penal Code Ann. § 825 (West 1985), arraignments must be conducted without unnecessary delay and, in any event, within two days of arrest. This 2-day requirement excludes from computation weekends and holidays. Thus, an individual arrested without a warrant late in the week may in some cases be held for as long as five days before receiving a probable cause determination. Over the Thanksgiving holiday, a 7-day delay is possible.

The parties dispute whether the combined probable cause/ arraignment procedure is available to all warrantless arrestees. Testimony by Riverside County District Attorney Grover Trask suggests that individuals arrested without warrants for felonies do not receive a probable cause determination until the preliminary hearing, which may not occur until 10 days after arraignment. 2 App. 298–299. Before this Court, however, the County represents that its policy is to provide probable cause determinations at arraignment for all persons arrested without a warrant, regardless of the nature of the charges against them. *Ibid. See also* Tr. of Oral Arg. 13. We need not resolve the factual inconsistency here. For present purposes, we accept the County's representation.

In August 1987, Donald Lee McLaughlin filed a complaint in the United States District Court for the Central District of California, seeking injunctive and declaratory relief on behalf of himself and " 'all others similarly situated.' " The complaint alleged that McLaughlin was then currently incarcerated in the Riverside County Jail and had not received a probable cause determination. He requested " 'an order and judgment requiring that the defendants and the County of Riverside provide in-custody arrestees, arrested without warrants, prompt probable cause, bail and arraignment hearings.' " Pet. for Cert. 6. Shortly thereafter, McLaughlin moved for class certification. The County moved to dismiss the complaint, asserting that McLaughlin lacked standing to bring the suit because he had failed to show, as required by Los Angeles v. Lyons, 461 U.S. 95 (1983), that he would again be subject to the allegedly unconstitutional conduct—i.e., a warrantless detention without a probable cause determination.

In light of the pending motion to dismiss, the District Court continued the hearing on the motion to certify the class. Various papers were submitted; then, in July 1988, the District Court accepted for filing a second amended complaint, which is the operative pleading here. From the record it appears that the District Court never explicitly ruled on defendants' motion to dismiss, but rather took it off the court's calendar in August 1988.

The second amended complaint named three additional plaintiffs— Johnny E. James, Diana Ray Simon, and Michael Scott Hyde— individually and as class representatives. The amended complaint alleged that each of the named plaintiffs had been arrested without a warrant, had received neither a prompt probable cause nor a bail hearing, and was still in custody. 1 App. 3. In November 1988, the District Court certified a class comprising "all present and future prisoners in the Riverside County Jail including those pretrial detainees arrested without warrants and held in the Riverside County Jail from August 1, 1987 to the present, and all such future detainees who have been or may be denied prompt probable cause, bail or arraignment hearings." 1 App. 7.

In March 1989, plaintiffs asked the District Court to issue a preliminary injunction requiring the County to provide all persons arrested without a warrant a judicial determination of probable cause within 36 hours of arrest. 1 App. 21. The District Court issued the injunction, holding that the County's existing practice violated this Court's decision in *Gerstein*. Without discussion, the District Court adopted a rule that the County provide probable cause determinations within 36 hours of arrest, except in exigent circumstances. The court "retained jurisdiction indefinitely" to ensure that the County established new procedures that complied with the injunction. 2 App. 333–334.

The United States Court of Appeals for the Ninth Circuit consolidated this case with another challenging an identical preliminary injunction issued against the County of San Bernardino. *See* McGregor v. County of San Bernardino, decided with McLaughlin v. County of Riverside, 888 F.2d 1276 (1989).

On November 8, 1989, the Court of Appeals affirmed the order granting the preliminary injunction against Riverside County. One aspect of the injunction against San Bernardino County was reversed by the Court of Appeals; that determination is not before us.

The Court of Appeals rejected Riverside County's *Lyons*-based standing argument, holding that the named plaintiffs had Article III standing to bring the class action for injunctive relief. 888 F.2d, at 1277.

It reasoned that, at the time plaintiffs filed their complaint, they were in custody and suffering injury as a result of defendants' allegedly unconstitutional action. The court then proceeded to the merits and determined that the County's policy of providing probable cause determinations at arraignment within 48 hours was "not in accord with *Gerstein*'s requirement of a determination 'promptly after arrest'" because no more than 36 hours were needed "to complete the administrative steps incident to arrest." *Id.*, at 1278.

The Ninth Circuit thus joined the Fourth and Seventh Circuits in interpreting *Gerstein* as requiring a probable cause determination immediately following completion of the administrative procedures incident to arrest. Llaguno v. Mingey, 763 F.2d 1560, 1567–1568 (CA7 1985) (en banc); Fisher v. Washington Metropolitan Area Transit Authority, 690 F.2d 1133, 1139–1141 (CA4 1982). By contrast, the Second Circuit understands *Gerstein* to "stres[s] the need for flexibility" and to permit States to combine probable cause determinations with other pretrial proceedings. Williams v. Ward, 845 F.2d 374, 386 (1988), cert. denied, 488 U.S. 1020 (1989). We granted certiorari to resolve this conflict among the Circuits as to what constitutes a "prompt" probable cause determination under *Gerstein*.

II

As an initial matter, the County renews its claim that plaintiffs lack standing. It explains that the main thrust of plaintiffs' suit is that they are entitled to "prompt" probable cause determinations and insists that this is, by definition, a time-limited violation. Once sufficient time has passed, the County argues, the constitutional violation is complete because a probable cause determination made after that point would no longer be "prompt." Thus, at least as to the named plaintiffs, there is no standing because it is too late for them to receive a prompt hearing and, under *Lyons*, they cannot show that they are likely to be subjected again to the unconstitutional conduct.

We reject the County's argument. . . . This case is easily distinguished from *Lyons,* in which the constitutionally objectionable practice ceased altogether before the plaintiff filed his complaint.

It is true, of course, that the claims of the named plaintiffs have since been rendered moot; eventually, they either received probable cause determinations or were released. Our cases leave no doubt, however, that by obtaining class certification, plaintiffs preserved the merits of the controversy for our review. In factually similar cases we have held that "the termination of a class representative's claim does not moot the claims of the unnamed members of the class." *See, e.g., Gerstein*, 420 U.S., at 110–111, n. 11, citing Sosna v. Iowa, 419 U.S. 393 (1975); Schall v. Martin, 467 U.S. 253, 256, n. 3 (1984). That the class was not certified until after the named plaintiffs' claims had become moot does not deprive us of jurisdiction. We recognized in *Gerstein* that "[s]ome claims are so inherently transitory that the trial court will not have even enough time to rule on a motion for class certification before the proposed representative's individual interest expires." United States Parole Comm'n v. Geraghty, 445 U.S. 388, 399 (1980), citing *Gerstein, supra,* 420 U.S., at 110, n. 11. In such cases, the "relation back" doctrine is properly invoked to preserve the merits of the case for judicial resolution. *See* Swisher v. Brady, 438 U.S. 204, 213–214, n. 11 (1978); *Sosna, supra,* 419 U.S., at 402. Accordingly, we proceed to the merits.

III

A

In *Gerstein,* this Court held unconstitutional Florida procedures under which persons arrested without a warrant could remain in police custody for 30 days or more without a judicial determination of probable cause. In reaching this conclusion we attempted to reconcile important competing interests. On the one hand, States have a strong interest in protecting public safety by taking into custody those persons who are reasonably suspected of having engaged in criminal activity, even where there has been no opportunity for a prior judicial determination of probable cause. 420 U.S., at 112. On the other hand, prolonged detention based on incorrect or unfounded suspicion may unjustly "imperil [a] suspect's job, interrupt his source of income, and impair his family relationships." *Id.,* at 114. We sought to balance these competing concerns by holding that States "must provide a fair and reliable determination of probable cause as a condition for any significant pretrial restraint of liberty, and this determination must be made by a judicial officer either before or promptly after arrest." *Id.,* at 125 (emphasis added).

The Court thus established a "practical compromise" between the rights of individuals and the realities of law enforcement. *Id.,* at 113. Under *Gerstein,* warrantless arrests are permitted but persons arrested without a warrant must promptly be brought before a neutral magistrate for a judicial determination of probable cause. *Id.,* at 114. Significantly, the Court stopped short of holding that jurisdictions were constitutionally compelled to provide a probable cause hearing immediately upon taking a suspect into custody and completing booking procedures. We acknowledged the burden that proliferation of pretrial proceedings places on the criminal justice system and recognized that the interests of everyone involved, including those persons who are arrested, might be disserved by introducing further procedural complexity into an already intricate system. *Id.,* at 119–123. Accordingly, we left it to the individual States to integrate prompt probable cause determinations into their differing systems of pretrial procedures. *Id.,* at 123–124.

In so doing, we gave proper deference to the demands of federalism. We recognized that "state systems of criminal procedure vary widely" in the nature and number of pretrial procedures they provide, and we noted that there is no single "preferred" approach. *Id.,* at 123. We explained further that "flexibility and experimentation by the States" with respect to integrating probable cause determinations was desirable and that each State should settle upon an approach "to accord with [the] State's pretrial procedure viewed as a whole." *Ibid.* Our purpose in *Gerstein* was to make clear that the Fourth Amendment requires every State to provide prompt determinations of probable cause, but that the Constitution does not impose on the States a rigid procedural framework. Rather, individual States may choose to comply in different ways.

Inherent in *Gerstein*'s invitation to the States to experiment and adapt was the recognition that the Fourth Amendment does not compel an immediate determination of probable cause upon completing the administrative steps incident to arrest. Plainly, if a probable cause hearing is constitutionally compelled the moment a suspect is finished being "booked," there is no room whatsoever for "flexibility and experimentation by the States." *Ibid.* Incorporating probable cause determinations "into the procedure for setting bail or fixing other conditions of pretrial release"—which *Gerstein* explicitly contemplated, *id.*, at 124—would be impossible. Waiting even a few hours so that a bail hearing or arraignment could take place at the same time as the probable cause determination would amount to a constitutional violation. Clearly, *Gerstein* is not that inflexible.

Notwithstanding *Gerstein*'s discussion of flexibility, the Court of Appeals for the Ninth Circuit held that no flexibility was permitted. It construed *Gerstein* as "requir[ing] a probable cause determination to be made as soon as the administrative steps incident to arrest were completed, and that such steps should require only a brief period." 888 F.2d, at 1278 (emphasis added) (internal quotation marks omitted). This same reading is advanced by the dissents. *See post,* at 1671 (opinion of MARSHALL, J.); *post* at 1672–1673, 1674 (opinion of SCALIA, J.). The foregoing discussion readily demonstrates the error of this approach. *Gerstein* held that probable cause determinations must be prompt—not immediate. The Court explained that "flexibility and experimentation" were "desirab[le]"; that "[t]here is no single preferred pretrial procedure"; and that "the nature of the probable cause determination usually will be shaped to accord with a State's pretrial procedure viewed as a whole." 420 U.S., at 123. The Court of Appeals and Justice SCALIA disregard these statements, relying instead on selective quotations from the Court's opinion. As we have explained, *Gerstein* struck a balance between competing interests; a proper understanding of the decision is possible only if one takes into account both sides of the equation.

Justice SCALIA claims to find support for his approach in the common law. He points to several statements from the early 1800's to the effect that an arresting officer must bring a person arrested without a warrant before a judicial officer " 'as soon as he reasonably can.' " *Post,* at 1672 (emphasis in original). This vague admonition offers no more support for the dissent's inflexible standard than does *Gerstein*'s statement that a hearing follow "promptly after arrest." 420 U.S., at 125.

As mentioned at the outset, the question before us today is what is "prompt" under *Gerstein*. We answer that question by recognizing that *Gerstein* struck a balance between competing interests.

B

Given that *Gerstein* permits jurisdictions to incorporate probable cause determinations into other pretrial procedures, some delays are inevitable. For example, where, as in Riverside County, the probable cause determination is combined with arraignment, there will be delays caused by paperwork and logistical problems. Records will have to be reviewed, charging documents drafted, appearance of counsel arranged, and appropriate bail determined. On weekends, when the number of arrests is often higher and available resources tend to be limited, arraignments may get pushed back even further. In our view, the Fourth Amendment permits a reasonable postponement of a probable cause determination while the police cope with the everyday problems of processing suspects through an overly burdened criminal justice system.

But flexibility has its limits; *Gerstein* is not a blank check. A State has no legitimate interest in detaining for extended periods individuals who have been arrested without probable cause. The Court recognized in *Gerstein* that a person arrested without a warrant is entitled to a fair and reliable determination of probable cause and that this determination must be made promptly.

Unfortunately, as lower court decisions applying *Gerstein* have demonstrated, it is not enough to say that probable cause determinations must be "prompt." This vague standard simply has not provided sufficient guidance. Instead, it has led to a flurry of systemic challenges to city and county practices, putting federal judges in the role of making legislative judgments and overseeing local jailhouse operations. See, e.g., McGregor v. County of San Bernardino, decided with McLaughlin v. County of Riverside, 888 F.2d 1276 (CA9 1989); Scott v. Gates, Civ. No. 84-8647 (CD Cal., Oct. 3, 1988); *See* also Bernard v. Palo Alto, 699 F.2d 1023 (CA9 1983); Sanders v. Houston, 543 F.Supp. 694 (SD Tex.1982), aff'd, 741 F.2d 1379 (CA5 1984); Lively v. Cullinane, 451 F.Supp. 1000 (DC 1978).

Our task in this case is to articulate more clearly the boundaries of what is permissible under the Fourth Amendment. Although we hesitate to announce that the Constitution compels a specific time limit, it is important to provide some degree of certainty so that States and counties may establish procedures with confidence that they fall within constitutional bounds. Taking into account the competing interests articulated in *Gerstein,* we believe that a jurisdiction that provides judicial determinations of probable cause within 48 hours of arrest will, as a general matter, comply with the promptness requirement of Gerstein. For this reason, such jurisdictions will be immune from systemic challenges.

This is not to say that the probable cause determination in a particular case passes constitutional muster simply because it is provided within 48 hours. Such a hearing may nonetheless violate *Gerstein* if the arrested individual can prove that his or her probable cause determination was delayed unreasonably. Examples of unreasonable delay are delays for the purpose of gathering additional evidence to justify the arrest, a delay motivated by ill will against the arrested individual, or delay for delay's sake. In evaluating whether the delay in a particular case is unreasonable, however, courts must allow a substantial degree of flexibility. Courts cannot ignore the often unavoidable delays in transporting arrested persons from one facility to another, handling late-night bookings where no magistrate is readily available, obtaining the presence of an arresting officer who may be busy processing other suspects or securing the premises of an arrest, and other practical realities.

Where an arrested individual does not receive a probable cause determination within 48 hours, the calculus changes. In such a case, the arrested individual does not bear the burden of proving an unreasonable delay. Rather, the burden shifts to the government to demonstrate the existence of a bona fide emergency or other extraordinary circumstance. The fact that in a particular case it may take longer than 48 hours to consolidate pretrial proceedings does not qualify as an extraordinary circumstance. Nor, for that matter, do intervening weekends. A jurisdiction that chooses to offer combined proceedings must do so as soon as is reasonably feasible, but in no event later than 48 hours after arrest.

Justice SCALIA urges that 24 hours is a more appropriate outer boundary for providing probable cause determinations. In arguing that any delay in probable cause hearings beyond completing the administrative steps incident to arrest and arranging for a magistrate is unconstitutional, Justice SCALIA, in effect, adopts the view of the Court of Appeals. Yet he ignores entirely the Court of Appeals' determination of the time required to complete those procedures. That court, better situated than this one, concluded that it takes 36 hours to process arrested persons in Riverside County. 888 F.2d, at 1278. In advocating a 24-hour rule, Justice SCALIA would compel Riverside County—and countless others across the Nation—to speed up its criminal justice mechanisms substantially, presumably by allotting local tax dollars to hire additional police officers and magistrates. There may be times when the Constitution compels such direct interference with local control, but this is not one. As we have explained, *Gerstein* clearly contemplated a reasonable accommodation between legitimate competing concerns. We do no more than recognize that such accommodation can take place without running afoul of the Fourth Amendment.

Everyone agrees that the police should make every attempt to minimize the time a presumptively innocent individual spends in jail. One way to do so is to provide a judicial determination of probable cause immediately upon completing the administrative steps incident to arrest—i.e., as soon as the suspect has been booked, photographed, and fingerprinted. As Justice SCALIA explains, several States, laudably, have adopted this approach. The Constitution does not compel so rigid a schedule, however. Under *Gerstein*, jurisdictions may choose to combine probable cause determinations with other pretrial proceedings, so long as they do so promptly. This necessarily means that only certain proceedings are candidates for combination. Only those proceedings that arise very early in the pretrial process—such as bail hearings and arraignments—may be chosen. Even then, every effort must be made to expedite the combined proceedings. *See* 420 U.S., at 124.

IV

For the reasons we have articulated, we conclude that Riverside County is entitled to combine probable cause determinations with arraignments. The record indicates, however, that the County's current policy and practice do not comport fully with the principles we have outlined. The County's current policy is to offer combined proceedings within two days, exclusive of Saturdays, Sundays, or holidays. As a result, persons arrested on Thursdays may have to wait until the following Monday before they receive a probable cause determination. The delay is even longer if there is an intervening holiday. Thus, the County's regular practice exceeds the 48-hour period we deem constitutionally permissible, meaning that the County is not immune from systemic challenges, such as this class action.

As to arrests that occur early in the week, the County's practice is that "arraignment[s] usually tak[e] place on the last day" possible. 1 App. 82. There may well be legitimate reasons for this practice; alternatively, this may constitute delay for delay's sake. We leave it to the Court of Appeals and the District Court, on remand, to make this determination.

The judgment of the Court of Appeals is vacated, and the case is remanded for further proceedings consistent with this opinion.

It is so ordered.

■ JUSTICE MARSHALL, with whom JUSTICE BLACKMUN and JUSTICE STEVENS join, dissenting.

In Gerstein v. Pugh, 420 U.S. 103 (1975), this Court held that an individual detained following a warrantless arrest is entitled to a "prompt" judicial determination of probable cause as a prerequisite to any further restraint on his liberty. *See id.*, at 114–116, 125. I agree with Justice SCALIA that a probable-cause hearing is sufficiently "prompt" under *Gerstein* only when provided immediately upon completion of the "administrative steps incident to arrest," *id.*, at 114. *See post*, at 1673. Because the Court of Appeals correctly held that the County of Riverside must provide probable-cause hearings as soon as it completes the administrative steps incident to arrest, *See* 888 F.2d 1276, 1278 (CA9

1989), I would affirm the judgment of the Court of Appeals. Accordingly, I dissent.

■ JUSTICE SCALIA, dissenting.

The story is told of the elderly judge who, looking back over a long career, observes with satisfaction that "when I was young, I probably let stand some convictions that should have been overturned, and when I was old, I probably set aside some that should have stood; so overall, justice was done." I sometimes think that is an appropriate analog to this Court's constitutional jurisprudence, which alternately creates rights that the Constitution does not contain and denies rights that it does. Compare Roe v. Wade, 410 U.S. 113 (1973) (right to abortion does exist), with Maryland v. Craig, 497 U.S. 836 (1990) (right to be confronted with witnesses, U.S. Const.Amdt. 6, does not). Thinking that neither the one course nor the other is correct, nor the two combined, I dissent from today's decision, which eliminates a very old right indeed.

I

The Court views the task before it as one of "balanc[ing] [the] competing concerns" of "protecting public safety," on the one hand, and avoiding "prolonged detention based on incorrect or unfounded suspicion," on the other hand, ante, at 1668. It purports to reaffirm the " 'practical compromise' " between these concerns struck in Gerstein v. Pugh, 420 U.S. 103 (1975), *ante,* at 1668. There is assuredly room for such an approach in resolving novel questions of search and seizure under the "reasonableness" standard that the Fourth Amendment sets forth. But not, I think, in resolving those questions on which a clear answer already existed in 1791 and has been generally adhered to by the traditions of our society ever since. As to those matters, the "balance" has already been struck, the "practical compromise" reached—and it is the function of the Bill of Rights to preserve that judgment, not only against the changing views of Presidents and Members of Congress, but also against the changing views of Justices whom Presidents appoint and Members of Congress confirm to this Court.

The issue before us today is of precisely that sort. As we have recently had occasion to explain, the Fourth Amendment's prohibition of "unreasonable seizures," insofar as it applies to seizure of the person, preserves for our citizens the traditional protections against unlawful arrest afforded by the common law. *See* California v. Hodari D., 499 U.S. 621 1991). One of those—one of the most important of those—was that a person arresting a suspect without a warrant must deliver the arrestee to a magistrate "as soon as he reasonably can." 2 M. Hale, Pleas of the Crown 95, n. 13 (1st Am. ed. 1847). *See also* 4 W. Blackstone, Commentaries * 289, * 293; Wright v. Court, 107 Eng.Rep. 1182 (K. B. 1825) ("[I]t is the duty of a person arresting any one on suspicion of felony to take him before a justice as soon as he reasonably can"); 1 R. Burn, Justice of the Peace 276–277 (1837) ("When a constable arrests a party for treason or felony, he must take him before a magistrate to be examined as soon as he reasonably can") (emphasis omitted). The practice in the United States was the same. *See* e.g., 5 Am.Jur.2d, Arrest, §§ 76, 77 (1962); Venable v. Huddy, 77 N.J.L. 351, 72 A. 10, 11 (1909); Atchison, T. & S.F.R. Co. v. Hinsdell, 76 Kan. 74, 76, 90 P. 800, 801 (1907); Ocean S.S. Co. v. Williams, 69 Ga. 251, 262 (1883); Johnson v. Mayor and City Council of Americus, 46 Ga. 80, 86–87 (1872); Low v. Evans, 16 Ind. 486, 489 (1861); Tubbs v. Tukey, 57 Mass. 438, 440 (1849) (warrant); Perkins, The Law of Arrest, 25 Iowa L.Rev. 201, 254 (1940). Cf. Pepper v. Mayes, 81 Ky. 673 (1884). It was clear, moreover, that the only element bearing upon the reasonableness of delay was not such circumstances as the pressing need to conduct further investigation, but the arresting officer's ability, once the prisoner had been secured, to reach a magistrate who could issue the needed warrant for further detention. 5 Am.Jur.2d, Arrest, *supra*, §§ 76, 77 (1962); 1 Restatement of Torts § 134, Comment b (1934); Keefe v. Hart, 213 Mass. 476, 482, 100 N.E. 558, 559 (1913); Leger v. Warren, 62 Ohio St. 500, 57 N.E. 506, 508 (1900); Burk v. Howley, 179 Pa. 539, 551, 36 A. 327, 329 (1897); Kirk & Son v. Garrett, 84 Md. 383, 405, 35 A. 1089, 1091 (1896); Simmons v. Vandyke, 138 Ind. 380, 384, 37 N.E. 973, 974 (1894) (dictum); Ocean S.S. Co. v. Williams, *supra*, at 263; Hayes v. Mitchell, 69 Ala. 452, 455 (1881); Kenerson v. Bacon, 41 Vt. 573, 577 (1869); Green v. Kennedy, 48 N.Y. 653, 654 (1871); Schneider v. McLane, 3 Keyes 568 (NY App. 1867); Annot., 51 L.R.A. 216 (1901). *Cf.* Wheeler v. Nesbitt, 24 How. 544, 552 (1860). Any detention beyond the period within which a warrant could have been obtained rendered the officer liable for false imprisonment. *See, e.g.,* Twilley v. Perkins, 77 Md. 252, 265, 26 A. 286, 289 (1893); Wiggins v. Norton, 83 Ga. 148, 152, 9 S.E. 607, 608–609 (1889); Brock v. Stimson, 108 Mass. 520 (1871); Annot., 98 A.L.R.2d 966 (1964).

We discussed and relied upon this common-law understanding in *Gerstein, see* 420 U.S., at 114–116, holding that the period of warrantless detention must be limited to the time necessary to complete the arrest and obtain the magistrate's review.

> "[A] policeman's on-the-scene assessment of probable cause provides legal justification for arresting a person suspected of crime, and for a brief period of detention to take the administrative steps incident to arrest. Once the suspect is in custody . . . the reasons that justify dispensing with the magistrate's neutral judgment evaporate." *Id.*, at 113–114 (emphasis added). . . .

Today, however, the Court discerns something quite different in *Gerstein*. It finds that the plain statements set forth above (not to mention the common-law tradition of liberty upon which they were based) were trumped by the implication of a later dictum in the case which, according to the Court, manifests a "recognition that the Fourth Amendment does not compel an immediate determination of probable cause upon completing the administrative steps incident to arrest." (emphasis added). Of course *Gerstein* did not say, nor do I contend, that an "immediate" determination is required. But what the Court today means by "not immediate" is that the delay can be attributable to something other than completing the administrative steps incident to arrest and arranging for the magistrate—namely, to the administrative convenience of combining the probable-cause determination with other state proceedings. The result, we learn later in the opinion, is that what *Gerstein* meant by "a brief period of detention to take the administrative steps incident to arrest" is two full days. I think it is clear that the case neither said nor meant any such thing.

Since the Court's opinion hangs so much upon *Gerstein*, it is worth quoting the allegedly relevant passage in its entirety.

> "Although we conclude that the Constitution does not require an adversary determination of probable cause, we recognize that state systems of criminal procedure vary widely. There is no single preferred pretrial procedure, and the nature of the probable cause determination usually will be shaped to accord with a State's pretrial procedure viewed as a whole. While we limit our holding to the precise requirement of the Fourth Amendment, we recognize the desirability of flexibility and experimentation by the States. It may be found desirable, for example, to make the probable cause determination at the suspect's first appearance before a judicial officer, . . . or the determination may be incorporated into the procedure for setting bail or fixing other conditions of pretrial release. In some States, existing procedures may satisfy the requirement of the Fourth Amendment. Others may require only minor adjustment, such as acceleration of existing preliminary hearings. Current proposals for criminal procedure reform suggest other ways of testing probable cause for detention. Whatever procedure a State may adopt, it must provide a fair and reliable determination of probable cause as a condition for any significant pretrial restraint of liberty, and this determination must be made by a judicial officer either before or promptly after arrest." 420 U.S., at 123–125 (footnotes omitted; emphasis added).

The Court's holding today rests upon the statement that "we recognize the desirability of flexibility and experimentation." But in its context that statement plainly refers to the nature of the hearing and not to its timing. That the timing is a given and a constant is plain from the italicized phrases, especially that which concludes the relevant passage. The timing is specifically addressed in the previously quoted passage of the opinion, which makes clear that "promptly after arrest" means upon completion of the "administrative steps incident to arrest." It is not apparent to me, as it is to the Court, that on these terms "[i]ncorporating probable cause determinations 'into the procedure for setting bail or fixing other conditions of pretrial release' . . . would be impossible," *ante,* at 1668; but it is clear that, if and when it is impossible, *Gerstein* envisioned that the procedural "experimentation," rather than the Fourth Amendment's requirement of prompt presentation to a magistrate, would have to yield.

Of course even if the implication of the dictum in *Gerstein* were what the Court says, that would be poor reason for keeping a wrongfully arrested citizen in jail contrary to the clear dictates of the Fourth Amendment. What is most revealing of the frailty of today's opinion is that it relies upon nothing but that implication from a dictum, plus its own (quite irrefutable because entirely value laden) "balancing" of the competing demands of the individual and the State. With respect to the point at issue here, different times and different places—even highly liberal times and places—have struck that balance in different ways. Some Western democracies currently permit the executive a period of detention without impartially adjudicated cause. In England, for example, the Prevention of Terrorism Act 1989, §§ 14(4), 5, permits suspects to be held without presentation and without charge for seven days. 12 Halsbury's Stat. 1294 (4th ed. 1989). It was the purpose of the Fourth Amendment to put this matter beyond time, place, and judicial predilection, incorporating the traditional common-law guarantees against unlawful arrest. The Court says not a word about these guarantees, and they are determinative. *Gerstein*'s approval of a "brief period" of delay to accomplish "administrative steps incident to an arrest" is already a questionable extension of the traditional formulation, though it probably has little practical effect and can perhaps be justified on de minimis grounds.[2] To expand *Gerstein*, however, into an authorization for 48-hour detention related neither to the obtaining of a magistrate nor the administrative "completion" of the arrest seems to me utterly unjustified. Mr. McLaughlin was entitled to have a prompt impartial determination that there was reason to deprive him of his liberty—not according to a schedule that suits the State's convenience in piggybacking various proceedings, but as soon as his arrest was completed and the magistrate could be procured.

II

I have finished discussing what I consider the principal question in this case, which is what factors determine whether the postarrest determination of probable cause has been (as the Fourth Amendment requires) "reasonably prompt." The Court and I both accept two of those factors, completion of the administrative steps incident to arrest and

---

[2]   Ordinarily, I think, there would be plenty of time for "administrative steps" while the arrangements for a hearing are being made. But if, for example, a magistrate is present in the precinct and entertaining probable-cause hearings at the very moment a wrongfully arrested person is brought in, I see no basis for intentionally delaying the hearing in order to subject the person to a cataloging of his personal effects, fingerprinting, photographing, etc. He ought not be exposed to those indignities if there is no proper basis for constraining his freedom of movement, and if that can immediately be determined.

arranging for a magistrate's probable-cause determination. Since we disagree, however, upon a third factor—the Court believing, as I do not, that "combining" the determination with other proceedings justifies a delay—we necessarily disagree as well on the subsequent question, which can be described as the question of the absolute time limit. Any determinant of "reasonable promptness" that is within the control of the State (as the availability of the magistrate, the personnel and facilities for completing administrative procedures incident to arrest, and the timing of "combined procedures" all are) must be restricted by some outer time limit, or else the promptness guarantee would be worthless. If, for example, it took a full year to obtain a probable-cause determination in California because only a single magistrate had been authorized to perform that function throughout the State, the hearing would assuredly not qualify as "reasonably prompt." At some point, legitimate reasons for delay become illegitimate.

I do not know how the Court calculated its outer limit of 48 hours. I must confess, however, that I do not know how I would do so either, if I thought that one justification for delay could be the State's "desire to combine." There are no standards for "combination," and as we acknowledged in *Gerstein* the various procedures that might be combined "vary widely" from State to State. 420 U.S., at 123. So as far as I can discern (though I cannot pretend to be able to do better), the Court simply decided that, given the administrative convenience of "combining," it is not so bad for an utterly innocent person to wait 48 hours in jail before being released.

If one eliminates (as one should) that novel justification for delay, determining the outer boundary of reasonableness is a more objective and more manageable task. We were asked to undertake it in *Gerstein*, but declined—wisely, I think, since we had before us little data to support any figure we might choose. As the Court notes, however, *Gerstein* has engendered a number of cases addressing not only the scope of the procedures "incident to arrest," but also their duration. The conclusions reached by the judges in those cases, and by others who have addressed the question, are surprisingly similar. I frankly would prefer even more information, and for that purpose would have supported reargument on the single question of an outer time limit. The data available are enough to convince me, however, that certainly no more than 24 hours is needed.[3]

---

[3]   The Court claims that the Court of Appeals "concluded that it takes 36 hours to process arrested persons in Riverside County." *Ante*, at 1670. The court concluded no such thing. It concluded that 36 hours (the time limit imposed by the District Court) was "ample" time to complete the arrest, 888 F.2d 1276, 1278 (CA9 1989), and that the county had provided no evidence to demonstrate the contrary. The District Court, in turn, had not made any evidentiary finding to the effect that 36 hours was necessary, but for unexplained reasons said that it "declines to adopt the 24 hour standard [generally applied by other courts], but adopts a 36 hour limit, except in exigent circumstances." McLaughlin v. County of Riverside, No. CV87-5597 RG (CD Cal., Apr. 19, 1989). 2 App. 332. Before this Court, moreover, the county has acknowledged that "nearly 90 percent of all cases . . . can be completed in 24 hours or less," Briefs for District Attorney, County of Riverside, as Amicus Curiae 16, and the examples given to explain the other 10 percent are entirely unpersuasive (heavy traffic on the Southern California freeways; the

With one exception, no federal court considering the question has regarded 24 hours as an inadequate amount of time to complete arrest procedures, and with the same exception every court actually setting a limit for a probable-cause determination based on those procedures has selected 24 hours. (The exception would not count Sunday within the 24-hour limit.) . . . Federal courts have reached a similar conclusion in applying Federal Rule of Criminal Procedure 5(a), which requires presentment before a federal magistrate "without unnecessary delay." See, e.g., Thomas, *The Poisoned Fruit of Pretrial Detention,* 61 N.Y.U.L.Rev. 413, 450, n. 238 (1986) (citing cases). And state courts have similarly applied a 24-hour limit under state statutes requiring presentment without "unreasonable delay." New York, for example, has concluded that no more than 24 hours is necessary from arrest to arraignment, People ex rel. Maxian v. Brown, 164 App.Div.2d, at 62–64, 561 N.Y.S.2d, at 421–422. Twenty-nine States have statutes similar to New York's, which require either presentment or arraignment "without unnecessary delay" or "forthwith"; eight States explicitly require presentment or arraignment within 24 hours; and only seven States have statutes explicitly permitting a period longer than 24 hours. [citation omitted] Since the States requiring a probable-cause hearing within 24 hours include both New York and Alaska, it is unlikely that circumstances of population or geography demand a longer period. Twenty-four hours is consistent with the American Law Institute's Model Code. ALI, Model Code of Pre-Arraignment Procedure § 310.1 (1975). And while the American Bar Association in its proposed rules of criminal procedure initially required that presentment simply be made "without unnecessary delay," it has recently concluded that no more than six hours should be required, except at night. Uniform Rules of Criminal Procedure, 10 U.L.A. App., Criminal Justice Standard 10–4.1 (Spec.Pamph.1987). Finally, the conclusions of these commissions and judges, both state and federal, are supported by commentators who have examined the question. See, e.g., . . . Note, 74 Minn.L.Rev., at 207–209.

In my view, absent extraordinary circumstances, it is an "unreasonable seizure" within the meaning of the Fourth Amendment for the police, having arrested a suspect without a warrant, to delay a determination of probable cause for the arrest either (1) for reasons unrelated to arrangement of the probable-cause determination or completion of the steps incident to arrest, or (2) beyond 24 hours after the arrest. Like the Court, I would treat the time limit as a presumption;

---

need to wait for arrestees who are properly detainable because they are visibly under the influence of drugs to come out of that influence before they can be questioned about other crimes; the need to take blood and urine samples promptly in drug cases) with one exception: awaiting completion of investigations and filing of investigation reports by various state and federal agencies. *Id.*, at 16–17. We have long held, of course, that delaying a probable-cause determination for the latter reason—effecting what Judge Posner has aptly called "imprisonment on suspicion, while the police look for evidence to confirm their suspicion," Llaguno v. Mingey, 763 F.2d 1560, 1568 (CA7 1985)—is improper. *See Gerstein,* 420 U.S., at 120, n.21, citing Mallory v. United States, 354 U.S. 449, 456 (1957).

when the 24 hours are exceeded the burden shifts to the police to adduce unforeseeable circumstances justifying the additional delay.

* * *

A few weeks before issuance of today's opinion there appeared in the Washington Post the story of protracted litigation arising from the arrest of a student who entered a restaurant in Charlottesville, Virginia, one evening, to look for some friends. Failing to find them, he tried to leave—but refused to pay a $5 fee (required by the restaurant's posted rules) for failing to return a red tab he had been issued to keep track of his orders. According to the story, he "was taken by police to the Charlottesville jail" at the restaurant's request. "There, a magistrate refused to issue an arrest warrant," and he was released. Washington Post, Apr. 29, 1991, p. 1. That is how it used to be; but not, according to today's decision, how it must be in the future. If the Fourth Amendment meant then what the Court says it does now, the student could lawfully have been held for as long as it would have taken to arrange for his arraignment, up to a maximum of 48 hours.

Justice Story wrote that the Fourth Amendment "is little more than the affirmance of a great constitutional doctrine of the common law." 3 J. Story, Commentaries on the Constitution 748 (1833). It should not become less than that. One hears the complaint, nowadays, that the Fourth Amendment has become constitutional law for the guilty; that it benefits the career criminal (through the exclusionary rule) often and directly, but the ordinary citizen remotely if at all. By failing to protect the innocent arrestee, today's opinion reinforces that view. The common-law rule of prompt hearing had as its primary beneficiaries the innocent—not those whose fully justified convictions must be overturned to scold the police; nor those who avoid conviction because the evidence, while convincing, does not establish guilt beyond a reasonable doubt; but those so blameless that there was not even good reason to arrest them. While in recent years we have invented novel applications of the Fourth Amendment to release the unquestionably guilty, we today repudiate one of its core applications so that the presumptively innocent may be left in jail. Hereafter a law-abiding citizen wrongfully arrested may be compelled to await the grace of a Dickensian bureaucratic machine, as it churns its cycle for up to two days—never once given the opportunity to show a judge that there is absolutely no reason to hold him, that a mistake has been made. In my view, this is the image of a system of justice that has lost its ancient sense of priority, a system that few Americans would recognize as our own.

I respectfully dissent.

Shadwick v. City of Tampa

407 U.S. 345 (1972)

■ MR. JUSTICE POWELL delivered the opinion for a unanimous Court.

The charter of Tampa, Florida, authorizes the issuance of certain arrest warrants by clerks of the Tampa Municipal Court. The sole question in this case is whether these clerks qualify as neutral and detached magistrates for purposes of the Fourth Amendment. We hold that they do.

Appellant was arrested for impaired driving on a warrant issued by a clerk of the municipal court. He moved the court to quash the warrnt on the ground that it was issued by a nonjudicial officer in violation of the Fourth and Fourteenth Amendments. When the motion was denied, he initiated proceedings in the Florida courts by means of that State's writ of common-law certiorari. The state proceedings culminated in the holding of the Florida Supreme Court that '(t)he clerk and deputy clerks of the municipal court of the City of Tampa are neutral and detached 'magistrates' . . . for the purpose of issuing arrest warrants within the requirements of the United States Constitution . . .' 250 So.2d 4, 5 (1971). We noted probable jurisdiction, 404 U.S. 1014 (1972).

I

A clerk of the municipal court is appointed by the city clerk from a classified list of civil servants and assigned to work in the municipal court. The statute does not specify the qualifications necessary for this job, but no law degree or special legal training is required. The clerk's duties are to receive traffic fines, prepare the court's dockets and records, fill out commitment papers and perform other routine clerical tasks. Apparently he may issue subpoenas. He may not, however, sit as a judge, and he may not issue a search warrant or even a felony or misdemeanor arrest warrant for violations of state laws. The only warrants he may issue are for the arrest of those charged with having breached municipal ordinances of the city of Tampa.

Appellant, contending that the Fourth Amendment requires that warrants be issued by 'judicial officers,' argues that even this limited warrant authority is constitutionally invalid. He reasons that warrant applications of whatever nature cannot be assured the discerning, independent review compelled by the Fourth Amendment when the review is performed by less than a judicial officer. It is less than clear, however, as to who would qualify as a 'judicial officer' under appellant's theory. There is some suggestion in appellant's brief that a judicial officer must be a lawyer or the municipal court judge himself. A more complete portrayal of appellant's position would be that the Tampa clerks are disqualified as judicial officers not merely because they are not lawyers or judges, but because they lack the institutional independence associated with the judiciary in that they are members of the civil service, appointed by the city clerk, 'an executive official,' and enjoy no statutorily specified tenure in office.

II

Past decisions of the Court has mentioned review by a 'judicial officer' prior to issuance of a warrant, Whiteley v. Warden, 401 U.S. 560, 564 (1971); Katz v. United States, 389 U.S. 347, 356 (1967); Wong Sun v. United States, 371 U.S. 471, 481–482 (1963); Jones v. United States, 362 U.S. 257, 270 (1960); Johnson v. United States, 333 U.S. 10, 14 (1948). In some cases the term 'judicial officer' appears to have been used interchangeably with that of 'magistrate.' *Katz v. United States, supra,* and *Johnson v. United States, supra.* In others, it was intended simply to underscore the now accepted fact that someone independent of the police and prosecution must determine probable cause. *Jones v. United States, supra; Wong Sun v. United States, supra.* The very term 'judicial officer' implies, of course, some connection with the judicial branch. But it has never been held that only a lawyer or judge could grant a warrant, regardless of the court system or the type of warrant involved. In *Jones, supra,* at 270–271 of 362 U.S., the Court implied that United States Commissioners, many of whom were not lawyers or judges, were nonetheless 'independent judicial officers.'

The Court frequently has employed the term 'magistrate' to denote those who may issue warrants. Coolidge v. New Hampshire, 403 U.S. 443, 449–453 (1971); *Whiteley v. Warden, supra,* at 566 of 401 U.S.; *Katz v. United States, supra,* at 356–357, of 389 U.S.; United States v. Ventresca, 380 U.S. 102 (1965); Giordenello v. United States, 357 U.S. 480, 486 (1958); *Johnson v. United States, supra,* at 13–14 of 333 U.S.; United States v. Lefkowitz, 285 U.S. 452, 464 (1932). Historically, a magistrate has been defined broadly as 'a public civil officer, possessing such power—legislative, executive, or judicial—as the government appointing him may ordain,' Compton v. Alabama, 214 U.S. 1, 7 (1909), or, in a narrower sense 'an inferior judicial officer, such as a justice of the peace.' Ibid. More recent definitions have not much changed.[7]

An examination of the Court's decisions reveals that the terms 'magistrate' and 'judicial officer' have been used interchangeably. Little attempt was made to define either term, to distinguish the one from the other, or to advance one as the definitive Fourth Amendment requirement. We find no commendment in either term, however, that all warrant authority must reside exclusively in a lawyer or judge. Such a

---

[7] In *Compton,* a notary public was deemed a 'magistrate,' but the Court has nowhere indicated that the term denotes solely a lawyer or judge. Webster's Dictionary (2d ed. 1957), defines magistrate as '(a) person clothed with power as a public civil officer; a public civil officer invested with executive or judicial powers . . .' or, more narrowly, '(a) magistrate of a class having summary, often criminal, jurisdiction, as a justice of the peace, or one of certain officials having a similar jurisdiction . . .' Random House Dictionary (1966) defines magistrate as (1) 'a civil officer charged with the administration of the law' and (2) 'a minor judicial officer, as a justice of the peace or a police justice, having jurisdiction to try minor criminal cases and to conduct preliminary examinations of persons charged with serious crimes.'

requirement would have been incongruous when even within the federal system warrants were until recently widely issued by nonlawyers.

To attempt to extract further significance from the above terminology would be both unnecessary and futile. The substance of the Constitution's warrant requirements does not turn on the labeling of the issuing party. The warrant traditionally has represented an independent assurance that a search and arrest will not proceed without probable cause to believe that a crime has been committed and that the person or place named in the warrant is involved in the crime. Thus, an issuing magistrate must meet two tests. He must be neutral and detached, and he must be capable of determining whether probable cause exists for the requested arrest or search. This Court long has insisted that inferences of probable cause be drawn by 'a neutral and detached magistrate instead of being judged by the officer engaged in the often competitive enterprise of ferreting out crime.' *Johnson v. United States, supra,* at 14 of 333 U.S.; *Giordenello v. United States, supra,* at 486 of 357 U.S. In *Coolidge v. New Hampshire, supra,* the Court last Term voided a search warrant issued by the state attorney general 'who was actively in charge of the investigation and later was to be chief prosecutor at trial.' *Id.,* at 450 of 403 U.S. If, on the other hand, detachment and capacity do conjoin, the magistrate has satisfied the Fourth Amendment's purpose.

III

The requisite detachment is present in the case at hand. Whatever else neutrality and detachment might entail, it is clear that they require severance and disengagement from activities of law enforcement. There has been no showing whatever here of partiality, or affiliation of these clerks with prosecutors or police. The record shows no connection with any law enforcement activity or authority which would distort the independent judgment the Fourth Amendment requires. Appellant himself expressly refused to allege anything to that effect. The municipal court clerk is assigned not to the police or prosecutor but to the municipal court judge for whom he does much of his work. In this sense, he may well be termed a 'judicial officer.' While a statutorily specified term of office and appointment by someone other than 'an executive authority' might be desirable, the absence of such features is hardly disqualifying. Judges themselves take office under differing circumstances. Some are appointed, but many are elected by legislative bodies or by the people. Many enjoy but limited terms and are subject to re-appointment or re-election. Most depend for their salary level upon the legislative branch. We will not elevate requirements for the independence of a municipal clerk to a level higher than that prevailing with respect to many judges. The clerk's neutrality has not been impeached: he is removed from prosecutor or police and works within the judicial branch subject to the supervision of the municipal court judge.

Appellant likewise has failed to demonstrate that these clerks lack capacity to determine probable cause. The clerk's authority extends only to the issuance of arrest warrants for breach of municipal ordinances. We presume from the nature of the clerk's position that he would be able to deduce from the facts on an affidavit before him whether there was probable cause to believe a citizen guilty of impaired driving, breach of peace, drunkenness, trespass, or the multiple other common offenses covered by a municipal code. There has been no showing that this is too difficult a task for a clerk to accomplish. Our legal system has long entrusted nonlawyers to evaluate more complex and significant factual data than that in the case at hand. Grand juries daily determine probable cause prior to rendering indictments, and trial juries assess whether guilt is proved beyond a reasonable doubt. The significance and responsibility of these lay judgments betray any belief that the Tampa clerks could not determine probable cause for arrest.

We decide today only that clerks of the municipal court may constitutionally issue the warrants in question. We have not considered whether the actual issuance was based upon an adequate showing of probable cause. Aguilar v. Texas, 378 U.S. 108 (1964). Appellant did not submit this question to the courts below, 237 So.2d 231 (1970), 250 So.2d 4 (1971), and we will not decide it here initially. The single question is whether power has been lawfully vested, not whether it has been constitutionally exercised.

Nor need we determine whether a State may lodge warrant authority in someone entirely outside the sphere of the judicial branch. Many persons may not qualify as the kind of 'public civil officers' we have come to associate with the term 'magistrate.' Had the Tampa clerk been entirely divorced from a judicial position, this case would have presented different considerations. Here, however, the clerk is an employee of the judicial branch of the city of Tampa, disassociated from the role of law enforcement. On the record in this case, the independent status of the clerk cannot be questioned.

What we do reject today is any per se invalidation of a state or local warrant system on the ground that the issuing magistrate is not a lawyer or judge. Communities may have sound reasons for delegating the responsibility of issuing warrants to competent personnel other than judges or lawyers. Many municipal courts face stiff and unrelenting caseloads. A judge pressured with the docket before him may give warrant applications more brisk and summary treatment than would a clerk. All this is not to imply that a judge or lawyer would not normally provide the most desirable review of warrant requests. But our federal system warns of converting desirable practice into constitutional commandment. It recognizes in plural and diverse state activities one key to national innovation and vitality. States are entitled to some flexibility and leeway in their designation of magistrates, so long as all are neutral and detached and capable of the probable-cause determination required of them.

We affirm the judgment of the Florida Supreme Court.

Affirmed.

3. INCIDENTAL SEARCH AUTHORITY—RIGHT TO FORCE ENTRY

United States v. Johnson
106 Fed. Appx. 363 (6th Cir. 2004)

■ SURHREINRICH, JUDGE.

The United States appeals the district court's order granting Defendant James Johnson's motion to suppress a shotgun found during a warrantless search of his residence. . . . We reverse.

I.

On the night of July 4, 2002, officers of the Grand Rapids police department responded to a report that a man was firing a shotgun from a porch of a home on Sigsbee in Grand Rapids, an area of two-story homes. The dispatch report indicated residents of the home included children. On arriving, officers saw a black male sitting on the front porch of 813 Sigsbee with a long gun on his lap. He was wearing a jersey bearing the number 05 and a bandana. As the officers watched, the man stood up, discharged the firearm into the air twice, and then reloaded it. The officers then heard someone say "police," and saw the man quickly turn and flee into the house through the front door.

The officers requested backup. Within minutes more officers arrived and surrounded the house. Several officers approached the front door and knocked numerous times, shouting to the occupants to answer the door. Although they heard muffled voices and rustling noises from within, the officers did not receive an answer. Not knowing the number of occupants in the house, whether they included children or if they had been taken hostage, or the identity of the shooter and whether he also lived there, the officers forced open the front door and entered the residence.

Upon entry, the officers immediately observed a shirtless, bareheaded black man, who was later identified as the shooter, and a woman in the kitchen area. The officers did not see the gun. Two officers immediately ran upstairs to search for the armed suspect and to determine if there were other occupants. In the meantime, other officers secured the man and the woman, having them lie on the living room floor, and then searched the remainder of the main floor for the armed suspect or additional occupants. During this search, and less than one minute after entry, officers discovered a loaded 12-gauge semiautomatic shotgun in a large pantry closet, adjacent to the kitchen, approximately eight to fifteen feet from where the man and woman had been found. The shotgun was within plain view when the closet door was opened. A short time later, the "05" jersey was found on the living room floor. No other persons were found in the home. This search lasted just two to three minutes.

Johnson was arrested at that point for violating state misdemeanor laws and city ordinances. The officers did not obtain an arrest warrant before entering the home to arrest Defendant. Nor did the officers obtain a search warrant prior to searching the house.

At the time of his arrest, the officers did not know Defendant was a convicted felon. Upon that discovery, on July 25, 2002, he was indicted on federal charges for being a felon in possession of a firearm in violation of 18 U.S.C. § 922(g). On February 25, 2003, Defendant filed a motion to suppress the gun evidence, arguing that the shotgun was found in an unconstitutional search and seizure. After a hearing, the district court granted Defendant's motion. The United States appeals.

II.

This Court reviews a district court's ruling on a suppression motion under a mixed standard of review. The district court's factual findings are reviewed for clear error, but we review its conclusions of law *de novo*. *Id.*

III.

In a confusing bench ruling that cited no authority, the district court initially concluded that the warrantless entry was justified because the officers "had the right to pursue the individual to reasonably ascertain who it was and make an arrest for the misdemeanor committed in their presence." The district court then found that officers determined "very quickly" that Defendant was the shooter. The court noted that, although Defendant was bare-chested, the jersey he had been wearing was lying on the floor. The district court also found that there was no reason to believe that there was anyone else in the house. Because the district court viewed this case as one involving a "protective sweep" to search for a weapon following an arrest, and because the arrest was for a misdemeanor and not for a felony, the court ruled that the warrantless search for the gun was unconstitutional. The court therefore suppressed the shotgun.

First, we think the district court misunderstood the nature of the protective sweep doctrine. Under the protective sweep doctrine, officers may quickly look into closets and other places in close proximity to the place of an arrest, after they have secured a suspect, to search for other persons who could launch an attack. *See* Maryland v. Buie, 494 U.S. 325 334 (1990). This may be done as a mere precaution and officers need not have reasonable suspicion or probable cause to do so. *Id.* Protective sweeps, therefore, generally involve searches for persons other than an arrestee. The district court cited no authority, and we have found none, to support the view that a protective sweep—under circumstances in which the officers have observed the suspect firing and reloading a shotgun and then fleeing into the house, the occupants of which are unknown to the officers—would be unconstitutional simply because the eventual arrest was only for a misdemeanor. However, searches of places within the arrestee's immediate area of control to find weapons are also permissible to protect officers from an arrestee who might gain possession of a nearby weapon. *See* Chimel v. California, 395 U.S. 752, 763 (1969).

Thus, even if the officers believed that they "had their man" when they seized defendant, they still had the authority to conduct a protective sweep to search for other persons. And, they were authorized to search the immediate vicinity for weapons. Here, the pantry closet was both large enough to hide a man and near enough to be accessible to Defendant. Under such facts, the officers would have discovered the shotgun during a valid protective search. It therefore would have been admissible under the protective sweep doctrine.

Nevertheless, we think this case is better characterized as one involving a search *for a suspect* where a gun was found in plain view incident to that search. We view the facts of this case as falling within the hot pursuit and risk of danger exceptions to the warrant requirement. The Fourth Amendment to the United States Constitution protects the people "against unreasonable searches and seizures." U.S. Const. amend. IV. Absent exigent circumstances, warrantless searches and warrantless seizures of evidence within a home are presumptively unreasonable. The exigent circumstances permitting warrantless entries of homes generally fall into four categories: "(1) hot pursuit of a fleeing felon, (2) imminent destruction of evidence, (3) the need to prevent a suspect's escape, and (4) a risk of danger to the police or others." *United States v. Rohrig,* 98 F.3d 1506, 1515 (6th Cir. 1996).[1] Importantly, seizures of items that are in plain view and made after entries under exceptions to the warrant requirement are legitimate. *See* Horton v. California, 496 U.S. 128, 134–35 (1990).

Here, the district court found that the officers determined "very quickly" that Defendant was the shooter, as if officers had immediately arrested Defendant and had no reason to look for anyone else. However, Defendant was only recognized as the shooter *after* the police determined no other persons were in the house and the shotgun had already been found. Upon entry, the man discovered in the kitchen was shirtless, bare-headed, and unarmed. Thus, there was ample reason for the officers to believe the actual suspect might be someone other than the arrestee and that he was somewhere else in the home. Indeed, it was entirely appropriate for the police to immediately continue looking for an armed

---

[1] In *Rohrig* we recognized that these are not the only exigencies. When one of the traditional exigent circumstances does not exist, warrantless entries into a home may nevertheless be justified by examining "(1) whether immediate government action was required, (2) whether the governmental interest was sufficiently compelling to justify a warrantless intrusion, and (3) whether the citizen's expectations of privacy was diminished in some way." *Id.* Here, immediate action was required because an armed man, who had already fired the shotgun and reloaded it, then fled into a house thought to be occupied. It was a compelling governmental interest to protect the occupants from harm, especially if they were children, as reported. And, defendant's expectation of privacy was diminished because he had fired his weapon outdoors where any passerby could witness his unlawful conduct.

man fitting the description of the man they had seen flee into the home. Moreover, although Defendant was secured immediately after entry into the home, no testimony established the timing of Defendant's arrest as the perpetrator prior to the continuation of the search for the suspect. In fact, when asked on cross-examination whether they were looking for the gun, one officer testified that he was looking for armed suspects or victims, thereby denying that he had been searching for the gun. The other officer also never testified that he had been searching for the gun, indicating instead that he was searching for other people including "victims and casualties." In sum, the district court's ruling is based on two erroneous factual assumptions: (1) that the officers knew immediately that they had the gunman, and (2) therefore, if they kept searching it must have been to look for the weapon. The facts clearly do not support such assumptions.

The facts instead support application of the first category of exigent circumstances—hot pursuit. *Warden v. Hayden,* 387 U.S. 294, 298–299 (1967) (involving hot pursuit of an armed felon into an occupied home). As our Supreme Court has made plain, "[t]he Fourth Amendment does not require police officers to delay in the course of an investigation if to do so would gravely endanger their lives or the lives of others." *Id.* at 298–299. The *Hayden* Court also made clear that the permissible scope of a search for an armed suspect in a home must at least "be as broad as may reasonably be necessary to prevent the dangers that the suspect in the house may resist or escape." *Id.* at 299. Although the Supreme Court has focused on the nature of the crime and upheld warrantless entries into homes in search of felons, as in *Hayden,* it has not completely foreclosed the possibility that such entries may be made to search for misdemeanants. See, *e.g.,* Welsh v. Wisconsin, 466 U.S. 740, 753 (1984) (noting that such entries are "rarely" sanctionable for minor offenses). Thus, the fact that this case involves the commission of misdemeanors, rather than the more usual situation involving felonies, does not render the hot pursuit doctrine inapplicable.

As in *Hayden,* this case involves the seizure of evidence found during a search for an armed suspect in the home into which he had fled after committing a crime. The police were not sure the man in the kitchen was the suspect they were looking for and reasonably continued their search for the suspect. Opening the door to a large pantry closet to look for him was reasonable because the closet was large enough to hide a man. The shotgun was in plain view once the door was opened. Thus, the warrantless entry in search of the suspect was constitutional under the exigency of hot pursuit. Because the shotgun was found and seized incident to the search for the gunman, as was the evidence in *Hayden,* it is admissible evidence.

Additionally, the fourth category of exigent circumstances—when there is a risk of danger to the police or others, *See* Minnesota v. Olson, 495 U.S. 91, 100 (1990),—also applies here. Under the circumstances of this case, the officers had ample justification for fearing for their own safety and especially the safety of others who might now be in the house with this reckless gunman. There had been a report of a man firing a gun from the porch in a residential neighborhood and that children resided there. Officers who responded to the call observed a man recklessly fire two shots into the air, reload the shotgun, and then flee into the house. The officers did not know whether the man lived at the house, whether there were other occupants inside, or whether such occupants were hostages. The man had already demonstrated his willingness to repeatedly fire the shotgun and had apparently fled into the house only upon becoming aware of the police. That the man turned and fled into the home armed, rather than dropping the weapon and talking to the officers, created the potential for the incident to escalate into a deadly confrontation that could have involved hostage-taking. From the officers' vantage point, this was a dangerous situation. Police are not required to wait for injury or death to occur in their presence before acting to protect people from a gunman who has amply demonstrated his propensity to use his weapon. Thus, the risk of danger was an exigent circumstance that also amply justified the officers' warrantless entry into the house and the seizure of the shotgun was permissible under *Horton*.

In sum, on these facts, we hold that the shotgun should not have been suppressed.[2]

IV.

For the foregoing reasons, we **REVERSE** the district court's order granting Defendant's motion to suppress and **REMAND** the case to the district court for further proceedings.

■ COLE, CIRCUIT JUDGE, dissenting.

The officers in this case violated Johnson's Fourth Amendment rights by entering his home without a warrant or permission. The majority concludes that this entry was justified by exigent circumstances. But such a conclusion is not supported by the law or the facts of this case.

The officers knew the following things: That discharging firearms into the air is common, albeit dangerous and illegal, on the Fourth of July, and that they had had various other such incidents reported that day; that a neighbor had reported a man firing a shotgun into the air from his porch; that the neighbor reported both that the man lived at the house and that there were children who lived there; that Officer Bauer saw Johnson fire the gun into the air; that Officer Bauer heard Johnson

---

[2] Even if the search in this case was unconstitutional, however, the shotgun is admissible evidence because it inevitably would have been discovered by lawful means. *See Nix v. Williams,* 467 U.S. 431, 444 (1984); *United States v. Kimes,* 246 F.3d 800, 804–805 (6th Cir. 2001). The officers had probable cause to believe that the shotgun was in the house because they had witnessed Defendant shoot it from the porch, reload it and then flee into the house with it. Had it not been found in the search for the suspect, the officers would have obtained a warrant after they secured the house. Inevitably, they would have found the shotgun upon opening the pantry closet door. Thus, application of the exclusionary rule would not be appropriate here.

to "say 'police' or something to that effect" before retreating into the house; and that discharge of a firearm within city limits is a misdemeanor city ordinance violation.

The officers certainly could have arrested Johnson even without a warrant because one of the officers had observed Johnson violate the misdemeanor city ordinance. Yet this alone does not sanction the officers' warrantless entry into Johnson's home.

The majority first asserts that the police's subsequent entry was justified by "hot pursuit." This exception to the Fourth Amendment arose in Warden v. Hayden, 387 U.S. 294 (1967). In *Hayden,* "[t]he police were informed that an armed robbery had taken place, and that the suspect had entered 2111 Cocoa Lane less than five minutes before they reached it." *Id.* at 299. The Supreme Court held that "[t]he Fourth Amendment does not require police officers to delay the course of an investigation if to do so would gravely endanger their lives or the lives of others." *Id.* The majority also suggests that this case falls under Minnesota v. Olson, 495 U.S. 91 (1990), which recognized that danger to police or others can be an exigent circumstance, even when pursuit is not hot.

There is a key, material difference between *Hayden* and the present case: here, the police knew that Johnson lived at the house. In *Hayden,* all that the officers knew was that an armed robbery suspect had fled into a house. It was reasonable for them to fear that the home he had entered was not his own, and that an individual fleeing the police into another's home after committing a felony posed a threat to the occupants of that home. In this case, however, the home that Johnson entered was his own, and the police knew this. Contrariwise, the majority states that "the officers did not know whether the man lived at the house." However, although Officer Cobb stated on direct examination that they did not know whether Johnson lived at the house, his memory was refreshed on cross-examination by a transcript from the police dispatch, in which the dispatcher had informed the officers that the man firing his gun lived at the house. Thus the officers did know, as Officer Cobb acknowledged, that Johnson lived at the house.

The officers' knowledge that Johnson lived at the house is crucial to this case because the permissibility of the police entry depends on the reasonableness of their determination that an emergency existed, sufficient to excuse the normal requirements of the Fourth Amendment. Both of the emergency rationales relied upon by the majority in justifying the warrantless entry depend upon it being reasonable for the police to conclude that Johnson posed a danger to the occupants of his home. However, such a conclusion was not reasonable. What the officers saw was a man fire a shot into the air—not at anyone or anything—from his own front porch, and retreat inside when he saw a police officer—but, notably, before the police attempted to arrest him. On this basis alone, the officers concluded that Johnson posed such a danger to his family that an exigent circumstance existed.

Yet, the City of Grand Rapids only considers firing a gun in the air to be a misdemeanor, and the State of Michigan does not criminalize this conduct at all. Thus, based on non-felonious conduct directed at neither person nor property, the police concluded that Johnson was an imminent threat to his family once he re-entered his home. The unreasonableness of this conclusion is exacerbated by the fact that the officers knew that it was the Fourth of July; knew that discharging firearms into the air on that day is a (dangerous and illegal) tradition; and knew that various other individuals had engaged in the same conduct on that day. While the fact that it was the Fourth of July in no way excuses Johnson's misdemeanant conduct, it makes it even less reasonable for the police to conclude that because he committed the misdemeanor of firing a gun into the air he posed some threat to his family inside the home.

Firing the gun in the air was undoubtedly reckless and showed a disregard for the safety of potential passers-by, but it is a significant leap to conclude, from the fact that Johnson would act recklessly, that he intended to harm his family or the police. The specific reckless conduct (firing the gun in the air) would not have recurred once Johnson entered the house (and if he exited to do it again, the police could simply have arrested him). That Johnson might commit other dangerous, deadly, or deranged behavior once in his home is pure conjecture, and the mere existential possibility that Johnson could have done anything imaginable is not enough to support the warrantless violation of his home.

Thus, it was not reasonable, as the majority concludes, for the officers to determine on this basis alone that Johnson posed an emergency threat to his family, such that the officers were excused from the normal requirement of obtaining a warrant, which they presumably could have acquired, before entering his home. Exigent circumstances did not justify the warrantless entry into the home, and the entry therefore violated the Fourth Amendment.

Mascorro v. Billings

656 F.3d 1198 (10th Cir. 2011)

■ O'BRIEN, CIRCUIT JUDGE.

Relying mostly on their version of events, Craig Billings, a Murray County Oklahoma deputy sheriff, and Steve Watkins and Tony Simpson, police officers with the City of Sulphur, Oklahoma police department, appeal from the district court's denial of their motion for summary judgment based on qualified immunity. But the Mascorros have a different version. Because, as the district court concluded, the issues are fact bound, we lack jurisdiction to consider the officers' arguments with respect to all but one claim of error. As the evidence and reasonable inferences regarding that single claim, hot pursuit of a traffic offender, taken in the light most favorable to the Mascorros demonstrates a violation of a clearly established constitutional right, we affirm.

I. FACTUAL BACKGROUND

Joshua Burchett is Christina Mascorro's son and Jose Mascorro's stepson. At the time of these events, Joshua was 17 years old. At 11:30 p.m. on July 23, 2007, Billings noticed Joshua was driving without taillights and turned around to pull him over. Joshua did not stop but drove two blocks to his parents' house, ran inside, and hid in the bathroom.

The front door is the only door to the Mascorro house. The Mascorros claim they woke to Billings kicking the door in a rage, swearing, threatening and ordering someone to open it and come outside. Christina testified to the following. She did not at first understand to whom Billings was referring. When Jose opened the door, Billings drew his gun, pointed it at Jose's head and yelled, "On your knees, mother f* * * *r!" (Appellant Billings Appendix at p. 115.) Christina raised her voice to ask Billings to calm down and tell them what he wanted because she could not understand him. Billings answered, "I want the mother F'er driving that car out here now." (Appellants Watkins & Simpson Appendix at 158.) After asking Billings what car he meant, Christina noticed her son's car in the driveway and said "That's my son's car. Oh, my gosh, what did he do?" (*Id.* at 158). Jose asked Billings if he had a warrant. As Christina started to turn away from the door Billings sprayed her in the face with pepper spray, and then stepped into the house and sprayed her again. Billings then sprayed Jose and Christopher, Christina's 14-year-old son, directly in the face as Christina retreated to the back bedroom to call 911. At some point after she completed her call, Officer Watkins retrieved her from the bedroom and led her outside.

According to Jose's testimony he retreated to the kitchen to try to wash the pepper spray from his face. "[A]s soon as [he] kn[e]w" another officer, later identified as Simpson, entered the kitchen and led him out of the house.[2] (Watkins and Simpson Appendix at p. 232.)

Billings informed Watkins and Simpson that Joshua had locked himself in the bathroom. The officers ordered Joshua to come out and, when he refused, Simpson drew his gun, kicked down the bathroom door, and took him into custody. The Mascorros contend Billings was visibly angry during the entire encounter, screaming at the top of his lungs and spitting with rage as he tried to speak and they did nothing to threaten or physically resist Billings in any way.

A number of other officers were present at the house when the Mascorros were taken outside. According to Christina's testimony, before Joshua was removed from the home, Billings approached her, pushed her up against a wall, and demanded to know where he was. When one of the officers suggested calling an ambulance Billings said, "No one is calling

---

[2]   Jose also filed a supplemental affidavit stating Watkins and Simpson were in the home seconds after Billings sprayed the Mascorros "so they had to be right behind [him]" when he used the pepper spray. (Appellants Watkins and Simpson Appendix at p. 263).

any ambulance." (Appellants Watkins & Simpson Appendix at p. 259). At some point, she requested an ambulance but Billings responded she did not need one. Nevertheless, an ambulance was called to the scene. Billings arrested Christina and Jose and cuffed them in the ambulance. Other officers escorted them with Christopher to the hospital. The three Mascorros were treated and released from the hospital, at which point officers took Christina and Jose to jail. They were both charged with obstructing a police officer in the performance of his duties and Christina was charged with aggravated assault and battery on a police officer because Billings alleged and subsequently testified that she poked him in the chest when he was standing at the front door before he sprayed her. They were released on bond later the same day. The state court eventually quashed the arrest and dismissed the charges, concluding Billings had entered the house illegally because no exigent circumstances justified his warrantless entry. When they returned home, they found their belongings strewn about, trash cans upended, and a hole kicked in one wall.

II. PROCEDURAL HISTORY

The Mascorros brought this action against Billings, Watkins and Simpson asserting claims of unlawful entry, excessive use of force, false arrest, false imprisonment, and malicious prosecution. Watkins and Simpson moved for dismissal on the excessive force and malicious prosecution claims. The district court dismissed the Mascorros' claims of malicious prosecution against Watkins and Simpson under Rule 12(b)(6) of the Federal Rules of Civil Procedure but left all other claims intact. The Mascorros moved for partial summary judgment and Billings, Simpson, and Watkins moved for summary judgment based on qualified immunity and other grounds. The district court denied the Mascorros' summary judgment motion. It granted Billings, Simpson, and Watkins' motions as to claims against them in their official capacities, but denied summary judgment on all other issues, including their qualified immunity defense. The officers brought this interlocutory appeal on the single issue of whether they are entitled to qualified immunity.

III. DISCUSSION

A. *Issues We Cannot Address*

The officers contend the district court erred in denying them qualified immunity on each of the Mascorros' claims. However, their arguments concerning the excessive force, false arrest, false imprisonment and (against Billings) malicious prosecution claims are based solely on their version of events. For instance, all the officers claim their actions were justified because the Mascorros refused to hand over their son to the police and Christina assaulted Billings. The Mascorros' version of events is different. Watkins and Simpson allege they arrived too late to be held responsible for Billings' use of force and the timing of their arrival made reliance on Billings' assertions at the scene reasonable.[5] Again, the Mascorros saw it differently. The district court properly determined genuine issues of material fact were present with respect to these claims. We lack jurisdiction as to them.[6]

B. *The Issue We Can Address*

As to the Mascorros' unlawful entry claim, however, the officers argue their entry into the home was justified by probable cause to arrest Joshua for a traffic offense coupled with the exigent circumstances necessarily attending the pursuit of a fleeing suspect.[7] The facts relating to this narrow aspect of the unlawful entry claim are not disputed and therefore we may address the purely legal issue of whether the officers are entitled to qualified immunity with respect to that claim.

To defeat the officers' claim of qualified immunity, the Mascorros must show (1) the officers violated their constitutional or statutory rights, and (2) the violated rights were clearly established at the time of the events in question. Shroff v. Spellman, 604 F.3d 1179, 1188 (10th Cir.2010). We have discretion to determine which prong of the immunity defense to address first, in light of the circumstances of the case at hand, and may resolve the question by finding either requirement is not met. Christensen v. Park City Mun. Corp., 554 F.3d 1271, 1277 (10th Cir.2009) (citing Pearson v. Callahan, 555 U.S. 223 (2009)).

C. *Warrantless Entry into a Home*

"It is a basic principle of Fourth Amendment law that searches and seizures inside a home without a warrant are presumptively unreasonable." Payton v. New York, 445 U.S. 573, 586 (1980) (quotation marks and citation omitted). "[T]he Fourth Amendment . . . prohibits police from effectuating a warrantless and non-consensual entry into a suspect's home to make a routine felony arrest." Howard v. Dickerson, 34 F.3d 978, 982 (10th Cir.1994) (citing *Payton,* 445 U.S. at 576. Even an arrest warrant does not give police carte blanche to enter any dwelling in search of the object of the warrant; while such a warrant permits entry

---

[5] It is not necessary that a police officer actually participate in the use of excessive force in order to be held liable under section 1983. Rather, an officer who is present at the scene and who fails to take reasonable steps to protect the victim of another officer's use of excessive force, can be held liable for his nonfeasance.

Mick v. Brewer, 76 F.3d 1127, 1136 (10th Cir.1996) (quoting Fundiller v. City of Cooper City, 777 F.2d 1436, 1441–42 (11th Cir.1985)). The district court concluded there was a question of fact regarding the timing of the officers' arrival, which calls into question whether, in fact, they had the opportunity to intervene at some point during the spraying and whether their subsequent acts were reasonable even if they lacked the opportunity to prevent the use of the pepper spray in the first instance.

[6] Orders denying qualified immunity are appealable to the extent that they resolve abstract issues of law. We will not hear an appeal when the question is the sufficiency of the evidence or the correctness of the district court's findings with respect to a genuine issue of material fact. An appeal is proper if the defendant sets off to show that the law was not clearly established at the time of the challenged action, or that qualified immunity is proper even under the plaintiff's version of the facts. Because we may review only legal issues, we must accept any facts that the district court assumed in denying summary judgment.

Amundsen v. Jones, 533 F.3d 1192, 1196 (10th Cir.2008) (citations and quotations omitted).

[7] This slim tendril of legitimate argument, buried as it is in larger, mostly improper, factual discussion, is the only reason we have not dismissed the appeal for lack of jurisdiction.

into the suspect's residence to effectuate an arrest, entry into a third party's home for the same purpose requires a search warrant. Steagald v. United States, 451 U.S. 204, 222 (1981). If, however, police have probable cause for an arrest, the existence of certain exigent circumstances may "overcome the presumption of unreasonableness that attaches to all warrantless home entries." Welsh v. Wisconsin, 466 U.S. 740, 750 (1984); *Howard,* 34 F.3d at 982. "To determine the existence of an exigency, a court must consider the gravity of the offense supporting arrest." *Howard,* 34 F.3d at 982 (citing *Welsh,* 466 U.S. at 753). "When the government's interest is only to arrest for a minor offense, that presumption of unreasonableness is difficult to rebut, and the government usually should be allowed to make such arrests only with a warrant issued upon probable cause by a neutral and detached magistrate." *Welsh,* 466 U.S. at 750 (footnote omitted). The burden is on the government to demonstrate the existence of exigent circumstances. *Id.* at 749.

The officers justify their warrantless entry into the Mascorro home by probable cause to arrest Joshua coupled with an exigent circumstance—pursuit of a fleeing suspect.[8] The Mascorros argue the "hot pursuit" of their son under these circumstances did not constitute the kind of exigent circumstance excusing the officers from obtaining a warrant before entering their home. They do not dispute the relevant facts: Joshua was driving without taillights and he continued driving toward the house when Billings turned around to follow him. And they have not refuted Billings' assertion of probable cause to arrest their son for the traffic offense.[9]

In United States v. Santana, 427 U.S. 38 (1976), the Supreme Court concluded the exigent circumstances, based in part on hot pursuit of a suspect, were sufficient to rebut the presumption of unreasonableness generally attending the warrantless entry into a home. The officers entered Santana's home immediately following a controlled drug transaction when she retreated into her house, still in possession of the drugs, after the officers identified themselves and attempted to arrest

---

[8] Simpson and Watkins argue their entry was justified by the need to aid the Mascorros; they arrived only after Billings told them he had used his pepper spray. However, the Mascorros dispute the timing of Watkins and Simpson's entry and any discussion on that point is not appropriate here. *See Amundsen,* 533 F.3d at 1196. Simpson and Watkins also argue that under the "fellow officer rule," they were deemed to have relied on information possessed by Billings. *See* Karr v. Smith, 774 F.2d 1029, 1031 (10th Cir.1985). The Mascorros' evidence puts Watkins and Simpson at the scene when they were sprayed and they have sufficiently raised a question of fact with respect to whether Watkins and Simpson witnessed enough to preclude their reliance on Billings' statements.

[9] The officers also argue their entry was justified because Joshua eluded an officer in violation of Okla. Stat. Ann. tit. 21, § 540A. However, the Mascorros claim Billings did not have probable cause to arrest Joshua for eluding a police officer because while Billings may have activated his emergency lights he never deployed his siren or any other "audible signal" (a requirement under Oklahoma law) to signal pursuit. *See* Aldridge v. State, 674 P.2d 553, 554 (Okla.Crim.App.1984). Those technicalities do not matter; whatever crime Joshua may have committed and for which he was pursued was a nonviolent misdemeanor raising no articulated concerns about possible destruction of evidence.

her. *Santana,* 427 U.S. at 42–43. Santana was in the threshold of her home when officers approached and they pursued her into the vestibule into which she retreated without closing the front door. *Id.* at 40. The Court noted the potential for destruction of evidence once Santana had seen the police and concluded "a suspect may not defeat an arrest which has been set in motion in a public place . . . by the expedient of escaping to a private place." *Id.* at 43.

Four years later the Court again addressed the issue of a warrantless arrest in a home. In *Payton v. New York,* it reiterated the requirement for police to have either a warrant or an ability to articulate exigent circumstances in order to enter a home even where circumstances would otherwise permit a warrantless arrest for a felony. 445 U.S. at 590. That is so because "the Fourth Amendment has drawn a firm line at the entrance to the house. Absent exigent circumstances, that threshold may not reasonably be crossed without a warrant." *Id.*

Again addressing the question of warrantless entry, in *Welsh v. Wisconsin,* the Supreme Court noted "the Court in [*Payton*] explicitly refused to consider the sort of emergency or dangerous situation, described in our cases as 'exigent circumstances,' that would justify a warrantless entry into a home for the purpose of either arrest or search." 466 U.S. at 742 (quotation omitted). Officers arrested Welsh in his home for a drunk driving offense after he left his vehicle at the scene of an accident. *Id.* at 740. The underlying exigency in *Welsh* was not pursuit, but preservation of evidence based on the need to collect blood and breath samples before alcohol dissipated from Welsh's system. *Id.* at 753. The Court decided the officers violated the Fourth Amendment by entering Welsh's home at night without a warrant to arrest him for a noncriminal traffic offense.[10] In so holding, the Court looked to the cases in which it had previously found exigent circumstances permitting such an entry, including *Santana.* The cases involved felonies, and the "decision in *Payton,* allowing warrantless home arrests upon a showing of probable cause and exigent circumstances, was also expressly limited to felony arrests." *Id.* at 749 n. 11. Because it concluded no exigent circumstances existed, the Court had "no occasion to consider whether the Fourth Amendment may impose an absolute ban on warrantless home arrests for certain minor offenses" but held the nature of the underlying offense was an important consideration when determining the reasonableness of a warrantless entry:

> [A]n important factor to be considered when determining whether **any** exigency exists is the gravity of the underlying offense for which the arrest is being made. . . . [A]pplication of the exigent-circumstances exception in the context of a home entry should rarely be sanctioned when there is a probable

---

[10] Driving under the influence was a "nonjailable traffic offense that constituted only a civil violation under the applicable state law" in Wisconsin at the time. *See Welsh,* 466 U.S. at 746 n.6.

cause to believe that only a minor offense ... has been committed.

Id. at 749 n. 11, 753 (emphasis added). . . . .

We do not find the circumstances here amount to the kind of exigency excusing an officer from obtaining a warrant before entering a home. The intended arrest was for a traffic misdemeanor committed by a minor, with whom the officer was well acquainted,[11] who had fled into his family home from which there was only one exit. The risk of flight or escape was somewhere between low and nonexistent. Moreover, there was no evidence which could have potentially been destroyed[12] and there were no officer or public safety concerns. There is nothing to indicate the sort of "real immediate and serious consequences" of postponing action to obtain a warrant required for a showing of exigent circumstances. *See Welsh,* 466 U.S. at 751. The warrantless entry based on hot pursuit was not justified.

D.   *Clearly Established Law*

. . . . The constitutional right was clearly established for purposes of qualified immunity if it would have been clear to a reasonable officer at the time the officers entered the Mascorro house that their entry was unlawful under the circumstances presented. Fogarty v. Gallegos, 523 F.3d 1147, 1155 (10th Cir.2008). For a right to be clearly established there must be Tenth Circuit or Supreme Court precedent close enough on point to make the unlawfulness of the officers' actions apparent. Weise v. Casper, 593 F.3d 1163, 1167 (10th Cir.2010). In the alternative, "the clearly established weight of authority from other courts must have found the law to be as the plaintiff maintains." *Id.* (quotations omitted).

Relevant precedent clearly prohibits police from routinely entering a person's home to effectuate a warrantless arrest (even if the officers have probable cause to believe the person committed a felony), *See Payton,* 445 U.S. at 576, and a minor offense does not permit warrantless entry into the home except in the most extraordinary of circumstances. *See Welsh,* 466 U.S. at 753 ("[I]t is difficult to conceive of a warrantless home arrest that would not be unreasonable under the Fourth Amendment when the underlying offense is extremely minor."). Our focus must be on whether an exception to bedrock constitutional

---

[11]   Billings testified he recognized Joshua because he previously had contact with him for drug violations and he was also a neighbor. From his testimony one might infer he knew Joshua was a minor.

[12]   In a hot pursuit case, warrantless entry is in part justified by the significant risk that the evidence would no longer be in the suspect's possession if the police waited until a warrant could be obtained. In such cases, however, the intrusion is also justified by the suspect's flight, which frustrates police efforts to make a legitimate warrantless arrest.

United States v. Aquino, 836 F.2d at 1271 (discussing *Santana* as "hot pursuit of a fleeing felon") (citation and quotation omitted). Billings claims his prior drug-related contact with Joshua led him to believe Joshua might have drugs concealed on his person but he offers nothing approaching probable cause to arrest Joshua for any drug crime. In any event, the district court found there was no basis for entry based on any imminent destruction of evidence and we will not consider the argument based on Billings' version of the facts.

principles clearly exists. There appears to be no relevant precedent announcing such an exception in cases such as this.

While hot pursuit of a felon might be sufficient, neither the Supreme Court nor this Court has ever found an entry into a person's home permissible based merely on the pursuit of a misdemeanant; additional circumstances have always dictated the result. *Santana* involved a hot pursuit of a fleeing felon as well as possible destruction of evidence and was decided before the Supreme Court's admonition in *Welsh* that the seriousness of the offense for which officers seek to effectuate an arrest is a vital component of **any** exigent circumstances justifying warrantless entry into the home.

We do not rely on generalities in our application of the "clearly established" standard here. The specific and identifiable facts of the relevant cases make clear the sort of exigent circumstances permitting officers to enter a suspect's home without a warrant in pursuit of the suspect—they must involve a serious offense coupled with the existence of an immediate and pressing concern such as destruction of evidence, officer or public safety, or the possibility of imminent escape. These officers do not even argue such concerns were present or that the traffic violation for which Billings had probable cause to arrest Joshua constituted a serious offense. No reasonable officer would have thought pursuit of a minor for a mere misdemeanor traffic offense constituted the sort of exigency permitting entry into a home without a warrant.

4. SEARCH INCIDENT TO ARREST

United States v. Brown

233 Fed. Appx. 564 (7th Cir. 2007)

■ Before HON. WILLIAM J. BAUER, CIRCUIT JUDGE, HON. JOHN L. COFFEY, CIRCUIT JUDGE and HON. ANN CLAIRE WILLIAMS, CIRCUIT JUDGE.

ORDER

During the course of a routine traffic stop, Datona Brown fled from the scene and assaulted two of the arresting officers from the Decatur, Illinois Police Department. After the officers were able to restrain Brown and take him into custody, they handcuffed and locked him in their squad car. Because of Brown's suspicious actions at the scene, the officers believed that he might be in possession of a controlled substance, they proceeded to search his person and the surrounding area. Shortly thereafter they discovered a brown bag containing crack cocaine on his person in the area of his crotch. Brown was charged with possession of five grams or more of cocaine base with intent to deliver, and he filed a motion to suppress both the cocaine and his incriminating statements to police. He now appeals and contests the district court's ruling that the search of his person was valid as incident to an arrest. We affirm.

During his patrol on September 20, 2003, Officer Christopher Hale observed Brown driving his automobile without a seatbelt,[1] and began to follow him. While being pursued, Brown accelerated his vehicle and drove through a stop sign, resulting in Officer Hale activating the warning lights on his vehicle after which Brown stopped his vehicle.

Hale approached Brown and informed him that he was going to give him two citations: one for failing to wear a seatbelt and another for running the stop sign. Hale walked back to his squad car to process the tickets. At about this time, Officer Roger Craig arrived as a backup to assist and Hale and Craig both approached Brown's car. Hale was on the driver's side and Craig on the passenger side. Hale advised Brown that he was of the opinion that he was attempting to flee when he accelerated his car and ran a stop sign. Hale asked Brown for permission to search his car and Brown refused, with Hale responding that he was going to request a canine sniff of the exterior of the car.

As Hale began to return to his squad car, Craig observed Brown reach inside his jacket pocket and, fearing that the suspect might be armed, he alerted Hale. The defendant immediately exited the car, pushing Hale aside and fled from the scene. Hale, in an attempt to restrain him, grabbed his coat, but Brown slipped out of his coat and bolted across the street. Hale chased Brown and wrestled him to the ground, while spraying him with pepper spray. While struggling, Hale observed Brown pull a small brown paper bag out of his shirt and clutch the bag in his right hand.

During the struggle Officer Craig jumped on both Hale and Brown, allowing Brown to escape and run a few more yards. The officers tackled Brown and he proceeded to resist arrest. During the ensuing fight, Brown kicked and punched Hale, all the while keeping his right hand strangely positioned beneath his body while he was on the ground. After the officers succeeded in restraining him, they patted him down and searched his person, including his pockets, but found nothing. The officers handcuffed him, locked him in the squad car, and conducted a search of the area, looking for the brown bag, but were still unable to locate it. Hale returned to the squad car and instituted another more thorough search of Brown's person, and at this time discovered a small brown bag, containing crack cocaine, in the crotch of Brown's pants. The officers took custody of the brown bag, transported it with Brown to the police station, where they read him his *Miranda* rights.

Before trial, Brown moved to suppress the introduction of the crack cocaine arguing that: (1) he was not under arrest at the time of the search; and (2) there was no justification for the search of Brown's crotch area. The district court denied the motion, finding that there was probable cause to arrest Brown and the search was valid as incident to

---

[1]　Driving without a seatbelt is a violation of Illinois law. *See* 645 Ill. Comp. Stat. 5/12–603.1 (2003).

that arrest. Thereafter, Brown entered a conditional plea of guilty while preserving his right to appeal the ruling on the suppression motion.

On appeal, Brown argues that the district court erred in holding that the search was valid as incident to his arrest. He now asks this court to rule that he was not "under arrest" in spite of the fact that the officers had tackled him, restrained him, handcuffed him, and locked him in the squad car. Instead, Brown somehow contends that he was only briefly detained in order to subdue him and prevent further flight until after the search, when he was arrested and taken to the police station. We review the district court's findings of fact for clear error and its determinations of law de novo.

We determine whether a suspect is under arrest after looking to the totality of the circumstances surrounding any restraint on the suspect's movements created by a police officer's use of physical force or the suspect's submission to an officer's show of authority. Those circumstances include whether a reasonable person in the suspect's position would have felt free to leave and whether the officers have acquired physical control over the suspect, either through the use of physical force or a show of physical force, i.e., placing their hands on their armed holsters. A suspect is under arrest when "a reasonable person in the suspect's position would have understood the situation to constitute a restraint on the freedom of movement of the degree which the law associates with formal arrest."

We use an objective standard in applying the case law to the facts. In this case, after Brown had initially fled the scene and assaulted the two arresting officers, and one of the officers had observed a suspicious bag, both officers were able to wrestle Brown to the ground, spray him with pepper spray, handcuff him, and lock him in the squad car. It is obvious that Brown was seized; his movements were restrained when he sat handcuffed and locked in the squad car and he clearly was not free to leave. Moreover, the officers had initially acquired physical control over him at the time they tackled him, sprayed him with pepper spray, and cuffed him. Obviously, any reasonable person in Brown's position at that time in the arrest scenario would have considered himself or herself restrained, beyond the limited—like stop, and under "arrest." Brown's argument that a reasonable person would not consider himself or herself "under arrest" after being tackled, handcuffed, and locked in the back of the squad car is preposterous.

Brown argues that he was not under arrest because, after restraining and locking him in the squad car, the officers failed to pronounce the magic word ("arrest") and explicitly advise him that he was under arrest. He cites not a scintilla of case law to support his self-serving theory. Officers do not have to formally advise the suspect that he or she is under arrest or complete other formalities of this notice in order to make an arrest valid. Dunaway v. New York, 442 U.S. 200, 212–13 (1979). Common sense dictates that he was under arrest. . . .

The case of United States v. Wilson, 2 F.3d 226 (7th Cir. 1993), on which Brown relies and argues that no arrest occurred, is inapposite. In *Wilson,* the police saw Wilson jump out of a moving car and thereafter fled from the police and hid under a porch. After ordering Wilson to come out from under the porch, the police used handcuffs to prevent further flight during the *Terry* stop, and this court held that the application of handcuffs alone under those circumstances did not constitute arrest. The court also emphasized the short length of the detention (less than one minute) in determining that there was no arrest.

Here, in contrast, Brown was observed operating a motor vehicle without a seatbelt, proceeded to accelerate his vehicle with the officer in pursuit, and ran a stop sign while fleeing the scene. Shortly thereafter he was apprehended, struggled with the police officers, was sprayed with pepper spray, and was once again apprehended after another struggle with the police officers. Thereafter, he was handcuffed and locked in a squad car. Obviously, Brown was restrained to a greater degree than the suspect in *Wilson*. Moreover, Brown remained handcuffed and locked in the squad car while the officers proceeded to search the surrounding area for contraband. Under these facts, the district court did not err in determining that Brown was under arrest and in custody.

Furthermore, unlike the suspect in *Wilson,* Brown had already given the officers probable cause to arrest him. . . . Here, Brown failed to wear his seat belt, ran a stop sign and fled from the scene, resisted arrest and struck two police officers. Certainly the facts as set forth herein were more than sufficient to establish probable cause that Brown had violated laws against resisting arrest and aggravated assault.

Brown goes on to argue that, even if he was arrested, the district court erred in holding that the search into Brown's crotch area was within the valid limits of a search incident to arrest. He claims that the search into his crotch area was overly-intrusive, and thus the officers were required to have some specific reason to believe that Brown was concealing contraband in his crotch area before they could proceed.

It is a "bright-line rule" that officers are allowed to and should thoroughly search suspects' clothing and bodies upon arrest, even if they do not suspect at that time that the person is armed or carrying contraband for the protection of themselves and others. A search incident to arrest is reasonable and proper because officers must recover any and all weapons from the suspect in order that they might protect themselves as well as others who might come in contact with him. They must also look for and preserve evidence of a crime that might otherwise be destroyed. *See* Gustafson v. Florida, 414 U.S. 260, 263–65 (1973); United States v. Robinson, 414 U.S. 218, 224–26 (1973); Chimel v. California, 395 U.S. 752 (1969). No additional justification is required. *See Gustafson,* 414 U.S. at 263–65; *Robinson,* 414 U.S. at 235.

As we have made clear, Brown was under arrest, and thus the officers did not need any further justification to search him.

Furthermore, even if cause for the search was required, Officer Hale believed that he saw Brown holding contraband during their struggle, and it was reasonable for him to continue to search Brown to find that contraband.

The next question we will deal with is whether the search was conducted in an overly intrusive manner. We have held that the intrusiveness of a search must be balanced against the need for the search. *See* United States v. Williams, 209 F.3d 940, 943–44 (7th Cir. 2000). *See also* Mary Beth G. v. City of Chicago, 723 F.2d 1263, 1270–73 (7th Cir. 1983) (holding that a valid arrest allows for a full search but not any search no matter how extreme or abusive). A search of the private areas of a suspect's body is reasonable if the suspect's private parts are not exposed to onlookers and in particular when an attempted flight from officers suggests that they must search immediately because the suspect is in all probability likely to conceal or destroy evidence. *Williams,* 209 F.3d at 943–44.

Here, Officer Hale early on had observed the suspect holding a small brown bag that he believed to contain contraband, but was initially unable to locate the bag either in Brown's clothing or in the immediate surrounding area during a search. As a result, a knowledgeable and experienced police officer would reasonably suspect that Brown had it hidden under his clothing. The search was neither more intrusive than necessary for the purpose, and at no time were Brown's body parts exposed to onlookers. The search was not intrusive.

AFFIRMED.

United States v. Tejada

524 F.3d 809 (7th Cir. 2008)

■ POSNER, CIRCUIT JUDGE.

The defendant pleaded guilty to federal drug offenses (and was sentenced to 120 months in prison), reserving however his claim that the drugs used in evidence against him had been seized in violation of the Fourth Amendment by DEA agents who did not have a search warrant. The district judge, after a hearing on the defendant's motion to suppress the evidence, ruled that the drugs had been seized as a lawful incident to his arrest and alternatively that they would inevitably have been discovered.

One of the agents, posing as a buyer of cocaine, met with the defendant in the parking lot of a restaurant and was shown by him a small blue travel bag containing the cocaine that the agent had agreed to buy. But the defendant told him that the sale would have to take place not there but in the defendant's apartment, which was nearby. The defendant drove from the parking lot, and the agent followed him to the apartment house and saw him enter an attic apartment by an exterior staircase and stand at the window holding the bag. Together with 12 to 15 other undercover agents, the agent entered the apartment house and forced open the door of the defendant's tiny apartment (400 square feet). When the defendant refused to obey their order to get down on the floor, they forced him down and handcuffed his hands behind his back. During the scuffle he reached for a gun in his waistband, but the agents seized it.

With the defendant handcuffed and face down on the floor, the agents did a protective sweep of the apartment to make sure that no one else was in it and that there were no weapons that the defendant might grab for. One of the places searched was an "entertainment center" in the living room. It seems, though the record is unclear and the district judge made no finding, that by this time the defendant was on the floor in the kitchen; but the kitchen was close to the entertainment center.

In the entertainment center was a closed cabinet, which the agents opened. And in the cabinet was the blue travel bag that the defendant had exhibited to the agent in the parking lot. The agents unzipped the bag and inside found another bag, which they opened, discovering cocaine. By the time they unzipped the blue travel bag, the agents knew there was no one else in the apartment besides themselves and the defendant.

The defendant was arrested lawfully, even though the arrest took place in his home and the police did not have a warrant. They could not have gotten a warrant in time and were therefore justified in arresting the defendant without one ("exigent circumstances"). The sale of the cocaine was originally to have taken place in the restaurant's parking lot, and had that happened the agent would have had the bag of cocaine and no need for a warrant. Unexpectedly, the defendant at the last minute insisted that the sale take place in his apartment. The agent decided to arrest the defendant on the spot. The defendant had shown him the drugs, so there was probable cause to arrest him. The agent gave a signal to fellow officers to assist with the arrest, but something went awry and they did not appear, so the agent went to the defendant's building and when he arrived he was able to signal to the other officers. Before they arrived, the defendant entered the building and went into his apartment—at which point the sound of the sirens of the arriving police cars could be heard. With the defendant alerted to their arrival, the police were justified in entering the apartment immediately.

As an incident to a lawful arrest, the police can search not only the person they have arrested to make sure he doesn't have a weapon but also and for the same purpose they can search the area within his immediate control—the area within grabbing distance—in which a weapon might be concealed that he could attempt to use against the officers or in which there might be evidence of his crime that he could destroy. Chimel v. California, 395 U.S. 752, 763 (1969); United States v. Thomas, 512 F.3d 383, 387 (7th Cir.2008). There is no doubt that the police were entitled to open the cabinet in the entertainment center. The defendant had identified himself as a dangerous person by resisting arrest and reaching for a gun even though he knew the crowd of officers were indeed law enforcement officers and not rival gangsters. He had a gun in his waistband; he might have other guns in the apartment— perhaps in the "entertainment center." The apartment was tiny, which meant not only that there were few other places in which to hide another gun or other guns but also that the defendant was within a few steps of the entertainment center. Handcuffed, lying face down on the floor, and surrounded by police, he was unlikely to be able to make a successful lunge for the entertainment center. But the police did not know how strong he was, and he seemed desperate.

So they could open the cabinet in the entertainment center. In it was the telltale blue travel bag. They knew it contained cocaine. It might also have contained a gun. But while it is conceivable though unlikely that the defendant could have made a successful lunge for the entertainment center and opened the cabinet and grabbed something inside it, it is inconceivable that having opened the cabinet door he would have had time to unzip the travel bag without being wrestled to the floor once again by the more than dozen police, who having ascertained that there was no one else in the apartment would not have been distracted from the task of re-subduing him.

But if this is wrong, what is inconceivable squared is that he could have unzipped not only the blue travel bag but also the bag inside it. That was the bag containing the cocaine used in evidence against him. The agents did not need to unzip that bag in order to protect themselves or prevent the destruction of evidence, and there is authority that that is enough to condemn the search. United States v. Lyons, 706 F.2d 321, 324–25, 330–31 (D.C.Cir.1983); United States v. Cueto, 611 F.2d 1056, 1062 (5th Cir.1980). Most cases, however, including our own United States v. Fleming, 677 F.2d 602, 607 (7th Cir.1982), deem such searches lawful. E.g., United States v. Williams, 483 F.3d 425, 430 (6th Cir.2007); United States v. Currence, 446 F.3d 554, 557 (4th Cir.2006); United States v. Hudson, 100 F.3d 1409, 1413–14, 1420 (9th Cir.1996); United States v. Turner, 926 F.2d 883, 887–88 (9th Cir.1991); see Myron Moskovitz, *A Rule in Search of a Reason: An Empirical Reexamination of Chimel and Belton*, 2002 Wis. L.Rev. 657, 682–85. *Hudson,* for example, a case factually similar to this one, upheld the search of a closed rifle case that had been next to the defendant in his bedroom when he was arrested, even though the search was conducted after he had been handcuffed and removed from the house.

These cases, going beyond *Chimel*, hold that if the search is limited to the area under the defendant's control at the time of his arrest, the fact that it is no longer under his control at the time of the search does not invalidate the search. *E.g., United States v. Currence, supra*, 446 F.3d at 557; *United States v. Hudson, supra*, 100 F.3d at 1419. Their rationale, as well explained in United States v. Abdul-Saboor, 85 F.3d 664, 669 (D.C.Cir.1996), is that if the police could lawfully have searched the defendant's grabbing radius at the moment of arrest, he has no legitimate complaint if, the better to protect themselves from him, they first put him outside that radius.

Were this rationale wrong or inapplicable, the defendant would find himself up against the doctrine of inevitable discovery. Nix v. Williams, 467 U.S. 431 (1984); United States v. Gravens, 129 F.3d 974, 979–80 (7th Cir.1997). It is true that cases such as United States v. Virden, 488 F.3d 1317, 1323 (11th Cir.2007); United States v. Conner, 127 F.3d 663, 667–68 (8th Cir.1997), and United States v. Mejia, 69 F.3d 309, 320 (9th Cir.1995), say that the doctrine should be confined to the situation in which the police are gathering evidence with a view toward obtaining a search warrant and it is certain or nearly so that had one of them not jumped the gun and searched without a warrant the investigation would have culminated in a successful warrant application. The agents in this case never had plans to obtain a search warrant. Against these cases it could be argued that the doctrine of inevitable discovery should apply in any case in which the police have probable cause to obtain a warrant; for if they would have obtained one had they asked, why should a defendant benefit from their failure to ask? But while that is mentioned as a possible rule in United States v. Elder, 466 F.3d 1090, 1091 (7th Cir.2006), it is not endorsed there and no court has embraced it. The obvious objection is that if it were adopted the police might never bother to apply for a warrant, in order to avoid the risk that the application would be denied. United States v. Johnson, 22 F.3d 674, 683 (6th Cir.1994); United States v. $639,558 in U.S. Currency, 955 F.2d 712, 710–21 (D.C.Cir.1992); Robert M. Bloom, Inevitable Discovery: *An Exception Beyond the Fruits,* 20 Am. J.Crim. L. 79, 96 (1992). But the opposite rule, which would allow the doctrine to be invoked only if the police were in the process of obtaining a warrant, would be equally untenable. It would confer a windfall, in violation of "the familiar rule of tort law," which has force in the criminal context as well (think of the doctrine of harmless error, Fed.R.Crim.P. 51(a)), "that a person can't complain about a violation of his rights if the same injury would have occurred even if they had not been violated." United States v. Johnson, 380 F.3d 1013, 1014 (7th Cir.2004); *see also* United States v. Stefonek, 179 F.3d 1030, 1035–36 (7th Cir.1999).

An attractive middle ground is to require the government, if it wants to use the doctrine of inevitable discovery to excuse its failure to have obtained a search warrant, to prove that a warrant would certainly, and not merely probably, have been issued had it been applied for. This was the approach taken in United States v. Buchanan, 910 F.2d 1571, 1573 (7th Cir.1990), and explained in *United States v. Elder, supra,* 466 F.3d at 1091: "when a warrant is sure to issue (if sought), the exclusionary 'remedy' is not a remedy, for no legitimate privacy interest has been invaded without good justification, but is instead a substantial punishment of the general public" (emphasis added). A requirement of sureness—of some approach to certainty—preserves the incentive of police to seek warrants where warrants are required without punishing harmless mistakes excessively. For we must bear in mind that the people who are punished when criminals escape justice are not the police; they are the people on whom criminals prey.

Judged by this intermediate test, inevitable discovery has been shown. The police unquestionably were lawfully in the apartment, and unquestionably entitled to open the cabinet in the entertainment center. And there in plain view was the blue travel bag that they knew contained cocaine. (Whether, though the bag itself did not reveal its contents, those contents could be thought in "plain view" because known with certainty, is an issue that has divided the circuits, *e.g.,* compare United States v. Gast, 405 F.3d 797, 801–02 (9th Cir.2005), with United States v. Williams, 41 F.3d 192, 197–98 (4th Cir.1994), and on which our court has not taken a position and need not do so in this case.) There isn't even the shadow of a doubt that had they applied for a warrant to search the bag, knowing what they knew, the warrant would have been issued. The case is remote from one in which the police, having probable cause to search a person's house, barge in and search without benefit of a warrant and defend their conduct by invoking inevitable discovery. If that defense prevailed, the requirement of obtaining a warrant to search a person's home would be out the window. The requirement of obtaining a warrant to search inside a container, when the container is known to contain contraband or other evidence of crime, is far from the core of the Fourth Amendment; as this case illustrates, there is a diminished risk of error or fabrication.

Affirmed.

Arizona v. Gant

556 U.S. 332 (2009)

■ JUSTICE STEVENS delivered the opinion of the Court.

After Rodney Gant was arrested for driving with a suspended license, handcuffed, and locked in the back of a patrol car, police officers searched his car and discovered cocaine in the pocket of a jacket on the backseat. Because Gant could not have accessed his car to retrieve weapons or evidence at the time of the search, the Arizona Supreme Court held that the search-incident-to-arrest exception to the Fourth Amendment's warrant requirement, as defined in Chimel v. California, 395 U.S. 752 (1969), and applied to vehicle searches in New York v. Belton, 453 U.S. 454 (1981), did not justify the search in this case. We agree with that conclusion.

Under *Chimel,* police may search incident to arrest only the space within an arrestee's " 'immediate control,' " meaning "the area from within which he might gain possession of a weapon or destructible evidence." 395 U.S., at 763. The safety and evidentiary justifications underlying *Chimel*'s reaching-distance rule determine *Belton*'s scope. Accordingly, we hold that *Belton* does not authorize a vehicle search incident to a recent occupant's arrest after the arrestee has been secured and cannot access the interior of the vehicle. Consistent with the holding in Thornton v. United States, 541 U.S. 615 (2004), and following the suggestion in Justice SCALIA's opinion concurring in the judgment in that case, *id.,* at 632, we also conclude that circumstances unique to the automobile context justify a search incident to arrest when it is reasonable to believe that evidence of the offense of arrest might be found in the vehicle.

I

On August 25, 1999, acting on an anonymous tip that the residence at 2524 North Walnut Avenue was being used to sell drugs, Tucson police officers Griffith and Reed knocked on the front door and asked to speak to the owner. Gant answered the door and, after identifying himself, stated that he expected the owner to return later. The officers left the residence and conducted a records check, which revealed that Gant's driver's license had been suspended and there was an outstanding warrant for his arrest for driving with a suspended license.

When the officers returned to the house that evening, they found a man near the back of the house and a woman in a car parked in front of it. After a third officer arrived, they arrested the man for providing a false name and the woman for possessing drug paraphernalia. Both arrestees were handcuffed and secured in separate patrol cars when Gant arrived. The officers recognized his car as it entered the driveway, and Officer Griffith confirmed that Gant was the driver by shining a flashlight into the car as it drove by him. Gant parked at the end of the driveway, got out of his car, and shut the door. Griffith, who was about 30 feet away, called to Gant, and they approached each other, meeting 10-to-12 feet from Gant's car. Griffith immediately arrested Gant and handcuffed him.

Because the other arrestees were secured in the only patrol cars at the scene, Griffith called for backup. When two more officers arrived, they locked Gant in the backseat of their vehicle. After Gant had been handcuffed and placed in the back of a patrol car, two officers searched his car: One of them found a gun, and the other discovered a bag of cocaine in the pocket of a jacket on the backseat.

Gant was charged with two offenses—possession of a narcotic drug for sale and possession of drug paraphernalia (*i.e.,* the plastic bag in which the cocaine was found). He moved to suppress the evidence seized from his car on the ground that the warrantless search violated the Fourth Amendment. Among other things, Gant argued that *Belton* did not authorize the search of his vehicle because he posed no threat to the officers after he was handcuffed in the patrol car and because he was arrested for a traffic offense for which no evidence could be found in his vehicle. When asked at the suppression hearing why the search was conducted, Officer Griffith responded: "Because the law says we can do it." App. 75.

The trial court rejected the State's contention that the officers had probable cause to search Gant's car for contraband when the search began, *id.,* at 18, 30, but it denied the motion to suppress. Relying on the fact that the police saw Gant commit the crime of driving without a license and apprehended him only shortly after he exited his car, the court held that the search was permissible as a search incident to arrest. *Id.,* at 37. A jury found Gant guilty on both drug counts, and he was sentenced to a 3-year term of imprisonment.

After protracted state-court proceedings, the Arizona Supreme Court concluded that the search of Gant's car was unreasonable within the meaning of the Fourth Amendment. The court's opinion discussed at length our decision in *Belton,* which held that police may search the passenger compartment of a vehicle and any containers therein as a contemporaneous incident of an arrest of the vehicle's recent occupant. 216 Ariz. 1, 3–4, 162 P.3d 640, 642–643 (2007) (citing 453 U.S., at 460). The court distinguished *Belton* as a case concerning the permissible scope of a vehicle search incident to arrest and concluded that it did not answer "the threshold question whether the police may conduct a search incident to arrest at all once the scene is secure." 216 Ariz., at 4, 162 P.3d, at 643. Relying on our earlier decision in *Chimel,* the court observed that the search-incident-to-arrest exception to the warrant requirement is justified by interests in officer safety and evidence preservation. 216 Ariz., at 4, 162 P.3d, at 643. When "the justifications underlying *Chimel* no longer exist because the scene is secure and the arrestee is handcuffed, secured in the back of a patrol car, and under the supervision of an officer," the court concluded, a "warrantless search of the arrestee's car cannot be justified as necessary to protect the officers at the scene or prevent the destruction of evidence." *Id.,* at 5, 162 P.3d, at 644. Accordingly, the court held that the search of Gant's car was unreasonable.

The dissenting justices would have upheld the search of Gant's car based on their view that "the validity of a *Belton* search . . . clearly does not depend on the presence of the *Chimel* rationales in a particular case." *Id.,* at 8, 162 P.3d, at 647. Although they disagreed with the majority's view of *Belton,* the dissenting justices acknowledged that "[t]he bright-line rule embraced in *Belton* has long been criticized and probably merits reconsideration." 216 Ariz., at 10, 162 P.3d, at 649. They thus "add[ed] their] voice[s] to the others that have urged the Supreme Court to revisit *Belton*." *Id.,* at 11, 163 P.3d, at 650.

The chorus that has called for us to revisit *Belton* includes courts, scholars, and Members of this Court who have questioned that decision's clarity and its fidelity to Fourth Amendment principles. We therefore granted the State's petition for certiorari. 552 U.S. ___ (2008).

II

Consistent with our precedent, our analysis begins, as it should in every case addressing the reasonableness of a warrantless search, with the basic rule that "searches conducted outside the judicial process, without prior approval by judge or magistrate, are *per se* unreasonable under the Fourth Amendment—subject only to a few specifically established and well-delineated exceptions." Katz v. United States, 389 U.S. 347, 357 (1967) (footnote omitted). Among the exceptions to the warrant requirement is a search incident to a lawful arrest. *See* Weeks v. United States, 232 U.S. 383, 392 2 (1914). The exception derives from interests in officer safety and evidence preservation that are typically implicated in arrest situations. *See* United States v. Robinson, 414 U.S. 218, 230–234 (1973); *Chimel,* 395 U.S., at 763. . . .

In *Belton,* we considered *Chimel*'s application to the automobile context. A lone police officer in that case stopped a speeding car in which Belton was one of four occupants. While asking for the driver's license and registration, the officer smelled burnt marijuana and observed an envelope on the car floor marked "Supergold"—a name he associated with marijuana. Thus having probable cause to believe the occupants had committed a drug offense, the officer ordered them out of the vehicle, placed them under arrest, and patted them down. Without handcuffing the arrestees,[1] the officer " 'split them up into four separate areas of the Thruway . . . so they would not be in physical touching area of each other' " and searched the vehicle, including the pocket of a jacket on the backseat, in which he found cocaine. 453 U.S., at 456.

The New York Court of Appeals found the search unconstitutional, concluding that after the occupants were arrested the vehicle and its contents were "safely within the exclusive custody and control of the police." State v. Belton, 50 N.Y.2d 447, 452, 429 N.Y.S.2d 574, 407 N.E.2d 420, 423 (1980). The State asked this Court to consider whether the exception recognized in *Chimel* permits an officer to search "a jacket found inside an automobile while the automobile's four occupants, all under arrest, are standing unsecured around the vehicle." Brief in No. 80–328, p. *i*. We granted certiorari because "courts ha[d] found no workable definition of 'the area within the immediate control of the arrestee' when that area arguably includes the interior of an automobile." 453 U.S., at 460.

. . . [W]e held that when an officer lawfully arrests "the occupant of an automobile, he may, as a contemporaneous incident of that arrest, search the passenger compartment of the automobile" and any containers

---

[1] The officer was unable to handcuff the occupants because he had only one set of handcuffs. *See* Brief for Petitioner in *New York v. Belton,* O.T.1980, No. 80-328, p. 3 (hereinafter Brief in No. 80-328).

therein. *Belton,* 453 U.S., at 460 (footnote omitted). That holding was based in large part on our assumption "that articles inside the relatively narrow compass of the passenger compartment of an automobile are in fact generally, even if not inevitably, within 'the area into which an arrestee might reach.' " *Ibid.*

The Arizona Supreme Court read our decision in *Belton* as merely delineating "the proper scope of a search of the interior of an automobile" incident to an arrest, *id.,* at 459. That is, *when* the passenger compartment is within an arrestee's reaching distance, *Belton* supplies the generalization that the entire compartment and any containers therein may be reached. On that view of *Belton,* the state court concluded that the search of Gant's car was unreasonable because Gant clearly could not have accessed his car at the time of the search. It also found that no other exception to the warrant requirement applied in this case.

Gant now urges us to adopt the reading of *Belton* followed by the Arizona Supreme Court.

III

Despite the textual and evidentiary support for the Arizona Supreme Court's reading of *Belton,* our opinion has been widely understood to allow a vehicle search incident to the arrest of a recent occupant even if there is no possibility the arrestee could gain access to the vehicle at the time of the search. This reading may be attributable to Justice Brennan's dissent in *Belton,* in which he characterized the Court's holding as resting on the "fiction . . . that the interior of a car is *always* within the immediate control of an arrestee who has recently been in the car." 453 U.S., at 466. Under the majority's approach, he argued, "the result would presumably be the same even if [the officer] had handcuffed Belton and his companions in the patrol car" before conducting the search. *Id.,* at 468.

Since we decided *Belton,* Courts of Appeals have given different answers to the question whether a vehicle must be within an arrestee's reach to justify a vehicle search incident to arrest,[2] but Justice Brennan's reading of the Court's opinion has predominated. As Justice O'Connor observed, "lower court decisions seem now to treat the ability to search a

---

[2] Compare United States v. Green, 324 F.3d 375, 379 (C.A.5 2003) (holding that *Belton* did not authorize a search of an arrestee's vehicle when he was handcuffed and lying facedown on the ground surrounded by four police officers 6-to-10 feet from the vehicle), United States v. Edwards, 242 F.3d 928, 938 (C.A.10 2001) (finding unauthorized a vehicle search conducted while the arrestee was handcuffed in the back of a patrol car), United States v. Vasey, 834 F.2d 782, 787 (C.A.9 1987) (finding unauthorized a vehicle search conducted 30-to-45 minutes after an arrest and after the arrestee had been handcuffed and secured in the back of a police car), with United States v. Hrasky, 453 F.3d 1099, 1102 (C.A.8 2006) (upholding a search conducted an hour after the arrestee was apprehended and after he had been handcuffed and placed in the back of a patrol car); United States v. Weaver, 433 F.3d 1104, 1106 (C.A.9 2006) (upholding a search conducted 10-to-15 minutes after an arrest and after the arrestee had been handcuffed and secured in the back of a patrol car), and United States v. White, 871 F.2d 41, 44 (C.A.6 1989) (upholding a search conducted after the arrestee had been handcuffed and secured in the back of a police cruiser).

vehicle incident to the arrest of a recent occupant as a police entitlement rather than as an exception justified by the twin rationales of *Chimel.*" *Thornton,* 541 U.S., at 624 (opinion concurring in part). Justice SCALIA has similarly noted that, although it is improbable that an arrestee could gain access to weapons stored in his vehicle after he has been handcuffed and secured in the backseat of a patrol car, cases allowing a search in "this precise factual scenario . . . are legion." *Id.,* at 628 (opinion concurring in judgment) (collecting cases).[3] Indeed, some courts have upheld searches under *Belton* "even when . . . the handcuffed arrestee has already left the scene." 541 U.S., at 628 (same).

Under this broad reading of *Belton,* a vehicle search would be authorized incident to every arrest of a recent occupant notwithstanding that in most cases the vehicle's passenger compartment will not be within the arrestee's reach at the time of the search. To read *Belton* as authorizing a vehicle search incident to every recent occupant's arrest would thus untether the rule from the justifications underlying the *Chimel* exception—a result clearly incompatible with our statement in *Belton* that it "in no way alters the fundamental principles established in the *Chimel* case regarding the basic scope of searches incident to lawful custodial arrests." 453 U.S., at 460, n. 3. Accordingly, we reject this reading of *Belton* and hold that the *Chimel* rationale authorizes police to search a vehicle incident to a recent occupant's arrest only when the arrestee is unsecured and within reaching distance of the passenger compartment at the time of the search.[4]

Although it does not follow from *Chimel,* we also conclude that circumstances unique to the vehicle context justify a search incident to a lawful arrest when it is "reasonable to believe evidence relevant to the crime of arrest might be found in the vehicle." *Thornton,* 541 U.S., at 632 (SCALIA, J., concurring in judgment). In many cases, as when a recent occupant is arrested for a traffic violation, there will be no reasonable basis to believe the vehicle contains relevant evidence. See, *e.g.,* Atwater v. Lago Vista, 532 U.S. 318, 324 (2001); Knowles v. Iowa, 525 U.S. 113, 118 (1998). But in others, including *Belton* and *Thornton,* the offense of arrest will supply a basis for searching the passenger compartment of an arrestee's vehicle and any containers therein.

---

[3] The practice of searching vehicles incident to arrest after the arrestee has been handcuffed and secured in a patrol car has not abated since we decided *Thornton.* See, *e.g.,* United States v. Murphy, 221 Fed.Appx. 715, 717 (C.A.10 2007); *Hrasky,* 453 F.3d, at 1100; *Weaver,* 433 F.3d, at 1105; United States v. Williams, 170 Fed.Appx. 399, 401 (C.A.6 2006); United States v. Dorsey, 418 F.3d 1038, 1041 (C.A.9 2005); United States v. Osife, 398 F.3d 1143, 1144 (C.A.9 2005); United States v. Sumrall, 115 Fed.Appx. 22, 24 (C.A.10 2004).

[4] Because officers have many means of ensuring the safe arrest of vehicle occupants, it will be the rare case in which an officer is unable to fully effectuate an arrest so that a real possibility of access to the arrestee's vehicle remains. *Cf.* 3 W. LaFave, Search and Seizure § 7.1(c), p. 525 (4th ed.2004) (hereinafter LaFave) (noting that the availability of protective measures "ensur[es] the nonexistence of circumstances in which the arrestee's 'control' of the car is in doubt"). But in such a case a search incident to arrest is reasonable under the Fourth Amendment.

Neither the possibility of access nor the likelihood of discovering offense-related evidence authorized the search in this case. Unlike in *Belton,* which involved a single officer confronted with four unsecured arrestees, the five officers in this case outnumbered the three arrestees, all of whom had been handcuffed and secured in separate patrol cars before the officers searched Gant's car. Under those circumstances, Gant clearly was not within reaching distance of his car at the time of the search. An evidentiary basis for the search was also lacking in this case. Whereas Belton and Thornton were arrested for drug offenses, Gant was arrested for driving with a suspended license—an offense for which police could not expect to find evidence in the passenger compartment of Gant's car. Cf. *Knowles,* 525 U.S., at 118. Because police could not reasonably have believed either that Gant could have accessed his car at the time of the search or that evidence of the offense for which he was arrested might have been found therein, the search in this case was unreasonable.

IV

The State does not seriously disagree with the Arizona Supreme Court's conclusion that Gant could not have accessed his vehicle at the time of the search, but it nevertheless asks us to uphold the search of his vehicle under the broad reading of *Belton* discussed above. The State argues that *Belton* searches are reasonable regardless of the possibility of access in a given case because that expansive rule correctly balances law enforcement interests, including the interest in a bright-line rule, with an arrestee's limited privacy interest in his vehicle.

For several reasons, we reject the State's argument. First, the State seriously undervalues the privacy interests at stake. Although we have recognized that a motorist's privacy interest in his vehicle is less substantial than in his home, s*ee* New York v. Class, 475 U.S. 106, 112–113 (1986), the former interest is nevertheless important and deserving of constitutional protection, *see Knowles,* 525 U.S., at 117. It is particularly significant that *Belton* searches authorize police officers to search not just the passenger compartment but every purse, briefcase, or other container within that space. A rule that gives police the power to conduct such a search whenever an individual is caught committing a traffic offense, when there is no basis for believing evidence of the offense might be found in the vehicle, creates a serious and recurring threat to the privacy of countless individuals. Indeed, the character of that threat implicates the central concern underlying the Fourth Amendment—the concern about giving police officers unbridled discretion to rummage at will among a person's private effects.[5]

At the same time as it undervalues these privacy concerns, the State exaggerates the clarity that its reading of *Belton* provides. Courts that have read *Belton* expansively are at odds regarding how close in time to

---

[5]   *See . . . See* 3 LaFave § 7.1(c), at 527 (observing that *Belton* creates the risk "that police will make custodial arrests which they otherwise would not make as a cover for a search which the Fourth Amendment otherwise prohibits") . . .

the arrest and how proximate to the arrestee's vehicle an officer's first contact with the arrestee must be to bring the encounter within *Belton*'s purview[6] and whether a search is reasonable when it commences or continues after the arrestee has been removed from the scene.[7] The rule has thus generated a great deal of uncertainty, particularly for a rule touted as providing a "bright line." *See* 3 LaFave, § 7.1(c), at 514–524.

Contrary to the State's suggestion, a broad reading of *Belton* is also unnecessary to protect law enforcement safety and evidentiary interests. Under our view, *Belton* and *Thornton* permit an officer to conduct a vehicle search when an arrestee is within reaching distance of the vehicle or it is reasonable to believe the vehicle contains evidence of the offense of arrest. Other established exceptions to the warrant requirement authorize a vehicle search under additional circumstances when safety or evidentiary concerns demand. For instance, Michigan v. Long, 463 U.S. 1032 (1983), permits an officer to search a vehicle's passenger compartment when he has reasonable suspicion that an individual, whether or not the arrestee, is "dangerous" and might access the vehicle to "gain immediate control of weapons." *Id.,* at 1049 (citing Terry v. Ohio, 392 U.S. 1, 21 (1968)). If there is probable cause to believe a vehicle contains evidence of criminal activity, United States v. Ross, 456 U.S. 798, 820–821 (1982), authorizes a search of any area of the vehicle in which the evidence might be found. Unlike the searches permitted by Justice SCALIA's opinion concurring in the judgment in *Thornton,* which we conclude today are reasonable for purposes of the Fourth Amendment, *Ross* allows searches for evidence relevant to offenses other than the offense of arrest, and the scope of the search authorized is broader. Finally, there may be still other circumstances in which safety or evidentiary interests would justify a search. Cf. Maryland v. Buie, 494 U.S. 325, 334 (1990) (holding that, incident to arrest, an officer may conduct a limited protective sweep of those areas of a house in which he reasonably suspects a dangerous person may be hiding).

These exceptions together ensure that officers may search a vehicle when genuine safety or evidentiary concerns encountered during the arrest of a vehicle's recent occupant justify a search. Construing *Belton* broadly to allow vehicle searches incident to any arrest would serve no

---

[6]   Compare United States v. Caseres, 533 F.3d 1064, 1072 (C.A.9 2008) (declining to apply *Belton* when the arrestee was approached by police after he had exited his vehicle and reached his residence), with Rainey v. Commonwealth, 197 S.W.3d 89, 94–95 (Ky.2006) (applying *Belton* when the arrestee was apprehended 50 feet from the vehicle), and Black v. State, 810 N.E.2d 713, 716 (Ind.2004) (applying *Belton* when the arrestee was apprehended inside an auto repair shop and the vehicle was parked outside).

[7]   Compare *McLaughlin,* 170 F.3d, at 890–891 (upholding a search that commenced five minutes after the arrestee was removed from the scene), United States v. Snook, 88 F.3d 605, 608 (C.A.8 1996) (same), and United States v. Doward, 41 F.3d 789, 793 (C.A.1 1994) (upholding a search that continued after the arrestee was removed from the scene), with United States v. Lugo, 978 F.2d 631, 634 (C.A.10 1992) (holding invalid a search that commenced after the arrestee was removed from the scene), and State v. Badgett, 200 Conn. 412, 427–428, 512 A.2d 160, 169 (1986) (holding invalid a search that continued after the arrestee was removed from the scene).

purpose except to provide a police entitlement, and it is anathema to the Fourth Amendment to permit a warrantless search on that basis. For these reasons, we are unpersuaded by the State's arguments that a broad reading of *Belton* would meaningfully further law enforcement interests and justify a substantial intrusion on individuals' privacy.[8]

V

Our dissenting colleagues argue that the doctrine of *stare decisis* requires adherence to a broad reading of *Belton* even though the justifications for searching a vehicle incident to arrest are in most cases absent. The doctrine of *stare decisis* is of course "essential to the respect accorded to the judgments of the Court and to the stability of the law," but it does not compel us to follow a past decision when its rationale no longer withstands "careful analysis." Lawrence v. Texas, 539 U.S. 558, 577 (2003).

We have never relied on *stare decisis* to justify the continuance of an unconstitutional police practice. And we would be particularly loath to uphold an unconstitutional result in a case that is so easily distinguished from the decisions that arguably compel it. The safety and evidentiary interests that supported the search in *Belton* simply are not present in this case. Indeed, it is hard to imagine two cases that are factually more distinct, as *Belton* involved one officer confronted by four unsecured arrestees suspected of committing a drug offense and this case involves several officers confronted with a securely detained arrestee apprehended for driving with a suspended license. This case is also distinguishable from *Thornton,* in which the petitioner was arrested for a drug offense. It is thus unsurprising that Members of this Court who concurred in the judgments in *Belton* and *Thornton* also concur in the decision in this case.[10]

We do not agree with the contention in Justice ALITO's dissent (hereinafter dissent) that consideration of police reliance interests requires a different result. Although it appears that the State's reading of *Belton* has been widely taught in police academies and that law enforcement officers have relied on the rule in conducting vehicle searches during the past 28 years,[11] many of these searches were not justified by the reasons underlying the *Chimel* exception. Countless

---

[8]   At least eight States have reached the same conclusion. Vermont, New Jersey, New Mexico, Nevada, Pennsylvania, New York, Oregon, and Wyoming have declined to follow a broad reading of *Belton* under their state constitutions. . . . And a Massachusetts statute provides that a search incident to arrest may be made only for the purposes of seizing weapons or evidence of the offense of arrest. *See* Commonwealth v. Toole, 389 Mass. 159, 161–162, 448 N.E.2d 1264, 1266–1267 (1983) (citing Mass. Gen. Laws, ch. 276, § 1 (West 2007)).

[10]   Justice STEVENS concurred in the judgment in *Belton,* 453 U.S., at 463, for the reasons stated in his dissenting opinion in Robbins v. California, 453 U.S. 420, 444 (1981), Justice THOMAS joined the Court's opinion in *Thornton,* 541 U.S. 615, and Justice SCALIA and Justice GINSBURG concurred in the judgment in that case, *id.,* at 625.

[11]   Because a broad reading of *Belton* has been widely accepted, the doctrine of qualified immunity will shield officers from liability for searches conducted in reasonable reliance on that understanding.

individuals guilty of nothing more serious than a traffic violation have had their constitutional right to the security of their private effects violated as a result. The fact that the law enforcement community may view the State's version of the *Belton* rule as an entitlement does not establish the sort of reliance interest that could outweigh the countervailing interest that all individuals share in having their constitutional rights fully protected. If it is clear that a practice is unlawful, individuals' interest in its discontinuance clearly outweighs any law enforcement "entitlement" to its persistence. Cf. Mincey v. Arizona, 437 U.S. 385, 393 (1978) ("[T]he mere fact that law enforcement may be made more efficient can never by itself justify disregard of the Fourth Amendment"). The dissent's reference in this regard to the reliance interests cited in Dickerson v. United States, 530 U.S. 428 (2000), is misplaced. *See post,* at 1728. In observing that *"Miranda* has become embedded in routine police practice to the point where the warnings have become part of our national culture," 530 U.S., at 443, the Court was referring not to police reliance on a rule requiring them to provide warnings but to the broader societal reliance on that individual right.

The dissent also ignores the checkered history of the search-incident-to-arrest exception. Police authority to search the place in which a lawful arrest is made was broadly asserted in Marron v. United States, 275 U.S. 192 (1927), and limited a few years later in Go-Bart Importing Co. v. United States, 282 U.S. 344 (1931), and United States v. Lefkowitz, 285 U.S. 452 (1932). The limiting views expressed in *Go-Bart* and *Lefkowitz* were in turn abandoned in Harris v. United States, 331 U.S. 145 (1947), which upheld a search of a four-room apartment incident to the occupant's arrest. Only a year later the Court in Trupiano v. United States, 334 U.S. 699, 708 (1948), retreated from that holding, noting that the search-incident-to-arrest exception is "a strictly limited" one that must be justified by "something more in the way of necessity than merely a lawful arrest." And just two years after that, in United States v. Rabinowitz, 339 U.S. 56 (1950), the Court again reversed course and upheld the search of an entire apartment. Finally, our opinion in *Chimel* overruled *Rabinowitz* and what remained of *Harris* and established the present boundaries of the search-incident-to-arrest exception. Notably, none of the dissenters in *Chimel* or the cases that preceded it argued that law enforcement reliance interests outweighed the interest in protecting individual constitutional rights so as to warrant fidelity to an unjustifiable rule.

The experience of the 28 years since we decided *Belton* has shown that the generalization underpinning the broad reading of that decision is unfounded. We now know that articles inside the passenger compartment are rarely "within 'the area into which an arrestee might reach,' " 453 U.S., at 460, and blind adherence to *Belton*'s faulty assumption would authorize myriad unconstitutional searches. The doctrine of *stare decisis* does not require us to approve routine constitutional violations.

VI

Police may search a vehicle incident to a recent occupant's arrest only if the arrestee is within reaching distance of the passenger compartment at the time of the search or it is reasonable to believe the vehicle contains evidence of the offense of arrest. When these justifications are absent, a search of an arrestee's vehicle will be unreasonable unless police obtain a warrant or show that another exception to the warrant requirement applies. The Arizona Supreme Court correctly held that this case involved an unreasonable search. Accordingly, the judgment of the State Supreme Court is affirmed.

It is so ordered.

■ JUSTICE SCALIA, concurring.

To determine what is an "unreasonable" search within the meaning of the Fourth Amendment, we look first to the historical practices the Framers sought to preserve; if those provide inadequate guidance, we apply traditional standards of reasonableness. *See* Virginia v. Moore, 553 U.S. ___, ___ (2008). Since the historical scope of officers' authority to search vehicles incident to arrest is uncertain, *see* Thornton v. United States, 541 U.S. 615, 629–631 (2004) (SCALIA, J., concurring in judgment), traditional standards of reasonableness govern. It is abundantly clear that those standards do not justify what I take to be the rule set forth in New York v. Belton, 453 U.S. 454 (1981), and *Thornton:* that arresting officers may always search an arrestee's vehicle in order to protect themselves from hidden weapons. When an arrest is made in connection with a roadside stop, police virtually always have a less intrusive and more effective means of ensuring their safety—and a means that is virtually always employed: ordering the arrestee away from the vehicle, patting him down in the open, handcuffing him, and placing him in the squad car.

Law enforcement officers face a risk of being shot whenever they pull a car over. But that risk is at its height at the time of the initial confrontation; and it is *not at all* reduced by allowing a search of the stopped vehicle after the driver has been arrested and placed in the squad car. I observed in *Thornton* that the government had failed to provide a single instance in which a formerly restrained arrestee escaped to retrieve a weapon from his own vehicle, 541 U.S., at 626; Arizona and its *amici* have not remedied that significant deficiency in the present case.

It must be borne in mind that we are speaking here only of a rule automatically permitting a search when the driver or an occupant is arrested. Where no arrest is made, we have held that officers may search the car if they reasonably believe "the suspect is dangerous and . . . may gain immediate control of weapons." Michigan v. Long, 463 U.S. 1032, 1049 (1983). In the no-arrest case, the possibility of access to weapons in the vehicle always exists, since the driver or passenger will be allowed to return to the vehicle when the interrogation is completed. The rule of *Michigan v. Long* is not at issue here.

Justice STEVENS acknowledges that an officer-safety rationale cannot justify all vehicle searches incident to arrest, but asserts that that is not the rule *Belton* and *Thornton* adopted. (As described above, I read those cases differently). Justice STEVENS would therefore retain the application of Chimel v. California, 395 U.S. 752 (1969), in the car-search context but would apply in the future what he believes our cases held in the past: that officers making a roadside stop may search the vehicle so long as the "arrestee is within reaching distance of the passenger compartment at the time of the search." *Ante,* at 1723. I believe that this standard fails to provide the needed guidance to arresting officers and also leaves much room for manipulation, inviting officers to leave the scene unsecured (at least where dangerous suspects are not involved) in order to conduct a vehicle search. In my view we should simply abandon the *Belton-Thornton* charade of officer safety and overrule those cases. I would hold that a vehicle search incident to arrest is *ipso facto* "reasonable" only when the object of the search is evidence of the crime for which the arrest was made, or of another crime that the officer has probable cause to believe occurred. Because respondent was arrested for driving without a license (a crime for which no evidence could be expected to be found in the vehicle), I would hold in the present case that the search was unlawful.

Justice ALITO insists that the Court must demand a good reason for abandoning prior precedent. That is true enough, but it seems to me ample reason that the precedent was badly reasoned and produces erroneous (in this case unconstitutional) results. *See* Payne v. Tennessee, 501 U.S. 808, 827 (1991). We should recognize *Belton*'s fanciful reliance upon officer safety for what it was: "a return to the broader sort of [evidence-gathering] search incident to arrest that we allowed before *Chimel*." *Thornton, supra,* at 631 (SCALIA, J., concurring in judgment; citations omitted).

Justice ALITO argues that there is no reason to adopt a rule limiting automobile-arrest searches to those cases where the search's object is evidence of the crime of arrest. *Post,* at 1731 (dissenting opinion). I disagree. This formulation of officers' authority both preserves the outcomes of our prior cases and tethers the scope and rationale of the doctrine to the triggering event. *Belton,* by contrast, allowed searches precisely when its exigency-based rationale was least applicable: The fact of the arrest in the automobile context makes searches on exigency grounds *less* reasonable, not more. I also disagree with Justice ALITO's conclusory assertion that this standard will be difficult to administer in practice, *post,* at 1729; the ease of its application in this case would suggest otherwise.

No other Justice, however, shares my view that application of *Chimel* in this context should be entirely abandoned. It seems to me unacceptable for the Court to come forth with a 4-to-1-to-4 opinion that leaves the governing rule uncertain. I am therefore confronted with the choice of either leaving the current understanding of *Belton* and *Thornton* in effect, or acceding to what seems to me the artificial narrowing of those cases adopted by Justice STEVENS. The latter, as I have said, does not provide the degree of certainty I think desirable in this field; but the former opens the field to what I think are plainly unconstitutional searches—which is the greater evil. I therefore join the opinion of the Court.

■ JUSTICE ALITO, with whom THE CHIEF JUSTICE and JUSTICE KENNEDY join, and with whom JUSTICE BREYER JOINS except as to Part II-E, dissenting.

Twenty-eight years ago, in New York v. Belton, 453 U.S. 454, 460 (1981), this Court held that "when a policeman has made a lawful custodial arrest of the occupant of an automobile, he may, as a contemporaneous incident of that arrest, search the passenger compartment of that automobile." (Footnote omitted.) Five years ago, in Thornton v. United States, 541 U.S. 615 (2004)—a case involving a situation not materially distinguishable from the situation here—the Court not only reaffirmed but extended the holding of *Belton,* making it applicable to recent occupants. Today's decision effectively overrules those important decisions, even though respondent Gant has not asked us to do so.

To take the place of the overruled precedents, the Court adopts a new two-part rule under which a police officer who arrests a vehicle occupant or recent occupant may search the passenger compartment if (1) the arrestee is within reaching distance of the vehicle at the time of the search or (2) the officer has reason to believe that the vehicle contains evidence of the offense of arrest. The first part of this new rule may endanger arresting officers and is truly endorsed by only four Justices; Justice SCALIA joins solely for the purpose of avoiding a "4-to-1-to 4 opinion." *Ante,* at 1725 (concurring opinion). The second part of the new rule is taken from Justice SCALIA's separate opinion in *Thornton* without any independent explanation of its origin or justification and is virtually certain to confuse law enforcement officers and judges for some time to come. The Court's decision will cause the suppression of evidence gathered in many searches carried out in good-faith reliance on well-settled case law, and although the Court purports to base its analysis on the landmark decision in Chimel v. California, 395 U.S. 752 (1969), the Court's reasoning undermines *Chimel*. I would follow *Belton,* and I therefore respectfully dissent. . . .

Riley v. California & United States v. Wurie

573 U.S. 373 (2014)

■ ROBERTS, C.J., delivered the opinion of the Court, in which SCALIA, KENNEDY, THOMAS, GINSBURG, BREYER, SOTOMAYOR, and KAGAN, JJ., joined. ALITO, J., filed an opinion concurring in part and concurring in the judgment.

■ CHIEF JUSTICE ROBERTS delivered the opinion of the Court.

These two cases raise a common question: whether the police may, without a warrant, search digital information on a cell phone seized from an individual who has been arrested.

I

A

In the first case, petitioner David Riley was stopped by a police officer for driving with expired registration tags. In the course of the stop, the officer also learned that Riley's license had been suspended. The officer impounded Riley's car, pursuant to department policy, and another officer conducted an inventory search of the car. Riley was arrested for possession of concealed and loaded firearms when that search turned up two handguns under the car's hood.

An officer searched Riley incident to the arrest and found items associated with the "Bloods" street gang. He also seized a cell phone from Riley's pants pocket. According to Riley's uncontradicted assertion, the phone was a "smart phone," a cell phone with a broad range of other functions based on advanced computing capability, large storage capacity, and Internet connectivity. The officer accessed information on the phone and noticed that some words (presumably in text messages or a contacts list) were preceded by the letters "CK"—a label that, he believed, stood for "Crip Killers," a slang term for members of the Bloods gang.

At the police station about two hours after the arrest, a detective specializing in gangs further examined the contents of the phone. The detective testified that he "went through" Riley's phone "looking for evidence, because . . . gang members will often video themselves with guns or take pictures of themselves with the guns." Although there was "a lot of stuff" on the phone, particular files that "caught [the detective's] eye" included videos of young men sparring while someone yelled encouragement using the moniker "Blood." The police also found photographs of Riley standing in front of a car they suspected had been involved in a shooting a few weeks earlier.

Riley was ultimately charged, in connection with that earlier shooting, with firing at an occupied vehicle, assault with a semiautomatic firearm, and attempted murder. The State alleged that Riley had committed those crimes for the benefit of a criminal street gang, an aggravating factor that carries an enhanced sentence. Prior to trial, Riley moved to suppress all evidence that the police had obtained from his cell phone. He contended that the searches of his phone violated the Fourth Amendment, because they had been performed without a warrant and were not otherwise justified by exigent circumstances. The trial court rejected that argument. At Riley's trial, police officers testified about the photographs and videos found on the phone, and some of the photographs were admitted into evidence. Riley was convicted on all three counts and received an enhanced sentence of 15 years to life in prison.

The California Court of Appeal affirmed. The court relied on the California Supreme Court's decision in People v. Diaz, 51 Cal.4th 84, 119 Cal.Rptr.3d 105, 244 P.3d 501 (2011), which held that the Fourth Amendment permits a warrantless search of cell phone data incident to an arrest, so long as the cell phone was immediately associated with the arrestee's person.

The California Supreme Court denied Riley's petition for review, and we granted certiorari.

B

In the second case, a police officer performing routine surveillance observed respondent Brima Wurie make an apparent drug sale from a car. Officers subsequently arrested Wurie and took him to the police station. At the station, the officers seized two cell phones from Wurie's person. The one at issue here was a "flip phone," a kind of phone that is flipped open for use and that generally has a smaller range of features than a smart phone. Five to ten minutes after arriving at the station, the officers noticed that the phone was repeatedly receiving calls from a source identified as "my house" on the phone's external screen. A few minutes later, they opened the phone and saw a photograph of a woman and a baby set as the phone's wallpaper. They pressed one button on the phone to access its call log, then another button to determine the phone number associated with the "my house" label. They next used an online phone directory to trace that phone number to an apartment building.

When the officers went to the building, they saw Wurie's name on a mailbox and observed through a window a woman who resembled the woman in the photograph on Wurie's phone. They secured the apartment while obtaining a search warrant and, upon later executing the warrant, found and seized 215 grams of crack cocaine, marijuana, drug paraphernalia, a firearm and ammunition, and cash.

Wurie was charged with distributing crack cocaine, possessing crack cocaine with intent to distribute, and being a felon in possession of a firearm and ammunition. *See* 18 U.S.C. § 922(g); 21 U.S.C. § 841(a). He moved to suppress the evidence obtained from the search of the apartment, arguing that it was the fruit of an unconstitutional search of his cell phone. The District Court denied the motion. Wurie was convicted on all three counts and sentenced to 262 months in prison.

A divided panel of the First Circuit reversed the denial of Wurie's motion to suppress and vacated Wurie's convictions for possession with intent to distribute and possession of a firearm as a felon. The court held that cell phones are distinct from other physical possessions that may be searched incident to arrest without a warrant, because of the amount of personal data cell phones contain and the negligible threat they pose to law enforcement interests.

We granted certiorari.

II

The Fourth Amendment provides:

"The right of the people to be secure in their persons, houses, papers, and effects, against unreasonable searches and seizures, shall not be violated, and no Warrants shall issue, but upon probable cause, supported by Oath or affirmation, and particularly describing the place to be searched, and the persons or things to be seized."

As the text makes clear, "the ultimate touchstone of the Fourth Amendment is 'reasonableness.' " Brigham City v. Stuart, 547 U.S. 398, 403 2006). Our cases have determined that "[w]here a search is undertaken by law enforcement officials to discover evidence of criminal wrongdoing, . . . reasonableness generally requires the obtaining of a judicial warrant." Vernonia School Dist. 47J v. Acton, 515 U.S. 646, 653 (1995). Such a warrant ensures that the inferences to support a search are "drawn by a neutral and detached magistrate instead of being judged by the officer engaged in the often competitive enterprise of ferreting out crime." Johnson v. United States, 333 U.S. 10, 14 (1948). In the absence of a warrant, a search is reasonable only if it falls within a specific exception to the warrant requirement. *See* Kentucky v. King, 563 U.S. ___, ___ (2011).

The two cases before us concern the reasonableness of a warrantless search incident to a lawful arrest. In 1914, this Court first acknowledged in dictum "the right on the part of the Government, always recognized under English and American law, to search the person of the accused when legally arrested to discover and seize the fruits or evidences of crime." Weeks v. United States, 232 U.S. 383, 392. Since that time, it has been well accepted that such a search constitutes an exception to the warrant requirement. Indeed, the label "exception" is something of a misnomer in this context, as warrantless searches incident to arrest occur with far greater frequency than searches conducted pursuant to a warrant. *See* 3 W. LaFave, Search and Seizure § 5.2(b), p. 132, and n. 15 (5th ed. 2012).

Although the existence of the exception for such searches has been recognized for a century, its scope has been debated for nearly as long. *See* Arizona v. Gant, 556 U.S. 332, 350 (2009) (noting the exception's "checkered history"). That debate has focused on the extent to which officers may search property found on or near the arrestee. Three related precedents set forth the rules governing such searches:

The first, Chimel v. California, 395 U.S. 752 (1969), laid the groundwork for most of the existing search incident to arrest doctrine. Police officers in that case arrested Chimel inside his home and proceeded to search his entire three-bedroom house, including the attic and garage. In particular rooms, they also looked through the contents of drawers.

The Court crafted the following rule for assessing the reasonableness of a search incident to arrest:

> "When an arrest is made, it is reasonable for the arresting officer to search the person arrested in order to remove any weapons that the latter might seek to use in order to resist arrest or effect his escape. Otherwise, the officer's safety might well be endangered, and the arrest itself frustrated. In addition, it is entirely reasonable for the arresting officer to search for and seize any evidence on the arrestee's person in order to prevent its concealment or destruction. . . . There is ample justification, therefore, for a search of the arrestee's person and the area 'within his immediate control'—construing that phrase to mean the area from within which he might gain possession of a weapon or destructible evidence."

The extensive warrantless search of Chimel's home did not fit within this exception, because it was not needed to protect officer safety or to preserve evidence.

Four years later, in United States v. Robinson, 414 U.S. 218 (1973), the Court applied the *Chimel* analysis in the context of a search of the arrestee's person. A police officer had arrested Robinson for driving with a revoked license. The officer conducted a patdown search and felt an object that he could not identify in Robinson's coat pocket. He removed the object, which turned out to be a crumpled cigarette package, and opened it. Inside were 14 capsules of heroin.

> [The Court of Appeals concluded that the search was unreasonable because Robinson was unlikely to have evidence of the crime of arrest on his person, and because it believed that extracting the cigarette package and opening it could not be justified as part of a protective search for weapons. This Court reversed, rejecting the notion that "case-by-case adjudication" was required to determine "whether or not there was present one of the reasons supporting the authority for a search of the person incident to a lawful arrest." As the Court explained, "[t]he authority to search the person incident to a lawful custodial arrest, while based upon the need to disarm and to discover evidence, does not depend on what a court may later decide was the probability in a particular arrest situation that

weapons or evidence would in fact be found upon the person of the suspect." Instead, a "custodial arrest of a suspect based on probable cause is a reasonable intrusion under the Fourth Amendment; that intrusion being lawful, a search incident to the arrest requires no additional justification."

The Court thus concluded that the search of Robinson was reasonable even though there was no concern about the loss of evidence, and the arresting officer had no specific concern that Robinson might be armed. In doing so, the Court did not draw a line between a search of Robinson's person and a further examination of the cigarette pack found during that search. It merely noted that, "[h]aving in the course of a lawful search come upon the crumpled package of cigarettes, [the officer] was entitled to inspect it." *Ibid.* A few years later, the Court clarified that this exception was limited to "personal property . . . immediately associated with the person of the arrestee." United States v. Chadwick, 433 U.S. 1, 15 538 (1977) (200-pound, locked footlocker could not be searched incident to arrest), abrogated on other grounds by California v. Acevedo, 500 U.S. 565 (1991).

The search incident to arrest trilogy concludes with *Gant,* which analyzed searches of an arrestee's vehicle. *Gant,* like *Robinson,* recognized that the *Chimel* concerns for officer safety and evidence preservation underlie the search incident to arrest exception. As a result, the Court concluded that *Chimel* could authorize police to search a vehicle "only when the arrestee is unsecured and within reaching distance of the passenger compartment at the time of the search." *Gant* added, however, an independent exception for a warrantless search of a vehicle's passenger compartment "when it is 'reasonable to believe evidence relevant to the crime of arrest might be found in the vehicle.'" *Ibid.* (quoting Thornton v. United States, 541 U.S. 615, 632 (2004) (SCALIA, J., concurring in judgment)). That exception stems not from *Chimel,* the Court explained, but from "circumstances unique to the vehicle context."

III

These cases require us to decide how the search incident to arrest doctrine applies to modern cell phones, which are now such a pervasive and insistent part of daily life that the proverbial visitor from Mars might conclude they were an important feature of human anatomy. A smart phone of the sort taken from Riley was unheard of ten years ago; a significant majority of American adults now own such phones. *See* A. Smith, Pew Research Center, Smartphone Ownership—2013 Update (June 5, 2013). Even less sophisticated phones like Wurie's, which have already faded in popularity since Wurie was arrested in 2007, have been around for less than 15 years. Both phones are based on technology nearly inconceivable just a few decades ago, when *Chimel* and *Robinson* were decided.

Absent more precise guidance from the founding era, we generally determine whether to exempt a given type of search from the warrant requirement "by assessing, on the one hand, the degree to which it intrudes upon an individual's privacy and, on the other, the degree to which it is needed for the promotion of legitimate governmental interests." Wyoming v. Houghton, 526 U.S. 295, 300 (1999). Such a balancing of interests supported the search incident to arrest exception in *Robinson,* and a mechanical application of *Robinson* might well support the warrantless searches at issue here.

But while *Robinson*'s categorical rule strikes the appropriate balance in the context of physical objects, neither of its rationales has much force with respect to digital content on cell phones. On the government interest side, *Robinson* concluded that the two risks identified in *Chimel*—harm to officers and destruction of evidence—are present in all custodial arrests. There are no comparable risks when the search is of digital data. In addition, *Robinson* regarded any privacy interests retained by an individual after arrest as significantly diminished by the fact of the arrest itself. Cell phones, however, place vast quantities of personal information literally in the hands of individuals. A search of the information on a cell phone bears little resemblance to the type of brief physical search considered in Robinson.

We therefore decline to extend *Robinson* to searches of data on cell phones, and hold instead that officers must generally secure a warrant before conducting such a search.

A

We first consider each *Chimel* concern in turn. In doing so, we do not overlook *Robinson*'s admonition that searches of a person incident to arrest, "while based upon the need to disarm and to discover evidence," are reasonable regardless of "the probability in a particular arrest situation that weapons or evidence would in fact be found." Rather than requiring the "case-by-case adjudication" that *Robinson* rejected, we ask instead whether application of the search incident to arrest doctrine to this particular category of effects would "untether the rule from the justifications underlying the Chimel exception," *Gant, supra,* at 343. *See also* Knowles v. Iowa, 525 U.S. 113, 119 (1998) (declining to extend *Robinson* to the issuance of citations, "a situation where the concern for officer safety is not present to the same extent and the concern for destruction or loss of evidence is not present at all").

1

Digital data stored on a cell phone cannot itself be used as a weapon to harm an arresting officer or to effectuate the arrestee's escape. Law enforcement officers remain free to examine the physical aspects of a phone to ensure that it will not be used as a weapon—say, to determine whether there is a razor blade hidden between the phone and its case.

Once an officer has secured a phone and eliminated any potential physical threats, however, data on the phone can endanger no one.

Perhaps the same might have been said of the cigarette pack seized from Robinson's pocket. Once an officer gained control of the pack, it was unlikely that Robinson could have accessed the pack's contents. But unknown physical objects may always pose risks, no matter how slight, during the tense atmosphere of a custodial arrest. The officer in *Robinson* testified that he could not identify the objects in the cigarette pack but knew they were not cigarettes. Given that, a further search was a reasonable protective measure. No such unknowns exist with respect to digital data. As the First Circuit explained, the officers who searched Wurie's cell phone "knew exactly what they would find therein: data. They also knew that the data could not harm them." 728 F.3d, at 10.

The United States and California both suggest that a search of cell phone data might help ensure officer safety in more indirect ways, for example by alerting officers that confederates of the arrestee are headed to the scene. There is undoubtedly a strong government interest in warning officers about such possibilities, but neither the United States nor California offers evidence to suggest that their concerns are based on actual experience. The proposed consideration would also represent a broadening of *Chimel*'s concern that an arrestee himself might grab a weapon and use it against an officer "to resist arrest or effect his escape." And any such threats from outside the arrest scene do not "lurk[ ] in all custodial arrests." *Chadwick,* 433 U.S., at 14–15. Accordingly, the interest in protecting officer safety does not justify dispensing with the warrant requirement across the board. To the extent dangers to arresting officers may be implicated in a particular way in a particular case, they are better addressed through consideration of case-specific exceptions to the warrant requirement, such as the one for exigent circumstances. *See, e.g.,* Warden, Md. Penitentiary v. Hayden, 387 U.S. 294, 298–299 (1967) ("The Fourth Amendment does not require police officers to delay in the course of an investigation if to do so would gravely endanger their lives or the lives of others.").

2

The United States and California focus primarily on the second *Chimel* rationale: preventing the destruction of evidence.

Both Riley and Wurie concede that officers could have seized and secured their cell phones to prevent destruction of evidence while seeking a warrant. That is a sensible concession. *See* Illinois v. McArthur, 531 U.S. 326, 331–333 (2001); *Chadwick, supra,* at 13, and n. 8. And once law enforcement officers have secured a cell phone, there is no longer any risk that the arrestee himself will be able to delete incriminating data from the phone.

The United States and California argue that information on a cell phone may nevertheless be vulnerable to two types of evidence destruction unique to digital data—remote wiping and data encryption. Remote wiping occurs when a phone, connected to a wireless network, receives a signal that erases stored data. This can happen when a third party sends a remote signal or when a phone is preprogrammed to delete data upon entering or leaving certain geographic areas (so-called "geofencing"). *See* Dept. of Commerce, National Institute of Standards and Technology, R. Ayers, S. Brothers, & W. Jansen, Guidelines on Mobile Device Forensics (Draft) 29, 31 (SP 800–101 Rev. 1, Sept. 2013) (hereinafter Ayers). Encryption is a security feature that some modern cell phones use in addition to password protection. When such phones lock, data becomes protected by sophisticated encryption that renders a phone all but "unbreakable" unless police know the password. Brief for United States as Amicus Curiae in No. 13–132, p. 11.

As an initial matter, these broader concerns about the loss of evidence are distinct from *Chimel*'s focus on a defendant who responds to arrest by trying to conceal or destroy evidence within his reach. With respect to remote wiping, the Government's primary concern turns on the actions of third parties who are not present at the scene of arrest. And data encryption is even further afield. There, the Government focuses on the ordinary operation of a phone's security features, apart from any active attempt by a defendant or his associates to conceal or destroy evidence upon arrest.

We have also been given little reason to believe that either problem is prevalent. The briefing reveals only a couple of anecdotal examples of remote wiping triggered by an arrest. *See* Brief for Association of State Criminal Investigative Agencies et al. as Amici Curiae in No. 13–132, pp. 9–10; *See* also Tr. of Oral Arg. in No. 13–132, p. 48. Similarly, the opportunities for officers to search a password-protected phone before data becomes encrypted are quite limited. Law enforcement officers are very unlikely to come upon such a phone in an unlocked state because most phones lock at the touch of a button or, as a default, after some very short period of inactivity. See, e.g., iPhone User Guide for iOS 7.1 Software 10 (2014) (default lock after about one minute). This may explain why the encryption argument was not made until the merits stage in this Court, and has never been considered by the Courts of Appeals.

Moreover, in situations in which an arrest might trigger a remote-wipe attempt or an officer discovers an unlocked phone, it is not clear that the ability to conduct a warrantless search would make much of a difference. The need to effect the arrest, secure the scene, and tend to other pressing matters means that law enforcement officers may well not be able to turn their attention to a cell phone right away. *See* Tr. of Oral Arg. in No. 13–132, at 50; *See also* Brief for United States as Amicus Curiae in No. 13–132, at 19. Cell phone data would be vulnerable to remote wiping from the time an individual anticipates arrest to the time any eventual search of the phone is completed, which might be at the station house hours later. Likewise, an officer who seizes a phone in an unlocked state might not be able to begin his search in the short time remaining before the phone locks and data becomes encrypted.

In any event, as to remote wiping, law enforcement is not without specific means to address the threat. Remote wiping can be fully prevented by disconnecting a phone from the network. There are at least two simple ways to do this: First, law enforcement officers can turn the phone off or remove its battery. Second, if they are concerned about encryption or other potential problems, they can leave a phone powered on and place it in an enclosure that isolates the phone from radio waves. *See* Ayers 30–31. Such devices are commonly called "Faraday bags," after the English scientist Michael Faraday. They are essentially sandwich bags made of aluminum foil: cheap, lightweight, and easy to use. *See* Brief for Criminal Law Professors as Amici Curiae 9. They may not be a complete answer to the problem, *see* Ayers 32, but at least for now they provide a reasonable response. In fact, a number of law enforcement agencies around the country already encourage the use of Faraday bags. See, e.g., Dept. of Justice, National Institute of Justice, Electronic Crime Scene Investigation: A Guide for First Responders 14, 32 (2d ed. Apr. 2008); Brief for Criminal Law Professors as Amici Curiae 4–6.

To the extent that law enforcement still has specific concerns about the potential loss of evidence in a particular case, there remain more targeted ways to address those concerns. If "the police are truly confronted with a 'now or never' situation,"—for example, circumstances suggesting that a defendant's phone will be the target of an imminent remote-wipe attempt—they may be able to rely on exigent circumstances to search the phone immediately. Missouri v. McNeely, 569 U.S. ___, ___ (2013) (quoting Roaden v. Kentucky, 413 U.S. 496, 505 (1973); some internal quotation marks omitted). Or, if officers happen to seize a phone in an unlocked state, they may be able to disable a phone's automatic-lock feature in order to prevent the phone from locking and encrypting data. *See* App. to Reply Brief in No. 13–132, p. 3a (diagramming the few necessary steps). Such a preventive measure could be analyzed under the principles set forth in our decision in *McArthur*, 531 U.S. 326, which approved officers' reasonable steps to secure a scene to preserve evidence while they awaited a warrant.

B

The search incident to arrest exception rests not only on the heightened government interests at stake in a volatile arrest situation, but also on an arrestee's reduced privacy interests upon being taken into police custody. Robinson focused primarily on the first of those rationales. But it also quoted with approval then-Judge Cardozo's account of the historical basis for the search incident to arrest exception: "Search of the person becomes lawful when grounds for arrest and accusation have been discovered, and the law is in the act of subjecting the body of the accused to its physical dominion." 414 U.S., at 232 (quoting People v. Chiagles, 237 N.Y. 193, 197, 142 N.E. 583, 584 (1923)); *see also* 414 U.S., at 237 (Powell, J., concurring) ("an individual lawfully subjected to a custodial arrest retains no significant Fourth Amendment interest in the privacy of his person"). Put simply, a patdown of Robinson's clothing and an inspection of the cigarette pack found in his pocket constituted only minor additional intrusions compared to the substantial government authority exercised in taking Robinson into custody. *See Chadwick,* 433 U.S., at 16, n. 10 (searches of a person are justified in part by "reduced expectations of privacy caused by the arrest").

The fact that an arrestee has diminished privacy interests does not mean that the Fourth Amendment falls out of the picture entirely. Not every search "is acceptable solely because a person is in custody." Maryland v. King, 569 U.S. ___, ___ (2013). To the contrary, when "privacy-related concerns are weighty enough" a "search may require a warrant, notwithstanding the diminished expectations of privacy of the arrestee." *Ibid.* One such example, of course, is *Chimel. Chimel* refused to "characteriz[e] the invasion of privacy that results from a top-to-bottom search of a man's house as 'minor.'" 395 U.S., at 766–767, n. 12. Because a search of the arrestee's entire house was a substantial invasion beyond the arrest itself, the Court concluded that a warrant was required.

Robinson is the only decision from this Court applying *Chimel* to a search of the contents of an item found on an arrestee's person. In an earlier case, this Court had approved a search of a zipper bag carried by an arrestee, but the Court analyzed only the validity of the arrest itself. *See* Draper v. United States, 358 U.S. 307, 310–311, 327 (1959). Lower courts applying *Robinson* and *Chimel,* however, have approved searches of a variety of personal items carried by an arrestee. See, e.g., United States v. Carrion, 809 F.2d 1120, 1123, 1128 (C.A.5 1987) (billfold and address book); United States v. Watson, 669 F.2d 1374, 1383–1384 (C.A.11 1982) (wallet); United States v. Lee, 501 F.2d 890, 892 (C.A.D.C.1974) (purse).

The United States asserts that a search of all data stored on a cell phone is "materially indistinguishable" from searches of these sorts of physical items. Brief for United States in No. 13–212, p. 26. That is like saying a ride on horseback is materially indistinguishable from a flight to the moon. Both are ways of getting from point A to point B, but little else justifies lumping them together. Modern cell phones, as a category, implicate privacy concerns far beyond those implicated by the search of a cigarette pack, a wallet, or a purse. A conclusion that inspecting the contents of an arrestee's pockets works no substantial additional intrusion on privacy beyond the arrest itself may make sense as applied to physical items, but any extension of that reasoning to digital data has to rest on its own bottom.

1

Cell phones differ in both a quantitative and a qualitative sense from other objects that might be kept on an arrestee's person. The term "cell phone" is itself misleading shorthand; many of these devices are in fact minicomputers that also happen to have the capacity to be used as a telephone. They could just as easily be called cameras, video players, rolodexes, calendars, tape recorders, libraries, diaries, albums, televisions, maps, or newspapers.

One of the most notable distinguishing features of modern cell phones is their immense storage capacity. Before cell phones, a search of a person was limited by physical realities and tended as a general matter to constitute only a narrow intrusion on privacy. *See* Kerr, Foreword: *Accounting for Technological Change*, 36 Harv. J.L. & Pub. Pol'y 403, 404–405 (2013). Most people cannot lug around every piece of mail they have received for the past several months, every picture they have taken, or every book or article they have read—nor would they have any reason to attempt to do so. And if they did, they would have to drag behind them a trunk of the sort held to require a search warrant in *Chadwick, supra,* rather than a container the size of the cigarette package in *Robinson*.

But the possible intrusion on privacy is not physically limited in the same way when it comes to cell phones. The current top-selling smart phone has a standard capacity of 16 gigabytes (and is available with up to 64 gigabytes). Sixteen gigabytes translates to millions of pages of text, thousands of pictures, or hundreds of videos. *See* Kerr, *supra*, at 404; Brief for Center for Democracy & Technology et al. as Amici Curiae 7–8. Cell phones couple that capacity with the ability to store many different types of information: Even the most basic phones that sell for less than $20 might hold photographs, picture messages, text messages, Internet browsing history, a calendar, a thousand-entry phone book, and so on. *See id.*, at 30; United States v. Flores-Lopez, 670 F.3d 803, 806 (C.A.7 2012). We expect that the gulf between physical practicability and digital capacity will only continue to widen in the future.

The storage capacity of cell phones has several interrelated consequences for privacy. First, a cell phone collects in one place many distinct types of information—an address, a note, a prescription, a bank statement, a video—that reveal much more in combination than any isolated record. Second, a cell phone's capacity allows even just one type of information to convey far more than previously possible. The sum of an individual's private life can be reconstructed through a thousand photographs labeled with dates, locations, and descriptions; the same cannot be said of a photograph or two of loved ones tucked into a wallet. Third, the data on a phone can date back to the purchase of the phone, or even earlier. A person might carry in his pocket a slip of paper reminding him to call Mr. Jones; he would not carry a record of all his communications with Mr. Jones for the past several months, as would routinely be kept on a phone.[1]

Finally, there is an element of pervasiveness that characterizes cell phones but not physical records. Prior to the digital age, people did not typically carry a cache of sensitive personal information with them as they went about their day. Now it is the person who is not carrying a cell phone, with all that it contains, who is the exception. According to one poll, nearly three-quarters of smart phone users report being within five feet of their phones most of the time, with 12% admitting that they even use their phones in the shower. *See* Harris Interactive, 2013 Mobile Consumer Habits Study (June 2013). A decade ago police officers searching an arrestee might have occasionally stumbled across a highly personal item such as a diary. *See, e.g.,* United States v. Frankenberry, 387 F.2d 337 (C.A.2 1967) (per curiam). But those discoveries were likely to be few and far between. Today, by contrast, it is no exaggeration to say that many of the more than 90% of American adults who own a cell phone keep on their person a digital record of nearly every aspect of their lives—from the mundane to the intimate. *See* Ontario v. Quon, 560 U.S. 746, 760 (2010). Allowing the police to scrutinize such records on a routine basis is quite different from allowing them to search a personal item or two in the occasional case.

Although the data stored on a cell phone is distinguished from physical records by quantity alone, certain types of data are also qualitatively different. An Internet search and browsing history, for example, can be found on an Internet-enabled phone and could reveal an individual's private interests or concerns—perhaps a search for certain symptoms of disease, coupled with frequent visits to WebMD. Data on a cell phone can also reveal where a person has been. Historic location information is a standard feature on many smart phones and can reconstruct someone's specific movements down to the minute, not only around town but also within a particular building. *See* United States v. Jones, 565 U.S. ___, ___ (2012) (SOTOMAYOR, J., concurring) ("GPS monitoring generates a precise, comprehensive record of a person's public movements that reflects a wealth of detail about her familial, political, professional, religious, and sexual associations.").

Mobile application software on a cell phone, or "apps," offer a range of tools for managing detailed information about all aspects of a person's life. There are apps for Democratic Party news and Republican Party news; apps for alcohol, drug, and gambling addictions; apps for sharing prayer requests; apps for tracking pregnancy symptoms; apps for planning your budget; apps for every conceivable hobby or pastime; apps for improving your romantic life. There are popular apps for buying or selling just about anything, and the records of such transactions may be

---

[1]   Because the United States and California agree that these cases involve searches incident to arrest, these cases do not implicate the question whether the collection or inspection of aggregated digital information amounts to a search under other circumstances.

accessible on the phone indefinitely. There are over a million apps available in each of the two major app stores; the phrase "there's an app for that" is now part of the popular lexicon. The average smart phone user has installed 33 apps, which together can form a revealing montage of the user's life. *See* Brief for Electronic Privacy Information Center as Amicus Curiae in No. 13–132, p. 9.

In 1926, Learned Hand observed (in an opinion later quoted in *Chimel*) that it is "a totally different thing to search a man's pockets and use against him what they contain, from ransacking his house for everything which may incriminate him." United States v. Kirschenblatt, 16 F.2d 202, 203 (C.A.2). If his pockets contain a cell phone, however, that is no longer true. Indeed, a cell phone search would typically expose to the government far more than the most exhaustive search of a house: A phone not only contains in digital form many sensitive records previously found in the home; it also contains a broad array of private information never found in a home in any form—unless the phone is.

2

To further complicate the scope of the privacy interests at stake, the data a user views on many modern cell phones may not in fact be stored on the device itself. Treating a cell phone as a container whose contents may be searched incident to an arrest is a bit strained as an initial matter. *See* New York v. Belton, 453 U.S. 454, 460, n. 4(1981) (describing a "container" as "any object capable of holding another object"). But the analogy crumbles entirely when a cell phone is used to access data located elsewhere, at the tap of a screen. That is what cell phones, with increasing frequency, are designed to do by taking advantage of "cloud computing." Cloud computing is the capacity of Internet-connected devices to display data stored on remote servers rather than on the device itself. Cell phone users often may not know whether particular information is stored on the device or in the cloud, and it generally makes little difference. *See* Brief for Electronic Privacy Information Center in No. 13–132, at 12–14, 20. Moreover, the same type of data may be stored locally on the device for one user and in the cloud for another.

The United States concedes that the search incident to arrest exception may not be stretched to cover a search of files accessed remotely—that is, a search of files stored in the cloud. *See* Brief for United States in No. 13–212, at 43–44. Such a search would be like finding a key in a suspect's pocket and arguing that it allowed law enforcement to unlock and search a house. But officers searching a phone's data would not typically know whether the information they are viewing was stored locally at the time of the arrest or has been pulled from the cloud.

Although the Government recognizes the problem, its proposed solutions are unclear. It suggests that officers could disconnect a phone from the network before searching the device—the very solution whose feasibility it contested with respect to the threat of remote wiping.

Alternatively, the Government proposes that law enforcement agencies "develop protocols to address" concerns raised by cloud computing. Reply Brief in No. 13–212, pp. 14–15. Probably a good idea, but the Founders did not fight a revolution to gain the right to government agency protocols. The possibility that a search might extend well beyond papers and effects in the physical proximity of an arrestee is yet another reason that the privacy interests here dwarf those in Robinson.

C

Apart from their arguments for a direct extension of *Robinson,* the United States and California offer various fallback options for permitting warrantless cell phone searches under certain circumstances. Each of the proposals is flawed and contravenes our general preference to provide clear guidance to law enforcement through categorical rules. "[I]f police are to have workable rules, the balancing of the competing interests . . . 'must in large part be done on a categorical basis—not in an ad hoc, case-by-case fashion by individual police officers.' " Michigan v. Summers, 452 U.S. 692, 705, n. 19 (1981) (quoting Dunaway v. New York, 442 U.S. 200, 219–220 (1979) (White, J., concurring)).

The United States first proposes that the *Gant* standard be imported from the vehicle context, allowing a warrantless search of an arrestee's cell phone whenever it is reasonable to believe that the phone contains evidence of the crime of arrest. But *Gant* relied on "circumstances unique to the vehicle context" to endorse a search solely for the purpose of gathering evidence. 556 U.S., at 343. Justice SCALIA's Thornton opinion, on which Gant was based, explained that those unique circumstances are "a reduced expectation of privacy" and "heightened law enforcement needs" when it comes to motor vehicles. 541 U.S., at 631; *see also Wyoming v. Houghton,* 526 U.S., at 303–304. For reasons that we have explained, cell phone searches bear neither of those characteristics.

At any rate, a *Gant* standard would prove no practical limit at all when it comes to cell phone searches. In the vehicle context, *Gant* generally protects against searches for evidence of past crimes. *See* 3 W. LaFave, Search and Seizure § 7.1(d), at 709, and n. 191. In the cell phone context, however, it is reasonable to expect that incriminating information will be found on a phone regardless of when the crime occurred. Similarly, in the vehicle context *Gant* restricts broad searches resulting from minor crimes such as traffic violations. *See id.,* § 7.1(d), at 713, and n. 204. That would not necessarily be true for cell phones. It would be a particularly inexperienced or unimaginative law enforcement officer who could not come up with several reasons to suppose evidence of just about any crime could be found on a cell phone. Even an individual pulled over for something as basic as speeding might well have locational data dispositive of guilt on his phone. An individual pulled over for reckless driving might have evidence on the phone that shows whether he was texting while driving. The sources of potential pertinent information are virtually unlimited, so applying the *Gant* standard to cell phones would in effect give "police officers unbridled discretion to rummage at will among a person's private effects." 556 U.S., at 345.

The United States also proposes a rule that would restrict the scope of a cell phone search to those areas of the phone where an officer reasonably believes that information relevant to the crime, the arrestee's identity, or officer safety will be discovered. This approach would again impose few meaningful constraints on officers. The proposed categories would sweep in a great deal of information, and officers would not always be able to discern in advance what information would be found where.

We also reject the United States' final suggestion that officers should always be able to search a phone's call log, as they did in Wurie's case. The Government relies on Smith v. Maryland, 442 U.S. 735 (1979), which held that no warrant was required to use a pen register at telephone company premises to identify numbers dialed by a particular caller. The Court in that case, however, concluded that the use of a pen register was not a "search" at all under the Fourth Amendment. *See id.*, at 745–746. There is no dispute here that the officers engaged in a search of Wurie's cell phone. Moreover, call logs typically contain more than just phone numbers; they include any identifying information that an individual might add, such as the label "my house" in Wurie's case.

Finally, at oral argument California suggested a different limiting principle, under which officers could search cell phone data if they could have obtained the same information from a pre-digital counterpart. *See* Tr. of Oral Arg. in No. 13–132, at 38–43; s*ee also Flores-Lopez,* 670 F.3d, at 807 ("If police are entitled to open a pocket diary to copy the owner's address, they should be entitled to turn on a cell phone to learn its number."). But the fact that a search in the pre-digital era could have turned up a photograph or two in a wallet does not justify a search of thousands of photos in a digital gallery. The fact that someone could have tucked a paper bank statement in a pocket does not justify a search of every bank statement from the last five years. And to make matters worse, such an analogue test would allow law enforcement to search a range of items contained on a phone, even though people would be unlikely to carry such a variety of information in physical form. In Riley's case, for example, it is implausible that he would have strolled around with video tapes, photo albums, and an address book all crammed into his pockets. But because each of those items has a pre-digital analogue, police under California's proposal would be able to search a phone for all of those items—a significant diminution of privacy.

In addition, an analogue test would launch courts on a difficult line-drawing expedition to determine which digital files are comparable to physical records. Is an e-mail equivalent to a letter? Is a voicemail equivalent to a phone message slip? It is not clear how officers could make these kinds of decisions before conducting a search, or how courts would apply the proposed rule after the fact. An analogue test would "keep defendants and judges guessing for years to come." Sykes v. United

States, 564 U.S. 1, ___ (2011) (SCALIA, J., dissenting) (discussing the Court's analogue test under the Armed Career Criminal Act).

IV

We cannot deny that our decision today will have an impact on the ability of law enforcement to combat crime. Cell phones have become important tools in facilitating coordination and communication among members of criminal enterprises, and can provide valuable incriminating information about dangerous criminals. Privacy comes at a cost.

Our holding, of course, is not that the information on a cell phone is immune from search; it is instead that a warrant is generally required before such a search, even when a cell phone is seized incident to arrest. Our cases have historically recognized that the warrant requirement is "an important working part of our machinery of government," not merely "an inconvenience to be somehow 'weighed' against the claims of police efficiency." Coolidge v. New Hampshire, 403 U.S. 443, 481 (1971). Recent technological advances similar to those discussed here have, in addition, made the process of obtaining a warrant itself more efficient. *See McNeely,* 569 U.S., at ___; *id.,* at ___ (ROBERTS, C.J., concurring in part and dissenting in part) (describing jurisdiction where "police officers can e-mail warrant requests to judges' iPads [and] judges have signed such warrants and e-mailed them back to officers in less than 15 minutes").

Moreover, even though the search incident to arrest exception does not apply to cell phones, other case-specific exceptions may still justify a warrantless search of a particular phone. "One well-recognized exception applies when " 'the exigencies of the situation" make the needs of law enforcement so compelling that [a] warrantless search is objectively reasonable under the Fourth Amendment.' " *Kentucky v. King,* 563 U.S., at ___, at 1856 (quoting Mincey v. Arizona, 437 U.S. 385, 394 (1978)). Such exigencies could include the need to prevent the imminent destruction of evidence in individual cases, to pursue a fleeing suspect, and to assist persons who are seriously injured or are threatened with imminent injury. 563 U.S., at ___. In *Chadwick,* for example, the Court held that the exception for searches incident to arrest did not justify a search of the trunk at issue, but noted that "if officers have reason to believe that luggage contains some immediately dangerous instrumentality, such as explosives, it would be foolhardy to transport it to the station house without opening the luggage." 433 U.S., at 15, n. 9.

In light of the availability of the exigent circumstances exception, there is no reason to believe that law enforcement officers will not be able to address some of the more extreme hypotheticals that have been suggested: a suspect texting an accomplice who, it is feared, is preparing to detonate a bomb, or a child abductor who may have information about the child's location on his cell phone. The defendants here recognize—indeed, they stress—that such fact-specific threats may justify a warrantless search of cell phone data The critical point is that, unlike the search incident to arrest exception, the exigent circumstances exception requires a court to examine whether an emergency justified a warrantless search in each particular case. *See* McNeely, *supra*, at ___.[2]

* * *

Our cases have recognized that the Fourth Amendment was the founding generation's response to the reviled "general warrants" and "writs of assistance" of the colonial era, which allowed British officers to rummage through homes in an unrestrained search for evidence of criminal activity. Opposition to such searches was in fact one of the driving forces behind the Revolution itself. In 1761, the patriot James Otis delivered a speech in Boston denouncing the use of writs of assistance. A young John Adams was there, and he would later write that "[e]very man of a crowded audience appeared to me to go away, as I did, ready to take arms against writs of assistance." 10 Works of John Adams 247–248 (C. Adams ed. 1856). According to Adams, Otis's speech was "the first scene of the first act of opposition to the arbitrary claims of Great Britain. Then and there the child Independence was born." *Id.*, at 248 (quoted in Boyd v. United States, 116 U.S. 616, 625 (1886)).

Modern cell phones are not just another technological convenience. With all they contain and all they may reveal, they hold for many Americans "the privacies of life," *Boyd, supra,* at 630. The fact that technology now allows an individual to carry such information in his hand does not make the information any less worthy of the protection for which the Founders fought. Our answer to the question of what police must do before searching a cell phone seized incident to an arrest is accordingly simple—get a warrant.

We reverse the judgment of the California Court of Appeal in No. 13–132 and remand the case for further proceedings not inconsistent with this opinion. We affirm the judgment of the First Circuit in No. 13–212.

It is so ordered.

■ JUSTICE ALITO, concurring in part and concurring in the judgment.

I agree with the Court that law enforcement officers, in conducting a lawful search incident to arrest, must generally obtain a warrant before searching information stored or accessible on a cell phone. I write separately to address two points.

I

A

First, I am not convinced at this time that the ancient rule on searches incident to arrest is based exclusively (or even primarily) on the

---

2 In Wurie's case, for example, the dissenting First Circuit judge argued that exigent circumstances could have justified a search of Wurie's phone. *See* 728 F.3d 1, 17 (2013) (opinion of Howard, J.) (discussing the repeated unanswered calls from "my house," the suspected location of a drug stash). But the majority concluded that the Government had not made an exigent circumstances argument. *See id.*, at 1. The Government acknowledges the same in this Court. *See* Brief for United States in No. 13–212, p. 28, n. 8.

need to protect the safety of arresting officers and the need to prevent the destruction of evidence. This rule antedates the adoption of the Fourth Amendment by at least a century. *See* T. Clancy, The Fourth Amendment: Its History and Interpretation 340 (2008); T. Taylor, Two Studies in Constitutional Interpretation 28 (1969); Amar, *Fourth Amendment First Principles,* 107 Harv. L. Rev. 757, 764 (1994). In Weeks v. United States, 232 U.S. 383, 392 (1914), we held that the Fourth Amendment did not disturb this rule. *See* also Taylor, *supra,* at 45; Stuntz, *The Substantive Origins of Criminal Procedure,* 105 Yale L.J. 393, 401 (1995) ("The power to search incident to arrest—a search of the arrested suspect's person . . .—was well established in the mid-eighteenth century, and nothing in . . . the Fourth Amendment changed that"). And neither in *Weeks* nor in any of the authorities discussing the old common-law rule have I found any suggestion that it was based exclusively or primarily on the need to protect arresting officers or to prevent the destruction of evidence. . . .

What ultimately convinces me that the rule is not closely linked to the need for officer safety and evidence preservation is that these rationales fail to explain the rule's well-recognized scope. It has long been accepted that written items found on the person of an arrestee may be examined and used at trial. But once these items are taken away from an arrestee (something that obviously must be done before the items are read), there is no risk that the arrestee will destroy them. Nor is there any risk that leaving these items unread will endanger the arresting officers.

The idea that officer safety and the preservation of evidence are the sole reasons for allowing a warrantless search incident to arrest appears to derive from the Court's reasoning in Chimel v. California, 395 U.S. 752 (1969), a case that involved the lawfulness of a search of the scene of an arrest, not the person of an arrestee. As I have explained, *Chimel's* reasoning is questionable, *see* Arizona v. Gant, 556 U.S. 332, 361–363 (2009) (ALITO, J., dissenting), and I think it is a mistake to allow that reasoning to affect cases like these that concern the search of the person of arrestees.

B

Despite my view on the point discussed above, I agree that we should not mechanically apply the rule used in the predigital era to the search of a cell phone. Many cell phones now in use are capable of storing and accessing a quantity of information, some highly personal, that no person would ever have had on his person in hard-copy form. This calls for a new balancing of law enforcement and privacy interests.

The Court strikes this balance in favor of privacy interests with respect to all cell phones and all information found in them, and this approach leads to anomalies. For example, the Court's broad holding favors information in digital form over information in hard-copy form. Suppose that two suspects are arrested. Suspect number one has in his pocket a monthly bill for his land-line phone, and the bill lists an incriminating call to a long-distance number. He also has in his a wallet a few snapshots, and one of these is incriminating. Suspect number two has in his pocket a cell phone, the call log of which shows a call to the same incriminating number. In addition, a number of photos are stored in the memory of the cell phone, and one of these is incriminating. Under established law, the police may seize and examine the phone bill and the snapshots in the wallet without obtaining a warrant, but under the Court's holding today, the information stored in the cell phone is out.

While the Court's approach leads to anomalies, I do not see a workable alternative. Law enforcement officers need clear rules regarding searches incident to arrest, and it would take many cases and many years for the courts to develop more nuanced rules. And during that time, the nature of the electronic devices that ordinary Americans carry on their persons would continue to change.

II

This brings me to my second point. While I agree with the holding of the Court, I would reconsider the question presented here if either Congress or state legislatures, after assessing the legitimate needs of law enforcement and the privacy interests of cell phone owners, enact legislation that draws reasonable distinctions based on categories of information or perhaps other variables.

The regulation of electronic surveillance provides an instructive example. After this Court held that electronic surveillance constitutes a search even when no property interest is invaded, see Katz v. United States, 389 U.S. 347, 353–359 (1967), Congress responded by enacting Title III of the Omnibus Crime Control and Safe Streets Act of 1968, 82 Stat. 211. See also 18 U.S.C. § 2510 et seq. Since that time, electronic surveillance has been governed primarily, not by decisions of this Court, but by the statute, which authorizes but imposes detailed restrictions on electronic surveillance. See ibid.

Modern cell phones are of great value for both lawful and unlawful purposes. They can be used in committing many serious crimes, and they present new and difficult law enforcement problems. See Brief for United States in No. 13–212, pp. 2–3. At the same time, because of the role that these devices have come to play in contemporary life, searching their contents implicates very sensitive privacy interests that this Court is poorly positioned to understand and evaluate. Many forms of modern technology are making it easier and easier for both government and private entities to amass a wealth of information about the lives of ordinary Americans, and at the same time, many ordinary Americans are choosing to make public much information that was seldom revealed to outsiders just a few decades ago.

In light of these developments, it would be very unfortunate if privacy protection in the 21st century were left primarily to the federal courts using the blunt instrument of the Fourth Amendment. Legislatures, elected by the people, are in a better position than we are to assess and respond to the changes that have already occurred and those that almost certainly will take place in the future.

5. LIMITS

Virginia v. Moore
553 U.S. 164 (2008)

■ JUSTICE SCALIA delivered the opinion of the Court.

We consider whether a police officer violates the Fourth Amendment by making an arrest based on probable cause but prohibited by state law.

I

On February 20, 2003, two City of Portsmouth police officers stopped a car driven by David Lee Moore. They had heard over the police radio that a person known as "Chubs" was driving with a suspended license, and one of the officers knew Moore by that nickname. The officers determined that Moore's license was in fact suspended, and arrested him for the misdemeanor of driving on a suspended license, which is punishable under Virginia law by a year in jail and a $2,500 fine, Va.Code Ann. §§ 18.2–11, 18.2–272, 46.2–301(C) (Lexis 2005). The officers subsequently searched Moore and found that he was carrying 16 grams of crack cocaine and $516 in cash.[1] See 272 Va. 717, 636 S.E.2d 395 (2006); 45 Va.App. 146, 609 S.E.2d 74 (2005).

Under state law, the officers should have issued Moore a summons instead of arresting him. Driving on a suspended license, like some other misdemeanors, is not an arrestable offense except as to those who "fail or refuse to discontinue" the violation, and those whom the officer reasonably believes to be likely to disregard a summons, or likely to harm themselves or others. Va.Code Ann. § 19.2–74 (Lexis 2004). The intermediate appellate court found none of these circumstances applicable, and Virginia did not appeal that determination. See 272 Va., at 720, n. 3, 636 S.E.2d, at 396–397, n. 3. Virginia also permits arrest for driving on a suspended license in jurisdictions where "prior general approval has been granted by order of the general district court," Va.Code Ann. § 46.2–936; Virginia has never claimed such approval was in effect in the county where Moore was arrested.

Moore was charged with possessing cocaine with the intent to distribute it in violation of Virginia law. He filed a pretrial motion to suppress the evidence from the arrest search. Virginia law does not, as a

---

[1] The arresting officers did not perform a search incident to arrest immediately upon taking Moore into custody, because each of them mistakenly believed that the other had done so. App. 54-55; See also id., at 33–34. They realized their mistake after arriving with Moore at Moore's hotel room, which they had obtained his consent to search, and they searched his person there. Ibid. Moore does not contend that this delay violated the Fourth Amendment.

general matter, require suppression of evidence obtained in violation of state law. *See* 45 Va.App., at 160–162, 609 S.E.2d, at 82 (Annunziata, J., dissenting). Moore argued, however, that suppression was required by the Fourth Amendment. The trial court denied the motion, and after a bench trial found Moore guilty of the drug charge and sentenced him to a 5-year prison term, with one year and six months of the sentence suspended. The conviction was reversed by a panel of Virginia's intermediate court on Fourth Amendment grounds, *id.*, at 149–150, 609 S.E.2d, at 76, reinstated by the intermediate court sitting en banc, 47 Va.App. 55, 622 S.E.2d 253 (2005), and finally reversed again by the Virginia Supreme Court, 272 Va., at 725, 636 S.E.2d, at 400. The Court reasoned that since the arresting officers should have issued Moore a citation under state law, and the Fourth Amendment does not permit search incident to citation, the arrest search violated the Fourth Amendment. *Ibid.* We granted certiorari.

II

The Fourth Amendment protects "against unreasonable searches and seizures" of (among other things) the person. In determining whether a search or seizure is unreasonable, we begin with history. We look to the statutes and common law of the founding era to determine the norms that the Fourth Amendment was meant to preserve. *See* Wyoming v. Houghton, 526 U.S. 295, 299 (1999); Wilson v. Arkansas, 514 U.S. 927, 931 (1995).

We are aware of no historical indication that those who ratified the Fourth Amendment understood it as a redundant guarantee of whatever limits on search and seizure legislatures might have enacted.[2] The immediate object of the Fourth Amendment was to prohibit the general warrants and writs of assistance that English judges had employed against the colonists, Boyd v. United States, 116 U.S. 616, 624–627 (1886); Payton v. New York, 445 U.S. 573, 583–584 (1980). That suggests, if anything, that founding-era citizens were skeptical of using the rules for search and seizure set by government actors as the index of reasonableness.

Joseph Story, among others, saw the Fourth Amendment as "little more than the affirmance of a great constitutional doctrine of the common law," 3 Commentaries on the Constitution of the United States § 1895, p. 748 (1833), which Story defined in opposition to statutes, *see*

---

[2] Atwater v. Lago Vista, 532 U.S. 318 (2001), rejected the view Justice GINSBURG advances that the legality of arrests for misdemeanors involving no breach of the peace "depended on statutory authorization." Post, at ___, n. 1 (opinion concurring in judgment). *Atwater* cited both of the sources on which Justice GINSBURG relies for a limited view of common-law arrest authority, but it also identified and quoted numerous treatises that described common-law authority to arrest for minor misdemeanors without limitation to cases in which a statute authorized arrest. *See* 532 U.S., at 330–332. *Atwater* noted that many statutes authorized arrest for misdemeanors other than breaches of the peace, but it concluded that the view of arrest authority as extending beyond breaches of the peace also reflected judge-made common law. *Id.*, at 330–331. Particularly since *Atwater* considered the materials on which Justice GINSBURG relies, we see no reason to revisit the case's conclusion.

Codification of the Common Law in The Miscellaneous Writings of Joseph Story 698, 699, 701 (W. Story ed. 1852). No early case or commentary, to our knowledge, suggested the Amendment was intended to incorporate subsequently enacted statutes. None of the early Fourth Amendment cases that scholars have identified sought to base a constitutional claim on a violation of a state or federal statute concerning arrest. *See* Davies, *Recovering the Original Fourth Amendment,* 98 Mich. L.Rev. 547, 613–614 (1999); *see also* T. Taylor, Two Studies in Constitutional Interpretation 44–45 (1969).

Of course such a claim would not have been available against state officers, since the Fourth Amendment was a restriction only upon federal power, *see* Barron ex rel. Tiernan v. Mayor of Baltimore, 7 Pet. 243 (1833). But early Congresses tied the arrest authority of federal officers to state laws of arrest. *See* United States v. Di Re, 332 U.S. 581, 589 (1948); United States v. Watson, 423 U.S. 411, 420 (1976). Moreover, even though several state constitutions also prohibited unreasonable searches and seizures, citizens who claimed officers had violated state restrictions on arrest did not claim that the violations also ran afoul of the state constitutions. The apparent absence of such litigation is particularly striking in light of the fact that searches incident to warrantless arrests (which is to say arrests in which the officer was not insulated from private suit) were, as one commentator has put it, "taken for granted" at the founding, Taylor, *supra*, at 45, as were warrantless arrests themselves, Amar, *Fourth Amendment First Principles,* 107 Harv. L.Rev. 757, 764 (1994).

There are a number of possible explanations of why such constitutional claims were not raised. Davies, for example, argues that actions taken in violation of state law could not qualify as state action subject to Fourth Amendment constraints. 98 Mich. L.Rev., at 660–663. Be that as it may, as Moore adduces neither case law nor commentaries to support his view that the Fourth Amendment was intended to incorporate statutes, this is "not a case in which the claimant can point to 'a clear answer [that] existed in 1791 and has been generally adhered to by the traditions of our society ever since.'" Atwater v. Lago Vista, 532 U.S. 318, 345 (2001) (alteration in original).

III

A

When history has not provided a conclusive answer, we have analyzed a search or seizure in light of traditional standards of reasonableness "by assessing, on the one hand, the degree to which it intrudes upon an individual's privacy and, on the other, the degree to which it is needed for the promotion of legitimate governmental interests." *Houghton,* 526 U.S., at 300; *see also Atwater,* 532 U.S., at 346. That methodology provides no support for Moore's Fourth Amendment claim. In a long line of cases, we have said that when an officer has probable cause to believe a person committed even a minor crime in his presence, the balancing of private and public interests is not in doubt. The arrest is constitutionally reasonable. *Id.*, at 354; *see also, e.g.,* Devenpeck v. Alford, 543 U.S. 146, 152 (2004); Gerstein v. Pugh, 420 U.S. 103, 111 (1975); Brinegar v. United States, 338 U.S. 160, 164 (1949).

Our decisions counsel against changing this calculus when a State chooses to protect privacy beyond the level that the Fourth Amendment requires. We have treated additional protections exclusively as matters of state law. In Cooper v. California, 386 U.S. 58 (1967), we reversed a state court that had held the search of a seized vehicle to be in violation of the Fourth Amendment because state law did not explicitly authorize the search. We concluded that whether state law authorized the search was irrelevant. States, we said, remained free "to impose higher standards on searches and seizures than required by the Federal Constitution," *id.*, at 62, but regardless of state rules, police could search a lawfully seized vehicle as a matter of federal constitutional law.

In California v. Greenwood, 486 U.S. 35 (1988), we held that search of an individual's garbage forbidden by California's Constitution was not forbidden by the Fourth Amendment. "[W]hether or not a search is reasonable within the meaning of the Fourth Amendment," we said, has never "depend[ed] on the law of the particular State in which the search occurs." *Id.*, at 43. While "[i]ndividual States may surely construe their own constitutions as imposing more stringent constraints on police conduct than does the Federal Constitution," *ibid.*, state law did not alter the content of the Fourth Amendment.

We have applied the same principle in the seizure context. Whren v. United States, 517 U.S. 806 (1996), held that police officers had acted reasonably in stopping a car, even though their action violated regulations limiting the authority of plainclothes officers in unmarked vehicles. We thought it obvious that the Fourth Amendment's meaning did not change with local law enforcement practices—even practices set by rule. While those practices "vary from place to place and from time to time," Fourth Amendment protections are not "so variable" and cannot "be made to turn upon such trivialities." *Id.*, at 815.

Some decisions earlier than these excluded evidence obtained in violation of state law, but those decisions rested on our supervisory power over the federal courts, rather than the Constitution. In *Di Re*, 332 U.S. 581, federal and state officers collaborated in an investigation that led to an arrest for a federal crime. The Government argued that the legality of an arrest for a federal offense was a matter of federal law. *Id.*, at 589. We concluded, however, that since Congress had provided that arrests with warrants must be made in accordance with state law, the legality of arrests without warrants should also be judged according to state-law standards. *Id.*, at 589–590. This was plainly not a rule we derived from the Constitution, however, because we repeatedly invited Congress to change it by statute—saying that state law governs the validity of a warrantless arrest "in [the] absence of an applicable federal statute," *id.*, at 589, and that the *Di Re* rule applies "except in those cases where Congress has enacted a federal rule," *id.*, at 589–590.

Later decisions did not expand the rule of *Di Re*. Johnson v. United States, 333 U.S. 10 (1948), relied on *Di Re* to suppress evidence obtained under circumstances identical in relevant respects to those in that case. *See* 333 U.S., at 12, 15, n. 5. And Michigan v. DeFillippo, 443 U.S. 31 (1979), upheld a warrantless arrest in a case where compliance with state law was not at issue. While our opinion said that "[w]hether an officer is authorized to make an arrest ordinarily depends, in the first instance, on state law," it also said that a warrantless arrest satisfies the Constitution so long as the officer has "probable cause to believe that the suspect has committed or is committing a crime." *Id.*, at 36. We need not pick and choose among the dicta: Neither *Di Re* nor the cases following it held that violations of state arrest law are also violations of the Fourth Amendment, and our more recent decisions, discussed above, have indicated that when States go above the Fourth Amendment minimum, the Constitution's protections concerning search and seizure remain the same.

B

We are convinced that the approach of our prior cases is correct, because an arrest based on probable cause serves interests that have long been seen as sufficient to justify the seizure. *Whren, supra,* at 817; *Atwater, supra,* at 354. Arrest ensures that a suspect appears to answer charges and does not continue a crime, and it safeguards evidence and enables officers to conduct an in-custody investigation. *See* W. LaFave, Arrest: The Decision to Take a Suspect into Custody 177–202 (1965).

Moore argues that a State has no interest in arrest when it has a policy against arresting for certain crimes. That is not so, because arrest will still ensure a suspect's appearance at trial, prevent him from continuing his offense, and enable officers to investigate the incident more thoroughly. State arrest restrictions are more accurately characterized as showing that the State values its interests in forgoing arrests more highly than its interests in making them, see, e.g., Dept. of Justice, National Institute of Justice, D. Whitcomb, B. Lewin, & M. Levine, Issues and Practices: Citation Release 17 (Mar.1984) (describing cost savings as a principal benefit of citation-release ordinances); or as showing that the State places a higher premium on privacy than the Fourth Amendment requires. A State is free to prefer one search-and-seizure policy among the range of constitutionally permissible options, but its choice of a more restrictive option does not render the less restrictive ones unreasonable, and hence unconstitutional.

If we concluded otherwise, we would often frustrate rather than further state policy. Virginia chooses to protect individual privacy and dignity more than the Fourth Amendment requires, but it also chooses not to attach to violations of its arrest rules the potent remedies that federal courts have applied to Fourth Amendment violations. Virginia does not, for example, ordinarily exclude from criminal trials evidence obtained in violation of its statutes. *See* 45 Va.App., at 161, 609 S.E.2d, at 82 (Annunziata, J., dissenting) (citing Janis v. Commonwealth, 22 Va.App. 646, 651, 472 S.E.2d 649, 652 (1996)). Moore would allow Virginia to accord enhanced protection against arrest only on pain of accompanying that protection with federal remedies for Fourth Amendment violations, which often include the exclusionary rule. States unwilling to lose control over the remedy would have to abandon restrictions on arrest altogether. This is an odd consequence of a provision designed to protect against searches and seizures.

Even if we thought that state law changed the nature of the Commonwealth's interests for purposes of the Fourth Amendment, we would adhere to the probable-cause standard. In determining what is reasonable under the Fourth Amendment, we have given great weight to the "essential interest in readily administrable rules." *Atwater,* 532 U.S., at 347. In *Atwater,* we acknowledged that nuanced judgments about the need for warrantless arrest were desirable, but we nonetheless declined to limit to felonies and disturbances of the peace the Fourth Amendment rule allowing arrest based on probable cause to believe a law has been broken in the presence of the arresting officer. *Id.,* at 346–347. The rule extends even to minor misdemeanors, we concluded, because of the need for a bright-line constitutional standard. If the constitutionality of arrest for minor offenses turned in part on inquiries as to risk of flight and danger of repetition, officers might be deterred from making legitimate arrests. *Id.,* at 351. We found little to justify this cost, because there was no "epidemic of unnecessary minor-offense arrests," and hence "a dearth of horribles demanding redress." *Id.,* at 353.

Incorporating state-law arrest limitations into the Constitution would produce a constitutional regime no less vague and unpredictable than the one we rejected in *Atwater.* The constitutional standard would be only as easy to apply as the underlying state law, and state law can be complicated indeed. The Virginia statute in this case, for example, calls on law enforcement officers to weigh just the sort of case-specific factors that *Atwater* said would deter legitimate arrests if made part of the constitutional inquiry. It would authorize arrest if a misdemeanor suspect fails or refuses to discontinue the unlawful act, or if the officer believes the suspect to be likely to disregard a summons. Va.Code Ann. § 19.2–74.A.1. *Atwater* specifically noted the "extremely poor judgment" displayed in arresting a local resident who would "almost certainly" have discontinued the offense and who had "no place to hide and no incentive to flee." 532 U.S., at 346–347. It nonetheless declined to make those considerations part of the constitutional calculus. *Atwater* differs from this case in only one significant respect: It considered (and rejected) federal constitutional remedies for all minor-misdemeanor arrests; Moore seeks them in only that subset of minor-misdemeanor arrests in which there is the least to be gained—that is, where the State has already acted to constrain officers' discretion and prevent abuse. Here we confront fewer horribles than in *Atwater*, and less of a need for redress.

Finally, linking Fourth Amendment protections to state law would cause them to "vary from place to place and from time to time," *Whren*, 517 U.S., at 815. Even at the same place and time, the Fourth Amendment's protections might vary if federal officers were not subject to the same statutory constraints as state officers. In Elkins v. United States, 364 U.S. 206, 210–212 (1960), we noted the practical difficulties posed by the "silver-platter doctrine," which had imposed more stringent limitations on federal officers than on state police acting independent of them. It would be strange to construe a constitutional provision that did not apply to the States at all when it was adopted to now restrict state officers more than federal officers, solely because the States have passed search-and-seizure laws that are the prerogative of independent sovereigns.

We conclude that warrantless arrests for crimes committed in the presence of an arresting officer are reasonable under the Constitution, and that while States are free to regulate such arrests however they desire, state restrictions do not alter the Fourth Amendment's protections.

IV

Moore argues that even if the Constitution allowed his arrest, it did not allow the arresting officers to search him. We have recognized, however, that officers may perform searches incident to constitutionally permissible arrests in order to ensure their safety and safeguard evidence. United States v. Robinson, 414 U.S. 218 (1973). We have described this rule as covering any "lawful arrest," *id.*, at 235, with constitutional law as the reference point. That is to say, we have equated a lawful arrest with an arrest based on probable cause: "A custodial arrest of a suspect based on probable cause is a reasonable intrusion under the Fourth Amendment; that intrusion being lawful, a search incident to the arrest requires no additional justification." *Ibid.* (emphasis added). Moore correctly notes that several important state-court decisions have defined the lawfulness of arrest in terms of compliance with state law. *See* Brief for Respondent 32–33 (citing People v. Chiagles, 237 N.Y. 193, 197, 142 N.E. 583, 584 (1923); People v. Defore, 242 N.Y. 13, 17–19, 150 N.E. 585, 586 (1926)). But it is not surprising that States have used "lawful" as shorthand for compliance with state law, while our constitutional decision in Robinson used "lawful" as shorthand for compliance with constitutional constraints.

The interests justifying search are present whenever an officer makes an arrest. A search enables officers to safeguard evidence, and, most critically, to ensure their safety during "the extended exposure which follows the taking of a suspect into custody and transporting him to the police station." *Robinson, supra*, at 234–235. Officers issuing citations do not face the same danger, and we therefore held in Knowles

v. Iowa, 525 U.S. 113 (1998), that they do not have the same authority to search. We cannot agree with the Virginia Supreme Court that *Knowles* controls here. The state officers arrested Moore, and therefore faced the risks that are "an adequate basis for treating all custodial arrests alike for purposes of search justification." *Robinson, supra,* at 235.

The Virginia Supreme Court may have concluded that *Knowles* required the exclusion of evidence seized from Moore because, under state law, the officers who arrested Moore should have issued him a citation instead. This argument might have force if the Constitution forbade Moore's arrest, because we have sometimes excluded evidence obtained through unconstitutional methods in order to deter constitutional violations. *See* Wong Sun v. United States, 371 U.S. 471, 484–485 (1963). But the arrest rules that the officers violated were those of state law alone, and as we have just concluded, it is not the province of the Fourth Amendment to enforce state law. That Amendment does not require the exclusion of evidence obtained from a constitutionally permissible arrest.

* * *

We reaffirm against a novel challenge what we have signaled for more than half a century. When officers have probable cause to believe that a person has committed a crime in their presence, the Fourth Amendment permits them to make an arrest, and to search the suspect in order to safeguard evidence and ensure their own safety. The judgment of the Supreme Court of Virginia is reversed, and the case is remanded for further proceedings not inconsistent with this opinion.

It is so ordered.

■ JUSTICE GINSBURG, concurring in the judgment.

I find in the historical record more support for Moore's position than the Court does.[1] Further, our decision in United States v. Di Re, 332 U.S. 581, 587–590 (1948), requiring suppression of evidence gained in a search incident to an unlawful arrest, seems to me pinned to the Fourth Amendment and not to our "supervisory power," And I am aware of no "long line of cases" holding that, regardless of state law, probable cause

---

[1] Under the common law prevailing at the end of the 19th century, it appears that arrests for minor misdemeanors, typically involving no breach of the peace, depended on statutory authorization. *See* Wilgus, *Arrest Without a Warrant,* 22 Mich. L.Rev. 541, 674 (1924) ("Neither [an officer] nor [a citizen], without statutory authority, may arrest [a defendant] for . . . a misdemeanor which is not a [breach of the peace]" (emphasis added)); 9 Halsbury, Laws of England §§ 608, 611–612, 615 (1909). *See also* Atwater v. Lago Vista, 532 U.S. 318, 342–345 (2001) (noting 19th-century decisions upholding statutes extending warrantless arrest authority to misdemeanors, other than breaches of the peace, committed in a police officer's presence); Wilgus, *supra,* at 551 (warrantless misdemeanor arrests "made under authority of a statute must conform strictly to its provisions; otherwise they will not be valid, and the one arresting becomes a trespasser").

renders every warrantless arrest for crimes committed in the presence of an arresting officer "constitutionally reasonable," *ante,* at 1604.[3]

Noting colonial hostility to general warrants and writs of assistance, the Court observes that "founding-era citizens were skeptical of using the rules for search and seizure set by government actors as the index of reasonableness." *Ante,* at 1604. The practices resisted by the citizenry, however, served to invade the people's privacy, not to shield it.

I agree with the Court's conclusion and its reasoning, however, to this extent. In line with the Court's decision in Atwater v. Lago Vista, 532 U.S. 318 (2001), Virginia could have made driving on a suspended license an arrestable offense. The Commonwealth chose not to do so. Moore asks us to credit Virginia law on a police officer's arrest authority, but only in part. He emphasizes Virginia's classification of driving on a suspended license as a nonarrestable misdemeanor. Moore would have us ignore, however, the limited consequences Virginia attaches to a police officer's failure to follow the Commonwealth's summons-only instruction. For such an infraction, the officer may be disciplined and the person arrested may bring a tort suit against the officer. But Virginia law does not demand the suppression of evidence seized by an officer who arrests when he should have issued a summons.

The Fourth Amendment, today's decision holds, does not put States to an all-or-nothing choice in this regard. A State may accord protection against arrest beyond what the Fourth Amendment requires, yet restrict the remedies available when police deny to persons they apprehend the extra protection state law orders. Because I agree that the arrest and search Moore challenges violated Virginia law, but did not violate the Fourth Amendment, I join the Court's judgment.

Tennessee v. Garner
471 U.S. 1 (1985)

■ JUSTICE WHITE delivered the opinion of the Court.

This case requires us to determine the constitutionality of the use of deadly force to prevent the escape of an apparently unarmed suspected felon. We conclude that such force may not be used unless it is necessary to prevent the escape and the officer has probable cause to believe that the suspect poses a significant threat of death or serious physical injury to the officer or others.

I

At about 10:45 p.m. on October 3, 1974, Memphis Police Officers Elton Hymon and Leslie Wright were dispatched to answer a "prowler

---

[3] Demonstrative of the "long line," the Court lists *Atwater*, 532 U.S., at 354, Devenpeck v. Alford, 543 U.S. 146, 152 (2004), Brinegar v. United States, 338 U.S. 160, 164 (1949), and Gerstein v. Pugh, 420 U.S. 103, 111 (1975). *Ante,* at 1604. But in all of these cases, unlike Moore's case, state law authorized the arrests. . . .

inside call." Upon arriving at the scene they saw a woman standing on her porch and gesturing toward the adjacent house.[1] She told them she had heard glass breaking and that "they" or "someone" was breaking in next door. While Wright radioed the dispatcher to say that they were on the scene, Hymon went behind the house. He heard a door slam and saw someone run across the backyard. The fleeing suspect, who was appellee-respondent's decedent, Edward Garner, stopped at a 6-feet-high chain link fence at the edge of the yard. With the aid of a flashlight, Hymon was able to see Garner's face and hands. He saw no sign of a weapon, and, though not certain, was "reasonably sure" and "figured" that Garner was unarmed. App. 41, 56; Record 219. He thought Garner was 17 or 18 years old and about 5'5" or 5'7" tall.[2] While Garner was crouched at the base of the fence, Hymon called out "police, halt" and took a few steps toward him. Garner then began to climb over the fence. Convinced that if Garner made it over the fence he would elude capture,[3] Hymon shot him. The bullet hit Garner in the back of the head. Garner was taken by ambulance to a hospital, where he died on the operating table. Ten dollars and a purse taken from the house were found on his body.[4]

In using deadly force to prevent the escape, Hymon was acting under the authority of a Tennessee statute and pursuant to Police Department policy. The statute provides that "[i]f, after notice of the intention to arrest the defendant, he either flee or forcibly resist, the officer may use all the necessary means to effect the arrest." Tenn.Code Ann. § 40–7–108 (1982).[5] The Department policy was slightly more restrictive than the statute, but still allowed the use of deadly force in cases of burglary. App. 140–144. The incident was reviewed by the Memphis Police Firearm's

---

[1]   The owner of the house testified that no lights were on in the house, but that a back door light was on. Record 160. Officer Hymon, though uncertain, stated in his deposition that there were lights on in the house. *Id.*, at 209.

[2]   In fact, Garner, an eighth-grader, was 15. He was 5' 4" tall and weighed somewhere around 100 or 110 pounds.

[3]   When asked at trial why he fired, Hymon stated:

"Well, first of all it was apparent to me from the little bit that I knew about the area at the time that he was going to get away because, number 1, I couldn't get to him. My partner then couldn't find where he was because, you know, he was late coming around. He didn't know where I was talking about. I couldn't get to him because of the fence here, I couldn't have jumped this fence and come up, consequently jumped this fence and caught him before he got away because he was already up on the fence, just one leap and he was already over the fence, and so there is no way that I could have caught him."

He also stated that the area beyond the fence was dark, that he could not have gotten over the fence easily because he was carrying a lot of equipment and wearing heavy boots, and that Garner, being younger and more energetic, could have outrun him.

[4]   Garner had rummaged through one room in the house, in which, in the words of the owner, "[a]ll the stuff was out on the floors, all the drawers was pulled out, and stuff was scattered all over." The owner testified that his valuables were untouched but that, in addition to the purse and the 10 dollars, one of his wife's rings was missing. The ring was not recovered.

[5]   Although the statute does not say so explicitly, Tennessee law forbids the use of deadly force in the arrest of a misdemeanant. *See* Johnson v. State, 173 Tenn. 134, 114 S.W.2d 819 (1938).

Review Board and presented to a grand jury. Neither took any action. *Id.*, at 57.

Garner's father then brought this action in the Federal District Court for the Western District of Tennessee, seeking damages under 42 U.S.C. § 1983 for asserted violations of Garner's constitutional rights. The complaint alleged that the shooting violated the Fourth, Fifth, Sixth, Eighth, and Fourteenth Amendments of the United States Constitution. It named as defendants Officer Hymon, the Police Department, its Director, and the Mayor and city of Memphis. After a 3-day bench trial, the District Court entered judgment for all defendants. It dismissed the claims against the Mayor and the Director for lack of evidence. It then concluded that Hymon's actions were authorized by the Tennessee statute, which in turn was constitutional. Hymon had employed the only reasonable and practicable means of preventing Garner's escape. Garner had "recklessly and heedlessly attempted to vault over the fence to escape, thereby assuming the risk of being fired upon." App. to Pet. for Cert. A10.

The Court of Appeals for the Sixth Circuit affirmed with regard to Hymon, finding that he had acted in good-faith reliance on the Tennessee statute and was therefore within the scope of his qualified immunity. 600 F.2d 52 (1979). It remanded for reconsideration of the possible liability of the city, however, in light of Monell v. New York City Dept. of Social Services, 436 U.S. 658 (1978), which had come down after the District Court's decision. The District Court was directed to consider whether a city enjoyed a qualified immunity, whether the use of deadly force and hollow point bullets in these circumstances was constitutional, and whether any unconstitutional municipal conduct flowed from a "policy or custom" as required for liability under *Monell.* 600 F.2d, at 54–55.

The District Court concluded that *Monell* did not affect its decision. While acknowledging some doubt as to the possible immunity of the city, it found that the statute, and Hymon's actions, were constitutional. Given this conclusion, it declined to consider the "policy or custom" question. App. to Pet. for Cert. A37–A39.

The Court of Appeals reversed and remanded. 710 F.2d 240 (1983). It reasoned that the killing of a fleeing suspect is a "seizure" under the Fourth Amendment, and is therefore constitutional only if "reasonable." The Tennessee statute failed as applied to this case because it did not adequately limit the use of deadly force by distinguishing between felonies of different magnitudes—"the facts, as found, did not justify the use of deadly force under the Fourth Amendment." *Id.*, at 246. Officers cannot resort to deadly force unless they "have probable cause . . . to believe that the suspect [has committed a felony and] poses a threat to the safety of the officers or a danger to the community if left at large."[7]

The court also found that "[a]n analysis of the facts of this case under the Due Process Clause" required the same result, because the statute was not narrowly drawn to further a compelling state interest. 710 F.2d, at 246–247. The court considered the generalized interest in effective law enforcement sufficiently compelling only when the suspect is dangerous. Finally, the court held, relying on Owen v. City of Independence, 445 U.S. 622 (1980), that the city was not immune.

The State of Tennessee, which had intervened to defend the statute, *see* 28 U.S.C. § 2403(b), appealed to this Court. The city filed a petition for certiorari. We noted probable jurisdiction in the appeal and granted the petition. 465 U.S. 1098 (1984).

II

Whenever an officer restrains the freedom of a person to walk away, he has seized that person. United States v. Brignoni-Ponce, 422 U.S. 873, 878 (1975). While it is not always clear just when minimal police interference becomes a seizure, *see* United States v. Mendenhall, 446 U.S. 544 (1980), there can be no question that apprehension by the use of deadly force is a seizure subject to the reasonableness requirement of the Fourth Amendment.

A

A police officer may arrest a person if he has probable cause to believe that person committed a crime. *E.g.,* United States v. Watson, 423 U.S. 411 (1976). Petitioners and appellant argue that if this requirement is satisfied the Fourth Amendment has nothing to say about how that seizure is made. This submission ignores the many cases in which this Court, by balancing the extent of the intrusion against the need for it, has examined the reasonableness of the manner in which a search or seizure is conducted. To determine the constitutionality of a seizure "[w]e must balance the nature and quality of the intrusion on the individual's Fourth Amendment interests against the importance of the governmental interests alleged to justify the intrusion." United States v. Place, 462 U.S. 696, 703 (1983); *see* Delaware v. Prouse, 440 U.S. 648, 654 (1979); United States v. Martinez-Fuerte, 428 U.S. 543, 555 (1976).

---

[7] The Court of Appeals concluded that the rule set out in the Model Penal Code "accurately states Fourth Amendment limitations on the use of deadly force against fleeing felons." 710 F.2d, at 247. The relevant portion of the Model Penal Code provides:

"The use of deadly force is not justifiable . . . unless (i) the arrest is for a felony; and (ii) the person effecting the arrest is authorized to act as a peace officer; or is assisting a person whom he believes to be authorized to act as a peace officer; and (iii) the actor believes that the force employed creates no substantial risk of injury to innocent persons; and (iv) the actor believes that (1) the crime for which the arrest is made involved conduct including the use or threatened use of deadly force; or (2) there is a substantial risk that the person to be arrested will cause death or serious bodily harm if his apprehension is delayed." American Law Institute, Model Penal Code § 3.07(2)(b) (Proposed Official Draft 1962).

We have described "the balancing of competing interests" as "the key principle of the Fourth Amendment." Michigan v. Summers, 452 U.S. 692, 700, n. 12 (1981). *See also* Camara v. Municipal Court, 387 U.S. 523, 536–537 (1967). Because one of the factors is the extent of the intrusion, it is plain that reasonableness depends on not only when a seizure is made, but also how it is carried out. United States v. Ortiz, 422 U.S. 891, 895 (1975); Terry v. Ohio, 392 U.S. 1, 28–29 (1968).

Applying these principles to particular facts, the Court has held that governmental interests did not support a lengthy detention of luggage, *United States v. Place, supra,* an airport seizure not "carefully tailored to its underlying justification," Florida v. Royer, 460 U.S. 491, 500 (1983) (plurality opinion), surgery under general anesthesia to obtain evidence, Winston v. Lee, 470 U.S. 753 (1985), or detention for fingerprinting without probable cause, Davis v. Mississippi, 394 U.S. 721 (1969); Hayes v. Florida, 470 U.S. 811 (1985). On the other hand, under the same approach it has upheld the taking of fingernail scrapings from a suspect, Cupp v. Murphy, 412 U.S. 291 (1973), an unannounced entry into a home to prevent the destruction of evidence, Ker v. California, 374 U.S. 23 (1963), administrative housing inspections without probable cause to believe that a code violation will be found, *Camara v. Municipal Court, supra,* and a blood test of a drunken-driving suspect, Schmerber v. California, 384 U.S. 757 (1966). In each of these cases, the question was whether the totality of the circumstances justified a particular sort of search or seizure.

B

The same balancing process applied in the cases cited above demonstrates that, notwithstanding probable cause to seize a suspect, an officer may not always do so by killing him. The intrusiveness of a seizure by means of deadly force is unmatched. The suspect's fundamental interest in his own life need not be elaborated upon. The use of deadly force also frustrates the interest of the individual, and of society, in judicial determination of guilt and punishment. Against these interests are ranged governmental interests in effective law enforcement. It is argued that overall violence will be reduced by encouraging the peaceful submission of suspects who know that they may be shot if they flee. Effectiveness in making arrests requires the resort to deadly force, or at least the meaningful threat thereof. "Being able to arrest such individuals is a condition precedent to the state's entire system of law enforcement." Brief for Petitioners 14.

The dissent emphasizes that subsequent investigation cannot replace immediate apprehension. We recognize that this is so, *see* n. 13, *infra*; indeed, that is the reason why there is any dispute. If subsequent arrest were assured, no one would argue that use of deadly force was justified. Thus, we proceed on the assumption that subsequent arrest is not likely. Nonetheless, it should be remembered that failure to apprehend at the scene does not necessarily mean that the suspect will never be caught.

In lamenting the inadequacy of later investigation, the dissent relies on the report of the President's Commission on Law Enforcement and Administration of Justice. It is worth noting that, notwithstanding its awareness of this problem, the Commission itself proposed a policy for use of deadly force arguably even more stringent than the formulation we adopt today. *See* President's Commission on Law Enforcement and Administration of Justice, Task Force Report: The Police 189 (1967). The Commission proposed that deadly force be used only to apprehend "perpetrators who, in the course of their crime threatened the use of deadly force, or if the officer believes there is a substantial risk that the person whose arrest is sought will cause death or serious bodily harm if his apprehension is delayed." In addition, the officer would have "to know, as a virtual certainty, that the suspect committed an offense for which the use of deadly force is permissible." *Ibid.*

Without in any way disparaging the importance of these goals, we are not convinced that the use of deadly force is a sufficiently productive means of accomplishing them to justify the killing of nonviolent suspects. *Cf. Delaware v. Prouse, supra,* 440 U.S., at 659. The use of deadly force is a self-defeating way of apprehending a suspect and so setting the criminal justice mechanism in motion. If successful, it guarantees that that mechanism will not be set in motion. And while the meaningful threat of deadly force might be thought to lead to the arrest of more live suspects by discouraging escape attempts,[9] the presently available evidence does not support this thesis.[10] The fact is that a majority of police departments in this country have forbidden the use of deadly force against nonviolent suspects. If those charged with the enforcement of the criminal law have abjured the use of deadly force in arresting

---

[9] We note that the usual manner of deterring illegal conduct—through punishment—has been largely ignored in connection with flight from arrest. Arkansas, for example, specifically excepts flight from arrest from the offense of "obstruction of governmental operations." The commentary notes that this "reflects the basic policy judgment that, absent the use of force or violence, a mere attempt to avoid apprehension by a law enforcement officer does not give rise to an independent offense." Ark.Stat.Ann. § 41–2802(3)(a) (1977) and commentary. In the few States that do outlaw flight from an arresting officer, the crime is only a misdemeanor. See, e.g., Ind.Code § 35–44–3–3 (1982). Even forceful resistance, though generally a separate offense, is classified as a misdemeanor. E.g., Ill.Rev.Stat., ch. 38, ¶ 31–1 (1984); Mont.Code Ann. § 45–7–301 (1984); N.H.Rev.Stat.Ann. § 642:2 (Supp.1983); Ore.Rev.Stat. § 162.315 (1983).

This lenient approach does avoid the anomaly of automatically transforming every fleeing misdemeanant into a fleeing felon—subject, under the common-law rule, to apprehension by deadly force—solely by virtue of his flight. However, it is in real tension with the harsh consequences of flight in cases where deadly force is employed. For example, Tennessee does not outlaw fleeing from arrest. The Memphis City Code does, § 22–34.1 (Supp.17, 1971), subjecting the offender to a maximum fine of $50, § 1–8 (1967). Thus, Garner's attempted escape subjected him to (a) a $50 fine, and (b) being shot.

[10] *See* Sherman, *Reducing Police Gun Use,* in Control in the Police Organization 98, 120–123 (M. Punch ed. 1983); Fyfe, *Observations on Police Deadly Force,* 27 Crime & Delinquency 376, 378–381 (1981); W. Geller & K. Karales, Split-Second Decisions 67 (1981); App. 84 (affidavit of William Bracey, Chief of Patrol, New York City Police Department). *See generally* Brief for Police Foundation et al. as Amici Curiae.

nondangerous felons, there is a substantial basis for doubting that the use of such force is an essential attribute of the arrest power in all felony cases. *See* Schumann v. McGinn, 307 Minn. 446, 472, 240 N.W.2d 525, 540 (1976) (Rogosheske, J., dissenting in part). Petitioners and appellant have not persuaded us that shooting nondangerous fleeing suspects is so vital as to outweigh the suspect's interest in his own life.

The use of deadly force to prevent the escape of all felony suspects, whatever the circumstances, is constitutionally unreasonable. It is not better that all felony suspects die than that they escape. Where the suspect poses no immediate threat to the officer and no threat to others, the harm resulting from failing to apprehend him does not justify the use of deadly force to do so. It is no doubt unfortunate when a suspect who is in sight escapes, but the fact that the police arrive a little late or are a little slower afoot does not always justify killing the suspect. A police officer may not seize an unarmed, nondangerous suspect by shooting him dead. The Tennessee statute is unconstitutional insofar as it authorizes the use of deadly force against such fleeing suspects.

It is not, however, unconstitutional on its face. Where the officer has probable cause to believe that the suspect poses a threat of serious physical harm, either to the officer or to others, it is not constitutionally unreasonable to prevent escape by using deadly force. Thus, if the suspect threatens the officer with a weapon or there is probable cause to believe that he has committed a crime involving the infliction or threatened infliction of serious physical harm, deadly force may be used if necessary to prevent escape, and if, where feasible, some warning has been given. As applied in such circumstances, the Tennessee statute would pass constitutional muster.

III

A

It is insisted that the Fourth Amendment must be construed in light of the common-law rule, which allowed the use of whatever force was necessary to effect the arrest of a fleeing felon, though not a misdemeanant. As stated in Hale's posthumously published Pleas of the Crown:

> "[I]f persons that are pursued by these officers for felony or the just suspicion thereof . . . shall not yield themselves to these officers, but shall either resist or fly before they are apprehended or being apprehended shall rescue themselves and resist or fly, so that they cannot be otherwise apprehended, and are upon necessity slain therein, because they cannot be otherwise taken, it is no felony." 2 M. Hale, Historia Placitorum Coronae 85 (1736).

See also 4 W. Blackstone, Commentaries *289. Most American jurisdictions also imposed a flat prohibition against the use of deadly force to stop a fleeing misdemeanant, coupled with a general privilege to use such force to stop a fleeing felon. . . . The State and city argue that because this was the prevailing rule at the time of the adoption of the Fourth Amendment and for some time thereafter, and is still in force in some States, use of deadly force against a fleeing felon must be "reasonable." It is true that this Court has often looked to the common law in evaluating the reasonableness, for Fourth Amendment purposes, of police activity. *See, e.g.,* United States v. Watson, 423 U.S. 411, 418–419 (1976); Gerstein v. Pugh, 420 U.S. 103, 111, 114 (1975); Carroll v. United States, 267 U.S. 132, 149–153 (1925). On the other hand, it "has not simply frozen into constitutional law those law enforcement practices that existed at the time of the Fourth Amendment's passage." Payton v. New York, 445 U.S. 573, 591, n. 33 (1980). Because of sweeping change in the legal and technological context, reliance on the common-law rule in this case would be a mistaken literalism that ignores the purposes of a historical inquiry.

B

It has been pointed out many times that the common-law rule is best understood in light of the fact that it arose at a time when virtually all felonies were punishable by death. "Though effected without the protections and formalities of an orderly trial and conviction, the killing of a resisting or fleeing felon resulted in no greater consequences than those authorized for punishment of the felony of which the individual was charged or suspected." American Law Institute, Model Penal Code § 3.07, Comment 3, p. 56 (Tentative Draft No. 8, 1958) (hereinafter Model Penal Code Comment). Courts have also justified the common-law rule by emphasizing the relative dangerousness of felons. *See, e.g., Schumann v. McGinn,* 307 Minn., at 458, 240 N.W.2d, at 533; *Holloway v. Moser, supra,* 193 N.C., at 187, 136 S.E., at 376 (1927).

Neither of these justifications makes sense today. Almost all crimes formerly punishable by death no longer are or can be. See, e.g., Enmund v. Florida, 458 U.S. 782 (1982); Coker v. Georgia, 433 U.S. 584 (1977). And while in earlier times "the gulf between the felonies and the minor offences was broad and deep," 2 Pollock & Maitland 467, n. 3; *Carroll v. United States, supra,* 267 U.S., at 158, today the distinction is minor and often arbitrary. Many crimes classified as misdemeanors, or nonexistent, at common law are now felonies. Wilgus, 22 Mich.L.Rev., at 572–573. These changes have undermined the concept, which was questionable to begin with, that use of deadly force against a fleeing felon is merely a speedier execution of someone who has already forfeited his life. They have also made the assumption that a "felon" is more dangerous than a misdemeanant untenable. Indeed, numerous misdemeanors involve conduct more dangerous than many felonies.[12]

---

[12] White-collar crime, for example, poses a less significant physical threat than, say, drunken driving. *See* Welsh v. Wisconsin, 466 U.S. 740; *id.,* at 755 (BLACKMUN, J., concurring). *See* Model Penal Code Comment, at 57.

There is an additional reason why the common-law rule cannot be directly translated to the present day. The common-law rule developed at a time when weapons were rudimentary. Deadly force could be inflicted almost solely in a hand-to-hand struggle during which, necessarily, the safety of the arresting officer was at risk. Handguns were not carried by police officers until the latter half of the last century. L. Kennett & J. Anderson, The Gun in America 150–151 (1975). Only then did it become possible to use deadly force from a distance as a means of apprehension. As a practical matter, the use of deadly force under the standard articulation of the common-law rule has an altogether different meaning—and harsher consequences—now than in past centuries. *See* Wechsler & Michael, *A Rationale for the Law of Homicide: I,* 37 Colum.L.Rev. 701, 741 (1937).[13]

One other aspect of the common-law rule bears emphasis. It forbids the use of deadly force to apprehend a misdemeanant, condemning such action as disproportionately severe. *See Holloway v. Moser,* 193 N.C., at 187, 136 S.E., at 376; *State v. Smith,* 127 Iowa, at 535, 103 N.W., at 945. *See generally* Annot., 83 A.L.R.3d 238 (1978).

In short, though the common-law pedigree of Tennessee's rule is pure on its face, changes in the legal and technological context mean the rule is distorted almost beyond recognition when literally applied.

C

In evaluating the reasonableness of police procedures under the Fourth Amendment, we have also looked to prevailing rules in individual jurisdictions. *See, e.g., United States v. Watson,* 423 U.S., at 421–422. The rules in the States are varied. *See generally* Comment, 18 Ga.L.Rev. 137, 140–144 (1983). Some 19 States have codified the common-law rule, though in two of these the courts have significantly limited the statute. Four States, though without a relevant statute, apparently retain the common-law rule. Two States have adopted the Model Penal Code's provision verbatim. Eighteen others allow, in slightly varying language, the use of deadly force only if the suspect has committed a felony involving the use or threat of physical or deadly force, or is escaping with a deadly weapon, or is likely to endanger life or inflict serious physical injury if not arrested. Louisiana and Vermont, though without statutes or case law on point, do forbid the use of deadly force to prevent any but

---

[13] It has been argued that sophisticated techniques of apprehension and increased communication between the police in different jurisdictions have made it more likely that an escapee will be caught than was once the case, and that this change has also reduced the "reasonableness" of the use of deadly force to prevent escape. E.g., Sherman, *Execution Without Trial: Police Homicide and the Constitution,* 33 Vand.L.Rev. 71, 76 (1980). We are unaware of any data that would permit sensible evaluation of this claim. Current arrest rates are sufficiently low, however, that we have some doubt whether in past centuries the failure to arrest at the scene meant that the police had missed their only chance in a way that is not presently the case. In 1983, 21% of the offenses in the Federal Bureau of Investigation crime index were cleared by arrest. Federal Bureau of Investigation, Uniform Crime Reports, Crime in the United States 159 (1984). The clearance rate for burglary was 15%. *Ibid.*

violent felonies. The remaining States either have no relevant statute or case law, or have positions that are unclear.

It cannot be said that there is a constant or overwhelming trend away from the common-law rule. In recent years, some States have reviewed their laws and expressly rejected abandonment of the common-law rule. Nonetheless, the long-term movement has been away from the rule that deadly force may be used against any fleeing felon, and that remains the rule in less than half the States.

This trend is more evident and impressive when viewed in light of the policies adopted by the police departments themselves. Overwhelmingly, these are more restrictive than the common-law rule. C. Milton, J. Halleck, J. Lardner, & G. Abrecht, Police Use of Deadly Force 45–46 (1977). The Federal Bureau of Investigation and the New York City Police Department, for example, both forbid the use of firearms except when necessary to prevent death or grievous bodily harm. *Id.*, at 40–41; App. 83. For accreditation by the Commission on Accreditation for Law Enforcement Agencies, a department must restrict the use of deadly force to situations where "the officer reasonably believes that the action is in defense of human life . . . or in defense of any person in immediate danger of serious physical injury." Commission on Accreditation for Law Enforcement Agencies, Inc., Standards for Law Enforcement Agencies 1–2 (1983) (italics deleted). A 1974 study reported that the police department regulations in a majority of the large cities of the United States allowed the firing of a weapon only when a felon presented a threat of death or serious bodily harm. Boston Police Department, Planning & Research Division, The Use of Deadly Force by Boston Police Personnel (1974), cited in Mattis v. Schnarr, 547 F.2d 1007, 1016, n. 19 (CA8 1976), vacated as moot sub nom. Ashcroft v. Mattis, 431 U.S. 171 (1977). Overall, only 7.5% of departmental and municipal policies explicitly permit the use of deadly force against any felon; 86.8% explicitly do not. K. Matulia, A Balance of Forces: A Report of the International Association of Chiefs of Police 161 (1982) (table). *See also* Record 1108–1368 (written policies of 44 departments). *See generally* W. Geller & K. Karales, Split-Second Decisions 33–42 (1981); Brief for Police Foundation et al. as Amici Curiae. In light of the rules adopted by those who must actually administer them, the older and fading common-law view is a dubious indicium of the constitutionality of the Tennessee statute now before us.

D

Actual departmental policies are important for an additional reason. We would hesitate to declare a police practice of long standing "unreasonable" if doing so would severely hamper effective law enforcement. But the indications are to the contrary. There has been no suggestion that crime has worsened in any way in jurisdictions that have adopted, by legislation or departmental policy, rules similar to that announced today. Amici noted that "[a]fter extensive research and consideration, [they] have concluded that laws permitting police officers to use deadly force to apprehend unarmed, non-violent fleeing felony suspects actually do not protect citizens or law enforcement officers, do not deter crime or alleviate problems caused by crime, and do not improve the crime-fighting ability of law enforcement agencies." *Id.*, at 11. The submission is that the obvious state interests in apprehension are not sufficiently served to warrant the use of lethal weapons against all fleeing felons.

Nor do we agree with petitioners and appellant that the rule we have adopted requires the police to make impossible, split-second evaluations of unknowable facts. *See* Brief for Petitioners 25; Brief for Appellant 11. We do not deny the practical difficulties of attempting to assess the suspect's dangerousness. However, similarly difficult judgments must be made by the police in equally uncertain circumstances. *See, e.g., Terry v. Ohio,* 392 U.S., at 20, 27. Nor is there any indication that in States that allow the use of deadly force only against dangerous suspects, the standard has been difficult to apply or has led to a rash of litigation involving inappropriate second-guessing of police officers' split-second decisions. Moreover, the highly technical felony/misdemeanor distinction is equally, if not more, difficult to apply in the field. An officer is in no position to know, for example, the precise value of property stolen, or whether the crime was a first or second offense. Finally, as noted above, this claim must be viewed with suspicion in light of the similar self-imposed limitations of so many police departments.

IV

The District Court concluded that Hymon was justified in shooting Garner because state law allows, and the Federal Constitution does not forbid, the use of deadly force to prevent the escape of a fleeing felony suspect if no alternative means of apprehension is available. This conclusion made a determination of Garner's apparent dangerousness unnecessary. The court did find, however, that Garner appeared to be unarmed, though Hymon could not be certain that was the case. Restated in Fourth Amendment terms, this means Hymon had no articulable basis to think Garner was armed.

In reversing, the Court of Appeals accepted the District Court's factual conclusions and held that "the facts, as found, did not justify the use of deadly force." 710 F.2d, at 246. We agree. Officer Hymon could not reasonably have believed that Garner—young, slight, and unarmed—posed any threat. Indeed, Hymon never attempted to justify his actions on any basis other than the need to prevent an escape. The District Court stated in passing that "[t]he facts of this case did not indicate to Officer Hymon that Garner was 'non-dangerous.'" This conclusion is not explained, and seems to be based solely on the fact that Garner had broken into a house at night. However, the fact that Garner was a suspected burglar could not, without regard to the other circumstances, automatically justify the use of deadly force. Hymon did not have probable cause to believe that Garner, whom he correctly believed to be unarmed, posed any physical danger to himself or others.

The dissent argues that the shooting was justified by the fact that Officer Hymon had probable cause to believe that Garner had committed a nighttime burglary. While we agree that burglary is a serious crime, we cannot agree that it is so dangerous as automatically to justify the use of deadly force. The FBI classifies burglary as a "property" rather than a "violent" crime. *See* Federal Bureau of Investigation, Uniform Crime Reports, Crime in the United States 1 (1984). Although the armed burglar would present a different situation, the fact that an unarmed suspect has broken into a dwelling at night does not automatically mean he is physically dangerous. This case demonstrates as much. *See also* Solem v. Helm, 463 U.S. 277, 296–297, and nn. 22–23 (1983). In fact, the available statistics demonstrate that burglaries only rarely involve physical violence. During the 10-year period from 1973–1982, only 3.8% of all burglaries involved violent crime. Bureau of Justice Statistics, Household Burglary 4 (1985).[23] *See also* T. Reppetto, Residential Crime 17, 105 (1974); Conklin & Bittner, *Burglary in a Suburb,* 11 Criminology 208, 214 (1973).

V

We wish to make clear what our holding means in the context of this case. The complaint has been dismissed as to all the individual defendants. The State is a party only by virtue of 28 U.S.C. § 2403(b) and is not subject to liability. The possible liability of the remaining defendants—the Police Department and the city of Memphis—hinges on Monell v. New York City Dept. of Social Services, 436 U.S. 658 (1978), and is left for remand. We hold that the statute is invalid insofar as it purported to give Hymon the authority to act as he did. As for the policy of the Police Department, the absence of any discussion of this issue by the courts below, and the uncertain state of the record, preclude any consideration of its validity.

The judgment of the Court of Appeals is affirmed, and the case is remanded for further proceedings consistent with this opinion.

So ordered.

■ JUSTICE O'CONNOR, with whom THE CHIEF JUSTICE and JUSTICE REHNQUIST join, dissenting.

---

[23]   The dissent points out that three-fifths of all rapes in the home, three-fifths of all home robberies, and about a third of home assaults are committed by burglars. *Post,* at 1709. These figures mean only that if one knows that a suspect committed a rape in the home, there is a good chance that the suspect is also a burglar. That has nothing to do with the question here, which is whether the fact that someone has committed a burglary indicates that he has committed, or might commit, a violent crime.

The dissent also points out that this 3.8% adds up to 2.8 million violent crimes over a 10-year period, as if to imply that today's holding will let loose 2.8 million violent burglars. The relevant universe is, of course, far smaller. At issue is only that tiny fraction of cases where violence has taken place and an officer who has no other means of apprehending the suspect is unaware of its occurrence.

The Court today holds that the Fourth Amendment prohibits a police officer from using deadly force as a last resort to apprehend a criminal suspect who refuses to halt when fleeing the scene of a nighttime burglary. This conclusion rests on the majority's balancing of the interests of the suspect and the public interest in effective law enforcement. Notwithstanding the venerable common-law rule authorizing the use of deadly force if necessary to apprehend a fleeing felon, and continued acceptance of this rule by nearly half the States, the majority concludes that Tennessee's statute is unconstitutional inasmuch as it allows the use of such force to apprehend a burglary suspect who is not obviously armed or otherwise dangerous. Although the circumstances of this case are unquestionably tragic and unfortunate, our constitutional holdings must be sensitive both to the history of the Fourth Amendment and to the general implications of the Court's reasoning. By disregarding the serious and dangerous nature of residential burglaries and the longstanding practice of many States, the Court effectively creates a Fourth Amendment right allowing a burglary suspect to flee unimpeded from a police officer who has probable cause to arrest, who has ordered the suspect to halt, and who has no means short of firing his weapon to prevent escape. I do not believe that the Fourth Amendment supports such a right, and I accordingly dissent. . . .

II

For purposes of Fourth Amendment analysis, I agree with the Court that Officer Hymon "seized" Garner by shooting him. Whether that seizure was reasonable and therefore permitted by the Fourth Amendment requires a careful balancing of the important public interest in crime prevention and detection and the nature and quality of the intrusion upon legitimate interests of the individual. United States v. Place, 462 U.S. 696, 703 (1983). In striking this balance here, it is crucial to acknowledge that police use of deadly force to apprehend a fleeing criminal suspect falls within the "rubric of police conduct . . . necessarily [involving] swift action predicated upon the on-the-spot observations of the officer on the beat." Terry v. Ohio, 392 U.S. 1, 20 (1968). The clarity of hindsight cannot provide the standard for judging the reasonableness of police decisions made in uncertain and often dangerous circumstances. Moreover, I am far more reluctant than is the Court to conclude that the Fourth Amendment proscribes a police practice that was accepted at the time of the adoption of the Bill of Rights and has continued to receive the support of many state legislatures. Although the Court has recognized that the requirements of the Fourth Amendment must respond to the reality of social and technological change, fidelity to the notion of constitutional—as opposed to purely judicial—limits on governmental action requires us to impose a heavy burden on those who claim that practices accepted when the Fourth Amendment was adopted are now constitutionally impermissible. See, e.g., United States v. Watson, 423 U.S. 411, 416–42 (1976); Carroll v. United States, 267 U.S. 132, 149–153

(1925). *Cf.* United States v. Villamonte-Marquez, 462 U.S. 579, 585 (1983) (noting "impressive historical pedigree" of statute challenged under Fourth Amendment).

The public interest involved in the use of deadly force as a last resort to apprehend a fleeing burglary suspect relates primarily to the serious nature of the crime. Household burglaries not only represent the illegal entry into a person's home, but also "pos[e] real risk of serious harm to others." Solem v. Helm, 463 U.S. 277, 315–316 (1983) (BURGER, C.J., dissenting). According to recent Department of Justice statistics, "[t]hree-fifths of all rapes in the home, three-fifths of all home robberies, and about a third of home aggravated and simple assaults are committed by burglars." Bureau of Justice Statistics Bulletin, Household Burglary 1 (January 1985). During the period 1973–1982, 2.8 million such violent crimes were committed in the course of burglaries. *Ibid.* Victims of a forcible intrusion into their home by a nighttime prowler will find little consolation in the majority's confident assertion that "burglaries only rarely involve physical violence." *Ante*, at 1707. Moreover, even if a particular burglary, when viewed in retrospect, does not involve physical harm to others, the "harsh potentialities for violence" inherent in the forced entry into a home preclude characterization of the crime as "innocuous, inconsequential, minor, or 'nonviolent.'" Solem v. Helm, *supra*, at 316 (BURGER, C.J., dissenting). *See also* Restatement of Torts § 131, Comment g (1934) (burglary is among felonies that normally cause or threaten death or serious bodily harm); R. Perkins & R. Boyce, Criminal Law 1110 (3d ed. 1982) (burglary is dangerous felony that creates unreasonable risk of great personal harm).

Because burglary is a serious and dangerous felony, the public interest in the prevention and detection of the crime is of compelling importance. Where a police officer has probable cause to arrest a suspected burglar, the use of deadly force as a last resort might well be the only means of apprehending the suspect. With respect to a particular burglary, subsequent investigation simply cannot represent a substitute for immediate apprehension of the criminal suspect at the scene. *See* President's Commission on Law Enforcement and Administration of Justice, Task Force Report: The Challenge of Crime in a Free Society 97 (1967). Indeed, the Captain of the Memphis Police Department testified that in his city, if apprehension is not immediate, it is likely that the suspect will not be caught. Although some law enforcement agencies may choose to assume the risk that a criminal will remain at large, the Tennessee statute reflects a legislative determination that the use of deadly force in prescribed circumstances will serve generally to protect the public. Such statutes assist the police in apprehending suspected perpetrators of serious crimes and provide notice that a lawful police order to stop and submit to arrest may not be ignored with impunity. *See, e.g.,* Wiley v. Memphis Police Department, 548 F.2d 1247, 1252–1253

(CA6), cert. denied, 434 U.S. 822 (1977); Jones v. Marshall, 528 F.2d 132, 142 (CA2 1975). . . .

Without questioning the importance of a person's interest in his life, I do not think this interest encompasses a right to flee unimpeded from the scene of a burglary. Cf. Payton v. New York, 445 U.S. 573, 617, n. 14 (1980) (WHITE, J., dissenting) ("[T]he policeman's hands should not be tied merely because of the possibility that the suspect will fail to cooperate with legitimate actions by law enforcement personnel"). The legitimate interests of the suspect in these circumstances are adequately accommodated by the Tennessee statute: to avoid the use of deadly force and the consequent risk to his life, the suspect need merely obey the valid order to halt.

A proper balancing of the interests involved suggests that use of deadly force as a last resort to apprehend a criminal suspect fleeing from the scene of a nighttime burglary is not unreasonable within the meaning of the Fourth Amendment. Admittedly, the events giving rise to this case are in retrospect deeply regrettable. No one can view the death of an unarmed and apparently nonviolent 15-year-old without sorrow, much less disapproval. Nonetheless, the reasonableness of Officer Hymon's conduct for purposes of the Fourth Amendment cannot be evaluated by what later appears to have been a preferable course of police action. The officer pursued a suspect in the darkened backyard of a house that from all indications had just been burglarized. The police officer was not certain whether the suspect was alone or unarmed; nor did he know what had transpired inside the house. He ordered the suspect to halt, and when the suspect refused to obey and attempted to flee into the night, the officer fired his weapon to prevent escape. The reasonableness of this action for purposes of the Fourth Amendment is not determined by the unfortunate nature of this particular case; instead, the question is whether it is constitutionally impermissible for police officers, as a last resort, to shoot a burglary suspect fleeing the scene of the crime.

III

Even if I agreed that the Fourth Amendment was violated under the circumstances of this case, I would be unable to join the Court's opinion. The Court holds that deadly force may be used only if the suspect "threatens the officer with a weapon or there is probable cause to believe that he has committed a crime involving the infliction or threatened infliction of serious physical harm." The Court ignores the more general implications of its reasoning. Relying on the Fourth Amendment, the majority asserts that it is constitutionally unreasonable to use deadly force against fleeing criminal suspects who do not appear to pose a threat of serious physical harm to others. *Ibid.* By declining to limit its holding to the use of firearms, the Court unnecessarily implies that the Fourth Amendment constrains the use of any police practice that is potentially lethal, no matter how remote the risk. Cf. Los Angeles v. Lyons, 461 U.S. 95 (1983). . . .

IV

The Court's opinion sweeps broadly to adopt an entirely new standard for the constitutionality of the use of deadly force to apprehend fleeing felons. Thus, the Court "lightly brushe[s] aside," *Payton v. New York, supra*, at 600, long-standing police practice that predates the Fourth Amendment and continues to receive the approval of nearly half of the state legislatures. I cannot accept the majority's creation of a constitutional right to flight for burglary suspects seeking to avoid capture at the scene of the crime. Whatever the constitutional limits on police use of deadly force in order to apprehend a fleeing felon, I do not believe they are exceeded in a case in which a police officer has probable cause to arrest a suspect at the scene of a residential burglary, orders the suspect to halt, and then fires his weapon as a last resort to prevent the suspect's escape into the night. I respectfully dissent.

Cardenas v. Fisher

307 Fed. Appx. 122 (10th Cir. 2009)

■ Before BRISCOE, TYMKOVICH, and GORSUCH, CIRCUIT JUDGES.

ORDER AND JUDGMENT**

■ TIMOTHY M. TYMOKOVICH, CIRCUIT JUDGE.

Matthew Fisher, an Albuquerque Police Department officer, asserts he is entitled to qualified immunity from a claim brought by Benjie Lorenzo Cardenas and Viola Prieto for constitutional violations under 42 U.S.C. § 1983. Fisher appeals from a district court order denying his summary judgment motion.

While we have jurisdiction to review interlocutory appeals under 28 U.S.C. § 1291, this jurisdiction is limited to reviewing issues of law. Because Fisher raises only sufficiency of the evidence issues, we DISMISS his appeal for lack of jurisdiction.

I. Background

The following facts are set forth in the light most favorable to Cardenas and Prieto as the nonmoving parties.

Late in the evening on December 3, 2005, Officer Fisher stopped a Honda Civic after it ran a stop sign near an apartment complex. The Civic's driver produced a driver's license with the name Isaac Romero, but he lacked any proof of insurance or registration. The driver's license photograph depicted a "Hispanic male with short, dark brown hair, a goatee, and a mustache," and the license indicated the driver was 5′8″ tall. The driver told Fisher he lived in the neighborhood, but the address

---

** This order and judgment is not binding precedent except under the doctrines of law of the case, res judicata and collateral estoppel. It may be cited, however, for its persuasive value consistent with Fed. R. App. P. 32.1 and 10th Cir. R. 32.1.

on the license was not nearby. In addition, the driver appeared to be drunk and was slurring his words.

Fisher took the driver's keys, placed them on the trunk of the Civic, and returned to the patrol car to begin his paperwork. While Fisher was writing the citation, the driver exited the car, grabbed the keys off the trunk, and ran toward the nearby apartment complex. Fisher reported what happened on his police radio and within five minutes two additional officers arrived. Together the officers knocked on doors in the apartment complex and questioned the residents about the person pictured on the confiscated driver's license.

Prieto and her adult son, Cardenas, lived in separate apartments in this complex. At the time of this incident, Cardenas was in his mother's apartment helping with Christmas decorations. Approximately ten minutes after the driver fled from the Civic, the officers knocked on the door of Prieto's apartment and Cardenas answered. Cardenas was a "Hispanic male with dark hair, a haircut similar to [the] driver's license photograph, and a mustache."

Unlike the driver of the Civic, though, Cardenas was 5'10" tall, was not wearing the clothes the driver of the Civic had been wearing, and appeared sober. Despite these differences, Fisher at first believed Cardenas was the person on the confiscated driver's license. He "grabbed Cardenas by the arms, twisted him around, and slapped him in handcuffs." The handcuffs were "extremely, extremely tight," and Cardenas "immediately felt pain in his arm, shoulder, and back." Despite Cardenas's complaints about the handcuffs' tightness, Fisher refused to loosen them.

Cardenas and Prieto repeatedly told Fisher that Cardenas was neither the driver nor the person on the driver's license. When the officers took Cardenas to his apartment, he produced a birth certificate, a New Mexico driver's license, a rent receipt, and a utility bill corroborating his identity. Fisher then searched Cardenas's apartment without permission and without a warrant.

Fisher eventually concluded Cardenas was not the man on the driver's license, but still believed Cardenas was the driver who had fled. The officers transported Cardenas to the police station and charged him with concealing identity, eluding a police officer, improper use of a license plate, and failure to register and maintain insurance. He was not charged with running a stop sign or for driving while intoxicated. Another officer released the handcuffs at the police station and reportedly observed that "[t]hose cuffs are on way too tight." Cardenas himself indicated he "was in physical discomfort on his whole left side, from his shoulder to his lower back, while in the squad car and at the jail."

The district court found that sufficient evidence supported the claim that Cardenas "sustained injuries as a result of the handcuffing, including bruises and abrasions around his wrists." *Id.* According to the district court, "Cardenas sought medical attention for his injuries a week or two after the incident and maintains that he was unable to work for approximately two months." *Id*. Cardenas was eventually acquitted on all charges, and following his acquittal he and Prieto brought this § 1983 suit against Fisher in federal court.

Fisher moved for summary judgment, claiming qualified immunity protected him from Cardenas's unlawful arrest and excessive use of force claims. The district court denied Fisher's summary judgment motion, and he now appeals that denial.

II. Discussion

Qualified immunity protects public officials "from undue interference with their duties and from potentially disabling threats of liability." Harlow v. Fitzgerald, 457 U.S. 800, 806 (1982). Plaintiffs seeking to overcome a qualified immunity defense must show that (1) the defendant violated a constitutional or statutory right, and (2) the right was clearly established at the time of the defendant's unlawful conduct. Meachum v. Frazier, 500 F.3d 1200 (10th Cir. 2007). In denying Fisher's summary judgment motion, the district court found Cardenas asserted sufficient facts that, if true, would constitute a violation of a clearly established constitutional right. . . .

As we explain in more detail below, Fisher requests that we review the record and separately weigh the sufficiency of Cardenas's proffered evidence—precisely what we are jurisdictionally prohibited from doing. Fisher argues that when properly reviewed, the facts show neither unlawful arrest nor excessive force. Regardless of the merits of these arguments, the Supreme Court's decisions in [Behrens v. Pelletier, 516 U.S. 299 (1996) and Johnson v. Jones, 515 U.S. 304, 316 (1995)] are clear that we simply lack jurisdiction to consider them at this interlocutory stage.

A. Unlawful Arrest

Fisher claims he is entitled to qualified immunity since he reasonably believed Cardenas had committed a crime when the arrest occurred. His reasonable belief would provide the probable cause needed to make the arrest lawful.

But the problem here is that Fisher fails to make a *legal* argument that the facts Cardenas asserts, even if true, do not amount to a constitutional violation. Instead, he essentially disagrees with the district court's conclusions that disputed facts remain for a jury on the probable cause question and that, "[o]n the facts as alleged by Plaintiff Cardenas, a reasonable officer in Defendant Fisher's position . . . would not have believed he had probable cause to suspect that it was Plaintiff Cardenas he had stopped." Fisher argues the district court improperly credited the testimony of certain eyewitnesses, failed to consider trustworthy identifying information Fisher had at the time, and failed to account for the similarities in appearance between the driver and Cardenas that would have made a mistake of identity reasonable.

These arguments relate to the sufficiency of the evidence, however, and we have no jurisdiction to address them in this interlocutory context. *See Behrens,* 516 U.S. at 313 ("[D]eterminations of evidentiary sufficiency at summary judgment are not immediately appealable merely because they happen to arise in a qualified-immunity case."). Because jurisdiction is wanting, we must dismiss the unlawful arrest argument.

B. Excessive Force During Arrest

Fisher next challenges the district court's denial of qualified immunity on the excessive force claim. He argues the amount of force used in arresting and handcuffing Cardenas was objectively reasonable.

"We analyze whether the force used to effectuate an arrest violates an individual's Fourth Amendment rights under the 'objective reasonableness' standard of the Fourth Amendment." Marquez v. City of Albuquerque, 399 F.3d 1216, 1220 (10th Cir. 2005) (quoting Graham v. Connor, 490 U.S. 386, 388 (1989)). This reasonableness inquiry turns on several factors, including the alleged crime's severity, the threat a suspect poses, and the suspect's efforts to resist or evade arrest. *Id.* In essence these factors "evaluate[ ] the force used in a given arrest or detention against the force reasonably necessary to effect a lawful arrest or detention under the circumstances of the case." Cortez v. McCauley, 478 U.S. 1108, 1126 (10th Cir. 2007). Unduly tight handcuffing can constitute excessive force if a plaintiff alleges: (1) "some actual injury that is not *de minimis,* be it physical or emotional," and (2) that the officer ignored the "plaintiff's timely complaints . . . that the handcuffs were too tight." *Id.* at 1129.

After applying these principles, the district court concluded that disputed facts existed relating to whether the amount of force used to effectuate the arrest was reasonable in these circumstances. Accepting Cardenas's allegations as true, though, the district court concluded sufficient facts existed for a constitutional excessive force claim. In finding that Cardenas alleged more than a *de minimis* injury, the court noted the significant pain he experienced while handcuffed, his need to seek medical attention for his wrists, and his inability to work "for two months as a result of his injuries."

Fisher's interlocutory challenge to the excessive force ruling suffers the same deficiencies as his challenge to the unlawful arrest ruling. In essence he asks us to reweigh the evidence and find that Fisher used an objectively reasonable amount of force to effect Cardenas's arrest. As we have already indicated, jurisdictional limits prevent us from reaching this factual question. Because Fisher asserts no cognizable legal challenge regarding the *de minimis* nature of the injury, we need not address the district court's conclusion that the facts alleged meet the *de minimis* standard imposed by *Cortez.* And, as the district court notes, any dispute about the seriousness of these alleged injuries, including medical and work records, will be fair game for trial. At that point "Cardenas will be required to come forward with evidence sufficient to prove actual injury that is not *de minimis*." *See also Forgarty,* 523 F.3d at 1159 (we are free to reconsider the record on appeal after trial to determine if the facts establish entitlement to qualified immunity).

Because jurisdiction is wanting, we must also dismiss Fisher's argument against the excessive force claim.

III. Conclusion

For the foregoing reasons, we DISMISS Fisher's interlocutory appeal.

CHAPTER 4

SEARCH FOR EVIDENCE

1. THE "REASONABLE EXPECTATION OF PRIVACY" TEST

United States v. Jones

565 U.S. 400 (2012)

■ SCALIA, J., delivered the opinion of the Court, in which ROBERTS, C.J., and KENNEDY, THOMAS, and SOTOMAYOR, JJ., joined. SOTOMAYOR, J., filed a concurring opinion. ALITO, J., filed an opinion concurring in the judgment, in which GINSBURG, BREYER, and KAGAN, JJ., joined.

■ JUSTICE SCALIA delivered the opinion of the Court.

We decide whether the attachment of a Global-Positioning-System (GPS) tracking device to an individual's vehicle, and subsequent use of that device to monitor the vehicle's movements on public streets, constitutes a search or seizure within the meaning of the Fourth Amendment.

I

In 2004 respondent Antoine Jones, owner and operator of a nightclub in the District of Columbia, came under suspicion of trafficking in narcotics and was made the target of an investigation by a joint FBI and Metropolitan Police Department task force. Officers employed various investigative techniques, including visual surveillance of the nightclub, installation of a camera focused on the front door of the club, and a pen register and wiretap covering Jones's cellular phone.

Based in part on information gathered from these sources, in 2005 the Government applied to the United States District Court for the District of Columbia for a warrant authorizing the use of an electronic tracking device on the Jeep Grand Cherokee registered to Jones's wife. A warrant issued, authorizing installation of the device in the District of Columbia and within 10 days.

On the 11th day, and not in the District of Columbia but in Maryland,[1] agents installed a GPS tracking device on the undercarriage of the Jeep while it was parked in a public parking lot. Over the next 28 days, the Government used the device to track the vehicle's movements, and once had to replace the device's battery when the vehicle was parked in a different public lot in Maryland. By means of signals from multiple satellites, the device established the vehicle's location within 50 to 100 feet, and communicated that location by cellular phone to a Government

---

[1] In this litigation, the Government has conceded noncompliance with the warrant and has argued only that a warrant was not required. United States v. Maynard, 615 F.3d 544, 566, n. * (C.A.D.C. 2010).

computer. It relayed more than 2,000 pages of data over the 4-week period.

The Government ultimately obtained a multiple-count indictment charging Jones and several alleged co-conspirators with, as relevant here, conspiracy to distribute and possess with intent to distribute five kilograms or more of cocaine and 50 grams or more of cocaine base, in violation of 21 U.S.C. §§ 841 and 846. Before trial, Jones filed a motion to suppress evidence obtained through the GPS device. The District Court granted the motion only in part, suppressing the data obtained while the vehicle was parked in the garage adjoining Jones's residence. 451 F.Supp.2d 71, 88 (2006). It held the remaining data admissible, because " '[a] person traveling in an automobile on public thoroughfares has no reasonable expectation of privacy in his movements from one place to another.' " *Ibid.* (quoting United States v. Knotts, 460 U.S. 276, 281 (1983)). Jones's trial in October 2006 produced a hung jury on the conspiracy count.

In March 2007, a grand jury returned another indictment, charging Jones and others with the same conspiracy. The Government introduced at trial the same GPS-derived locational data admitted in the first trial, which connected Jones to the alleged conspirators' stash house that contained $850,000 in cash, 97 kilograms of cocaine, and 1 kilogram of cocaine base. The jury returned a guilty verdict, and the District Court sentenced Jones to life imprisonment.

The United States Court of Appeals for the District of Columbia Circuit reversed the conviction because of admission of the evidence obtained by warrantless use of the GPS device which, it said, violated the Fourth Amendment. United States v. Maynard, 615 F.3d 544 (2010). The D.C. Circuit denied the Government's petition for rehearing en banc, with four judges dissenting. 625 F.3d 766 (2010). We granted certiorari.

II

A

The Fourth Amendment provides in relevant part that "[t]he right of the people to be secure in their persons, houses, papers, and effects, against unreasonable searches and seizures, shall not be violated." It is beyond dispute that a vehicle is an "effect" as that term is used in the Amendment. *United States v. Chadwick,* 433 U.S. 1, 12 (1977). We hold that the Government's installation of a GPS device on a target's vehicle,[2] and its use of that device to monitor the vehicle's movements, constitutes a "search."

---

[2] As we have noted, the Jeep was registered to Jones's wife. The Government acknowledged, however, that Jones was "the exclusive driver." *Id.,* at 555, n. * (internal quotation marks omitted). If Jones was not the owner he had at least the property rights of a bailee. The Court of Appeals concluded that the vehicle's registration did not affect his ability to make a Fourth Amendment objection, *ibid.,* and the Government has not challenged that determination here. We therefore do not consider the Fourth Amendment significance of Jones's status.

It is important to be clear about what occurred in this case: The Government physically occupied private property for the purpose of obtaining information. We have no doubt that such a physical intrusion would have been considered a "search" within the meaning of the Fourth Amendment when it was adopted. Entick v. Carrington, 95 Eng. Rep. 807 (C.P. 1765), is a "case we have described as a 'monument of English freedom' 'undoubtedly familiar' to 'every American statesman' at the time the Constitution was adopted, and considered to be 'the true and ultimate expression of constitutional law' " with regard to search and seizure. Brower v. County of Inyo, 489 U.S. 593, 596 (1989) (quoting Boyd v. United States, 116 U.S. 616, 626 (1886)). In that case, Lord Camden expressed in plain terms the significance of property rights in search-and-seizure analysis:

> "[O]ur law holds the property of every man so sacred, that no man can set his foot upon his neighbour's close without his leave; if he does he is a trespasser, though he does no damage at all; if he will tread upon his neighbour's ground, he must justify it by law." *Entick, supra,* at 817.

The text of the Fourth Amendment reflects its close connection to property, since otherwise it would have referred simply to "the right of the people to be secure against unreasonable searches and seizures"; the phrase "in their persons, houses, papers, and effects" would have been superfluous.

Consistent with this understanding, our Fourth Amendment jurisprudence was tied to common-law trespass, at least until the latter half of the 20th century. Kyllo v. United States, 533 U.S. 27, 31 (2001); Kerr, *The Fourth Amendment and New Technologies: Constitutional Myths and the Case for Caution,* 102 Mich. L.Rev. 801, 816 (2004). Thus, in Olmstead v. United States, 277 U.S. 438 (1928), we held that wiretaps attached to telephone wires on the public streets did not constitute a Fourth Amendment search because "[t]here was no entry of the houses or offices of the defendants," *id.,* at 464.

Our later cases, of course, have deviated from that exclusively property-based approach. In Katz v. United States, 389 U.S. 347, 351 1967), we said that "the Fourth Amendment protects people, not places," and found a violation in attachment of an eavesdropping device to a public telephone booth. Our later cases have applied the analysis of Justice Harlan's concurrence in that case, which said that a violation occurs when government officers violate a person's "reasonable expectation of privacy," *id.,* at 360. *See, e.g.,* Bond v. United States, 529 U.S. 334 (2000); California v. Ciraolo, 476 U.S. 207 (1986); Smith v. Maryland, 442 U.S. 735 (1979).

The Government contends that the Harlan standard shows that no search occurred here, since Jones had no "reasonable expectation of privacy" in the area of the Jeep accessed by Government agents (its underbody) and in the locations of the Jeep on the public roads, which were visible to all. But we need not address the Government's contentions, because Jones's Fourth Amendment rights do not rise or fall with the *Katz* formulation. At bottom, we must "assur[e] preservation of that degree of privacy against government that existed when the Fourth Amendment was adopted." *Kyllo, supra,* at 34. As explained, for most of our history the Fourth Amendment was understood to embody a particular concern for government trespass upon the areas ("persons, houses, papers, and effects") it enumerates.[3] *Katz* did not repudiate that understanding. Less than two years later the Court upheld defendants' contention that the Government could not introduce against them conversations between *other* people obtained by warrantless placement of electronic surveillance devices in their homes. The opinion rejected the dissent's contention that there was no Fourth Amendment violation "unless the conversational privacy of the homeowner himself is invaded."[4] Alderman v. United States, 394 U.S. 165, 176 (1969). "[W]e [do not] believe that *Katz,* by holding that the Fourth Amendment protects persons and their private conversations, was intended to withdraw any of the protection which the Amendment extends to the home. . . ." *Id.,* at 180.

More recently, in Soldal v. Cook County, 506 U.S. 56 (1992), the Court unanimously rejected the argument that although a "seizure" had occurred "in a 'technical' sense" when a trailer home was forcibly removed, *id.,* at 62, no Fourth Amendment violation occurred because law enforcement had not "invade[d] the [individuals'] privacy," *id.,* at 60. *Katz,* the Court explained, established that "property rights are not the sole measure of Fourth Amendment violations," but did not "snuf[f] out the previously recognized protection for property." 506 U.S., at 64. As Justice Brennan explained in his concurrence in *Knotts, Katz* did not erode the principle "that, when the Government *does* engage in physical intrusion of a constitutionally protected area in order to obtain information, that intrusion may constitute a violation of the Fourth Amendment." 460 U.S., at 286 (opinion concurring in judgment). We have embodied that preservation of past rights in our very definition of "reasonable expectation of privacy" which we have said to be an

---

[3] Justice ALITO's concurrence (hereinafter concurrence) doubts the wisdom of our approach because "it is almost impossible to think of late-18th-century situations that are analogous to what took place in this case." (opinion concurring in judgment). But in fact it posits a situation that is not far afield—a constable's concealing himself in the target's coach in order to track its movements. *Ibid.* There is no doubt that the information gained by that trespassory activity would be the product of an unlawful search—whether that information consisted of the conversations occurring in the coach, or of the destinations to which the coach traveled.

In any case, it is quite irrelevant whether there was an 18th-century analog. Whatever new methods of investigation may be devised, our task, at a minimum, is to decide whether the action in question would have constituted a "search" within the original meaning of the Fourth Amendment. Where, as here, the Government obtains information by physically intruding on a constitutionally protected area, such a search has undoubtedly occurred.

[4] Thus, the concurrence's attempt to recast *Alderman* as meaning that individuals have a "legitimate expectation of privacy in all conversations that [take] place under their roof," is foreclosed by the Court's opinion. The Court took as a given that the homeowner's "conversational privacy" had not been violated.

expectation "that has a source outside of the Fourth Amendment, either by reference to concepts of real or personal property law or to understandings that are recognized and permitted by society." Minnesota v. Carter, 525 U.S. 83, 88 (1998) (internal quotation marks omitted). *Katz* did not narrow the Fourth Amendment's scope.[5]

The Government contends that several of our post-*Katz* cases foreclose the conclusion that what occurred here constituted a search. It relies principally on two cases in which we rejected Fourth Amendment challenges to "beepers," electronic tracking devices that represent another form of electronic monitoring. The first case, *Knotts,* upheld against Fourth Amendment challenge the use of a "beeper" that had been placed in a container of chloroform, allowing law enforcement to monitor the location of the container. 460 U.S., at 278. We said that there had been no infringement of Knotts' reasonable expectation of privacy since the information obtained—the location of the automobile carrying the container on public roads, and the location of the off-loaded container in open fields near Knotts' cabin—had been voluntarily conveyed to the public.[6] *Id.,* at 281–282. But as we have discussed, the *Katz* reasonable-expectation-of-privacy test has been *added to,* not *substituted for,* the common-law trespassory test. The holding in *Knotts* addressed only the former, since the latter was not at issue. The beeper had been placed in the container before it came into Knotts' possession, with the consent of the then-owner. 460 U.S., at 278. Knotts did not challenge that installation, and we specifically declined to consider its effect on the Fourth Amendment analysis. *Id.,* at 279, n.* *. *Knotts* would be relevant, perhaps, if the Government were making the argument that what would otherwise be an unconstitutional search is not such where it produces only public information. The Government does not make that argument, and we know of no case that would support it.

The second "beeper" case, United States v. Karo, 46 U.S. 705 (1984), does not suggest a different conclusion. There we addressed the question left open by *Knotts,* whether the installation of a beeper in a container

---

[5] The concurrence notes that post-*Katz* we have explained that " 'an actual trespass is neither necessary nor sufficient to establish a constitutional violation.' " (quoting United States v. Karo, 468 U.S. 705, 713 (1984)). That is undoubtedly true, and undoubtedly irrelevant. *Karo* was considering whether a seizure occurred, and as the concurrence explains, a seizure of property occurs, not when there is a trespass, but "when there is some meaningful interference with an individual's possessory interests in that property." (internal quotation marks omitted). Likewise with a search. Trespass alone does not qualify, but there must be conjoined with that what was present here: an attempt to find something or to obtain information.

Related to this, and similarly irrelevant, is the concurrence's point that, if analyzed separately, neither the installation of the device nor its use would constitute a Fourth Amendment search. *See ibid.* Of course not. A trespass on "houses" or "effects," or a *Katz* invasion of privacy, is not alone a search unless it is done to obtain information; and the obtaining of information is not alone a search unless it is achieved by such a trespass or invasion of privacy.

[6] *Knotts* noted the "limited use which the government made of the signals from this particular beeper," 460 U.S., at 284; and reserved the question whether "different constitutional principles may be applicable" to "dragnet-type law enforcement practices" of the type that GPS tracking made possible here, *ibid.*

amounted to a search or seizure. 468 U.S., at 713. As in *Knotts,* at the time the beeper was installed the container belonged to a third party, and it did not come into possession of the defendant until later. 468 U.S., at 708. Thus, the specific question we considered was whether the installation *"with the consent of the original owner* constitute[d] a search or seizure . . . when the container is delivered to a buyer having no knowledge of the presence of the beeper." *Id.,* at 707 (emphasis added). We held not. The Government, we said, came into physical contact with the container only before it belonged to the defendant Karo; and the transfer of the container with the unmonitored beeper inside did not convey any information and thus did not invade Karo's privacy. *See id.,* at 712. That conclusion is perfectly consistent with the one we reach here. Karo accepted the container as it came to him, beeper and all, and was therefore not entitled to object to the beeper's presence, even though it was used to monitor the container's location. *Cf.* On Lee v. United States, 343 U.S. 747, 751–752 (1952) (no search or seizure where an informant, who was wearing a concealed microphone, was invited into the defendant's business). Jones, who possessed the Jeep at the time the Government trespassorily inserted the information-gathering device, is on much different footing.

The Government also points to our exposition in New York v. Class, 475 U.S. 106 (1986), that "[t]he exterior of a car . . . is thrust into the public eye, and thus to examine it does not constitute a 'search.'" *Id.,* at 114. That statement is of marginal relevance here since, as the Government acknowledges, "the officers in this case did *more* than conduct a visual inspection of respondent's vehicle," Brief for United States 41 (emphasis added). By attaching the device to the Jeep, officers encroached on a protected area. In *Class* itself we suggested that this would make a difference, for we concluded that an officer's momentary reaching into the interior of a vehicle did constitute a search.[7] 475 U.S., at 114–115.

Finally, the Government's position gains little support from our conclusion in Oliver v. United States, 466 U.S. 170 (1984), that officers' information-gathering intrusion on an "open field" did not constitute a Fourth Amendment search even though it was a trespass at common law, *id.,* at 183. Quite simply, an open field, unlike the curtilage of a home, *See* United States v. Dunn, 480 U.S. 294 (1987), is not one of those protected areas enumerated in the Fourth Amendment. *Oliver, supra,* at 176–177. *See also* Hester v. United States, 265 U.S. 57, 59 (1924). The

---

[7]   The Government also points to Cardwell v. Lewis, 417 U.S. 583 (1974), in which the Court rejected the claim that the inspection of an impounded vehicle's tire tread and the collection of paint scrapings from its exterior violated the Fourth Amendment. Whether the plurality said so because no search occurred or because the search was reasonable is unclear. Compare *id.,* at 591 (opinion of Blackmun, J.) ("[W]e fail to comprehend what expectation of privacy was infringed"), with *id.,* at 592 ("Under circumstances such as these, where probable cause exists, a warrantless examination of the exterior of a car is not unreasonable . . .").

Government's physical intrusion on such an area—unlike its intrusion on the "effect" at issue here—is of no Fourth Amendment significance.[8]

B

The concurrence begins by accusing us of applying "18th-century tort law." That is a distortion. What we apply is an 18th-century guarantee against unreasonable searches, which we believe must provide *at a minimum* the degree of protection it afforded when it was adopted. The concurrence does not share that belief. It would apply *exclusively Katz*'s reasonable-expectation-of-privacy test, even when that eliminates rights that previously existed.

The concurrence faults our approach for "present[ing] particularly vexing problems" in cases that do not involve physical contact, such as those that involve the transmission of electronic signals. We entirely fail to understand that point. For unlike the concurrence, which would make *Katz* the *exclusive* test, we do not make trespass the exclusive test. Situations involving merely the transmission of electronic signals without trespass would *remain* subject to *Katz* analysis.

In fact, it is the concurrence's insistence on the exclusivity of the *Katz* test that needlessly leads us into "particularly vexing problems" in the present case. This Court has to date not deviated from the understanding that mere visual observation does not constitute a search. *See Kyllo,* 533 U.S., at 31–32. We accordingly held in *Knotts* that "[a] person traveling in an automobile on public thoroughfares has no reasonable expectation of privacy in his movements from one place to another." 460 U.S., at 281. Thus, even assuming that the concurrence is correct to say that "[t]raditional surveillance" of Jones for a 4-week period "would have required a large team of agents, multiple vehicles, and perhaps aerial assistance," our cases suggest that such visual observation is constitutionally permissible. It may be that achieving the same result through electronic means, without an accompanying trespass, is an unconstitutional invasion of privacy, but the present case does not require us to answer that question.

And answering it affirmatively leads us needlessly into additional thorny problems. The concurrence posits that "relatively short-term monitoring of a person's movements on public streets" is okay, but that "the use of longer term GPS monitoring in investigations *of most offenses*" is no good. (emphasis added). That introduces yet another novelty into our jurisprudence. There is no precedent for the proposition that whether a search has occurred depends on the nature of the crime being investigated. And even accepting that novelty, it remains unexplained

---

[8]   Thus, our theory is not that the Fourth Amendment is concerned with "*any* technical trespass that led to the gathering of evidence." (ALITO, J., concurring in judgment) (emphasis added). The Fourth Amendment protects against trespassory searches only with regard to those items ("persons, houses, papers, and effects") that it enumerates. The trespass that occurred in *Oliver* may properly be understood as a "search," but not one "in the constitutional sense." 466 U.S., at 170, 183.

why a 4-week investigation is "surely" too long and why a drug-trafficking conspiracy involving substantial amounts of cash and narcotics is not an "extraordinary offens[e]" which may permit longer observation. What of a 2-day monitoring of a suspected purveyor of stolen electronics? Or of a 6-month monitoring of a suspected terrorist? We may have to grapple with these "vexing problems" in some future case where a classic trespassory search is not involved and resort must be had to *Katz* analysis; but there is no reason for rushing forward to resolve them here.

III

The Government argues in the alternative that even if the attachment and use of the device was a search, it was reasonable—and thus lawful—under the Fourth Amendment because "officers had reasonable suspicion, and indeed probable cause, to believe that [Jones] was a leader in a large-scale cocaine distribution conspiracy." Brief for United States 50–51. We have no occasion to consider this argument. The Government did not raise it below, and the D.C. Circuit therefore did not address it. *See* 625 F.3d, at 767 (Ginsburg, Tatel, and Griffith, JJ., concurring in denial of rehearing en banc). We consider the argument forfeited. *See* Sprietsma v. Mercury Marine, 537 U.S. 51, 56, n. 4 (2002).

* * *

The judgment of the Court of Appeals for the D.C. Circuit is affirmed.

It is so ordered.

■ JUSTICE SOTOMAYOR, concurring.

I join the Court's opinion because I agree that a search within the meaning of the Fourth Amendment occurs, at a minimum, "[w]here, as here, the Government obtains information by physically intruding on a constitutionally protected area." *Ante,* at n. 3. In this case, the Government installed a Global Positioning System (GPS) tracking device on respondent Antoine Jones' Jeep without a valid warrant and without Jones' consent, then used that device to monitor the Jeep's movements over the course of four weeks. The Government usurped Jones' property for the purpose of conducting surveillance on him, thereby invading privacy interests long afforded, and undoubtedly entitled to, Fourth Amendment protection. See, *e.g.,* Silverman v. United States, 365 U.S. 505, 511–512 (1961).

Of course, the Fourth Amendment is not concerned only with trespassory intrusions on property. *See, e.g.,* Kyllo v. United States, 533 U.S. 27, 31–33 (2001). Rather, even in the absence of a trespass, "a Fourth Amendment search occurs when the government violates a subjective expectation of privacy that society recognizes as reasonable." *Id.,* at 33; *See also* Smith v. Maryland, 442 U.S. 735, 740–741(1979); Katz v. United States, 389 U.S. 347, 361 (1967) (Harlan, J., concurring). In *Katz,* this Court enlarged its then-prevailing focus on property rights by announcing that the reach of the Fourth Amendment does not "turn upon the presence or absence of a physical intrusion." *Id.,* at 353. As the majority's opinion makes clear, however, *Katz*'s reasonable-expectation-of-privacy test augmented, but did not displace or diminish, the common-law trespassory test that preceded it. Thus, "when the Government *does* engage in physical intrusion of a constitutionally protected area in order to obtain information, that intrusion may constitute a violation of the Fourth Amendment." *United States v. Knotts,* 460 U.S. 276, 286 (1983) (Brennan, J., concurring in judgment); *see also, e.g., Rakas v. Illinois,* 439 U.S. 128, 144, n. 12 (1978). Justice ALITO's approach, which discounts altogether the constitutional relevance of the Government's physical intrusion on Jones' Jeep, erodes that longstanding protection for privacy expectations inherent in items of property that people possess or control. By contrast, the trespassory test applied in the majority's opinion reflects an irreducible constitutional minimum: When the Government physically invades personal property to gather information, a search occurs. The reaffirmation of that principle suffices to decide this case.

Nonetheless, as Justice ALITO notes, physical intrusion is now unnecessary to many forms of surveillance. With increasing regularity, the Government will be capable of duplicating the monitoring undertaken in this case by enlisting factory- or owner-installed vehicle tracking devices or GPS-enabled smartphones. *See* United States v. Pineda-Moreno, 617 F.3d 1120, 1125 (C.A.9 2010) (Kozinski, C.J., dissenting from denial of rehearing en banc). In cases of electronic or other novel modes of surveillance that do not depend upon a physical invasion on property, the majority opinion's trespassory test may provide little guidance. But "[s]ituations involving merely the transmission of electronic signals without trespass would *remain* subject to *Katz* analysis.". As Justice ALITO incisively observes, the same technological advances that have made possible nontrespassory surveillance techniques will also affect the *Katz* test by shaping the evolution of societal privacy expectations. Under that rubric, I agree with Justice ALITO that, at the very least, "longer term GPS monitoring in investigations of most offenses impinges on expectations of privacy."

In cases involving even short-term monitoring, some unique attributes of GPS surveillance relevant to the *Katz* analysis will require particular attention. GPS monitoring generates a precise, comprehensive record of a person's public movements that reflects a wealth of detail about her familial, political, professional, religious, and sexual associations. *See, e.g.,* People v. Weaver, 12 N.Y.3d 433, 441–442, 882 N.Y.S.2d 357, 909 N.E.2d 1195, 1199 (2009) ("Disclosed in [GPS] data . . . will be trips the indisputably private nature of which takes little imagination to conjure: trips to the psychiatrist, the plastic surgeon, the abortion clinic, the AIDS treatment center, the strip club, the criminal defense attorney, the by-the-hour motel, the union meeting, the mosque, synagogue or church, the gay bar and on and on"). The Government can store such records and efficiently mine them for information years into the future. *Pineda-Moreno,* 617 F.3d, at 1124 (opinion of Kozinski, C.J.). And because GPS monitoring is cheap in comparison to conventional surveillance techniques and, by design, proceeds surreptitiously, it evades the ordinary checks that constrain abusive law enforcement practices: "limited police resources and community hostility." Illinois v. Lidster, 540 U.S. 419, 426 (2004).

Awareness that the Government may be watching chills associational and expressive freedoms. And the Government's unrestrained power to assemble data that reveal private aspects of identity is susceptible to abuse. The net result is that GPS monitoring—by making available at a relatively low cost such a substantial quantum of intimate information about any person whom the Government, in its unfettered discretion, chooses to track—may "alter the relationship between citizen and government in a way that is inimical to democratic society." United States v. Cuevas-Perez, 640 F.3d 272, 285 (C.A.7 2011) (Flaum, J., concurring).

I would take these attributes of GPS monitoring into account when considering the existence of a reasonable societal expectation of privacy in the sum of one's public movements. I would ask whether people reasonably expect that their movements will be recorded and aggregated in a manner that enables the Government to ascertain, more or less at will, their political and religious beliefs, sexual habits, and so on. I do not regard as dispositive the fact that the Government might obtain the fruits of GPS monitoring through lawful conventional surveillance techniques. *See Kyllo,* 533 U.S., at 35, n. 2; majority opinion *ante* (leaving open the possibility that duplicating traditional surveillance "through electronic means, without an accompanying trespass, is an unconstitutional invasion of privacy"). I would also consider the appropriateness of entrusting to the Executive, in the absence of any oversight from a coordinate branch, a tool so amenable to misuse, especially in light of the Fourth Amendment's goal to curb arbitrary exercises of police power to and prevent "a too permeating police surveillance," United States v. Di Re, 332 U.S. 581, 595 (1948).

More fundamentally, it may be necessary to reconsider the premise that an individual has no reasonable expectation of privacy in information voluntarily disclosed to third parties. *E.g., Smith,* 442 U.S., at 742; United States v. Miller, 425 U.S. 435, 443 (1976). This approach is ill suited to the digital age, in which people reveal a great deal of information about themselves to third parties in the course of carrying out mundane tasks. People disclose the phone numbers that they dial or text to their cellular providers; the URLs that they visit and the e-mail addresses with which they correspond to their Internet service providers; and the books, groceries, and medications they purchase to online retailers. Perhaps, as Justice ALITO notes, some people may find the "tradeoff" of privacy for convenience "worthwhile," or come to accept this "diminution of privacy" as "inevitable," and perhaps not. I for one doubt that people would accept without complaint the warrantless disclosure to the Government of a list of every Web site they had visited in the last week, or month, or year. But whatever the societal expectations, they can attain constitutionally protected status only if our Fourth Amendment jurisprudence ceases to treat secrecy as a prerequisite for privacy. I would not assume that all information voluntarily disclosed to some member of the public for a limited purpose is, for that reason alone, disentitled to Fourth Amendment protection. *See Smith,* 442 U.S., at 749 (Marshall, J., dissenting) ("Privacy is not a discrete commodity, possessed absolutely or not at all. Those who disclose certain facts to a bank or phone company for a limited business purpose need not assume that this information will be released to other persons for other purposes"); *See also Katz,* 389 U.S., at 351–352 ("[W]hat [a person] seeks to preserve as private, even in an area accessible to the public, may be constitutionally protected").

Resolution of these difficult questions in this case is unnecessary, however, because the Government's physical intrusion on Jones' Jeep supplies a narrower basis for decision. I therefore join the majority's opinion.

■ JUSTICE ALITO, with whom JUSTICE GINSBURG, JUSTICE BREYER, and JUSTICE KAGAN join, concurring in the judgment.

This case requires us to apply the Fourth Amendment's prohibition of unreasonable searches and seizures to a 21st-century surveillance technique, the use of a Global Positioning System (GPS) device to monitor a vehicle's movements for an extended period of time. Ironically, the Court has chosen to decide this case based on 18th-century tort law. By attaching a small GPS device[1] to the underside of the vehicle that respondent drove, the law enforcement officers in this case engaged in conduct that might have provided grounds in 1791 for a suit for trespass to chattels.[2] And for this reason, the Court concludes, the installation and use of the GPS device constituted a search.

This holding, in my judgment, is unwise. It strains the language of the Fourth Amendment; it has little if any support in current Fourth Amendment case law; and it is highly artificial.

I would analyze the question presented in this case by asking whether respondent's reasonable expectations of privacy were violated by the long-term monitoring of the movements of the vehicle he drove.

---

[1] Although the record does not reveal the size or weight of the device used in this case, there is now a device in use that weighs two ounces and is the size of a credit card. Tr. of Oral Arg. 27.

[2] At common law, a suit for trespass to chattels could be maintained if there was a violation of "the dignitary interest in the inviolability of chattels," but today there must be "some actual damage to the chattel before the action can be maintained." W. Keeton, D. Dobbs, R. Keeton, & D. Owen, Prosser & Keeton on Law of Torts 87 (5th ed.1984) (hereinafter Prosser & Keeton). Here, there was no actual damage to the vehicle to which the GPS device was attached.

I

A

The Fourth Amendment prohibits "unreasonable searches and seizures," and the Court makes very little effort to explain how the attachment or use of the GPS device fits within these terms. The Court does not contend that there was a seizure. A seizure of property occurs when there is "some meaningful interference with an individual's possessory interests in that property," United States v. Jacobsen, 466 U.S. 109, 113 (1984), and here there was none. Indeed, the success of the surveillance technique that the officers employed was dependent on the fact that the GPS did not interfere in any way with the operation of the vehicle, for if any such interference had been detected, the device might have been discovered.

The Court does claim that the installation and use of the GPS constituted a search, but this conclusion is dependent on the questionable proposition that these two procedures cannot be separated for purposes of Fourth Amendment analysis. If these two procedures are analyzed separately, it is not at all clear from the Court's opinion why either should be regarded as a search. It is clear that the attachment of the GPS device was not itself a search; if the device had not functioned or if the officers had not used it, no information would have been obtained. And the Court does not contend that the use of the device constituted a search either. On the contrary, the Court accepts the holding in United States v. Knotts, 460 U.S. 276 (1983), that the use of a surreptitiously planted electronic device to monitor a vehicle's movements on public roads did not amount to a search.

The Court argues—and I agree—that "we must 'assur[e] preservation of that degree of privacy against government that existed when the Fourth Amendment was adopted.'" *Ante,* (quoting Kyllo v. United States, 533 U.S. 27, 34 (2001)). But it is almost impossible to think of late-18th-century situations that are analogous to what took place in this case. (Is it possible to imagine a case in which a constable secreted himself somewhere in a coach and remained there for a period of time in order to monitor the movements of the coach's owner?[3]) The Court's theory seems to be that the concept of a search, as originally understood, comprehended any technical trespass that led to the gathering of evidence, but we know that this is incorrect. At common law, any unauthorized intrusion on private property was actionable, *see* Prosser & Keeton 75, but a trespass on open fields, as opposed to the "curtilage" of a home, does not fall within the scope of the Fourth Amendment because private property outside the curtilage is not part of a "hous[e]" within the meaning of the Fourth Amendment. *See* Oliver v.

---

[3] The Court suggests that something like this might have occurred in 1791, but this would have required either a gigantic coach, a very tiny constable, or both—not to mention a constable with incredible fortitude and patience.

United States, 466 U.S. 170 (1984); Hester v. United States, 265 U.S. 57 (1924).

B

The Court's reasoning in this case is very similar to that in the Court's early decisions involving wiretapping and electronic eavesdropping, namely, that a technical trespass followed by the gathering of evidence constitutes a search. In the early electronic surveillance cases, the Court concluded that a Fourth Amendment search occurred when private conversations were monitored as a result of an "unauthorized physical penetration into the premises occupied" by the defendant. Silverman v. United States, 365 U.S. 505, 509 (1961). In *Silverman,* police officers listened to conversations in an attached home by inserting a "spike mike" through the wall that this house shared with the vacant house next door. *Id.,* at 506. This procedure was held to be a search because the mike made contact with a heating duct on the other side of the wall and thus "usurp[ed] . . . an integral part of the premises." *Id.,* at 511.

By contrast, in cases in which there was no trespass, it was held that there was no search. Thus, in Olmstead v. United States, 277 U.S. 438 (1928), the Court found that the Fourth Amendment did not apply because "[t]he taps from house lines were made in the streets near the houses." *Id.,* at 457. Similarly, the Court concluded that no search occurred in Goldman v. United States, 316 U.S. 129 (1942), where a "detectaphone" was placed on the outer wall of defendant's office for the purpose of overhearing conversations held within the room.

This trespass-based rule was repeatedly criticized. In *Olmstead,* Justice Brandeis wrote that it was "immaterial where the physical connection with the telephone wires was made." 277 U.S., at 479 (dissenting opinion). Although a private conversation transmitted by wire did not fall within the literal words of the Fourth Amendment, he argued, the Amendment should be understood as prohibiting "every unjustifiable intrusion by the government upon the privacy of the individual." *Id.,* at 478. *See also, e.g., Silverman, supra,* at 513 (Douglas, J., concurring) ("The concept of 'an unauthorized physical penetration into the premises,' on which the present decision rests seems to me beside the point. Was not the wrong . . . done when the intimacies of the home were tapped, recorded, or revealed? The depth of the penetration of the electronic device—even the degree of its remoteness from the inside of the house—is not the measure of the injury"); *Goldman, supra,* at 139 (Murphy, J., dissenting) ("[T]he search of one's home or office no longer requires physical entry, for science has brought forth far more effective devices for the invasion of a person's privacy than the direct and obvious methods of oppression which were detested by our forebears and which inspired the Fourth Amendment").

Katz v. United States, 389 U.S. 347 (1967), finally did away with the old approach, holding that a trespass was not required for a Fourth

Amendment violation. *Katz* involved the use of a listening device that was attached to the outside of a public telephone booth and that allowed police officers to eavesdrop on one end of the target's phone conversation. This procedure did not physically intrude on the area occupied by the target, but the *Katz* Court, "repudiate[ed]" the old doctrine, Rakas v. Illinois, 439 U.S. 128 (1978), and held that "[t]he fact that the electronic device employed . . . did not happen to penetrate the wall of the booth can have no constitutional significance," 389 U.S., at 353 ("[T]he reach of th[e] [Fourth] Amendment cannot turn upon the presence or absence of a physical intrusion into any given enclosure"); *see Rakas, supra,* at 143 (describing *Katz* as holding that the "capacity to claim the protection for the Fourth Amendment depends not upon a property right in the invaded place but upon whether the person who claims the protection of the Amendment has a legitimate expectation of privacy in the invaded place"); *Kyllo, supra,* at 32 ("We have since decoupled violation of a person's Fourth Amendment rights from trespassory violation of his property"). What mattered, the Court now held, was whether the conduct at issue "violated the privacy upon which [the defendant] justifiably relied while using the telephone booth." *Katz, supra,* at 353.

Under this approach, as the Court later put it when addressing the relevance of a technical trespass, "an actual trespass is neither necessary *nor sufficient* to establish a constitutional violation." United States v. Karo, 468 U.S. 705, 713 (1984) (emphasis added). *Ibid.* ("Compar[ing] Katz v. United States, 389 U.S. 347 (1967) (no trespass, but Fourth Amendment violation), with Oliver v. United States, 466 U.S. 170 (1984) (trespass, but no Fourth Amendment violation)"). In *Oliver*, the Court wrote:

> "The existence of a property right is but one element in determining whether expectations of privacy are legitimate. 'The premise that property interests control the right of the Government to search and seize has been discredited.' *Katz,* 389 U.S., at 353, (quoting Warden v. Hayden, 387 U.S. 294, 304 (1967); some internal quotation marks omitted)." 466 U.S., at 183.

II

The majority suggests that two post-*Katz* decisions—Soldal v. Cook County, 506 U.S. 56 (1992), and Alderman v. United States, 394 U.S. 165 (1969)—show that a technical trespass is sufficient to establish the existence of a search, but they provide little support.

In *Soldal,* the Court held that towing away a trailer home without the owner's consent constituted a seizure even if this did not invade the occupants' personal privacy. But in the present case, the Court does not find that there was a seizure, and it is clear that none occurred.

In *Alderman,* the Court held that the Fourth Amendment rights of homeowners were implicated by the use of a surreptitiously planted listening device to monitor third-party conversations that occurred within their home. *See* 394 U.S., at 176–180. *Alderman* is best understood to mean that the homeowners had a legitimate expectation of privacy in all conversations that took place under their roof. *See Rakas,* 439 U.S., at 144, n. 12 (citing *Alderman* for the proposition that "the Court has not altogether abandoned use of property concepts in determining the presence or absence of the privacy interests protected by that Amendment"); 439 U.S., at 153 (Powell, J., concurring) (citing *Alderman* for the proposition that "property rights reflect society's explicit recognition of a person's authority to act as he wishes in certain areas, and therefore should be considered in determining whether an individual's expectations of privacy are reasonable"); *Karo, supra,* at 732 (Stevens, J., concurring in part and dissenting in part) (citing *Alderman* in support of the proposition that "a homeowner has a reasonable expectation of privacy in the contents of his home, including items owned by others").

In sum, the majority is hard pressed to find support in post-*Katz* cases for its trespass-based theory.

III

Disharmony with a substantial body of existing case law is only one of the problems with the Court's approach in this case.

I will briefly note four others. First, the Court's reasoning largely disregards what is really important (the *use* of a GPS for the purpose of long-term tracking) and instead attaches great significance to something that most would view as relatively minor (attaching to the bottom of a car a small, light object that does not interfere in any way with the car's operation). Attaching such an object is generally regarded as so trivial that it does not provide a basis for recovery under modern tort law. *See* Prosser & Keeton § 14, at 87 (harmless or trivial contact with personal property not actionable); D. Dobbs, Law of Torts 124 (2000) (same). But under the Court's reasoning, this conduct may violate the Fourth Amendment. By contrast, if long-term monitoring can be accomplished without committing a technical trespass—suppose, for example, that the Federal Government required or persuaded auto manufacturers to include a GPS tracking device in every car—the Court's theory would provide no protection.

Second, the Court's approach leads to incongruous results. If the police attach a GPS device to a car and use the device to follow the car for even a brief time, under the Court's theory, the Fourth Amendment applies. But if the police follow the same car for a much longer period using unmarked cars and aerial assistance, this tracking is not subject to any Fourth Amendment constraints.

In the present case, the Fourth Amendment applies, the Court concludes, because the officers installed the GPS device after respondent's wife, to whom the car was registered, turned it over to respondent for his exclusive use. But if the GPS had been attached prior to that time, the Court's theory would lead to a different result. The Court proceeds on the assumption that respondent "had at least the property rights of a bailee," *ante,* at n. 2, but a bailee may sue for a trespass to chattel only if the injury occurs during the term of the bailment. *See* 8A Am.Jur.2d, Bailment § 166, pp. 685–686 (2009). So if the GPS device had been installed before respondent's wife gave him the keys, respondent would have no claim for trespass—and, presumably, no Fourth Amendment claim either.

Third, under the Court's theory, the coverage of the Fourth Amendment may vary from State to State. If the events at issue here had occurred in a community property State or a State that has adopted the Uniform Marital Property Act, respondent would likely be an owner of the vehicle, and it would not matter whether the GPS was installed before or after his wife turned over the keys. In non-community-property States, on the other hand, the registration of the vehicle in the name of respondent's wife would generally be regarded as presumptive evidence that she was the sole owner. *See* 60 C.J. S., Motor Vehicles § 231, pp. 398–399 (2002); 8 Am.Jur.2d, Automobiles § 1208, pp. 859–860 (2007).

Fourth, the Court's reliance on the law of trespass will present particularly vexing problems in cases involving surveillance that is carried out by making electronic, as opposed to physical, contact with the item to be tracked. For example, suppose that the officers in the present case had followed respondent by surreptitiously activating a stolen vehicle detection system that came with the car when it was purchased. Would the sending of a radio signal to activate this system constitute a trespass to chattels? Trespass to chattels has traditionally required a physical touching of the property. *See* Restatement (Second) of Torts § 217 and Comment *e* (1963 and 1964); Dobbs, *supra,* at 123. . . .

IV

A

The *Katz* expectation-of-privacy test avoids the problems and complications noted above, but it is not without its own difficulties. It involves a degree of circularity, *see Kyllo,* 533 U.S., at 34, and judges are apt to confuse their own expectations of privacy with those of the hypothetical reasonable person to which the *Katz* test looks. *See* Minnesota v. Carter, 525 U.S. 83, 97 (1998) (SCALIA, J., concurring). In addition, the *Katz* test rests on the assumption that this hypothetical reasonable person has a well-developed and stable set of privacy expectations. But technology can change those expectations. Dramatic technological change may lead to periods in which popular expectations are in flux and may ultimately produce significant changes in popular attitudes. New technology may provide increased convenience or security at the expense of privacy, and many people may find the tradeoff worthwhile. And even if the public does not welcome the diminution of privacy that new technology entails, they may eventually reconcile themselves to this development as inevitable.

On the other hand, concern about new intrusions on privacy may spur the enactment of legislation to protect against these intrusions. This is what ultimately happened with respect to wiretapping. After *Katz,* Congress did not leave it to the courts to develop a body of Fourth Amendment case law governing that complex subject. Instead, Congress promptly enacted a comprehensive statute, *see* 18 U.S.C. §§ 2510–2522 (2006 ed. and Supp. IV), and since that time, the regulation of wiretapping has been governed primarily by statute and not by case law.[7] In an ironic sense, although *Katz* overruled *Olmstead,* Chief Justice Taft's suggestion in the latter case that the regulation of wiretapping was a matter better left for Congress, *see* 277 U.S., at 465–466, has been borne out.

B

Recent years have seen the emergence of many new devices that permit the monitoring of a person's movements. In some locales, closed-circuit television video monitoring is becoming ubiquitous. On toll roads, automatic toll collection systems create a precise record of the movements of motorists who choose to make use of that convenience. Many motorists purchase cars that are equipped with devices that permit a central station to ascertain the car's location at any time so that roadside assistance may be provided if needed and the car may be found if it is stolen.

Perhaps most significant, cell phones and other wireless devices now permit wireless carriers to track and record the location of users—and as of June 2011, it has been reported, there were more than 322 million wireless devices in use in the United States. For older phones, the accuracy of the location information depends on the density of the tower network, but new "smart phones," which are equipped with a GPS device, permit more precise tracking. For example, when a user activates the GPS on such a phone, a provider is able to monitor the phone's location and speed of movement and can then report back real-time traffic conditions after combining ("crowdsourcing") the speed of all such phones on any particular road. Similarly, phone-location-tracking services are offered as "social" tools, allowing consumers to find (or to avoid) others who enroll in these services. The availability and use of these and other new devices will continue to shape the average person's expectations about the privacy of his or her daily movements.

V

In the pre-computer age, the greatest protections of privacy were neither constitutional nor statutory, but practical. Traditional surveillance for any extended period of time was difficult and costly and

---

[7] *See* Kerr, The *Fourth Amendment and New Technologies: Constitutional Myths and the Case for Caution,* 102 Mich. L.Rev. 801, 850–851 (2004) (hereinafter Kerr).

therefore rarely undertaken. The surveillance at issue in this case—
constant monitoring of the location of a vehicle for four weeks—would
have required a large team of agents, multiple vehicles, and perhaps
aerial assistance. Only an investigation of unusual importance could
have justified such an expenditure of law enforcement resources. Devices
like the one used in the present case, however, make long-term
monitoring relatively easy and cheap. In circumstances involving
dramatic technological change, the best solution to privacy concerns may
be legislative. *See, e.g.,* Kerr, 102 Mich. L.Rev., at 805–806. A legislative
body is well situated to gauge changing public attitudes, to draw detailed
lines, and to balance privacy and public safety in a comprehensive way.

To date, however, Congress and most States have not enacted
statutes regulating the use of GPS tracking technology for law
enforcement purposes. The best that we can do in this case is to apply
existing Fourth Amendment doctrine and to ask whether the use of GPS
tracking in a particular case involved a degree of intrusion that a
reasonable person would not have anticipated.

Under this approach, relatively short-term monitoring of a person's
movements on public streets accords with expectations of privacy that
our society has recognized as reasonable. *See Knotts,* 460 U.S., at 281–
282. But the use of longer term GPS monitoring in investigations of most
offenses impinges on expectations of privacy. For such offenses, society's
expectation has been that law enforcement agents and others would
not—and indeed, in the main, simply could not—secretly monitor and
catalogue every single movement of an individual's car for a very long
period. In this case, for four weeks, law enforcement agents tracked every
movement that respondent made in the vehicle he was driving. We need
not identify with precision the point at which the tracking of this vehicle
became a search, for the line was surely crossed before the 4-week mark.
Other cases may present more difficult questions. But where uncertainty
exists with respect to whether a certain period of GPS surveil lance is
long enough to constitute a Fourth Amendment search, the police may
always seek a warrant. We also need not consider whether prolonged
GPS monitoring in the context of investigations involving extraordinary
offenses would similarly intrude on a constitutionally protected sphere of
privacy. In such cases, long-term tracking might have been mounted
using previously available techniques.

For these reasons, I conclude that the lengthy monitoring that
occurred in this case constituted a search under the Fourth Amendment.
I therefore agree with the majority that the decision of the Court of
Appeals must be affirmed.

a. "OPEN FIELDS"

United States v. Vankesteren

553 F.3d 286 (4th Cir. 2009)

■ GREGORY, CIRCUIT JUDGE:

The appellant in this case, Steve Vankesteren, invites us to consider the application of the Fourth Amendment to a product of modern surveillance technology: namely, a hidden, fixed-range, motion-activated video camera placed in the appellant's open fields. We find that the protective wall of the Fourth Amendment does not shield the appellant from the Commonwealth's use of such a camera, and we therefore affirm the decision of the district court.

I.

Appellant Vankesteren is a farmer on the Eastern Shore of Virginia. In December 2006, the Virginia Department of Game and Inland Fisheries ("VDGIF") received a telephone call alerting them that a protected bird was trapped in a cage in Vankesteren's fields near a public road. Steve Garvis, an agent with VDGIF, responded to the call and observed a trap that was one-to-two feet high and contained five leghold traps-one on top of the cage and four surrounding it. The trap was uncovered and set, and it contained one live and one dead pigeon inside. Garvis had allegedly seen a similar trap on Appellant's property in 2003 and on the internet being advertised for the purpose of hawk trapping. In January 2007, Garvis contacted the VDGIF's Special Operations Division in order to obtain video surveillance of the trap. Such cameras were used because there were only five VDGIF special agents in the Commonwealth. The camera had a viewing area of twelve-by-twelve feet, ran only during daylight hours, and was motion activated. On January 11, 2007, Garvis and the special operations agents installed the camera without a warrant.

On January 24, 2007, Special Operations Agent Gene Agnese notified Garvis that he had obtained surveillance footage of two birds being trapped and killed at the site of the camera. Vankesteren killed the first bird on January 17. Garvis could not identify the bird in the footage with certainty, but he narrowed the possibilities to a red-tailed hawk, broad-wing hawk, or red-shouldered hawk. Vankesteren killed the second bird with an ax on January 20, and Garvis identified the bird in that footage as a red-tailed hawk. Agnese advised Garvis that their carcasses were likely along the hedgerow by the trap, just outside the camera's viewing area. On January 25, 2007, Garvis went to the area and located the carcasses. He identified both of the birds by their markings as red-tailed hawks. One of the hawks had sustained severe head damage, consistent with the video footage, and the other carcass was of an immature red-tailed hawk. The birds had not been eaten and had not begun decomposing.

On January 30, 2007, Garvis and Agent Dan Rolince of the U.S. Fish and Wildlife Service met with Vankesteren at his residence. He admitted to catching some hawks by accident and placing their carcasses by the hedgerow. Vankesteren was charged in the U.S. District Court for the Eastern District of Virginia with two counts of taking or possessing a migratory bird without a permit, in violation of 16 U.S.C. § 703 (2006) and 50 C.F.R. § 21.11 (2008). Vankesteren appeared pro se before a magistrate judge on August 7, 2007. The judge refused to suppress the video surveillance footage and found the appellant guilty on both counts, imposing a $500 fine for each count, along with a $10 special assessment and $25 processing fee. Vankesteren appealed the magistrate judge's ruling, but the district court found no error and entered a final judgment against him on December 21, 2007. Vankesteren subsequently appealed to this Court.

II.

This Court has jurisdiction pursuant to 28 U.S.C. § 1291 (2000). "In reviewing a denial of a suppression motion, the court reviews the district court's factual findings for clear error and the district court's legal conclusions de novo." United States v. Johnson, 114 F.3d 435, 439 (4th Cir.1997). We review the sufficiency of evidence on appeal by viewing it and all inferences "in the light most favorable to the Government." United States v. Bursey, 416 F.3d 301, 306 (4th Cir.2005). Findings of law are reviewed de novo, and findings of fact are reviewed for clear error. *Id.*

A.

Vankesteren largely conceded in oral argument that the VDGIF placed its camera in a constitutionally unprotected open field, but a review of the Supreme Court's open-fields doctrine is nonetheless essential to our consideration of this case. In Hester v. United States, 265 U.S. 57, 59 (1924), the Supreme Court first held that the protection of the Fourth Amendment did not extend to open fields. In that case, revenue officers went to Hester's house and observed an illegal moonshine transaction from fifty to one-hundred yards away on Hester's land. *Id.* at 58. The Court found no Fourth Amendment violation. *Id.* at 59.

The open-fields doctrine was clarified in Oliver v. United States, 466 U.S. 170 (1984). There, the Supreme Court considered two cases in which marijuana was being grown in wooded areas on the defendants' properties. In one instance, the police walked around a locked gate with a "No Trespassing" sign, passed a barn and parked camper, and continued after someone shouted at them to leave. A mile from the defendant's house, they found the marijuana field. *Id.* at 173. In the other case, police followed a path between the defendant's residence and the neighboring house into the woods until they saw two marijuana patches surrounded by chicken wire. Upholding both searches, the Court held that "an individual may not legitimately demand privacy for activities conducted out of doors in fields, except in the area immediately surrounding the home [the curtilage]." *Id.* at 178. The Court further noted, "An open field need be neither 'open' nor a 'field' as those terms are used in common speech. For example . . . a thickly wooded area nonetheless may be an open field as that term is used in construing the Fourth Amendment." *Id.* at 180 n. 11.

In United States v. Dunn, 480 U.S. 294 (1987), the Supreme Court considered a case that involved property that was approximately fifty yards from the main residence and on which officers took the following actions:

> [They] crossed over the perimeter fence and one interior fence. Standing approximately midway between the residence and the barns, the DEA agent smelled what he believed to be phenylacetic acid, the odor coming from the direction of the barns. The officers approached the smaller of the barns— crossing over a barbed wire fence—and, looking into the barn, observed only empty boxes. The officers then proceeded to the larger barn, crossing another barbed wire fence as well as a wooden fence that enclosed the front portion of the barn. The officers walked under the barn's overhang to the locked wooden gates and, shining a flashlight through the netting on top of the gates, peered into the barn.

Id. at 297–98. Once more, the Court found that there was no Fourth Amendment violation. *Id.* at 301.

The *Dunn* Court established four factors to consider when resolving questions about the boundaries of curtilage: "the proximity of the area claimed to be curtilage to the home, whether the area is included within an enclosure surrounding the home, the nature of the uses to which the area is put, and the steps taken by the resident to protect the area from observation by people passing by." *Id.* at 301; *accord* United States v. Breza, 308 F.3d 430, 435 (4th Cir.2002). Applying the factors, the Court found that the barn was sixty yards from the house, it was outside the fence surrounding the house, police had objective data—aerial photographs—that showed the barn was not being used for intimate activities, and there was no indication that the interior fences were designed to keep people out. *Dunn*, 480 U.S. at 302–03.

Given the facts of these Supreme Court decisions, Vankesteren has little on which to base his case. Vankesteren's fields were located a mile or more from his home, the land was being used for farming and not intimate activities, VDGIF had received a report of a trapped protected bird, and there is no indication in the record that Vankesteren had taken any steps to protect his field from observation. Therefore, under the Supreme Court's jurisprudence, the subject land must be classified as open fields and not curtilage, and Vankesteren has no reasonable expectation of privacy in those open fields.

As noted previously, Vankesteren has essentially conceded this point. Vankesteren instead stakes his case on the argument that hidden surveillance cameras are subject to a higher degree of Fourth Amendment scrutiny. He cites cases in support of that proposition; yet, none of these cases involve open fields where the defendant presumably has no reasonable expectation of privacy.

In United States v. Taketa, 923 F.2d 665 (9th Cir.1991), the Ninth Circuit found that a DEA agent had a reasonable expectation of privacy in his office, and that expectation was violated through the use of hidden video surveillance. In so finding, however, the court noted, "Video surveillance does not in itself violate a reasonable expectation of privacy. Videotaping of suspects in public places, such as banks, does not violate the fourth amendment; the police may record what they normally may view with the naked eye." *Id.* at 677. In United States v. Nerber, 222 F.3d 597 (9th Cir.2000), the Ninth Circuit suppressed hidden video surveillance, but did so because it found that drug dealers had a legitimate expectation of privacy in their hotel room after police informants left.

The Fifth Circuit considered a closer case in United States v. Cuevas-Sanchez, 821 F.2d 248 (5th Cir.1987). There, the police placed a camera on top of a power pole overlooking the defendant's ten-foot-high fence surrounding his back yard. The court found that the defendant had a reasonable expectation of privacy that would have been violated because the fence surrounded his curtilage. However, because the police properly obtained a court order for the surveillance, the court affirmed his conviction. *Id.* at 251–52. This case also does not help Vankesteren because VDGIF's camera was not placed within or even near the curtilage of his home.

Vankesteren then attempts to distinguish his case from United States v. McIver, 186 F.3d 1119 (9th Cir.1999), the most directly relevant case on this issue. In that case, law enforcement agents placed unmanned, motion-activated surveillance cameras onto land in a national forest in order to monitor a patch of marijuana plants. The agents used the footage from the cameras in order to identify and track down the defendants in the case. The court held that the placement of the cameras on public land, open to all, did not violate the defendants' Fourth Amendment rights. *Id.* at 1125–26.

While McIver involved public land and this case involves private land, the effect is still the same: just as one would not have a reasonable expectation of privacy in a national forest, the foregoing cases demonstrate that Vankesteren had no reasonable expectation of privacy in the open fields where he killed the hawks. Those fields were located a mile or more from his home, near a public road, and as evidenced by the phone call reporting the trap, the land was accessible to other members of the public. Vankesteren notes that he felt comfortable enough to relieve himself there, but that is of no consequence under our jurisprudence.[1]

The idea of a video camera constantly recording activities on one's property is undoubtedly unsettling to some. Individuals might engage in any number of intimate activities on their wooded property or open field—from romantic trysts under a moonlit sky to relieving oneself, as in Mr. Vankesteren's case—and do so under the belief that they are not being observed. But the protection of the Fourth Amendment is not predicated upon these subjective beliefs. "[O]pen fields do not provide the setting for those intimate activities that the Amendment is intended to shelter from government interference or surveillance." *Oliver*, 466 U.S. at 179. Anyone could have walked onto Vankesteren's property, including a VDGIF agent, and observed his traps. Under our jurisprudence, VDGIF could have stationed agents to surveil Vankesteren's property twenty-four hours a day. *See id.* at 178–81; *McIver*, 186 F.3d at 1125. That the agents chose to use a more resource-efficient surveillance method does not change our Fourth Amendment analysis.

Since Vankesteren had no legitimate expectation of privacy, the agents were free, as on public land, to use video surveillance to capture what any passerby would have been able to observe. As the Supreme Court noted in Dow Chemical Co. v. United States, 476 U.S. 227, 238 (1986), when it was assessing the constitutionality of aerial surveillance by the EPA:

> It may well be, as the Government concedes, that surveillance of private property by using highly sophisticated surveillance equipment not generally available to the public, such as satellite technology, might be constitutionally proscribed absent a warrant. . . . [But t]he mere fact that human vision is enhanced somewhat, at least to the degree here, does not give rise to constitutional problems.

(internal footnote omitted). Likewise, the placement of a video camera in an open field does not portend the arrival of the Orwellian state that the appellant would have us fear. We are not dealing in this case with a camera that took, for instance, thermal images of Vankesteren's home[2] or that was equipped with an automatic guidance system that allowed it to roam about Vankesteren's property, possibly into protected Fourth Amendment areas. Instead, this camera was in a fixed location, was focused on a limited area of Vankesteren's fields, was activated only by motion, and recorded only during the daylight hours. Essentially, the camera did little more than the agents themselves could have physically done, and its use was therefore not unconstitutional. . . .

---

[1] Indeed, if Fourth Amendment protection were to be predicated upon where one felt comfortable enough to eliminate, our search and seizure jurisprudence would be turned on its head.

[2] *See* Kyllo v. United States, 533 U.S. 27 (2001).

AFFIRMED

b. MAGIC BULLETS

Florida v. Jardines
569 U.S. 1 (2013)

■ JUSTICE SCALIA delivered the opinion of the Court.

We consider whether using a drug-sniffing dog on a homeowner's porch to investigate the contents of the home is a "search" within the meaning of the Fourth Amendment.

I

In 2006, Detective William Pedraja of the Miami-Dade Police Department received an unverified tip that marijuana was being grown in the home of respondent Joelis Jardines. One month later, the Department and the Drug Enforcement Administration sent a joint surveillance team to Jardines' home. Detective Pedraja was part of that team. He watched the home for fifteen minutes and saw no vehicles in the driveway or activity around the home, and could not see inside because the blinds were drawn. Detective Pedraja then approached Jardines' home accompanied by Detective Douglas Bartelt, a trained canine handler who had just arrived at the scene with his drug-sniffing dog. The dog was trained to detect the scent of marijuana, cocaine, heroin, and several other drugs, indicating the presence of any of these substances through particular behavioral changes recognizable by his handler.

Detective Bartelt had the dog on a six-foot leash, owing in part to the dog's "wild" nature, App. to Pet. for Cert. A–35, and tendency to dart around erratically while searching. As the dog approached Jardines' front porch, he apparently sensed one of the odors he had been trained to detect, and began energetically exploring the area for the strongest point source of that odor. As Detective Bartelt explained, the dog "began tracking that airborne odor by . . . tracking back and forth," engaging in what is called "bracketing," "back and forth, back and forth." Id., at A–33 to A–34. Detective Bartelt gave the dog "the full six feet of the leash plus whatever safe distance [he could] give him" to do this—he testified that he needed to give the dog "as much distance as I can." Id., at A–35. And Detective Pedraja stood back while this was occurring, so that he would not "get knocked over" when the dog was "spinning around trying to find" the source. Id., at A–38.

After sniffing the base of the front door, the dog sat, which is the trained behavior upon discovering the odor's strongest point. Detective Bartelt then pulled the dog away from the door and returned to his vehicle. He left the scene after informing Detective Pedraja that there had been a positive alert for narcotics.

On the basis of what he had learned at the home, Detective Pedraja applied for and received a warrant to search the residence. When the warrant was executed later that day, Jardines attempted to flee and was arrested; the search revealed marijuana plants, and he was charged with trafficking in cannabis.

At trial, Jardines moved to suppress the marijuana plants on the ground that the canine investigation was an unreasonable search. The trial court granted the motion, and the Florida Third District Court of Appeal reversed. On a petition for discretionary review, the Florida Supreme Court quashed the decision of the Third District Court of Appeal and approved the trial court's decision to suppress, holding (as relevant here) that the use of the trained narcotics dog to investigate Jardines' home was a Fourth Amendment search unsupported by probable cause, rendering invalid the warrant based upon information gathered in that search. 73 So.3d 34 (2011).

We granted certiorari, limited to the question of whether the officers' behavior was a search within the meaning of the Fourth Amendment.

II

The Fourth Amendment provides in relevant part that the "right of the people to be secure in their persons, houses, papers, and effects, against unreasonable searches and seizures, shall not be violated." The Amendment establishes a simple baseline, one that for much of our history formed the exclusive basis for its protections: When "the Government obtains information by physically intruding" on persons, houses, papers, or effects, "a 'search' within the original meaning of the Fourth Amendment" has "undoubtedly occurred." United States v. Jones, 565 U.S. ___, ___, n. 3 (2012). By reason of our decision in Katz v. United States, 389 U.S. 347 (1967), property rights "are not the sole measure of Fourth Amendment violations," Soldal v. Cook County, 506 U.S. 56, 64 (1992)—but though *Katz* may add to the baseline, it does not subtract anything from the Amendment's protections "when the Government does engage in [a] physical intrusion of a constitutionally protected area," United States v. Knotts, 460 U.S. 276, 286 (1983) (Brennan, J., concurring in the judgment).

That principle renders this case a straightforward one. The officers were gathering information in an area belonging to Jardines and immediately surrounding his house—in the curtilage of the house, which we have held enjoys protection as part of the home itself. And they gathered that information by physically entering and occupying the area to engage in conduct not explicitly or implicitly permitted by the homeowner.

A

The Fourth Amendment "indicates with some precision the places and things encompassed by its protections": persons, houses, papers, and effects. Oliver v. United States, 466 U.S. 170, 176 (1984). The Fourth

Amendment does not, therefore, prevent all investigations conducted on private property; for example, an officer may (subject to *Katz*) gather information in what we have called "open fields"—even if those fields are privately owned—because such fields are not enumerated in the Amendment's text. Hester v. United States, 265 U.S. 57 (1924).

But when it comes to the Fourth Amendment, the home is first among equals. At the Amendment's "very core" stands "the right of a man to retreat into his own home and there be free from unreasonable governmental intrusion." Silverman v. United States, 365 U.S. 505, 511 (1961). This right would be of little practical value if the State's agents could stand in a home's porch or side garden and trawl for evidence with impunity; the right to retreat would be significantly diminished if the police could enter a man's property to observe his repose from just outside the front window.

We therefore regard the area "immediately surrounding and associated with the home"—what our cases call the curtilage—as "part of the home itself for Fourth Amendment purposes." *Oliver, supra,* at 180. That principle has ancient and durable roots. Just as the distinction between the home and the open fields is "as old as the common law," *Hester, supra,* at 59, so too is the identity of home and what Blackstone called the "curtilage or homestall," for the "house protects and privileges all its branches and appurtenants." 4 W. Blackstone, Commentaries on the Laws of England 223, 225 (1769). This area around the home is "intimately linked to the home, both physically and psychologically," and is where "privacy expectations are most heightened." California v. Ciraolo, 476 U.S. 207, 213 (1986).

While the boundaries of the curtilage are generally "clearly marked," the "conception defining the curtilage" is at any rate familiar enough that it is "easily understood from our daily experience." *Oliver,* 466 U.S., at 182, n. 12. Here there is no doubt that the officers entered it: The front porch is the classic exemplar of an area adjacent to the home and "to which the activity of home life extends." *Ibid.*

B

Since the officers' investigation took place in a constitutionally protected area, we turn to the question of whether it was accomplished through an unlicensed physical intrusion.[1] While law enforcement officers need not "shield their eyes" when passing by the home "on public thoroughfares," *Ciraolo,* 476 U.S., at 213, an officer's leave to gather information is sharply circumscribed when he steps off those thoroughfares and enters the Fourth Amendment's protected areas. In permitting, for example, visual observation of the home from "public

---

[1] At oral argument, the State and its amicus the Solicitor General argued that Jardines conceded in the lower courts that the officers had a right to be where they were. This misstates the record. Jardines conceded nothing more than the unsurprising proposition that the officers could have lawfully approached his home to knock on the front door in hopes of speaking with him. Of course, that is not what they did.

navigable airspace," we were careful to note that it was done "in a physically nonintrusive manner." *Ibid.* Entick v. Carrington, 2 Wils. K.B. 275, 95 Eng. Rep. 807 (K.B. 1765), a case "undoubtedly familiar" to "every American statesman" at the time of the Founding, Boyd v. United States, 116 U.S. 616, 626 (1886), states the general rule clearly: "[O]ur law holds the property of every man so sacred, that no man can set his foot upon his neighbour's close without his leave." 2 Wils. K.B., at 291, 95 Eng. Rep., at 817. As it is undisputed that the detectives had all four of their feet and all four of their companion's firmly planted on the constitutionally protected extension of Jardines' home, the only question is whether he had given his leave (even implicitly) for them to do so. He had not.

"A license may be implied from the habits of the country," notwithstanding the "strict rule of the English common law as to entry upon a close." McKee v. Gratz, 260 U.S. 127, 136 (1922) (Holmes, J.). We have accordingly recognized that "the knocker on the front door is treated as an invitation or license to attempt an entry, justifying ingress to the home by solicitors, hawkers and peddlers of all kinds." Breard v. Alexandria, 341 U.S. 622, 626 (1951). This implicit license typically permits the visitor to approach the home by the front path, knock promptly, wait briefly to be received, and then (absent invitation to linger longer) leave. Complying with the terms of that traditional invitation does not require fine-grained legal knowledge; it is generally managed without incident by the Nation's Girl Scouts and trick-or-treaters.[2] Thus, a police officer not armed with a warrant may approach a home and knock, precisely because that is "no more than any private citizen might do." Kentucky v. King, 563 U.S. ___ (2011).

But introducing a trained police dog to explore the area around the home in hopes of discovering incriminating evidence is something else. There is no customary invitation to do that. An invitation to engage in canine forensic investigation assuredly does not inhere in the very act of hanging a knocker.[3] To find a visitor knocking on the door is routine (even

---

[2]   With this much, the dissent seems to agree—it would inquire into " 'the appearance of things,' " *post*, at 1422 (opinion of ALITO, J.), what is "typica[l]" for a visitor, *ibid.*, what might cause "alarm" to a "resident of the premises," *ibid.*, what is "expected" of "ordinary visitors," *ibid.*, and what would be expected from a " 'reasonably respectful citizen,' " *post*, at 1423. These are good questions. But their answers are incompatible with the dissent's outcome, which is presumably why the dissent does not even try to argue that it would be customary, usual, reasonable, respectful, ordinary, typical, nonalarming, etc., for a stranger to explore the curtilage of the home with trained drug dogs.

[3]   The dissent insists that our argument must rest upon "the particular instrument that Detective Bartelt used to detect the odor of marijuana"—the dog. *post*, at 1424. It is not the dog that is the problem, but the behavior that here involved use of the dog. We think a typical person would find it " 'a cause for great alarm' " (the kind of reaction the dissent quite rightly relies upon to justify its no-night-visits rule, *post*, at 1422) to find a stranger snooping about his front porch with or without a dog. The dissent would let the police do whatever they want by way of gathering evidence so long as they stay on the base-path, to use a baseball analogy—so long as they "stick to the path that is typically used to approach a front door, such as a paved walkway." *Ibid.* From that vantage point they can presumably peer into the house through binoculars with impunity. That is not the law, as even the State concedes. *See* Tr. of Oral Arg. 6.

if sometimes unwelcome); to spot that same visitor exploring the front path with a metal detector, or marching his bloodhound into the garden before saying hello and asking permission, would inspire most of us to—well, call the police. The scope of a license—express or implied—is limited not only to a particular area but also to a specific purpose. Consent at a traffic stop to an officer's checking out an anonymous tip that there is a body in the trunk does not permit the officer to rummage through the trunk for narcotics. Here, the background social norms that invite a visitor to the front door do not invite him there to conduct a search.[4]

The State points to our decisions holding that the subjective intent of the officer is irrelevant. *See* Ashcroft v. al-Kidd, 563 U.S. ___ (2011); Whren v. United States, 517 U.S. 806 (1996). But those cases merely hold that a stop or search that is objectively reasonable is not vitiated by the fact that the officer's real reason for making the stop or search has nothing to do with the validating reason. Thus, the defendant will not be heard to complain that although he was speeding the officer's real reason for the stop was racial harassment. *See id.*, at 810, 813. Here, however, the question before the court is precisely whether the officer's conduct was an objectively reasonable search. As we have described, that depends upon whether the officers had an implied license to enter the porch, which in turn depends upon the purpose for which they entered. Here, their behavior objectively reveals a purpose to conduct a search, which is not what anyone would think [they] had license to do.

III

The State argues that investigation by a forensic narcotics dog by definition cannot implicate any legitimate privacy interest. The State cites for authority our decisions in United States v. Place, 462 U.S. 696 (1983), United States v. Jacobsen, 466 U.S. 109 (1984), and Illinois v. Caballes, 543 U.S. 405 (2005), which held, respectively, that canine inspection of luggage in an airport, chemical testing of a substance that had fallen from a parcel in transit, and canine inspection of an automobile during a lawful traffic stop, do not violate the "reasonable expectation of privacy" described in *Katz*.

Just last Term, we considered an argument much like this. Jones held that tracking an automobile's whereabouts using a physically-mounted GPS receiver is a Fourth Amendment search. The Government argued that the *Katz* standard "show[ed] that no search occurred," as the defendant had "no 'reasonable expectation of privacy'" in his whereabouts on the public roads, *Jones,* 565 U.S., at—a proposition with at least as much support in our case law as the one the State marshals

---

[4] The dissent argues, citing *King,* that "gathering evidence—even damning evidence—is a lawful activity that falls within the scope of the license to approach." *Post,* at 1423. That is a false generalization. What *King* establishes is that it is not a Fourth Amendment search to approach the home in order to speak with the occupant, because all are invited to do that. The mere "purpose of discovering information," *post,* at 1424, in the course of engaging in that permitted conduct does not cause it to violate the Fourth Amendment. But no one is impliedly invited to enter the protected premises of the home in order to do nothing but conduct a search.

here. *See, e.g.,* United States v. Knotts, 460 U.S. 276, 278 (1983). But because the GPS receiver had been physically mounted on the defendant's automobile (thus intruding on his "effects"), we held that tracking the vehicle's movements was a search: a person's "Fourth Amendment rights do not rise or fall with the Katz formulation." *Jones, supra,* at ___. The Katz reasonable-expectations test "has been added to, not substituted for," the traditional property-based understanding of the Fourth Amendment, and so is unnecessary to consider when the government gains evidence by physically intruding on constitutionally protected areas. *Jones, supra,* at ___.

Thus, we need not decide whether the officers' investigation of Jardines' home violated his expectation of privacy under *Katz*. One virtue of the Fourth Amendment's property-rights baseline is that it keeps easy cases easy. That the officers learned what they learned only by physically intruding on Jardines' property to gather evidence is enough to establish that a search occurred.

For a related reason we find irrelevant the State's argument (echoed by the dissent) that forensic dogs have been commonly used by police for centuries. This argument is apparently directed to our holding in Kyllo v. United States, 533 U.S. 27 (2001), that surveillance of the home is a search where "the Government uses a device that is not in general public use" to "explore details of the home that would previously have been unknowable without physical intrusion." *Id.*, at 40 (emphasis added). But the implication of that statement (inclusio unius est exclusio alterius) is that when the government uses a physical intrusion to explore details of the home (including its curtilage), the antiquity of the tools that they bring along is irrelevant.

* * *

The government's use of trained police dogs to investigate the home and its immediate surroundings is a "search" within the meaning of the Fourth Amendment. The judgment of the Supreme Court of Florida is therefore affirmed.

It is so ordered.

■ JUSTICE KAGAN, with whom JUSTICE GINSBURG and JUSTICE SOTOMAYOR join, concurring.

For me, a simple analogy clinches this case—and does so on privacy as well as property grounds. A stranger comes to the front door of your home carrying super-high-powered binoculars. *See ante,* at 1416, n. 3. He doesn't knock or say hello. Instead, he stands on the porch and uses the binoculars to peer through your windows, into your home's furthest corners. It doesn't take long (the binoculars are really very fine): In just a couple of minutes, his uncommon behavior allows him to learn details of your life you disclose to no one. Has your "visitor" trespassed on your property, exceeding the license you have granted to members of the public to, say, drop off the mail or distribute campaign flyers? Yes, he has. And has he also invaded your "reasonable expectation of privacy," by nosing into intimacies you sensibly thought protected from disclosure? Katz v. United States, 389 U.S. 347, 360 (1967) (Harlan, J., concurring). Yes, of course, he has done that too.

That case is this case in every way that matters. Here, police officers came to Joelis Jardines' door with a super-sensitive instrument, which they deployed to detect things inside that they could not perceive unassisted. The equipment they used was animal, not mineral. But contra the dissent, *see post,* at 1420 (opinion of ALITO, J.) (noting the ubiquity of dogs in American households), that is of no significance in determining whether a search occurred. Detective Bartelt's dog was not your neighbor's pet, come to your porch on a leisurely stroll. As this Court discussed earlier this Term, drug-detection dogs are highly trained tools of law enforcement, geared to respond in distinctive ways to specific scents so as to convey clear and reliable information to their human partners. *See* Florida v. Harris, 568 U.S. ___ (2013). They are to the poodle down the street as high-powered binoculars are to a piece of plain glass. Like the binoculars, a drug-detection dog is a specialized device for discovering objects not in plain view (or plain smell). And as in the hypothetical above, that device was aimed here at a home—the most private and inviolate (or so we expect) of all the places and things the Fourth Amendment protects. Was this activity a trespass? Yes, as the Court holds today. Was it also an invasion of privacy? Yes, that as well.

The Court today treats this case under a property rubric; I write separately to note that I could just as happily have decided it by looking to Jardines' privacy interests. A decision along those lines would have looked . . . well, much like this one. It would have talked about " 'the right of a man to retreat into his own home and there be free from unreasonable governmental intrusion.' " *Ante,* at 1414 (quoting Silverman v. United States, 365 U.S. 505, 511 (1961)). It would have insisted on maintaining the "practical value" of that right by preventing police officers from standing in an adjacent space and "trawl[ing] for evidence with impunity." *Ante*, at 1414. It would have explained that " 'privacy expectations are most heightened' " in the home and the surrounding area. *Ante,* at 1414–1415 (quoting California v. Ciraolo, 476 U.S. 207, 213 (1986)). And it would have determined that police officers invade those shared expectations when they use trained canine assistants to reveal within the confines of a home what they could not otherwise have found there. *See ante,* at 1415–1416, and nn. 2–3.

It is not surprising that in a case involving a search of a home, property concepts and privacy concepts should so align. The law of property "naturally enough influence[s]" our "shared social expectations" of what places should be free from governmental incursions. Georgia v. Randolph, 547 U.S. 103, 111 (2006); *See* Rakas v. Illinois, 439 U.S. 128, 143, n. 12 (1978). And so the sentiment "my home is my own," while originating in property law, now also denotes a common understanding—

extending even beyond that law's formal protections—about an especially private sphere. Jardines' home was his property; it was also his most intimate and familiar space. The analysis proceeding from each of those facts, as today's decision reveals, runs mostly along the same path.

I can think of only one divergence: If we had decided this case on privacy grounds, we would have realized that Kyllo v. United States, 533 U.S. 27 (2001), already resolved it.[1] The *Kyllo* Court held that police officers conducted a search when they used a thermal-imaging device to detect heat emanating from a private home, even though they committed no trespass. Highlighting our intention to draw both a "firm" and a "bright" line at "the entrance to the house," *id.*, at 40, we announced the following rule:

> "Where, as here, the Government uses a device that is not in general public use, to explore details of the home that would previously have been unknowable without physical intrusion, the surveillance is a 'search' and is presumptively unreasonable without a warrant." *Ibid.*

That "firm" and "bright" rule governs this case: The police officers here conducted a search because they used a "device . . . not in general public use" (a trained drug-detection dog) to "explore details of the home" (the presence of certain substances) that they would not otherwise have discovered without entering the premises.

And again, the dissent's argument that the device is just a dog cannot change the equation. As *Kyllo* made clear, the "sense-enhancing" tool at issue may be "crude" or "sophisticated," may be old or new (drug-detection dogs actually go back not "12,000 years" or "centuries," *post*, at 1420, 1424, 1428, but only a few decades), may be either smaller or bigger than a breadbox; still, "at least where (as here)" the device is not "in general public use," training it on a home violates our "minimal expectation of privacy"—an expectation "that exists, and that is acknowledged to be reasonable." 533 U.S., at 34, 36. That does not mean the device is off-limits, as the dissent implies, *see post*, at 1425–1426; it just means police officers cannot use it to examine a home without a warrant or exigent circumstance. *See* Brigham City v. Stuart, 547 U.S. 398, 403–404 (2006) (describing exigencies allowing the warrantless search of a home).

The dissent's other principal reason for concluding that no violation of privacy occurred in this case—that police officers themselves might detect an aroma wafting from a house—works no better. If officers can smell drugs coming from a house, they can use that information; a human

---

[1]   The dissent claims, alternatively, that Illinois v. Caballes, 543 U.S. 405, 409–410 (2005), controls this case (or nearly does). *See post,* at 1424, 1425. But *Caballes* concerned a drug-detection dog's sniff of an automobile during a traffic stop. *See also* Florida v. Harris, 568 U.S. ___ (2013). And we have held, over and over again, that people's expectations of privacy are much lower in their cars than in their homes. *See, e.g.,* Arizona v. Gant, 556 U.S. 332, 345 (2009); Wyoming v. Houghton, 526 U.S. 295, 303 (1999); New York v. Class, 475 U.S. 106, 115 (1986); Cardwell v. Lewis, 417 U.S. 583, 590–591 (1974) (plurality opinion).

sniff is not a search, we can all agree. But it does not follow that a person loses his expectation of privacy in the many scents within his home that (his own nose capably tells him) are not usually detectible by humans standing outside. And indeed, *Kyllo* already decided as much. In response to an identical argument from the dissent in that case, *see* 533 U.S., at 43 (Stevens, J., dissenting) (noting that humans can sometimes detect "heat emanating from a building"), the *Kyllo* Court stated: "The dissent's comparison of the thermal imaging to various circumstances in which outside observers might be able to perceive, without technology, the heat of the home . . . is quite irrelevant. The fact that equivalent information could sometimes be obtained by other means does not make lawful the use of means that violate the Fourth Amendment. . . . In any event, [at the time in question,] no outside observer could have discerned the relative heat of Kyllo's home without thermal imaging." *Id.*, at 35, n. 2.

With these further thoughts, suggesting that a focus on Jardines' privacy interests would make an "easy cas[e] easy" twice over, I join the Court's opinion in full.

■ JUSTICE ALITO, with whom THE CHIEF JUSTICE, JUSTICE KENNEDY, and JUSTICE BREYER join, dissenting.

The Court's decision in this important Fourth Amendment case is based on a putative rule of trespass law that is nowhere to be found in the annals of Anglo-American jurisprudence.

The law of trespass generally gives members of the public a license to use a walkway to approach the front door of a house and to remain there for a brief time. This license is not limited to persons who intend to speak to an occupant or who actually do so. (Mail carriers and persons delivering packages and flyers are examples of individuals who may lawfully approach a front door without intending to converse.) Nor is the license restricted to categories of visitors whom an occupant of the dwelling is likely to welcome; as the Court acknowledges, this license applies even to "solicitors, hawkers and peddlers of all kinds." *Ante,* at 1415 (internal quotation marks omitted). And the license even extends to police officers who wish to gather evidence against an occupant (by asking potentially incriminating questions).

According to the Court, however, the police officer in this case, Detective Bartelt, committed a trespass because he was accompanied during his otherwise lawful visit to the front door of respondent's house by his dog, Franky. Where is the authority evidencing such a rule? Dogs have been domesticated for about 12,000 years;[1] they were ubiquitous in both this country and Britain at the time of the adoption of the Fourth Amendment;[2] and their acute sense of smell has been used in law

---

[1]   See, e.g., Sloane, Dogs in War, Police Work and on Patrol, 46 J. Crim. L., C. & P.S. 385 (1955–1956) (hereinafter Sloane).

[2]   M. Derr, A Dog's History of America 68–92 (2004); K. Olsen, Daily Life in 18th-Century England 32–33 (1999).

enforcement for centuries.[3] Yet the Court has been unable to find a single case—from the United States or any other common-law nation—that supports the rule on which its decision is based. Thus, trespass law provides no support for the Court's holding today.

The Court's decision is also inconsistent with the reasonable-expectations-of-privacy test that the Court adopted in Katz v. United States, 389 U.S. 347 (1967). A reasonable person understands that odors emanating from a house may be detected from locations that are open to the public, and a reasonable person will not count on the strength of those odors remaining within the range that, while detectible by a dog, cannot be smelled by a human.

For these reasons, I would hold that no search within the meaning of the Fourth Amendment took place in this case, and I would reverse the decision below.

I

The opinion of the Court may leave a reader with the mistaken impression that Detective Bartelt and Franky remained on respondent's property for a prolonged period of time and conducted a far-flung exploration of the front yard. *See ante*, at 1414 ("trawl for evidence with impunity"), 1416 ("marching his bloodhound into the garden"). But that is not what happened.

Detective Bartelt and Franky approached the front door via the driveway and a paved path—the route that any visitor would customarily use 4—and Franky was on the kind of leash that any dog owner might employ. As Franky approached the door, he started to track an airborne odor. He held his head high and began "bracketing" the area (pacing back and forth) in order to determine the strongest source of the smell. App. 95–96. Detective Bartelt knew "the minute [he] observed" this behavior that Franky had detected drugs. *Id.*, at 95. Upon locating the odor's strongest source, Franky sat at the base of the front door, and at this point, Detective Bartelt and Franky immediately returned to their patrol car. *Id.*, at 98.

The Court notes that Franky was on a 6-foot leash, but such a leash is standard equipment for ordinary dog owners. See, e.g., J. Stregowski, Four Dog Leash Varieties, http://dogs.about.com/od/toyssupplies/tp/Dog-Leashes.htm (all Internet materials as visited Mar. 21, 2013, and available in Clerk of Court's case file).

A critical fact that the Court omits is that, as respondent's counsel explained at oral argument, this entire process—walking down the driveway and front path to the front door, waiting for Franky to find the strongest source of the odor, and walking back to the car—took approximately a minute or two. Tr. of Oral Arg. 57–58. Thus, the amount of time that Franky and the detective remained at the front porch was

---

3   Sloane 388–389.

even less. The Court also fails to mention that, while Detective Bartelt apparently did not personally smell the odor of marijuana coming from the house, another officer who subsequently stood on the front porch, Detective Pedraja, did notice that smell and was able to identify it. App. 81.

II

The Court concludes that the conduct in this case was a search because Detective Bartelt exceeded the boundaries of the license to approach the house that is recognized by the law of trespass, but the Court's interpretation of the scope of that license is unfounded.

A

It is said that members of the public may lawfully proceed along a walkway leading to the front door of a house because custom grants them a license to do so. Breard v. Alexandria, 341 U.S. 622, 626 (1951); Lakin v. Ames, 64 Mass. 198, 220 (1852); J. Bishop, Commentaries on the Non-Contract Law § 823, p. 378 (1889). This rule encompasses categories of visitors whom most homeowners almost certainly wish to allow to approach their front doors—friends, relatives, mail carriers, persons making deliveries. But it also reaches categories of visitors who are less universally welcome—"solicitors," "hawkers," "peddlers," and the like. The law might attempt to draw fine lines between categories of welcome and unwelcome visitors, distinguishing, for example, between tolerable and intolerable door-to-door peddlers (Girl Scouts selling cookies versus adults selling aluminum siding) or between police officers on agreeable and disagreeable missions (gathering information about a bothersome neighbor versus asking potentially incriminating questions). But the law of trespass has not attempted such a difficult taxonomy. *See* Desnick v. American Broadcasting Cos., 44 F.3d 1345, 1351 (C.A.7 1995) ("[C]onsent to an entry is often given legal effect even though the entrant has intentions that if known to the owner of the property would cause him for perfectly understandable and generally ethical or at least lawful reasons to revoke his consent"); cf. Skinner v. Ogallala Public School Dist., 262 Neb. 387, 402, 631 N.W.2d 510, 525 (2001) ("[I]n order to determine if a business invitation is implied, the inquiry is not a subjective assessment of why the visitor chose to visit the premises in a particular instance"); Crown Cork & Seal Co. v. Kane, 213 Md. 152, 159, 131 A.2d 470, 473–474 (1957) (noting that "there are many cases in which an invitation has been implied from circumstances, such as custom," and that this test is "objective in that it stresses custom and the appearance of things" as opposed to "the undisclosed intention of the visitor").

Of course, this license has certain spatial and temporal limits. A visitor must stick to the path that is typically used to approach a front door, such as a paved walkway. A visitor cannot traipse through the garden, meander into the backyard, or take other circuitous detours that veer from the pathway that a visitor would customarily use. See, e.g., Robinson v. Virginia, 47 Va.App. 533, 549–550, 625 S.E.2d 651, 659

(2006) (en banc); United States v. Wells, 648 F.3d 671, 679–680 (C.A.8 2011) (police exceeded scope of their implied invitation when they bypassed the front door and proceeded directly to the back yard); State v. Harris, 919 S.W.2d 619, 624 (Tenn.Crim.App.1995) ("Any substantial and unreasonable departure from an area where the public is impliedly invited exceeds the scope of the implied invitation . . ." (internal quotation marks and brackets omitted)); 1 W. LaFave, Search and Seizure § 2.3(c), p. 578 (2004) (hereinafter LaFave); *id.*, § 2.3(f), at 600–603 ("[W]hen the police come on to private property to conduct an investigation or for some other legitimate purpose and restrict their movements to places visitors could be expected to go (e.g., walkways, driveways, porches), observations made from such vantage points are not covered by the Fourth Amendment" (footnotes omitted)).

Nor, as a general matter, may a visitor come to the front door in the middle of the night without an express invitation. *See* State v. Cada, 129 Idaho 224, 233, 923 P.2d 469, 478 (App.1996) ("Furtive intrusion late at night or in the predawn hours is not conduct that is expected from ordinary visitors. Indeed, if observed by a resident of the premises, it could be a cause for great alarm").

Similarly, a visitor may not linger at the front door for an extended period. *See* 9 So.3d 1, 11 (Fla.App.2008) (case below) (Cope, J., concurring in part and dissenting in part) ("[T]here is no such thing as squatter's rights on a front porch. A stranger may not plop down uninvited to spend the afternoon in the front porch rocking chair, or throw down a sleeping bag to spend the night, or lurk on the front porch, looking in the windows"). The license is limited to the amount of time it would customarily take to approach the door, pause long enough to see if someone is home, and (if not expressly invited to stay longer), leave.

As I understand the law of trespass and the scope of the implied license, a visitor who adheres to these limitations is not necessarily required to ring the doorbell, knock on the door, or attempt to speak with an occupant. For example, mail carriers, persons making deliveries, and individuals distributing flyers may leave the items they are carrying and depart without making any attempt to converse. A pedestrian or motorist looking for a particular address may walk up to a front door in order to check a house number that is hard to see from the sidewalk or road. A neighbor who knows that the residents are away may approach the door to retrieve an accumulation of newspapers that might signal to a potential burglar that the house is unoccupied.

As the majority acknowledges, this implied license to approach the front door extends to the police. *See ante,* at 1415. As we recognized in Kentucky v. King, 563 U.S. ___ (2011), police officers do not engage in a search when they approach the front door of a residence and seek to engage in what is termed a "knock and talk," i.e., knocking on the door and seeking to speak to an occupant for the purpose of gathering evidence. *See id.*, at ___ ("When law enforcement officers who are not armed with a warrant knock on a door, they do no more than any private citizen might do"). *See also* 1 LaFave § 2.3(e), at 592 ("It is not objectionable for an officer to come upon that part of the property which has been opened to public common use" (internal quotation marks omitted)). Even when the objective of a "knock and talk" is to obtain evidence that will lead to the homeowner's arrest and prosecution, the license to approach still applies. In other words, gathering evidence— even damning evidence—is a lawful activity that falls within the scope of the license to approach. And when officers walk up to the front door of a house, they are permitted to see, hear, and smell whatever can be detected from a lawful vantage point. California v. Ciraolo, 476 U.S. 207, 213 (1986) ("The Fourth Amendment protection of the home has never been extended to require law enforcement officers to shield their eyes when passing by a home on public thoroughfares"); *Cada, supra,* at 232, 923 P.2d, at 477 ("[P]olice officers restricting their activity to [areas to which the public is impliedly invited] are permitted the same intrusion and the same level of observation as would be expected from a reasonably respectful citizen" (internal quotation marks omitted)); 1 LaFave §§ 2.2(a), 2.3(c), at 450–452, 572–577.

B

Detective Bartelt did not exceed the scope of the license to approach respondent's front door. He adhered to the customary path; he did not approach in the middle of the night; and he remained at the front door for only a very short period (less than a minute or two).

The Court concludes that Detective Bartelt went too far because he had the "objectiv[e] . . . purpose to conduct a search." *Ante,* at 1417 (emphasis added). What this means, I take it, is that anyone aware of what Detective Bartelt did would infer that his subjective purpose was to gather evidence. But if this is the Court's point, then a standard "knock and talk" and most other police visits would likewise constitute searches. With the exception of visits to serve warrants or civil process, police almost always approach homes with a purpose of discovering information. That is certainly the objective of a "knock and talk." The Court offers no meaningful way of distinguishing the "objective purpose" of a "knock and talk" from the "objective purpose" of Detective Bartelt's conduct here.

The Court contends that a "knock and talk" is different because it involves talking, and "all are invited" to do that. *Ante,* at 1416, n. 4 (emphasis deleted). But a police officer who approaches the front door of a house in accordance with the limitations already discussed may gather evidence by means other than talking. The officer may observe items in plain view and smell odors coming from the house. *Ciraolo, supra,* at 213; *Cada,* 129 Idaho, at 232, 923 P.2d, at 477; 1 LaFave §§ 2.2(a), 2.3(c), at 450–452, 572–577. So the Court's "objective purpose" argument cannot stand.

What the Court must fall back on, then, is the particular instrument that Detective Bartelt used to detect the odor of marijuana, namely, his dog. But in the entire body of common-law decisions, the Court has not found a single case holding that a visitor to the front door of a home commits a trespass if the visitor is accompanied by a dog on a leash. On the contrary, the common law allowed even unleashed dogs to wander on private property without committing a trespass. G. Williams, Liability for Animals 136–146 (1939); J. Ingham, A Treatise on Property in Animals Wild and Domestic and the Rights and Responsibilities Arising Therefrom 277–278 (1900). *Cf.* B. Markesinis & S. Deakin, Tort Law 511 (4th ed. 1999).

The Court responds that "[i]t is not the dog that is the problem, but the behavior that here involved use of the dog." *Ante,* at 1416, n. 3. But where is the support in the law of trespass for this proposition? Dogs' keen sense of smell has been used in law enforcement for centuries. The antiquity of this practice is evidenced by a Scottish law from 1318 that made it a crime to "disturb a tracking dog or the men coming with it for pursuing thieves or seizing malefactors." K. Brown et al., The Records of the Parliaments of Scotland to 1707, (St Andrews, 2007–2013), online at http://www.rps.ac.uk/mss/1318/9. If bringing a tracking dog to the front door of a home constituted a trespass, one would expect at least one case to have arisen during the past 800 years. But the Court has found none.

For these reasons, the real law of trespass provides no support for the Court's holding today. While the Court claims that its reasoning has "ancient and durable roots," *ante,* at 1414, its trespass rule is really a newly struck counterfeit.

III

The concurring opinion attempts to provide an alternative ground for today's decision, namely, that Detective Bartelt's conduct violated respondent's reasonable expectations of privacy. But we have already rejected a very similar, if not identical argument, *see* Illinois v. Caballes, 543 U.S. 405, 409–410 (2005), and in any event I see no basis for concluding that the occupants of a dwelling have a reasonable expectation of privacy in odors that emanate from the dwelling and reach spots where members of the public may lawfully stand.

It is clear that the occupant of a house has no reasonable expectation of privacy with respect to odors that can be smelled by human beings who are standing in such places. *See* United States v. Johns, 469 U.S. 478, 482 (1985) ("After the officers came closer and detected the distinct odor of marihuana, they had probable cause to believe that the vehicles contained contraband"); United States v. Ventresca, 380 U.S. 102, 111 (1965) (scent of fermenting mash supported probable cause for warrant); United States v. Johnston, 497 F.2d 397, 398 (C.A.9 1974) (there is no "reasonable expectation of privacy from drug agents with inquisitive nostrils"). And I would not draw a line between odors that can be smelled by humans and those that are detectible only by dogs.

Consider the situation from the point of view of the occupant of a building in which marijuana is grown or methamphetamine is manufactured. Would such an occupant reason as follows? "I know that odors may emanate from my building and that atmospheric conditions, such as the force and direction of the wind, may affect the strength of those odors when they reach a spot where members of the public may lawfully stand. I also know that some people have a much more acute sense of smell than others,[6] and I have no idea who might be standing in one of the spots in question when the odors from my house reach that location. In addition, I know that odors coming from my building, when they reach these locations, may be strong enough to be detected by a dog. But I am confident that they will be so faint that they cannot be smelled by any human being." Such a finely tuned expectation would be entirely unrealistic, and I see no evidence that society is prepared to recognize it as reasonable.

In an attempt to show that respondent had a reasonable expectation of privacy in the odor of marijuana wafting from his house, the concurrence argues that this case is just like Kyllo v. United States, 533 U.S. 27 (2001), which held that police officers conducted a search when they used a thermal imaging device to detect heat emanating from a house. *Ante,* at 1419 (opinion of KAGAN, J.). This Court, however, has already rejected the argument that the use of a drug-sniffing dog is the same as the use of a thermal imaging device. *See Caballes,* 543 U.S., at 409–410. The very argument now advanced by the concurrence appears in Justice Souter's *Caballes* dissent. *See id.,* at 413, and n. 3. But the Court was not persuaded.

Contrary to the interpretation propounded by the concurrence, *Kyllo* is best understood as a decision about the use of new technology. The *Kyllo* Court focused on the fact that the thermal imaging device was a form of "sense-enhancing technology" that was "not in general public use," and it expressed concern that citizens would be "at the mercy of advancing technology" if its use was not restricted. 533 U.S., at 34–35. A dog, however, is not a new form of "technology" or a "device." And, as noted, the use of dogs' acute sense of smell in law enforcement dates back many centuries.

The concurrence suggests that a *Kyllo*-based decision would be "much like" the actual decision of the Court, but that is simply not so. The holding of the Court is based on what the Court sees as a " 'physical intrusion of a constitutionally protected area.' " *Ante,* at 1414 (quoting United States v. Knotts, 460 U.S. 276, 286 (1983) (BRENNAN, J., concurring in judgment)). As a result, it does not apply when a dog alerts

---

[6] Some humans naturally have a much more acute sense of smell than others, and humans can be trained to detect and distinguish odors that could not be detected without such training. *See* E. Hancock, A Primer on Smell, http://www.jhu.edu/jhumag/996web/smell.html. Some individuals employed in the perfume and wine industries, for example, have an amazingly acute sense of smell. *Ibid.*

while on a public sidewalk or street or in the corridor of a building to which the dog and handler have been lawfully admitted.

The concurrence's *Kyllo*-based approach would have a much wider reach. When the police used the thermal imaging device in *Kyllo*, they were on a public street, 533 U.S., at 29 and "committed no trespass." *Ante*, at 1419. Therefore, if a dog's nose is just like a thermal imaging device for Fourth Amendment purposes, a search would occur if a dog alerted while on a public sidewalk or in the corridor of an apartment building. And the same would be true if the dog was trained to sniff, not for marijuana, but for more dangerous quarry, such as explosives or for a violent fugitive or kidnapped child. I see no ground for hampering legitimate law enforcement in this way.

IV

The conduct of the police officer in this case did not constitute a trespass and did not violate respondent's reasonable expectations of privacy. I would hold that this conduct was not a search, and I therefore respectfully dissent.

c. THE ASSUMPTION OF RISK AND THIRD PARTY DOCTRINES

United States v. White

401 U.S. 745 (1971)

■ MR. JUSTICE WHITE announced the judgment of the Court and an opinion in which THE CHIEF JUSTICE, MR. JUSTICE STEWART, and MR. JUSTICE BLACKMUN join.

In 1966, respondent James A. White was tried and convicted under two consolidated indictments charging various illegal transactions in narcotics violative of 26 U.S.C. § 4705(a) and 21 U.S.C. § 174. He was fined and sentenced as a second offender to 25-year concurrent sentences. The issue before us is whether the Fourth Amendment bars from evidence the testimony of governmental agents who related certain conversations which had occurred between defendant White and a government informant, Harvey Jackson, and which the agents overheard by monitoring the frequency of a radio transmitter carried by Jackson and concealed on his person.[1] On four occasions the conversations took place in Jackson's home; each of these conversations was overheard by an agent concealed in a kitchen closet with Jackson's consent and by a second agent outside the house using a radio receiver. Four other conversations—one in respondent's home, one in a restaurant, and two in Jackson's car—were overheard by the use of radio equipment. The

---

[1] White argues that Jackson, though admittedly 'cognizant' of the presence of transmitting devices on his person, did not voluntarily consent thereto. Because the court below did not reach the issue of Jackson's consent, we decline to do so. Similarly, we do not consider White's claim that the Government's actions violated state law.

prosecution was unable to locate and produce Jackson at the trial and the trial court overruled objections to the testimony of the agents who conducted the electronic surveillance. The jury returned a guilty verdict and defendant appealed.

The Court of Appeals read Katz v. United States, 389 U.S. 347 (1967), as overruling On Lee v. United States, 343 U.S. 747 (1952), and interpreting the Fourth Amendment to forbid the introduction of the agents' testimony in the circumstances of this case. Accordingly, the court reversed but without adverting to the fact that the transactions at issue here had occurred before *Katz* was decided in this Court. In our view, the Court of Appeals misinterpreted both the *Katz* case and the Fourth Amendment and in any event erred in applying the *Katz* case to events that occurred before that decision was rendered by this Court.

I

Until *Katz v. United States*, neither wiretapping nor electronic eavesdropping violated a defendant's Fourth Amendment rights 'unless there has been an official search and seizure of his person, or such a seizure of his papers or his tangible material effects, or an actual physical invasion of his house 'or curtilage' for the purpose of making a seizure.' Olmstead v. United States, 277 U.S. 438, 466 (1928); Goldman v. United States, 316 U.S. 129, 135–136 (1942). But where 'eavesdropping was accomplished by means of an unauthorized physical penetration into the premises occupied' by the defendant, although falling short of a 'technical trespass under the local property law,' the Fourth Amendment was violated and any evidence of what was seen and heard, as well as tangible objects seized, was considered the inadmissible fruit of an unlawful invasion. Silverman v. United States, 365 U.S. 505, 509 (1961); *see also* Wong Sun v. United States, 371 U.S. 471(1963); Berger v. New York, 388 U.S. 41, 52 (1967); Alderman v. United States, 394 U.S. 165, 177–178 (1969).

Katz v. United States, however, finally swept away doctrines that electronic eavesdropping is permissible under the Fourth Amendment unless physical invasion of a constitutionally protected area produced the challenged evidence. In that case government agents, without petitioner's consent or knowledge, attached a listening device to the outside of a public telephone booth and recorded the defendant's end of his telephone conversations. In declaring the recordings inadmissible in evidence in the absence of a warrant authorizing the surveillance, the Court overruled *Olmstead* and *Goldman* and held that the absence of physical intrusion into the telephone booth did not justify using electronic devices in listening to and recording Katz' words, thereby violating the privacy on which he justifiably relied while using the telephone in those circumstances.

The Court of Appeals understood *Katz* to render inadmissible against White the agents' testimony concerning conversations that Jackson broadcast to them. We cannot agree. *Katz* involved no revelation to the Government by a party to conversations with the defendant nor did the Court indicate in any way that a defendant has a justifiable and constitutionally protected expectation that a person with whom he is conversing will not then or later reveal the conversation to the police.

Hoffa v. United States, 385 U.S. 293 (1966), which was left undisturbed by *Katz*, held that however strongly a defendant may trust an apparent colleague, his expectations in this respect are not protected by the Fourth Amendment when it turns out that the colleague is a government agent regularly communicating with the authorities. In these circumstances, 'no interest legitimately protected by the Fourth Amendment is involved,' for that amendment affords no protection to 'a wrongdoer's misplaced belief that a person to whom he voluntarily confides his wrongdoing will not reveal it.' *Hoffa v. United States,* at 302. No warrant to 'search and seize' is required in such circumstances, nor is it when the Government sends to defendant's home a secret agent who conceals his identity and makes a purchase of narcotics from the accused, Lewis v. United States, 385 U.S. 206 (1966), or when the same agent, unbeknown to the defendant, carries electronic equipment to record the defendant's words and the evidence so gathered is later offered in evidence. Lopez v. United States, 373 U.S. 427 (1963).

Conceding that *Hoffa*, *Lewis*, and *Lopez* remained unaffected by *Katz*,[3] the Court of Appeals nevertheless read both *Katz* and the Fourth Amendment to require a different result if the agent not only records his conversations with the defendant but instantaneously transmits them electronically to other agents equipped with radio receivers. Where this occurs, the Court of Appeals held, the Fourth Amendment is violated and the testimony of the listening agents must be excluded from evidence.

To reach this result it was necessary for the Court of Appeals to hold that *On Lee v. United States* was no longer good law. In that case, which involved facts very similar to the case before us, the Court first rejected claims of a Fourth Amendment violation because the informer had not trespassed when he entered the defendant's premises and conversed with him. To this extent the Court's rationale cannot survive *Katz*. *See* 389 U.S., at 352–353. But the Court announced a second and independent ground for its decision; for it went on to say that overruling *Olmstead* and *Goldman* would be of no aid to *On Lee* since he 'was talking confidentially and indiscreetly with one he trusted, and he was overheard. * * * It would be a dubious service to the genuine liberties protected by the Fourth Amendment to make them bedfellows with spurious liberties improvised by farfetched analogies which would liken eavesdropping on a conversation, with the connivance of one of the parties, to an unreasonable search or seizure. We find no violation of the Fourth Amendment here.' 343 U.S., at 753–754. We see no indication in *Katz* that the Court meant to disturb that understanding of the Fourth

---

[3]   It follows from our opinion that we reject respondent's contentions that Lopez should be overruled.

Amendment or to disturb the result reached in the *On Lee* case, nor are we now inclined to overturn this view of the Fourth Amendment.

Concededly a police agent who conceals his police connections may write down for official use his conversations with a defendant and testify concerning them, without a warrant authorizing his encounters with the defendant and without otherwise violating the latter's Fourth Amendment rights. *Hoffa v. United States*, 385 U.S., at 300–303. For constitutional purposes, no different result is required if the agent instead of immediately reporting and transcribing his conversations with defendant, either (1) simultaneously records them with electronic equipment which he is carrying on his person, *Lopez v. United States, supra*; (2) or carries radio equipment which simultaneously transmits the conversations either to recording equipment located elsewhere or to other agents monitoring the transmitting frequency. *On Lee v. United States, supra.* If the conduct and revelations of an agent operating without electronic equipment do not invade the defendant's constitutionally justifiable expectations of privacy, neither does a simultaneous recording of the same conversations made by the agent or by others from transmissions received from the agent to whom the defendant is talking and whose trustworthiness the defendant necessarily risks.

Our problem is not what the privacy expectations of particular defendants in particular situations may be or the extent to which they may in fact have relied on the discretion of their companions. Very probably, individual defendants neither know nor suspect that their colleagues have gone or will go to the police or are carrying recorders or transmitters. Otherwise, conversation would cease and our problem with these encounters would be nonexistent or far different from those now before us. Our problem, in terms of the principles announced in *Katz*, is what expectations of privacy are constitutionally 'justifiable'—what expectations the Fourth Amendment will protect in the absence of a warrant. So far, the law permits the frustration of actual expectations of privacy by permitting authorities to use the testimony of those associates who for one reason or another have determined to turn to the police, as well as by authorizing the use of informants in the manner exemplified by *Hoffa* and *Lewis*. If the law gives no protection to the wrongdoer whose trusted accomplice is or becomes a police agent, neither should it protect him when that same agent has recorded or transmitted the conversations which are later offered in evidence to prove the State's case. *See* Lopez v. United States, 373 U.S. 427 (1963).

Inescapably, one contemplating illegal activities must realize and risk that his companions may be reporting to the police. If he sufficiently doubts their trustworthiness, the association will very probably end or never materialize. But if he has no doubts, or allays them, or risks what doubt he has, the risk is his. In terms of what his course will be, what he will or will not do or say, we are unpersuaded that he would distinguish between probably informers on the one hand and probable informers with transmitters on the other. Given the possibility or probability that one of his colleagues is cooperating with the police, it is only speculation to assert that the defendant's utterances would be substantially different or his sense of security any less if he also thought it possible that the suspected colleague is wired for sound. At least there is no persuasive evidence that the difference in this respect between the electronically equipped and the unequipped agent is substantial enough to require discrete constitutional recognition, particularly under the Fourth Amendment which is ruled by fluid concepts of 'reasonableness.'

Nor should we be too ready to erect constitutional barriers to relevant and probative evidence which is also accurate and reliable. An electronic recording will many times produce a more reliable rendition of what a defendant has said than will the unaided memory of a police agent. It may also be that with the recording in existence it is less likely that the informant will change his mind, less chance that threat or injury will suppress unfavorable evidence and less chance that cross-examination will confound the testimony. Considerations like these obviously do not favor the defendant, but we are not prepared to hold that a defendant who has no constitutional right to exclude the informer's unaided testimony nevertheless has a Fourth Amendment privilege against a more accurate version of the events in question.

It is thus untenable to consider the activities and reports of the police agent himself, though acting without a warrant, to be a 'reasonable' investigative effort and lawful under the Fourth Amendment but to view the same agent with a recorder or transmitter as conducting an 'unreasonable' and unconstitutional search and seizure. Our opinion is currently shared by Congress and the Executive Branch, Title III, Omnibus Crime Control and Safe Streets Act of 1968, 82 Stat. 212, 18 U.S.C. § 2510 et seq. (1964 ed., Supp. V), and the American Bar Association. Project on Standards for Criminal Justice, Electronic Surveillance § 4.1 (Approved Draft 1971). It is also the result reached by prior cases in this Court. *On Lee, supra*; *Lopez v. United States, supra*.

No different result should obtain where, is in *On Lee* and the instant case, the informer disappears and is unavailable at trial; for the issue of whether specified events on a certain day violate the Fourth Amendment should not be determined by what later happens to the informer. His unavailability at trial and proffering the testimony of other agents may raise evidentiary problems or pose issues of prosecutorial misconduct with respect to the informer's disappearance, but they do not appear critical to deciding whether prior events invaded the defendant's Fourth Amendment rights.

II

The Court of Appeals was in error for another reason. In Desist v. United States, 394 U.S. 244 (1969), we held that our decision in *Katz v. United States* applied only to those electronic surveillances that occurred subsequent to the date of that decision. Here the events in question took place in late 1965 and early 1966, long prior to *Katz*. We adhere to the rationale of *Desist, see* Williams v. United States, 401 U.S. 646. It was error for the Court of Appeals to dispose of this case based on its understanding of the principles announced in the *Katz* case. The court should have judged this case by the pre-*Katz* law and under that law, as *On Lee* clearly holds, the electronic surveillance here involved did not violate White's rights to be free from unreasonable searches and seizures.

The judgment of the Court of Appeals is reversed.

It is so ordered.

Judgment of Court of Appeals reversed.

■ MR. JUSTICE BLACK, while adhering to his views expressed in Linkletter v. Walker, 381 U.S. 618, 640 (1965), concurs in the judgment of the Court for the reasons set forth in his dissent in Katz v. United States, 389 U.S. 347, 364 (1967).

■ MR. JUSTICE BRENNAN, concurring in the result.

I agree that Desist v. United States, 394 U.S. 244 (1969), requires reversal of the judgment of the Court of Appeals. Therefore, a majority of the Court supports disposition of this case on that ground. However, my Brothers DOUGLAS, HARLAN, and WHITE also debate the question whether On Lee v. United States, 343 U.S. 747 (1952), may any longer be regarded as sound law. My Brother WHITE argues that On Lee is still sound law. My Brothers DOUGLAS and HARLAN argue that it is not. Neither position commands the support of a majority of the Court. For myself, I agree with my Brothers DOUGLAS and HARLAN. But I go further. It is my view that the reasoning of both my Brothers DOUGLAS and HARLAN compels the conclusion that Lopez v. United States, 373 U.S. 427 (1963), is also no longer sound law. In other words, it is my view that current Fourth Amendment jurisprudence interposes a warrant requirement not only in cases of third-party electronic monitoring (the situation in *On Lee* and in this case) but also in cases of electronic recording by a government agent of a face-to-face conversation with a criminal suspect, which was the situation in *Lopez*. For I adhere to the dissent in *Lopez*, 373 U.S., at 446–471, in which, to quote my Brother HARLAN, *post,* at 1139 n. 12, 'the doctrinal basis of our subsequent Fourteenth Amendment decisions may be said to have had its genesis.' Katz v. United States, 389 U.S. 347 (1967), adopted that 'doctrinal basis' and thus, it seems to me, agreed with the argument in the *Lopez* dissent that 'subsequent decisions and subsequent experience have sapped whatever vitality (*On Lee*) may once have had; that it should now be regarded as overruled' and that the situation in I 'is rationally indistinguishable.' 373 U.S., at 447. The reasons in support of those conclusions are set forth fully in the *Lopez* dissent and need not be repeated here. It suffices to say that for those reasons I remain of the view that the Fourth Amendment imposes the warrant requirement in both the *On Lee* and *Lopez* situations.

■ MR. JUSTICE DOUGLAS, dissenting.

I

The issue in this case is clouded and concealed by the very discussion of it in legalistic terms. What the ancients knew as 'eavesdropping,' we now call 'electronic surveillance'; but to equate the two is to treat man's first gunpowder on the same level as the nuclear bomb. Electronic surveillance is the greatest leveler of human privacy ever known. How most forms of it can be held 'reasonable' within the meaning of the Fourth Amendment is a mystery. To be sure, the Constitution and Bill of Rights are not to be read as covering only the technology known in the 18th century. Otherwise its concept of 'commerce' would be hopeless when it comes to the management of modern affairs. At the same time the concepts of privacy which the Founders enshrined in the Fourth Amendment vanish completely when we slavishly allow an all-powerful government, proclaiming law and order, efficiency, and other benign purposes, to penetrate all the walls and doors which men need to shield them from the pressures of a turbulent life around them and give them the health and strength to carry on.

That is why a 'strict construction' of the Fourth Amendment is necessary if every man's liberty and privacy are to be constitutionally honored.

When Franklin D. Roosevelt on May 21, 1940, authorized wiretapping in cases of 'fifth column' activities and sabotage and limited it 'insofar as possible to aliens,' he said that 'under ordinary and normal circumstances wire-tapping by Government agents should not be carried on for the excellent reason that it is almost bound to lead to abuse of civil rights. . . .

II

We held in Berger v. New York, 388 U.S. 41, that wiretapping is a search and seizure within the meaning of the Fourth Amendment and therefore must meet its requirements, viz., there must be a prior showing of probable cause, the warrant authorizing the wiretap must particularly describe 'the place to be searched, and the persons or things to be seized,' and that it may not have the breadth, generality, and long life of the general warrant against which the Fourth Amendment was aimed.

In Katz v. United States, 389 U.S. 347, we held that an electronic device, used without trespass onto any given enclosure (there a telephone booth), was a search for which a Fourth Amendment warrant was needed.[1] Mr. Justice Stewart, speaking for the Court, said: 'Wherever a

---

[1] *See* Greenawalt, *The Consent Problem in Wiretapping & Eavesdropping: Surreptitious Monitoring With the Consent of a Participant in a Conversation*, 68 Col.L.Rev. 189; Kitch, *Katz v. United States: The Limits of the Fourth Amendment,* 1968 Sup.Ct.Rev. 133; Note, *Police Undercover Agents: New Threat to First Amendment Freedoms,* 37 Geo.Wash.L.Rev. 634; Comment, *Electronic Surveillance: The New Standards,* 35 Brooklyn L.Rev. 49.The relaxing of constitutional requirements by the Executive Branch is apparent from the Appendices to this dissent.

man may be, he is entitled to know that he will remain free from unreasonable searches and seizures.' *Id.*, at 359. As a result of *Berger* and of *Katz,* both wiretapping and electronic surveillance through a 'bug' or other device are now covered by the Fourth Amendment.

There were prior decisions representing an opposed view. In On Lee v. United States, 343 U.S. 747, an undercover agent with a radio transmitter concealed on his person interviewed the defendant whose words were heard over a radio receiver by another agent down the street. The idea, discredited by *Katz,* that there was no violation of the Fourth Amendment because there was no trespass, was the core of the *On Lee* decision. *Id.*, at 751–754.

Lopez v. United States, 373 U.S. 427, was also pre-*Berger* and pre-*Katz.* The government agent there involved carried a pocket wire recorder which the Court said 'was not planted by means of an unlawful physical invasion of petitioner's premises under circumstances which would violate the Fourth Amendment.' *Id.*, at 439. . . .

It is urged by the Department of Justice that *On Lee* be established as the controlling decision in this field. I would stand by *Berger* and *Katz* and reaffirm the need for judicial supervision[2] under the Fourth Amendment of the use of electronic surveillance which, uncontrolled, promises to lead us into a police state.

These were wholly pre-arranged episodes of surveillance. The first was in the informant's home to which respondent had been invited. The second was also in the informer's home, the next day. The third was four days later at the home of the respondent. The fourth was in the informer's car two days later. Twelve days after that a meeting in the informer's home was intruded upon. The sixth occurred at a street rendezvous. The seventh was in the informer's home and the eighth in a restaurant owned by respondent's mother-law. So far as time is concerned there is no excuse for not seeking a warrant. And while there is always an effort involved in preparing affidavits or other evidence in support of a showing a probable cause, that burden was given constitutional sanction in the Fourth Amendment against the activities of the agents of George III. It was designed not to protect criminals but to protect everyone's privacy.

On Lee and *Lopez* are of a vintage opposed to *Berger* and *Katz.* However they may be explained, they are products of the old common-law notions of trespass. *Katz,* on the other hand, emphasized that with few exceptions 'searches conducted outside the judicial process, without prior approval by judge or magistrate, are per se unreasonable under the Fourth Amendment. * * *' 389 U.S., at 357.

■ MR. JUSTICE HARLAN, dissenting.

---

[2]   Osborn v. United States, 385 U.S. 323 was held to be in that tradition, as the federal district judges, prior to the use of the recording device by the agent and with full knowledge of the alleged law violation involved, 'authorized the use of a recording device for the narrow and particularized purpose of ascertaining the truth' of the charge. *Id.*, at 330.

The uncontested facts of this case squarely challenge the continuing viability of On Lee v. United States, 343 U.S. 747 (1952). As the plurality opinion of Mr. Justice White itself makes clear, important constitutional developments since *On Lee* mandate that we reassess that case, which has continued to govern official behavior of this sort in spite of the subsequent erosion of its doctrinal foundations. With all respect, my agreement with the plurality opinion ends at that point.

I think that a perception of the scope and role of the Fourth Amendment, as elucidated by this Court since *On Lee* was decided, and full comprehension of the precise issue at stake lead to the conclusion that *On Lee* can no longer be regarded as sound law. Nor do I think the date we decided Katz v. United States, 389 U.S. 347 (1967), can be deemed controlling both for the reasons discussed in my dissent in Desist v. United States, 394 U.S. 244, 256 (1969), and my separate opinion in Mackey v. United States (and companion cases), 401 U.S. 667, 675 (1971) (the case defore us being here on direct review), and because, in my view, it requires no discussion of the holding in *Katz*, as distinguished from its underlying rationale as to the reach of the Fourth Amendment, to comprehend the constitutional infirmity of *On Lee*.

I

Before turning to matters of precedent and policy, several preliminary observations should be made. We deal here with the constitutional validity of instantaneous third-party electronic eavesdropping, conducted by federal law enforcement officers, without any prior judicial approval of the technique utilized, but with the consent and cooperation of a participant in the conversation,[1] and where the substance of the matter electronically overheard is related in a federal criminal trial by those who eavesdropped as direct, not merely corroborative, evidence of the guilt of the nonconsenting party.[2] The magnitude of the issue at hand is evidenced not simply by the obvious doctrinal difficulty of weighing such activity in the Fourth Amendment balance, but also, and more importantly, by the prevalence of police utilization of this technique. Professor Westin has documented in careful detail the numerous devices that make technologically feasible the Orwellian Big Brother. Of immediate relevance is his observation that ' 'participant recording,' in which one participant in a conversation or meeting, either a police officer or a co-operating party, wears a concealed device that records the conversation or broadcasts it to others nearby * * * is used tens of thousands of times each year throughout the country,

---

[1] I agree with the plurality opinion, *ante,* at 1123 n. 1, that the issue of the informer's consent to utilization of this technique is not properly before us. Whether persons can, consistent with constitutional prohibitions, by tricked or coerced into transmitting their conversations, with or without prior judicial approval, and, if not, whether other parties to the conversation would have standing to object to the admission against them of evidence so obtained, cf. Alderman v. United States, 394 U.S. 165 (1969), are questions upon which I express no opinion

[2] In the case at hand agents were also surreptitiously placed in respondent's home at various times. No testimony by these agents was offered at trial.

particularly in cases involving extortion, conspiracy, narcotics, gambling, prostitution, corruption by police officials * * * and similar crimes.'

Moreover, as I shall undertake to show later in this opinion, the factors that must be reckoned with in reaching constitutional conclusions respecting the use of electronic eavesdropping as a tool of law enforcement are exceedingly subtle and complex. They have provoked sharp differences of opinion both within and without the judiciary, and the entire problem has been the subject of continuing study by various governmental and nongovernmental bodies.

Finally, given the importance of electronic eavesdropping as a technique for coping with the more deep-seated kinds of criminal activity, and the complexities that are encountered in striking a workable constitutional balance between the public and private interests at stake, I believe that the courts should proceed with specially measured steps in this field. More particularly, I think this Court should not foreclose itself from reconsidering doctrines that would prevent the States from seeking, independently of the niceties of federal restrictions as they may develop, solutions to such vexing problems, *see* Mapp v. Ohio, 367 U.S. 643 (1961), and Ker v. California, 374 U.S. 23 (1963), and *see also* Berger v. New York, 388 U.S. 41 (1967); Baldwin v. New York, 399 U.S. 66 (1970) (dissenting opinion); California v. Green, 399 U.S. 149, 172 (1970) (concurring opinion). I also think that in the adjudication of federal cases, the Court should leave ample room for congressional developments.

II

On these premises I move to the problem of third-party 'bugging.' To begin by tracing carefully the evolution of Fourth Amendment doctrine in post-*On Lee* decisions has proved useful in several respects. It serves to cast in perspective both the issue involved here and the imperative necessity for reconsidering *On Lee* afresh. Additionally, a full exposition of the dynamics of the decline of the trespass rationale underlying *On Lee* strikingly illuminates the deficiencies of the plurality opinion's retroactivity analysis.

A

On Lee involved circumstances virtually identical to those now before us. There, Government agents enlisted the services of Chin Poy, a former friend of Lee, who was suspected of engaging in illegal narcotics traffic. Poy was equipped with a 'minifon' transmitting device which enabled outside Government agents to monitor Poy's conversations with Lee. In the privacy of his laundry, Lee made damaging admissions to Poy which were overheard by the agents and later related at trial. Poy did not testify. Mr. Justice Jackson, writing for five Justices, held the testimony admissible. Without reaching the question of whether a conversation could be the subject of a 'seizure' for Fourth Amendment purposes, as yet an unanswered if not completely open question, the

Court concluded that in the absence of a trespass, no constitutional violation had occurred.

The validity of the trespass rationale was questionable even at the time the decision was rendered. In this respect *On Lee* rested on common-law notions and looked to a waning era of Fourth Amendment jurisprudence. Three members of the Court refused to join with Justice Jackson, and within 10 years the Court expressly disavowed an approach to Fourth Amendment questions that looked to common-law distinctions. *See, e.g.,* Jones v. United States, 362 U.S. 257 (1960); Silverman v. United States, 365 U.S. 505 (1961); Lanza v. New York, 370 U.S. 139 (1962).

It is, of course, true that the opinion in *On Lee* drew some support from a brief additional assertion that 'eavesdropping on a conversation, with the connivance of one of the parties' raises no Fourth Amendment problem. 343 U.S., at 754. But surely it is a misreading of that opinion to view this unelaborated assertion as a wholly independent ground for decision. At the very least, this rationale needs substantial buttressing if it is to persist in our constitutional jurisprudence after the decisions I discuss below. Indeed, the plurality opinion in the present case, in greatly elaborating the point, tacitly recognizes the analytic inability of this bare hypothesis to support a rule of law so profoundly important to the proper administration of justice. Moreover, if this was the true rationale of *On Lee* from the outset, it is difficult to see the relevance of *Desist* to the resolution of the instant case, for *Katz* surely does not speak directly to the continued viability of that ground for decision. *See Katz v. United States*, 389 U.S., at 363 n. (White, J., concurring).

By 1963, when we decided *Lopez v. United States*, 373 U.S. 427 four members of the Court were prepared to pronounce *On Lee* and Olmstead v. United States, 277 U.S. 438 (1928), dead. The pyre, they reasoned, had been stoked by decisions like Wong Sun v. United States, 371 U.S. 471 (1963), which, on the one hand, expressly brought verbal communication within the sweep of the Fourth Amendment, and, on the other, reinforced our *Silverman* and *Jones* decisions which 'refused to crowd the Fourth Amendment into the mold of local property law,' 373 U.S., at 460 (Brennan, J., dissenting).

Although the Court's decision in *Lopez* is cited by the Government as a reaffirmation of *On Lee*, it can hardly be thought ot have nurtured the questionable rationale of that decision or its much-criticized ancestor, *Olmstead*. To the discerning lawyer *Lopez* could only give pause, not comfort. While the majority opinion, of which I was the author, declined to follow the course favored by the dissenting and concurring Justices by sounding the death knell for *Olmstead* and *On Lee*, our holding, despite an allusion to the absence of 'an unlawful * * * invasion of a constitutionally protected area,' 373 U.S., at 438–439., at 1388, was bottomed on two premises: the corroborative use that was made of the tape recordings, which increased reliability in the fact-finding process, and the absence of a 'risk' not fairly assumed by petitioner. The tape recording was made by a participant in the conversation and the opinion emphasized this absence of a third-party intrusion, expressly noting that there was no 'electronic eavesdropping on a private conversation which government agents could not otherwise have overheard.' 373 U.S., at 440.[10] As I point out in Part III of this opinion, it is one thing to subject the average citizen to the risk that participants in a conversation with him will subsequently divulge its contents to another, but quite a different matter to foist upon him the risk that unknown third parties may be simultaneously listening in. . . .

Viewed in perspective, then, *Katz* added no new dimension to the law. At most it was a formal dispatch of *Olmstead* and the notion that such problems may usefully be resolved in the light of trespass doctrine, and, of course, it freed from speculation what was already evident, that *On Lee* was completely open to question.

B

But the decisions of this Court since *On Lee* do more than demonstrate that the doctrine of that case is wholly open for reconsideration, and has been since well before *Katz* was decided. They also establish sound general principles for application of the Fourth Amendment that were either dimly perceived or not fully worked out at the time of *On Lee*. I have already traced some of these principles in Part II-A, *supra*: that verbal communication is protected by the Fourth Amendment, that the reasonableness of a search does not depend on the presence or absence of a trespass, and that the Fourth Amendment is principally concerned with protecting interests of privacy, rather than property rights.

Especially when other recent Fourth Amendment decisions, not otherwise so immediately relevant, are read with those already discussed, the primacy of an additional general principle becomes equally evident: official investigatory action that impinges on privacy must typically, in order to be constitutionally permissible, be subjected to the warrant requirement. . . .

"Over and again this Court has emphasized that the mandate of the (Fourth) Amendment requires adherence to judicial processes,' *United States v. Jeffers*, 342 U.S. 48, 51, and that searches conducted outside the judicial process, without prior approval by judge or magistrate, are per se unreasonable under the Fourth Amendment—subject only to a few specifically established and well-delineated exceptions.' *Katz v. United States*, 389 U.S., at 356–357.The warrant procedure need not always entail an inquiry into the existence of probable cause in the usual sense.

---

[10] 'Stripped to its essentials, petitioner's argument amounts to saying that he has a constitutional right to rely on possible flaws in the agent's memory, or to challenge the agent's credibility without being beset by corroborating evidence that is not susceptible of impeachment. For no other argument can justify excluding an accurate version of a conversation that the agent could testify to from memory. We think the risk that petitioner took in offering a bribe to Davis fairly included the risk that the offer would be accurately reproduced in court, whether by faultless memory or mechanical recording.' 373 U.S., at 439.

Cf. Camara v. Municipal Court. For example, where an informer is being sent in to investigate a dangerous crime, and there is reason to believe his person would be in danger, monitoring might be justified and a warrant issued even though no probable cause existed to believe the particular meeting would provide evidence of particular criminal activity. *Cf.* Warden v. Hayden, 387 U.S. 294, 298 (1967); McDonald v. United States, 335 U.S., at 455–456; Johnson v. United States, 333 U.S., at 14–15; Ker v. California, 374 U.S. 23 (1963); Trupiano v. United States, 334 U.S. 699 (1948), all taking the view that exceptions to the warrant requirement may be made in narrowly defined special circumstances.

The scope and meaning of the rule have emerged with even greater clarity by virtue of our holdings setting the boundaries for the exceptions. Recently, in Chimel v. California, 395 U.S. 752 (1969), we reiterated the importance of the prior independent determination of a neutral magistrate and underscored its centrality to the reasonableness requirement of the Fourth Amendment, and abandoned the holdings of Harris v. United States, 331 U.S. 145 (1947), and United States v. Rabinowitz, 339 U.S. 56 (1950). We were concerned by the breadth of searches occasioned by the *Rabinowitz* rule which frequently proved to be an invitation to a hunting expedition. Searches incident to arrest, we held, must be confined to a locus no greater than necessary to prevent injury to the arresting officer or destruction of evidence. 395 U.S., at 763, 767; *cf.* Terry v. Ohio, 392 U.S. 1 (1968).

To complete the tapestry, the strands of doctrine reflected in the search cases must be interwoven with the Court's other contemporary holdings. Most significant are *Terry v. Ohio, supra,* and Davis v. Mississippi, 394 U.S. 721 (1969), which were also harbingers of the new thrust in Fourth Amendment doctrine. There the Court rejected the contention that only an arrest triggered the 'incident-to-arrest' exception to the warrant requirement of the Fourth Amendment, and held that any restraint of the person, however brief and however labeled, was subject to a reasonableness examination. 392 U.S., at 19. The controlling principle is 'to recognize that the Fourth Amendment governs all intrusions by agents of the public upon personal security, and to make the scope of the particular intrusion, in light of all the exigencies of the case, a central element in the analysis of reasonableness.' 392 U.S., at 18 n. 15. *See also Davis v. Mississippi,* 394 U.S., at 727.

III

A

That the foundations of *On Lee* have been destroyed does not, of course, mean that its result can no longer stand. Indeed, the plurality opinion today fastens upon our decisions in *Lopez,* Lewis v. United States, 385 U.S. 206 (1966), and Hoffa v. United States, 385 U.S. 293 (1966), to resist the undercurrents of more recent cases emphasizing the warrant procedure as a safeguard to privacy. But this category provides insufficient support. In each of these cases the risk the general populace faced was different from that surfaced by the instant case. No surreptitious third ear was present, and in each opinion that fact was carefully noted.

In *Lewis,* a federal agent posing as a potential purchaser of narcotics gained access to petitioner's home and there consummated an illegal sale, the fruits of which were admitted at trial along with the testimony of the agent. Chief Justice Warren, writing for the majority, expressly distinguished the third-party overhearing involved, by way of example, in a case like *Silverman v. United States, supra,* nothing that 'there, the conduct proscribed was that of eavesdroppers, unknown and unwanted intruders who furtively listened to conversations occurring in the privacy of a house.' 385 U.S., at 212. Similarly in *Hoffa,* Mr. Justice Stewart took care to mention that 'surreptitious' monitoring was not there before the Court, and so too in *Lopez, supra.*

The plurality opinion seeks to erase the crucial distinction between the facts before us and these holdings by the following reasoning: if A can relay verbally what is revealed to him by B (as in *Lewis* and *Hoffa*), or record and later divulge it (as in *Lopez*), what difference does it make if A conspires with another to betray B by contemporaneously transmitting to the other all that is said? The contention is, in essence, an argument that the distinction between third-party monitoring and other undercover techniques is one of form and not substance. The force of the contention depends on the evaluation of two separable but intertwined assumptions: first, that there is no greater invasion of privacy in the third-party situation, and, second, that uncontrolled consensual surveillance in an electronic age is a tolerable technique of law enforcement, given the values and goals of our political system.

The first of these assumptions takes as a point of departure the so-called 'risk analysis' approach of *Lewis,* and *Lopez,* and to a lesser extent *On Lee,* or the expectations approach of *Katz.* While these formulations represent an advance over the unsophisticated trespass analysis of the common law, they too have their limitations and can, ultimately, lead to the substitution of words for analysis. The analysis must, in my view, transcend the search for subjective expectations or legal attribution of assumptions of risk. Our expectations, and the risks we assume, are in large part reflections of laws that translate into rules the customs and values of the past and present.

Since it is the task of the law to form and project, as well as mirror and reflect, we should not, as judges, merely recite the expectations and risks without examining the desirability of saddling them upon society. The critical question, therefore, is whether under our system of government, as reflected in the Constitution, we should impose on our citizens the risks of the electronic listener or observer without at least the protection of a warrant requirement.

This question must, in my view, be answered by assessing the nature of a particular practice and the likely extent of its impact on the individual's sense of security balanced against the utility of the conduct as a technique of law enforcement. For those more extensive intrusions that significantly jeopardize the sense of security which is the paramount concern of Fourth Amendment liberties, I am of the view that more than self-restraint by law enforcement officials is required and at the least warrants should be necessary. Cf. *Terry v. Ohio, supra*; *Davis v. Mississippi, supra*.

B

The impact of the practice of third-party bugging, must, I think, be considered such as to undermine that confidence and sense of security in dealing with one another that is characteristic of individual relationships between citizens in a free society. It goes beyond the impact on privacy occasioned by the ordinary type of 'informer' investigation upheld in Lewis and Hoffa. The argument of the plurality opinion, to the effect that it is irrelevant whether secrets are revealed by the mere tattletale or the transistor, ignores the differences occasioned by third-party monitoring and recording which insures full and accurate disclosure of all that is said, free of the possibility of error and oversight that inheres in human reporting.

Authority is hardly required to support the proposition that words would be measured a good deal more carefully and communication inhibited if one suspected his conversations were being transmitted and transcribed. Were third-party bugging a prevalent practice, it might well smother that spontaneity—reflected in frivolous, impetuous, sacrilegious, and defiant discourse—that liberates daily life. Much offhand exchange is easily forgotten and one may count on the obscurity of his remarks, protected by the very fact of a limited audience, and the likelihood that the listener will either overlook or forget what is said, as well as the listener's inability to reformulate a conversation without having to contend with a documented record. All these values are sacrificed by a rule of law that permits official monitoring of private discourse limited only by the need to locate a willing assistant.

It matters little that consensual transmittals are less obnoxious than wholly clandestine eavesdrops. This was put forward as justification for the conduct in Boyd v. United States, 116 U.S. 616 (1886), where the Government relied on mitigating aspects of the conduct in question. The Court, speaking through Mr. Justice Bradley, declined to countenance literalism:

> 'Though the proceeding in question is divested of many of the aggravating incidents of actual search and seizure, yet, as before said, it contains their substance and essence, and effects their substantial purpose. It may be that it is the obnoxious thing in its mildest and least repulsive form; but illegitimate and unconstitutional practices get their first footing in that way, namely, by silent approaches and slight deviations from legal modes of procedure.' 116 U.S. 616, at 635.

Finally, it is too easy to forget—and, hence, too often forgotten—that the issue here is whether to interpose a search warrant procedure between law enforcement agencies engaging in electronic eavesdropping and the public generally. By casting its 'risk analysis' solely in terms of the expectations and risks that 'wrongdoers' or 'one contemplating illegal activities' ought to bear, the plurality opinion, I think, misses the mark entirely. *On Lee* does not simply mandate that criminals must daily run the risk of unknown eavesdroppers prying into their private affairs; it subjects each and every law-abiding member of society to that risk. The very purpose of interposing the Fourth Amendment warrant requirement is to redistribute the privacy risks throughout society in a way that produces the results the plurality opinion ascribes to the *On Lee* rule. Abolition of *On Lee* would not end electronic eavesdropping. It would prevent public officials from engaging in that practice unless they first had probable cause to suspect an individual of involvement in illegal activities and had tested their version of the facts before a detached judicial officer. The interest *On Lee* fails to protect is the expectation of the ordinary citizen, who has never engaged in illegal conduct in his life, that he may carry on his private discourse freely, openly, and spontaneously without measuring his every word against the connotations it might carry when instantaneously heard by others unknown to him and unfamiliar with his situation or analyzed in a cold, formal record played days, months, or years after the conversation. Interposition of a warrant requirement is designed not to shield 'wrongdoers,' but to secure a measure of privacy and a sense of personal security throughout our society.

The Fourth Amendment does, of course, leave room for the employment of modern technology in criminal law enforcement, but in the stream of current developments in Fourth Amendment law I think it must be held that third-party electronic monitoring, subject only to the self-restraint of law enforcement officials, has no place in our society.

IV

I reach these conclusions notwithstanding seemingly contrary views espoused by both Congress and an American Bar Association study group. Both the ABA study and Title III of the Omnibus Crime Control and Safe Streets Act of 1968, 82 Stat. 212, 18 U.S.C. § 2510 et seq. (1964 ed., Supp. V), appear to reflect little more than this Court's prior decisions. Indeed, the comprehensive provisions of Title III are evidence of the extent of congressional concern with the impact of electronic surveillance on the right to privacy. This concern is further manifested in the introductory section of the Senate Committee Report. Although § 2511(2)(c) exempts consensual and participant monitoring by law enforcement agents from the general prohibitions against surveillance without prior judicial authorization and makes the fruits admissible in court, *see* § 2515, congressional malaise with such conduct is evidenced by the contrastingly limited endorsement of consensual surveillance carried out by private individuals.[27] While individual Congressmen expressed concern about and criticized the provisions for unsupervised consensual electronic surveillance contained in § 2511, the Senate Committee Report comment, to the effect that '(i)t (§ 2511(2)(c)) largely reflects existing law,' S.Rep.No.1097, 90th Cong., 2d Sess., 93–94 (1968), followed by citations to *On Lee* and *Lopez*, strongly suggests that the provisions represent not intractable approval of these practices, but rather an intention to adopt these holdings and to leave to the courts the task of determining their viability in light of later holdings such as *Berger*, *Osborn*, and *Katz*.

I find in neither the ABA study nor Title III any justification for ignoring the identifiable difference—albeit an elusive one in the present state of knowledge—between the impact on privacy of single-party informer bugging and third-party bugging, which in my opinion justifies drawing the constitutional line at this juncture between the two as regards the necessity for obtaining a warrant. Recognition of this difference is, at the very least, necessary to preserve the openness which is at the core of our traditions and is secure only in a society that tolerates official invasion of privacy simply in circumscribed situations.

The Fourth Amendment protects these traditions, and places limitations on the means and circumstances by which the Government may collect information about its citizens by intruding into their personal lives. The spirit of the principle is captured by the oft-quoted language of *Boyd v. United States*, 116 U.S., at 630:

> 'The principles laid down in this opinion (speaking of Entick v. Carrington, 19 How.St. Tr. 1029 (1765)) affect the very essence of constitutional liberty and security. They reach farther than the concrete form of the case then before the court, with its adventitious circumstances; they apply to all invasions on the part of the government and its employes of the sanctity of a man's home and the privacies of life. It is not the breaking of his doors, and the rummaging of his drawers, that constitutes the essence of the offence; but it is the invasion of his indefeasible right of personal security. * * *'

What this means is that the burden of guarding privacy in a free society should not be on its citizens; it is the Government that must justify its need to electronically eavesdrop. . . .

I would hold that *On Lee* is no longer good law and affirm the judgment below.

■ MR. JUSTICE MARSHALL, dissenting.

---

[27] *See* § 2511(2)(d), which prohibits nongovernmental recording and listening when the 'communication is intercepted for the purpose of committing any criminal or tortious act in violation of the Constitution or laws of the United States or of any State or for the purpose of committing any other injurious act.'

I am convinced that the correct view of the Fourth Amendment in the area of electronic surveillance is one that brings the safeguards of the warrant requirement to bear on the investigatory activity involved in this case. In this regard I agree with the dissents of Mr. Justice DOUGLAS and Mr. Justice HARLAN. In short, I believe that On Lee v. United States, 343 U.S. 747 (1952), cannot be considered viable in light of the constitutional principles articulated in Katz v. United States, 389 U.S. 347 (1967), and other cases. And for reasons expressed by Mr. Justice Fortas in dissent in Desist v. United States, 394 U.S. 244 (1969), I do not think we should feel constrained to employ a discarded theory of the Fourth Amendment in evaluating the governmental intrusions challenged here.

2. HISTORICAL NOTE: ORIGINS OF THE THIRD PARTY DOCTRINE

Warrants do not require the target of the investigation to do anything other than step aside and let the officers conduct the search described in the warrant. Subpoenas (as the word, meaning "under penalty," suggests) compel the respondent to provide evidence, whether testimony, records, or physical evidence. Subpoenas to the target of the investigation are "first party" subpoenas.

Under *Boyd,* a first-party subpoena for documents held by the target could be quashed on *both* Fourth and Fifth Amendment grounds. As a Fourth Amendment matter, warrants for "papers" were "reasonable" only when the papers were contraband—stolen goods, obscene matter, or instruments of crime like illegal lottery tickets. A subpoena doing the same work as a warrant was forbidden. As a Fifth Amendment matter, the long-standing doctrine of *The King v. Purnell* treated court-ordered production of documents from the target in a criminal prosecution as compelled self-incrimination.

The Supreme Court has abandoned *Boyd*'s central premises. In Hale v. Henkel, 201 U.S. 43 (1906), the Court held that a corporate officer who had received transactional immunity could be held in contempt for failing to produce records of his corporate employer. The corporation was not a "person" for purposes of the self-incrimination clause, and Hale himself had immunity. The Fifth Amendment, therefore, did not bar enforcing the subpoena for the corporation's records.

Hale maintained so much of *Boyd* as equated subpoenas with search warrants. *Hale,* however, rejected the proposition that *any* compelled production of lawfully-possessed documents was "unreasonable." The *Hale* Court held that a subpoena for all of the corporation's records would violate the Fourth Amendment. *See id.* at 77 ("A general subpoena of this description is equally indefensible as a search warrant would be if couched in similar terms.") (citing, *inter alia,* Ex Parte Brown, 72 Mo. 83 (1880)).

After *Hale,* the Court continued to hold seizure of documents was unreasonable, even when there was probable cause to view the papers as evidence, unless the papers were illegally possessed. *See* Marron v. United States, 275 U.S. 192 (1927) (upholding seizure of documents found at prohibition-era speakeasy, including the utility bills, as instrumentalities of crime rather than "private papers"). As *Marron* suggests, an expansive view of instrumentalities took a big bite out of *Boyd* and *Entick.*

Eventually the Court repudiated *Boyd's* special regard for "papers." In Warden v. Hayden, 387 U.S. 294 (1967), the Court held that the clothes worn by a robber during the robbery could be seized, subject to return after trial, even if they were not contraband, fruits or instrumentalities. In Andressen v. Maryland, 427 U.S. 463 (1976), the Court upheld the seizure of business records under a warrant to seize records relating to the sale of a named piece of real estate, in connection with a fraud investigation. The Court not only approved the warrant, but also upheld the seizure of documents not named in the warrant that tended to prove a different, but factually related, fraud offense. *Andressen* treated the records as indistinguishable from the clothing at issue in *Hayden.* Today, "papers" are subject to the same Fourth Amendment rules as "effects." *See, e.g.,* F.R. Crim. Pro. 41(e)(2)(b) ("A warrant under Rule 41(e)(2)(a) may authorize the seizure of electronic storage media or the seizure or copying of electronically stored information.").

The third-party situation arises when the evidence sought by investigators is in the custody of a person other than the target of the investigation. A warrant for evidence held by third-parties is lawful so long as it satisfies the Fourth Amendment's warrant clause. *See, e.g.,* Zurcher v. Stanford Daily, 436 U.S. 547 (1978) (upholding warrant to search newspaper office for photographs of protest demonstration). What, however, about a subpoena to a non-suspect for evidence, when the investigators cannot satisfy the probable-cause-particular description formula?

This issue first arose in the context of subpoenas for telegrams. The telegraph company (a service provider, we would say today) received the text of a message from the sender (the paying customer). A human operator then transmitted the message using Morse code to another human operator, who translated the Morse into text. A messenger would then deliver the message to the recipient.

Neither a search warrant nor a subpoena directed to Western Union invaded any property rights of the senders or the recipients. Nor was there any recognized privilege for messenger services, as distinct from legal services. *Ex parte Jackson,* discussed in *Olmstead, supra* Chapter 1, held that warrantless searches of sealed mail were illegal. Many cases, however, upheld subpoenas for telegrams for use in criminal investigations. *See, e.g.,* In re Storror, 63 F. 564 (N.D. Cal. 1894); United

States v. Babcock, 24 F. Cas. 908 (C.C.E.D. Mo. 1876). The distinction between letters and telegrams might have rested on the government's unique obligation to maintain the postal system. *See* Anuj C. Desai, *Wiretapping Before the Wires: The Post Office and the Birth of Communications Privacy,* 60 Stan. L. Rev. 553, 583 (2007).

The distinction between mail and telegrams might, however, have been either an illusion or a mistake. The telegram cases took pains to insist that subpoenas for telegrams be as specific as possible. *See ex parte Brown, supra,* 72 Mo. At 94 ("To permit an indiscriminate search among all the papers in one's possession for no particular paper, but some paper, which may throw some light on some issue involved in the trial of some cause pending, would lead to consequences that can be contemplated only with horror, and such a process is not to be tolerated among a free people."; *in re Storror, supra,* 63 F. at 94 (subpoena describes telegrams sought "with such particularity as appears to be practicable."). At the time these cases were decided, warrants for lawfully-possessed papers were still illegal (*Andressen* follows *Brown* by one hundred years). So one might read the telegram cases as anticipating warrants for papers, by authorizing subpoenas for papers provided the subpoena provided the same safeguards as the warrant process.

Alternatively, the cases approving subpoenas for telegrams might have been a mistake. None was decided by the Supreme Court, although *Hale* did cite *Brown* (*Brown* being a notable instance of a court insisting on warrant-like particularity for subpoenas). Judge Cooley, in his renowned Treatise on the Constitutional Limitations, condemned subpoeanas for telegrams as abominations. *See* Thomas M. Cooley, Treatise on the Constitutional Limitations 372–373 n.2 (5th ed. 1883):

> T]he public could not be entitled to a man's private correspondence, whether obtainable by seizing it in the mails, or by compelling the operator of the telegraph to testify to it, or by requiring his servants to take from his desks his private letters and journals, and bring them into court on *subpoena duces tecum.* Any such compulsory process to obtain it seems a most arbitrary and unjustifiable seizure of private papers; such an "unreasonable seizure" as directly condemned by the Constitution.

For Cooley, it made no difference that the sender voluntarily shared the message content with Western Union operators:

> [The telegraph] is used as a means of correspondence, and as a valuable, and in many cases, indispensable, substitute for the postal facilities; and the communication is made, not because the party desires to put the operator in possession of facts, but because transmission without it is impossible. It is not voluntary in any other sense than this, that the party makes it rather than deprive himself of the benefits of this great invention and improvement. *Id.*

When the Supreme Court did consider subpoenas for records held by third-parties, it approved court-ordered production, without probable cause, of credit card records and of telephone company records of the numbers called by the suspect. *See Smith* and *Miller,* discussed in *Carpenter* below. *Carpenter* itself, however, echoes many of the points Judge Cooley made—points that are forcefully challenged by the *Carpenter* dissenters.

Carpenter v. United States
138 S.Ct. 2206 (2018)

■ ROBERTS, C.J., delivered the opinion of the Court, in which GINSBURG, BREYER, SOTOMAYOR, and KAGAN, JJ., joined. KENNEDY, J., filed a dissenting opinion, in which THOMAS and ALITO, JJ., joined. THOMAS, J., filed a dissenting opinion. ALITO, J., filed a dissenting opinion, in which THOMAS, J., joined. GORSUCH, J., filed a dissenting opinion.

■ CHIEF JUSTICE ROBERTS delivered the opinion of the Court.

This case presents the question whether the Government conducts a search under the Fourth Amendment when it accesses historical cell phone records that provide a comprehensive chronicle of the user's past movements.

I

A

There are 396 million cell phone service accounts in the United States—for a Nation of 326 million people. Cell phones perform their wide and growing variety of functions by connecting to a set of radio antennas called "cell sites." Although cell sites are usually mounted on a tower, they can also be found on light posts, flagpoles, church steeples, or the sides of buildings. Cell sites typically have several directional antennas that divide the covered area into sectors.

Cell phones continuously scan their environment looking for the best signal, which generally comes from the closest cell site. Most modern devices, such as smartphones, tap into the wireless network several times a minute whenever their signal is on, even if the owner is not using one of the phone's features. Each time the phone connects to a cell site, it generates a time-stamped record known as cell-site location information (CSLI). The precision of this information depends on the size of the geographic area covered by the cell site. The greater the concentration of cell sites, the smaller the coverage area. As data usage from cell phones has increased, wireless carriers have installed more cell sites to handle the traffic. That has led to increasingly compact coverage areas, especially in urban areas.

Wireless carriers collect and store CSLI for their own business purposes, including finding weak spots in their network and applying "roaming" charges when another carrier routes data through their cell sites. In addition, wireless carriers often sell aggregated location records to data brokers, without individual identifying information of the sort at issue here. While carriers have long retained CSLI for the start and end of incoming calls, in recent years phone companies have also collected location information from the transmission of text messages and routine data connections. Accordingly, modern cell phones generate increasingly vast amounts of increasingly precise CSLI.

B

In 2011, police officers arrested four men suspected of robbing a series of Radio Shack and (ironically enough) T-Mobile stores in Detroit. One of the men confessed that, over the previous four months, the group (along with a rotating cast of getaway drivers and lookouts) had robbed nine different stores in Michigan and Ohio. The suspect identified 15 accomplices who had participated in the heists and gave the FBI some of their cell phone numbers; the FBI then reviewed his call records to identify additional numbers that he had called around the time of the robberies.

Based on that information, the prosecutors applied for court orders under the Stored Communications Act to obtain cell phone records for petitioner Timothy Carpenter and several other suspects. That statute, as amended in 1994, permits the Government to compel the disclosure of certain telecommunications records when it "offers specific and articulable facts showing that there are reasonable grounds to believe" that the records sought "are relevant and material to an ongoing criminal investigation." 18 U.S.C. § 2703(d). Federal Magistrate Judges issued two orders directing Carpenter's wireless carriers—MetroPCS and Sprint—to disclose "cell/site sector [information] for [Carpenter's] telephone[ ] at call origination and at call termination for incoming and outgoing calls" during the four-month period when the string of robberies occurred. App. to Pet. for Cert. 60a, 72a. The first order sought 152 days of cell-site records from MetroPCS, which produced records spanning 127 days. The second order requested seven days of CSLI from Sprint, which produced two days of records covering the period when Carpenter's phone was "roaming" in northeastern Ohio. Altogether the Government obtained 12,898 location points cataloging Carpenter's movements—an average of 101 data points per day.

Carpenter was charged with six counts of robbery and an additional six counts of carrying a firearm during a federal crime of violence. *See* 18 U.S.C. §§ 924(c), 1951(a). Prior to trial, Carpenter moved to suppress the cell-site data provided by the wireless carriers. He argued that the Government's seizure of the records violated the Fourth Amendment because they had been obtained without a warrant supported by probable cause. The District Court denied the motion. App. to Pet. for Cert. 38a–39a.

At trial, seven of Carpenter's confederates pegged him as the leader of the operation. In addition, FBI agent Christopher Hess offered expert testimony about the cell-site data. Hess explained that each time a cell phone taps into the wireless network, the carrier logs a time-stamped record of the cell site and particular sector that were used. With this information, Hess produced maps that placed Carpenter's phone near four of the charged robberies. In the Government's view, the location records clinched the case: They confirmed that Carpenter was "right where the . . . robbery was at the exact time of the robbery." App. 131 (closing argument). Carpenter was convicted on all but one of the firearm counts and sentenced to more than 100 years in prison.

The Court of Appeals for the Sixth Circuit affirmed. 819 F.3d 880 (2016). The court held that Carpenter lacked a reasonable expectation of privacy in the location information collected by the FBI because he had shared that information with his wireless carriers. Given that cell phone users voluntarily convey cell-site data to their carriers as "a means of establishing communication," the court concluded that the resulting business records are not entitled to Fourth Amendment protection. *Id.,* at 888 (quoting Smith v. Maryland, 442 U.S. 735, 741 (1979)).

We granted certiorari. 582 U.S. ___ (2017).

II

A

The Fourth Amendment protects "[t]he right of the people to be secure in their persons, houses, papers, and effects, against unreasonable searches and seizures." The "basic purpose of this Amendment," our cases have recognized, "is to safeguard the privacy and security of individuals against arbitrary invasions by governmental officials." Camara v. Municipal Court of City and County of San Francisco, 387 U.S. 523, 528 (1967). The Founding generation crafted the Fourth Amendment as a "response to the reviled 'general warrants' and 'writs of assistance' of the colonial era, which allowed British officers to rummage through homes in an unrestrained search for evidence of criminal activity." Riley v. California, 573 U.S. ___, ___ (2014). In fact, as John Adams recalled, the patriot James Otis's 1761 speech condemning writs of assistance was "the first act of opposition to the arbitrary claims of Great Britain" and helped spark the Revolution itself. *Id.,* at ___–___ (quoting 10 Works of John Adams 248 (C. Adams ed. 1856)).

For much of our history, Fourth Amendment search doctrine was "tied to common-law trespass" and focused on whether the Government "obtains information by physically intruding on a constitutionally protected area." United States v. Jones, 565 U.S. 400, 405, 406, n. 3 (2012). More recently, the Court has recognized that "property rights are not the sole measure of Fourth Amendment violations." Soldal v. Cook County, 506 U.S. 56, 64 (1992). In Katz v. United States, 389 U.S. 347, 351 (1967), we established that "the Fourth Amendment protects people, not places," and expanded our conception of the Amendment to protect certain expectations of privacy as well. When an individual "seeks to preserve something as private," and his expectation of privacy is "one that society is prepared to recognize as reasonable," we have held that official intrusion into that private sphere generally qualifies as a search and requires a warrant supported by probable cause. *Smith,* 442 U.S., at 740 (internal quotation marks and alterations omitted).

Although no single rubric definitively resolves which expectations of privacy are entitled to protection,[1] the analysis is informed by historical understandings "of what was deemed an unreasonable search and seizure when [the Fourth Amendment] was adopted." Carroll v. United States, 267 U.S. 132, 149 (1925). On this score, our cases have recognized some basic guideposts. First, that the Amendment seeks to secure "the privacies of life" against "arbitrary power." Boyd v. United States, 116 U.S. 616, 630 (1886). Second, and relatedly, that a central aim of the Framers was "to place obstacles in the way of a too permeating police surveillance." United States v. Di Re, 332 U.S. 581, 595 (1948).

We have kept this attention to Founding-era understandings in mind when applying the Fourth Amendment to innovations in surveillance tools. As technology has enhanced the Government's capacity to encroach upon areas normally guarded from inquisitive eyes, this Court has sought to "assure [ ] preservation of that degree of privacy against government that existed when the Fourth Amendment was adopted." Kyllo v. United States, 533 U.S. 27, 34 (2001). For that reason, we rejected in *Kyllo* a "mechanical interpretation" of the Fourth Amendment and held that use of a thermal imager to detect heat radiating from the side of the defendant's home was a search. *Id.,* at 35. Because any other conclusion would leave homeowners "at the mercy of advancing technology," we determined that the Government—absent a warrant—could not capitalize on such new sense-enhancing technology to explore what was happening within the home. *Ibid.*

Likewise in *Riley,* the Court recognized the "immense storage capacity" of modern cell phones in holding that police officers must generally obtain a warrant before searching the contents of a phone. 573 U.S., at ___. We explained that while the general rule allowing warrantless searches incident to arrest "strikes the appropriate balance in the context of physical objects, neither of its rationales has much force

---

[1] Justice KENNEDY believes that there is such a rubric—the "property-based concepts" that *Katz* purported to move beyond. *Post,* at 2224 (dissenting opinion). But while property rights are often informative, our cases by no means suggest that such an interest is "fundamental" or "dispositive" in determining which expectations of privacy are legitimate. *Post,* at 2227–2228. Justice THOMAS (and to a large extent Justice GORSUCH) would have us abandon *Katz* and return to an exclusively property-based approach. *Post,* at 2235–2236, 2244–2246 (THOMAS J., dissenting); *post,* at 2264–2266 (GORSUCH, J., dissenting). *Katz* of course "discredited" the "premise that property interests control," 389 U.S., at 353, and we have repeatedly emphasized that privacy interests do not rise or fall with property rights, see, *e.g.,* United States v. Jones, 565 U.S. 400, 411 (2012) (refusing to "make trespass the exclusive test"); Kyllo v. United States, 533 U.S. 27, 32 (2001) ("We have since decoupled violation of a person's Fourth Amendment rights from trespassory violation of his property."). Neither party has asked the Court to reconsider *Katz* in this case.

with respect to" the vast store of sensitive information on a cell phone. *Id.*, at ___.

B

The case before us involves the Government's acquisition of wireless carrier cell-site records revealing the location of Carpenter's cell phone whenever it made or received calls. This sort of digital data—personal location information maintained by a third party—does not fit neatly under existing precedents. Instead, requests for cell-site records lie at the intersection of two lines of cases, both of which inform our understanding of the privacy interests at stake.

The first set of cases addresses a person's expectation of privacy in his physical location and movements. In United States v. Knotts, 460 U.S. 276 (1983), we considered the Government's use of a "beeper" to aid in tracking a vehicle through traffic. Police officers in that case planted a beeper in a container of chloroform before it was purchased by one of Knotts's co-conspirators. The officers (with intermittent aerial assistance) then followed the automobile carrying the container from Minneapolis to Knotts's cabin in Wisconsin, relying on the beeper's signal to help keep the vehicle in view. The Court concluded that the "augment[ed]" visual surveillance did not constitute a search because "[a] person traveling in an automobile on public thoroughfares has no reasonable expectation of privacy in his movements from one place to another." *Id.*, at 281, 282. Since the movements of the vehicle and its final destination had been "voluntarily conveyed to anyone who wanted to look," Knotts could not assert a privacy interest in the information obtained. *Id.*, at 281.

This Court in *Knotts,* however, was careful to distinguish between the rudimentary tracking facilitated by the beeper and more sweeping modes of surveillance. The Court emphasized the "limited use which the government made of the signals from this particular beeper" during a discrete "automotive journey." *Id.*, at 284, 285. Significantly, the Court reserved the question whether "different constitutional principles may be applicable" if "twenty-four hour surveillance of any citizen of this country [were] possible." *Id.*, at 283–284.

Three decades later, the Court considered more sophisticated surveillance of the sort envisioned in *Knotts* and found that different principles did indeed apply. In *United States v. Jones,* FBI agents installed a GPS tracking device on Jones's vehicle and remotely monitored the vehicle's movements for 28 days. The Court decided the case based on the Government's physical trespass of the vehicle. 565 U.S., at 404–405. At the same time, five Justices agreed that related privacy concerns would be raised by, for example, "surreptitiously activating a stolen vehicle detection system" in Jones's car to track Jones himself, or conducting GPS tracking of his cell phone. *Id.*, at 426, 428 (ALITO, J., concurring in judgment); *id.*, at 415 (SOTOMAYOR, J., concurring). Since GPS monitoring of a vehicle tracks "every movement" a person makes in that vehicle, the concurring Justices concluded that "longer term GPS monitoring in investigations of most offenses impinges on expectations of privacy"—regardless whether those movements were disclosed to the public at large. *Id.,* at 430 (opinion of Alito, J.); *id.,* at 415 (opinion of Sotomayor, J.).[2]

In a second set of decisions, the Court has drawn a line between what a person keeps to himself and what he shares with others. We have previously held that "a person has no legitimate expectation of privacy in information he voluntarily turns over to third parties." *Smith,* 442 U.S., at 743–744. That remains true "even if the information is revealed on the assumption that it will be used only for a limited purpose." United States v. Miller, 425 U.S. 435, 443 (1976). As a result, the Government is typically free to obtain such information from the recipient without triggering Fourth Amendment protections.

This third-party doctrine largely traces its roots to *Miller.* While investigating Miller for tax evasion, the Government subpoenaed his banks, seeking several months of canceled checks, deposit slips, and monthly statements. The Court rejected a Fourth Amendment challenge to the records collection. For one, Miller could "assert neither ownership nor possession" of the documents; they were "business records of the banks." *Id.,* at 440. For another, the nature of those records confirmed Miller's limited expectation of privacy, because the checks were "not confidential communications but negotiable instruments to be used in commercial transactions," and the bank statements contained information "exposed to [bank] employees in the ordinary course of business." *Id.,* at 442. The Court thus concluded that Miller had "take[n] the risk, in revealing his affairs to another, that the information [would] be conveyed by that person to the Government." *Id.,* at 443.

Three years later, *Smith* applied the same principles in the context of information conveyed to a telephone company. The Court ruled that the Government's use of a pen register—a device that recorded the outgoing phone numbers dialed on a landline telephone—was not a search. Noting the pen register's "limited capabilities," the Court "doubt[ed] that people in general entertain any actual expectation of privacy in the numbers they dial." 442 U.S., at 7427. Telephone subscribers know, after all, that the numbers are used by the telephone company "for a variety of legitimate business purposes," including routing calls. *Id.,* at 743. And at any rate, the Court explained, such an expectation "is not one that society is prepared to recognize as

---

[2] Justice KENNEDY argues that this case is in a different category from *Jones* and the dragnet-type practices posited in *Knotts* because the disclosure of the cell-site records was subject to "judicial authorization." *Post,* at 2230–2232. That line of argument conflates the threshold question whether a "search" has occurred with the separate matter of whether the search was reasonable. The subpoena process set forth in the Stored Communications Act does not determine a target's expectation of privacy. And in any event, neither *Jones* nor *Knotts* purported to resolve the question of what authorization may be required to conduct such electronic surveillance techniques. *But see Jones,* 565 U.S., at 430 (ALITO, J., concurring in judgment) (indicating that longer term GPS tracking may require a warrant).

reasonable." *Ibid.* (internal quotation marks omitted). When Smith placed a call, he "voluntarily conveyed" the dialed numbers to the phone company by "expos[ing] that information to its equipment in the ordinary course of business." *Id.,* at 744 (internal quotation marks omitted). Once again, we held that the defendant "assumed the risk" that the company's records "would be divulged to police." *Id.,* at 745.

III

The question we confront today is how to apply the Fourth Amendment to a new phenomenon: the ability to chronicle a person's past movements through the record of his cell phone signals. Such tracking partakes of many of the qualities of the GPS monitoring we considered in *Jones.* Much like GPS tracking of a vehicle, cell phone location information is detailed, encyclopedic, and effortlessly compiled.

At the same time, the fact that the individual continuously reveals his location to his wireless carrier implicates the third-party principle of *Smith* and *Miller.* But while the third-party doctrine applies to telephone numbers and bank records, it is not clear whether its logic extends to the qualitatively different category of cell-site records. After all, when *Smith* was decided in 1979, few could have imagined a society in which a phone goes wherever its owner goes, conveying to the wireless carrier not just dialed digits, but a detailed and comprehensive record of the person's movements.

We decline to extend *Smith* and *Miller* to cover these novel circumstances. Given the unique nature of cell phone location records, the fact that the information is held by a third party does not by itself overcome the user's claim to Fourth Amendment protection. Whether the Government employs its own surveillance technology as in *Jones* or leverages the technology of a wireless carrier, we hold that an individual maintains a legitimate expectation of privacy in the record of his physical movements as captured through CSLI. The location information obtained from Carpenter's wireless carriers was the product of a search.[3]

A

A person does not surrender all Fourth Amendment protection by venturing into the public sphere. To the contrary, "what [one] seeks to preserve as private, even in an area accessible to the public, may be constitutionally protected." *Katz,* 389 U.S., at 351–352. A majority of this Court has already recognized that individuals have a reasonable

---

[3] The parties suggest as an alternative to their primary submissions that the acquisition of CSLI becomes a search only if it extends beyond a limited period. *See* Reply Brief 12 (proposing a 24-hour cutoff); Brief for United States 55–56 (suggesting a seven-day cutoff). As part of its argument, the Government treats the seven days of CSLI requested from Sprint as the pertinent period, even though Sprint produced only two days of records. Brief for United States 56. Contrary to Justice KENNEDY's assertion, *post,* at 2233, we need not decide whether there is a limited period for which the Government may obtain an individual's historical CSLI free from Fourth Amendment scrutiny, and if so, how long that period might be. It is sufficient for our purposes today to hold that accessing seven days of CSLI constitutes a Fourth Amendment search.

expectation of privacy in the whole of their physical movements. *Jones,* 565 U.S., at 430 (ALITO, J., concurring in judgment); *id.,* at 415 (SOTOMAYOR, J., concurring). Prior to the digital age, law enforcement might have pursued a suspect for a brief stretch, but doing so "for any extended period of time was difficult and costly and therefore rarely undertaken." *Id.,* at 429 (opinion of Alito, J.). For that reason, "society's expectation has been that law enforcement agents and others would not—and indeed, in the main, simply could not—secretly monitor and catalogue every single movement of an individual's car for a very long period." *Id.,* at 430.

Allowing government access to cell-site records contravenes that expectation. Although such records are generated for commercial purposes, that distinction does not negate Carpenter's anticipation of privacy in his physical location. Mapping a cell phone's location over the course of 127 days provides an all-encompassing record of the holder's whereabouts. As with GPS information, the time-stamped data provides an intimate window into a person's life, revealing not only his particular movements, but through them his "familial, political, professional, religious, and sexual associations." *Id.,* at 415 (opinion of SOTOMAYOR, J.). These location records "hold for many Americans the 'privacies of life.'" *Riley,* 573 U.S., at ___ (quoting *Boyd,* 116 U.S., at 630). And like GPS monitoring, cell phone tracking is remarkably easy, cheap, and efficient compared to traditional investigative tools. With just the click of a button, the Government can access each carrier's deep repository of historical location information at practically no expense.

In fact, historical cell-site records present even greater privacy concerns than the GPS monitoring of a vehicle we considered in *Jones.* Unlike the bugged container in *Knotts* or the car in *Jones,* a cell phone— almost a "feature of human anatomy," *Riley,* 573 U.S., at ___ tracks nearly exactly the movements of its owner. While individuals regularly leave their vehicles, they compulsively carry cell phones with them all the time. A cell phone faithfully follows its owner beyond public thoroughfares and into private residences, doctor's offices, political headquarters, and other potentially revealing locales. *See id.,* at ___ (noting that "nearly three-quarters of smart phone users report being within five feet of their phones most of the time, with 12% admitting that they even use their phones in the shower"); contrast Cardwell v. Lewis, 417 U.S. 583, 590 (1974) (plurality opinion) ("A car has little capacity for escaping public scrutiny."). Accordingly, when the Government tracks the location of a cell phone it achieves near perfect surveillance, as if it had attached an ankle monitor to the phone's user.

Moreover, the retrospective quality of the data here gives police access to a category of information otherwise unknowable. In the past, attempts to reconstruct a person's movements were limited by a dearth of records and the frailties of recollection. With access to CSLI, the Government can now travel back in time to retrace a person's whereabouts, subject only to the retention polices of the wireless carriers, which currently maintain records for up to five years. Critically, because location information is continually logged for all of the 400 million devices in the United States—not just those belonging to persons who might happen to come under investigation—this newfound tracking capacity runs against everyone. Unlike with the GPS device in *Jones,* police need not even know in advance whether they want to follow a particular individual, or when.

Whoever the suspect turns out to be, he has effectively been tailed every moment of every day for five years, and the police may—in the Government's view—call upon the results of that surveillance without regard to the constraints of the Fourth Amendment. Only the few without cell phones could escape this tireless and absolute surveillance.

The Government and Justice KENNEDY contend, however, that the collection of CSLI should be permitted because the data is less precise than GPS information. Not to worry, they maintain, because the location records did "not on their own suffice to place [Carpenter] at the crime scene"; they placed him within a wedge-shaped sector ranging from one-eighth to four square miles. Brief for United States 24; *see post,* at 2232–2233. Yet the Court has already rejected the proposition that "inference insulates a search." *Kyllo,* 533 U.S., at 36. From the 127 days of location data it received, the Government could, in combination with other information, deduce a detailed log of Carpenter's movements, including when he was at the site of the robberies. And the Government thought the CSLI accurate enough to highlight it during the closing argument of his trial. App. 131.

At any rate, the rule the Court adopts "must take account of more sophisticated systems that are already in use or in development." *Kyllo,* 533 U.S., at 36. While the records in this case reflect the state of technology at the start of the decade, the accuracy of CSLI is rapidly approaching GPS-level precision. As the number of cell sites has proliferated, the geographic area covered by each cell sector has shrunk, particularly in urban areas. In addition, with new technology measuring the time and angle of signals hitting their towers, wireless carriers already have the capability to pinpoint a phone's location within 50 meters. Brief for Electronic Frontier Foundation et al. as *Amici Curiae* 12 (describing triangulation methods that estimate a device's location inside a given cell sector).

Accordingly, when the Government accessed CSLI from the wireless carriers, it invaded Carpenter's reasonable expectation of privacy in the whole of his physical movements.

B

The Government's primary contention to the contrary is that the third-party doctrine governs this case. In its view, cell-site records are fair game because they are "business records" created and maintained by the wireless carriers. The Government (along with Justice KENNEDY) recognizes that this case features new technology, but asserts that the legal question nonetheless turns on a garden-variety request for information from a third-party witness. Brief for United States 32–34; *post,* at 2229–2231.

The Government's position fails to contend with the seismic shifts in digital technology that made possible the tracking of not only Carpenter's location but also everyone else's, not for a short period but for years and years. Sprint Corporation and its competitors are not your typical witnesses. Unlike the nosy neighbor who keeps an eye on comings and goings, they are ever alert, and their memory is nearly infallible. There is a world of difference between the limited types of personal information addressed in *Smith* and *Miller* and the exhaustive chronicle of location information casually collected by wireless carriers today. The Government thus is not asking for a straightforward application of the third-party doctrine, but instead a significant extension of it to a distinct category of information. The third-party doctrine partly stems from the notion that an individual has a reduced expectation of privacy in information knowingly shared with another. But the fact of "diminished privacy interests does not mean that the Fourth Amendment falls out of the picture entirely." *Riley,* 573 U.S., at ___. *Smith* and *Miller,* after all, did not rely solely on the act of sharing. Instead, they considered "the nature of the particular documents sought" to determine whether "there is a legitimate 'expectation of privacy' concerning their contents." *Miller,* 425 U.S., at 442. *Smith* pointed out the limited capabilities of a pen register; as explained in *Riley,* telephone call logs reveal little in the way of "identifying information." *Smith,* 442 U.S., at 742; *Riley,* 573 U.S., at ___. *Miller* likewise noted that checks were "not confidential communications but negotiable instruments to be used in commercial transactions." 425 U.S., at 442. In mechanically applying the third-party doctrine to this case, the Government fails to appreciate that there are no comparable limitations on the revealing nature of CSLI.

The Court has in fact already shown special solicitude for location information in the third-party context. In *Knotts,* the Court relied on *Smith* to hold that an individual has no reasonable expectation of privacy in public movements that he "voluntarily conveyed to anyone who wanted to look." *Knotts,* 460 U.S., at 281; *see id.,* at 283 (discussing *Smith*). But when confronted with more pervasive tracking, five Justices agreed that longer term GPS monitoring of even a vehicle traveling on public streets constitutes a search. *Jones,* 565 U.S., at 430 (ALITO, J., concurring in judgment); *id.,* at 415 (SOTOMAYOR, J., concurring). Justice GORSUCH wonders why "someone's location when using a phone" is sensitive, *post,* at 2262, and Justice KENNEDY assumes that a person's discrete movements "are not particularly private," *post,* at 2232. Yet this case is not about "using a phone" or a person's movement at a particular time. It is about a detailed chronicle of a person's physical presence compiled every day, every moment, over several years. Such a chronicle implicates privacy concerns far beyond those considered in *Smith* and *Miller*.

Neither does the second rationale underlying the third-party doctrine—voluntary exposure—hold up when it comes to CSLI. Cell phone location information is not truly "shared" as one normally understands the term. In the first place, cell phones and the services they provide are "such a pervasive and insistent part of daily life" that carrying one is indispensable to participation in modern society. *Riley,* 573 U.S., at ___. Second, a cell phone logs a cell-site record by dint of its operation, without any affirmative act on the part of the user beyond powering up. Virtually any activity on the phone generates CSLI, including incoming calls, texts, or e-mails and countless other data connections that a phone automatically makes when checking for news, weather, or social media updates. Apart from disconnecting the phone from the network, there is no way to avoid leaving behind a trail of location data. As a result, in no meaningful sense does the user voluntarily "assume[ ] the risk" of turning over a comprehensive dossier of his physical movements. *Smith,* 442 U.S., at 745.

We therefore decline to extend *Smith* and *Miller* to the collection of CSLI. Given the unique nature of cell phone location information, the fact that the Government obtained the information from a third party does not overcome Carpenter's claim to Fourth Amendment protection. The Government's acquisition of the cell-site records was a search within the meaning of the Fourth Amendment.

* * *

Our decision today is a narrow one. We do not express a view on matters not before us: real-time CSLI or "tower dumps" (a download of information on all the devices that connected to a particular cell site during a particular interval). We do not disturb the application of *Smith* and *Miller* or call into question conventional surveillance techniques and tools, such as security cameras. Nor do we address other business records that might incidentally reveal location information. Further, our opinion does not consider other collection techniques involving foreign affairs or national security. As Justice Frankfurter noted when considering new innovations in airplanes and radios, the Court must tread carefully in such cases, to ensure that we do not "embarrass the future." *Northwest Airlines, Inc. v. Minnesota,* 322 U.S. 292, 300 (1944).[4]

IV

Having found that the acquisition of Carpenter's CSLI was a search, we also conclude that the Government must generally obtain a warrant

---

[4] Justice GORSUCH faults us for not promulgating a complete code addressing the manifold situations that may be presented by this new technology—under a constitutional provision turning on what is "reasonable," no less. *Post,* at 2266–2268. Like Justice GORSUCH, we "do not begin to claim all the answers today," *post,* at 2268, and therefore decide no more than the case before us.

supported by probable cause before acquiring such records. Although the "ultimate measure of the constitutionality of a governmental search is 'reasonableness,' " our cases establish that warrantless searches are typically unreasonable where "a search is undertaken by law enforcement officials to discover evidence of criminal wrongdoing." *Vernonia School Dist. 47J v. Acton,* 515 U.S. 646, 652–653 (1995). Thus, "[i]n the absence of a warrant, a search is reasonable only if it falls within a specific exception to the warrant requirement." *Riley,* 573 U.S., at ___.

The Government acquired the cell-site records pursuant to a court order issued under the Stored Communications Act, which required the Government to show "reasonable grounds" for believing that the records were "relevant and material to an ongoing investigation." 18 U.S.C. § 2703(d). That showing falls well short of the probable cause required for a warrant. The Court usually requires "some quantum of individualized suspicion" before a search or seizure may take place. *United States v. Martinez-Fuerte,* 428 U.S. 543, 560–561 (1976). Under the standard in the Stored Communications Act, however, law enforcement need only show that the cell-site evidence might be pertinent to an ongoing investigation—a "gigantic" departure from the probable cause rule, as the Government explained below. App. 34. Consequently, an order issued under Section 2703(d) of the Act is not a permissible mechanism for accessing historical cell-site records. Before compelling a wireless carrier to turn over a subscriber's CSLI, the Government's obligation is a familiar one—get a warrant.

Justice ALITO contends that the warrant requirement simply does not apply when the Government acquires records using compulsory process. Unlike an actual search, he says, subpoenas for documents do not involve the direct taking of evidence; they are at most a "constructive search" conducted by the target of the subpoena. *Post,* at 2252–2253. Given this lesser intrusion on personal privacy, Justice ALITO argues that the compulsory production of records is not held to the same probable cause standard. In his view, this Court's precedents set forth a categorical rule—separate and distinct from the third-party doctrine—subjecting subpoenas to lenient scrutiny without regard to the suspect's expectation of privacy in the records. *Post,* at 2250–2257.

But this Court has never held that the Government may subpoena third parties for records in which the suspect has a reasonable expectation of privacy. Almost all of the examples Justice ALITO cites, *see post,* at 2253–2255, contemplated requests for evidence implicating diminished privacy interests or for a corporation's own books.[5] The lone

---

[5] *See United States v. Dionisio,* 410 U.S. 1, 14 (1973) ("No person can have a reasonable expectation that others will not know the sound of his voice"); *Donovan v. Lone Steer, Inc.,* 464 U.S. 408, 411 (1984) (payroll and sales records); *California Bankers Assn. v. Shultz,* 416 U.S. 21, 67 (1974) (Bank Secrecy Act reporting requirements); *See v. Seattle,* 387 U.S. 541, 544 (1967) (financial books and records); *United States v. Powell,* 379 U.S. 48, 49, 57 (1964) (corporate tax records); *McPhaul v. United States,* 364 U.S. 372, 374, 382 (1960) (books and records of an organization); *United States v. Morton Salt Co.,* 338 U.S. 632, 634 (1950) (Federal Trade Commission reporting requirement); *Oklahoma Press Publishing Co. v. Walling,* 327 U.S. 186,

exception, of course, is *Miller,* where the Court's analysis of the third-party subpoena merged with the application of the third-party doctrine. 425 U.S., at 444 (concluding that Miller lacked the necessary privacy interest to contest the issuance of a subpoena to his bank).

Justice ALITO overlooks the critical issue. At some point, the dissent should recognize that CSLI is an entirely different species of business record—something that implicates basic Fourth Amendment concerns about arbitrary government power much more directly than corporate tax or payroll ledgers. When confronting new concerns wrought by digital technology, this Court has been careful not to uncritically extend existing precedents. *See Riley,* 573 U.S., at ___ ("A search of the information on a cell phone bears little resemblance to the type of brief physical search considered [in prior precedents].").

If the choice to proceed by subpoena provided a categorical limitation on Fourth Amendment protection, no type of record would ever be protected by the warrant requirement. Under Justice ALITO's view, private letters, digital contents of a cell phone—any personal information reduced to document form, in fact—may be collected by subpoena for no reason other than "official curiosity." United States v. Morton Salt Co., 338 U.S. 632, 652 (1950). Justice KENNEDY declines to adopt the radical implications of this theory, leaving open the question whether the warrant requirement applies "when the Government obtains the modern-day equivalents of an individual's own 'papers' or 'effects,' even when those papers or effects are held by a third party." *Post,* at 2230 (citing United States v. Warshak, 631 F.3d 266, 283–288 (C.A.6 2010)). That would be a sensible exception, because it would prevent the subpoena doctrine from overcoming any reasonable expectation of privacy. If the third-party doctrine does not apply to the "modern-day equivalents of an individual's own 'papers' or 'effects,'" then the clear implication is that the documents should receive full Fourth Amendment protection. We simply think that such protection should extend as well to a detailed log of a person's movements over several years.

This is certainly not to say that all orders compelling the production of documents will require a showing of probable cause. The Government will be able to use subpoenas to acquire records in the overwhelming majority of investigations. We hold only that a warrant is required in the rare case where the suspect has a legitimate privacy interest in records held by a third party.

Further, even though the Government will generally need a warrant to access CSLI, case-specific exceptions may support a warrantless search of an individual's cell-site records under certain circumstances. "One well-recognized exception applies when " 'the exigencies of the situation" make the needs of law enforcement so compelling that [a]

189, 204–208 1946) (payroll records); Hale v. Henkel, 201 U.S. 43, 45, 75 (1906) (corporate books and papers).

warrantless search is objectively reasonable under the Fourth Amendment.'" Kentucky v. King, 563 U.S. 452, 460 (2011) (quoting Mincey v. Arizona, 437 U.S. 385, 394 (1978)). Such exigencies include the need to pursue a fleeing suspect, protect individuals who are threatened with imminent harm, or prevent the imminent destruction of evidence. 563 U.S., at 460, and n. 3.

As a result, if law enforcement is confronted with an urgent situation, such fact-specific threats will likely justify the warrantless collection of CSLI. Lower courts, for instance, have approved warrantless searches related to bomb threats, active shootings, and child abductions. Our decision today does not call into doubt warrantless access to CSLI in such circumstances. While police must get a warrant when collecting CSLI to assist in the mine-run criminal investigation, the rule we set forth does not limit their ability to respond to an ongoing emergency.

* * *

As Justice Brandeis explained in his famous dissent, the Court is obligated—as "[s]ubtler and more far-reaching means of invading privacy have become available to the Government"—to ensure that the "progress of science" does not erode Fourth Amendment protections. Olmstead v. United States, 277 U.S. 438, 473–474 (1928). Here the progress of science has afforded law enforcement a powerful new tool to carry out its important responsibilities. At the same time, this tool risks Government encroachment of the sort the Framers, "after consulting the lessons of history," drafted the Fourth Amendment to prevent. *Di Re*, 332 U.S., at 595.

We decline to grant the state unrestricted access to a wireless carrier's database of physical location information. In light of the deeply revealing nature of CSLI, its depth, breadth, and comprehensive reach, and the inescapable and automatic nature of its collection, the fact that such information is gathered by a third party does not make it any less deserving of Fourth Amendment protection. The Government's acquisition of the cell-site records here was a search under that Amendment.

The judgment of the Court of Appeals is reversed, and the case is remanded for further proceedings consistent with this opinion.

It is so ordered.

■ JUSTICE KENNEDY, with whom JUSTICE THOMAS and JUSTICE ALITO join, dissenting.

This case involves new technology, but the Court's stark departure from relevant Fourth Amendment precedents and principles is, in my submission, unnecessary and incorrect, requiring this respectful dissent.

The new rule the Court seems to formulate puts needed, reasonable, accepted, lawful, and congressionally authorized criminal investigations at serious risk in serious cases, often when law enforcement seeks to prevent the threat of violent crimes. And it places undue restrictions on the lawful and necessary enforcement powers exercised not only by the Federal Government, but also by law enforcement in every State and locality throughout the Nation. Adherence to this Court's longstanding precedents and analytic framework would have been the proper and prudent way to resolve this case.

The Court has twice held that individuals have no Fourth Amendment interests in business records which are possessed, owned, and controlled by a third party. United States v. Miller, 425 U.S. 435 (1976); Smith v. Maryland, 442 U.S. 735 (1979). This is true even when the records contain personal and sensitive information. So when the Government uses a subpoena to obtain, for example, bank records, telephone records, and credit card statements from the businesses that create and keep these records, the Government does not engage in a search of the business's customers within the meaning of the Fourth Amendment.

In this case petitioner challenges the Government's right to use compulsory process to obtain a now-common kind of business record: cell-site records held by cell phone service providers. The Government acquired the records through an investigative process enacted by Congress. Upon approval by a neutral magistrate, and based on the Government's duty to show reasonable necessity, it authorizes the disclosure of records and information that are under the control and ownership of the cell phone service provider, not its customer. Petitioner acknowledges that the Government may obtain a wide variety of business records using compulsory process, and he does not ask the Court to revisit its precedents. Yet he argues that, under those same precedents, the Government searched his records when it used court-approved compulsory process to obtain the cell-site information at issue here.

Cell-site records, however, are no different from the many other kinds of business records the Government has a lawful right to obtain by compulsory process. Customers like petitioner do not own, possess, control, or use the records, and for that reason have no reasonable expectation that they cannot be disclosed pursuant to lawful compulsory process.

The Court today disagrees. It holds for the first time that by using compulsory process to obtain records of a business entity, the Government has not just engaged in an impermissible action, but has conducted a search of the business's customer. The Court further concludes that the search in this case was unreasonable and the Government needed to get a warrant to obtain more than six days of cell-site records.

In concluding that the Government engaged in a search, the Court unhinges Fourth Amendment doctrine from the property-based concepts that have long grounded the analytic framework that pertains in these cases. In doing so it draws an unprincipled and unworkable line between cell-site records on the one hand and financial and telephonic records on the other. According to today's majority opinion, the Government can acquire a record of every credit card purchase and phone call a person makes over months or years without upsetting a legitimate expectation of privacy. But, in the Court's view, the Government crosses a constitutional line when it obtains a court's approval to issue a subpoena for more than six days of cell-site records in order to determine whether a person was within several hundred city blocks of a crime scene. That distinction is illogical and will frustrate principled application of the Fourth Amendment in many routine yet vital law enforcement operations.

It is true that the Cyber Age has vast potential both to expand and restrict individual freedoms in dimensions not contemplated in earlier times. *See* Packingham v. North Carolina, 582 U.S. ___, ___–___ (2017). For the reasons that follow, however, there is simply no basis here for concluding that the Government interfered with information that the cell phone customer, either from a legal or commonsense standpoint, should have thought the law would deem owned or controlled by him. . . .

. . . And law enforcement officers are not alone in their reliance on subpoenas to obtain business records for legitimate investigations. Subpoenas also are used for investigatory purposes by state and federal grand juries, *See* United States v. Dionisio, 410 U.S. 1 (1973), state and federal administrative agencies, *see Oklahoma Press, supra,* and state and federal legislative bodies, *see* McPhaul v. United States, 364 U.S. 372 (1960).

B

Carpenter does not question these traditional investigative practices. And he does not ask the Court to reconsider *Miller* and *Smith.* Carpenter argues only that, under *Miller* and *Smith,* the Government may not use compulsory process to acquire cell-site records from cell phone service providers.

There is no merit in this argument. Cell-site records, like all the examples just discussed, are created, kept, classified, owned, and controlled by cell phone service providers, which aggregate and sell this information to third parties. As in *Miller,* Carpenter can "assert neither ownership nor possession" of the records and has no control over them. 425 U.S., at 440.

Carpenter argues that he has Fourth Amendment interests in the cell-site records because they are in essence his personal papers by operation of 47 U.S.C. § 222. That statute imposes certain restrictions on how providers may use "customer proprietary network information"—a term that encompasses cell-site records. §§ 222(c), (h)(1)(A). The statute in general prohibits providers from disclosing personally identifiable cell-site records to private third parties. § 222(c)(1). And it allows customers to request cell-site records from the provider. § 222(c)(2).

Carpenter's argument is unpersuasive, however, for § 222 does not grant cell phone customers any meaningful interest in cell-site records. The statute's confidentiality protections may be overridden by the interests of the providers or the Government. The providers may disclose the records "to protect the[ir] rights or property" or to "initiate, render, bill, and collect for telecommunications services." §§ 222(d)(1), (2). They also may disclose the records "as required by law"—which, of course, is how they were disclosed in this case. § 222(c)(1). Nor does the statute provide customers any practical control over the records. Customers do not create the records; they have no say in whether or for how long the records are stored; and they cannot require the records to be modified or destroyed. Even their right to request access to the records is limited, for the statute "does not preclude a carrier from being reimbursed by the customers . . . for the costs associated with making such disclosures." H.R.Rep. No. 104–204, pt. 1, p. 90 (1995). So in every legal and practical sense the "network information" regulated by § 222 is, under that statute, "proprietary" to the service providers, not Carpenter. The Court does not argue otherwise.

Because Carpenter lacks a requisite connection to the cell-site records, he also may not claim a reasonable expectation of privacy in them. He could expect that a third party—the cell phone service provider—could use the information it collected, stored, and classified as its own for a variety of business and commercial purposes.

All this is not to say that *Miller* and *Smith* are without limits. *Miller* and *Smith* may not apply when the Government obtains the modern-day equivalents of an individual's own "papers" or "effects," even when those papers or effects are held by a third party. *See* ex parte Jackson, 96 U.S. 727, 733 (1878) (letters held by mail carrier); United States v. Warshak, 631 F.3d 266, 283–288 (C.A.6 2010) (e-mails held by Internet service provider). As already discussed, however, this case does not involve property or a bailment of that sort. Here the Government's acquisition of cell-site records falls within the heartland of *Miller* and *Smith*.

In fact, Carpenter's Fourth Amendment objection is even weaker than those of the defendants in *Miller* and *Smith*. Here the Government did not use a mere subpoena to obtain the cell-site records. It acquired the records only after it proved to a Magistrate Judge reasonable grounds to believe that the records were relevant and material to an ongoing criminal investigation. *See* 18 U.S.C. § 2703(d). So even if § 222 gave Carpenter some attenuated interest in the records, the Government's conduct here would be reasonable under the standards governing subpoenas. *See Donovan,* 464 U.S., at 415.

Under *Miller* and *Smith,* then, a search of the sort that requires a warrant simply did not occur when the Government used court-approved compulsory process, based on a finding of reasonable necessity, to compel a cell phone service provider, as owner, to disclose cell-site records.

III

The Court rejects a straightforward application of *Miller* and *Smith*. It concludes instead that applying those cases to cell-site records would work a "significant extension" of the principles underlying them, *ante,* at 2219, and holds that the acquisition of more than six days of cell-site records constitutes a search, *ante,* at 2217, n. 3.

In my respectful view the majority opinion misreads this Court's precedents, old and recent, and transforms *Miller* and *Smith* into an unprincipled and unworkable doctrine. The Court's newly conceived constitutional standard will cause confusion; will undermine traditional and important law enforcement practices; and will allow the cell phone to become a protected medium that dangerous persons will use to commit serious crimes.

A

The Court errs at the outset by attempting to sidestep *Miller* and *Smith*. The Court frames this case as following instead from United States v. Knotts, 460 U.S. 276 (1983), and United States v. Jones, 565 U.S. 400 (2012). Those cases, the Court suggests, establish that "individuals have a reasonable expectation of privacy in the whole of their physical movements." *Ante,* at 2214–2216, 2217.

Knotts held just the opposite: "A person traveling in an automobile on public thoroughfares has no reasonable expectation of privacy in his movements from one place to another." 460 U.S., at 281. True, the Court in *Knotts* also suggested that "different constitutional principles may be applicable" to "dragnet-type law enforcement practices." *Id.,* at 284. But by dragnet practices the Court was referring to " 'twenty-four hour surveillance of any citizen of this country . . . without judicial knowledge or supervision.' " *Id.,* at 283.

Those "different constitutional principles" mentioned in *Knotts,* whatever they may be, do not apply in this case. Here the Stored Communications Act requires a neutral judicial officer to confirm in each case that the Government has "reasonable grounds to believe" the cell-site records "are relevant and material to an ongoing criminal investigation." 18 U.S.C. § 2703(d). This judicial check mitigates the Court's concerns about " 'a too permeating police surveillance.' " *Ante,* at 2214 (quoting United States v. Di Re, 332 U.S. 581, 595 (1948)). Here, even more so than in *Knotts,* "reality hardly suggests abuse." 460 U.S., at 284.

The Court's reliance on *Jones* fares no better. In *Jones* the Government installed a GPS tracking device on the defendant's automobile. The Court held the Government searched the automobile because it "physically occupied private property [of the defendant] for the purpose of obtaining information." 565 U.S., at 404. So in *Jones* it was "not necessary to inquire about the target's expectation of privacy in his vehicle's movements." Grady v. North Carolina, 575 U.S. ___, ___ (2015) (per curiam).

Despite that clear delineation of the Court's holding in *Jones,* the Court today declares that *Jones* applied the " 'different constitutional principles' " alluded to in *Knotts* to establish that an individual has an expectation of privacy in the sum of his whereabouts. *Ante,* at 2215, 2217–2218. For that proposition the majority relies on the two concurring opinions in *Jones,* one of which stated that "longer term GPS monitoring in investigations of most offenses impinges on expectations of privacy." 565 U.S., at 430 (ALITO, J., concurring). But *Jones* involved direct governmental surveillance of a defendant's automobile without judicial authorization—specifically, GPS surveillance accurate within 50 to 100 feet. *Id.,* at 402–403. Even assuming that the different constitutional principles mentioned in *Knotts* would apply in a case like *Jones*—a proposition the Court was careful not to announce in *Jones, supra,* at 412–413—those principles are inapplicable here. Cases like this one, where the Government uses court-approved compulsory process to obtain records owned and controlled by a third party, are governed by the two majority opinions in *Miller* and *Smith.*

B

. . . . But suppose the Court were correct to say that *Miller* and *Smith* rest on so imprecise a foundation. Still the Court errs, in my submission, when it concludes that cell-site records implicate greater privacy interests—and thus deserve greater Fourth Amendment protection— than financial records and telephone records.

Indeed, the opposite is true. A person's movements are not particularly private. As the Court recognized in *Knotts,* when the defendant there "traveled over the public streets he voluntarily conveyed to anyone who wanted to look the fact that he was traveling over particular roads in a particular direction, the fact of whatever stops he made, and the fact of his final destination." 460 U.S., at 281–282. Today expectations of privacy in one's location are, if anything, even less reasonable than when the Court decided *Knotts* over 30 years ago. Millions of Americans choose to share their location on a daily basis, whether by using a variety of location-based services on their phones, or by sharing their location with friends and the public at large via social media.

And cell-site records, as already discussed, disclose a person's location only in a general area. The records at issue here, for example, revealed Carpenter's location within an area covering between around a dozen and several hundred city blocks. "Areas of this scale might encompass bridal stores and Bass Pro Shops, gay bars and straight ones, a Methodist church and the local mosque." 819 F.3d 880, 889 (C.A.6 2016). These records could not reveal where Carpenter lives and works, much less his " 'familial, political, professional, religious, and sexual associations.'" *Ante,* at 2217 (quoting *Jones, supra,* at 415 (SOTOMAYOR, J., concurring)).

By contrast, financial records and telephone records do "'revea[l] . . . personal affairs, opinions, habits and associations.'" *Miller,* 425 U.S., at 451 (Brennan, J., dissenting); *see Smith,* 442 U.S., at 751 (Marshall, J., dissenting). What persons purchase and to whom they talk might disclose how much money they make; the political and religious organizations to which they donate; whether they have visited a psychiatrist, plastic surgeon, abortion clinic, or AIDS treatment center; whether they go to gay bars or straight ones; and who are their closest friends and family members. The troves of intimate information the Government can and does obtain using financial records and telephone records dwarfs what can be gathered from cell-site records.

Still, the Court maintains, cell-site records are "unique" because they are "comprehensive" in their reach; allow for retrospective collection; are "easy, cheap, and efficient compared to traditional investigative tools"; and are not exposed to cell phone service providers in a meaningfully voluntary manner. *Ante,* at 2216–2218, 2220, 2223. But many other kinds of business records can be so described. Financial records are of vast scope. Banks and credit card companies keep a comprehensive account of almost every transaction an individual makes on a daily basis. "With just the click of a button, the Government can access each [company's] deep repository of historical [financial] information at practically no expense." *Ante,* at 2218. And the decision whether to transact with banks and credit card companies is no more or less voluntary than the decision whether to use a cell phone. Today, just as when *Miller* was decided, "'it is impossible to participate in the economic life of contemporary society without maintaining a bank account.'" 425 U.S., at 451 (BRENNAN, J., dissenting). But this Court, nevertheless, has held that individuals do not have a reasonable expectation of privacy in financial records.

Perhaps recognizing the difficulty of drawing the constitutional line between cell-site records and financial and telephonic records, the Court posits that the accuracy of cell-site records "is rapidly approaching GPS-level precision." *Ante,* at 2219. That is certainly plausible in the era of cyber technology, yet the privacy interests associated with location information, which is often disclosed to the public at large, still would not outweigh the privacy interests implicated by financial and telephonic records.

Perhaps more important, those future developments are no basis upon which to resolve this case. In general, the Court "risks error by elaborating too fully on the Fourth Amendment implications of emerging technology before its role in society has become clear." Ontario v. Quon, 560 U.S. 746, 759 (2010). That judicial caution, prudent in most cases, is imperative in this one.

Technological changes involving cell phones have complex effects on crime and law enforcement. Cell phones make crimes easier to coordinate and conceal, while also providing the Government with new investigative tools that may have the potential to upset traditional privacy expectations. *See* Kerr, *An Equilibrium-Adjustment Theory of the Fourth Amendment*, 125 Harv. L. Rev 476, 512–517 (2011). How those competing effects balance against each other, and how property norms and expectations of privacy form around new technology, often will be difficult to determine during periods of rapid technological change. In those instances, and where the governing legal standard is one of reasonableness, it is wise to defer to legislative judgments like the one embodied in § 2703(d) of the Stored Communications Act. *See Jones,* 565 U.S., at 430 (ALITO, J., concurring). In § 2703(d) Congress weighed the privacy interests at stake and imposed a judicial check to prevent executive overreach. The Court should be wary of upsetting that legislative balance and erecting constitutional barriers that foreclose further legislative instructions. *See Quon, supra,* at 759. The last thing the Court should do is incorporate an arbitrary and outside limit—in this case six days' worth of cell-site records—and use it as the foundation for a new constitutional framework. The Court's decision runs roughshod over the mechanism Congress put in place to govern the acquisition of cell-site records and closes off further legislative debate on these issues.

C

The Court says its decision is a "narrow one." *Ante,* at 2220. But its reinterpretation of *Miller* and *Smith* will have dramatic consequences for law enforcement, courts, and society as a whole.

Most immediately, the Court's holding that the Government must get a warrant to obtain more than six days of cell-site records limits the effectiveness of an important investigative tool for solving serious crimes. As this case demonstrates, cell-site records are uniquely suited to help the Government develop probable cause to apprehend some of the Nation's most dangerous criminals: serial killers, rapists, arsonists, robbers, and so forth. *See* also, *e.g., Davis,* 785 F.3d, at 500–501 (armed robbers); Brief for Alabama et al. as *Amici Curiae* 21–22 (serial killer). These records often are indispensable at the initial stages of investigations when the Government lacks the evidence necessary to obtain a warrant. *See United States v. Pembrook,* 876 F.3d 812, 816–819 (C.A.6 2017). And the long-term nature of many serious crimes, including serial crimes and terrorism offenses, can necessitate the use of significantly more than six days of cell-site records. The Court's arbitrary 6-day cutoff has the perverse effect of nullifying Congress' reasonable framework for obtaining cell-site records in some of the most serious criminal investigations.

The Court's decision also will have ramifications that extend beyond cell-site records to other kinds of information held by third parties, yet the Court fails "to provide clear guidance to law enforcement" and courts on key issues raised by its reinterpretation of *Miller* and *Smith*. *Riley v. California*, 573 U.S. ___, ___ (2014).

First, the Court's holding is premised on cell-site records being a "distinct category of information" from other business records. *Ante*, at 2219. But the Court does not explain what makes something a distinct category of information. Whether credit card records are distinct from bank records; whether payment records from digital wallet applications are distinct from either; whether the electronic bank records available today are distinct from the paper and microfilm records at issue in *Miller*; or whether cell-phone call records are distinct from the home-phone call records at issue in *Smith*, are just a few of the difficult questions that require answers under the Court's novel conception of *Miller* and *Smith*.

Second, the majority opinion gives courts and law enforcement officers no indication how to determine whether any particular category of information falls on the financial-records side or the cell-site-records side of its newly conceived constitutional line. The Court's multifactor analysis—considering intimacy, comprehensiveness, expense, retrospectivity, and voluntariness—puts the law on a new and unstable foundation.

Third, even if a distinct category of information is deemed to be more like cell-site records than financial records, courts and law enforcement officers will have to guess how much of that information can be requested before a warrant is required. The Court suggests that less than seven days of location information may not require a warrant. *See ante*, at 2217, n. 3; *see* also *ante*, at 2220–2221 (expressing no opinion on "real-time CSLI," tower dumps, and security-camera footage). But the Court does not explain why that is so, and nothing in its opinion even alludes to the considerations that should determine whether greater or lesser thresholds should apply to information like IP addresses or website browsing history.

Fourth, by invalidating the Government's use of court-approved compulsory process in this case, the Court calls into question the subpoena practices of federal and state grand juries, legislatures, and other investigative bodies, as Justice ALITO's opinion explains. *See post*, at 2247–2257 (dissenting opinion). Yet the Court fails even to mention the serious consequences this will have for the proper administration of justice.

In short, the Court's new and uncharted course will inhibit law enforcement and "keep defendants and judges guessing for years to come." *Riley*, 573 U.S., at ___ (internal quotation marks omitted).

* * *

This case should be resolved by interpreting accepted property principles as the baseline for reasonable expectations of privacy. Here the Government did not search anything over which Carpenter could assert ownership or control. Instead, it issued a court-authorized subpoena to a third party to disclose information it alone owned and controlled. That should suffice to resolve this case.

Having concluded, however, that the Government searched Carpenter when it obtained cell-site records from his cell phone service providers, the proper resolution of this case should have been to remand for the Court of Appeals to determine in the first instance whether the search was reasonable. Most courts of appeals, believing themselves bound by *Miller* and *Smith,* have not grappled with this question. And the Court's reflexive imposition of the warrant requirement obscures important and difficult issues, such as the scope of Congress' power to authorize the Government to collect new forms of information using processes that deviate from traditional warrant procedures, and how the Fourth Amendment's reasonableness requirement should apply when the Government uses compulsory process instead of engaging in an actual, physical search.

These reasons all lead to this respectful dissent.

APPENDIX

"(d) REQUIREMENTS FOR COURT ORDER.—A court order for disclosure under subsection (b) or (c) may be issued by any court that is a court of competent jurisdiction and shall issue only if the governmental entity offers specific and articulable facts showing that there are reasonable grounds to believe that the contents of a wire or electronic communication, or the records or other information sought, are relevant and material to an ongoing criminal investigation. In the case of a State governmental authority, such a court order shall not issue if prohibited by the law of such State. A court issuing an order pursuant to this section, on a motion made promptly by the service provider, may quash or modify such order, if the information or records requested are unusually voluminous in nature or compliance with such order otherwise would cause an undue burden on such provider."

■ JUSTICE THOMAS, dissenting.

This case should not turn on "whether" a search occurred. *Ante,* at 2223–2224. It should turn, instead, on *whose* property was searched. The Fourth Amendment guarantees individuals the right to be secure from unreasonable searches of "*their* persons, houses, papers, and effects." (Emphasis added.) In other words, "*each* person has the right to be secure against unreasonable searches . . . in *his own* person, house, papers, and effects." Minnesota v. Carter, 525 U.S. 83, 92 (1998) (Scalia, J., concurring). By obtaining the cell-site records of MetroPCS and Sprint, the Government did not search Carpenter's property. He did not create the records, he does not maintain them, he cannot control them, and he cannot destroy them. Neither the terms of his contracts nor any provision of law makes the records his. The records belong to MetroPCS and Sprint.

The Court concludes that, although the records are not Carpenter's, the Government must get a warrant because Carpenter had a reasonable "expectation of privacy" in the location information that they reveal. *Ante,* at 2216–2217. I agree with Justice KENNEDY, Justice ALITO, Justice GORSUCH, and every Court of Appeals to consider the question that this is not the best reading of our precedents.

The more fundamental problem with the Court's opinion, however, is its use of the "reasonable expectation of privacy" test, which was first articulated by Justice Harlan in Katz v. United States, 389 U.S. 347, 360–361 (1967) (concurring opinion). The *Katz* test has no basis in the text or history of the Fourth Amendment. And, it invites courts to make judgments about policy, not law. Until we confront the problems with this test, *Katz* will continue to distort Fourth Amendment jurisprudence. I respectfully dissent.

II

Under the *Katz* test, a "search" occurs whenever "government officers violate a person's 'reasonable expectation of privacy.'" *Jones, supra,* at 406. The most glaring problem with this test is that it has "no plausible foundation in the text of the Fourth Amendment." *Carter,* 525 U.S., at 97 (opinion of Scalia, J.). The Fourth Amendment, as relevant here, protects "[t]he right of the people to be secure in their persons, houses, papers, and effects, against unreasonable searches." By defining "search" to mean "any violation of a reasonable expectation of privacy," the *Katz* test misconstrues virtually every one of these words.

A

The *Katz* test distorts the original meaning of "searc[h]"—the word in the Fourth Amendment that it purports to define, *see ante,* at 2213–2214; *Smith, supra.* Under the *Katz* test, the government conducts a search anytime it violates someone's "reasonable expectation of privacy." That is not a normal definition of the word "search."

At the founding, "search" did not mean a violation of someone's reasonable expectation of privacy. The word was probably not a term of art, as it does not appear in legal dictionaries from the era. And its ordinary meaning was the same as it is today: " '[t]o look over or through for the purpose of finding something; to explore; to examine by inspection; as, to *search* the house for a book; to *search* the wood for a thief.' " Kyllo v. United States, 533 U.S. 27, 32, n. 1 (2001) (quoting N. Webster, An American Dictionary of the English Language 66 (1828) (reprint 6th ed. 1989)); accord, 2 S. Johnson, A Dictionary of the English Language (5th ed. 1773) ("Inquiry by looking into every suspected place"); N. Bailey, An Universal Etymological English Dictionary (22d ed. 1770) ("a seeking after, a looking for, & c."); 2 J. Ash, The New and Complete Dictionary of the English Language (2d ed. 1795) ("An enquiry, an examination, the act of seeking, an enquiry by looking into every suspected place; a quest; a pursuit"); T. Sheridan, A Complete Dictionary of the English Language (6th ed. 1796) (similar). The word "search" was not associated with "reasonable expectation of privacy" until Justice Harlan coined that phrase in 1967. The phrase "expectation(s) of privacy" does not appear in the pre-*Katz* federal or state case reporters, the papers of prominent Founders, early congressional documents and debates, collections of early American English texts, or early American newspapers.

B

The *Katz* test strays even further from the text by focusing on the concept of "privacy." The word "privacy" does not appear in the Fourth Amendment (or anywhere else in the Constitution for that matter). Instead, the Fourth Amendment references "[t]he right of the people to be secure." It then qualifies that right by limiting it to "persons" and three specific types of property: "houses, papers, and effects." By connecting the right to be secure to these four specific objects, "[t]he text of the Fourth Amendment reflects its close connection to property." *Jones, supra,* at 405. "[P]rivacy," by contrast, "was not part of the political vocabulary of the [founding]. Instead, liberty and privacy rights were understood largely in terms of property rights." Cloud, *Property Is Privacy: Locke and Brandeis in the Twenty-First Century,* 55 Am. Crim. L. Rev. 37, 42 (2018).

Of course, the founding generation understood that, by securing their property, the Fourth Amendment would often protect their privacy as well. *See, e.g., Boyd, supra,* at 630 (explaining that searches of houses invade "the privacies of life"); Wilkes v. Wood, 19 How. St. Tr. 1153, 1154 (C.P. 1763) (argument of counsel contending that seizures of papers implicate "our most private concerns"). But the Fourth Amendment's attendant protection of privacy does not justify *Katz*'s elevation of privacy as the *sine qua non* of the Amendment. *See* T. Clancy, The Fourth Amendment: Its History and Interpretation § 3.4.4, p. 78 (2008) ("[The *Katz* test] confuse[s] the reasons for exercising the protected right with the right itself. A purpose of exercising one's Fourth Amendment rights might be the desire for privacy, but the individual's motivation is not the right protected"); cf. *United States v. Gonzalez-Lopez,* 548 U.S. 140, 145 (2006) (rejecting "a line of reasoning that 'abstracts from the right to its purposes, and then eliminates the right' "). As the majority opinion in *Katz* recognized, the Fourth Amendment "cannot be translated into a general constitutional 'right to privacy,' " as its protections "often have nothing to do with privacy at all." 389 U.S., at 350. Justice Harlan's focus on privacy in his concurrence—an opinion that was issued between Griswold v. Connecticut, 381 U.S. 479 (1965), and Roe v. Wade, 410 U.S. 113 (1973)—reflects privacy's status as the organizing constitutional idea of the 1960's and 1970's. The organizing constitutional idea of the founding era, by contrast, was property. . . .

C

In shifting the focus of the Fourth Amendment from property to privacy, the *Katz* test also reads the words "persons, houses, papers, and effects" out of the text. At its broadest formulation, the *Katz* test would find a search "*wherever* an individual may harbor a reasonable 'expectation of privacy.'" *Terry,* 392 U.S., at 9 (emphasis added). The Court today, for example, does not ask whether cell-site location records are "persons, houses, papers, [or] effects" within the meaning of the Fourth Amendment.[8] Yet "persons, houses, papers, and effects" cannot mean "anywhere" or "anything." *Katz*'s catchphrase that "the Fourth Amendment protects people, not places," is not a serious attempt to reconcile the constitutional text. *See Carter,* 525 U.S., at 98, n. 3 (opinion of Scalia, J.). The Fourth Amendment obviously protects people; "[t]he question . . . is what protection it affords to those people." *Katz,* 389 U.S., at 361 (Harlan, J., concurring). The Founders decided to protect the people from unreasonable searches and seizures of four specific things— persons, houses, papers, and effects. They identified those four categories as "the objects of privacy protection to which the *Constitution* would extend, leaving further expansion to the good judgment . . . of the people through their representatives in the legislature." *Carter, supra,* at 97–98 (opinion of Scalia, J.).

This limiting language was important to the founders. Madison's first draft of the Fourth Amendment used a different phrase: "their persons, their houses, their papers, and their *other property*." 1 Annals of Cong. 452 (1789) (emphasis added). In one of the few changes made to Madison's draft, the House Committee of Eleven changed "other property" to "effects." *See* House Committee of Eleven Report (July 28, 1789), in N. Cogan, The Complete Bill of Rights 334 (2d ed. 2015). This change might have narrowed the Fourth Amendment by clarifying that it does not protect real property (other than houses). *See* Oliver v. United States, 466 U.S. 170, 177, and n. 7 (1984); Davies, *Recovering the Original Fourth Amendment,* 98 Mich. L. Rev. 547, 709–714 (1999) (Davies). Or the change might have broadened the Fourth Amendment by clarifying that it protects commercial goods, not just personal possessions. *See* Donahue at 1301. Or it might have done both. Whatever its ultimate effect, the change reveals that the Founders understood the phrase "persons, houses, papers, and effects" to be an important measure of the Fourth Amendment's overall scope. *See* Davies 710. The *Katz* test, however, displaces and renders that phrase entirely "superfluous." *Jones,* 565 U.S., at 405. . . .

III

That the *Katz* test departs so far from the text of the Fourth Amendment is reason enough to reject it. But the *Katz* test also has proved unworkable in practice. Jurists and commentators tasked with deciphering our jurisprudence have described the *Katz* regime as "an unpredictable jumble," "a mass of contradictions and obscurities," "all

---

[8]　The answer to that question is not obvious. Cell-site location records are business records that mechanically collect the interactions between a person's cell phone and the company's towers; they are not private papers and do not reveal the contents of any communications. Cf. Schnapper, *Unreasonable Searches and Seizures of Papers,* 71 Va. L. Rev. 869, 923–924 (1985) (explaining that business records that do not reveal "personal or speech-related confidences" might not satisfy the original meaning of "papers").

over the map," "riddled with inconsistency and incoherence," "a series of inconsistent and bizarre results that [the Court] has left entirely undefended," "unstable," "chameleon-like," " 'notoriously unhelpful,' " "a conclusion rather than a starting point for analysis," "distressingly unmanageable," "a dismal failure," "flawed to the core," "unadorned fiat," and "inspired by the kind of logic that produced Rube Goldberg's bizarre contraptions."[10] Even Justice Harlan, four years after penning his concurrence in *Katz,* confessed that the test encouraged "the substitution of words for analysis." *United States v. White,* 401 U.S. 745, 786 (1971) (dissenting opinion).

After 50 years, it is still unclear what question the *Katz* test is even asking. This Court has steadfastly declined to elaborate the relevant considerations or identify any meaningful constraints. *See, e.g., ante,* at 2213–2214 ("[N]o single rubric definitively resolves which expectations of privacy are entitled to protection"); O'Connor v. Ortega, 480 U.S. 709, 715 (1987) (plurality opinion) ("We have no talisman that determines in all cases those privacy expectations that society is prepared to accept as reasonable"); *Oliver,* 466 U.S., at 177 ("No single factor determines whether an individual legitimately may claim under the Fourth Amendment that a place should be free of government intrusion").

Justice Harlan's original formulation of the *Katz* test appears to ask a descriptive question: Whether a given expectation of privacy is "one that society is prepared to recognize as 'reasonable.' " 389 U.S., at 361. As written, the *Katz* test turns on society's actual, current views about the reasonableness of various expectations of privacy.

But this descriptive understanding presents several problems. For starters, it is easily circumvented. If, for example, "the Government were suddenly to announce on nationwide television that all homes henceforth would be subject to warrantless entry," individuals could not realistically expect privacy in their homes. *Smith,* 442 U.S., at 740, n. 5; *see also* Chemerinsky, *Rediscovering Brandeis's Right to Privacy,* 45 Brandeis L.J. 643, 650 (2007*)* ("[Under *Katz,* t]he government seemingly can deny privacy just by letting people know in advance not to expect any"). A purely descriptive understanding of the *Katz* test also risks

---

[10] Kugler & Strahilevitz, *Actual Expectations of Privacy, Fourth Amendment Doctrine, and the Mosaic Theory,* 2015 S.Ct. Rev. 205, 261; Bradley, *Two Models of the Fourth Amendment,* 83 Mich. L. Rev. 1468 (1985); Kerr, *Four Models of Fourth Amendment Protection,* 60 Stan. L. Rev. 503, 505 (2007); Solove, *Fourth Amendment Pragmatism,* 51 Boston College L. Rev. 1511 (2010); Wasserstom & Seidman, *The Fourth Amendment as Constitutional Theory,* 77 Geo. L.J. 19, 29 (1988); Colb, *What Is a Search? Two Conceptual Flaws in Fourth Amendment Doctrine and Some Hints of a Remedy,* 55 Stan. L. Rev. 119, 122 (2002); Clancy, The Fourth Amendment: Its History and Interpretation § 3.3.4, p. 65 (2008); Minnesota v. Carter, 525 U.S. 83, 97 (1998) (Scalia, J., dissenting); State v. Campbell, 306 Ore. 157, 164, 759 P.2d 1040, 1044 (1988); Wilkins, *Defining the "Reasonable Expectation of Privacy": an Emerging Tripartite Analysis,* 40 Vand. L. Rev. 1077, 1107 (1987); Yeager, *Search, Seizure and the Positive Law: Expectations of Privacy Outside the Fourth Amendment,* 84 J.Crim. L. & C. 249, 251 (1993); Thomas, *Time Travel, Hovercrafts, and the Framers: James Madison Sees the Future and Rewrites the Fourth Amendment,* 80 Notre Dame L. Rev. 1451, 1500 (2005); Rakas v. Illinois, 439 U.S. 128, 165 (1978) (White, J., dissenting); Cloud, *Rube Goldberg Meets the Constitution: The Supreme Court, Technology, and the Fourth Amendment,* 72 Miss. L.J. 5, 7 (2002).

"circular[ity]." *Kyllo,* 533 U.S., at 34. While this Court is supposed to base its decisions on society's expectations of privacy, society's expectations of privacy are, in turn, shaped by this Court's decisions. *See* Posner, *The Uncertain Protection of Privacy by the Supreme Court,* 1979 S.Ct. Rev. 173, 188 ("[W]hether [a person] will or will not have [a reasonable] expectation [of privacy] will depend on what the legal rule is").

To address this circularity problem, the Court has insisted that expectations of privacy must come from outside its Fourth Amendment precedents, "either by reference to concepts of real or personal property law or to understandings that are recognized and permitted by society." *Rakas v. Illinois,* 439 U.S. 128, 144, n. 12 (1978). But the Court's supposed reliance on "real or personal property law" rings hollow. The whole point of *Katz* was to " 'discredi[t]' " the relationship between the Fourth Amendment and property law, 389 U.S., at 353, and this Court has repeatedly downplayed the importance of property law under the *Katz* test, see, *e.g.,* United States v. Salvucci, 448 U.S. 83, 91 (1980) ("[P]roperty rights are neither the beginning nor the end of this Court's inquiry [under *Katz*]"); Rawlings v. Kentucky, 448 U.S. 98, 105 (1980) ("[This Court has] emphatically rejected the notion that 'arcane' concepts of property law ought to control the ability to claim the protections of the Fourth Amendment"). Today, for example, the Court makes no mention of property law, except to reject its relevance. *See ante,* at 2214, and n. 1.

As for "understandings that are recognized or permitted in society," this Court has never answered even the most basic questions about what this means. *See* Kerr, *Four Models of Fourth Amendment Protection,* 60 Stan. L. Rev. 503, 504–505 (2007). For example, our precedents do not explain who is included in "society," how we know what they "recogniz[e] or permi[t]," and how much of society must agree before something constitutes an "understanding."

Here, for example, society might prefer a balanced regime that prohibits the Government from obtaining cell-site location information unless it can persuade a neutral magistrate that the information bears on an ongoing criminal investigation. That is precisely the regime Congress created under the Stored Communications Act and Telecommunications Act. *See* 47 U.S.C. § 222(c)(1); 18 U.S.C. §§ 2703(c)(1)(B), (d). With no sense of irony, the Court invalidates this regime today—the one that society actually created "in the form of its elected representatives in Congress." 819 F.3d 880, 890 (2016).

Truth be told, this Court does not treat the *Katz* test as a descriptive inquiry. Although the *Katz* test is phrased in descriptive terms about society's views, this Court treats it like a normative question—whether a particular practice *should* be considered a search under the Fourth Amendment. Justice Harlan thought this was the best way to understand his test. *See White,* 401 U.S., at 786 (dissenting opinion) (explaining that courts must assess the "desirability" of privacy expectations and ask whether courts "should" recognize them by "balanc[ing]" the "impact on the individual's sense of security . . . against the utility of the conduct as a technique of law enforcement"). And a normative understanding is the only way to make sense of this Court's precedents, which bear the hallmarks of subjective policymaking instead of neutral legal decisionmaking. "[T]he only thing the past three decades have established about the *Katz* test" is that society's expectations of privacy "bear an uncanny resemblance to those expectations of privacy that this Court considers reasonable." *Carter,* 525 U.S., at 97 (opinion of Scalia, J.). Yet, "[t]hough we know ourselves to be eminently reasonable, self-awareness of eminent reasonableness is not really a substitute for democratic election." Sosa v. Alvarez-Machain, 542 U.S. 692, 750 (2004) (Scalia, J., concurring in part and concurring in judgment). . . .

Because the *Katz* test is a failed experiment, this Court is dutybound to reconsider it. Until it does, I agree with my dissenting colleagues' reading of our precedents. Accordingly, I respectfully dissent.

■ JUSTICE ALITO, with whom JUSTICE THOMAS joins, dissenting.

I share the Court's concern about the effect of new technology on personal privacy, but I fear that today's decision will do far more harm than good. The Court's reasoning fractures two fundamental pillars of Fourth Amendment law, and in doing so, it guarantees a blizzard of litigation while threatening many legitimate and valuable investigative practices upon which law enforcement has rightfully come to rely.

First, the Court ignores the basic distinction between an actual search (dispatching law enforcement officers to enter private premises and root through private papers and effects) and an order merely requiring a party to look through its own records and produce specified documents. The former, which intrudes on personal privacy far more deeply, requires probable cause; the latter does not. Treating an order to produce like an actual search, as today's decision does, is revolutionary. It violates both the original understanding of the Fourth Amendment and more than a century of Supreme Court precedent. Unless it is somehow restricted to the particular situation in the present case, the Court's move will cause upheaval. Must every grand jury subpoena *duces tecum* be supported by probable cause? If so, investigations of terrorism, political corruption, white-collar crime, and many other offenses will be stymied. And what about subpoenas and other document-production orders issued by administrative agencies? See, *e.g.,* 15 U.S.C. § 57b–1(c) (Federal Trade Commission); §§ 77s(c), 78u(a)–(b) (Securities and Exchange Commission); 29 U.S.C. § 657(b) (Occupational Safety and Health Administration); 29 C.F.R. § 1601.16(a)(2) (2017) (Equal Employment Opportunity Commission).

Second, the Court allows a defendant to object to the search of a third party's property. This also is revolutionary. The Fourth Amendment protects "[t]he right of the people to be secure in *their* persons, houses, papers, and effects" (emphasis added), not the persons, houses, papers, and effects of others. Until today, we have been careful to heed this fundamental feature of the Amendment's text. This was true when the Fourth Amendment was tied to property law, and it remained true after Katz v. United States, 389 U.S. 347 (1967), broadened the Amendment's reach.

By departing dramatically from these fundamental principles, the Court destabilizes long-established Fourth Amendment doctrine. We will be making repairs—or picking up the pieces—for a long time to come.

I

Today the majority holds that a court order requiring the production of cell-site records may be issued only after the Government demonstrates probable cause. *See ante,* at 2220–2221. That is a serious and consequential mistake. The Court's holding is based on the premise that the order issued in this case was an actual "search" within the meaning of the Fourth Amendment, but that premise is inconsistent with the original meaning of the Fourth Amendment and with more than a century of precedent.

A

The order in this case was the functional equivalent of a subpoena for documents, and there is no evidence that these writs were regarded as "searches" at the time of the founding. Subpoenas *duces tecum* and other forms of compulsory document production were well known to the founding generation. Blackstone dated the first writ of subpoena to the reign of King Richard II in the late 14th century, and by the end of the 15th century, the use of such writs had "become the daily practice of the [Chancery] court." 3 W. Blackstone, Commentaries on the Laws of England 53 (G. Tucker ed. 1803) (Blackstone). Over the next 200 years, subpoenas would grow in prominence and power in tandem with the Court of Chancery, and by the end of Charles II's reign in 1685, two important innovations had occurred.

First, the Court of Chancery developed a new species of subpoena. Until this point, subpoenas had been used largely to compel attendance and oral testimony from witnesses; these subpoenas correspond to today's subpoenas *ad testificandum.* But the Court of Chancery also improvised a new version of the writ that tacked onto a regular subpoena an order compelling the witness to bring certain items with him. By issuing these so-called subpoenas *duces tecum,* the Court of Chancery could compel the production of papers, books, and other forms of physical evidence, whether from the parties to the case or from third parties. Such subpoenas were sufficiently commonplace by 1623 that a leading treatise on the practice of law could refer in passing to the fee for a *"Sub poena of Ducas tecum"* (seven shillings and two pence) without needing to elaborate further. T. Powell, The Attourneys Academy 79 (1623). Subpoenas *duces tecum* would swell in use over the next century as the rules for their application became ever more developed and definite. *See, e.g.,* 1 G. Jacob, The Compleat Chancery-Practiser 290 (1730) ("The

Subpoena duces tecum is awarded when the Defendant has confessed by his Answer that he hath such Writings in his Hands as are prayed by the Bill to be discovered or brought into Court").

Second, although this new species of subpoena had its origins in the Court of Chancery, it soon made an appearance in the work of the common-law courts as well. One court later reported that "[t]he Courts of Common law . . . employed the same or similar means . . . from the time of Charles the Second at least." Amey v. Long, 9 East. 473, 484, 103 Eng. Rep. 653, 658 (K.B. 1808).

By the time Blackstone published his Commentaries on the Laws of England in the 1760's, the use of subpoenas *duces tecum* had bled over substantially from the courts of equity to the common-law courts. Admittedly, the transition was still incomplete: In the context of jury trials, for example, Blackstone complained about "the want of a compulsive power for the production of books and papers belonging to the parties." Blackstone 381; *see also, e.g., Entick v. Carrington,* 19 State Trials 1029, 1073 (K.B. 1765) ("I wish some cases had been shewn, where the law forceth evidence out of the owner's custody by process. [But] where the adversary has by force or fraud got possession of your own proper evidence, there is no way to get it back but by action"). But Blackstone found some comfort in the fact that at least those documents "[i]n the hands of third persons . . . can generally be obtained by rule of court, or by adding a clause of requisition to the writ of *subpoena,* which is then called a *subpoena duces tecum.*" Blackstone 381; *see also, e.g.,* Leeds v. Cook, 4 Esp. 256, 257, 170 Eng. Rep. 711 (N.P. 1803) (third-party subpoena *duces tecum*); Rex v. Babb, 3 T.R. 579, 580, 100 Eng. Rep. 743, 744 (K.B. 1790) (third-party document production). One of the primary questions outstanding, then, was whether common-law courts would remedy the "defect[s]" identified by the Commentaries, and allow parties to use subpoenas *duces tecum* not only with respect to third parties but also with respect to each other. Blackstone 381.

That question soon found an affirmative answer on both sides of the Atlantic. In the United States, the First Congress established the federal court system in the Judiciary Act of 1789. As part of that Act, Congress authorized "all the said courts of the United States . . . in the trial of actions at law, on motion and due notice thereof being given, to require the parties to produce books or writings in their possession or power, which contain evidence pertinent to the issue, in cases and under circumstances where they might be compelled to produce the same by the ordinary rules of proceeding in chancery." § 15, 1 Stat. 82. From that point forward, federal courts in the United States could compel the production of documents regardless of whether those documents were held by parties to the case or by third parties.

In Great Britain, too, it was soon definitively established that common-law courts, like their counterparts in equity, could subpoena documents held either by parties to the case or by third parties. After proceeding in fits and starts, the King's Bench eventually held in *Amey v. Long* that the "writ of subpoena duces tecum [is] a writ of compulsory obligation and effect in the law." 9 East., at 486, 103 Eng. Rep., at 658. Writing for a unanimous court, Lord Chief Justice Ellenborough explained that "[t]he right to resort to means competent to compel the production of written, as well as oral, testimony seems essential to the very existence and constitution of a Court of Common Law." *Id.*, at 484, 103 Eng. Rep., at 658. Without the power to issue subpoenas *duces tecum*, the Lord Chief Justice observed, common-law courts "could not possibly proceed with due effect." *Ibid.*

The prevalence of subpoenas *duces tecum* at the time of the founding was not limited to the civil context. In criminal cases, courts and prosecutors were also using the writ to compel the production of necessary documents. In Rex v. Dixon, 3 Burr. 1687, 97 Eng. Rep. 1047 (K.B. 1765), for example, the King's Bench considered the propriety of a subpoena *duces tecum* served on an attorney named Samuel Dixon. Dixon had been called "to give evidence before the grand jury of the county of Northampton" and specifically "to produce three vouchers . . . in order to found a prosecution by way of indictment against [his client] Peach . . . for forgery." *Id.*, at 1687, 97 Eng. Rep., at 1047–1048. Although the court ultimately held that Dixon had not needed to produce the vouchers on account of attorney-client privilege, none of the justices expressed the slightest doubt about the general propriety of subpoenas *duces tecum* in the criminal context. *See id.*, at 1688, 97 Eng. Rep., at 1048. As Lord Chief Justice Ellenborough later explained, "[i]n that case no objection was taken to the writ, but to the special circumstances under which the party possessed the papers; so that the Court may be considered as recognizing the general obligation to obey writs of that description in other cases." *Amey, supra*, at 485, 103 Eng. Rep., at 658; *See also* 4 J. Chitty, Practical Treatise on the Criminal Law 185 (1816) (template for criminal subpoena *duces tecum*).

As *Dixon* shows, subpoenas *duces tecum* were routine in part because of their close association with grand juries. Early American colonists imported the grand jury, like so many other common-law traditions, and they quickly flourished. *See* United States v. Calandra, 414 U.S. 338, 342–343 (1974). Grand juries were empaneled by the federal courts almost as soon as the latter were established, and both they and their state counterparts actively exercised their wide-ranging common-law authority. *See* R. Younger, The People's Panel 47–55 (1963). Indeed, "the Founders thought the grand jury so essential . . . that they provided in the Fifth Amendment that federal prosecution for serious crimes can only be instituted by 'a presentment or indictment of a Grand Jury.' " *Calandra, supra*, at 343.

Given the popularity and prevalence of grand juries at the time, the Founders must have been intimately familiar with the tools they used— including compulsory process—to accomplish their work. As a matter of tradition, grand juries were "accorded wide latitude to inquire into violations of criminal law," including the power to "compel the production of evidence or the testimony of witnesses as [they] conside[r] appropriate." *Ibid.* Long before national independence was achieved, grand juries were already using their broad inquisitorial powers not only to present and indict criminal suspects but also to inspect public buildings, to levy taxes, to supervise the administration of the laws, to advance municipal reforms such as street repair and bridge maintenance, and in some cases even to propose legislation. Younger, *supra,* at 5–26. Of course, such work depended entirely on grand juries' ability to access any relevant documents.

Grand juries continued to exercise these broad inquisitorial powers up through the time of the founding. *See* Blair v. United States, 250 U.S. 273, 280 (1919) ("At the foundation of our Federal Government the inquisitorial function of the grand jury and the compulsion of witnesses were recognized as incidents of the judicial power"). In a series of lectures delivered in the early 1790's, Justice James Wilson crowed that grand juries were "the peculiar boast of the common law" thanks in part to their wide-ranging authority: "All the operations of government, and of its ministers and officers, are within the compass of their view and research." 2 J. Wilson, The Works of James Wilson 534, 537 (R. McCloskey ed. 1967). That reflected the broader insight that "[t]he grand jury's investigative power must be broad if its public responsibility is adequately to be discharged." *Calandra, supra,* at 344.

Compulsory process was also familiar to the founding generation in part because it reflected "the ancient proposition of law" that " ' "the public . . . has a right to every man's evidence." ' " United States v. Nixon, 418 U.S. 683, 709 (1974); *see also ante,* at 2228 (KENNEDY, J., dissenting). As early as 1612, "Lord Bacon is reported to have declared that 'all subjects, without distinction of degrees, owe to the King tribute and service, not only of their deed and hand, but of their knowledge and discovery.' " *Blair, supra,* at 279–280. That duty could be "onerous at times," yet the Founders considered it "necessary to the administration of justice according to the forms and modes established in our system of government." *Id.,* at 281. *See also Calandra, supra,* at 345.

B

Talk of kings and common-law writs may seem out of place in a case about cell-site records and the protections afforded by the Fourth Amendment in the modern age. But this history matters, not least because it tells us what was on the minds of those who ratified the Fourth Amendment and how they understood its scope. That history makes it abundantly clear that the Fourth Amendment, as originally understood, did not apply to the compulsory production of documents at all.

The Fourth Amendment does not regulate all methods by which the Government obtains documents. Rather, it prohibits only those "searches and seizures" of "persons, houses, papers, and effects" that are "unreasonable." Consistent with that language, "at least until the latter half of the 20th century" "our Fourth Amendment jurisprudence was tied to common-law trespass." United States v. Jones, 565 U.S. 400, 405 (2012). So by its terms, the Fourth Amendment does not apply to the compulsory production of documents, a practice that involves neither any physical intrusion into private space nor any taking of property by agents of the state. Even Justice Brandeis—a stalwart proponent of construing the Fourth Amendment liberally—acknowledged that "under any ordinary construction of language," "there is no 'search' or 'seizure' when a defendant is required to produce a document in the orderly process of a court's procedure." Olmstead v. United States, 277 U.S. 438, 476 (1928) (dissenting opinion).[1]

Nor is there any reason to believe that the Founders intended the Fourth Amendment to regulate courts' use of compulsory process. American colonists rebelled against the Crown's physical invasions of their persons and their property, not against its acquisition of information by any and all means. As Justice Black once put it, "[t]he Fourth Amendment was aimed directly at the abhorred practice of breaking in, ransacking and searching homes and other buildings and seizing people's personal belongings without warrants issued by magistrates." *Katz,* 389 U.S., at 367 (dissenting opinion). More recently, we have acknowledged that "the Fourth Amendment was the founding generation's response to the reviled 'general warrants' and 'writs of assistance' of the colonial era, which allowed British officers to rummage through homes in an unrestrained search for evidence of criminal activity." Riley v. California, 573 U.S. ___, ___ (2014). . . .

Compliance with a subpoena *duces tecum* requires none of that. A subpoena *duces tecum* permits a subpoenaed individual to conduct the search for the relevant documents himself, without law enforcement officers entering his home or rooting through his papers and effects. As a result, subpoenas avoid the many incidental invasions of privacy that necessarily accompany any actual search. And it was *those* invasions of privacy—which, although incidental, could often be extremely intrusive and damaging—that led to the adoption of the Fourth Amendment.

Neither this Court nor any of the parties have offered the slightest bit of historical evidence to support the idea that the Fourth Amendment

---

[1] Any other interpretation of the Fourth Amendment's text would run into insuperable problems because it would apply not only to subpoenas *duces tecum* but to all other forms of compulsory process as well. If the Fourth Amendment applies to the compelled production of documents, then it must also apply to the compelled production of testimony—an outcome that we have repeatedly rejected and which, if accepted, would send much of the field of criminal procedure into a tailspin. *See, e.g.,* United States v. Dionisio, 410 U.S. 1, 9 (1973) ("It is clear that a subpoena to appear before a grand jury is not a 'seizure' in the Fourth Amendment sense, even though that summons may be inconvenient or burdensome"); United States v. Calandra, 414 U.S. 338, 354 (1974) ("Grand jury questions . . . involve no independent governmental invasion of one's person, house, papers, or effects"). As a matter of original understanding, a subpoena *duces tecum* no more effects a "search" or "seizure" of papers within the meaning of the Fourth Amendment than a subpoena *ad testificandum* effects a "search" or "seizure" of a person.

originally applied to subpoenas *duces tecum* and other forms of compulsory process. . . .

C

Of course, our jurisprudence has not stood still since 1791. We now evaluate subpoenas *duces tecum* and other forms of compulsory document production under the Fourth Amendment, although we employ a reasonableness standard that is less demanding than the requirements for a warrant. But the road to that doctrinal destination was anything but smooth, and our initial missteps—and the subsequent struggle to extricate ourselves from their consequences—should provide an object lesson for today's majority about the dangers of holding compulsory process to the same standard as actual searches and seizures.

For almost a century after the Fourth Amendment was enacted, this Court said and did nothing to indicate that it might regulate the compulsory production of documents. But that changed temporarily when the Court decided Boyd v. United States, 116 U.S. 616 (1886), the first—and, until today, the only—case in which this Court has ever held the compulsory production of documents to the same standard as actual searches and seizures.

The *Boyd* Court held that a court order compelling a company to produce potentially incriminating business records violated both the Fourth and the Fifth Amendments. The Court acknowledged that "certain aggravating incidents of actual search and seizure, such as forcible entry into a man's house and searching amongst his papers, are wanting" when the Government relies on compulsory process. *Id.*, at 622. But it nevertheless asserted that the Fourth Amendment ought to "be liberally construed," *id.*, at 635, and further reasoned that compulsory process "effects the sole object and purpose of search and seizure" by "forcing from a party evidence against himself," *id.*, at 622. "In this regard," the Court concluded, "the Fourth and Fifth Amendments run almost into each other." *Id.*, at 630. Having equated compulsory process with actual searches and seizures and having melded the Fourth Amendment with the Fifth, the Court then found the order at issue unconstitutional because it compelled the production of property to which the Government did not have superior title. *See id.*, at 622–630.

In a concurrence joined by Chief Justice Waite, Justice Miller agreed that the order violated the Fifth Amendment, *id.*, at 639, but he strongly protested the majority's invocation of the Fourth Amendment. He explained: "[T]here is no reason why this court should assume that the action of the court below, in requiring a party to produce certain papers . . ., authorizes an unreasonable search or seizure of the house, papers, or effects of that party. There is in fact no search and no seizure." *Ibid*. "If the mere service of a notice to produce a paper . . . is a search," Justice Miller concluded, "then a change has taken place in the meaning of words, which has not come within my reading, and which I think was unknown at the time the Constitution was made." *Id.*, at 641.

Although *Boyd* was replete with stirring rhetoric, its reasoning was confused from start to finish in a way that ultimately made the decision unworkable. *See* 3 W. LaFave, J. Israel, N. King, & O. Kerr, Criminal Procedure § 8.7(a) (4th ed. 2015). Over the next 50 years, the Court would gradually roll back *Boyd's* erroneous conflation of compulsory process with actual searches and seizures.

That effort took its first significant stride in *Hale v. Henkel,* 201 U.S. 43 (1906), where the Court found it "quite clear" and "conclusive" that "the search and seizure clause of the Fourth Amendment was not intended to interfere with the power of courts to compel, through a *subpoena duces tecum,* the production, upon a trial in court, of documentary evidence." *Id.,* at 73. Without that writ, the Court recognized, "it would be 'utterly impossible to carry on the administration of justice.'" *Ibid.*

Hale, however, did not entirely liberate subpoenas *duces tecum* from Fourth Amendment constraints. While refusing to treat such subpoenas as the equivalent of actual searches, *Hale* concluded that they must not be unreasonable. And it held that the subpoena *duces tecum* at issue was "far too sweeping in its terms to be regarded as reasonable." *Id.,* at 76. The *Hale* Court thus left two critical questions unanswered: Under the Fourth Amendment, what makes the compulsory production of documents "reasonable," and how does that standard differ from the one that governs actual searches and seizures?

The Court answered both of those questions definitively in *Oklahoma Press Publishing Co. v. Walling,* 327 U.S. 186 (1946), where we held that the Fourth Amendment regulates the compelled production of documents, but less stringently than it does full-blown searches and seizures. *Oklahoma Press* began by admitting that the Court's opinions on the subject had "perhaps too often . . . been generative of heat rather than light," "mov[ing] with variant direction" and sometimes having "highly contrasting" "emphasis and tone." *Id.,* at 202. "The primary source of misconception concerning the Fourth Amendment's function" in this context, the Court explained, "lies perhaps in the identification of cases involving so-called 'figurative' or 'constructive' search with cases of actual search and seizure." *Ibid.* But the Court held that "the basic distinction" between the compulsory production of documents on the one hand, and actual searches and seizures on the other, meant that two different standards had to be applied. *Id.,* at 204.

Having reversed *Boyd's* conflation of the compelled production of documents with actual searches and seizures, the Court then set forth the relevant Fourth Amendment standard for the former. When it comes to "the production of corporate or other business records," the Court held that the Fourth Amendment "at the most guards against abuse only by way of too much indefiniteness or breadth in the things required to be 'particularly described,' if also the inquiry is one the demanding agency is authorized by law to make and the materials specified are relevant."

Oklahoma Press, supra, at 208. Notably, the Court held that a showing of probable cause was not necessary so long as "the investigation is authorized by Congress, is for a purpose Congress can order, and the documents sought are relevant to the inquiry." *Id.,* at 209. . . .

D

Today, however, the majority inexplicably ignores the settled rule of *Oklahoma Press* in favor of a resurrected version of *Boyd.* That is mystifying. This should have been an easy case regardless of whether the Court looked to the original understanding of the Fourth Amendment or to our modern doctrine.

As a matter of original understanding, the Fourth Amendment does not regulate the compelled production of documents at all. Here the Government received the relevant cell-site records pursuant to a court order compelling Carpenter's cell service provider to turn them over. That process is thus immune from challenge under the original understanding of the Fourth Amendment.

As a matter of modern doctrine, this case is equally straightforward. As Justice KENNEDY explains, no search or seizure of Carpenter or his property occurred in this case. *Ante,* at 2226–2235; s*ee also* Part II, *infra.* But even if the majority were right that the Government "searched" Carpenter, it would at most be a "figurative or constructive search" governed by the *Oklahoma Press* standard, not an "actual search" controlled by the Fourth Amendment's warrant requirement.

. . . .That is what makes the majority's opinion so puzzling. It decides that a "search" of Carpenter occurred within the meaning of the Fourth Amendment, but then it leaps straight to imposing requirements that— until this point—have governed only *actual* searches and seizures. *See ante,* at 2220–2221. Lost in its race to the finish is any real recognition of the century's worth of precedent it jeopardizes. For the majority, this case is apparently no different from one in which Government agents raided Carpenter's home and removed records associated with his cell phone.

Against centuries of precedent and practice, all that the Court can muster is the observation that "this Court has never held that the Government may subpoena third parties for records in which the suspect has a reasonable expectation of privacy." *Ante,* at 2221. Frankly, I cannot imagine a concession more damning to the Court's argument than that. As the Court well knows, the reason that we have never seen such a case is because—until today—defendants categorically had no "reasonable expectation of privacy" and no property interest in records belonging to third parties. By implying otherwise, the Court tries the nice trick of seeking shelter under the cover of precedents that it simultaneously perforates.

Not only that, but even if the Fourth Amendment permitted someone to object to the subpoena of a third party's records, the Court cannot explain why that individual should be entitled to *greater* Fourth

Amendment protection than the party actually being subpoenaed. When parties are subpoenaed to turn over their records, after all, they will at most receive the protection afforded by *Oklahoma Press* even though they will own and have a reasonable expectation of privacy in the records at issue. Under the Court's decision, however, the Fourth Amendment will extend greater protections to someone else who is not being subpoenaed and does not own the records. That outcome makes no sense, and the Court does not even attempt to defend it. . . .

II

Compounding its initial error, the Court also holds that a defendant has the right under the Fourth Amendment to object to the search of a third party's property. This holding flouts the clear text of the Fourth Amendment, and it cannot be defended under either a property-based interpretation of that Amendment or our decisions applying the reasonable-expectations-of-privacy test adopted in *Katz,* 389 U.S. 347. By allowing Carpenter to object to the search of a third party's property, the Court threatens to revolutionize a second and independent line of Fourth Amendment doctrine. . . .

For all these reasons, there is no plausible ground for maintaining that the information at issue here represents Carpenter's "papers" or "effects."[6]

B

In the days when this Court followed an exclusively property-based approach to the Fourth Amendment, the distinction between an individual's Fourth Amendment rights and those of a third party was clear cut. We first asked whether the object of the search—say, a house, papers, or effects—belonged to the defendant, and, if it did, whether the Government had committed a "trespass" in acquiring the evidence at issue. *Jones,* 565 U.S., at 411, n.8. . . . .

In the end, the Court never explains how its decision can be squared with the fact that the Fourth Amendment protects only "[t]he right of the people to be secure in *their* persons, houses, papers, and effects." (Emphasis added.)

* * *

Although the majority professes a desire not to " 'embarrass the future,' " *ante,* at 2220, we can guess where today's decision will lead.

One possibility is that the broad principles that the Court seems to embrace will be applied across the board. All subpoenas *duces tecum* and all other orders compelling the production of documents will require a demonstration of probable cause, and individuals will be able to claim a protected Fourth Amendment interest in any sensitive personal

---

[6]   Thus, this is not a case in which someone has entrusted papers that he or she owns to the safekeeping of another, and it does not involve a bailment. Cf. *post,* at 2268–2269 (GORSUCH, J., dissenting).

information about them that is collected and owned by third parties. Those would be revolutionary developments indeed.

The other possibility is that this Court will face the embarrassment of explaining in case after case that the principles on which today's decision rests are subject to all sorts of qualifications and limitations that have not yet been discovered. If we take this latter course, we will inevitably end up "mak[ing] a crazy quilt of the Fourth Amendment." *Smith, supra,* at 745.

All of this is unnecessary. In the Stored Communications Act, Congress addressed the specific problem at issue in this case. The Act restricts the misuse of cell-site records by cell service providers, something that the Fourth Amendment cannot do. The Act also goes beyond current Fourth Amendment case law in restricting access by law enforcement. It permits law enforcement officers to acquire cell-site records only if they meet a heightened standard and obtain a court order. If the American people now think that the Act is inadequate or needs updating, they can turn to their elected representatives to adopt more protective provisions. Because the collection and storage of cell-site records affects nearly every American, it is unlikely that the question whether the current law requires strengthening will escape Congress's notice.

Legislation is much preferable to the development of an entirely new body of Fourth Amendment caselaw for many reasons, including the enormous complexity of the subject, the need to respond to rapidly changing technology, and the Fourth Amendment's limited scope. The Fourth Amendment restricts the conduct of the Federal Government and the States; it does not apply to private actors. But today, some of the greatest threats to individual privacy may come from powerful private companies that collect and sometimes misuse vast quantities of data about the lives of ordinary Americans. If today's decision encourages the public to think that this Court can protect them from this looming threat to their privacy, the decision will mislead as well as disrupt. And if holding a provision of the Stored Communications Act to be unconstitutional dissuades Congress from further legislation in this field, the goal of protecting privacy will be greatly disserved.

The desire to make a statement about privacy in the digital age does not justify the consequences that today's decision is likely to produce.

■ JUSTICE GORSUCH, dissenting.

In the late 1960s this Court suggested for the first time that a search triggering the Fourth Amendment occurs when the government violates an "expectation of privacy" that "society is prepared to recognize as 'reasonable.'" Katz v. United States, 389 U.S. 347, 361 (1967) (Harlan, J., concurring). Then, in a pair of decisions in the 1970s applying the *Katz* test, the Court held that a "reasonable expectation of privacy" *doesn't* attach to information shared with "third parties." *See* Smith v. Maryland,

442 U.S. 735, 743–744 (1979); United States v. Miller, 425 U.S. 435, 443 (1976). By these steps, the Court came to conclude, the Constitution does nothing to limit investigators from searching records you've entrusted to your bank, accountant, and maybe even your doctor.

What's left of the Fourth Amendment? Today we use the Internet to do most everything. Smartphones make it easy to keep a calendar, correspond with friends, make calls, conduct banking, and even watch the game. Countless Internet companies maintain records about us and, increasingly, *for* us. Even our most private documents—those that, in other eras, we would have locked safely in a desk drawer or destroyed— now reside on third party servers. *Smith* and *Miller* teach that the police can review all of this material, on the theory that no one reasonably expects any of it will be kept private. But no one believes that, if they ever did.

What to do? It seems to me we could respond in at least three ways. The first is to ignore the problem, maintain *Smith* and *Miller,* and live with the consequences. If the confluence of these decisions and modern technology means our Fourth Amendment rights are reduced to nearly nothing, so be it. The second choice is to set *Smith* and *Miller* aside and try again using the *Katz* "reasonable expectation of privacy" jurisprudence that produced them. The third is to look for answers elsewhere.

*

Start with the first option. *Smith* held that the government's use of a pen register to record the numbers people dial on their phones doesn't infringe a reasonable expectation of privacy because that information is freely disclosed to the third party phone company. 442 U.S., at 743–744. *Miller* held that a bank account holder enjoys no reasonable expectation of privacy in the bank's records of his account activity. That's true, the Court reasoned, "even if the information is revealed on the assumption that it will be used only for a limited purpose and the confidence placed in the third party will not be betrayed." 425 U.S., at 443. Today the Court suggests that *Smith* and *Miller* distinguish between *kinds* of information disclosed to third parties and require courts to decide whether to "extend" those decisions to particular classes of information, depending on their sensitivity. *See ante,* at 2216–2221. But as the Sixth Circuit recognized and Justice KENNEDY explains, no balancing test of this kind can be found in *Smith* and *Miller. See ante,* at 2231–2232 (dissenting opinion). Those cases announced a categorical rule: Once you disclose information to third parties, you forfeit any reasonable expectation of privacy you might have had in it. And even if *Smith* and *Miller* did permit courts to conduct a balancing contest of the kind the Court now suggests, it's still hard to see how that would help the petitioner in this case. Why is someone's location when using a phone so much more sensitive than who he was talking to (*Smith*) or what financial transactions he engaged in (*Miller*)? I do not know and the Court does not say.

The problem isn't with the Sixth Circuit's application of *Smith* and *Miller* but with the cases themselves. Can the government demand a copy of all your e-mails from Google or Microsoft without implicating your Fourth Amendment rights? Can it secure your DNA from 23andMe without a warrant or probable cause? *Smith* and *Miller* say yes it can— at least without running afoul of *Katz*. But that result strikes most lawyers and judges today—me included—as pretty unlikely. In the years since its adoption, countless scholars, too, have come to conclude that the "third-party doctrine is not only wrong, but horribly wrong." Kerr, *The Case for the Third-Party Doctrine*, 107 Mich. L. Rev. 561, 563, n. 5, 564 (2009) (collecting criticisms but defending the doctrine (footnotes omitted)). The reasons are obvious. "As an empirical statement about subjective expectations of privacy," the doctrine is "quite dubious." Baude & Stern, *The Positive Law Model of the Fourth Amendment*, 129 Harv. L. Rev. 1821, 1872 (2016). People often *do* reasonably expect that information they entrust to third parties, especially information subject to confidentiality agreements, will be kept private. Meanwhile, if the third party doctrine is supposed to represent a normative assessment of when a person should expect privacy, the notion that the answer might be "never" seems a pretty unattractive societal prescription. *Ibid.*

What, then, is the explanation for our third party doctrine? The truth is, the Court has never offered a persuasive justification. The Court has said that by conveying information to a third party you " 'assum[e] the risk' " it will be revealed to the police and therefore lack a reasonable expectation of privacy in it. *Smith, supra,* at 744. But assumption of risk doctrine developed in tort law. It generally applies when "by contract or otherwise [one] expressly agrees to accept a risk of harm" or impliedly does so by "manifest[ing] his willingness to accept" that risk and thereby "take[s] his chances as to harm which may result from it." Restatement (Second) of Torts §§ 496B, 496C(1), and Comment *b* (1965); *see also* 1 D. Dobbs, P. Hayden, & E. Bublick, Law of Torts §§ 235–236, pp. 841–850 (2d ed. 2017). That rationale has little play in this context. Suppose I entrust a friend with a letter and he promises to keep it secret until he delivers it to an intended recipient. In what sense have I agreed to bear the risk that he will turn around, break his promise, and spill its contents to someone else? More confusing still, what have I done to "manifest my willingness to accept" the risk that the government will pry the document from my friend and read it *without* his consent?

One possible answer concerns knowledge. I know that my friend *might* break his promise, or that the government *might* have some reason to search the papers in his possession. But knowing about a risk doesn't mean you assume responsibility for it. Whenever you walk down the sidewalk you know a car may negligently or recklessly veer off and hit you, but that hardly means you accept the consequences and absolve the driver of any damage he may do to you. Epstein, *Privacy and the Third Hand: Lessons From the Common Law of Reasonable Expectations*, 24

Berkeley Tech. L.J. 1199, 1204 (2009); *see* W. Keeton, D. Dobbs, R. Keeton, & D. Owen, Prosser & Keeton on Law of Torts 490 (5th ed.1984).

Some have suggested the third party doctrine is better understood to rest on consent than assumption of risk. "So long as a person knows that they are disclosing information to a third party," the argument goes, "their choice to do so is voluntary and the consent valid." Kerr, *supra,* at 588. I confess I still don't see it. Consenting to give a third party access to private papers that remain my property is not the same thing as consenting to a *search of those papers by the government*. Perhaps there are exceptions, like when the third party is an undercover government agent. *See* Murphy, *The Case Against the Case Against the Third-Party Doctrine: A Response to Epstein and Kerr,* 24 Berkeley Tech. L.J. 1239, 1252 (2009); cf. Hoffa v. United States, 385 U.S. 293 (1966). But otherwise this conception of consent appears to be just assumption of risk relabeled—you've "consented" to whatever risks are foreseeable.

Another justification sometimes offered for third party doctrine is clarity. You (and the police) know exactly how much protection you have in information confided to others: none. As rules go, "the king always wins" is admirably clear. But the opposite rule would be clear too: Third party disclosures *never* diminish Fourth Amendment protection (call it "the king always loses"). So clarity alone cannot justify the third party doctrine.

In the end, what do *Smith* and *Miller* add up to? A doubtful application of *Katz* that lets the government search almost whatever it wants whenever it wants. The Sixth Circuit had to follow that rule and faithfully did just that, but it's not clear why we should.

*

There's a second option. What if we dropped *Smith* and *Miller*'s third party doctrine and retreated to the root *Katz* question whether there is a "reasonable expectation of privacy" in data held by third parties? Rather than solve the problem with the third party doctrine, I worry this option only risks returning us to its source: After all, it was *Katz* that produced *Smith* and *Miller* in the first place. . . .

Even taken on its own terms, *Katz* has never been sufficiently justified. In fact, we still don't even know what its "reasonable expectation of privacy" test *is*. Is it supposed to pose an empirical question (what privacy expectations do people *actually* have) or a normative one (what expectations *should* they have)? Either way brings problems. If the test is supposed to be an empirical one, it's unclear why judges rather than legislators should conduct it. Legislators are responsive to their constituents and have institutional resources designed to help them discern and enact majoritarian preferences. Politically insulated judges come armed with only the attorneys' briefs, a few law clerks, and their own idiosyncratic experiences. They are hardly the representative group you'd expect (or want) to be making empirical judgments for hundreds of millions of people. Unsurprisingly, too, judicial judgments often fail to reflect public views. *See* Slobogin & Schumacher, *Reasonable Expectations of Privacy and Autonomy in Fourth Amendment Cases: An Empirical Look at "Understandings Recognized and Permitted by Society,"* 42 Duke L.J. 727, 732, 740–742 (1993). Consider just one example. Our cases insist that the seriousness of the offense being investigated does *not* reduce Fourth Amendment protection. Mincey v. Arizona, 437 U.S. 385, 393–394 (1978). Yet scholars suggest that most people *are* more tolerant of police intrusions when they investigate more serious crimes. *See* Blumenthal, Adya, & Mogle, *The Multiple Dimensions of Privacy: Testing Lay "Expectations of Privacy,"* 11 U. Pa. J. Const. L. 331, 352–353 (2009). And I very much doubt that this Court would be willing to adjust its *Katz* cases to reflect these findings even if it believed them.

Maybe, then, the *Katz* test should be conceived as a normative question. But if that's the case, why (again) do judges, rather than legislators, get to determine whether society *should be* prepared to recognize an expectation of privacy as legitimate? Deciding what privacy interests *should be* recognized often calls for a pure policy choice, many times between incommensurable goods—between the value of privacy in a particular setting and society's interest in combating crime. Answering questions like that calls for the exercise of raw political will belonging to legislatures, not the legal judgment proper to courts. *See* The Federalist No. 78, p. 465 (C. Rossiter ed. 1961) (A. Hamilton). When judges abandon legal judgment for political will we not only risk decisions where "reasonable expectations of privacy" come to bear "an uncanny resemblance to those expectations of privacy" shared by Members of this Court. Minnesota v. Carter, 525 U.S. 83, 97 (1998) (Scalia, J., concurring). We also risk undermining public confidence in the courts themselves.

My concerns about *Katz* come with a caveat. *Sometimes,* I accept, judges may be able to discern and describe existing societal norms. See, *e.g.,* Florida v. Jardines, 569 U.S. 1, 8 (2013) (inferring a license to enter on private property from the " 'habits of the country' " (quoting McKee v. Gratz, 260 U.S. 127 (1922))); Sachs, *Finding Law,* 107 Cal. L. Rev. (forthcoming 2019), online at https://ssrn.com/abstract=3064443 (as last visited June 19, 2018). That is particularly true when the judge looks to positive law rather than intuition for guidance on social norms. *See Byrd v. United States,* 584 U.S. ___, ___–___ (2018) ("general property-based concept[s] guid[e] the resolution of this case"). So there may be *some* occasions where *Katz* is capable of principled application—though it may simply wind up approximating the more traditional option I will discuss in a moment. Sometimes it may also be possible to apply *Katz* by analogizing from precedent when the line between an existing case and a new fact pattern is short and direct. But so far this Court has declined to tie itself to any significant restraints like these. *See ante,* at 2214, n. 1

("[W]hile property rights are often informative, our cases by no means suggest that such an interest is 'fundamental' or 'dispositive' in determining which expectations of privacy are legitimate"). . . .

The Court's application of these principles supplies little more direction. The Court declines to say whether there is any sufficiently limited period of time "for which the Government may obtain an individual's historical [location information] free from Fourth Amendment scrutiny." *Ante,* at 2217, n. 3; *see ante,* at 2216–2219. But then it tells us that access to seven days' worth of information *does* trigger Fourth Amendment scrutiny—even though here the carrier "produced only two days of records." *Ante,* at 2217, n. 3. Why is the relevant fact the seven days of information the government *asked for* instead of the two days of information the government *actually saw?* Why seven days instead of ten or three or one? And in what possible sense did the government "search" five days' worth of location information it was never even sent? We do not know.

Later still, the Court adds that it can't say whether the Fourth Amendment is triggered when the government collects "real-time CSLI or 'tower dumps' (a download of information on all the devices that connected to a particular cell site during a particular interval)." *Ante,* at 2220. But what distinguishes historical data from real-time data, or seven days of a single person's data from a download of *everyone*'s data over some indefinite period of time? Why isn't a tower dump the *paradigmatic* example of "too permeating police surveillance" and a dangerous tool of "arbitrary" authority—the touchstones of the majority's modified *Katz* analysis? On what possible basis could such mass data collection survive the Court's test while collecting a single person's data does not? Here again we are left to guess. At the same time, though, the Court offers some firm assurances. It tells us its decision does *not* "call into question conventional surveillance techniques and tools, such as security cameras." *Ibid.* That, however, just raises more questions for lower courts to sort out about what techniques qualify as "conventional" and why those techniques would be okay *even if* they lead to "permeating police surveillance" or "arbitrary police power."

Nor is this the end of it. After finding a reasonable expectation of privacy, the Court says there's still more work to do. Courts must determine whether to "extend" *Smith* and *Miller* to the circumstances before them. *Ante,* at 2216, 2219–2220. So apparently *Smith* and *Miller* aren't quite left for dead; they just no longer have the clear reach they once did. How do we measure their new reach? The Court says courts now must conduct a *second Katz*-like balancing inquiry, asking whether the fact of disclosure to a third party outweighs privacy interests in the "category of information" so disclosed. *Ante,* at 2218, 2219–2220. But how are lower courts supposed to weigh these radically different interests? Or assign values to different categories of information? All we know is that historical cell-site location information (for seven days, anyway) escapes

Smith and *Miller's* shorn grasp, while a lifetime of bank or phone records does not. As to any other kind of information, lower courts will have to stay tuned.

In the end, our lower court colleagues are left with two amorphous balancing tests, a series of weighty and incommensurable principles to consider in them, and a few illustrative examples that seem little more than the product of judicial intuition. In the Court's defense, though, we have arrived at this strange place not because the Court has misunderstood *Katz*. Far from it. We have arrived here because this is where *Katz* inevitably leads.

*

There is another way. From the founding until the 1960s, the right to assert a Fourth Amendment claim didn't depend on your ability to appeal to a judge's personal sensibilities about the "reasonableness" of your expectations or privacy. It was tied to the law. *Jardines,* 569 U.S., at 11; United States v. Jones, 565 U.S. 400, 405 (2012). The Fourth Amendment protects "the right of the people to be secure in their persons, houses, papers and effects, against unreasonable searches and seizures." True to those words and their original understanding, the traditional approach asked if a house, paper or effect was *yours* under law. No more was needed to trigger the Fourth Amendment. Though now often lost in *Katz's* shadow, this traditional understanding persists. *Katz* only "supplements, rather than displaces the traditional property-based understanding of the Fourth Amendment." *Byrd,* 584 U.S., at ___, 138 S.Ct., at 1526 (internal quotation marks omitted); *Jardines, supra,* at 11 (same); Soldal v. Cook County, 506 U.S. 56, 64 (1992) (*Katz* did not "snuf[f] out the previously recognized protection for property under the Fourth Amendment").

Beyond its provenance in the text and original understanding of the Amendment, this traditional approach comes with other advantages. Judges are supposed to decide cases based on "democratically legitimate sources of law"—like positive law or analogies to items protected by the enacted Constitution—rather than "their own biases or personal policy preferences." Pettys, *Judicial Discretion in Constitutional Cases,* 26 J.L. & Pol. 123, 127 (2011). A Fourth Amendment model based on positive legal rights "carves out significant room for legislative participation in the Fourth Amendment context," too, by asking judges to consult what the people's representatives have to say about their rights. Baude & Stern, 129 Harv. L. Rev., at 1852. Nor is this approach hobbled by *Smith* and *Miller,* for those cases are just *limitations* on *Katz,* addressing only the question whether individuals have a reasonable expectation of privacy in materials they share with third parties. Under this more traditional approach, Fourth Amendment protections for your papers and effects do not automatically disappear just because you share them with third parties.

Given the prominence *Katz* has claimed in our doctrine, American courts are pretty rusty at applying the traditional approach to the Fourth Amendment. We know that if a house, paper, or effect is yours, you have a Fourth Amendment interest in its protection. But what kind of legal interest is sufficient to make something *yours*? And what source of law determines that? Current positive law? The common law at 1791, extended by analogy to modern times? Both? *See Byrd, supra,* at ___–___ (THOMAS, J., concurring); *cf.* Re, *The Positive Law Floor,* 129 Harv. L. Rev. Forum 313 (2016). Much work is needed to revitalize this area and answer these questions. I do not begin to claim all the answers today, but (unlike with *Katz*) at least I have a pretty good idea what the questions *are*. And it seems to me a few things can be said.

First, the fact that a third party has access to or possession of your papers and effects does not necessarily eliminate your interest in them. Ever hand a private document to a friend to be returned? Toss your keys to a valet at a restaurant? Ask your neighbor to look after your dog while you travel? You would not expect the friend to share the document with others; the valet to lend your car to his buddy; or the neighbor to put Fido up for adoption. Entrusting your stuff to others is a *bailment*. A bailment is the "delivery of personal property by one person (the *bailor*) to another (the *bailee*) who holds the property for a certain purpose." Black's Law Dictionary 169 (10th ed. 2014); J. Story, Commentaries on the Law of Bailments § 2, p. 2 (1832) ("a bailment is a delivery of a thing in trust for some special object or purpose, and upon a contract, expressed or implied, to conform to the object or purpose of the trust"). A bailee normally owes a legal duty to keep the item safe, according to the terms of the parties' contract if they have one, and according to the "implication[s] from their conduct" if they don't. 8 C.J. S., Bailments § 36, pp. 468–469 (2017). A bailee who uses the item in a different way than he's supposed to, or against the bailor's instructions, is liable for conversion. *Id.,* § 43, at 481; *See* Goad v. Harris, 207 Ala. 357, 92 So. 546 (1922); Knight v. Seney, 290 Ill. 11, 17, 124 N.E. 813, 815–816 (1919); Baxter v. Woodward, 191 Mich. 379, 385, 158 N.W. 137, 139 (1916). This approach is quite different from *Smith* and *Miller*'s (counter)-intuitive approach to reasonable expectations of privacy; where those cases extinguish Fourth Amendment interests once records are given to a third party, property law may preserve them.

Our Fourth Amendment jurisprudence already reflects this truth. In Ex parte Jackson, 96 U.S. 727, 24 L.Ed. 877 (1878), this Court held that sealed letters placed in the mail are "as fully guarded from examination and inspection, except as to their outward form and weight, as if they were retained by the parties forwarding them in their own domiciles." *Id.,* at 733. The reason, drawn from the Fourth Amendment's text, was that "[t]he constitutional guaranty of the right of the people to be secure in their papers against unreasonable searches and seizures extends to *their papers,* thus closed against inspection, *wherever they may be*." *Ibid.*

(emphasis added). It did not matter that letters were bailed to a third party (the government, no less). The sender enjoyed the same Fourth Amendment protection as he does "when papers are subjected to search in one's own household." *Ibid.*

These ancient principles may help us address modern data cases too. Just because you entrust your data—in some cases, your modern-day papers and effects—to a third party may not mean you lose any Fourth Amendment interest in its contents. Whatever may be left of *Smith* and *Miller,* few doubt that e-mail should be treated much like the traditional mail it has largely supplanted—as a bailment in which the owner retains a vital and protected legal interest. *See ante,* at 2230 (KENNEDY, J., dissenting) (noting that enhanced Fourth Amendment protection may apply when the "modern-day equivalents of an individual's own 'papers' or 'effects' . . . are held by a third party" through "bailment"); *ante,* at 2259, n. 6 (ALITO, J., dissenting) (reserving the question whether Fourth Amendment protection may apply in the case of "bailment" or when "someone has entrusted papers he or she owns . . . to the safekeeping of another"); United States v. Warshak, 631 F.3d 266, 285–286 (C.A.6 2010) (relying on an analogy to *Jackson* to extend Fourth Amendment protection to e-mail held by a third party service provider).

Second, I doubt that complete ownership or exclusive control of property is always a necessary condition to the assertion of a Fourth Amendment right. Where houses are concerned, for example, individuals can enjoy Fourth Amendment protection without fee simple title. Both the text of the Amendment and the common law rule support that conclusion. "People call a house 'their' home when legal title is in the bank, when they rent it, and even when they merely occupy it rent free." *Carter,* 525 U.S., at 95–96 (Scalia, J., concurring). That rule derives from the common law. Oystead v. Shed, 13 Mass. 520, 523 (1816) (explaining, citing "[t]he very learned judges, *Foster, Hale,* and *Coke,*" that the law "would be as much disturbed by a forcible entry to arrest a boarder or a servant, who had acquired, by contract, express or implied, a right to enter the house at all times, and to remain in it as long as they please, as if the object were to arrest the master of the house or his children"). That is why tenants and resident family members—though they have no legal title—have standing to complain about searches of the houses in which they live. Chapman v. United States, 365 U.S. 610, 616–617 (1961), Bumper v. North Carolina, 391 U.S. 543, 548, n. 11 (1968).

Another point seems equally true: just because you *have* to entrust a third party with your data doesn't necessarily mean you should lose all Fourth Amendment protections in it. Not infrequently one person comes into possession of someone else's property without the owner's consent. Think of the finder of lost goods or the policeman who impounds a car. The law recognizes that the goods and the car still belong to their true owners, for "where a person comes into lawful possession of the personal property of another, even though there is no formal agreement between the property's owner and its possessor, the possessor will become a constructive bailee when justice so requires." Christensen v. Hoover, 643 P.2d 525, 529 (Colo.1982) (en banc); Laidlaw, *Principles of Bailment*, 16 Cornell L.Q. 286 (1931). At least some of this Court's decisions have already suggested that use of technology is functionally compelled by the demands of modern life, and in that way the fact that we store data with third parties may amount to a sort of involuntary bailment too. *See ante*, at 2217–2218 (majority opinion); *Riley v. California*, 573 U.S. ___, ___ (2014).

Third, positive law may help provide detailed guidance on evolving technologies without resort to judicial intuition. State (or sometimes federal) law often creates rights in both tangible and intangible things. *See* Ruckelshaus v. Monsanto Co., 467 U.S. 986, 1001 (1984). In the context of the Takings Clause we often ask whether those state-created rights are sufficient to make something someone's property for constitutional purposes. *See id.*, at 1001–1003; Louisville Joint Stock Land Bank v. Radford, 295 U.S. 555, 590–595 (1935). A similar inquiry may be appropriate for the Fourth Amendment. Both the States and federal government are actively legislating in the area of third party data storage and the rights users enjoy. See, *e.g.*, Stored Communications Act, 18 U.S.C. § 2701 *et seq.*; Tex. Prop.Code Ann. § 111.004(12) (West 2017) (defining "[p]roperty" to include "property held in any digital or electronic medium"). State courts are busy expounding common law property principles in this area as well. *E.g.*, Ajemian v. Yahoo!, Inc., 478 Mass. 169, 170, 84 N.E.3d 766, 768 (2017) (e-mail account is a "form of property often referred to as a 'digital asset' "); *Eysoldt v. ProScan Imaging*, 194 Ohio App.3d 630, 638, 2011–Ohio–2359, 957 N.E.2d 780, 786 (2011) (permitting action for conversion of web account as intangible property). If state legislators or state courts say that a digital record has the attributes that normally make something property, that may supply a sounder basis for judicial decisionmaking than judicial guesswork about societal expectations.

Fourth, while positive law may help establish a person's Fourth Amendment interest there may be some circumstances where positive law cannot be used to defeat it. *Ex parte Jackson* reflects that understanding. There this Court said that "[n]o law of Congress" could authorize letter carriers "to invade the secrecy of letters." 96 U.S., at 733. So the post office couldn't impose a regulation dictating that those mailing letters surrender all legal interests in them once they're deposited in a mailbox. If that is right, *Jackson* suggests the existence of a constitutional floor below which Fourth Amendment rights may not descend. Legislatures cannot pass laws declaring your house or papers to be your property except to the extent the police wish to search them without cause. As the Court has previously explained, "we must 'assur[e] preservation of that degree of privacy against government that existed when the Fourth Amendment was adopted.' " *Jones*, 565 U.S., at 406 (quoting *Kyllo v. United States,* 533 U.S. 27, 34 (2001)). Nor does this mean protecting only the specific rights known at the founding; it means protecting their modern analogues too. So, for example, while thermal imaging was unknown in 1791, this Court has recognized that using that technology to look inside a home constitutes a Fourth Amendment "search" of that "home" no less than a physical inspection might. *Id.,* at 40.

Fifth, this constitutional floor may, in some instances, bar efforts to circumvent the Fourth Amendment's protection through the use of subpoenas. No one thinks the government can evade *Jackson*'s prohibition on opening sealed letters without a warrant simply by issuing a subpoena to a postmaster for "all letters sent by John Smith" or, worse, "all letters sent by John Smith concerning a particular transaction." So the question courts will confront will be this: What other kinds of records are sufficiently similar to letters in the mail that the same rule should apply?

It may be that, as an original matter, a subpoena requiring the recipient to produce records wasn't thought of as a "search or seizure" by the government implicating the Fourth Amendment, *see ante,* at 2247–2253 (opinion of ALITO, J.), but instead as an act of compelled self-incrimination implicating the Fifth Amendment, *see United States v. Hubbell,* 530 U.S. 27, 49–55 (2000) (THOMAS, J., dissenting); Nagareda, *Compulsion "To Be a Witness" and the Resurrection of* Boyd, 74 N.Y.U. L. Rev. 1575, 1619, and n. 172 (1999). But the common law of searches and seizures does not appear to have confronted a case where private documents equivalent to a mailed letter were entrusted to a bailee and then subpoenaed. As a result, "[t]he common-law rule regarding subpoenas for documents held by third parties entrusted with information from the target is . . . unknown and perhaps unknowable." Dripps, *Perspectives on The Fourth Amendment Forty Years Later: Toward the Realization of an Inclusive Regulatory Model,* 100 Minn. L. Rev. 1885, 1922 (2016). Given that (perhaps insoluble) uncertainty, I am content to adhere to *Jackson* and its implications for now.

To be sure, we must be wary of returning to the doctrine of *Boyd v. United States,* 116 U.S. 616. *Boyd* invoked the Fourth Amendment to restrict the use of subpoenas even for ordinary business records and, as Justice ALITO notes, eventually proved unworkable. *See ante,* at 2253 (dissenting opinion); 3 W. LaFave, J. Israel, N. King, & O. Kerr, Criminal Procedure § 8.7(a), pp. 185–187 (4th ed. 2015). But if we were to overthrow *Jackson* too and deny Fourth Amendment protection to *any* subpoenaed materials, we would do well to reconsider the scope of the Fifth Amendment while we're at it. Our precedents treat the right against self-incrimination as applicable only to testimony, not the production of incriminating evidence. *See* Fisher v. United States, 425 U.S. 391, 401 (1976). But there is substantial evidence that the privilege against self-incrimination was also originally understood to protect a person from being forced to turn over potentially incriminating evidence. Nagareda, *supra,* at 1605–1623; Rex v. Purnell, 96 Eng. Rep. 20 (K.B. 1748); Slobogin, Privacy at Risk 145 (2007).

*

What does all this mean for the case before us? To start, I cannot fault the Sixth Circuit for holding that *Smith* and *Miller* extinguish any *Katz*-based Fourth Amendment interest in third party cell-site data. That is the plain effect of their categorical holdings. Nor can I fault the Court today for its implicit but unmistakable conclusion that the rationale of *Smith* and *Miller* is wrong; indeed, I agree with that. The Sixth Circuit was powerless to say so, but this Court can and should. At the same time, I do not agree with the Court's decision today to keep *Smith* and *Miller* on life support and supplement them with a new and multilayered inquiry that seems to be only *Katz*-squared. Returning there, I worry, promises more trouble than help. Instead, I would look to a more traditional Fourth Amendment approach. Even if *Katz* may still supply one way to prove a Fourth Amendment interest, it has never been the only way. Neglecting more traditional approaches may mean failing to vindicate the full protections of the Fourth Amendment.

Our case offers a cautionary example. It seems to me entirely possible a person's cell-site data could qualify as *his* papers or effects under existing law. Yes, the telephone carrier holds the information. But 47 U.S.C. § 222 designates a customer's cell-site location information as "customer proprietary network information" (CPNI), § 222(h)(1)(A), and gives customers certain rights to control use of and access to CPNI about themselves. The statute generally forbids a carrier to "use, disclose, or permit access to individually identifiable" CPNI without the customer's consent, except as needed to provide the customer's telecommunications services. § 222(c)(1). It also requires the carrier to disclose CPNI "upon affirmative written request by the customer, to any person designated by the customer." § 222(c)(2). Congress even afforded customers a private cause of action for damages against carriers who violate the Act's terms. § 207. Plainly, customers have substantial legal interests in this information, including at least some right to include, exclude, and control its use. Those interests might even rise to the level of a property right.

The problem is that we do not know anything more. Before the district court and court of appeals, Mr. Carpenter pursued only a *Katz* "reasonable expectations" argument. He did not invoke the law of property or any analogies to the common law, either there or in his petition for certiorari. Even in his merits brief before this Court, Mr. Carpenter's discussion of his positive law rights in cell-site data was cursory. He offered no analysis, for example, of what rights state law might provide him in addition to those supplied by § 222. In these circumstances, I cannot help but conclude—reluctantly—that Mr. Carpenter forfeited perhaps his most promising line of argument.

Unfortunately, too, this case marks the second time this Term that individuals have forfeited Fourth Amendment arguments based on positive law by failing to preserve them. *See Byrd,* 584 U.S., at ___. Litigants have had fair notice since at least *United States v. Jones* (2012) and *Florida v. Jardines* (2013) that arguments like these may vindicate Fourth Amendment interests even where *Katz* arguments do not. Yet the arguments have gone unmade, leaving courts to the usual *Katz* handwaving. These omissions do not serve the development of a sound or fully protective Fourth Amendment jurisprudence.

3. THE "WARRANT REQUIREMENT"

a. OVERVIEW OF THE "REQUIREMENT" AND THE "EXIGENT CIRCUMSTANCES" EXCEPTION

Mincey v. Arizona
437 U.S. 385 (1978)

■ MR. JUSTICE STEWART delivered the opinion of the Court.

On the afternoon of October 28, 1974, undercover police officer Barry Headricks of the Metropolitan Area Narcotics Squad knocked on the door of an apartment in Tucson, Ariz., occupied by the petitioner, Rufus Mincey. Earlier in the day, Officer Headricks had allegedly arranged to purchase a quantity of heroin from Mincey and had left, ostensibly to obtain money. On his return he was accompanied by nine other plainclothes policemen and a deputy county attorney. The door was opened by John Hodgman, one of three acquaintances of Mincey who were in the living room of the apartment. Officer Headricks slipped inside and moved quickly into the bedroom. Hodgman attempted to slam the door in order to keep the other officers from entering, but was pushed back against the wall. As the police entered the apartment, a rapid volley of shots was heard from the bedroom. Officer Headricks emerged and collapsed on the floor. When other officers entered the bedroom they found Mincey lying on the floor, wounded and semiconscious. Officer Headricks died a few hours later in the hospital.

The petitioner was indicted for murder, assault, and three counts of narcotics offenses. He was tried at a single trial and convicted on all the charges. At his trial and on appeal, he contended that evidence used against him had been unlawfully seized from his apartment without a warrant and that statements used to impeach his credibility were inadmissible because they had not been made voluntarily. The Arizona Supreme Court reversed the murder and assault convictions on state-law grounds, but affirmed the narcotics convictions. 115 Ariz. 472, 566 P.2d 273. It held that the warrantless search of a homicide scene is permissible under the Fourth and Fourteenth Amendments and that Mincey's statements were voluntary. We granted certiorari to consider these substantial constitutional questions. 434 U.S. 902.

I

The first question presented is whether the search of Mincey's apartment was constitutionally permissible. After the shooting, the narcotics agents, thinking that other persons in the apartment might have been injured, looked about quickly for other victims. They found a young woman wounded in the bedroom closet and Mincey apparently unconscious in the bedroom, as well as Mincey's three acquaintances (one of whom had been wounded in the head) in the living room. Emergency assistance was requested, and some medical aid was administered to Officer Headricks. But the agents refrained from further investigation, pursuant to a Tucson Police Department directive that police officers should not investigate incidents in which they are involved. They neither searched further nor seized any evidence; they merely guarded the suspects and the premises.

Within 10 minutes, however, homicide detectives who had heard a radio report of the shooting arrived and took charge of the investigation. They supervised the removal of Officer Headricks and the suspects, trying to make sure that the scene was disturbed as little as possible, and then proceeded to gather evidence. Their search lasted four days, during which period the entire apartment was searched, photographed, and diagrammed. The officers opened drawers, closets, and cupboards, and inspected their contents; they emptied clothing pockets; they dug bullet fragments out of the walls and floors; they pulled up sections of the carpet and removed them for examination. Every item in the apartment was closely examined and inventoried, and 200 to 300 objects were seized. In short, Mincey's apartment was subjected to an exhaustive and intrusive search. No warrant was ever obtained.

The petitioner's pretrial motion to suppress the fruits of this search was denied after a hearing. Much of the evidence introduced against him at trial (including photographs and diagrams, bullets and shell casings, guns, narcotics, and narcotics paraphernalia) was the product of the four-day search of his apartment. On appeal, the Arizona Supreme Court reaffirmed previous decisions in which it had held that the warrantless search of the scene of a homicide is constitutionally permissible. It stated its ruling as follows:

> "We hold a reasonable, warrantless search of the scene of a homicide—or of a serious personal injury with likelihood of death where there is reason to suspect foul play—does not violate the Fourth Amendment to the United States Constitution where the law enforcement officers were legally on the premises in the first instance. . . . For the search to be reasonable, the purpose must be limited to determining the circumstances of death and the scope must not exceed that purpose. The search must also begin within a reasonable period

following the time when the officials first learn of the murder (or potential murder)." 115 Ariz., at 482, 566 P.2d, at 283.

Since the investigating homicide detectives knew that Officer Headricks was seriously injured, began the search promptly upon their arrival at the apartment, and searched only for evidence either establishing the circumstances of death or "relevant to motive and intent or knowledge (narcotics, e. g.)," *id.*, at 483, 566 P.2d, at 284, the court found that the warrantless search of the petitioner's apartment had not violated the Fourth and Fourteenth Amendments.

We cannot agree. The Fourth Amendment proscribes all unreasonable searches and seizures, and it is a cardinal principle that "searches conducted outside the judicial process, without prior approval by judge or magistrate, are per se unreasonable under the Fourth Amendment—subject only to a few specifically established and well-delineated exceptions." Katz v. United States, 389 U.S. 347, 357 (footnotes omitted); *see also* South Dakota v. Opperman, 428 U.S. 364, 381(POWELL, J., concurring); Coolidge v. New Hampshire, 403 U.S. 443, 481; Vale v. Louisiana, 399 U.S. 30, 34; Terry v. Ohio, 392 U.S. 1, 20; Trupiano v. United States, 334 U.S. 699, 705. The Arizona Supreme Court did not hold that the search of the petitioner's apartment fell within any of the exceptions to the warrant requirement previously recognized by this Court, but rather that the search of a homicide scene should be recognized as an additional exception.

Several reasons are advanced by the State to meet its "burden. . . to show the existence of such an exceptional situation" as to justify creating a new exception to the warrant requirement. *See Vale v. Louisiana, supra*, 399 U.S., at 34; United States v. Jeffers, 342 U.S. 48, 51. None of these reasons, however, persuades us of the validity of the generic exception delineated by the Arizona Supreme Court.

The first contention is that the search of the petitioner's apartment did not invade any constitutionally protected right of privacy. *See Katz v. United States, supra*. This argument appears to have two prongs. On the one hand, the State urges that by shooting Officer Headricks, Mincey forfeited any reasonable expectation of privacy in his apartment. We have recently rejected a similar waiver argument in Michigan v. Tyler, 436 U.S. 499, 505–506; it suffices here to say that this reasoning would impermissibly convict the suspect even before the evidence against him was gathered.[5] On the other hand, the State contends that the police entry to arrest Mincey was so great an invasion of his privacy that the additional intrusion caused by the search was constitutionally irrelevant. But this claim is hardly tenable in light of the extensive nature of this search. It is one thing to say that one who is legally taken into police

---

[5] Moreover, this rationale would be inapplicable if a homicide occurred at the home of the victim or of a stranger, yet the Arizona cases indicate that a warrantless search in such a case would also be permissible under the "murder scene exception." *Cf. State v. Sample, supra*, 107 Ariz., at 409, 489 P.2d, at 46.

custody has a lessened right of privacy in his person. *See* United States v. Edwards, 415 U.S. 800, 808–809; United States v. Robinson, 414 U.S. 218. It is quite another to argue that he also has a lessened right of privacy in his entire house. Indeed this very argument was rejected when it was advanced to support the warrantless search of a dwelling where a search occurred as "incident" to the arrest of its occupant. Chimel v. California, 395 U.S. 752, 766 n.12. Thus, this search cannot be justified on the ground that no constitutionally protected right of privacy was invaded.

The State's second argument in support of its categorical exception to the warrant requirement is that a possible homicide presents an emergency situation demanding immediate action. We do not question the right of the police to respond to emergency situations. Numerous state and federal cases have recognized that the Fourth Amendment does not bar police officers from making warrantless entries and searches when they reasonably believe that a person within is in need of immediate aid. Similarly, when the police come upon the scene of a homicide they may make a prompt warrantless search of the area to see if there are other victims or if a killer is still on the premises. Cf. Michigan v. Tyler, *supra*, 436 U.S., at 509–510. "The need to protect or preserve life or avoid serious injury is justification for what would be otherwise illegal absent an exigency or emergency." Wayne v. United States, 115 U.S.App.D.C. 234, 241, 318 F.2d 205, 212 (opinion of Burger, J.). And the police may seize any evidence that is in plain view during the course of their legitimate emergency activities. Michigan v. Tyler, *supra*, 436 U.S., at 509–510; Coolidge v. New Hampshire, 403 U.S., at 465–466.

But a warrantless search must be "strictly circumscribed by the exigencies which justify its initiation," *Terry v. Ohio,* 392 U.S., at 25–26, and it simply cannot be contended that this search was justified by any emergency threatening life or limb. All the persons in Mincey's apartment had been located before the investigating homicide officers arrived there and began their search. And a four-day search that included opening dresser drawers and ripping up carpets can hardly be rationalized in terms of the legitimate concerns that justify an emergency search.

Third, the State points to the vital public interest in the prompt investigation of the extremely serious crime of murder. No one can doubt the importance of this goal. But the public interest in the investigation of other serious crimes is comparable. If the warrantless search of a homicide scene is reasonable, why not the warrantless search of the scene of a rape, a robbery, or a burglary? "No consideration relevant to the Fourth Amendment suggests any point of rational limitation" of such a doctrine. *Chimel v. California, supra,* 395 U.S., at 766.

Moreover, the mere fact that law enforcement may be made more efficient can never by itself justify disregard of the Fourth Amendment.

Cf. Coolidge v. New Hampshire, supra, at 481. The investigation of crime would always be simplified if warrants were unnecessary. But the Fourth Amendment reflects the view of those who wrote the Bill of Rights that the privacy of a person's home and property may not be totally sacrificed in the name of maximum simplicity in enforcement of the criminal law. *See* United States v. Chadwick, 433 U.S. 1, 6–11. For this reason, warrants are generally required to search a person's home or his person unless "the exigencies of the situation" make the needs of law enforcement so compelling that the warrantless search is objectively reasonable under the Fourth Amendment. McDonald v. United States, 335 U.S. 451, 456; Johnson v. United States, 333 U.S. 10, 14–15. *See, e.g., Chimel v. California, supra* (search of arrested suspect and area within his control for weapons or evidence); Warden v. Hayden, 387 U.S. 294, 298–300 ("hot pursuit" of fleeting suspect); Schmerber v. California, 384 U.S. 757, 770–771 (imminent destruction of evidence); *see also supra,* at 2413–2414.

Except for the fact that the offense under investigation was a homicide, there were no exigent circumstances in this case, as, indeed, the Arizona Supreme Court recognized. 115 Ariz., at 482, 566 P.2d, at 283. There was no indication that evidence would be lost, destroyed, or removed during the time required to obtain a search warrant. Indeed, the police guard at the apartment minimized that possibility. And there is no suggestion that a search warrant could not easily and conveniently have been obtained. We decline to hold that the seriousness of the offense under investigation itself creates exigent circumstances of the kind that under the Fourth Amendment justify a warrantless search.

Finally, the State argues that the "murder scene exception" is constitutionally permissible because it is narrowly confined by the guidelines set forth in the decision of the Arizona Supreme Court, *see supra,* at 2411–2412.[8] In light of the extensive search that took place in this case it may be questioned what protection the guidelines afford a person in whose home a homicide or assault occurs. Indeed, these so-called guidelines are hardly so rigidly confining as the State seems to assert. They confer unbridled discretion upon the individual officer to interpret such terms as "reasonable . . . search," "serious personal injury with likelihood of death where there is reason to suspect foul play," and "reasonable period." It is precisely this kind of judgmental assessment of the reasonableness and scope of a proposed search that the Fourth Amendment requires be made by a neutral and objective magistrate, not a police officer. *See, e.g.,* United States v. United States District Court, 407 U.S. 297, 316; *Coolidge v. New Hampshire, supra,* at 449–453; Mancusi v. DeForte, 392 U.S. 364, 371; Wong Sun v. United States, 371 U.S. 471, 481–482.

---

[8] The State also relies on the fact that observance of these guidelines can be enforced by a motion to suppress evidence. But the Fourth Amendment "is designed to prevent, not simply to redress, unlawful police action." Chimel v. California, 395 U.S. 752, 766 n. 12.

It may well be that the circumstances described by the Arizona Supreme Court would usually be constitutionally sufficient to warrant a search of substantial scope. But the Fourth Amendment requires that this judgment in each case be made in the first instance by a neutral magistrate.

"The point of the Fourth Amendment, which often is not grasped by zealous officers, is not that it denies law enforcement the support of the usual inferences which reasonable men draw from evidence. Its protection consists in requiring that those inferences be drawn by a neutral and detached magistrate instead of being judged by the officer engaged in the often competitive enterprise of ferreting out crime." *Johnson v. United States, supra*, at 13–14.

In sum, we hold that the "murder scene exception" created by the Arizona Supreme Court is inconsistent with the Fourth and Fourteenth Amendments—that the warrantless search of Mincey's apartment was not constitutionally permissible simply because a homicide had recently occurred there.[9]

O'Brien v. City of Grand Rapids

23 F.3d 990, 997 (6th Cir. 1994)

"Exigent circumstances," something of a term of art, denotes the existence of " 'real immediate and serious consequences' " that would certainly occur were a police officer to " 'postpone[] action to get a warrant.' " Welsh v. Wisconsin, 466 U.S. 740, 751 (1984) (quoting McDonald v. United States, 335 U.S. 451, 459–60 (1948) (Jackson, J., concurring)). The phrase has been understood by the Supreme Court to comprise, generally, two separate sets of circumstances: 1) "the imminent destruction of vital evidence," Wong Sun v. United States, 371 U.S. 471, 484 (1963), and 2) the " 'need to protect or preserve life or avoid serious injury,' " Mincey v. Arizona, 437 U.S. 385, 392 (1978) (citation omitted), either of police officers themselves or of others, *Hayden*, 387 U.S. at 299.

Examples of "exigent circumstances" exceptions to the warrant requirement abound in Supreme Court case law: 1) the "automobile exception," Carroll v. United States, 267 U.S. 132 (1925); 2) search incident to arrest, Chimel v. California, 395 U.S. 752 (1969); 3) "inventory" searches, Illinois v. Lafayette, 462 U.S. 640 (1983); 4) "hot pursuit," *Hayden*, 387 U.S. 294; 5) "stop and frisk," Terry v. Ohio, 392 U.S. 1 (1968); 6) "border searches," United States v. Montoya de Hernandez, 473 U.S. 531 (1985); 7) "plain view," *Coolidge*, 403 U.S. 443; 8) "school searches," New Jersey v. T.L.O., 469 U.S. 325 (1985); 9) "consent searches," United States v. Mendenhall, 446 U.S. 544 (1980);

---

[9]   To what extent, if any, the evidence found in Mincey's apartment was permissibly seized under established Fourth Amendment standards will be for the Arizona courts to resolve on remand.

and 10) "administrative searches," Donovan v. Dewey, 452 U.S. 594 (1981).

b. SEARCH INCIDENT TO ARREST

See Chapter III, Section 4.

c. VEHICLE EXCEPTION

United States v. Kelly
592 F.3d 586 (4th Cir. 2010)

■ WILKINSON, CIRCUIT JUDGE:

We are asked to review David Kelly's convictions for conspiracy to distribute and possess with intent to distribute drugs and three counts of drug possession with intent to distribute. Kelly's principal claim is that the police violated the Fourth Amendment by conducting a warrantless search of an automobile parked on the street in front of his residence. He contends that the automobile exception to the warrant requirement does not apply here because the police were armed, had the only two individuals at his residence under arrest, and possessed the key to the ignition—thus eliminating any immediate threat that the vehicle would be driven away.

We reject Kelly's attempt to create an exception to the automobile exception. The exception, as carefully crafted by the Supreme Court, does not have an exigency requirement apart from the inherent mobility of the automobile. Consequently, if the police have probable cause, the justification to conduct a warrantless search does not vanish once the police have established some degree of control over the automobile. After careful consideration, we also reject Kelly's other claims and affirm his convictions.

I.

A.

Federal agents and local narcotics investigators conducted a year-long investigation into the drug dealing activities of David Kelly and other co-conspirators. During the investigation, they learned that Kelly had distributed multiple kilograms of cocaine in and around Hampton Roads, Virginia and that his main cocaine supplier was a Hispanic male from New York City. In addition, they learned that Kelly drove several vehicles, including a dark green Lexus sedan.

On September 19, 2006, a federal magistrate issued arrest warrants for Kelly and two of his co-conspirators. The magistrate also issued search warrants for Kelly's residence and a commercial building he owned. The warrant for his residence did not refer to any of his vehicles.

On September 20, 2006, a police officer conducted surveillance at Kelly's residence from 5:00 a.m. until 8:00 p.m. in preparation for the execution of the warrants. She spotted three vehicles owned by Kelly and his girlfriend: two Chevrolet sports utility vehicles parked in the lot of the residence and an Infiniti parked along the street. There was no sign, however, of Kelly or the Lexus at any point that day. On the morning of September 21, the officer resumed her surveillance and immediately noticed that Kelly's Lexus was parked on the street in front of the residence. She also saw Kelly come out of the residence to jump-start the Infiniti, which his girlfriend then drove away.

Around noon of that day, a search team executed the warrant at Kelly's residence. Once inside, the team arrested Kelly and a man whom they unexpectedly discovered. The man identified himself as Jose Jiminez and told the police that he was from New York City. In his possession was a bag containing travel items, such as underwear, soap, and toothpaste. Based on these facts, the officers immediately suspected that Jiminez was Kelly's cocaine supplier and that the two of them had arrived the previous night in the Lexus.

After waiving his Miranda rights, Kelly was placed in a police cruiser and questioned by the officers. Kelly initially denied that there were any drugs in either the residence or his three vehicles parked outside. But after learning that a K–9 unit was on its way, Kelly nodded his head "yes" when asked if there was cocaine in the vehicles. He did not, however, specify which of the three vehicles contained the cocaine.

Subsequently, the K–9 unit arrived at the residence. A specially trained officer led a drug detection dog around the Lexus, and the dog alerted positively by turning its head and scratching at the driver's door. Using Kelly's car keys to open the vehicle, the officers searched the passenger compartment but did not find any drugs. They then searched the trunk and discovered a backpack containing five kilograms of cocaine and 856 tablets of ecstasy. The dog also alerted on Kelly's two sports utility vehicles, and the officers processed all three vehicles for forfeiture under Virginia state law.

B.

On March 7, 2007, a grand jury returned an indictment against Kelly and two co-defendants, both of whom subsequently pled guilty to various charges. Kelly was charged with conspiracy to distribute and possess with intent to distribute cocaine and cocaine base in violation of 21 U.S.C. § 846, two counts of possession with intent to distribute cocaine in violation of 21 U.S.C. § 841(a)(1) and 18 U.S.C. § 2, and one count of possession with intent to distribute ecstasy in violation of 21 U.S.C. § 841(a)(1) and 18 U.S.C. § 2.

Prior to trial, Kelly moved to suppress the evidence seized from his Lexus, claiming that the warrantless search of the vehicle violated the Fourth Amendment. Following a suppression hearing, the district court denied the motion. It held that the automobile exception to the warrant requirement applied and that the police had probable cause to search the vehicle, including its trunk, based on the totality of the circumstances. It stressed three factors supporting probable cause: (1) the presence of an individual that fit the description of Kelly's cocaine supplier, (2) Kelly's admission that there was cocaine in the vehicles, and (3) the drug detection dog's positive alert on the Lexus.

Kelly pled not guilty, and a jury trial began on May 13, 2008. The government put on evidence that Kelly had been involved in a drug conspiracy since sometime around 2000. Several cooperating co-conspirators testified that they personally purchased cocaine from Kelly, set up cocaine deals between Kelly and others, or otherwise witnessed Kelly distributing cocaine. Notably, Jose Jiminez explained that he brokered deals for cocaine and, on one occasion, ecstasy between Kelly and suppliers in New York City. Jiminez testified that he would travel to Virginia, stay at Kelly's residence while Kelly distributed the drugs, and then transport some of the money back to New York City to pay the suppliers. The last of these drug deals, Jiminez testified, ended when the police arrested him and Kelly at Kelly's residence. The government then presented witnesses and evidence regarding the seizure of drugs from the Lexus in 2006.

On May 16, 2008, the jury convicted Kelly of all counts. Subsequently, the district court imposed a sentence of life imprisonment, ten years supervised release, and a special assessment of $400.

On appeal, Kelly challenges the district court's denial of his motion to suppress the evidence seized from the Lexus. He also appeals the district court's denial of his motion for a mistrial based on prosecutorial misconduct and challenges the sufficiency of the evidence introduced at trial. We address each claim in turn and set forth additional facts as they become necessary.

II.

A.

We first address the district court's denial of Kelly's motion to suppress. Kelly challenges both elements of the district court's holding: that (1) the automobile exception to the warrant requirement applies here and (2) the police had probable cause to search the Lexus, including its trunk. We review the district court's legal determinations de novo and its factual determinations for clear error. Because the district court denied Kelly's motion, we construe the evidence in the light most favorable to the government. United States v. Branch, 537 F.3d 328, 337 (4th Cir.2008).

We begin our analysis with a brief review of the law governing automobile searches. The Fourth Amendment generally requires the police to obtain a warrant before conducting a search. There is a well-established exception to this requirement, however, for automobile searches. See, e.g., Carroll v. United States, 267 U.S. 132, 153 (1925). Under this exception, "[i]f a car is readily mobile and probable cause exists to believe it contains contraband, the Fourth Amendment thus permits police to search the vehicle without more." Pennsylvania v. Labron, 518 U.S. 938, 940 (1996) (per curiam). The scope of a search pursuant to this exception is as broad as a magistrate could authorize. United States v. Ross, 456 U.S. 798, 825 (1982). Thus, once police have probable cause, they may search "every part of the vehicle and its contents that may conceal the object of the search." Id.

There are two justifications for the automobile exception. The Supreme Court's early cases were based on the mobility of the automobile. Unlike homes or other structures, cars "can be quickly moved out of the locality or jurisdiction in which the warrant must be sought." *Carroll,* 267 U.S. at 153. This rationale for the automobile exception is not one whose utility has diminished with time. *Carroll,* the seminal case, was decided in 1925, and the speeds at which automobiles are capable of traveling have only increased since that day. *See* Scott v. Harris, 550 U.S. 372, 375 (2007) (describing a car chase "at speeds exceeding 85 miles per hour").

More recent cases provide a second justification for the exception. "Besides the element of mobility, less rigorous warrant requirements govern because the expectation of privacy with respect to one's automobile is significantly less than that relating to one's home or office." South Dakota v. Opperman, 428 U.S. 364, 367 (1976). It is true, of course, that cars harbor personal effects and that some vehicles, mobile homes for example, blend the properties of automobiles and residences. But, unlike a home, a car has not been termed an owner's castle and, again unlike a home, an automobile ventures out in public. This lesser expectation of privacy thus stems from the fact that cars as movable public objects are subject to "pervasive schemes of regulation." California v. Carney, 471 U.S. 386, 392.

Kelly first contends that the automobile exception does not apply here because the police exercised control over the vehicle and had therefore eliminated any potential exigencies. As he points out, the officers at the scene were armed, had both Kelly and Jiminez handcuffed and under arrest, and possessed the keys to the Lexus. He further contends that he was placed in a police cruiser and that four to seven officers were present at the residence. Under these circumstances, he argues, there was not "even the slightest possibility that any potential evidence in the Lexus might be in danger of imminent destruction," and the police should have obtained a warrant before conducting the search. Br. of Appellant at 13–14. In essence, Kelly urges us to recognize an exception to the automobile exception when the police have significantly reduced the likelihood that a car will be driven away.

As an initial matter, we note that officers may not have had as much control over this situation as Kelly suggests. They had no way of knowing whether Kelly's girlfriend or one of his co-conspirators would arrive at the residence during the time it took them to secure a warrant, nor did they know whether there was a spare set of keys to the Lexus. Moreover, the Lexus was parked along a road where it was easily accessible to others.

But even if Kelly is correct that there was little risk that the Lexus would be driven away, it matters not. It is well established that the exception "does not have a separate exigency requirement" apart from the inherent mobility of the automobile. Maryland v. Dyson, 527 U.S. 465, 467 (1999) (per curiam). This is because "[e]ven in cases where an automobile [is] not immediately mobile, the lesser expectation of privacy resulting from its use as a readily mobile vehicle justifie[s] application of the vehicular exception." *Carney,* 471 U.S. at 391. Thus, reviewing courts need not determine the probability in each case that someone would have driven the car away during the time it would have taken the police to secure a warrant. Michigan v. Thomas, 458 U.S. 259, 261 (1982) (per curiam). Instead, the exception applies as long as a car is "readily mobile" in the sense that it is "being used on the highways" or is "readily capable of such use" rather than, say, "elevated on blocks." *Carney,* 471 U.S. at 392–93, 394 n.3.

Following this precedent, we have previously declined to carve out exceptions to the automobile exception based on the degree of control police exercise over a vehicle. In United States v. Brookins, 345 F.3d 231 (4th Cir.2003), for example, we applied the exception to the search of an unoccupied vehicle parked in a driveway even though the police could have blocked the vehicle from escaping. Id. at 237–38. Likewise, in United States v. Gastiaburo, 16 F.3d 582 (4th Cir.1994), we applied the exception after the police had impounded a vehicle, rendering it "virtually impossible for anyone to drive the car away or tamper with its contents." Id. at 586. As these cases recognize, "the justification to conduct a warrantless search under the automobile exception does not disappear merely because the car has been immobilized." Id.

These cases also reflect the well-recognized need to provide "clear and unequivocal guidelines to the law enforcement profession" in the context of automobile searches. *See* California v. Acevedo, 500 U.S. 565, 577 (1991) (internal quotations omitted). As this very case illustrates, whether the police exercise control over an automobile sufficient to eliminate any exigencies may turn on a number of imponderable factors. Were the applicability of the automobile exception to turn on such factors, it would be hard for courts to administer the exception in a coherent and predictable manner. The result would be a series of finely spun legal distinctions that would render the exception difficult for police to follow in quickly developing situations. Would the police, for example, have sufficient control over a vehicle solely because the driver was sitting in a police car? Would they have control if there were six or seven officers at the scene? Two or three? What about a passenger or two? Would the police have control if the driver had a flat tire by the roadside or if he parked his car in a driveway where the police could block his getaway? Would they have control if they possessed the keys to the ignition? And so on. Given the reduced privacy interests at stake, such doctrinal complexities are particularly undesirable in this context.

For these reasons, we reject Kelly's attempt to create an exception to the automobile exception. Turning to the facts here, there is no doubt that Kelly's Lexus was operational and therefore readily mobile. Consequently, the police were not required to obtain a warrant before searching the car or the containers therein.

C.

We now turn to whether the police had probable cause to conduct the warrantless search of the Lexus. Probable cause is "not readily, or even usefully, reduced to a neat set of legal rules." Illinois v. Gates, 462 U.S. 213, 232 (1983). However, the Supreme Court has described it as "existing where the known facts and circumstances are sufficient to warrant a man of reasonable prudence in the belief that contraband or evidence of a crime will be found." Ornelas v. United States, 517 U.S. 690, 696 (1996). When assessing probable cause, we must examine the facts "from the standpoint of an objectively reasonable police officer," giving "due weight to inferences drawn from those facts by . . . local law enforcement officers." Id. at 696, 699.

Here, Kelly acknowledges that the police had probable cause based on the drug detection dog's positive alert and for good reason. *See* Florida v. Royer, 460 U.S. 491, 506 (1983) ("[A] positive result [from a dog] would have resulted in . . . probable cause"); United States v. Jeffus, 22 F.3d 554, 557 (4th Cir.1994) (finding probable cause based on a positive alert); see also United States v. Place, 462 U.S. 696, 707 (1983); United States v. Branch, 537 F.3d 328, 340 n. 2 (4th Cir.2008). But Kelly challenges the scope of the ensuing search. Although the dog's alert at the driver's door may have provided probable cause to search the passenger compartment, he argues, it did not provide probable cause to search the trunk, which was a few feet away from the exact spot of the alert. We disagree.

To be sure, probable cause to search one compartment or container within a car does not invariably provide probable cause to search the entire vehicle. See California v. Acevedo, 500 U.S. 565, 580 (1991). But it does not follow, as Kelly would have it, that a dog's alert at one compartment cannot give probable cause to search another compartment simply because the latter is a few feet away. Unsurprisingly, Kelly cites no authority supporting such a bold proposition. The only case on which he relies notes instead that a "dog's alerting [at a driver's door] was sufficiently close to the trunk to give [the officer] probable cause to believe it contained contraband," United States v. Carter, 300 F.3d 415, 422 (4th Cir.2002). Kelly points us to no features of his car that would allow us to deviate from *Carter*'s ultimate holding.

Probable cause is simply not so exacting a standard that it requires a dog to be able to pinpoint the location of drugs within a foot or two. Instead, it is a "commonsense" conception that deals with "the factual and practical considerations of everyday life." *Ornelas,* 517 U.S. at 695 (internal quotation omitted). Dogs, of course, react not to the presence of drugs themselves but to their odors. And, as the K–9 officer in this case explained, odors travel within a car and seep through loose seals into the outside environment. Consequently, he continued, it is not uncommon for dogs to alert at the doors of vehicles where the seals tend to be heavily worn. Given these practical realities, we think it was reasonable to conclude that the odor which the dog detected may have travelled from the trunk, which is after all a logical place for drugs to be stored.

The district court alluded to several additional factors here. The first was the presence of an individual whom the police believed to be Kelly's drug supplier. . . .

Second, Kelly nodded "yes" when asked if there was cocaine in the vehicles parked outside the residence. To be sure, he did not specify which of the three vehicles contained cocaine, but there was a fair probability that the drugs would be found in the Lexus, which had been driven the most recently.

There can thus be no question that the district court properly upheld the search of the Lexus for drugs, and the trunk and the backpack therein were logical places for the officers to look. Accordingly, we affirm the district court's denial of Kelly's motion to suppress.*

. . . For the foregoing reasons, the judgment of the district court is AFFIRMED.

United States v. Camou

773 F.3d 932 (9th Cir. 2014)

■ PREGERSON, CIRCUIT JUDGE:

Chad Camou appeals the district court's denial of his motion to suppress images of child pornography found on his cell phone during a warrantless search. We have jurisdiction pursuant to 28 U.S.C. § 1291. We reverse.

FACTUAL & PROCEDURAL BACKGROUND

I.   Camou's Arrest and the Seizure of Camou's Cell Phone at 10:40 p.m.

On August 1, 2009, United States Border Patrol agents stopped a truck belonging to Chad Camou at a primary inspection checkpoint on

---

* The government also contends that the evidence from the Lexus is admissible even if the police lacked probable cause because the police would have inevitably discovered the evidence when conducting an inventory search prior to impounding the vehicle. Because we find that the police did have probable cause, we need not reach this issue.

Highway 86 in Westmorland, California. Camou was driving the truck, while his girlfriend, Ashley Lundy, sat in the passenger seat. Agents at the checkpoint grew suspicious when Lundy did not make eye contact, so they asked Camou if they could open the door to the truck. Once they opened the door, the agents saw Alejandro Martinez-Ramirez (Martinez-Ramirez), an undocumented immigrant, lying on the floor behind the truck's front seats. Consequently, at about 10:40 p.m., agents arrested and handcuffed Camou, Lundy, and Martinez-Ramirez. At the same time, agents also seized Camou's truck and a cell phone found in the cab of the truck. Agents then moved Camou, Lundy, and Martinez-Ramirez into the checkpoint's security offices for booking.

II. Agents Processed, Booked, and Interviewed Camou at the Security Offices

Once at the checkpoint's security offices, Border Patrol agents processed and booked Camou and Lundy. At some point during the booking process, Border Patrol Agent Andrew Baldwin inventoried Camou's cell phone as "seized property and evidence."

Agents then began to interview Camou and Lundy. Lundy was given *Miranda* warnings. It is unclear whether Camou was given *Miranda* warnings or whether he said anything to the agents at this point. Neither Camou nor Lundy asked for an attorney.

During Lundy's initial interview with Border Patrol Agent Richard Walla, Lundy waived her *Miranda* rights and explained that, before she and Camou picked up Martinez-Ramirez, Camou had received a phone call from Jessie, a.k.a. "Mother Teresa." "Mother Teresa" arranged for Camou to pick up Martinez-Ramirez in Calexico, California and transport him to either Palm Desert, California or Coachella, California. During Lundy's interview, Camou's cell phone rang several times. The caller identification screen on the phone displayed the phone number that Lundy had identified as belonging to "Mother Teresa." Agents asked Camou if the cell phone belonged to him. Camou replied, "Yes."

Border Patrol Agents Jason Masney and Ciudad Real attempted to further interview Martinez-Ramirez, Camou, and Lundy. Martinez-Ramirez told the agents that he had been in the car for about forty minutes and that Camou had planned to take him to Los Angeles. Camou invoked his right to remain silent. Lundy, meanwhile, agreed to answer more questions. She told the agents that she and Camou had been smuggling undocumented immigrants about eight times per month for about nine months. She explained that Camou would receive phone calls from smugglers on his cell phone both before and after passing the Highway 86 checkpoint.

III. Warrantless Search of Camou's Cell Phone at 12:00 a.m.

At 12:00 a.m., one hour and twenty minutes after Camou's arrest, Agent Walla searched Camou's cell phone. In his subsequent report, Agent Walla claimed he was looking for evidence of "known smuggling organizations and information related to the case." Agent Walla did not assert that the search was necessary to prevent the destruction of evidence or to ensure his or anyone else's safety.

Agent Walla searched the call logs of the cell phone and discovered several recent calls from "Mother Teresa." Agent Walla closed the call logs screen and opened the videos stored on the phone's internal memory. He saw several videos that appeared to be taken near the Calexico, California Port of Entry. He then closed the videos and opened the photographs, which were also stored on the phone's internal memory. He "scrolled quickly through about 170 of the images before stopping. Of the images he viewed, about 30 to 40 were child pornography. Walla was disturbed by the images and stopped reviewing the contents of the phone."

After stopping the search, Agent Walla called U.S. Immigration and Customs Enforcement, the Imperial County Sheriff's Office, and the FBI to pursue child pornography charges against Camou. Assistant United States Attorney John Weis at the El Centro Sector Prosecutions Office did not pursue alien smuggling charges against Camou because Weis decided that the smuggling case against Camou "did not meet prosecution guidelines." Weis informed Border Patrol agents of his decision the same day Camou's cell phone was searched by Agent Walla.

Several days later, on August 5, 2009, the FBI executed a federal warrant to search Camou's cell phone for child pornography. Pursuant to the warrant, the FBI found several hundred images of child pornography on the cell phone.

IV. District Court Proceedings

A grand jury indicted Camou for possession of child pornography in violation of 18 U.S.C. § 2252(a)(4)(B). Camou moved the district court to suppress the child pornography images found on his cell phone, arguing that the warrantless search of his cell phone at the checkpoint's security offices violated his Fourth Amendment rights. The district court denied Camou's motion. The district court found that the search of the phone was a lawful search incident to arrest and, even if the search was unconstitutional, the good faith and inevitable discovery exceptions to the exclusionary rule were satisfied.

Camou entered a conditional guilty plea to possession of child pornography in violation of 18 U.S.C. § 2252(a)(4)(B). Camou was sentenced to thirty-seven months in prison followed by five years of supervised release. Camou is currently serving his prison sentence. Camou appeals the district court's denial of his motion to suppress.

STANDARD OF REVIEW

We review de novo the district court's denial of a motion to suppress. United States v. Song Ja Cha, 597 F.3d 995, 999 (9th Cir.2010). We review the district court's underlying factual findings for clear error. *Id*. We review de novo the application of the good faith and inevitable discovery exceptions to the exclusionary rule. United States v. Krupa, 658 F.3d 1174, 1179 (9th Cir.2011).

DISCUSSION

Camou argues that the warrantless search of his cell phone was unconstitutional because the search was not incident to arrest, and no other exceptions to the warrant requirement apply. Camou also argues that the exclusionary rule bars the admissibility of the images found on his phone. We agree.

I.   Search Incident to Arrest

A search incident to a lawful arrest is an exception to the general rule that warrantless searches violate the Fourth Amendment. The exception allows a police officer making a lawful arrest to conduct a search of the area within the arrestee's "immediate control," that is, "the area from within which [an arrestee] might gain possession of a weapon or destructible evidence." Chimel v. California, 395 U.S. 752, 763 (1969) (internal quotation marks omitted), *abrogated on other grounds by* Arizona v. Gant, 556 U.S. 332, 344 (2009).

The first requirement of a search incident to arrest is that the search be limited to the arrestee's person or areas in the arrestee's "immediate control" at the time of arrest. *Gant,* 556 U.S. at 339; *Chimel,* 395 U.S. at 763; United States v. Turner, 926 F.2d 883, 887 (9th Cir.1991). The "immediate control" requirement ensures that a search incident to arrest will not exceed the rule's two original purposes of protecting arresting officers and preventing the arrestee from destroying evidence: "If there is no possibility that an arrestee could reach into the area that law enforcement officers seek to search, both justifications for the search-incident-to-arrest exception are absent and the rule does not apply." *Gant,* 556 U.S. at 339.[1]

The second requirement of a search incident to arrest is that the search be spatially and temporally incident to the arrest. *See* United States v. Chadwick, 433 U.S. 1, 15 (1977), *abrogated on other grounds by* California v. Acevedo, 500 U.S. 565, 580 (1991); United States v. Hudson, 100 F.3d 1409, 1419 (9th Cir.1996). The Supreme Court has held that "warrantless searches of luggage or other property seized at the time of an arrest cannot be justified as incident to that arrest . . . *if the search is remote in time or place from the arrest.* . . ." *Chadwick,* 433 U.S. at 15 (emphasis added). We have interpreted the temporal requirement to mean that the search must be "roughly contemporaneous with the

---

[1]   One exception to the immediate control requirement, however, occurs in the vehicle context. Where the search incident to arrest is of a vehicle, the Supreme Court has held: "Although it does not follow from *Chimel,* we also conclude that circumstances unique to the vehicle context justify a search incident to lawful arrest when it is '*reasonable to believe evidence relevant to the crime of the arrest might be found in the vehicle.*' " *Gant,* 556 U.S. at 343 (emphasis added) (quoting Thornton v. United States, 541 U.S. 615, 632 (2004) (Scalia, J., concurring in judgment)).

arrest." United States v. Smith, 389 F.3d 944, 951 (9th Cir.2004) (per curiam).

We have summed up the two general requirements of a valid search incident to arrest as follows: "The determination of the validity of a search incident to arrest in this circuit is a two-fold inquiry: (1) was the searched item 'within the arrestee's immediate control when he was arrested'; (2) did 'events occurring after the arrest but before the search ma[k]e the search unreasonable'?" United States v. Maddox, 614 F.3d 1046, 1048 (9th Cir.2010) (quoting United States v. Turner, 926 F.2d 883, 887 (9th Cir.1991)).

We need not decide whether the government meets the first requirement of search incident to arrest because the government cannot show that the second requirement—that the search be spatially and temporally incident to the arrest—is met.

Agent Walla's search of Camou's cell phone was too far removed in time from Camou's arrest to be incident to that arrest. As stated above, we have interpreted the temporal requirement to mean that the search must be "roughly contemporaneous with the arrest." *Smith,* 389 F.3d at 951. To determine whether this contemporaneity requirement is met, we have stated that the focus is "upon whether the arrest and search are so separated in time or by intervening acts that the latter cannot be said to have been incident to the former." *Id.* In some cases, we have "relied on the number of minutes that passed between the arrest and the search. . . . In other cases, we have relied on a more impressionistic sense of the flow of events that begins with the arrest and ends with the search." United States v. Caseres, 533 F.3d 1064, 1073 (9th Cir.2008).

In *Caseres,* we found that a search of the arrestee-defendant's car was not incident to arrest for two independent reasons: (1) the "arrest was not spatially related to the vehicle" because Caseres, the arrestee, was a block and a half away from his car at the time of his arrest; and (2) "the search . . . was too far removed in time from the arrest to be considered as truly incidental to [the] arrest." *Id.* at 1072, 1074. We noted that, while it was unclear from the record how much time passed between arrest and search, the district court reasonably found the search was conducted "well after" the arrest. *Id.* at 1074. In holding that the search was too temporally removed from the arrest, we reasoned that the "arrest and the search were separated not only by substantial time, but also by a string of intervening events that signaled that the exigencies of the situation had dissipated." *Id.* The intervening events we noted were: police questioning of Caseres, conversations between police, and police moving back and forth between the site of the arrest and Caseres's car. *Id.*

In *Maddox,* we similarly held that the warrantless search of an arrestee-defendant's car was not incident to arrest, but in so holding we relied solely on intervening events between the arrest and search. 614 F.3d at 1048. In *Maddox,* after Maddox ignored the officer's request to exit his car following a stop for reckless driving, the officer seized Maddox's key chain and cell phone and threw them on the front seat. *Id.* at 1047. The officer arrested and handcuffed Maddox and placed him in the back of the patrol car. *Id.* He then returned to Maddox's car, reached inside, and grabbed the key chain and cell phone. *Id.* The key chain included a metal vial with a screw top. *Id.* The officer unscrewed the metal vial's top and discovered methamphetamine inside. *Id.* We held that the intervening event of Maddox being handcuffed and placed in the back of a patrol car rendered the search unreasonable. *Id.* at 1048–49; *see also* United States v. Vasey, 834 F.2d 782, 787–88 (9th Cir.1987) (holding that the warrantless search of Vasey's car was not incident to arrest where the search occurred thirty to forty-five minutes after Vasey was arrested; Vasey was handcuffed and placed in the back of the patrol car before the search; and officers "conducted several conversations with Vasey" between arrest and search); United States v. Monclavo-Cruz, 662 F.2d 1285, 1288 (9th Cir.1981) (holding that the warrantless search of an arrestee's purse at the station house, about an hour after she was arrested next to her car, was not sufficiently contemporaneous with the arrest to be incident to arrest).[2]

Here, Agent Walla's search of Camou's cell phone was not roughly contemporaneous with Camou's arrest and, therefore, was not incident to arrest. First, one hour and twenty minutes passed between Camou's arrest and Agent Walla's search of the cell phone. This delay is longer than the thirty to forty-five minutes in *Vasey* and the one hour in *Monclavo-Cruz;* and the searches in those two cases were deemed not sufficiently contemporaneous with arrest.

Second, a string of intervening acts occurred between Camou's arrest and the search of his cell phone that make the one hour and twenty minute delay even more unreasonable: (1) Camou and Lundy were restrained with handcuffs; (2) Camou and Lundy were moved from the checkpoint area to the security offices; (3) Camou and Lundy were processed; (4) agents moved Camou's cell phone from the vehicle into the security offices, inventoried the phone as a seized item, and moved the phone into the interview rooms; (5) Camou and Lundy were interviewed as part of the booking process; (6) Martinez-Ramirez was interviewed; and (7) Agents Masney and Real interviewed Lundy for a second time and tried to interview Camou, who invoked his right to remain silent. These intervening acts include the same sort of intervening acts in *Caseres*—police questioning the arrestee, conversations between police, and police moving between the site of the arrest and the site of search—

---

[2] We briefly note that, by citing to United States v. Johns, 469 U.S. 478 (1985), the government incorrectly conflates two different search and seizure doctrines: search incident to arrest and the vehicle exception to the warrant requirement. As *Johns* did not concern a search incident to arrest, *Johns's* holding allowing a three-day delay in searching seized items does not help the government's search incident to arrest argument. We revisit the government's *Johns* argument in the next section when analyzing whether the vehicle exception to the warrant requirement applies.

as well as the intervening acts of *Maddox* and *Vasey*—police handcuffing the arrestee and placing him under police control. And here we also have the additional intervening acts of police booking the arrestee, police questioning the material witness, Martinez-Ramirez, and police moving the item to be searched—i.e., Camou's cell phone—from the site of the arrest to the security offices.

Given both the passage of one hour and twenty minutes between arrest and search and the seven intervening acts between arrest and search that signaled the arrest was over, we conclude that the search of the phone was not roughly contemporaneous with arrest and, therefore, was not a search incident to arrest.

II. Two Other Exceptions to the Warrant Requirement: the Exigency Exception & the Vehicle Exception

Several of the government's arguments more properly fall under the exigency and vehicle exceptions. For the reasons explained below, we conclude that neither of these exceptions is met.

A. The Exigency Exception

Under the exigency exception, officers may make a warrantless search if: (1) they have probable cause to believe that the item or place to be searched contains evidence of a crime, and (2) they are facing exigent circumstances that require immediate police action. *See* Warden, Md. Penitentiary v. Hayden, 387 U.S. 294, 298–301 (1967) (upholding a warrantless search where "the exigencies of the situation made that course imperative"). We have defined exigent circumstances as "those circumstances that would cause a reasonable person to believe that entry [or search] . . . was necessary to prevent physical harm to the officers or other persons, the destruction of relevant evidence, the escape of the suspect, or some other consequence improperly frustrating legitimate law enforcement efforts." United States v. McConney, 728 F.2d 1195, 1199 (9th Cir.1984) (en banc), *overruled on other grounds by* Estate of Merchant v. Comm'r, 947 F.2d 1390, 1392–93 (9th Cir.1991). To be reasonable, a search under this exception must be limited in scope so that it is "strictly circumscribed by the exigencies which justify its initiation." Mincey v. Arizona, 437 U.S. 385, 393 (1978) (internal quotation marks omitted); *see also* United States v. Reyes-Bosque, 596 F.3d 1017, 1029 (9th Cir.2010) ("In order to prove that the exigent circumstances doctrine justified a warrantless search, the government must [also] show that . . . the search's scope and manner were reasonable to meet the need.").

After we submitted this case, the Supreme Court granted the petition for writ of certiorari in Riley v. California, ___ U.S. ___ (2014), on January 17, 2014, to answer the following question: "Whether evidence admitted at petitioner's trial was obtained in a search of petitioner's cell phone that violated petitioner's Fourth Amendment rights." We then vacated submission of this case pending the Supreme Court's decision in *Riley*. On June 25, 2014, the Supreme Court issued its unanimous decision in Riley v. California, ___ U.S. ___ (2014), holding that "a warrant is generally required before . . . a search [of a cell phone], even when a cell phone is seized incident to arrest." *Id.* at 2493. The Court went on, however, to note that "other case-specific exceptions may still justify a warrantless search of a particular phone." *Id.* at 2494. Specifically, the exigency exception "could include the need to prevent the imminent destruction of evidence in individual cases, to pursue a fleeing suspect, and to assist persons who are seriously injured or are threatened with imminent injury." *Id.*

Even if there was probable cause to search Camou's cell phone, we conclude that the government failed to meet the second prong of the exigency exception: exigent circumstances that require immediate police action.

The government argues that "the volatile nature of call logs and other cell phone information with the passing of time" presented an exigent circumstance. *Riley* forecloses this argument. There, the Court determined that "once law enforcement officers have secured a cell phone, there is no longer any risk that the arrestee himself will be able to delete incriminating data from the phone." *Riley,* 134 S.Ct. at 2486. And although "information on a cell phone may nevertheless be vulnerable to . . . remote wiping," there is "little reason to believe that [this] problem is prevalent." *Id.* And, "as to remote wiping, law enforcement is not without specific means to address the threat. Remote wiping can be fully prevented by disconnecting the phone from the network." *Id.* at 2487. When "the police are truly confronted with a 'now or never' situation—for example, circumstances suggesting that a defendant's phone will be the target of an imminent remote-wipe attempt—they may be able to rely on exigent circumstances to search the phone immediately." *Id.* (internal quotation marks omitted). Here, the search of Camou's cell phone occurred one hour and twenty minutes after his arrest. This was not an "imminent" "now or never situation" such that the exigency exception would apply. Moreover, the record does not indicate that Agent Walla believed the call logs on Camou's cell phone were volatile and that a search of Camou's phone was necessary to prevent the loss of recent call data.

And even if we were to assume that the exigencies of the situation permitted a search of Camou's cell phone to prevent the loss of call data, the search's scope was impermissibly overbroad. The search in this case went beyond contacts and call logs to include a search of hundreds of photographs and videos stored on the phone's internal memory. Thus, Agent Walla exceeded the scope of any possible exigency by extending the search beyond the call logs to examine the phone's photographs and videos. *See* State v. Carroll, 322 Wis.2d 299, 778 N.W.2d 1, 12 (2010) (holding that the exigency exception justified the answering of an incoming call on the defendant's cell phone but did not justify a search of images stored on the phone "because there were no exigent circumstances at the time requiring [the officer] to review the gallery or other data stored on the phone. That data was not in immediate danger of disappearing before [the officer] could obtain a warrant."). We therefore conclude that the search of Camou's cell phone is not excused under the exigency exception to the warrant requirement.

B. The Vehicle Exception

Another exception to the Fourth Amendment's warrant requirement is the vehicle exception. Carroll v. United States, 267 U.S. 132, 153–54 (1925). Under the vehicle exception, officers may search a vehicle and any containers found therein without a warrant, so long as they have probable cause. California v. Acevedo, 500 U.S. 565, 580 (1991); United States v. Ross, 456 U.S. 798, 821–22 (1982). Unlike search incident to arrest, the vehicle exception is not rooted in arrest and the *Chimel* rationales of preventing arrestees from harming officers and destroying evidence. Instead, the vehicle exception is motivated by the supposedly lower expectation of privacy individuals have in their vehicles as well as the mobility of vehicles, which allows evidence contained within those vehicles to be easily concealed from the police. *Carroll,* 267 U.S. at 153; California v. Carney, 471 U.S. 386, 390–91 (1985).

As the Supreme Court noted in *Arizona v. Gant,* the permissible scope of a vehicle exception search is "broader" than that of a search incident to arrest: "If there is probable cause to believe a vehicle contains evidence of criminal activity, [*Ross*] authorizes a search of any area of the vehicle in which the evidence might be found. . . . *Ross* allows searches for evidence relevant to offenses other than the offense of arrest." 556 U.S. 332, 347 (2009) (citing *Ross,* 456 U.S. at 820–21). Moreover, unlike searches incident to arrest, searches of vehicles and containers pursuant to the vehicle exception need not be conducted right away. United States v. Johns, 469 U.S. 478, 487–88 (1985). So long as the officers had probable cause to believe the car had evidence of criminal activity when they seized a container from inside the car, they may delay searching it. *Id.* Delays, however, must be "reasonable in light of all the circumstances." United States v. Albers, 136 F.3d 670, 674 (9th Cir.1998) (upholding as reasonable a seven—to ten-day delay in viewing videotapes and film seized from a houseboat).

We assume that the agents had probable cause to believe Camou's truck contained evidence of criminal activity once they saw Martinez-Ramirez lying down behind the seats of the truck. If the vehicle exception applied in this case, pursuant to *Johns* and *Albers,* the one hour and twenty minute delay between the seizure of Camou's cell phone and the search of its contents would not invalidate the search. We hold, however, that cell phones are not containers for purposes of the vehicle exception.

In *New York v. Belton,* the Supreme Court defined "container" as "any object capable of holding another object" and explained that in the vehicle context, containers "include[ ] closed or open glove compartments, consoles, or other receptacles located anywhere within the passenger compartment, as well as luggage, boxes, bags, clothing, and the like." 453 U.S. 454, 460 n. 4 (1981), *overruled on other grounds by Gant,* 556 U.S. at 350–51. In *United States v. Ross,* the Supreme Court provided "paper bags, locked trunks, lunch buckets, and orange crates" as examples of containers. 456 U.S. 798, 821–22 (1982).

Then, in *Riley,* the Supreme Court examined the definition of "container" as it would apply to cell phones and the search incident to arrest exception. The Court found:

> Treating a cell phone as a container whose contents may be searched incident to an arrest is a bit strained as an initial matter. But the analogy crumbles entirely when a cell phone is used to access data located elsewhere, at the tap of a screen.

134 S.Ct. 2473, 2491 (2014) (citation omitted).

The Court then addressed the government's proposal that cell phone searches incident to arrest be analyzed under the *Gant* standard imported from the vehicle context:

> [A] *Gant* standard would prove no practical limit at all when it comes to cell phone searches. In the vehicle context, *Gant* generally protects against searches for evidence of past crimes. In the cell phone context, however, it is reasonable to expect that incriminating information will be found on a phone regardless of when the crime occurred. . . . The sources of potential pertinent information are virtually unlimited, so applying the *Gant* standard to cell phones would in effect give police officers unbridled discretion to rummage at will among a person's private effects.

Id. at 2492 (internal quotation marks omitted).

Given the Court's extensive analysis of cell phones as "containers" and cell phone searches in the vehicle context, we find no reason not to extend the reasoning in *Riley* from the search incident to arrest exception to the vehicle exception. Just as "[c]ell phones differ in both a quantitative and a qualitative sense from other objects that might be kept on an arrestee's person," so too do cell phones differ from any other object officers might find in a vehicle. *Id.* at 2489. Today's cell phones are unlike any of the container examples the Supreme Court has provided in the vehicle context. Whereas luggage, boxes, bags, clothing, lunch buckets, orange crates, wrapped packages, glove compartments, and locked trunks are capable of physically "holding another object," *see Belton,* 453 U.S. at 460 n. 4, "[m]odern cell phones, as a category, implicate privacy concerns far beyond those implicated by the search of a cigarette pack, a wallet, or a purse," *Riley,* 134 S.Ct. at 2488–89. In fact, "a cell phone search would typically expose to the government far *more* than the most exhaustive search of a house." *Id.* at 2491 (emphasis in original).

We further note that the privacy intrusion of searching a cell phone without a warrant is of particular concern in the vehicle exception context because the allowable scope of the search is broader than that of an exigency search, or a search incident to arrest. Whereas exigency searches are circumscribed by the specific exigency at hand and searches incident to arrest are limited to areas within the arrestee's immediate control or to evidence relevant to the crime of arrest, vehicle exception searches allow for evidence relevant to criminal activity broadly. If cell phones are considered containers for purposes of the vehicle exception, officers would often be able to sift through all of the data on cell phones found in vehicles because they would not be restrained by any limitations of exigency or relevance to a specific crime.

We therefore conclude that cell phones are *non*-containers for purposes of the vehicle exception to the warrant requirement, and the search of Camou's cell phone cannot be justified under that exception.

III. Inevitable Discovery and the Good Faith Exceptions to the Exclusionary Rule

The government argues that, even if the warrantless search of Camou's cell phone was unconstitutional, the photographs found as a result of the search should not be suppressed because the inevitable discovery and good faith exceptions to the exclusionary rule are met. We disagree with the government and find that neither exception is met.

A. Inevitable Discovery

The exclusionary rule allows courts to suppress evidence obtained as a result of an unconstitutional search or seizure. Mapp v. Ohio, 367 U.S. 643, 655 (1961); Weeks v. United States, 232 U.S. 383, 393 (1914). But if the government can establish by a preponderance of the evidence that the unlawfully obtained information "ultimately or inevitably would have been discovered by lawful means," the exclusionary rule will not apply. Nix v. Williams, 467 U.S. 431, 444 (1984). We have "never applied the inevitable discovery exception so as to excuse the failure to obtain a search warrant where the police had probable cause but simply did not attempt to obtain a warrant." United States v. Young, 573 F.3d 711, 723 (9th Cir.2009) (quoting United States v. Mejia, 69 F.3d 309, 320 (9th Cir.1995)). As we reasoned in *Mejia,* "[i]f evidence were admitted notwithstanding the officers' unexcused failure to obtain a warrant, simply because probable cause existed, then there would never be *any* reason for officers to seek a warrant." 69 F.3d at 320.

Here, the government argues that a warrant to search Camou's cell phone for evidence of smuggling activity inevitably would have been sought and approved, and therefore that the inevitable discovery doctrine applies. This argument fails for two independent reasons.

First, the government has not proved by a preponderance of the evidence that it would have applied for a warrant to search Camou's phone for evidence of alien smuggling activity. In fact, the record points to the opposite conclusion: that no search warrant would have been sought and thus that no search warrant would have been approved. Camou was ultimately charged only with possession of child pornography, not with alien smuggling. Border Patrol agents knew the day Agent Walla searched Camou's cell phone that Camou would not be charged with alien smuggling. The Sector Prosecutions Office informed the agents that day that "prosecution was declined" in the smuggling case against Camou because the case "did not meet prosecution guidelines." Because the reasonable conclusion from the record is that no search warrant would have been sought, the inevitable discovery exception to the exclusionary rule is not satisfied.

Second, and more importantly, *Mejia* governs this case. By asking this court to conclude that the inevitable discovery exception applies here because a search warrant would have issued, the government is asking us to "excuse the failure to obtain a search warrant where the police had probable cause but simply did not attempt to obtain a warrant." *Mejia,* 69 F.3d at 320. Under *Mejia,* this is impermissible and the inevitable discovery exception to the exclusionary rule is not satisfied. . . .

CONCLUSION

For the foregoing reasons, we **REVERSE** the district court's denial of Camou's motion to suppress.

d. INVENTORY SEARCHES

United States v. Lopez
547 F.3d 364 (2d Cir. 2008)

■ LEVAL, CIRCUIT JUDGE:

Defendant Ricardo Lopez appeals from the judgment of the United States District Court for the Southern District of New York (Sidney Stein J.) convicting him at a bench trial of possession of cocaine with intent to distribute, in violation of 21 U.S.C. §§ 812, 841(a)(1) and (b)(1)(C), and possession of two firearms in furtherance of a drug trafficking crime, in violation of 18 U.S.C. § 924(c)(1)(A)(i). The court sentenced Lopez to ten months of imprisonment on the cocaine count, plus a mandatory consecutive term of sixty months on the firearm count, as well as three years of supervised release and a $200 special assessment. Defendant contends that the district court made two errors: first, in finding that the warrantless search of Lopez's car was justifiable as an inventory search, notwithstanding that the procedure for the search was not governed in all aspects by a standardized police department policy and the officer conducting the search did not make a complete list of the car's contents; and second, in admitting expert testimony by a narcotics detective that cocaine and cutting materials found in Lopez's car suggested distribution.

We affirm.

Background

I.   The Evidence at Trial

The evidence presented at Lopez's trial, seen in the light most favorable to the government, *see* United States v. Rommy, 506 F.3d 108, 128 (2d Cir.2007), showed the following.

a.   Lopez's Arrest

On August 3, 2005, at approximately 3:30 a.m., Police Officer Lorrie Arroyo and Sergeant Stacy Barrett of the New York City Police Department ("NYPD") were patrolling in a police vehicle in the Hunts Point neighborhood of the Bronx, watching out for prostitution and auto theft. They observed a car parked on the right side of Faile Street. Two people were in the car, with the passenger door open and the engine running. The officers slowed as they passed the car and overheard the occupants arguing. They parked their car and got out to investigate. Arroyo approached the driver's side of the car; Barrett the passenger's side. The driver, the defendant Lopez, told them he had been arguing with his girlfriend. The passenger identified herself as Griselle Lopez. (Ricardo Lopez and Griselle are neither married to each other nor otherwise related.) Griselle told the police she was just hanging out with her boyfriend. Arroyo smelled alcohol and noticed that the defendant's eyes were bloodshot and his speech was slurred. She asked him if he had been drinking, and he responded, "Yes, one cup." Arroyo decided to arrest him for driving while intoxicated. She asked him to step out of the car and frisked him. She found a bulge in his rear right pants pocket, which seemed heavier than a wallet. Arroyo asked him what was in his pocket. He replied that it was a gun. Officer Arroyo then reached into the defendant's pocket, recovered a handgun and a wallet, and alerted Barrett that the defendant had a gun.

Meanwhile, Sgt. Barrett had asked Griselle to get out of the car. The sergeant asked for her identification. She replied that it was in the car. Two other officers who had arrived on the scene stood with Griselle while Barrett went to get Griselle's bag from the car. Sgt. Barrett located a bag near the front passenger seat and asked Griselle if it was hers, and if so, whether the sergeant could look in it for a driver's license or some other form of identification. Griselle confirmed that it was her bag and gave the sergeant permission to search it for identification. Barrett observed a wallet in the bag. On removing it, she saw a clear glass container of white powdery substance, which she believed to be cocaine. Barrett then arrested Griselle.

The defendant and Ms. Lopez were taken to the 41st Precinct station house in separate police cars. Officer Fischer, one of the other officers who had arrived on the scene, took over the defendant's car and drove it to the station.

b.   The Searches of Lopez's Car

At the 41st Precinct, Officer Arroyo and Sgt. Barrett conducted an inventory search of the defendant's car. According to Arroyo's testimony, inventory searches are standard in the NYPD when a car is seized upon the arrest of an intoxicated driver, both to protect the property of the owner and to protect the police. "[Y]ou have to do a total inventory search of the vehicle," she testified. "Everything has to come out." In searching the car, Arroyo found two glassines of cocaine in the middle console between the two front seats, as well as a bottle of liquor in the driver's side door. From the trunk, the officers removed plastic bags, canvas bags, a beach chair and umbrella, and some audio speakers. Arroyo then found a small green toiletry bag "tucked away" on the driver's side of the trunk. In it she discovered thirteen glassines of cocaine, as well as cocaine-related paraphernalia: a scale, a strainer with cocaine residue, a wooden masher with cocaine residue, two spoons with cocaine residue, more than one hundred empty glassines, and a jar of a white powdery substance that looked like cocaine. The officers then locked the gun, the bottle of liquor, the two glassines from the front middle console, and the green bag with its contents in a desk in their office. They drove the defendant to the 45th Precinct-which was, according to Officer Arroyo, an area hub for alcohol screening-where he was given a breathalyzer test and found to be legally impaired. At approximately 8:00 a.m., he was brought back to the 41st Precinct and returned to his cell. Shortly thereafter, Sgt. Barrett's shift ended and she went home.

Upon returning to the 41st Precinct, Arroyo noticed that Griselle was wearing jewelry. Arroyo asked her if someone could pick up the jewelry for her. Griselle arranged to have her daughter come to the station to get it. The daughter agreed also to take the defendant's belongings. Arroyo asked another officer, Officer Rivera, to make a list of the jewelry and have the daughter sign for it when the jewelry was handed over to her. Arroyo then went back to Lopez's car and began to place the contents into large plastic bags to give to Griselle's daughter. In the process of emptying the car, Arroyo looked in the glove compartment, where she found a loaded .38 caliber gun. Barrett testified that she had opened the glove compartment during the first search of the car, but became distracted when Arroyo asked her for a flashlight and failed to search it. Arroyo returned to the 41st Precinct to voucher the newly discovered gun and then turned over the noncontraband property to Griselle's daughter.

The list created by the officers identified items such as Griselle's pocketbook and jewelry. The beach chair, the umbrella, the audio speakers, etc.-items which Arroyo considered to be of no substantial value-were covered by a general catch-all description: "the belongings from the vehicle." Officer Arroyo explained that it was her practice to itemize objects in an inventory list only when they are "worth something." "If I handed off something smaller, say like car items, antifreeze, I wouldn't make a list, because it is worth nothing." Sgt. Barrett testified that it was her practice to make a complete list of returned property to be signed by the recipient. Sgt. Barrett testified that a written inventory of seized items-including "noncontraband evidence"-is supposed to be made as part of an inventory search. However, Sgt. Barrett also testified that the absence of a list of "noncontraband property" was not a violation of police regulations.

II.   District Court Proceedings

Prior to trial, Lopez waived his right to a jury trial and moved to suppress the drugs, drug paraphernalia, and gun recovered from the car, as well as his post-arrest statements. The motion to suppress the evidence found in the search of the automobile was on the ground that the warrantless search could not be justified as an inventory search because the officers did not prepare an inventory list of the items found and did not adhere to any prescribed standard procedure for the conduct of inventory searches. The motion to suppress his statements was on the ground that the delay in arraigning him before a magistrate judge was unreasonable.

The court conducted a combined bench trial and evidentiary hearing on the suppression motions. After the trial-hearing, the court denied both motions. As for the delay between Lopez's arrest and arraignment, the court found that it was reasonable in routine arrest processing. (This ruling is not challenged on appeal.) The court found that the inventory searches were reasonable because Officer Arroyo and Sgt. Barrett searched the car systematically, acted in good faith, and understood the proper purposes of an inventory search. With respect to whether the officers followed a standardized procedure, the district court observed that although "[n]o written rules or regulations were introduced into evidence at the trial . . . both officers, Arroyo and Barrett, testified that such procedures did exist." Noting the two officers' slightly different views, the court expressed doubt whether the dictates of Department procedure as to how seized property should be listed had been "rigorously followed." In the absence of any evidence of bad faith on the part of the police, the court concluded that minor deviations from any required listing procedures would not invalidate an inventory search.

Discussion

I.   The Inventory Search

Lopez's first argument on appeal is that the district court erred in denying his motion to suppress the items seized from the car. Lopez contends that the warrantless search violated the standards of the Fourth Amendment because the government failed to establish that it was a valid inventory search. According to the defendant's arguments, the search could not qualify as an inventory search because its conduct was not dictated by a standardized policy and because the police did not create a complete inventory list of the objects found. We believe the defendant's arguments are based on a misunderstanding of Supreme Court precedent.

It is well recognized in Supreme Court precedent that, when law enforcement officials take a vehicle into custody, they may search the vehicle and make an inventory of its contents without need for a search warrant and without regard to whether there is probable cause to suspect that the vehicle contains contraband or evidence of criminal conduct. *See* Illinois v. Lafayette, 462 U.S. 640, 643(1983) ("[An] inventory search constitutes a well-defined exception to the warrant requirement" under the Fourth Amendment (citing South Dakota v. Opperman, 428 U.S. 364 (1976))). This is because "[t] he policies behind the warrant requirement are not implicated in an inventory search, nor is the related concept of probable cause." Colorado v. Bertine, 479 U.S. 367, 371 (1987) (internal citation omitted). Such a search is not done to detect crime or to serve criminal prosecutions. It is done for quite different reasons: (1) to protect the owner's property while it is in police custody; (2) to protect the police against spurious claims of lost or stolen property; and (3) to protect the police from potential danger. Opperman, 428 U.S. at 369; *see also Bertine,* 479 U.S. at 372. The service of these objectives is wholly independent of whether the contents of the car figure in any way in a criminal investigation or prosecution.

The Supreme Court has, however, recognized the danger to privacy interests protected by the Fourth Amendment if officers were at liberty in their discretion to conduct warrantless investigative searches when they suspected criminal activity, which searches they would subsequently justify by labeling them as "inventory searches." *See* Florida v. Wells, 495 U.S. 1, 4 (1990). Accordingly, the Court has stressed the importance, in determining the lawfulness of an inventory search, that it be conducted under "standardized procedures." *See Bertine,* 479 U.S. at 374 & n. 6; *Lafayette,* 462 U.S. at 648; *Opperman,* 428 U.S. at 374–75. In *Bertine,* the Court upheld the lawfulness of the inventory search, concluding that, "as in *Lafayette,* reasonable police regulations relating to inventory procedures administered in good faith satisfy the Fourth Amendment, even though courts might as a matter of hindsight be able to devise equally reasonable rules requiring a different procedure." 479 U.S. at 374. Our court has noted that a consideration in determining the reasonableness of an inventory search is whether the officials conducting the search "act[ed] in good faith pursuant to 'standardized criteria . . . or established routine.'" United States v. Thompson, 29 F.3d 62, 65 (2d Cir.1994) (quoting *Wells,* 495 U.S. at 4).

Lopez contends that the search of his car in this case failed to conform to these requirements. According to his argument, the testimony of Officer Arroyo and Sgt. Barrett showed that there is no standardized procedure in the New York City Police Department. Barrrett testified that it was proper procedure to list all items found in an impounded vehicle. Officer Arroyo said it was her practice to list only items of value, grouping others under a general catch-all. Arroyo added, "Some cops don't make any list at all, some cops may list everything. It is not written anywhere that we have to make any type of a list." Because the search conducted in his case under Officer Arroyo's direction did not result in a complete list of the contents of the car, Lopez argues further that the search necessarily failed to meet the requirement that the objective of the search must be to produce an inventory.

In our view, the argument misunderstands the Supreme Court's requirements. It is true, without doubt, that the Court has stressed the need for a standardized policy. The Court has made it clear that a standardized policy is required so that inventory searches do not become "a ruse for a general rummaging in order to discover incriminating evidence." *Wells*, 495 U.S. at 4. The evidence adduced at the trial satisfied this standard. The unchallenged testimony of both Officer Arroyo and Sgt. Barrett established that there is a uniform standardized policy in the New York City Police Department to do a complete inventory search of the contents when a car is impounded. Arroyo testified, "[Y]ou have to do a total inventory of the vehicle. Everything has to come out." Sgt. Barrett confirmed that it is the responsibility of the officer to conduct an inventory search of an impounded car in order "to see if there were any items that needed to be safeguarded." This evidence was unchallenged and was credited by the district court. Accordingly, the purposes of the Supreme Court's requirement of a standardized policy were satisfied.

The lack of standardization that serves as the basis of Lopez's argument concerns whether the inventory list produced must include an itemization of every object found in the car, or whether items of small value may be omitted or grouped under a general category. We do not understand the Supreme Court's requirement of a standardized policy to extend to this issue because it has no bearing on the reason for the requirement of standardization. A standardized policy is needed to ensure that inventory searches do not become "a ruse for a general rummaging in order to discover incriminating evidence." *Wells,* 495 U.S. at 4. While the Supreme Court referred to the need for a standardized policy, we do not think the Court meant that every detail of search procedure must be governed by a standardized policy. We doubt, for example, that the Court intended a requirement of standardized policy as to the order in which different parts of the car are searched, or whether officers performing the search need to report the results on a standardized form, or whether the search should be conducted by the officers responsible for the impoundment decision. A standardized policy governing those questions would do nothing to safeguard the interests protected by the Fourth Amendment. Nor do we think the Court intended to require uniformity as to whether insignificant items of little or no value must be explicitly itemized. Once again, departmental uniformity on that issue would have no bearing on protecting the privacy interests of the public from unreasonable police intrusion. On the other hand, when a police department adopts a standardized policy governing the search of the contents of impounded vehicles, the owners and occupants of those vehicles are protected against the risk that officers will use selective discretion, searching only when they suspect criminal activity and then seeking to justify the searches as conducted for inventory purposes. As we understand the Supreme Court's objective, this is the kind of issue the Supreme Court had in mind in requiring that an inventory search be governed by a standardized policy. The evidence offered by the government and accepted by the district court satisfied that requirement.

Nor do we find merit in Lopez's argument that the failure to itemize each object found in the car, instead of covering items of lesser value under a general catch-all category of "personal belongings," is incompatible with the Supreme Court's warning that "inventory searches should be designed to produce an inventory." *Wells*, 495 U.S. at 4. The search did produce an inventory. The concept of an inventory does not demand the separate itemization of every single object. A conventional family automobile is likely to contain a bunch of road maps, pens and a notepad, a bottle opener, packs of chewing gum or candy, clip-on sunshades, a pack of tissues, a vanilla-scented deodorizer, DVDs and children's games, a baby bottle and a soiled baby blanket, an old sock, a sweater, windshield cleaning fluid, jumper cables, a tow rope, a tire iron and jack, a first aid kit, and emergency flares, not to mention empty candy wrappers and wads of chewed gum. That an officer might use a catch-all to cover objects of little or no value in no way casts doubt on the officer's claim that the purpose of the search was to make an inventory. It would serve no useful purpose to require separate itemization of each object found, regardless of its value, as a precondition to accepting a search as an inventory search. Such an obligation would furthermore interfere severely with the enforcement of the criminal laws by requiring irrational, unjustified suppression of evidence of crime where officers, conducting a bona fide search of an impounded vehicle, found evidence of serious crime but, in making their inventory, failed to distinguish between the maps of Connecticut and New York, or failed to list separately the soiled baby blanket or a pack of gum. Imposing a requirement to identify each item separately, regardless of lack of value, would furthermore add considerable administrative burden without in any way advancing the purposes of the Fourth Amendment to protect the public from "unreasonable searches and seizures." U.S. Const. amend. IV.

Finally, noting the Supreme Court's statement in *Bertine* that "reasonable police regulations relating to inventory searches administered in good faith satisfy the Fourth Amendment . . .," 479 U.S. at 374, Lopez argues that in his case the procedures were not administered in good faith because the officers were motivated by the expectation of finding criminal evidence in his car. We believe this also misunderstands the Court's explanations. The Fourth Amendment does not permit police officers to disguise warrantless, investigative searches as inventory searches. *See id.* at 371–72. However, the Supreme Court has not required an absence of expectation of finding criminal evidence as a prerequisite to a lawful inventory search. When officers, following standardized inventory procedures, seize, impound, and search a car in circumstances that suggest a probability of discovering criminal evidence, the officers will inevitably be motivated in part by criminal investigative objectives. Such motivation, however, cannot reasonably disqualify an inventory search that is performed under standardized procedures for legitimate custodial purposes. *See Opperman,* 428 U.S. at 369; *see also Bertine,* 479 U.S. at 372. Under the Supreme Court's precedents, if a search of an impounded car for inventory purposes is conducted under standardized procedures, that search falls under the inventory exception to the warrant requirement of the Fourth Amendment, notwithstanding a police expectation that the search will reveal criminal evidence. If good faith is a prerequisite of an inventory search, the expectation and motivation to find criminal evidence do not constitute bad faith.

In the present case, while the officers may well have had an investigative motivation to search Lopez's car, the circumstances called for the impoundment of his car, as Lopez was arrested for driving it while intoxicated, and the impoundment required the conduct of an inventory search. We find no reason to doubt that the Supreme Court's standards for the conduct of a warrantless inventory search were fully satisfied. We therefore affirm the district court's denial of the motion to suppress the evidence found in the impounded car.

e.   "PLAIN VIEW"

Horton v. California
496 U.S. 128 (1990)

■ STEVENS, J., delivered the opinion of the Court, in which REHNQUIST, C.J., and WHITE, BLACKMUN, O'CONNOR, SCALIA, and KENNEDY, JJ., joined. BRENNAN, J., filed a dissenting opinion in which MARSHALL, J., joined, *post,* p. 496 U. S. 142.

■ JUSTICE STEVENS delivered the opinion of the Court.

In this case, we revisit an issue that was considered, but not conclusively resolved, in Coolidge v. New Hampshire, 403 U. S. 443 (1971): Whether the warrantless seizure of evidence of crime in plain view is prohibited by the Fourth Amendment if the discovery of the evidence was not inadvertent. We conclude that even though inadvertence is a characteristic of most legitimate "plain view" seizures, it is not a necessary condition.

I

Petitioner was convicted of the armed robbery of Erwin Wallaker, the treasurer of the San Jose Coin Club. When Wallaker returned to his home after the Club's annual show, he entered his garage and was accosted by two masked men, one armed with a machine gun and the other with an electrical shocking device, sometimes referred to as a "stun gun." The two men shocked Wallaker, bound and handcuffed him, and robbed him of jewelry and cash. During the encounter, sufficient conversation took place to enable Wallaker subsequently to identify petitioner's distinctive voice. His identification was partially corroborated by a witness who saw the robbers leaving the scene, and by evidence that petitioner had attended the coin show.

Sergeant LaRault, an experienced police officer, investigated the crime and determined that there was probable cause to search petitioner's home for the proceeds of the robbery and for the weapons used by the robbers. His affidavit for a search warrant referred to police reports that described the weapons as well as the proceeds, but the warrant issued by the Magistrate only authorized a search for the proceeds, including three specifically described rings.

Pursuant to the warrant, LaRault searched petitioner's residence, but he did not find the stolen property. During the course of the search, however, he discovered the weapons in plain view and seized them. Specifically, he seized an Uzi machine gun, a .38 caliber revolver, two stun guns, a handcuff key, a San Jose Coin Club advertising brochure, and a few items of clothing identified by the victim.[1] LaRault testified that, while he was searching for the rings, he also was interested in finding other evidence connecting petitioner to the robbery. Thus, the seized evidence was not discovered "inadvertently."

The trial court refused to suppress the evidence found in petitioner's home and, after a jury trial, petitioner was found guilty and sentenced to prison. The California Court of Appeal affirmed. App. 43. It rejected petitioner's argument that our decision in *Coolidge* required suppression of the seized evidence that had not been listed in the warrant because its discovery was not inadvertent. App. 52–53. The court relied on the California Supreme Court's decision in North v. Superior Court, 8 Cal.3d 301, 104 Cal.Rptr. 833, 502 P.2d 1305 (1972). In that case, the court noted that the discussion of the inadvertence limitation on the "plain view" doctrine in Justice Stewart's opinion in *Coolidge* had been joined by only three other Members of this Court, and therefore was not binding on it.[2]

---

[1] Although the officer viewed other handguns and rifles, he did not seize them because there was no probable cause to believe they were associated with criminal activity. App. 30; *see* Arizona v. Hicks, 480 U. S. 321, 480 U. S. 327 (1987).

[2] "In *Coolidge*, the police arrested a murder suspect in his house and thereupon seized his automobile and searched it later at the police station, finding physical evidence that the victim had been inside the vehicle. The record disclosed that the police had known for some time of the probable role of the car in the crime, and there were no 'exigent circumstances' to justify a warrantless search. Accordingly, the plurality opinion of Justice Stewart concluded that the

The California Supreme Court denied petitioner's request for review. App. 78.

Because the California courts' interpretation of the "plain view" doctrine conflicts with the view of other courts, and because the unresolved issue is important, we granted certiorari, 493 U.S. 889 (1989).

II

. . . .The right to security in person and property protected by the Fourth Amendment may be invaded in quite different ways by searches and seizures. A search compromises the individual interest in privacy; a seizure deprives the individual of dominion over his or her person or property. United States v. Jacobsen, 466 U. S. 109, 113 (1984). The "plain view" doctrine is often considered an exception to the general rule that warrantless searches are presumptively unreasonable,[4] but this characterization overlooks the important difference between searches and seizures.[5] If an article is already in plain view, neither its observation nor its seizure would involve any invasion of privacy. *Arizona v. Hicks,* 480 U. S. 321 (1987); Illinois v. Andreas, 463 U. S. 765, 463 U. S. 771 (1983). A seizure of the article, however, would obviously invade the owner's possessory interest. Maryland v. Macon, 472 U. S. 463, 472 U. S. 469 (1985); *Jacobsen,* 466 U.S. at413. If "plain view" justifies an exception from an otherwise applicable warrant requirement, therefore, it must be an exception that is addressed to the concerns that are implicated by seizures, rather than by searches.

The criteria that generally guide "plain view" seizures were set forth in Coolidge v. New Hampshire, 403 U. S. 443 (1971). The Court held that

---

seizure could not be justified on the theory that the vehicle was itself the 'instrumentality' of the crime and was discovered 'in plain view' of the officers. Justice Stewart was of the opinion that the 'plain view' doctrine is applicable only to the inadvertent discovery of incriminating evidence."

"If the plurality opinion in *Coolidge* were entitled to binding effect as precedent, we would have difficulty distinguishing its holding from the instant case, for the discovery of petitioner's car was no more 'inadvertent' than in *Coolidge*. However, that portion of Justice Stewart's plurality opinion which proposed the adoption of new restrictions to the 'plain view' rule was signed by only four members of the court (Stewart, J., Douglas, J., Brennan, J., and Marshall, J.). Although concurring in the judgment, Justice Harlan declined to join in that portion of the opinion, and the four remaining justices expressly disagreed with Justice Stewart on this point." North v. Superior Court, 8 Cal.3d 301, 307–308, 104 Cal.Rptr. 833, 836, 502 P.2d 1305, 1308 (1972) (citations omitted).

    [4] "We reaffirm the basic rule of Fourth Amendment jurisprudence stated by Justice Stewart for a unanimous Court in Mincey v. Arizona, 437 U. S. 385, 437 U. S. 390:

"The Fourth Amendment proscribes all unreasonable searches and seizures, and it is a cardinal principle that 'searches conducted outside the judicial process, without prior approval by judge or magistrate, are *per se* unreasonable under the Fourth Amendment—subject only to a few specifically established and well-delineated exceptions.' " "Katz v. United States, 389 U. S. 347, 389 U. S. 357 (footnotes omitted)." United States v. Ross, 456 U. S. 798, 456 U. S. 824–825 (1982).

    [5] "It is important to distinguish 'plain view,' as used in *Coolidge* to justify seizure of an object, from an officer's mere observation of an item left in plain view. Whereas the latter generally involves no Fourth Amendment search, *see infra* at 740; Katz v. United States, 389 U. S. 347 (1967), the former generally does implicate the Amendment's limitations upon seizures of personal property." Texas v. Brown, 460 U. S. 730, 460 U. S. 738, n. 4 (1983) (opinion of REHNQUIST, J.).

the seizure of two automobiles parked in plain view on the defendant's driveway in the course of arresting the defendant violated the Fourth Amendment. Accordingly, particles of gun powder that had been subsequently found in vacuum sweepings from one of the cars could not be introduced in evidence against the defendant. The State endeavored to justify the seizure of the automobiles, and their subsequent search at the police station, on four different grounds, including the "plain view" doctrine.[6] The scope of that doctrine as it had developed in earlier cases was fairly summarized in these three paragraphs from Justice Stewart's opinion:

> "It is well established that, under certain circumstances, the police may seize evidence in plain view without a warrant. But it is important to keep in mind that, in the vast majority of cases, any evidence seized by the police will be in plain view, at least at the moment of seizure. The problem with the 'plain view' doctrine has been to identify the circumstances in which plain view has legal significance, rather than being simply the normal concomitant of any search, legal or illegal."

> "An example of the applicability of the 'plain view' doctrine is the situation in which the police have a warrant to search a given area for specified objects, and in the course of the search come across some other article of incriminating character. Cf. Go-Bart Importing Co. v. United States, 282 U. S. 344; United States v. Lefkowitz, 285 U. S. 452; Steele v. United States, 267 U. S. 498; Stanley v. Georgia, 394 U. S. 557, 394 U. S. 571 (STEWART, J., concurring in result). Where the initial intrusion that brings the police within plain view of such an article is supported, not by a warrant, but by one of the recognized exceptions to the warrant requirement, the seizure is also legitimate. Thus the police may inadvertently come across evidence while in 'hot pursuit' of a fleeing suspect. *Warden v. Hayden, supra*; cf. Hester v. United States, 265 U. S. 57. And an object that comes into view during a search incident to arrest that is appropriately limited in scope under existing law may be seized without a warrant. Chimel v. California, 395 U.S. at 762–763. Finally, the 'plain view' doctrine has been applied where a police officer is not searching for evidence against the accused, but nonetheless inadvertently comes across an incriminating object. Harris v. United States, 390 U. S. 234; Frazier v. Cupp, 394 U. S. 731; Ker v. California, 374 U.S. at 374 U. S. 43. *Cf.* Lewis v. United States, 385 U. S. 206."

---

[6]   The State primarily contended that the seizures were authorized by a warrant issued by the Attorney General, but the Court held the warrant invalid because it had not been issued by "a neutral and detached magistrate." 403 U.S. at 403 U. S. 449–453. In addition, the State relied on three exceptions from the warrant requirement: (1) search incident to arrest; (2) the automobile exception; and (3) the "plain view" doctrine. *id.* at 403 U. S. 453–473.

"What the 'plain view' cases have in common is that the police officer in each of them had a prior justification for an intrusion in the course of which he came inadvertently across a piece of evidence incriminating the accused. The doctrine serves to supplement the prior justification—whether it be a warrant for another object, hot pursuit, search incident to lawful arrest, or some other legitimate reason for being present unconnected with a search directed against the accused—and permits the warrantless seizure. Of course, the extension of the original justification is legitimate only where it is immediately apparent to the police that they have evidence before them; the 'plain view' doctrine may not be used to extend a general exploratory search from one object to another until something incriminating at last emerges."

Id. at 403 U. S. 465–466 (footnote omitted). Justice Stewart then described the two limitations on the doctrine that he found implicit in its rationale: First, "that plain view alone is never enough to justify the warrantless seizure of evidence," *id.* at 468; and second, "that the discovery of evidence in plain view must be inadvertent." *Id.* at 469.

Justice Stewart's analysis of the "plain view" doctrine did not command a majority, and a plurality of the Court has since made clear that the discussion is "not a binding precedent." Texas v. Brown, 460 U.S. at 737 (opinion of REHNQUIST, J.). Justice Harlan, who concurred in the Court's judgment and in its response to the dissenting opinions, 403 U.S. at 473–484, did not join the plurality's discussion of the "plain view" doctrine. *See id.* at 464–473. The decision nonetheless is a binding precedent. Before discussing the second limitation, which is implicated in this case, it is therefore necessary to explain why the first adequately supports the Court's judgment.

It is, of course, an essential predicate to any valid warrantless seizure of incriminating evidence that the officer did not violate the Fourth Amendment in arriving at the place from which the evidence could be plainly viewed. There are, moreover, two additional conditions that must be satisfied to justify the warrantless seizure. First, not only must the item be in plain view, its incriminating character must also be "immediately apparent." *Id.* at 466; *see also Arizona v. Hicks,* 480 U.S. at 326–327. Thus, in *Coolidge,* the cars were obviously in plain view, but their probative value remained uncertain until after the interiors were swept and examined microscopically. Second, not only must the officer be lawfully located in a place from which the object can be plainly seen, but he or she must also have a lawful right of access to the object itself.[7] As

---

[7] "This is simply a corollary of the familiar principle discussed above, that no amount of probable cause can justify a warrantless search or seizure absent exigent circumstances. Incontrovertible testimony of the senses that an incriminating object is on premises belonging to a criminal suspect may establish the fullest possible measure of probable cause. But even where the object is contraband, this Court has repeatedly stated and enforced the basic rule that the police may not enter and make a warrantless seizure. Taylor v. United States, 286 U.

the Solicitor General has suggested, Justice Harlan's vote in *Coolidge* may have rested on the fact that the seizure of the cars was accomplished by means of a warrantless trespass on the defendant's property. In all events, we are satisfied that the absence of inadvertence was not essential to the Court's rejection of the State's "plain view" argument in *Coolidge*.

III

Justice Stewart concluded that the inadvertence requirement was necessary to avoid a violation of the express constitutional requirement that a valid warrant must particularly describe the things to be seized. He explained:

> "The rationale of the exception to the warrant requirement, as just stated, is that a plain-view seizure will not turn an initially valid (and therefore limited) search into a 'general' one, while the inconvenience of procuring a warrant to cover an inadvertent discovery is great. But where the discovery is anticipated, where the police know in advance the location of the evidence and intend to seize it, the situation is altogether different. The requirement of a warrant to seize imposes no inconvenience whatever, or at least none which is constitutionally cognizable in a legal system that regards warrantless searches as 'per se unreasonable' in the absence of 'exigent circumstances.' "

> "If the initial intrusion is bottomed upon a warrant that fails to mention a particular object, though the police know its location and intend to seize it, then there is a violation of the express constitutional requirement of 'Warrants . . . particularly describing . . . [the] things to be seized.' "

403 U. S. at 469–471.

We find two flaws in this reasoning. First, even-handed law enforcement is best achieved by the application of objective standards of conduct, rather than standards that depend upon the subjective state of mind of the officer. The fact that an officer is interested in an item of evidence and fully expects to find it in the course of a search should not invalidate its seizure if the search is confined in area and duration by the terms of a warrant or a valid exception to the warrant requirement. If the officer has knowledge approaching certainty that the item will be found, we see no reason why he or she would deliberately omit a particular description of the item to be seized from the application for a search warrant.[9] Specification of the additional item could only permit

---

S. 1; Johnson v. United States, 333 U. S. 10; McDonald v. United States, 335 U. S. 451; Jones v. United States, 357 U. S. 493, 357 U. S. 497–498; Chapman v. United States, 365 U. S. 610; Trupiano v. United States, 334 U. S. 699."

[9] "If the police have probable cause to search for a photograph as well as a rifle and they proceed to seek a warrant, they could have no possible motive for deliberately including the rifle but omitting the photograph. Quite the contrary is true. Only oversight or careless mistake

the officer to expand the scope of the search. On the other hand, if he or she has a valid warrant to search for one item and merely a suspicion concerning the second, whether or not it amounts to probable cause, we fail to see why that suspicion should immunize the second item from seizure if it is found during a lawful search for the first. The hypothetical case put by Justice WHITE in his dissenting opinion in *Coolidge* is instructive:

> "Let us suppose officers secure a warrant to search a house for a rifle. While staying well within the range of a rifle search, they discover two photographs of the murder victim, both in plain sight in the bedroom. Assume also that the discovery of the one photograph was inadvertent, but finding the other was anticipated. The Court would permit the seizure of only one of the photographs. But in terms of the 'minor' peril to Fourth Amendment values, there is surely no difference between these two photographs: the interference with possession is the same in each case and the officers' appraisal of the photograph they expected to see is no less reliable than their judgment about the other. And in both situations, the actual inconvenience and danger to evidence remain identical if the officers must depart and secure a warrant."

Id. at 516.

Second, the suggestion that the inadvertence requirement is necessary to prevent the police from conducting general searches, or from converting specific warrants into general warrants, is not persuasive, because that interest is already served by the requirements that no warrant issue unless it "particularly describ[es] the place to be searched and the persons or things to be seized," *See* Maryland v. Garrison, 480 U. S. 79, 84 (1987); Steele v. United States No. 1, 267 U. S. 498, 503 (1925), and that a warrantless search be circumscribed by the exigencies which justify its initiation. *See, e.g.,* Maryland v. Buie, 494 U. S. 325, 332–334 (1990); Mincey v. Arizona, 437 U. S. 385, 393 (1978). Scrupulous adherence to these requirements serves the interests in limiting the area and duration of the search that the inadvertence requirement inadequately protects. Once those commands have been satisfied and the officer has a lawful right of access, however, no additional Fourth Amendment interest is furthered by requiring that the discovery of evidence be inadvertent. If the scope of the search exceeds that permitted by the terms of a validly issued warrant or the character of the relevant exception from the warrant requirement, the subsequent seizure is unconstitutional without more. Thus, in the case of a search incident to a lawful arrest,

---

would explain the omission in the warrant application if the police were convinced they had probable cause to search for the photograph." *Coolidge,* 403 U.S. at 517 (WHITE, J., dissenting).

> "[i]f the police stray outside the scope of an authorized *Chimel* search, they are already in violation of the Fourth Amendment, and evidence so seized will be excluded; adding a second reason for excluding evidence hardly seems worth the candle."

Coolidge, 403 U.S. at 517. Similarly, the object of a warrantless search of an automobile also defines its scope:

> "The scope of a warrantless search of an automobile thus is not defined by the nature of the container in which the contraband is secreted. Rather, it is defined by the object of the search and the places in which there is probable cause to believe that it may be found. Just as probable cause to believe that a stolen lawnmower may be found in a garage will not support a warrant to search an upstairs bedroom, probable cause to believe that undocumented aliens are being transported in a van will not justify a warrantless search of a suitcase. Probable cause to believe that a container placed in the trunk of a taxi contains contraband or evidence does not justify a search of the entire cab."

United States v. Ross, 456 U. S. 798, 824 (1982).

In this case, the scope of the search was not enlarged in the slightest by the omission of any reference to the weapons in the warrant. Indeed, if the three rings and other items named in the warrant had been found at the outset—or if petitioner had them in his possession and had responded to the warrant by producing them immediately—no search for weapons could have taken place. Again, Justice WHITE's dissenting opinion in *Coolidge* is instructive:

> "Police with a warrant for a rifle may search only places where rifles might be, and must terminate the search once the rifle is found; the inadvertence rule will in no way reduce the number of places into which they may lawfully look."

403 U.S. at 517.

As we have already suggested, by hypothesis the seizure of an object in plain view does not involve an intrusion on privacy.[11] If the interest in privacy has been invaded, the violation must have occurred before the object came into plain view, and there is no need for an inadvertence limitation on seizures to condemn it. The prohibition against general searches and general warrants serves primarily as a protection against unjustified intrusions on privacy. But reliance on privacy concerns that support that prohibition is misplaced when the inquiry concerns the

---

[11] Even if the item is a container, its seizure does not compromise the interest in preserving the privacy of its contents, because it may only be opened pursuant to either a search warrant, *See Smith v. Ohio,* 494 U. S. 541 (1990); *United States v. Place,* 462 U. S. 696, 462 U. S. 701 (1983); *Arkansas v. Sanders,* 442 U. S. 753 (1979); *United States v. Chadwick,* 433 U. S. 1 (1977); *United States v. Van Leeuwen,* 397 U. S. 249 (1970); *Ex parte Jackson,* 96 U. S. 727, 96 U. S. 733 (1878), or one of the well-delineated exceptions to the warrant requirement. *See Colorado v. Bertine,* 479 U. S. 367 (1987); *United States v. Ross,* 456 U. S. 798 (1982).

scope of an exception that merely authorizes an officer with a lawful right of access to an item to seize it without a warrant.

In this case, the items seized from petitioner's home were discovered during a lawful search authorized by a valid warrant. When they were discovered, it was immediately apparent to the officer that they constituted incriminating evidence. He had probable cause not only to obtain a warrant to search for the stolen property, but also to believe that the weapons and handguns had been used in the crime he was investigating. The search was authorized by the warrant, the seizure was authorized by the "plain view" doctrine. The judgment is affirmed.

▪ JUSTICE BRENNAN, with whom JUSTICE MARSHALL joins, dissenting.

I remain convinced that Justice Stewart correctly articulated the plain view doctrine in Coolidge v. New Hampshire, 403 U. S. 443 (1971). The Fourth Amendment permits law enforcement officers to seize items for which they do not have a warrant when those items are found in plain view and (1) the officers are lawfully in a position to observe the items, (2) the discovery of the items is "inadvertent," and (3) it is immediately apparent to the officers that the items are evidence of a crime, contraband, or otherwise subject to seizure. In eschewing the inadvertent discovery requirement, the majority ignores the Fourth Amendment's express command that warrants particularly describe not only the *places* to be searched but also the *things* to be seized.

4. REQUIREMENTS OF A VALID WARRANT

a. "PROBABLE CAUSE"

Illinois v. Gates
462 U.S. 213 (1983)

▪ JUSTICE REHNQUIST delivered the opinion of the Court.

Respondents Lance and Susan Gates were indicted for violation of state drug laws after police officers, executing a search warrant, discovered marijuana and other contraband in their automobile and home. Prior to trial the Gates' moved to suppress evidence seized during this search. The Illinois Supreme Court, 85 Ill.2d 376, 53 Ill.Dec. 218, 423 N.E.2d 887 (1981) affirmed the decisions of lower state courts, 82 Ill.App.3d 749, 38 Ill.Dec. 62, 403 N.E.2d 77 (1980) granting the motion. It held that the affidavit submitted in support of the State's application for a warrant to search the Gates' property was inadequate under this Court's decisions in Aguilar v. Texas, 378 U.S. 108 (1964) and Spinelli v. United States, 393 U.S. 410 (1969).

We granted certiorari to consider the application of the Fourth Amendment to a magistrate's issuance of a search warrant on the basis of a partially corroborated anonymous informant's tip. After receiving briefs and hearing oral argument on this question, however, we requested the parties to address an additional question:

> "Whether the rule requiring the exclusion at a criminal trial of evidence obtained in violation of the Fourth Amendment, Mapp v. Ohio, 367 U.S. 643 (1961); Weeks v. United States, 232 U.S. 383 (1914), should to any extent be modified, so as, for example, not to require the exclusion of evidence obtained in the reasonable belief that the search and seizure at issue was consistent with the Fourth Amendment."

We decide today, with apologies to all, that the issue we framed for the parties was not presented to the Illinois courts and, accordingly, do not address it. Rather, we consider the question originally presented in the petition for certiorari, and conclude that the Illinois Supreme Court read the requirements of our Fourth Amendment decisions too restrictively.

II

We now turn to the question presented in the State's original petition for certiorari, which requires us to decide whether respondents' rights under the Fourth and Fourteenth Amendments were violated by the search of their car and house. A chronological statement of events usefully introduces the issues at stake. Bloomingdale, Ill., is a suburb of Chicago located in DuPage County. On May 3, 1978, the Bloomingdale Police Department received by mail an anonymous handwritten letter which read as follows:

> "This letter is to inform you that you have a couple in your town who strictly make their living on selling drugs. They are Sue and Lance Gates, they live on Greenway, off Bloomingdale Rd. in the condominiums. Most of their buys are done in Florida. Sue his wife drives their car to Florida, where she leaves it to be loaded up with drugs, then Lance flys down and drives it back. Sue flys back after she drops the car off in Florida. May 3 she is driving down there again and Lance will be flying down in a few days to drive it back. At the time Lance drives the car back he has the trunk loaded with over $100,000.00 in drugs. Presently they have over $100,000.00 worth of drugs in their basement.

> They brag about the fact they never have to work, and make their entire living on pushers.

> I guarantee if you watch them carefully you will make a big catch. They are friends with some big drugs dealers, who visit their house often.

> Lance & Susan Gates

> Greenway

> in Condominiums"

The letter was referred by the Chief of Police of the Bloomingdale Police Department to Detective Mader, who decided to pursue the tip.

Mader learned, from the office of the Illinois Secretary of State, that an Illinois driver's license had been issued to one Lance Gates, residing at a stated address in Bloomingdale. He contacted a confidential informant, whose examination of certain financial records revealed a more recent address for the Gates, and he also learned from a police officer assigned to O'Hare Airport that "L. Gates" had made a reservation on Eastern Airlines flight 245 to West Palm Beach, Fla., scheduled to depart from Chicago on May 5 at 4:15 p.m.

Mader then made arrangements with an agent of the Drug Enforcement Administration for surveillance of the May 5 Eastern Airlines flight. The agent later reported to Mader that Gates had boarded the flight, and that federal agents in Florida had observed him arrive in West Palm Beach and take a taxi to the nearby Holiday Inn. They also reported that Gates went to a room registered to one Susan Gates and that, at 7:00 a.m. the next morning, Gates and an unidentified woman left the motel in a Mercury bearing Illinois license plates and drove northbound on an interstate frequently used by travelers to the Chicago area. In addition, the DEA agent informed Mader that the license plate number on the Mercury registered to a Hornet station wagon owned by Gates. The agent also advised Mader that the driving time between West Palm Beach and Bloomingdale was approximately 22 to 24 hours.

Mader signed an affidavit setting forth the foregoing facts, and submitted it to a judge of the Circuit Court of DuPage County, together with a copy of the anonymous letter. The judge of that court thereupon issued a search warrant for the Gates' residence and for their automobile. The judge, in deciding to issue the warrant, could have determined that the modus operandi of the Gates had been substantially corroborated. As the anonymous letter predicted, Lance Gates had flown from Chicago to West Palm Beach late in the afternoon of May 5th, had checked into a hotel room registered in the name of his wife, and, at 7:00 a.m. the following morning, had headed north, accompanied by an unidentified woman, out of West Palm Beach on an interstate highway used by travelers from South Florida to Chicago in an automobile bearing a license plate issued to him.

At 5:15 a.m. on March 7th, only 36 hours after he had flown out of Chicago, Lance Gates, and his wife, returned to their home in Bloomingdale, driving the car in which they had left West Palm Beach some 22 hours earlier. The Bloomingdale police were awaiting them, searched the trunk of the Mercury, and uncovered approximately 350 pounds of marijuana. A search of the Gates' home revealed marijuana, weapons, and other contraband. The Illinois Circuit Court ordered suppression of all these items, on the ground that the affidavit submitted to the Circuit Judge failed to support the necessary determination of probable cause to believe that the Gates' automobile and home contained the contraband in question. This decision was affirmed in turn by the

Illinois Appellate Court and by a divided vote of the Supreme Court of Illinois.

The Illinois Supreme Court concluded—and we are inclined to agree—that, standing alone, the anonymous letter sent to the Bloomingdale Police Department would not provide the basis for a magistrate's determination that there was probable cause to believe contraband would be found in the Gates' car and home. The letter provides virtually nothing from which one might conclude that its author is either honest or his information reliable; likewise, the letter gives absolutely no indication of the basis for the writer's predictions regarding the Gates' criminal activities. Something more was required, then, before a magistrate could conclude that there was probable cause to believe that contraband would be found in the Gates' home and car. *See* Aguilar v. Texas, 378 U.S. 108, 109, n. 1 (1964); Nathanson v. United States, 290 U.S. 41 (1933).

The Illinois Supreme Court also properly recognized that Detective Mader's affidavit might be capable of supplementing the anonymous letter with information sufficient to permit a determination of probable cause. *See* Whiteley v. Warden, 401 U.S. 560, 567 (1971). In holding that the affidavit in fact did not contain sufficient additional information to sustain a determination of probable cause, the Illinois court applied a "two-pronged test," derived from our decision in Spinelli v. United States, 393 U.S. 410 (1969).[3] The Illinois Supreme Court, like some others, apparently understood *Spinelli* as requiring that the anonymous letter satisfy each of two independent requirements before it could be relied on. J.A., at 5. According to this view, the letter, as supplemented by Mader's affidavit, first had to adequately reveal the "basis of knowledge" of the letter writer—the particular means by which he came by the information given in his report. Second, it had to provide facts sufficiently establishing either the "veracity" of the affiant's informant, or,

---

[3] In *Spinelli,* police officers observed Mr. Spinelli going to and from a particular apartment, which the telephone company said contained two telephones with stated numbers. The officers also were "informed by a confidential reliable informant that William Spinelli [was engaging in illegal gambling activities]" at the apartment, and that he used two phones, with numbers corresponding to those possessed by the police. The officers submitted an affidavit with this information to a magistrate and obtained a warrant to search Spinelli's apartment. We held that the magistrate could have made his determination of probable cause only by "abdicating his constitutional function," *id.,* at 416. The Government's affidavit contained absolutely no information regarding the informant's reliability. Thus, it did not satisfy *Aguilar's* requirement that such affidavits contain "some of the underlying circumstances" indicating that "the informant . . . was 'credible' " or that "his information [was] 'reliable.' " *Aguilar, supra,* 378 U.S., at 114. In addition, the tip failed to satisfy Aguilar's requirement that it detail "some of the underlying circumstances from which the informant concluded that . . . narcotics were where he claimed they were. We also held that if the tip concerning Spinelli had contained "sufficient detail" to permit the magistrate to conclude "that he [was] relying on something more substantial than a casual rumor circulating in the underworld or an accusation based merely on an individual's general reputation," 393 U.S., at 416, then he properly could have relied on it; we thought, however, that the tip lacked the requisite detail to permit this "self-verifying detail" analysis.

alternatively, the "reliability" of the informant's report in this particular case.

The Illinois court, alluding to an elaborate set of legal rules that have developed among various lower courts to enforce the "two-pronged test,"[4] found that the test had not been satisfied. First, the "veracity" prong was not satisfied because, "there was simply no basis [for] . . . conclud[ing] that the anonymous person [who wrote the letter to the Bloomingdale Police Department] was credible." J.A., at 7a. The court indicated that corroboration by police of details contained in the letter might never satisfy the "veracity" prong, and in any event, could not do so if, as in the present case, only "innocent" details are corroborated. In addition, the letter gave no indication of the basis of its writer's knowledge of the Gates' activities. The Illinois court understood Spinelli as permitting the detail contained in a tip to be used to infer that the informant had a reliable basis for his statements, but it thought that the anonymous letter failed to provide sufficient detail to permit such an inference. Thus, it concluded that no showing of probable cause had been made.

We agree with the Illinois Supreme Court that an informant's "veracity," "reliability" and "basis of knowledge" are all highly relevant in determining the value of his report. We do not agree, however, that these elements should be understood as entirely separate and independent requirements to be rigidly exacted in every case,[5] which the opinion of the Supreme Court of Illinois would imply. Rather, as detailed below, they should be understood simply as closely intertwined issues that may usefully illuminate the commonsense, practical question whether there is "probable cause" to believe that contraband or evidence is located in a particular place.

---

[4] *See, e.g.,* Stanley v. State, 19 Md.App. 507, 313 A.2d 847 (Md.App.1974). In summary, these rules posit that the "veracity" prong of the Spinelli test has two "spurs"—the informant's "credibility" and the "reliability" of his information. Various interpretations are advanced for the meaning of the "reliability" spur of the "veracity" prong. Both the "basis of knowledge" prong and the "veracity" prong are treated as entirely separate requirements, which must be independently satisfied in every case in order to sustain a determination of probable cause. *See* n. 5, infra. Some ancillary doctrines are relied on to satisfy certain of the foregoing requirements. For example, the "self-verifying detail" of a tip may satisfy the "basis of knowledge" requirement, although not the "credibility" spur of the "veracity" prong. *See* J.A. 10a. Conversely, corroboration would seem not capable of supporting the "basis of knowledge" prong, but only the "veracity" prong. *Id.,* at 12a.

The decision in *Stanley,* while expressly approving and conscientiously attempting to apply the "two-pronged test" observes that "[t]he built-in subtleties [of the test] are such, however, that a slipshod application calls down upon us the fury of Murphy's Law." 313 A.2d, at 860 (footnote omitted). The decision also suggested that it is necessary "to evolve analogous guidelines [to hearsay rules employed in trial settings] for the reception of hearsay in a probable cause setting." *Id.,* at 857.

[5] The entirely independent character that the *Spinelli* prongs have assumed is indicated both by the opinion of the Illinois Supreme Court in this case, and by decisions of other courts. One frequently cited decision, Stanley v. State, 19 Md.App. 507, 313 A.2d 847, 861 (Md.App.1974), remarks that "the dual requirements represented by the 'two-pronged test' are 'analytically severable' and an 'overkill' on one prong will not carry over to make up for a deficit on the other prong." *See also* n. 9, *infra.*

III

This totality-of-the-circumstances approach is far more consistent with our prior treatment of probable cause than is any rigid demand that specific "tests" be satisfied by every informant's tip. Perhaps the central teaching of our decisions bearing on the probable cause standard is that it is a "practical, nontechnical conception." Brinegar v. United States, 338 U.S. 160, 176 (1949). "In dealing with probable cause, . . . as the very name implies, we deal with probabilities. These are not technical; they are the factual and practical considerations of everyday life on which reasonable and prudent men, not legal technicians, act." *Id.*, at 175. Our observation in United States v. Cortez, 449 U.S. 411, 418 (1981), regarding "particularized suspicion," is also applicable to the probable cause standard:

> As our language indicates, we intended neither a rigid compartmentalization of the inquiries into an informant's "veracity," "reliability" and "basis of knowledge," nor that these inquiries be elaborate exegeses of an informant's tip. Rather, we required only that some facts bearing on two particular issues be provided to the magistrate. . . .
>
> The process does not deal with hard certainties, but with probabilities. Long before the law of probabilities was articulated as such, practical people formulated certain common-sense conclusions about human behavior; jurors as factfinders are permitted to do the same—and so are law enforcement officers. Finally, the evidence thus collected must be seen and weighed not in terms of library analysis by scholars, but as understood by those versed in the field of law enforcement.

As these comments illustrate, probable cause is a fluid concept—turning on the assessment of probabilities in particular factual contexts—not readily, or even usefully, reduced to a neat set of legal rules. Informants' tips doubtless come in many shapes and sizes from many different types of persons. As we said in Adams v. Williams, 407 U.S. 143, 147 (1972), "Informants' tips, like all other clues and evidence coming to a policeman on the scene may vary greatly in their value and reliability." Rigid legal rules are ill-suited to an area of such diversity. "One simple rule will not cover every situation." *Ibid.*[7]

---

[7] The diversity of informants' tips, as well as the usefulness of the totality-of-the-circumstances approach to probable cause, is reflected in our prior decisions on the subject. In Jones v. United States, 362 U.S. 257, 271 (1960), we held that probable cause to search petitioners' apartment was established by an affidavit based principally on an informant's tip. The unnamed informant claimed to have purchased narcotics from petitioners at their apartment; the affiant stated that he had been given correct information from the informant on a prior occasion. This, and the fact that petitioners had admitted to police officers on another occasion that they were narcotics users, sufficed to support the magistrate's determination of probable cause.

Likewise, in Rugendorf v. United States, 376 U.S. 528 (1964), the Court upheld a magistrate's determination that there was probable cause to believe that certain stolen property would be

Moreover, the "two-pronged test" directs analysis into two largely independent channels—the informant's "veracity" or "reliability" and his "basis of knowledge." *See* nn. 4 and 5 *supra*. There are persuasive arguments against according these two elements such independent status. Instead, they are better understood as relevant considerations in the totality-of-the-circumstances analysis that traditionally has guided probable cause determinations: a deficiency in one may be compensated for, in determining the overall reliability of a tip, by a strong showing as to the other, or by some other indicia of reliability. *See, e.g.,* Adams v. Williams, *supra,* 407 U.S., at 146–147; Harris v. United States, 403 U.S. 573 (1971).

If, for example, a particular informant is known for the unusual reliability of his predictions of certain types of criminal activities in a locality, his failure, in a particular case, to thoroughly set forth the basis of his knowledge surely should not serve as an absolute bar to a finding of probable cause based on his tip. *See* United States v. Sellers, 483 F.2d 37 (CA5 1973). Likewise, if an unquestionably honest citizen comes forward with a report of criminal activity—which if fabricated would subject him to criminal liability—we have found rigorous scrutiny of the basis of his knowledge unnecessary. *Adams v. Williams, supra.* Conversely, even if we entertain some doubt as to an informant's motives, his explicit and detailed description of alleged wrongdoing, along with a statement that the event was observed first-hand, entitles his tip to greater weight than might otherwise be the case. Unlike a totality-of-the-circumstances analysis, which permits a balanced assessment of the relative weights of all the various indicia of reliability (and unreliability) attending an informant's tip, the "two-pronged test" has encouraged an excessively technical dissection of informants' tips,[9] with undue attention

---

found in petitioner's apartment. The affidavit submitted to the magistrate stated that certain furs had been stolen, and that a confidential informant, who previously had furnished confidential information, said that he saw the furs in petitioner's home. Moreover, another confidential informant, also claimed to be reliable, stated that one Schweihs had stolen the furs. Police reports indicated that petitioner had been seen in Schweihs' company and a third informant stated that petitioner was a fence for Schweihs.

   [9] Some lower court decisions, brought to our attention by the State, reflect a rigid application of such rules. In Bridger v. State, 503 S.W.2d 801 (Tex.Cr.App.1974), the affiant had received a confession of armed robbery from one of two suspects in the robbery; in addition, the suspect had given the officer $800 in cash stolen during the robbery. The suspect also told the officer that the gun used in the robbery was hidden in the other suspect's apartment. A warrant issued on the basis of this was invalidated on the ground that the affidavit did not satisfactorily describe how the accomplice had obtained his information regarding the gun.

Likewise, in People v. Palanza, 55 Ill.App.3d 1028, 13 Ill.Dec. 752, 371 N.E.2d 687 (Ill.App.1978), the affidavit submitted in support of an application for a search warrant stated that an informant of proven and uncontested reliability had seen, in specifically described premises, "a quantity of a white crystalline substance which was represented to the informant by a white male occupant of the premises to be cocaine. Informant has observed cocaine on numerous occasions in the past and is thoroughly familiar with its appearance. The informant states that the white crystalline powder he observed in the above described premises appeared to him to be cocaine." The warrant issued on the basis of the affidavit was invalidated because "There is no indication as to how the informant or for that matter any other person could tell whether a white substance was cocaine and not some other substance such as sugar or salt." *Id.,* 13 Ill.Dec., at 754, 371 N.E.2d, at 689.

being focused on isolated issues that cannot sensibly be divorced from the other facts presented to the magistrate.

As early as Locke v. United States, 7 Cranch. 339, 348 (1813), Chief Justice Marshall observed, in a closely related context, that "the term 'probable cause,' according to its usual acceptation, means less than evidence which would justify condemnation. . . . It imports a seizure made under circumstances which warrant suspicion." More recently, we said that "the quanta . . . of proof" appropriate in ordinary judicial proceedings are inapplicable to the decision to issue a warrant. *Brinegar, supra*, 338 U.S., at 173. Finely-tuned standards such as proof beyond a reasonable doubt or by a preponderance of the evidence, useful in formal trials, have no place in the magistrate's decision. While an effort to fix some general, numerically precise degree of certainty corresponding to "probable cause" may not be helpful, it is clear that "only the probability, and not a prima facie showing, of criminal activity is the standard of probable cause." *Spinelli, supra*, 393 U.S., at 419. *See* Model Code of Pre-Arraignment Procedure § 210.1(7) (Proposed Off. Draft 1972); W. LaFave, Search and Seizure, § 3.2(3) (1978).

We also have recognized that affidavits "are normally drafted by nonlawyers in the midst and haste of a criminal investigation. Technical requirements of elaborate specificity once exacted under common law pleading have no proper place in this area." *Ventresca, supra*, 380 U.S., at 108. Likewise, search and arrest warrants long have been issued by persons who are neither lawyers nor judges, and who certainly do not remain abreast of each judicial refinement of the nature of "probable cause." *See* Shadwick v. City of Tampa, 407 U.S. 345, 348–350 (1972). The rigorous inquiry into the *Spinelli* prongs and the complex superstructure of evidentiary and analytical rules that some have seen implicit in our Spinelli decision, cannot be reconciled with the fact that many warrants are—quite properly, *ibid.*—issued on the basis of nontechnical, common-sense judgments of laymen applying a standard less demanding than those used in more formal legal proceedings. Likewise, given the informal, often hurried context in which it must be applied, the "built-in subtleties," Stanley v. State, 19 Md.App. 507, 313 A.2d 847, 860 (Md.App.1974), of the "two-pronged test" are particularly unlikely to assist magistrates in determining probable cause.

Similarly, we have repeatedly said that after-the-fact scrutiny by courts of the sufficiency of an affidavit should not take the form of de novo review. A magistrate's "determination of probable cause should be paid great deference by reviewing courts." *Spinelli, supra*, 393 U.S., at 419. "A grudging or negative attitude by reviewing courts toward warrants," *Ventresca, supra*, 380 U.S., at 108, is inconsistent with the Fourth

---

Finally, in People v. Brethauer, 174 Colo. 29, 482 P.2d 369 (Colo.1971), an informant, stated to have supplied reliable information in the past, claimed that L.S.D. and marijuana were located on certain premises. The affiant supplied police with drugs, which were tested by police and confirmed to be illegal substances. The affidavit setting forth these, and other, facts was found defective under both prongs of *Spinelli*.

Amendment's strong preference for searches conducted pursuant to a warrant "courts should not invalidate . . . warrant[s] by interpreting affidavit [s] in a hypertechnical, rather than a commonsense, manner." *Id.*, at 109.

If the affidavits submitted by police officers are subjected to the type of scrutiny some courts have deemed appropriate, police might well resort to warrantless searches, with the hope of relying on consent or some other exception to the warrant clause that might develop at the time of the search. In addition, the possession of a warrant by officers conducting an arrest or search greatly reduces the perception of unlawful or intrusive police conduct, by assuring "the individual whose property is searched or seized of the lawful authority of the executing officer, his need to search, and the limits of his power to search." United States v. Chadwick, 433 U.S. 1, 9 (1977). Reflecting this preference for the warrant process, the traditional standard for review of an issuing magistrate's probable cause determination has been that so long as the magistrate had a "substantial basis for . . . conclud[ing]" that a search would uncover evidence of wrongdoing, the Fourth Amendment requires no more. Jones v. United States, 362 U.S. 257, 271 (1960). *See* United States v. Harris, 403 U.S. 573, 577–583 (1971). We think reaffirmation of this standard better serves the purpose of encouraging recourse to the warrant procedure and is more consistent with our traditional deference to the probable cause determinations of magistrates than is the "two-pronged test."

Finally, the direction taken by decisions following *Spinelli* poorly serves "the most basic function of any government": "to provide for the security of the individual and of his property." Miranda v. Arizona, 384 U.S. 436, 539 (1966) (WHITE, J., dissenting). The strictures that inevitably accompany the "two-pronged test" cannot avoid seriously impeding the task of law enforcement, see, e.g., n. 9 *supra*. If, as the Illinois Supreme Court apparently thought, that test must be rigorously applied in every case, anonymous tips seldom would be of greatly diminished value in police work. Ordinary citizens, like ordinary witnesses, *see* Federal Rules of Evidence 701, Advisory Committee Note (1976), generally do not provide extensive recitations of the basis of their everyday observations. Likewise, as the Illinois Supreme Court observed in this case, the veracity of persons supplying anonymous tips is by hypothesis largely unknown, and unknowable. As a result, anonymous tips seldom could survive a rigorous application of either of the *Spinelli* prongs. Yet, such tips, particularly when supplemented by independent police investigation, frequently contribute to the solution of otherwise "perfect crimes." While a conscientious assessment of the basis for crediting such tips is required by the Fourth Amendment, a standard that leaves virtually no place for anonymous citizen informants is not.

For all these reasons, we conclude that it is wiser to abandon the "two-pronged test" established by our decisions in Aguilar and Spinelli.[11] In its place we reaffirm the totality-of-the-circumstances analysis that traditionally has informed probable cause determinations. *See Jones v. United States, supra; United States v. Ventresca, supra; Brinegar v. United States, supra.* The task of the issuing magistrate is simply to make a practical, common-sense decision whether, given all the circumstances set forth in the affidavit before him, including the "veracity" and "basis of knowledge" of persons supplying hearsay information, there is a fair probability that contraband or evidence of a crime will be found in a particular place. And the duty of a reviewing court is simply to ensure that the magistrate had a "substantial basis for . . . conclud[ing]" that probable cause existed. *Jones v. United States, supra,* 362 U.S., at 271. We are convinced that this flexible, easily applied standard will better achieve the accommodation of public and private interests that the Fourth Amendment requires than does the approach that has developed from *Aguilar* and *Spinelli.*

Our earlier cases illustrate the limits beyond which a magistrate may not venture in issuing a warrant. A sworn statement of an affiant that "he has cause to suspect and does believe that" liquor illegally brought into the United States is located on certain premises will not do. Nathanson v. United States, 290 U.S. 41 (1933). An affidavit must provide the magistrate with a substantial basis for determining the existence of probable cause, and the wholly conclusory statement at issue in Nathanson failed to meet this requirement. An officer's statement that "affiants have received reliable information from a credible person and believe" that heroin is stored in a home, is likewise inadequate. Aguilar v. Texas, 378 U.S. 108 (1964). As in *Nathanson,* this is a mere conclusory statement that gives the magistrate virtually no basis at all for making a judgment regarding probable cause. Sufficient information must be presented to the magistrate to allow that official to determine probable cause; his action cannot be a mere ratification of the bare conclusions of others. In order to ensure that such an abdication of the magistrate's duty does not occur, courts must continue to conscientiously review the sufficiency of affidavits on which warrants are issued. But when we move beyond the "bare bones" affidavits present in cases such as *Nathanson*

---

[11] The Court's decision in *Spinelli* has been the subject of considerable criticism, both by members of this Court and others. Justice BLACKMUN, concurring in United States v. Harris, 403 U.S. 573, 585–586 (1971), noted his long-held view "that *Spinelli* . . . was wrongly decided" by this Court. Justice Black similarly would have overruled that decision. *Ibid.* Likewise, a noted commentator has observed that "[t]he *Aguilar-Spinelli* formulation has provoked apparently ceaseless litigation." 8A Moore's Federal Practice ¶ 41.04 (1981).

Whether the allegations submitted to the magistrate in *Spinelli* would, under the view we now take, have supported a finding of probable cause, we think it would not be profitable to decide. There are so many variables in the probable cause equation that one determination will seldom be a useful "precedent" for another. Suffice it to say that while we in no way abandon *Spinelli's* concern for the trustworthiness of informers and for the principle that it is the magistrate who must ultimately make a finding of probable cause, we reject the rigid categorization suggested by some of its language.

and *Aguilar*, this area simply does not lend itself to a prescribed set of rules, like that which had developed from *Spinelli*. Instead, the flexible, common-sense standard articulated in *Jones, Ventresca,* and *Brinegar* better serves the purposes of the Fourth Amendment's probable cause requirement. . . .

Justice BRENNAN's dissent . . . suggests that "words such as 'practical,' 'nontechnical,' and 'common sense,' as used in the Court's opinion, are but code words for an overly-permissive attitude towards police practices in derogation of the rights secured by the Fourth Amendment." Infra, p. 2359. An easy, but not a complete, answer to this rather florid statement would be that nothing we know about Justice Rutledge suggests that he would have used the words he chose in *Brinegar* in such a manner. More fundamentally, no one doubts that "under our Constitution only measures consistent with the Fourth Amendment may be employed by government to cure [the horrors of drug trafficking],"; but this agreement does not advance the inquiry as to which measures are, and which measures are not, consistent with the Fourth Amendment. "Fidelity" to the commands of the Constitution suggests balanced judgment rather than exhortation. The highest "fidelity" is achieved neither by the judge who instinctively goes furthest in upholding even the most bizarre claim of individual constitutional rights, any more than it is achieved by a judge who instinctively goes furthest in accepting the most restrictive claims of governmental authorities. The task of this Court, as of other courts, is to "hold the balance true," and we think we have done that in this case.

IV

Our decisions applying the totality-of-the-circumstances analysis outlined above have consistently recognized the value of corroboration of details of an informant's tip by independent police work. In *Jones v. United States, supra,* 362 U.S., at 269, we held that an affidavit relying on hearsay "is not to be deemed insufficient on that score, so long as a substantial basis for crediting the hearsay is presented." We went on to say that even in making a warrantless arrest an officer "may rely upon information received through an informant, rather than upon his direct observations, so long as the informant's statement is reasonably corroborated by other matters within the officer's knowledge." *Ibid.* Likewise, we recognized the probative value of corroborative efforts of police officials in *Aguilar*—the source of the "two-pronged test"—by observing that if the police had made some effort to corroborate the informant's report at issue, "an entirely different case" would have been presented. *Aguilar, supra,* 378 U.S., at 109, n. 1.

Our decision in Draper v. United States, 358 U.S. 307 (1959), however, is the classic case on the value of corroborative efforts of police officials. There, an informant named Hereford reported that Draper would arrive in Denver on a train from Chicago on one of two days, and that he would be carrying a quantity of heroin. The informant also supplied a fairly detailed physical description of Draper, and predicted that he would be wearing a light colored raincoat, brown slacks and black shoes, and would be walking "real fast." *Id.*, at 309. Hereford gave no indication of the basis for his information.[12]

On one of the stated dates police officers observed a man matching this description exit a train arriving from Chicago; his attire and luggage matched Hereford's report and he was walking rapidly. We explained in *Draper* that, by this point in his investigation, the arresting officer "had personally verified every facet of the information given him by Hereford except whether petitioner had accomplished his mission and had the three ounces of heroin on his person or in his bag. And surely, with every other bit of Hereford's information being thus personally verified, [the officer] had 'reasonable grounds' to believe that the remaining unverified bit of Hereford's information—that Draper would have the heroin with him—was likewise true," *id.*, at 313.

The showing of probable cause in the present case was fully as compelling as that in *Draper*. Even standing alone, the facts obtained through the independent investigation of Mader and the DEA at least suggested that the Gates were involved in drug trafficking. In addition to being a popular vacation site, Florida is well-known as a source of narcotics and other illegal drugs. *See* United States v. Mendenhall, 446 U.S. 544, 562 (1980) (POWELL, J., concurring); DEA, Narcotics Intelligence Estimate, The Supply of Drugs to the U.S. Illicit Market From Foreign and Domestic Sources 10 (1979). Lance Gates' flight to Palm Beach, his brief, overnight stay in a motel, and apparent immediate return north to Chicago in the family car, conveniently awaiting him in West Palm Beach, is as suggestive of a pre-arranged drug run, as it is of an ordinary vacation trip.

In addition, the magistrate could rely on the anonymous letter, which had been corroborated in major part by Mader's efforts—just as had occurred in *Draper*.[13] The Supreme Court of Illinois reasoned that Draper involved an informant who had given reliable information on previous occasions, while the honesty and reliability of the anonymous

---

[12]   The tip in *Draper* might well not have survived the rigid application of the "two-pronged test" that developed following *Spinelli*. The only reference to Hereford's reliability was that he had "been engaged as a 'special employee' of the Bureau of Narcotics at Denver for about six months, and from time to time gave information to [the police] for small sums of money, and that [the officer] had always found the information given by Hereford to be accurate and reliable." 358 U.S., at 309. Likewise, the tip gave no indication of how Hereford came by his information. At most, the detailed and accurate predictions in the tip indicated that, however Hereford obtained his information, it was reliable.

[13]   The Illinois Supreme Court thought that the verification of details contained in the anonymous letter in this case amounted only to "the corroboration of innocent activity," J.A. 12a, and that this was insufficient to support a finding of probable cause. We are inclined to agree, however, with the observation of Justice Moran in his dissenting opinion that "In this case, just as in *Draper*, seemingly innocent activity became suspicious in the light of the initial tip." J.A. 18a. And it bears noting that all of the corroborating detail established in *Draper, supra*, was of entirely innocent activity—a fact later pointed out by the Court in both Jones v. United States, 362 U.S. 257, 269–270 (1960), and Ker v. California, 374 U.S. 23, 36 (1963).

informant in this case were unknown to the Bloomingdale police. While this distinction might be an apt one at the time the police department received the anonymous letter, it became far less significant after Mader's independent investigative work occurred. The corroboration of the letter's predictions that the Gates' car would be in Florida, that Lance Gates would fly to Florida in the next day or so, and that he would drive the car north toward Bloomingdale all indicated, albeit not with certainty, that the informant's other assertions also were true. "Because an informant is right about some things, he is more probably right about other facts," *Spinelli, supra*, 393 U.S., at 427 (WHITE, J., concurring)— including the claim regarding the Gates' illegal activity. This may well not be the type of "reliability" or "veracity" necessary to satisfy some views of the "veracity prong" of *Spinelli,* but we think it suffices for the practical, common-sense judgment called for in making a probable cause determination. It is enough, for purposes of assessing probable cause, that "corroboration through other sources of information reduced the chances of a reckless or prevaricating tale," thus providing "a substantial basis for crediting the hearsay." *Jones v. United States, supra*, 362 U.S., at 269, 271.

This is perfectly reasonable. As discussed previously, probable cause requires only a probability or substantial chance of criminal activity, not an actual showing of such activity. By hypothesis, therefore, innocent behavior frequently will provide the basis for a showing of probable cause; to require otherwise would be to sub silentio impose a drastically more rigorous definition of probable cause than the security of our citizens demands. We think the Illinois court attempted a too rigid classification of the types of conduct that may be relied upon in seeking to demonstrate probable cause. *See* Brown v. Texas, 443 U.S. 47, 52, n.2 (1979). In making a determination of probable cause the relevant inquiry is not whether particular conduct is "innocent" or "guilty," but the degree of suspicion that attaches to particular types of non-criminal acts.

Finally, the anonymous letter contained a range of details relating not just to easily obtained facts and conditions existing at the time of the tip, but to future actions of third parties ordinarily not easily predicted. The letter writer's accurate information as to the travel plans of each of the Gates was of a character likely obtained only from the Gates themselves, or from someone familiar with their not entirely ordinary travel plans. If the informant had access to accurate information of this type a magistrate could properly conclude that it was not unlikely that he also had access to reliable information of the Gates' alleged illegal activities.[14] Of course, the Gates' travel plans might have been learned

---

[14] The dissent seizes on one inaccuracy in the anonymous informant's letter—its statement that Sue Gates would fly from Florida to Illinois, when in fact she drove—and argues that the probative value of the entire tip was undermined by this allegedly "material mistake." We have never required that informants used by the police be infallible, and can see no reason to impose such a requirement in this case. Probable cause, particularly when police have obtained a warrant, simply does not require the perfection the dissent finds necessary. Likewise, there is no force to the dissent's argument that the Gates' action in leaving their home unguarded

from a talkative neighbor or travel agent; under the "two-pronged test" developed from *Spinelli*, the character of the details in the anonymous letter might well not permit a sufficiently clear inference regarding the letter writer's "basis of knowledge." But, as discussed previously, probable cause does not demand the certainty we associate with formal trials. It is enough that there was a fair probability that the writer of the anonymous letter had obtained his entire story either from the Gates or someone they trusted. And corroboration of major portions of the letter's predictions provides just this probability. It is apparent, therefore, that the judge issuing the warrant had a "substantial basis for . . . conclud[ing]" that probable cause to search the Gates' home and car existed. The judgment of the Supreme Court of Illinois therefore must be Reversed.

■ JUSTICE WHITE, concurring.

Since a majority of the Court deems it inappropriate to address the good faith issue, I briefly address the question that the Court does reach—whether the warrant authorizing the search and seizure of respondents' car and home was constitutionally valid. Abandoning the "two-pronged test" of Aguilar v. Texas, 378 U.S. 108 (1964), and Spinelli v. United States, 393 U.S. 410 (1969), the Court upholds the validity of the warrant under a new "totality of the circumstances" approach. Although I agree that the warrant should be upheld, I reach this conclusion in accordance with the *Aguilar-Spinelli* framework. . . .

In the present case, it is undisputed that the anonymous tip, by itself, did not furnish probable cause. The question is whether those portions of the affidavit describing the results of the police investigation of the respondents, when considered in light of the tip, "would permit the suspicions engendered by the informant's report to ripen into a judgment that a crime was probably being committed." *Spinelli, supra*, at 418. The Illinois Supreme Court concluded that the corroboration was insufficient to permit such a ripening. . . .

In my view, the lower court's characterization of the Gates' activity here as totally "innocent" is dubious. In fact, the behavior was quite suspicious. I agree with the Court that Lance Gates' flight to Palm Beach,

---

undercut the informant's claim that drugs were hidden there. Indeed, the line-by-line scrutiny that the dissent applies to the anonymous letter is akin to that we find inappropriate in reviewing magistrate's decisions. The dissent apparently attributes to the magistrate who issued the warrant in this case the rather implausible notion that persons dealing in drugs always stay at home, apparently out of fear that to leave might risk intrusion by criminals. If accurate, one could not help sympathizing with the self-imposed isolation of people so situated. In reality, however, it is scarcely likely that the magistrate ever thought that the anonymous tip "kept one spouse" at home, much less that he relied on the theory advanced by the dissent. The letter simply says that Sue would fly from Florida to Illinois, without indicating whether the Gates' made the bitter choice of leaving the drugs in their house, or those in their car, unguarded. The magistrate's determination that there might be drugs or evidence of criminal activity in the Gates' home was well-supported by the less speculative theory, noted in text, that if the informant could predict with considerable accuracy the somewhat unusual travel plans of the Gates, he probably also had a reliable basis for his statements that the Gates' kept a large quantity of drugs in their home and frequently were visited by other drug traffickers there.

an area known to be a source of narcotics, the brief overnight stay in a motel, and apparent immediate return North, suggest a pattern that trained law-enforcement officers have recognized as indicative of illicit drug-dealing activity.

As in *Draper*, the police investigation in the present case satisfactorily demonstrated that the informant's tip was as trustworthy as one that would alone satisfy the *Aguilar* tests. The tip predicted that Sue Gates would drive to Florida, that Lance Gates would fly there a few days after May 3, and that Lance would then drive the car back. After the police corroborated these facts, the magistrate could reasonably have inferred, as he apparently did, that the informant, who had specific knowledge of these unusual travel plans, did not make up his story and that he obtained his information in a reliable way. It is theoretically possible, as respondents insist, that the tip could have been supplied by a "vindictive travel agent" and that the Gates' activities, although unusual, might not have been unlawful.[24] But *Aguilar* and *Spinelli*, like our other cases, do not require that certain guilt be established before a warrant may properly be issued. "[O]nly the probability, and not a prima facie showing, of criminal activity is the standard of probable cause." *Spinelli, supra*, at 419 (citing Beck v. Ohio, 379 U.S. 89, 96 (1964)). I therefore conclude that the judgment of the Illinois Supreme Court invalidating the warrant must be reversed.

The Court agrees that the warrant was valid, but, in the process of reaching this conclusion, it overrules the *Aguilar-Spinelli* tests and replaces them with a "totality of the circumstances" standard. As shown above, it is not at all necessary to overrule *Aguilar-Spinelli* in order to reverse the judgment below. Therefore, because I am inclined to believe that, when applied properly, the *Aguilar-Spinelli* rules play an appropriate role in probable cause determinations, and because the Court's holding may foretell an evisceration of the probable cause standard, I do not join the Court's holding. . . .

■ JUSTICE BRENNAN, with whom JUSTICE MARSHALL joins, dissenting.

Although I join Justice STEVENS' dissenting opinion and agree with him that the warrant is invalid even under the Court's newly announced "totality of the circumstances" test, *see post*, at 2361–2362, and n. 8, I write separately to dissent from the Court's unjustified and ill-advised rejection of the two-prong test for evaluating the validity of a warrant based on hearsay announced in Aguilar v. Texas, 378 U.S. 108 (1964), and refined in Spinelli v. United States, 393 U.S. 410 (1969). . . .

In any event, there certainly is no basis for treating anonymous informants as presumptively reliable. Nor is there any basis for assuming that the information provided by an anonymous informant has

---

[24] It is also true, as Justice STEVENS points out, post, at 2360, n. 3, that the fact that respondents were last seen leaving West Palm Beach on a northbound interstate highway is far from conclusive proof that they were heading directly to Bloomington.

been obtained in a reliable way. If we are unwilling to accept conclusory allegations from the police, who are presumptively reliable, or from informants who are known, at least to the police, there cannot possibly be any rational basis for accepting conclusory allegations from anonymous informants.

To suggest that anonymous informants' tips are subject to the tests established by *Aguilar* and *Spinelli* is not to suggest that they can never provide a basis for a finding of probable cause. It is conceivable that police corroboration of the details of the tip might establish the reliability of the informant under *Aguilar's* veracity prong, as refined in *Spinelli,* and that the details in the tip might be sufficient to qualify under the "self-verifying detail" test established by *Spinelli* as a means of satisfying *Aguilar's* basis of knowledge prong. The *Aguilar* and *Spinelli* tests must be applied to anonymous informants' tips, however, if we are to continue to insure that findings of probable cause, and attendant intrusions, are based on information provided by an honest or credible person who has acquired the information in a reliable way.[6]

In cases in which the police rely on information obtained from an anonymous informant, the police, by hypothesis, cannot obtain further information from the informant regarding the facts and circumstances on which the informant based his conclusion. When the police seek a warrant based solely on an anonymous informants' tip, therefore, they are providing the magistrate with all the information on which they have based their conclusion. In this respect, the command of *Aguilar* and *Spinelli* has been met and the process value identified above has been served. But *Aguilar* and *Spinelli* advance other values which argue for their application even to anonymous informants' tips. They structure the magistrate's probable cause inquiry and, more importantly, they guard against findings of probable cause, and attendant intrusions, based on anything other than information which magistrates reasonably can conclude has been obtained in a reliable way by an honest or credible person.

In light of the important purposes served by *Aguilar* and *Spinelli*, I would not reject the standards they establish. If anything, I simply would make more clear that *Spinelli*, properly understood, does not depart in any fundamental way from the test established by *Aguilar*. For reasons

---

[6] *Aguilar* and *Spinelli* inform the police of what information they have to provide and magistrates of what information they should demand. This advances the important process value, which is intimately related to substantive Fourth Amendment concerns, of having magistrates, rather than police, or informants, determine whether there is probable cause to support the issuance of a warrant. We want the police to provide magistrates with the information on which they base their conclusions so that magistrates can perform their important function. When the police rely on facts about which they have personal knowledge, requiring them to disclose those facts to magistrates imposes no significant burden on the police. When the police rely on information obtained from confidential informants, requiring the police to disclose the facts on which the informants based their conclusions imposes a more substantial burden on the police, but it is one that they can meet because they presumably have access to their confidential informants.

I shall next state, I do not find persuasive the Court's justifications for rejecting the test established by Aguilar and refined by Spinelli.

II

In rejecting the *Aguilar-Spinelli* standards, the Court suggests that a "totality-of-the-circumstances approach is far more consistent with our prior treatment of probable cause than is any rigid demand that specific 'tests' be satisfied by every informant's tip." In support of this proposition the Court relies on several cases that purportedly reflect this approach, and on the "practical, nontechnical," nature of probable cause.

[O]ne can concede that probable cause is a "practical, nontechnical" concept without betraying the values that *Aguilar* and *Spinelli* reflect. As noted, *see supra*, at 2347, *Aguilar* and *Spinelli* require the police to provide magistrates with certain crucial information. They also provide structure for magistrates' probable cause inquiries. In so doing, *Aguilar* and *Spinelli* preserve the role of magistrates as independent arbiters of probable cause, insure greater accuracy in probable cause determinations, and advance the substantive value of precluding findings of probable cause, and attendant intrusions, based on anything less than information from an honest or credible person who has acquired his information in a reliable way. Neither the standards nor their effects are inconsistent with a "practical, nontechnical" conception of probable cause. Once a magistrate has determined that he has information before him that he can reasonably say has been obtained in a reliable way by a credible person, he has ample room to use his common sense and to apply a practical, nontechnical conception of probable cause.

It also should be emphasized that cases such as Nathanson v. United States, 290 U.S. 41 (1933), and Giordenello v. United States, 357 U.S. 480 (1958), discussed *supra*, at 2352, directly contradict the Court's suggestion, that a strong showing on one prong of the *Aguilar* test should compensate for a deficient showing on the other. If the conclusory allegations of a presumptively reliable police officer are insufficient to establish probable cause, there is no conceivable reason why the conclusory allegations of an anonymous informant should not be insufficient as well. Moreover, contrary to the Court's implicit suggestion, *Aguilar* and *Spinelli* do not stand as an insuperable barrier to the use of even anonymous informants' tips to establish probable cause. It is no justification for rejecting them outright that some courts may have employed an overly technical version of the *Aguilar-Spinelli* standards, *see ante*, at n. 9.

The Court also insists that the *Aguilar-Spinelli* standards must be abandoned because they are inconsistent with the fact that non-lawyers frequently serve as magistrates. To the contrary, the standards help to structure probable cause inquiries and, properly interpreted, may actually help a non-lawyer magistrate in making a probable cause determination. Moreover, the *Aguilar* and *Spinelli* tests are not inconsistent with deference to magistrates' determinations of probable cause. *Aguilar* expressly acknowledged that reviewing courts "will pay substantial deference to judicial determinations of probable cause. . . ." 378 U.S., at 111. In *Spinelli*, the Court noted that it was not retreating from the proposition that magistrates' determinations of probable cause "should be paid great deference by reviewing courts. . . ." 393 U.S., at 419. It is also noteworthy that the language from United States v. Ventresca, 380 U.S. 102, 108–109 (1965), which the Court repeatedly quotes, *see ante,* at 2330, 2331, and n. 10, brackets the following passage, which the Court does not quote:

> "This is not to say that probable cause can be made out by affidavits which are purely conclusory, stating only the affiant's or an informer's belief that probable cause exists without detailing any of the 'underlying circumstances' upon which that belief is based. *See* Aguilar v. Texas, *supra.* Recital of some of the underlying circumstances in the affidavit is essential if the magistrate is to perform his detached function and not serve merely as a rubber stamp for the police. However, where these circumstances are detailed, where reason for crediting the source of the information is given, and when a magistrate has found probable cause, the courts should not invalidate the warrant by interpreting the affidavit in a hypertechnical, rather than a commonsense, manner." 380 U.S., at 108–109.[9]

At the heart of the Court's decision to abandon *Aguilar* and *Spinelli* appears to be its belief that "the direction taken by decisions following *Spinelli* poorly serves 'the most basic function of any government: to provide for the security of the individual and of his property.' " This conclusion rests on the judgment that *Aguilar* and *Spinelli* "seriously imped[e] the task of law enforcement," *ibid.*, and render anonymous tips valueless in police work. *Ibid.* Surely, the Court overstates its case. But of particular concern to all Americans must be that the Court gives virtually no consideration to the value of insuring that findings of probable cause are based on information that a magistrate can

---

[9]   The Court also argues that "[i]f the affidavits submitted by police officers are subjected to the type of scrutiny some courts have deemed appropriate, police might well resort to warrantless searches, with the hope of relying on consent or some other exception to the warrant clause that might develop at the time of the search." *Ante,* at 2331. If the Court is suggesting, as it appears to be, that the police will intentionally disregard the law, it need only be noted in response that the courts are not helpless to deal with such conduct. Moreover, as was noted in Coolidge v. New Hampshire, 403 U.S. 443 (1971):

> "[T]he most basic constitutional rule in this area is that 'searches conducted outside the judicial process, without prior approval by judge or magistrate, are per se unreasonable under the Fourth Amendment—subject only to a few specifically established and well-delineated exceptions.' The exceptions are 'jealously and carefully drawn,' and there must be 'a showing by those who seek exemption . . . that the exigencies of the situation made that course imperative.' '[T]he burden is on those seeking the exemption to show the need for it.' " *Id.*, at 454–455 (plurality opinion) (footnotes omitted).

It therefore would appear to be not only inadvisable, but also unavailing, for the police to conduct warrantless searches in "the hope of relying on consent or some other exception to the warrant clause that might develop at the time of the search." *Ante*, at 2331.

reasonably say has been obtained in a reliable way by an honest or credible person. I share Justice WHITE's fear that the Court's rejection of *Aguilar* and *Spinelli* and its adoption of a new totality-of-the-circumstances test, *ante,* at 2332, "may foretell an evisceration of the probable cause standard. . . ."

■ JUSTICE STEVENS, with whom JUSTICE BRENNAN joins, dissenting.

The fact that Lance and Sue Gates made a 22-hour nonstop drive from West Palm Beach, Florida, to Bloomingdale, Illinois, only a few hours after Lance had flown to Florida provided persuasive evidence that they were engaged in illicit activity. That fact, however, was not known to the magistrate when he issued the warrant to search their home.

What the magistrate did know at that time was that the anonymous informant had not been completely accurate in his or her predictions. The informant had indicated that "Sue drives their car to Florida where she leaves it to be loaded up with drugs. . . . Sue flies back after she drops the car off in Florida." App. 1a (emphasis added). Yet Detective Mader's affidavit reported that she "left the West Palm Beach area driving the Mercury northbound." App. 12a.

The discrepancy between the informant's predictions and the facts known to Detective Mader is significant for three reasons. First, it cast doubt on the informant's hypothesis that the Gates already had "over $100,000 worth of drugs in their basement," App. 1a. The informant had predicted an itinerary that always kept one spouse in Bloomingdale, suggesting that the Gates did not want to leave their home unguarded because something valuable was hidden within. That inference obviously could not be drawn when it was known that the pair was actually together over a thousand miles from home.

Second, the discrepancy made the Gates' conduct seem substantially less unusual than the informant had predicted it would be. It would have been odd if, as predicted, Sue had driven down to Florida on Wednesday, left the car, and flown right back to Illinois. But the mere facts that Sue was in West Palm Beach with the car,[1] that she was joined by her husband at the Holiday Inn on Friday,[2] and that the couple drove north

---

[1]   The anonymous note suggested that she was going down on Wednesday, App. 1a, but for all the officers knew she had been in Florida for a month. App. 10b-13b.

[2]   Lance does not appear to have behaved suspiciously in flying down to Florida. He made a reservation in his own name and gave an accurate home phone number to the airlines. Compare Florida v. Royer, ___ U.S. ___, ___, n. 2, (1983); United States v. Mendenhall, 446 U.S. 544, 548 (1980) (Stewart, J., announcing the judgment). And Detective Mader's affidavit does not report that he did any of the other things drug couriers are notorious for doing, such as paying for the ticket in cash, *Royer, supra,* 460 U.S., at ___, n. 2, dressing casually, *ibid.*, looking pale and nervous, *ibid.*; *Mendenhall, supra,* 446 U.S., at 548, improperly filling out baggage tags, *Royer, supra,* 460 U.S., at ___, n. 2, carrying American Tourister luggage, *ibid.*, not carrying any luggage, Mendenhall, *supra,* 446 U.S., at 564–565, (POWELL, J., concurring in part and concurring in the judgment), or changing airlines en route, *ibid.*

together the next morning[3] are neither unusual nor probative of criminal activity.

Third, the fact that the anonymous letter contained a material mistake undermines the reasonableness of relying on it as a basis for making a forcible entry into a private home.

Of course, the activities in this case did not stop when the magistrate issued the warrant. The Gates drove all night to Bloomingdale, the officers searched the car and found 400 pounds of marijuana, and then they searched the house. However, none of these subsequent events may be considered in evaluating the warrant,[6] and the search of the house was legal only if the warrant was valid. Vale v. Louisiana, 399 U.S. 30, 33–35 (1970). I cannot accept the Court's casual conclusion that, before the Gates arrived in Bloomingdale, there was probable cause to justify a valid entry and search of a private home. No one knows who the informant in this case was, or what motivated him or her to write the note. Given that the note's predictions were faulty in one significant respect, and were corroborated by nothing except ordinary innocent activity, I must surmise that the Court's evaluation of the warrant's validity has been colored by subsequent events.

Although the foregoing analysis is determinative as to the house search, the car search raises additional issues because "there is a constitutional difference between houses and cars." Chambers v. Maroney, 399 U.S. 42, 52 (1970) . . . .

In apologizing for its belated realization that we should not have ordered reargument in this case, the Court today shows high regard for the appropriate relationship of this Court to state courts. When the Court discusses the merits, however, it attaches no weight to the conclusions of the Circuit Judge of DuPage County, Illinois, of the three judges of the Second District of the Illinois Appellate Court, or of the five justices of the Illinois Supreme Court, all of whom concluded that the warrant was not based on probable cause. In a fact-bound inquiry of this sort, the judgment of three levels of state courts, all of whom are better able to evaluate the probable reliability of anonymous informants in Bloomingdale, Illinois, than we are, should be entitled to at least a presumption of accuracy.[8]

---

[3]   Detective Mader's affidavit hinted darkly that the couple had set out upon "that interstate highway commonly used by travelers to the Chicago area." But the same highway is also commonly used by travelers to Disney World, Sea World, and Ringling Brothers and Barnum and Bailey Circus World. It is also the road to Cocoa Beach, Cape Canaveral, and Washington, D.C. I would venture that each year dozens of perfectly innocent people fly to Florida, meet a waiting spouse, and drive off together in the family car.

[6]   It is a truism that "a search warrant is valid only if probable cause has been shown to the magistrate and that an inadequate showing may not be rescued by post-search testimony on information known to the searching officers at the time of the search." Rice v. Wolff, 513 F.2d 1280 (CA8 1975).

[8]   The Court holds that what were heretofore considered two independent "prongs"— "veracity" and "basis of knowledge"—are now to be considered together as circumstances whose totality must be appraised. *Ante,* at 2329. "A deficiency in one may be compensated for, in

b. "NEUTRAL AND DETACHED" MAGISTRATE

State v. Brown

444 S.E.2d 47 (W. Va. 1994)

■ MILLER, JUSTICE:

In this appeal from a habeas corpus proceeding, we consider whether the Circuit Court of Jefferson County was correct in holding that a search warrant issued by a magistrate was void because the magistrate was married to the chief of police and one of his officers had procured the warrant.

The lower court determined that because the magistrate was married to the chief of police there was a violation of Canon 3C(1) and 3C(1)(d) of the Judicial Code of Ethics. The former provision requires the recusal of a judge if his impartiality might reasonably be questioned; the latter requires disqualification where the judge's spouse has an interest in the proceeding.[3] We have not had occasion to consider this particular question.

Initially, we note that independent of the Judicial Code of Ethics, the United States Supreme Court has interpreted the Fourth Amendment to the United States Constitution to require that a search warrant be issued by a "neutral and detached magistrate." *See* Johnson v. United States, 333 U.S. 10, 14 (1948). In Shadwick v. City of Tampa, 407 U.S. 345, 350 (1972), the Supreme Court held that the office of magistrate, in order to satisfy the neutral and detached standard "require[s] severance and disengagement from activities of law enforcement." By way of illustration, the Supreme Court in *Shadwick* pointed to its earlier case of Coolidge v. New Hampshire, 403 U.S. 443, 450 (1971), where it voided a search warrant issued by the state's attorney general because he " 'was

---

determining the overall reliability of a tip, by a strong showing as to the other, or by some other indicia of reliability." *Ibid.* Yet in this case, the lower courts found neither factor present. App. 12a. And the supposed "other indicia" in the affidavit take the form of activity that is not particularly remarkable. I do not understand how the Court can find that the "totality" so far exceeds the sum of its "circumstances."

[3] The applicable provisions in 1992 of the Judicial Code of Ethics, which were in effect at the time the warrant was issued, were in Canon 3C(1) and 3C(1)(d):

"C.   Disqualification

"(1)   A judge should disqualify himself in a proceeding in which his impartiality might reasonably be questioned, including but not limited to instances where:

* * *

"(d)   he or his spouse, or a person within the third degree of relationship to either of them, or the spouse of such a person:

(i)   is a party to the proceeding, or an officer, director, or trustee of a party;

(ii)   is acting as a lawyer in the proceeding;

(iii)   is known by the judge to have an interest that could be substantially affected by the outcome of the proceeding;

(iv)   is to the judge's knowledge likely to be a material witness in the proceeding[.]"

Similar provisions now are found in Canon 3E(1)(c) and 3E(1)(d) of the Code of Judicial Conduct, which became effective January 1, 1993.

actively in charge of the investigation and later was to be chief prosecutor at trial.'" 407 U.S. at 350. Similarly, in LO-JI Sales, Inc. v. New York, 442 U.S. 319, 327 (1979), the magistrate was found not to be neutral and detached when he "allowed himself to become a member, if not the leader, of the search party which was essentially a police operation." In Connally v. Georgia, 429 U.S. 245 (1977), the Supreme Court determined that a magistrate who was compensated based on a fee for the warrants issued could not be considered neutral and detached. It relied on its earlier case of Tumey v. Ohio, 273 U.S. 510 (1927), which invalidated on due process principles the payment of the village mayor when he acted as a judge from costs collected in criminal cases brought before him in which there was a conviction.

We afforded the same protection for a neutral and detached magistrate under our search and seizure constitutional provision in Syllabus Point 2 of State v. Dudick, 158 W.Va. 629, 213 S.E.2d 458 (1975):

> "The constitutional guarantee under W.Va. Const., Article III, § 6 that no search warrant will issue except on probable cause goes to substance and not to form; therefore, where it is conclusively proved that a magistrate acted as a mere agent of the prosecutorial process and failed to make an independent evaluation of the circumstances surrounding a request for a warrant, the warrant will be held invalid and the search will be held illegal."

See also State v. Schofield, 175 W.Va. 99, 331 S.E.2d 829 (1985); State v. Wotring, 167 W.Va. 104, 279 S.E.2d 182 (1981).

As the foregoing law indicates, where there is a lack of neutrality and detachment in the issuance of the search warrant, it is void. Aside from the constitutional requirements for a neutral and detached magistrate as to warrants, similar standards are imposed by Canon 3C of the Judicial Code of Ethics relating to the disqualification of a judge. The Code defines those situations when a judge may be precluded from presiding over a case. The underlying rationale for requiring disqualification is based on principles of due process. As we recognized in Louk v. Haynes, 159 W.Va. 482, 499, 223 S.E.2d 780, 791 (1976):

> "Due process requires that the appearance of justice be satisfied. The United States Supreme Court has stated:
>
> "'A fair trial in a fair tribunal is a basic requirement of due process. Fairness of course requires an absence of actual bias in the trial of cases. But our system of law has always endeavored to prevent even the probability of unfairness. To this end no man can be a judge in his own case and no man is permitted to try cases where he has an interest in the outcome. That interest cannot be defined with precision. Circumstances and relationships must be considered. This Court has said, however,

that "[e]very procedure which would offer a possible temptation to the average man as a judge . . . not to hold the balance nice, clear and true between the State and the accused, denies the latter due process of law." Tumey v. Ohio, 273 U.S. 510, 532 (1927).' In Re Murchison, 349 U.S. 133, 136 (1955)."

(Emphasis and ellipsis in *Murchison*).

Canon 3C(1) contains an initial general admonition that "[a] judge should disqualify himself in a proceeding in which his impartiality might reasonably be questioned[.]" This admonition is followed by a number of specific instances when disqualification is required. Canon 3C(1) also recognizes that the enumerated instances are not to be considered as exclusive as it states that disqualification "includ[es] but [is] not limited to instances where: . . .

The general standard under Canon 3C(1) to determine whether a judge should be disqualified because the judge's impartiality might reasonably be questioned is analogous to the rule contained in Syllabus Point 14, in part, of *Louk v. Haynes*, *supra*:

> "[W]here a challenge to a judge's impartiality is made for substantial reasons which indicate that the circumstances offer a possible temptation to the average man as a judge not to hold the balance nice, clear and true between the State and the accused, a judge should recuse himself."

In this case, in addition to the general disqualification standard, it is claimed that the more specific disqualification test contained in Canon 3C(1)(d)(iii) applies. This provision requires disqualification if the judge's spouse has "an interest that could be substantially affected by the outcome of the proceeding[.]"[10] This disqualification is claimed to apply if Chief Boober appeared before his wife to seek a warrant. It also is claimed that he would be acting as "a party to the proceeding," and Magistrate Boober would be disqualified under Canon 3C(1)(d)(i). This claim is based on the fact that Chief Boober would have executed the affidavit for the warrant. We have no case law on this point, but we agree with cases from other jurisdictions that support the disqualification.

For example, the Louisiana court in State v. LaCour, 493 So.2d 756 (La.Ct.App.1986), set aside a criminal conviction because it found that the judge should have disqualified himself because his son was prosecuting the defendant on another criminal charge in a different county. The Nevada Supreme Court reached the same disqualification

---

[10] Note 3, *supra*, contains the entire text of Canon 3C(1)(d)(iii). The provision covers not only a spouse, but any "person within the third degree of relationship to either of them, or the spouse of such a person [.]" Under Canon 3C(3)(a), "the degree of relationship is calculated according to the civil law system[.]" The official commentary under this section states:

"According to the civil law system, the third degree of relationship test would, for example, disqualify the judge if his or his spouse's father, grandfather, uncle, brother, or niece's husband were a party or lawyer in the proceeding, but would not disqualify him if a cousin were a party or lawyer in the proceeding."

conclusion in Hoff v. Eighth Judicial District Court, 79 Nev. 108, 378 P.2d 977 (1963), where the judge's son was the prosecuting attorney in the same district. *See also* Adams v. State, 269 Ark. 548, 601 S.W.2d 881 (1980) (prosecutor was the nephew of the judge). Cf. Black v. State, 187 So.2d 815 (Miss.1966) (sole prosecuting witness was close relative of judge).

In Smith v. Beckman, 683 P.2d 1214 (Colo.Ct.App.1984), the judge's wife was an assistant prosecutor. The record showed that the prosecutor's office had screened her from cases that were before her husband. The court concluded that his disqualification in all criminal cases was warranted because of the appearance of impropriety:

> "Therefore, the possibility that the facts alleged may give rise to the appearance of impropriety must always receive the highest consideration in ruling on a motion for disqualification. *See* People v. Botham, 629 P.2d 589 (Colo.1981). It is of paramount importance that our judges meticulously avoid any appearance of partiality, not only to secure the confidence of litigants before their courts, but to retain public respect." 683 P.2d at 1216.

The critical point in the court's view was the perception of the closeness created by the marital relationship:

> "The circumstances here are such that an appearance of impropriety is created by the close nature of the marriage relationship. A husband and wife generally conduct their personal and financial affairs as a partnership. In addition to living together, a husband and wife are also perceived to share confidences regarding their personal lives and employment situations. Generally, the public views married people as 'a couple,' as 'a partnership,' and as participants in a relationship more intimate than any other kind of relationship between individuals. In our view the existence of a marriage relationship between a judge and a deputy district attorney in the same county is sufficient to establish grounds for disqualification, even though no other facts call into question the judge's impartiality." 683 P.2d at 1216.

Moreover, in State v. Holloway, 66 N.C.App. 491, 311 S.E.2d 707 (1984), the court of appeals held that the defendant had been improperly foreclosed from presenting evidence at the trial court level showing that the search warrant was not issued by a neutral and detached magistrate. This claim was based on the assertion that the magistrate was dating the officer who sought the warrant. The Supreme Court of North Carolina reversed this holding on the basis that the defendant had not filed a proper affidavit to challenge the warrant. State v. Holloway, 311 N.C. 573, 319 S.E.2d 261 (1984).[13] Following this decision, the defendant filed

---

[13] Justice Exum of the North Carolina Supreme Court dissented, with Justice Copeland and Justice Frye joining him. Justice Exum stated, in part:

a petition for a writ of habeas corpus in the federal district court which awarded the writ to allow the defendant an opportunity to show that the magistrate was not neutral and detached. Holloway v. Woodard, 655 F.Supp. 1245 (W.D.N.C.1987).

We believe that the foregoing cases and the language in Canon 3C(1) and 3C(1)(d)(i) of the Judicial Code of Ethics relating to the disqualification of a judicial official when his or her impartiality might reasonably be questioned if the official's spouse is a party to the proceeding would foreclose a magistrate from issuing a warrant sought by his or her spouse who is a police officer. However, this situation did not occur here.

The search warrant was issued at the request of Sergeant R.R. Roberts of the Ranson police force. At the hearing below, Magistrate Boober testified that she was the on-call magistrate for emergency matters that might occur after 4:00 p.m. and before 8:00 a.m. the next morning when the magistrate office would be open for normal business.

Magistrate Boober also stated that she was not related to Sergeant Roberts and had no contact with him except through the magistrate system. She also stated that she made an independent review of the affidavit for the search warrant. Her husband's name did not appear on the affidavit nor was there any discussion about her husband with Sergeant Roberts.

There was no evidence to show any actual bias or partiality on the part of Magistrate Boober. The entire argument centered on an implied partiality because of the magistrate's relationship to Chief Boober. We indicated earlier that any criminal matters which the magistrate's husband is involved with cannot be brought before her because of their spousal relationship. We decline to extend such a per se rule with regard to the other members of the Ranson police force. The fact that a magistrate's spouse is the chief of police of a small police force[14] does not automatically disqualify the magistrate, who is otherwise neutral and detached, from issuing a warrant sought by another member of such police force. However, a small police force coupled with the chief's active role in a given case may create an appearance of impropriety that would

---

"I note, too, that whether a magistrate issuing a search warrant is neutral and detached is an issue more crucial than ever in light of United States v. Leon, [468] U.S. [897 (1984)]. *Leon* holds that evidence seized pursuant to a warrant issued by a 'detached and neutral magistrate but ultimately found to be unsupported by probable cause' is admissible under the Fourth Amendment. Gone is the Fourth Amendment's probable cause requirement insofar as it protects a citizen from being convicted on the basis of evidence seized in its absence pursuant to a warrant. Now under the Fourth Amendment when a warrant is required all that stands between the state's ability to search for and seize evidence and use it in court and the 'right of the people to be secure in their persons, houses, papers, and effects against unreasonable searches and seizures' is a 'detached and neutral magistrate.'" 311 N.C. at 579–80, 319 S.E.2d at 265.

[14] The 1993 West Virginia Blue Book at 904 gives the population of the City of Ranson at 2,890. According to the Brief of Appellee, Eustace Brown, there are six other police officers in addition to the Chief of Police.

warrant a right to challenge the validity of a search warrant. Certainly, prudence dictates that Magistrate Boober's involvement with warrants from the Ranson police force should be severely curtailed. . . .

Finally, we are asked to extend the rule of necessity to allow Magistrate Boober to handle warrants when she is the on-call magistrate. The rule of necessity is an exception to the disqualification of a judge. It allows a judge who is otherwise disqualified to handle the case to preside if there is no provision that allows another judge to hear the matter. This rule of necessity is summarized in 46 Am.Jur.2d Judges § 89 (1969):

> "The majority view is that the rule of disqualification must yield to the demands of necessity, and a judge or an officer exercising judicial functions may act in a proceeding wherein he is disqualified by interest, relationship, or the like, if his jurisdiction is exclusive and there is no legal provision for calling in a substitute, so that his refusal to act would destroy the only tribunal in which relief could be had and thus prevent a determination of the proceeding." (Footnote omitted).

The rule of necessity is an exception to the general rule precluding a disqualified judge from hearing a matter. Therefore, it is strictly construed and applied only when there is no other person having jurisdiction to handle the matter that can be brought in to hear it, as stated in 46 Am.Jur.2d Judges § 90 (1969):

> "The application of the rule permitting a disqualified judge to act where no other judge is available can be justified only by strict and imperious necessity, since the rule is an exception to the greater rule of disqualification resting on sound public policy. Under the doctrine, a disqualified judge may sit where no decision is possible if he does not sit, as in the case of an appellate court where there is no method provided by constitution or statute to have another person sit as judge of the court if a member is disqualified." (Footnotes omitted).

In this case, Magistrate Boober sought to invoke the rule on the basis that one of the other magistrates was out of town and the third magistrate had a policy of refusing to come out when not on regular on-call duty. Acknowledgement is made that a circuit judge has jurisdiction to issue warrants under W.Va.Code, 62–1–10. However, no attempt was made to contact the circuit judge. . . .

We are not cited nor have we found a case that is analogous to the case at hand where the rule of necessity has been authorized. As earlier discussed, the rule of necessity should be used only sparingly to circumvent a disqualification. We would not sanction the use of the rule were it to be offered if Chief Boober appeared seeking the search warrant. In the case of the other police officers from Ranson, we decline to utilize the rule simply because we do not find that Magistrate Boober is automatically barred from issuing warrants at their request. There may be circumstances that can be shown that would cast a shadow over the magistrate's impartiality. In that event, a motion to suppress the evidence obtained under the warrant may be made, and the issue will be resolved at a hearing.

For the foregoing reasons, we reverse the judgment of the Circuit Court of Jefferson County which suppressed the evidence obtained under the search warrant. The matter is remanded for a further hearing with regard to the warrant if the relators below desire to challenge it on the basis that there are additional facts, other than her marriage to Chief Boober, that demonstrate Magistrate Boober was not neutral and detached.

Reversed and Remanded.

c. "PARTICULARLY DESCRIBING . . . ."

Levenduski v. State
876 N.E.2d 798 (2007)

■ MAY, JUDGE.

Casey Levenduski asserts the trial court should have suppressed evidence of methamphetamine production found in his home because police conducted an unlawful warrantless search of his property and then improperly obtained a search warrant based on that warrantless search. As the evidence was obtained pursuant to an overly broad "catch-all" provision of the warrant, it should have been suppressed even if the warrant was properly obtained. We therefore reverse and remand.

FACTS AND PROCEDURAL HISTORY

In August of 2003, a Crawford County deputy sheriff and a conservation officer went to Levenduski's home to execute an arrest warrant. There was no response when the deputy knocked on the front door. The officers heard a sound from a wooded area behind the residence and they thought Levenduski might be trying to leave on an all-terrain vehicle. They walked down a mowed path that led to a footpath and through a fencerow. At the end of the footpath near what was described as a "grown up fence row area," they found two pots with three marijuana plants in them. The deputy did not know who owned the property where the plants were found. The officers also found pots and potting soil in Levenduski's yard.

The deputy left to get a search warrant on the premise the empty pots probably had been used to grow marijuana and there might be marijuana in the residence. A state police officer arrived at Levenduski's home and the deputy contacted him and asked him to measure how far the plants were from the home. While taking the measurements, the officer found two dead marijuana plants in a wooded area about twelve feet from a garage. The state police officer told the deputy what he had found.

The deputy obtained a search warrant and returned to the home where three other officers were waiting. The warrant authorized police to enter Levenduski's house and search for marijuana, hashish, "instruments used to manufacture, introduce into the body or deal marijuana," (App. at 28), money records, notes, documents, or videotapes "relating to the use, dealing, or manufacture of marijuana," (*id.*), instruments used in growing or processing marijuana, paraphernalia "and any other item of contraband which are [sic] evidence of a crime." (*Id.*)

The officers knocked on the front door and received no response, then kicked the door in and entered the house. Levenduski was inside and the police found various items related to the production of methamphetamine.

Levenduski was charged with six offenses. One was dismissed, and he was found not guilty of possession of marijuana and possession of paraphernalia. He was found guilty of Class C felony possession of methamphetamine, Class B felony dealing in methamphetamine, and Class C felony possession of chemical reagents or precursors with intent to manufacture.

DISCUSSION AND DECISION

The Fourth Amendment to the United States Constitution and Article I, Section 11 of the Indiana Constitution provide "the right of the people to be secure in their persons, houses, papers and effects, against unreasonable searches and seizures. . . ." U.S. Const, amend. IV; Ind. Const., art. 1 § 11. Created to protect one's right to privacy, this protection against unreasonable, state-sponsored searches and seizures is a principal mode of discouraging lawless police conduct. Jones v. State, 655 N.E.2d 49, 54 (Ind.1995), reh'g denied. Consequently, evidence obtained through an unreasonable search and seizure is not admissible. *Id.* An agent of the government must obtain a search warrant from a neutral, detached magistrate before undertaking a search of a person or private property, except under special circumstances fitting within certain carefully-drawn and well-delineated exceptions. *Id.* . . .

Validity of the "General" Warrant as to Methamphetamine Evidence

The Fourth Amendment to the United States Constitution requires search warrants to "particularly describ[e] the place to be searched, and the persons or things to be seized." U.S. Const. amend. IV.

> General warrants, of course, are prohibited by the Fourth Amendment. The problem posed by the general warrant is not that of intrusion per se, but of a general, exploratory rummaging in a person's belongings. The Fourth Amendment addresses the problem by requiring a "particular description" of the things to be seized. This requirement makes general searches impossible

and prevents the seizure of one thing under a warrant describing another. As to what is to be taken, nothing is left to the discretion of the officer executing the warrant.

Andresen v. Maryland, 427 U.S. 463, 480 (1976) (internal quotations and citations omitted). A warrant that leaves the executing officer with discretion is invalid. Warren v. State, 760 N.E.2d 608, 610 (Ind.2002).

In *Warren*, police obtained a warrant for an apartment where Warren lived with someone who had been killed during the commission of a crime. The police discovered identification cards and driver's licenses that led them to focus their investigation on Warren.

The warrant listed the items to be seized as "guns, ammunition, gun parts, lists of acquaintances, blood, microscop0ic [sic] or trace evidence, silver duct tape, white cord and *any other indicia of criminal activity including but not limited to books, records, documents, or any other such items.*" *Id.* (emphasis supplied). Warren argued the warrant was therefore "without any practical limit as to the items for which a search may be conducted." *Id.* He challenged the search warrant as granting "unbridled discretion to the police regarding the items sought in violation of the search and seizure clauses of the United States and Indiana Constitutions." *Id.* Our Supreme Court agreed the phrase "any other indicia of criminal activity including but not limited to books, records, documents, or any other such items" granted the officer "unlawful unbridled discretion to conduct a general exploratory search." *Id.*

However, in Warren's case the infirmity of the "catchall language" did not doom the entire warrant; rather, it required suppression of only the evidence seized pursuant to that general part of the warrant and not the suppression of evidence obtained pursuant to the valid specific portions of the warrant. *Id.* The identification cards and driver's licenses were not seized pursuant to the "catchall" language because they were included within the "lists of acquaintances" described in the search warrant. They were properly seized because they were "particularly described" in the warrant. *Id.*

In the case before us, by contrast, all the methamphetamine-related evidence Levenduski sought to suppress was obtained pursuant to the illegal "catchall" provision in the warrant and should accordingly have been suppressed. The warrant authorized police to enter Levenduski's house and search for marijuana, hashish, "instruments used to manufacture, introduce into the body or deal marijuana," (App. at 28) (emphasis supplied), money records, notes, documents, or videotapes "relating to the use, dealing, or manufacture of marijuana," (*id.*) (emphasis supplied), instruments used in growing or processing marijuana, paraphernalia "and any other item of contraband which are [sic] evidence of a crime." (*Id.*) (emphasis supplied). As to the evidence unrelated to marijuana or hashish, the warrant was invalid to the extent it "[left] the executing officer with discretion," *Warren*, 760 N.E.2d at 610, and the trial court should have granted Levenduski's motion to suppress that evidence.

The State acknowledges the language in the warrant purporting to authorize a search for and seizure of "any other item of contraband which are [sic] evidence of a crime" is "perhaps a bit too general in its description of the items permitted to be searched for by the warrant." (Br. of the Appellee at 19.) But it asserts the discovery and seizure of the methamphetamine was reasonable because the "methamphetamine evidence" was discovered "primarily in plain view." (*Id.* at 19–20.) It was not. . . . .

Levenduski was charged with possession of only two precursors—iodine and red phosphorous—but this testimony does not indicate such were in plain view. There was evidence red phosphorous was confiscated at the scene by the Clandestine Lab Team, but no testimony it was ever in "plain view." Police testified foil with "burnt residue" (*id.* at 154, 155), was found in plain view, but there was no testimony the "residue" was methamphetamine or either of the precursors. Police testified they saw, in a cabinet with an open door, certain items they characterized as "a precursor or reagent," (*id.* at 155), but those were not the precursors Levenduski was charged with and convicted of possessing. There was testimony iodine was found in a box or bag inside the garage, but no indication the contents of the box or bag were in plain view.

The State has not demonstrated the evidence obtained pursuant to the illegal "catch-all" provision of the search warrant was found in plain view. It therefore should have been suppressed. *See* Chandler v. State, 816 N.E.2d 464, 468 (Ind.Ct.App.2004):

> Nor is there evidence the marijuana was in plain view. Officer James Walsh testified some marijuana 'was found in the middle bedroom' and 'in the living room.' There was no direct testimony this marijuana was in plain view; as the State bears that burden of proof, we will not presume it was.

(Internal citations and footnote omitted). In *Chandler* there was "a passing reference to the marijuana in the living room being found 'on the coffee table,'" *id.* n. 7, but we noted "the record does not indicate whether it was in plain view, obscured by other objects, or hidden inside a container. Given that dearth of information, we decline to hold that an item on a table is presumptively 'in plain view.'" *Id.*

CONCLUSION

We reverse the denial of Levenduski's motion to suppress, and we remand.

Reversed and remanded.

d. VERACITY OF THE AFFIDAVIT

People v. Gales

618 N.E.2d 847 (Ill. App. 1993)

■ JUSTICE MURRAY delivered the opinion of the court:

Defendant, Bernard Gales (Gales), was charged by indictment with possession with intent to deliver cocaine, armed violence and unlawful possession of a weapon by a felon. Pretrial hearings were held on various defense motions. Defendant and Reginald Gales (Reginald) were tried by a jury, and codefendant, Russell Smalley (Smalley), was simultaneously tried by the trial judge. The jury found defendant guilty of possession with intent to deliver between 100 and 400 grams of cocaine and unlawful use of a weapon. Defendant was sentenced to concurrent terms of 30 years' imprisonment for the drug conviction and five years' imprisonment for the weapon possession conviction in the Illinois Department of Corrections.

THE "*FRANKS*" HEARING[1]

Defendant filed a motion to quash the warrant and suppress evidence. Based on affidavits attached to the motion, the trial court found that defendant had made a sufficient preliminary showing to warrant an evidentiary hearing. Over the State's objection, the trial judge granted defendant's motion for a *Franks* hearing.

At the hearing Roxanne Boatman testified that during March 1989, she was the manager of Service Optical in Naperville. On March 18, 1989, Boatman received an employment application from, and interviewed, defendant. On Saturday March 25, 1989, defendant arrived at the store at approximately 8:30 a.m. for a training session. He left at approximately 5:30 p.m.

Michael Thornton testified that he lived at 5357 South May, a two flat, during March 1989. He leased the first-floor apartment and basement area. On March 25, 1989, the basement door was nailed shut and barricaded with 2 × 4's to prevent break-ins. Inside the apartment an old stove was pushed against the basement door. Although Thornton knew defendant, they were not friends, having had a conflict about a girlfriend. To his knowledge, Gales had never been inside either Thornton's apartment or the basement. Thornton did not allow defendant to use the 5357 May apartment at any time on March 25, 1989, nor did Thornton recall seeing Gales at all that day. On the evening of March 24 he was home with his infant son. On the evening of March 25 he was also home, except for 30 minutes that he was at his mother's home. At approximately 9:30 p.m. on March 25, 1989, police officers entered 5357 South May through the basement door that Thornton testified was

---

[1] "*Franks* hearing" is a hearing contemplated by the case of Franks v. Delaware (1978), 438 U.S. 15, where an attack is made on the truthfulness of a search warrant.

barricaded. On that date Thornton was arrested for a narcotics violation. When Thornton saw the basement door again on the 26th the door was torn down.

Officer Robert Schaefer was called to testify by the defense. On March 25, 1989, Officer Schaefer, a 14-year veteran of the Chicago police department, obtained search warrants for the premises at 5350 and 5357 South May. The search warrants were executed at 9:30 that evening.

Schaefer claimed that he spoke to a confidential informant at 1:00 p.m. on March 25, 1989. He started work at 5:30 but he reported early that day, around 5:00 p.m. As soon as he got to work, he began typing out the warrant affidavit. Schaefer did not takes notes during the conversation he had with the confidential informant. Schaefer testified that the informant had his home telephone number and had contacted him at home at approximately 1 p.m. on March 25, 1989. He spoke with him for approximately 10–15 minutes. Ordinarily an informant would be given a beeper number, rather than a home phone number, but Schaefer testified that he did not have a beeper at that time. An objection was sustained when Schaefer was asked what time of day the informant went to 5357 South May. Included in the complaint for search warrant was information that Schaefer had known the confidential informant for 18 months and the fact that the informant had given Schaefer information on at least five occasions, two of which had occurred within the last six months and on each occasion contraband was recovered and arrests were made. Schaefer had thrown away all of his notes for the years preceding 1989 and could not produce the names of any other persons who were arrested as a result of this informant's work.

Schaefer testified that on March 25, 1989, the informant went to 5357 South May where he met Bernard Gales. Gales gave the informant some cannabis which the informant smoked. Gales then took the informant over to 5350 South May to the first-floor apartment where the informant purchased cannabis. The informant left Gales and went to a different location where the informant again smoked some marijuana, and as a result of ingesting this marijuana into his system he enjoyed the same high he always enjoyed when smoking marijuana.

Defendant's wife, LaSauna Gales, testified that in March 1989 she lived with defendant and their daughter in the first-floor apartment at 5350 South May. On March 25, 1989, she was home when the police raided their apartment. The police searched their apartment and she and Gales were arrested and taken to the police station. While at the station, Officer Schaefer handed her a card with his name on it. He told Mrs. Gales to beep him at the number listed on the card, and if she could provide some good information it would help her husband. Mrs. Gales produced the card Schaefer gave her. Printed on the card were his name, two police station phone numbers and a beeper number.

Defendant testified that on March 24, 1989, he was home with his wife and daughter. He went to bed around 10 p.m. that evening. On

March 25, 1989, he got up and left his home around 7:20 a.m. to go to a job training session at Service Optical in Naperville. Defendant arrived in Naperville at 8:30 a.m. and spent all day in training with Roxanne Boatman. He drove directly home after leaving Service Optical. He arrived home at approximately 6:30 p.m. and watched a basketball game on television. From the time he went to bed on the evening of the 24th until he left his home the following morning at 7:30 a.m. no one came into his home. His home is across the street from 5357 South May and he was familiar with that building.

Upon being recalled to testify, Officer Schaefer testified that he was one of the officers who executed the search warrant at 5357 South May on March 25, 1989. Other Chicago police officers placed defendant under arrest after executing a search warrant at the first-floor apartment at 5350 South May. When confronted with the business card with a beeper number on it, Schaefer responded that he had utilized a beeper that had that number in 1989. He did not recall if the number was his beeper number or one of his partner's beeper numbers because at that point in time he had to use other people's beeper numbers until he could obtain one for himself. Officer Schaefer continued to maintain that the informant had his home phone number; he had given him his home phone number instead of his pager number when he first meet the informant, because he did not have a beeper at that time. Cannabis was recovered in the basement at 5357 South May and cocaine was recovered at 5350 South May.

The State moved for a directed finding. The defense asserted that the affidavits submitted by the defendant accounted for all of the day of March 25th up to the time the warrant was executed. Defendant renewed his request that the trial court order production of the informant before defendant rested his case on the motion to quash. Defendant also pointed out that Officer Schaefer claimed he had no notes of his alleged conversation with the informant and that Ms. Boatman, a neutral witness, accounted for all of the time between 8:30 a.m. and 5:30 p.m. on March 25, 1989. The trial court denied defendant's request for the production of the informant.

When announcing its holding, the trial court stated that defendant had to prove by a preponderance of the evidence that Officer Schaefer lied or acted with reckless indifference to the truth when he prepared the warrant affidavit. Without disclosing what questions were asked or answers given, the trial judge explained that he had met and interviewed the confidential informant alone. The informant had been presented to him by Officer Schaefer and an assistant State's Attorney. Other than a greeting, the trial judge did not speak to Officer Schaefer at that time. The trial judge went to another location to speak with the informant; the conversation took place off-the-record, neither the attorneys nor a court reporter were present. The trial judge indicated that suggested questions were submitted by the defense, and he asked those that he thought were appropriate. The trial court found: that the affiant (Schaefer) knew the area; that he had seen the buildings in question though he had never checked them out or been in them; and the affiant had seen and spoken with the defendant on several occasions, although he had never arrested him. The trial court further found that there was, in fact, a confidential informant in this case and that the confidential informant gave the affiant the information that appears in the search warrant. The trial court also found that the defendant by his own testimony was available at home from midnight until 7:30 a.m. on the date in question and that neither the affidavit nor the complaint indicates the time of the purchase. In addition, the trial judge found the affiant had given his home number to the confidential informant, that on the date in question the affiant did not carry or have in his possession a beeper, and the affiant was, in fact, contacted at home by phone by the confidential informant. The trial court found that the defendant failed to prove by a preponderance of the evidence that the affiant either in reckless disregard of the truth or knowingly and intentionally made false statements in the warrant affidavit. Noting the exception of the defense, the court denied the defendant's motion to quash and granted the State's motion for a directed finding. The trial judge took no notes during his conversation with the informant and defendant's request for a summary of the trial judge's meeting with the informant was denied. . . .

For the following reasons we affirm the decision of the trial court.

OPINION

I

Defendant argues that his motion to produce the informant should have been sustained since defendant filed detailed affidavits contradicting the warrant affidavit and the warrant affidavit consisted of the uncorroborated statements of an untrustworthy drug addict. The defendant contends: (A) the *Franks* standard of review is different when the informant is a presumptively unreliable drug addict as opposed to a presumptively reliable citizen; (B) once defendant made a substantial preliminary showing sufficient to mandate a Franks evidentiary hearing, the court should have ordered the production of the informant; and (C) when an in camera hearing is held the trial court must allow defense counsel to be present and an accurate record must be kept.

In *Franks,* the United States Supreme Court recognized that although an affidavit supporting a search warrant is presumed valid, a defendant has a limited right to challenge the veracity of the affidavit. The court held that "where the defendant makes a substantial preliminary showing that a false statement knowingly and intentionally, or with reckless disregard for the truth, was included by the affiant in the warrant affidavit, and if the allegedly false statement is necessary to the finding of probable cause, the fourth amendment requires that a hearing be held at the defendant's request." (Franks v. Delaware (1978), 438 U.S. 154, 155–56.) The determination as to whether there has been a substantial showing sufficient to warrant a hearing must be made by the trial judge, and to a degree the decision on the issue will be final. (People v. Lucente (1987), 116 Ill.2d 133, 152, 107 Ill.Dec. 214, 506 N.E.2d 1269; *see also* McCray v. Illinois (1967), 386 U.S. 300.) At the hearing, "the defendant must prove his claim of perjury by a preponderance of the evidence." (*Lucente*, 116 Ill.2d at 151, 107 Ill.Dec. 214, 506 N.E.2d 1269) However, *Franks* does not require that the defendant disprove every other possibility at the preliminary stage. (People v. Gomez (1992), 236 Ill.App.3d 283, 289, 177 Ill.Dec. 632, 603 N.E.2d 702.) "In ruling on a motion to suppress, it is the trial court's province to determine the credibility of witnesses and the weight to be given their testimony, and its findings will not be disturbed upon review [unless they are] contrary to the manifest weight of the evidence." People v. Myers (1978), 66 Ill.App.3d 934, 935, 23 Ill.Dec. 722, 384 N.E.2d 516.

A.

Defendant argues that the *Franks* standard of review is different when the informant is a presumptively unreliable drug addict as opposed to a presumptively reliable citizen. Defendant points out in *Franks*, the sources of the information in the warrant application were ordinary citizens who were presumptively reliable. (*See* People v. Adams (1989), 131 Ill.2d 387, 137 Ill.Dec. 616, 546 N.E.2d 561.) Defendant maintains a warrant which is based on the alleged observations of a drug addicted informant must be tested by a different standard than *Franks* established. Defendant argues when a government agent, especially one who is not presumptively reliable, is the source of the information, a different standard must apply otherwise circumvention of the warrant requirement is easily facilitated by having one government agent (the informant) provide false, misleading or inaccurate information to the police officer affiant who then includes the false statement in the warrant application.

We find no support for defendant's argument. [The court concludes that the affidavit established probable cause under the *Gates* totality-of-the-circumstances approach.]

B.

The defendant argues that once defendant made a substantial preliminary showing sufficient to mandate a Franks evidentiary hearing, the court should have ordered the production of the informant. Defendant claims he submitted evidence which directly contradicted the information in the affidavit for search warrant: (1) defendant's affidavit as to his whereabouts on March 25, 1989; (2) Ms. Boatman's affidavit stating defendant was in a training session with her from 8:30 a.m. until 5:30 p.m. on March 25, 1989; (3) the time sheets from Service Optical; and (4) the affidavit of Thornton which indicated that Thornton lived in the building where the alleged drug transaction occurred on March 25, 1989, that no drugs were sold, that defendant was not present there on that day, and that the doors were nailed shut at the location of the alleged drug transaction. Defendant contends that after the hearing, he had done all that he could do except call the informant as a witness. He claims to have rebutted all the information contained in the affidavit by showing: (1) his whereabouts on March 25th through three witnesses; (2) that the informant was a drug user; (3) that the police officer could not substantiate the informant's prior reliability; (4) that it was physically impossible for the events to have occurred as the informant allegedly indicated; and (5) that the affiant police officer's testimony was inconsistent.

The State maintains that since defendant's delivery to the confidential informant was not an issue at trial, the defendant's request for disclosure of the informant related only to the preliminary issue of probable cause and not the fundamental question of defendant's guilt or innocence. Accordingly, the State maintains that the trial judge's determination that disclosure of the confidential informant's identity was not needed and should not be disturbed. *See* People v. Elworthy (1991), 214 Ill.App.3d 914, 922–23, 158 Ill.Dec. 614, 620–21, 574 N.E.2d 727, 733–34.

The State points out that the informant's information was shown to be credible. Officer Schaefer testified that the informant told him he purchased an amount of cannabis from defendant and another person at 5357 South May. Pursuant to the search warrants, the officers discovered a large amount of cannabis at that address. Finally, as the trial court also noted, there was no information as to the hour that the informant made the purchase from the defendant, thus the fact that defendant was not home all day does not in necessarily contradict Officer Schaefer's testimony. (Officer Schaefer testified that informant told him at 1 p.m. that he had made the purchase that day.)

The State argues if the trial judge had permitted the presence of both the State and the defense counsel at the interview it would have exposed the informant's identity to them and destroyed the informant's confidentiality and similarly, the keeping of a record of the interview would have destroyed the informant's credibility.

Supreme Court Rule 412(j)(ii) provides:

"Disclosure of an informant's identity shall not be required where his identity is a prosecution secret and a failure to disclose will not infringe the constitutional rights of the accused. Disclosure shall not be denied hereunder of the identity of witnesses to be produced at a hearing or trial." (Ill.Rev.Stat.1991, ch. 110A, par. 412(j)(ii).)

In People v. McBee (1992), 228 Ill.App.3d 769, 773, 170 Ill.Dec. 685, 593 N.E.2d 574, the court stated:

"It is well settled that strong public policy reasons favoring nondisclosure of an informant must be balanced against a defendant's need for disclosure in order to prepare his defense [citation], or where disclosure is essential for a fair determination of a cause. [Citation.] However, if the issue is one of probable cause, and guilt or innocence is not at stake, the nondisclosure of an informer's identity is not error. [Citation.] Whatever the circumstances, defendant must show a need for disclosure."

In determining whether a confidential informant's identity should be disclosed, a court should balance "the strong public policy reasons favoring it against a defendant's need for disclosure in order to prepare his defense." (People v. Witherspoon (1991), 216 Ill.App.3d 323, 331, 160 Ill.Dec. 76, 576 N.E.2d 1030.) The identity of a confidential informant can be withheld if he is not a participant or a material witness to the essential elements of the offense. (People v. Velez (1990), 204 Ill.App.3d 318, 326, 149 Ill.Dec. 783, 562 N.E.2d 247.) It is the defendant's burden to establish that the informant can testify to facts bearing on the charged offense. (*Witherspoon,* 216 Ill.App.3d at 331, 160 Ill.Dec. 76, 576 N.E.2d 1030.) The State is generally not required to disclose the identity of the informant unless the failure to do so would infringe defendant's constitutional rights. (People v. Elworthy (1991), 214 Ill.App.3d 914, 921, 158 Ill.Dec. 614, 620, 574 N.E.2d 727, 733.) The Supreme Court in *Franks* specifically stated that the "deliberate falsity or reckless disregard whose impeachment is permitted today is only that of the affiant, not of any nongovernmental informant." Franks, 438 U.S. at 171; *see also Lucente,* 116 Ill.2d at 148, 107 Ill.Dec. at 220, 506 N.E.2d at 1275.

The court in People v. Velez (1990), 204 Ill.App.3d 318, 326, 149 Ill.Dec. 783, 562 N.E.2d 247 stated:

"Our supreme court, in People v. Lewis (1974), 57 Ill.2d 232, 235, 311 N.E.2d 685, has adopted the *Roviaro* standard, holding that disclosure would be required when an informant acted in the dual role of informant participant. (Roviaro v. United States (1957), 353 U.S. 53, 64–65.) Where an informant's knowledge is potentially significant on the issue of the defendant's guilt or innocence, the defendant is prejudiced by the State's denial of production. [Citation.] Contrarily, where the unnamed informant was neither a participant nor material witness to the essential elements of the offense, the informant is not a crucial witness and his identity can be withheld. [Citations.] Finally, where the informant could not have testified to any fact bearing on the charged offense, but merely provided information to law enforcement officials, his disclosure is not required. * * *. The balancing of rights test, as enunciated in Roviaro, calls for balancing the public interest in protecting the flow of information against the individual's right to prepare his defense. (*Roviaro,* 353 U.S. at 60–62.) In Illinois the factors considered by the courts under this test are whether the request for disclosure related to the fundamental question of guilt or innocence rather than to the preliminary issue of probable cause, where the informant played an active role in the criminal occurrence, as opposed to being a mere tipster, and whether it has been shown that the informant's life or safety would likely be jeopardized by disclosure of his identity."

The informants' information in the present case was only used to support the search warrant. Defendant's delivery to the confidential informant was not an issue at trial. The informant did not participate in the crimes defendant was charged with committing. The informant played no material role as a participant in defendant's possession of the controlled substance, nor could he have provided any testimony concerning the charged offense. He was not present when the defendant was arrested. The informant simply provided information to Officer Schaefer. The informant's testimony would have had no significant value on the issue of defendant's guilt or innocence. Thus, the burden was on the defendant to show that disclosure of the informant's identity was necessary to prepare their defense. No such showing was made. Therefore, the trial court properly denied the defense motion to produce the informant.

C.

The defendant argues that when an in camera hearing is held the trial court must allow defense counsel to be present and an accurate record must be kept. Defendant argues that once the court determines that an in camera hearing should be held some provisions must be made to maintain and preserve a record of that hearing to insure the proceeding is not rendered unreviewable.

The State argues that the trial judge interviewed the informant in chambers, and corroborated the officer's testimony. The State maintains that the trial judge properly conducted the interview outside of the presence of defendant or defense counsel, because if the trial judge had either permitted the presence of defendant or defense counsel at the interview or had the trial judge kept a record of the interview, the informant's identity would have been exposed and the informant's confidentiality destroyed. We believe the trial judge was within his discretion to maintain the confidentiality of the informant in this case. (*See* Ill.Rev.Stat.1991, ch. 110A, par. 412(j)(ii).) Although the trial court did not indicate what the specific questions or answers were, he did indicate the scope of his interview prior to ruling. In essence the trial court found that the informant corroborated the information in Officer Schaefer's warrant affidavit. We believe that the trial court's comments on the record, provided a summary of the in camera interview, while preserving the confidentiality of the informant.

Moreover, if there was any error, we find that it was harmless. The standard of review in a *Franks* case is whether the affiant police officer knowingly and intentionally, or with reckless disregard for the truth, made a false statement in a warrant affidavit. (Franks v. Delaware

(1978), 438 U.S. 154.) We find sufficient support in the record to find that the trial court properly denied the motion to quash without considering the information obtained in the interview with the informant.

AFFIRMED.

5. MANNER OF EXECUTION

a. "KNOCK AND ANNOUNCE"

Whittier v. Kobayashi

581 F.3d 1304 (11th Cir. 2009)

■ PER CURIAM:

Daniel Kobayashi, an officer with the City of Sunrise, Florida, Police Department, appeals the district court's order denying in part his motion for summary judgment. Kobayashi was a member of a Special Weapons and Tactics (SWAT) team that conducted a raid on Plaintiff-Appellee Marlene Whittier's home, which she shared with her son, Anthony Diotaiuto. During the raid, Diotaiuto was shot and killed. Whittier brought a 42 U.S.C. § 1983 action, both individually and as personal representative for Diotaiuto's estate, against several members of the SWAT team alleging, inter alia, Kobayashi violated her son's Fourth Amendment rights when he entered her home without first knocking and announcing the SWAT team's presence. After extensive discovery, Kobayashi moved for summary judgment, arguing he was entitled to qualified immunity and no genuine issue of material fact existed as to whether a knock and announce occurred. The district court denied his motion as to Whittier's knock-and-announce claim. Because Kobayashi is entitled to qualified immunity, we now reverse.

I. FACTS

In July 2005, one of Anthony Diotaiuto's neighbors informed the City of Sunrise Police Department (Sunrise police) that Diotaiuto was selling large quantities of cannabis and cocaine from his residence. Based upon this information, law enforcement began an investigation of Diotaiuto's drug activity, which included surveillance of the Whittier/Diotaiuto residence and a "controlled buy" of marijuana by a confidential informant. In addition to evidence that Diotaiuto was selling illegal narcotics in his home, the investigation also revealed Diotaiuto carried a handgun on his person at all times and kept a loaded shotgun in his bedroom closet.

On August 3, 2005, a state circuit judge signed a warrant for the Sunrise police to search the Whittier/Diotaiuto home. Based upon Diotaiuto's drug activity and possession of firearms, the Sunrise police classified the warrant as "high risk," which the Sunrise police define as "involving acts of violence or potential acts of violence." The Sunrise police use a SWAT team in the service of all "high risk" warrants, and thus a SWAT team was assembled to serve the warrant on the Whittier/Diotaiuto residence.

In preparation for the service of the warrant, the Sunrise police made a SWAT operational plan. This plan indicated Diotaiuto sold illegal narcotics from his home, had a criminal history, and possessed two firearms—a semi-automatic handgun carried on his person and a shotgun kept in his bedroom closet. The plan also called for an eight-man SWAT team to execute the warrant; Kobayashi was designated as the team leader and was responsible for knocking and announcing the presence of the SWAT team prior to entry. The members of the SWAT team received and reviewed the information in the operational plan during a briefing that was held in the early morning hours of August 5, 2005.

Following the briefing, at just after 6:00 a.m. on that same day, the SWAT team arrived at the Whittier/Diotaiuto residence to execute the warrant. According to the testimony of the officers, Kobayashi approached the door, knocked loudly several times, and announced the presence of the Sunrise police and the search warrant. Fourteen police officers present at the scene testified they heard a knock and announce. Only a single officer did not hear a knock and announce. Despite the fact that nearly every officer present heard a loud and forceful knock and announce, not a single neighbor heard a knock or an announcement of the police presence. At least three neighbors testified they were listening and would have been able to hear such an announcement if it had occurred.

Next, Kobayashi signaled for the breach team to open the front door. After the door was pried open, the SWAT team entered the home and encountered Diotaiuto, whom Kobayashi instructed to "get on the ground." Diotaiuto did not comply with the order and instead ran to his bedroom. Two SWAT team officers followed in pursuant, kicked open the bedroom door, and followed Diotaiuto inside. According to the testimony of the officers, Diotaiuto entered his closet, racked a gun, and pointed it at the officers. Both officers were yelling at Diotaiuto to put the gun down. They then opened fire, and Diotaiuto fell back into the closet. From a seated position in the closet, Diotaiuto began to raise his gun again. Both officers yelled at Diotaiuto to drop the gun; their commands, however, were disregarded. The officers fired again, and Diotaiuto was killed.

II. STANDARD OF REVIEW

This Court reviews "de novo a district court's disposition of a summary judgment motion based on qualified immunity, applying the same legal standards as the district court." Durruthy v. Pastor, 351 F.3d 1080, 1084 (11th Cir.2003). We resolve all issues of material fact in favor of the plaintiff, and then, under that version of the facts, determine the legal question of whether the defendant is entitled to qualified immunity. *Id.*

III. DISCUSSION

"Qualified immunity protects government officials performing discretionary functions from suits in their individual capacities unless their conduct violates 'clearly established statutory or constitutional rights of which a reasonable person would have known.'" Dalrymple v. Reno, 334 F.3d 991, 994 (11th Cir.2003) (quoting Hope v. Pelzer, 536 U.S. 730, 739 (2002)). "[T]o receive qualified immunity, an official must first establish that 'he was acting within the scope of his discretionary authority when the allegedly wrongful acts occurred.'" McCullough v. Antolini, 559 F.3d 1201, 1205 (11th Cir.2009) (quoting Lee v. Ferraro, 284 F.3d 1188, 1194 (11th Cir.2002)).

"If the official was acting within the scope of his discretionary authority . . . the burden shifts to the plaintiff to show that the official is not entitled to qualified immunity." Skop v. City of Atlanta, 485 F.3d 1130, 1136–37 (11th Cir.2007). "To overcome qualified immunity, the plaintiff must satisfy a two prong test; he must show that: (1) the defendant violated a constitutional right, and (2) this right was clearly established at the time of the alleged violation." Holloman ex rel. Holloman v. Harland, 370 F.3d 1252, 1264 (11th Cir.2004). "The relevant, dispositive inquiry in determining whether a right is clearly established is whether it would be clear to a reasonable officer that his conduct was unlawful in the situation he confronted." Saucier v. Katz, 533 U.S. 194, 202 (2001).

Whittier asserts Kobayashi entered her and her son's residence without first knocking and announcing the SWAT team's presence in violation of the Fourth Amendment. The Fourth Amendment protects "[t]he right of the people to be secure in their persons, houses, papers, and effects, against unreasonable searches and seizures." U.S. Const. amend. IV. In Wilson v. Arkansas, 514 U.S. 927, 929 (1995), the Supreme Court held the Fourth Amendment reasonableness inquiry incorporated the common law requirement that officers, when executing a search warrant, must knock on a door and announce their identity before attempting a forcible entry into a home. The Court, however, recognized "[t]he Fourth Amendment's flexible requirement of reasonableness should not be read to mandate a rigid rule of announcement that ignores countervailing law enforcement interests," *id.* at 934, and noted the knock-and-announce requirement could give way "under circumstances presenting a threat of physical violence," or "where police officers have reason to believe that evidence would likely be destroyed if advance notice were given," *id.* at 936.

Following *Wilson,* some courts created a blanket exception to the knock-and-announce requirement in felony drug cases, based in part on the generalization that these cases often involve a threat of violence and destruction of drugs. *See* Richards v. Wisconsin, 520 U.S. 385, 392 (1997).

In *Richards v. Wisconsin,* however, the Supreme Court rejected such a categorical exception and instead adopted a case-by-case approach for determining if law enforcement acted reasonably in entering a residence without first knocking and announcing: "In order to justify a 'no-knock' entry, the police must have a reasonable suspicion that knocking and announcing their presence, under the particular circumstances, would be dangerous or futile, or that it would inhibit the effective investigation of the crime by, for example, allowing the destruction of evidence." *Id.* at 394. The Court acknowledged, however, "[t]his showing is not high." *Id.*

Both *Wilson* and *Richards* were criminal cases in which the defendants had moved to suppress evidence based upon alleged Fourth Amendment violations. In the context of qualified immunity, this Court has stated "the issue is not whether reasonable suspicion existed in fact, but whether the officer had 'arguable' reasonable suspicion." Jackson v. Sauls, 206 F.3d 1156, 1166 (11th Cir.2000). In other words, we analyze whether a reasonable officer could have had reasonable suspicion that exigent circumstances, such as a threat of violence and/or destruction of evidence, existed to justify the no-knock entry. *See* Brent v. Ashley, 247 F.3d 1294, 1303 (11th Cir.2001) (discussing the arguable reasonable suspicion standard within the context of strip searches). In undertaking the arguable reasonable suspicion inquiry, this Court must examine the totality of the circumstances to determine whether an officer had a "particularized and objective" basis to support his suspicion. *Id.* at 1304. Whether the officer's suspicion ends up being mistaken is immaterial so long as it was reasonable. *Id.* at 1303.

Within the context of warrantless searches, we have held the mere presence of contraband, without more, does not give rise to exigent circumstances. United States v. Tobin, 923 F.2d 1506, 1510 (11th Cir.1991). At the same time, however, we have also repeatedly noted the dangerous, and often violent, combination of drugs and firearms, see, e.g., United States v. Hromada, 49 F.3d 685, 689 (11th Cir.1995) ("Guns and violence go hand-in-hand with illegal drug operations."), and several of our sister circuits have concluded this combination may give rise to reasonable suspicion of danger and justify a no-knock entry, see United States v. Stevens, 439 F.3d 983, 988–89 (8th Cir.2006) (affirming a magistrate judge's conclusion that a no-knock search was justified based upon the presence of drugs and a sawed-off shotgun in a common area of the house); United States v. Washington, 340 F.3d 222, 227 (5th Cir.2003) (stating information that "the suspect was selling drugs and was typically armed . . . . exceeds the level this circuit has found sufficient to establish a reasonable suspicion of danger").

In this case, we conclude Kobayashi is entitled to qualified immunity because a reasonable officer could have had reasonable suspicion that knocking and announcing his presence would have been dangerous under the circumstances facing the SWAT team.[1] Those circumstances included serving a search warrant on the home of a suspected drug dealer (Diotaiuto), who had ready access to firearms and occupied the premises when the SWAT team arrived to serve the warrant. Indeed, based upon the information available to the SWAT team, Diotaiuto (1) received and sold narcotics, including cocaine and marijuana, at his residence; (2) had a criminal history; (3) carried a concealed semi-automatic handgun on his person; and (4) possessed a shotgun that he kept in his bedroom. This information, which was contained in the SWAT team's operational plan and received and reviewed by the members of the team, provided a "particularized and objective" basis for a reasonable officer to suspect the situation had a potential for violence and to believe exigent circumstances existed to justify a no-knock entry.

The fact that the operational plan called for a knock and announce prior to entry does not alter our analysis. Even assuming the operational plan, which was prepared prior to the service of the warrant, speaks for what Kobayashi actually believed as he stood outside the Whittier/Diotaiuto residence, Kobayashi's subjective beliefs regarding the circumstances are irrelevant to the qualified immunity inquiry. *See* Harlow v. Fitzgerald, 457 U.S. 800, 817–18 (1982) (discarding the subjective component of the qualified immunity inquiry and adopting the "objective reasonableness" standard); *Jackson,* 206 F.3d at 1165 ("[T]he standard for determining if an officer violated clearly established law is an objective one and does not include inquiry into the officer's subjective intent or beliefs."). Moreover, we have held an officer is entitled to qualified immunity even when he reasonably, but mistakenly, believes reasonable suspicion is present, *See Brent*, 247 F.3d at 1303; it makes little sense to not afford the same protection to an officer who, sensitive to the rights citizens enjoy under the Constitution, initially, but mistakenly, believes the situation involves a constitutional protection, but later learns it does not.

IV. CONCLUSION

In sum, we conclude Kobayashi is entitled to qualified immunity on Whittier's knock-and-announce claim. Accordingly, we reverse the district court's order denying his motion for summary judgment as to this claim.[3]

---

[1] We are aware that Kobayashi maintains he did actually knock and announce the SWAT team's presence and that fourteen officers have testified to that effect. Whether a knock and announcement actually occurred, however, is irrelevant to our analysis of arguable reasonable suspicion, and thus the outcome in this case is the same under both Kobayashi's and Whittier's versions of the facts.

[3] Because we conclude Kobayashi is entitled to summary judgment on the basis of qualified immunity, we need not address the second issue he raises on appeal—that is, whether he is entitled to summary judgment on the ground that no genuine issue of material fact existed as to whether a knock and announce actually occurred. We note, however, we likely would not have jurisdiction to consider this issue on an interlocutory appeal, as it is not a part of, or inextricably intertwined with, the core qualified immunity issue. *See* Behrens v. Pelletier, 516 U.S. 299, 312–13 (1996); Koch v. Rugg, 221 F.3d 1283, 1295–96 (11th Cir.2000).

REVERSED.

b. INCIDENTAL DETENTION AND SEARCH POWERS

Muehler v. Mena

544 U.S. 93 (2005)

■ REHNQUIST, C. J., delivered the opinion of the Court, in which O'CONNOR, SCALIA, KENNEDY, and THOMAS, JJ., joined. KENNEDY, J., filed a concurring opinion. STEVENS, J., filed an opinion concurring in the judgment, in which SOUTER, GINSBURG, and BREYER, JJ., joined.

■ CHIEF JUSTICE REHNQUIST delivered the opinion of the Court.

Respondent Iris Mena was detained in handcuffs during a search of the premises that she and several others occupied. Petitioners were lead members of a police detachment executing a search warrant of these premises. She sued the officers under Rev. Stat. § 1979, 42 U.S.C. § 1983, and the District Court found in her favor. The Court of Appeals affirmed the judgment, holding that the use of handcuffs to detain Mena during the search violated the Fourth Amendment and that the officers' questioning of Mena about her immigration status during the detention constituted an independent Fourth Amendment violation. Mena v. Simi Valley, 332 F.3d 1255 (C.A.9 2003). We hold that Mena's detention in handcuffs for the length of the search was consistent with our opinion in Michigan v. Summers, 452 U.S. 692 (1981), and that the officers' questioning during that detention did not violate her Fourth Amendment rights.

* * *

Based on information gleaned from the investigation of a gang-related, driveby shooting, petitioners Muehler and Brill had reason to believe at least one member of a gang—the West Side Locos—lived at 1363 Patricia Avenue. They also suspected that the individual was armed and dangerous, since he had recently been involved in the driveby shooting. As a result, Muehler obtained a search warrant for 1363 Patricia Avenue that authorized a broad search of the house and premises for, among other things, deadly weapons and evidence of gang membership. In light of the high degree of risk involved in searching a house suspected of housing at least one, and perhaps multiple, armed gang members, a Special Weapons and Tactics (SWAT) team was used to secure the residence and grounds before the search.

At 7 a.m. on February 3, 1998, petitioners, along with the SWAT team and other officers, executed the warrant. Mena was asleep in her bed when the SWAT team, clad in helmets and black vests adorned with badges and the word "POLICE," entered her bedroom and placed her in handcuffs at gunpoint. The SWAT team also handcuffed three other individuals found on the property. The SWAT team then took those individuals and Mena into a converted garage, which contained several beds and some other bedroom furniture. While the search proceeded, one or two officers guarded the four detainees, who were allowed to move around the garage but remained in handcuffs.

Aware that the West Side Locos gang was composed primarily of illegal immigrants, the officers had notified the Immigration and Naturalization Service (INS) that they would be conducting the search, and an INS officer accompanied the officers executing the warrant. During their detention in the garage, an officer asked for each detainee's name, date of birth, place of birth, and immigration status. The INS officer later asked the detainees for their immigration documentation. Mena's status as a permanent resident was confirmed by her papers.

The search of the premises yielded a .22 caliber handgun with .22 caliber ammunition, a box of .25 caliber ammunition, several baseball bats with gang writing, various additional gang paraphernalia, and a bag of marijuana. Before the officers left the area, Mena was released.

In her § 1983 suit against the officers she alleged that she was detained "for an unreasonable time and in an unreasonable manner" in violation of the Fourth Amendment. In addition, she claimed that the warrant and its execution were overbroad, that the officers failed to comply with the "knock and announce" rule, and that the officers had needlessly destroyed property during the search. The officers moved for summary judgment, asserting that they were entitled to qualified immunity, but the District Court denied their motion. The Court of Appeals affirmed that denial, except for Mena's claim that the warrant was overbroad; on this claim the Court of Appeals held that the officers were entitled to qualified immunity. Mena v. Simi Valley, 226 F.3d 1031 (C.A.9 2000). After a trial, a jury, pursuant to a special verdict form, found that Officers Muehler and Brill violated Mena's Fourth Amendment right to be free from unreasonable seizures by detaining her both with force greater than that which was reasonable and for a longer period than that which was reasonable. The jury awarded Mena $10,000 in actual damages and $20,000 in punitive damages against each petitioner for a total of $60,000.

The Court of Appeals affirmed the judgment on two grounds. 332 F.3d 1255 (C.A.9 2003). Reviewing the denial of qualified immunity de novo, *id.*, at 1261, n. 2, it first held that the officers' detention of Mena violated the Fourth Amendment because it was objectively unreasonable to confine her in the converted garage and keep her in handcuffs during the search. In the Court of Appeals' view, the officers should have released Mena as soon as it became clear that she posed no immediate threat. The court additionally held that the questioning of Mena about her immigration status constituted an independent Fourth Amendment violation. The Court of Appeals went on to hold that those rights were clearly established at the time of Mena's questioning, and thus the officers were not entitled to qualified immunity. We granted certiorari, and now vacate and remand.

* * *

In Michigan v. Summers, 452 U.S. 692 (1981), we held that officers executing a search warrant for contraband have the authority "to detain the occupants of the premises while a proper search is conducted." Such detentions are appropriate, we explained, because the character of the additional intrusion caused by detention is slight and because the justifications for detention are substantial. We made clear that the detention of an occupant is "surely less intrusive than the search itself," and the presence of a warrant assures that a neutral magistrate has determined that probable cause exists to search the home. Against this incremental intrusion, we posited three legitimate law enforcement interests that provide substantial justification for detaining an occupant: "preventing flight in the event that incriminating evidence is found"; "minimizing the risk of harm to the officers"; and facilitating "the orderly completion of the search," as detainees' "self-interest may induce them to open locked doors or locked containers to avoid the use of force."

Mena's detention was, under *Summers*, plainly permissible.[1] An officer's authority to detain incident to a search is categorical; it does not depend on the "quantum of proof justifying detention or the extent of the intrusion to be imposed by the seizure." *Id.*, at 705, n. 19. Thus, Mena's detention for the duration of the search was reasonable under Summers because a warrant existed to search 1363 Patricia Avenue and she was an occupant of that address at the time of the search.

Inherent in *Summers'* authorization to detain an occupant of the place to be searched is the authority to use reasonable force to effectuate the detention. *See* Graham v. Connor, 490 U.S. 386, 396 (1989) ("Fourth Amendment jurisprudence has long recognized that the right to make an arrest or investigatory stop necessarily carries with it the right to use some degree of physical coercion or threat thereof to effect it"). Indeed, *Summers* itself stressed that the risk of harm to officers and occupants is minimized "if the officers routinely exercise unquestioned command of the situation." 452 U.S., at 703.

The officers' use of force in the form of handcuffs to effectuate Mena's detention in the garage, as well as the detention of the three other occupants, was reasonable because the governmental interests outweigh the marginal intrusion. *See Graham, supra*, at 396–397 The imposition of correctly applied handcuffs on Mena, who was already being lawfully detained during a search of the house, was undoubtedly a separate

---

[1]   In determining whether a Fourth Amendment violation occurred we draw all reasonable factual inferences in favor of the jury verdict, but as we made clear in Ornelas v. United States, 517 U.S. 690, 697–699 (1996), we do not defer to the jury's legal conclusion that those facts violate the Constitution.

intrusion in addition to detention in the converted garage.[2] The detention was thus more intrusive than that which we upheld in *Summers. See* 452 U.S., at 701–702 (concluding that the additional intrusion in the form of a detention was less than that of the warrant-sanctioned search); Maryland v. Wilson, 519 U.S. 408, 413–414 (1997) (concluding that the additional intrusion from ordering passengers out of a car, which was already stopped, was minimal).

But this was no ordinary search. The governmental interests in not only detaining, but using handcuffs, are at their maximum when, as here, a warrant authorizes a search for weapons and a wanted gang member resides on the premises. In such inherently dangerous situations, the use of handcuffs minimizes the risk of harm to both officers and occupants. Cf. *Summers, supra,* at 702–703 (recognizing the execution of a warrant to search for drugs "may give rise to sudden violence or frantic efforts to conceal or destroy evidence"). Though this safety risk inherent in executing a search warrant for weapons was sufficient to justify the use of handcuffs, the need to detain multiple occupants made the use of handcuffs all the more reasonable. *Cf. Maryland v. Wilson, supra,* at 414 (noting that "danger to an officer from a traffic stop is likely to be greater when there are passengers in addition to the driver in the stopped car").

Mena argues that, even if the use of handcuffs to detain her in the garage was reasonable as an initial matter, the duration of the use of handcuffs made the detention unreasonable. The duration of a detention can, of course, affect the balance of interests under *Graham.* However, the 2- to 3-hour detention in handcuffs in this case does not outweigh the government's continuing safety interests. As we have noted, this case involved the detention of four detainees by two officers during a search of a gang house for dangerous weapons. We conclude that the detention of Mena in handcuffs during the search was reasonable.

The Court of Appeals also determined that the officers violated Mena's Fourth Amendment rights by questioning her about her immigration status during the detention. 332 F.3d, at 1264–1266. This holding, it appears, was premised on the assumption that the officers were required to have independent reasonable suspicion in order to question Mena concerning her immigration status because the questioning constituted a discrete Fourth Amendment event. But the

---

[2] In finding the officers should have released Mena from the handcuffs, the Court of Appeals improperly relied upon the fact that the warrant did not include Mena as a suspect. *See* Mena v. Simi Valley, 332 F.3d 1255, 1263, n. 5 (C.A.9 2003). The warrant was concerned not with individuals but with locations and property. In particular, the warrant in this case authorized the search of 1363 Patricia Avenue and its surrounding grounds for, among other things, deadly weapons and evidence of street gang membership. In this respect, the warrant here resembles that at issue in Michigan v. Summers, 452 U.S. 692 (1981), which allowed the search of a residence for drugs without mentioning any individual, including the owner of the home whom police ultimately arrested. *See* People v. Summers, 407 Mich. 432, 440–443, 286 N.W.2d 226, 226–227 (1979), rev'd, Michigan v. Summers, *supra. Summers* makes clear that when a neutral magistrate has determined police have probable cause to believe contraband exists, "[t]he connection of an occupant to [a] home" alone "justifies a detention of that occupant." 452 U.S., at 703–704.

premise is faulty. We have "held repeatedly that mere police questioning does not constitute a seizure." *Florida v. Bostick*, 501 U.S. 429, 434 (1991); *see also* INS v. Delgado, 466 U.S. 210, 212 (1984). "[E]ven when officers have no basis for suspecting a particular individual, they may generally ask questions of that individual; ask to examine the individual's identification; and request consent to search his or her luggage." *Bostick, supra,* at 434–435 (citations omitted). As the Court of Appeals did not hold that the detention was prolonged by the questioning, there was no additional seizure within the meaning of the Fourth Amendment. Hence, the officers did not need reasonable suspicion to ask Mena for her name, date and place of birth, or immigration status. . . .

In summary, the officers' detention of Mena in handcuffs during the execution of the search warrant was reasonable and did not violate the Fourth Amendment. Additionally, the officers' questioning of Mena did not constitute an independent Fourth Amendment violation. Mena has advanced in this Court, as she did before the Court of Appeals, an alternative argument for affirming the judgment below. She asserts that her detention extended beyond the time the police completed the tasks incident to the search. Because the Court of Appeals did not address this contention, we too decline to address it.

The judgment of the Court of Appeals is therefore vacated, and the case is remanded for further proceedings consistent with this opinion.

It is so ordered.

■ JUSTICE KENNEDY, concurring.

I concur in the judgment and in the opinion of the Court. It does seem important to add this brief statement to help ensure that police handcuffing during searches becomes neither routine nor unduly prolonged.

The safety of the officers and the efficacy of the search are matters of first concern, but so too is it a matter of first concern that excessive force is not used on the persons detained, especially when these persons, though lawfully detained under Michigan v. Summers, 452 U.S. 692 (1981), are not themselves suspected of any involvement in criminal activity. The use of handcuffs is the use of force, and such force must be objectively reasonable under the circumstances, Graham v. Connor, 490 U.S. 386 (1989).

The reasonableness calculation under *Graham* is in part a function of the expected and actual duration of the search. If the search extends to the point when the handcuffs can cause real pain or serious discomfort, provision must be made to alter the conditions of detention at least long enough to attend to the needs of the detainee. This is so even if there is no question that the initial handcuffing was objectively reasonable. The restraint should also be removed if, at any point during the search, it would be readily apparent to any objectively reasonable officer that removing the handcuffs would not compromise the officers' safety or risk interference or substantial delay in the execution of the search. The time spent in the search here, some two to three hours, certainly approaches, and may well exceed, the time beyond which a detainee's Fourth Amendment interests require revisiting the necessity of handcuffing in order to ensure the restraint, even if permissible as an initial matter, has not become excessive.

That said, under these circumstances I do not think handcuffing the detainees for the duration of the search was objectively unreasonable. As I understand the record, during much of this search 2 armed officers were available to watch over the 4 unarmed detainees, while the other 16 officers on the scene conducted an extensive search of a suspected gang safe house. Even if we accept as true—as we must—the factual assertions that these detainees posed no readily apparent danger and that keeping them handcuffed deviated from standard police procedure, it does not follow that the handcuffs were unreasonable. Where the detainees outnumber those supervising them, and this situation could not be remedied without diverting officers from an extensive, complex, and time-consuming search, the continued use of handcuffs after the initial sweep may be justified, subject to adjustments or temporary release under supervision to avoid pain or excessive physical discomfort. Because on this record it does not appear the restraints were excessive, I join the opinion of the Court.

■ JUSTICE STEVENS, with whom JUSTICE SOUTER, JUSTICE GINSBURG, and JUSTICE BREYER join, concurring in the judgment.

The jury in this case found that the two petitioners violated Iris Mena's Fourth Amendment right to be free from unreasonable seizure by detaining her with greater force and for a longer period of time than was reasonable under the circumstances. In their post-trial motion in the District Court, petitioners advanced three legal arguments: (1) They were entitled to qualified immunity because the unconstitutionality of their conduct was not clearly established;[1] (2) the judge's instruction to the jury was erroneous;[2] and (3) the evidence was not sufficient to support the jury's award of punitive damages. The trial judge's

---

[1] The Court of Appeals' conclusion that the officers were not entitled to qualified immunity was not challenged in the petition for certiorari and is therefore waived.

[2] The trial judge instructed the jury as follows:

" 'Generally, a police officer carrying out a search authorized by a warrant may detain occupants of the residence during the search, so long as the detention is reasonable.

" 'In determining the reasonableness of a detention conducted in connection with a search, you may look to all the circumstances, including the severity of the suspected crime, whether the person being detained is the subject of the investigation, whether such person poses an immediate threat to the security of the police or others or to the ability of the police to conduct the search, and whether such person is actively resisting arrest or attempting to flee. A detention may be unreasonable if it is unnecessarily painful, degrading, prolonged or if it involves an undue invasion of privacy. A police officer is required to release an individual detained in connection with a lawful search as soon as the officers' right to conduct the search ends or the search itself is concluded, whichever is sooner.' " Mena v. Simi Valley, 332 F.3d 1255, 1267–1268 (C.A.9 2003) (alterations omitted; one paragraph break added).

thoughtful explanation of his reasons for denying the motion does not address either of the issues the Court discusses today.

In its opinion affirming the judgment, the Court of Appeals made two mistakes. First, as the Court explains, it erroneously held that the immigration officers' questioning of Mena about her immigration status was an independent violation of the Fourth Amendment. Second, instead of merely deciding whether there was sufficient evidence in the record to support the jury's verdict, the Court of Appeals appears to have ruled as a matter of law that the officers should have released her from the handcuffs sooner than they did. I agree that it is appropriate to remand the case to enable the Court of Appeals to consider whether the evidence supports Mena's contention that she was held longer than the search actually lasted. In doing so, the Court of Appeals must of course accord appropriate deference to the jury's reasonable factual findings, while applying the correct legal standard. *See* Ornelas v. United States, 517 U.S. 690, 699 (1996).

In my judgment, however, the Court's discussion of the amount of force used to detain Mena pursuant to Michigan v. Summers, 452 U.S. 692 (1981), is analytically unsound. Although the Court correctly purports to apply the "objective reasonableness" test announced in Graham v. Connor, 490 U.S. 386 (1989), it misapplies that test. Given the facts of this case—and the presumption that a reviewing court must draw all reasonable inferences in favor of supporting the verdict—I think it clear that the jury could properly have found that this 5-foot-2-inch young lady posed no threat to the officers at the scene, and that they used excessive force in keeping her in handcuffs for up to three hours. Although Summers authorizes the detention of any individual who is present when a valid search warrant is being executed, that case does not give officers carte blanche to keep individuals who pose no threat in handcuffs throughout a search, no matter how long it may last. On remand, I would therefore instruct the Court of Appeals to consider whether the evidence supports Mena's contention that the petitioners used excessive force in detaining her when it considers the length of the Summers detention.

I

As the Court notes, the warrant in this case authorized the police to enter the Mena home to search for a gun belonging to Raymond Romero that may have been used in a gang-related driveby shooting. Romero, a known member of the West Side Locos gang, rented a room from the Mena family. The house, described as a " 'poor house,' " was home to several unrelated individuals who rented from the Menas. Each resident had his or her own bedroom, which could be locked with a padlock on the outside, and each had access to the living room and kitchen. In addition, several individuals lived in trailers in the back yard and also had access to the common spaces in the Mena home.

In addition to Romero, police had reason to believe that at least one other West Side Locos gang member had lived at the residence, although Romero's brother told police that the individual had returned to Mexico. The officers in charge of the search, petitioners Muehler and Brill, had been at the same residence a few months earlier on an unrelated domestic violence call, but did not see any other individuals they believed to be gang members inside the home on that occasion.

In light of the fact that the police believed that Romero possessed a gun and that there might be other gang members at the residence, petitioner Muehler decided to use a Special Weapons and Tactics (SWAT) team to execute the warrant. As described in the majority opinion, eight members of the SWAT team forcefully entered the home at 7 a.m. In fact, Mena was the only occupant of the house, and she was asleep in her bedroom. The police woke her up at gunpoint, and immediately handcuffed her. At the same time, officers served another search warrant at the home of Romero's mother, where Romero was known to stay several nights each week. In part because Romero's mother had previously cooperated with police officers, they did not use a SWAT team to serve that warrant. Romero was found at his mother's house; after being cited for possession of a small amount of marijuana, he was released.

Meanwhile, after the SWAT team secured the Mena residence and gave the "all clear," police officers transferred Mena and three other individuals (who had been in trailers in the back yard) to a converted garage.[4] To get to the garage, Mena, who was still in her bedclothes, was forced to walk barefoot through the pouring rain. The officers kept her and the other three individuals in the garage for up to three hours while they searched the home. Although she requested them to remove the handcuffs, they refused to do so. For the duration of the search, two officers guarded Mena and the other three detainees. A .22-caliber handgun, ammunition, and gang-related paraphernalia were found in Romero's bedroom, and other gang-related paraphernalia was found in the living room. Officers found nothing of significance in Mena's bedroom.[5]

II

In analyzing the quantum of force used to effectuate the *Summers* detention, the Court rightly employs the "objective reasonableness" test

---

[4] The other individuals were a 55-year-old Latina female, a 40-year-old Latino male who was removed from the scene by the Immigration and Naturalization Service (INS), and a white male who appears to be in his early 30's and who was cited for possession of a small amount of marijuana.

[5] One of the justifications for our decision in Michigan v. Summers, 452 U.S. 692 (1981), was the fact that the occupants may be willing to "open locked doors or locked containers to avoid the use of force that is not only damaging to property but may also delay the completion of the task at hand." *Id.*, at 703. Mena, however, was never asked to assist the officers, although she testified that she was willing to do so. See 3 Tr. 42 (June 14, 2001). Instead, officers broke the locks on several cabinets and dressers to which Mena possessed the keys.

of *Graham*. Under *Graham,* the trier of fact must balance " 'the nature and quality of the intrusion on the individual's Fourth Amendment interests' against the countervailing governmental interests at stake." 490 U.S., at 396. The District Court correctly instructed the jury to take into consideration such factors as " 'the severity of the suspected crime, whether the person being detained is the subject of the investigation, whether such person poses an immediate threat to the security of the police or others or to the ability of the police to conduct the search, and whether such person is actively resisting arrest or attempting to flee.' " *See* n. 2, *supra.* The District Court also correctly instructed the jury to consider whether the detention was prolonged and whether Mena was detained in handcuffs after the search had ended. Many of these factors are taken from *Graham* itself, and the jury instruction reflects an entirely reasonable construction of the objective reasonableness test in the *Summers* context.

Considering those factors, it is clear that the SWAT team's initial actions were reasonable. When officers undertake a dangerous assignment to execute a warrant to search property that is presumably occupied by violence-prone gang members, it may well be appropriate to use both overwhelming force and surprise in order to secure the premises as promptly as possible. In this case the decision to use a SWAT team of eight heavily armed officers and to execute the warrant at 7 a.m. gave the officers maximum protection against the anticipated risk. As it turned out, there was only one person in the house—Mena—and she was sound asleep. Nevertheless, "[t]he 'reasonableness' of a particular use of force must be judged from the perspective of a reasonable officer on the scene, rather than with the 20/20 vision of hindsight." *Graham,* 490 U.S., at 396. At the time they first encountered Mena, the officers had no way of knowing her relation to Romero, whether she was affiliated with the West Side Locos, or whether she had any weapons on her person. Further, the officers needed to use overwhelming force to immediately take command of the situation; by handcuffing Mena they could more quickly secure her room and join the other officers. It would be unreasonable to expect officers, who are entering what they believe to be a high risk situation, to spend the time necessary to determine whether Mena was a threat before they handcuffed her. To the extent that the Court of Appeals relied on the initial actions of the SWAT team to find that there was sufficient evidence to support the jury's verdict, it was in error.

Whether the well-founded fears that justified the extraordinary entry into the house should also justify a prolonged interruption of the morning routine of a presumptively innocent person, however, is a separate question and one that depends on the specific facts of the case. This is true with respect both to how the handcuffs were used, and to the totality of the circumstances surrounding the detention, including whether Mena was detained in handcuffs after the search had concluded.

With regard to the handcuffs, police may use them in different ways.[6] Here, the cuffs kept Mena's arms behind her for two to three hours. She testified that they were " 'real uncomfortable' " and that she had asked the officers to remove them, but that they had refused. Moreover, she was continuously guarded by two police officers who obviously made flight virtually impossible even if the cuffs had been removed.

A jury could reasonably have found a number of facts supporting a conclusion that the prolonged handcuffing was unreasonable. No contraband was found in Mena's room or on her person. There were no indications suggesting she was or ever had been a gang member, which was consistent with the fact that during the police officers' last visit to the home, no gang members were present. She fully cooperated with the officers and the INS agent, answering all their questions. She was unarmed, and given her small size, was clearly no match for either of the two armed officers who were guarding her. In sum, there was no evidence that Mena posed any threat to the officers or anyone else.

The justifications offered by the officers are not persuasive. They have argued that at least six armed officers were required to guard the four detainees, even though all of them had been searched for weapons. Since there were 18 officers at the scene, and since at least 1 officer who at one point guarded Mena and the other three residents was sent home after offering to assist in the search, it seems unlikely that lack of resources was really a problem. While a court should not ordinarily question the allocation of police officers or resources, a jury could have reasonably found that this is a case where ample resources were available.

The jury may also have been skeptical of testimony that the officers in fact feared for their safety given that the actual suspect of the shooting had been found at the other location and promptly released. Additionally, while the officers testified that as a general matter they would not release an individual from handcuffs while searching a residence, the SWAT team's tactical plan for this particular search arguably called for them to do just that, since it directed that "[a]ny subjects encountered will be handcuffed and detained until they can be patted down, their location noted, [field identified], and released by Officer Muehler or Officer R. Brill.". The tactical plan suggests that they can, and often do, release individuals who are not related to the search. The SWAT team leader testified that handcuffs are not always required when executing a search.

In short, under the factors listed in *Graham* and those validly presented to the jury in the jury instructions, a jury could have reasonably found from the evidence that there was no apparent need to

---

[6] For instance, a suspect may be handcuffed to a fixed object, to a custodian, or her hands may simply be linked to one another. The cuffs may join the wrists either in the front or the back of the torso. They can be so tight that they are painful, particularly when applied for prolonged periods. While they restrict movement, they do not necessarily preclude flight if the prisoner is not kept under constant surveillance.

handcuff Mena for the entire duration of the search and that she was detained for an unreasonably prolonged period. She posed no threat whatsoever to the officers at the scene. She was not suspected of any crime and was not a person targeted by the search warrant. She had no reason to flee the scene and gave no indication that she desired to do so. Viewing the facts in the light most favorable to the jury's verdict, as we are required to do, there is certainly no obvious factual basis for rejecting the jury's verdict that the officers acted unreasonably, and no obvious basis for rejecting the conclusion that, on these facts, the quantum of force used was unreasonable as a matter of law.

III

Police officers' legitimate concern for their own safety is always a factor that should weigh heavily in balancing the relevant *Graham* factors. But, as Officer Brill admitted at trial, if that justification were always sufficient, it would authorize the handcuffing of every occupant of the premises for the duration of every *Summers* detention. Nothing in either the *Summers* or the *Graham* opinion provides any support for such a result. Rather, the decision of what force to use must be made on a case-by-case basis. There is evidence in this record that may well support the conclusion that it was unreasonable to handcuff Mena throughout the search. On remand, therefore, I would instruct the Ninth Circuit to consider that evidence, as well as the possibility that Mena was detained after the search was completed, when deciding whether the evidence in the record is sufficient to support the jury's verdict.

6. ELECTRONIC SURVEILLANCE WARRANTS

U.S. Department of Justice, U.S. Attorneys Manual, Criminal Resource Manual

https://www.justice.gov/jm/crm-1-99 (as of Nov. 14, 2019)

27. Electronic Surveillance

Discussed below are the requirements of each of the three documents comprising a Title III application: the Application, the Affidavit, and the Order. These requirements, which are set forth in 18 U.S.C. § 2518, are applicable to requests to the court for an order authorizing the interception of oral, wire, and/or electronic communications.

28. Electronic Surveillance—Title III Applications

The Application should meet the following requirements:

A. It must be prepared by an applicant identified as a law enforcement or investigative officer. The application must be in writing, signed by the United States Attorney, an Assistant United States Attorney, and made under oath. It must be presented to a Federal district court or court of appeals judge and be accompanied by the Department's authorization memorandum signed by an appropriate Department official and a copy of the most recent Attorney General's Order designating that official to authorize Title III applications. The application may not be presented to a magistrate. *See* 18 U.S.C. §§ 2510(9) and 2516(1); *see also In re United States of America*, 10 F.3d 931, 935–38 (2d Cir. 1993).

B.   It must identify the type of communications to be intercepted. "Wire communications" include "aural transfers" (involving the human voice) that are transmitted, at least in part by wire, between the point of origin and the point of reception, i.e., telephone calls. 18 U.S.C. § 2510(1). This includes cellular phones, cordless phones, voice mail, and voice pagers, as well as traditional landline telephones. "Oral communications" are communications between people who are together under circumstances where the parties enjoy a reasonable expectation of privacy. 18 U.S.C. § 2510(2). "Electronic communications" include text messages, email, non-voice computer and Internet transmissions, faxes, communications over digital-display paging devices, and, in some cases, satellite transmissions. Communications over tone-only paging devices, data from tracking devices (as defined by 18 U.S.C. § 3117), and electronic funds transfer information are not electronic communications under Title III. 18 U.S.C. § 2510(12).

C.   It must identify the specific Federal offenses for which there is probable cause to believe are being committed. The offenses that may be the predicate for a wire or oral interception order are limited to only those set forth in 18 U.S.C. § 2516(1). In the case of electronic communications, a request for interception may be based on any Federal felony, pursuant to 18 U.S.C. § 2516(3).

D.   It must provide a particular description of the nature and location of the facilities from which, or the place where, the interception is to occur. An exception to this is the roving interception provision set forth in 18 U.S.C. § 2518(11)(a) and (b). The specific requirements of the roving provision are discussed in JM 9-7.111. Briefly, in the case of a roving oral interception, the application must show, and the court order must indicate, that it is impractical to specify the location(s) where oral communications of a particular named subject are to be intercepted. 18 U.S.C. § 2518(11)(a)(ii) and (iii). In the case of a roving wire or electronic interception, the application must state, and the court order must indicate, that a particular named subject's actions could have the effect of thwarting interception from a specified facility. 18 U.S.C. § 2518(11)(b)(ii) and (iii). The accompanying DOJ document authorizing the roving interception must be signed by an official at the level of an Assistant Attorney General (including Acting AAG) or higher. 18 U.S.C. § 2518(11)(a)(i) and (b)(i). Further guidance on roving interceptions may be found on the DOJNet site of the Electronic Surveillance Unit (ESU), Office of Enforcement Operations (OEO).

E. It must identify, with specificity, those persons known to be committing the offenses and whose communications are to be intercepted. In *United States v. Donovan*, 429 U.S. 413, 422–32 (1977), the Supreme Court held that 18 U.S.C. § 2518(1)(b)(iv) requires the government to name all individuals whom it has probable cause to believe are engaged in the offenses under investigation, and whose conversations it expects to intercept over or from within the targeted facilities. It is the Criminal Division's policy to name as subjects *all* persons whose involvement in the alleged offenses is indicated, even if not all those persons are expected to be intercepted over the target facility or at the target location.

F. It must contain a statement affirming that normal investigative procedures have been tried and failed, are reasonably unlikely to succeed if tried, or are too dangerous to employ. 18 U.S.C. § 2518(1)(c). The applicant may then state that a complete discussion of attempted alternative investigative techniques is set forth in the accompanying affidavit.

G. It must contain a statement affirming that the affidavit contains a complete statement of the facts—to the extent known to the applicant and the official approving the application—concerning all previous applications that have been made to intercept the oral, wire, or electronic communications of any of the named subjects or involving the target facility or location. 18 U.S.C. § 2518(1)(e).

H. In an oral (and occasionally in a wire or electronic) interception, it must contain a request that the court issue an order authorizing investigative agents to make all necessary surreptitious and/or forcible entries to install, maintain, and remove electronic interception devices in or from the targeted premises (or device). When effecting this portion of the order, the applicant should notify the court as soon as practicable after each surreptitious entry.

I. When requesting the interception of wire communications over a cellular telephone, it should contain a request that the authorization and court order apply not only to the target telephone identified therein, but also to: 1) any change in *one* of several potential identifying numbers for the phone, including the electronic serial number (ESN), International Mobile Subscriber Identity (IMSI) number, International Mobile Equipment Identification (IMEI) number, Mobile Equipment Identifier (MEID) number, or Urban Fleet Mobile Identification

(UFMI) number; and 2) any changed target telephone number when the other identifying number has remained the same. Model continuity language for each type of identifier may be obtained from ESU. With regard to a landline phone, it should request that the authorization and court order apply not only to the target telephone number identified therein, but also to any changed telephone number subsequently assigned to the same cable, pair, and binding posts used by the target landline telephone. No continuity language should be included when the target telephone is a Voice Over Internet Protocol (VoIP) phone. The application should also request that the authorization apply to background conversations intercepted in the vicinity of the target phone while the phone is in use. *See United States v. Baranek*, 903 F.2d 1068, 1070–72 (6th Cir. 1990).

J.   It must contain, when concerning the interception of wire communications, a request that the court issue an order directly to the service provider, as defined in 18 U.S.C. § 2510(15), to furnish the investigative agency with all information, facilities, and technical assistance necessary to facilitate the ordered interception. 18 U.S.C. § 2511(2)(a)(ii). The application should also request that the court direct service providers and their agents and employees not to disclose the contents of the court order or the existence of the investigation. *Id.*

K.   For original and spinoff applications, it should contain a request that the court's order authorize the requested interception until all relevant communications have been intercepted, not to exceed a period of thirty (30) days from the earlier of the day on which the interception begins or ten (10) days after the order is entered. 18 U.S.C. § 2518(5). For extensions, it should contain a request that the thirty-day period be measured from the date of the court's order.

L.   It should contain a statement affirming that all interceptions will be minimized in accordance with Chapter 119 of Title 18, United States Code, as described further in the affidavit. 18 U.S.C. § 2518(5).

29. Electronic Surveillance—Title III Affidavits

The Affidavit must meet the following requirements:

A.   It must be sworn and attested to by an investigative or law enforcement officer as defined in 18 U.S.C. § 2510(7). Criminal Division policy requires that the affiant be a member of one of the following agencies: FBI, DEA, ICE/HSI, ATF, U.S. Secret Service, U.S. Marshals Service, or U.S. Postal Inspection Service. Criminal Division policy precludes the use of multiple affiants except when it is indicated clearly which affiant swears to which part of the affidavit, or states that each affiant swears to the entire affidavit. If a State or local law enforcement officer is the affiant in a Federal electronic surveillance affidavit, the enforcement officer must be *deputized* as a Federal officer of the agency responsible for the offenses under investigation. 18 U.S.C. § 2516(1).

B.   It must identify the target subjects, describe the facility or location that is the subject of the proposed electronic surveillance, and list the alleged offenses. 18 U.S.C. § 2518(1). If any of the alleged offenses are not listed predicate offenses under 18 U.S.C. § 2516(1), that fact should be noted.

C.   It must establish probable cause that the named subjects are using the targeted facility or location to commit the stated offenses. Any background information needed to understand fully the instant investigation should be set forth briefly at the beginning of this section. The focus, however, should be on recent and current criminal activity by the subjects, with an emphasis on their use of the target facility or location. This is generally accomplished through information from a confidential informant, cooperating witness, or undercover agent, combined with pen register or telephone toll information for the target phone or physical surveillance of the target premises. Criminal Division policy requires that the affidavit demonstrate criminal use of the target facility or premises within six months from the date of Department approval. For wire communications, where probable cause is demonstrated by consensually recorded calls or calls intercepted over another wiretap, the affidavit should include some direct quotes of the calls, with appropriate characterization. Criminal Division policy dictates that that pen register or telephone toll information for the target telephone, or physical surveillance of the targeted premises, standing alone, is generally insufficient to establish probable cause. Generally, probable cause to establish criminal use of the facilities or premises requires independent evidence of use of the facilities or premises in addition to pen register or surveillance information, often in the form of informant or undercover information. It is preferable that all informants used in the affidavit to establish probable cause be qualified according to the "Aguilar-Spinelli" standards (*Aguilar v. Texas*, 378 U.S. 108 (1964) and *Spinelli v. United States*, 393 U.S. 410 (1969)), rather than those set forth in the Supreme Court decision of *Illinois v. Gates*, 463 U.S. 1237 (1983). Under some circumstances, criminal use of the target facility within six months of Department approval may be established in the absence of consensually recorded communications or prior interceptions when use of the phone may be tied to a significant event, such as a narcotics transaction or a seizure, through phone records.

In addition to criminal use within six months, the affidavit must also show recent use of the facility or premises within 21 days from the date on which the Department authorizes the filing of the application. For wire and electronic communications, the affidavit must contain records showing contact between the facility and at least one other criminally relevant facility that demonstrates necessity for the wiretap within 21 days of Department approval. The affidavit must clearly and specifically demonstrate how the other facility is criminally relevant and state the date range for the contacts and the date of the most recent contact. The date range for all pen register/ phone records data must be updated to within 10 days of submission to OEO. For extension requests, the affidavit should include some direct quotes of wire communications (and/or electronic communications, if applicable), with appropriate characterization, including one from within seven days of Department approval, or an explanation of the failure to obtain such results and the continued need to conduct interceptions. (When the application requests authorization to intercept oral communications within a location, it is often helpful to include a diagram of the target location as an attachment to the affidavit.)

D. It must explain the need for the proposed electronic surveillance and provide a detailed discussion of the other investigative procedures that have been tried and failed, are reasonably unlikely to succeed if tried, or are too dangerous to employ. 18 U.S.C. § 2518(1)(e). This is to ensure that highly intrusive electronic surveillance techniques are not resorted to in situations where traditional investigative techniques would suffice to expose the crime. *United States v. Kahn*, 415 U.S. 143 (1974). It need not be shown that no other investigative avenues are available, only that they have been tried and proven inadequate or have been considered and rejected for reasons described. *See, e.g., United States v. Foy*, 641 F.3d 455, 464 (10th Cir. 2011); *United States v. Cartagena*, 593 F.3d 104, 109–111 (1st Cir. 2010); *United States v. Concepcion*, 579 F.3d 214, 218–220 (2d Cir. 2009). There should also be a discussion as to why electronic surveillance is the technique most likely to succeed. When drafting this section of the affidavit, the discussion of these and other investigative techniques should be augmented with facts particular to the specific investigation and subjects. General declarations and conclusory statements about the exhaustion of alternative techniques will not suffice.

It is most important that this section be tailored to the facts of the specific case and be more than a recitation of "boiler plate." The affidavit must discuss the particular problems involved in the investigation in order to fulfill the requirement of 18 U.S.C. § 2518(1)(c). The affidavit should explain specifically why other normally utilized investigative techniques, such as physical surveillance or the use of informants and undercover agents, are inadequate in the particular case. For example, if physical surveillance is impossible or unproductive because the suspects live in remote areas or will likely be alerted to law enforcement presence (by counter-surveillance or other means), the affidavit should set forth those facts clearly. If the informants refuse to testify or cannot penetrate the hierarchy of the criminal organization involved, the affidavit should explain why that is so in this particular investigation. If undercover agents cannot be used because the suspects deal only with trusted associates/family, the affidavit must so state and include the particulars. Conclusory generalizations about the difficulties of using a particular investigative technique will not suffice. It is not enough, for example, to state that the use of undercover agents is always difficult in organized crime cases because crime families, in general, deal only with trusted associates. While the affidavit may contain a general statement regarding the impossibility of using undercover agents in organized crime cases, it must also demonstrate that the particular subject or subjects in the instant case deal only with known associates. The key is to tie the inadequacy of a specific investigative technique to the particular facts underlying the investigation. *See, e.g., Foy*, 641 F.3d at 464 *United States v. Blackmon*, 273 F.3d 1204, 1210–1212 (9th Cir. 2001); *United States v. Uribe*, 890 F.2d 554 (1st Cir. 1989).

E.   It must contain a full and complete statement of any known previous applications made to any judge (federal, state, or foreign) for authorization to intercept, or for approval of interceptions of, wire, oral, or electronic communications involving any of the same persons, facilities, or places specified in the application. This statement should include the date, jurisdiction, and disposition of previous applications, as well as their relevance, if any, to the instant investigation. All relevant electronic surveillance ("ELSUR") databases must be checked, including that of the agency conducting the investigation. In narcotics investigations, Criminal Division policy provides that the DEA, FBI, and ICE databases be searched. In investigations involving firearms offenses, ATF ELSUR databases should be checked. In joint investigations, all participating agencies' databases should be checked; in all other cases when it is likely that more than one agency may have investigated the subjects, multiple indices checks should likewise be made. It is recommended that all ELSUR searches be updated to within 45 days of submission of an application to OEO. The duty to disclose prior applications under 18 U.S.C. § 2518(1)(e) covers all persons named in the application, and not just those designated as "principal targets." *United States v. Bianco*, 998 F.2d 1112 (2d Cir. 1993).

F. It must contain a statement of the period of time for which the interception is to be maintained. The statute provides that an order may be granted for not more than thirty days or until the objectives of the investigation are achieved, whichever occurs first. 18 U.S.C. § 2518(5). If the violations are continuing, facts sufficient to justify interception for the full thirty-day period must be provided, or the court may order monitoring to cease once initial, criminal conversations are intercepted. This may be accomplished by showing, through informant or undercover investigation, pen register analysis, physical surveillance, or other law enforcement investigation, that a pattern of criminal activity exists and is likely to continue. If it is clear that the interceptions will terminate after a limited number of days, then the time requested should also be so limited in accordance with the facts of the case.

The statute also provides for a ten-day grace period, before the thirty-day period begins to run. 18 U.S.C. § 2518(5). This statutory grace period allows for delays by the service provider in establishing interception capability. The ten-day grace period applies only to the *initial* installation of equipment or establishment of interceptions, and may not be used in an extension application, or in an original application when the equipment is already installed. Some courts have consulted Rule 45 of the Federal Rules of Criminal Procedure for guidance on the method to calculate the thirty-day period under the statute, and have held that the thirty-day period begins to run on the date after the order was signed, even if the interception started on the same day that it was signed. *See United States v. Smith*, 223 F.3d 554, 575 (7th Cir. 2000); *United States v. Villegas*, 1993 WL 535013, at *11–12 (S.D.N.Y. Dec. 22, 1993); *United States v. Gerena*, 695 F. Supp. 649, 658 (D. Conn. 1988); *United States v. Sklaroff*, 323 F. Supp. 296, 317 (S.D. Fla. 1971); *but see United States v. Gangi*, 33 F. Supp. 2d 303, 310–11 (S.D.N.Y. 1999); *United States v. Pichardo*, 1999 WL 649020, at * 3 (S.D.N.Y. Aug. 25, 1999). In an abundance of caution, however, OEO recommends that the thirty-day period be calculated from the date and time that the order is signed. OEO further suggests that an applicant adhere to established practice regarding the calculation of the thirty-day period in the applicant's particular district.

G. It must contain a statement affirming that monitoring agents will minimize all non-pertinent interceptions in accordance with Chapter 119 of Title 18, United States Code, as well as additional standard minimization language and other language addressing any specific minimization problems (e.g., steps to be taken to avoid the interception of privileged communications, such as attorney-client communications) in the instant case. (18 U.S.C. § 2518(5) permits non-officer government personnel or individuals acting under contract with the government to monitor conversations pursuant to the interception order. These individuals must be acting under the supervision of an investigative or law enforcement officer when monitoring communications, and the affidavit should note the fact that these individuals will be used as monitors pursuant to 18 U.S.C. § 2518(5).)

When communications are intercepted that relate to any offense not enumerated in the authorization order, the monitoring agent should report it immediately to the Assistant United States Attorney, who should notify the court at the earliest opportunity. Approval by the issuing judge should be sought for the continued interception of such conversations. While 18 U.S.C. § 2517(1) and (2) permit use or disclosure of this information without first obtaining a court order, 18 U.S.C. § 2517(5) requires a disclosure order before the information may be used in any proceeding (e.g., before a grand jury).

All wire and oral communications must be minimized in real time. The statute permits after-the-fact minimization for wire and oral communications only when the intercepted communications are in code, or in a foreign language when a foreign language expert is not reasonably available. 18 U.S.C. § 2518(5). In either event, the minimization must be accomplished as soon as practicable after the interception. Such after-the-fact minimization can be accomplished by an interpreter who listens to and minimizes the communications after they have been recorded, giving only the pertinent communications to the supervising agent. The process utilized must protect the suspect's privacy interests to approximately the same extent as would contemporaneous minimization, properly applied. *United States v. David*, 940 F.2d 722 (1st Cir. 1991); *United States v. Simels*, 2009 WL 1924746, at *6–*9 (E.D.N.Y. Jul. 2, 2009). After-the-fact minimization provisions should be applied in light of the "reasonableness" standard established by the Supreme Court in *United States v. Scott*, 436 U.S. 128 (1978). After-the-fact minimization is a necessity for the interception of electronic communications, such as those in the form of text messages, email, or faxes. In such cases, all communications should be recorded and then examined by a monitoring agent to determine their relevance to the investigation. Further dissemination is then limited to those communications by the subjects or their confederates that are criminal in nature. Further guidance regarding the minimization of text messages may be found on ESU's DOJNet site.

    H.   A judge may only enter an order approving interceptions "within the territorial jurisdiction of the court in which the judge is sitting (and outside that jurisdiction but within the United States in the case of a mobile interception device authorized by a Federal court within such jurisdiction)." 18 U.S.C. § 2518(3). Interceptions occur at the site of the target facility or location and at the site where the communications are first heard/reviewed and minimized (e.g. the wire room). *United States v. Rodriguez*, 968 F.2d 130, 136 (2d Cir. 1992); *see also United States v. Luong*, 471 F.3d 1107, 1109 (9th Cir. 2006); *United States v. Denman*, 100 F.3d 399, 403 (5th Cir. 1996).

Department policy requires that a Title III order be obtained in the district where the wireroom is located. This policy change is intended to ensure that all Title III interceptions occur within the territorial jurisdiction of the authorizing court, as required by 18 U.S.C. § 2518(3). Use of a regional wireroom will only be considered in exceptional circumstances, and must be discussed with the reviewing ESU attorney on a case-by-case basis.

In cases involving interceptions over a stationary facility or at a fixed location, the order may be obtained in the district where the target facility or location is located.

30. Electronic Surveillance—Title III Orders

The Order must meet the following requirements:

The authorizing language of the order should mirror the requesting language of the application and affidavit, stating that there is probable cause to believe that the named subjects are committing particular Title III predicate offenses (or, in the case of electronic communications, any Federal felony), that particular communications concerning those offenses will be obtained through interception, and that normal investigative techniques have been tried and have failed, or are reasonably unlikely to succeed if tried, or are too dangerous to employ. 18 U.S.C. § 2518(3) and (4). The court then orders (again tracking the language of the application and affidavit) that agents of the investigative agency are authorized to intercept wire, oral, or electronic communications over the described facility or at the described premises. *Id.* The order should also contain language specifying the length of time the interception may be conducted, and, if necessary, authorizing surreptitious and/or forcible entry to effectuate the purpose of the order. *Id.* The order may also contain language mandating the government to make periodic progress reports (pursuant to 18 U.S.C. § 2518(6)), and ordering the sealing of those as well as the order, application and affidavit. In the case of a roving interception, the court must make a specific finding that the requirements of 18 U.S.C. § 2518(11)(a) and/or (b) have been demonstrated adequately. Any other special requests, such as enforceability of the order as to changed service providers without further order of the court, should also be authorized specifically in the order.

The court should also issue a technical assistance order to the communications service provider. 18 U.S.C. § 2518(4). This is a redacted order that requires the telephone company or other service provider to assist the agents in effecting the electronic surveillance. OEO does not review redacted service provider orders. An order to seal all of the pleadings should also be sought at this time.

The Application, Affidavit, and Order should be sent via email to OEO at ESU.Requests@usdoj.gov. Submissions must include a completed Title III cover sheet that includes the signature of a supervising attorney who reviewed and approved the Title III papers. Criminal Division policy requires that all Title III submissions be approved by a supervising attorney other than the attorney submitting the application. That supervisory attorney must sign the Title III cover sheet, demonstrating that he or she has reviewed the affidavit, application, and draft order included in the submission packet, and that, in light of the overall investigative plan for the matter, and taking into account applicable Department policies and procedures, he or she supports the request and approves of it. The Title III cover sheet, with a space for the supervisor's signature, may be found on ESU's DOJNet site.

Spinoff requests (e.g., additional applications to conduct electronic surveillance over a new facility or at a new location in the same investigation) and extension requests are reviewed in the same manner as described above. While the exigencies of investigative work occasionally make the normally required lead time impossible, the timeliness with which an application is reviewed and authorized is largely under the control of the Assistant United States Attorney handling the case. When coordinating an investigation or planning extension requests, it is important to allow sufficient time for the Title III application to be reviewed by OEO. OEO strongly recommends that extension requests be submitted up to a week in advance of the date on which the interception period expires.

7. CONSENT SEARCHES

United States v. Price

558 F.3d 270 (3d Cir. 2009)

OPINION OF THE COURT

■ CHAGARES, CIRCUIT JUDGE.

John Joseph Price, Jr. entered a conditional plea of guilty to methamphetamine manufacturing and possession and now appeals two aspects of his proceedings. First, he argues that the District Court erred in refusing to suppress evidence because the Government violated his Fourth Amendment rights. In particular, Price contends that a consent to search his house was not voluntary and that evidence seized from his basement pursuant to a later-obtained warrant should be suppressed. Second, Price argues that notwithstanding his waiver of appeal, the Government abused its discretion by refusing to request an additional offense level reduction of one point for acceptance of responsibility under § 3E1.1(b) of the Sentencing Guidelines. Because we agree with the

District Court's decisions regarding the motion to suppress and its sentence, we will affirm.

I.

A.

On April 5, 2002, Price sold approximately 1/4 gram of methamphetamine to Randall Schirra, an undercover agent with the Pennsylvania Attorney General's office. As a result of this sale, the Commonwealth issued a warrant for Price's arrest, but he eluded capture for more than two years. On October 5, 2004, Price's luck ran out, for on that date, law enforcement officers from both the Attorney General's office and the Pennsylvania State Police went to Price's place of work—a garage off of Route 97 in Erie, PA. Schirra had source information that Price would be there.

The agents found Price in a small office near the back of the garage. They handcuffed him and removed him from the building. A search of Price conducted incident to the arrest revealed "items indicative of methamphetamine trafficking, including plastic baggies with methamphetamine residue and pH papers used to gauge the acidity of the methamphetamine production process." Appendix (App.) 61.

B.

Outside the garage, Price told Schirra that he was supposed to pick up his kids, and since his wife was working, the children would be home alone. Price lived with his common-law wife, Debbie Fischer, and two children (a girl, age 14, the daughter of Price, and a boy, age 9, the son of Price and Fischer) at 8350 Page Road in Wattsburg, Pennsylvania. Schirra testified at the suppression hearing that he told Price that officers would "check on the childrens['] safety [and] contact his wife." App. 132. Schirra also testified, however, that he wanted to get consent to search the Page Road residence to see if Price operated a methamphetamine lab there. The officers had "quite a bit of information gleaned from sources, unidentified informants and concerned citizens about Mr. Price's involvement in methamphetamine" at the Page Road residence. App. 152.

Leaving Price in the custody of a state trooper, Schirra and two other state officers, Trooper Ron Wilson and Agent Tim Albeck, drove to Price's Page Road residence. The two children answered Schirra's knock on the door and confirmed that no adult was home. They gave the officers Fischer's number at work. Wilson called Fischer, and she drove home from work to the house. On her way home, Fischer ran out of gas, so Albeck picked her up and brought her to the house.

C.

More officers arrived on the scene, but Schirra and Wilson had those officers stay down the road, away from the Page Road residence, so that only three or four officers were present when Schirra, Wilson, and

Fischer first conversed in the driveway/front yard area of the home. Wilson testified that they minimize the number of officers on the scene "so that . . . the people are not overwhelmed with law enforcement's presence whenever they give or do not give consent. So it's not-so that they're more relaxed and they don't feel coerced at all." App. 174.

Schirra and Wilson explained to Fischer that Price had been arrested, and that the authorities "had prior information that Mr. Price was involved in manufacturing methamphetamine at the residence. And that we would like to have consent to search to make sure it was a safe environment for her and her children." App. 113. Wilson also mentioned that the agents had information that there was a stolen All Terrain Vehicle (ATV) on the premises.

These were the only reasons the officers gave Fischer for why they wanted to search the house and property—to protect the safety of her and her children from any methamphetamine production, and to look for the ATV. The officers did not tell Fischer that she had the right to not consent, did not tell her that anything found could incriminate her or Price, and did not present her with a written consent form (which included all of that information). Schirra did not present Fischer with a written consent form because, in his words, "I didn't have one on me."[1]

Without hesitation, Fischer verbally consented to having the agents look around the house and the property. Fischer did not appear to be under the influence of drugs or alcohol, seemed to understand what the officers were telling her, and did not appear especially agitated or afraid. Schirra observed that "she was a little nervous," but "relatively normal." App. 161.

Schirra followed Fischer into the house. Wilson remained outside, and began walking around the curtilage, looking for the ATV. He eventually found the stolen four-wheeled vehicle under a pile of car seats and covers near an outbuilding.

D.

Just off of the living room, as one entered the house, was a room with a padlock on the door. Fischer explained that she and Price slept in this room. Schirra asked Fischer if she had a key. She answered affirmatively, produced a key, and unlocked the door. As she did so, Fischer told Schirra that she and Price used methamphetamine (but did not manufacture it), and that there "might be some pipes" in the bedroom. App. 115. Schirra searched the room and found two glass pipes and a baggie containing sodium hypophosphite in the drawers of a nightstand near the bed.[2] "At

---

[1] Schirra did not have a consent form with him because he works undercover—as does Agent Wilson—and so it is critical not to have any police-related paperwork in their respective cars.

[2] Sodium hypophosphite is a salt of hypophosphorous acid. Its legitimate uses include electroless nickel plating, fire retardation, and the catalysis of polymers. But many methamphetamine producers also use phosphorus chemicals—most commonly red phosphorous, but also white phosphorous or hypophosphorous acids like sodium

that point," Schirra testified, "she asked me to stop searching the house part. Because we found that stuff and she thought she was going to get in trouble."[3]

Schirra obliged, and left the house. His "prior information about Mr. Price's manufacturing methamphetamine," however, "always said [Price] was cooking in the garage, in the basement area of the home." App. 124. Therefore, as he was leaving the house, he asked Fischer how one could get to the basement. Fischer replied that there was no access to the basement from within the house and then "asked [Schirra] to follow her outside." App. 126. As the two walked around the side of the house, they reconnected with Wilson.

E.

Schirra asked if Fischer would give the agents consent to search the basement. Without responding verbally, Fischer "directed [the officers] down to the side of the house where you get into the basement . . . and she said that she didn't have the key for it, that only Mr. Price had the key for it." App. 117–18. Schirra again asked if the agents "could [ ] have permission to search the basement. She said if you could get in, you could search it, but she had no key to get in." App. 126. Fischer added that she did not want them to "do any damage to the doors." App. 118. Wilson testified that Fischer did not hesitate to offer consent for him to pick the lock because "I wouldn't have gone in if she had" hesitated. App. 161.

Although she did not have a key, Fischer indicated to the agents that she used the basement to do laundry, and that the family stored various items, such as Christmas decorations, in the basement. App. 146. Schirra did not ask Fischer how she accessed the basement if she did not own a key. He was not sure if she ever possessed a key and just did not have it that day, or if she never had a key.

Wilson then picked the lock of the basement door with a pocketknife, entered the basement briefly, and came out. Wilson only went "a half dozen steps in . . . [j]ust to make sure that it was secure, that it was safe. So that somebody wasn't hiding in there with a gun." App. 172. Schirra entered the basement after Wilson exited. Immediately inside, on the right, lay an open bag containing numerous Sudafed blister packets, as well as "some other chemicals and items that were used in the manufacture of methamphetamine." App. 119. Schirra exited the

---

hypophosphite—as catalysts in the conversion of ephedrine or pseudoephedrine to methamphetamine precursor, which is one step in the process of methamphetamine production. As compared to red phosphorous, "white phosphorus and hypophosphorous acid methods of illicit methamphetamine production are significantly more hazardous. . . . The hypophosphorous acid method is . . . extremely hazardous since it produces phosphine gas. If not confined within the reaction vessel, ingestion of this poisonous gas can result in death." Control of Red Phosphorus, White Phosphorus and Hypophosphorous Acid (and Its Salts) as List I Chemicals, 65 Fed.Reg. 57577, 57578 (proposed Sept. 25, 2000) (to be codified at 21 C.F.R. pt. 1310).

[3] Fischer's exact words at this point are the subject of some dispute. Although Schirra twice said that she asked him to stop searching "the house part," he amended that later, saying that Fischer asked him to stop searching only the drawers of the nightstand. App. 141-42.

basement, and told Fischer that she and the children had to leave the house "because it was a[ ] potential hazard for the kids because there was [sic] chemicals in there." App. 120. He also recommended that Fischer and the children seek medical treatment.

Schirra then asked Fischer to sign a written consent form. She refused. Schirra stated that he asked Fischer to sign a form after going into the basement "[b]ecause other officers had arrived [who] had written consents on their person." App. 122. Moreover, the signed form would have "save[d] me time. . . . It's faster for me to react to a hazardous area with a consent search than applying [for] and obtaining a search warrant." App. 149. If Fischer had signed the consent form, Schirra would have "felt comfortable securing the residence and treating the hazardous environment immediately, rather than having to wait such a long time to obtain a search warrant." App. 122. Because Fischer did not consent, however, Schirra posted officers outside the house and left to apply for a search warrant.

F.

A Magistrate Judge issued a warrant at 2:10 a.m. on October 6, 2004 after reviewing Schirra's Application and Affidavit for Search Warrant (warrant application). The warrant applied to "a one story single family ranch style residence with a basement and garage accessible from the outside" at "8350 Page Road, Wattsburg." App. 53. It permitted a search for "[m]ethamphetamine and any other illegal controlled substance, any and all devices used to store, manufacture, and/or ingest methamphetamine or any controlled substance"; "[c]hemicals, laboratory equipment and other apparatus used in the production, storage or transportation of methamphetamine, listed chemicals and other controlled substances"; any documents relating to controlled substance transactions; and any type of firearms. App. 56.

G.

The police returned to the Page Road residence later the same day and seized numerous chemicals related to methamphetamine manufacture from the basement, including 671 grams of sodium hypophosphite. On November 9, 2004, a grand jury indicted Price on seven counts relating to the manufacture and possession of methamphetamine. On May 4, 2006, after a hearing on Price's motion to suppress the fruits of the search, the District Court granted the motion in part and denied it in part. On June 16, 2006, Price entered a conditional plea of guilty to Count One of the indictment, reserving the right to appeal the denied portion of his suppression motion to this Court.

The Presentence Report calculated Price's Base Offense Level at 28. After a two-level downward adjustment for acceptance of responsibility, Price's Total Offense Level was 26. This offense level, combined with a criminal history category of V, produced a Guidelines range of 110–137 months. On October 10, 2006, the District Court sentenced Price to 115 months of imprisonment. This appeal followed.

II.

. . . . Price preserved his suppression argument, and so we review the District Court's factual determinations for clear error and exercise plenary review over the application of the law to those facts. . . . We review de novo the legal question of whether Price waived his right to appeal the calculation of his Guidelines range. *See* United States v. Khattak, 273 F.3d 557, 560 (3d Cir.2001).

III.

Price argues that the Government's actions in obtaining evidence at his Page Road residence violated his Fourth Amendment rights and that the District Court should have granted his motion to suppress that evidence. First, Price contends that the initial[5] consent to search his house was not voluntary and, therefore, the evidence discovered in his bedroom (two glass pipes with suspected methamphetamine residue and a baggie containing sodium hypophosphite) should have been suppressed. Second, Price contends that evidence seized from the basement of his house pursuant to the warrant should be suppressed because the warrant application did not establish probable cause when the allegedly tainted evidence from his bedroom and the prior warrantless search of the basement is excised from the warrant application.

A.

The Fourth Amendment to the Constitution provides: "The right of the people to be secure in their persons, houses, papers, and effects, against unreasonable searches and seizures, shall not be violated, and no Warrants shall issue, but upon probable cause. . . ." "The touchstone of the Fourth Amendment is reasonableness." Florida v. Jimeno, 500 U.S. 248, 250 (1991). Therefore, the Fourth Amendment does not prohibit all searches—only those that are unreasonable. *See* Illinois v. Rodriguez, 497 U.S. 177, 183 (1990). The general rule is that the warrantless entry into a person's house is unreasonable per se. *See* Payton v. New York, 445 U.S. 573, 586 (1980). This rule, however, is subject to several "jealously and carefully drawn" exceptions. Jones v. United States, 357 U.S. 493, 499 (1958).

"It is . . . well settled that one of the specifically established exceptions to the requirements of both a warrant and probable cause is a search that is conducted pursuant to consent." Schneckloth v. Bustamonte, 412 U.S. 218, 219 (1973). The Supreme Court has "long approved consensual searches because it is no doubt reasonable for the police to conduct a search once they have been permitted to do so." *Jimeno,* 500 U.S. at 250–51. To justify a search based on consent, the

---

[5] The "initial" consent for purposes of our discussion refers to Fischer's consent to search the living area of the Page Road residence—including the bedroom—as opposed to the basement.

Government "has the burden of proving that the consent was, in fact, freely and voluntarily given." Bumper v. North Carolina, 391 U.S. 543, 548 (1968). This burden "is not satisfied by showing a mere submission to a claim of lawful authority." Florida v. Royer, 460 U.S. 491, 497 (1983).

There is "no talismanic definition of 'voluntariness,' mechanically applicable to the host of situations where the question has arisen." *Schneckloth*, 412 U.S. at 224. Instead, we determine the voluntariness of a consent by examining the totality of the circumstances. *See id.* at 227. Both "the characteristics of the accused and the details of the interrogation" are useful to determine whether, under all the circumstances, a consent to search was voluntary, and no case should "turn[ ] on the presence or absence of a single controlling criterion."[6] *Id.* at 226.

Factors to consider include: the age, education, and intelligence of the subject; whether the subject was advised of his or her constitutional rights; the length of the encounter; the repetition or duration of the questioning; and the use of physical punishment. *See id.*; *see also* United States v. Kim, 27 F.3d 947, 955 (3d Cir.1994). We have further identified as relevant "the setting in which the consent was obtained [and] the parties' verbal and non-verbal actions." United States v. Givan, 320 F.3d 452, 459 (3d Cir.2003).

The District Court found Fischer's initial consent voluntary.[7] The Court noted that Fischer was an adult, apparently of average intelligence, who had previous experience with the criminal justice system. Moreover, "the atmosphere surrounding the encounter was not hostile," since the officers drove her to the Page Road residence after her car ran out of gas, the officers did not have their guns drawn when they asked for Fischer's consent, Fischer was not verbally or physically threatened, and only two officers, Schirra and Wilson, discussed Fischer's initial consent with her in the driveway.

Price attacks the validity of the initial consent on two grounds.[8] First, he alleges that because Fischer was not informed of her right to refuse consent, her consent was involuntary. Specifically, he argues that if the officers had shown Fischer a consent form and asked her to sign it, "she would have been advised of her rights concerning consent and would likely not have signed prior to the search, just as she had refused to sign the form when it was presented to her after the search was over." Price Reply Br. at 1. Second, Price contends that the officers lied to Fischer when they told her that they wanted to search to protect her safety and

---

[6] Fourth Amendment tests nearly always involve examination of the totality of the circumstances, because the Amendment "recognizes that no single set of legal rules can capture the ever changing complexity of human life." Georgia v. Randolph, 547 U.S. 103, 125 (2006) (Breyer, J., concurring).

[7] The District Court's determination of voluntariness is a finding of fact. *See* Schneckloth, 412 U.S. at 227. As such, we review for clear error.

[8] Price does not argue that Fischer was without authority to give the initial consent.

that of her children; rather, the officers' true intention was to look for evidence of a methamphetamine lab. This alleged deception, according to Price, supports a finding of involuntariness.[9]

We hold that the District Court's determination of voluntariness was not clearly erroneous in light of the totality of the circumstances. First, *Schneckloth* contradicts Price's contention that the lack of a consent form, without more, means that Fischer consented involuntarily. The *Schneckloth* Court held that "[w]hile knowledge of the right to refuse consent is one factor to be taken into account, the [G]overnment need not establish such knowledge as the sine qua non of an effective consent." *Schneckloth,* 412 U.S. at 227. The Court explicitly considered—and rejected—the possibility of mandating *Miranda*-like warnings for all consensual searches. *See id.* at 231 (concluding that it would "be thoroughly impractical to impose on the normal consent search the detailed requirements of an effective warning").

Our leading case on the voluntariness of consent supports this conclusion and provides an instructive comparison for our case. In *Kim,* 27 F.3d 947, a 39-year-old male was traveling from Los Angeles to Chicago on an Amtrak train. Two DEA agents knocked on Kim's sleeper car, looked at Kim's ticket, and then stated that they were with the DEA and that the DEA had problems with people smuggling drugs on similar trains. Without telling him that he could refuse, one agent asked if Kim would consent to have his luggage searched, to which Kim "readily replied 'Sure'." *Id.* at 950. The agents arrested Kim after they found drugs in his luggage.

We held that the consent was voluntary, observing that Schneckloth held clearly that the Government is not "required to advise the defendant of his right to refuse consent before eliciting his consent." *Id.* at 955. We found it important that Kim replied to the agents' request "readily" and that Kim was cooperative during the entire interaction: "Kim's demeanor was no doubt a strong indication of voluntariness. . . . Moreover, the whole encounter was short, lasting only several minutes," and only one officer was visible to Kim. *Id.* "There was no repeated and prolonged questioning. Nor did [the agent] ask Kim direct, probing, or incriminating questions." *Id.* We concluded that "particularly in the face of strong evidence of voluntariness," it was not significant that the agents did not advise Kim of his right to refuse consent. *Id.*

The instant case is analogous to *Kim.* Even more than in *Kim,* the circumstances of the encounter were low-key. Fischer was asked for consent as she stood on her own property. Most officers on the scene were deliberately kept away so as not to overwhelm her. The officers who were

---

[9] Price also notes that after he was arrested, the Government did not ask him for consent to search his home. Instead of obtaining a search warrant for the Page Road residence, the officers went to the house, and when Fischer eventually arrived, they told her that Price had been arrested and that they wanted her consent to search only to make sure that the house was safe for her and her children. But, critically, this is irrelevant to the voluntariness of Fischer's consent, and so will not be considered.

there did not have their guns drawn. No one threatened, coerced, or promised anything to Fischer. At no point was she arrested, handcuffed, or even touched. Schirra and Wilson both testified that Fischer granted the initial consent to search the house without any reluctance or hesitation whatsoever. There was no prolonged questioning, and the officers did not ask any incriminating questions before seeking consent to search. Moreover, as the District Court set forth, Fischer's age, intelligence, and education were at least average, and she had previous experience with the criminal justice system. In sum, every factor, save one (that she was not advised of her right to refuse consent),[10] favors a finding of voluntary consent. Under these circumstances, Fischer's consent was voluntary, and this is true notwithstanding that Fischer was not advised of her right to refuse consent.

Next, as the District Court found, Price's suggestion that the officers' only concern was to uncover a methamphetamine lab at the Page Road residence is belied by the record. No doubt, the police certainly were looking for a methamphetamine lab. But the agents—indisputably—also wanted to make sure that Fischer and the two children were not placed in danger by the chemicals associated with any such operation. Even after the agents had completed their work at the house, and even after Fischer had refused to sign the consent form, Schirra "advised her that she had to get her kids out, she would have to leave because it was a very potential hazard [sic] for the kids because there was [sic] chemicals in there. They posed an explosive hazard, plus the chemicals smell." App. 120. Schirra also advised Fischer to seek a medical examination for her and for her children. We agree with the District Court that the agents had two motives for seeking consent—to find the methamphetamine lab they thought might be there, and also to safeguard the well-being of Fischer and her children. The officers' statement of reasons for desiring the search does not alter our conclusion that Fischer's consent was voluntary under the totality of the circumstances.

Accordingly, the District Court did not err in refusing to suppress the evidence—two glass pipes with suspected methamphetamine residue and a baggie containing sodium hypophosphite—obtained in Price's bedroom following the initial consent.

B.

Price also argues that the evidence obtained pursuant to the search warrant should have been suppressed. He claims that if the warrant application is stripped of evidence obtained in: (1) his bedroom pursuant to the initial consent (we considered and rejected this challenge *supra*, section III(A)), and (2) the basement pursuant to the warrantless search,

---

[10] As the District Court observed, however, "[a]lthough [Fischer] was not advised of her right to refuse consent . . . her subsequent revocation of consent indicates her awareness of that right." App. 5.

then "what remains does not amount to probable cause to support a search." Price Br. at 29.

The parties dispute vigorously three issues related to the warrantless search of the basement: First, did Fischer withdraw the initial consent to search that she had provided to Schirra and Wilson in the driveway, and if so, what was the extent of the revocation? Second, even if Fischer revoked her consent to search the house, and even if that revocation applied to the basement as well, did Fischer later consent voluntarily to a search of the basement? Third, even if Fischer voluntarily consented to the basement search, did she have the authority to consent to such a search?

These are all difficult issues, but we need not resolve any of them. Rather, we hold that the search warrant application contained probable cause from independent sources even after excising all the evidence found in the basement. Thus, even assuming Fischer did not consent to the basement search, or did not have authority to consent, the "independent source" rule applies here and vitiates any taint from the initial, assumed illegal, entry.

The independent source doctrine serves as an exception to the exclusionary rule and permits the introduction of "evidence initially discovered during, or as a consequence of, an unlawful search, but later obtained independently from activities untainted by the initial illegality." Murray v. United States, 487 U.S. 533, 537 (1988); *see* United States v. Perez, 280 F.3d 318, 336 (3d Cir.2002); United States v. Herrold, 962 F.2d 1131, 1140 (3d Cir.1992).

In *Murray,* law enforcement agents improperly forced entry into a warehouse and observed burlap-wrapped bales, later found to contain marijuana, in plain view. The agents left the warehouse without disturbing the bales, and did not reenter until they had obtained a search warrant for the warehouse. In applying for the warrant, the agents did not mention the prior entry and did not rely on any observations made during that entry. A magistrate issued a warrant and the agents then conducted a second search of the warehouse and seized the burlap bales containing the marijuana.

The Court observed that the proper remedy for police error or misconduct relating to evidence is to "put[-] the police in the same, not a worse, position that they would have been in if no police error or misconduct had occurred." 487 U.S. at 537 (emphasis in original) (quotation marks omitted). Accordingly, "[w]hen the challenged evidence has an independent source, exclusion of such evidence would put the police in a worse position than they would have been in absent any error or violation." *Id.* (quotation marks omitted). . . .

Price contends that if, indeed, the police would have applied for a warrant even without the allegedly tainted material, they should have applied for a warrant before conducting their search. But the question is not what the police should have done. Instead, the issue is whether the police would have applied for a warrant without the material tainted by a warrantless search.

The answer is yes. Indeed, the facts of this case closely track the facts in *Herrold*. As in *Herrold*, it seems impossible that the police would not have applied for a warrant to search the basement of the house, knowing that: 1) confidential informants told the police that Price was operating a methamphetamine laboratory in the basement of the Page Road residence; 2) Price had sold Schirra methamphetamine in the past; 3) when arrested, Price had pH papers and baggies containing methamphetamine residue; and 4) Price's bedroom contained glass pipes with methamphetamine residue and a baggie of sodium hypophosphite.

The second question is whether the warrant application contained probable cause without the information gleaned from the basement. The District Court determined that even "assuming that the contraband found in the basement area should not have been included in the affidavit in support of the search warrant, . . . the warrant was independently supportable by other information contained therein." App. 17. "Thus, even if all references to the contraband found in the basement area were excised from the affidavit," the District Court held that "the affidavit would still support a broad search of the premises for the evidence outlined in the warrant." App. 18. We agree with the holding of the District Court. . . .

Without any reference to the evidence obtained pursuant to the warrantless basement search, the warrant application would still include at least three key pieces of information about Price's activities: 1) that Price sold Schirra 1/4 gram of methamphetamine on April 5, 2002; 2) that Schirra arrested Price on October 5, 2004, and that when searched, Price possessed "items indicative of methamphetamine trafficking, including plastic baggies with methamphetamine residue and pH papers used to gauge the acidity of the methamphetamine production process"; and 3) that after searching Price's bedroom, Schirra found two glass pipes that were consistent with the ingestion of methamphetamine. *See generally* App. 217 (Government noting to the District Court the illegality of possessing drug paraphernalia in Pennsylvania, and representing that possession of glass pipes alone would support a search of Price's premises).[11] The warrant application also explains that people who are involved in methamphetamine distribution often have, in their homes, drugs, large quantities of money, and evidence of financial transactions, as well as documentation concerning illegal narcotics, such as "recipes" for making methamphetamine and other substances.

Based on the evidence set forth above, as well as the warrant application's statements regarding the characteristics of those who are

---

[11] The warrant application did not mention the baggie of sodium hypophosphite obtained in Price's bedroom.

involved in methamphetamine production, it is clear that there was probable cause for the warrant to be issued without any reference to the evidence found in the basement of the Page Road residence during the warrantless search. Accordingly, we will affirm the District Court's refusal to suppress the evidence discovered in the basement pursuant to the search warrant.

8. THE "SPECIAL NEEDS" DOCTRINE

Cassidy v. Chertoff
471 F.3d 67 (2d Cir. 2006)

■ SOTOMAYOR, CIRCUIT JUDGE.

Plaintiffs-appellants Michael Cassidy and Robert J. Cabin appeal from a judgment of the United States District Court for the District of Vermont (Murtha, J.) granting defendants-appellants Michael Chertoff, Thomas H. Collins, Glenn Wiltshire, and Lake Champlain Transportation Company's ("LCT") motion to dismiss the plaintiffs' claim that LCT's practice of searching the carry-on baggage of randomly selected passengers and inspecting randomly selected vehicles, including their trunks, pursuant to the Maritime Transportation Security Act of 2002 ("MTSA"), 46 U.S.C. §§ 70101–70119 (2006), violated plaintiffs' Fourth Amendment rights. For the reasons that follow, we reject plaintiffs' contention that the searches at issue in this case violated their Fourth Amendment rights and affirm the judgment of the district court.

BACKGROUND

In the wake of the September 11, 2001 terrorist attacks, Congress enacted the MTSA to detect and deter a potential "transportation security incident," which Congress defined as a "security incident resulting in a significant loss of life, environmental damage, transportation system disruption, or economic disruption in a particular area." 46 U.S.C. § 70101(6). Because the resolution of this appeal depends, in significant part, on the MTSA and the regulations enacted pursuant to it, we begin by discussing the statutory background in some detail.

The MTSA contains a set of nationwide directives for increasing both vessel and port security. First, it requires the Secretary of the Department of Homeland Security ("DHS") to "conduct an assessment of vessel types . . . on or adjacent to the waters subject to the jurisdiction of the United States to identify those vessel types . . . that pose a high risk of being involved in a transportation security incident." *Id.* § 70102(a). Based on the information gathered in this initial assessment, the Secretary must then "conduct a detailed vulnerability assessment of . . . [such] vessels" to identify, inter alia, possible threats to critical assets and infrastructure as well as existing weaknesses in passenger and cargo security protection systems. *Id.* § 70102(b). After these vulnerability assessments have been made, the MTSA requires the owners and operators of vessels "that the Secretary believes may be involved in a transportation security incident" to prepare a security plan "for deterring a transportation incident to the maximum extent practicable." *Id.* § 70103(c)(1)–(2).

The Coast Guard conducted the initial nationwide vulnerability assessment on behalf of the Secretary. See Implementation of National Maritime Security Initiatives, 68 Fed.Reg. 39,240, 39,243 (July 1, 2003) (to be codified at 33 C.F.R. pts. 101, 102, 103 et al., 46 C.F.R. pts. 2, 31, 71, et al.). This assessment was aimed at "determin[ing] risks associated with specific threat scenarios against various classes of targets within the Marine Transportation System." *Id.* at 39,244. In order to determine the susceptibility of various segments of the commercial maritime community to terrorist attack, Coast Guard analysts considered, inter alia, the likelihood that a particular type of vessel would be a terrorist target or would be used as a weapon itself; the plausibility of terrorists actually carrying out various hypothetical attack scenarios; the risk associated with a given attack against a given target; and the likelihood and consequences of various attack scenarios. *Id.* at 39,244–45; *see also id.* at 39,243–50 (describing the methods of assessment employed by the Coast Guard in making the determinations required by the MTSA).

Based on this assessment, the Coast Guard determined that certain maritime vessels, including those that weigh more than 100 gross register tons or are licensed to carry more than 150 passengers "are at a high risk of a transportation security incident." *Id.* at 39,246; see also 33 C.F.R. § 104.105(a) (codifying the Coast Guard's above determination). Under the MTSA implementing regulations, vessels that fall into the high-risk category are required to adopt certain security measures to "[d]eter the unauthorized introduction of dangerous substances and devices, including any device intended to damage or destroy persons, vessels, facilities, or ports." 33 C.F.R. § 104.265(a)(1). To determine what security measures are required for such high-risk vessels, a vessel owner must prepare a Vessel Security Assessment ("VSA"), which is "an analysis that examines and evaluates the vessel and its operations taking into account possible threats, vulnerabilities, consequences, and existing protective measures, procedures and operations," *id.* § 101.105, by collecting specified background information and carrying out an onsite survey of the vessel to check existing protective measures, procedures, and operations for a variety of factors. *Id.* § 104.305(a)–(b). When complete, the VSA is used by the vehicle's owner or operator to devise a Vessel Security Plan ("VSP"), which is a "plan developed to ensure the application of security measures designed to protect the vessel and the facility that the vessel is servicing or interacting with." *Id.* § 101.105. The VSP must be submitted to the Coast Guard for review and approval. *Id.* § 104.410. Owners of a vessel operating under a VSP must "[s]creen persons, baggage (including carry-on items), personal effects, and vehicles for dangerous substances and devices at the rate specified in the approved Vessel Security Plan." *Id.* § 104.265(e)(1). Owners must also "[c]heck the identification of any person seeking to board the vessel." *Id.* § 104.265(e)(3).

Owners and operators of high-risk vessels are permitted a certain measure of flexibility within this general framework. They may opt out of "identification checks and passenger screening requirements." *Id.* § 104.292(b). In place of these search requirements, vessel owners "may ensure security measures are implemented that include":

(1) Searching selected areas prior to embarking passengers and prior to sailing; and

(2) Implementing one or more of the following:

(i) Performing routine security patrols;

(ii) Providing additional closed-circuit television to monitor passenger areas; or

(iii) Securing all non-passenger areas.

Id. In fact, a vessel owner or operator may, with the express permission of the Coast Guard, opt out of any regulatory requirement contained in a VSP so long as the Coast Guard has determined that "the waiver will not reduce the overall security of the vessel." *Id.* § 104.130 (stating that the owner or operator of a high-risk vessel is permitted to "apply for a waiver of any requirement . . . that the owner or operator considers unnecessary in light of the nature or operating conditions of the vessel"). The regulations also permit owners and operators to propose an "equivalent" to any of the security measures required by a VSP. *Id.* § 104.135. Finally, instead of implementing a VSP, a vessel owner or operator may fulfill the requirements of the MTSA by implementing an Alternative Security Program ("ASP"). *Id.* § 104.140(c). An ASP is "a third-party or industry organization developed standard that the [Coast Guard] Commandant has determined provides an equivalent level of security to that established by" the agency's regulations. *Id.* § 101.105. Vessel owners and operators who adopt an ASP must still develop and make available for Coast Guard inspection a vessel-specific security assessment report. *Id.* §§ 101. 120(b)(4), 104.120. To date, the Coast Guard has approved a number of ASPs through publication in the Code of Federal Regulations, *see* 33 C.F.R. § 101.125, including the program that LCT adopted, which was devised by the Passenger Vessel Association. *See id.* § 101.125(c).

The parties agree that an ASP is a classified document, subject to the same "sensitive security information" designation that applies to a VSP. *See id.* § 104.400(c) (stating that VSPs are subject to protection as "sensitive security information"). Because the ASP designed by the Passenger Vessel Association is classified and has not been entered into evidence, we will assume, for the purpose of reviewing the district court's decision to grant defendants' motion to dismiss, that the searches alleged by the plaintiffs are either required or permitted by LCT's security program.

Plaintiffs Michael Cassidy and Robert J. Cabin, both residents of Vermont, are commuters who ride LCT ferries and were subject to random searches pursuant to the ferry company's ASP. They traveled to their jobs in New York via the LCT ferry between Grand Isle, Vermont and Plattsburgh, New York several times a week. The ferries that operate on this route weigh more than 100 gross register tons and are therefore subject to the MTSA's regulations for high-risk vessels. Cassidy usually crosses on the ferry in his car while Cabin, who mostly commutes by bicycle, always carries with him a backpack or small bike pack.

Shortly before July 1, 2004, LCT posted a notice at its ticket booths warning passengers that "[a]s a result of the September 11, 2001, terrorist attacks on the United States," LCT had been required by DHS and the Coast Guard "to conduct random screening of persons, cargo, vehicles, or carry-on baggage." The notice further explained that compliance with the search policy was mandatory and that "anyone refusing to submit to security screening will not be allowed to board [LCT] ferries." LCT also placed large plastic signs near its ticket booth and ferry boarding areas stating that its facilities and boats were subject to security regulations issued by DHS and the Coast Guard; that all vehicles, baggage, and personal items were subject to screening at any time; and that failure to observe these requirements could result in immediate removal from the ferry or detention by law enforcement authorities.

On July 1, 2004, LCT ferry attendants began selecting passengers to be searched. Based on observations made by plaintiffs and other witnesses, LCT's security program appears to involve the following protocols. Foot and bicycle passengers are asked to open their carry-on items and present them for visual inspection. Car passengers are asked to open their trunks or tailgates so that the attendant may visually inspect the car's interior; attendants do not appear to search containers in either the trunks or interiors of vehicles. On occasion, attendants will ask the driver to open the car's windows to permit a visual scan of the interior.

Cassidy has been asked to open the trunk of his car on a number of occasions when attempting to board the ferry. Cabin has been asked to open his bike pack on at least one occasion. Cassidy and Cabin acquiesced to these demands because commuting via LCT ferries is a practical necessity for both of them. (Cassidy stated in his complaint that the only feasible alternative—traversing Lake Champlain via Rouse's Point Bridge—would double his daily commute time from two hours to four.) Moreover, plaintiffs wish to avoid any repercussions that may attend refusal to acquiesce to LCT's boarding requirements; plaintiffs allege that LCT records the license numbers of vehicles whose drivers refuse to consent to a trunk search and communicates this information to attendants at all of its loading docks, where the offending vehicle is barred from boarding any LCT ferry until its driver submits to a search. In addition, 33 C.F.R. § 104.265(e) provides that some type of report, as required by undisclosed DHS and Coast Guard directives, must be made if a person refuses to consent to a search. Plaintiffs allege that they acquiesced to LCT's unconstitutional searches in order to avoid such repercussions.

Plaintiffs brought the instant suit on October 4, 2004, seeking injunctive and declaratory relief against defendants for Fourth Amendment violations. Defendants moved to dismiss the complaint under Rule 12(b)(6) of the Federal Rules of Civil Procedure, and the district court granted the motion after determining that the searches conducted by LCT "advance a 'special governmental need' to provide domestic security [and thus] are not proscribed by the Fourth Amendment." The district court explained that "Congress has determined that ferries like those which operate on Lake Champlain may be vulnerable to terrorist incidents and, therefore, should be subject to new, more comprehensive security measures designed to protect public safety and secure commercial interests." The court found that "[r]andom, warrantless searches further these goals by deterring potential security breaches," and that the searches here are reasonable because "they are conducted in a manner no more intrusive than is necessary to achieve the compelling government interest of protecting the safety of passengers and deterring terrorist attacks on maritime vessels." The court found further that the plaintiffs voluntarily elected to ride LCT ferries and consented to the required searches. The court also concluded that plaintiffs had a diminished expectation of privacy when attempting to board the ferries because such search procedures are akin to those that passengers have been accustomed to expect, and which have been found constitutional, in the airline industry. Plaintiffs filed this timely appeal.[1]

DISCUSSION

We review de novo a district court's grant of a motion to dismiss; we accept as true the factual allegations in the complaint and draw all inferences in the plaintiffs' favor.

Plaintiffs contend that LCT's policy of requiring passengers to submit to security checks before boarding ferries on two of its Lake Champlain routes violates their Fourth Amendment rights. The Fourth Amendment to the United States Constitution provides that the federal government shall not violate "[t]he right of the people to be secure in their persons, houses, papers, and effects, against unreasonable searches and seizures." U.S. Const. amend. IV. Although a wholly private search falls outside the scope of the Fourth Amendment, Burdeau v. McDowell, 256

---

[1] After oral argument, plaintiffs filed a motion for leave to file supplemental briefs regarding the impact of our decision in Mac Wade v. Kelly, 460 F.3d 260 (2d Cir.2006), in which a panel of this Court upheld suspicionless searches of subway passengers' carry-on baggage as constitutional. We granted the motion and the parties have submitted their supplemental briefs.

U.S. 465, 475 (1921), a search conducted by private individuals at the instigation of a government officer or authority constitutes a governmental search for purposes of the Fourth Amendment. See Skinner v. Ry. Labor Executives' Ass'n, 489 U.S. 602, 614 (1989). LCT implemented its security policy in order to satisfy the requirements imposed by the MTSA and such law's implementing regulations on owners and operators of ferries that weigh over 100 gross register tons. The ASP adopted by LCT was approved by the Coast Guard—and published in the Code of Federal Regulations, 33 C.F.R. § 101.125(c)—as an adequate means of fulfilling the requirements imposed by the MTSA. The parties agree that the government's significant involvement in LCT's contested search policy brings these searches within the ambit of the Fourth Amendment.

"[T]he ultimate measure of the constitutionality of a governmental search is 'reasonableness.'" Vernonia Sch. Dist. 47J v. Acton, 515 U.S. 646, 652 (1995). Courts judge the reasonableness of a search "by balancing its intrusion on the individual's Fourth Amendment interests against its promotion of legitimate governmental interests." *Id.* at 652–53 (internal quotation marks omitted). When law enforcement officials undertake a search to discover evidence of criminal wrongdoing, the Supreme Court has held that reasonableness generally requires those officials to obtain a search warrant. *See Skinner,* 489 U.S. at 619. Such warrants cannot be obtained without a showing of probable cause. *Id.*

In a limited set of circumstances, however, the Supreme Court has held that a search warrant, and the requisite showing of probable cause, are not required. A search unsupported by probable cause may be constitutional "when special needs, beyond the normal need for law enforcement, make the warrant and probable-cause requirement impracticable." Griffin v. Wisconsin, 483 U.S. 868, 873 (1987) (internal quotation marks omitted). Indeed, the Supreme Court and this Court have upheld warrantless, suspicionless searches in a variety of circumstances in which the government's actions were motivated by "special needs." *See, e.g.,* Illinois v. Lidster, 540 U.S. 419 (2004) (upholding highway checkpoint stops erected in the course of investigating a fatal hit-and-run accident); Vernonia, 515 U.S. at 650 (upholding random drug testing by school officials of students who participate in interscholastic sports); Mich. Dep't of State Police v. Sitz, 496 U.S. 444 (1990) (upholding highway checkpoint stops designed to detect drunk drivers); Nat'l Treasury Employees Union v. Von Raab, 489 U.S. 656 (1989) (upholding drug tests for United States Customs Service employees who seek transfer or promotion to certain positions and those who carry firearms); *Skinner,* 489 U.S. at 608–13 (1989) (upholding drug and alcohol tests by railroad companies of railroad employees who are involved in train accidents or violate certain safety rules); United States v. Martinez-Fuerte, 428 U.S. 543 (1976) (upholding brief stops for questioning at a fixed Border Patrol checkpoint); Nicholas v. Goord, 430

F.3d 652 (2d Cir.2005) (upholding a statute that requires certain classes of convicted felons to provide DNA samples to be maintained in a state database); United States v. Edwards, 498 F.2d 496 (2d Cir.1974) (Friendly, J.) (upholding suspicionless searches of the persons and carry-on luggage of all passengers seeking to board an airplane). Most recently, we upheld a random, suspicionless search regime of subway passengers' baggage as constitutional under the special needs doctrine. MacWade v. Kelly, 460 F.3d 260 (2d Cir.2006).

In Chandler v. Miller, 520 U.S. 305 (1997), the Supreme Court discussed the rubric courts must use to determine whether a particular governmental search falls within the "closely guarded category of constitutionally permissible suspicionless searches." *Id.* at 309. The Court explained that when " 'special needs'—concerns other than crime detection or ordinary evidence gathering—are alleged in justification of a Fourth Amendment intrusion, courts must undertake a context-specific inquiry, examining closely the competing private and public interests advanced by the parties." *Id.* at 314. In applying the special needs doctrine, courts must assess the constitutionality of the challenged conduct by weighing "the government conduct—in light of the special need and against the privacy interest advanced"—through the examination of three factors: (1) the nature of the privacy interest involved; (2) the character and degree of the governmental intrusion; and (3) the nature and immediacy of the government's needs, and the efficacy of its policy in addressing those needs. Palmieri v. Lynch, 392 F.3d 73, 81 (2d Cir.2004); *see also* United States v. Lifshitz, 369 F.3d 173, 183–84 (2d Cir.2004). We examine each of these three factors in turn.

I.   Plaintiffs' Privacy Interest

Plaintiffs assert that they have a full privacy interest in protecting their carry-on baggage and automobiles from random, suspicionless searches. They contend that members of the public have an undiminished expectation of privacy when they board ferries on Lake Champlain. Plaintiffs further argue that the searches LCT conducts on its loading docks differ from searches the government conducts at international borders and traffic checkpoints because borders between countries, unlike rural loading docks, are obviously sensitive locations that implicate a diminished expectation of privacy.

A.   Plaintiffs' Expectation of Privacy in Their Carry-on Baggage

Plaintiffs assert that passengers with carry-on baggage retain an undiminished privacy interest in such baggage because plaintiffs experienced LCT's searches as a substantial intrusion on their privacy and because Bond v. United States, 529 U.S. 334 (2000), "definitively reaffirmed the protected privacy interest in the contents of hand luggage." While we do not read *Bond* as broadly as plaintiffs suggest, we agree with plaintiffs that they enjoy a full expectation of privacy in their carry-on baggage.

The Supreme Court has held that "[t]he Fourth Amendment does not protect all subjective expectations of privacy, but only those that society recognizes as 'legitimate.' What expectations are legitimate varies, of course, with context, depending, for example, upon whether the individual asserting the privacy interest is at home, at work, in a car, or in a public park." *Vernonia,* 515 U.S. at 654 (citations omitted). Two key cases have applied this test to passengers' carry-on luggage in the mass transport context and refused to find any diminished privacy expectations regarding such luggage. In *Bond,* the Supreme Court determined that travelers on an intracity bus enjoyed a full expectation of privacy in their carry-on items because they did not "expect that other passengers or bus employees will, as a matter of course, feel the bag in an exploratory manner," and that expectation was objectively reasonable. 529 U.S. at 338–39. In *MacWade,* we confronted the question of whether a legitimate privacy interest existed as to searches of "items in a closed, opaque bag," 460 F.3d at 272, carried by subway passengers, and found a full privacy interest in such bags, *id.* at 272–73.

It is clear that *Bond* reaffirmed the general privacy interest that individuals enjoy in relation to their bags, but we hesitate to accede to the plaintiffs' assertion that *Bond* precludes a finding of a diminished expectation of privacy in such bags in any context. Instead, as with any privacy analysis, the Supreme Court has cautioned that privacy expectations necessarily depend on context. *Vernonia,* 515 U.S. at 654. We do, however, agree with plaintiffs that in this specific context, *MacWade* is particularly persuasive here because it concerned the privacy interests of individuals commuting on mass transportation. First, plaintiffs have clearly evinced—and the government does not deny—a subjective privacy interest in the carry-on bags that they take with them onto the ferry. *MacWade,* 460 F.3d at 272. Second, given that we found it objectively reasonable for subway riders to expect that their carry-on bags will not be "opened and [their] contents visually inspected or physically manipulated," *id.* at 273, we see little reason to alter that analysis as applied here to ferry passengers.

Finally, we are not convinced by the government's argument that our airport search cases alter the privacy interest calculus here. In *United States v. Edwards,* we upheld pre-boarding, suspicionless searches of airline passengers, holding that to brand them "as unreasonable would go beyond any fair interpretation of the Fourth Amendment." 498 F.2d at 500. But airplanes are very different creatures from the more quotidian commuting methods at issue in *MacWade* and the instant case, and society has long accepted a heightened level of security and privacy intrusion with regard to air travel. Moreover, *Edwards* did not specifically determine or discuss the privacy interest involved, and we are wary of extending its analysis to a markedly different factual context.[2]

For the foregoing reasons, we find that the privacy interests of LCT's ferry passengers in their carry-on luggage are undiminished.[3]

B. Plaintiffs' Expectation of Privacy in Their Automobiles

We turn now to the question of whether plaintiffs have a full privacy interest in their automobiles, including the trunks of such vehicles. It has long been recognized that "[t]he search of an automobile is far less intrusive on the rights protected by the Fourth Amendment than the search of one's person or of a building." *Cardwell v. Lewis*, 417 U.S. 583, 590 (1974) (internal quotation marks omitted); *see also Martinez-Fuerte*, 428 U.S. at 561 ("[O]ne's expectation of privacy in an automobile and of freedom in its operation are significantly different from the traditional expectation of privacy and freedom in one's residence."). The Supreme Court has held that "[o]ne has a lesser expectation of privacy in a motor vehicle" because it "travels public thoroughfares where its occupants and its contents are in plain view," *Cardwell*, 417 U.S. at 590 and because the "pervasive regulation of vehicles" diminishes one's expectation of privacy in an automobile, *California v. Carney*, 471 U.S. 386, 392 (1985). Even plaintiffs concede—and the Supreme Court has recognized—that there may be a diminished expectation of privacy regarding the part of the search that involves ferry attendants looking through car windows. *See Texas v. Brown*, 460 U.S. 730, 740 (1983) ("There is no legitimate expectation of privacy shielding that portion of the interior of an automobile which may be viewed from outside the vehicle by either inquisitive passersby or diligent police officers." (internal citations omitted)).

Plaintiffs contend, nevertheless, that they have a full privacy interest in the trunks of their cars and that LCT ferry attendants violate this interest when they ask passengers to open their trunks. Plaintiffs note that the Supreme Court has not upheld a suspicionless search regime that involved the opening and examination of motor vehicle compartments outside of the border or customs context. We are mindful, nonetheless, that the Supreme Court has stated:

---

[2] We do not read *MacWade* or *Bond*'s privacy analysis (nor our discussion here) to suggest that *Edwards* no longer remains good law. Indeed, the Supreme Court, we observe, has specifically noted in its special needs jurisprudence that *Edwards* is a "leading case." *Von Raab*, 489 U.S. at 675 n.3 (citing *Edwards* and condoning "the Federal Government's practice of requiring the search of all passengers seeking to board commercial airliners, as well as the search of their carry-on luggage, without any basis for suspecting any particular passenger of an untoward motive").

[3] Although plaintiffs contend that LCT's searches were unconstitutional, they concede that they acquiesced in the searches and did not experience any of the repercussions that might attend refusal to submit to a search. Cassidy and Cabin are therefore not representative of hypothetical plaintiffs claiming that their rights were violated as a result of their refusal to submit to LCT's searches. Our opinion does not address the constitutionality of any repercussions that might be visited upon a person who withholds consent.

> [E]ven when enclosed "repository" areas have been involved, we
> have concluded that the lesser expectations of privacy warrant
> application of the exception. We have applied the exception in
> the context of a locked car trunk, Cady v. Dombrowski, 413 U.S.
> 433, 442 (1973), a sealed package in a car trunk, United States
> v. Ross, 456 U.S. 798, 806 (1982), a closed compartment under
> the dashboard, Chambers v. Maroney, 399 U.S. 42 (1970), the
> interior of a vehicle's upholstery, Carroll v. United States, 267
> U.S. 132 (1925), or sealed packages inside a covered pickup
> truck, United States v. Johns, 469 U.S. 478 (1985).

Carney, 471 U.S. at 391–92. While the above-cited cases involved
warrantless searches where probable cause existed, the Court clearly
found an exception to the warrant requirement because of the lesser
expectations of privacy attendant to automobiles. This would suggest
that the vehicle owners might also have diminished privacy interests in
their vehicles' trunks, in the narrow factual context presented in the
instant case, where randomly selected automobile drivers, who seek to
board a ferry, are simply asked to open their trunks briefly for security
purposes.

It is clear that there are significant questions here regarding the
level of the privacy interest implicated in trunk searches. Given that we
have already found an undiminished privacy interest in plaintiffs' carry-
on baggage, the government will have to demonstrate that the other two
factors of the special needs analysis outweigh plaintiffs' privacy interests
to establish the constitutionality of its searches. Thus, regardless of how
we resolve the issue of the expectation of privacy in the plaintiffs'
automobile trunks, the government must overcome the full privacy
expectations plaintiffs enjoy in their carry-on bags here. Accordingly, we
need not reach the privacy expectation plaintiffs possess in the trunks of
their motor vehicles and will assume but expressly not hold that
plaintiffs have demonstrated that they enjoy a full expectation of privacy
in their vehicles' trunks.

Finally, plaintiffs' briefs focus on the searches of carry-on bags and
motor vehicles' trunks. To the extent that their complaint can be read to
challenge the visual inspection of a vehicle's interior through its
windows, the parties do not appear to dispute that, as we noted above,
there is a diminished expectation of privacy in that context. This does not
alter our analysis of the searches' constitutionality.

II.   The Character and Degree of the Governmental Intrusion

Because an undiminished privacy interest is not itself dispositive in
special needs cases but is merely one among three factors to be weighed,
MacWade, 460 F.3d at 272, we must next examine the screening at issue
and determine whether searches, which consist of random visual
inspections by ferry attendants of vehicles' trunks as well as the carry-
on baggage of bicyclists and pedestrians, are minimally or substantially
intrusive. In making this examination, courts have looked to various

factors, including, inter alia, the duration of the search or stop, *see Lidster,* 540 U.S. at 427; *Sitz,* 496 U.S. at 451–52; *Martinez-Fuerte,* 428 U.S. at 546–47, 558, the manner in which government agents determine which individuals to search, *see Lidster,* 540 U.S. at 428, *Martinez-Fuerte,* 428 U.S. at 559, the notice given to individuals that they are subject to search and the opportunity to avoid the search by exiting the premises, *see MacWade,* 460 F.3d at 273; *Edwards,* 498 F.2d at 500, as well as the methods employed in the search, *see Sitz,* 496 U.S. at 451; *Martinez-Fuerte,* 428 U.S. at 558.

On the basis of these factors, it is clear that the searches in this case are, by any measure, minimally intrusive. As recounted by plaintiffs, the duration of the stops or searches have been "cursory" and of the short duration which the Supreme Court has long held to be minimally intrusive. *Lidster,* 540 U.S. at 427 (upholding brief stops of vehicles at checkpoint and questioning of drivers); *Sitz,* 496 U.S. at 451 (same); *Martinez-Fuerte,* 428 U.S. at 546–47, 558, (same). Plaintiffs have not alleged that the government has given unbridled discretion to LCT employees to carry out searches in a discriminatory or arbitrary manner. *Lidster,* 540 U.S. at 428 ("[T]here is no allegation here that the police acted in a discriminatory or otherwise unlawful manner while questioning motorists during stops."); *Martinez-Fuerte,* 428 U.S. at 559 (discussing the intrusiveness of roving patrols that presented "a grave danger [of] unreviewable discretion," but finding that a fixed checkpoint greatly reduced the possibility of abuse). Other factors similarly weigh in the government's favor in this inquiry. For instance, the methods used to conduct the searches at issue are limited to visual inspections of vehicles and their trunks and brief examinations of the contents of carry-on baggage. *See Sitz,* 496 U.S. at 451 (brief visual inspections); *Martinez-Fuerte,* 428 U.S. at 558 (same); *Edwards,* 498 F.2d at 500 (brief examination of contents of carry-on luggage). Ample notice is given to individuals seeking to board LCT ferries that they are subject to search and that they may avoid the search by exiting the premises. *See MacWade,* 460 F.3d at 273 ("[P]assengers receive notice of the searches and may decline to be searched so long as they leave the subway. . . ."); *Edwards,* 498 F.2d at 499–500 (finding notice central to upholding the constitutionality of airport searches where large signs had been posted near the boarding gates warning: "PASSENGERS AND BAGGAGE SUBJECT TO SEARCH"). Such notice helps "reduc[e] to a minimum any unsettling show of authority that may be associated with unexpected intrusions on privacy." *Von Raab,* 489 U.S. at 672 n. 2 (internal citation and quotation marks omitted); *see also Edwards,* 498 F.2d at 501 ("The point is . . . that in order to bring itself within the test of reasonableness applicable to airport searches, the Government must give the citizen fair warning, before he enters the area of search, that he is at liberty to proceed no further."). Notice also serves to eliminate any stigma associated with the search. *Id.* at 500 ("The search of carry-on baggage, applied to everyone, involves not the slightest stigma. More than a million Americans subject themselves to it daily . . . .") (internal citation omitted).

Plaintiffs argue that the searches in the above cases are inapposite because they did not involve opening trunks. The drivers brought to the "secondary inspection area" in *Martinez-Fuerte* for more intense questioning of their residency status were, however, almost certainly subjected to a greater intrusion of their privacy than the ferry passengers who have to open their trunks for a brief visual inspection by a ferry attendant. 428 U.S. at 547 (upholding brief questioning in a "secondary inspection area" which lasted on average between three and five minutes). And even if the intrusions in this case were more significant than those in the Supreme Court's checkpoint cases, they are certainly less intrusive than the search at issue in *Edwards*. In *Edwards,* we found pre-boarding baggage searches at airports to be minimally intrusive, even when a Deputy United States Marshal searched a woman's bag, found a package with a pair of slacks wrapped around it, removed the slacks, and looked inside the package. 498 F.2d at 499–500; *see also MacWade,* 460 F.3d at 273 (holding that random searches of subway passengers' carry-on bags, which include the visual inspection of the contents of such bags, to be minimal).

Nor does plaintiffs' assertion that magnetometer searches are less intrusive than visual searches alter the fact that the level of intrusion visited on the plaintiffs in this case was minimal. The Supreme Court has "repeatedly stated that reasonableness under the Fourth Amendment does not require employing the least intrusive means" to accomplish the government's ends. Bd. of Educ. of Indep. Sch. Dist. No. 92 of Pottawatomie County v. Earls, 536 U.S. 822, 837 (2002); *see also Vernonia,* 515 U.S. at 663; *Skinner,* 489 U.S. at 629 n. 9. Thus, what matters in this case is not whether the defendants could have satisfied the requirements of the MTSA by devising a less intrusive means of searching passengers, but whether the means they chose unconstitutionally trenched on plaintiffs' privacy interests in an unreasonable way. As our decision today makes clear, we cannot say, after having balanced the "special needs" factors, that plaintiffs' Fourth Amendment rights have been violated.[6]

---

[6] Plaintiffs take issue with the fact that the MTSA allowed LCT to implement the ASP designed by the Passenger Vessel Association that imposed relatively little cost on the ferry company when the company could instead have adopted other less intrusive, but more costly security measures. That LCT took cost into account in determining how to fulfill the requirements of the MTSA does not in and of itself render LCT's policy constitutionally suspect. All governmental search procedures, whether conducted by the government or by a private entity at the instigation of the government, take cost into account. An inexpensive search policy, like any search policy, runs afoul of the Fourth Amendment only insofar as it is unreasonable. Similarly, it is clear that a private entity, empowered by the government to conduct a search, need not choose the least restrictive means to avoid a violation of the Fourth Amendment. *See, e.g., Skinner,* 489 U.S. at 611, 625–27 (finding no constitutional violation where a private entity was granted substantial discretion by statute to conduct breath and urine tests on certain employees).

Finally, plaintiffs make a slippery-slope argument, claiming that because the threat of terrorism is omnipresent, there is no clear limit to the government power to conduct suspicionless searches. This is a legitimate concern. As we discuss in the next section, however, it is not a concern implicated by the facts in this case, where the government has imposed security requirements only on the nation's largest ferries after making extensive findings about the risk these vessels present in relation to terrorism and, as noted, the scope of the searches is rather limited. Having thus found that the visual inspection of vehicles and their trunks along with the search of carry-on baggage at issue here are minimally intrusive, we weigh this factor in the government's favor.

III. The Government's Special Needs and the Efficacy of the Searches

A. The Government's Special Need

Our next task in the special needs analysis requires us to determine the "nature and immediacy of the governmental concern at issue here." *Vernonia,* 515 U.S. at 660. The Supreme Court has cautioned that the government's asserted special need must "describe[ ] an interest that appears important enough to justify the particular search at hand," *id.* at 661, and we have expressly mandated that "a close and substantial relationship" exist between the degree of intrusiveness and the governmental need asserted, *Lifshitz,* 369 F.3d at 184, 186.

The Supreme Court has indeed "been reluctant to ratify implausible or overbroad assertions of 'special needs.' " *Id.* at 185, 369 F.3d 173. In *Chandler v. Miller,* for example, the Court struck down a drug testing regime imposed upon candidates for state office in Georgia because it found that "the proffered special need for drug testing" was not substantial where Georgia "assert[ed] no evidence of a drug problem among the State's elected officials, [and] those officials typically do not perform high-risk, safety-sensitive tasks." 520 U.S. at 318, 322. The Court concluded that the government's asserted need was merely "symbolic, not 'special.' " Id. at 322.

The Court has also emphasized that the government's asserted "special need" must not be isomorphic with law enforcement needs, but rather go beyond them. *See, e.g.,* Ferguson v. City of Charleston, 532 U.S. 67, 80 (2001) (striking down a public hospital's policy of ordering drug screens for maternity patients suspected of cocaine use because "the central and indispensable feature of the policy from its inception was the use of law enforcement to coerce the patients into substance abuse treatment"); City of Indianapolis v. Edmond, 531 U.S. 32, 42, 47 (2000) (invalidating an Indianapolis drug checkpoint program because its "primary purpose" was "to uncover evidence of ordinary criminal wrongdoing," and noting that, "[w]hile reasonableness under the Fourth Amendment is predominantly an objective inquiry, our special needs . . . cases demonstrate that purpose is often relevant when suspicionless intrusions pursuant to a general scheme are at issue"). The Court differentiated the drug checkpoint in *Edmond* from the immigration checkpoint in *Martinez-Fuerte* by emphasizing the difficulty of effectively containing illegal immigration at the border and noting that this problem was distinct from, and went beyond, regular law enforcement needs. *See Edmond,* 531 U.S. at 38–39.

Plaintiffs make three principal arguments that the searches at issue here do not constitute a special need under our caselaw. They first argue that the special needs doctrine only applies where those searched comprise a "well-defined target class." They next contend that the government has proffered only an abstract, unsubstantiated need that does not justify the searches at issue. Finally, plaintiffs assert that this Court should not defer to the Coast Guard's determinations of the terrorism risk in deciding this case. We discuss each argument in turn.

1.   The Special Needs Doctrine Does Not Require a "Well-Defined Target Class."

As a threshold matter, plaintiffs contend that this case does not involve "special needs" because LCT's search policy is not aimed at a "well-defined target class." Although it is true that some "special needs" searches target well-defined groups—i.e., high school students who participate in competitive extracurricular activities, *see Earls*, 536 U.S. at 825, or a particular group of United States Customs Service employees, *see Von Raab,* 489 U.S. at 659—neither the Supreme Court nor this Court has ever held that a "well-defined target class" is a requisite showing in a "special needs" case. In fact, the baggage screening and checkpoint cases make it clear that such targeting is not required in order for the government to establish a "special need." *See, e.g., Sitz*, 496 U.S. at 455 (permitting sobriety checkpoints); *Martinez-Fuerte*, 428 U.S. at 561–64 (permitting immigration-control checkpoints); *MacWade,* 460 F.3d at 275 (permitting random, suspicionless searches at subway stations); *Edwards,* 498 F.2d at 499–500 (permitting pre-boarding baggage inspection at airports). This argument is without merit.

2.   The Government Has Demonstrated a "Special Need."

Plaintiffs further contend that defendants have adduced only an "abstract or general" need to justify the implementation of searches aboard the Lake Champlain ferries and that is insufficient to excuse the invasion of their privacy.

It is clear to the Court that the prevention of terrorist attacks on large vessels engaged in mass transportation and determined by the Coast Guard to be at heightened risk of attack constitutes a "special need." Preventing or deterring large-scale terrorist attacks present problems that are distinct from standard law enforcement needs and indeed go well beyond them. *See MacWade*, 460 F.3d at 272 ("[P]reventing a terrorist from bombing the subways constitutes a special need that is distinct from ordinary post hoc criminal investigation."); *Nicholas,* 430 F.3d at 661 (explaining that "[w]hat unifies [the Supreme Court's "special needs"] cases, despite their varied contexts, is that in each instance, the Court found that the suspicionless-search regime at issue served some special need distinct from normal law-enforcement needs"). There is also an obvious nexus between protecting a ferry and guarding against the threat of terrorism through minimally intrusive searches of vehicles and carry-on baggage. Indeed, as in the case of airline hijacking, a large ferry commandeered by a terrorist becomes a weapon, or as in the case of subway bombing, the ferry becomes a death trap. Either way, the government has a "special need" to prevent such potentially disastrous situations from developing, and courts have readily acknowledged the special government need in protecting citizens in the mass transportation context. *See, e.g., Skinner,* 489 U.S. at 608–13 (testing railroad employees for drugs and alcohol when safety incidents occur); *MacWade,* 460 F.3d at 271–72; United States v. Hartwell, 436 F.3d 174, 179 (3d Cir.2006) (Alito, J.) (pre-boarding search of airline passengers' carry-on baggage); *Edwards,* 498 F.2d at 500 (same); United States v. Davis, 482 F.2d 893, 910 (9th Cir.1973) (same).

Plaintiffs contend that even if the government has a "special need" to protect large ferries in major metropolitan areas, it does not have a "special need" to protect the ferries on Lake Champlain, where there is no obvious terrorist threat. The Supreme Court, however, has held that the government need not adduce a specific threat in order to demonstrate a "special need." *See Earls,* 536 U.S. at 835–36 (noting that "this Court has not required a particularized or pervasive . . . problem [to occur] before allowing the government to conduct" suspicionless searches where there is a real threat of substantial harm to society). In *Von Raab,* the Court pointed to the federal government's practice of requiring the search of all airline passengers seeking to board commercial airlines as an illustration of this point. The *Von Raab* Court quoted approvingly the following passage in Judge Friendly's opinion in *Edwards*:

> When the risk is the jeopardy to hundreds of human lives and millions of dollars of property inherent in the pirating or blowing up of a large airplane, that danger alone meets the test of reasonableness, so long as the search is conducted in good faith for the purpose of preventing hijacking or like damage and with reasonable scope and the passenger has been given advance notice of his liability to such a search so that he can avoid it by choosing not to travel by air. United States v. Edwards, 498 F.2d 496, 500 (2d Cir.1974) (emphasis in original).

Von Raab, 489 U.S. at 675 n.3. The *Von Raab* Court then noted that although airline searches "were adopted in response to an observable national and international hijacking crisis," the Court

> would not suppose that, if the validity of these searches be conceded, the Government would be precluded from conducting them absent a demonstration of danger as to any particular airport or airline. It is sufficient that the Government have a

compelling interest in preventing an otherwise pervasive
societal problem from spreading to the particular context.

Id. (emphasis added). Although the plaintiffs may be correct that Lake
Champlain ferries are a less obvious terrorist target than ferries in, for
example, New York City or Los Angeles, the airline cases make it clear
that the government, in its attempt to counteract the threat of terrorism,
need not show that every airport or every ferry terminal is threatened by
terrorism in order to implement a nationwide security policy that
includes suspicionless searches.

As the Supreme Court noted in *Von Raab*: If the government has
determined that airports fall into a high-risk category and require special
protection from terrorist attack, it does not matter whether a regional
airport in a small city is perceived to be less susceptible to attack than
an international airport in a major city. *See id.* at 675 n.3. Here, the Coast
Guard, pursuant to a Congressional directive, conducted a risk analysis
to determine which vessels "pose a high risk of being involved in a
transportation security incident." 46 U.S.C. § 70102(a). This analysis
involved various factors, including the susceptibility of various segments
of the commercial maritime industry as targets and as weapons
themselves, the plausibility of a terrorist actually carrying out the
various attack scenarios contemplated, the risk associated with a given
attack against a given target, the likelihood of various attack scenarios,
and the consequences of various attack scenarios. *See* 68 Fed.Reg. at
39,243–50. Based on this assessment, the Coast Guard concluded that
vessels weighing over 100 gross register tons "are at a high risk of being
involved in a transportation security incident" and should therefore be
subject to the regulations at issue in this case. *Id.* at 39,246. Whether
these large vessels dock at urban or rural ports is therefore beside the
point; the government need not demonstrate the existence of a specific
danger to a particular port or ferry in order to establish a special
governmental need justifying suspicionless searches of ferry passengers.

3.   The Government's Determinations of "High Risk" Are Entitled to
Deference.

Expert determinations by the Coast Guard, like the one discussed
above, which are based on an explicit Congressional delegation of
legislative authority (in this case, 46 U.S.C. §§ 70102(a), 70103(c)(1)–(2))
are entitled to significant deference. *See* Chevron U.S.A. Inc. v. Natural
Res. Def. Council, Inc., 467 U.S. 837, 843–44 (1984) (deference
appropriate where Congress expressly delegated authority to agency to
"elucidate a specific provision of the statute by regulation"). Plaintiffs
argue that deference is not due in this case because LCT's security plan
was submitted only to the regional Coast Guard authority and thus does
not constitute the sort of agency action entitled to deference. In support
of this proposition, plaintiffs cite United States v. Mead Corp., 533 U.S.
218 (2001). At issue in *Mead* were a statute providing that the United
States Customs Service should prescribe rules establishing procedures

for the issuance of tariff classification rulings, and regulations promulgated by Customs providing for tariff rulings via "ruling letters" that set tariff classifications for particular imports. *Id.* at 221–22. Under the regulations, any of the forty-six port-of-entry Customs offices could issue ruling letters. *Id.* at 224. The *Mead* Court held that a tariff classification ruling by the United States Customs Service was not entitled to Chevron deference because "the terms of the congressional delegation give no indication that Congress meant to delegate authority to Customs to issue classification rulings with the force of law." *Id.* at 231–32. The Court further held that "the agency practice itself [gave no] indication that Customs ever set out with a lawmaking pretense in mind when it undertook to make classifications like these. . . . Indeed, to claim that classifications have legal force is to ignore the reality that 46 different Customs offices issue 10,000 to 15,000 of them each year." *Id.* at 233.

It is clear that the Coast Guard is entitled to deference on its determinations that 100-ton vessels are at "high risk" of terrorist attack; even plaintiffs acknowledge as much. They instead seek to analogize the instant case to *Mead* by suggesting that the ASP under which LCT operates is akin to a tariff classification ruling made by a local Customs office. *Mead,* however, is inapposite to the instant case. Here, the Coast Guard was acting under an explicit congressional delegation of legislative authority when it determined that increased security was required on the nation's largest ferries, and the regulations it devised were clearly intended to have the force of law. The MTSA requires the owners and operators of specified maritime vessels to implement a Coast-Guard approved security plan. ASPs, such as the one implemented by LCT, are approved at a national level by the Coast Guard Commandant if he or she finds that they provide a level of security equivalent to that established by the agency's regulations. 33 C.F.R. §§ 101–105. To date, the Coast Guard has approved only a few ASPs, including the Passenger Vessel Association program adopted by LCT. Id. § 101.125(c). Thus, contrary to the plaintiff's suggestion, LCT's ASP bears little resemblance to the thousands of tariff classification rulings issued by dozens of local Customs offices each year, and we owe significant deference to the Coast Guard's determination that ferries weighing over 100 gross register tons fall into a high-risk category.

Finally, even were we to accept plaintiffs' reading of *Mead,* it is unclear exactly what portion of our analysis here would change. The "high risk" designation, as we have already held, applies to LCT ferries on Lake Champlain as much as it does to the Staten Island Ferry. Plaintiffs are thus left to challenge the ASP, but it is simply a detailed plan of the security procedures that LCT has implemented to comply with the MTSA. As this opinion makes clear, we have not deferred to the government in examining the searches as authorized by the ASP, but have analyzed de novo the constitutional privacy interests involved as well as the nature of the government's intrusion. Given this scrutiny, plaintiffs' challenge here would still fail were we to follow their application of *Mead*. We accordingly find that the government has proffered an important, even compelling, special need here, having determined that ferries such as the ones operated by LCT are at a high risk of terrorist attack.

B. The Efficacy of the Searches

We now conclude the special needs analysis by examining the efficacy of the searches at issue here. We are mindful that the requirement that a court assess the efficacy of challenged searches and seizures in a "special needs" case is "not meant to transfer from politically accountable officials to the courts the decision as to which among reasonable alternatives law enforcement techniques should be employed to deal with a serious public danger. . . . [T]he choice among such reasonable alternatives remains with the governmental officials who have a unique understanding of, and responsibility for, limited public resources." *Sitz*, 496 U.S. at 453–54; *see also* Mollica v. Volker, 229 F.3d 366, 370 (2d Cir.2000) ("[T]he effectiveness inquiry involves only the question whether the [search] is a 'reasonable method of deterring the prohibited conduct;' the test does not require that the [search] be 'the most effective measure.' ") (quoting Maxwell v. City of New York, 102 F.3d 664, 667 (2d Cir.1996)). In this case, the government determined that the ASP devised by the Passenger Vessel Association and adopted by LCT was a reasonable means of fulfilling the requirements of the MTSA. Thus, our task is to determine not whether LCT's ASP was optimally effective, but whether it was reasonably so.[7]

Congress made clear in the MTSA that the central purpose of random security screening on high-risk maritime vessels is to "deter[ ] a transportation security incident," 46 U.S.C. § 70103(a). The Secretary then determined that the statutory purpose would be served by "[d]eter[ring] the unauthorized introduction of dangerous substances and devices" onto such vessels. 33 C.F.R. § 104.265(a)(1). When evaluated in this context, the ASP adopted by LCT appears to be reasonably calculated to serve its goal of deterring potential terrorists because "[i]t provides a gauntlet, random as it is, that persons bent on mischief must traverse." United States v. Green, 293 F.3d 855, 862 (5th Cir.2002); *see also id.* (finding that a military base commander's decision that stopping every sixth car can be effective at preventing terrorism or keeping the roads and personnel of the installation safe from unlicensed drivers was "common sense" because it preserved scarce governmental resources and deterred individuals from attacking the base); *cf. Von Raab*, 489 U.S. at

---

[7]   LCT's security measures were probably not optimally effective. As plaintiffs note, LCT's search policy applies to carry-on baggage, but not baggage stored in cars, and exempts tractor trailer trucks from search altogether. Furthermore, LCT's policy allows passengers to board the ferry with knives and guns, which may increase the risk that the ferry will be hijacked. Our task, however, is to determine not whether we could devise a superior plan, but whether LCT's security policy was reasonably effective in accomplishing its goals.

675 n.3 ("Nor would we think, in view of the obvious deterrent purpose of these searches, that the validity of the Government's airport screening program necessarily turns on whether significant numbers of putative air pirates are actually discovered by the searches conducted under the program.") (emphasis added); *Davis,* 482 F.2d at 908 (purpose of airport screening is deterrence). Indeed, in *MacWade,* we expressly observed that deterrence "need not be reduced to a quotient before a court may recognize a search program as effective." 460 F.3d at 274.

Plaintiffs contend, however, that the government cannot intrude on privacy rights merely for symbolic purposes. In support of this argument, plaintiffs cite the Supreme Court's holding in *Chandler v. Miller,* that suspicionless drug testing of candidates for state office cannot be justified by the government's desire to communicate a message that "the candidates, if elected, would be fit to serve their constituents free from the influence of illegal drugs." 520 U.S. at 321. The *Chandler* Court found that Georgia had not shown that candidates for state office were engaged in drug abuse and that a merely symbolic purpose that did not address an actual need could not justify a nontrivial invasion of privacy. Here, by contrast, the government is not seeking to convey a message that it disapproves of terrorism, but rather to deter an actual terrorist attack on a vessel that the Coast Guard has determined to be at an elevated risk of such attack. Unfortunately, the government's efforts to prevent terrorism in this case are not merely symbolic.

Plaintiffs further contend that the screening policy at issue in this case is not reasonably calculated to further Congress's aim of deterring a terrorist attack because it is not sufficiently thorough. The Supreme Court has been skeptical of challenges to the constitutionality of searches under the Fourth Amendment that suggest that a security policy's randomness or insufficient thoroughness contributes to its constitutional deficiencies:

> [P]etitioners' objection is based on those features of the . . . program . . . that contribute significantly to diminish the program's intrusion on privacy. . . . Thus, under petitioners' view, the testing program would be more likely to be constitutional if it were more pervasive and more invasive of privacy.

Von Raab, 489 U.S. at 676 n.4 (citations and internal quotation marks omitted). In this case, Congress directed the Coast Guard to identify vessel types posing a high risk of being involved in a terrorist attack. 46 U.S.C. § 70102(a). The Coast Guard was then charged with implementing the statutory directive to "establish[ ] and maintain[ ] physical security [and] passenger and cargo security." *Id.* § 70103(c)(3)(C). Although the security policy implemented by LCT may not be maximally effective in preventing terrorist attacks on its ferries, it is minimally intrusive, and we cannot say, particularly in light of the deference we owe to the Coast Guard, that it does not constitute a "reasonable method of deterring the prohibited conduct." *Mollica*, 229 F.3d at 370 (internal quotation marks omitted). Indeed, "[a]n unexpected change of plans," resulting from "a would-be bomber declin[ing] a search" may "well stymie an attack, disrupt the synchronicity of multiple bombings, or at least reduce casualties." *MacWade*, 460 F.3d at 275.

Having determined that LCT's practice of searching carry-on baggage and vehicles of randomly selected passengers is justified by a special governmental need and that such searches are a reasonable method to discourage prohibited conduct, we weigh this factor heavily in the government's favor.

CONCLUSION

While plaintiffs enjoy undiminished privacy expectations in their carry-on baggage and we presume such undiminished expectation in the trunks of their vehicles, we find that the remaining two factors under the "special needs" doctrine weigh heavily in the government's favor. Indeed, given that both the intrusions on plaintiffs' privacy interests are minimal and the measures adopted by LCT are reasonably efficacious in serving the government's undisputedly important special need to protect ferry passengers and crew from terrorist acts, we find no constitutional violation. Accordingly, we affirm the district court's judgment granting defendants' motion to dismiss.

City of Los Angeles, Calif. v. Patel
576 U.S. 409, 135 S.Ct. 2443 (2015)

■ JUSTICE SOTOMAYOR delivered the opinion of the Court.

Respondents brought a Fourth Amendment challenge to a provision of the Los Angeles Municipal Code that compels "[e]very operator of a hotel to keep a record" containing specified information concerning guests and to make this record "available to any officer of the Los Angeles Police Department for inspection" on demand. Los Angeles Municipal Code §§ 41.49(2), (3)(a), (4) (2015). The questions presented are whether facial challenges to statutes can be brought under the Fourth Amendment and, if so, whether this provision of the Los Angeles Municipal Code is facially invalid. We hold facial challenges can be brought under the Fourth Amendment. We further hold that the provision of the Los Angeles Municipal Code that requires hotel operators to make their registries available to the police on demand is facially unconstitutional because it penalizes them for declining to turn over their records without affording them any opportunity for precompliance review.

I

A

Los Angeles Municipal Code (LAMC) § 41.49 requires hotel operators to record information about their guests, including: the guest's name and address; the number of people in each guest's party; the make, model, and license plate number of any guest's vehicle parked on hotel property; the guest's date and time of arrival and scheduled departure date; the room number assigned to the guest; the rate charged and amount collected for the room; and the method of payment. § 41.49(2). Guests without reservations, those who pay for their rooms with cash, and any guests who rent a room for less than 12 hours must present photographic identification at the time of check-in, and hotel operators are required to record the number and expiration date of that document. § 41.49(4). For those guests who check in using an electronic kiosk, the hotel's records must also contain the guest's credit card information. § 41.49(2)(b). This information can be maintained in either electronic or paper form, but it must be "kept on the hotel premises in the guest reception or guest check-in area or in an office adjacent" thereto for a period of 90 days. § 41.49(3)(a).

Section 41.49(3)(a)—the only provision at issue here—states, in pertinent part, that hotel guest records "shall be made available to any officer of the Los Angeles Police Department for inspection," provided that "[w]henever possible, the inspection shall be conducted at a time and in a manner that minimizes any interference with the operation of the business." A hotel operator's failure to make his or her guest records available for police inspection is a misdemeanor punishable by up to six months in jail and a $1,000 fine. § 11.00(m) (general provision applicable to entire LAMC).

B

In 2003, respondents, a group of motel operators along with a lodging association, sued the city of Los Angeles (City or petitioner) in three consolidated cases challenging the constitutionality of § 41.49(3)(a). They sought declaratory and injunctive relief. The parties "agree[d] that the sole issue in the . . . action [would be] a facial constitutional challenge" to § 41.49(3)(a) under the Fourth Amendment. App. 195. They further stipulated that respondents have been subjected to mandatory record inspections under the ordinance without consent or a warrant. *Id.,* at 194–195.

Following a bench trial, the District Court entered judgment in favor of the City, holding that respondents' facial challenge failed because they lacked a reasonable expectation of privacy in the records subject to inspection. A divided panel of the Ninth Circuit affirmed on the same grounds. 686 F.3d 1085 (2012). On rehearing en banc, however, the Court of Appeals reversed. 738 F.3d 1058, 1065 (2013).

The en banc court first determined that a police officer's nonconsensual inspection of hotel records under § 41.49 is a Fourth Amendment "search" because "[t]he business records covered by § 41.49 are the hotel's private property" and the hotel therefore "has the right to exclude others from prying into the[ir] contents." *Id.,* at 1061. Next, the court assessed "whether the searches authorized by § 41.49 are reasonable." *Id.*, at 1063. Relying on Donovan v. Lone Steer, Inc., 464 U.S. 408 (1984), and See v. Seattle, 387 U.S. 541 (1967), the court held that § 41.49 is facially unconstitutional "as it authorizes inspections" of hotel records "without affording an opportunity to 'obtain judicial review of the reasonableness of the demand prior to suffering penalties for refusing to comply.'" 738 F.3d, at 1065 (quoting *See*, 387 U.S., at 545).

Two dissenting opinions were filed. The first dissent argued that facial relief should rarely be available for Fourth Amendment challenges, and was inappropriate here because the ordinance would be constitutional in those circumstances where police officers demand access to hotel records with a warrant in hand or exigent circumstances justify the search. 738 F.3d, at 1065–1070 (opinion of Tallman, J.). The second dissent conceded that inspections under § 41.49 constitute Fourth Amendment searches, but faulted the majority for assessing the reasonableness of these searches without accounting for the weakness of the hotel operators' privacy interest in the content of their guest registries. *Id.*, at 1070–1074 (opinion of Clifton, J.).

We granted certiorari, 574 U.S. ___ (2014), and now affirm.

II

We first clarify that facial challenges under the Fourth Amendment are not categorically barred or especially disfavored.

A

A facial challenge is an attack on a statute itself as opposed to a particular application. While such challenges are "the most difficult . . . to mount successfully," United States v. Salerno, 481 U.S. 739, 745 (1987), the Court has never held that these claims cannot be brought under any otherwise enforceable provision of the Constitution. *Cf.* Fallon, *Fact and Fiction About Facial Challenges*, 99 Cal. L.Rev. 915, 918 (2011) (pointing to several Terms in which "the Court adjudicated more facial challenges on the merits than it did as-applied challenges"). Instead, the Court has allowed such challenges to proceed under a diverse array of constitutional provisions. *See, e.g.,* Sorrell v. IMS Health Inc., 564 U.S. ___ (2011) (First Amendment); District of Columbia v. Heller, 554 U.S. 570 (2008) (Second Amendment); Chicago v. Morales, 527 U.S. 41 (1999) (Due Process Clause of the Fourteenth Amendment); Kraft Gen. Foods, Inc. v. Iowa Dept. of Revenue and Finance, 505 U.S. 71 (1992) (Foreign Commerce Clause).

Fourth Amendment challenges to statutes authorizing warrantless searches are no exception. Any claim to the contrary reflects a misunderstanding of our decision in Sibron v. New York, 392 U.S. 40 (1968). In *Sibron,* two criminal defendants challenged the constitutionality of a statute authorizing police to, among other things, "stop any person abroad in a public place whom [they] reasonably suspec[t] is committing, has committed or is about to commit a felony." *Id.*, at 43 (quoting then N.Y. Code Crim. Proc. § 180–a). The Court held that the search of one of the defendants under the statute violated the Fourth Amendment, 392 U.S., at 59, 62but refused to opine more broadly on the statute's validity, stating that "[t]he constitutional validity of a warrantless search is pre-eminently the sort of question which can only be decided in the concrete factual context of the individual case." *Id.,* at 59.

This statement from *Sibron*—which on its face might suggest an intent to foreclose all facial challenges to statutes authorizing warrantless searches—must be understood in the broader context of that case. In the same section of the opinion, the Court emphasized that the "operative categories" of the New York law at issue were "susceptible of a wide variety of interpretations," *id.,* at 60, and that "[the law] was passed too recently for the State's highest court to have ruled upon many of the questions involving potential intersections with federal constitutional guarantees," *id.,* at 60, n. 20. *Sibron* thus stands for the simple proposition that claims for facial relief under the Fourth Amendment are unlikely to succeed when there is substantial ambiguity as to what conduct a statute authorizes: Where a statute consists of "extraordinarily elastic categories," it may be "impossible to tell" whether and to what extent it deviates from the requirements of the Fourth Amendment. *Id.,* at 59, 61, n. 20.

This reading of *Sibron* is confirmed by subsequent precedents. Since *Sibron,* the Court has entertained facial challenges under the Fourth Amendment to statutes authorizing warrantless searches. See, *e.g.,* Vernonia School District 47J v. Acton, 515 U.S. 646, 648 (1995) ("We granted certiorari to decide whether" petitioner's student athlete drug testing policy "violates the Fourth and Fourteenth Amendments to the United States Constitution"); Skinner v. Railway Labor Executives' Assn., 489 U.S. 602, 633, n.10 (1989) ("[R]espondents have challenged the administrative scheme on its face. We deal therefore with whether the [drug] tests contemplated by the regulation can *ever* be conducted"); *cf.* Illinois v. Krull, 480 U.S. 340, 354 (1987) ("[A] person subject to a statute authorizing searches without a warrant or probable cause may bring an action seeking a declaration that the statute is unconstitutional and an injunction barring its implementation"). Perhaps more importantly, the Court has on numerous occasions declared statutes facially invalid under the Fourth Amendment. For instance, in Chandler v. Miller, 520 U.S. 305, 308–309 (1997), the Court struck down a Georgia statute requiring candidates for certain state offices to take and pass a drug test, concluding that this "requirement . . . [did] not fit within the closely guarded category of constitutionally permissible suspicionless searches." Similar examples abound. *See, e.g.,* Ferguson v. Charleston, 532 U.S. 67, 86 (2001) (holding that a hospital policy authorizing "nonconsensual, warrantless, and suspicionless searches" contravened the Fourth Amendment); Payton v. New York, 445 U.S. 573, 574, 576 (1980) (holding that a New York statute "authoriz[ing] police officers to enter a private residence without a warrant and with force, if necessary, to make a routine felony arrest" was "not consistent with the Fourth Amendment"); Torres v. Puerto Rico, 442 U.S. 465, 466 (1979) (holding that a Puerto Rico statute authorizing "police to search the luggage of any person arriving in Puerto Rico from the United States" was unconstitutional because it failed to require either probable cause or a warrant).

B

Petitioner principally contends that facial challenges to statutes authorizing warrantless searches must fail because such searches will never be unconstitutional in all applications. *Cf. Salerno,* 481 U.S., at 745 (to obtain facial relief the party seeking it "must establish that no set of circumstances exists under which the [statute] would be valid"). In particular, the City points to situations where police are responding to an emergency, where the subject of the search consents to the intrusion, and where police are acting under a court-ordered warrant. *See* Brief for Petitioner 19–20. While petitioner frames this argument as an objection to respondents' challenge in this case, its logic would preclude facial relief in every Fourth Amendment challenge to a statute authorizing warrantless searches. For this reason alone, the City's argument must fail: The Court's precedents demonstrate not only that facial challenges to statutes authorizing warrantless searches can be brought, but also that they can succeed. *See* Part II-A, *supra.*

Moreover, the City's argument misunderstands how courts analyze facial challenges. Under the most exacting standard the Court has prescribed for facial challenges, a plaintiff must establish that a "law is unconstitutional in all of its applications." Washington State Grange v. Washington State Republican Party, 552 U.S. 442, 449 (2008). But when assessing whether a statute meets this standard, the Court has considered only applications of the statute in which it actually authorizes or prohibits conduct. For instance, in Planned Parenthood of Southeastern Pa. v. Casey, 505 U.S. 833 (1992), the Court struck down a provision of Pennsylvania's abortion law that required a woman to notify her husband before obtaining an abortion. Those defending the statute argued that facial relief was inappropriate because most women voluntarily notify their husbands about a planned abortion and for them the law would not impose an undue burden. The Court rejected this argument, explaining: The "[l]egislation is measured for consistency with the Constitution by its impact on those whose conduct it affects. . . . The proper focus of the constitutional inquiry is the group for whom the law is a restriction, not the group for whom the law is irrelevant." *Id.,* at 894.

Similarly, when addressing a facial challenge to a statute authorizing warrantless searches, the proper focus of the constitutional inquiry is searches that the law actually authorizes, not those for which it is irrelevant. If exigency or a warrant justifies an officer's search, the subject of the search must permit it to proceed irrespective of whether it is authorized by statute. Statutes authorizing warrantless searches also do no work where the subject of a search has consented. Accordingly, the constitutional "applications" that petitioner claims prevent facial relief here are irrelevant to our analysis because they do not involve actual applications of the statute.

III

Turning to the merits of the particular claim before us, we hold that § 41.49(3)(a) is facially unconstitutional because it fails to provide hotel operators with an opportunity for precompliance review.

A

The Fourth Amendment protects "[t]he right of the people to be secure in their persons, houses, papers, and effects, against unreasonable searches and seizures." It further provides that "no Warrants shall issue, but upon probable cause." Based on this constitutional text, the Court has repeatedly held that " 'searches conducted outside the judicial process, without prior approval by [a] judge or [a] magistrate [judge], are *per se* unreasonable . . . subject only to a few specifically established and well-delineated exceptions.' " Arizona v. Gant, 556 U.S. 332, 338 (2009) (quoting Katz v. United States, 389 U.S. 347, 357 (1967)). This rule "applies to commercial premises as well as to homes." Marshall v. Barlow's, Inc., 436 U.S. 307, 312.

Search regimes where no warrant is ever required may be reasonable where " 'special needs . . . make the warrant and probable-cause requirement impracticable,' " *Skinner,* 489 U.S., at 619 (quoting Griffin v. Wisconsin, 483 U.S. 868, 873 (1987) (some internal quotation marks omitted)), and where the "primary purpose" of the searches is "[d]istinguishable from the general interest in crime control," Indianapolis v. Edmond, 531 U.S. 32, 44 (2000). Here, we assume that the searches authorized by § 41.49 serve a "special need" other than conducting criminal investigations: They ensure compliance with the recordkeeping requirement, which in turn deters criminals from operating on the hotels' premises.[2] The Court has referred to this kind of search as an "administrative searc[h]." Camara v. Municipal Court of City and County of San Francisco, 387 U.S. 523, 534 (1967). Thus, we consider whether § 41.49 falls within the administrative search exception to the warrant requirement.

The Court has held that absent consent, exigent circumstances, or the like, in order for an administrative search to be constitutional, the subject of the search must be afforded an opportunity to obtain precompliance review before a neutral decisionmaker. See *See,* 387 U.S., at 545; *Lone Steer,* 464 U.S., at 415 (noting that an administrative search may proceed with only a subpoena where the subpoenaed party is

---

[2] Respondents contend that § 41.49's principal purpose instead is to facilitate criminal investigation. Brief for Respondents 44–47. Because we find that the searches authorized by § 41.49 are unconstitutional even if they serve the City's asserted purpose, we decline to address this argument.

sufficiently protected by the opportunity to "question the reasonableness of the subpoena, before suffering any penalties for refusing to comply with it, by raising objections in an action in district court"). And, we see no reason why this minimal requirement is inapplicable here. While the Court has never attempted to prescribe the exact form an opportunity for precompliance review must take, the City does not even attempt to argue that § 41.49(3)(a) affords hotel operators any opportunity whatsoever. Section 41.49(3)(a) is, therefore, facially invalid.

A hotel owner who refuses to give an officer access to his or her registry can be arrested on the spot. The Court has held that business owners cannot reasonably be put to this kind of choice. *Camara,* 387 U.S., at 533 (holding that "broad statutory safeguards are no substitute for individualized review, particularly when those safeguards may only be invoked at the risk of a criminal penalty"). Absent an opportunity for precompliance review, the ordinance creates an intolerable risk that searches authorized by it will exceed statutory limits, or be used as a pretext to harass hotel operators and their guests. Even if a hotel has been searched 10 times a day, every day, for three months, without any violation being found, the operator can only refuse to comply with an officer's demand to turn over the registry at his or her own peril.

To be clear, we hold only that a hotel owner must be afforded an *opportunity* to have a neutral decisionmaker review an officer's demand to search the registry before he or she faces penalties for failing to comply. Actual review need only occur in those rare instances where a hotel operator objects to turning over the registry. Moreover, this opportunity can be provided without imposing onerous burdens on those charged with an administrative scheme's enforcement. For instance, respondents accept that the searches authorized by § 41.49(3)(a) would be constitutional if they were performed pursuant to an administrative subpoena. Tr. of Oral Arg. 36–37. These subpoenas, which are typically a simple form, can be issued by the individual seeking the record—here, officers in the field—without probable cause that a regulation is being infringed. *See See,* 387 U.S., at 544 ("[T]he demand to inspect may be issued by the agency"). Issuing a subpoena will usually be the full extent of an officer's burden because "the great majority of businessmen can be expected in normal course to consent to inspection without warrant." *Barlow's, Inc.,* 436 U.S., at 316. Indeed, the City has cited no evidence suggesting that without an ordinance authorizing on-demand searches, hotel operators would regularly refuse to cooperate with the police.

In those instances, however, where a subpoenaed hotel operator believes that an attempted search is motivated by illicit purposes, respondents suggest it would be sufficient if he or she could move to quash the subpoena before any search takes place. Tr. of Oral Arg. 38–39. A neutral decisionmaker, including an administrative law judge, would then review the subpoenaed party's objections before deciding whether the subpoena is enforceable. Given the limited grounds on which a motion to quash can be granted, such challenges will likely be rare. And, in the even rarer event that an officer reasonably suspects that a hotel operator may tamper with the registry while the motion to quash is pending, he or she can guard the registry until the required hearing can occur, which ought not take long. Riley v. California, 573 U.S. (2014) (police may seize and hold a cell phone "to prevent destruction of evidence while seeking a warrant"); Illinois v. McArthur, 531 U.S. 326, 334 (2001) (citing cases upholding the constitutionality of "temporary restraints where [they are] needed to preserve evidence until police could obtain a warrant"). Cf. Missouri v. McNeely, 569 U.S. ___ (2013) (noting that many States have procedures in place for considering warrant applications telephonically).[3]

Procedures along these lines are ubiquitous. A 2002 report by the Department of Justice "identified approximately 335 existing administrative subpoena authorities held by various [federal] executive branch entities." Office of Legal Policy, Report to Congress on the Use of Administrative Subpoena Authorities by Executive Branch Agencies and Entities 3, online at http://www.justice.gov/archive/olp/rpt_to_congress.htm (All Internet materials as visited June 19, 2015, and available in Clerk of Court's case file). Their prevalence confirms what common sense alone would otherwise lead us to conclude: In most contexts, business owners can be afforded at least an opportunity to contest an administrative search's propriety without unduly compromising the government's ability to achieve its regulatory aims.

Of course administrative subpoenas are only one way in which an opportunity for precompliance review can be made available. But whatever the precise form, the availability of precompliance review alters the dynamic between the officer and the hotel to be searched, and reduces the risk that officers will use these administrative searches as a pretext to harass business owners.

Finally, we underscore the narrow nature of our holding. Respondents have not challenged and nothing in our opinion calls into question those parts of § 41.49 that require hotel operators to maintain guest registries containing certain information. And, even absent legislative action to create a procedure along the lines discussed above, see *supra,* at 2452–2453, police will not be prevented from obtaining access to these documents. As they often do, hotel operators remain free to consent to searches of their registries and police can compel them to turn them over if they have a proper administrative warrant—including one that was issued *ex parte*—or if some other exception to the warrant requirement applies, including exigent circumstances.[4]

---

[3] Justice SCALIA professes to be baffled at the idea that we could suggest that in certain circumstances, police officers may seize something that they cannot immediately search. *Post,* at 2461–2462 (dissenting opinion). But that is what this Court's cases have explicitly endorsed, including *Riley* just last Term.

[4] In suggesting that our holding today will somehow impede law enforcement from achieving its important aims, Justice SCALIA relies on instances where hotels were used as

B

Rather than arguing that § 41.49(3)(a) is constitutional under the general administrative search doctrine, the City and Justice SCALIA contend that hotels are "closely regulated," and that the ordinance is facially valid under the more relaxed standard that applies to searches of this category of businesses. Brief for Petitioner 28–47; *post,* at 2459. They are wrong on both counts.

Over the past 45 years, the Court has identified only four industries that "have such a history of government oversight that no reasonable expectation of privacy . . . could exist for a proprietor over the stock of such an enterprise," *Barlow's, Inc.,* 436 U.S., at 313. Simply listing these industries refutes petitioner's argument that hotels should be counted among them. Unlike liquor sales, Colonnade Catering Corp. v. United States, 397 U.S. 72 (1970), firearms dealing, United States v. Biswell, 406 U.S. 311, 311–312 (1972), mining, Donovan v. Dewey, 452 U.S. 594 (1981), or running an automobile junkyard, New York v. Burger, 482 U.S. 691 (1987), nothing inherent in the operation of hotels poses a clear and significant risk to the public welfare. See, *e.g., id.,* at 709 ("Automobile junkyards and vehicle dismantlers provide the major market for stolen vehicles and vehicle parts"); *Dewey,* 452 U.S., at 602 (describing the mining industry as "among the most hazardous in the country").[5]

Moreover, "[t]he clear import of our cases is that the closely regulated industry . . . is the exception." *Barlow's, Inc.,* 436 U.S., at 313. To classify hotels as pervasively regulated would permit what has always been a narrow exception to swallow the rule. The City wisely refrains from arguing that § 41.49 itself renders hotels closely regulated. Nor do any of the other regulations on which petitioner and Justice SCALIA rely—regulations requiring hotels to, *inter alia,* maintain a license, collect taxes, conspicuously post their rates, and meet certain sanitary standards—establish a comprehensive scheme of regulation that distinguishes hotels from numerous other businesses. *See* Brief for Petitioner 33–34 (citing regulations); *post,* at 2460 (same). All businesses in Los Angeles need a license to operate. LAMC §§ 21.03(a), 21.09(a). While some regulations apply to a smaller set of businesses, *See, e.g.* Cal.Code Regs., tit. 25, § 40 (2015) (requiring linens to be changed between rental guests), online at http://www.oal.ca.gov/ccr.htm, these can hardly be said to have created a " 'comprehensive' " scheme that puts hotel owners on notice that their " 'property will be subject to periodic inspections undertaken for specific purposes,' " *Burger,* 482 U.S., at 705, n.16 (quoting *Dewey,* 452 U.S., at 600). Instead, they are more akin to the

---

"prisons for migrants smuggled across the border and held for ransom" or as "rendezvous sites where child sex workers meet their clients on threat of violence from their procurers." *See post,* at 2457. It is hard to imagine circumstances more exigent than these.

[5] Justice SCALIA's effort to depict hotels as raising a comparable degree of risk rings hollow. *See post,* at 2457, 2463–2464. Hotels—like practically all commercial premises or services—can be put to use for nefarious ends. But unlike the industries that the Court has found to be closely regulated, hotels are not intrinsically dangerous.

widely applicable minimum wage and maximum hour rules that the Court rejected as a basis for deeming "the entirety of American interstate commerce" to be closely regulated in *Barlow's, Inc.* 436 U.S., at 314. If such general regulations were sufficient to invoke the closely regulated industry exception, it would be hard to imagine a type of business that would not qualify. *See* Brief for Google Inc. as *Amicus Curiae* 16–17; Brief for the Chamber of Commerce of United States of America as *Amicus Curiae* 12–13.

Petitioner attempts to recast this hodgepodge of regulations as a comprehensive scheme by referring to a "centuries-old tradition" of warrantless searches of hotels. Brief for Petitioner 34–36. History is relevant when determining whether an industry is closely regulated. See, *e.g., Burger,* 482 U.S., at 707. The historical record here, however, is not as clear as petitioner suggests. The City and Justice SCALIA principally point to evidence that hotels were treated as public accommodations. Brief for Petitioner 34–36; *post,* at 2459–2460, and n.1. For instance, the Commonwealth of Massachusetts required innkeepers to " 'furnish[ ] . . . suitable provisions and lodging, for the refreshment and entertainment of strangers and travellers, pasturing and stable room, hay and provender . . . for their horses and cattle.' " Brief for Petitioner 35 (quoting An Act For The Due Regulation Of Licensed Houses (1786), reprinted in Acts and Laws of the Commonwealth of Massachusetts 209 (1893)). But laws obligating inns to provide suitable lodging to all paying guests are not the same as laws subjecting inns to warrantless searches. Petitioner also asserts that "[f]or a long time, [hotel] owners left their registers open to widespread inspection." Brief for Petitioner 51. Setting aside that modern hotel registries contain sensitive information, such as driver's licenses and credit card numbers for which there is no historic analog, the fact that some hotels chose to make registries accessible to the public has little bearing on whether government authorities could have viewed these documents on demand without a hotel's consent.

Even if we were to find that hotels are pervasively regulated, § 41.49 would need to satisfy three additional criteria to be reasonable under the Fourth Amendment: (1) "[T]here must be a 'substantial' government interest that informs the regulatory scheme pursuant to which the inspection is made"; (2) "the warrantless inspections must be 'necessary' to further [the] regulatory scheme"; and (3) "the statute's inspection program, in terms of the certainty and regularity of its application, [must] provid[e] a constitutionally adequate substitute for a warrant." *Burger,* 482 U.S., at 702–703 (internal quotation marks omitted). We assume petitioner's interest in ensuring that hotels maintain accurate and complete registries might fulfill the first of these requirements, but conclude that § 41.49 fails the second and third prongs of this test.

The City claims that affording hotel operators any opportunity for precompliance review would fatally undermine the scheme's efficacy by giving operators a chance to falsify their records. Brief for Petitioner 41–

42. The Court has previously rejected this exact argument, which could be made regarding any recordkeeping requirement. *See Barlow's, Inc.,* 436 U.S., at 320 ("[It is not] apparent why the advantages of surprise would be lost if, after being refused entry, procedures were available for the [Labor] Secretary to seek an *ex parte* warrant to reappear at the premises without further notice to the establishment being inspected"); *cf. Lone Steer,* 464 U.S., at 411, 415 (affirming use of administrative subpoena which provided an opportunity for precompliance review as a means for obtaining "payroll and sales records"). We see no reason to accept it here.

As explained above, nothing in our decision today precludes an officer from conducting a surprise inspection by obtaining an *ex parte* warrant or, where an officer reasonably suspects the registry would be altered, from guarding the registry pending a hearing on a motion to quash. *See Barlow's, Inc.,* 436 U.S., at 319–321; *Riley,* 573 U.S., at ___. Justice SCALIA's claim that these procedures will prove unworkable given the large number of hotels in Los Angeles is a red herring. *See post,* at 2462. While there are approximately 2,000 hotels in Los Angeles, *ibid.,* there is no basis to believe that resort to such measures will be needed to conduct spot checks in the vast majority of them. *See supra,* at 2452–2453.

Section 41.49 is also constitutionally deficient under the "certainty and regularity" prong of the closely regulated industries test because it fails sufficiently to constrain police officers' discretion as to which hotels to search and under what circumstances. While the Court has upheld inspection schemes of closely regulated industries that called for searches at least four times a year, *Dewey,* 452 U.S., at 604 or on a "regular basis," *Burger,* 482 U.S., at 711, § 41.49 imposes no comparable standard.

* * *

For the foregoing reasons, we agree with the Ninth Circuit that § 41.49(3)(a) is facially invalid insofar as it fails to provide any opportunity for precompliance review before a hotel must give its guest registry to the police for inspection. Accordingly, the judgment of the Ninth Circuit is affirmed.

It is so ordered.

■ JUSTICE SCALIA, with whom THE CHIEF JUSTICE and JUSTICE THOMAS join, dissenting.

The city of Los Angeles, like many jurisdictions across the country, has a law that requires motels, hotels, and other places of overnight accommodation (hereinafter motels) to keep a register containing specified information about their guests. Los Angeles Municipal Code (LAMC) § 41.49(2) (2015). The purpose of this recordkeeping requirement is to deter criminal conduct, on the theory that criminals will be unwilling to carry on illicit activities in motel rooms if they must provide identifying information at check-in. Because this deterrent effect will only be accomplished if motels actually do require guests to provide the required information, the ordinance also authorizes police to conduct random spot checks of motels' guest registers to ensure that they are properly maintained. § 41.49(3). The ordinance limits these spot checks to the four corners of the register, and does not authorize police to enter any nonpublic area of the motel. To the extent possible, police must conduct these spot checks at times that will minimize any disruption to a motel's business.

The parties do not dispute the governmental interests at stake. Motels not only provide housing to vulnerable transient populations, they are also a particularly attractive site for criminal activity ranging from drug dealing and prostitution to human trafficking. Offering privacy and anonymity on the cheap, they have been employed as prisons for migrants smuggled across the border and held for ransom, *See* Sanchez, *Immigrant Smugglers Become More Ruthless*, Washington Post, June 28, 2004, p. A3; Wagner, Human Smuggling, Arizona Republic, July 23, 2006, p. A1, and rendezvous sites where child sex workers meet their clients on threat of violence from their procurers.

Nevertheless, the Court today concludes that Los Angeles's ordinance is "unreasonable" inasmuch as it permits police to flip through a guest register to ensure it is being filled out without first providing an opportunity for the motel operator to seek judicial review. Because I believe that such a limited inspection of a guest register is eminently reasonable under the circumstances presented, I dissent. . . .

One exception to normal warrant requirements applies to searches of closely regulated businesses. "[W]hen an entrepreneur embarks upon such a business, he has voluntarily chosen to subject himself to a full arsenal of governmental regulation," and so a warrantless search to enforce those regulations is not unreasonable. Marshall v. Barlow's, Inc., 436 U.S. 307, 313 (1978). Recognizing that warrantless searches of closely regulated businesses may nevertheless *become* unreasonable if arbitrarily conducted, we have required laws authorizing such searches to satisfy three criteria: (1) There must be a " 'substantial' government interest that informs the regulatory scheme pursuant to which the inspection is made"; (2) "the warrantless inspections must be 'necessary to further [the] regulatory scheme' "; and (3) " 'the statute's inspection program, in terms of the certainty and regularity of its application, [must] provid[e] a constitutionally adequate substitute for a warrant.' " New York v. Burger, 482 U.S. 691, 702–703 (1987).

Los Angeles's ordinance easily meets these standards.

A

In determining whether a business is closely regulated, this Court has looked to factors including the duration of the regulatory tradition, *id.,* at 705–707; Colonnade Catering Corp. v. United States, 397 U.S. 72, 75–77 (1970), Donovan v. Dewey, 452 U.S. 594, 606 (1981); the comprehensiveness of the regulatory regime, *Burger, supra,* at 704–705; *Dewey, supra,* at 606; and the imposition of similar regulations by other jurisdictions, *Burger, supra,* at 705. These factors are not talismans, but shed light on the expectation of privacy the owner of a business may reasonably have, which in turn affects the reasonableness of a warrantless search. *See Barlow's, supra,* at 313.

Reflecting the unique public role of motels and their commercial forebears, governments have long subjected these businesses to unique public duties, and have established inspection regimes to ensure compliance. As Blackstone observed, "Inns, in particular, being intended for the lodging and receipt of travellers, may be indicted, suppressed, and the inn-keepers fined, if they refuse to entertain a traveller without a very sufficient cause: for thus to frustrate the end of their institution is held to be disorderly behavior." 4 W. Blackstone, Commentaries on the Laws of England 168 (1765). Justice Story similarly recognized "[t]he soundness of the public policy of subjecting particular classes of persons to extraordinary responsibility, in cases where an extraordinary confidence is necessarily reposed in them, and there is an extraordinary temptation to fraud, or danger of plunder." J. Story, Commentaries on the Law of Bailments § 464, pp. 487–488 (5th ed. 1851). Accordingly, in addition to the obligation to receive any paying guest, "innkeepers are bound to take, not merely ordinary care, but uncommon care, of the goods, money, and baggage of their guests," *id.,* § 470, at 495, as travellers "are obliged to rely almost implicitly on the good faith of innholders, whose education and morals are none of the best, and who might have frequent opportunities of associating with ruffians and pilferers," *id.,* § 471, at 498.

These obligations were not merely aspirational. At the time of the founding, searches—indeed, warrantless searches—of inns and similar places of public accommodation were commonplace. For example, although Massachusetts was perhaps the State most protective against government searches, "the state code of 1788 still allowed tithingmen to search public houses of entertainment on every Sabbath without any sort of warrant." W. Cuddihy, Fourth Amendment: Origins and Original Meaning 602–1791, 743 (2009).

As this evidence demonstrates, the regulatory tradition governing motels is not only longstanding, but comprehensive. And the tradition continues in Los Angeles. The City imposes an occupancy tax upon transients who stay in motels, LAMC § 21.7.3, and makes the motel owner responsible for collecting it, § 21.7.5. It authorizes city officials "to enter [a motel], free of charge, during business hours" in order to "inspect and examine" them to determine whether these tax provisions have been complied with. §§ 21.7.9, 21.15. It requires all motels to obtain a "Transient Occupancy Registration Certificate," which must be displayed on the premises. § 21.7.6. State law requires motels to "post in a conspicuous place . . . a statement of rate or range of rates by the day for lodging," and forbids any charges in excess of those posted rates. Cal. Civ.Code Ann. § 1863 (West 2010). Hotels must change bed linens between guests, Cal.Code Regs., tit. 25, § 40 (2015), and they must offer guests the option not to have towels and linens laundered daily, LAMC § 121.08. "Multiuse drinking utensils" may be placed in guest rooms only if they are "thoroughly washed and sanitized after each use" and "placed in protective bags." Cal.Code Regs., tit. 17, § 30852. And state authorities, like their municipal counterparts, "may at reasonable times enter and inspect any hotels, motels, or other public places" to ensure compliance. § 30858.

The regulatory regime at issue here is thus substantially *more* comprehensive than the regulations governing junkyards in *Burger,* where licensing, inventory-recording, and permit-posting requirements were found sufficient to qualify the industry as closely regulated. 482 U.S., at 704–705. The Court's suggestion that these regulations are not sufficiently targeted to motels, and are "akin to . . . minimum wage and maximum hour rules," *ante,* at 2455, is simply false. The regulations we have described above reach into the "minutest detail[s]" of motel operations, *Barlow's, supra,* at 314, and those who enter that business today (like those who have entered it over the centuries) do so with an expectation that they will be subjected to especially vigilant governmental oversight.

Finally, this ordinance is not an outlier. The City has pointed us to more than 100 similar register-inspection laws in cities and counties across the country, Brief for Petitioner 36, and n. 3, and that is far from exhaustive. In all, municipalities in at least 41 States have laws similar to Los Angeles's, Brief for National League of Cities et al. as *Amici Curiae* 16–17, and at least 8 States have their own laws authorizing register inspections, Brief for California et al. as *Amici Curiae* 12–13.

This copious evidence is surely enough to establish that "[w]hen a [motel operator] chooses to engage in this pervasively regulated business . . . he does so with the knowledge that his business records . . . will be subject to effective inspection." United States v. Biswell, 406 U.S. 311, 316 (1972). And *that* is the relevant constitutional test—not whether this regulatory superstructure is "the same as laws subjecting inns to warrantless searches," or whether, as an historical matter, government authorities not only required these documents to be kept but permitted them to be viewed on demand without a motel's consent. *Ante,* at 2455–2456.

The Court's observation that "[o]ver the past 45 years, the Court has identified only four industries" as closely regulated, *ante,* at 2454, is neither here nor there. Since we first concluded in *Colonnade Catering* that warrantless searches of closely regulated businesses are reasonable, we have only identified *one* industry as *not* closely regulated, *see Barlow's,* 436 U.S., at 313–314. The Court's statistic thus tells us more about how this Court exercises its discretionary review than it does about the number of industries that qualify as closely regulated. At the same time, lower courts, which do not have the luxury of picking the cases they hear, have identified many more businesses as closely regulated under the test we have announced: pharmacies, *United States v. Gonsalves,* 435 F.3d 64, 67 (C.A.1 2006); massage parlors, *Pollard v. Cockrell,* 578 F.2d 1002, 1014 (C.A.5 1978); commercial-fishing operations, *United States v. Raub,* 637 F.2d 1205, 1208–1209 (C.A.9 1980); day-care facilities, *Rush v. Obledo,* 756 F.2d 713, 720–721 (C.A.9 1985); nursing homes, *People v. Firstenberg,* 92 Cal.App.3d 570, 578–580, 155 Cal.Rptr. 80, 84–86 (1979); jewelers, *People v. Pashigian,* 150 Mich.App. 97, 100–101, 388 N.W.2d 259, 261–262 (1986) (*per curiam*); barbershops, *Stogner v. Kentucky,* 638 F.Supp. 1, 3 (W.D.Ky.1985); and yes, even rabbit dealers, *Lesser v. Espy,* 34 F.3d 1301, 1306–1307 (C.A.7 1994). Like automobile junkyards and catering companies that serve alcohol, many of these businesses are far from "intrinsically dangerous," cf. *ante,* at 2455, n.5. This should come as no surprise. The reason closely regulated industries may be searched without a warrant has nothing to do with the risk of harm they pose; rather, it has to do with the expectations of those who enter such a line of work. *See Barlow's, supra,* at 313.

B

The City's ordinance easily satisfies the remaining *Burger* requirements: It furthers a substantial governmental interest, it is necessary to achieving that interest, and it provides an adequate substitute for a search warrant.

Neither respondents nor the Court question the substantial interest of the City in deterring criminal activity. *See* Brief for Respondents 34–41; *ante,* at 2455. The private pain and public costs imposed by drug dealing, prostitution, and human trafficking are beyond contention, and motels provide an obvious haven for those who trade in human misery.

Warrantless inspections are also necessary to advance this interest. Although the Court acknowledges that law enforcement can enter a motel room without a warrant when exigent circumstances exist, *see ante,* at 2454, n. 4, the whole reason criminals use motel rooms in the first place is that they offer privacy and secrecy, so that police will never come to discover these exigencies. The recordkeeping requirement, which all parties admit is permissible, therefore operates by *deterring* crime. Criminals, who depend on the anonymity that motels offer, will balk when confronted with a motel's demand that they produce identification. And a motel's evasion of the recordkeeping requirement fosters crime. In San Diego, for example, motel owners were indicted for collaborating with members of the Crips street gang in the prostitution of underage girls; the motel owners "set aside rooms apart from the rest of their legitimate customers where girls and women were housed, charged the gang members/pimps a higher rate for the rooms where 'dates' or 'tricks' took place, and warned the gang members of inquiries by law enforcement." Office of the Attorney General, Cal. Dept. of Justice, The

State of Human Trafficking in California 25 (2012). The warrantless inspection requirement provides a necessary incentive for motels to maintain their registers thoroughly and accurately: They never know when law enforcement might drop by to inspect.

Respondents and the Court acknowledge that *inspections* are necessary to achieve the purposes of the recordkeeping regime, but insist that *warrantless* inspections are not. They have to acknowledge, however, that the motel operators who conspire with drug dealers and procurers may demand precompliance judicial review simply as a pretext to buy time for making fraudulent entries in their guest registers. The Court therefore must resort to arguing that warrantless inspections are not "necessary" because other alternatives exist.

9. BORDER SEARCHES

United States v. Cano

934 F.3d 1002 (9th Cir. 2019)

OPINION

■ BYBEE, CIRCUIT JUDGE:

Defendant-Appellant Miguel Cano was arrested for carrying cocaine as he attempted to cross into the United States from Mexico at the San Ysidro Port of Entry. Following his arrest, a Customs and Border Protection official seized Cano's cell phone and searched it, first manually and then using software that accesses all text messages, contacts, call logs, media, and application data. When Cano moved to suppress the evidence obtained from the warrantless searches of his cell phone, the district court held that the searches were valid under the border search exception to the Fourth Amendment's warrant requirement.

Applying United States v. Cotterman, 709 F.3d 952 (9th Cir. 2013) (en banc), we conclude that *manual* cell phone searches may be conducted by border officials without reasonable suspicion but that *forensic* cell phone searches require reasonable suspicion. We clarify *Cotterman* by holding that "reasonable suspicion" in this context means that officials must reasonably suspect that the cell phone contains digital contraband. We further conclude that cell phone searches at the border, whether manual or forensic, must be limited in scope to a search for digital contraband. In this case, the officials violated the Fourth Amendment when their warrantless searches exceeded the permissible scope of a border search. Accordingly, we hold that most of the evidence from the searches of Cano's cell phone should have been suppressed. We also conclude that Cano's *Brady* claims are unpersuasive. Because we vacate Cano's conviction, we do not reach his claim of prosecutorial misconduct.

We reverse the district court's order denying Cano's motion to suppress and vacate Cano's conviction.

I. THE BACKGROUND

A. *The Facts*

Defendant-Appellant Miguel Cano worked in the flooring and carpet installation trade and lived with his wife and children in the Mission Hills community north of Los Angeles. In the summer of 2016, however, Cano moved from Los Angeles to Tijuana, Mexico, where he stayed with his cousin Jose Medina. While staying with Medina, Cano crossed the border into the United States six times, sometimes remaining in the United States for less than thirty minutes. On two of those trips, Cano was referred to secondary inspection, but no contraband was found.

On July 25, 2016, Cano arrived at the San Ysidro Port of Entry from Tijuana. In primary inspection, Cano stated that "he was living in Mexico, working in San Diego, but going to LA on that day." Pursuant to a random Customs and Border Protection (CBP) computer referral, Cano was referred to secondary inspection, where a narcotic-detecting dog alerted to the vehicle's spare tire. A CBP official removed the spare tire from the undercarriage of the truck and discovered 14 vacuum-sealed packages inside, containing 14.03 kilograms (30.93 pounds) of cocaine.

Cano was arrested, and a CBP official administratively seized his cell phone. The CBP officials called Homeland Security Investigations (HSI), which dispatched Agents Petonak and Medrano to investigate. After arriving, Agent Petonak "briefly" and manually reviewed Cano's cell phone, noticing a "lengthy call log" but no text messages. Agent Petonak later stated that the purpose of this manual search was "two-pronged": "to find some brief investigative leads in the current case," and "to see if there's evidence of other things coming across the border."

Agent Petonak proceeded to question Cano, who waived his *Miranda* rights and agreed to talk. During that interview, Cano denied any knowledge of the cocaine. Cano stated that he had moved to Tijuana to look for work in nearby San Diego, because work was slow in Los Angeles. He also said he had crossed the border every day for the previous three weeks looking for work. He told Agent Petonak that he was headed to a carpet store in Chula Vista that day to seek work. When pressed, Cano was not able to provide the name or address of the store, claiming that he intended to look it up on Google after crossing the border. Cano also explained that he did not have his flooring tools with him in his pickup truck so as to avoid problems with border crossings; Cano intended to drive to Los Angeles to retrieve his tools if he located work in San Diego.

During the interrogation, Agent Petonak specifically asked Cano about the lack of text messages on his cell phone. Cano responded that his cousin had advised him to delete his text messages "just in case" he got pulled over in Mexico and police were to check his cell phone. Cano stated that he erased his messages to avoid "any problems" with the Mexican police.

While Agent Petonak questioned Cano, Agent Medrano conducted a second manual search of the cell phone. Agent Medrano browsed the call log and wrote down some of the phone numbers on a piece of paper. He also noticed two messages that arrived after Cano had reached the border, and he took a photograph of the messages. The first message stated, "Good morning," and the second message stated, "Primo, are you coming to the house?" Agent Medrano gave all of this information—the recorded list of calls and the photograph—to Agent Petonak.

Finally, Agent Medrano conducted a "logical download" of the phone using Cellebrite software. A Cellebrite search enables the user to access text messages, contacts, call logs, media, and application data on a cell phone and to select which types of data to download. It does not, however, allow the user to access data stored within third-party applications. Agent Medrano typically does not select the option to download photographs.

After Agent Petonak interviewed Cano, he reviewed the results of the Cellebrite download of Cano's phone by Agent Medrano. The Cellebrite results revealed that Cano had sent no text messages, and it listed all the calls made by Cano. Agent Petonak later concluded that none of the phone numbers in the call log corresponded to carpeting stores in San Diego.

B. *The Proceedings*

Cano was indicted for importing cocaine. Before trial, Cano moved to suppress any evidence obtained from Agents Petonak and Medrano's warrantless searches of his cell phone at the border. The district court denied Cano's motion, ruling that the manual searches and the Cellebrite search of Cano's phone were valid border searches. During trial, the government introduced evidence that resulted from the manual searches of the phone and from Agent Medrano's Cellebrite download of the phone.[1]

In preparation for trial, Cano indicated his intent to present a third-party culpability defense claiming that his cousin, Jose Medina, was responsible for placing the drugs in Cano's spare tire without Cano's knowledge. Cano proffered evidence that Medina had a key to Cano's car and had driven it shortly before Cano's attempted border crossing, that Medina had a criminal record including a conviction for cocaine possession, that Medina was a member of a Chicago-based gang called the Latin Kings, and that the Latin Kings sold cocaine within the United

---

[1] Some—but not all—of the evidence was available through alternative channels. For example, the government introduced a call log, unchallenged by Cano, that the government received from Cano's phone company. Similarly, the government later obtained a warrant to search the phone, and an agent conducted further searches. Because the government introduced at trial much evidence pre-dating those events, and because the government has not argued that any Fourth Amendment error was harmless, those later events do not affect our Fourth Amendment analysis of the warrantless searches. *United States v. Rodriguez*, 880 F.3d 1151, 1163 (9th Cir. 2018)

States and were involved with a cartel that trafficked drugs across the border.

Following Cano's implication of Medina, the government contacted Medina and promised him immunity and immigration papers in exchange for his cooperation. Medina initially denied being involved with drugs, but later contacted the government on his own and offered to help them with the "biggest RICO case" and "drug seizures of 20 to 25 kilograms at a time." All of this information was made available to Cano.

As part of his defense, Cano sought additional discovery from HSI, the Federal Bureau of Investigation (FBI), and the Drug Enforcement Agency (DEA) . . . .

The case proceeded to trial and Cano presented his third-party culpability defense. The first trial resulted in a hung jury and a mistrial. On retrial, Cano again relied on his third-party culpability defense. The second trial resulted in Cano's conviction. This appeal followed, in which Cano raises three issues: (1) whether the warrantless searches of his cell phone violated the Fourth Amendment and whether the resulting evidence should be suppressed; (2) whether the government's non-disclosure of materials that may have been held by the DEA and FBI violated his right to due process under *Brady* and Federal Rule of Criminal Procedure 16; and (3) whether the government raised an improper propensity inference in its closing argument. We address Cano's first two arguments in turn. Because we conclude that the district court erred in denying Cano's motion to suppress, we vacate Cano's conviction and do not reach his claim of prosecutorial misconduct.

II.   THE WARRANTLESS SEARCH OF CANO'S CELL PHONE

The Fourth Amendment protects "[t]he right of the people to be secure in their persons, houses, papers, and effects, against unreasonable searches and seizures." U.S. Const. amend. IV. Ordinarily, before conducting a search, police must obtain a warrant issued by a judicial officer based "upon probable cause, supported by Oath or affirmation, and particularly describing the place to be searched, and the persons or things to be seized." *Id.* Warrants are generally required "unless 'the exigencies of the situation' make the needs of law enforcement so compelling that the warrantless search is objectively reasonable under the Fourth Amendment." Mincey v. Arizona, 437 U.S. 385, 393–94 (1978) (citation omitted). Consequently, "searches conducted outside the judicial process, without prior approval by judge or magistrate, are *per se* unreasonable under the Fourth Amendment—subject only to a few specifically established and well-delineated exceptions." Katz v. United States, 389 U.S. 347, 357 (1967) (footnote omitted). Such "specifically established and well-delineated exceptions" include exigent circumstances, searches incident to arrest, vehicle searches, and border searches. *See* Arizona v. Gant, 556 U.S. 332, 343 (2009) (vehicle searches); Brigham City v. Stuart, 547 U.S. 398, 403 (2006) (exigent circumstances; listing other exceptions, including warrantless entry to fight a fire, to prevent the imminent destruction of evidence, or in "hot pursuit" of a fleeing suspect); United States v. Ramsey, 431 U.S. 606, 616 (1977) (border searches); Weeks v. United States, 232 U.S. 383, 392 (1914) (searches incident to arrest), *overruled in part on other grounds by* Mapp v. Ohio, 367 U.S. 643 (1961).

Exceptions to the warrant requirement are subject to two important constraints. First, any search conducted under an exception must be within the *scope* of the exception. Second, some searches, even when conducted within the scope of the exception, are so *intrusive* that they require additional justification, up to and including probable cause and a warrant.

The first constraint is illustrated by the Supreme Court's decision in Riley v. California, 573 U.S. 373 (2014), a case involving the search incident to arrest exception. In *Riley*, the Court addressed "whether the police may, without a warrant, search digital information on a cell phone seized from an individual who has been arrested"; in other words, whether cell phones fell within the scope of the search incident to arrest exception. *Id.* at 378. The Court began by recognizing the increasing role in our lives of "minicomputers that also happen to have the capacity to be used as a telephone"; "[m]odern cell phones, as a category, implicate privacy concerns far beyond those implicated by the search of a cigarette pack, a wallet, or a purse." *Id.* at 393. Acknowledging that "it has been well accepted that [a search incident to lawful arrest] constitutes an exception to the warrant requirement," *id.* at 382, the Court pointed out that such searches serve two purposes: (1) to secure "the officer's safety" and (2) to "prevent . . . concealment or destruction [of evidence]," *id.* at 383 (citation omitted). The Court then considered whether a cell phone search qualified as a search incident to arrest by considering "whether application of the search incident to arrest doctrine to [cell phones] would 'untether the rule from the justifications underlying the . . . exception.'" *Id.* at 386 (quoting *Gant*, 556 U.S. at 343).

The Court concluded that neither purpose for the search incident to arrest exception justified the search of a cell phone. The Court rejected the government's argument that searching a cell phone incident to arrest would "help ensure officer safety in . . . indirect ways, for example by alerting officers that confederates of the arrestee are headed to the scene." *Id.* at 387. The Court reasoned that the government's position "would . . . represent a broadening" of the exception's foundational concern that "an *arrestee himself* might grab a weapon and use it against an officer." *Id.* at 387–88. The Court observed that "once law enforcement officers have secured a cell phone, there is no longer any risk that the arrestee himself will be able to delete incriminating data from the phone," *id.* at 388, and police have means to ensure that data cannot be wiped from the phone remotely, *id.* at 390. The Court concluded "not that the information on a cell phone is immune from search; [but rather] that a warrant is generally required before such a search, even when a cell phone is seized incident to arrest." *Id.* at 401.

The second constraint on warrantless searches is illustrated by the Court's decision in United States v. Montoya de Hernandez, 473 U.S. 531 (1985). Montoya was stopped at Los Angeles International Airport and referred to secondary inspection. *Id.* at 533. She had arrived from Bogota and was carrying $5,000 in cash. *Id.* She had no credit cards and no hotel reservations. *Id.* at 533–34. Because border officials suspected that Montoya may have swallowed cocaine-filled balloons, Montoya was held in the customs office and, after a magistrate judge issued an order, taken to a hospital for a rectal examination. *Id.* at 534–35. Over the next four days, she passed 88 balloons containing cocaine. *Id.* at 536. Montoya argued that the search she was subjected to, though a border search, was so intrusive that it could not be conducted without a high level of particularized suspicion. *Id.* at 536–37. The Court balanced her privacy interests against the interests of the government at the border and concluded that, while routine searches may be conducted at the border without any showing of suspicion, a more intrusive, nonroutine search must be supported by "reasonable suspicion." *Id.* at 537–41; *see also* United States v. Flores-Montano, 541 U.S. 149, 152 (2004) (suggesting that nonroutine searches are limited to "highly intrusive searches of the person" involving "dignity and privacy interests").

Cano recognizes that he was subject to search at the border, but Cano and amicus Electronic Frontier Foundation ("EFF") raise two categorical challenges and one as-applied challenge to the searches conducted here. First, EFF argues that any warrantless search of a cell phone falls outside the scope of the border search exception. Second, EFF argues that even if the search is within the scope of the border search exception, a warrantless cell phone search is so intrusive that it requires probable cause. We address these categorical challenges in Part II.A. Third, Cano asserts that, even if cell phones are generally subject to search at the border, the manual and forensic searches of *his* cell phone exceeded the "well delineated" scope of the border search. We address this as-applied question in Part II.B. Finally, the government argues that even if the border search exceeded the limits of the Fourth Amendment, the search was conducted in good faith, and the evidence is admissible. We consider the good faith exception in Part II.C.

A.   *Border Searches and Cell Phones*

"[B]order searches constitute a 'historically recognized exception to the Fourth Amendment's general principle that a warrant be obtained.'" *Cotterman*, 709 F.3d at 957 (quoting *Ramsey*, 431 U.S. at 621). Indeed, border searches typically do not require any particularized suspicion, so long as they are "routine inspections and searches of individuals or conveyances seeking to cross our borders." Almeida-Sanchez v. United States, 413 U.S. 266, 272 (1973); *see* United States v. Seljan, 547 F.3d 993, 999 (9th Cir. 2008) (en banc). Such searches are "reasonable simply by virtue of the fact they occur at the border." *Ramsey*, 431 U.S. at 616. The exception is "rooted in 'the long-standing right of the sovereign to protect itself by stopping and examining persons and property crossing into this country,' " *Cotterman*, 709 F.3d at 960 (quoting *Ramsey*, 431 U.S. at 616), to "prevent[ ] the entry of unwanted persons and effects," *id.* (quoting *Flores-Montano*, 541 U.S. at 152).

The sovereign's right to conduct suspicionless searches at the border "does not mean, however, that at the border 'anything goes.' " *Id.* (quoting *Seljan*, 547 F.3d at 1000). Rather, the border search exception is a "narrow exception" that is limited in two important ways. *Id.* (citation omitted). First, "[t]he authorizing statute limits the persons who may legally conduct a 'border search' to 'persons authorized to board or search vessels.' " United States v. Soto-Soto, 598 F.2d 545, 549 (9th Cir. 1979) (citing 19 U.S.C. § 482).[4] This includes customs and immigration officials, but not general law enforcement officers such as FBI agents. *Id.*; *see* United States v. Diamond, 471 F.2d 771, 773 (9th Cir. 1973) (stating that "customs agents are not general guardians of the public peace"). Second, a border search must be conducted "in enforcement of customs laws." *Soto-Soto*, 598 F.2d at 549. A border search must be conducted to "enforce importation laws," and not for "general law enforcement purposes." *Id.* A general search cannot be "justif[ied] . . . on the mere basis that it occurred at the border." *Id.* (affirming the suppression of evidence where an FBI agent stopped and searched the vehicle of an alien to determine whether the car had been stolen).

1.   Cell Phone Data as Contraband

As we discussed briefly above, the Supreme Court has identified two principal purposes behind warrantless border searches: First, to identify "[t]ravellers . . . entitled to come in" and, second, to verify their "belongings as effects which may be lawfully brought in." Carroll v. United States, 267 U.S. 132, 154 (1925); *see Ramsey*, 431 U.S. at 620

---

4   Section 482 now reads in relevant part:

Any of the officers or persons authorized to board or search vessels may stop, search, and examine . . . any vehicle, beast, or person, on which or whom he or they shall suspect there is merchandise which is subject to duty, or shall have been introduced into the United States in any manner contrary to law . . . . [and may] seize and secure the same for trial.

19 U.S.C. § 482(a); *see id.* § 1467 ("[T]he appropriate customs officer for [a] port or place of arrival may . . . enforce, cause inspection, examination, and search to be made of the persons, baggage, and merchandise discharged or unladen from [an arriving] vessel . . . ."); *id.* § 1496 ("The appropriate customs officer may cause an examination to be made of the baggage of any persons arriving in the United States in order to ascertain what articles are contained therein and whether subject to duty, free of duty, or prohibited . . . ."); *id.* § 1582 ("[A]ll persons coming into the United States from foreign countries shall be liable to detention and search by authorized officers or agents . . . .").

The Court has described § 482 as granting the executive "plenary authority to conduct routine searches and seizures at the border, without probable cause or a warrant." *Montoya de Hernandez*, 473 U.S. at 537. We have held that the "outer limits of authority delegated by [§ 482 are] available only in border searches." Corngold v. United States, 367 F.2d 1, 3 (9th Cir. 1966) (en banc).

("The border-search exception is grounded in the recognized right of the sovereign to control . . . who and what may enter the country.").

EFF argues that applying the border search exception to a cell phone's data would "untether" the exception from the purposes underlying it. EFF contends that a border search encompasses only a search for illegal persons and *physical contraband* located on the body of the applicant for admission or among his effects. Because digital data on a cell phone cannot conceal objects such as drugs, guns, or smuggled persons, EFF asserts that digital cell phone searches are always beyond the scope of the border search exception.

We agree with EFF that the purpose of the border search is to interdict contraband, but we disagree with its premise that cell phones cannot contain contraband. Although cell phone data cannot hide physical objects,[5] the data can contain *digital contraband*. The best example is child pornography. *See* United States v. Molina-Isidoro, 884 F.3d 287, 295 n.3 (5th Cir. 2018) (Costa, J., specially concurring) ("One type of contraband that can be stored within the data of a cell phone . . . is child pornography."). And because cell phones may ultimately be released into the interior, even if the owner has been detained, the United States has a strong interest in preventing the entry of such material. *See, e.g.*, United States v. Vergara, 884 F.3d 1309, 1311 (11th Cir.) (2018) (describing how agents returned one of the defendant's phones to a family member after defendant had been arrested for possessing child pornography on his other two phones). We find no basis for the proposition that the border search exception is limited to searching for physical contraband. At the very least, a cell phone that has photos stored on it is the equivalent of photographs, magazines, and books.[6] *See Riley*, 573 U.S. at 394; *Cotterman*, 709 F.3d at 964. The contents may be digital when they are on the phone, but the physicality of the phone itself and the possibility that the phone's contents can be printed or shared electronically gives border officials sufficient reason to inspect it at the border. We conclude that cell phones—including the phones' data—are subject to search at the border.

2.   Forensic Cell Phone Searches as an Intrusive Search

The second question we must address in response to amicus EFF is whether forensic searches of a cell phone are so intrusive that they require reasonable suspicion or even probable cause. We answered this

---

[5]   No one contests that a border official could, consistent with the Fourth Amendment, examine the physical body of a cell phone to see if the phone itself is contraband—because, for example, it is a pirated copy of a patented U.S. phone—or if the phone itself presents a physical threat to officers. *See Riley*, 573 U.S. at 387 ("Law enforcement officers remain free to examine the physical aspects of a phone to ensure that it will not be used as a weapon—say, to determine whether there is a razor blade hidden between the phone and its case."). The dispute here concerns only whether border officials may search the digital data contained within the phone.

[6]   We need not address here questions surrounding the use of "cloud computing," where the phone gives access to, but does not contain in its own memory, digital data stored in the cloud. *See Riley*, 573 U.S. at 397–98; *Cotterman*, 709 F.3d at 965 & n.12.

question in our en banc decision in *Cotterman*, but with respect to laptop computers.[7] *Cotterman*, 709 F.3d at 962–68. Cotterman was a United States citizen returning to the United States from Mexico. *Id.* at 957. When he reached the port of entry, border officials noted that Cotterman had various convictions for sexual conduct with children. *Id.* Concerned that Cotterman might be involved in child sex tourism, officials conducted a brief search of his laptop computers and digital cameras and noted that the laptops had password-protected files. *Id.* at 958. The officials detained the computers for several days in order to run a comprehensive forensic search of the hard drive, which revealed hundreds of images of child pornography. *Id.* at 958–59. For us, "the legitimacy of the initial search of Cotterman's electronic devices at the border [was] not in doubt," *id.* at 960, "[t]he difficult question . . . [was] the reasonableness, without a warrant, of the forensic examination that comprehensively analyzed the hard drive of the computer," *id.* at 961.

We acknowledged the "substantial personal privacy interests" in "[e]lectronic devices . . . capable of storing warehouses full of information." *Id.* at 964. At the same time, we recognized "the important security concerns that prevail at the border" and the legitimacy of "[t]he effort to interdict child pornography." *Id.* at 966. We held that a routine, manual search of files on a laptop computer—"a quick look and unintrusive search"—is reasonable "even without particularized suspicion," but that officials must "possess a particularized and objective basis for suspecting the person stopped of criminal activity" to engage in a forensic examination, which is "essentially a computer strip search." *Id.* at 960–61, 966, 967 (citation omitted). We concluded that reasonable suspicion was "a modest, workable standard that is already applied in the extended border search, *Terry* stop, and other contexts." *Id.* at 966; *see id.* at 968 (defining reasonable suspicion as "a particularized and objective basis for suspecting the particular person stopped of criminal activity" (quoting United States v. Cortez, 449 U.S. 411, 417–18 (1981))).

We think that *Cotterman*'s reasoning applies equally to cell phones. In large measure, we anticipated the Supreme Court's reasoning in *Riley*, 573 U.S. at 393–97, when we recognized in *Cotterman* that digital devices "contain the most intimate details of our lives" and "the uniquely sensitive nature of data on electronic devices carries with it a significant expectation of privacy," *Cotterman*, 709 F.3d at 965–66; *see Riley*, 573 U.S. at 385 (describing cell phones as "a pervasive and insistent part of daily life" that, "as a category, implicate privacy concerns far beyond those implicated by the search of a cigarette pack, a wallet, or a purse"). The Court's view of cell phones in *Riley* so closely resembles our own

---

[7] Although *Cotterman* referred to "electronic devices" generally, *see* 709 F.3d at 962–68, our holding was limited to the "examination of Cotterman's computer," *id.* at 968, and did not address cell phones. We mentioned cell phones only once—in the first paragraph of the introduction describing the modern "digital world." *Id.* at 956.

analysis of laptop computers in *Cotterman* that we find no basis to distinguish a forensic cell phone search from a forensic laptop search.[8]

Nor do we believe that *Riley* renders the *Cotterman* standard insufficiently protective. *Riley*, of course, held that "a warrant is generally required" before searching a cell phone, "even when a cell phone is seized incident to arrest." 573 U.S. at 401. But here we deal with the border search exception—not the search incident to arrest exception—and the difference in context is critical. In light of the government's enhanced interest in protecting the "integrity of the border" and the individual's decreased expectation of privacy, the Court has emphasized that "the Fourth Amendment's balance of reasonableness is qualitatively different at the international border than in the interior" and is "struck much more favorably to the Government." *Montoya de Hernandez*, 473 U.S. at 538–40. As a result, post-*Riley*, no court has required more than reasonable suspicion to justify even an intrusive border search. *See* United States v. Wanjiku, 919 F.3d 472, 485 (7th Cir. 2019) ("[N]o circuit court, before or after *Riley*, has required more than reasonable suspicion for a border search of cell phones or electronically-stored data."); *Touset*, 890 F.3d at 1234 ("*Riley*, which involved the search-incident-to-arrest exception, does not apply to searches at the border."); *Molina-Isidoro*, 884 F.3d at 291 ("For border searches both routine and not, no case has required a warrant."); *id.* at 293 ("The bottom line is that only two of the many federal cases addressing border searches of electronic devices have ever required any level of suspicion. They both required only reasonable suspicion and that was for the more intrusive forensic search."); *see also* United States v. Kolsuz, 890 F.3d 133, 137 (4th Cir. 2018) (concluding that a "forensic examination of Kolsuz's phone must be considered a nonroutine border search, requiring some measure of individualized suspicion" but declining to decide whether the standard should be reasonable suspicion or probable cause).

Accordingly, we hold that manual searches of cell phones at the border are reasonable without individualized suspicion, whereas the forensic examination of a cell phone requires a showing of reasonable suspicion. *See Cotterman*, 709 F.3d at 968.

B.   *The Searches of Cano's Cell Phone and the Scope of the Border Search Exception*

Having concluded that border officials may conduct suspicionless manual searches of cell phones, but must have reasonable suspicion before they conduct a forensic search, we still must address the core of Cano's argument: whether the manual and forensic searches of his cell

---

[8]   We note that the Eleventh Circuit disagreed with *Cotterman* in *United States v. Touset*, 890 F.3d 1227, 1234 (11th Cir. 2018). The court held that no level of suspicion was required to conduct a forensic search of a cell phone. *Id.* at 1234–35. Nevertheless, the *Touset* court held, in the alternative, that the forensic search of various electronic devices seized at the border were supported by reasonable suspicion. *Id.* at 1237. As with most cell phone search cases, in *Touset* border agents were looking for child pornography.

phone were not searches for digital contraband, but searches for evidence of a crime, and thus exceeded the proper scope of a border search.

1.   The Border Exception and the Search for Contraband

As a threshold matter, Cano argues that border searches are limited in both purpose and scope to searches for contraband.[9] In response, the government argues that searches for evidence that would aid in prosecuting past and preventing future border-related crimes are tethered to the purpose of the border search exception—namely, interdicting foreign contraband—and thus fall within its scope.

This is a close question, but we think Cano has the better of the argument. There is a difference between a search for contraband and a search for evidence of border-related crimes, although the distinction may not be apparent. *Cotterman* helps us focus on the difference. There, border officials had been alerted that Cotterman had a criminal record of sex abuse of minors and might be involved in "child sex tourism." *Cotterman*, 709 F.3d at 957. The officials seized his laptop and subjected it to searches for child pornography, which they found. In *Cotterman*, the child pornography was contraband subject to seizure at the border. As contraband, the child pornography is *also* evidence of various crimes, including possession of child pornography, 18 U.S.C. § 2252A(a)(5)(B), and importation of obscene material, 18 U.S.C. § 1462(a). But nothing in *Cotterman* authorized border officials to conduct a search for evidence that Cotterman was involved in sex-related crimes generally.

Border officials are authorized to seize "*merchandise* which . . . shall have been introduced into the United States in any manner contrary to law." 19 U.S.C. § 482(a) (emphasis added). The photos on Cotterman's laptop computer were such merchandise. 18 U.S.C. § 2252(a). But border officials have no general authority to search for crime. This is true even if there is a possibility that such crimes may be perpetrated at the border in the future. So, for example, if U.S. officials reasonably suspect that a

---

[9]   Cano emphasizes that the officials who arrested him were looking for evidence of a crime, not contraband that could be seized at the border, and this renders the search unconstitutional. He points to Officers Petonak and Medrano, who searched Cano's cell phone, and who testified that their searches had a dual purpose: "to find some brief investigative leads in the current case" and "to see if there[ ] [was] evidence of other things coming across the border." Because the agents acknowledged that they sought evidence to use against Cano in building a criminal case, Cano argues that the court should treat the search as one conducted for "general law enforcement purposes" rather than a border search.

Cano's focus on the officials' subjective motivations is misplaced, however. As the district court recognized, "courts have repeatedly held that the Fourth Amendment's reasonableness analysis is 'predominantly an objective inquiry.'" *See* Whren v. United States, 517 U.S. 806, 813 (1996) (upholding a "pretextual" stop because "[s]ubjective intentions play no role in ordinary . . . Fourth Amendment analysis"). We have upheld border searches of persons seeking entry even when those searches were conducted "at the behest" of DEA agents seeking criminal evidence. *See* United States v. Schoor, 597 F.2d 1303, 1305–06 (9th Cir. 1979) (holding a border search reasonable where it was conducted "at the behest" of DEA agents and included a search for certain items of evidence in addition to a search for contraband). Thus, the mere fact that Officers Petonak and Medrano subjectively hoped to find "investigative leads" pertaining to the seized shipment of cocaine does not render their searches of Cano's phone beyond the border search exception.

person who has presented himself at the border may be engaged in price fixing, *see* 15 U.S.C. § 1, they may not conduct a forensic search of his phone or laptop. Evidence of price fixing—texts or emails, for example— is not itself contraband whose importation is prohibited by law. Such emails may be evidence of a crime, but they are not contraband, and there is no law prohibiting the importation of mere evidence of crime.

We recognize that our analysis is in tension with the Fourth Circuit's decision in *Kolsuz.* Kolsuz was detained at Washington Dulles International Airport when customs agents discovered firearm parts in his luggage. *Kolsuz*, 890 F.3d at 138–39. Kolsuz was arrested and his cell phone seized. *Id.* at 139. The agents subjected the phone to a month-long forensic search, producing a 896-page report. *Id.* Kolsuz challenged the search, which the district court upheld and the Fourth Circuit affirmed. *Id.* at 139–42. The court approved the forensic search because the agents had "reason to believe . . . that Kolsuz was attempting to export firearms illegally" and that "their search would reveal not only evidence of the export violation they already had detected, but also 'information related to other ongoing attempts to export illegally various firearm parts.'" *Id.* at 143 (quoting the district court; citation omitted). According to the Fourth Circuit, "[t]he justification behind the border search exception is broad enough to accommodate not only the direct interception of contraband as it crosses the border, but also *the prevention and disruption of ongoing efforts to export contraband illegally.*" *Id.* (emphasis added).[10]

We agree with much of the Fourth Circuit's discussion of foundational principles, but we respectfully disagree with the final step approving the search for further evidence that Kolsuz was smuggling weapons. Our disagreement focuses precisely on the critical question that we previously identified: Does the proper scope of a border search include the power to search for *evidence* of contraband that is *not* present at the border? Or, put differently, can border agents conduct a warrantless search for evidence of past or future border-related crimes? We think that the answer must be "no." The "[d]etection of . . . contraband is the strongest historic rationale for the border-search exception." *Molina-Isidoro*, 884 F.3d at 295 (Costa, J., specially concurring). Indeed, "every border-search case the Supreme Court has decided involved searches to locate *items being smuggled*" rather than evidence. *Id.* (emphasis added); *see Montoya de Hernandez*, 473 U.S. at 537 (the border search is "to prevent the introduction of contraband into this country"); United States v. 12 200-Foot Reels of Super 8mm. Film, 413 U.S. 123, 125 (1973) (border

---

[10] As support for this proposition, the Fourth Circuit cited two district court cases originating within our circuit. Both of those cases addressed fact-patterns almost identical to Cano's, and in each case the district court held that the border-search exception was not limited to searching for contraband directly. *See* United States v. Mendez, 240 F. Supp. 3d 1005, 1007– 08 (D. Ariz. 2017); United States v. Ramos, 190 F. Supp. 3d 992, 999 (S.D. Cal. 2016). In neither case was the issue appealed to our circuit. Thus, Cano's case presents the first opportunity for us to consider the matter.

searches are "necessary to prevent smuggling and to prevent prohibited articles from entry"); United States v. Thirty-Seven Photographs, 402 U.S. 363, 376 (1971) ("Customs officers characteristically inspect luggage and their power to do so is not questioned in this case; it is an old practice and is intimately associated with excluding illegal articles from the country"). In fact, the Court has long "draw[n] a sharp distinction between searches for contraband and those for evidence that may reveal the importation of contraband." *Molina-Isidoro*, 884 F.3d at 296 (Costa, J., specially concurring). The classic statement on the distinction between seizing goods at the border because their importation is prohibited and seizing goods at the border because they may be useful in prosecuting crimes is found in *Boyd v. United States*:

> Is a search and seizure, or, what is equivalent thereto, a compulsory production of a man's private papers, to be used in evidence against him in a proceeding to forfeit his property for alleged fraud against the revenue laws—is such a proceeding for such a purpose an *"unreasonable* search and seizure" within the meaning of the fourth amendment of the constitution? . . . . The search for and seizure of stolen or forfeited goods, or goods liable to duties and concealed to avoid the payment thereof, are totally different things from a search for and seizure of a man's private books and papers for the purpose of obtaining information therein contained, or of using them as evidence against him. The two things differ *toto coelo*.

116 U.S. 616, 622–23 (1886), *overruled in part on other grounds by* Warden, Md. Penitentiary v. Hayden, 387 U.S. 294 (1967); *see also id.* at 633 (stating that compelling a man to produce the evidence against himself not only violates the Fifth Amendment, but makes the seizure of his "books and papers" unreasonable under the Fourth Amendment).

Although we continue to acknowledge that "[t]he Government's interest in preventing the entry of unwanted persons and effects is at its zenith at the international border" and that "the expectation of privacy is less at the border than it is in the interior," *Flores-Montano*, 541 U.S. at 152, 154, we hold that the border search exception authorizes warrantless searches of a cell phone only to determine whether the phone contains contraband. A broader search cannot be "justified by the particular purposes served by the exception." *Florida v. Royer*, 460 U.S. 491, 500 (1983).

2.   The Impact of a Limited Scope for Border Searches

Our conclusion that the border search exception is restricted in scope to searches for contraband implicates two practical limitations on warrantless border searches. First, border officials are limited to searching for contraband only; they may not search in a manner untethered to the search for contraband. The Supreme Court has repeatedly emphasized that "[t]he scope of the search must be 'strictly tied to and justified by' the circumstances which rendered its initiation permissible." *Terry v. Ohio*, 392 U.S. 1, 19 (1968).

The validity of the manual searches conducted by Agents Petonak and Medrano *at their inception* is beyond dispute. Manual searches of a cell phone at the border can be conducted without any suspicion whatsoever, *see Cotterman*, 709 F.3d at 960, and both agents were officers of HSI and thus had authority to conduct border searches, *Soto-Soto*, 598 F.2d at 548–49. As the Supreme Court explained in *Terry*, however, "a search which is reasonable at its inception may violate the Fourth Amendment by virtue of its intolerable intensity and scope." 392 U.S. at 18.

Once Cano was arrested, Agent Petonak briefly searched Cano's phone and observed that there were no text messages. The observation that the phone contained no text messages falls comfortably within the scope of a search for digital contraband. Child pornography may be sent via text message, so the officers acted within the scope of a permissible border search in accessing the phone's text messages.

Agent Medrano conducted a second manual search of the phone log and text messages on Cano's phone. Medrano, however, did more than thumb through the phone consistent with a search for contraband. He also recorded phone numbers found in the call log, and he photographed two messages received after Cano had reached the border. Those actions have no connection whatsoever to digital contraband. Criminals may hide contraband in unexpected places, so it was reasonable for the two HSI officers to open the phone's call log to verify that the log contained a list of phone numbers and not surreptitious images or videos. But the border search exception does not justify Agent Medrano's recording of the phone numbers and text messages for further processing, because that action has no connection to ensuring that the phone lacks digital contraband. Accordingly, to the extent that Agent Medrano's search of Cano's phone went beyond a verification that the phone lacked digital contraband, the search exceeded the proper scope of a border search and was unreasonable as a border search under the Fourth Amendment.[11]

---

[11] The fact of Cano's arrest does not affect our analysis. The border search does not lose its identity as such once Cano was arrested. The United States retains a strong interest in preventing contraband from entering the United States, whether it is brought in inadvertently, smuggled, or admitted into the United States once its owner is arrested. *See* United States v. Ickes, 393 F.3d 501, 503–05 (4th Cir. 2005) (upholding the post-arrest search of a laptop computer at the border where the officials had reason to suspect the computer carried child pornography); *see also* United States v. Bates, 526 F.2d 966, 967–68 (5th Cir. 1976) (per curiam) (upholding a search of the defendant's vehicle after he had been arrested at the border for violating his bond in connection with a previous drug crime under both the search incident to arrest *and* the border search exception).

The government has not argued that the forensic search of Cano's phone can be justified as a search incident to lawful arrest. Such an argument is foreclosed by *Riley. See Riley*, 573 U.S. at 388–91. Nor has the government argued that once Medrano saw the phone numbers in the call log and the text messages that he could record them consistent with the plain view exception. *See* United States v. Comprehensive Drug Testing, 621 F.3d 1162, 1175–77 (9th Cir. 2010) (en

Second, because the border search exception is limited in scope to searches for contraband, border officials may conduct a forensic cell phone search only when they reasonably suspect that the cell phone contains contraband. We have held that a "highly intrusive" search—such as a forensic cell phone search—requires some level of particularized suspicion. *Cotterman*, 709 F.3d at 963, 968; *see Flores-Montano*, 541 U.S. at 152. But that just begs the question: Particularized suspicion of what? Contraband? Or evidence of future border-related crimes? Having concluded above that border searches are limited in scope to searches for contraband and do not encompass searches for evidence of past or future border-related crimes, we think the answer here is clear: to conduct a more intrusive, forensic cell phone search border officials must reasonably suspect that the cell phone to be searched itself contains contraband.

Were we to rule otherwise, the government could conduct a full forensic search of every electronic device of anyone arrested at the border, for the probable cause required to justify an arrest at the border will always satisfy the lesser reasonable suspicion standard needed to justify a forensic search. As the Court pointed out in *Riley*, modern cell phones are "minicomputers" with "immense storage capacity." 573 U.S. at 393. Such phones "carry a cache of sensitive personal information"—"[t]he sum of an individual's private life"—such that a search of a cell phone may give the government not only "sensitive records previously found in the home," but a "broad array of private information never found in a home in any form—unless the phone is." *Id.* at 393–97. Were we to give the government unfettered access to cell phones, we would enable the government to evade the protections laid out in *Riley* "on the mere basis that [the searches] occurred at the border." *Soto-Soto*, 598 F.2d at 549.

Moreover, in cases such as this, where the individual suspected of committing the border-related crime has already been arrested, there is no reason why border officials cannot obtain a warrant before conducting their forensic search. This "is particularly true in light of 'advances' in technology that now permit 'the more expeditious processing of warrant applications.' " Birchfield v. North Dakota, ___ U.S. ___ (2016) (quoting Missouri v. McNeely, 569 U.S. 141, 154 (2013)); *see Riley*, 573 U.S. at 401. Indeed, in most cases the time required to obtain a warrant would seem trivial compared to the hours, days, and weeks needed to complete a forensic electronic search. *See, e.g.*, *Wanjiku*, 919 F.3d at 477 (noting that a forensic "preview" takes one to three hours; the full examination "could take months"); *Kolsuz*, 890 F.3d at 139 (describing how the forensic search "lasted for a full month, and yielded an 896-page report"); *Cotterman*, 709 F.3d at 959 (describing how the first forensic search was conducted over five days; additional evidence was found "[o]ver the next few months"). We therefore conclude that border officials may conduct a

banc) (per curiam), *overruled in part on other grounds as recognized by* Demaree v. Pederson, 887 F.3d 870, 876 (9th Cir. 2018) (per curiam).

forensic cell phone search only when they reasonably suspect that the cell phone to be searched itself contains contraband.

Applied here, if the Cellebrite search of Cano's cell phone qualifies as a forensic search, the entire search was unreasonable under the Fourth Amendment.[12] Although Agents Petonak and Medrano had reason to suspect that Cano's phone would contain evidence leading to additional drugs, the record does not give rise to any objectively reasonable suspicion that the digital data in the phone contained contraband.[13] Absent reasonable suspicion, the border search exception did not authorize the agents to conduct a warrantless forensic search of Cano's phone, and evidence obtained through a forensic search should be suppressed.

C. *Good Faith Exception*

We next consider whether the evidence uncovered by the searches is nevertheless allowed by the good faith exception. Having held that the manual searches partially violated the Fourth Amendment and having held that, if the Cellebrite search of Cano's phone was a forensic search, it violated the Fourth Amendment, we must determine whether the appropriate remedy is suppression of the evidence. The exclusionary rule is "a 'prudential' doctrine"; it is " 'not a personal constitutional right,' nor is it designed to 'redress the injury' occasioned by an unconstitutional search." Davis v. United States, 564 U.S. 229, 236 (2011) (quoting Stone v. Powell, 428 U.S. 465, 486 (1976)). Because "[e]xclusion exacts a heavy toll on both the judicial system and society at large," we invoke the rule when we are confident that it will "deter future Fourth Amendment violations." *Id.* at 236–37. The exclusionary rule does not deter such violations "when the police conduct a search in objectively reasonable reliance on binding judicial precedent." *Id.* at 239. We have said that the good faith exception applies only to searches where "binding appellate precedent . . . 'specifically authorizes' the police's search." United States v. Lara, 815 F.3d 605, 613 (9th Cir. 2016) (quoting *Davis*, 564 U.S. at 232). It is not sufficient for the question to be "unclear" or for the government's position to be "plausibly . . . permissible." *Id.* at 613–14. At the same time, the "precedent [does not have] to constitute a factual match with the circumstances of the search in question for the good-faith

---

[12] Whether the Cellebrite search constitutes a forensic search is disputed. Because the district court passed on the issue without deciding it, because neither party has briefed the question to us, and because we are vacating Defendant's conviction, we decline to reach the merits of the parties' dispute. *See* ASSE Int'l, Inc. v. Kerry, 803 F.3d 1059, 1079 (9th Cir. 2015).

[13] Indeed, the detection-of-contraband justification would rarely seem to apply to an electronic search of a cell phone outside the context of child pornography. The courts of appeals have just begun to confront the difficult questions attending cell phone searches at the border. Most of the cases have involved child pornography. *See, e.g., Wanjiku*, 919 F.3d 472; *Touset*, 890 F.3d 1227; *Molina-Isidoro*, 884 F.3d 287; *Vergara*, 884 F.3d 1309; *Cotterman*, 709 F.3d 952. Among the courts of appeals, only the Fourth Circuit has addressed the question outside the context of pornography. *Kolsuz*, 890 F.3d 133 (exportation of firearms parts); *see also* United States v. Kim, 103 F. Supp. 3d 32 (D.D.C. 2015) (exports in violation of Iranian trade embargo); United States v. Saboonchi, 990 F. Supp. 2d 536 (D. Md. 2014) (same).

exception to apply" so as not to "make the good-faith exception a nullity." United States v. Lustig, 830 F.3d 1075, 1082 (9th Cir. 2016).

The government points to *Cotterman* as support for the good faith of the officials. We fail to see how border officials could believe that *Cotterman* was "binding appellate precedent" authorizing their search. Although we have concluded that *Cotterman* is still good law after *Riley*, the officials could not rely on *Cotterman* to justify a search for *evidence*; *Cotterman* was a search for *contraband* that the government has a right to seize at the border. Here, the officials' search was objectively tied only to proving their case against Cano and finding *evidence* of future crimes. Searching for evidence and searching for contraband are not the same thing.

We understand that border officials might have thought that their actions were reasonable, and we recognize that border officials have to make in-the-moment decisions about how to conduct their business— whether or not they have written guidance from the courts. But as we understand the *Davis* rule, the good faith exception to the exclusionary rule applies only when the officials have relied on "*binding* appellate precedent." *See Lara*, 815 F.3d at 613; *see also Wanjiku*, 919 F.3d at 485– 86 (finding that agents had reasonable suspicion to search the defendant's cell phone, laptop, and portable hard drive for child pornography; holding that, if probable cause was required, the officials acted in good faith). This is a rapidly developing area, not an area of settled law. Even if our decision in *Cotterman* rendered the searches "plausibly . . . permissible," it did not "specifically authorize" the cell phone searches at issue here. *Lara*, 815 F.3d at 613–14.

* * *

In sum, the manual searches and the Cellebrite search of Cano's cell phone exceeded the scope of a valid border search. Because the good faith exception does not apply, most of the evidence obtained from the searches of Cano's cell phone should have been suppressed. We thus reverse the district court's order denying Cano's motion to suppress, and we vacate Cano's conviction. On any retrial, the district court should determine whether any additional evidence from the warrantless searches of Cano's cell phone should be suppressed, either because the Cellebrite search qualifies as a forensic search, which the government lacked reasonable suspicion to conduct, or because the evidence exceeds the proper scope of a border search. . . .

IV. CONCLUSION

We **REVERSE** the district court's order denying Cano's motion to suppress and **VACATE** Cano's conviction.

CHAPTER 5

FOURTH AMENDMENT REMEDIES

1. HABEAS CORPUS

L.A.E. v. Davis

263 Ga. 473, 435 S.E.2d 216 (Ga. 1993)

Petitioner L.A.E. is a juvenile. He was arrested and charged with a capital felony on Saturday, March 20, 1993. On Tuesday, March 23, the juvenile court conducted a detention hearing within the 72-hour period required by OCGA § 15–11–21(c), and concluded that there existed probable cause to detain petitioner. OCGA § 15–11–18. On March 24, 1993, petitioner's counsel filed this application for habeas corpus, alleging that OCGA § 15–11–21(c), which requires a probable cause hearing in a juvenile case to be conducted within 72 hours, was unconstitutional under the authority of County of Riverside v. McLaughlin, 500 U.S. 44 (1991). In *County of Riverside* the U.S. Supreme Court held "that a jurisdiction that provides judicial determinations of probable cause within 48 hours of arrest will, as a general matter, comply with the promptness requirement" of Gerstein v. Pugh, 420 U.S. 103 (1975) and the Fourth Amendment to the U.S. Constitution. 500 U.S. at ___.

The habeas court denied the petition, concluding that *County of Riverside* does not apply here because "the state's interest in promoting the welfare of the child as *parens patriae* makes a juvenile proceeding fundamentally different from an adult criminal proceeding."

We find it unnecessary to decide whether the requirements of *Riverside* are applicable to a case involving a juvenile. Because petitioner did not file his petition for habeas corpus until after a probable cause determination had been made, the issue of whether this determination was timely is moot. *County of Riverside, supra,* 500 U.S. at ___;[1] McCranie v. Mullis, 221 Ga. 617, 146 S.E.2d 723 (1966).

Judgment affirmed.

---

[1] In *County of Riverside* the U.S. Supreme Court noted that the claims of the named petitioners were moot because the petitioners had either received probable cause determinations or been released. However, the Court held that because the claims in that case had been certified as a class action, "the termination of a class representative's claim does not moot the claims of the unnamed members of the class." *Id.*

2. DAMAGE ACTIONS UNDER STATE TORT LAW

Spears v. Akron Police Department

2010 WL 625822 (Ohio Ct. App. Feb. 24, 2010)

Appellants, City of Akron ("City") and Kevin Kabellar ("Officer Kabellar"), appeal the ruling of Summit County Court of Common Pleas which denied in part their summary judgment motion based upon sovereign immunity. For reasons set forth below, we affirm in part and reverse in part.

I.

Appellee, Gerald Spears, and his wife, Appellee, Dottie Spears, were involved in a multi-vehicle automobile accident on Friday March 24, 2007. Mr. Spears was the driver. He had a couple of drinks at his Aunt's house prior the accident. Paramedics and police were dispatched to the scene. The paramedic who responded to the Spears' vehicle noted that Mr. Spears was uncooperative and "observed that [Mr. Spears] had been drinking[.]" Officer Kabellar "observed a strong odor of alcohol about [Mr. Spears'] person [and] also observed Mr. Spears staggering and his eyes were bloodshot."

Officer Kabellar administered field sobriety tests to Mr. Spears. Mr. Spears did not complete all of the tests and the officer placed him under arrest. The parties hold different views of what took place during the process of arresting and transporting Mr. Spears to the police station. Mr. Spears alleged that Officer Kabellar's actions resulted in an injury to his left wrist. The police took Mrs. Spears home and Mrs. Spears had her daughter take her to the hospital. At the police station, Mr. Spears participated in the mobility tests, but refused to take a Breathalyzer test. Mr. Spears was then taken to the detoxification center and was later picked up there by his son and taken to the hospital to meet his wife. Mr. Spears contacted his physician concerning the injury to his left wrist that Monday. The physician referred Mr. Spears to a hand specialist who initiated conservative treatment; however, ultimately Mr. Spears was required to undergo surgery.

Mr. and Mrs. Spears filed a five-count complaint against the Akron Police Department, the City, Officer Kabellar and a John Doe Officer for (1) assault-excessive force; (2) battery-excessive force; (3) intentional infliction of emotional distress; (4) reckless infliction of emotional distress; and (5) loss of consortium. The City, Akron Police Department, and Officer Kabellar moved for summary judgment on all claims based primarily upon sovereign immunity. The trial court granted the motion as to the Akron Police Department, finding that as an entity it was not capable of being sued. The trial court also granted summary judgment as to the Spears' claim for intentional infliction of emotional distress. The trial court denied the motion with respect to the claims against the City and Officer Kabellar for assault and battery and with respect to Mrs.

Spears' claim for loss of consortium. The City and Officer Kabellar have timely appealed, raising three assignments of error for our review.

II.

ASSIGNMENT OR ERROR I

"THE TRIAL COURT ERRED IN NOT GRANTING IMMUNITY TO THE CITY OF AKRON PURSUANT TO R.C. [ ]2744.02(A) FOR THE INTENTIONAL TORT CLAIMS OF ASSAULT AND BATTERY[.]"

The City argues that the trial court erred by denying the City's motion for summary judgment on the claims of assault and battery, as the City is immune pursuant to R.C. 2744.02(A). We agree.

Initially we note that "when a trial court denies a motion in which a political subdivision or its employee seeks immunity under R.C. Chapter 2744, that order denies the benefit of an alleged immunity and thus is a final, appealable order pursuant to R.C. 2744.02(C)." Hubbell v. City of Xenia, 115 Ohio St.3d 77, 873 N.E.2d 878, 2007-Ohio-4839, at ¶ 27.

This Court reviews an order ruling on a motion for summary judgment de novo. Grafton v. Ohio Edison Co. (1996), 77 Ohio St.3d 102, 105, 671 N.E.2d 241. We apply the same standard as the trial court, viewing the facts of the case in the light most favorable to the non-moving party and resolving any doubt in favor of the non-moving party. Viock v. Stowe-Woodward Co. (1983), 13 Ohio App.3d 7, 12, 467 N.E.2d 1378.

Pursuant to Civil Rule 56(C), summary judgment is proper if:

"(1) No genuine issue as to any material fact remains to be litigated; (2) the moving party is entitled to judgment as a matter of law; and (3) it appears from the evidence that reasonable minds can come to but one conclusion, and viewing such evidence most strongly in favor of the party against whom the motion for summary judgment is made, that conclusion is adverse to that party." Temple v. Wean United, Inc. (1977), 50 Ohio St.2d 317, 327, 364 N.E.2d 267.

The party moving for summary judgment bears the initial burden of informing the trial court of the basis for the motion and pointing to parts of the record that show the absence of a genuine issue of material fact. Dresher v. Burt (1996), 75 Ohio St.3d 280, 292–93, 662 N.E.2d 264. Specifically, the moving party must support the motion by pointing to some evidence in the record of the type listed in Civ.R. 56(C). *Id.* Once this burden is satisfied, the non-moving party bears the burden of offering specific facts to show a genuine issue for trial. *Id.* at 293, 662 N.E.2d 264. The nonmoving party may not rest upon the mere allegations and denials in the pleadings but instead must point to or submit some evidentiary material that demonstrates a genuine dispute over a material fact. Henkle v. Henkle (1991), 75 Ohio App.3d 732, 735, 600 N.E.2d 791.

In order to determine whether a political subdivision is immune from liability, we engage in a three-tiered analysis. Cater v. City of Cleveland (1998), 83 Ohio St.3d 24, 28, 697 N.E.2d 610. The first tier sets forth the premise that:

> "[e]xcept as provided in division (B) of this section, a political subdivision is not liable in damages in a civil action for injury, death, or loss to person or property allegedly caused by an act or omission of the political subdivision or an employee of the political subdivision in connection with a governmental or proprietary function." R.C. 2744.02(A)(1).

Pursuant to the second tier, we determine whether one of the five exceptions to immunity outlined in R.C. 2744.02(B) applies to hold the political subdivision liable for damages. *Cater,* 83 Ohio St.3d at 28, 697 N.E.2d 610. Lastly, immunity may be restored, and the political subdivision will not be liable, if one of the defenses enumerated in R.C. 2744.03(A) applies. *Id.*

Here the City argued in its motion for summary judgment that the City was immune pursuant to R.C. 2744.02(A), as the provision of police services was a governmental function, and that none of the exceptions found in R.C. 2744.02(B) was applicable. Mr. and Mrs. Spears made no argument in response with respect to the immunity of the City. The trial court denied the City immunity, concluding that while "[Mr. Spears] has not identified any of the above exceptions [to immunity] as being applicable in this case[,][ ] [Mr. Spears] claims that Officer Kabellar, an employee of the City of Akron is liable. If [ ] Officer Kabellar is liable, then the City may be as well." We disagree.

"Chapter 2744 of the Ohio Revised Code grants immunity to political subdivisions for injuries caused by any act or omission unless an exception applies. R.C. 2744.02(A)(1). The City of Akron is a political subdivision under Chapter 2744. R.C. 2744.01(F). The exceptions to political subdivision immunity include, in general terms: (1) the negligent operation of a motor vehicle; (2) the negligent performance of proprietary functions; (3) the negligent failure to maintain public roads; (4) negligence on the grounds of a public building; and (5) liability that is expressly imposed by statute. R.C. 2744.02(B)(1)–(5)." Watson v. Akron, 9th Dist. No. 24077, 2008-Ohio-4995, at ¶ 12.

"The provision or nonprovision of police * * * services or protection" is a governmental function, R.C. 2744.01(C)(2)(a), and therefore pursuant to R.C. 2744.02(A)(1), the City is entitled to immunity for the provision of such services, absent an exception. *See, also,* Weibel v. Akron (May 8, 1991), 9th Dist. No. 14878, at *1. As pointed out by the City, "[i]n Ohio, a political subdivision may not be held liable for intentional torts unless 'liability is expressly imposed upon the political subdivision by a section of the Revised Code.'" *Watson* at ¶ 14, quoting R.C. 2774.02(B)(5). Mr. Spears did not argue in the trial court, and does not argue here, that any of the above-listed exceptions applies to his case. In fact, Mr. Spears provided no argument refuting the City's contention that it was entitled to immunity. Therefore, the trial court erred in denying the City's motion for summary judgment pertaining to Mr. Spears' claims for assault and battery.

ASSIGNMENT OF ERROR II

"THE TRIAL COURT ERRED IN NOT GRANTING IMMUNITY TO OFFICER KEVIN KABELLAR PURSUANT TO R.C. [ ]2744.03(A)(6) FOR THE INTENTIONAL TORT CLAIMS OF ASSAULT AND BATTERY."

The City and Officer Kabellar argue that Officer Kabellar was entitled to the benefits of immunity, and that the trial court erred in denying their motion for summary judgment. Specifically, the City and Officer Kabellar argue that Mr. Spears has not provided evidence that Officer Kabellar acted "with malicious purpose, in bad faith, or in a wanton or reckless manner." R.C. 2744.03(A)(6)(b). Mr. and Mrs. Spears contend the opposite is true. Issues regarding malice, bad faith, recklessness and wanton conduct are generally questions left to the jury to resolve. Shadoan v. Summit Cty. Children Servs. Bd., 9th Dist. No. 21486, 2003-Ohio-5775, at ¶ 14.

The three-tiered analysis of liability applicable to a political subdivision does not apply when determining whether an employee of the political subdivision will be liable for harm caused to an individual. Cramer v. Auglaize Acres, 113 Ohio St.3d 266, 865 N.E.2d 9, 2007-Ohio-1946, at ¶ 17. Pursuant to R.C. 2744.03(A)(6), an employee of a political subdivision is immune from liability unless:

"(a) The employee's acts or omissions were manifestly outside the scope of the employee's employment or official responsibilities;

"(b) The employee's acts or omissions were with malicious purpose, in bad faith, or in a wanton or reckless manner;

"(c) Civil liability is expressly imposed upon the employee by a section of the Revised Code. Civil liability shall not be construed to exist under another section of the Revised Code merely because that section imposes a responsibility or mandatory duty upon an employee, because that section provides for a criminal penalty, because of a general authorization in that section that an employee may sue and be sued, or because the section uses the term 'shall' in a provision pertaining to an employee."

The issue before us is whether there remains a genuine issue of material fact concerning Officer Kabellar's actions with respect to Mr. Spears. The City and Officer Kabellar maintain that there is no evidence that Officer Kabellar acted with a "malicious purpose, in bad faith, or in a wanton or reckless manner[.]" R.C. 2744.03(A)(6)(b).

One acts with a malicious purpose if one willfully and intentionally acts with a purpose to cause harm. Piro v. Franklin Twp. (1995), 102 Ohio App.3d 130, 139, 656 N.E.2d 1035. Malice includes "the willful and intentional design to do injury, or the intention or desire to harm another through conduct which is unlawful or unjustified." (Internal quotations omitted.) *Shadoan* at ¶ 12. Bad faith is defined as a "dishonest purpose, moral obliquity, conscious wrongdoing, or breach of a known duty through some ulterior motive or ill will." (Internal quotations and citations omitted.) Lindsey v. Summit Cty. Children Services Bd., 9th Dist. No. 24352, 2009-Ohio-2457, at ¶ 16. A person acts wantonly if that person acts with a complete "failure to exercise any care whatsoever." Fabrey v. McDonald Police Dept. (1994), 70 Ohio St.3d 351, 356, 639 N.E.2d 31. One acts recklessly if one is aware that one's conduct "creates an unreasonable risk of physical harm to another[.]" (Internal quotations and citation omitted.) Thompson v. McNeill (1990), 53 Ohio St.3d 102, 104, 559 N.E.2d 705. Recklessness is more than mere negligence in that the person "must be conscious that his [or her] conduct will in all probability result in injury." *Fabrey,* 70 Ohio St.3d at 356, 639 N.E.2d 31.

We conclude there remains a genuine issue of material fact concerning Officer Kabellar's conduct, and thus the trial court did not err in denying Officer Kabellar the benefit of immunity. Officer Kabellar's and Mr. and Mrs. Spears' version of the events differ to a significant extent on several important facts. . . .

Given the above evidence presented to the trial court there is a genuine issue of material fact concerning whether Officer Kabellar's actions were done with a "malicious purpose, in bad faith, or in a wanton or reckless manner[.]" R.C. 2744.03(A)(6)(b). If the facts as presented by Mr. and Mrs. Spears are true, if nothing else, it could reasonably be determined that Officer Kabellar's actions in arresting Mr. Spears were reckless in that he was aware that his conduct "create[d] an unreasonable risk of physical harm to [Mr. Spears][,]" *Thompson,* 53 Ohio St.3d at 104, 559 N.E.2d 705, or were done with a malicious purpose in that Officer Kabellar could be perceived as willfully and intentionally acting with a purpose to cause harm. *Piro,* 102 Ohio App.3d at 139, 656 N.E.2d 1035. While a jury could find the Officer's actions reasonable under the circumstances, a jury could also find that slamming a suspect's face into a police car, forcibly grabbing him by the neck and arm and then applying handcuffs too tightly or allowing them to remain too tight when the officer was not confronted by a physically combative suspect could constitute reckless or malicious behavior on the part of the officer. As reasonable minds could differ on whether Officer Kabellar's conduct was reckless or done with malicious purpose, summary judgment was inappropriate. *See, e.g.,* Ruth v. Jennings (1999), 136 Ohio App.3d 370, 375–376, 736 N.E.2d 917 (even assuming appellant was resisting arrest, the facts required "further inquiry to determine whether the actions of the arresting officers were reasonable under the circumstances, or whether the officers acted in a malicious, willful or wanton manner[ ]"); MacNamara v. Gustin (June 4, 1999), 2d Dist. No. 17575, at *6 ("Assuming the truth of Judy MacNamara's assertions that one of the officers had tightened the handcuffs after she had explained that they were too tight, that her shoulder had 'popped,' and that she had injured her shoulder while being shoved into the police cruiser, reasonable minds could conclude that Officers Gustin and Colvin had acted with a malicious purpose, in bad faith, or in a reckless manner.").

ASSIGNMENT OF ERROR III

"THE TRIAL COURT ERRED IN NOT DISMISSING DOTTIE SPEARS' DERIVATIVE LOSS OF CONSORTIUM CLAIM[.]"

In the City's and Officer Kabellar's third assignment of error they allege that the trial court erred in not granting them summary judgment on Mrs. Spears' consortium claim because it is a derivative claim and all of Mr. Spears' claims fail. We disagree.

"A claim for loss of consortium is derivative and, but for the primary cause of action by the plaintiff, would not exist." Bradley v. Sprenger Enterprises, Inc., 9th Dist. No. 07CA009238, 2008-Ohio-1988, at ¶ 14. However, as we agreed with the trial court's determination that Mr. Spears' claims for assault and battery against Officer Kabellar survive summary judgment, the loss of consortium claim survives as well. *See* Moss v. Lorain Cty. Bd. of Mental Retardation, 9th Dist. No. 09CA009550, 2009-Ohio-6931, at ¶ 32.

III.

The City's and Officer Kabellar's first assignment of error is sustained and the remaining assignments of error are overruled. The judgment of the Summit County Court of Common Pleas is affirmed in part and reversed in part.

Judgment affirmed in part, reversed in part, and cause remanded.

Timmons v. Metropolitan Government of Nashville and Davidson County

307 S.W.3d 735 (Tenn. Ct. App. June 15, 2009)

■ FRANK G. CLEMENT, JR.

Plaintiff filed this Governmental Tort Liability Act action against the Metropolitan Government of Nashville and Davidson County for injuries sustained during his arrest for driving under the influence following a vehicular accident. Plaintiff contends the police officers who arrested him were negligent in failing to recognize that he was not intoxicated but in diabetic shock, in failing to recognize that he could be restrained and handcuffed while standing, instead of in the prone position, and that he sustained a spiral, comminuted fracture of the humerus while an officer was pulling his right arm behind his back in an effort to cuff his hands. Following a bench trial, the trial court found the officers were negligent in the manner in which they assessed the threat posed by Plaintiff and were negligent in the decision to handcuff him in the prone position, which caused his injuries. The trial court, therefore, held the Metropolitan Government liable for the officers' negligence, assessed 100% of the fault to the officers, and awarded Plaintiff $140,000 in damages. On appeal, the Metropolitan Government insists it is immune from liability because the officers' actions were not the result of negligence but, it contends, the officers' consciously and volitionally used an excessive amount of force that constituted the intentional tort of battery. Alternatively, the Government contends, if it is liable under a negligence theory, the trial court erred by apportioning no fault to Plaintiff. We have determined the evidence does not preponderate against the trial court's findings that Plaintiff's injuries resulted from the officers' negligent acts and omissions, that the Metropolitan Government is liable for the officers' negligence, that Plaintiff was not contributorily negligent, and that Plaintiff is entitled to recover damages in the amount of $140,000. Accordingly, we affirm the trial court in all respects.

This action arises from the events that occurred on the evening of March 6, 2004, after Plaintiff, Ronald Timmons, had eaten dinner at his sister's residence. After dinner, at approximately 7:00 p.m., he started driving to his home, which was approximately four miles from her house. While driving, Mr. Timmons, a Type I diabetic, began to experience the symptoms of insulin shock.[1] In an effort to regulate his blood sugar, Mr. Timmons stopped at a convenience store to buy a candy bar, which he ate, and then waited at the store fifteen minutes for the symptoms to subside. When the symptoms began to subside, Mr. Timmons resumed his drive home; however, shortly thereafter, he again experienced the symptoms of insulin shock. Believing he could drive home safely, Mr. Timmons continued his drive toward his home, but he never made it. While driving on Dickerson Pike, Mr. Timmons "blacked out" and began driving down the wrong side of the road, causing motorists to make 911 calls to inform the police. Before the police could respond, Mr. Timmons was involved in an accident; the property damage to both vehicles was minor and no one sustained injuries in the collision.

Metropolitan Police Officer Corey Wilson was the first officer to arrive at the scene. When Officer Wilson arrived, he found Mr. Timmons sitting in the driver's seat clutching the steering wheel with both hands; Mr. Timmons' frame was rigid, he was completely unresponsive to Officer Wilson's inquiries, and Mr. Timmons' eyes appeared red and watery. Based upon these observations and Mr. Timmons' non-responsiveness, Officer Wilson believed Mr. Timmons was intoxicated. Because Mr. Timmons would not respond or cooperate, Officer Wilson called for the

---

[1] "Insulin shock" is a medical condition where the body reacts to excessively large amounts of insulin in the bloodstream producing an abnormal fall in the person's level of blood sugar. Symptoms include nervousness, trembling, sweating, and paleness.

assistance of additional officers. When the second officer, Officer Thornton, arrived at the scene, he did not realize Officer Wilson was already at the scene. As a consequence, Officer Thornton approached the vehicle and ordered Mr. Timmons to get out of the vehicle. As before, Mr. Timmons did not respond to Officer Thornton, nor comply with any of his instructions. Officer Thornton then attempted, unsuccessfully, to pull Mr. Timmons out of the vehicle. Within a few minutes, fifteen police vehicles, an ambulance, and a fire truck arrived at the scene.

In the interim, and despite Officer Thornton's repeated efforts, Mr. Timmons remained in the driver's seat, rigid, unresponsive, and vigorously clutching the steering wheel with both his hands. When Officer Jacob Pilarski arrived, he entered the vehicle on the passenger side in an attempt to push Mr. Timmons toward Officer Thornton, as Officer Thornton attempted to pull Mr. Timmons out of the vehicle on the driver's side using a technique called "soft empty hand control." As Officer Thornton pulled Mr. Timmons' hands from the steering wheel in an attempt to pull him from the vehicle, Mr. Timmons, in what the trial court found was a reflexive action, immediately pulled his hands back in the vehicle. Finally, Officer Thornton succeeded in pulling Mr. Timmons from the vehicle. At the moment Mr. Timmons was removed from the vehicle, Officer Pilarski immediately went to the driver's side of the vehicle, grabbed Mr. Timmons from Officer Thornton's grasp, and with the help of an unidentified officer, placed Mr. Timmons face down on the ground in what is known as the "prone position."[2]

With Mr. Timmons face down in the prone position, Officer Pilarski straddled Mr. Timmons in order to handcuff him. Officer Pilarski pulled Mr. Timmons' left arm behind him and placed a handcuff on his wrist. As Officer Pilarski unsuccessfully attempted to place a handcuff on Mr. Timmons' right wrist, he believed Mr. Timmons was resisting arrest because Mr. Timmons' right arm was rigid underneath Mr. Timmons' body, and Mr. Timmons was not cooperating. After a few failed attempts to remove Mr. Timmons' right arm from underneath Mr. Timmons' body, Officer Pilarski requested assistance from Officer Wilson, who was 6 feet 7 inches tall and weighed 220 pounds. While other officers were assisting in securing Mr. Timmons' legs, which "flopped and flailed" about, Officer Wilson pulled Mr. Timmons' right arm from underneath Mr. Timmons' body, and as he was attempting to place the right hand behind Mr. Timmons' back, Mr. Timmons sustained a "spiral, comminuted fracture" of his right humerus. None of the officers realized that Mr. Timmons was injured and they proceeded to place the handcuffs on Mr. Timmons' right wrist and then placed Mr. Timmons in the back of a police car for

---

[2]   Officer Pilarski's and Officer Thornton's testimony differed in some respects at trial. Officer Thornton stated that it was Officer Pilarski who took Mr. Timmons to the ground. Officer Pilarski testified that it was not him and that he was unaware who had taken Mr. Timmons to the ground, and that Mr. Timmons was already on the ground when he reached the driver's side of the vehicle. The trial court found Officer Thornton's version of events to be more credible, a decision which is entitled to great weight on appeal.

transport to jail. While Mr. Timmons was in the police car at the scene, paramedics examined him to see if he had sustained injuries during the vehicular accident. It was during this examination that the paramedics determined that Mr. Timmons was in shock and that he had sustained an injury to his right arm, whereupon Mr. Timmons was transported to receive medical care.

On January 14, 2005, Mr. Timmons filed this action against the Metropolitan Government alleging that the Metropolitan Government's employees, the police officers, were negligent in failing to recognize that he was in diabetic shock and were negligent in using force against a "helpless and unconscious man." Following discovery, the Metropolitan Government filed for summary judgment, which the trial court granted. Mr. Timmons appealed that judgment and this Court determined that there was a genuine dispute concerning material facts regarding whether the police officers acted reasonably under the circumstances; this Court reversed the grant of summary judgment and remanded the matter for trial. See Timmons v. Metropolitan Government of Nashville, No. M2006-01828-COA-R3-CV, 2007 WL 2405132 (Tenn.Ct.App. Aug. 23, 2007).

On remand, a bench trial was held over a period of three days, following which the trial court determined that Mr. Timmons' injuries were the result of the officers' negligent acts and omissions, for which the Metropolitan Government was liable, and awarded a judgment in favor of Mr. Timmons in the amount of $140,000, plus $2,722.65 in discretionary costs. The trial court's findings were set forth pursuant to Tenn. R. Civ. P. 52.01 in a detailed Memorandum Opinion dated June 23, 2008. In pertinent part, the trial court found that the force employed by Officer Wilson, who pulled Mr. Timmons' right arm from underneath his body, was not excessive force, that the force used to handcuff Mr. Timmons was the result of another officer's negligent decision to place him in the prone position, and that the injuries sustained by Mr. Timmons were the result of the negligent decision to place Mr. Timmons in the prone position which necessitated the use of the more risky "prone handcuffing" technique. The trial court also found that Mr. Timmons was not contributorily negligent because he was incapacitated due to insulin shock, that Mr. Timmons was essentially unconscious and unable to comprehend the officers' questions or to voluntarily communicate, and that Mr. Timmons was not being combative or actively resisting the officers. Following the entry of a judgment in accordance with the foregoing findings, the Metropolitan Government filed this appeal.

ANALYSIS

On appeal, the Metropolitan Government argues that the trial court erred in holding it responsible under a negligence theory because, it contends, its employees, the police officers, acted consciously and volitionally when they used an unreasonable amount of force which constituted the intentional tort of battery for which the Metropolitan Government retains immunity under the Governmental Tort Liability

Act. The Metropolitan Government also argues that the trial court erred in assigning no portion of fault to Mr. Timmons for his injuries based upon his conscious decision to continue driving when he felt the onset of insulin shock and for his resistance to the police officers' attempts to remove him from his vehicle. . . .

THE GOVERNMENTAL TORT LIABILITY ACT

The Tennessee Governmental Tort Liability Act (the Act) codifies the general common law rule that " 'all governmental entities shall be immune from suit for any injury which may result from the activities of such governmental entities,' Tenn.Code Ann. § 29–20–201(a), subject to statutory exceptions in the Act's provisions." Limbaugh v. Coffee Med. Ctr., 59 S.W.3d 73, 79 (Tenn.2001). But for certain enumerated exceptions, Tenn.Code Ann. § 29–20–205 of the Act provides a general waiver of immunity from suit for personal injury claims for injuries proximately caused by a negligent act or omission of an employee acting within the scope of his employment. *Id.* One of the enumerated exceptions is the intentional tort exception, which includes the intentional tort of battery. *Id.* Accordingly, the Metropolitan Government may be held liable for the actions of its police officers if the acts or omissions of the officers caused injury to Mr. Timmons while the officers were acting within the scope of their employment. *See id.* Conversely, the Metropolitan Government is immune from liability, and cannot be held liable for injuries sustained by Mr. Timmons if the injuries were the result of the intentional tort of battery by the officers. *See id.*

MR. TIMMONS' CLAIM OF NEGLIGENCE

Mr. Timmons' negligence claim centers on what he contends were the negligent acts and omissions of two police officers: Officer Pilarski who made the decision to place Mr. Timmons on the ground in the prone position, which necessitated that he be handcuffed pursuant to the prone cuffing technique, and Officer Wilson who was attempting to place the handcuff on Mr. Timmons' right wrist when the humerus in his right arm fractured.

A negligence cause of action has five essential elements: (1) a legally recognized duty owed by the defendant to the plaintiff, (2) the defendant's breach of that duty, (3) an injury or loss, (4) causation in fact, and (5) legal cause. Biscan v. Brown, 160 S.W.3d 462, 478 (Tenn.2005); Draper v. Westerfield, 181 S.W.3d 283, 290 (Tenn.2005); Foster v. Bue, 749 S.W.2d 736, 741 (Tenn.1988).

The first element of duty is "the legal obligation owed by defendant to plaintiff to conform to a reasonable person standard of care for the protection against unreasonable risks of harm." McCall v. Wilder, 913 S.W.2d 150, 153 (Tenn.1995). "[T]he existence or nonexistence of a duty owed to plaintiff is entirely a question of law for the Court." Carson v. Headrick, 900 S.W.2d 685, 690 (Tenn.1995). It is undisputed that the police officers had a duty to abide by the applicable policies and procedures of the Metropolitan Police Department as they attempted to arrest and handcuff Mr. Timmons.

The 2001 Lesson Plan for the Metropolitan Nashville Police Department Training Division was introduced as evidence of the Department's applicable policies and procedures. In the section entitled "Defensive Tactics: Removing/Placing Subjects: Vehicle," the Plan instructs officers "to remove a resisting, drunken subject from a vehicle" and handcuff them by placing the subject's chest against the vehicle for support. This technique is to be employed if the subject being arrested is not believed to be a high risk to the arresting officers or others. Alternatively, the Defensive Tactics section instructs that it is appropriate for officers to employ the "prone cuffing" technique—where the subject is placed on the ground face down—when "the subject being arrested is *though[t]* to be a high risk to officers or others." (emphasis added). There are four instances when the "prone position" is considered appropriate: when the subject is a violent felon, is armed, has a history of resisting arrest, or actively resists arrest. The section also instructs that the "crime or danger must be serious enough to warrant placing the subject on the ground." Mr. Timmons was not a violent felon, he was not armed, and he did not have a history of resisting arrest. Accordingly, we find, as a matter of law, that the police officers had a duty to evaluate whether Mr. Timmons was actively resisting arrest before deciding to employ the prone handcuffing technique.

With that determination, the question is whether the officers failed to exercise reasonable care under the circumstances in making the decision to employ the prone handcuffing technique. *See McCall,* 913 S.W.2d at 153 (quoting W. Keeton, *Prosser and Keeton on the Law of Torts,* § 356 (5th ed. 1984)) (holding that what a defendant, or its employees acting in the scope of their employment, must do, or must not do, "is a question of the standard of conduct required to satisfy the duty"). The standard of conduct is the "standard of reasonable care in light of the apparent risk." *Id.* (citing Pittman v. Upjohn Co., 890 S.W.2d 425, 428 (Tenn.1994) ("As in all cases, there is a duty to exercise reasonable care under the circumstances."); *Bradshaw v. Daniel,* 854 S.W.2d 865, 870 (Tenn.1993) ("All persons have a duty to use reasonable care to refrain from conduct that will foreseeably cause injury to others."); Prosser and Keeton, § 356). Defendants who do not exercise reasonable care breach their duty. *Id.* at 153–54 (citing Doe v. Linder Const. Co., Inc., 845 S.W.2d 173, 178 (Tenn.1992)).

As the Department's policies instruct, the only policy justification for the use of the prone handcuffing technique would be that the officers reasonably *thought* Mr. Timmons was "actively resisting" their attempts to place him under arrest for driving under the influence. While the officers were attempting to extract Mr. Timmons from his vehicle, which took a great deal of effort by two officers, most of the officers believed that Mr. Timmons was passively resisting arrest, meaning they did not believe that he was "actively" resisting arrest. Officer Pilarski, however, believed Mr. Timmons was actively resisting arrest. These differing opinions are evident by the reports made by officers following the arrest. The Police Department's "Use of Force" form, commonly referred to as "Form 108," was completed by three of the officers and filed with the Department following this unfortunate incident. The Use of Force form is to be completed following any incident in which officers use force. The form provides boxes for the officers to check to indicate the subject's level of resistance. Two of the officers reported that Mr. Timmons was passively resisting arrest. Officer Pilarski checked two boxes, indicating that he believed Mr. Timmons exhibited both passive resistance and active resistance. Officer Thornton, the one who extracted Mr. Timmons from the vehicle, additionally testified at trial that he did not believe Mr. Timmons was actively resisting.

The trial court made the express factual finding that Mr. Timmons did not actively resist arrest. The record fully supports the trial court's finding that Mr. Timmons was not intending to resist arrest; he was simply suffering from the effects of insulin shock and was unaware of his actions or the officers' instructions. The record also supports the trial court's finding that Mr. Timmons was not "actively resisting" the officers; instead he was merely exhibiting "reflexive reactions" by rigidly sitting in his car, resisting the officers' repeated efforts to remove him from the car, and "pulling his arms" toward his body as they removed his hands from the steering wheel, which he was firmly grasping. Accordingly, we affirm the trial court's conclusion that Officer Pilarski negligently evaluated the resistance and threat posed by Mr. Timmons, which led to the erroneous conclusion that Mr. Timmons was actively resisting arrest and the decision to place Mr. Timmons on the ground, thereby necessitating the use of the prone handcuffing technique.

A defendant's negligent conduct is the cause in fact of the plaintiff's injury "if, as a factual matter, it directly contributed to the plaintiff's injury and without it plaintiff's injury would not have occurred." T.P.I.-Civil 3.21 (8th ed. 2008) (citing Hale v. Ostrow, 166 S.W.3d 713, 718–19 (Tenn.2005)). An actor's conduct is the legal cause of a person's injury if the actor's conduct was "a substantial factor in bringing about the harm," and if there is no "legal rule or policy that would operate to relieve the actor from liability." Lowery v. Franks, No. 02A01-9612-CV-00304, 1997 WL 566114, at *5 (Tenn.Ct.App. Sept. 10, 1997) (citing McClenahan v. Cooley, 806 S.W.2d 767, 775 (Tenn.1991)). Additionally, the harm that occurred must have been reasonably foreseeable by a person of ordinary intelligence and prudence. Id. (citing McClenahan, 806 S.W.2d at 775).

We find Officer Pilarski's negligent evaluation of the type of resistance and the threat Mr. Timmons posed to the officers significant because testimony presented at trial reveals the importance of evaluating subjects to determine whether they were intoxicated or suffering from a medical ailment. That testimony also revealed the significantly greater risks associated with the prone handcuffing technique, meaning the risks of injury to the subject being handcuffed in the prone position as opposed to the standing position. Based on the evidence in the record, we affirm the trial court's finding that the use of the prone handcuffing technique posed additional risks of injury to Mr. Timmons and that injury from the use of the prone handcuffing technique was foreseeable.

The decision to place Mr. Timmons on the ground and handcuff him in the prone position was also a substantial factor in bringing about the injuries he sustained. When the decision was made to place Mr. Timmons on the ground, this led to his right arm being beneath his body, which led to Officer Wilson having to exert more force to pull Mr. Timmons' right arm behind his back, which is when the fracture to the right arm occurred. The record reveals that it was reasonably foreseeable that Mr. Timmons might be injured by being handcuffed in the prone position, and it is undisputed that Mr. Timmons suffered a "spiral, comminuted fracture" as the prone handcuffing technique was being employed. Therefore, the negligent decision that necessitated that Mr. Timmons be handcuffed in the prone position was both the cause-in-fact and the legal cause of his injuries.

We acknowledge the vigorous argument presented by the Metropolitan Government that the actions by the police officers constituted the intentional tort of battery, not a negligent act. This argument is principally based on the decision in City of Mason v. Banks, 581 S.W.2d 621 (Tenn.1979). In *Banks,* the Court addressed whether a municipal corporation was required to indemnify an employee of the police department against whom judgment was recovered from conduct occurring within the scope of the officer's employment. *Id.* at 622. The dispositive "factual issue" in *Banks* was whether the officer "engaged in willful wrongdoing," or "whether he was justified, although negligent, in using force that ultimately blinded respondent in his left eye." *Id.* at 623. We find the facts of this case are distinguishable from those in *Banks,* and therefore, *Banks* is not controlling.

There are two key distinctions between *Banks* and this case. In *Banks,* the officer used a "blackjack" to subdue the subject, who was attempting to escape from the police car where he had been placed following his arrest.[4] *Id.* The *Banks* Court commented:

> It is clear from the record that [the officer] intended to hit respondent in the head with his blackjack; it was his voluntary and conscious act. He was privileged to use only that force necessary to effect the arrest and was liable for the amount of the force that was excessive. See Restatement (Second) of Torts

---

[4]   In Banks, the underlying action from which the suit to indemnify arose was a 42 U.S.C. § 1983 action. Banks, 581 S.W.2d at 626. Notably, while "isolated incidents of negligence" are not cognizable under § 1983, excessive force actions when a "policeman's conduct was conscious, volitional, and purposeful" have been held actionable under § 1983. *Id.* at 626–27.

§§ 71, 133. *Hence [the officer] was liable for the damages caused by his excessive and unprivileged use of force under the intentional tort of battery.*

Id. at 626 (emphasis added). The officer's actions in *Banks* were found to be "willful" and "excessive." *Id.* Here, the trial court found that Mr. Timmons' injuries were the result of the officer's negligent evaluation of the extent of Mr. Timmons' resistance to being arrested. As a result of the negligent assessment of the extent of Mr. Timmons' resistance, the officers followed a Department policy which authorized handcuffing the subject in the prone position. Mr. Timmons' injuries flowed from the negligent assessment concerning his resistance to being arrested, not from an intentional decision to use excessive force. Furthermore, the trial court in *Banks* made the factual determination that the police officer used "excessive force in effecting the arrest" and, therefore, the municipality was not liable. *Id.* at 626. Here, the trial court made the opposite finding, holding that the injuries were the result of the officers' negligence and that the officers did not use "excessive force." As a consequence, to prevail on this issue the Metropolitan Government must establish that the evidence preponderates against the trial court's finding that the officer's were negligent and that the force used was "excessive." We have determined the evidence does not preponderate against the trial court's findings. Based on the foregoing, Mr. Timmons has successfully established each of the essential elements of a negligence claim against the Metropolitan Government, and the Metropolitan Government has failed to establish that the evidence preponderates against the findings that the officers' actions constituted negligence and that they did not intentionally use excessive force.

COMPARATIVE FAULT

We now consider the contention that the trial court erred by finding that Mr. Timmons was not comparatively negligent. The Metropolitan Government argues that Mr. Timmons was comparatively negligent in two ways. One, Mr. Timmons was negligent when he continued driving despite feeling the onset of an episode of insulin shock. Two, Mr. Timmons was negligent by resisting the officers' attempts to remove him from his car and handcuff him.

Pursuant to the comparative fault doctrine, the court may compare the fault of the tortfeasor to the fault of the plaintiff. Lewis v. State, 73 S.W.3d 88, 94 (Tenn.Ct.App.2001). "If the plaintiff's own negligence is less [than the tortfeasor's fault], [the plaintiff] may recover, but the damages he can collect are reduced in proportion to the percentage of the total negligence that can be attributed to [the plaintiff]." *Id.* The degree of fault of each party in producing the injury is a circumstance for the finder of fact to consider and determine. *Id.* at 94–95 (quoting Prince v. St. Thomas Hospital, 945 S.W.2d 731 at 736 (Tenn.Ct.App.1996)). The apportionment of fault by the trier of fact is entitled to a presumption of correctness on appeal. *Id.* at 95.

The trial court found that "the decision by Mr. Timmons to continue driving had nothing to do with the negligence of the officers in deciding to throw him on the ground and use the prone handcuffing technique." The trial court further found that a conscious decision was required to be comparatively at fault, and as Mr. Timmons was suffering from the effects of insulin shock and "essentially unconscious," no fault could be attributed to him. Based upon these and other findings, the trial court apportioned 100% of the fault against the police officers, and thus against their employer, the Metropolitan Government.

The Metropolitan Government asserts that Mr. Timmons is comparatively at fault due to his decision to continue driving despite experiencing the symptoms of insulin shock. We believe the facts of this case are analogous to that in the matter of Mercer v. Vanderbilt, 134 S.W.3d 121, 125 (Tenn.2004). *Mercer* was a medical malpractice case wherein a patient's negligence was the cause of injuries and the need for medical attention at Vanderbilt Hospital, where he was taken following the accident. *Id.* The patient was injured in a vehicle accident of his own fault, a result of his driving while under the influence of alcohol. The patient suffered severe brain damage while being treated at the hospital, which was due to the negligence of hospital personnel who deprived him of oxygen. *Id.* at 126. In its assessment of the fault of the hospital versus that of the patient, the court noted that patients, even those who negligently injure themselves, are entitled to subsequent non-negligent medical treatment. *Id.* (quoting Fritts v. McKinne, 934 P.2d 371, 374 (Okla.Civ.App.1996) (quoting Martin v. Reed, 200 Ga.App. 775, 409 S.E.2d 874, 877 (1991)). The court went on to state that such a patient was also entitled to "an undiminished recovery if such subsequent non-negligent treatment is not afforded." *Id.* (quoting *Fritts,* 934 P.2d at 374) (quoting *Martin,* 409 S.E.2d at 877)). Upon that reasoning, the *Mercer* court held that "a patient's negligent conduct that occurs prior to a health care provider's negligent treatment and provides only the occasion for the health care provider's subsequent negligence may not be compared to the negligence of the health care provider." *Mercer,* 134 S.W.3d at 130.

In this case, Mr. Timmons was suffering the effects of insulin shock. Although insulin shock was the cause of the wreck and the reason for the police officers to come to the scene, Mr. Timmons' medical condition, and his acts and omissions while essentially unconscious, cannot constitute acts of negligence. When the police arrived, and at all times material thereafter, Mr. Timmons was not conscious, and due to his medical condition he was not aware of his actions. We, therefore, find that the evidence does not preponderate against the trial court's finding that Mr. Timmons was not at fault as it pertained to the injuries he suffered while being handcuffed in the prone position.

IV CONCLUSION

The judgment of the trial court is affirmed in all respects, and this matter is remanded with costs of appeal assessed against the Metropolitan Government of Nashville and Davidson County.

Niderstadt v. Town of Carrizozo

182 P.3d 769 (N.M. App. 2008)

■ FRY, JUDGE.

{1} Plaintiff filed suit in federal court against the Town of Carrizozo's employee, police officer Johnny Rivera, in his individual capacity, for violation of Plaintiff's constitutional rights and for other torts. When Rivera asked the Town of Carrizozo (the Town) to provide a defense for him, the Town refused, and Rivera mounted a pro se defense. Plaintiff and Rivera ultimately settled the federal case such that Rivera agreed to having judgment entered against him in favor of Plaintiff in the amount of $60,000, and Rivera assigned to Plaintiff all of his claims against the Town, including claims for its failure to defend him.

{2} Plaintiff, as Rivera's assignee, then filed the present case against the Town, seeking (1) a declaratory judgment that the Town must satisfy the judgment against Rivera, and (2) damages for the Town's alleged bad faith failure to defend Rivera in the federal lawsuit. The Town filed a motion to dismiss based on Plaintiff's failure to give the Town written notice of Plaintiff's claims against Rivera pursuant to the New Mexico Tort Claims Act (TCA), NMSA 1978, §§ 41–4–1 to –29 (1976, as amended through 2007). The district court granted the motion, and Plaintiff appeals. We reverse and hold that Plaintiff's failure to give notice under the TCA does not release the Town from its statutory duties under the TCA to defend and indemnify Rivera.

BACKGROUND

{3} In the federal case, Plaintiff alleged that on August 28, 2003, Rivera approached him as he sat on the porch of his mother's home in the town of Carrizozo, New Mexico. Rivera, with the intent to arrest Plaintiff, grabbed Plaintiff's hair, slammed him into the ground, and twisted his arm behind his back. Plaintiff allegedly suffered both physical and psychological injuries as a result of Rivera's actions.

{4} Plaintiff filed the original action in United States District Court for the District of New Mexico for "violation of his civil rights under 42 U.S.C. § 1983 [(2000)], and for assault, battery, false arrest, and false imprisonment, under the New Mexico Tort Claims Act." The complaint in the federal action named Rivera in his individual capacity and alleged that Rivera was "[a]t all times material . . . acting within the scope of his employment as a law enforcement officer and under color of state law." Plaintiff did not name the Town or any other governmental entity as a defendant in the federal action.

{5} After Rivera was served with the complaint in the federal action on August 10, 2004, he notified his superior officer, Chief Angelo Vega, of the complaint, and Vega told Rivera he would "look into it." Rivera followed up with Vega, inquiring about the Town providing Rivera with a defense, and Vega informed Rivera that "the matter was being 'taken care of.'" Vega gave Rivera the name and telephone number of the Town's attorney, David Stevens. Rivera called Stevens' office, which instructed Rivera to forward a copy of the complaint, and Rivera complied. Someone in Stevens' office called Rivera to inform him that the Town would not be providing Rivera with a defense, and Rivera then received a brief memorandum from Stevens confirming that fact. Both the Town Clerk and the Mayor of Carrizozo admitted in their affidavits that they saw a copy of the complaint in the federal action on August 26, 2004. According to Stevens' affidavit, the Town, the Mayor, and Vega were all informed of the existence of the complaint on August 26, 2004, and a "decision was made not to provide [ ] Rivera a defense."

{6} When the Town denied Rivera's request for a defense, Rivera proceeded pro se and filed a response to the federal complaint and a consent to proceed before a federal magistrate. Counsel for Plaintiff sent a letter to Stevens and the Town to confirm that they had received notice of the complaint and inquiring whether the Town planned to defend Rivera. Stevens, on behalf of the Town, responded to Plaintiff's counsel directly and stated that the Town would not be providing Rivera with a defense.

{7} At a conference with the federal magistrate, Plaintiff and Rivera negotiated a settlement, which resolved all of Plaintiff's claims. The settlement provided that Rivera would allow judgment to be taken against him by Plaintiff in the amount of $60,000. In addition, Rivera assigned to Plaintiff all of Rivera's claims against the Town. Plaintiff's counsel sent another letter to Stevens notifying him of the settlement and requesting that Stevens contact the Town's insurer to pay the judgment. Counsel for Plaintiff also indicated that the Town had a duty to defend and indemnify Rivera pursuant to the TCA. § 41–4–4(B), (D).

{8} Plaintiff, as Rivera's assignee, brought the instant action against the Town in state district court. Plaintiff sought both a declaratory judgment that the Town had duties to defend and indemnify Rivera and damages for the Town's alleged bad faith failure to defend. The Town filed a motion to dismiss based on Plaintiff's failure to serve a written notice of tort claim pursuant to the TCA, Section 41–4–16(A), within ninety days of the incident. Plaintiff opposed the motion to dismiss and filed a motion for summary judgment. The district court denied Plaintiff's motion for summary judgment and granted the Town's motion to dismiss for failure to provide notice under the TCA. Plaintiff now appeals.

DISCUSSION

{9} In determining the applicable standard of review, we observe that the district court apparently considered matters outside the pleadings in ruling on the Town's motion to dismiss. The Town attached two affidavits to its motion to dismiss. "[W]here matters outside the pleadings are considered on a motion to dismiss for failure to state a claim, the motion becomes one for summary judgment." Gulf Ins. Co. v. Cottone, 2006-NMCA-150, ¶ 7, 140 N.M. 728, 148 P.3d 814 (internal quotation marks and citation omitted). We therefore treat the district court's order as a summary judgment and consider whether the Town was entitled to judgment as a matter of law, which is a legal question subject to de novo review. *Id.* This question also requires us to interpret the language of the TCA. Interpretation of a statute is also a question of law that we review de novo. Morgan Keegan Mortgage Co. v. Candelaria, 1998-NMCA-008, ¶ 5, 124 N.M. 405, 951 P.2d 1066.

{10} On appeal, Plaintiff argues that (1) he did not have to provide the Town with written notice of his claim against Rivera pursuant to Section 41–4–16(A) because Plaintiff's claim was against Rivera in his individual capacity, not against the Town itself; (2) the Town had a statutory duty to defend Rivera pursuant to Section 41–4–4(B); and (3) the Town had a duty to pay the judgment against Rivera pursuant to Section 41–4–4(D). In analyzing Plaintiff's contentions, we will focus most of our attention on the TCA itself. However, in order to provide context, we begin by setting out several principles applicable to 42 U.S.C. § 1983 claims, because Plaintiff's primary claim against Rivera was such a claim.

42 U.S.C. § 1983 Claims

{11} In Plaintiff's original federal action, he alleged, among other claims, that Rivera violated his federal constitutional rights, and he sought relief under 42 U.S.C. § 1983. Plaintiff named Rivera individually as the only defendant in order to impose "*personal* liability upon a government official for actions he [took] under color of state law." Kentucky v. Graham, 473 U.S. 159, 165 (1985) (emphasis added). By contrast, if Plaintiff had instead sued Rivera in his official capacity, this would have been a way of pleading an action against Rivera's employer, the Town. *Id.* (stating that "[o]fficial-capacity suits . . . generally represent only another way of pleading an action against an entity of which an officer is an agent" (internal quotation marks and citation omitted)). However, it is difficult to prevail under a 42 U.S.C. § 1983 claim against a governmental entity itself. In order to do so, a plaintiff must show more than just that the entity's agent violated the plaintiff's rights; the plaintiff must also demonstrate that the injury to the plaintiff resulted from the "execution of a government's policy or custom, whether made by its lawmakers or by those whose edicts or acts may fairly be said to represent official policy." Monell v. New York City Dep't of Soc. Servs., 436 U.S. 658, 694 (1978).

{12} Given these principles, it is clear that Plaintiff could bring a 42 U.S.C. § 1983 action only against Rivera, and not against the Town, unless he had some evidence that the Town had a policy or custom permitting or condoning assaults by its police officers. Because Plaintiff did not name the Town in the federal action, we assume he did not have such evidence. With this in mind, we turn to an analysis of the relevant provisions of the TCA.

The Tort Claims Act

{13} There are three primary provisions of the TCA that govern this case: Section 41–4–16, which we will refer to as the "notice provision"; Section 41–4–4(B), which we will refer to as the "employee defense provision"; and Section 41–4–4(D), which we will refer to as the "employee indemnification provision." Overarching these three provisions is the TCA's legislative declaration, which provides the lens through which we must view all other parts of the TCA. *See* Grine v. Peabody Natural Res., 2006-NMSC-031, 17, 140 N.M. 30, 139 P.3d 190 (explaining that a court, in construing a statute, must seek to achieve the intent of the legislature).

{14} The legislative declaration states, in pertinent part:

> A. The legislature recognizes the inherently unfair and inequitable results which occur in the strict application of the doctrine of sovereign immunity. On the other hand, the legislature recognizes that while a private party may readily be held liable for his torts within the chosen ambit of his activity, the area within which the government has the power to act for the public good is almost without limit, and therefore government should not have the duty to do everything that might be done. Consequently, it is declared to be the public policy of New Mexico that governmental entities and public employees shall only be liable within the limitations of the Tort Claims Act and in accordance with the principles established in that act.

§ 41–4–2(A) (citation omitted). Through this declaration, the legislature expressed its intent to achieve balance between the public policy supporting compensation of those injured by public employees and the public policy militating in favor of limiting government liability. Cobos v. Doña Ana County Hous. Auth., 1998-NMSC-049, ¶ 6, 126 N.M. 418, 970 P.2d 1143.

{15} The TCA's notice provision states:

> A. Every person who claims damages from the state or any local public body under the Tort Claims Act shall cause to be presented to the risk management division for claims against the state, the mayor of the municipality for claims against the municipality, . . . within ninety days after an occurrence giving rise to a claim for which immunity has been waived under the Tort Claims Act, a written notice stating the time, place and circumstances of the loss or injury.
>
> B. No suit or action for which immunity has been waived under the Tort Claims Act shall be maintained and no court

shall have jurisdiction to consider any suit or action against the state or any local public body unless notice has been given as required by this section, or unless the governmental entity had actual notice of the occurrence.

§ 41–4–16(A), (B) (citation omitted). We observe that Subsection (A) establishes notice requirements applicable to anyone claiming damages "from the state or any local public body," and that Subsection (B) sets out the consequences for failure to provide such notice. *Id.* Those consequences are that no one may maintain an "action against the state or any local public body." *Id.* Significantly, the notice provision says nothing about persons who claim damages from or file actions solely against individual governmental employees.

{16} The TCA's employee defense provision states:

> B. Unless an insurance carrier provides a defense, a governmental entity shall provide a defense, including costs and attorneys' fees, for any public employee when liability is sought for:
>
>> (1) any tort alleged to have been committed by the public employee while acting within the scope of his duty; or
>>
>> (2) any violation of property rights or any rights, privileges or immunities secured by the constitution and laws of the United States or the constitution and laws of New Mexico when alleged to have been committed by the public employee while acting within the scope of his duty.

§ 41–4–4(B). We note that Subsection (B)(2) would include a claim under 42 U.S.C. § 1983. *See* Risk Mgmt. Div. v. McBrayer, 2000-NMCA-104, ¶ 7, 129 N.M. 778, 14 P.3d 43 (explaining that Section 41–4–4(B)(2) addresses the defense of public employees accused of civil rights violations).

{17} In addition, the TCA's employee indemnification provision states:

> D. A governmental entity shall pay any settlement or any final judgment entered against a public employee for:
>
>> (1) any tort that was committed by the public employee while acting within the scope of his duty; or
>>
>> (2) a violation of property rights or any rights, privileges or immunities secured by the constitution and laws of the United States or the constitution and laws of New Mexico that occurred while the public employee was acting within the scope of his duty.

§ 41–4–4(D).

{18} Plaintiff asserts that the employee defense and indemnification provisions require that the Town defend and indemnify its employee, Rivera. The Town argues that the notice provision acts as a limit on a governmental entity's duties under the employee defense and indemnification provisions, and that when a plaintiff fails to give the appropriate written notice of a claim, the entity is released from its statutory duties to provide a defense to and indemnify its employee.

{19} In construing a statute, we seek to achieve the intent of the legislature. *Grine,* 2006-NMSC-031, ¶ 17, 140 N.M. 30, 139 P.3d 190. "We look first to the plain meaning of the statute's words, and we construe the provisions of the Act together to produce a harmonious whole." *Id.* (internal quotation marks and citation omitted). We do not read a statute in such a way that "would lead to injustice, absurdity, or contradiction." Otero v. State, 105 N.M. 731, 733, 737 P.2d 90, 92 (Ct.App.1987).

{20} As we noted earlier in this opinion, the language of the notice provision does not include language suggesting that notice must be given by a claimant who is suing only a governmental employee. Rather, the language requires a "person who claims damages from the state or any local public body" to give written notice within ninety days of an occurrence. § 41–4–16(A). If such notice is not given, the claimant may not maintain an action and no court shall have jurisdiction to consider an action "against the state or any local public body." § 41–4–16(B).

{21} This Court interpreted the notice provision as being inapplicable to a governmental employee in Martinez v. City of Clovis, 95 N.M. 654, 656, 625 P.2d 583, 585 (Ct.App.1980). In that case, the plaintiff sued the City of Clovis and a Clovis police officer for damages the plaintiff sustained in a collision with the officer. *Id.* at 655, 625 P.2d at 584. In holding that the notice of claim provision did not apply to the plaintiff's claims against the employee police officer, we made reference to the TCA's employee defense and indemnification provisions and observed that

> merely because [the employee defense and indemnification provision] imposes upon the governmental entity for which the employee works the obligation to provide a defense to its employee and pay any settlement or judgment reached, it does not convert a public employee . . . into a local public body, a governmental entity, or the state or state agency [for purposes of the notice provision].

Id. at 656, 625 P.2d at 585 (internal quotation marks and citation omitted); *See also* Frappier v. Mergler, 107 N.M. 61, 65, 752 P.2d 253, 257 (Ct.App.1988) (holding that notice provision does not apply to individual governmental employees).

{22} The Town argues that *Martinez* does not apply because its holding was limited in *Otero.* In *Otero,* the plaintiff, on behalf of the plaintiff's decedent, originally brought suit in federal court against a state penitentiary guard in his individual capacity, alleging federal civil rights violations under 42 U.S.C. § 1983. *Otero,* 105 N.M. at 732, 737 P.2d at 91. In the federal lawsuit, the plaintiff served the guard with process, but the guard made no appearance in the suit, and a default judgment was entered against him. *Id.* Neither the state nor any other governmental entity had actual notice of the federal lawsuit, and the plaintiff did not file a written notice of claim pursuant to Section 41–4–16. *Id.* The plaintiff then brought suit in the state district court, asking that the state and the department of finance and administration (DFA) be required to pay the default judgment under the TCA's employee defense provision. *Id.* The district court entered summary judgment in favor of the state and DFA.

{23} In construing the TCA, this Court in *Otero* affirmed the district court. *Id.* at 734, 737 P.2d at 93. We held that even though the notice provision does not require that notice be given to a governmental entity employer when an individual employee is sued, "it does not necessarily follow that the state must pay [the] plaintiff's judgment." *Id.* at 732–33, 737 P.2d at 91–92. We further stated that

> [i]n the context of a carefully drafted statute that: waives immunity; contains means for covering the risks; provides methods for those entities covering the risks to investigate and defend claims; and contains other stringent limitations on payment, the legislature surely could not have intended that governmental entities pay judgments arising out of the default of one alleged to be a public employee when the governmental entity did not have the benefit of any of the statutory provisions integral to the whole scheme.

Id. at 733, 737 P.2d at 92.

{24} At first glance, *Otero* seems determinative of the issue presented in this case. However, we note two meaningful distinctions between the facts of *Otero* and the present case. First, in *Otero,* the plaintiff failed to provide written notice *and* the governmental entities did not have actual notice of the lawsuit. *Id.* at 732, 737 P.2d at 91. In this case, Plaintiff concedes that he did not provide the statutory notice, but he argues that the Town had actual notice of the lawsuit because Rivera sought a defense from his employer soon after he was served in the federal action. Indeed, the attorney for the Town said that a "decision was made not to provide Mr. Rivera a defense." Thus, unlike the governmental entity defendants in *Otero,* the Town had the "opportunity to participate [in and] defend the lawsuit." *Id.* at 733, 737 P.2d at 92.

{25} The second distinction between this case and *Otero* is that in *Otero* the plaintiff, after obtaining a default judgment in the federal action against the state employee, brought suit in state court solely to require the employer to pay the judgment. *Id.* at 732, 737 P.2d at 91. Like the plaintiff in *Otero,* Plaintiff here won a judgment in the federal action. This case, however, was not brought merely to obtain payment of the judgment from the Town. As an assignee of Rivera, Plaintiff also claims damages for the Town's bad faith failure to defend him. This fact highlights the tension between the competing policies embodied in our TCA. Although *Otero* stressed the importance of not exposing a governmental entity to liability for claims of which it had no statutory or actual notice, we believe the TCA also reflects the important policy of protecting a governmental employee from the expense and stress of mounting a defense and satisfying a judgment. By requiring governmental employers to defend and indemnify their employees, the TCA advances the legislature's intent that the TCA balance the limiting of governmental liability against the policy favoring compensation of those injured by governmental employees. See *Cobos,* 1998-NMSC-049, ¶ 6, 126 N.M. 418, 970 P.2d 1143. We therefore distinguish this case from *Otero.*

{26} We do not overrule the holding in *Otero.* Its holding would apply if an employee failed to notify and request a defense from his or her governmental employer if the employee were sued individually. However, under the circumstances of this case, where the employer does not dispute that its employee was acting within the scope of his employment, and where the employee notified his employer that a suit had been filed against him, asked the employer to provide a defense, and followed up on the request, all within the time for filing an answer to the complaint, the TCA requires the employer to defend and indemnify its employee.

{27} The Town argues that reading Section 41–4–4 as requiring it to defend and indemnify Rivera allows Plaintiff, by creative lawyering, to circumvent the notice provision, thus leading to "an absurdity . . . clearly contrary to the legislature's intent." We disagree. The employee defense and indemnification provisions are not connected to the notice provision, as the Town suggests. The TCA's employee defense and indemnification provisions deal with the relationship between the governmental entity and its agents, employees, and officers in the event the employee is faced with a lawsuit for his or her actions in "the scope of duty," whereas the notice provision governs the responsibility of a claimant to give the governmental entity notice when the claimant seeks damages from the entity.

CONCLUSION

{28} For the foregoing reasons, we reverse the summary judgment entered in favor of the Town. We remand for entry of summary judgment in Plaintiff's favor declaring that the Town had a duty to defend Rivera and has a duty to pay the judgment against Rivera, and for further proceedings consistent with this opinion. We express no opinion about the viability of Plaintiff's claim for bad faith failure to defend.

3. THE CONSTITUTIONAL TORT ACTION UNDER 42 U.S.C. § 1983

42 U.S.C. § 1983 Civil Action for Deprivation of Rights

Every person who, under color of any statute, ordinance, regulation, custom, or usage, of any State or Territory or the District of Columbia, subjects, or causes to be subjected, any citizen of the United States or other person within the jurisdiction thereof to the deprivation of any rights, privileges, or immunities secured by the Constitution and laws, shall be liable to the party injured in an action at law, suit in equity, or other proper proceeding for redress, except that in any action brought against a judicial officer for an act or omission taken in such officer's judicial capacity, injunctive relief shall not be granted unless a declaratory decree was violated or declaratory relief was unavailable. For the purposes of this section, any Act of Congress applicable exclusively to the District of Columbia shall be considered to be a statute of the District of Columbia.

Presidential Proclamation Calling Attention to the Act Commonly Known as the Ku Klux Law, and Enjoining Obedience Thereto
May 3, 1871

The Act of congress, entitled "An act to enforce the provisions of the fourteenth amendment to the Constitution of the United States, and for other purposes," Approved April 20, A.D. 1871, being a law of extraordinary public importance, I consider it my duty to issue this my proclamation calling the attention of the people of the United States thereto; enjoining upon all good citizens, and especially upon all public officers, to be zealous in the enforcement thereof, and warning all persons to abstain from committing any of the acts thereby prohibited.

This law of Congress applies to all parts of the United States, and will be enforced everywhere, to the extent of the powers vested in the Executive. But inasmuch as the necessity therefor is well known to have been caused chiefly by persistent violations of the rights of citizens of the United States by combinations of lawless and disaffected persons in certain localities lately the theater of insurrection and military conflict, I do particularly exhort the people of those parts of the country to suppress all such combinations by their own voluntary efforts through the agency of local laws, and to maintain the rights of all citizens of the United States, and to secure to all such citizens the equal protection of the laws. . . .

The failure of local communities to furnish such means for the attainment of results so earnestly desired imposes upon the national

Government the duty of putting forth all its energies for the protection of its citizens of every race and color, and for the restoration of peace and order throughout the entire country.

—U.S. Grant

Poolaw v. Marcantel

565 F.3d 721 (10th Cir. 2009)

■ LUCEERO, CIRCUIT JUDGE.

This case requires us to address the extent to which a familial connection to a suspect supports either probable cause for a search warrant or reasonable suspicion for an investigative detention. Following the murder of Bernalillo County Sheriff's Deputy James McGrane, Lieutenant Gregg Marcantel and Detective Timothy Hix obtained a warrant and ordered the search of property belonging to Rick and Cindy Poolaw, the parents-in-law of the primary suspect, Michael Paul Astorga. Marcantel later ordered the stop of Chara Poolaw, Astorga's sister-in-law. The search and stop were based on little more than the Poolaws' status as Astorga's in-laws.

Although we are sympathetic to the urgency of the officers' search for Astorga, we conclude that these actions violated the Fourth Amendment. Adhering to established Supreme Court precedent and the unanimous case law of this and other courts, we hold that a familial relationship is insufficiently particularized to justify invading an individual's reasonable expectation of privacy. Applying this rule to the present case, we conclude that the Poolaws' status as Astorga's in-laws, combined with the meager additional facts known to Marcantel and Hix, were insufficient to support a finding of either probable cause to search the property or reasonable suspicion to detain Chara.1 Further, because these Fourth Amendment principles were clearly established at the time of their actions, Marcantel and Hix are not entitled to qualified immunity. We have jurisdiction under 28 U.S.C. § 1291, Mitchell v. Forsyth, 472 U.S. 511, 530 (1985), and we affirm.

I

A

In the early hours of March 22, 2006, Bernalillo County Sheriff's Deputy James McGrane was shot and killed while conducting a traffic stop. Bernalillo County Sheriff's Office ("BCSO") investigators determined that the truck Deputy McGrane had stopped belonged to Astorga, who was also wanted in connection with the November 2005 homicide of Candido Martinez. Based on this information, the investigators identified Astorga as the primary suspect in the McGrane homicide, and a manhunt ensued.

BCSO investigators discovered that Astorga had been in the area of the McGrane homicide on the night in question and that he lived at # 31

Lark Road, approximately fifteen miles south of where McGrane was killed. Neighbors of # 31 Lark Road told investigators that a man matching Astorga's description had recently moved in with his "pregnant girlfriend." Upon canvassing the area, officers also found the vehicle Deputy McGrane had stopped the night he was killed parked in the vicinity of Astorga's address.

Investigators then sought out Marcella because Astorga had listed her as his spouse and emergency contact when he had been arrested in the past. After detectives failed to locate Marcella at her known address, Lieutenant Marcantel telephoned Rick, a retired New Mexico State Police officer and acquaintance. Rick confirmed that Marcella was his daughter and that she was pregnant by Astorga. He also told Marcantel that she had spent the night of March 21 at Rick and Cindy's home. Throughout the day, Rick called Marcantel to tell him that Marcella was no longer at the house, that she had uncharacteristically called in sick to work, and, then, that he had ultimately located her.

At the time of the investigation, Rick lived at 343 Calle Del Banco with Cindy and their daughter Chara. Two days after the McGrane homicide, Astorga remained at large. BCSO investigators, including Marcantel and Hix, decided that the Poolaws' property should be searched. Hix prepared an affidavit seeking a warrant to search the Poolaws' property ("the Hix affidavit"), in which he provided a general description of the McGrane homicide and investigation. In the affidavit, Hix gave specific information explaining why Astorga was identified as the suspect. He then asserted a connection between Astorga and the Poolaws' property:

> On previous arrests, Michael Paul Astorga listed Marcella Astorga as his spouse and emergency contact. Police detectives have had contact with Ms. Marcella Astorga, and know her as Marcella Poolaw, and that she is currently pregnant BCSO Lieutenant G. Marcantel recognized the name Poolaw and contacted Rick Poolaw at approximately 0830 hours and confirmed he had a daughter named Marcella Poolaw and she was pregnant by Michael Paul Astorga. Rick advised Lieutenant Marcantel that when he left home (343 Calle Del Banco, described above to be searched) that morning, Marcella had got up and was getting ready for work (indicating that she resides there at least part time). Rick Poolaw told Lieutenant Marcantel he would attempt to locate his daughter. Rick later contacted Lieutenant Marcantel and advised him that he had contacted Marcella's place of employment, and was told she had called in sick. Rick stated that Marcella had not indicated to him that she was sick and that it was very unusual for her not to show up for work. Rick stated that he would continue to attempt to locate Marcella. Based on the apparent fact that Marcella Poolaw (Astorga) resides at least part time at 343 Calle Del Banco

(described above to be searched) it would be reasonable to assume that her husband, Michael Astorga, resides there at least part time as well and may have left or hidden evidence related to this crime at this residence. It is also reasonable to assume that, because the entire property is owned by Michael Astorga's in-laws, that he may have secreted himself or any evidence within any of the structures on the property.

In addition, the affidavit included the facts that Astorga was recently seen by neighbors moving in at # 31 Lark Road with his "girlfriend" and that "[d]etectives attempted to contact [Marcella] at her residence located at 9820 Edith NW, but she was not there." A New Mexico state court judge issued a warrant on the afternoon of March 24.

That same evening, BCSO officers—but not Marcantel or Hix—executed the warrant on the Poolaws' property under the supervision of then-Sergeant Scott Baird. During the search, Rick and Cindy were handcuffed outside their home.

A few days later, Marcantel learned that Chara had called Cindy and had asked whether she could "get in trouble" for having a gun. Based on "the fact that Chara was a loved one of Michael Paul Astorga's wife" and "her admission that she had a gun," Marcantel ordered her stopped to determine whether the gun was the McGrane homicide weapon. Chara was detained, handcuffed, and held in a squad car while her car was searched. After the gun found in her car was determined not to be the murder weapon, she was released.

B

Alleging that the search and seizures violated the Fourth Amendment, Rick, Cindy, and Chara ("the Poolaws") brought this § 1983 action in the United States District Court for the District of New Mexico. Named as defendants were Bernalillo County Sheriff Darren White, Lieutenant Marcantel, Detective Hix, and the Bernalillo County Board of Commissioners. First, the Poolaws alleged that the detentions of Rick, Cindy, and Chara constituted unreasonable seizures ("Claim I"). Second, the Poolaws alleged that the defendants had unreasonably searched their property ("Claim II"). In their answer, the defendants raised a number of affirmative defenses, including qualified immunity.

On the undisputed facts, the Poolaws moved for partial summary judgment, arguing that the warrant to search their property lacked probable cause on its face or, in the alternative, omitted material information negating probable cause, and thus the search and incidental seizure of Rick and Cindy violated the Fourth Amendment. In addition, they argued that Marcantel lacked probable cause to order Chara's detention, and thus, the stop was unconstitutional. Defendants responded and filed their own motion for partial summary judgment based on qualified immunity.

In a single order, the district court granted summary judgment in favor of the Poolaws on Claims I and II, denying Marcantel and Hix qualified immunity. Poolaw v. White, Mem. Op. and Order, No. CIV 06-923, at 13 (D.N.M. Sept. 26, 2007) ("Sept.2007 Order"). Reviewing the Hix affidavit, the district court found that it established only that Marcella was married to Astorga, that she stayed overnight at Rick and Cindy's home and did not go to work the next day, and that Astorga was on the run. *Id.* at 7. Regarding Astorga's connection to the property, the court concluded that the affidavit "provided only inferences and assumptions of dubious reliability," which were "simply not enough to provide probable cause to violate the Poolaws' right of privacy in their home." *Id.* at 8–9. In addition, the court found that Chara's status as Astorga's sister-in-law and her conversation with Cindy about a gun did not create reasonable suspicion of criminal activity justifying Chara's detention. *Id.* at 12–13. Concluding that these Fourth Amendment principles were clearly established when the incidents occurred, the court denied qualified immunity. Marcantel and Hix now appeal.

II

Orders granting partial summary judgment or denying summary judgment are generally not final appealable orders under 28 U.S.C. § 1291, but we have jurisdiction to review a denial of qualified immunity if the denial turned on a question of law. Liberty Mut. Ins. Co. v. Wetzel, 424 U.S. 737, 744 (1976) (a grant of partial summary judgment on liability but not damages is not final); Fogarty v. Gallegos, 523 F.3d 1147, 1153 (10th Cir.2008) (a denial of qualified immunity on summary judgment is appealable to the extent it turns on a question of law). We review the denial of a summary judgment motion raising qualified immunity de novo, Roska ex rel. Roska v. Sneddon, 437 F.3d 964, 971 (10th Cir.2006), applying the same standard as the district court. When a defendant raises an affirmative defense of qualified immunity, the burden rests with the plaintiff to show that the defendant's actions fall outside the scope of the immunity. *See* Weigel v. Broad, 544 F.3d 1143, 1151 (10th Cir.2008). In determining whether the plaintiff has made that showing, the district court considers whether the facts taken in the light most favorable to the plaintiff show that the defendant's conduct violated a constitutional right. *Fogarty,* 523 F.3d at 1155 (quoting Saucier v. Katz, 533 U.S. 194, 201 (2001)). If that initial inquiry is satisfied, the court considers whether the right violated was clearly established. *Id.*

A

Marcantel and Hix contend that the search of the Poolaws' property was constitutional because it was authorized by a warrant supported by probable cause. Marcantel and Hix argue in the alternative that even if the search violated the Poolaws' rights, they cannot be held liable under § 1983 because they were not present when the warrant was executed. We disagree with both contentions.

1

If the Hix affidavit established probable cause for the search, the search of the Poolaws' property was constitutional. We review the district court's ruling on the sufficiency of the warrant de novo, but we pay great deference to the probable cause determination made by the judge who issued the warrant. United States v. Perrine, 518 F.3d 1196, 1201 (10th Cir.2008). We will uphold a warrant if the issuing judge had a "substantial basis for . . . conclud[ing] that a search would uncover evidence of wrongdoing." Illinois v. Gates, 462 U.S. 213, 236 (1983) (quotations omitted); accord United States v. Grimmett, 439 F.3d 1263, 1268 (10th Cir.2006).

"In determining whether probable cause exists to issue a warrant, the issuing judge must decide whether, given the totality of the circumstances, there is a fair probability that contraband or evidence of a crime will be found in a particular place." *Grimmett,* 439 F.3d at 1270 (quotation omitted); *see also* United States v. Harris, 369 F.3d 1157, 1165 (10th Cir.2004) ("Probable cause exists when the facts presented in the affidavit would warrant a man of reasonable caution to believe that evidence of a crime will be found at the place to be searched." (quotation omitted)). But, a court may not "arrive at probable cause simply by piling hunch upon hunch." United States v. Valenzuela, 365 F.3d 892, 897 (10th Cir.2004). We assess the validity of the warrant "on the basis of the information that the officers disclosed, or had a duty to discover and to disclose, to the issuing [judge]," Maryland v. Garrison, 480 U.S. 79, 85 (1987); *see* Wilkins v. DeReyes, 528 F.3d 790, 802 (10th Cir.2008), looking both at the facts that support probable cause and those that militate against it, *Valenzuela,* 365 F.3d at 897.

Marcantel and Hix do not contend that facts outside the affidavit, but known to the issuing judge, supported its issuance, thus we confine our review to the Hix affidavit. *See* Aguilar v. Texas, 378 U.S. 108, 109 n.1 (1964) ("It is elementary that in passing on the validity of a warrant, the reviewing court may consider only information brought to the magistrate's attention."), overruled on other grounds by *Gates,* 462 U.S. at 238. Although it describes the progress of the McGrane homicide investigation, less than a page of the Hix affidavit links the investigation to the Poolaws' property. The district court characterized the warrant as "issued because [the Poolaws'] daughter was married to Astorga, she stayed overnight at their house and did not go to work the next morning, and Astorga was on the run." Sept.2007 Order, at 7. As Marcantel and Hix note, the affidavit also mentions that Astorga had listed Marcella as his emergency contact when arrested previously and that she was pregnant by him. Marcantel and Hix claim that the district court erred in concluding that these facts did not provide a substantial basis for the warrant.

We start our analysis with the inarguable proposition that "mere propinquity to others independently suspected of criminal activity does not, without more, give rise to probable cause." Ybarra v. Illinois, 444 U.S. 85, 91 (1979). In *Ybarra,* the proximity at issue was physical, but propinquity is specifically defined as nearness in "kindred or parentage." Black's Law Dictionary 1255 (8th ed.2004). In *United States v. Vazquez-Pulido,* this court accepted the proposition that "mere propinquity" includes sibling relationships when reviewing probable cause to arrest. 155 F.3d 1213, 1216 (10th Cir.1998) (citing *Ybarra,* 444 U.S. at 91). We see no reason to distinguish between probable cause to arrest, the issue in *Vazquez-Pulido,* and probable cause to search, the issue here. Our sibling circuits to address the question have held that a search warrant resting primarily on a "familial relation" is "so lacking in indicia of probable cause as to render official belief in its existence entirely unreasonable." United States v. Herron, 215 F.3d 812, 814 (8th Cir.2000); *see also* Walczyk v. Rio, 496 F.3d 139, 162–63 (2d Cir.2007) (a warrant inaccurately implying that the defendant had lived with his mother recently did not establish probable cause to search the mother's home).

District courts directly addressing whether a familial relationship constitutes probable cause have also uniformly held that it does not. United States v. Fernandez-Morris, 99 F.Supp.2d 1358, 1368 (S.D.Fla.1999) (one's status as the father of a suspect is insufficient to establish probable cause); Timberlake ex rel. Timberlake v. Benton, 786 F.Supp. 676, 686 (M.D.Tenn.1992) (one's status as the girlfriend or sister of a suspect is insufficient to establish probable cause); Doe v. City of Chicago, 580 F.Supp. 146, 150–51 (N.D.Ill.1983) (one's status as the child of a suspect is insufficient to establish probable cause). Based on *Ybarra,* *Vazquez-Pulido,* the plain meaning of propinquity, and the unanimity of the case law from other jurisdictions, we discern a clear rule: A familial relationship to someone suspected of criminal activity, without more, does not constitute probable cause to search or arrest.

Therefore, we must consider whether the additional facts linking Astorga to the Poolaws' property provide the additional particularized information necessary to establish probable cause. From the face of the affidavit, the following additional facts are relevant: (1) Astorga listed Marcella as his spouse and emergency contact during previous arrests; (2) Marcella was pregnant; (3) Marcella spent the night of the McGrane homicide at Rick and Cindy's home; (4) Marcella called in sick to work the next day, which was unusual for her; (5) Marcella resided with Astorga at # 31 Lark Road; and (6) detectives also had a residence for her listed as 9820 Edith NW.

We agree with the district court that the affidavit fails to establish the "apparent fact" or "reasonable . . . assum[ption]" that either Marcella or Astorga resided "at least part time" with the Poolaws. Rather, these are unsupported conclusions that Hix leapt to knowing only that Marcella had spent a single night there. An overnight stay is not part-time residency. Further, the actual facts in the affidavit militate against either conclusion: Marcella and Astorga lived at a different address, # 31

Lark Road, a fact confirmed by neighbors and Marcella herself, and the only alternative residence known to BCSO detectives was 9820 Edith NW. Certainly, a single night indicated a possibility that Marcella lived at her parents' part time, but a possibility is not the probability that the Fourth Amendment requires. *Grimmett*, 439 F.3d at 1270.

Further, the connection between the Poolaws' property and Astorga-the actual suspect and the would-be source of evidence of criminal activity-is even more attenuated. It relies on the assumption that if Marcella had contact with the property, so too did Astorga. The affidavit establishes a close familial connection between Astorga and Marcella, and it connects Marcella to the property because she stayed there the night of the McGrane homicide. But linking Marcella to the property is not equivalent to linking the McGrane homicide to the property; to find probable cause, it is the latter connection that must be established. *See* United States v. Gonzales, 399 F.3d 1225, 1231 (10th Cir.2005). Further circumstances described in the affidavit-that Marcella had uncharacteristically called in sick to work-do not rise to a fair probability that such a connection exists, particularly in light of the fact that Astorga and Marcella resided elsewhere. *See Harris,* 369 F.3d at 1165.

No fact in the Hix affidavit suggests that Marcella had any contact with Astorga or that Astorga had any contact with the Poolaws' property during which time Astorga could have hidden evidence of the McGrane homicide.8 Rather, following its description of Marcella's connection to the property, the Hix affidavit enters into pure speculation:

> Based on the apparent fact that Marcella Poolaw (Astorga) resides at least part time at 343 Calle Del Banco . . . it would be reasonable to assume that her husband, Michael Astorga, resides there at least part time as well and may have left or hidden evidence related to this crime at this residence. It is also reasonable to assume that, because the entire property is owned by Michael Astorga's in-laws, that he may have secreted himself or any evidence within any of the structures on the property (emphases added).

Thus, the ultimate conclusion that Astorga or evidence of the McGrane homicide would be found at the Poolaws' property was based on a mere hunch that Astorga lived there, piled upon the hunch that Marcella lived at the property. *See Valenzuela,* 365 F.3d at 897; s*ee also Gonzales,* 399 F.3d at 1229–30 (an officer cannot reasonably rely upon a warrant containing "no facts explaining how the address was linked to [the defendant] . . . or the suspected criminal activity, or why the officer thought the items to be seized would be located at the residence").

Nonetheless, Marcantel and Hix argue that "[l]aw enforcement officers know and are trained that fugitives like Astorga will run to their family and friends," and that this experience is sufficient to establish a substantial nexus between Astorga and the Poolaws' property. Appellant's Br. at 14. Marcantel and Hix claim that our precedent does not require law enforcement officers to obtain direct evidence or possess personal knowledge that evidence or contraband is located on property to be searched; rather, they contend that officers can rely on training and experience to establish the required nexus. They cite *United States v. $149,442.43 in U.S. Currency* for the proposition that "[c]ourts often rely on the opinion of police officers as to where contraband may be kept." 965 F.2d 868, 874 (10th Cir.1992) (citations omitted). But unlike the affidavit at issue in *$149,442.43 in U.S. Currency*, the Hix affidavit does not mention any training or experience regarding where fugitives hide. Even if Hix had included such training in the affidavit, an officer's expertise cannot be invoked to nullify the Supreme Court's holding that mere propinquity is insufficient to establish probable cause. *Ybarra*, 444 U.S. at 91. Considering the totality of the circumstances and the lack of specific information linking Astorga to the Poolaws' property, we conclude that there was not probable cause to issue the search warrant. *See Grimmett*, 439 F.3d at 1270.

Because there was no probable cause to issue the warrant, the search of the Poolaws' property violated their Fourth Amendment rights. Moreover, because the "search [wa]s illegal and not supported by probable cause, the justification for using the search as the foundation for the seizure disappears because it was the connection of the individual with a location suspected of harboring criminal activity that provided the reasonable basis for the seizure." Jacobs v. City of Chicago, 215 F.3d 758, 772 (7th Cir.2000) (citation omitted); *see also* Michigan v. Summers, 452 U.S. 692, 703 (1981) ("[A] detention represents only an incremental intrusion on personal liberty when the search of a home has been authorized by a valid warrant." (emphasis added)). Because Marcantel and Hix do not assert independent cause or suspicion for the detention of Rick and Cindy while their property was searched, this seizure also violated their constitutional rights. *Jacobs,* 215 F.3d at 772.

2

We next consider Marcantel and Hix's assertion that even if the search and seizure violated the Poolaws' Fourth Amendment rights, they cannot be liable under § 1983 because they were not present during its execution. While a supervisory relationship alone is insufficient for liability under § 1983, Duffield v. Jackson, 545 F.3d 1234, 1239 (10th Cir.2008), an officer need not execute a search personally to be liable. *See* Snell v. Tunnell, 920 F.2d 673, 700–01 (10th Cir.1990). Rather, a defendant may be liable if a plaintiff can show that an "affirmative link exists between the [constitutional] deprivation and either the [officer's] personal participation, his exercise of control or direction, or his failure to supervise." Green v. Branson, 108 F.3d 1296, 1302 (10th Cir.1997) (quotation omitted). That showing can be made with "deliberate, intentional act[s]" that "caused or contributed to the . . . violation." Jenkins v. Wood, 81 F.3d 988, 994–95 (10th Cir.1996) (quotation omitted).

> For liability under section 1983, direct participation is not necessary. Any official who "causes" a citizen to be deprived of her constitutional rights can also be held liable. The requisite causal connection is satisfied if the defendant set in motion a series of events that the defendant knew or reasonably should have known would cause others to deprive the plaintiff of her constitutional rights.

Snell, 920 F.2d at 700 (quoting Conner v. Reinhard, 847 F.2d 384, 396–97 (7th Cir.1988)); *see also* Buck v. City of Albuquerque, 549 F.3d 1269, 1279–80 (10th Cir.2008).

In order for the plaintiffs to prevail on their claims, therefore, they must show that Marcantel and Hix set in motion a series of events they knew or reasonably should have known would result in the search of the Poolaws' property and the seizure of Rick and Cindy. Given that Marcantel ordered the search and Hix swore out the affidavit, it strains credulity that they would not have known these clearly intentional acts would lead directly to the search. On the record before us, however, it is far less clear whether they knew or reasonably should have known that these actions would cause the seizure, and the district court gave this question perfunctory analysis. Nonetheless, viewing the record and drawing the reasonable inferences therefrom in the light most favorable to the Poolaws, as we must, *Weigel,* 544 F.3d at 1151, we conclude that a reasonable jury could find Marcantel and Hix knew or reasonably should have known the Poolaws would be seized incident to the search. In particular, Sergeant Baird testified in his deposition that it was BCSO standard procedure to handcuff the people present in a home during a search, and there is no evidence in the record that Marcantel and Hix believed an exception would occur during this particular search. For these reasons, Marcantel and Hix are not entitled to qualified immunity on summary judgment despite not being present when the Poolaws' Fourth Amendment rights were violated.

B

Because Marcantel and Hix violated the Poolaws' constitutional rights, we must inquire whether the rights were clearly established such that a reasonable person in the position of Marcantel or Hix would have been aware that the search and seizure were unconstitutional when they occurred. *Weigel,* 544 F.3d at 1153. Because the defendants assert that they are entitled to qualified immunity on the undisputed facts, this is a question of law. *See* Keylon v. City of Albuquerque, 535 F.3d 1210, 1217–18 (10th Cir.2008).

> Ordinarily, in order for the law to be clearly established, there must be a Supreme Court or Tenth Circuit decision on point, or the clearly established weight of authority from other courts must have found the law to be as the plaintiff maintains. The plaintiff is not required to show, however, that the very act

in question previously was held unlawful in order to establish
an absence of qualified immunity.

544 F.3d at 1153 (quotations omitted). Our inquiry is whether the
contour of the divide is "sufficiently clear that a reasonable official would
understand that what he is doing violates that right." Hope v. Pelzer, 536
U.S. 730, 739 (2002) (quotation omitted).

This court has unambiguously held that probable cause cannot be
established, as noted, "simply by piling hunch upon hunch." *Valenzuela,*
365 F.3d at 897. As explained above, the only link between the McGrane
homicide and the Poolaws' property was the unjustified conclusion that
Marcella lived there at least part time and the follow-on conjecture that
Astorga lived there as well. It is clearly established in our Fourth
Amendment jurisprudence that probable cause for a warrant requires a
fair probability that the evidence sought would be found on the property.
Grimmett, 439 F.3d at 1268, 1270. As we held in *Gonzales,* the necessity
of a nexus between the suspected criminal activity and the particular
place to be searched is so well established that in the absence of such a
connection, "the affidavit and resulting warrant are so lacking in indicia
of probable cause as to render official belief in its existence entirely
unreasonable." 399 F.3d at 1231 (quotation omitted).

Specifically, it is clearly established that mere propinquity is
insufficient to establish probable cause. *Ybarra,* 444 U.S. at 91. That
neither the Supreme Court nor the Tenth Circuit has explicitly held that
propinquity includes parents-in-law and sisters-in-law is immaterial
given the plain meaning of propinquity and the unanimity of courts
holding that a familial relationship does not establish probable cause. *See*
York v. City of Las Cruces, 523 F.3d 1205, 1211–12 (10th Cir.2008)
("[T]he clearly established weight of authority from other courts"
establishes a right for the purposes of qualified immunity.). Under the
clearly established standards for what constitutes probable cause, no
reasonable officer could have believed that the meager facts related to
the Poolaws' property described in the Hix affidavit established more
than a possibility that evidence of the McGrane homicide would be found
there. The affidavit was "so lacking in indicia of probable cause as to
render official belief in its existence unreasonable." Malley v. Briggs, 475
U.S. 335, 345 (1986). Thus, Marcantel and Hix could not have
"reasonably but mistakenly conclude[d] that probable cause [wa]s
present," and they are not entitled to qualified immunity. Cortez v.
McCauley, 478 F.3d 1108, 1120 (10th Cir.2007) (en banc).

The dissent presses the point that because Marcantel and Hix
sought and obtained a search warrant from a judge, they should be
entitled to qualified immunity unless they intentionally misled the judge.
Dissenting Op. at 745–46. This conclusion is misguided for two reasons.

First, it is clearly established that "employ[ing] a reasonable process
in seeking the warrant" does not relieve officers of their constitutional
duty to "exercise their own professional judgment" as to the existence of

probable cause. *Gonzales,* 399 F.3d at 1230. The very case on which the dissent relies stands for the proposition that the issuance of a warrant by a magistrate does not immunize officers:

> It is true that in an ideal system an unreasonable request for a warrant would be harmless, because no judge would approve it. But ours is not an ideal system, and it is possible that a magistrate, working under docket pressures, will fail to perform as a magistrate should. We find it reasonable to require the officer applying for the warrant to minimize this danger by exercising reasonable professional judgment.

Malley, 475 U.S. at 345–46. Thus, it is not conclusive, as the dissent suggests, that "[a] law trained judge found the affidavit sufficient to establish probable cause and issued the warrant," Dissenting Op. at 742, as the issuance of the warrant simply does not control the outcome of our inquiry into the officers' exercise of their own professional judgment. Malley, 475 U.S. at 345–46.

Second, it is beyond question that an officer's duty to exercise his independent professional judgment is not met simply because he lacks subjective bad faith. Rather, the inquiry is an objective one: "whether a reasonably well-trained officer in [the defendant's] position would have known that his affidavit failed to establish probable cause and that he should not have applied for the warrant." *Malley,* 475 U.S. at 345; accord *Keylon,* 535 F.3d at 1218 ("After Harlow [v. Fitzgerald, 457 U.S. 800 (1982)], qualified immunity does not depend on the officer's subjective, good faith belief that he was not violating clearly established federal law, but instead the defense now hinges on whether that belief was reasonable."); Bruning v. Pixler, 949 F.2d 352, 356 (10th Cir.1991) ("The subjective component [of qualified immunity] focused on the good faith of the official and relieved him from liability if he did not actually know his conduct was unconstitutional and did not act with malicious intent. *Harlow* eliminated any consideration of the defendant's intent as it relates to his knowledge of the law. . . ."). Whether the officers intentionally misled the judge is simply of no moment unless such intent is an element of the plaintiffs' claims, which it is not here. *See Bruning,* 949 F.2d at 356; Meyer v. Bd. of County Comm'rs of Harper County, 482 F.3d 1232, 1242 (10th Cir.2007) ("Subjective good faith or bad faith of government actors is ordinarily irrelevant to the objective inquiry whether a reasonable officer would have realized that his conduct was unlawful."). As we explain above, given the absence of a factual connection other than Marcella between Astorga and the Poolaws' property, an officer could not reasonably apply for a search warrant believing that probable cause existed.

We thus affirm the district court's denial of Marcantel and Hix's motion for summary judgment related to the search of the Poolaws' property and the resulting detention of Rick and Cindy.

III

Marcantel also asserts that he is entitled to qualified immunity for the detention of Chara because he did not violate her Fourth Amendment right to be free from unreasonable seizures. He acknowledges that he ordered the stop, but asserts that it was based on reasonable suspicion. We disagree: Chara's status as Astorga's sister-in-law and her conversation with Cindy about a gun did not establish a reasonable suspicion that she was committing or had committed a crime.

A

. . . Marcantel argues that he had reasonable suspicion to believe that Chara had the McGrane homicide weapon in her car when he ordered the stop. He relies on three facts for this conclusion: (1) Chara told her mother she was anxious about having a gun in her car, (2) Chara was Astorga's sister-in-law, and (3) the McGrane homicide weapon had not been found.

Because it is lawful to carry a gun in a vehicle in New Mexico, N.M. Stat. § 30–7–2(A)(2); United States v. King, 990 F.2d 1552, 1563 n. 5 (10th Cir.1993); State v. Gutierrez, 136 N.M. 18, 94 P.3d 18, 22 (N.M.Ct.App.2004), Chara's admission that she had a gun does not weigh heavily in our reasonable suspicion calculus—particularly in light of the fact that Marcantel knew the Poolaws legally owned firearms. We next weigh Chara's anxiety during the phone call, but in light of the fact that her home had just been searched by a team of law enforcement, we consider such anxiety to be akin to nervousness during a police encounter. " 'We have repeatedly held that nervousness is of limited significance in determining reasonable suspicion and that the government's repetitive reliance on . . . nervousness . . . as a basis for reasonable suspicion . . . must be treated with caution.' " United States v. Wood, 106 F.3d 942, 948 (10th Cir.1997) (quoting United States v. Fernandez, 18 F.3d 874, 879 (10th Cir.1994)) (alterations original). Given the paucity of additional information on which Marcantel based his decision, this case is quite unlike those in which this court has identified significant additional factors supporting the connection between nervousness and reasonable suspicion. *See, e.g.,* United States v. AlcarazArellano, 441 F.3d 1252, 1260 (10th Cir.2006) (defendant had implausible travel plans and suspiciously purchased a used vehicle); United States v. Bradford, 423 F.3d 1149, 1157–58 (10th Cir.2005) ("[Defendant's] answers to basic questions were evasive and conflicting at best, and the story she told defied common sense, particularly the financial illogic of purchasing a series of one-way plane tickets and one-way car-rentals."); *see also* United States v. Santos, 403 F.3d 1120, 1127 (10th Cir.2005) ("[N]ervousness is a sufficiently common-indeed natural-reaction to confrontation with the police that unless it is unusually severe or persistent, or accompanied by other, more probative, grounds for reasonable suspicion, it is of limited significance in determining whether reasonable suspicion exists." (quotations and citations omitted)). Thus, on the facts of this case, we give little weight to Chara's anxiety.

Because we examine the totality of the circumstances, we add the final relevant fact to our calculus: Chara was Astorga's sister-in-law. As above, we consider that "'a person's mere propinquity to others independently suspected of criminal activity,' create[s] neither probable cause nor reasonable suspicion." United States v. Tehrani, 49 F.3d 54, 59 (2d Cir.1995) (quoting *Ybarra,* 444 U.S. at 91). *Ybarra* itself rejected the argument that propinquity alone was sufficient to justify an investigative detention. 444 U.S. at 91–93. Thus, our holding above applies equally to the stop of Chara: Without more, a familial connection to a suspect does not establish reasonable suspicion.

Marcantel does not argue that he knew of anything beyond mere propinquity connecting Chara and Astorga. Because the status of an individual, rather than her behavior, cannot be particularized to a specific accusation, we are wary of giving it much weight. *See* United States v. Freeman, 479 F.3d 743, 749 (10th Cir.2007). In *Freeman,* we held that the defendant's parolee status and criminal history, even when combined with his agitation and his girlfriend's sudden movement, did not create reasonable suspicion without other particularized objective facts. *Id.* Chara's status as Astorga's sister-in-law, when combined with nothing more than her possession of a firearm and her anxiety, similarly fails to establish reasonable suspicion. Thus, because Marcantel did not reasonably suspect that Chara was involved in the McGrane homicide, he violated her Fourth Amendment right to be free from unreasonable seizures by ordering the stop.

B

Marcantel does not challenge whether the law regarding Chara's stop is clearly established, but we consider it because it is a question of law on which the plaintiffs bear the burden of proof. *See Weigel,* 544 F.3d at 1151. That "mere propinquity" does not create reasonable suspicion is clearly established, and its contours encompass familial relationships. *See supra* Part II.B. Further, it is clearly established that nervous behavior is of minimal significance in determining reasonable suspicion. *Wood,* 106 F.3d at 948. Thus, Chara's stop violated her clearly established Fourth Amendment rights. For that reason, we affirm the district court's denial of Marcantel's motion for summary judgment based on qualified immunity with respect to the detention of Chara.

IV

AFFIRMED.

■ O'BRIEN, CIRCUIT JUDGE, dissenting.

Regrettably, I can find comfort in no part of the majority opinion. Contrary to its views: 1) there was probable cause to search the Poolaw property; 2) even if probable cause had been lacking no constitutional violation occurred because the search was conducted in good faith reliance upon a warrant issued by a detached and impartial judge; 3) because the search of the Poolaw property was lawful the seizure of Rick and Cindy Poolaw incident to that search violated no constitutional rights; 4) we have jurisdiction to conduct an interlocutory review of the summary judgment entered in favor of the Poolaws on the seizure issue and should reverse; 5) the stop of Chara Poolaw was proper based upon reasonable suspicion of criminal activity; and 6) at no time did Marcantel and Hix act contrary to clearly established law. I respectfully dissent. . . . .

2.   The *Leon* Doctrine

. . . *Leon* recognized four situations in which an officer cannot be found to have relied on a warrant in good faith: 1) the issuing judge "was misled by information in an affidavit that the affiant knew was false or would have known was false except for his reckless disregard of the truth"; 2) the issuing judge "wholly abandoned his judicial role"; 3) the warrant was "so facially deficient-i.e., in failing to particularize the place to be searched or the things to be seized-that the executing officers cannot reasonably presume it to be valid"; and 4) "[the] affidavit [is] so lacking in probable cause as to render official belief in its existence entirely unreasonable." *Leon,* 468 U.S. at 923 (emphasis added) (quotations omitted). In summary the Court said: "In the absence of an allegation that the magistrate abandoned his detached and neutral role, suppression is appropriate only if the officers were dishonest or reckless in preparing their affidavit or could not have harbored an objectively reasonable belief in the existence of probable cause." *Id.* at 926 It then applied the newly minted test to Leon's arguments:

> Officer Rombach's application for a warrant clearly was supported by much more than a "bare bones" affidavit. The affidavit related the results of an extensive investigation and, as the opinions of the divided panel of the Court of Appeals make clear, provided evidence sufficient to create disagreement among thoughtful and competent judges as to the existence of probable cause. Under these circumstances, the officers' reliance on the magistrate's determination of probable cause was objectively reasonable, and application of the extreme sanction of exclusion is inappropriate.

Id.

The *Leon* doctrine applies not only to suppression issues in criminal cases but in qualified immunity cases as well. In *Malley,* the Supreme Court held "the same standard of objective reasonableness that we applied in the context of a suppression hearing in Leon . . . defines the qualified immunity accorded an officer whose request for a warrant allegedly caused an unconstitutional [search]." 475 U.S. at 344. "Only where the warrant application is so lacking in indicia of probable cause as to render official belief in its existence unreasonable will the shield of immunity be lost." *Id.* at 344–45 (citation omitted). Elaborating, the Court said:

> In *Leon,* we stated that our good-faith inquiry is confined to the objectively ascertainable question whether a reasonably well-trained officer would have known that the search was illegal despite the magistrate's authorization. The analogous question in [a § 1983 qualified immunity] case is whether a reasonably well-trained officer in petitioner's position would have known that his affidavit failed to establish probable cause and that he should not have applied for the warrant. If such was the case, the officer's application for a warrant was not objectively reasonable [and he is not entitled to immunity].

Id. at 345 (emphasis added); *see also* Groh v. Ramirez, 540 U.S. 551, 565 n. 8 (2004); Davis v. Gracey, 111 F.3d 1472, 1480 (10th Cir.1997); Beard v. City of Northglenn, Colo., 24 F.3d 110, 114 n. 3 (10th Cir.1994).

The first three *Leon* factors are not in play; the only question is whether Marcantel and Hix could have "harbored an objectively reasonable belief in the existence of probable cause." *Leon,* 468 U.S. at 926. The answer is yes. At most it is debatable whether the warrant should have issued. Surely this is not a case where the officers "should not have applied for the warrant." *Malley,* 475 U.S. at 345. While not conclusive evidence of the officers' reasonable belief, a law trained judge found the affidavit sufficient to establish probable cause and issued the warrant. Moreover the officers also consulted counsel with respect to the adequacy of the affidavit before it was presented to the judge. In such circumstances the threshold over which the officers must pass to avoid suppression of evidence in a criminal case or to be entitled to qualified immunity in a civil case is quite low.

This circuit has applied a different rubric to the "bare bones" affidavit mentioned in *Leon.* Under our case law if a search warrant was erroneously issued, we nevertheless uphold the search if there is a minimal nexus between the place searched and the suspected criminal activity or evidence. United States v. Gonzales, 399 F.3d 1225, 1231 (10th Cir.2005). "[T]here must be some factual basis connecting the place to be searched to the defendant or suspected criminal activity. When this connection is wholly absent, the affidavit and resulting warrant are so lacking in indicia of probable cause as to render official belief in its existence entirely unreasonable." *Id.* (quotations omitted). The affidavit in this case certainly satisfies the reasonable nexus (or "bare bones") test. As explained above, the affidavit provides detailed facts connecting Astorga to Marcella, connecting Marcella to the Poolaw property on the very night Astorga went on the run, and demonstrating unusual, even suspicious, behavior by Marcella. Common sense supplies the motive for Astorga to contact Marcella and for her to assist him. The affidavit also establishes an opportunity for Marcella to have contacted Astorga (during the early morning hours of March 22 and later that day when her whereabouts were suspiciously unknown from early morning until 1:30 p.m.) Moreover, it is not an unwarranted leap of logic to assume Marcella could have contacted Astorga between March 22 and March 24 (the date of the affidavit) or to embrace the possibility that Marcella returned to her parents' property after she had contact with Astorga.

"Just as reviewing courts give 'great deference' to the decisions of judicial officers who make probable-cause determinations, police officers should be entitled to rely upon the probable-cause determination of a neutral magistrate when defending an attack on their good faith for either seeking or executing a warrant." United States v. Corral-Corral, 899 F.2d 927, 939 (10th Cir.1990); *see also Malley,* 475 U.S. at 346 n. 9 ("It is a sound presumption that the magistrate is more qualified than the police officer to make a probable cause determination, and it goes without saying that where a magistrate acts mistakenly in issuing a warrant but within the range of professional competence of a magistrate, the officer who requested the warrant cannot be held liable.") (citation and quotations omitted). "This is particularly true, where, as here, with the benefit of hindsight and thoughtful reflection, reviewing judges still cannot agree on the sufficiency of the affidavit." Corral-Corral, 899 F.2d at 939; *see also Arnsberg,* 757 F.2d at 981 (granting qualified immunity to officers for invalid arrest warrant where reasonable officers could disagree with court's probable cause assessment: "It would be plainly unreasonable to rule that the arresting officers . . . must take issue with the considered judgment of . . . the federal magistrate. [Such a rule] would . . . mean that lay officers must at their own risk second-guess the legal assessments of trained lawyers. The Constitution does not require that allocation of law enforcement duties."). "If judges . . . disagree on a constitutional question, it is unfair to subject police to money damages for picking the losing side of the controversy." *Wilson,* 526 U.S. at 618.

If the search was erroneously authorized the consequences of the error ought not be visited on Marcantel and Hix, who followed proper procedure in obtaining the warrant, which, in turn, was executed in good faith by other officers. *Leon,* 468 U.S. at 921 ("Once [a] warrant issues, there is literally nothing more the policeman can do in seeking to comply with the law. Penalizing the officer for the magistrate's error, rather than his own, cannot logically contribute to the deterrence of Fourth Amendment violations.") (citation and quotations omitted).

B.   Clearly Established Law

Assuming, arguendo, a constitutional violation occurred, Marcantel and Hix are entitled to qualified immunity because the law at the time of the search did not fairly warn their conduct was unlawful. *See* Hope v. Pelzer, 536 U.S. 730, 741 (2002) (for the law to be clearly established, the law at the time of the incident must have provided the law enforcement officers with "fair warning" that their conduct was unconstitutional). "Ordinarily, in order for the law to be clearly established, there must be a Supreme Court or Tenth Circuit decision on point, or the clearly established weight of authority from other courts must have found the law to be as the plaintiff maintains." Medina v. City & County of Denver, 960 F.2d 1493, 1498 (10th Cir.1992).

Conducting a *de novo* review of the affidavit the majority has concluded it does not supply probable cause to search (actually the majority must be saying no reasonable officer or judge would think the affidavit was sufficient). To justify that conclusion it says: 1) the law requires "more" than a showing of a family relationship to establish probable cause and 2) the "more" required was insufficient in this case because it consisted of piling inference upon inference, a practice forbidden by our case law. With all due respect, I think the majority has lost focus. The piling of inference upon inference, if it occurred, was judge error, not officer error. And the "more" required, to the extent it finds expression in our cases or in common sense, has been met by reasonable inferences drawn from facts recited in the affidavit. Our concern should center on whether the officers violated clearly established law in seeking the warrant, not whether the affidavit is ultimately satisfying to this Court. . . .

The law encourages, generally demands, officers obtain a warrant before conducting a search, especially of a home. *See* Payton v. New York, 445 U.S. 573, 586 (1980) ("It is a basic principle of Fourth Amendment law that searches and seizures inside a home without a warrant are presumptively unreasonable.") (quotations omitted); *Franks,* 438 U.S. at 164 ("The bulwark of Fourth Amendment protection, of course, is the Warrant Clause, requiring that, absent certain exceptions, police obtain a warrant from a neutral and disinterested magistrate before embarking upon a search."). Courts reward officers who obtain warrants. *See Ventresca,* 380 U.S. at 106 ("[I]n a doubtful or marginal case a search under a warrant may be sustainable where without one it would fall."). That reward may be most unsatisfying for officers who followed proper procedure and exhibited objective good faith in obtaining a search warrant only to find themselves being forced to trial in a civil suit for damages because a judge may have erred in issuing the warrant. . . .

In any event, the test is not whether the officers were incorrect in their assessment of probable cause or whether the judge was wrong to issue the warrant. It is whether the officers' request and the judge's response were reasonable. Even if the officers were mistaken, their mistake was reasonable. The protection of qualified immunity extends to such reasonable mistakes, whether they are ones of law, fact or a combination thereof. *Id.* at 815; *see also* Saucier v. Katz, 533 U.S. 194, 205 (2001) ("The concern of the immunity inquiry is to acknowledge that reasonable mistakes can be made as to the legal constraints on particular police conduct. . . . If the officer's mistake as to what the law requires is reasonable, however, the officer is entitled to the immunity defense."), overruled on other grounds by Pearson v. Callahan, 555 U.S. 223 (2009); Cortez v. McCauley, 478 F.3d 1108, 1120 (10th Cir.2007) (en banc)

("[L]aw enforcement officials who reasonably but mistakenly conclude that probable cause is present are entitled to immunity.").

II. SEIZURE OF RICK AND CINDY POOLAW

A. Constitutional Violation

In addition to other claims the Poolaws brought an excessive force claim against Marcantel and Hix (who were not present when the search warrant was executed) which they voluntarily dismissed. The only remaining issue is the constitutionality of Rick and Cindy Poolaws' seizure incidental to the search.

Because the search of the Poolaw property was constitutionally reasonable, the seizure of Rick and Cindy during that search was also reasonable. *See* Michigan v. Summers, 452 U.S. 692, 705 (1981) ("[F]or Fourth Amendment purposes, we hold that a warrant to search for contraband founded on probable cause implicitly carries with it the limited authority to detain the occupants of the premises while a proper search is conducted."); *see also* Muehler v. Mena, 544 U.S. 93, 98 (2005) ("Mena's detention for the duration of the search was reasonable under Summers because a warrant existed to search 1363 Patricia Avenue and she was an occupant of that address at the time of the search."). Whether or not these officers knew or should have known the Poolaws would be seized incident to the search is immaterial because their seizure was lawful. There was no constitutional violation.

B. Jurisdiction

The district court denied qualified immunity to these officers. It also concluded "any detention at all [of the Poolaws] was ipso facto unreasonable" because the search was unconstitutional and so entered summary judgment against the officers on the Poolaws' seizure claim (as to liability only). (R.App. at 326 n. 7.) The officers appealed from both rulings.

The majority refuses to address the summary judgment entered in favor of the Poolaws on the seizure issue, concluding we lack jurisdiction to consider it: "We note that in this interlocutory appeal, the court has jurisdiction solely to review the issues of law raised by the denial of qualified immunity to Marcantel and Hix. Mitchell, 472 U.S. at 530. . . . However, qualified immunity is immunity to suit, not a defense to liability. *Id.* at 526." (Majority Op. at 733 n. 11.) That strikes me as incorrect.

The complete quote from *Mitchell v. Forsyth* is this: "The entitlement [to qualified immunity] is an immunity from suit rather than a mere defense to liability. . . ." 472 U.S. 511, 526 (1985) (emphasis added). "[I]t is effectively lost if [the] case is erroneously permitted to go to trial." *Id.* The summary judgment entered in favor of the Poolaws and against the officers (finding them liable) deprives them of a "defense to liability" *Id.* They are entitled to interlocutory review of that decision. Refusing to consider that appeal also improperly runs the risk of forcing them to trial twice, contrary to the intent and purpose of qualified immunity.

These officers must now face a trial on damages where they will be foreclosed from presenting evidence or argument on liability. When that trial is concluded and the officers appeal we will reverse because the summary judgment on liability was improvidently granted-genuine issues of material fact exist as to liability (as I explain infra at 750–51). The issue will then return to the district court for a trial on liability and damages. The officers will unnecessarily face two trials. This is a needless and wasteful exercise. If the trial judge entered summary judgment in error we should correct it now. If he was correct we should affirm. Deciding, rather than avoiding, the issue saves time, expense and aggravation for all parties and all courts. The matter should be approached in a practical way, which is the justification for pendent appellate jurisdiction.

We have pendent appellate jurisdiction over the partial grant of the Poolaws' motion for summary judgment; the record is adequate to decide the issue and the summary judgment is inextricably intertwined with the denial of the officers' motion for partial summary judgment based on qualified immunity. . . .

III. STOP OF CHARA

. . . While it may be legal to carry a gun in a vehicle in New Mexico, it certainly is not legal to conceal the fruits of a crime. *See* N.M. Stat. Ann. §§ 30–22–4 ("Harboring or aiding a felon consists of any person, not standing in the relation of husband or wife, parent or grandparent, child or grandchild, brother or sister by consanguinity or affinity, who knowingly conceals any offender or gives such offender any other aid, knowing that he has committed a felony, with the intent that he escape or avoid arrest, trial, conviction or punishment."); 30–22–5 ("Tampering with evidence consists of destroying, changing, hiding, placing or fabricating any physical evidence with intent to prevent the apprehension, prosecution or conviction of any person or to throw suspicion of the commission of a crime upon another."). A reasonable officer could logically infer from Chara's comment to her mother that the gun Chara had was no "ordinary" gun. *See Arvizu,* 534 U.S. at 273 ("[Reasonable suspicion] allows officers to draw on their own experience and specialized training to make inferences from and deductions about the cumulative information available to them that might well elude an untrained person.") (quotations omitted). "[We] must defer to the ability of a trained law enforcement officer to distinguish between innocent and suspicious actions." United States v. Karam, 496 F.3d 1157, 1162 (10th Cir.2007) (quotations omitted). "Reasonable suspicion requires a dose of reasonableness and simply does not require an officer to rule out every possible lawful explanation for suspicious circumstances before effecting a brief stop to investigate further." United States v. Cortez-Galaviz, 495 F.3d 1203, 1208 (10th Cir.200) (2008).

The facts known to Marcantel supplied reasonable suspicion to stop Chara in order to investigate further. Whether the duration or intensity of the seizure of Chara was excessive is not before us. Neither is the voluntariness of her consent to search her vehicle.

IV. CONCLUSION

I would reverse the district court and extend qualified immunity to Marcantel and Hix on the unlawful search and unlawful seizure claims made by Rick and Cindy Poolaw. In the alternative I would reverse the grant of summary judgment to the Poolaws on the seizure claim and remand for trial on the issue of liability as well as damages. I would also reverse and extend qualified immunity on the claim that the stop of Chara violated her constitutional rights.

42 U.S.C. § 1988

(b) Attorney's fees

In any action or proceeding to enforce a provision of sections 1981, 1981a, 1982, 1983, 1985, and 1986 of this title, title IX of Public Law 92–318 [20 U.S.C.A. § 1681 et seq.], the Religious Freedom Restoration Act of 1993 [42 U.S.C.A. § 2000bb et seq.], the Religious Land Use and Institutionalized Persons Act of 2000 [42 U.S.C.A. § 2000cc et seq.], title VI of the Civil Rights Act of 1964 [42 U.S.C.A. § 2000d et seq.], or section 13981 of this title, the court, in its discretion, may allow the prevailing party, other than the United States, a reasonable attorney's fee as part of the costs, except that in any action brought against a judicial officer for an act or omission taken in such officer's judicial capacity such officer shall not be held liable for any costs, including attorney's fees, unless such action was clearly in excess of such officer's jurisdiction.

(c) Expert fees

In awarding an attorney's fee under subsection (b) of this section in any action or proceeding to enforce a provision of section 1981 or 1981a of this title, the court, in its discretion, may include expert fees as part of the attorney's fee.

Poy v. Boutselis

352 F.3d 479 (1st Cir. 2003)

■ COFFIN, SENIOR CIRCUIT JUDGE.

These appeals arise out of an incident on February 16, 1997 involving plaintiff Phaly Poy in an arrest, a scuffle with a Lowell, Massachusetts, police officer, defendant Boutselis, a booking at the police station, and emergency hospital treatment for a laceration. Plaintiff was charged with several offenses, including disturbing the peace and assault and battery. After being acquitted by a jury, he brought suit on February 16, 2000 against Boutselis and another officer present at the scene,

Conroy, and the Lowell Chief of Police, Davis, as well as the city of Lowell, citing 42 U.S.C. § 1983, and a variety of state claims. Also included as a defendant was one Neov, owner of the premises where the incident occurred and the temporary employer of Boutselis.

After denial of a motion to dismiss on statute of limitations grounds, a seven day jury trial in 2002 resulted in a verdict for plaintiff against defendant Boutselis in his personal capacity, granting him $5,000 to compensate for the use of excessive force, $5,000 to compensate for severe emotional distress, and $25,000 in punitive damages. In addition, the court allowed prejudgment interest in the amount of $31,013.33. All other claims against all parties were dismissed. Post trial, the district court denied Boutselis' motion for new trial and declined to award any counsel fees to any party.

Both plaintiff and Boutselis have appealed. Boutselis has challenged the rejection of his statute of limitations defense, the denial of his motion for a new trial, and denial of defendant Conroy's motion for attorney's fees. Poy appeals from the court's refusal to award him attorney's fees and costs. We affirm the court's rulings as to Boutselis and Conroy; we vacate the court's orders denying Poy's motions for attorney's fees and costs and remand for reconsideration in light of this opinion.

We first describe the incident giving rise to these cases, giving the version of facts and inferences favorable to plaintiff-appellant Poy. We then discuss defendant-appellant Boutselis' appeal, following with our deliberations as to Poy's appeal.

I.   The Incident

At about 11:30 p.m. on February 16, 1997, Poy, a 24-year-old man of Cambodian origin, and three friends went to a club, The Golden Swan, and proceeded along a hallway to a dance or function room. Barred from entering by a doorman, Poy looked inside to see if he knew anyone there. Soon officer Boutselis, specially employed by the club owner Neov, approached Poy, telling him in abusive language to leave before "I fucking pound your fucking head." As Poy was peacefully leaving, Boutselis pushed him from behind. Poy fell on the floor. Boutselis, six feet tall and weighing 240 pounds, sat on him, struck him above his right eye, and handcuffed his hands behind him, the right hand being brought over his shoulder and the left hand being drawn across his back and up. Two of Poy's friends testified that Boutselis, using the handcuffs as brass knuckles, repeatedly hit Poy on the head.

Poy was dragged to a police van and taken to the police station, helped by a policewoman to sign his name, and was charged with four counts: disorderly conduct; assault and battery on a police officer; assault and battery with a dangerous weapon; and resisting arrest. He was then taken to a hospital where he received five stitches to close a laceration over his right eye, leaving a scar observed by the jury. He returned to the police station where he remained for a number of hours until he was bailed. Poy testified that he felt pain lasting some two months in his shoulder, back, wrist, and head, and had difficulty sleeping and eating.

The above account is diametrically contradicted by the testimony of Officer Boutselis at every critical point-provocation, resistance, efforts to subdue, and extent of injury. But the jury was not required to accept his version.

II.   Appeal of Boutselis

A.   Statute of Limitations

Boutselis argues that Poy's suit, filed on the third anniversary of the key events, was one day late. Boutselis urges us to reject both Mass. R. Civ. P. 6(a) and Fed.R.Civ.P. 6(a) by counting the limitations period of three years inclusive of the date of accrual, so that the final day for bringing suit would fall one day before the third anniversary. It is an argument which upon analysis reveals less than meets the eye.

The argument begins with the recitation of propositions accepted by both parties: a § 1983 claim, according to 42 U.S.C. § 1988, borrows the appropriate state law governing limitations unless contrary to federal law, Wilson v. Garcia, 471 U.S. 261, 267 (1984); since the claims against Boutselis were for the use of excessive force, assault, battery, etc., the limitations period for personal injury is the appropriate analogue, *id.* at 273; the Massachusetts statute governing personal injury claims is Mass. Gen. Laws ch. 260, § 2A, providing that actions shall be commenced "within three years next after the cause of action accrues." Federal law controls the determination of when the cause of action accrues, Guzman-Rivera v. Rivera-Cruz, 29 F.3d 3, 5 (1st Cir.1994). Both federal and Massachusetts law agree that a § 1983 claim accrues when a plaintiff knows or has reason to know of his injury. *See* Nieves v. McSweeney, 241 F.3d 46, 52 (1st Cir.2001); Riley v. Presnell, 565 N.E.2d 780, 784, 409 Mass. 239, 243 (1991).

Massachusetts begins counting on the day following the day of the incident, with the last day for filing suit being the anniversary date of the event, in accordance with Mass. R. Civ. P. 6(a). *See* Ciampa v. January, 1992 Mass.App. Div. 204 (1992). We refer to Rule 6(a) as the Massachusetts application rule.

At this point, appellant advances two parallel arguments—both strained—in support of his contention that the claim is time barred.

First, Boutselis argues that while we may borrow the limitations period in Mass. Gen. Laws ch. 260 § 2A, we are prohibited from borrowing the application rule in Mass. R. Civ. P. 6(a). Under Boutselis' reading of precedent, borrowing the Massachusetts application rule contradicts the Supreme Court's directive in West v. Conrail, 481 U.S. 35, 39 (1987), which advised federal courts that if a state statute of limitations must be borrowed for a federal cause of action, the court is to borrow "no more than necessary." Second, even if we were permitted to borrow the state rule of application, Boutselis maintains that

Massachusetts utilizes a different application rule for § 1983 claims than for those arising under state law.

With respect to his first argument—that we may not borrow the Massachusetts application rule—Boutselis attempts to derail as precedent our opinion in Carreras-Rosa v. Alves-Cruz, 127 F.3d 172 (1st Cir.1997), but in doing so contradicts the Supreme Court's decision in *Wilson*, 471 U.S. at 269, which holds that "the length of the limitations period, and closely related questions of tolling and application, are to be governed by state law." In *Carreras*, we recognized *Wilson*'s teaching and looked to a Puerto Rico statute and a ruling of the Puerto Rico Supreme Court to determine the timeliness of a § 1983 action. *See Carreras*, 127 F.3d at 174. Boutselis suggests, however, that this holding encompasses only those instances in which a state statute, rather than a rule of procedure, sets forth the application rule. In advancing this pained distinction, he also ignores our disagreement in Carreras with dicta equating "the date of accrual with the first day of the limitations period," *id.* at 175.

Boutselis' second argument urges us to hold that Massachusetts uses a different rule of application for § 1983 claims than for claims arising under state law. Boutselis concedes that Massachusetts generally excludes the accrual date in calculating the limitations period of tort claims, *see Ciampa*, 1992 Mass.App. Div. at 204, but he maintains that under Pagliuca v. City of Boston, 626 N.E.2d 625, 35 Mass.App.Ct. 820 (1994), the statute of limitations for § 1983 claims begins running on (and therefore is inclusive of) the date of the wrongful acts. In *Pagliuca*, the court was dealing with the question of whether a § 1983 action accrues on the date of the wrongful acts or a later date when the effects of the acts were felt. Its decision about the beginning and ending dates of the limitations period cited no Massachusetts authority and relied solely on our decision in Altair v. Pesquera de Busquets, 769 F.2d 30, 32 (1st Cir.1985). We specifically abrogated *Altair* in *Carreras*, 127 F.3d at 174, borrowing instead the Puerto Rico law which calculated the limitations period exclusive of the date of accrual.

Most importantly, Boutselis ignores the strong indication of a beginning date in the "next after" language of Mass. Gen. Laws ch. 260 § 2A as well as longstanding Massachusetts precedent excluding the date of accrual from the calculation of the limitations period. *See* Pierce v. Tiernan, 280 Mass. 180, 182, 182 N.E. 292, 293 (1932) (interpreting prior Mass. Gen. Laws. ch. 260 § 4, which contained the same "next after" language as the current Mass. Gen. Laws. ch. 260 § 2A, to mean that in "computing [the] limit of time, the day upon which the cause of action accrued is to be excluded"); *see also* Bemis v. Leonard, 118 Mass. 502, 506 (1875) ("In this Commonwealth, the general rule, as applied in a variety of circumstances, and now well established, is, that in computing time from the date . . . the day of the date is to be excluded.").

We thus hold that in determining the accrual and limitations period of a § 1983 claim, we borrow Mass. Gen. Laws ch. 260, § 2A as well as Mass. R. Civ. P. 6(a). We note also that there cannot be any inconsistency with federal law since the rules of the two jurisdictions are identical. *See Wilson,* 471 U.S. at 269; *Carreras,* 127 F.3d at 174 n.1. The district court therefore did not err in finding that Poy's anniversary date filing was timely.

B.   Motion for New Trial

In his motion for a new trial, Boutselis made one allegation, namely, that the amount of damages for the intentional or reckless infliction of emotional distress ($5,000) and for punitive damages ($25,000) was excessive and the result of prejudice or sympathy. In the memorandum submitted to the district court, the argument widened to an assertion of a complete absence of evidence supporting two jury findings. With reference to the state law claim involving emotional distress, appellant argued that there was no medical or psychiatric evidence, and no testimony from the plaintiff specifically mentioning emotional distress. With reference to the § 1983 claim for punitive damages, appellant argued that the jury had made a special finding that he, Boutselis, had not acted maliciously and sadistically for the purpose of causing harm, that there was no evidence of evil intent, and that the incident was an isolated one. The district court denied the motion, ruling that there was "a genuine dispute of fact for decision by the jury."

Appellant faces a formidable burden in trying to persuade us to reverse a district judge's denial of a motion for new trial. Our review of such an issue is "extremely circumscribed." Correa v. Hospital San Francisco, 69 F.3d 1184, 1194 (1st Cir.1995). In assessing whether or not there is a reasonable basis for the jury's decision, we take "both the facts and the reasonable inferences therefrom in the light most hospitable to the jury's verdict." *Id.* at 1188.

First of all, both the claims for intentional or reckless infliction of emotional distress and for punitive damages require proof of similarly extreme conduct. The former requires evidence of conduct that is "extreme and outrageous." Nancy P. v. D'Amato, 517 N.E.2d 824, 827, 401 Mass. 516, 518 (1988). The latter requires either evidence of evil intent or "reckless or callous indifference to the federally protected rights of others." Smith v. Wade, 461 U.S. 30, 56 (1983). In this case the jury answered a carefully constructed series of questions. After it had found that Boutselis had used excessive physical force, despite an absence of resistance, threats, or attempt to flee on the part of Poy, it went on to find that his conduct "violated contemporary standards of decency and is repugnant to the conscience of the community," was "unnecessarily wanton or excessive," extended "beyond the scope of his capacity as a police officer," and took place "with reckless disregard for the likelihood that it would cause Poy to suffer severe emotional distress." We agree with the district court that at the very least the evidence presented factual questions as to Boutselis' conduct which could be and were resolved by the jury.

As for the evidence of resulting emotional distress, although there was no medical or psychiatric evidence, there was considerable testimony, not only from plaintiff but from two other witnesses, of the following facts: Poy was struck repeatedly on his face and back, being knocked to the floor and pinioned by Boutselis; his hands were locked behind him and handcuffs were used as brass knuckles, striking him repeatedly on the forehead; a resulting wound required sutures at a hospital and left visible evidence of a scar which the jury observed; the incident was followed by two months of pain in his shoulder, back, wrist, and head. A jury could reasonably infer from such humiliation, long continued pain, and facial disfigurement a condition of severe emotional distress. *Cf.* Wagenmann v. Adams, 829 F.2d 196, 216 (1st Cir.1987)(upholding compensatory damages of $225,000 for a 36-hour incident involving false arrest, bringing of charges, handcuffing, thrusting into police vehicle, arraignment, and a night in a mental hospital, but no physical injury).

On this record, the district court's denial of the motion for new trial is far from an abuse of discretion, not to mention "a manifest abuse of discretion." Joia v. Jo-Ja Service Corp., 817 F.2d 908, 918 (1st Cir.1987).

III. Appeal of Poy

The question posed by this appeal is whether, on the facts of this case, the district court was within its discretion in denying any attorney's fee award at all to Poy, although he obtained a verdict and not insignificant money damages against a city police officer.

A. Proceedings Below

The proceedings leading to this appeal involve several hearings. The first was held shortly after the conclusion of the jury trial, on October 18, 2002, to consider motions for attorney's fees. Poy's two attorneys each submitted a motion containing statements totaling some $98,631 and covering over four and a half years of representation by the senior counsel as well as work in preparation for the recent trial by the junior counsel. The court expressed its reactions that both motions were excessive, commented on what it thought wasteful duplication of lawyer presence and effort by Poy's team, questioned the apparent inappropriateness of including fees for the pursuit of claims on behalf of the disappearing Em and against officer Conroy, and heard an argument that Poy's lawyers' records did not appear to be contemporaneous in two specific entries in which conversations with Boutselis' attorney Freda were noted at a time prior to his association with his present firm. The court then set another date for further presentations, giving an opportunity for counsel to amend their affidavits.

Poy's counsel responded to the court's invitation with several submissions. One was from junior counsel Miller, affirming that all billing records had been reviewed and a good faith attempt made to locate errors and exclude excessive items. He rehearsed the work performed, principally in discovery, depositions, meeting with plaintiffs, and trial. He asserted that plaintiff Em's claims and claims against the city of Lowell involved the "common core of facts" and "related legal theories" deemed legitimate in successful claims by plaintiffs in Aubin v. Fudala, 782 F.2d 287, 291 (1st Cir.1986). Finally, he signified his willingness to take a ten percent cut, reducing his request from $44,102 to $39,611.

Poy's senior attorney, Wernick, explained the allocation of work between him, with 25 years experience, and Miller, with six, in which discovery matters were handled largely by Miller, and depositions largely by Wernick. Both were in attendance at trial as were the two lawyer teams representing Boutselis and the city. Attorney Wernick also voluntarily reduced his request from $63,562 to $47,206, saying this was a ten percent cut. In reality this would be a cut in excess of 25 percent and is clearly an error. A third submission addressed the two entries recording a conversation with Boutselis' attorney Freda at a time prior to his association with his firm. Photocopies of the original time records were submitted purporting to show that conversations with an unnamed Boutselis attorney had indeed been made on the cited dates.

A second hearing was soon held, on November 15, 2002. In replying to counsel's query why the court was not inclined to award any attorney's fees to either party, though plaintiff had prevailed against Boutselis, the court said, "[B]ecause you prevailed in part, but only in part, and very substantially did not prevail. Each of you overclaimed very, very substantially." Instead of spending a great deal of time with more submissions and repetitive arguments, the court concluded, "I should simply say that since neither of you prevailed in the sense that justifies an award of attorney's fees or costs, I will not give it to either side as between the plaintiff and Boutselis."

A third hearing was held on January 10, 2003. In the course of it the court said, "[T]here is not any prevailing party in the sense required for an attorney's fees award in this case because each party won in some significant respect and lost in some significant respect." The court further affirmed that this was the only basis of its decision. When its memorandum and order memorializing the results of the hearing was issued, however, Poy's request for attorney's fees was disposed of because the request was "plainly excessive," and even considering the attorneys' voluntary ten percent reduction, the fault had not been remedied. A second basis for denying fees in toto was that "there are strong indications the records given to this court were not contemporaneous records." The court also denied plaintiff all his costs except the $150 filing fee, partly because they were not listed in 28 U.S.C. § 1920(1) and partly because deposition transcripts were not shown to be necessary or paid for.

B.   Law of Prevailing Parties

We begin with the threshold principle enunciated by the Supreme Court in Hensley v. Eckerhart, 461 U.S. 424, 433 (1983), endorsing our formulation in Nadeau v. Helgemoe, 581 F.2d 275, 278–279 (1st Cir.1978), that "plaintiffs may be considered 'prevailing parties' for attorney's fees purposes if they succeed on any significant issue in litigation which achieves some of the benefit the parties sought in bringing suit." We have noted the permissive phrasing but have concluded that "awards in favor of prevailing civil rights plaintiffs are virtually obligatory." Gay Officers Action League v. Puerto Rico, 247 F.3d 288, 293 (1st Cir.2001). Prevailing party status, we have recognized, might be denied if success on a claim was "purely technical or *de minimis*," *id.* at 294 (quoting Tex. State Teachers Ass'n v. Garland Indep. Sch. Dist., 489 U.S. 782, 792 (1989)). Another basis for denying fees to a prevailing plaintiff is the presence of "special circumstances [which] would render such an award unjust." Hensley, 461 U.S. at 429 (quoting Newman v. Piggie Park Enters., 390 U.S. 400, 402 (1968)). In such a case, we require "findings of fact and conclusions of law identifying the special circumstances and explaining why an award would be inappropriate." de Jesus v. Banco Popular de Puerto Rico, 918 F.2d 232, 234 (1st Cir.1990).

Appellee Boutselis invokes Lewis v. Kendrick, 944 F.2d 949 (1st Cir.1991), where we reversed an award of attorney's fees to a plaintiff who had been awarded $1,000 compensatory damages in connection with a false arrest. The circumstances of that case demonstrate a coalescence of extremes in terms of litigation judgment, expenditure of time, and overclaiming: an incident involving merely a 15-minute investigation by police, an hour and three quarters detention awaiting bail, and the fastening of handcuffs too tightly, resulting in a demand for $250,000 in actual damages and $50,000 in punitive damages, and an initial request for $132,788 in attorney's fees for a time record of 952 hours, or half a billing year. Even so, total denial of fees caused then Judge Breyer to dissent, recommending at least a token fee. *See id.* at 956.

In the light of these precedents, we now look at this case. We are in sympathy with the plight of the district court, which is faced with a tedious and unpleasant task. It must determine time reasonably spent, the reasonable rates applicable, assess the significance of any success, and finally ascertain if special circumstances trump such calculations. There is no easy way. In this process counsel have an obligation to "make a good faith effort to exclude from a fee request hours that are excessive, redundant, or otherwise unnecessary." *Hensley,* 461 U.S. at 434. But in the end, the biases, pressures, self interest, and perspective of parties and their counsel make the task of the trial court central and indispensable.

Our task now is to review the district court's decision for "manifest abuse of discretion." *Gay Officers Action League,* 247 F.3d at 292. "Apart from mistakes of law . . . we will set aside a fee award only if it clearly appears that the trial court ignored a factor deserving significant weight, relied upon an improper factor, or evaluated all the proper factors (and no improper ones), but made a serious mistake in weighing them." *Id.* at 292–93.

C. The Record

The basic requirement that a plaintiff prevail on a significant issue is clearly met. The district court recognized this in commenting that "each party won in some significant respect and lost in some significant respect." Poy's victory was for his core claim of false arrest, the use of excessive force, and the infliction of emotional distress against the one individual whose acts were in issue. He obtained $10,000 in compensatory damages and two and one half times that amount in punitive damages. This was not only a personal victory but a recognition that professional, civil standards must be vigilantly maintained in law enforcement. To the extent that the district court may have deemed plaintiff's success de minimis, we disagree, deeming this a defect in weighing.

But before this could be considered serious, we must see whether the observations of the district court rise to the level of special circumstances sufficient to deny any attorney's fee as unjust. We look at the record to ascertain the extent to which the district court's views of overclaiming, unsuccessful claims, and lack of contemporaneous records are supported.

We have looked at the fee applications submitted to us. In form they appear quite meticulous and disclose fairly the object and amount of the time spent. We think it likely, from our somewhat removed vantage point, that the plaintiff's explanation of the misnaming of the attorney representing Boutselis in two entries reveals only an inadvertence in preparing the fee application from original records. We have no indication of any other instance suggesting lack of contemporaneity.

Although Poy's attorneys volunteered a ten percent reduction in their fee to respond to the court's concerns, this was not tied to any attempt to excise redundant or unnecessary work, unlike the more responsive action of counsel in *Gay Officers Action League,* 247 F.3d at 292. It may have been viewed merely as a token gesture. Nevertheless, the significance of the proffered reduction is borne out by further scrutiny of the fee applications. Much has been made of plaintiff Em's early abandonment of his case and of the failure of plaintiff to prevail in his claims against the city and its chief of police. In reviewing the fee applications, we deleted all time attributed to either Em's claims or claims against the city. This revealed a total fee attribution to these two sets of claims in the amount of some $8,400. As for claims against officer Conroy, a matter of some concern to the district court, our review indicates almost no time charges addressed to them. The proffered ten percent reduction in fee, according to our admittedly preliminary calculation, amounts to approximately $10,750 or well in excess of the unsuccessful claims by or against dismissed parties.

A number of state causes of action and defendant parties were dismissed. They include assault and battery on the part of officers Boutselis and Conroy. It appears to us that whatever work was relevant to these claims arguably may have had to be done in connection with plaintiff's claims of false arrest, excessive force and emotional distress against Boutselis. There were three claims against Neov, the owner of the site of the incident, The Golden Swan, for negligent hiring (of Boutselis) and supervision, respondeat superior, and premises liability. We have found no indication of time spent or charges allocated to supporting these claims. And the claims of unconstitutional policy or custom and negligence against the chief and the city, even if unrelated to plaintiff's claims against Boutselis, may fall within the proffered ten percent reduction. These are only our preliminary impressions; definitive resolution of the issue of relatedness is better left to the informed judgment of the district court.

Another area of concern to the district court was the possibility of wasteful redundancy of effort by plaintiff's two attorneys. Attorney Wernick explained that in pre-trial matters such as discovery, most of the work was done by his junior, Miller. He himself did most of the deposition work. While the district court may eventually reject this explanation, it is at least facially plausible. There remains the important and intense period of trial when both were in attendance much of the time. The requested fees for this period are indeed very substantial. We note, however, that both the city (including Chief Davis) and Boutselis were at the same time represented by teams of two attorneys. We cannot improve on the advice we gave in *Gay Officers Action League,* 247 F.3d at 297: "[A] court should not hesitate to discount hours if it sees signs that a prevailing party has overstaffed a case. . . .On the other hand . . . [g]iven the complexity of modern litigation, the deployment of multiple attorneys is sometimes an eminently reasonable tactic." In short, the district court must weigh and consider the claim of overstaffing, using its intimate knowledge of the case, and make specific findings thereon.

As a result of this analysis and based on this record, we see no "special circumstances" justifying the elevation of this case to that rarified level of irresponsible litigation strategy, minimal accomplishment, and intolerable overclaiming which merits denial of any fees whatsoever to a prevailing party. In short, our conclusion is that a serious mistake in weighing was made, aided by the complete discounting of the relevant prevailing party factor.

We therefore must remand this issue to the district court for consideration in accordance with this opinion. It should examine any claim of interrelatedness between work done on unsuccessful claims and the claims on which plaintiff was successful. It should examine the reasonableness of time spent and rates charged, including the possibility of overstaffing. Counsel are urged to be as forthcoming and cooperative as possible. In the final analysis, the court must make its judgment and support it with sufficient specificity. We add that it should also review plaintiff's request for reimbursement of costs, not being restricted to the specifications of 28 U.S.C. § 1920, *See* System Management, Inc. v. Loiselle, 154 F.Supp.2d 195, 204 (D.Mass.2001) (holding that "reasonable out-of-pocket expenses incurred by the attorney and normally charged to the client" could be awarded pursuant to statutory authority of § 1988).

We therefore vacate the sections of the court's order of January 10, 2003 relating to plaintiff's request for fees and costs, as well as Boutselis' motion to reduce any attorney's fees awarded to plaintiff. We remand the case to the district court for determination of an appropriate attorney's fee for plaintiff. This shall not alter the date of judgment concerning the awards of damages, but we suggest that the amount of prejudgment interest be revisited to insure accuracy.

Appellant is entitled to his reasonable attorney's fees and costs on appeal.

Affirmed in part, vacated in part, and remanded.

Angiolillo v. Collier County
394 Fed. Appx. 609 (10th Cir. 2010)

Vincent D. Angiolillo filed this § 1983 and state law action against Collier County, its Sheriff, and five employees of the Collier County Sheriff's Department ("Defendants"), alleging claims of false arrest, malicious prosecution, conspiracy, and state law malicious prosecution. The district court either dismissed or granted summary judgment to Defendants on all claims. Angiolillo now appeals, raising three issues for our review. First, Angiolillo argues that the district court abused its discretion in denying his motion to file a second amended complaint. Second, he argues that the court erred in granting summary judgment to Defendants Bates, Celiberti, and Hurley. And third he argues that the district court erred in awarding attorney's fees to Defendants. After thorough review of the parties' briefs and the record on appeal, we affirm on all grounds.

I.   Denial of Motion to Amend

. . . The district court's deadline to amend pleadings expired on February 20, 2009, as delineated in its Case Management and Scheduling Order. Angiolillo filed his motion for leave to amend on June 11, 2009, nearly four months after the court's deadline. Therefore, Rule 16(b)'s good cause requirement governed the court's decision whether to grant Angiolillo's motion for leave to amend. We agree with the district court that Angiolillo failed to demonstrate good cause.

II.   Summary Judgment in Favor of Defendants
Bates, Celiberti, Hurley

The district court granted summary judgment to Defendants Bates, Celiberti, and Hurley, concluding that Defendants were entitled to qualified immunity on Angiolillo's false arrest claim and that Angiolillo failed to raise a genuine issue of material fact on his § 1983 malicious prosecution claim. "We review the district court's grant of summary judgment de novo, viewing all evidence and any reasonable inferences that might be drawn therefrom in the light most favorable to the non-moving party." Rine v. Imagitas, Inc., 590 F.3d 1215, 1222 (11th Cir.2009). Upon review, we affirm.

A. False Arrest

... Angiolillo was arrested for violating the terms of a Temporary Injunction for Protection Against Dating Violence, which prohibited him from contacting a woman whose full legal name is "Crystal" either in person or by phone, from using another person to contact her, or from frequenting a bar called JD Jags. Angiolillo received a similar temporary injunction against Crystal. The evidence submitted to the State Attorney's office, which led to its issuance of the capias warrant for Angiolollo's arrest, included the following items: (1) an investigative report stating that on May 12, 2007, Crystal (who is a realtor) received four phone calls from someone named "Lisa" purporting to express interest in a piece of real estate but that when Crystal returned the call she heard Angiolillo's voice stating, "GOT HER!," accompanied by cheering and laughing; (2) a recording of the May 12, 2007, phone call by Crystal, which captured the background noise on the open line and Angiolollo's voice stating "SHE'S FUCKED ... SHE CAN' HEAR NOTHING ... SHE'S LEAVING A MESSAGE ...."; (3) an investigative report stating that Angiolillo had contacted the Sheriff's office to report that Crystal had violated the injunction order by calling his phone and leaving a message and a notation that no such message was recorded on Angiolillo's phone; (4) an investigative report stating that on May 27, 2007, Crystal reported that two of her friends, Judith Simon and Reuben Thompson, saw Angiolillo drive within 50–60 feet of the front door of JD Jags; and (5) statements by Simon and Thompson as to the same. Based on this evidence, the district court concluded that arguable probable cause existed to arrest Angiolillo, and thus Defendants Bates, Celiberti, and Hurley—the agents responsible for the investigation and providing the evidence to the State Attorney's Office—were entitled to qualified immunity from liability for Angiolillo's alleged false arrest. ...

Even accepting all of Angiolillo's statements as true, and disregarding the unsworn statements of Simon and Thompson that Angiolillo approached JD Jags in his car, the remaining undisputed evidence in the record is sufficient to establish arguable probable cause that Angiolillo used a third party, "Lisa," to contact Crystal—conduct that expressly violates the terms of the temporary injunction. First, Crystal's victim statement reported that when she returned "Lisa's" phone call, she heard Angiolillo's voice saying, "We got her!" Second, Defendants obtained from Crystal a recording of the open line, which captures Angiolillo's voice making statements suggesting he intended to capture a message from Crystal on the phone line via the use of a "Boost" phone, a fact which was eventually corroborated by examining Angiolillo's and Crystal's phone records. Finally, Angiolillo subsequently contacted the Sheriff's Office claiming that Crystal had violated her temporary injunction by calling his phone number and leaving a message but that no such message was found. In sum, we conclude that a reasonable officer in the same position of the Assistant State Attorney issuing the capias warrant for Angiolillo's arrest "could have believed that probable cause existed to arrest Plaintiff." *Brown,* 608 F.3d at 734. Accordingly, we affirm the district court's grant of summary judgment to Defendants Bates, Celiberti, and Hurley on Angiolillo's false-arrest claim.

B.   Malicious Prosecution

"To establish a federal malicious prosecution claim under § 1983, a plaintiff must prove (1) the elements of the common law tort of malicious prosecution, and (2) a violation of her Fourth Amendment right to be free from unreasonable seizures." Kingsland v. City of Miami, 382 F.3d 1220, 1234 (11th Cir.2004). "Under Florida law, a plaintiff must establish each of six elements to support a claim of malicious prosecution: (1) an original judicial proceeding against the present plaintiff was commenced or continued; (2) the present defendant was the legal cause of the original proceeding; (3) the termination of the original proceeding constituted a bona fide termination of that proceeding in favor of the present plaintiff; (4) there was an absence of probable cause for the original proceeding; (5) there was malice on the part of the present defendant; and (6) the plaintiff suffered damages as a result of the original proceeding." *Id.* Because we agree with the district court that there was probable cause for Angiolillo's arrest, he is unable to establish the fourth element of a common law claim for malicious prosecution under Florida law. Accordingly, Defendants were entitled to summary judgment on Angiolillo's § 1983 malicious prosecution claim.

III. Attorney's Fees

A court may award attorney's fees under § 1988 to a prevailing defendant where the court finds that "the plaintiff's action was frivolous, unreasonable, or without foundation, even though not brought in subjective bad faith." Hughes v. Rowe, 449 U.S. 5, 14 (1980) (quoting Christiansburg Garment Co. v. EEOC, 434 U.S. 412, 421 (1978)). Our circuit considers the following factors in determining whether a claim is frivolous: "(1) whether the plaintiff established a prima facie case; (2) whether the defendant offered to settle; and (3) whether the trial court dismissed the case prior to trial or held a full-blown trial on the merits." Sullivan v. Sch. Bd. of Pinellas County, 773 F.2d 1182, 1189 (11th Cir.1985). We review an award of attorney's fees and costs for abuse of discretion. Gray ex rel. Alexander v. Bostic, 570 F.3d 1321, 1324 (11th Cir.2009). Abuse-of-discretion review requires us to "affirm unless we find that the district court has made a clear error of judgment, or has applied the wrong legal standard." United States v. Frazier, 387 F.3d 1244, 1259 (11th Cir.2004) (en banc).

The district court, adopting the Magistrate Judge's report and recommendation, made the ultimate determination that Angiolillo's lawsuit was frivolous and awarded Defendants' attorney's fees. The court specifically concluded that Angiolillo failed to establish a prima facie case; Defendants did not offer to settle; and the district court dismissed the majority of Angiolillo's claims with prejudice early in the litigation upon the filing of various motions to dismiss and Angiolillo's few remaining claims with prejudice on summary judgment. Thus, the district court did not apply "the wrong legal standard." *Id.* On appeal, Angiolillo renews the same two objections to the Magistrate Judge's report as he raised before the district court. Neither of these objections persuade us that the district court "made a clear error of judgment." *Id.*

First, Angiolillo argues that the Magistrate Judge violated the "sanctity of the mediation process" by determining that Defendants did not offer to settle because local rules require that any information derived from a mediation may not be made known to the Court. *See* Rule M.D. Fla. L.R. 9.07(b). As the district court stated in its response to this argument below, the Magistrate Judge did not violate Rule 9.07(b) by determining that Defendants did not offer to settle. Rule 9.07(b) protects parties participating in mediation from the use of any statement made during mediation proceedings as an admission against their interest.FN3 The Magistrate Judge did not use any statement made by Angiolillo during mediation as an admission against his interest in violation of Rule 9.07(b).

Second, Angiolillo disputes the Magistrate Judge's determination that he failed to establish a prima facie case by arguing that certain statements made by the Magistrate Judge are unsupported by the record. Angiolillo argues that if the Magistrate Judge had correctly stated the record, which allegedly demonstrates that he contested the allegation that he violated the temporary injunction by driving by JD Jags and that he amended his complaint only once, as opposed to twice, upon consent of the district court, Defendants would have failed to satisfy Sullivan's first prong. We agree with the district court; these discrete factual disputes do not undermine the district court's ultimate determination that Angiolillo failed to establish a prima facie case.

To the contrary, our independent review of the record demonstrates that the district court was completely warranted in concluding that "Angiolillo [did] not even attempt to shoulder his burden to establish that genuine issues of fact remain on his [malicious prosecution] claim." In his response to Defendants' Motion for Summary Judgment, Angiolillo recites the elements for a prima facie case of malicious prosecution and, in a conclusory fashion, contends that these elements have been satisfied. He engages in no discussion demonstrating how the evidence supports his satisfaction of those elements. With respect to his false arrest claim, although he did put forth some argument in an attempt to undermine the conclusion that probable cause existed for his arrest, he did not provide any evidence to that effect. Angiolillo may have argued that Defendants' hypothesis that "Lisa's" phone was a "Boost" phone linked to Angiollio was "unsupported," but the record demonstrates the opposite. This hypothesis was derived directly from Crystal's victim statement, the audio recording of Angiolillo's voice, and Angiolillo's report that Crystal had violated the injunction by calling his cell phone. Furthermore, this "unsupported hypothesis" was ultimately confirmed after Angiolillo's arrest. We have sustained findings of frivolity where a motion for summary judgment has been granted in instances in which the plaintiff did not introduce any evidence in support of his claim. *See* Roper v. Edwards, 815 F.2d 1474, 1478 (11th Cir.1987) ("With this total absence of credible evidence to support their claims, the Ropers' action was frivolous, and the court's award of fees to Cochran was clearly justified."). Rather than offering substantive evidence in support of his claims, Angiolillo's submissions to the district court are replete with exclamatory statements and hyperbolic accusations, in many cases wholly unsupported by substantive legal argument.

Moreover, this case stands in stark contrast to the narrow circumstances in which we have reversed an award of attorney's fees to a prevailing defendant. *See, e.g.,* Walker v. NationsBank of Florida N.A., 53 F.3d 1548, 1559 (11th Cir.1995) (holding that "a plaintiff's claim should not be considered groundless or without foundation for the purpose of awarding fees to a prevailing defendant when the claims are meritorious enough to receive careful attention and review"). In *Walker,* the district court on two occasions denied the defendants' summary judgment motions and the case proceeded to trial. Here, almost all of Angiolillo's claims were dismissed early in this litigation on various motions to dismiss, and in its summary judgment order the district court concluded that Angiolillo's arguments were not only unpersuasive but almost nonexistent. Angiolillo's case did not present claims meritorious enough to receive the district court's "careful attention and review." *Id.*

In sum, we conclude that the district court did not clearly err in finding Angiolillo's claims "frivolous, unreasonable, or without foundation." *Hughes,* 449 U.S. at 14 (quoting *Christiansburg,* 434 U.S. at 421). Accordingly, we uphold the district court's award of attorney's fees to Defendants pursuant to § 1988.

AFFIRMED.

Town of Newton v. Rumery
480 U.S. 386 (1987)

■ JUSTICE POWELL announced the judgment of the Court and delivered the opinion of the Court with respect to Parts I, II, III-A, IV, and V, and an opinion with respect to Part III-B, in which THE CHIEF JUSTICE, JUSTICE WHITE, and JUSTICE SCALIA join.

The question in this case is whether a court properly may enforce an agreement in which a criminal defendant releases his right to file an action under 42 U.S.C. § 1983 in return for a prosecutor's dismissal of pending criminal charges.

I

In 1983, a grand jury in Rockingham County, New Hampshire, indicted David Champy for aggravated felonious sexual assault. Respondent Bernard Rumery, a friend of Champy's, read about the charges in a local newspaper. Seeking information about the charges, he telephoned Mary Deary, who was acquainted with both Rumery and Champy. Coincidentally, Deary had been the victim of the assault in question and was expected to be the principal witness against Champy. The record does not reveal directly the date or substance of this conversation between Rumery and Deary, but Deary apparently was disturbed by the call. On March 12, according to police records, she called David Barrett, the Chief of Police for the town of Newton. She told him that Rumery was trying to force her to drop the charges against Champy. Rumery talked to Deary again on May 11. The substance of this conversation also is disputed. Rumery claims that Deary called him and that she raised the subject of Champy's difficulties. According to the police records, however, Deary told Chief Barrett that Rumery had threatened that, if Deary went forward on the Champy case, she would "end up like" two women who recently had been murdered in Lowell, Massachusetts. Barrett arrested Rumery and accused him of tampering with a witness in violation of N.H.Rev.Stat.Ann. § 641:5(I)(b) (1986), a Class B felony.

Rumery promptly retained Stephen Woods, an experienced criminal defense attorney.[1] Woods contacted Brian Graf, the Deputy County Attorney for Rockingham County. He warned Graf that he "had better [dismiss] these charges, because we're going to win them and after that we're going to sue." After further discussions, Graf and Woods reached an agreement, under which Graf would dismiss the charges against Rumery if Rumery would agree not to sue the town, its officials, or Deary for any harm caused by the arrest. All parties agreed that one factor in Graf's decision not to prosecute Rumery was Graf's desire to protect

---

[1]   By the time this case was litigated in the District Court, Woods had become the County Attorney for Rockingham County.

Deary from the trauma she would suffer if she were forced to testify. As the prosecutor explained in the District Court:

"I had been advised by Chief Barrett that Mary Deary did not want to testify against Mr. Rumery. The witness tampering charge would have required Mary Deary to testify. . . .

"I think that was a particularly sensitive type of case where you are dealing with a victim of an alleged aggravated felonious sexual assault." *Id.*, at 52 (deposition of Brian Graf).

See also App. to Pet. for Cert. B–2 (District Court's findings of fact); App. 20 (deposition of defense counsel Woods).

Woods drafted an agreement in which Rumery agreed to release any claims he might have against the town, its officials, or Deary if Graf agreed to dismiss the criminal charges (the release-dismissal agreement). After Graf approved the form of the agreement, Woods presented it to Rumery. Although Rumery's recollection of the events was quite different, the District Court found that Woods discussed the agreement with Rumery in his office for about an hour and explained to Rumery that he would forgo all civil actions if he signed the agreement. Three days later, on June 6, 1983, Rumery returned to Woods' office and signed the agreement. The criminal charges were dropped.

Ten months later, on April 13, 1984, Rumery filed an action under § 1983 in the Federal District Court for the District of New Hampshire. He alleged that the town and its officers had violated his constitutional rights by arresting him, defaming him, and imprisoning him falsely. The defendants filed a motion to dismiss, relying on the release-dismissal agreement as an affirmative defense. Rumery argued that the agreement was unenforceable because it violated public policy. The court rejected Rumery's argument and concluded that a "release of claims under section 1983 is valid . . . if it results from a decision that is voluntary, deliberate and informed." The court found that Rumery

"is a knowledgeable, industrious individual with vast experience in the business world. . . . [H]e intelligently and carefully, after weighing all the factors, concluded that it would be in his best interest and welfare to sign the covenant. He was also represented by a very competent attorney with more than ordinary expertise in the sometimes complex area of criminal law."

The court then dismissed Rumery's suit.

On appeal, the Court of Appeals for the First Circuit reversed. It adopted a *per se* rule invalidating release-dismissal agreements. The court stated:

"It is difficult to envision how release agreements, negotiated in exchange for a decision not to prosecute, serve the public interest. Enforcement of such covenants would tempt prosecutors to trump up charges in reaction to a defendant's civil rights claim, suppress evidence of police misconduct, and leave unremedied deprivations of constitutional rights." 778 F.2d 66, 69 (1985).

Because the case raises a question important to the administration of criminal justice, we granted the town's petition for a writ of certiorari.). We reverse.

II

We begin by noting the source of the law that governs this case. The agreement purported to waive a right to sue conferred by a federal statute. The question whether the policies underlying that statute may in some circumstances render that waiver unenforceable is a question of federal law. We resolve this question by reference to traditional common-law principles, as we have resolved other questions about the principles governing § 1983 actions. *E.g., Pulliam v. Allen,* 466 U.S. 522, 539–540 (1984). The relevant principle is well established: a promise is unenforceable if the interest in its enforcement is outweighed in the circumstances by a public policy harmed by enforcement of the agreement.[2]

III

The Court of Appeals concluded that the public interests related to release-dismissal agreements justified a *per se* rule of invalidity. We think the court overstated the perceived problems and also failed to credit the significant public interests that such agreements can further. Most importantly, the Court of Appeals did not consider the wide variety of factual situations that can result in release-dismissal agreements. Thus, although we agree that in some cases these agreements may infringe important interests of the criminal defendant and of society as a whole, we do not believe that the mere possibility of harm to these interests calls for a *per se* rule.

A

Rumery's first objection to release-dismissal agreements is that they are inherently coercive. He argues that it is unfair to present a criminal defendant with a choice between facing criminal charges and waiving his right to sue under § 1983. We agree that some release-dismissal agreements may not be the product of an informed and voluntary decision. The risk, publicity, and expense of a criminal trial may intimidate a defendant, even if he believes his defense is meritorious. But this possibility does not justify invalidating *all* such agreements. In other contexts criminal defendants are required to make difficult choices that effectively waive constitutional rights. For example, it is well settled that plea bargaining does not violate the Constitution even though a guilty

---

[2] Cf. Restatement (Second) of Contracts § 178(1) (1981). See also *Crampton v. Ohio,* decided with *McGautha v. California,* 402 U.S. 183, 213, 91 S.Ct. 1454, 1470, 28 L.Ed.2d 711 (1971) ("The threshold question is whether compelling [a defendant to decide whether to waive constitutional rights] impairs to an appreciable extent any of the policies behind the rights involved").

plea waives important constitutional rights. See *Brady v. United States,* 397 U.S. 742, 752–753 (1970); *Santobello v. New York,* 404 U.S. 257, 264 (1971) (Douglas, J., concurring).[3] We see no reason to believe that release-dismissal agreements pose a more coercive choice than other situations we have accepted. *E.g., Corbitt v. New Jersey,* 439 U.S. 212 (1978) (upholding a statute that imposed higher sentences on defendants who went to trial than on those who entered guilty pleas). As Justice Harlan explained:

"The criminal process, like the rest of the legal system, is replete with situations requiring 'the making of difficult judgments' as to which course to follow. *McMann v. Richardson,* 397 U.S. [759], at 769 (1970)]. Although a defendant may have a right, even of constitutional dimensions, to follow whichever course he chooses, the Constitution does not by that token always forbid requiring him to choose." *Crampton v. Ohio,* decided with *McGautha v. California,* 402 U.S. 183, 213 (1971).

In many cases a defendant's choice to enter into a release-dismissal agreement will reflect a highly rational judgment that the certain benefits of escaping criminal prosecution exceed the speculative benefits of prevailing in a civil action. Rumery's voluntary decision to enter this agreement exemplifies such a judgment. Rumery is a sophisticated businessman. He was not in jail and was represented by an experienced criminal lawyer, who drafted the agreement. Rumery considered the agreement for three days before signing it. The benefits of the agreement to Rumery are obvious: he gained immunity from criminal prosecution in consideration of abandoning a civil suit that he may well have lost.

Because Rumery voluntarily waived his right to sue under § 1983, the public interest opposing involuntary waiver of constitutional rights is no reason to hold this agreement invalid. Moreover, we find that the possibility of coercion in the making of similar agreements insufficient by itself to justify a *per se* rule against release-dismissal bargains. If there is such a reason, it must lie in some external public interest necessarily injured by release-dismissal agreements.

B

As we noted above, the Court of Appeals held that all release-dismissal agreements offend public policy because it believed these agreements "tempt prosecutors to trump up charges in reaction to a defendant's civil rights claim, suppress evidence of police misconduct, and leave unremedied deprivations of constitutional rights." 778 F.2d, at 69. We can agree that in some cases there may be a substantial basis for

---

[3]   We recognize that the analogy between plea bargains and release-dismissal agreements is not complete. The former are subject to judicial oversight. Moreover, when the State enters a plea bargain with a criminal defendant, it receives immediate and tangible benefits, such as promptly imposed punishment without the expenditure of prosecutorial resources, see *Brady v. United States,* 397 U.S., at 752. Also, the defendant's agreement to plead to some crime tends to ensure some satisfaction of the public's interest in the prosecution of crime and confirms that the prosecutor's charges have a basis in fact. The benefits the State may realize in particular cases from release-dismissal agreements may not be as tangible, but they are not insignificant.

this concern. It is true, of course, that § 1983 actions to vindicate civil rights may further significant public interests. But it is important to remember that Rumery had no public duty to institute a § 1983 action merely to further the public's interest in revealing police misconduct. Congress has confined the decision to bring such actions to the injured individuals, not to the public at large. Thus, we hesitate to elevate more diffused public interests above Rumery's considered decision that he would benefit personally from the agreement.

We also believe the Court of Appeals misapprehended the range of public interests arguably affected by a release-dismissal agreement. The availability of such agreements may threaten important public interests. They may tempt prosecutors to bring frivolous charges, or to dismiss meritorious charges, to protect the interests of other officials.[4] But a *per se* rule of invalidity fails to credit other relevant public interests and improperly assumes prosecutorial misconduct.[5] The vindication of constitutional rights and the exposure of official misconduct are not the only concerns implicated by § 1983 suits. No one suggests that all such suits are meritorious. Many are marginal and some are frivolous. Yet even when the risk of ultimate liability is negligible, the burden of defending such lawsuits is substantial. Counsel may be retained by the official, as well as the governmental entity. Preparation for trial, and the trial itself, will require the time and attention of the defendant officials, to the detriment of their public duties. In some cases litigation will extend over a period of years. This diversion of officials from their normal duties and the inevitable expense of defending even unjust claims is distinctly not in the public interest. To the extent release-dismissal agreements protect public officials from the burdens of defending such unjust claims, they further this important public interest.

A *per se* rule invalidating release-dismissal agreements also assumes that prosecutors will seize the opportunity for wrongdoing. In recent years the Court has considered a number of claims that prosecutors have acted improperly. *E.g., Wayte v. United States,* 470 U.S. 598 (1985); *United States v. Goodwin,* 457 U.S. 368 (1982); *Bordenkircher v. Hayes,* 434 U.S. 357 (1978). Our decisions in those cases uniformly have recognized that courts normally must defer to prosecutorial decisions as to whom to prosecute. The reasons for judicial deference are well known. Prosecutorial charging decisions are rarely simple. In addition to assessing the strength and importance of a case, prosecutors also must consider other tangible and intangible factors, such as

---

[4]   Actions taken for these reasons properly have been recognized as unethical. See ABA Model Code of Professional Responsibility, Disciplinary Rule 7–105 (1980).

[5]   Prosecutors themselves rarely are held liable in § 1983 actions. See *Imbler v. Pachtman,* 424 U.S. 409 (1976) (discussing prosecutorial immunity). Also, in many States and municipalities—perhaps in most—prosecutors are elected officials and are entirely independent of the civil authorities likely to be defendants in § 1983 suits. There may be situations, of course, when a prosecutor is motivated to protect the interests of such officials or of police. But the constituency of an elected prosecutor is the public, and such a prosecutor is likely to be influenced primarily by the general public interest.

government enforcement priorities. See *Wayte v. United States,* 470 U.S., at 607. Finally, they also must decide how best to allocate the scarce resources of a criminal justice system that simply cannot accommodate the litigation of every serious criminal charge.[6] Because these decisions "are not readily susceptible to the kind of analysis the courts are competent to undertake," we have been "properly hesitant to examine the decision whether to prosecute." *Id.,* at 607–608.

Against this background of discretion, the mere opportunity to act improperly does not compel an assumption that all—or even a significant number of—release-dismissal agreements stem from prosecutors abandoning "the independence of judgment required by [their] public trust," *Imbler v. Pachtman,* 424 U.S. 409 (1976).[7] Rather, tradition and experience justify our belief that the great majority of prosecutors will be faithful to their duty. Indeed, the merit of this view is illustrated by this case, where the only evidence of prosecutorial misconduct is the agreement itself.

Because release-dismissal agreements may further legitimate prosecutorial and public interests, we reject the Court of Appeals' holding that all such agreements are invalid *per se.*[8]

IV

Turning to the agreement presented by this case, we conclude that the District Court's decision to enforce the agreement was correct. As we have noted, *supra,* at 1193, it is clear that Rumery voluntarily entered the agreement. Moreover, in this case the prosecutor had an independent, legitimate reason to make this agreement directly related to his prosecutorial responsibilities. The agreement foreclosed both the civil and criminal trials concerning Rumery, in which Deary would have been a key witness. She therefore was spared the public scrutiny and embarrassment she would have endured if she had had to testify in either

---

[6] In 1985, the federal district courts disposed of 47,360 criminal cases. Of these, only 6,053, or about 12.8%, ended after a trial. Annual Report of the Director of the Administrative Office of the U.S. Courts 374 (1985). As we have recognized, if every serious criminal charge were evaluated through a full-scale criminal trial, "the States and the Federal Government would need to multiply by many times the number of judges and court facilities," *Santobello v. New York,* 404 U.S. 257, 260 (1971).

[7] Of course, the Court has found that certain actions are so likely to result from prosecutorial misconduct that it has " 'presume[d]' an improper vindictive motive," *United States v. Goodwin,* 457 U.S. 368, 373 (1982). *E.g., Blackledge v. Perry,* 417 U.S. (1974) (holding that it violates the Due Process Clause for a prosecutor to increase charges in response to a defendant's exercise of his right to appeal). But the complexity of pretrial decisions by prosecutors suggests that judicial evaluation of those decisions should be especially deferential. Thus, the Court has never accepted such a blanket claim with respect to pretrial decisions. See *United States v. Goodwin, supra; Bordenkircher v. Hayes,* 434 U.S. 357 (1978).

[8] Justice STEVENS' evaluation of the public interests associated with release-dismissal agreements relies heavily on his view that Rumery is a completely innocent man. He rests this conclusion on the testimony Rumery and his attorney presented to the District Court, but fails to acknowledge that the District Court's factual findings gave little credence to this testimony. Justice STEVENS also gives great weight to the fact that Rumery "must be presumed to be innocent.". But this is not a criminal case. This is a civil case, in which Rumery bears the ultimate burden of proof.

of those cases.[9] Both the prosecutor and the defense attorney testified in the District Court that this was a significant consideration in the prosecutor's decision. *Supra,* at 1191.

In sum, we conclude that this agreement was voluntary, that there is no evidence of prosecutorial misconduct, and that enforcement of this agreement would not adversely affect the relevant public interests.[10]

V

We reverse the judgment of the Court of Appeals and remand the case to the District Court for dismissal of the complaint.

It is so ordered.

■ JUSTICE O'CONNOR, concurring in part and concurring in the judgment.

I join in Parts I, II, III-A, IV, and V of the Court's opinion. More particularly, I join the Court in disapproving the Court of Appeals' broad holding that a criminal defendant's promise not to sue local governments and officials for constitutional violations arising out of his arrest and prosecution, given in exchange for the prosecutor's agreement to dismiss pending criminal charges, is void as against public policy under all circumstances. I agree with the Court that a case-by-case approach appropriately balances the important interests on both sides of the question of the enforceability of these agreements, and that on the facts of this particular case Bernard Rumery's covenant not to sue is enforceable. I write separately, however, in order to set out the factors that lead me to conclude that this covenant should be enforced and to emphasize that it is the burden of those relying upon such covenants to establish that the agreement is neither involuntary nor the product of an abuse of the criminal process. . . .

Many factors may bear on whether a release was voluntary and not the product of overreaching, some of which come readily to mind. The knowledge and experience of the criminal defendant and the circumstances of the execution of the release, including, importantly, whether the defendant was counseled, are clearly relevant. The nature of the criminal charges that are pending is also important, for the greater the charge, the greater the coercive effect. The existence of a legitimate criminal justice objective for obtaining the release will support its

---

[9]   Cf. ABA Standards for Criminal Justice 14–1.8(a)(iii) (2d ed. 1980) (following a guilty plea, it is proper for the sentencing judge to consider that the defendant "by making public trial unnecessary, has demonstrated genuine consideration for the victims . . . by . . . prevent[ing] unseemly public scrutiny or embarrassment").

[10]   We note that two Courts of Appeals have applied a voluntariness standard to determine the enforceability of agreements entered into *after* trial, in which the defendants released possible § 1983 claims in return for sentencing considerations. See *Bushnell v. Rossetti,* 750 F.2d 298 (CA4 1984); *Jones v. Taber,* 648 F.2d 1201 (CA9 1981). We have no occasion in this case to determine whether an inquiry into voluntariness alone is sufficient to determine the enforceability of release-dismissal agreements. We also note that it would be helpful to conclude release-dismissal agreements under judicial supervision. Although such supervision is not essential to the validity of an otherwise-proper agreement, it would help ensure that the agreements did not result from prosecutorial misconduct.

validity. And, importantly, the possibility of abuse is clearly mitigated if the release-dismissal agreement is executed under judicial supervision.

Close examination of all the factors in this case leads me to concur in the Court's decision that this covenant not to sue is enforceable. There is ample evidence in the record concerning the circumstances of the execution of this agreement. Testimony of the prosecutor, defense counsel, and Rumery himself leave little doubt that the agreement was entered into voluntarily. While the charge pending against Rumery was serious—subjecting him to up to seven years in prison, N.H.Rev.Stat.Ann. § 641:5(I)(b) (1986)—it is one of the lesser felonies under New Hampshire law, and a long prison term was probably unlikely given the absence of any prior criminal record and the weaknesses in the case against Rumery. Finally, as the Court correctly notes, the prosecutor had a legitimate reason to enter into this agreement directly related to his criminal justice function. The prosecutor testified that:

"I had been advised by Chief Barrett that Mary Deary did not want to testify against Mr. Rumery. The witness tampering charge would have required Mary Deary to testify. She would have been the primary source of evidence against Mr. Rumery. There was still considerable concern about Mary Deary because the David Champy case was still pending.

"I think that was a particular sensitive type of case where you are dealing with a victim of an alleged aggravated felonious sexual assault. And I think I was taking into consideration the fact that I had her as a victim of one case, and now, the State was in a position of perhaps having to force her to testify against her will perhaps causing more trauma or upset to her forcing her to go through more things than what I felt comfortable with doing. So that was one of the considerations I was taking into play at that time, that I had been informed that Mary Deary did not want to go forward with the prosecution, that she felt she had gone through enough."

Thus, Mary Deary's emotional distress, her unwillingness to testify against Rumery, presumably in later civil as well as criminal proceedings, and the necessity of her testimony in the pending sexual assault case against David Champy all support the prosecutor's judgment that the charges against Rumery should be dropped if further injury to Deary, and therefore the Champy case, could thereby be avoided.

Against the convincing evidence that Rumery voluntarily entered into the agreement and that it served the public interest, there is only Rumery's blanket claim that agreements such as this one are inherently coercive. While it would have been preferable, and made this an easier case, had the release-dismissal agreement been concluded under some form of judicial supervision, I concur in the Court's judgment, and all but Part III-B of its opinion, that Rumery's § 1983 suit is barred by his valid, voluntary release.

■ JUSTICE STEVENS, with whom JUSTICE BRENNAN, JUSTICE MARSHALL and JUSTICE BLACKMUN join, dissenting.

The question whether the release-dismissal agreement signed by respondent is unenforceable is much more complex than the Court's opinion indicates. A complete analysis of the question presented by this case cannot end with the observation that respondent made a knowing and voluntary choice to sign a settlement agreement. Even an intelligent and informed, but completely innocent, person accused of crime should not be required to choose between a threatened indictment and trial, with their attendant publicity and the omnipresent possibility of wrongful conviction, and surrendering the right to a civil remedy against individuals who have violated his or her constitutional rights. Moreover, the prosecutor's representation of competing and possibly conflicting interests compounds the dangerous potential of release-dismissal agreements. To explain my disagreement with the majority, I shall first discuss the dilemma confronted by respondent at the time his lawyer advised him to sign the agreement, then comment on the three different interests the prosecutor represented, and finally discuss the plurality's evaluation of the relevant public interests in this case.

I

Respondent is an innocent man. As a matter of law, he must be presumed to be innocent. As a matter of fact, the uncontradicted sworn testimony of respondent, and his lawyer, buttressed by the circumstantial evidence,[3] overwhelmingly attest to his innocence. There was no written statement by the alleged victim, sworn or unsworn, implicating respondent in any criminal activity. The charge that respondent had threatened the victim was reported to the police by the victim's daughter, and the substance of the conversation as summarized in Chief Barrett's report was based in part on his conversation with the daughter, in part on conversations between another police officer and the victim, and in part on his own conversation with the victim when she was in a state of extreme emotional distress. Respondent was never indicted, and the warrant for his arrest was issued on the basis of a sketchy statement by Chief Barrett. Even the assistant prosecutor who was in charge of the case was surprised to learn that Chief Barrett had arrested respondent on the basis of the information in the police report. Thus, when the Newton police officers arrested respondent in his home they had not even obtained a written statement from the complaining witness. Prior to the arrest, and prior to the police chief's press conference concerning it, respondent was a respected member of a small community who had never been arrested, even for a traffic offense.

---

[3]   It may well be true that respondent expressed the opinion to his alleged victim that it would be in her best interest not to press criminal charges against a mutual friend. It seems highly improbable, however, in a telephone conversation that she initiated after they had not communicated with one another for approximately two months, that he suddenly threatened her life and gave her an ultimatum that would expire at 11 o'clock the following morning.

A few days before respondent was scheduled for a probable-cause hearing on the charge of witness tampering, respondent's attorney advised him to sign a covenant not to sue the town of Newton, its police officers, or the witness Deary in exchange for dismissal of the charge against him. The advice was predicated on the lawyer's judgment that the value of a dismissal outweighed the harmful consequences of an almost certain indictment on a felony charge together with the risk of conviction in a case in which the outcome would depend on the jury's assessment of the relative credibility of respondent and his alleged victim. The lawyer correctly advised respondent that even if he was completely innocent, there could be no guarantee of acquittal. He therefore placed a higher value on his client's interest in terminating the criminal proceeding promptly than on the uncertain benefits of pursuing a civil remedy against the town and its police department. After delaying a decision for three days, respondent reluctantly followed his lawyer's advice.

From respondent's point of view, it is unquestionably true that the decision to sign the release-dismissal agreement was, as the Court emphasizes, "voluntary, deliberate, and informed." It reflected "a highly rational judgment that the certain benefits of escaping criminal prosecution exceed the speculative benefits of prevailing in a civil action." As the plurality iterates and reiterates, respondent made a "considered decision that he would benefit personally from the agreement." I submit, however, that the deliberate and rational character of respondent's decision is not a sufficient reason for concluding that the agreement is enforceable. Otherwise, a promise to pay a state trooper $20 for not issuing a ticket for a traffic violation, or a promise to contribute to the police department's retirement fund in exchange for the dismissal of a felony charge, would be enforceable. Indeed, I would suppose that virtually all contracts that courts refuse to enforce nevertheless reflect perfectly rational decisions by the parties who entered into them. There is nothing irrational about an agreement to bribe a police officer, to enter into a wagering arrangement, to pay usurious rates of interests, or to threaten to indict an innocent man in order to induce him to surrender something of value.

The "voluntary, deliberate, and informed" character of a defendant's decision generally provides an acceptable basis for upholding the validity of a plea bargain. But it is inappropriate to assume that the same standard determines the validity of a quite different agreement to forgo a civil remedy for the violation of the defendant's constitutional rights in exchange for complete abandonment of a criminal charge.

The net result of every plea bargain is an admission of wrongdoing by the defendant and the imposition of a criminal sanction with its attendant stigma. Although there may be some cases in which an innocent person pleads guilty to a minor offense to avoid the risk of conviction on a more serious charge, it is reasonable to presume that such cases are rare and represent the exception rather than the rule. See Fed.Rule Crim.Proc. 11(f) (court may not enter judgment on a guilty plea unless it is satisfied the plea has a factual basis). Like a plea bargain, an agreement by the suspect to drop § 1983 charges and to pay restitution to the victim in exchange for the prosecutor's termination of criminal proceedings involves an admission of wrongdoing by the defendant. The same cannot be said about an agreement that completely exonerates the defendant. Not only is such a person presumptively innocent as a matter of law; as a factual matter the prosecutor's interest in obtaining a covenant not to sue will be strongest in those cases in which he realizes that the defendant was innocent and was wrongfully accused. Moreover, the prosecutor will be most willing—indeed, he is ethically obligated—to drop charges when he believes that probable cause as established by the available, admissible evidence is lacking.

The plea bargain represents a practical compromise between the prosecutor and the defendant that takes into account the burdens of litigation and its probable outcome, as well as society's interest in imposing appropriate punishment upon an admitted wrongdoer. The defendant admits wrongdoing for conduct upon which the guilty plea is based and avoids further prosecution; the prosecutor need not go to trial; and an admitted wrongdoer is punished, all under close judicial supervision. See Fed.Rule Crim.Proc. 11(e). By simultaneously establishing and limiting the defendant's criminal liability, plea bargains delicately balance individual and social advantage. This mutuality of advantage does not exist in release-dismissal agreements. A defendant entering a release-dismissal agreement is forced to waive claims based on official conduct under color of state law, in exchange merely for the assurance that the State will not prosecute him for conduct for which he has made no admission of wrongdoing. The State is spared the necessity of going to trial, but its willingness to drop the charge completely indicates that it might not have proceeded with the prosecution in any event.[11] No social interest in the punishment of wrongdoers is satisfied; the only interest vindicated is that of resolving once and for all the question of § 1983 liability.

Achieving this result has no connection with the give-and-take over the defendant's wrongdoing that is the essence of the plea-bargaining process, and thus cannot be justified by reference to the principles of mutual advantage that support plea bargaining. Although the outcome of a criminal proceeding may affect the value of the civil claim, as a matter of law the claims are quite distinct. Even a guilty defendant may be entitled to receive damages for physical abuse, and conversely, the fact that a defendant is ultimately acquitted is entirely consistent with the

---

[11] In this case the prosecutor had been advised that the witness Deary was unwilling to testify against respondent. He may also have known that she would not testify against Champy, her alleged assailant, on the sexual assault charge.

possibility that the police had probable cause to arrest him and did not violate any of his constitutional rights.

The plurality assumes that many § 1983 suits "are marginal and some are frivolous." Whether that assumption is correct or incorrect, the validity of each ought to be tested by the adversary process. Experience teaches us that *some* § 1983 suits in which release-dismissal agreements are sought are meritorious.[14] Whatever the true value of a § 1983 claim may be, a defendant who is required to give up such a claim in exchange for a dismissal of a criminal charge is being forced to pay a price that is unrelated to his possible wrongdoing as reflected in that charge. Indeed, if the defendant is forced to abandon a claim that has a value of $1,000, the price that he pays is the functional equivalent of a $1,000 payment to a police department's retirement benefit fund.

Thus, even though respondent's decision in this case was deliberate, informed, and voluntary, this observation does not address two distinct objections to enforcement of the release-dismissal agreement. The prosecutor's offer to drop charges if the defendant accedes to the agreement is inherently coercive; moreover, the agreement exacts a price unrelated to the character of the defendant's own conduct.

II

When the prosecutor negotiated the agreement with respondent, he represented three potentially conflicting interests. His primary duty, of course, was to represent the sovereign's interest in the evenhanded and effective enforcement of its criminal laws. See *Berger v. United States,* 295 U.S. 78, 88 (1935). In addition, as the covenant demonstrates, he sought to represent the interests of the town of Newton and its Police Department in connection with their possible civil liability to respondent. Finally, as the inclusion of Mary Deary as a covenantee indicates, the prosecutor also represented the interest of a potential witness who allegedly accused both respondent and a mutual friend of separate instances of wrongdoing.

If we view the problem from the standpoint of the prosecutor's principal client, the State of New Hampshire, it is perfectly clear that the release-dismissal agreement was both unnecessary and unjustified. For both the prosecutor and the State of New Hampshire enjoy absolute immunity from common-law and § 1983 liability arising out of a prosecutor's decision to initiate criminal proceedings. See *Imbler v. Pachtman,* 424 U.S. 409, 427(1976). The agreement thus gave the State and the prosecutor no protection that the law did not already provide.

---

[14] See, *e.g., Dixon v. District of Columbia,* 129 U.S.App.D.C. 341, 394 F.2d 966 (1968) (prosecutor may not file charges when defendant reneged on agreement not to sue); *MacDonald v. Musick,* 425 F.2d 373 (CA9) (prosecutor may not condition dismissal of charges on defendant's admission of probable cause which would preclude enforcement of civil claim against arresting officers), cert. denied, 400 U.S. 852, 91 S.Ct. 54, 27 L.Ed.2d 90 (1970); *Boyd v. Adams,* 513 F.2d 83 (CA7 1975) (postarrest release of § 1983 claim, executed while on conditional bail, is void as against public policy).

The record in this case indicates that an important reason for obtaining the covenant was "[t]o protect the police department." There is, however, an obvious potential conflict between the prosecutor's duty to enforce the law and his objective of protecting members of the Police Department who are accused of unlawful conduct. The public is entitled to have the prosecutor's decision to go forward with a criminal case, or to dismiss it, made independently of his concerns about the potential damages liability of the Police Department. It is equally clear that this separation of functions cannot be achieved if the prosecutor may use the threat of criminal prosecution as a weapon to obtain a favorable termination of a civil claim against the police.

In negotiating a release-dismissal agreement, the prosecutor inevitably represents both the public and the police. When release agreements are enforceable, consideration of the police interest in avoiding damages liability severely hampers the prosecutor's ability to conform to the strictures of professional responsibility in deciding whether to prosecute. In particular, the possibility that the suspect will execute a covenant not to sue in exchange for a decision not to prosecute may well encourage a prosecutor to bring or to continue prosecutions in violation of his or her duty to "refrain from prosecuting a charge that the prosecutor knows is not supported by probable cause." ABA Model Rules of Professional Conduct, Rule 3.8(a) (1984).[16]

This ethical obligation of every prosecutor is consistent with the general and fundamental rule that "[a] lawyer should exercise independent professional judgment on behalf of a client." ABA Model Code of Professional Responsibility, Canon 5 (1980). Every attorney should avoid situations in which he is representing potentially conflicting interests. See *id.*, at Ethical Consideration 5–2. As we noted in *Imbler v. Pachtman,* prosecutorial immunity from § 1983 lawsuits "does not leave the public powerless to deter misconduct or to punish that which occurs," in large part because "a prosecutor stands perhaps unique, among officials whose acts could deprive persons of constitutional rights, in his amenability to professional discipline by an association of his peers." 424 U.S., at 429 (footnote omitted).[17]

---

[16] See also ABA Model Code of Professional Responsibility, Disciplinary Rule 7–103 (1980) ("A public prosecutor or other government lawyer shall not institute or cause to be instituted criminal charges when he knows or it is obvious that the charges are not supported by probable cause"), and Ethical Consideration 7–14 ("A government lawyer who has discretionary power relative to litigation should refrain from instituting or continuing litigation that is obviously unfair"); ABA Standards for Criminal Justice 3–3.9(a) (2d ed. 1980) ("It is unprofessional conduct for a prosecutor to institute, or cause to be instituted, or to permit the continued pendency of criminal charges when it is known that the charges are not supported by probable cause").

[17] As the Court of Appeals for the Ninth Circuit has observed:

"It is no part of the proper duty of a prosecutor to use a criminal prosecution to forestall a civil proceeding by the defendant against policemen, even where the civil case arises from the events that are also the basis for the criminal charge. We do not mean that the prosecutor cannot present such a criminal charge. What he cannot do is condition a voluntary dismissal of a charge

The prosecutor's potential conflict of interest increases in magnitude in direct proportion to the seriousness of the charges of police wrongdoing. Yet a rule that determines the enforceability of a release-dismissal agreement by focusing entirely on the quality of the defendant's decision to sign the agreement cannot detect the seriousness of this conflict of interest because it cannot distinguish the meritorious § 1983 claims from the frivolous ones. On the other hand, if the merits of the claim must be evaluated in each case in order to decide whether the agreement should be enforced, the agreement would not serve the goal of saving the litigation costs associated with a trial of the claim itself. The efficiency argument on behalf of enforcing a release-dismissal agreement thus requires inattention to conflicts of interest in precisely those circumstances in which the agreement to be enforced is most likely to have been exacted by a prosecutor serving the interests of more than one constituency.

At bottom, the Court's holding in this case seems to rest on concerns related to the potential witness, Mary Deary.[18] As is true with the prosecutor's concerns for police liability, there is a potential conflict between the public interest represented by the prosecutor and the private interests of a recalcitrant witness. As a general matter there is no reason to fashion a rule that either requires or permits a prosecutor always to defer to the interests of a witness. The prosecutor's law enforcement responsibilities will sometimes diverge from those interests; there will be cases in which the prosecutor has a plain duty to obtain critical testimony despite the desire of the witness to remain anonymous or to avoid a courtroom confrontation with an offender. There may be other cases in which a witness has given false or exaggerated testimony for malicious reasons. It would plainly be unwise for the Court to hold that a release-dismissal agreement is enforceable simply because it affords protection to a potential witness.

Arguably a special rule should be fashioned for witnesses who are victims of sexual assaults. The trauma associated with such an assault leaves scars that may make it especially difficult for a victim to press charges or to testify publicly about the event. It remains true, however, that uncorroborated, unsworn statements by persons who claim to have been victims of any crime, including such an assault, may be inaccurate, exaggerated, or incomplete—and sometimes even malicious. It is even more clear that hearsay descriptions of statements by such persons may be unreliable. Rather than adopting a general rule that upholds a

---

upon a stipulation by the defendant that is designed to forestall the latter's civil case." *MacDonald v. Musick,* 425 F.2d, at 375.

[18] Despite a good deal of unfortunate language in its opinion, in the final analysis the Court merely rejects a *per se* rule invalidating all release-dismissal agreements and holds that this particular agreement is enforceable. See *ante,* at 1195; see also Justice O'CONNOR's opinion, *ante,* at 1194 (concurring in part and in the judgment). If the interest in protecting the potential witness were not present, presumably the author of the Court's opinion would adhere to the views he expressed in *Bordenkircher v. Hayes,* 434 U.S. 357, 372–373 (1978) (POWELL, J., dissenting).

release-dismissal agreement whenever the criminal charge was based on a statement by the alleged victim of a sexual assault, I believe the Court should insist upon a "close examination" of the facts that purportedly justified the agreement.

Thus, in this case Justice O'CONNOR has suggested that three special facts support the conclusion that the prosecutor was legitimately interested in protecting the witness Deary from "further injury": (1) her "emotional distress"; (2) her unwillingness to testify against Rumery; and (3) the necessity of her testimony in the pending sexual assault case against Champy. Each of these facts merits a brief comment.

The only evidence of Deary's emotional distress in the record is found in Chief Barrett's report of his telephone conversation on the afternoon of May 11, 1983. While he was talking to Deary's daughter he "could hear an intense argument and sobbing in the background"; after he was finally able to talk to Deary herself, he characterized her conversation as "hysterical, distra[u]ght, and terrified." It is, of course, reasonable to assume that Deary's emotional distress may have affected her unwillingness to testify against either Champy or Rumery, and thereby influenced the prosecutor's decision to dismiss the witness tampering charge. But the testimony of the prosecutor, who appears only to have talked to her about the sexual assault charge, does not even mention the possibility that she might have to testify in any civil litigation.

Deary's unwillingness to testify against Rumery is perfectly obvious.[19] That fact unquestionably supports the prosecutor's decision to dismiss the charge against respondent, but it is not a sufficient reason for exonerating police officers from the consequences of actions that they took when they must have known that Deary was unwilling to testify. For it was the precipitate character of the police decision to make an arrest without first obtaining a written statement from the witness and contrary to the expectations—and presumably the advice—of the prosecutor that created the risk that the victim might have to testify in open court.[20]

The need for Deary's testimony in the pending sexual assault case against Champy simply cannot justify denying this respondent a remedy for a violation of his Fourth Amendment rights. Presumably, if there had been an actual trial of the pending charge against Champy,[21] that trial

---

[19] Indeed, that fact must have been obvious to the police before they arrested respondent. For it was Deary's daughter, not Deary herself, who advised the police of Deary's call to respondent on May 11. Since the allegedly incriminating version of that call is based on two police officers' summary of what they had been told by Deary and her daughter—rather than a coherent statement by Deary herself—it is reasonable to assume that Deary was unwilling to provide the police with a statement of her recollection of exactly what was said in her conversation with respondent.

[20] Moreover, it is by no means apparent that testimony in a § 1983 action arising out of Rumery's telephone conversations with Deary would require any inquiry about the facts of the underlying assault or about the victim's relationship with Champy, the alleged assailant.

[21] Champy pleaded guilty to a lesser included offense and the felony charge against him was dismissed without a trial.

would have concluded long before Deary would have been required to testify in any § 1983 litigation.

It may well be true that a full development of all the relevant facts would provide a legitimate justification for enforcing the release-dismissal agreement. In my opinion, however, the burden of developing those facts rested on the defendants in the § 1983 litigation, and that burden has not been met by mere conjecture and speculation concerning the emotional distress of one reluctant witness.

III

Because this is the first case of this kind that the Court has reviewed, I am hesitant to adopt an absolute rule invalidating all such agreements.[22] I am, however, persuaded that the federal policies reflected in the enactment and enforcement of § 1983 mandate a strong presumption against the enforceability of such agreements and that the presumption is not overcome in this case by the facts or by any of the policy concerns discussed by the plurality. . . .

Accordingly, although I am not prepared to endorse all of the reasoning of the Court of Appeals, I would affirm its judgment.

4. NOTE ON INSTITUTIONAL COMPETENCE AND SYSTEMIC FEEDBACK LOOPS

Scholars sympathetic to the Warren Court's imposition of federal constitutional procedural rights on criminal procedure in the states point out that legislatures generally have given free rein to police and prosecutors. Coercive police practices—stops, arrests, and interrogations—affect relatively few individuals, a disproportionate number drawn from racial and ethnic minorities. Majoritarian democratic processes are unlikely to give fair consideration to the interests of this (literally) suspect class. Donald A. Dripps, *Criminal Procedure, Footnote Four, and the Theory of Public Choice; Or, Why Don't*

---

[22] It seems likely, however, that the costs of having courts determine the validity of release-dismissal agreements will outweigh the benefits that most agreements can be expected to provide. A court may enforce such an agreement only after a careful inquiry into the circumstances under which the plaintiff signed the agreement and into the legitimacy of the prosecutor's objective in entering into the agreement. See *ante,* at 1195; *ante,* at 1195, 1197 (O'CONNOR, J., concurring in part and in judgment). This inquiry will occupy a significant amount of the court's and the parties' time, and will subject prosecutorial decisionmaking to judicial review. But the only benefit most of these agreements will provide is another line of defense for prosecutors and police in § 1983 actions. This extra protection is unnecessary because prosecutors already enjoy absolute immunity, see *supra,* at 1195, and because police have been afforded qualified immunity, see *Harlow v. Fitzgerald,* 457 U.S. 800 (1982). Thus, the vast majority of "marginal or frivolous" § 1983 suits can be dismissed under existing standards with little more burden on the defendants than is entailed in defending a release-dismissal agreement. Moreover, there is an oddly suspect quality to this extra protection; the agreement is one that a public official signs, presumably in good faith, but that a court must conclude is invalid unless that official proves otherwise. *Ante,* at 1195 (O'CONNOR, J., concurring in part and in judgment). In most cases, if social and judicial resources are to be expended at all, they would seem better spent on an evaluation of the merits of the § 1983 claim rather than on a detour into the enforceability of a release-dismissal agreement.

Legislatures Give a Damn About the Rights of the Accused?, 44 Syracuse L. Rev. 1079, 1093–94 (1993); Michael J. Klarman, *The Puzzling Resistance to Political Process Theory*, 77 Va. L. Rev. 747, 766 (1991); Carol S. Steiker, *Second Thoughts About First Principles*, 107 Harv. L. Rev. 820, 850 (1994).

The same political incentives that apply to criminal procedure also apply to legislation defining crimes and setting penalties. The Supreme Court, however, has recognized only modest constitutional limits on the substantive criminal law. As *Rumery* recognizes, there are terms of trade between procedural rights and substantive liabilities. Plea bargaining is, in essence, exchanging the defendant's procedural right to trial for the prosecution's surrender of some of the punishment the substantive law authorizes. *See* Frank H. Easterbrook, *Criminal Procedure as a Market System,* 12 J. Legal Stud. 289 (1983).

Professor Stuntz characterized this division of constitutional labor as

> less a careful balance than a vicious circle. Countermajoritarian criminal procedure tends to encourage legislatures to pass overbroad criminal statutes and to underfund defense counsel. These actions in turn tend to mask the costs of procedural rules, thereby encouraging courts to make more such rules. That raises legislatures' incentive to overcriminalize and underfund. So the circle goes. This is a necessary consequence of a system with extensive, judicially defined regulation of the criminal process, coupled with extensive legislative authority over everything else.

William J. Stuntz, *The Uneasy Relationship Between Criminal Procedure and Criminal Justice,* 107 Yale L.J. 1, 54 (1997). Court-imposed procedural rules might thus actually *encourage* legislatures to adopt wider criminal statutes carrying higher penalties. *See* William J. Stuntz, The Collapse of American Criminal Justice 242 (2011) ("The Court's decisions probably exacerbated both crime and punishment trends, but the trends themselves had other causes . . . .But if the Justices did not cause the backlash, they made a large contribution to it.").

Various scholars have challenged the claim that court decisions favoring civil liberties induced more punitive policies from legislatures. *See* Stephen J. Schulhofer, *Criminal Justice, Local Democracy, and Constitutional Rights* 111 Mich. L. Rev. 1045 (2013) (reviewing *Collapse*); Donald A. Dripps, *Does Liberal Procedure Cause Punitive Substance? Preliminary Evidence from Some Natural Experiments,* 87 S. Cal. L. Rev. 459 (2014); David Alan Sklansky, *Killer Seatbelts and Criminal Procedure,* 119 Harv. L. Rev. F. 56 (2006).

Whether or not pro-defense procedural rulings set off a punitive feedback loop, the reality is that terms of trade exist between procedural rights and substantive liabilities. Not only must lawyers, on both sides, litigate suppression motions and civil rights lawsuits with a thorough knowledge of the often complex law. They must also estimate the chances for success before advising the client about the pros and cons of plea bargains and civil settlements. To serve their clients well, they must argue passionately, but think dispassionately.

5. *BIVENS* ACTIONS AGAINST FEDERAL OFFICERS

Big Cats of Serenity Springs v. Rhodes

843 F.3d 853 (10th Cir. 2016)

Opinion

■ TYMKOVICH, CHIEF JUDGE.

Big Cats of Serenity Springs is a Colorado-based non-profit that provides housing, food, and veterinary care for exotic animals. The facility is regulated by the United States Department of Agriculture's Animal and Plant Health Inspection Service (APHIS), established pursuant to the Animal Welfare Act. Three APHIS inspectors accompanied by El Paso County sheriff's deputies broke into the Big Cats facility without its permission to perform an unannounced inspection of two tiger cubs. But at the time the inspectors entered the facility, the cubs were at a veterinarian's office receiving treatment, just as Big Cats had promised the APHIS inspectors the previous day.

Big Cats and its directors sued the APHIS inspectors for the unauthorized entry pursuant to Bivens v. Six Unknown Narcotics Agents, 403 U.S. 388 (1971) and 42 U.S.C. § 1983, asserting the entry was an illegal search under the Fourth Amendment. The district court denied the APHIS inspectors' motion to dismiss the complaint and they filed an interlocutory appeal challenging the court's failure to grant qualified immunity. This court has jurisdiction over the interlocutory appeal from the district court's order under 28 U.S.C. § 1291. *See* Mitchell v. Forsyth, 472 U.S. 511, 535 (1985). Additionally, the court has jurisdiction over the question of whether a *Bivens* remedy exists because it was sufficiently implicated by the qualified immunity defense. *See* *Wilkie v. Robbins*, 551 U.S. 537, 549 n.4 (2007).

We affirm in part and reverse in part. Big Cats' complaint has stated a claim for relief under *Bivens*. No APHIS inspector would reasonably have believed unauthorized forcible entry of the Big Cats facility was permissible, and therefore Big Cats and its directors may have a claim for violation of their Fourth Amendment right to be free from an unreasonable search. But we reverse on Big Cats' civil rights claim because the federal inspectors are not liable under § 1983 in the circumstances here.

I.   Background

We start by explaining the regulatory scheme that applies to Big Cats' business and then address the relevant factual and procedural background.

A.   The Animal Welfare Act

Big Cats is a licensed wild animal exhibitor under the Animal Welfare Act, 7 U.S.C. §§ 2131–59 (AWA). Under the AWA, a facility must meet care and sanitation standards issued by the United States Department of Agriculture (USDA). 7 U.S.C. § 2143(a). Among other things, the regulations require licensees to handle animals safely, 9 C.F.R. § 2.131, provide adequate veterinary care, *id.* at § 2.40, and mark animals for identification, *id.* at § 2.50.

To enforce these standards, the AWA authorizes the USDA to "make such investigations or inspections as [the USDA] deems necessary." 7 U.S.C. § 2146(a). It grants the USDA access to licensees' facilities, animals, and records "at all reasonable times." *Id.* The corresponding regulations require a licensed organization to allow inspectors "during business hours . . . to enter its place of business . . . [and] inspect and photograph the facilities, property and animals, as the APHIS officials consider necessary to enforce the provisions of the Act. . . ." 9 C.F.R. § 2.126.

Violations by licensees, whether by providing substandard care or refusing inspection, are sanctioned through an administrative process. 7 U.S.C. § 2149. Licensees are subject to license suspension, civil penalties up to $10,000, and in some instances, imprisonment for up to one year. *Id.* Licensed organizations can appeal a final order to a federal Court of Appeals to "enjoin, set aside, suspend (in whole or in part), or determine the validity of the Secretary's order." *Id.* at § 2149(c).

B.   The Incident

The following allegations are from Big Cats' complaint, and we take them as true for purposes of our analysis. Weise v. Casper, 507 F.3d 1260, 1269–70 (10th Cir. 2007).

After a routine inspection of Big Cats' Serenity Springs Wildlife Center in early April 2013, APHIS inspectors determined that the care of an injured tiger cub was substandard and issued a citation requiring Big Cats to provide veterinary care. But when an inspector conducted a follow-up visit the next week, she found that the injury had worsened, and issued another citation. Big Cats denied both allegations and contested both citations, claiming they were part of a "pattern of harassing behavior" by the inspectors. App. 51.

On May 6, APHIS inspectors conducted another follow-up inspection. The inspectors claimed the cub's injuries had worsened, and also noticed that a different cub was suffering from an injured hind leg. Although Big Cats claimed the cubs had been treated and were receiving appropriate medications, the inspectors again cited Big Cats for failure to use "appropriate methods to prevent, control, diagnose, and treat diseases and injuries." 9 C.F.R. § 2.40(b)(2). The inspectors required the cubs to be evaluated as soon as possible, but "not later than 8:00 AM on 5/7/2013." App. 37.

During the inspection, Big Cats' founder and director, Nick Sculac, asked whether the cubs could be examined on May 8, because he had already scheduled an in-facility visit for that day with his contract veterinarian. But the APHIS officials would not approve a one-day delay. So even though transportation to a clinic risked further injury according to two of Big Cats' contract veterinarians, it was Mr. Sculac's only option to meet the citation's 8:00 a.m. requirement. He arrived, with the cubs, at the veterinary clinic at 7:00 a.m. on May 7.

Meanwhile, around 8:00 a.m., three APHIS personnel arrived at the Serenity Springs Wildlife Center only to find the facility closed. After unsuccessfully trying to reach Mr. Sculac on his cell phone, the inspectors decided to forcibly enter the facility. They contacted the El Paso County Sheriff's Office at 8:45 a.m., requesting urgent assistance in entering the facility. Two sheriff's deputies arrived at the facility and were told by the inspectors that they had a court order to seize the cubs. The deputies cut the outer gate's chains, and the inspectors entered the facility. They then cut the locks off an inner gate to access the pens, where they encountered an employee. The employee was "shocked and alarmed to suddenly see three [APHIS personnel] and two heavily armed police officers appear inside the locked, private facility." App. 17. After she informed them the cubs were at the veterinary clinic, the inspectors left and went to the clinic.

C. Procedural History

Big Cats and its directors filed a lawsuit against the APHIS inspectors, alleging a Fourth Amendment *Bivens* claim and a statutory claim under 42 U.S.C. § 1983. The district court denied the government's motion to dismiss, concluding the inspectors were not entitled to qualified immunity because their conduct—forcible entry without permission— violated clearly established Fourth Amendment constitutional law. The inspectors bring this interlocutory appeal from the denial of qualified immunity.

II. Analysis

The government makes two arguments: first, it contends neither *Bivens* nor § 1983 apply to the APHIS inspectors' unauthorized entry into Big Cats' facility; and, second, even if the inspectors' conduct was unlawful, it argues that the inspectors are still entitled to qualified immunity because the violation was not clearly established under federal law.

Since this is the denial of a Rule 12(b)(6) motion, our review is *de novo*, accepting "all well-pleaded allegations 'of the complaint as true and

consider[ing] them in the light most favorable to the nonmoving party.'"
Butler v. Rio Rancho Pub. Sch. Bd. of Educ., 341 F.3d 1197, 1199 (10th
Cir. 2003) (quoting Sutton v. Utah State Sch. for the Deaf & Blind, 173
F.3d 1226, 1236 (10th Cir. 1999)). "To survive a motion to dismiss, a
complaint must allege facts that, if true, 'state a claim to relief that is
plausible on its face.' A claim is facially plausible when the allegations
give rise to a reasonable inference that the defendant is liable." Mayfield
v. Bethards, 826 F.3d 1252, 1255 (10th Cir. 2016) (quoting Wilson v.
Montano, 715 F.3d 847, 852 (10th Cir. 2013)). In the context of qualified
immunity, we may not dismiss a complaint for failure to state a claim
unless it appears beyond doubt that plaintiffs cannot prove a set of facts
that would entitle them to relief. *Id.*

We address the *Bivens* and § 1983 claims in turn.

A.   Bivens

The government first contends that a *Bivens* cause of action is not
available under the Animal Welfare Act. It argues a *Bivens* remedy is not
available where the AWA provides parties with an alternative remedy
for misconduct. But as we explain, the AWA does not allow forcible entry
to a licensee's facility, nor does it provide licensees any relief from such
conduct. A *Bivens* claim is Big Cats' only available relief for an
unconstitutional search of its premises.

The Constitution does not ordinarily provide a private right of action
for constitutional violations by federal officials. Nonetheless, the
Supreme Court in *Bivens* approved a judicially-implied cause of action
allowing individuals to seek damages for unconstitutional conduct by
federal officials. 403 U.S. 388 (1971). According to the Court, "[t]hat
damages may be obtained for injuries consequent upon a violation of the
Fourth Amendment by federal officials should hardly seem a surprising
proposition." *Bivens*, 403 U.S. at 395. " '[I]t is well settled that where
legal rights have been invaded, and a federal statute provides for a
general right to sue for such invasion, federal courts may use any
available remedy to make good the wrong done.' " *Id.* at 396 (alterations
omitted) (quoting Bell v. Hood, 327 U.S. 678, 684 (1946)).

In several cases following *Bivens*, the Supreme Court extended the
doctrine from the Fourth Amendment context to other types of
constitutional claims. In Davis v. Passman, 442 U.S. 228 (1979), the
Court held that a federal Congressional employee could bring a *Bivens*
action pursuant to the "equal protection" element of the Due Process
clause of the Fifth Amendment. *See id.* at 248–49. And then in Carlson
v. Green, 446 U.S. 14 1980), the Court allowed the plaintiffs to pursue a
Bivens claim against federal prison officials for failure to provide
adequate medical treatment in violation of the Eighth Amendment's
cruel and unusual punishment clause. *See id.* at 17–18.

Davis and *Carlson* represent the high-water mark in the Court's
Bivens jurisprudence. Since those cases, the Court has steadfastly

retreated from a broad application of the doctrine, refusing to extend implied causes of action to other constitutional provisions, and cabining the contexts in which it will allow *Bivens* claims to proceed. *See* Richard H. Fallon, Jr. et al., Hart & Wechsler's The Federal Courts and the Federal System 770–72 (7th ed. 2015); *see also* Correctional Serv. Corp v. Malesko, 534 U.S. 61, 66–71 (2001) (collecting cases). The Court recognizes that a judicially-implied cause of action risks infringing on Congress's power to make law, and has explained that

> any freestanding damages remedy for a claimed constitutional violation [based on *Bivens*] has to represent a judgment about the best way to implement a constitutional guarantee; it is not an automatic entitlement no matter what other means there may be to vindicate a protected interest, and in most instances we have found a *Bivens* remedy unjustified.

Wilkie v. Robbins, 551 U.S. 537, 550 (2007). Thus, where Congress has already constructed a "constitutionally adequate" alternative remedy for federal misconduct, courts ought not step in by implying a *Bivens* cause of action. *See* Bush v. Lucas, 462 U.S. 367, 379 n.14 (1983) (declining to find new substantive legal liability to permit federal employee to recover damages from his supervisor after supervisor improperly disciplined him for exercising his First Amendment rights); *see also* Correctional Serv. Corp. v. Malesko, 534 U.S. 61 (2001) (claims against private prisons); FDIC v. Meyer, 510 U.S. 471 (1994) (claims against federal agencies); Schweiker v. Chilicky, 487 U.S. 412, 425 (1988) (Fifth Amendment claim against former government officials arising out of delays in receipt of Social Security benefits); United States v. Stanley, 483 U.S. 669 (1987) (declining to extend *Bivens* remedies to harms arising out of military service); Chappell v. Wallace, 462 U.S. 296 (1983) (same).

Yet *Bivens* still remains available in some circumstances, and our circuit has allowed *Bivens* claims in a variety of factual scenarios—based on violations of the First, Fourth, and Eighth Amendments. *See* Smith v. United States, 561 F.3d 1090 (10th Cir. 2009) (Eighth Amendment claim against prison officials); Oxendine v. Kaplan, 241 F.3d 1272 (10th Cir. 2001) (same); Nat'l Commodity & Barter Ass'n v. Archer, 31 F.3d 1521 (10th Cir. 1994) (First and Fourth Amendment claims against IRS agents).

Nonetheless, the Supreme Court requires courts evaluating *Bivens* causes of action to carefully consider the facts and context. The analysis proceeds along a two-step analytical framework. First, we examine whether an "alternative, existing process for protecting the [plaintiff's] interest amounts to a convincing reason for the Judicial Branch to refrain from providing a new and freestanding remedy in damages." *Wilkie*, 551 U.S. at 550. Second, in the absence of an alternative remedy, we will consider whether "special factors" counsel hesitation before authorizing a new kind of federal litigation. *Id.* In evaluating this consideration, courts "weigh[ ] reasons for and against the creation of a new cause of action, the way common law judges have always done." *Id.* at 554.

Relying on these principles, the government contends the AWA provides a comprehensive "alternative, existing process" that protects Big Cats' constitutional interests and therefore counsels against an implied *Bivens* cause of action. It argues that because Big Cats may administratively challenge an adverse inspection report, it must therefore resolve any alleged Fourth Amendment claims through that process. Moreover, the government contends that even if the AWA does not provide a fully adequate remedial scheme, special factors weigh against a *Bivens* claim here.

We consider each argument in turn.

1.   *Alternative Remedy*

The Supreme Court has explained that where an " 'alternative, existing process' [is] capable of protecting the constitutional interests at stake," the courts should refrain from augmenting the process with an implied damages remedy. Minneci v. Pollard, 565 U.S. 118 (2012) (quoting *Wilkie*, 551 U.S. at 550). "The point of examining the existing process is to determine whether Congress has explicitly or implicitly indicated 'that the Court's power should not be exercised.' " De La Paz v. Coy, 786 F.3d 367, 375 (5th Cir. 2015), *cert. filed*, (Jan. 12, 2016) (quoting *Bush*, 462 U.S. at 378). Congress may explicitly "indicate its intent[ ] by statutory language, by clear legislative history, or perhaps even by the statutory remedy itself, that the Court's power should not be exercised." *Bush*, 462 U.S. at 378. But Congress may also *implicitly* indicate intent "by creating a process that provides 'an avenue for some redress' " for injured persons, and "[i]n these instances, 'bedrock principles of separation of powers' show that 'Congress expected the Judiciary to stay its *Bivens* hand' and instead apply the statutory remedy." Koprowski v. Baker, 822 F.3d 248, 262 (6th Cir. 2016) (Sutton, J., dissenting) (quoting *Malesko*, 534 U.S. at 69; *Wilkie*, 551 U.S. at 554). Thus, in analyzing whether a *Bivens* claim is precluded by an alternative remedy, courts must consider the nature and extent of the statutory scheme created by Congress, and assess the significance of that scheme in light of the factual background of the case at hand. *See Wilkie*, 551 U.S. at 551.

Several cases illustrate this analysis. For example, in *Minneci* the Court considered whether prisoners could bring a *Bivens* claim against employees of a privately owned federal prison. The Court found no right of action because a claim "for physical or related emotional harm suffered as a result of [inadequate medical care is] the kind of conduct that state tort law typically forbids." . . . Similarly, in the Fifth Amendment context, the Court determined that Title II of the Social Security Act is a constitutionally adequate substitute for a Due Process challenge based on wrongful termination of disability benefits. Even though the Act did not provide full compensatory relief, Congress had sufficiently "addressed the problems created by state agencies' wrongful termination of disability benefits," making a *Bivens* remedy unnecessary. Schweiker, 487 U.S. at 429.[1]

But in the prototypical Fourth Amendment context, the Court has so far rejected the notion that state tort law can adequately protect a citizen's "absolute right to be free from unreasonable searches." *Bivens*, 403 U.S. at 392. According to the Court, the Fourth Amendment proscribes a broader range of conduct than what state law typically condemns, and, moreover, state law in some cases may be "inconsistent or even hostile" to the interests protected by the Fourth Amendment. *Bivens*, 403 U.S. at 392–94; *see also id.* at 410 (Harlan, J., concurring in the judgment) ("For people in Bivens' shoes, it is damages or nothing.").[2]

The government does not rely on state law as an alternative source of relief for Big Cats. Instead, it argues that we should conclude Congress has designed a comprehensive statutory scheme that provides meaningful remedies for victims, such that a *Bivens* remedy is unwarranted. It contends the regulatory scheme need not provide "complete relief," but should reflect Congress's meaningful intention to "provide[ ] what it considers adequate remedial mechanisms for constitutional violations that may occur in the course of [the statute's] administration." *Schweiker*, 487 U.S. at 423. Under the AWA, a licensee may administratively challenge an adverse inspection report under the Administrative Procedure Act. Thus, the government maintains that even though the AWA has no express compensatory mechanism to remedy constitutional claims, a Fourth Amendment claim is "*capable* of being addressed in the remedial process" by way of rejection of inspection violations predicated on illegal conduct. Reply Br. at 10 (emphasis added).

This reading of the AWA seriously misconstrues its regulatory scope and is not faithful to the Supreme Court's case law considering alternative remedies. The Court tells us the operative "question [is] whether any alternative, existing process for protecting the interest amounts to a convincing reason for the Judicial Branch to refrain from providing a new and freestanding remedy in damages." *Wilkie*, 551 U.S. at 550. In other words, the appropriate consideration is whether an alternate, existing process demonstrates Congress's *intent* to exclude a damages remedy. *Schweiker*, 487 U.S. at 435. Evidence of that intent would be a scheme that provides adequate deterrence of constitutional

---

[1] The Court suggested an Eighth Amendment *Bivens* claim would be permitted in *Malesko*, 534 U.S. at 70, because a prisoner may lack "any alternative remedy" for harms caused by a federal prison officer's unconstitutional conduct.

[2] One court recently found Congress supplanted an implied Fourth Amendment *Bivens* remedy. In *De La Paz*, 786 F.3d at 377, the Fifth Circuit found Congress supplanted Fourth Amendment claims in the immigration context where: (1) illegally seized evidence could be suppressed in deportation hearings; (2) the government had a process for reviewing alleged Fourth Amendment violations by employees; and (3) Congress has enacted an "elaborate remedial system" of immigration laws that has been in place for decades.

violations and at least *some* form of relief for the harm. *Malesko*, 534 U.S. at 70.

But Big Cats' challenge is based on a violation of the constitutional right to be free from an unreasonable search, not the propriety of the licensing citation. Nor does the AWA appeals process provide a mechanism for relief for misconduct by inspection agents themselves, it only allows for a licensee to challenge the factual basis for the citation—here Big Cats' failure to "allow APHIS officials access to conduct inspections." App. 91; *see also* Aple. Br. 28–29 (citing United States Dep't of Agric., *Animal Care: Appeals Process* (2014) (demonstrating grounds for appeal with no mechanism to assert constitutional violations)). In fact, should an APHIS inspector unlawfully enter and search a business, but find nothing to cite, that business would have no basis to challenge the inspector's behavior. Moreover, while it is true that judicial review under the APA may, in some circumstances, foreclose a *Bivens* claim, even if we accept the government's characterization of the existing AWA administrative scheme, we fail to see the APA as an " 'alternative, existing process' capable of protecting the constitutional interests at stake." *Minneci*, 132 S.Ct. at 623 (citation omitted). While there is no need for congruent remedies or even money damages to deny a *Bivens* remedy, there must be more than nothing. Here, the AWA and administrative review provide no relief for the conduct alleged by Big Cats.

Even if the AWA provided some form of alternative relief, it would be hard to square this case with circuit precedent. In Smith v. United States, 561 F.3d 1090, 1103 (10th Cir. 2009), we found Congress had not displaced a *Bivens* remedy based on an Eighth Amendment claim even where a statutory scheme substantially occupied the field of inmate injury. We concluded the Inmate Accident Compensation Act (IACA), which provides compensation for federal inmates who suffer work-related injuries, did not provide an adequate remedial scheme, since the IACA operates a no-fault compensation system that provided no " 'forum where the allegedly unconstitutional conduct would come to light.' " *Smith*, 561 F.3d at 1103 (quoting Bagola v. Kindt, 131 F.3d 632, 642–43 (7th Cir. 1997)); *see also Koprowski*, 822 F.3d at 255 ("Under the [IACA] scheme, all that matters is the nature of the injury, not the underlying conduct."). In finding such a system offers "very little deterrent effect for constitutional harms," we held the IACA did not provide an adequate, alternative process to protect prisoners' Eighth Amendment rights. *Smith*, 561 F.3d at 1103; *see also Koprowski*, 822 F.3d at 252; *Bagola*, 131 F.3d at 644; Vaccaro v. Dobre, 81 F.3d 854, 857 (9th Cir. 1996) (same).

If anything, the scheme in *Smith* offered a more meaningful remedy for plaintiffs to redress their injuries than the AWA does in this case. *See Koprowski*, 822 F.3d at 264 (Sutton, J., dissenting) ("Taken together, these [IACA] alternatives allow an injured inmate to receive money for the injury *and* order the officials to obey the Constitution, demonstrating that Congress paid 'careful attention' to this precise injury. . . . They also offer injured inmates extensive review procedures, which further 'safeguard their rights.' " (alteration and citation omitted)). In this case, unlike the IACA, the AWA provides no compensatory mechanism for unconstitutional conduct, whether it be damages or dismissal of inspection violations. And even if unconstitutional searches were exposed, the appeals process does not describe any recourse. The only recourse the government suggests is that evidence improperly gathered would be ruled impermissible to support a citation. But the citation for failure to provide access is not ameliorated by inspectors' subsequent conduct—no evidence was gathered. Putting aside that no remedy appears in the statute, regulations, or in internal administrative guidance, even if it did, the government does not explain how the exclusion of evidence provides accountability, or—in other words—gives APHIS officials "skin in the game" to deter illegal conduct. *See Koprowski*, 822 F.3d at 255. In short, because nothing in the AWA provides licensees protection from Fourth Amendment violations in the circumstances alleged here, we cannot hold that an alternative, existing process excludes a *Bivens* remedy.

2. *Special Factors*

The Supreme Court also counsels that a *Bivens* action is not available where the government demonstrates "special factors" that weigh against an implied remedy. This requires "weighing reasons for and against the creation of a new cause of action, the way common law judges have always done," and whether those reasons "counsel[ ] hesitation before authorizing a new kind of federal litigation." *Wilkie*, 551 U.S. at 550, 554.

Wilkie again is illustrative. There, the Court found the risk of a floodgate of spurious claims against BLM officials would undermine the functioning of the agency, as well as the elusive nature of the proposed cause of action counseled hesitation: "We think accordingly that any damages remedy for actions by Government employees who push too hard for the Government's benefit may come better, if at all, through legislation." *Id.* at 562.

The Court similarly found special factors precluded a *Bivens* action in *Chappell*, where the Court held that "the unique disciplinary structure of the Military Establishment and Congress' activity in the field constitute 'special factors' which dictate that it would be inappropriate to provide enlisted military personnel a *Bivens*-type remedy against their superior officers." 462 U.S. at 304; *see also Schweiker* at 414 (finding that design of the Social Security Act's administrative and judicial scheme was a special factor counseling against finding a *Bivens* remedy). In *Bush*, the Court also rejected a *Bivens* remedy for the plaintiff's First Amendment violation on the basis of a special factors analysis, because the case involved policy questions in an area that had received significant congressional scrutiny. *Id.* at 423.

Here, the government argues that the animal inspection context militates against a *Bivens* remedy because the AWA already provides a series of remedies. Aplt. Br. at 26. But as we explained above, the AWA does not provide an adequate remedy for illegal searches. Additionally, this is not the case where "indications [of] congressional inaction" support an inference that the *Bivens* action has been supplanted. *Chilicky*, 487 U.S. at 423. APHIS inspectors are not subject to a comprehensive disciplinary scheme crafted by Congress or the Executive Branch. Nor are there any concerns about a workable cause of action. Fourth Amendment *Bivens* causes of action have been routinely applied to the conduct of federal officials in a variety of contexts, including ATF agents, *Groh v. Ramirez*, 540 U.S. 551 (2004); federal marshals and FBI agents, Harris v. Roderick, 126 F.3d 1189 (9th Cir. 1997); and IRS special agents, Nat'l Commodity & Barter Ass'n v. Archer, 31 F.3d 1521 (10th Cir. 1994).

If we were writing on a blank slate, we might be persuaded that *Bivens* is a relic of another era, and that Congress is perfectly capable of policing federal misconduct. But given our case law, Supreme Court precedent, and the factual context present here, we are constrained to find that Big Cats may proceed. Big Cats alleges a garden-variety constitutional violation (hardly a new context), the regulatory scheme is plainly unavailable to remedy the alleged misconduct, and no special factors place AWA inspectors outside *Bivens*. We therefore agree with the district court that Big Cats' *Bivens* claim may go forward unless the inspectors are entitled to qualified immunity.

3. *Qualified Immunity*

Public officials enjoy "qualified immunity in civil actions that are brought against them in their individual capacities and that arise out of the performance of their duties." Pahls v. Thomas, 718 F.3d 1210, 1227 (10th Cir. 2013). To overcome qualified immunity, a plaintiff must show that: (1) the public official violated the plaintiff's constitutional rights; and (2) these rights were clearly established at the time of the alleged violation. *Id.* "This standard, by design, 'gives government officials breathing room to make reasonable but mistaken judgments about open legal questions.'" *Id.* (quoting Ashcroft v. al-Kidd, 563 U.S. 731 (2011)). Although the purpose of a *Bivens* action is to deter individual federal officers from committing constitutional violations, "the threat of litigation and liability will adequately deter federal officers for *Bivens* purposes no matter that they may enjoy qualified immunity." *Malesko*, 534 U.S. at 70.

We first discuss the contours of a Fourth Amendment violation in the regulatory context and then consider whether the law was clearly established so that a reasonable APHIS inspector would have known he could not forcibly enter the Serenity Springs Wildlife Center without authorization.

a. *Constitutional Violation*

The Fourth Amendment protects the right to be free from unreasonable searches and seizures. U.S. Const. amend. IV. "[S]earches conducted outside the judicial process, without prior approval by judge or magistrate, are *per se* unreasonable under the Fourth Amendment—subject only to a few specifically established and well-delineated exceptions." Arizona v. Gant, 556 U.S. 332, 338 (2009) (quoting Katz v. United States, 389 U.S. 347, 357 (1967)).

It is well established that the Fourth Amendment applies not only to private homes and individuals, but also to commercial premises. *New York v. Burger*, 482 U.S. 691, 699 (1987). An owner or operator of a business thus has a reasonable expectation of privacy in commercial property, *see id.* at 702; *see also Katz*, 389 U.S. at 360–62 (Harlan, J., concurring), and that expectation includes not only traditional police searches, but also administrative inspections to enforce regulations, *Burger*, 482 U.S. at 699.

The Supreme Court has recognized, however, that an expectation of privacy in commercial property is "different from, and indeed less than, a similar expectation in an individual's home." *Id.* at 700. The expectation of privacy is particularly low for the narrow class of heavily or "closely regulated" businesses—such as those that sell firearms and liquor—because the business owner has voluntarily decided to "subject himself to a full arsenal of governmental regulation." *Marshall v. Barlow's, Inc.*, 436 U.S. 307, 313 (1978). Without elaborate enforcement schemes, the regulation of those industries would be ineffective. Thus, for closely regulated businesses, warrantless administrative searches of commercial premises—including surprise inspections—do not *per se* violate the Fourth Amendment. *See* 5 Wayne R. LaFave, Search and Seizure: A Treatise on the Fourth Amendment § 10.2(f) (5th ed. 2012); 2 William E. Ringel, Searches and Seizures, Arrests and Confessions § 14:8 (2d ed. Nov. 2016 Update).

A closely regulated industry is still protected by the Fourth Amendment, however, and warrantless searches of those businesses are unreasonable if arbitrarily conducted. *See* Ringel, *supra*, § 14:8. To guard against unreasonable administrative searches, in *Burger* the Supreme Court articulated several criteria the government must meet to justify warrantless inspections: (1) the government must prove a *substantial interest* that justifies warrantless inspections; (2) the warrantless inspections must be *necessary to further the regulatory scheme*; and (3) the inspection program must be *sufficiently certain and regular* to provide a constitutionally adequate substitute for a warrant. *Burger*, 482 U.S. at 702–03; *see also* United States v. Mitchell, 518 F.3d 740, 751 (10th Cir. 2008) (applying the *Burger* three-part test).

We assume the AWA fits within the analytical framework of *Burger*, an assumption Big Cats does not challenge. The government has a substantial interest in animal safety and welfare and surprise inspections help further those interests. And the regulations implementing the AWA allow routine inspections of regulated premises during "business hours" with protections for businesses to have the inspections conducted by authorized personnel. 9 C.F.R. § 2.126(a).

But the fact that the AWA might authorize warrantless inspections is not the end of the story. The question remains as to whether government officials may *forcibly* enter commercial premises in pursuit of their regulatory duties.

The Supreme Court addressed this question in Colonnade Catering Corp. v. United States, 397 U.S. 72 (1970). In that case, the Court considered a situation in which an IRS agent suspected a tavern of violating federal liquor excise tax laws. After the owner denied access to a locked liquor storage room, the agent broke the lock and entered the room, finding illicit goods. The store owner sued, seeking to suppress the seized liquor as evidence of misconduct.

The Supreme Court held that the IRS agent violated the Fourth Amendment. In reaching this conclusion, the Court considered the government's argument that the statutory scheme allowed tax inspectors to forcibly enter regulated premises. The relevant statute allowed inspectors to: (1) "enter during business hours the premises (including places of storage) of any dealer for the purpose of inspecting or examining any records or other documents required to be kept," 26 U.S.C. § 5146(b) (1964); and (2) "enter, in the daytime, any building or place where any articles or objects subject to tax are made, produced, or kept, so far as it may be necessary for the purpose of examining said articles," *id.* at § 7606. The Court rejected the government's contention that the statute authorized breaking into closed facilities without a warrant, noting Congress's lack of explicit authorization to use force to further lawful inspections and the statutory provision for civil penalties for businesses refusing entry. 26 U.S.C. § 7342 (1964).

The government argues that although the AWA is silent about warrantless searches, rules promulgated under the AWA permit warrantless forcible entry under *Burger* and *Colonnade*. Specifically, it points to the regulations governing the confiscation of animals as authority. 9 C.F.R. § 2.129. Under these regulations, where an inspector believes an animal is "suffering" due to the exhibitor's failure to comply with USDA regulations, an APHIS official shall "notify the [ ] exhibitor . . . and request that the condition be corrected and that adequate care be given to alleviate the animal's suffering or distress." 9 C.F.R. § 2.129(a). Then, if the exhibitor "refuses to comply with this request, the APHIS official may confiscate the animal(s) for care, treatment, or disposal . . . if, in the opinion of the [APHIS] Administrator, the circumstances indicate the animals' health is in danger." *Id.* The regulations also provide APHIS officials with guidance in the case of entry in premises where the owner is unavailable. An inspector "shall [then] contact a local police or other law officer to accompany him to the premises and shall provide for adequate care when necessary to alleviate the animals' suffering." *Id.* at § 2.129(b).[5] The government argues that "authorization for forcible entry is implicit" in these regulations considering: (1) the local law enforcement provision; and (2) that inspectors would be unable to discharge their responsibilities unless authorized to forcibly enter a facility. Aplt. Br. at 40–41.

But § 2.129 does not apply here. By its plain language, the regulation applies to circumstances where: (1) the licensee "refuses to comply" with an official request to correct the animal's suffering; and (2) the APHIS administrator certifies that "the circumstances indicate the animal's health is in danger." 9 C.F.R. § 2.129(a). Here, the factual allegations in the complaint state that Big Cats never refused to comply with a request for care or that the inspectors sought and received an opinion from the APHIS Administrator that forcible entry was necessary.

In fact, according to the complaint, the inspectors themselves did not think they were engaged in a confiscation under this provision. In their internal report on the incident, they characterized their visit as a "routine inspection" and that they were denied access pursuant to the inspection regulation, App. 90–91, a regulation that only allows APHIS officials to enter a business to inspect records, photograph animals, and document noncompliance with the Act, 9 C.F.R. § 2.126(a). These regulations do not give a whiff of support for unannounced forcible entry of a business.

In sum, the AWA regulatory scheme is similar to the scheme that the Court found inadequate in *Colonnade* to protect constitutional rights. Absent statutory authorization, the inspectors had no basis to forcibly enter the establishment without a warrant. Accordingly, Big Cats has adequately alleged that the APHIS inspectors' unauthorized entry violated their Fourth Amendment rights and that the AWA did not authorize the warrantless search.

b.   Clearly Established

Under qualified immunity, even if the inspectors violated the Fourth Amendment, they are entitled to immunity if no clearly established law would have informed them that a warrantless forcible search was improper. "A Government official's conduct violates clearly established

---

[5]   That provision states in relevant part that, where an APHIS official finds an animal is:

(a)   suffering as a result of a failure of the . . . carrier to comply with any provision of the regulations or the standards set forth in this subchapter, the APHIS official shall make a reasonable effort to notify the . . . carrier of the condition of the animal(s) and request that the condition be corrected and that adequate care be given to alleviate the animal's suffering or distress. . . . In the event that the . . . carrier refuses to comply with this request, the APHIS official may confiscate the animal(s) for care, treatment, or disposal as indicated in paragraph (b) of this section, if, in the opinion of the Administrator, the circumstances indicate the animal's health is in danger.

(b)   In the event that the APHIS official is unable to locate or notify the dealer, exhibitor, intermediate handler, or carrier as required in this section, the APHIS official shall contact a local police or other law officer to accompany him to the premises and shall provide for adequate care when necessary to alleviate the animal's suffering.

law when, at the time of the challenged conduct, 'the contours of a right are sufficiently clear' that every 'reasonable official would have understood that what he is doing violates that right.'" *al-Kidd*, 131 S.Ct. at 2083 (alterations omitted) (quoting Anderson v. Creighton, 483 U.S. 635, 640 (1987)). But the plaintiff must show a Supreme Court or Tenth Circuit decision on point, or the clearly established weight of authority from other courts must supply the requisite notice. Columbian Fin. Corp. v. Stork, 811 F.3d 390, 396 (10th Cir. 2016).

Colonnade is squarely on point. The inspection provisions allowed access at reasonable times for surprise inspections but nowhere allowed or authorized the use of force. Moreover, both inspection schemes provided penalties to enforce compliance. For the tax statutes in *Colonnade*, Congress required a fine for any person "who refuses to admit any officer or employee of the Treasury Department" acting under the tax statute. Similarly, under the AWA, licensed businesses face civil penalties up to $10,000 for violating the statute or corresponding regulations, thus obviating the need for forcible entry. 7 U.S.C. § 2149(b). Thus, the AWA's scheme is like that in *Colonnade*, which for fifty years has stood for the proposition that a warrant is required for forcible entry into closed premises.

The government argues the AWA goes further than the scheme in *Colonnade* or even *Burger*, making misconduct less obvious to inspectors. It contends, moreover, the regulations provide for forcible entry in cases of veterinary emergency to conduct a confiscation. As discussed above, where inspectors believe an animal is suffering and the exhibitor refuses to provide adequate care, the inspector may confiscate the animal if the APHIS Administrator determines the animal's health is in danger. 9 C.F.R. § 2.129(a). But, according to the complaint, at no point did Big Cats refuse to provide veterinary care, nor did the APHIS Administrator determine the tiger cubs were in danger. They also knew that both of Big Cats' contract veterinarians "believed [a] one-day delay [in examination] was preferable to transporting the animals," App. 53, obviating the basis to believe care was urgent. And, in any event, the inspectors did not rely on the confiscation regulations to justify their entry into the premises, which they described as a "routine inspection" in the report filed after the incident. It is also worth noting that neither the AWA regulations nor applicable Animal Care Inspection Guide suggest that forcible entry is a permissible technique. *See* Supp. App. 2–19; Aplt. Br. at 27. In fact, the Guide instructs agents to "not enter facilities with locked gates and/or No Trespassing signs." Supp. App. 2. The Guide further recommends law enforcement assistance only to provide security for personal safety, and not to suggest they are necessary to facilitate forcible entry. *Id.* And further at odds with the government's position, the Guide states "There may be times during a confiscation operation" when inspectors should involve legal counsel "in the acquisition or service of a subpoena or warrant." United States Dep't of Agric., *Animal Welfare Inspection Guide*

8–28 (2013); *see* Aplt. Br. at 27. Thus, we see no factual or regulatory basis for a reasonable inspection agent to use force to enter a licensee's premises absent an emergency or exigent circumstances.[6]

Because we see no meaningful difference between the *Colonnade* inspection scheme and the one here, reasonable APHIS inspectors should have known they could not forcibly enter a business facility to perform an inspection, absent a warrant or an exception to the warrant requirement. Big Cats alleges facts showing that the agents cut the locks to conduct a non-emergency inspection where the regulations did not provide for forcible entry. The law is clearly established that inspection officials cannot enter business premises without a warrant in those circumstances.

B. Section 1983

We turn lastly to the question of whether Big Cats can sue the APHIS inspectors under § 1983 of the Civil Rights Act. Big Cats contends the inspectors are subject to liability under § 1983 "because they acted under color of state law when they induced deputies to cut chains and enter the premises. . . ." App. 57. We disagree.

Section 1983 is not directed at conduct by federal officials. Instead, it provides a remedy against state actors who violate a federal right, pursuant to state authority. Fallon, *supra*, at 986; Monroe v. Pape, 365 U.S. 167, 171–76 (1961), *overruled in part on other grounds*, Monell v. Dep't. of Soc. Servs., 436 U.S. 658 (1978). For this reason, federal employees are rarely § 1983 defendants, and "actions of the Federal Government and its officers are at least facially exempt from [§ 1983] proscriptions." District of Columbia v. Carter, 409 U.S. 418, 424–25 (1973). But in some cases, federal officials may in fact act under "color of state law" for § 1983 purposes.

The paradigmatic example is when federal officials conspire with state officials to infringe a protected constitutional right. Martinez v. Winner, 771 F.2d 424, 441 (10th Cir. 1985) ("Federal officials ordinarily are not suable under § 1983, which requires action under color of state law, but they may be liable under § 1983 where, as here, they are charged with conspiring with state officers or employees."), *vacated on other grounds*, 800 F.2d 230 (10th Cir. 1986). Most courts agree that conspiracy with state actors is a requirement to finding that federal actors jointly acted under color of state law. Strickland ex rel. Strickland v. Shalala, 123 F.3d 863, 866–67 (6th Cir. 1997) ("[C]ourts finding that a *federal* official has acted under color of state law have done so only when there is evidence that federal and state officials engaged in a conspiracy or

---

[6] This is an appeal from a motion to dismiss. It is possible that after discovery in this case we may see a different factual posture. Our task here is based on the allegations in the complaint. If the landscape changes after discovery, the government is entitled to seek summary judgment on qualified immunity. For purposes of our analysis, the legal posture here does not support a finding of a veterinary emergency or other exigent circumstances.

'symbiotic' venture to violate a person's rights under the Constitution or federal law.").

Big Cats alleges the federal employees "acted jointly" with the deputies when they represented they had a court order to seize the cubs, and that "[r]elying on the USDA's representations, the deputies cut the chains." App. 54–55. These are insufficient allegations to establish a conspiracy. "[U]nder established case law, the fundamental characteristic of a conspiracy is a joint commitment to an 'endeavor which, if completed, would satisfy all of the elements of the underlying substantive criminal offense.'" Ocasio v. United States, ___ U.S. ___ (2016) (alteration and citation omitted). The complaint must allege (1) an agreement between two or more persons, with (2) an intent to achieve an unlawful act. Wayne R. LaFave, 2 Subst. Crim. L. § 12.2 (2d ed. 2003); see also United States v. Hill, 786 F.3d 1254, 1266 (10th Cir. 2015) (citing the elements of a conspiracy),. The allegations of the complaint make it clear the El Paso County sheriff's deputies were not engaged in an agreement with the inspectors to pursue an unlawful act. Read most favorably to Big Cats, the most that can be said is that the deputies were facilitating entry to the Big Cats premises on the false representation and mistaken impression that the inspectors had a court order to enter the facility. There was no agreement to violate law; indeed, the El Paso County incident report in the record states the deputies thought their actions were supported by a court order and a need to check on the cubs' welfare.

To hold federal officials subject to § 1983 liability based on joint action, plaintiff must at least allege that federal and state actors shared a "common, unconstitutional goal," or point to a "substantial degree of cooperative action" or "overt and significant state participation." See Schaffer v. Salt Lake City Corp., 814 F.3d 1151, 1157 (10th Cir. 2016) (quoting Gallagher v. Neil Young Freedom Concert, 49 F.3d 1442, 1454 (10th Cir. 1995)); see also Sigmon v. CommunityCare HMO, Inc., 234 F.3d 1121, 1126 (10th Cir. 2000) (requiring conspiracy such that the state and non-state actors "'share[d] a common, unconstitutional goal'" (quoting Anaya v. Crossroads Managed Care Sys., 195 F.3d 584, 596 (10th Cir. 1999))).[8]

The district court nonetheless concluded the "enlistment of state law enforcement" was sufficient to hold federal officers liable under § 1983. The court and the government rely on an unpublished district court case

---

[8]   A plaintiff may well need to allege a higher level of coordination to show federal officers, rather than private parties, acted under color of state law. This is for several reasons. First, plaintiffs must overcome the presumption that Congress did not intend for federal officers to be subject to § 1983 litigation. *Carter*, 409 U.S. 418, 424–25. Second, plaintiffs must overcome the presumption that where federal and state actors come together, they are acting pursuant to supreme law. *See* Arar v. Ashcroft, 585 F.3d 559, 568 (2d Cir. 2009) (en banc) ("[S]ince 'federal officials typically act under color of *federal* law,' they are rarely deemed to have acted under color of state law." (citation omitted)). We need not resolve exactly what this showing looks like, however, because plaintiffs fail to meet any existing analysis that would prove these non-state actors acted under color of state law.

from California for support, Reynoso v. City & County. of San Francisco, No. C 10–00984 SI, 2012 WL 646232 (N.D. Cal. Feb. 28, 2012). In that case, San Francisco police officers entered the plaintiff's residence to search for drugs. But the court found substantial concerted action by the state and federal officials. "After the premises was secured, the ATF agents 'merely substituted themselves for the agents of the City and County of San Francisco in the break-in of plaintiffs' home and took up the search and seizure initiated by the City and County of San Francisco authorities.'" *Id.* at *6 (citation omitted). Because the federal defendants were significant participants in the *state scheme*, those federal defendants' actions could "'fairly be attributed to the state.'" *Id.* at *5–6 (quoting Cabrera v. Martin, 973 F.2d 735, 742–43 (9th Cir. 1992)).

The circumstances here are quite different. The deputies were not actively engaged in pursuing a common law enforcement objective. Nor were they attempting to vindicate any state or county interest. They were only operating under the false assumption that the entry was authorized under federal law and pursuant to court order.

In sum, the complaint does not allege the federal and state actors shared an unconstitutional goal. Nor do we find sufficient state cooperation, considering the local deputies' entire involvement consisted of complying with the requests of the APHIS inspectors. More accurately, the federal officials are better seen as acting under color of *federal* law— the AWA—when they instructed the state officials to cut the locks.

Because the federal officials did not act under color of state law, the district court erred in denying the government's motion to dismiss the § 1983 claim.

III. Conclusion

Big Cats may proceed with its *Bivens* claim because no inspector would have reasonably believed he could forcibly enter the business premises of a licensee in these circumstances. We therefore AFFIRM the district court's order denying the government's motion to dismiss the *Bivens* claim. We REVERSE the court's order denying the government's motion to dismiss the § 1983 claim, however, because the federal officials did not act under color of state law.

6. THE EXCLUSIONARY RULE

a. STANDING

Atkins v. Commonwealth
57 Va.App. 2, 698 S.E.2d 249 (2010)

■ FRANK, JUDGE.

Kentora Delvontae Atkins, appellant, was convicted, in a bench trial, of possession of heroin, in violation of Code § 18.2–250, possession of a firearm while in possession of heroin, in violation of Code § 18.2–308.4(B), and possession of a firearm by a convicted felon, in violation of Code § 18.2–308.2. On appeal, he contends the trial court erred in: 1) finding he had no standing to challenge the search of the automobile in which he was a passenger; 2) denying his motion to suppress the heroin and the gun; 3) finding the evidence sufficient to prove he possessed the firearm while simultaneously in possession of heroin; 4) denying his motion to dismiss the felony firearm indictment for containing a fatal variance, and 5) finding the evidence sufficient to prove possession of a firearm by a convicted felon. For the reasons stated, we affirm.

BACKGROUND

Special Agent P.N. Gallaccio of the Virginia State Police and Norfolk Police Officer W.K. Winningear, on September 3, 2008, stopped a vehicle for a defective equipment violation because the license plate bulb was burned out. While the stop was in progress, appellant, the right rear passenger, "turned around" several times and Gallaccio lost sight of appellant's head "as if he was bending over in the seat."

After approaching the car, Gallaccio asked appellant for identification. Appellant stated that he had none. Gallaccio asked the front seat passenger for her identification, and she gave him a driver's license. Appellant then handed his license to Gallaccio. Gallaccio noticed that appellant did not appear nervous at that time. Gallaccio gave the licenses to Officer Winningear. It was then discovered that the front female passenger had outstanding warrants. For that reason, she was removed from the car. During this time, appellant was "constantly turning around and observing [the police] and [their] actions."

While appellant was still in the car, Gallaccio watched him as he tried to light a cigarette. Gallaccio observed that appellant was having difficulty doing so because he was "shaking unbelievably in his seat." Gallaccio testified, "in my 13 years of experience watching traffic stops, I'd never seen anybody struggle to light a cigarette as much as [appellant] did."

Winningear returned appellant's license to him and asked the driver for consent to search the vehicle. The driver did not consent. The officers told the occupants they were going to screen the vehicle with a drug dog.[2] At that point, the officers asked appellant and the driver to get out of the car.

After the driver got out of the vehicle, he and Officer Winningear engaged in a brief conversation before the driver abruptly retrieved his keys from the console and started the engine. In trying to keep the driver from leaving, Winningear struggled with the driver, and the driver fled. The driver was not apprehended that evening.

---

[2]   Winningear, a canine handler, had his dog, Rock, with him at the time of the stop.

When appellant got out of the car, Gallaccio observed needle marks on appellant's arms. He also saw that appellant's hands were "balled up," there was "tension in his arms," and he appeared nervous. When asked why, appellant responded, "because cops around here beat people up for no reason." Appellant then placed his hands in his pockets. Gallaccio advised him to take his hands out of his pockets and that he was going to pat him down for weapons. Appellant was instructed to walk to the back of the police vehicle, but he continued to walk past that vehicle. When he was passing another police vehicle, Special Agent Gallaccio grabbed him by the back of his shirt because he "thought something was afoot." Gallaccio testified that he thought appellant was going to run. As Gallaccio grabbed him, appellant took his hands out of his pockets and dropped a white pill bottle that contained eleven capsules of heroin. After a brief struggle with appellant, Gallaccio placed appellant under arrest.

At the suppression hearing, Gallaccio testified without objection that he searched the vehicle "incident to arrest." He also testified at trial that he searched the car because the driver ran, so the car was going to have to be towed and he was "inventorying the vehicle."

Inside the car, the officers recovered one firearm from under the driver's seat. Another firearm was found in the back seat area under the right passenger seat. The barrel was facing forward "with the magazine port facing toward the right as if someone was sitting there and stuck it right there." Gallaccio testified that he believed it would have been visible to someone sitting in the rear passenger seat. A DNA test was performed on the gun found in the back seat area, and no DNA was recovered.

This appeal follows.

ANALYSIS

Standing

Appellant argues that the trial court erred in ruling that he did not have standing to challenge the illegal search of the vehicle and the seizure of the weapons. As a result of the court's ruling, reasons appellant, the guns recovered from the car were erroneously admitted into evidence. The Commonwealth argues that the trial court properly found that Rakas v. Illinois, 439 U.S. 128 (1978), prevents appellant, as a passenger, from challenging the search of the vehicle.

At oral argument, we asked counsel to file supplemental briefs to address the applicability of *Rakas* and Brendlin v. California, 551 U.S. 249132 (2007).

At the suppression hearing, the Commonwealth initially raised the argument that appellant, as a passenger, would not have standing to challenge the search of the vehicle pursuant to *Rakas*. Appellant agreed, stating that he has "very little standing to contest the search." The trial court, citing *Rakas,* ruled that appellant, as a passenger, could not challenge the search and recovery of the firearms. Appellant responded, "yes, sir." In a timely filed motion to vacate, appellant cited *Brendlin* and contended that contrary to the trial court's ruling, appellant does have standing to contest the search of the vehicle and the seizure of the weapon.

We agree with the trial court that *Rakas* controls. Rakas was a passenger in an automobile in which police found a box of rifle shells in a locked glove compartment and a sawed-off rifle under the front passenger seat. 439 U.S. at 130. The Supreme Court rejected Rakas' argument that simply being a passenger in the vehicle afforded him standing to contest the search of the vehicle. *Id.* at 148. Rakas neither owned nor leased the vehicle. *Id.* at 140. Significantly, the Supreme Court found Rakas "asserted neither a property nor a possessory interest in the automobile, nor an interest in the property seized." *Id.* at 148. The Court then concluded:

> Judged by the foregoing analysis, petitioners' claims must fail. They asserted neither a property nor a possessory interest in the automobile, nor an interest in the property seized. And as we have previously indicated, the fact that they were "legitimately on [the] premises" in the sense that they were in the car with the permission of its owner is not determinative of whether they had a legitimate expectation of privacy in the particular areas of the automobile searched.
>
> * * * * * *
>
> But here petitioners' claim is one which would fail even in an analogous situation in a dwelling place, since they made no showing that they had any legitimate expectation of privacy in the glove compartment or area under the seat of the car in which they were merely passengers. Like the trunk of an automobile, these are areas in which a passenger *qua* passenger simply would not normally have a legitimate expectation of privacy.

Id. at 148–49 (citations omitted).

Appellant argues *Brendlin* supports his position. We find that his reliance is misplaced. *Brendlin* does not address a defendant passenger's right to contest the search of the vehicle; *Brendlin* addresses only a passenger's challenge to the stop itself. The Supreme Court concluded a passenger may bring a Fourth Amendment challenge to the legality of a traffic stop because the passenger is seized as a result of the traffic stop. *Brendlin,* 551 U.S. at 255. The Court reasoned, "A traffic stop necessarily curtails the travel a passenger has chosen just as much as it halts the driver, diverting both from the stream of traffic to the side of the road. . . ." *Id.* at 257. The Court added,

> If the likely wrongdoing is not the driving, the passenger will reasonably feel subject to suspicion owing to close association; but even when the wrongdoing is only bad driving, the passenger will expect to be subject to some scrutiny, and his

attempt to leave the scene would be so obviously likely to prompt an objection from the officer that no passenger would feel free to leave in the first place.

Id. By its own language, *Brendlin* does not address whether a passenger can challenge the legality of a search of the vehicle in which he is a passenger.

Appellant further cites Arizona v. Johnson, ___ U.S. ___ (2009), to support his contention. However, *Johnson* simply reiterates the *Brendlin* ruling that "[a] passenger therefore has standing to challenge a stop's constitutionality."

Under *Rakas,* we begin our analysis by noting that appellant bears the burden of proving that he has standing to assert the constitutional right. *Abell v. Commonwealth,* 221 Va. 607, 614, 272 S.E.2d 204, 208 (1980). In keeping with *Rakas,* "[t]he test is whether the appellant objectively had a reasonable expectation of privacy at the time and place of the disputed search." *McCoy v. Commonwealth,* 2 Va.App. 309, 311, 343 S.E.2d 383, 385 (1986). In determining whether an expectation of privacy is objectively reasonable, a court looks to the totality of the circumstances,

> "includ[ing] whether the defendant has a possessory interest in . . . the place searched, whether he has the right to exclude others from that place, whether he has exhibited a subjective expectation that it would remain free from governmental invasion, whether he took normal precautions to maintain his privacy and whether he was legitimately on the premises."

Id. at 312, 343 S.E.2d at 385 (quoting United States v. Haydel, 649 F.2d 1152, 1155 (5th Cir.1981)). *See also* Barnes v. Commonwealth, 234 Va. 130, 135, 360 S.E.2d 196, 200 (1987) (discussing that defendant failed to meet his burden where he showed he had permission to be present in the place searched but did not have a key, did not keep property there, and could not exclude others) (1988).

The Commonwealth argues, and we agree, that appellant asserted neither a property nor a possessory interest in the vehicle. Because appellant asserted a Fourth Amendment violation, it was his burden to show he had standing to challenge the search of the vehicle. At no point did he claim any interest in the vehicle or in the weapons found inside. From this record, it is clear that appellant did not own the vehicle and was in the vehicle to purchase heroin. All that appellant has shown is that he was a passenger in the vehicle.

Appellant contends Arnold v. Commonwealth, 17 Va.App. 313, 437 S.E.2d 235 (1993), modifies *Rakas.* We disagree. In *Arnold,* we held that a passenger had an expectation of privacy in a shopping bag found on the vehicle's floor at his feet. *Id.* at 316, 437 S.E.2d at 237. We distinguished *Rakas* in two respects. First, we found that in *Rakas,* the question was "a narrow one: Did the search of their friend's automobile after they had left it violate any Fourth Amendment right of the petitioners?" *Id.* We further distinguished *Rakas* because there, "the defendants asserted no interest in the property seized." *Id.*

Also of note in *Arnold,* Arnold never denied ownership of the items seized. In the instant case, unlike Arnold, appellant denied any interest in the weapon seized. While such a denial is not determinative of the issue, it clearly is a factor as part of the totality of the circumstances.

Under a totality of the circumstances approach, we find appellant did not have standing to challenge the search of the vehicle. He made no showing that he had a possessory interest in the car, that he had the right to exclude others from the vehicle, that he had exhibited a subjective expectation that the vehicle and its contents would remain free from governmental invasion, that he exercised control over the vehicle, or that appellant took any precautions to maintain his privacy. As in *Rakas,* appellant has not shown he has a legitimate expectation of privacy in the area under the seat where the guns were located. Appellant was nothing more than a temporary passenger in another's vehicle.

Appellant's contention that simply being a legitimate passenger affords him an expectation of privacy was clearly rejected in *Rakas.* "[T]he fact that they were 'legitimately on [the] premises' in the sense that they were in the car with the permission of its owner is not determinative of whether they had a legitimate expectation of privacy in the particular areas of the automobile searched." *Rakas,* 439 U.S. at 148.

Since we conclude appellant failed to meet his burden, we do not address the legality of the seizure of the weapon in the vehicle. We find the trial court did not err in determining appellant had no standing to challenge the search of the vehicle and the seizure of the weapon.

Carter v. State

2010 WL 3928492 (Tx. App. Oct. 7, 2010)

■ EVELYN V. KEYES, JUSTICE.

After the trial court denied his motion to suppress evidence, appellant, Quincy Rashard Carter, pled guilty to possessing between four and 200 grams of cocaine. The trial court assessed punishment at three years' confinement. In four issues, appellant contends that the trial court erred in denying his motion to suppress because (1) he had an objectively reasonable expectation of privacy in his girlfriend's hotel room, and thus has standing to challenge the search; (2) the first search was unreasonable because the arresting officer did not observe a violation of law; (3) the plain view doctrine did not justify the second search because the arresting officer was not in a lawful position and appellant did not commit any criminal activity in plain view; and (4) any consent to search, if given, was involuntary and thus did not support a warrantless search.

We hold that appellant lacks standing to challenge the search of his girlfriend's hotel room and therefore affirm.

Background

While on patrol during the evening of April 6, 2008, Texas City Police Department Officer L. Crouch observed Stephanie Falcon standing next to the passenger-side window of a car stopped outside of the Bay Motel, apparently soliciting a ride. According to Officer Crouch, the Bay Motel is a "well known area" for prostitutes to "hang out" and solicit rides, and he had previously encountered Falcon regarding solicitation of a ride offenses and other city warrants. Once Falcon noticed Officer Crouch's patrol car, she immediately walked back toward the Bay Motel entrance, and Officer Crouch watched her enter room fourteen of the motel. Officer Crouch followed Falcon to her room, intending to investigate further. While standing approximately five feet from the window, Officer Crouch looked through a two-inch gap in the curtains and observed appellant sitting at a table close to the window, "holding a razor blade in one hand and a large rock substance in the other hand."

Officer Crouch withdrew from the window and contacted his supervisor, Sergeant W. Creel, and Officer P. Slaton for assistance. Sergeant Creel and Officer Slaton both agreed with Officer Crouch that a gap in the blinds and curtains existed, and the officers could see movement in the room behind the blinds. According to Officer Slaton, she could walk by the window and "clearly" see appellant sitting at the table "without having to actually look inside" the room. The officers then contacted the on-call district attorney, who informed them that they needed to obtain either consent to search the motel room from the room's renter or a search warrant. The officers obtained the receipt for room fourteen from the Bay Motel manager. The receipt indicated that Falcon alone rented the room.

After Sergeant Creel knocked on the door, the officers heard Falcon ask who was there, and, without identifying themselves as police officers, Sergeant Creel asked the occupants to open the door. Falcon opened the door and Officer Crouch observed appellant leaving the bathroom and another male, Joey Johnson, standing just behind the door. Officer Crouch told Falcon that he saw her commit a violation outside the motel, and the officers asked the occupants to step outside the room, which they did voluntarily. Officer Crouch then asked Falcon if she rented the room alone or with another person, and she confirmed that she rented the room solely in her name.

Officer Crouch mentioned to Falcon that, as he came to her room to investigate her earlier violation, he observed appellant holding a razor blade and a "rocky substance." He asked whether Falcon would give her consent to search the room for "any illegal narcotics or narcotic paraphernalia." Falcon agreed, and all three officers witnessed her signing the "consent to search" form. Sergeant Creel informed Falcon that if she or one of her guests had any narcotics or paraphernalia in the room, she should tell him before the officers searched and found it themselves. Falcon told him that, as far as she knew, there was nothing illegal in her room. Officer Crouch testified that he did not hear appellant say anything about the search, none of the officers asked him for consent to search, and appellant never mentioned that he did not want the officers to search the room. Officer Slaton did not recall hearing appellant either say anything about the search or tell the officers to leave, although she did hear appellant or Johnson state that he had just arrived at the room and did not know what was going on.

After the officers obtained Falcon's consent, officers from the Special Crimes Unit searched the motel room. The officers found female clothing and personal articles in the dresser, but no male clothing or personal items anywhere in the room. On the table at which Officer Crouch initially saw appellant sitting, the officers discovered small particles of a "white rocky substance" that later field-tested positive for crack cocaine. The officers also found a small baggie of marijuana and numerous small, empty baggies in the trash can behind appellant's chair. The search also uncovered a large bag of crack cocaine hidden in the toilet tank. The officers then arrested appellant, Falcon, and Johnson, and the State charged appellant with possession of a controlled substance with intent to deliver.

The next morning, Detective R. Johnston interviewed appellant. Appellant told Detective Johnston that Falcon, his girlfriend, rented the room. When Detective Johnston asked appellant who consented to the search, appellant answered that both he and Falcon consented, although only Falcon signed the official consent form. Appellant further stated that, while in the room, he held a rock of crack-cocaine and cut pieces off of it. Detective Johnston gave appellant the opportunity to review his statement and make changes; appellant initialed each question and answer and signed each page of the statement.

Appellant testified on his own behalf at the suppression hearing. When asked by defense counsel whether he was staying with a woman at the Bay Motel on April 6, appellant stated that he was not staying there, but rather he and Johnson were just visiting. According to appellant, he and Johnson had "just arrived [at the room]" before the search, and they had not been to the room before. Appellant testified that he did not know that cocaine was present in the room, he did not shave a rock of cocaine with a razor while in the room, and the blinds and curtains did not have an opening large enough to see through. Appellant believed that the police ordered Johnson, Falcon, and himself out of the room, and he did not think that he had a choice whether to obey. Appellant also testified that he mentioned his objections to the search to both Officer Crouch and Sergeant Creel, and when he told them that Falcon rented the room, the officers ignored his objections and asked her for consent to search.

On cross-examination, appellant testified that he did not see Falcon give her consent to search. When asked about the discrepancies between his statement made to Detective Johnston and his testimony at the suppression hearing, he replied that his post-arrest statement was incorrect. According to appellant, Johnston told him to "hurry up and sign [his] initials by it because the Galveston County chain was coming to carry [him] to Galveston County," and thus he did not have the opportunity to read over the statement before initialing and signing. Appellant believed that Johnston "made up" almost everything contained in the statement and "conspired" with the other officers to "put this case on [appellant] or make [him] look like [he] was a drug dealer."

The trial court denied appellant's motion to suppress evidence and made the following findings of fact:

> (1) Officer Crouch observed a violation of law near the [Bay Motel]. As he proceeded closer to Apartment 14 to investigate, he observed a separate law violation: a person within Apartment 14 appeared to be possessing cocaine.

> (2) Officer Crouch determined that Stephanie Falcon had rented the apartment and obtained a signed consent form from her to search the apartment. There was no testimony that any other person had rented Apartment 14. The Defendant testified he was a mere visitor on the premises.

The trial court also made the following conclusions of law:

> (1) The Defendant has no standing to challenge the search of the premises where the alleged contraband was found because he was not the person who rented the premises.

> (2) A signed consent form was obtained by the Texas City Police Department from the person who rented the apartment and that gave officers the legal right to conduct a search of the premises.

After the trial court denied his motion to suppress, appellant, who had been indicted for possession of a controlled substance with intent to deliver, pled guilty to the reduced charge of possession of a controlled substance. The trial court assessed punishment at three years' confinement.

Discussion

Appellant contends that the trial court erred in denying his motion to suppress evidence because (1) Officer Crouch did not have reasonable suspicion to believe that Falcon committed a violation of law, and therefore his first search at the room's window was unreasonable; (2) the plain view doctrine does not justify the search of the motel room because Crouch was not lawfully in position when he allegedly saw appellant with crack cocaine and appellant did not commit any criminal activity in plain view; and (3) Falcon's consent to search, if given, was involuntary and thus does not support a warrantless search of the room.

We must first determine whether appellant has standing to challenge the validity of the search. A defendant seeking to suppress evidence under the Fourth Amendment must show that he had a legitimate expectation of privacy in the place that the government invaded. Luna v. State, 268 S.W.3d 594, 603 (Tex.Crim.App.2008); Granados v. State, 85 S.W.3d 217, 222–23 (Tex.Crim.App.2002) (citing Rakas v. Illinois, 439 U.S. 128 (1978)). The defendant bears the burden of demonstrating standing to challenge the legality of the search. *See Granados,* 85 S.W.3d at 223; Weaver v. State, 265 S.W.3d 523, 532 (Tex.App.-Houston [1st Dist.] 2008, pet. ref'd). The defendant must show that he had a subjective expectation of privacy in the place invaded that society is prepared to recognize as reasonable. *Granados,* 85 S.W.3d at 223.

In considering whether an appellant has demonstrated an objectively reasonable expectation of privacy, we examine the totality of the circumstances, including whether: (1) the defendant had a property or possessory interest in the place invaded; (2) he was legitimately in the place invaded; (3) he had complete dominion or control and the right to exclude others; (4) prior to the intrusion, he took normal precautions customarily taken by those seeking privacy; (5) he put the place to some private use; (6) his claim of privacy is consistent with historical notions of privacy. *Id.*; Rodriguez v. State, 313 S.W.3d 403, 407 (Tex.App.-Houston [1st Dist.] 2009, no pet.). This list of factors is not exhaustive, nor is any one factor dispositive of an assertion of privacy. *Granados,* 85 S.W.3d at 223.

The Court of Criminal Appeals has held that "an 'overnight guest' has a legitimate expectation of privacy in his host's home." *Luna,* 268 S.W.3d at 603 (citing Minnesota v. Olson, 495 U.S. 91, 98 (1990)). We have also previously held that "an overnight guest of a registered hotel guest shares the registered guest's reasonable expectation of privacy in the room." Wilson v. State, 98 S.W.3d 265, 269 (Tex.App.-Houston [1st Dist.] 2002, pet. ref'd) (citing Stoner v. California, 376 U.S. 483, 490 (1964) and *Olson,* 495 U.S. at 99–100. Although the Court of Criminal Appeals has previously held that a more casual visitor, rather than an overnight guest, does not have a reasonable expectation of privacy in another's home, it failed to adopt a rule that a non-overnight guest can never have standing to challenge a search of his host's home. *See* Villarreal v. State, 935 S.W.2d 134, 137 n.4 (Tex.Crim.App.1996) (plurality op.).

In *Villarreal,* the defendant spent an hour or two at an associate's house to arrange a business transaction, returned approximately two hours later, and "rush[ed] into the residence to avoid arrest" after the police officers monitoring the house identified themselves and warned Villarreal and two others to stop unloading packages from their vehicle. *Id.* at 136, 139. In the ensuing search of the house, officers discovered marijuana, firearms, a large quantity of cash, cocaine, and drug paraphernalia. *Id.* at 136. In holding that Villarreal's subjective expectation of privacy was not one that society was prepared to recognize as objectively reasonable, the plurality relied on Villarreal's failure to present evidence that: (1) he had a property or possessory interest in, or unrestricted access to, the house; (2) he had dominion or control over the residence or the right to exclude others; and (3) he intended to stay overnight at the house. *Id.* at 139. Under these circumstances, this "casual visitor" did not have standing to challenge the search of the house. *Id.* at 137, 139.

Appellant contends that his expectation of privacy in Falcon's hotel room was objectively reasonable because he was legitimately in the room, he believed that he had to power to exclude others from the room as demonstrated by his attempt to refuse entrance to the police, he tried to ensure his privacy by closing the curtains and blinds, the room was not open to the public, and the "expectation of privacy of a boyfriend and girlfriend behind closed doors" is consistent with historical notions of privacy.

The evidence presented at the suppression hearing, however, does not support appellant's contention that he has standing to challenge the search. Appellant testified that he was not staying with Falcon, but was only a visitor who had "just arrived" at the hotel room with Johnson before the search. Appellant stated that the curtains and blinds were closed, but Sergeant Creel and Officers Crouch and Slaton all testified that they could see into the room through a gap in the curtains. According to Officer Slaton, the gap in the curtains was wide enough that one could walk by the window and clearly see in "without having to actually look inside." Although appellant may have believed that he had the power to exclude others from the room, he also acknowledged that Falcon rented the room solely in her name and because he was "just a visitor," he had "no authority over giving a consent to search ... that room." Thus, because Falcon alone rented the room, appellant lacked "complete dominion or control" over the room. *See Granados,* 85 S.W.3d at 223.

Appellant also testified that he made his objections to the search known to both Officer Crouch and Sergeant Creel, and, instead of heeding his wish, they asked Falcon for her consent. This testimony not only contradicts the testimony of Officer Crouch, who stated that none of the officers ever asked appellant for consent to search and that appellant never gave any indication that he did not want the officers to search the room, but it also contradicts appellant's post-arrest statement, in which he informed Detective Johnston that both he and Falcon agreed to the search. Appellant argued that this statement was patently false and entirely made up by Johnston as part of a "conspiracy" to make it appear as though appellant was a drug dealer. However, at a suppression hearing, the trial court is the sole judge of the weight and credibility of the evidence and may choose to believe or disbelieve all or part of a witness's testimony. See *St. George,* 237 S.W.3d at 725; *Green,* 934

S.W.2d at 98; *see also Weaver,* 265 S.W.3d at 534 ("However, the trial court, as judge of demeanor and credibility, could have chosen to not believe appellant's unsubstantiated testimony."). The trial court reasonably could have chosen to believe the testimony of Sergeant Creel and Officers Crouch and Slaton, and chosen not to believe appellant's self-serving and unsubstantiated testimony.

Appellant also presented no evidence that he intended to stay overnight with Falcon in the room or that he contemplated anything other than a brief visit to her motel room with another friend. *See* Gouldsby v. State, 202 S.W.3d 329, 335 (Tex.App.-Texarkana 2006, pet. ref'd) (holding that reliance on *Olson*'s overnight guest doctrine is "misplaced" when defendant presents no evidence that he was overnight guest on night of search, although he had stayed overnight on previous occasions). Appellant testified that he had never been to the room before, and the officers conducting the search of the room found only female clothing and personal articles. *See* Hollis v. State, 219 S.W.3d 446, 458 (Tex.App.-Austin 2007, no pet.) (considering, among other factors, defendant's failure to keep personal belongings at another's property when making determination that defendant did not share owner's reasonable expectation of privacy); Smith v. State, 176 S.W.3d 907, 914 (Tex.App.-Dallas 2005, pet. ref'd) (holding same).

Appellant did not testify regarding his purpose for visiting Falcon's room or regarding what he did while in the room. The only testimony concerning appellant's activities inside the room came from Officer Crouch, who stated that he saw appellant shaving a rock, which later tested positive for crack cocaine, with a razor blade. Although appellant contends that "the expectation of privacy of a boyfriend and girlfriend behind closed doors together is consistent with historical notions of privacy," appellant visited his girlfriend's room with a third party, Johnson, and appellant cites no authority that the boyfriend-girlfriend relationship alone is sufficient to extend Falcon's reasonable expectation of privacy to appellant, when the evidence presented suggests that appellant intended only a brief visit to the room for an unspecified purpose. *See* Davidson v. State, 249 S.W.3d 709, 726 (Tex.App.-Austin 2008, pet. ref'd) ("As in *Villarreal,* appellant presented no evidence that she was anything other than a guest with indeterminate access to the property.").

Based on the evidence presented, we conclude that appellant did not meet his burden to demonstrate that he had an objectively reasonable expectation of privacy in Falcon's motel room. Accordingly, appellant lacks standing to challenge the legality of the officers' search of the motel room. We hold that the trial court did not abuse its discretion in denying appellant's motion to suppress evidence.[2]

---

[2] Because we hold that appellant lacks standing to contest the search, we do not address appellant's remaining contentions on appeal.

Conclusion

We hold that appellant lacks standing to contest the legality of the search of the motel room, and therefore affirm the judgment of the trial court.

b. ATTENUATION, INDEPENDENT SOURCE, AND INEVITABLE DISCOVERY

Utah v. Strieff

579 U.S. ___, 136 S.Ct. 2056 (2016)

■ JUSTICE THOMAS delivered the opinion of the Court.

To enforce the Fourth Amendment's prohibition against "unreasonable searches and seizures," this Court has at times required courts to exclude evidence obtained by unconstitutional police conduct. But the Court has also held that, even when there is a Fourth Amendment violation, this exclusionary rule does not apply when the costs of exclusion outweigh its deterrent benefits. In some cases, for example, the link between the unconstitutional conduct and the discovery of the evidence is too attenuated to justify suppression. The question in this case is whether this attenuation doctrine applies when an officer makes an unconstitutional investigatory stop; learns during that stop that the suspect is subject to a valid arrest warrant; and proceeds to arrest the suspect and seize incriminating evidence during a search incident to that arrest. We hold that the evidence the officer seized as part of the search incident to arrest is admissible because the officer's discovery of the arrest warrant attenuated the connection between the unlawful stop and the evidence seized incident to arrest.

I

This case began with an anonymous tip. In December 2006, someone called the South Salt Lake City police's drug-tip line to report "narcotics activity" at a particular residence. App. 15. Narcotics detective Douglas Fackrell investigated the tip. Over the course of about a week, Officer Fackrell conducted intermittent surveillance of the home. He observed visitors who left a few minutes after arriving at the house. These visits were sufficiently frequent to raise his suspicion that the occupants were dealing drugs.

One of those visitors was respondent Edward Strieff. Officer Fackrell observed Strieff exit the house and walk toward a nearby convenience store. In the store's parking lot, Officer Fackrell detained Strieff, identified himself, and asked Strieff what he was doing at the residence.

As part of the stop, Officer Fackrell requested Strieff's identification, and Strieff produced his Utah identification card. Officer Fackrell relayed Strieff's information to a police dispatcher, who reported that Strieff had an outstanding arrest warrant for a traffic violation. Officer

Fackrell then arrested Strieff pursuant to that warrant. When Officer Fackrell searched Strieff incident to the arrest, he discovered a baggie of methamphetamine and drug paraphernalia.

The State charged Strieff with unlawful possession of methamphetamine and drug paraphernalia. Strieff moved to suppress the evidence, arguing that the evidence was inadmissible because it was derived from an unlawful investigatory stop. At the suppression hearing, the prosecutor conceded that Officer Fackrell lacked reasonable suspicion for the stop but argued that the evidence should not be suppressed because the existence of a valid arrest warrant attenuated the connection between the unlawful stop and the discovery of the contraband.

The trial court agreed with the State and admitted the evidence. The court found that the short time between the illegal stop and the search weighed in favor of suppressing the evidence, but that two countervailing considerations made it admissible. First, the court considered the presence of a valid arrest warrant to be an " 'extraordinary intervening circumstance.' " App. to Pet. for Cert. 102 (quoting United States v. Simpson, 439 F.3d 490, 496 (C.A.8 2006)). Second, the court stressed the absence of flagrant misconduct by Officer Fackrell, who was conducting a legitimate investigation of a suspected drug house.

Strieff conditionally pleaded guilty to reduced charges of attempted possession of a controlled substance and possession of drug paraphernalia, but reserved his right to appeal the trial court's denial of the suppression motion. The Utah Court of Appeals affirmed. 2012 UT App ¶ 245, 286 P.3d 317.

The Utah Supreme Court reversed. 2015 UT ¶ 2, 357 P.3d 532. It held that the evidence was inadmissible because only "a voluntary act of a defendant's free will (as in a confession or consent to search)" sufficiently breaks the connection between an illegal search and the discovery of evidence. *Id.,* at 536. Because Officer Fackrell's discovery of a valid arrest warrant did not fit this description, the court ordered the evidence suppressed. *Ibid.*

We granted certiorari to resolve disagreement about how the attenuation doctrine applies where an unconstitutional detention leads to the discovery of a valid arrest warrant. 576 U.S. ___ (2015). Compare, *e.g.,* United States v. Green, 111 F.3d 515, 522–523 (C.A.7 1997) (holding that discovery of the warrant is a dispositive intervening circumstance where police misconduct was not flagrant), with, *e.g.,* State v. Moralez, 297 Kan. 397, 415, 300 P.3d 1090, 1102 (2013) (assigning little significance to the discovery of the warrant). We now reverse.

II

A

The Fourth Amendment protects "[t]he right of the people to be secure in their persons, houses, papers, and effects, against unreasonable searches and seizures." Because officers who violated the Fourth

Amendment were traditionally considered trespassers, individuals subject to unconstitutional searches or seizures historically enforced their rights through tort suits or self-help. Davies, *Recovering the Original Fourth Amendment,* 98 Mich. L. Rev. 547, 625 (1999). In the 20th century, however, the exclusionary rule—the rule that often requires trial courts to exclude unlawfully seized evidence in a criminal trial—became the principal judicial remedy to deter Fourth Amendment violations. *See, e.g.,* Mapp v. Ohio, 367 U.S. 643, 655 (1961).

Under the Court's precedents, the exclusionary rule encompasses both the "primary evidence obtained as a direct result of an illegal search or seizure" and, relevant here, "evidence later discovered and found to be derivative of an illegality," the so-called " 'fruit of the poisonous tree.' " Segura v. United States, 468 U.S. 796, 804 (1984). But the significant costs of this rule have led us to deem it "applicable only . . . where its deterrence benefits outweigh its substantial social costs." Hudson v. Michigan, 547 U.S. 586, 591 (2006) (internal quotation marks omitted). "Suppression of evidence . . . has always been our last resort, not our first impulse." *Ibid.*

We have accordingly recognized several exceptions to the rule. Three of these exceptions involve the causal relationship between the unconstitutional act and the discovery of evidence. First, the independent source doctrine allows trial courts to admit evidence obtained in an unlawful search if officers independently acquired it from a separate, independent source. See Murray v. United States, 487 U.S. 533, 537 (1988). Second, the inevitable discovery doctrine allows for the admission of evidence that would have been discovered even without the unconstitutional source. *See* Nix v. Williams, 467 U.S. 431, 443–444 (1984). Third, and at issue here, is the attenuation doctrine: Evidence is admissible when the connection between unconstitutional police conduct and the evidence is remote or has been interrupted by some intervening circumstance, so that "the interest protected by the constitutional guarantee that has been violated would not be served by suppression of the evidence obtained." *Hudson, supra,* at 593.

B

Turning to the application of the attenuation doctrine to this case, we first address a threshold question: whether this doctrine applies at all to a case like this, where the intervening circumstance that the State relies on is the discovery of a valid, pre-existing, and untainted arrest warrant. The Utah Supreme Court declined to apply the attenuation doctrine because it read our precedents as applying the doctrine only "to circumstances involving an independent act of a defendant's 'free will' in confessing to a crime or consenting to a search." 357 P.3d, at 544. In this Court, Strieff has not defended this argument, and we disagree with it, as well. The attenuation doctrine evaluates the causal link between the government's unlawful act and the discovery of evidence, which often has nothing to do with a defendant's actions. And the logic of our prior attenuation cases is not limited to independent acts by the defendant.

It remains for us to address whether the discovery of a valid arrest warrant was a sufficient intervening event to break the causal chain between the unlawful stop and the discovery of drug-related evidence on Strieff's person. The three factors articulated in Brown v. Illinois, 422 U.S. 590 (1975), guide our analysis. First, we look to the "temporal proximity" between the unconstitutional conduct and the discovery of evidence to determine how closely the discovery of evidence followed the unconstitutional search. *Id.,* at 603. Second, we consider "the presence of intervening circumstances." *Id.,* at 603–604. Third, and "particularly" significant, we examine "the purpose and flagrancy of the official misconduct." *Id.,* at 604. In evaluating these factors, we assume without deciding (because the State conceded the point) that Officer Fackrell lacked reasonable suspicion to initially stop Strieff. And, because we ultimately conclude that the warrant breaks the causal chain, we also have no need to decide whether the warrant's existence alone would make the initial stop constitutional even if Officer Fackrell was unaware of its existence.

1

The first factor, temporal proximity between the initially unlawful stop and the search, favors suppressing the evidence. Our precedents have declined to find that this factor favors attenuation unless "substantial time" elapses between an unlawful act and when the evidence is obtained. Kaupp v. Texas, 538 U.S. 626, 633 (2003) (*per curiam*). Here, however, Officer Fackrell discovered drug contraband on Strieff's person only minutes after the illegal stop. *See* App. 18–19. As the Court explained in *Brown,* such a short time interval counsels in favor of suppression; there, we found that the confession should be suppressed, relying in part on the "less than two hours" that separated the unconstitutional arrest and the confession. 422 U.S., at 604.

In contrast, the second factor, the presence of intervening circumstances, strongly favors the State. In *Segura,* 468 U.S. 796, the Court addressed similar facts to those here and found sufficient intervening circumstances to allow the admission of evidence. There, agents had probable cause to believe that apartment occupants were dealing cocaine. *Id.,* at 799–800. They sought a warrant. In the meantime, they entered the apartment, arrested an occupant, and discovered evidence of drug activity during a limited search for security reasons. *Id.,* at 800–801. The next evening, the Magistrate Judge issued the search warrant. *Ibid.* This Court deemed the evidence admissible notwithstanding the illegal search because the information supporting the warrant was "wholly unconnected with the [arguably illegal] entry and was known to the agents well before the initial entry." *Id.,* at 814.

Segura, of course, applied the independent source doctrine because the unlawful entry "did not contribute in any way to discovery of the evidence seized under the warrant." *Id.,* at 815. But the *Segura* Court suggested that the existence of a valid warrant favors finding that the connection between unlawful conduct and the discovery of evidence is "sufficiently attenuated to dissipate the taint." *Ibid.* That principle applies here.

In this case, the warrant was valid, it predated Officer Fackrell's investigation, and it was entirely unconnected with the stop. And once Officer Fackrell discovered the warrant, he had an obligation to arrest Strieff. "A warrant is a judicial mandate to an officer to conduct a search or make an arrest, and the officer has a sworn duty to carry out its provisions." United States v. Leon, 468 U.S. 897, 920, n.21 (1984) (internal quotation marks omitted). Officer Fackrell's arrest of Strieff thus was a ministerial act that was independently compelled by the pre-existing warrant. And once Officer Fackrell was authorized to arrest Strieff, it was undisputedly lawful to search Strieff as an incident of his arrest to protect Officer Fackrell's safety. *See* Arizona v. Gant, 556 U.S. 332, 339 (2009) (explaining the permissible scope of searches incident to arrest).

Finally, the third factor, "the purpose and flagrancy of the official misconduct," *Brown, supra,* at 604, also strongly favors the State. The exclusionary rule exists to deter police misconduct. Davis v. United States, 564 U.S. 229, 236–237 (2011). The third factor of the attenuation doctrine reflects that rationale by favoring exclusion only when the police misconduct is most in need of deterrence—that is, when it is purposeful or flagrant.

Officer Fackrell was at most negligent. In stopping Strieff, Officer Fackrell made two good-faith mistakes. First, he had not observed what time Strieff entered the suspected drug house, so he did not know how long Strieff had been there. Officer Fackrell thus lacked a sufficient basis to conclude that Strieff was a short-term visitor who may have been consummating a drug transaction. Second, because he lacked confirmation that Strieff was a short-term visitor, Officer Fackrell should have asked Strieff whether he would speak with him, instead of demanding that Strieff do so. Officer Fackrell's stated purpose was to "find out what was going on [in] the house." App. 17. Nothing prevented him from approaching Strieff simply to ask. *See* Florida v. Bostick, 501 U.S. 429, 434 (1991) ("[A] seizure does not occur simply because a police officer approaches an individual and asks a few questions"). But these errors in judgment hardly rise to a purposeful or flagrant violation of Strieff's Fourth Amendment rights.

While Officer Fackrell's decision to initiate the stop was mistaken, his conduct thereafter was lawful. The officer's decision to run the warrant check was a "negligibly burdensome precautio[n]" for officer safety. Rodriguez v. United States, 575 U.S. ___, ___ (2015). And Officer Fackrell's actual search of Strieff was a lawful search incident to arrest. *See Gant, supra,* at 339.

Moreover, there is no indication that this unlawful stop was part of any systemic or recurrent police misconduct. To the contrary, all the evidence suggests that the stop was an isolated instance of negligence that occurred in connection with a bona fide investigation of a suspected drug house. Officer Fackrell saw Strieff leave a suspected drug house. And his suspicion about the house was based on an anonymous tip and his personal observations.

Applying these factors, we hold that the evidence discovered on Strieff's person was admissible because the unlawful stop was sufficiently attenuated by the pre-existing arrest warrant. Although the illegal stop was close in time to Strieff's arrest, that consideration is outweighed by two factors supporting the State. The outstanding arrest warrant for Strieff's arrest is a critical intervening circumstance that is wholly independent of the illegal stop. The discovery of that warrant broke the causal chain between the unconstitutional stop and the discovery of evidence by compelling Officer Fackrell to arrest Strieff. And, it is especially significant that there is no evidence that Officer Fackrell's illegal stop reflected flagrantly unlawful police misconduct.

2

We find Strieff's counterarguments unpersuasive.

First, he argues that the attenuation doctrine should not apply because the officer's stop was purposeful and flagrant. He asserts that Officer Fackrell stopped him solely to fish for evidence of suspected wrongdoing. But Officer Fackrell sought information from Strieff to find out what was happening inside a house whose occupants were legitimately suspected of dealing drugs. This was not a suspicionless fishing expedition "in the hope that something would turn up." Taylor v. Alabama, 457 U.S. 687, 691 (1982).

Strieff argues, moreover, that Officer Fackrell's conduct was flagrant because he detained Strieff without the necessary level of cause (here, reasonable suspicion). But that conflates the standard for an illegal stop with the standard for flagrancy. For the violation to be flagrant, more severe police misconduct is required than the mere absence of proper cause for the seizure. *See, e.g., Kaupp,* 538 U.S., at 628 (finding flagrant violation where a warrantless arrest was made in the arrestee's home after police were denied a warrant and at least some officers knew they lacked probable cause). Neither the officer's alleged purpose nor the flagrancy of the violation rise to a level of misconduct to warrant suppression.

Second, Strieff argues that, because of the prevalence of outstanding arrest warrants in many jurisdictions, police will engage in dragnet searches if the exclusionary rule is not applied. We think that this outcome is unlikely. Such wanton conduct would expose police to civil liability. *See* 42 U.S.C. § 1983; Monell v. New York City Dept. of Social Servs., 436 U.S. 658, 690 (1978); *see also Segura,* 468 U.S., at 812. And in any event, the *Brown* factors take account of the purpose and flagrancy of police misconduct. Were evidence of a dragnet search presented here, the application of the *Brown* factors could be different. But there is no evidence that the concerns that Strieff raises with the criminal justice system are present in South Salt Lake City, Utah.

3

We hold that the evidence Officer Fackrell seized as part of his search incident to arrest is admissible because his discovery of the arrest warrant attenuated the connection between the unlawful stop and the evidence seized from Strieff incident to arrest. The judgment of the Utah Supreme Court, accordingly, is reversed.

It is so ordered.

■ JUSTICE SOTOMAYOR, with whom JUSTICE GINSBURG joins as to Parts I, II, and III, dissenting.

The Court today holds that the discovery of a warrant for an unpaid parking ticket will forgive a police officer's violation of your Fourth Amendment rights. Do not be soothed by the opinion's technical language: This case allows the police to stop you on the street, demand your identification, and check it for outstanding traffic warrants—even if you are doing nothing wrong. If the officer discovers a warrant for a fine you forgot to pay, courts will now excuse his illegal stop and will admit into evidence anything he happens to find by searching you after arresting you on the warrant. Because the Fourth Amendment should prohibit, not permit, such misconduct, I dissent. . . .

II

It is tempting in a case like this, where illegal conduct by an officer uncovers illegal conduct by a civilian, to forgive the officer. After all, his instincts, although unconstitutional, were correct. But a basic principle lies at the heart of the Fourth Amendment: Two wrongs don't make a right. *See* Weeks v. United States, 232 U.S. 383, 392 (1914). When "lawless police conduct" uncovers evidence of lawless civilian conduct, this Court has long required later criminal trials to exclude the illegally obtained evidence. *Terry,* 392 U.S., at 12; Mapp v. Ohio, 367 U.S. 643, 655 (1961). For example, if an officer breaks into a home and finds a forged check lying around, that check may not be used to prosecute the homeowner for bank fraud. We would describe the check as " 'fruit of the poisonous tree.' " Wong Sun v. United States, 371 U.S. 471, 488 (1963). Fruit that must be cast aside includes not only evidence directly found by an illegal search but also evidence "come at by exploitation of that illegality." *Ibid.*

This "exclusionary rule" removes an incentive for officers to search us without proper justification. *Terry,* 392 U.S., at 12. It also keeps courts from being "made party to lawless invasions of the constitutional rights of citizens by permitting unhindered governmental use of the fruits of such invasions." *Id.,* at 13. When courts admit only lawfully obtained evidence, they encourage "those who formulate law enforcement polices, and the officers who implement them, to incorporate Fourth Amendment ideals into their value system." Stone v. Powell, 428 U.S. 465, 492 (1976). But when courts admit illegally obtained evidence as well, they reward "manifest neglect if not an open defiance of the prohibitions of the Constitution." *Weeks,* 232 U.S., at 394.

Applying the exclusionary rule, the Utah Supreme Court correctly decided that Strieff's drugs must be excluded because the officer exploited his illegal stop to discover them. The officer found the drugs only after learning of Strieff's traffic violation; and he learned of Strieff's traffic violation only because he unlawfully stopped Strieff to check his driver's license.

The court also correctly rejected the State's argument that the officer's discovery of a traffic warrant unspoiled the poisonous fruit. The State analogizes finding the warrant to one of our earlier decisions, *Wong Sun v. United States.* There, an officer illegally arrested a person who, days later, voluntarily returned to the station to confess to committing a crime. 371 U.S., at 491. Even though the person would not have confessed "but for the illegal actions of the police," *id.,* at 488, we noted that the police did not exploit their illegal arrest to obtain the confession, *id.,* at 491. Because the confession was obtained by "means sufficiently distinguishable" from the constitutional violation, we held that it could be admitted into evidence. *Id.,* at 488, 491. The State contends that the search incident to the warrant-arrest here is similarly distinguishable from the illegal stop.

But *Wong Sun* explains why Strieff's drugs must be excluded. We reasoned that a Fourth Amendment violation may not color every investigation that follows but it certainly stains the actions of officers who exploit the infraction. We distinguished evidence obtained by innocuous means from evidence obtained by exploiting misconduct after considering a variety of factors: whether a long time passed, whether there were "intervening circumstances," and whether the purpose or flagrancy of the misconduct was "calculated" to procure the evidence. Brown v. Illinois, 422 U.S. 590, 603–604 (1975).

These factors confirm that the officer in this case discovered Strieff's drugs by exploiting his own illegal conduct. The officer did not ask Strieff to volunteer his name only to find out, days later, that Strieff had a warrant against him. The officer illegally stopped Strieff and immediately ran a warrant check. The officer's discovery of a warrant was not some intervening surprise that he could not have anticipated. Utah lists over 180,000 misdemeanor warrants in its database, and at the time of the arrest, Salt Lake County had a "backlog of outstanding warrants" so large that it faced the "potential for civil liability." *See* Dept. of Justice, Bureau of Justice Statistics, Survey of State Criminal History Information Systems, 2014 (2015) (Systems Survey) (Table 5a), online at https://www.ncjrs.gov/pdffiles1/bjs/grants/249799.pdf   (all   Internet materials as last visited June 16, 2016); Inst. for Law and Policy Planning, Salt Lake County Criminal Justice System Assessment 6.7 (2004), online at http://www.slco.org/cjac/resources/SaltLake CJSAfinal.pdf. The officer's violation was also calculated to procure evidence. His sole reason for stopping Strieff, he acknowledged, was investigative—he wanted to discover whether drug activity was going on in the house Strieff had just exited. App. 17.

The warrant check, in other words, was not an "intervening circumstance" separating the stop from the search for drugs. It was part and parcel of the officer's illegal "expedition for evidence in the hope that something might turn up." *Brown*, 422 U.S., at 605. Under our precedents, because the officer found Strieff's drugs by exploiting his own constitutional violation, the drugs should be excluded. . . . .

IIIB

Most striking about the Court's opinion is its insistence that the event here was "isolated," with "no indication that this unlawful stop was part of any systemic or recurrent police misconduct." *Ante,* at ___–___. Respectfully, nothing about this case is isolated.

Outstanding warrants are surprisingly common. When a person with a traffic ticket misses a fine payment or court appearance, a court will issue a warrant. See, *e.g.,* Brennan Center for Justice, Criminal Justice Debt 23 (2010), online at https://www.brennancenter.org/sites/default/files/legacy/Feesänd%20Fines%20FINAL.pdf. When a person on probation drinks alcohol or breaks curfew, a court will issue a warrant. See, *e.g.,* Human Rights Watch, Profiting from Probation 1, 51 (2014), online at https://www.hrw.org/report/2014/02/05/profiting-probation/americas-offender-funded-probation-industry. The States and Federal Government maintain databases with over 7.8 million outstanding warrants, the vast majority of which appear to be for minor offenses. *See* Systems Survey (Table 5a). Even these sources may not track the "staggering" numbers of warrants, " 'drawers and drawers' " full, that many cities issue for traffic violations and ordinance infractions. Dept. of Justice, Civil Rights Div., Investigation of the Ferguson Police Department 47, 55 (2015) (Ferguson Report), online at https://www. justice.gov/sites/default/files/opa/press-releases/attachments/2015/03/04/ ferguson_police_department_report.pdf. The county in this case has had a "backlog" of such warrants. *See supra,* at ___. The Department of Justice recently reported that in the town of Ferguson, Missouri, with a population of 21,000, 16,000 people had outstanding warrants against them. Ferguson Report, at 6, 55.

Justice Department investigations across the country have illustrated how these astounding numbers of warrants can be used by police to stop people without cause. In a single year in New Orleans, officers "made nearly 60,000 arrests, of which about 20,000 were of people with outstanding traffic or misdemeanor warrants from neighboring parishes for such infractions as unpaid tickets." Dept. of Justice, Civil

Rights Div., Investigation of the New Orleans Police Department 29 (2011), online at https://www.justice.gov/sites/default/files/crt/legacy/2011/03/17/nopd_report.pdf. In the St. Louis metropolitan area, officers "routinely" stop people—on the street, at bus stops, or even in court—for no reason other than "an officer's desire to check whether the subject had a municipal arrest warrant pending." Ferguson Report, at 49, 57. In Newark, New Jersey, officers stopped 52,235 pedestrians within a 4-year period and ran warrant checks on 39,308 of them. Dept. of Justice, Civil Rights Div., Investigation of the Newark Police Department 8, 19, n. 15 (2014), online at https://www.justice.gov/sites/default/files/crt/legacy/2014/07/22/newark_ findings_7–22–14.pdf. The Justice Department analyzed these warrant-checked stops and reported that "approximately 93% of the stops would have been considered unsupported by articulated reasonable suspicion." *Id.*, at ___, n. 7.

I do not doubt that most officers act in "good faith" and do not set out to break the law. That does not mean these stops are "isolated instance[s] of negligence," however. *Ante,* at ___. Many are the product of institutionalized training procedures. The New York City Police Department long trained officers to, in the words of a District Judge, "stop and question first, develop reasonable suspicion later." Ligon v. New York, 925 F.Supp.2d 478, 537–538 (S.D.N.Y.), stay granted on other grounds, 736 F.3d 118 (C.A.2 2013). The Utah Supreme Court described as " 'routine procedure' or 'common practice' " the decision of Salt Lake City police officers to run warrant checks on pedestrians they detained without reasonable suspicion. State v. Topanotes, 2003 UT 30, ¶ 2, 76 P.3d 1159, 1160. In the related context of traffic stops, one widely followed police manual instructs officers looking for drugs to "run at least a warrants check on all drivers you stop. Statistically, narcotics offenders are . . . more likely to fail to appear on simple citations, such as traffic or trespass violations, leading to the issuance of bench warrants. Discovery of an outstanding warrant gives you cause for an immediate custodial arrest and search of the suspect." C. Remsberg, Tactics for Criminal Patrol 205–206 (1995); C. Epp et al., Pulled Over 23, 33–36 (2014).

The majority does not suggest what makes this case "isolated" from these and countless other examples. Nor does it offer guidance for how a defendant can prove that his arrest was the result of "widespread" misconduct. Surely it should not take a federal investigation of Salt Lake County before the Court would protect someone in Strieff's position.

IV

Writing only for myself, and drawing on my professional experiences, I would add that unlawful "stops" have severe consequences much greater than the inconvenience suggested by the name. This Court has given officers an array of instruments to probe and examine you. When we condone officers' use of these devices without adequate cause, we give them reason to target pedestrians in an arbitrary manner. We also risk treating members of our communities as second-class citizens.

Although many Americans have been stopped for speeding or jaywalking, few may realize how degrading a stop can be when the officer is looking for more. This Court has allowed an officer to stop you for whatever reason he wants—so long as he can point to a pretextual justification after the fact. Whren v. United States, 517 U.S. 806, 813 (1996). That justification must provide specific reasons why the officer suspected you were breaking the law, *Terry,* 392 U.S., at 21, but it may factor in your ethnicity, United States v. Brignoni-Ponce, 422 U.S. 873, 886–887 (1975), where you live, Adams v. Williams, 407 U.S. 143, 147 (1972), what you were wearing, United States v. Sokolow, 490 U.S. 1, 4–5 (1989), and how you behaved, Illinois v. Wardlow, 528 U.S. 119, 124–125 (2000). The officer does not even need to know which law you might have broken so long as he can later point to any possible infraction—even one that is minor, unrelated, or ambiguous. Devenpeck v. Alford, 543 U.S. 146, 154–155 (2004); Heien v. North Carolina, 574 U.S. ___ (2014).

The indignity of the stop is not limited to an officer telling you that you look like a criminal. *See* Epp, Pulled Over, at 5. The officer may next ask for your "consent" to inspect your bag or purse without telling you that you can decline. *See* Florida v. Bostick, 501 U.S. 429, 438 (1991). Regardless of your answer, he may order you to stand "helpless, perhaps facing a wall with [your] hands raised." *Terry,* 392 U.S., at 17. If the officer thinks you might be dangerous, he may then "frisk" you for weapons. This involves more than just a pat down. As onlookers pass by, the officer may " 'feel with sensitive fingers every portion of [your] body. A thorough search [may] be made of [your] arms and armpits, waistline and back, the groin and area about the testicles, and entire surface of the legs down to the feet.' " *Id.,* at 17, n.13.

The officer's control over you does not end with the stop. If the officer chooses, he may handcuff you and take you to jail for doing nothing more than speeding, jaywalking, or "driving [your] pickup truck . . . with [your] 3-year-old son and 5-year-old daughter . . . without [your] seatbelt fastened." Atwater v. Lago Vista, 532 U.S. 318, 323–324 (2001). At the jail, he can fingerprint you, swab DNA from the inside of your mouth, and force you to "shower with a delousing agent" while you "lift [your] tongue, hold out [your] arms, turn around, and lift [your] genitals." Florence v. Board of Chosen Freeholders of County of Burlington, 566 U.S. ___, ___–___ (2012); Maryland v. King, 569 U.S. ___, ___ (2013). Even if you are innocent, you will now join the 65 million Americans with an arrest record and experience the "civil death" of discrimination by employers, landlords, and whoever else conducts a background check. Chin, *The New Civil Death,* 160 U. Pa. L. Rev. 1789, 1805 (2012); *See* J. Jacobs, The Eternal Criminal Record 33–51 (2015); Young & Petersilia, Keeping Track, 129 Harv. L. Rev. 1318, 1341–1357 (2016). And, of course, if you fail to pay bail or appear for court, a judge will issue a warrant to render you "arrestable on sight" in the future. A. Goffman, On the Run 196 (2014).

This case involves a *suspicionless* stop, one in which the officer initiated this chain of events without justification. As the Justice Department notes, *supra,* at ___, many innocent people are subjected to the humiliations of these unconstitutional searches. The white defendant in this case shows that anyone's dignity can be violated in this manner. *See* M. Gottschalk, Caught 119–138 (2015). But it is no secret that people of color are disproportionate victims of this type of scrutiny. *See* M. Alexander, The New Jim Crow 95–136 (2010). For generations, black and brown parents have given their children "the talk"—instructing them never to run down the street; always keep your hands where they can be seen; do not even think of talking back to a stranger—all out of fear of how an officer with a gun will react to them. See, *e.g.,* W.E.B. Du Bois, The Souls of Black Folk (1903); J. Baldwin, The Fire Next Time (1963); T. Coates, Between the World and Me (2015).

By legitimizing the conduct that produces this double consciousness, this case tells everyone, white and black, guilty and innocent, that an officer can verify your legal status at any time. It says that your body is subject to invasion while courts excuse the violation of your rights. It implies that you are not a citizen of a democracy but the subject of a carceral state, just waiting to be cataloged.

We must not pretend that the countless people who are routinely targeted by police are "isolated." They are the canaries in the coal mine whose deaths, civil and literal, warn us that no one can breathe in this atmosphere. *See* L. Guinier & G. Torres, The Miner's Canary 274–283 (2002). They are the ones who recognize that unlawful police stops corrode all our civil liberties and threaten all our lives. Until their voices matter too, our justice system will continue to be anything but.

I dissent.

■ JUSTICE KAGAN, with whom JUSTICE GINSBURG joins, dissenting.

If a police officer stops a person on the street without reasonable suspicion, that seizure violates the Fourth Amendment. And if the officer pats down the unlawfully detained individual and finds drugs in his pocket, the State may not use the contraband as evidence in a criminal prosecution. That much is beyond dispute. The question here is whether the prohibition on admitting evidence dissolves if the officer discovers, after making the stop but before finding the drugs, that the person has an outstanding arrest warrant. Because that added wrinkle makes no difference under the Constitution, I respectfully dissent. . . .

The majority's misapplication of *Brown*'s three-part inquiry creates unfortunate incentives for the police—indeed, practically invites them to do what Fackrell did here. Consider an officer who, like Fackrell, wishes to stop someone for investigative reasons, but does not have what a court would view as reasonable suspicion. If the officer believes that any evidence he discovers will be inadmissible, he is likely to think the unlawful stop not worth making—precisely the deterrence the exclusionary rule is meant to achieve. But when he is told of today's decision? Now the officer knows that the stop may well yield admissible evidence: So long as the target is one of the many millions of people in this country with an outstanding arrest warrant, anything the officer finds in a search is fair game for use in a criminal prosecution. The officer's incentive to violate the Constitution thus increases: From here on, he sees potential advantage in stopping individuals without reasonable suspicion—exactly the temptation the exclusionary rule is supposed to remove. Because the majority thus places Fourth Amendment protections at risk, I respectfully dissent.

State v. Le

103 Wash.App. 354, 12 P.3d 653 (Wa. App. 2000)

■ BAKER, J.

While investigating a residential burglary call, a police officer saw a young Asian male exiting the front door of the home. Officers gave chase but were unable to locate or track the suspect. Soon thereafter, acting on a tip, officers forcibly entered the home of Tan Le and arrested him without a search warrant or an arrest warrant. The first officer was called to Le's residence and there identified Le as the suspect she had seen fleeing the scene of the crime approximately three hours earlier. The trial court suppressed all physical evidence discovered in Le's home as fruits of an illegal search, but refused to suppress the officer's postarrest identification of Le, reasoning that the officers had probable cause to arrest him and there was an independent basis for her identification. Le was found guilty of residential burglary, and now appeals.

We hold that Le was illegally arrested and that the officer's postarrest identification of Le should have been suppressed. However, because the in-court identification was admissible, and because the postarrest identification was harmless error, we affirm the conviction.

I

Police officer Diana Nollette responded to a burglary in progress call placed by a man who saw two young Asian males jump over his neighbors' fence. Officer Nollette and other officers set up a perimeter around the home and announced their presence. Officer Nollette saw an Asian male fleeing the residence. She gave chase until she lost him, then returned to the house.

At that point, a second Asian male stepped out of the front door of the house. Officer Nollette ordered the suspect to stop, and he turned and looked directly at her for approximately ten seconds before running away. She gave chase until she lost sight of him, then broadcast a description of the suspect. A K–9 officer was called in to assist with the search. Meanwhile, the homeowner told police that he believed a firearm was missing from his home.

Officer Michael Lewis and his tracking dog arrived on the scene and searched the area. Ninety minutes into the search, the officer saw a nearby residence with the front door open. Officer Lewis and the tracking dog searched the house but did not find anyone there. Unable to locate a suspect, they terminated the search and left the scene.

Approximately 15 minutes later, a local resident called 911 and indicated that a "young man" had just run through his yard and into the house that had just been searched by Officer Lewis. No further description of the suspect was given. Police returned to the house and found the front door closed and locked. One of the officers saw someone inside running toward the rear of the residence. Although he lacked a search warrant, Officer Lewis and his tracking dog entered the home through an unlocked window and searched the house. Officer Lewis noticed a number of locked doors in the basement of the residence. Unable to determine whether the house was empty, Officer Lewis waited until a superior officer arrived. Still lacking a warrant, the superior officer gave permission to break into the locked rooms. As Officer Lewis kicked in one door, he heard a voice coming from another room and ordered the occupant to come out. The suspect exited the room and was immediately arrested. That person was defendant Tan Le, who resided at the home where the arrest took place.

Officer Nollette was called to the scene, where she identified Le as the second person she had chased from the burglarized residence approximately three hours earlier. She indicated that Le was not wearing the same clothing that he wore when she saw him fleeing the scene of the crime, but she was certain that he was the same person. Officers seized some clothing from the residence during the search.

Le was charged with residential burglary and theft of a firearm. At a CrR 3.6 hearing prior to trial, Le moved to suppress all physical evidence seized from his residence as fruits of an illegal search. In addition, Le moved to suppress Officer Nollette's identification of him as the fruit of an illegal arrest. The trial court granted Le's motion to suppress physical evidence, finding that the warrantless search of Le's home was illegal and that the "hot pursuit" and "exigent circumstances" exceptions were inapplicable. However, the court refused to suppress Officer Nollette's postarrest identification of Le as fruit of the poisonous tree, concluding that the arrest was properly supported by probable cause and the officer had an independent basis for her identification. The trial court later permitted Officer Nollette to identify Le in court. The jury acquitted Le of theft of a firearm, but found him guilty of residential burglary. Le appeals.

II

We review a trial court's decision to admit or exclude evidence for an abuse of discretion. A trial court abuses its discretion when its decision is manifestly unreasonable or based on untenable grounds.

Le argues that Officer Nollette's postarrest identification of him should have been suppressed as the fruit of an illegal arrest. If the arrest was legal, then the officer's postarrest identification of Le would clearly be permissible. Therefore, as a preliminary matter, we must first determine whether Le was illegally arrested. . . .

We hold that Le was illegally arrested.

The principal issue before us in this case is whether Officer Nollette's postarrest identification of Le should have been suppressed under the exclusionary rule as the fruit of an illegal arrest. Le argues that the postarrest identification should have been excluded because the State may not exploit an illegal arrest to obtain incriminating evidence. The State argues that the identification was admissible despite any extraneous procedural illegalities because Officer Nollette observed Le prior to the illegal search, and thus there was an independent basis for the pretrial identification. Unfortunately, both parties greatly oversimplify the required analysis.

The exclusionary rule requires courts to suppress evidence obtained through violation of a defendant's constitutional rights. The purpose of the rule is to deter police from exploiting their illegal conduct and to protect individual rights. Under the "fruit of the poisonous tree" doctrine, the exclusionary rule applies to evidence derived directly and indirectly from the illegal police conduct.[11] Derivative evidence will be excluded unless it was not obtained by exploitation of the initial illegality or by means sufficiently distinguishable to be purged of the primary taint.[12] To prove that the evidence was purged of taint, the State must show either that: (1) intervening circumstances have attenuated the link between the illegality and the evidence; (2) the evidence was discovered through a source independent from the illegality; or (3) the evidence would inevitably have been discovered through legitimate means.

Although Washington courts have addressed the issue of whether in-court identifications are admissible, the related issue of whether postarrest identification evidence is a tainted fruit of an illegal arrest is one of first impression in Washington. Elsewhere, this issue has caused courts "particular difficulty."[17]

Professor LaFave urges that an identification following an illegal arrest should be excluded as direct evidence, unless the identification is sufficiently attenuated from the primary illegality. Courts following this approach have applied essentially the same attenuation analysis used in *Brown v. Illinois*[19] to determine the connection between an illegal arrest and a confession. These factors include: (1) temporal proximity; (2) the

---

[11] Wong Sun v. United States, 371 U.S. 471, 484–85 (1963).

[12] Wong Sun, 371 U.S. at 488.

[17] 4 Wayne R. LaFave, Search and Seizure § 11.4(g), at 431 (2d ed. 1987).

[19] 422 U.S. 590 (1975).

presence of intervening circumstances; and (3) the purpose and flagrancy of the official misconduct.

Here, the postarrest identification was not attenuated from the illegal arrest. Regarding the first and second factors, the officer's identification of Le occurred almost immediately after his illegal arrest, and there were no intervening circumstances (such as bringing the defendant into court) which might have purged the taint. As for the third factor, the apparent purpose of the illegality was to arrest Le immediately without bothering to obtain a warrant. The trial court found no reason why the officers could not have contained the house for a brief time further so that a warrant could be obtained, and expressed its concern that the officers gave no excuse for their failure to do so. The Fourth Amendment requirement to obtain a warrant is not a mere administrative inconvenience. It is a fundamental protection against unreasonable searches and seizures. We hold that the officer's postarrest identification of Le was not sufficiently attenuated to purge the primary taint.

We next determine whether any of the exceptions to the exclusionary rule purged that identification of its taint. Not all courts have agreed on this issue. One court held that the "inevitable discovery" exception excused the illegal police conduct because the illegal arrest merely hastened the inevitable confrontation rather than influencing its outcome.[22] But this reasoning is not persuasive, for it erases the taint by conveniently assuming that the police would eventually effect a lawful arrest of the defendant. More importantly, such a result would eviscerate the exclusionary rule by readily excusing police failure to obtain a warrant. Similarly, based on the "independent source" doctrine, another court held that a pretrial identification was admissible because it emanated from the victim's recollections of the crime that occurred prior to the illegal arrest.[23] But the victim's pretrial identification of the defendant was made possible only because of the illegal arrest. Applying the independent source doctrine under these circumstances would likewise permit the police to ignore the requirement for an arrest warrant, secure in the knowledge that the victim's postarrest identification of the defendant will still be admissible.

Nevertheless, relying heavily on *United States v. Crews*,[24] the State urges this court to apply the independent source doctrine to validate both the postarrest and in-court identifications of Le. In *Crews*, the police seized a robbery suspect on pretextual reasons, photographed him at police headquarters, and released him. The photographs were shown to the robbery victims, who identified the suspect as the robber. The defendant was then taken into custody, where the victims identified him at a court-ordered lineup. The trial court ruled that the initial seizure

---

[22] Commonwealth of Pennsylvania v. Garvin, 448 Pa. 258, 293 A.2d 33 (1972).

[23] State of Missouri v. Lynch, 528 S.W.2d 454 (Mo.App.1975).

[24] 445 U.S. 463 (1980)

was an illegal arrest, and accordingly suppressed the photographic and lineup identifications, but permitted the victims to identify the defendant in court. The circuit court of appeals reversed, holding that one of the robbery victim's in-court identification should have been suppressed as fruit of the unlawful police activity.

The United States Supreme Court reversed and reinstated the conviction, reasoning that a victim's in-court identification has three distinct elements: (1) the victim is present at trial; (2) the victim possesses the knowledge of and the ability to reconstruct the prior criminal occurrence and to identify the defendant from observations at the time of the crime; and (3) the defendant is physically present. The Court concluded that none of these elements had been obtained by exploitation of the defendant's Fourth Amendment rights. First, the victim's identity and cooperation were obtained prior to the illegal police activity. Second, the illegal arrest did not infect the victim's ability to give accurate identification testimony based upon her observations at the time of the robbery:

Based upon her observations at the time of the robbery, the victim constructed a mental image of her assailant. At trial, she retrieved this mnemonic representation, compared it to the figure of the defendant, and positively identified him as the robber. No part of this process was affected by respondent's illegal arrest.[28]

The Court acknowledged that under some circumstances, the intervening photographic and lineup identifications could affect the reliability of the in-court identification and render it inadmissible, but under the facts of that case the trial court found that the victim's in-court identification of the defendant rested on an independent recollection of her initial encounter. In support of this conclusion, the Court noted that the victim viewed the assailant at close range under well-lit conditions and with no distractions for five to ten minutes; that he closely matched her description of him; that she immediately identified him in pretrial identification procedures; and that she first identified him only a week after the initial encounter.

Third, the defendant's presence at trial was not obtained by exploitation of his rights because an illegal arrest, without more, is not a bar to prosecution. Thus, "[r]espondent is not himself a suppressible 'fruit,' and the illegality of his detention cannot deprive the Government of the opportunity to prove his guilt through the introduction of evidence wholly untainted by the police misconduct."[30]

Clearly, *Crews* provides the correct analytical framework where the pretrial identification was inadmissible and the issue is whether the in-court identification must also be excluded. But the *Crews* analysis did not address the admissibility of pretrial identifications, because in *Crews* the

---

[28] *Crews,* 445 U.S. at 472.

[30] *Crews,* 445 U.S. at 474.

United States Supreme Court simply accepted the trial court's finding that the pretrial photographic and lineup identifications were properly suppressed. Here, in contrast, Le challenges the postarrest identification.

The State contends that the *Crews* analysis validates both the postarrest and in-court identifications of Le because Officer Nollette's initial observation of Le before the arrest served as an independent source of information that allowed her to identify him after the arrest. We disagree. As the *Crews* court explained, in-court identifications are composed of the victim's presence in the courtroom, the victim's independent, prearrest recollection of the defendant's face, and the defendant's presence in the courtroom. This allows the victim to retrieve her untainted, prearrest mental image of the defendant and compare it to the defendant in order to produce the identification. The defendant's presence is not affected by the Fourth Amendment violation because an illegal arrest is not a bar to prosecution.[31] Thus, the independent source—the victim's mental image—is connected with the defendant's legal presence in the courtroom to produce the identification. But, where the identification is made outside of the courtroom (at the scene of the crime, at the stationhouse, or at a lineup), the identification is nonetheless tainted because it could not have been made unless the defendant's presence was secured by the illegal arrest. The key difference is the defendant's location. In the courtroom, the defendant is barred from arguing that his presence is unlawful. But at a pretrial identification made possible only by the illegal arrest, the State has no comparable argument to purge the taint of the illegal arrest arising from the defendant's presence. This analysis best enforces the deterrence purposes of the exclusionary rule.

It is also worth noting that in *Crews,* the reliability of the witness's testimony was of paramount importance because she had observed the defendant via photographs and a lineup, and that evidence was later excluded as fruit of the illegal arrest. In this context, the Court needed to carefully examine whether the witness's in-court identification arose from a source untainted by that excluded evidence. In other words, was the witness's lawful in-court identification tainted by her observation of him in the lineup? Or was her prearrest observation of the defendant an untainted "independent source" of information that made her in-court identification reliable?

Thus, the Court was concerned with the reliability of the witness's in-court identification, which might have been tainted by the excluded pretrial identifications were it not for the independent source of her recollections. The independent source of information served to show that the in-court identification was not affected by the excluded pretrial identifications. In contrast, where the pretrial identification is being

---

[31] It can be argued that the defendant's presence in the courtroom is tainted because he would not be there but for the illegal arrest. But the *Crews* court rejected the notion that the defendant himself is a suppressible fruit. Crews, 445 U.S. at 474.

challenged, the taint arises directly from the illegal arrest. This taint is not purged by the "independent source" of information. To so hold would eviscerate the very purpose of the exclusionary rule by excusing the illegality of the arrest and accepting the assertion that the victim's recollection of the defendant at the scene of the crime was an "independent source."[32]

We conclude that the postarrest identification of Le was not attenuated from the primary illegality. Because the independent source analysis of *Crews* applies to in-court identifications but not to pretrial identifications, there are no applicable exceptions to the exclusionary rule. The testimony of Officer Nollette regarding her postarrest identification of Le was fruit of the poisonous tree, and should have been excluded. And, although counsel for Le indicated at oral argument that Le no longer challenges the admissibility of the in-court identification, we note in passing that it was admissible under *Crews*.

III

. . . . After excluding Officer Nollette's inadmissible postarrest identification testimony, we conclude that the remaining evidence meets this constitutional harmless error standard. Officer Nollette testified that she got a very good look at Le before he fled the scene of the burglary. Officer Nollette observed Le from a short distance in broad daylight for approximately ten seconds before he ran away. She then readily identified him in court approximately six months later. Furthermore, one of Le's neighbors testified that he called 911 when he saw a "young man" running through his yard and into the house Officer Lewis had recently searched. The house turned out to be Le's house, and the sole person apprehended there was Le. This evidence is sufficiently overwhelming to lead to a finding of guilt. Thus, we affirm the conviction despite the error.

AFFIRMED.

c. COLLATERAL PROCEEDINGS

Logan v. Commonwealth

279 Va. 288, 688 S.E.2d 275 (Va. 2010)

■ Opinion by SENIOR JUSTICE CHARLES S. RUSSELL

This appeal requires us to revisit the question of the application of the exclusionary rule to probation revocation proceedings. Reaffirming our holding in Anderson v. Commonwealth, 251 Va. 437, 470 S.E.2d 862

---

[32] The *Crews* Court seemed to acknowledge this issue in a footnote:

"Respondent contends that the 'independent source' test of United States v. Wade and Stovall v. Denno, although derived from an identical formulation in Wong Sun, seeks only to determine whether the in-court identification is sufficiently reliable to satisfy due process, and is thus inapplicable in the context of this Fourth Amendment violation. We agree that a satisfactory resolution of the reliability issue does not provide a complete answer to the considerations underlying Wong Sun, but note only that in the present case both concerns are met." *Crews,* 445 U.S. at 473 (citations omitted).

(1996), we hold that the exclusionary rule is not applicable in probation revocation proceedings absent a showing of bad faith on the part of the police.

Facts and Proceedings

On August 22, 2003, Danville Police Officer Jerry L. Pace followed James Gregory Logan into a rooming house under the mistaken apprehension that Logan was a man named Chappell for whom there was an outstanding felony warrant. Logan, a resident of the rooming house, was standing on the second-floor landing of a stairway leading upward from the entrance hall. Officer Pace saw Logan hand a piece of crack cocaine to another person and arrested him for possession of cocaine. This event gave rise to a ramified chain of proceedings leading to the present appeal.

Logan's motion to suppress the Commonwealth's evidence on Fourth Amendment grounds was denied by the Circuit Court of the City of Danville, which held that Logan had no expectation of privacy in the common areas of the rooming house. He was convicted of possession of cocaine and sentenced to four years and six months imprisonment, with three years suspended. That conviction was reversed by the Court of Appeals sitting en banc on the ground that the evidence obtained pursuant to the officer's warrantless entry into the rooming house violated Logan's rights under the Fourth Amendment. *Logan v. Commonwealth*, 47 Va.App. 168, 622 S.E.2d 771 (2005)[1] (*Logan II*). The Commonwealth did not appeal that reversal.

At all times pertinent to *Logan II*, Logan was on probation for an earlier conviction, in the same circuit court, for distribution of cocaine as an accommodation in 2001 (*Logan I*). In that case he was sentenced, on March 15, 2002, to five years imprisonment. The sentence was suspended, conditioned upon Logan's serving one year and five months imprisonment, followed by 12 months of supervised probation, with Logan to be of good behavior for three years and six months after his release from probation.

After the conviction in *Logan II*, the officer supervising Logan's probation under *Logan I* reported to the court that Logan had not been of good behavior based upon the facts leading to his conviction in *Logan II*. Logan was brought before the court on a rule to show cause and counsel was appointed for him, but the revocation hearing was continued until the Court of Appeals decided *Logan II*. After the Court of Appeals reversed the conviction in *Logan II*, Logan's counsel moved the circuit court to dismiss the rule to show cause, contending that the Commonwealth's effort to revoke Logan's probation from *Logan I* was now based solely upon a conviction that had been vacated. The

---

[1] The Court of Appeals, en banc, affirmed the prior decision of a panel of the Court, but did so on the narrow ground that the Commonwealth had conceded that the rooming house was not open to the general public. *Id.*

Commonwealth asked the court to revoke probation notwithstanding the reversal, based not upon the conviction but upon Logan's failure to be of good behavior. The circuit court denied the motion to dismiss and entered an order revoking suspension of the sentence imposed in *Logan I.*

Logan appealed the revocation order to the Court of Appeals. A panel of that Court held, based upon federal decisions, that the exclusionary rule is never applicable in probation revocation proceedings. Logan v. Commonwealth, 50 Va.App. 518, 524, 651 S.E.2d 403, 406 (2007). We awarded Logan an appeal from that judgment and reversed it, remanding the case to the Court of Appeals for consideration of Logan's contention that the circuit court had erred in finding that Officer Pace had not acted in bad faith. In so ruling, we held that the Court of Appeals' reliance on federal decisions was misplaced and that the application of the exclusionary rule to probation revocation proceedings continued to be as we expressed it in *Anderson.* Logan v. Commonwealth, 276 Va. 533, 535–36, 666 S.E.2d 346, 347–48 (2008).

Upon remand, the Court of Appeals held that the record contained no evidence to support a finding that Officer Pace had acted in bad faith. The officer testified that he had been in the rooming house on prior occasions and had seen no signs to indicate that it was not open to the general public.[2] The Court concluded that, although the Commonwealth later conceded that the rooming house was not in fact open to the general public, "[the fact that the officer] was mistaken, however, does not mean that he acted in bad faith." Logan v. Commonwealth, 53 Va.App. 520, 526, 673 S.E.2d 496, 499 (2009). The Court of Appeals affirmed the circuit court's determination that Officer Pace's actions did not warrant the exclusion of his evidence at the probation revocation hearing. *Id.* at 527, 673 S.E.2d at 499. We awarded Logan an appeal.

Analysis

In *Anderson,* we said:

> We hold that the exclusionary rule is not applicable in a probation revocation proceeding absent a showing of bad faith on the part of the police. There is a strong public interest in receiving all evidence relevant to the question whether a probationer has complied with the conditions of probation. Application of the exclusionary rule in a probation revocation proceeding would frustrate the remedial and protective purposes of the probation system, because a court would not be permitted to consider relevant evidence of the probationer's rehabilitation or regression.

---

2 Another witness testified that there were signs at and near the front door saying "No Trespassing" and "Ring or Knock to Enter." Officer Pace testified that the only signs he saw said merely "Rooms." He said that when he entered, "it was a storm door, and there's a wooden door on the inside, but at that particular time it was standing open."

251 Va. at 440, 470 S.E.2d at 863. We continue to adhere to that holding. In *Anderson,* we explained the difference between the application of the exclusionary rule in a criminal trial and its application in probation revocation proceedings. The rule is a judicially-created remedy, not an individual's constitutional right. The purpose of the rule is to deter future unlawful police conduct. Exclusion of unlawfully seized evidence at trial makes its seizure profitless to the police. Excluding it in a probation revocation proceeding will ordinarily serve only to impede the search for truth where the inquiry is whether the defendant has violated the terms of his probation. *Id.*

The circuit court made an express factual finding that the officer did not act in bad faith. Such findings are binding upon appeal unless they are plainly wrong or without evidence to support them because the credibility of witnesses and the weight accorded to evidence are matters solely for the fact-finder, who has an opportunity to see and hear that evidence as it is presented. Elliott v. Commonwealth, 277 Va. 457, 462–63, 675 S.E.2d 178, 181 (2009).

"Bad faith," in Fourth Amendment jurisprudence, is not the mere opposite of "good faith," as those terms have been judicially defined. In applying the bad faith exception stated in *Anderson,* exclusion of proof is warranted only upon a showing of conscious wrongdoing by an officer. Absence of the objective "good faith" required for certain constitutional exceptions to the warrant requirement is not sufficient to trigger the exclusionary rule in probation revocation proceedings. The United States Supreme Court has repeatedly refused to apply Fourth Amendment exclusion standards to probation revocation proceedings. Pennsylvania Bd. of Prob. & Parole v. Scott, 524 U.S. 357, 363–64 (1998).

A "good faith" analysis, in Fourth Amendment cases, turns upon a purely objective determination: the conclusion an objective police officer would reasonably have drawn under the circumstances known to him at the time of the search rather than the officer's subjective motivation or state of mind. Brigham City v. Stuart, 547 U.S. 398, 404 (2006); Illinois v. Krull, 480 U.S. 340, 349–50 (1987); United States v. Leon, 468 U.S. 897, 922 n.23 (1984); Robinson v. Commonwealth, 273 Va. 26, 34–38, 639 S.E.2d 217, 222–24 (2007).

A "bad faith" analysis, by contrast, turns almost entirely upon the subjective motivation or state of mind of the police officer making the search. In order to invoke the exclusionary rule in a probation revocation case, the evidence must show that the officer making the search was motivated by bias, personal animus, a desire to harass, a conscious intent to circumvent the law, or a similar improper motive. See Commonwealth v. Michaliga, 947 A.2d 786, 792–93 (Pa.Super.2008) (bad faith is not simply bad judgment or negligence but rather it implies conscious wrongdoing); Spencer v. State, 293 Ga.App. 450, 667 S.E.2d 223, 225 (2008) (police must not act in bad faith or in an arbitrary or capricious manner when searching a probationer); Plue v. State, 721 N.E.2d 308,

310 (Ind.Ct.App.1999) (evidence seized illegally will be excluded in a revocation proceeding if seized as part of a continuing plan of police harassment).

The record in the present case is devoid of evidence that would tend to show any such motivation on the part of Officer Pace. Therefore, applying the rule in *Anderson,* we will affirm the judgment of the Court of Appeals insofar as it upholds the revocation of Logan's probation and suspended sentence.

Four months after we had remanded this case to the Court of Appeals for reconsideration of Logan's bad faith claim, the Supreme Court of the United States decided Herring v. United States, 555 U.S. 135 (2009). That case involved the application of the exclusionary rule to evidence seized in a search that violated the Fourth Amendment because the police were mistakenly told that the defendant was wanted on an outstanding warrant in an adjoining county, when in fact that warrant had been recalled but the adjoining county's database had not been updated to show the recall. *Herring* involved the application of the exclusionary rule to evidence offered at a criminal trial, not a probation revocation proceeding. On remand, the Court of Appeals nevertheless applied the reasoning of *Herring* to the question of bad faith we had directed it to consider. That application may be read to substitute an objective "good faith" test for the admissibility, in probation revocation proceedings, of evidence that has been seized in violation of the Fourth Amendment.

Because we adhere to the requirement that bad faith must be shown in order to trigger the application of the exclusionary rule in probation revocation proceedings, we expressly overrule the opinion of the Court of Appeals in Logan v. Commonwealth, 53 Va.App. 520, 673 S.E.2d 496 (2009), insofar as it may be read to suggest that our holding in *Anderson* is in any way altered.

Affirmed.

d. IMPEACHMENT

Wilkes v. United States

631 A.2d 880 (D.C. App. 1993)

■ *TERRY,* ASSOCIATE JUDGE:

Appellant Wilkes was convicted of armed second-degree murder and related offenses. At trial he raised an insanity defense and relied primarily on the expert testimony of a psychiatrist. To impeach that testimony, the government cross-examined the psychiatrist about two statements which the police had taken from Wilkes in violation of Miranda v. Arizona, 384 U.S. 436 694 (1966). Later, in rebuttal, the government introduced the statements through the testimony of two police officers. The government also presented three experts of its own, two psychiatrists and a psychologist, whose testimony was based in part on those statements and the conclusions they drew from them. Wilkes argues that the court erred in allowing the jury to learn of his statements in this manner, citing James v. Illinois, 493 U.S. 307 (1990). We conclude that *James* is distinguishable and does not control this case. We hold, following a consistent line of Supreme Court cases beginning with Walder v. United States, 347 U.S. 62 (1954), and extending through *Michigan v. Harvey,* 494 U.S. 344 (1990), that evidence of the statements was properly heard by the jury. Accordingly, we affirm the convictions.

I

Thomas Wilkes started dating Johnetta McLean in late 1988. By April 1989, however, problems in the relationship had resulted in at least two angry confrontations between Wilkes and McLean at the office of McLean's employer. Then, in early May, Wilkes apparently began stalking McLean.

On May 19, 1989, Wilkes followed McLean and a co-worker, Michelle Williams, after they left work and were driving home at about 5:00 p.m. Wilkes pulled alongside McLean's car, which was traveling south on the Anacostia Freeway (Interstate Route 295), and engaged in a brief conversation with her. When McLean asked Wilkes if he would be following her all day, he replied, "No." Wilkes then positioned his car behind McLean's car and rear-ended her three or four times, forcing McLean's car off the road and into a ditch in the median strip. Wilkes stopped his car, walked over to McLean's car, and fired one or two shots toward it. McLean's car suddenly started and moved backwards out of the ditch and across the road, then went up an embankment, hit a fence, and became lodged against a tree. Wilkes came across the road to McLean's car, then raised his arm and fired four more shots at the driver's window. Three of those shots struck McLean. Wilkes then turned to fire at Williams. She tried to get down on the floor, but before she could do so, Wilkes fired once at her. The bullet struck her spinal cord, causing instant paralysis. After firing another shot in Williams' direction, he walked back across the road to his car and drove off. McLean died from the gunshot wounds to her head and chest. Williams survived, permanently paralyzed from the chest down.

Williams identified Wilkes to the police by name as the assailant. The next day Wilkes was arrested on a warrant by Metropolitan Police Sergeant Bobby Craig and other officers. Sergeant Craig briefly questioned him in the course of executing the warrant, but without advising him of his *Miranda* rights. Moments after entering Wilkes' apartment, Craig asked him where the murder weapon was, and Wilkes replied that he had "thrown it in a dumpster out in Virginia on Duke Street near to where he had parked the car." Wilkes was taken immediately to police headquarters, where Detective Robert Vacin of the Homicide Squad questioned him for approximately an hour before giving him any *Miranda* warnings. During this initial portion of his interrogation Wilkes described his relationship with Johnetta McLean. He also said "I did it" to Detective Vacin three times during this period, but he never explained what "it" was.

When Wilkes began to relate the events of the previous day, Detective Vacin interrupted and read him his *Miranda* rights. Wilkes did not then formally waive those rights. When he asked what crime he was being charged with, Vacin replied that the crime was murder, and Wilkes became upset. Detective Vacin testified that, on the basis of Wilkes' conduct at the time, "it wasn't clear in my mind that he was waiving his rights." The interview nevertheless continued for approximately one more hour. During this second portion of the interrogation Wilkes told Vacin that he had disposed of the gun in a dumpster or trash can outside a Peoples Drug Store in Alexandria, Virginia. Detective Vacin then asked Wilkes again whether he was willing to waive his *Miranda* rights, but Wilkes expressly declined to do so and said that he wanted an attorney present before he would answer any more questions. Vacin then ceased the interrogation.

After a pre-trial hearing on the admissibility of Wilkes' statements to Sergeant Craig and Detective Vacin, the court concluded that the statements, although voluntarily made, had been taken in violation of *Miranda* and therefore could not be used in the government's case in chief. The court also ruled, however, that since the statements were voluntary, they would be "admissible for impeachment purposes on rebuttal" if Wilkes testified inconsistently with them.

At trial Wilkes relied on the defense of insanity. The thrust of his defense was that he was afflicted with a mental disorder which resulted in blackouts and severe headaches, that he suffered from this disorder at the time of the shooting, that it caused him to have no recollection whatever of the crimes, and that he was therefore not criminally responsible for his conduct. Defense counsel called several family members and friends to testify about such blackout episodes in Wilkes' past.[5]

Also testifying was Michael Washington, a longtime friend of Wilkes. Washington said that Wilkes called him between 7:00 and 8:00 p.m. on May 19 at a bowling alley in Virginia where Washington played as a member of a bowling league. Wilkes told Washington that he was in Virginia but did not know how he had gotten there. Later that same night, at approximately 1:00 a.m., Wilkes telephoned his sister, Faye

---

[5] One defense witness, Wilkes' former supervisor, testified that on one occasion at work Wilkes "appeared to be passed out." The witness said that Wilkes was lying down with his eyes open, but that "he had actually no recognition." Another witness, Kevin Whitaker, described other such episodes. For example, Whitaker testified that one evening in 1978 Wilkes appeared at his home carrying a crowbar, but he could not recall how or why he had come to Whitaker's home or why he had a crowbar in his possession.

Wilkes. She testified that her brother did not sound like himself and that at first he seemed confused and did not recognize her voice.

The defense also relied on the expert testimony of Dr. George Saiger, a psychiatrist, who opined that Wilkes suffered from a "dissociative disorder" on May 19, 1989.[6] Dr. Saiger explained that this rare disorder involves a "disturbance in the usual integrated functioning of the psychological processes of memory, identity, and consciousness." As a result of this mental disease, the doctor concluded, Wilkes "was in a different state of awareness such that he was not able to either control his behavior or realize all the implications of what he was doing, including the illegality."

The prosecutor sought permission to cross-examine Dr. Saiger about the statements Wilkes gave to the police after his arrest because the doctor had testified that his opinion was based in part upon Wilkes' statements to him that he lacked any memory of the events surrounding the charged offenses.[8] Over defense counsel's objection,[9] the court allowed the prosecutor to use the statements for the limited purpose of asking Dr. Saiger, in the form of a hypothetical question, whether his diagnosis would be different "if the defendant told someone, police officers, the day after the murder that he dumped the car and gun in Virginia and that he then came back in the city, knew the police were looking for him." The court allowed the hypothetical question with the understanding that all facts assumed in it would be presented in the government's rebuttal case.

Thus, according to Wilkes' statements to Dr. Saiger, the memory lapse lasted from shortly before 5:00 p.m. (when he went to meet Johnetta McLean at work) until "some hours later" (when he found himself in Virginia).

Dr. Saiger then testified that he had based his diagnosis of Wilkes' condition "in large part" on Wilkes' statement to him that he had no memory of the shootings. The significance of this information with

---

[6]   This diagnosis was based on an interview with Wilkes, interviews with his family, an extensive review of Wilkes' medical history, and documents prepared by the police in connection with their investigation.

[8]   Dr. Saiger had testified to Wilkes' limited memory of the circumstances of the crime:

He described, with fair definiteness of recall, events earlier that day which included plans to meet up with the woman who became the victim. He states with . . . some emphasis that he does not remember anything beyond going to try to meet her and finding himself later in Virginia, even quite in contrast with the wealth of detail about what he had done earlier. He [was] emphatic when I questioned him about the possibility that he didn't remember because he was intoxicated. He was very insistent that not that day, not any day did he use alcohol or drugs. But it seems to have been a lapse of memory and consciousness that was unaffected by physical cause and which terminated abruptly some hours later.

[9]   The objection was based on two grounds, involuntariness and remoteness. Because the court had previously concluded that the statements were voluntary, that objection was overruled. As to remoteness, the court reasoned that "if the day after the incident [Wilkes] had some memory of what had occurred in the afternoon of the incident, that seems to me to be relevant to the opinions this witness has expressed. . . ." The court therefore overruled this objection as well.

respect to the diagnosis is not in dispute. Dr. Saiger readily acknowledged that if Wilkes "did remember [the events constituting the offenses] and lied when he said he didn't, the diagnosis would definitely be reconsidered."

The government's rebuttal case consisted primarily of expert testimony about Wilkes' mental condition as well as testimony from Sergeant Craig and Detective Vacin about the previously excluded statements. There were three expert witnesses, Drs. Kenneth Rogers and Neil Blumberg, both psychiatrists, and Dr. Mitchell Hugonnet, a clinical psychologist. All three unanimously concluded that Wilkes was not suffering from a mental disorder at the time of the crimes. Each doctor considered Wilkes' statements to Sergeant Craig and Detective Vacin, among other things, in arriving at that conclusion. The court gave a limiting instruction after the testimony of each of the two police officers. For example, after Sergeant Craig's testimony, the court told the jury:

Statements of the defendant to the doctor may be discredited or impeached by showing that the defendant has previously made statements which are inconsistent with what he told the doctor. The prior statement is admitted into evidence solely for your consideration in evaluating the credibility of the defendant's statement to the doctor and the reliability of the opinion which the doctor based in part on those statements.

The defendant's statement to the detective is not considered as evidence of the defendant's guilt of the offense for which he is charged. You may consider it-you may not consider it, rather, as establishing the truth of any facts contained in it, and you must not draw any inference of guilt against the defendant just from his statements.

Another officer, Detective Gary Queen, testified about the search of the area near the drug store and the recovery of the car but not the gun.

Before preparing final jury instructions, the court decided to address once again the admissibility of Wilkes' statements to Sergeant Craig and Detective Vacin. After hearing argument by counsel on this question, the court reiterated its earlier ruling that the statements could be used to rebut Dr. Saiger's diagnosis. The court explained its decision, in part, as follows:

The admission of this evidence provides valuable aid to the jury in assessing the weight of the doctors' opinions which is important to the truth finding process. It is certainly only speculative to suggest that impermissible police conduct would be encouraged by allowing the testimony in.

* * * * * *

So my conclusion is that this evidence is admissible by analogy to *Harris v. New York,* but it is not the impeaching evidence as such, that is, it is not a matter of defendant's credibility, but it is a matter solely for the jury to take into account in determining what weight to give to the opinions of the various experts.

In its final charge, the court instructed the jury about how it should assess Wilkes' statements to the police:

> Now the evidence in this case included the testimony of two detectives concerning various statements that were allegedly made by the defendant on the day of his arrest, May 20, 1989, the day after the offenses charged.

> The Government has contended that those statements were not consistent with some of the statements which the expert witnesses say the defendant made to them with respect to the defendant's memory of the events of May 19, 1989. Again, it is for you to determine whether the statements were consistent or not.

> The detectives' testimony in this regard is admitted into evidence solely for your consideration in evaluating the weight to be given to the experts' opinions on the question of the defendant's sanity, insofar as those expert opinions may have been based in part upon the defendant's statement to the experts.

> You are not to consider the two detectives' testimony at all in determining whether the Government has established beyond a reasonable doubt that the defendant committed the acts constituting the alleged offenses.

> Only if you first determine without considering their testimony that the Government has proven every element of the offenses charged beyond a reasonable doubt, so that you then must go on to consider the defense of insanity, may you then consider the testimony of two detectives in determining whether or not the defendant is not guilty by reason of insanity.

II

Wilkes contends that the use of his statements to the police to rebut the diagnosis of his expert violated his Fifth Amendment privilege against self-incrimination, and that he is therefore entitled to a new trial. The government argues, on the other hand, that the Fifth Amendment is simply not implicated in the determination of a defendant's sanity. For two reasons, we cannot accept the government's argument. First, the validity of its underlying premise is suspect. *See* Estelle v. Smith, 451 U.S. 454, 465 (1981). Second, the cases relied upon by the government address a factually and legally distinguishable issue, namely, the constitutionality of the use of statements made during compelled psychiatric examinations. Thus we must consider in this case whether the admission of Wilkes' statements, concededly taken in violation of *Miranda,* for the purpose of rebutting his expert's opinion on the issue of his sanity violated his rights under the Fifth Amendment.

In Walder v. United States, 347 U.S. 62 (1954), the Supreme Court created a narrow exception to its earlier holding in Agnello v. United States, 269 U.S. 20 (1925), in which the Court had reiterated the rule that illegally seized evidence must be excluded for all purposes. "The essence of a provision forbidding the acquisition of evidence in a certain way is not merely that evidence so acquired shall not be used before the Court but that it shall not be used at all." Silverthorne Lumber Co. v. United States, 251 U.S. 385, 392 (1920), quoted in *Agnello,* 269 U.S. at 35; *see also* Weeks v. United States, 232 U.S. 383 (1914). Despite the exclusionary rule, however, the Court in *Walder* allowed the government to introduce unlawfully seized evidence to rebut Walder's perjured testimony.

Walder had been previously arrested for purchasing and possessing heroin, but on that occasion a court had suppressed the seized narcotics on the ground that their seizure had violated his Fourth Amendment rights. The government thereupon dismissed its case. Two years later Walder was arrested again on similar charges. At the trial in the second case, he testified in his own defense and categorically denied ever having sold, distributed, or even possessed narcotics. The trial court allowed the government to impeach Walder on cross-examination with questions about the drugs seized from his home in the previously dismissed case. It was beyond dispute that the Constitution barred the use of illegally seized evidence to secure a conviction. *See* 347 U.S. at 64–65 (citing *Silverthorne* and *Weeks*). Accordingly, the Supreme Court said, Walder had a right to "deny all the elements of the case against him without giving leave to the Government to introduce by way of rebuttal evidence illegally secured by it, and therefore not available for its case in chief." *Id.* at 65. But Walder's sweeping denial of any prior involvement with illegal drugs, a matter collateral to the charged offenses, went too far. In upholding the admission of the evidence about the earlier drug case and affirming Walder's conviction, the Supreme Court held that the exclusionary rule did not justify "letting the defendant affirmatively resort to perjurious testimony in reliance on the Government's disability to challenge his credibility." *Id.* (footnote omitted). The Court explained:

> It is one thing to say that the Government cannot make an affirmative use of evidence unlawfully obtained. It is quite another to say that the defendant can turn the illegal method by which evidence in the Government's possession was obtained to his own advantage, and provide himself with a shield against contradiction of his untruths. Such an extension of the *Weeks* doctrine would be a perversion of the Fourth Amendment.

Id.

The *Walder* impeachment exception was first applied in the context of a *Miranda* violation in Harris v. New York, 401 U.S. 222 (1971). The defendant in *Harris* was impeached at trial with statements he had made to the police, taken in violation of *Miranda,* after he had testified in his own defense and had denied committing the crimes with which he was charged. The Court upheld the impeachment, ruling that evidence barred under *Miranda,* though unavailable to the government in its case in chief, need not be barred for all purposes. While *Walder* was limited by its facts to the permissibility of impeachment on collateral matters, the Court in *Harris* saw no "difference in principle" requiring it to reach a different result simply because the challenged impeachment bore directly on the defendant's guilt. 401 U.S. at 225.

> Every criminal defendant is privileged to testify in his own defense, or to refuse to do so. But that privilege cannot be construed to include the right to commit perjury. . . . The shield provided by *Miranda* cannot be perverted into a license to use perjury by way of a defense, free from the risk of confrontation with prior inconsistent statements.

Id. at 225–226 (citations omitted). The Court explicitly rejected the argument that the policies underlying the exclusionary rule, without more, were of sufficient force to carry the day:

> The impeachment process here undoubtedly provided valuable aid to the jury in assessing petitioner's credibility, and the benefits of this process should not be lost, in our view, because of the speculative possibility that impermissible police conduct will be encouraged thereby. Assuming that the exclusionary rule has a deterrent effect on proscribed police conduct, sufficient deterrence flows when the evidence in question is made unavailable to the prosecution in its case in chief.

Id. at 225.

The impeachment exception evolved further in the Court's decisions in Oregon v. Hass, 420 U.S. 714 (1975), and United States v. Havens, 446 U.S. 620 (1980). In *Hass* statements made by the defendant after he was properly advised of his *Miranda* rights, but was told that he could not speak with an attorney until later, were excluded from the prosecution's case in chief. After Hass testified in his own defense, directly contradicting the substance of the excluded statements, the prosecutor was allowed to call a police officer on rebuttal to testify about those statements even though they had previously been suppressed. The Supreme Court expressly pointed out that Hass' contradictory testimony was made after he knew the officer's testimony would be excluded. As in *Harris,* the Court held that "the shield provided by *Miranda* is not to be perverted to a license to testify inconsistently, or even perjuriously, free from the risk of confrontation with prior inconsistent utterances." 420 U.S. at 722. Similarly, in *Havens* the trial court had permitted the introduction of illegally seized evidence (a T-shirt which had been used to conceal cocaine) to impeach the defendant's credibility with respect to statements he had made on cross-examination about the T-shirt. The Court found no reason to distinguish the case before it from *Walder, Harris,* and *Hass:*

> In terms of impeaching a defendant's seemingly false statements with his prior inconsistent utterances or with other reliable evidence available to the government, we see no difference of constitutional magnitude between the defendant's statements on direct examination and his answers to questions put to him on cross-examination that are plainly within the scope of the defendant's direct examination. Without this opportunity, the normal function of cross-examination would be severely impeded.

446 U.S. at 627.

The Supreme Court's next significant decision on the scope of the impeachment exception was James v. Illinois, 493 U.S. 307 (1990), in which one group of teenagers was robbed by another group of teenagers. One person was killed and another was seriously injured when a member of the first group fired a gun into the second group. The next day the police arrested fifteen-year-old Darryl James for the shooting. At the time of his arrest, James was sitting under a hair dryer in his mother's beauty parlor. His hair was black and curly when he was arrested, but he acknowledged to the police that on the previous day it was reddish-brown and was combed straight. In response to police questioning, James stated that he had dyed and curled his hair to change his appearance. These statements were excluded at trial because they were the product of an arrest without probable cause and therefore were taken in violation of James' rights under the Fourth Amendment.

At trial James was positively identified by several members of the rival group even though, according to their testimony, his hair had been "reddish" and "slicked back" at the time of the shooting. He did not testify in his own defense. However, the defense did call a witness who testified, contrary to the state's witnesses, that on the day of the shooting James' hair had been black and curly. The prosecutor, over objection, was permitted to impeach the credibility of this witness with James' illegally obtained statements to the police. In its rebuttal case, the state presented testimony from a detective about James' statements, and he was ultimately convicted on both charged counts. The Supreme Court reversed.[13]

In the very first paragraph of its opinion, the Supreme Court in *James* made clear that the holding of the case should be read as a response to a state court's effort to create an exception to the exclusionary rule so broad that it virtually swallowed the rule. The Court said:

> The impeachment exception to the exclusionary rule permits the prosecution in a criminal proceeding to introduce illegally

---

[13] The Illinois Appellate Court reversed James' convictions after concluding that the admission of the suppressed statements was improper. People v. James, 153 Ill.App.3d 131, 505 N.E.2d 1118, 106 Ill.Dec. 327 (1987). The Illinois Supreme Court reversed the Appellate Court and reinstated the judgment of conviction. People v. James, 123 Ill.2d 523, 528 N.E.2d 723, 124 Ill.Dec. 35 (1988).

obtained evidence to impeach the defendant's own testimony. The Illinois Supreme Court extended this exception to permit the prosecution to impeach the testimony of *all* defense witnesses with illegally obtained evidence. . . . Finding this extension inconsistent with the balance of values underlying our previous applications of the exclusionary rule, we reverse.

493 U.S. at 309 (emphasis in original; citation omitted). Seizing on the italicized word *"all,"* Wilkes contends that the Court barred impeachment of *"all* defense witnesses," other than the defendant himself, with excluded evidence. Under Wilkes' reading of *James,* it was improper for the trial court in this case to admit his excluded statements to the police to rebut Dr. Saiger's opinion about his mental condition.

We conclude that Wilkes, in urging this wooden interpretation of *James,* misconstrues that decision. Wilkes assumes from his reading of the phrase *"all* defense witnesses" that only a defendant can be impeached by excluded evidence. *James* does not sweep so broadly. We think it more reasonable, and far less dramatic, to read *James* as principally rejecting an overly broad principle rather than establishing one of its own. The Court explained in *James* that "the truth-seeking rationale . . . of *Walder* and its progeny does not apply to other witnesses [*i.e.,* defense witnesses other than the defendant] with equal force." *Id.* at 317. We read this language as nothing more than a rejection of the idea that *"all* defense witnesses" can be treated as a homogeneous group for the purpose of determining the scope of the impeachment exception. Thus the Court makes clear that there is no shorthand way to apply to *"all* defense witnesses" *en masse* the balancing approach that is crucial to the impeachment exception. The Illinois court erred in doing so, but the Supreme Court engaged in a balancing process which must guide our decision in the present case as well.

Balancing the truth-seeking function of a trial with the deterrent function of the exclusionary rule, the *James* Court concluded that the broad exception to the exclusionary rule espoused by the Illinois Supreme Court would do more violence to the latter than it would benefit the former. In reaching this conclusion, the Court emphasized that the purpose of the impeachment exception is to discourage defendants "in the first instance from 'affirmatively resort[ing] to perjurious testimony.' " *Id.* at 314 (quoting *Walder, supra,* 347 U.S. at 65). The exception enables defendants to testify truthfully and avoid admission of the suppressed evidence, provided they do not open the door by contradicting the suppressed evidence. Hence the impeachment exception, properly applied, accommodates competing societal and individual interests. The Court did not see similar benefits flowing from the significantly expanded version of the impeachment exception adopted by the Illinois Supreme Court. In fact, it found that such expansion would be detrimental because it would both chill a defendant's ability to present a competent defense[14] and significantly weaken the exclusionary rule's deterrent effect on police misconduct.[15]

Walder and its progeny have emphasized and re-emphasized "the importance of arriving at truth in criminal trials" as a central factor in determining the proper scope of the impeachment exception following a violation of *Miranda*. For example, in *Havens* the Court wrote:

> There is no gainsaying that arriving at the truth is a fundamental goal of our legal system. We have repeatedly insisted that when defendants testify, they must testify truthfully or suffer the consequences. . . . This is true even though a defendant is compelled to testify against his will. . . . It is essential, therefore, to the proper functioning of the adversary system that when a defendant takes the stand, the government be permitted proper and effective cross-examination in an attempt to elicit the truth.

446 U.S. at 626–627 (citations omitted); *see also Oregon v. Hass, supra,* 420 U.S. at 722; *Harris v. New York, supra,* 401 U.S. at 225. This theme is echoed in later cases as well. *See, e.g.,* Illinois v. Krull, 480 U.S. 340, 347 (1987) (courts must consider "costs of withholding reliable information from the truth-seeking process" in evaluating proposed exceptions to the exclusionary rule); Jenkins v. Anderson, 447 U.S. 231, 238 (1980) ("Once a defendant decides to testify, '[t]he interests of the other party and regard for the function of the courts of justice to ascertain the truth become relevant, and prevail in the balance of considerations determining the scope and the limits of the privilege against self-incrimination'" (citation omitted)). Most recently, in Michigan v. Harvey, 494 U.S. 344 (1990)—decided two months after *James v. Illinois*—the Court declared:

> We have *never* prevented use by the prosecution of relevant voluntary statements by a defendant, particularly when the violations alleged by a defendant relate only to procedural safeguards that are "not themselves rights protected by the Constitution" . . . but are instead measures designed to ensure that the constitutional rights are protected. In such cases, we

---

[14] The Court theorized that such a rule could chill a defendant's ability to present his or her best defense because the defendant would have to weigh the risk of calling a witness who, although able to "offer truthful and favorable testimony," might somehow inadvertently open the door to the admission of the excluded evidence while giving that testimony. 493 U.S. at 315. The Court suggested further that the government might "brandish such evidence as a sword with which to dissuade defendants from presenting a meaningful defense through other witnesses." *Id.* at 317.

[15] The Court feared that such deterrence would be reduced because the Illinois Supreme Court's holding would "vastly increase the number of occasions on which such evidence could be used." 493 U.S. at 318. The Court perceived as well that the police "would recognize that obtaining evidence through illegal means stacks the deck heavily in the prosecution's favor" and that it would become "far more than a 'speculative possibility' that police misconduct will be encouraged by permitting such use of illegally obtained evidence." *Id.*

have decided that the "search for truth in a criminal case" outweighs the "speculative possibility" that exclusion of evidence might deter future violations of rules not compelled directly by the Constitution in the first place.

Id. at 351–352 (citations omitted; emphasis added).

III

Thus directed by the Supreme Court to strike a balance between the truth-seeking function of a trial and the deterrent function of the exclusionary rule,[17] we conclude that the trial court here did not commit error in permitting Wilkes' expert to be questioned about Wilkes' statements. That expert, Dr. Saiger, had recounted in detail what Wilkes had told him (*see* note 8, *supra*), and on cross-examination he testified that he had based his diagnosis "in large part" on Wilkes' statements to him that he had no memory of the shootings. The doctor conceded that if Wilkes did remember what happened on May 19 "and lied when he said he didn't, the diagnosis would definitely be reconsidered." Thus the excluded statements, directly contradicting what Wilkes had told Dr. Saiger, provided the most relevant information available with which to probe the factual basis of Dr. Saiger's opinion. We hold that the truth-seeking function of this trial "was better served by [allowing Dr. Saiger to be cross-examined about the statements] than the deterrent function would have been by [their] exclusion." *Martinez v. United States, supra* note 17, 566 A.2d at 1059.

The truth-seeking process would be frustrated even further by excluding the testimony of the three government experts, which Wilkes also seeks, at least in part. The testimony of each was premised to a considerable extent on the excluded statements. If that testimony were kept from the jury, none of these experts-who were charged with responsibility for assessing Wilkes' mental condition at the time of the crimes-would be able to form an opinion based on information which Dr. Saiger conceded was critical to an accurate diagnosis. We do not think the truth-seeking function of a trial would be served, even marginally, if the medical experts on either side of the case were required to render opinions on complicated issues of mental disability while ignorant of facts essential to a valid diagnosis. Such a result would be beyond the pale of reasonableness and is certainly not mandated by the Fifth Amendment or the decisions of the Supreme Court.

Moreover, as the Court emphasized in *James,* an important purpose of the impeachment exception is to discourage defendants "in the first instance from 'affirmatively resort[ing] to perjurious testimony.'" 493 U.S. at 314 (quoting *Walder, supra,* 347 U.S. at 65). Such discouragement is best achieved here by upholding the admission of Wilkes' statements.

---

[17] *See* Martinez v. United States, 566 A.2d 1049, 1055–1056 (D.C.1989) ("case-by-case balancing" required), cert. denied, 498 U.S. 1030 (1991); Tate v. United States, 109 U.S.App.D.C. 13, 15, 283 F.2d 377, 379 (1960).

Obviously, no one can be 100 percent certain whether Wilkes' apparent mental disorder is feigned or real. Nevertheless, this is probably the only situation (we can think of no other) in which the threat of a perjury prosecution is of no value. A doctor who accurately recounts what his patient has told him, and in so doing properly discloses to the fact-finder the basis for his opinion, does not commit perjury simply by relating untruths told to him by his patient. Thus this case is readily distinguishable from *James,* for example, in which the Court recognized that most defense witnesses (other than the defendant) are sufficiently deterred from committing perjury by the threat of being prosecuted for it. No analogous threat hangs over the head of a defendant who knows that his untruths will simply be relied upon and repeated to the jury on his behalf by his psychiatrist. . . .

Nor are we persuaded that allowing statements which have been excluded under *Miranda* to be used for rebutting an insanity defense would chill a defendant's ability to raise the best defense available. A defendant may still avoid admission of the suppressed evidence if he or she does not open the door by telling something to a psychiatrist that is contradicted by that evidence. In this regard, the application of the impeachment exception which we uphold in this case is simply not of the same breadth, and consequently cannot be charged with the same infirmities, as the broad rule adopted by the Illinois court and rejected by the Supreme Court in *James.* Our holding is limited to the factual context of a case such as this, in which the defendant offers the testimony of a psychiatrist (or other expert) to support an insanity defense. We do not think that such a defendant should be allowed to lie to the psychiatrist and get away with it when there is evidence tending to show that he lied *and that the psychiatrist's diagnosis was based on that lie.*

Finally, we do not believe that our decision today will encourage improper police conduct to an extent that would offset the benefits to the truth-seeking process. The Supreme Court has made clear that "the speculative possibility that impermissible police conduct will be encouraged" is an insufficient predicate upon which to hold that the Fifth Amendment was violated. *Oregon v. Hass, supra,* 420 U.S. at 722–723; *accord, Michigan v. Harvey, supra,* 494 U.S. at 352 (reaffirming *Hass*); *United States v. Havens, supra,* 446 U.S. at 627 (same). Police misconduct is not likely to increase as a result of our decision today because the police have no way of knowing, at the time someone is arrested and questioned, whether an insanity defense will be raised much later at the suspect's trial. Even if the police, at this preliminary stage of the case, could guess that such a defense might be possible, it would be unreasonable to expect that they would violate the suspect's rights by engaging in misconduct based on such a "speculative possibility."

Summing up, we hold that when a defendant offers the testimony of an expert in the course of presenting an insanity defense and the expert's opinion is based, to any appreciable extent, on statements made to the expert by the defendant, the government may offer evidence excluded under *Miranda*-either by way of impeachment (*i.e.,* during cross-examination of the expert) or in rebuttal (*i.e.,* by showing independently that the statements made to the expert were false)-for consideration by the fact-finder in assessing the expert's opinion. That is all that happened in this case, and accordingly Wilkes' convictions are

> *Affirmed.*

■ FARRELL, ASSOCIATE JUDGE, dissenting:

... [A]s the government concedes, a broad argument that *Miranda's* exclusionary rule should not apply to the insanity defense (*i.e.,* beyond the "guilt" phase of trial) would have to overcome Estelle v. Smith, 451 U.S. 454 (1980). Moreover, immunizing this class of cases from suppression for *Miranda* violations undoubtedly lowers the incentive to police to respect an arrestee's constitutional right to silence when, for example, the bizarre nature of the criminal conduct suggests the strong likelihood of an insanity defense. *E.g.,* United States v. Hinckley, 217 U.S.App.D.C. 262, 672 F.2d 115 (1982). The government therefore advances a narrower argument-but still one drawing from the peculiarity of the insanity defense-that under the *Walder, Harris, Hass,* and *Havens* line of cases, discussed by the majority, a defendant should not be able to place his own version of his mental state at the time of the offense before the jury through the testimony of defense psychiatric witnesses without the government being able to confront those witnesses with other statements he has made that may present a very different picture, and even affect their opinion. It is this argument, as I understand it, that the majority accepts.

However one might judge this argument if we were writing on a clean slate, I believe it is foreclosed by James v. Illinois, 493 U.S. 3071990). *James,* of course, was not an "insanity" case. Nonetheless, I do not think *James* can fairly be read as rejecting only a *categorical* rule that the impeachment exception of *Walder* and its progeny applies alike to defense witnesses and testifying defendants-but leaving open case-by-case application of the exception to defense witnesses (other than the defendant) in particular contexts, such as the insanity defense.

In *James,* the Illinois Supreme Court had concluded that,

> in order to deter the defendant from engaging in perjury "by proxy," the impeachment exception to the exclusionary rule ought to be expanded to allow the State to introduce illegally obtained evidence to impeach the testimony of defense witnesses *other than the defendant himself.*

James, 493 U.S. at 311 (emphasis added). The United States Supreme Court narrowly (5–4) rejected this conclusion. It is true that, at the beginning of its opinion, the Court summarized the holding of the Illinois court as "extend[ing the impeachment] exception to permit the prosecution to impeach the testimony of *all* defense witnesses with illegally obtained evidence." *Id.* at 309 (emphasis by Supreme Court). But what the Court meant by "all" is made clear by the rest of the opinion, beginning with the summary of the state court's conclusion quoted above: "*all* defense witnesses" means "witnesses other than the defendant himself." The Court later summed up the Illinois decision again as holding "that our balancing approach in *Walder* and its progeny justifies expanding the scope of the impeachment exception to permit prosecutors to use illegally obtained evidence to impeach the credibility *of defense witnesses.*" *Id.* at 313 (emphasis added). The Court replied: "We disagree." It went on to explain why "the truth-seeking rationale supporting the impeachment of defendants in *Walder* and its progeny does not apply *to other witnesses* with equal force." *Id.* at 317 (emphasis added). Moreover, in discussing the purpose of the exclusionary rule to deter police misconduct, the Court compared the situation addressed by *Harris*—where "[l]aw enforcement officers will think it unlikely that *the defendant* will first decide to testify at trial and will also open the door inadvertently to admission of any illegally obtained evidence"—with the proposed expansion of "the impeachment exception to *all* defense witnesses," *id.* at 318 (latter emphasis by Court); the latter would "vastly increase the number of occasions on which such evidence could be used," since, for example, "[d]efense witnesses easily outnumber testifying defendants. . . ." *Id.* The Court concluded that "[o]ur previous recognition of an impeachment exception *limited to the testimony of defendants* reflects a careful weighing of the competing values." *Id.* at 320 (emphasis added). The Court thus "adhere[d] to the line drawn in our previous cases" rather than "expanding the exception to encompass the testimony of all defense witnesses." *Id.* The four dissenting Justices, unsurprisingly, saw the majority as "adopt[ing] a sweeping rule that the testimony of witnesses other than the defendant may never be rebutted with excludable evidence." *Id.* at 324 (Kennedy, J., dissenting).

If, as the majority concludes here, the Supreme Court in *James* was merely rejecting the notion "that '*all* defense witnesses' can be treated as a homogeneous group for the purpose of determining the scope of the impeachment exception," *ante* at 887, one might have expected it-before reversing the judgment of the Illinois Supreme Court-to explain why impeachment of the particular defense witness in *James,* or impeachment of that particular sub-class of witnesses, was improper; yet the Court's legal discussion is all but silent about the particular impeachment of the defense witness in that case. Similarly, if the Court were only rejecting "an overly broad principle" announced by the Illinois court "rather than establishing one of its own," *ante* at 887, one might have expected it to make clear that on remand the Illinois court was free to engage in a more focused or particularized balancing and conceivably still hold that the impeachment of the defense witness in that case was proper. Instead the Court, succinctly, held "that the Illinois Supreme Court erred in affirming James' convictions despite the prosecutor's use of illegally obtained statements to impeach a defense witness' testimony."

493 U.S. at 320. There is no suggestion that on the ordered remand "for further proceedings not inconsistent with this opinion," *id.*, the state court was free to uphold the challenged impeachment if it could fairly place the witness in a narrower category than "all defense witnesses."

In short, I do not believe the Supreme Court has left it open to us "to strike a balance between the truth-seeking function of a trial and the deterrent function of the exclusionary rule," *ante* at 889, each time the prosecution desires to impeach a defense witness (other than the defendant) with illegally obtained evidence. Were we free to conduct that balancing, I might agree with the majority that the deterrent effect of a perjury charge-stressed in *James*-has little application to "a defendant who knows that his untruths will simply be relied upon and repeated to the jury on his behalf by his psychiatrist."[3] In other respects too impeachment of a psychiatric witness may present a special case. But I believe *James* forecloses this sort of case-by-case balancing of interests where proposed impeachment of a witness other than the defendant is involved. . . .

The government implies that, given the psychiatrist's reliance on appellant's statements and transmittal of them to the jury, this case is really about impeachment of the defendant himself rather than a defense witness. That argument differs only in degree, not kind, from the "proxy" theory rejected in *James, see* 493 U.S. at 311. Appellant's statements to his psychiatrist have little significance *except* as they formed a vital part of the basis for the expert's conclusion, a fact the trial judge recognized in admitting appellant's statements to the police only for their effect upon the weight of the psychiatrist's conclusion. This was classic impeachment of a witness other than the defendant.

The categorical distinction *James* draws between defendant testimony and testimony of defense witnesses is itself debatable. *See* J.L. Kainen, *The Impeachment Exception to the Exclusionary Rules: Policies, Principles, and Politics,* 44 STANFORD L.REV. 1301, 1312–21 (1992). But, for the reasons stated, *James* leaves no doubt that the government's recourse in defending the impeachment that took place here lies with the Supreme Court and not the lower courts.

---

[3]   Appellant, of course, rejects the notion of "psychiatrist as mouthpiece" in insanity cases, pointing out that the very role of the psychiatrist at all faithful to his profession is not to take and "repeat" anything the defendant tells him at face value; indeed, the "truth" of what the defendant tells him may be the very opposite of what the defendant says. In appellant's view, the professional oath and reputation of a medical doctor serve as the equivalent and more of the oath a lay witness (not acting as a "conduit") swears to tell the truth.

e. GOOD FAITH—AND THE FUTURE OF THE EXCLUSIONARY RULE

Herring v. United States
555 U.S. 135 (2009)

■ CHIEF JUSTICE ROBERTS delivered the opinion of the Court.

The Fourth Amendment forbids "unreasonable searches and seizures," and this usually requires the police to have probable cause or a warrant before making an arrest. What if an officer reasonably believes there is an outstanding arrest warrant, but that belief turns out to be wrong because of a negligent bookkeeping error by another police employee? The parties here agree that the ensuing arrest is still a violation of the Fourth Amendment, but dispute whether contraband found during a search incident to that arrest must be excluded in a later prosecution.

Our cases establish that such suppression is not an automatic consequence of a Fourth Amendment violation. Instead, the question turns on the culpability of the police and the potential of exclusion to deter wrongful police conduct. Here the error was the result of isolated negligence attenuated from the arrest. We hold that in these circumstances the jury should not be barred from considering all the evidence.

I

On July 7, 2004, Investigator Mark Anderson learned that Bennie Dean Herring had driven to the Coffee County Sheriff's Department to retrieve something from his impounded truck. Herring was no stranger to law enforcement, and Anderson asked the county's warrant clerk, Sandy Pope, to check for any outstanding warrants for Herring's arrest. When she found none, Anderson asked Pope to check with Sharon Morgan, her counterpart in neighboring Dale County. After checking Dale County's computer database, Morgan replied that there was an active arrest warrant for Herring's failure to appear on a felony charge. Pope relayed the information to Anderson and asked Morgan to fax over a copy of the warrant as confirmation. Anderson and a deputy followed Herring as he left the impound lot, pulled him over, and arrested him. A search incident to the arrest revealed methamphetamine in Herring's pocket, and a pistol (which as a felon he could not possess) in his vehicle. App. 17-23.

There had, however, been a mistake about the warrant. The Dale County sheriff's computer records are supposed to correspond to actual arrest warrants, which the office also maintains. But when Morgan went to the files to retrieve the actual warrant to fax to Pope, Morgan was unable to find it. She called a court clerk and learned that the warrant had been recalled five months earlier. Normally when a warrant is recalled the court clerk's office or a judge's chambers calls Morgan, who enters the information in the sheriff's computer database and disposes of the physical copy. For whatever reason, the information about the recall of the warrant for Herring did not appear in the database. Morgan immediately called Pope to alert her to the mixup, and Pope contacted Anderson over a secure radio. This all unfolded in 10 to 15 minutes, but Herring had already been arrested and found with the gun and drugs, just a few hundred yards from the sheriff's office. *Id.*, at 26, 35–42, 54–55.

Herring was indicted in the District Court for the Middle District of Alabama for illegally possessing the gun and drugs, violations of 18 U.S.C. § 922(g)(1) and 21 U.S.C. § 844(a). He moved to suppress the evidence on the ground that his initial arrest had been illegal because the warrant had been rescinded. The Magistrate Judge recommended denying the motion because the arresting officers had acted in a good-faith belief that the warrant was still outstanding. Thus, even if there were a Fourth Amendment violation, there was "no reason to believe that application of the exclusionary rule here would deter the occurrence of any future mistakes." App. 70. The District Court adopted the Magistrate Judge's recommendation, 451 F.Supp.2d 1290 (2005), and the Court of Appeals for the Eleventh Circuit affirmed, 492 F.3d 1212 (2007).

The Eleventh Circuit found that the arresting officers in Coffee County "were entirely innocent of any wrongdoing or carelessness." *id.*, at 1218. The court assumed that whoever failed to update the Dale County sheriff's records was also a law enforcement official, but noted that "the conduct in question [wa]s a negligent failure to act, not a deliberate or tactical choice to act." *Ibid.* Because the error was merely negligent and attenuated from the arrest, the Eleventh Circuit concluded that the benefit of suppressing the evidence "would be marginal or nonexistent," *ibid.* (internal quotation marks omitted), and the evidence was therefore admissible under the good-faith rule of United States v. Leon, 468 U.S. 897 (1984).

Other courts have required exclusion of evidence obtained through similar police errors, *e.g.*, Hoay v. State, 348 Ark. 80, 86–87, 71 S.W.3d 573, 577 (2002), so we granted Herring's petition for certiorari to resolve the conflict. We now affirm the Eleventh Circuit's judgment.

II

When a probable-cause determination was based on reasonable but mistaken assumptions, the person subjected to a search or seizure has not necessarily been the victim of a constitutional violation. The very phrase "probable cause" confirms that the Fourth Amendment does not demand all possible precision. And whether the error can be traced to a mistake by a state actor or some other source may bear on the analysis. For purposes of deciding this case, however, we accept the parties' assumption that there was a Fourth Amendment violation. The issue is whether the exclusionary rule should be applied.

A

The Fourth Amendment protects "[t]he right of the people to be secure in their persons, houses, papers, and effects, against unreasonable searches and seizures," but "contains no provision expressly precluding the use of evidence obtained in violation of its commands," Arizona v. Evans, 514 U.S. 1, 10 (1995). Nonetheless, our decisions establish an exclusionary rule that, when applicable, forbids the use of improperly obtained evidence at trial. See, *e.g.,* Weeks v. United States, 232 U.S. 383, 398 (1914). We have stated that this judicially created rule is "designed to safeguard Fourth Amendment rights generally through its deterrent effect." United States v. Calandra, 414 U.S. 338, 348 (1974).

In analyzing the applicability of the rule, *Leon* admonished that we must consider the actions of all the police officers involved. 468 U.S., at 923, n.24 ("It is necessary to consider the objective reasonableness, not only of the officers who eventually executed a warrant, but also of the officers who originally obtained it or who provided information material to the probable-cause determination"). The Coffee County officers did nothing improper. Indeed, the error was noticed so quickly because Coffee County requested a faxed confirmation of the warrant.

The Eleventh Circuit concluded, however, that somebody in Dale County should have updated the computer database to reflect the recall of the arrest warrant. The court also concluded that this error was negligent, but did not find it to be reckless or deliberate. 492 F.3d, at 1218.[1] That fact is crucial to our holding that this error is not enough by itself to require "the extreme sanction of exclusion." *Leon, supra,* at 916.

1. The fact that a Fourth Amendment violation occurred—*i.e.,* that a search or arrest was unreasonable—does not necessarily mean that the exclusionary rule applies. Illinois v. Gates, 462 U.S. 213, 223 (1983). Indeed, exclusion "has always been our last resort, not our first impulse," Hudson v. Michigan, 547 U.S. 586, 591 (2006), and our precedents establish important principles that constrain application of the exclusionary rule.

First, the exclusionary rule is not an individual right and applies only where it " 'result[s] in appreciable deterrence.' " *Leon, supra,* at 909 (quoting United States v. Janis, 428 U.S. 433, 454 (1976)). We have repeatedly rejected the argument that exclusion is a necessary consequence of a Fourth Amendment violation. *Leon, supra,* at 905–906; *Evans, supra,* at 13–14; *Pennsylvania Bd. of Probation and Parole v. Scott,* 524 U.S. 357, 363 (1998). Instead we have focused on the efficacy

---

[1] At an earlier point in its opinion, the Eleventh Circuit described the error as " 'at the very least negligent,' " 492 F.3d 1212, 1217 (2007) (quoting Michigan v. Tucker, 417 U.S. 433, 447 (1974)). But in the next paragraph, it clarified that the error was "a negligent failure to act, not a deliberate or tactical choice to act," 492 F.3d, at 1218. The question presented treats the error as a "negligen[t]" one, see Pet. for Cert. i; Brief in Opposition (I), and both parties briefed the case on that basis.

of the rule in deterring Fourth Amendment violations in the future. *See Calandra, supra,* at 347–355; Stone v. Powell, 428 U.S. 465, 486 (1976).[2]

In addition, the benefits of deterrence must outweigh the costs. *Leon, supra,* at 910. "We have never suggested that the exclusionary rule must apply in every circumstance in which it might provide marginal deterrence." *Scott, supra,* at 368. "[T]o the extent that application of the exclusionary rule could provide some incremental deterrent, that possible benefit must be weighed against [its] substantial social costs." Illinois v. Krull, 480 U.S. 340, 352–353 (1987) (internal quotation marks omitted). The principal cost of applying the rule is, of course, letting guilty and possibly dangerous defendants go free—something that "offends basic concepts of the criminal justice system." *Leon, supra,* at 908. "[T]he rule's costly toll upon truth-seeking and law enforcement objectives presents a high obstacle for those urging [its] application." *Scott, supra,* at 364–365 (internal quotation marks omitted); *see also* United States v. Havens, 446 U.S. 620, 626–627 (1980); United States v. Payner, 447 U.S. 727, 734 (1980).

These principles are reflected in the holding of *Leon*: When police act under a warrant that is invalid for lack of probable cause, the exclusionary rule does not apply if the police acted "in objectively reasonable reliance" on the subsequently invalidated search warrant. 468 U.S., at 922. We (perhaps confusingly) called this objectively reasonable reliance "good faith." *Ibid.,* n.23. In a companion case, Massachusetts v. Sheppard, 468 U.S. 981 (1984), we held that the exclusionary rule did not apply when a warrant was invalid because a judge forgot to make "clerical corrections" to it. *Id.,* at 991.

Shortly thereafter we extended these holdings to warrantless administrative searches performed in good-faith reliance on a statute later declared unconstitutional. *Krull, supra,* at 349–350. Finally, in *Evans,* 514 U.S. 1, we applied this good-faith rule to police who reasonably relied on mistaken information in a court's database that an arrest warrant was outstanding. We held that a mistake made by a judicial employee could not give rise to exclusion for three reasons: The exclusionary rule was crafted to curb police rather than judicial misconduct; court employees were unlikely to try to subvert the Fourth Amendment; and "most important, there [was] no basis for believing that application of the exclusionary rule in [those] circumstances" would have any significant effect in deterring the errors. *Id.,* at 15. *Evans* left unresolved "whether the evidence should be suppressed if police

---

[2] Justice GINSBURG's dissent champions what she describes as " 'a more majestic conception' of . . . the exclusionary rule," post, at 707 (quoting Arizona v. Evans, 514 U.S. 1, 18 (1995) (STEVENS, J., dissenting)), which would exclude evidence even where deterrence does not justify doing so. Majestic or not, our cases reject this conception, *see, e.g.,* United States v. Leon, 468 U.S. 897, 921, n.22 (1984), and perhaps for this reason, her dissent relies almost exclusively on previous dissents to support its analysis.

personnel were responsible for the error,"[3] an issue not argued by the State in that case, *id.,* at 16, n.5, but one that we now confront.

2. The extent to which the exclusionary rule is justified by these deterrence principles varies with the culpability of the law enforcement conduct. As we said in *Leon,* "an assessment of the flagrancy of the police misconduct constitutes an important step in the calculus" of applying the exclusionary rule. 468 U.S., at 911. Similarly, in *Krull* we elaborated that "evidence should be suppressed 'only if it can be said that the law enforcement officer had knowledge, or may properly be charged with knowledge, that the search was unconstitutional under the Fourth Amendment.' " 480 U.S., at 348–349 (quoting United States v. Peltier, 422 U.S. 531, 542 (1975)).

Anticipating the good-faith exception to the exclusionary rule, Judge Friendly wrote that "[t]he beneficent aim of the exclusionary rule to deter police misconduct can be sufficiently accomplished by a practice . . . outlawing evidence obtained by flagrant or deliberate violation of rights." *The Bill of Rights as a Code of Criminal Procedure,* 53 Calif. L.Rev. 929, 953 (1965) (footnotes omitted); *see also Brown v. Illinois,* 422 U.S. 590, 610–611 (1975) (Powell, J., concurring in part) ("[T]he deterrent value of the exclusionary rule is most likely to be effective" when "official conduct was flagrantly abusive of Fourth Amendment rights").

Indeed, the abuses that gave rise to the exclusionary rule featured intentional conduct that was patently unconstitutional. In *Weeks,* 232 U.S. 383, a foundational exclusionary rule case, the officers had broken into the defendant's home (using a key shown to them by a neighbor), confiscated incriminating papers, then returned again with a U.S. Marshal to confiscate even more. *Id.,* at 386. Not only did they have no search warrant, which the Court held was required, but they could not have gotten one had they tried. They were so lacking in sworn and particularized information that "not even an order of court would have justified such procedure." *Id.,* at 393–394. Silverthorne Lumber Co. v. United States, 251 U.S. 385 (1920), on which petitioner repeatedly relies, was similar; federal officials "without a shadow of authority" went to the defendants' office and "made a clean sweep" of every paper they could find. *Id.,* at 390. Even the Government seemed to acknowledge that the "seizure was an outrage." *Id.,* at 391.

Equally flagrant conduct was at issue in Mapp v. Ohio, 367 U.S. 643 (1961), which overruled Wolf v. Colorado, 338 U.S. 25 (1949), and extended the exclusionary rule to the States. Officers forced open a door to Ms. Mapp's house, kept her lawyer from entering, brandished what

---

[3] We thus reject Justice BREYER's suggestion that *Evans* was entirely "premised on a distinction between judicial errors and police errors," post, at 710 (dissenting opinion). Were that the only rationale for our decision, there would have been no reason for us expressly and carefully to leave police error unresolved. In addition, to the extent *Evans* is viewed as presaging a particular result here, it is noteworthy that the dissent's view in that case was that the distinction Justice BREYER regards as determinative was instead "artificial." 514 U.S., at 29 (GINSBURG, J., dissenting).

the court concluded was a false warrant, then forced her into handcuffs and canvassed the house for obscenity. 367 U.S., at 644–645. *See* Friendly, *supra,* at 953, and n.127 ("[T]he situation in *Mapp*" featured a "flagrant or deliberate violation of rights"). An error that arises from nonrecurring and attenuated negligence is thus far removed from the core concerns that led us to adopt the rule in the first place. And in fact since *Leon,* we have never applied the rule to exclude evidence obtained in violation of the Fourth Amendment, where the police conduct was no more intentional or culpable than this.

3.   To trigger the exclusionary rule, police conduct must be sufficiently deliberate that exclusion can meaningfully deter it, and sufficiently culpable that such deterrence is worth the price paid by the justice system. As laid out in our cases, the exclusionary rule serves to deter deliberate, reckless, or grossly negligent conduct, or in some circumstances recurring or systemic negligence. The error in this case does not rise to that level.[4]

Our decision in Franks v. Delaware, 438 U.S. 154 (1978), provides an analogy. Cf. *Leon, supra,* at 914. In *Franks,* we held that police negligence in obtaining a warrant did not even rise to the level of a Fourth Amendment violation, let alone meet the more stringent test for triggering the exclusionary rule. We held that the Constitution allowed defendants, in some circumstances, "to challenge the truthfulness of factual statements made in an affidavit supporting the warrant," even after the warrant had issued. 438 U.S., at 155–156. If those false statements were necessary to the Magistrate Judge's probable-cause determination, the warrant would be "voided." *Ibid.* But we did not find all false statements relevant: "There must be allegations of deliberate falsehood or of reckless disregard for the truth," and "[a]llegations of negligence or innocent mistake are insufficient." *Id.,* at 171.

Both this case and *Franks* concern false information provided by police. Under *Franks,* negligent police miscommunications in the course of acquiring a warrant do not provide a basis to rescind a warrant and render a search or arrest invalid. Here, the miscommunications occurred in a different context—after the warrant had been issued and recalled— but that fact should not require excluding the evidence obtained.

The pertinent analysis of deterrence and culpability is objective, not an "inquiry into the subjective awareness of arresting officers," Reply Brief for Petitioner 4–5. *See also post,* at 710, n.7 (GINSBURG, J., dissenting). We have already held that "our good-faith inquiry is confined to the objectively ascertainable question whether a reasonably well trained officer would have known that the search was illegal" in light of

---

4   We do not quarrel with Justice GINSBURG's claim that "liability for negligence . . . creates an incentive to act with greater care," post, at 708, and we do not suggest that the exclusion of this evidence could have no deterrent effect. But our cases require any deterrence to "be weighed against the 'substantial social costs exacted by the exclusionary rule,'" Illinois v. Krull, 480 U.S. 340, 352–353 (1987) (quoting Leon, 468 U.S., at 907), and here exclusion is not worth the cost.

"all of the circumstances." *Leon,* 468 U.S., at 922, n.23. These circumstances frequently include a particular officer's knowledge and experience, but that does not make the test any more subjective than the one for probable cause, which looks to an officer's knowledge and experience, Ornelas v. United States, 517 U.S. 690, 699–700 (1996), but not his subjective intent, Whren v. United States, 517 U.S. 806, 812–813 (1996).

4. We do not suggest that all recordkeeping errors by the police are immune from the exclusionary rule. In this case, however, the conduct at issue was not so objectively culpable as to require exclusion. In *Leon* we held that "the marginal or nonexistent benefits produced by suppressing evidence obtained in objectively reasonable reliance on a subsequently invalidated search warrant cannot justify the substantial costs of exclusion." 468 U.S., at 922. The same is true when evidence is obtained in objectively reasonable reliance on a subsequently recalled warrant.

If the police have been shown to be reckless in maintaining a warrant system, or to have knowingly made false entries to lay the groundwork for future false arrests, exclusion would certainly be justified under our cases should such misconduct cause a Fourth Amendment violation. We said as much in *Leon,* explaining that an officer could not "obtain a warrant on the basis of a 'bare bones' affidavit and then rely on colleagues who are ignorant of the circumstances under which the warrant was obtained to conduct the search." *Id.,* at 923, n.24, (citing Whiteley v. Warden, Wyo. State Penitentiary, 401 U.S. 560, 568 (1971)). Petitioner's fears that our decision will cause police departments to deliberately keep their officers ignorant, Brief for Petitioner 37–39, are thus unfounded.

The dissent also adverts to the possible unreliability of a number of databases not relevant to this case. *Post,* at 708–709. In a case where systemic errors were demonstrated, it might be reckless for officers to rely on an unreliable warrant system. *See Evans,* 514 U.S., at 17 (O'Connor, J., concurring) ("Surely it would *not* be reasonable for the police to rely . . . on a recordkeeping system . . . that *routinely* leads to false arrests" (second emphasis added)); *Hudson,* 547 U.S., at 604 (KENNEDY, J., concurring) ("If a *widespread pattern* of violations were shown . . . there would be reason for grave concern" (emphasis added)). But there is no evidence that errors in Dale County's system are routine or widespread. Officer Anderson testified that he had never had reason to question information about a Dale County warrant, App. 27, and both Sandy Pope and Sharon Morgan testified that they could remember no similar miscommunication ever happening on their watch, *id.,* at 33, 61–62. That is even less error than in the database at issue in *Evans,* where we also found reliance on the database to be objectively reasonable. 514 U.S., at 15 (similar error "every three or four years"). Because no such showings were made here, see 451 F.Supp.2d, at 1292,[5] the Eleventh Circuit was correct to affirm the denial of the motion to suppress.

* * *

Petitioner's claim that police negligence automatically triggers suppression cannot be squared with the principles underlying the exclusionary rule, as they have been explained in our cases. In light of our repeated holdings that the deterrent effect of suppression must be substantial and outweigh any harm to the justice system, e.g., *Leon,* 468 U.S., at 909–910, we conclude that when police mistakes are the result of negligence such as that described here, rather than systemic error or reckless disregard of constitutional requirements, any marginal deterrence does not "pay its way." *Id.,* at 907–908, n.6 (internal quotation marks omitted). In such a case, the criminal should not "go free because the constable has blundered." *People v. Defore,* 242 N.Y. 13, 21, 150 N.E. 585, 587 (1926) (opinion of the Court by Cardozo, J.).

The judgment of the Court of Appeals for the Eleventh Circuit is affirmed.

It is so ordered.

■ JUSTICE GINSBURG, with whom JUSTICE STEVENS, JUSTICE SOUTER, and JUSTICE BRYER joins, dissenting.

Petitioner Bennie Dean Herring was arrested, and subjected to a search incident to his arrest, although no warrant was outstanding against him, and the police lacked probable cause to believe he was engaged in criminal activity. The arrest and ensuing search therefore violated Herring's Fourth Amendment right "to be secure . . . against unreasonable searches and seizures." The Court of Appeals so determined, and the Government does not contend otherwise. The exclusionary rule provides redress for Fourth Amendment violations by placing the government in the position it would have been in had there been no unconstitutional arrest and search. The rule thus strongly encourages police compliance with the Fourth Amendment in the future. The Court, however, holds the rule inapplicable because careless recordkeeping by the police—not flagrant or deliberate misconduct— accounts for Herring's arrest.

I would not so constrict the domain of the exclusionary rule and would hold the rule dispositive of this case: "[I]f courts are to have any power to discourage [police] error of [the kind here at issue], it must be through the application of the exclusionary rule." Arizona v. Evans, 514

---

[5] Justice GINSBURG notes that at an earlier suppression hearing Morgan testified— apparently in confusion—that there had been miscommunications "[s]everal times." Post, at 706, n.2 (quoting App. to Pet. for Cert. 17a). When she later realized that she had misspoken, Morgan emphatically corrected the record. App. 61-62. Noting this, the District Court found that "Morgan's 'several times' statement is confusing and essentially unhelpful," and concluded that there was "no credible evidence of routine problems with disposing of recalled warrants." 451 F.Supp.2d, at 1292. This factual determination, supported by the record and credited by the Court of Appeals, see 492 F.3d, at 1219, is of course entitled to deference.

U.S. 1, 22–23 (1995) (STEVENS, J., dissenting). The unlawful search in this case was contested in court because the police found methamphetamine in Herring's pocket and a pistol in his truck. But the "most serious impact" of the Court's holding will be on innocent persons "wrongfully arrested based on erroneous information [carelessly maintained] in a computer data base." *Id.,* at 22.

I

A warrant for Herring's arrest was recalled in February 2004, apparently because it had been issued in error. *See* Brief for Petitioner 3, n. 1 (citing App. 63). The warrant database for the Dale County Sheriff's Department, however, does not automatically update to reflect such changes. App. 39-40, 43, 45. A member of the Dale County Sheriff's Department—whom the parties have not identified—returned the hard copy of the warrant to the County Circuit Clerk's office, but did not correct the Department's database to show that the warrant had been recalled. *Id.,* at 60. The erroneous entry for the warrant remained in the database, undetected, for five months.

On a July afternoon in 2004, Herring came to the Coffee County Sheriff's Department to retrieve his belongings from a vehicle impounded in the Department's lot. *Id.,* at 17. Investigator Mark Anderson, who was at the Department that day, knew Herring from prior interactions: Herring had told the district attorney, among others, of his suspicion that Anderson had been involved in the killing of a local teenager, and Anderson had pursued Herring to get him to drop the accusations. *Id.,* at 63–64. Informed that Herring was in the impoundment lot, Anderson asked the Coffee County warrant clerk whether there was an outstanding warrant for Herring's arrest. *Id.,* at 18. The clerk, Sandy Pope, found no warrant. *Id.,* at 19.

Anderson then asked Pope to call the neighboring Dale County Sheriff's Department to inquire whether a warrant to arrest Herring was outstanding there. Upon receiving Pope's phone call, Sharon Morgan, the warrant clerk for the Dale County Department, checked her computer database. As just recounted, that Department's database preserved an error. Morgan's check therefore showed—incorrectly—an active warrant for Herring's arrest. *Id.,* at 41. Morgan gave the misinformation to Pope, *ibid.,* who relayed it to Investigator Anderson, *id.,* at 35. Armed with the report that a warrant existed, Anderson promptly arrested Herring and performed an incident search minutes before detection of the error.

The Court of Appeals concluded, and the Government does not contest, that the "failure to bring the [Dale County Sheriff's Department] records up to date [was] 'at the very least negligent.'" 492 F.3d 1212, 1217 (C.A.11 2007) (quoting Michigan v. Tucker, 417 U.S. 433, 447 (1974)). And it is uncontested here that Herring's arrest violated his Fourth Amendment rights. The sole question presented, therefore, is whether evidence the police obtained through the unlawful search should have been suppressed.[1] The Court holds that suppression was unwarranted because the exclusionary rule's "core concerns" are not raised by an isolated, negligent recordkeeping error attenuated from the arrest. *Ante,* at 702, 704.[2] In my view, the Court's opinion underestimates the need for a forceful exclusionary rule and the gravity of recordkeeping errors in law enforcement.

II

A

The Court states that the exclusionary rule is not a defendant's right, *ante,* at 700; rather, it is simply a remedy applicable only when suppression would result in appreciable deterrence that outweighs the cost to the justice system, *ante,* at 704. *See* also *ante,* at 702 ("[T]he exclusionary rule serves to deter deliberate, reckless, or grossly negligent conduct, or in some circumstances recurring or systemic negligence.").

The Court's discussion invokes a view of the exclusionary rule famously held by renowned jurists Henry J. Friendly and Benjamin Nathan Cardozo. Over 80 years ago, Cardozo, then seated on the New York Court of Appeals, commented critically on the federal exclusionary rule, which had not yet been applied to the States. He suggested that in at least some cases the rule exacted too high a price from the criminal justice system. *See* People v. Defore, 242 N.Y. 13, 24–25, 150 N.E. 585, 588–589 (1926). In words often quoted, Cardozo questioned whether the criminal should "go free because the constable has blundered." *Id.,* at 21, 150 N.E., at 587.

Judge Friendly later elaborated on Cardozo's query. "The sole reason for exclusion," Friendly wrote, "is that experience has demonstrated this to be the only effective method for deterring the police from violating the Constitution." *The Bill of Rights as a Code of Criminal Procedure,* 53 Calif. L.Rev. 929, 951 (1965). He thought it excessive, in light of the rule's aim to deter police conduct, to require exclusion when the constable had merely "blundered"—when a police officer committed a technical error in an on-the-spot judgment, *id.,* at 952, or made a "slight and unintentional miscalculation," *id.,* at 953. As the Court recounts, Judge Friendly suggested that deterrence of police improprieties could be "sufficiently accomplished" by confining the rule to "evidence obtained by flagrant or deliberate violation of rights." *Ibid.; ante,* at 702.

---

[1] That the recordkeeping error occurred in Dale County rather than Coffee County is inconsequential in the suppression analysis. As the Court notes, "we must consider the actions of all the police officers involved." Ante, at 699. *See also* United States v. Leon, 468 U.S. 897, 923, n.24 (1984).

[2] It is not altogether clear how "isolated" the error was in this case. When the Dale County Sheriff's Department warrant clerk was first asked: "[H]ow many times have you had or has Dale County had problems, any problems with communicating about warrants," she responded: "Several times." App. to Pet. for Cert. 17a (internal quotation marks omitted).

B

Others have described "a more majestic conception" of the Fourth Amendment and its adjunct, the exclusionary rule. *Evans,* 514 U.S., at 18 (STEVENS, J., dissenting). Protective of the fundamental "right of the people to be secure in their persons, houses, papers, and effects," the Amendment "is a constraint on the power of the sovereign, not merely on some of its agents." *Ibid.* (internal quotation marks omitted); *See* Stewart, *The Road to* Mapp v. Ohio *and Beyond: The Origins, Development and Future of the Exclusionary Rule in Search-and-Seizure Cases,* 83 Colum. L.Rev. 1365 (1983). I share that vision of the Amendment.

The exclusionary rule is "a remedy necessary to ensure that" the Fourth Amendment's prohibitions "are observed in fact." *Id.,* at 1389; *see* Kamisar, *Does (Did) (Should) The Exclusionary Rule Rest On A "Principled Basis" Rather Than An "Empirical Proposition"?* 16 Creighton L.Rev. 565, 600 (1983). The rule's service as an essential auxiliary to the Amendment earlier inclined the Court to hold the two inseparable. *See* Whiteley v. Warden, Wyo. State Penitentiary, 401 U.S. 560, 568–569 (1971). Cf. Olmstead v. United States, 277 U.S. 438, 469–471 (1928) (Holmes, J., dissenting); *id.,* at 477–479, 483–485 (Brandeis, J., dissenting).

Beyond doubt, a main objective of the rule "is to deter—to compel respect for the constitutional guaranty in the only effectively available way—by removing the incentive to disregard it." Elkins v. United States, 364 U.S. 206, 217 (1960). But the rule also serves other important purposes: It "enabl[es] the judiciary to avoid the taint of partnership in official lawlessness," and it "assur[es] the people—all potential victims of unlawful government conduct—that the government would not profit from its lawless behavior, thus minimizing the risk of seriously undermining popular trust in government." United States v. Calandra, 414 U.S. 338, 357 (1974) (Brennan, J., dissenting). *See also* Terry v. Ohio, 392 U.S. 1, 13 (1968) ("A rule admitting evidence in a criminal trial, we recognize, has the necessary effect of legitimizing the conduct which produced the evidence, while an application of the exclusionary rule withholds the constitutional imprimatur."); Kamisar, *supra,* at 604 (a principal reason for the exclusionary rule is that "the Court's aid should be denied 'in order to maintain respect for law [and] to preserve the judicial process from contamination'" (quoting *Olmstead,* 277 U.S., at 484 (Brandeis, J., dissenting)).

The exclusionary rule, it bears emphasis, is often the only remedy effective to redress a Fourth Amendment violation. *See* Mapp v. Ohio, 367 U.S. 643, 652 (1961) (noting "the obvious futility of relegating the Fourth Amendment to the protection of other remedies"); Amsterdam, *Perspectives on the Fourth Amendment,* 58 Minn. L.Rev. 349, 360 (1974) (describing the exclusionary rule as "the primary instrument for enforcing the [F]ourth [A]mendment"). Civil liability will not lie for "the vast majority of [F]ourth [A]mendment violations—the frequent infringements motivated by commendable zeal, not condemnable malice." Stewart, 83 Colum. L.Rev., at 1389. Criminal prosecutions or administrative sanctions against the offending officers and injunctive relief against widespread violations are an even farther cry. *See id.,* at 1386–1388.

III

The Court maintains that Herring's case is one in which the exclusionary rule could have scant deterrent effect and therefore would not "pay its way." *Ante,* at 704 (internal quotation marks omitted). I disagree.

A

The exclusionary rule, the Court suggests, is capable of only marginal deterrence when the misconduct at issue is merely careless, not intentional or reckless. *See ante,* at 702, 703. The suggestion runs counter to a foundational premise of tort law—that liability for negligence, *i.e.,* lack of due care, creates an incentive to act with greater care. The Government so acknowledges. *See* Brief for United States 21; *cf.* Reply Brief 12.

That the mistake here involved the failure to make a computer entry hardly means that application of the exclusionary rule would have minimal value. "Just as the risk of *respondeat superior* liability encourages employers to supervise . . . their employees' conduct [more carefully], so the risk of exclusion of evidence encourages policymakers and systems managers to monitor the performance of the systems they install and the personnel employed to operate those systems." *Evans,* 514 U.S., at 29, n.5 (GINSBURG, J., dissenting).

Consider the potential impact of a decision applying the exclusionary rule in this case. As earlier observed, *see supra,* at 698, the record indicates that there is no electronic connection between the warrant database of the Dale County Sheriff's Department and that of the County Circuit Clerk's office, which is located in the basement of the same building. App. 39-40, 43, 45. When a warrant is recalled, one of the "many different people that have access to th[e] warrants," *id.,* at 60, must find the hard copy of the warrant in the "two or three different places" where the department houses warrants, *id.,* at 41, return it to the Clerk's office, and manually update the Department's database, *see id.,* at 60. The record reflects no routine practice of checking the database for accuracy, and the failure to remove the entry for Herring's warrant was not discovered until Investigator Anderson sought to pursue Herring five months later. Is it not altogether obvious that the Department could take further precautions to ensure the integrity of its database? The Sheriff's Department "is in a position to remedy the situation and might well do so if the exclusionary rule is there to remove the incentive to do otherwise." 1 W. LaFave, Search and Seizure § 1.8(e), p. 313 (4th ed.2004). *See also Evans,* 514 U.S., at 21 (STEVENS, J., dissenting).

B

Is the potential deterrence here worth the costs it imposes? *See ante,* at 702. In light of the paramount importance of accurate recordkeeping in law enforcement, I would answer yes, and next explain why, as I see it, Herring's motion presents a particularly strong case for suppression.

Electronic databases form the nervous system of contemporary criminal justice operations. In recent years, their breadth and influence have dramatically expanded. Police today can access databases that include not only the updated National Crime Information Center (NCIC), but also terrorist watchlists, the Federal Government's employee eligibility system, and various commercial databases. Brief for Electronic Privacy Information Center (EPIC) et al. as *Amicus Curiae* 6. Moreover, States are actively expanding information sharing between jurisdictions. *Id.,* at 8–13. As a result, law enforcement has an increasing supply of information within its easy electronic reach. *See* Brief for Petitioner 36–37.

The risk of error stemming from these databases is not slim. Herring's *amici* warn that law enforcement databases are insufficiently monitored and often out of date. Brief for *Amicus* EPIC 13–28. Government reports describe, for example, flaws in NCIC databases,[3] terrorist watchlist databases,[4] and databases associated with the Federal Government's employment eligibility verification system.[5]

Inaccuracies in expansive, interconnected collections of electronic information raise grave concerns for individual liberty. "The offense to the dignity of the citizen who is arrested, handcuffed, and searched on a public street simply because some bureaucrat has failed to maintain an accurate computer data base" is evocative of the use of general warrants that so outraged the authors of our Bill of Rights. *Evans,* 514 U.S., at 23 (STEVENS, J., dissenting).

C

The Court assures that "exclusion would certainly be justified" if "the police have been shown to be reckless in maintaining a warrant system, or to have knowingly made false entries to lay the groundwork for future false arrests." *Ante,* at 703. This concession provides little comfort.

---

[3] *See* Dept. of Justice, Bureau of Justice Statistics, P. Brien, Improving Access to and Integrity of Criminal History Records, NCJ 200581 (July 2005), available at http://www.ojp. usdoj.gov/bjs/pub/pdf/iaichr.pdf (All Internet materials as visited Jan. 12, 2009, and included in Clerk of Court's case file.).

[4] *See* Dept. of Justice, Office of Inspector General, Audit of the U.S. Department of Justice Terrorist Watchlist Nomination Processes, Audit Rep. 08-16 (Mar.2008), http://www.usdoj.gov/ oig/reports/plus/a0816/final.pdf.

[5] *See* Social Security Admin., Office of Inspector General, Congressional Response Report: Accuracy of the Social Security Administration's Numident File, A-08-06-26100 (Dec.2006), http://www.ssa.gov/oig/ADOBEPDF/A-08-06-26100.pdf.

First, by restricting suppression to bookkeeping errors that are deliberate or reckless, the majority leaves Herring, and others like him, with no remedy for violations of their constitutional rights. *See supra,* at 700–701. There can be no serious assertion that relief is available under 42 U.S.C. § 1983. The arresting officer would be sheltered by qualified immunity, *see* Harlow v. Fitzgerald, 457 U.S. 800 (1982), and the police department itself is not liable for the negligent acts of its employees, *see* Monell v. New York City Dept. of Social Servs., 436 U.S. 658 (1978). Moreover, identifying the department employee who committed the error may be impossible.

Second, I doubt that police forces already possess sufficient incentives to maintain up-to-date records. The Government argues that police have no desire to send officers out on arrests unnecessarily, because arrests consume resources and place officers in danger. The facts of this case do not fit that description of police motivation. Here the officer wanted to arrest Herring and consulted the Department's records to legitimate his predisposition. *See* App. 17-19.[6]

Third, even when deliberate or reckless conduct is afoot, the Court's assurance will often be an empty promise: How is an impecunious defendant to make the required showing? If the answer is that a defendant is entitled to discovery (and if necessary, an audit of police databases), *See* Tr. of Oral Arg. 57–58, then the Court has imposed a considerable administrative burden on courts and law enforcement.[7]

V

Negligent recordkeeping errors by law enforcement threaten individual liberty, are susceptible to deterrence by the exclusionary rule, and cannot be remedied effectively through other means. Such errors present no occasion to further erode the exclusionary rule. The rule "is needed to make the Fourth Amendment something real; a guarantee that does not carry with it the exclusion of evidence obtained by its violation is a chimera." *Calandra,* 414 U.S., at 361 (Brennan, J., dissenting). In keeping with the rule's "core concerns," *ante,* at 702, suppression should have attended the unconstitutional search in this case.

* * *

For the reasons stated, I would reverse the judgment of the Eleventh Circuit.

■ JUSTICE BREYER, with whom JUSTICE SOUTER joins, dissenting.

---

[6] It has been asserted that police departments have become sufficiently "professional" that they do not need external deterrence to avoid Fourth Amendment violations. *See* Tr. of Oral Arg. 24–25; cf. Hudson v. Michigan, 547 U.S. 586, 598–599 (2006). But professionalism is a sign of the exclusionary rule's efficacy—not of its superfluity.

[7] It is not clear how the Court squares its focus on deliberate conduct with its recognition that application of the exclusionary rule does not require inquiry into the mental state of the police. *See ante,* at 703; Whren v. United States, 517 U.S. 806, 812–813 (1996).

I agree with Justice GINSBURG and join her dissent. I write separately to note one additional supporting factor that I believe important. In Arizona v. Evans, 514 U.S. 1 (1995), we held that recordkeeping errors made by a court clerk do not trigger the exclusionary rule, so long as the police reasonably relied upon the court clerk's recordkeeping. *Id.,* at 14; *id.,* at 16–17 (O'Connor, J., concurring). The rationale for our decision was premised on a distinction between judicial errors and police errors, and we gave several reasons for recognizing that distinction.

First, we noted that "the exclusionary rule was historically designed as a means of deterring *police* misconduct, not mistakes by court employees." *Id.,* at 14 (emphasis added). *Second,* we found "no evidence that court employees are inclined to ignore or subvert the Fourth Amendment or that lawlessness among these actors requires application of the extreme sanction of exclusion." *Id.,* at 14–15. *Third,* we recognized that there was "no basis for believing that application of the exclusionary rule . . . [would] have a significant effect on court employees responsible for informing the police that a warrant has been quashed. Because court clerks are not adjuncts to the law enforcement team engaged in the often competitive enterprise of ferreting out crime, they have no stake in the outcome of particular criminal prosecutions." *Id.,* at 15 (citation omitted). Taken together, these reasons explain why police recordkeeping errors should be treated differently than judicial ones.

Other cases applying the "good faith" exception to the exclusionary rule have similarly recognized the distinction between police errors and errors made by others, such as judicial officers or legislatures. *See* United States v. Leon, 468 U.S. 897 (1984) (police reasonably relied on magistrate's issuance of warrant); Massachusetts v. Sheppard, 468 U.S. 981 (1984) (same); Illinois v. Krull, 480 U.S. 340 (1987) (police reasonably relied on statute's constitutionality).

Distinguishing between police recordkeeping errors and judicial ones not only is consistent with our precedent, but also is far easier for courts to administer than THE CHIEF JUSTICE's case-by-case, multifactored inquiry into the degree of police culpability. I therefore would apply the exclusionary rule when police personnel are responsible for a recordkeeping error that results in a Fourth Amendment violation.

The need for a clear line, and the recognition of such a line in our precedent, are further reasons in support of the outcome that Justice GINSBURG's dissent would reach.

Davis v. United States
564 U.S. 229 (2011)

The Fourth Amendment protects the right to be free from "unreasonable searches and seizures," but it is silent about how this right is to be enforced. To supplement the bare text, this Court created the exclusionary rule, a deterrent sanction that bars the prosecution from introducing evidence obtained by way of a Fourth Amendment violation. The question here is whether to apply this sanction when the police conduct a search in compliance with binding precedent that is later overruled. Because suppression would do nothing to deter police misconduct in these circumstances, and because it would come at a high cost to both the truth and the public safety, we hold that searches conducted in objectively reasonable reliance on binding appellate precedent are not subject to the exclusionary rule.

I

The question presented arises in this case as a result of a shift in our Fourth Amendment jurisprudence on searches of automobiles incident to arrests of recent occupants.

A

.... In State v. Gant, 216 Ariz. 1, 162 P.3d 640 (2007), the Arizona Supreme Court considered an automobile search conducted after the vehicle's occupant had been arrested, handcuffed, and locked in a patrol car. The court distinguished *Belton* as a case in which "four unsecured" arrestees "presented an immediate risk of loss of evidence and an obvious threat to [a] lone officer's safety." 216 Ariz., at 4, 162 P.3d, at 643. The court held that where no such "exigencies exis[t]"—where the arrestee has been subdued and the scene secured—the rule of Belton does not apply. 216 Ariz., at 4, 162 P.3d, at 643.

This Court granted certiorari in *Gant, see* 552 U.S. 1230, (2008), and affirmed in a 5-to-4 decision. Arizona v. Gant, 556 U.S. 332 (2009). Four of the Justices in the majority agreed with the Arizona Supreme Court that *Belton*'s holding applies only where "the arrestee is unsecured and within reaching distance of the passenger compartment at the time of the search." 556 U.S., at 343. The four dissenting Justices, by contrast, understood Belton to have explicitly adopted the simple, bright-line rule stated in the *Belton* Court's opinion. 556 U.S., at 357–358 (opinion of ALITO, J.); s*ee Belton*, 453 U.S., at 460 ("[W]e hold that when a policeman has made a lawful custodial arrest of the occupant of an automobile, he may, as a contemporaneous incident of that arrest, search the passenger compartment of that automobile" (footnote omitted)). To limit *Belton* to cases involving unsecured arrestees, the dissenters thought, was to overrule the decision's clear holding. *Gant, supra,* at 357–358. Justice SCALIA, who provided the fifth vote to affirm in *Gant*, agreed with the dissenters' understanding of *Belton*'s holding. 556 U.S., at 351–352 (concurring opinion). Justice SCALIA favored a more explicit and complete overruling of *Belton*, but he joined what became the majority opinion to avoid "a 4-to-1-to-4" disposition. 556 U.S., at 354. As a result, the Court adopted a new, two-part rule under which an automobile search incident to a recent occupant's arrest is constitutional (1) if the arrestee is within reaching distance of the vehicle during the search, or (2) if the police have reason to believe that the vehicle contains "evidence relevant to the crime of arrest." *Id.*, at 343 (citing *Thornton, supra*, at 632 (SCALIA, J., concurring in judgment); internal quotation marks omitted).

B

The search at issue in this case took place a full two years before this Court announced its new rule in *Gant*. On an April evening in 2007, police officers in Greenville, Alabama, conducted a routine traffic stop that eventually resulted in the arrests of driver Stella Owens (for driving while intoxicated) and passenger Willie Davis (for giving a false name to police). The police handcuffed both Owens and Davis, and they placed the arrestees in the back of separate patrol cars. The police then searched the passenger compartment of Owens's vehicle and found a revolver inside Davis's jacket pocket.

Davis was indicted in the Middle District of Alabama on one count of possession of a firearm by a convicted felon. *See* 18 U.S.C. § 922(g)(1). In his motion to suppress the revolver, Davis acknowledged that the officers' search fully complied with "existing Eleventh Circuit precedent." App. 13–15. Like most courts, the Eleventh Circuit had long read *Belton* to establish a bright-line rule authorizing substantially contemporaneous vehicle searches incident to arrests of recent occupants. *See* United States v. Gonzalez, 71 F.3d 819, 822, 824–827 (C.A.11 1996) (upholding automobile search conducted after the defendant had been "pulled from the vehicle, handcuffed, laid on the ground, and placed under arrest"). Davis recognized that the District Court was obligated to follow this precedent, but he raised a Fourth Amendment challenge to preserve "the issue for review" on appeal. App. 15. The District Court denied the motion, and Davis was convicted on the firearms charge.

While Davis's appeal was pending, this Court decided *Gant*. The Eleventh Circuit, in the opinion below, applied *Gant*'s new rule and held that the vehicle search incident to Davis's arrest "violated [his] Fourth Amendment rights." 598 F.3d 1259, 1263 (CA11 2010). As for whether this constitutional violation warranted suppression, the Eleventh Circuit viewed that as a separate issue that turned on "the potential of exclusion to deter wrongful police conduct." *Id.*, at 1265 (quoting Herring v. United States, 555 U.S. 135, 137 (2009); internal quotation marks omitted). The court concluded that "penalizing the [arresting] officer" for following binding appellate precedent would do nothing to "dete[r] . . . Fourth Amendment violations." 598 F.3d, at 1265–1266 (bracketing and internal quotation marks omitted). It therefore declined to apply the exclusionary rule and affirmed Davis's conviction. We granted certiorari.

II

. . . . Real deterrent value is a "necessary condition for exclusion," but it is not "a sufficient" one. Hudson v. Michigan, 547 U.S. 586, 596 (2006). The analysis must also account for the "substantial social costs" generated by the rule. *Leon, supra,* at 907. Exclusion exacts a heavy toll on both the judicial system and society at large. *Stone,* 428 U.S., at 490–491. It almost always requires courts to ignore reliable, trustworthy evidence bearing on guilt or innocence. *Ibid.* And its bottom-line effect, in many cases, is to suppress the truth and set the criminal loose in the community without punishment. *See Herring, supra,* at 141. Our cases hold that society must swallow this bitter pill when necessary, but only as a "last resort." *Hudson, supra,* at 591. For exclusion to be appropriate, the deterrence benefits of suppression must outweigh its heavy costs. *See Herring, supra,* at 141; *Leon, supra,* at 910.

Admittedly, there was a time when our exclusionary-rule cases were not nearly so discriminating in their approach to the doctrine. "Expansive dicta" in several decisions, *see Hudson, supra,* at 591, suggested that the rule was a self-executing mandate implicit in the Fourth Amendment itself. *See* Olmstead v. United States, 277 U.S. 438, 462 (1928) (remarking on the "striking outcome of the *Weeks* case" that "the Fourth Amendment, although not referring to or limiting the use of evidence in courts, really forbade its introduction"); *Mapp, supra,* at 655 ("[A]ll evidence obtained by searches and seizures in violation of the Constitution is, by that same authority, inadmissible in a state court"). As late as our 1971 decision in Whiteley v. Warden, Wyo. State Penitentiary, 401 U.S. 560, 568–569, the Court "treated identification of a Fourth Amendment violation as synonymous with application of the exclusionary rule." Arizona v. Evans, 514 U.S. 1, 13 (1995). In time, however, we came to acknowledge the exclusionary rule for what it undoubtedly is—a "judicially created remedy" of this Court's own making. *Calandra, supra,* at 348. We abandoned the old, "reflexive" application of the doctrine, and imposed a more rigorous weighing of its costs and deterrence benefits. *Evans, supra,* at 13; *see, e.g., Calandra, supra; Janis, supra; Stone, supra*; INS v. Lopez-Mendoza, 468 U.S. 1032 (1984); United States v. Havens, 446 U.S. 620 (1980). In a line of cases beginning with United States v. Leon, 468 U.S. 897, we also recalibrated our cost-benefit analysis in exclusion cases to focus the inquiry on the "flagrancy of the police misconduct" at issue.

The basic insight of the *Leon* line of cases is that the deterrence benefits of exclusion "var[y] with the culpability of the law enforcement conduct" at issue. *Herring,* 555 U.S., at 143. When the police exhibit "deliberate," "reckless," or "grossly negligent" disregard for Fourth Amendment rights, the deterrent value of exclusion is strong and tends to outweigh the resulting costs. But when the police act with an objectively "reasonable good-faith belief" that their conduct is lawful, *Leon, supra,* at 909 (internal quotation marks omitted), or when their conduct involves only simple, "isolated" negligence, *Herring, supra,* at 137, the " 'deterrence rationale loses much of its force,' " and exclusion cannot "pay its way." *See Leon, supra,* at 919, 908, n.6, (quoting United States v. Peltier, 422 U.S. 531, 539 (1975)).

The Court has over time applied this "good-faith" exception across a range of cases. *Leon* itself, for example, held that the exclusionary rule does not apply when the police conduct a search in "objectively reasonable reliance" on a warrant later held invalid. The error in such a case rests with the issuing magistrate, not the police officer, and "punish[ing] the errors of judges" is not the office of the exclusionary rule. *Id.,* at 916; *see also* Massachusetts v. Sheppard, 468 U.S. 981, 990 (1984) (companion case declining to apply exclusionary rule where warrant held invalid as a result of judge's clerical error).

Other good-faith cases have sounded a similar theme. Illinois v. Krull, 480 U.S. 340 (1987), extended the good-faith exception to searches conducted in reasonable reliance on subsequently invalidated statutes. *Id.,* at 349–350 ("legislators, like judicial officers, are not the focus of the rule"). In *Arizona v. Evans, supra,* the Court applied the good-faith exception in a case where the police reasonably relied on erroneous information concerning an arrest warrant in a database maintained by judicial employees. *Id.,* at 14. Most recently, in Herring v. United States, 555 U.S. 135, we extended *Evans* in a case where police employees erred in maintaining records in a warrant database. "[I]solated," "nonrecurring" police negligence, we determined, lacks the culpability required to justify the harsh sanction of exclusion. 555 U.S., at 137, 144.

III

The question in this case is whether to apply the exclusionary rule when the police conduct a search in objectively reasonable reliance on binding judicial precedent. At the time of the search at issue here, we had not yet decided Arizona v. Gant, 556 U.S. 332, and the Eleventh Circuit had interpreted our decision in New York v. Belton, 453 U.S. 454, to establish a bright-line rule authorizing the search of a vehicle's passenger compartment incident to a recent occupant's arrest. *Gonzalez,* 71 F.3d, at 825. The search incident to Davis's arrest in this case followed the Eleventh Circuit's *Gonzalez* precedent to the letter. Although the search turned out to be unconstitutional under *Gant,* all agree that the officers' conduct was in strict compliance with then-binding Circuit law and was not culpable in any way. *See* Brief for Petitioner 49 ("suppression" in this case would "impl[y] no assignment of blame").

Under our exclusionary-rule precedents, this acknowledged absence of police culpability dooms Davis's claim. Police practices trigger the harsh sanction of exclusion only when they are deliberate enough to yield "meaningfu[l]" deterrence, and culpable enough to be "worth the price paid by the justice system." *Herring,* 555 U.S., at 144. The conduct of the officers here was neither of these things. The officers who conducted the search did not violate Davis's Fourth Amendment rights deliberately, recklessly, or with gross negligence. Nor does this case involve any "recurring or systemic negligence" on the part of law enforcement. The police acted in strict compliance with binding precedent, and their behavior was not wrongful. Unless the exclusionary rule is to become a strict-liability regime, it can have no application in this case.

Indeed, in 27 years of practice under *Leon*'s good-faith exception, we have "never applied" the exclusionary rule to suppress evidence obtained as a result of nonculpable, innocent police conduct. *Herring, supra,* at 144. If the police in this case had reasonably relied on a warrant in conducting their search, *see Leon, supra,* or on an erroneous warrant record in a government database, *Herring, supra,* the exclusionary rule would not apply. And if Congress or the Alabama Legislature had enacted a statute codifying the precise holding of the Eleventh Circuit's decision in *Gonzalez*[4], we would swiftly conclude that " '[p]enalizing the officer for the legislature's error . . . cannot logically contribute to the deterrence of Fourth Amendment violations.' " *See Krull,* 480 U.S., at 350. The same should be true of Davis's attempt here to " '[p]enaliz[e] the officer for the [appellate judges'] error.' "

About all that exclusion would deter in this case is conscientious police work. Responsible law-enforcement officers will take care to learn "what is required of them" under Fourth Amendment precedent and will conform their conduct to these rules. *Hudson,* 547 U.S., at 599. But by the same token, when binding appellate precedent specifically authorizes a particular police practice, well-trained officers will and should use that tool to fulfill their crime-detection and public-safety responsibilities. An officer who conducts a search in reliance on binding appellate precedent does no more than " 'ac[t] as a reasonable officer would and should act' " under the circumstances. *Leon,* 468 U.S., at 920 (quoting *Stone,* 428 U.S., at 539–540 (White, J., dissenting)). The deterrent effect of exclusion in such a case can only be to discourage the officer from " 'do[ing] his duty.' " 468 U.S., at 920.

That is not the kind of deterrence the exclusionary rule seeks to foster. We have stated before, and we reaffirm today, that the harsh sanction of exclusion "should not be applied to deter objectively reasonable law enforcement activity." *Id.,* at 919. Evidence obtained during a search conducted in reasonable reliance on binding precedent is not subject to the exclusionary rule.

IV

■ JUSTICE BREYER's dissent and Davis argue that, although the police conduct in this case was in no way culpable, other considerations

---

[4] Cf. Kan. Stat. Ann. § 22–2501(c) (2007) ("When a lawful arrest is effected a law enforcement officer may reasonably search the person arrested and the area within such person's immediate presence for the purpose of . . . [d]iscovering the fruits, instrumentalities, or evidence of a crime"). The Kansas Supreme Court recently struck this provision down in light of Arizona v. Gant, 556 U.S. 332 (2009). State v. Henning, 289 Kan. 136, 137, 209 P.3d 711, 714 (2009). But it has applied Illinois v. Krull, 480 U.S. 340 (1987), and the good-faith exception to searches conducted in reasonable reliance on the statute. *See* State v. Daniel, 291 Kan. 490, 497–504, 242 P.3d 1186, 1191–1195 (2010).

should prevent the good-faith exception from applying. We are not persuaded.

A

1

The principal argument of both the dissent and Davis is that the exclusionary rule's availability to enforce new Fourth Amendment precedent is a retroactivity issue, *see* Griffith v. Kentucky, 479 U.S. 314 (1987), not a good-faith issue. They contend that applying the good-faith exception where police have relied on overruled precedent effectively revives the discarded retroactivity regime of Linkletter v. Walker, 381 U.S. 618 (1965).

In *Linkletter*, we held that the retroactive effect of a new constitutional rule of criminal procedure should be determined on a case-by-case weighing of interests. For each new rule, *Linkletter* required courts to consider a three-factor balancing test that looked to the "purpose" of the new rule, "reliance" on the old rule by law enforcement and others, and the effect retroactivity would have "on the administration of justice." 381 U.S., at 636. After "weigh[ing] the merits and demerits in each case," courts decided whether and to what extent a new rule should be given retroactive effect. *Id.*, at 629. In *Linkletter* itself, the balance of interests prompted this Court to conclude that Mapp v. Ohio, 367 U.S. 643—which incorporated the exclusionary rule against the States—should not apply retroactively to cases already final on direct review. 381 U.S., at 639–640. The next year, we extended *Linkletter* to retroactivity determinations in cases on direct review. *See* Johnson v. New Jersey, 384 U.S. 719, 733 (1966) (holding that Miranda v. Arizona, 384 U.S. 436 (1966), and Escobedo v. Illinois, 378 U.S. 478 (1964), applied retroactively only to trials commenced after the decisions were released).

Over time, *Linkletter* proved difficult to apply in a consistent, coherent way. Individual applications of the standard "produced strikingly divergent results," *See* Danforth v. Minnesota, 552 U.S. 264, 273 (2008), that many saw as "incompatible" and "inconsistent." Desist v. United States, 394 U.S. 244, 258 (1969) (Harlan, J., dissenting). Justice Harlan in particular, who had endorsed the *Linkletter* standard early on, offered a strong critique in which he argued that "basic judicial" norms required full retroactive application of new rules to all cases still subject to direct review. 394 U.S., at 258–259; *see also* Mackey v. United States, 401 U.S. 667, 675–702 (1971) (Harlan, J., concurring in part and dissenting in part). Eventually, and after more than 20 years of toil under *Linkletter,* the Court adopted Justice Harlan's view and held that newly announced rules of constitutional criminal procedure must apply "retroactively to all cases, state or federal, pending on direct review or not yet final, with no exception." *Griffith, supra,* at 328.

2

The dissent and Davis argue that applying the good-faith exception in this case is "incompatible" with our retroactivity precedent under *Griffith.* We think this argument conflates what are two distinct doctrines.

Our retroactivity jurisprudence is concerned with whether, as a categorical matter, a new rule is available on direct review as a potential ground for relief. Retroactive application under *Griffith* lifts what would otherwise be a categorical bar to obtaining redress for the government's violation of a newly announced constitutional rule. *See Danforth, supra,* at 271, n.5 (noting that it may "make more sense to speak in terms of the 'redressability' of violations of new rules, rather than the 'retroactivity' of such new rules"). Retroactive application does not, however, determine what "appropriate remedy" (if any) the defendant should obtain. *See Powell v. Nevada,* 511 U.S. 79, 84 (1994) (noting that it "does not necessarily follow" from retroactive application of a new rule that the defendant will "gain . . . relief"). Remedy is a separate, analytically distinct issue. Cf. American Trucking Assns., Inc. v. Smith, 496 U.S. 167, 189 (1990) (plurality opinion) ("[T]he Court has never equated its retroactivity principles with remedial principles"). As a result, the retroactive application of a new rule of substantive Fourth Amendment law raises the question whether a suppression remedy applies; it does not answer that question. *See Leon,* 468 U.S., at 906 ("Whether the exclusionary sanction is appropriately imposed in a particular case . . . is 'an issue separate from the question whether the Fourth Amendment rights of the party seeking to invoke the rule were violated by police conduct' ").

When this Court announced its decision in *Gant,* Davis's conviction had not yet become final on direct review. *Gant* therefore applies retroactively to this case. Davis may invoke its newly announced rule of substantive Fourth Amendment law as a basis for seeking relief. *See Griffith, supra,* at 326, 328. The question, then, becomes one of remedy, and on that issue Davis seeks application of the exclusionary rule. But exclusion of evidence does not automatically follow from the fact that a Fourth Amendment violation occurred. *See Evans,* 514 U.S., at 13–14. The remedy is subject to exceptions and applies only where its "purpose is effectively advanced." *Krull,* 480 U.S., at 347.

The dissent and Davis recognize that at least some of the established exceptions to the exclusionary rule limit its availability in cases involving new Fourth Amendment rules. Suppression would thus be inappropriate, the dissent and Davis acknowledge, if the inevitable-discovery exception were applicable in this case. *See* Reply Brief for Petitioner 22 ("Doctrines such as inevitable discovery, independent source, attenuated basis, [and] standing . . . sharply limit the impact of newly-announced rules"). The good-faith exception, however, is no less an established limit on the remedy of exclusion than is inevitable discovery. Its application here neither contravenes *Griffith* nor denies retroactive effect to *Gant*.[5]

It is true that, under the old retroactivity regime of *Linkletter,* the Court's decisions on the "retroactivity problem in the context of the exclusionary rule" did take into account whether "law enforcement officers reasonably believed in good faith" that their conduct was in compliance with governing law. *Peltier,* 422 U.S., at 535–537. As a matter of retroactivity analysis, that approach is no longer applicable. *See Griffith,* 479 U.S. 314. It does not follow, however, that reliance on binding precedent is irrelevant in applying the good-faith exception to the exclusionary rule. When this Court adopted the good-faith exception in *Leon,* the Court's opinion explicitly relied on *Peltier* and imported its reasoning into the good-faith inquiry. *See* 468 U.S., at 918–919. That reasonable reliance by police was once a factor in our retroactivity cases does not make it any less relevant under our *Leon* line of cases.

B

Davis also contends that applying the good-faith exception to searches conducted in reliance on binding precedent will stunt the development of Fourth Amendment law. With no possibility of suppression, criminal defendants will have no incentive, Davis maintains, to request that courts overrule precedent.

1

This argument is difficult to reconcile with our modern understanding of the role of the exclusionary rule. We have never held that facilitating the overruling of precedent is a relevant consideration in an exclusionary-rule case. Rather, we have said time and again that the sole purpose of the exclusionary rule is to deter misconduct by law enforcement.

We have also repeatedly rejected efforts to expand the focus of the exclusionary rule beyond deterrence of culpable police conduct. In *Leon,* for example, we made clear that "the exclusionary rule is designed to deter police misconduct rather than to punish the errors of judges." 468 U.S., at 916; s*ee id.,* at 918 ("If exclusion of evidence obtained pursuant to a subsequently invalidated warrant is to have any deterrent effect . . . it must alter the behavior of individual law enforcement officers or the policies of their departments"). *Krull* too noted that "legislators, like

---

[5]   The dissent argues that the good-faith exception is "unlike . . . inevitable discovery" because the former applies in all cases where the police reasonably rely on binding precedent, while the latter "applies only upon occasion." Post, at 2437. We fail to see how this distinction makes any difference. The same could be said—indeed, the same was said—of searches conducted in reasonable reliance on statutes. *See Krull,* 480 U.S., at 368–369 (O'Connor, J., dissenting) (arguing that result in *Krull* was inconsistent with Griffith). When this Court strikes down a statute on Fourth Amendment grounds, the good-faith exception may prevent the exclusionary rule from applying "in every case pending when [the statute] is overturned." This result does not make the Court's newly announced rule of Fourth Amendment law any less retroactive. It simply limits the applicability of a suppression remedy. *See Krull, supra,* at 354–355, n.11.

judicial officers, are not the focus" of the exclusionary rule. 480 U.S., at 350. And in *Evans,* we said that the exclusionary rule was aimed at deterring "police misconduct, not mistakes by court employees." 514 U.S., at 14. These cases do not suggest that the exclusionary rule should be modified to serve a purpose other than deterrence of culpable law-enforcement conduct.

2

And in any event, applying the good-faith exception in this context will not prevent judicial reconsideration of prior Fourth Amendment precedents. In most instances, as in this case, the precedent sought to be challenged will be a decision of a Federal Court of Appeals or State Supreme Court. But a good-faith exception for objectively reasonable reliance on binding precedent will not prevent review and correction of such decisions. This Court reviews criminal convictions from 12 Federal Courts of Appeals, 50 state courts of last resort, and the District of Columbia Court of Appeals. If one or even many of these courts uphold a particular type of search or seizure, defendants in jurisdictions in which the question remains open will still have an undiminished incentive to litigate the issue. This Court can then grant certiorari, and the development of Fourth Amendment law will in no way be stunted.[8]

Davis argues that Fourth Amendment precedents of this Court will be effectively insulated from challenge under a good-faith exception for reliance on appellate precedent. But this argument is overblown. For one thing, it is important to keep in mind that this argument applies to an exceedingly small set of cases. Decisions overruling this Court's Fourth Amendment precedents are rare. Indeed, it has been more than 40 years since the Court last handed down a decision of the type to which Davis refers. Chimel v. California, 395 U.S. 752 (overruling United States v. Rabinowitz, 339 U.S. 56 (1950), and Harris v. United States, 331 U.S. 145 (1947)). And even in those cases, Davis points out that no fewer than eight separate doctrines may preclude a defendant who successfully challenges an existing precedent from getting any relief. Brief for Petitioner 50. Moreover, as a practical matter, defense counsel in many cases will test this Court's Fourth Amendment precedents in the same way that *Belton* was tested in *Gant*—by arguing that the precedent is distinguishable. *See* Brief for Respondent in Arizona v. Gant, O.T.2008, No. 07–542, pp. 22–29.[9]

---

[8] The dissent does not dispute this point, but it claims that the good-faith exception will prevent us from "rely[ing] upon lower courts to work out Fourth Amendment differences among themselves." Post, at 2438. If that is correct, then today's holding may well lead to more circuit splits in Fourth Amendment cases and a fuller docket of Fourth Amendment cases in this Court. *See* this Court's Rule 10. Such a state of affairs is unlikely to result in ossification of Fourth Amendment doctrine.

[9] Where the search at issue is conducted in accordance with a municipal "policy" or "custom," Fourth Amendment precedents may also be challenged, without the obstacle of the good-faith exception or qualified immunity, in civil suits against municipalities. *See* 42 U.S.C. § 1983; Los Angeles County v. Humphries, 562 U.S. 29, (2010) (citing Monell v. New York City Dept. of Social Servs., 436 U.S. 658, 690–691 (1978)).

At most, Davis's argument might suggest that—to prevent Fourth Amendment law from becoming ossified—the petitioner in a case that results in the overruling of one of this Court's Fourth Amendment precedents should be given the benefit of the victory by permitting the suppression of evidence in that one case. Such a result would undoubtedly be a windfall to this one random litigant. But the exclusionary rule is "not a personal constitutional right." *Stone,* 428 U.S., at 486. It is a "judicially created" sanction, *Calandra,* 414 U.S., at 348, specifically designed as a "windfall" remedy to deter future Fourth Amendment violations. *See Stone, supra,* at 490. The good-faith exception is a judicially created exception to this judicially created rule. Therefore, in a future case, we could, if necessary, recognize a limited exception to the good-faith exception for a defendant who obtains a judgment over-ruling one of our Fourth Amendment precedents. *Cf.* Friendly, *The Bill of Rights as a Code of Criminal Procedure,* 53 Cal. L.Rev. 929, 952–953 (1965) ("[T]he same authority that empowered the Court to supplement the amendment by the exclusionary rule a hundred and twenty-five years after its adoption, likewise allows it to modify that rule as the lessons of experience may teach" (internal quotation marks and footnotes omitted)).[10]

But this is not such a case. Davis did not secure a decision overturning a Supreme Court precedent; the police in his case reasonably relied on binding Circuit precedent. *See United States v. Gonzalez,* 71 F.3d 819. That sort of blameless police conduct, we hold, comes within the good-faith exception and is not properly subject to the exclusionary rule.

* * *

It is one thing for the criminal "to go free because the constable has blundered." People v. Defore, 242 N.Y. 13, 21, 150 N.E. 585, 587 (1926) (Cardozo, J.). It is quite another to set the criminal free because the constable has scrupulously adhered to governing law. Excluding evidence in such cases deters no police misconduct and imposes substantial social costs. We therefore hold that when the police conduct a search in objectively reasonable reliance on binding appellate precedent, the

---

[10] Davis contends that a criminal defendant will lack Article III standing to challenge an existing Fourth Amendment precedent if the good-faith exception to the exclusionary rule precludes the defendant from obtaining relief based on police conduct that conformed to that precedent. This argument confuses weakness on the merits with absence of Article III standing. *See* ASARCO Inc. v. Kadish, 490 U.S. 605, 624 (1989) (standing does not " 'depen[d] on the merits of [a claim]' "). And as a practical matter, the argument is also overstated. In many instances, as in *Gant,* see 556 U.S., at ___, defendants will not simply concede that the police conduct conformed to the precedent; they will argue instead that the police conduct did not fall within the scope of the precedent.

In any event, even if some criminal defendants will be unable to challenge some precedents for the reason that Davis suggests, that provides no good reason for refusing to apply the good-faith exception. As noted, the exclusionary rule is not a personal right, *see Stone,* 428 U.S., at 486, 490, and therefore the rights of these defendants will not be impaired. And because (at least in almost all instances) the precedent can be challenged by others, Fourth Amendment case law will not be insulated from reconsideration.

exclusionary rule does not apply. The judgment of the Court of Appeals for the Eleventh Circuit is

Affirmed.

■ JUSTICE SOTOMAYOR, concurring in the judgment.

. . . . whether exclusion would result in appreciable deterrence in the circumstances of this case is a different question from whether exclusion would appreciably deter Fourth Amendment violations when the governing law is unsettled. The Court's answer to the former question in this case thus does not resolve the latter one.

■ JUSTICE BREYER, with whom JUSTICE GINSBURG joins, dissenting.

In 2009, in Arizona v. Gant, 556 U.S. 332, this Court held that a police search of an automobile without a warrant violates the Fourth Amendment if the police have previously removed the automobile's occupants and placed them securely in a squad car. The present case involves these same circumstances, and it was pending on appeal when this Court decided Gant. Because *Gant* represents a "shift" in the Court's Fourth Amendment jurisprudence, we must decide whether and how *Gant's* new rule applies here.

I

I agree with the Court about whether *Gant's* new rule applies. It does apply. . . . . After 22 years of struggling with its *Linkletter* approach, . . . the Court decided in *Griffith* that *Linkletter* had proved unfair and unworkable. It then substituted a clearer approach, stating that "a new rule for the conduct of criminal prosecutions is to be applied retroactively to all cases, state or federal, pending on direct review or not yet final, with no exception for cases in which the new rule constitutes a 'clear break' with the past." 479 U.S., at 328. The Court today, following *Griffith,* concludes that *Gant's* new rule applies here. And to that extent I agree with its decision.

II

The Court goes on, however, to decide how *Gant's* new rule will apply. And here it adds a fatal twist. While conceding that, like the search in *Gant*, this search violated the Fourth Amendment, it holds that, unlike Gant, this defendant is not entitled to a remedy. That is because the Court finds a new "good faith" exception which prevents application of the normal remedy for a Fourth Amendment violation, namely, suppression of the illegally seized evidence. Weeks v. United States, 232 U.S. 383 (1914); Mapp v. Ohio, 367 U.S. 643 (1961). Leaving Davis with a right but not a remedy, the Court "keep[s] the word of promise to our ear" but "break[s] it to our hope."

A

At this point I can no longer agree with the Court. A new "good faith" exception and this Court's retroactivity decisions are incompatible. For one thing, the Court's distinction between (1) retroactive application of a new rule and (2) availability of a remedy is highly artificial and runs counter to precedent. To determine that a new rule is retroactive is to determine that, at least in the normal case, there is a remedy. As we have previously said, the "source of a 'new rule' is the Constitution itself, not any judicial power to create new rules of law"; hence, "[w]hat we are actually determining when we assess the 'retroactivity' of a new rule is not the temporal scope of a newly announced right, but whether a violation of the right that occurred prior to the announcement of the new rule will entitle a criminal defendant to the relief sought." Danforth v. Minnesota, 552 U.S. 264, 271 (2008). The Court's "good faith" exception (unlike, say, inevitable discovery, a remedial doctrine that applies only upon occasion) creates "a categorical bar to obtaining redress" in every case pending when a precedent is overturned.

For another thing, the Court's holding re-creates the very problems that led the Court to abandon *Linkletter*'s approach to retroactivity in favor of *Griffith*'s. One such problem concerns workability. The Court says that its exception applies where there is "objectively reasonable" police "reliance on binding appellate precedent." But to apply the term "binding appellate precedent" often requires resolution of complex questions of degree. Davis conceded that he faced binding anti-*Gant* precedent in the Eleventh Circuit. But future litigants will be less forthcoming. Indeed, those litigants will now have to create distinctions to show that previous Circuit precedent was not "binding" lest they find relief foreclosed even if they win their constitutional claim.

At the same time, Fourth Amendment precedents frequently require courts to "slosh" their "way through the factbound morass of 'reasonableness.'" Scott v. Harris, 550 U.S. 372, 383 (2007). Suppose an officer's conduct is consistent with the language of a Fourth Amendment rule that a court of appeals announced in a case with clearly distinguishable facts? Suppose the case creating the relevant precedent did not directly announce any general rule but involved highly analogous facts? What about a rule that all other jurisdictions, but not the defendant's jurisdiction, had previously accepted? What rules can be developed for determining when, where, and how these different kinds of precedents do, or do not, count as relevant "binding precedent"? The *Linkletter*-like result is likely complex legal argument and police force confusion. *See* Williams v. United States, 401 U.S. 646, 656 (1971) (opinion of Harlan, J.) (describing trying to follow *Linkletter* decisions as "almost as difficult" as trying to follow "the tracks made by a beast of prey in search of its intended victim").

Another such problem concerns fairness. Today's holding, like that in *Linkletter*, "violates basic norms of constitutional adjudication." *Griffith, supra,* at 322. It treats the defendant in a case announcing a new rule one way while treating similarly situated defendants whose cases are pending on appeal in a different way. Justice Harlan explained why this approach is wrong when he said:

"We cannot release criminals from jail merely because we think one case is a particularly appropriate one [to announce a constitutional doctrine] . . . . Simply fishing one case from the stream of appellate review, using it as a vehicle for pronouncing new constitutional standards, and then permitting a stream of similar cases subsequently to flow by unaffected by that new rule constitute an indefensible departure from [our ordinary] model of judicial review." *Williams, supra,* at 679.

And in *Griffith,* the Court "embraced to a significant extent the comprehensive analysis presented by Justice Harlan." 479 U.S., at 322.

Of course, the Court may, as it suggests, avoid this unfairness by refusing to apply the exclusionary rule even to the defendant in the very case in which it announces a "new rule." But that approach would make matters worse. What would then happen in the lower courts? How would courts of appeals, for example, come to reconsider their prior decisions when other circuits' cases lead them to believe those decisions may be wrong? Why would a defendant seek to overturn any such decision? After all, if the (incorrect) circuit precedent is clear, then even if the defendant wins (on the constitutional question), he loses (on relief). *See* Stovall v. Denno, 388 U.S. 293, 301 (1967). To what extent then could this Court rely upon lower courts to work out Fourth Amendment differences among themselves—through circuit reconsideration of a precedent that other circuits have criticized? *See* Arizona v. Evans, 514 U.S. 1, 23, n.1 (1995) (GINSBURG, J., dissenting).

B

Perhaps more important, the Court's rationale for creating its new "good faith" exception threatens to undermine well-settled Fourth Amendment law. The Court correctly says that pre-Gant Eleventh Circuit precedent had held that a *Gant*-type search was constitutional; hence the police conduct in this case, consistent with that precedent, was "innocent." But the Court then finds this fact sufficient to create a new "good faith" exception to the exclusionary rule. It reasons that the "sole purpose" of the exclusionary rule "is to deter future Fourth Amendment violations," (internal quotation marks and brackets omitted). Those benefits are sufficient to justify exclusion where "police exhibit deliberate, reckless, or grossly negligent disregard for Fourth Amendment rights," *ibid.* (internal quotation marks omitted). But those benefits do not justify exclusion where, as here, the police act with "simple, isolated negligence" or an "objectively reasonable good-faith belief that their conduct is lawful," *ibid.* (internal quotation marks omitted).

If the Court means what it says, what will happen to the exclusionary rule, a rule that the Court adopted nearly a century ago for federal courts, Weeks v. United States, 232 U.S. 383, and made applicable to state courts a half century ago through the Fourteenth Amendment, Mapp v. Ohio, 367 U.S. 643? The Court has thought of that rule not as punishment for the individual officer or as reparation for the individual defendant but more generally as an effective way to secure enforcement of the Fourth Amendment's commands. *Weeks, supra,* at 393 (without the exclusionary rule, the Fourth Amendment would be "of no value," and "might as well be stricken from the Constitution"). This Court has deviated from the "suppression" norm in the name of "good faith" only a handful of times and in limited, atypical circumstances: where a magistrate has erroneously issued a warrant, United States v. Leon, 468 U.S. 897 (1984); where a database has erroneously informed police that they have a warrant, Arizona v. Evans, 514 U.S. 1 (1995), Herring v. United States, 555 U.S. 135 (2009); and where an unconstitutional statute purported to authorize the search, Illinois v. Krull, 480 U.S. 340 (1987). *See Herring, supra,* at 142 ("good faith" exception inaptly named).

The fact that such exceptions are few and far between is understandable. Defendants frequently move to suppress evidence on Fourth Amendment grounds. In many, perhaps most, of these instances the police, uncertain of how the Fourth Amendment applied to the particular factual circumstances they faced, will have acted in objective good faith. Yet, in a significant percentage of these instances, courts will find that the police were wrong. And, unless the police conduct falls into one of the exceptions previously noted, courts have required the suppression of the evidence seized. 1 W. LaFave, Search and Seizure § 1.3, pp. 103–104 (4th ed.2004) ("good faith" exception has not yet been applied to warrantless searches and seizures beyond the "rather special situations" of *Evans, Herring,* and *Krull*). See Valdes, *Frequency and Success: An Empirical Study of Criminal Law Defenses, Federal Constitutional Evidentiary Claims, and Plea Negotiations,* 153 U. Pa. L.Rev. 1709, 1728 (2005) (suppression motions are filed in approximately 7% of criminal cases; approximately 12% of suppression motions are successful); LaFave, *supra,* at 64 ("Surely many more Fourth Amendment violations result from carelessness than from intentional constitutional violations"); Stewart, *The Road* to Mapp v. Ohio *and Beyond: The Origins, Development and Future of the Exclusionary Rule in Search-and-Seizure Cases,* 83 Colum. L.Rev. 1365, 1389 (1983) ("[T]he vast majority of fourth amendment violations . . . [are] motivated by commendable zeal, not condemnable malice").

But an officer who conducts a search that he believes complies with the Constitution but which, it ultimately turns out, falls just outside the Fourth Amendment's bounds is no more culpable than an officer who follows erroneous "binding precedent." Nor is an officer more culpable where circuit precedent is simply suggestive rather than "binding," where it only describes how to treat roughly analogous instances, or where it just does not exist. Thus, if the Court means what it now says, if it would place determinative weight upon the culpability of an individual officer's conduct, and if it would apply the exclusionary rule only where a Fourth Amendment violation was "deliberate, reckless, or grossly negligent," then the "good faith" exception will swallow the exclusionary rule. Indeed, our broad dicta in *Herring*—dicta the Court repeats and expands upon today—may already be leading lower courts in this direction. *See* United States v. Julius, 610 F.3d 60, 66–67 (C.A.2 2010) (assuming warrantless search was unconstitutional and remanding for District Court to "perform the cost/benefit analysis required by *Herring*" and to consider "whether the degree of police culpability in this case rose beyond mere . . . negligence" before ordering suppression); United States v. Master, 614 F.3d 236, 243 (C.A.6 2010) ("[T]he *Herring* Court's emphasis seems weighed more toward preserving evidence for use in obtaining convictions, even if illegally seized . . . unless the officers engage in 'deliberate, reckless, or grossly negligent conduct'" (quoting Herring, *supra*, at 144)). Today's decision will doubtless accelerate this trend.

Any such change (which may already be underway) would affect not "an exceedingly small set of cases," but a very large number of cases, potentially many thousands each year. *See* Valdes, *supra*, at 1728. And since the exclusionary rule is often the only sanction available for a Fourth Amendment violation, the Fourth Amendment would no longer protect ordinary Americans from "unreasonable searches and seizures." *See* Wolf v. Colorado, 338 U.S. 25, 41 (1949) (Murphy, J., dissenting) (overruled by Mapp v. Ohio, 367 U.S. 643, (1961)) (In many circumstances, "there is but one alternative to the rule of exclusion. That is no sanction at all"); *Herring, supra,* at 152 (GINSBURG, J., dissenting) (the exclusionary rule is "an essential auxiliary" to the Fourth Amendment). It would become a watered-down Fourth Amendment, offering its protection against only those searches and seizures that are egregiously unreasonable.

III

In sum, I fear that the Court's opinion will undermine the exclusionary rule. And I believe that the Court wrongly departs from *Griffith* regardless. Instead I would follow *Griffith,* apply *Gant's* rule retroactively to this case, and require suppression of the evidence. Such an approach is consistent with our precedent, and it would indeed affect no more than "an exceedingly small set of cases."

For these reasons, with respect, I dissent.

f. COMPARATIVE NOTE—THE EXCLUSIONARY RULE IN CANADA

All free societies strike some sort of balance between liberty and security. While comparisons across systems—even those like the U.S. and the Canadian that share many common features—must be made carefully, much can be learned by considering how different systems deal with regulating the police. Countless comparisons are possible. An entire course might be devoted to Comparative Criminal Procedure. As one of many possible illustrations, consider Canada's approach to the exclusionary rule.

Constitution Act, 1982, Part I (Canadian Charter of Rights and Liberties)

8. Everyone has the right to be secure against unreasonable search or seizure.

9. Everyone has the right not to be arbitrarily detained or imprisoned. . . .

24. (1) Anyone whose rights or freedoms, as guaranteed by this Charter, have been infringed or denied may apply to a court of competent jurisdiction to obtain such remedy as the court considers appropriate and just in the circumstances.

(2) Where, in proceedings under subsection (1), a court concludes that evidence was obtained in a manner that infringed or denied any rights or freedoms guaranteed by this Charter, the evidence shall be excluded if it is established that, having regard to all the circumstances, the admission of it in the proceedings would bring the administration of justice into disrepute.

The Queen v. Grant
2009 SCC 32 (Supreme Court of Canada)

■ McLACHLIN C.J.C., CHARRON J. (LeBEL, FISH, ABELLA JJ. concurring): The threshold question in this case was whether the accused was detained before he produced the firearm and was arrested. While the accused may not have been physically detained, psychological constraint amounting to detention had been recognized. The officer's preliminary questioning was a legitimate exercise of police powers. Once the encounter changed from ascertaining the accused's identity to determining whether he "had anything he shouldn't", it took on the character of an interrogation and became inherently intimidating. The evidence supported the accused's contention that a reasonable person in his position would conclude that his right to choose how to act had been removed by the police, therefore the accused was detained. The officers agreed at trial that they did not have legal grounds or reasonable suspicion to detain the accused, therefore the detention was arbitrary and in breach of s. 9 of the Charter, as was his s. 10(b) right to counsel. Since the firearm was discovered as a result of statements taken in breach of the Charter, it was derivative evidence. The court was then required to consider whether the evidence was to be excluded under s. 24(2) of the Charter.

The role of the court in considering a s. 24(2) application was to balance three lines of inquiry to determine whether the admission of the evidence would bring the administration of justice into disrepute. While the previous framework had brought a measure of certainty to the s. 24(2) inquiry, the general rule of inadmissibility of all non-discoverable conscriptive evidence was not consistent with the requirement that the court consider "all the circumstances" in determining admissibility. A review of the previous framework led to the conclusion that clarification was required of the criteria relevant to determining when in "all the circumstances", admission of evidence obtained by a Charter breach would bring the administration of justice into disrepute.

Under the revised approach to s. 24(2), the first consideration in whether to exclude evidence was the seriousness of the conduct which led to the discovery of the evidence. The more severe or deliberate the conduct that led to the Charter violation, the more likely the court should be to exclude the evidence to maintain public confidence in the rule of law. This inquiry requires an evaluation of the seriousness of the state conduct that led to the breach. In this case, while the police were in error in detaining the accused, the mistake was understandable, was not done in bad faith, and was neither deliberate nor egregious, therefore the effect of admitting the evidence would not greatly undermine public confidence in the rule of law.

The second consideration was whether the admission of the evidence would bring the administration of justice into disrepute from the perspective of society's interest in respect for Charter rights. The more serious the impact on the accused's interests, the greater the risk that the admission of the evidence could breed public cynicism and bring the administration of justice into disrepute. In this case, the initial Charter violation was arbitrary detention under s. 9, and the second violation was a breach of the accused's s. 10(b) right to counsel. While the impact of the initial breach was not severe, it was more than minimal since it deprived the accused of his freedom to make an informed choice as to how to respond to the police. Furthermore, since discoverability remained a factor in assessing the impact of the breaches on the accused's Charter rights, the fact that the evidence was non-discoverable aggravated the impact of the breach on the accused's interest in being able to make an informed decision on speaking with the police without having the opportunity to seek legal advice. The impact of the infringement of the accused's rights under ss. 9 and 10(b) of the Charter was significant.

The third and final consideration was the effect of admitting the evidence on the public interest in having the case adjudicated on its merits. This required a consideration of the reliability of the evidence and its importance to the proper adjudication of the case. In this case, the gun was highly reliable evidence and was essential to a determination on the merits. Since the officers were operating in circumstances of legal uncertainty, this tipped the balance in favour of admission of the evidence.

On the issue of whether the accused "transferred" the firearm as defined in s. 84 of the Code, it was determined that Parliament did not intend s. 100(1) of the Code to address the simple movement of a firearm from one place to another. While the accused's offence was serious and potentially very dangerous, on the evidence, he did not commit the crime of trafficking, and the appeal on this ground was allowed and an acquittal entered.

7. INSTITUTIONAL REFORM LITIGATION

City of Los Angeles v. Lyons

461 U.S. 95 (1983)

■ JUSTICE WHITE delivered the opinion of the Court.

The issue here is whether respondent Lyons satisfied the prerequisites for seeking injunctive relief in the federal district court.

I

This case began on February 7, 1977, when respondent, Adolph Lyons, filed a complaint for damages, injunction, and declaratory relief in the United States District Court for the Central District of California. The defendants were the City of Los Angeles and four of its police officers. The complaint alleged that on October 6, 1976, at 2 a.m., Lyons was stopped by the defendant officers for a traffic or vehicle code violation and that although Lyons offered no resistance or threat whatsoever, the officers, without provocation or justification, seized Lyons and applied a "chokehold"[1]—either the "bar arm control" hold or the "carotid-artery control" hold or both—rendering him unconscious and causing damage to his larynx. Counts I through IV of the complaint sought damages against the officers and the City. Count V, with which we are principally concerned here, sought a preliminary and permanent injunction against the City barring the use of the control holds. That count alleged that the city's police officers, "pursuant to the authorization, instruction and encouragement of defendant City of Los Angeles, regularly and routinely apply these choke holds in innumerable situations where they are not threatened by the use of any deadly force whatsoever," that numerous persons have been injured as the result of the application of the chokeholds, that Lyons and others similarly situated are threatened with irreparable injury in the form of bodily injury and loss of life, and that Lyons "justifiably fears that any contact he has with Los Angeles police officers may result in his being choked and strangled to death without

---

[1] The police control procedures at issue in this case are referred to as "control holds," "chokeholds," "strangleholds," and "neck restraints." All these terms refer to two basic control procedures: the "carotid" hold and the "bar arm" hold. In the "carotid" hold, an officer positioned behind a subject places one arm around the subject's neck and holds the wrist of that arm with his other hand. The officer, by using his lower forearm and bicep muscle, applies pressure concentrating on the carotid arteries located on the sides of the subject's neck. The "carotid" hold is capable of rendering the subject unconscious by diminishing the flow of oxygenated blood to the brain. The "bar arm" hold, which is administered similarly, applies pressure at the front of the subject's neck. "Bar arm" pressure causes pain, reduces the flow of oxygen to the lungs, and may render the subject unconscious.

provocation, justification or other legal excuse." Lyons alleged the threatened impairment of rights protected by the First, Fourth, Eighth and Fourteenth Amendments. Injunctive relief was sought against the use of the control holds "except in situations where the proposed victim of said control reasonably appears to be threatening the immediate use of deadly force." Count VI sought declaratory relief against the City, *i.e.,* a judgment that use of the chokeholds absent the threat of immediate use of deadly force is a *per se* violation of various constitutional rights.

The District Court, by order, granted the City's motion for partial judgment on the pleadings and entered judgment for the City on Count V and VI. The Court of Appeals reversed the judgment for the City on Count V and VI, holding over the City's objection that despite our decisions in O'Shea v. Littleton, 414 U.S. 488 (1974), and Rizzo v. Goode, 423 U.S. 362 (1976), Lyons had standing to seek relief against the application of the chokeholds. 615 F.2d 1243. The Court of Appeals held that there was a sufficient likelihood that Lyons would again be stopped and subjected to the unlawful use of force to constitute a case or controversy and to warrant the issuance of an injunction, if the injunction was otherwise authorized. We denied certiorari. 449 U.S. 934.

On remand, Lyons applied for a preliminary injunction. Lyons pressed only the Count V claim at this point. *See* n.6, *infra.* The motion was heard on affidavits, depositions and government records. The District Court found that Lyons had been stopped for a traffic infringement and that without provocation or legal justification the officers involved had applied a "department-authorized chokehold which resulted in injuries to the plaintiff." The court further found that the department authorizes the use of the holds in situations where no one is threatened by death or grievous bodily harm, that officers are insufficiently trained, that the use of the holds involves a high risk of injury or death as then employed, and that their continued use in situations where neither death nor serious bodily injury is threatened "is unconscionable in a civilized society." The court concluded that such use violated Lyons' substantive due process rights under the Fourteenth Amendment. A preliminary injunction was entered enjoining "the use of both the carotid-artery and bar arm holds under circumstances which do not threaten death or serious bodily injury." An improved training program and regular reporting and record keeping were also ordered.[3] The Court of Appeals affirmed in a brief *per curiam* opinion stating that the District Court had not abused its discretion in entering a preliminary injunction. 656 F.2d 417 (1981). We granted certiorari, 455 U.S. 937 (1982), and now reverse.

---

[3]   By its terms, the injunction was to continue in force until the court approved the training program to be presented to it. It is fair to assume that such approval would not be given if the program did not confine the use of the strangleholds to those situations in which their use, in the view of the District Court, would be constitutional. Because of successive stays entered by the Court of Appeals and by this Court, the injunction has not gone into effect.

II

Since our grant of certiorari, circumstances pertinent to the case have changed. Originally, Lyons' complaint alleged that at least two deaths had occurred as a result of the application of chokeholds by the police. His first amended complaint alleged that 10 chokehold-related deaths had occurred. By May, 1982, there had been five more such deaths. On May 6, 1982, the Chief of Police in Los Angeles prohibited the use of the bar-arm chokehold in any circumstances. A few days later, on May 12, 1982, the Board of Police Commissioners imposed a six-month moratorium on the use of the carotid-artery chokehold except under circumstances where deadly force is authorized.

Based on these events, on June 3, 1982, the City filed in this Court a Memorandum Suggesting a Question of Mootness, reciting the facts but arguing that the case was not moot. Lyons in turn filed a motion to dismiss the writ of certiorari as improvidently granted. We denied that motion but reserved the question of mootness for later consideration.

In his brief and at oral argument, Lyons has reasserted his position that in light of changed conditions, an injunctive decree is now unnecessary because he is no longer subject to a threat of injury. He urges that the preliminary injunction should be vacated. The City, on the other hand, while acknowledging that subsequent events have significantly changed the posture of this case, again asserts that the case is not moot because the moratorium is not permanent and may be lifted at any time.

We agree with the City that the case is not moot, since the moratorium by its terms is not permanent. Intervening events have not "irrevocably eradicated the effects of the alleged violation." *County of Los Angeles v. Davis,* 440 U.S. 625, 631642 (1979). We nevertheless hold, for another reason, that the federal courts are without jurisdiction to entertain Lyons' claim for injunctive relief.

III

It goes without saying that those who seek to invoke the jurisdiction of the federal courts must satisfy the threshhold requirement imposed by Article III of the Constitution by alleging an actual case or controversy. Plaintiffs must demonstrate a "personal stake in the outcome" in order to "assure that concrete adverseness which sharpens the presentation of issues" necessary for the proper resolution of constitutional questions. *Baker v. Carr,* 369 U.S. 186, 204 (1962). Abstract injury is not enough. The plaintiff must show that he "has sustained or is immediately in danger of sustaining some direct injury" as the result of the challenged official conduct and the injury or threat of injury must be both "real and immediate," not "conjectural" or "hypothetical."

In O'Shea v. Littleton, 414 U.S. 488 (1974), we dealt with a case brought by a class of plaintiffs claiming that they had been subjected to discriminatory enforcement of the criminal law. Among other things, a county magistrate and judge were accused of discriminatory conduct in various respects, such as sentencing members of plaintiff's class more harshly than other defendants. The Court of Appeals reversed the dismissal of the suit by the District Court, ruling that if the allegations were proved, an appropriate injunction could be entered.

We reversed for failure of the complaint to allege a case or controversy. 414 U.S., at 493. Although it was claimed in that case that particular members of the plaintiff class had actually suffered from the alleged unconstitutional practices, we observed that "[p]ast exposure to illegal conduct does not in itself show a present case or controversy regarding injunctive relief . . . if unaccompanied by any continuing, present adverse effects." *Id.*, at 495–496. Past wrongs were evidence bearing on "whether there is a real and immediate threat of repeated injury." *Id.*, at 496. But the prospect of future injury rested "on the likelihood that [plaintiffs] will again be arrested for and charged with violations of the criminal law and will again be subjected to bond proceedings, trial, or sentencing before petitioners." *Ibid.* The most that could be said for plaintiffs' standing was "that *if* [plaintiffs] proceed to violate an unchallenged law and *if* they are charged, held to answer, and tried in any proceedings before petitioners, they will be subjected to the discriminatory practices that petitioners are alleged to have followed." *Id.*, at 497. We could not find a case or controversy in those circumstances: the threat to the plaintiffs was not "sufficiently real and immediate to show an existing controversy simply because they anticipate violating lawful criminal statutes and being tried for their offenses. . . ." *Id.*, at 496. It was to be assumed "that [plaintiffs] will conduct their activities within the law and so avoid prosecution and conviction as well as exposure to the challenged course of conduct said to be followed by petitioners." *Id.*, at 497.

We further observed that case or controversy considerations "obviously shade into those determining whether the complaint states a sound basis for equitable relief," 414 U.S., at 499, and went on to hold that even if the complaint presented an existing case or controversy, an adequate basis for equitable relief against petitioners had not been demonstrated:

> "[Plaintiffs] have failed, moreover, to establish the basic requisites of the issuance of equitable relief in these circumstances—the likelihood of substantial and immediate irreparable injury, and the inadequacy of remedies at law. We have already canvassed the necessarily conjectural nature of the threatened injury to which [plaintiffs] are allegedly subjected. And if any of the [plaintiffs] are ever prosecuted and face trial, or if they are illegally sentenced, there are available state and federal procedures which could provide relief from the wrongful conduct alleged." 414 U.S., at 502.

Another relevant decision for present purposes is Rizzo v. Goode, 423 U.S. 362 (1976), a case in which plaintiffs alleged widespread illegal and unconstitutional police conduct aimed at minority citizens and against City residents in general. The Court reiterated the holding in *O'Shea* that past wrongs do not in themselves amount to that real and immediate threat of injury necessary to make out a case or controversy. The claim of injury rested upon "what one or a small, unnamed minority of policemen might do to them in the future because of that unknown policeman's perception" of departmental procedures. 423 U.S., at 372. This hypothesis was "even more attenuated than those allegations of future injury found insufficient in *O'Shea* to warrant [the] invocation of federal jurisdiction." *Ibid.* The Court also held that plaintiffs' showing at trial of a relatively few instances of violations by individual police officers, without any showing of a deliberate policy on behalf of the named defendants, did not provide a basis for equitable relief. . . .

We note also our *per curiam* opinion in Ashcroft v. Mattis, 431 U.S. 171 (1977). There, the father of a boy who had been killed by the police sought damages and a declaration that the Missouri statute which authorized police officers to use deadly force in apprehending a person who committed a felony was unconstitutional. Plaintiff alleged that he had another son, who "*if* ever arrested or brought under an attempt at arrest on suspicion of a felony, *might* flee or give the appearance of fleeing, and would therefore be *in danger* of being killed by these defendants or other police officers . . ." 431 U.S., at 172–173, n.2. We ruled that "[s]uch speculation is insufficient to establish the existence of a present, live controversy." *Ibid.*

IV

No extension of *O'Shea* and *Rizzo* is necessary to hold that respondent Lyons has failed to demonstrate a case or controversy with the City that would justify the equitable relief sought.[6] Lyons' standing to seek the injunction requested depended on whether he was likely to suffer future injury from the use of the chokeholds by police officers. Count V of the complaint alleged the traffic stop and choking incident five months before. That Lyons may have been illegally choked by the police on October 6, 1976, while presumably affording Lyons standing to claim damages against the individual officers and perhaps against the City, does nothing to establish a real and immediate threat that he would again be stopped for a traffic violation, or for any other offense, by an officer or officers who would illegally choke him into unconsciousness without any provocation or resistance on his part. The additional allegation in the complaint that the police in Los Angeles routinely apply chokeholds in situations where they are not threatened by the use of

---

[6] The City states in its brief that on remand from the Court of Appeals' first judgment "the parties agreed and advised the district court that the respondent's damages claim could be severed from his effort to obtain equitable relief." Brief for Petitioner 8 n. 7. Respondent does not suggest otherwise. This case, therefore, as it came to us, is on all fours with O'Shea and should be judged as such.

deadly force falls far short of the allegations that would be necessary to establish a case or controversy between these parties.

In order to establish an actual controversy in this case, Lyons would have had not only to allege that he would have another encounter with the police but also to make the incredible assertion either, (1) that *all* police officers in Los Angeles *always* choke any citizen with whom they happen to have an encounter, whether for the purpose of arrest, issuing a citation or for questioning or, (2) that the City ordered or authorized police officers to act in such manner. Although Count V alleged that the City authorized the use of the control holds in situations where deadly force was not threatened, it did not indicate why Lyons might be realistically threatened by police officers who acted within the strictures of the City's policy. If, for example, chokeholds were authorized to be used only to counter resistance to an arrest by a suspect, or to thwart an effort to escape, any future threat to Lyons from the City's policy or from the conduct of police officers would be no more real than the possibility that he would again have an encounter with the police and that either he would illegally resist arrest or detention or the officers would disobey their instructions and again render him unconscious without any provocation.[7]

Under *O'Shea* and *Rizzo,* these allegations were an insufficient basis to provide a federal court with jurisdiction to entertain Count V of the complaint. This was apparently the conclusion of the District Court in dismissing Lyons' claim for injunctive relief. Although the District Court

---

[7] The centerpiece of Justice Marshall's dissent is that Lyons had standing to challenge the City's policy because to recover damages he would have to prove that what allegedly occurred on October 6, 1976, was pursuant to City authorization. We agree completely that for Lyons to succeed in his damages action, it would be necessary to prove that what happened to him—that is, as alleged, he was choked without any provocation or legal excuse whatsoever—was pursuant to a City policy. For several reasons, however, it does not follow that Lyons had standing to seek the injunction prayed for in Count V.

First, Lyons alleges in Count II of his first amended complaint that on October 6, 1976, the officers were carrying out official policies of the City. That allegation was incorporated by reference in Count V. That policy, however, is described in paragraphs 20 and 23 of Count V as authorizing the use of chokeholds "in situations where [the officers] are threatened by far less than deadly force." This is not equivalent to the unbelievable assertion that the City either orders or authorizes application of the chokeholds where there is no resistance or other provocation.

Second, even if such an allegation is thought to be contained in the complaint, it is belied by the record made on the application for preliminary injunction.

Third, even if the complaint must be read as containing an allegation that officers are authorized to apply the chokeholds where there is no resistance or other provocation, it does not follow that Lyons has standing to seek an injunction against the application of the restraint holds in situations that he has not experienced, as for example, where the suspect resists arrest or tries to escape but does not threaten the use of deadly force. Yet that is precisely the scope of the injunction that Lyons prayed for in Count V.

Fourth, and in any event, to have a case or controversy with the City that could sustain Count V, Lyons would have to credibly allege that he faced a realistic threat from the future application of the City's policy. Justice Marshall nowhere confronts this requirement—the necessity that Lyons demonstrate that he, himself, will not only again be stopped by the police but will be choked without any provocation or legal excuse. Justice Marshall plainly does not agree with that requirement, and he was in dissent in *O'Shea v. Littleton.* We are at issue in that respect.

acted without opinion or findings, the Court of Appeals interpreted its action as based on lack of standing, *i.e.*, that under *O'Shea* and *Rizzo,* Lyons must be held to have made an "insufficient showing that the police were likely to do this to the plaintiff again." 615 F.2d, at 1246. For several reasons—each of them infirm, in our view—the Court of Appeals thought reliance on *O'Shea* and *Rizzo* was misplaced and reversed the District Court.

First, the Court of Appeals thought that Lyons was more immediately threatened than the plaintiffs in those cases since, according to the Court of Appeals, Lyons need only be stopped for a minor traffic violation to be subject to the strangleholds. But even assuming that Lyons would again be stopped for a traffic or other violation in the reasonably near future, it is untenable to assert, and the complaint made no such allegation, that strangleholds are applied by the Los Angeles police to every citizen who is stopped or arrested regardless of the conduct of the person stopped. We cannot agree that the "odds," 615 F.2d, at 1247, that Lyons would not only again be stopped for a traffic violation but would also be subjected to a chokehold without any provocation whatsoever are sufficient to make out a federal case for equitable relief. We note that five months elapsed between October 6, 1976, and the filing of the complaint, yet there was no allegation of further unfortunate encounters between Lyons and the police.

Of course, it may be that among the countless encounters between the police and the citizens of a great city such as Los Angeles, there will be certain instances in which strangleholds will be illegally applied and injury and death unconstitutionally inflicted on the victim. As we have said, however, it is no more than conjecture to suggest that in every instance of a traffic stop, arrest, or other encounter between the police and a citizen, the police will act unconstitutionally and inflict injury without provocation or legal excuse. And it is surely no more than speculation to assert either that Lyons himself will again be involved in one of those unfortunate instances, or that he will be arrested in the future and provoke the use of a chokehold by resisting arrest, attempting to escape, or threatening deadly force or serious bodily injury.

Second, the Court of Appeals viewed *O'Shea* and *Rizzo* as cases in which the plaintiffs sought "massive structural" relief against the local law enforcement systems and therefore that the holdings in those cases were inapposite to cases such as this where the plaintiff, according to the Court of Appeals, seeks to enjoin only an "established," "sanctioned" police practice assertedly violative of constitutional rights. *O'Shea* and *Rizzo,* however, cannot be so easily confined to their facts. If Lyons has made no showing that he is realistically threatened by a repetition of his experience of October, 1976, then he has not met the requirements for seeking an injunction in a federal court, whether the injunction contemplates intrusive structural relief or the cessation of a discrete practice.

The Court of Appeals also asserted that Lyons "had a live and active claim" against the City "if only for a period of a few seconds" while the stranglehold was being applied to him and that for two reasons the claim had not become moot so as to disentitle Lyons to injunctive relief: First, because under normal rules of equity, a case does not become moot merely because the complained of conduct has ceased; and second, because Lyons' claim is "capable of repetition but evading review" and therefore should be heard. We agree that Lyons had a live controversy with the City. Indeed, he still has a claim for damages against the City that appears to meet all Article III requirements. Nevertheless, the issue here is not whether that claim has become moot but whether Lyons meets the preconditions for asserting an injunctive claim in a federal forum. The equitable doctrine that cessation of the challenged conduct does not bar an injunction is of little help in this respect, for Lyons' lack of standing does not rest on the termination of the police practice but on the speculative nature of his claim that he will again experience injury as the result of that practice even if continued.

The rule that a claim does not become moot where it is capable of repetition, yet evades review, is likewise inapposite. Lyons' claim that he was illegally strangled remains to be litigated in his suit for damages; in no sense does that claim "evade" review. Furthermore, the capable-of-repetition doctrine applies only in exceptional situations, and generally only where the named plaintiff can make a reasonable showing that he will again be subjected to the alleged illegality. DeFunis v. Odegaard, 416 U.S. 312, 319 (1974). As we have indicated, Lyons has not made this demonstration.

The record and findings made on remand do not improve Lyons' position with respect to standing. The District Court, having been reversed, did not expressly address Lyons' standing to seek injunctive relief, although the City was careful to preserve its position on this question. There was no finding that Lyons faced a real and immediate threat of again being illegally choked. The City's policy was described as authorizing the use of the strangleholds "under circumstances where no one is threatened with death or grievous bodily harm." That policy was not further described, but the record before the court contained the department's existing policy with respect to the employment of chokeholds. Nothing in that policy, contained in a Police Department manual, suggests that the chokeholds, or other kinds of force for that matter, are authorized absent some resistance or other provocation by the arrestee or other suspect.[9] On the contrary, police officers were

---

[9] The dissent notes that a LAPD training officer stated that the police are authorized to employ the control holds whenever an officer "feels" that there is about to be a bodily attack. Post, at 1673. The dissent's emphasis on the word "feels" apparently is intended to suggest that LAPD officers are authorized to apply the holds whenever they "feel" like it. If there is a distinction between permitting the use of the holds when there is a "threat" of serious bodily harm, and when the officer "feels" or believes there is about to be a bodily attack, the dissent has failed to make it clear. The dissent does not, because it cannot, point to any written or oral pronouncement by the LAPD or any evidence showing a pattern of police behavior that would

instructed to use chokeholds only when lesser degrees of force do not suffice and then only "to gain control of a suspect who is violently resisting the officer or trying to escape." App. 230.

Our conclusion is that the Court of Appeals failed to heed *O'Shea, Rizzo,* and other relevant authority, and that the District Court was quite right in dismissing Count V.

V

Lyons fares no better if it be assumed that his pending damages suit affords him Article III standing to seek an injunction as a remedy for the claim arising out of the October 1976 events. The equitable remedy is unavailable absent a showing of irreparable injury, a requirement that cannot be met where there is no showing of any real or immediate threat that the plaintiff will be wronged again—a "likelihood of substantial and immediate irreparable injury." *O'Shea v. Littleton,* 414 U.S., at 502. The speculative nature of Lyons' claim of future injury requires a finding that this prerequisite of equitable relief has not been fulfilled.

Nor will the injury that Lyons allegedly suffered in 1976 go unrecompensed; for that injury, he has an adequate remedy at law. Contrary to the view of the Court of Appeals, it is not at all "difficult" under our holding "to see how anyone can ever challenge police or similar administrative practices." 615 F.2d, at 1250. The legality of the violence to which Lyons claims he was once subjected is at issue in his suit for damages and can be determined there.

Absent a sufficient likelihood that he will again be wronged in a similar way, Lyons is no more entitled to an injunction than any other citizen of Los Angeles; and a federal court may not entertain a claim by any or all citizens who no more than assert that certain practices of law enforcement officers are unconstitutional. *Cf.* Warth v. Seldin, 422 U.S. 490 (1975); Schlesinger v. Reservists to Stop the War, 418 U.S. 208 (1974); United States v. Richardson, 418 U.S. 166 (1974). This is not to suggest that such undifferentiated claims should not be taken seriously by local authorities. Indeed, the interest of an alert and interested citizen is an essential element of an effective and fair government, whether on the local, state or national level. A federal court, however, is not the proper forum to press such claims unless the requirements for entry and the prerequisites for injunctive relief are satisfied.

We decline the invitation to slight the preconditions for equitable relief; for as we have held, recognition of the need for a proper balance between state and federal authority counsels restraint in the issuance of injunctions against state officers engaged in the administration of the states' criminal laws in the absence of irreparable injury which is both great and immediate. *O'Shea,* 414 U.S., at 499; Younger v. Harris, 401 U.S. 37 (1971). Mitchum v. Foster, 407 U.S. 225 (1972) held that suits

---

indicate that the official policy would permit the application of the control holds on a suspect that was not offering, or threatening to offer, physical resistance.

brought under 42 U.S.C. § 1983 are exempt from the flat ban against the issuance of injunctions directed at state court proceedings, 28 U.S.C. § 2283. But this holding did not displace the normal principles of equity, comity and federalism that should inform the judgment of federal courts when asked to oversee state law enforcement authorities. In exercising their equitable powers federal courts must recognize "[t]he special delicacy of the adjustment to be preserved between federal equitable power and State administration of its own law." Stefanelli v. Minard, 342 U.S. 117, 120 (1951); *O'Shea v. Littleton,* 414 U.S., at 500. *See also Rizzo v. Goode,* 423 U.S., at 380; Cleary v. Bolger, 371 U.S. 392 (1963); Wilson v. Schnettler, 365 U.S. 381 (1961); Pugach v. Dollinger, 365 U.S. 458 (1961). The Court of Appeals failed to apply these factors properly and therefore erred in finding that the District Court had not abused its discretion in entering an injunction in this case.

As we noted in *O'Shea,* 414 U.S., at 503, withholding injunctive relief does not mean that the "federal law will exercise no deterrent effect in these circumstances." If Lyons has suffered an injury barred by the Federal Constitution, he has a remedy for damages under § 1983. Furthermore, those who deliberately deprive a citizen of his constitutional rights risk conviction under the federal criminal laws. *Ibid.*

Beyond these considerations the state courts need not impose the same standing or remedial requirements that govern federal court proceedings. The individual states may permit their courts to use injunctions to oversee the conduct of law enforcement authorities on a continuing basis. But this is not the role of a federal court absent far more justification than Lyons has proffered in this case.

The judgment of the Court of Appeals is accordingly

Reversed.

■ JUSTICE MARSHALL, with whom JUSTICE BRENNAN, JUSTICE BLACKMUN, and JUSTICE STEVENS join, dissenting

The District Court found that the City of Los Angeles authorizes its police officers to apply life-threatening chokeholds to citizens who pose no threat of violence, and that respondent, Adolph Lyons, was subjected to such a chokehold. The Court today holds that a federal court is without power to enjoin the enforcement of the City's policy, no matter how flagrantly unconstitutional it may be. Since no one can show that he will be choked in the future, no one—not even a person who, like Lyons, has almost been choked to death—has standing to challenge the continuation of the policy. The City is free to continue the policy indefinitely as long as it is willing to pay damages for the injuries and deaths that result. I dissent from this unprecedented and unwarranted approach to standing.

There is plainly a "case or controversy" concerning the constitutionality of the City's chokehold policy. The constitutionality of that policy is directly implicated by Lyons' claim for damages against the

City. The complaint clearly alleges that the officer who choked Lyons was carrying out an official policy, and a municipality is liable under 42 U.S.C. § 1983 for the conduct of its employees only if they acted pursuant to such a policy. Monell v. New York City Dept. of Social Services, 436 U.S. 658, 694 (1978). Lyons therefore has standing to challenge the City's chokehold policy and to obtain whatever relief a court may ultimately deem appropriate. None of our prior decisions suggests that his requests for particular forms of relief raise any additional issues concerning his standing. Standing has always depended on whether a plaintiff has a "personal stake in the outcome of the controversy," Baker v. Carr, 369 U.S. 186, 204 (1962), not on the "precise nature of the relief sought." Jenkins v. McKeithen, 395 U.S. 411, 423 (1969) (opinion of MARSHALL, J., joined by WARREN, C.J., and BRENNAN, J.).

I

A

Respondent Adolph Lyons is a 24-year-old Negro male who resides in Los Angeles. According to the uncontradicted evidence in the record,[1] at about 2:30 A.M. on October 6, 1976, Lyons was pulled over to the curb by two officers of the Los Angeles Police Department (LAPD) for a traffic infraction because one of his taillights was burned out. The officers greeted him with drawn revolvers as he exited from his car. Lyons was told to face his car and spread his legs. He did so. He was then ordered to clasp his hands and put them on top of his head. He again complied. After one of the officers completed a pat-down search, Lyons dropped his hands, but was ordered to place them back above his head, and one of the officers grabbed Lyons' hands and slammed them onto his head. Lyons complained about the pain caused by the ring of keys he was holding in his hand. Within five to ten seconds, the officer began to choke Lyons by applying a forearm against his throat. As Lyons struggled for air, the officer handcuffed him, but continued to apply the chokehold until he blacked out. When Lyons regained consciousness, he was lying face down on the ground, choking, gasping for air, and spitting up blood and dirt. He had urinated and defecated. He was issued a traffic citation and released.

On February 7, 1977, Lyons commenced this action under 42 U.S.C. § 1983 against the individual officers and the City, alleging violations of his rights under the Fourth, Eighth, and Fourteenth Amendments to the Constitution and seeking damages and declaratory and injunctive relief. He claimed that he was subjected to a chokehold without justification and that defendant officers were "carrying out the official policies, customs and practices of the Los Angeles Police Department and the City

---

[1] The following summary of the evidence is taken from Lyons' deposition and his "Notice of Application and Application for Preliminary Injunction and Declaratory Relief; Points and Authorities." Pp. 3–4. Although petitioners' answer contains a general denial of the allegations set forth in the complaint, petitioners have never presented any evidence to challenge Lyons' account. Brief for Petitioner at 8.

of Los Angeles." Count II, ¶ 13.[2] These allegations were included or incorporated in each of the counts in which the City was named as a defendant. *See* Counts II through VI. Lyons alleged that the City authorizes the use of chokeholds "in innumerable situations where the police are not threatened by the use of any deadly force whatsoever." Count V, ¶ 22.

B

Although the City instructs its officers that use of a chokehold does not constitute deadly force, since 1975 no less than 16 persons have died following the use of a chokehold by an LAPD police officer. Twelve have been Negro males.[3] The evidence submitted to the District Court established that for many years it has been the official policy of the City to permit police officers to employ chokeholds in a variety of situations where they face no threat of violence. In reported "altercations" between LAPD officers and citizens the chokeholds are used more frequently than any other means of physical restraint. Between February 1975 and July 1980, LAPD officers applied chokeholds on at least 975 occasions, which represented more than three-quarters of the reported altercations.[6]

It is undisputed that chokeholds pose a high and unpredictable risk of serious injury or death. Chokeholds are intended to bring a subject under control by causing pain and rendering him unconscious. Depending on the position of the officer's arm and the force applied, the victim's voluntary or involuntary reaction, and his state of health, an officer may inadvertently crush the victim's larynx, trachea, or thyroid. The result may be death caused by either cardiac arrest or asphyxiation. An LAPD officer described the reaction of a person to being choked as "do[ing] the chicken," Exh. 44, p. 93, in reference apparently to the reactions of a chicken when its neck is wrung. The victim experiences extreme pain. His face turns blue as he is deprived of oxygen, he goes into spasmodic convulsions, his eyes roll back, his body wriggles, his feet kick up and down, and his arms move about wildly.

---

[2]   Count I of the first amended complaint also stated a claim against the individual officers for damages. ¶ 8.

[3]   Thus in a City where Negro males constitute 9% of the population, they have accounted for 75% of the deaths resulting from the use of chokeholds. In addition to his other allegations, Lyons alleged racial discrimination in violation of the Equal Protection Clause of the Fourteenth Amendment. ¶¶ 10, 15, 23, 24, 25, 30.Of the 16 deaths, 10 occurred prior to the District Court's issuance of the preliminary injunction, although at that time the parties and the Court were aware of only nine. On December 24, 1980, the Court of Appeals stayed the preliminary injunction pending appeal. Four additional deaths occurred during the period prior to the grant of a further stay pending filing and disposition of a petition for certiorari, 453 U.S. 1308 (1981) (REHNQUIST, J., in chambers), and two more deaths occurred thereafter.

[6]   Statement of Officer Pascal K. Dionne, App. 259. These figures undoubtedly understate the frequency of the use of chokeholds since, as Officer Dionne, a witness for the City, testified, the figures compiled do not include all altercations between police officers and citizens. *Id.*, at 241. Officer Dionne's Statement does not define "altercation" and does not indicate when "altercation reports" must be filed by an officer. The City does not maintain a record of injuries to suspects.

Although there has been no occasion to determine the precise contours of the City's chokehold policy, the evidence submitted to the District Court provides some indications. LAPD training officer Terry Speer testified that an officer is authorized to deploy a chokehold whenever he *"feels* that there's about to be a bodily attack made on him." App. 381 (emphasis added). A training bulletin states that "[c]ontrol holds . . . allow officers to subdue *any* resistance by the suspects." Exh. 47, p. 1 (emphasis added). In the proceedings below the City characterized its own policy as authorizing the use of chokeholds "to gain control of a suspect who is violently resisting the officer *or trying to escape,"* to "subdue *any* resistance by suspects," and to permit an officer, "where . . . resisted, but *not necessarily threatened with serious bodily harm or death,* . . . to subdue a suspect who forcibly resists an officer." (Emphasis added.)

The training given LAPD officers provides additional revealing evidence of the City's chokehold policy. Officer Speer testified that in instructing officers concerning the use of force, the LAPD does not distinguish between felony and misdemeanor suspects. App. 379. Moreover, the officers are taught to maintain the chokehold until the suspect goes limp, App. 387; Pet.App.H. 51a, despite substantial evidence that the application of a chokehold invariably induces a "flight or flee" syndrome, producing an *involuntary* struggle by the victim which can easily be misinterpreted by the officer as willful resistance that must be overcome by prolonging the chokehold and increasing the force applied. In addition, officers are instructed that the chokeholds can be safely deployed for up to three or four minutes. App. 387-388; Pet.App.H. 48a. Robert Jarvis, the City's expert who has taught at the Los Angeles Police Academy for the past twelve years, admitted that officers are never told that the bar-arm control can cause death if applied for just two seconds. App. 388. Of the nine deaths for which evidence was submitted to the District Court, the average duration of the choke where specified was approximately 40 seconds.

C

In determining the appropriateness of a preliminary injunction, the District Court recognized that the City's policy is subject to the constraints imposed by the Due Process Clause of the Fourteenth Amendment. The Court found that "[d]uring the course of this confrontation, said officers, without provocation or legal justification, applied a *Department-authorized* chokehold which resulted in injuries to plaintiff." (Emphasis added). The Court found that the "City of Los Angeles and the Department authorize the use of these holds under circumstances where no one is threatened by death or grievous bodily harm." The Court concluded that the use of the chokeholds constitutes "deadly force," and that the City may not constitutionally authorize the use of such force "in situations where death or serious bodily harm is not threatened." On the basis of this conclusion, the District Court entered a preliminary injunction enjoining "the use of both the carotid-artery and bar arm holds under circumstances which do not threaten death or serious bodily injury." As the Court of Appeals noted, "[a]ll the trial judge has done, so far, is to tell the city that its police officers may not apply life threatening strangleholds to persons stopped in routine police work unless the application of such force is necessary to prevent serious bodily harm to an officer." 656 F.2d 417, 418 (1981).

II

At the outset it is important to emphasize that Lyons' entitlement to injunctive relief and his entitlement to an award of damages both depend upon whether he can show that the City's chokehold policy violates the Constitution. An indispensable prerequisite of municipal liability under 42 U.S.C. § 1983 is proof that the conduct complained of is attributable to an unconstitutional official policy or custom. Polk Cty. v. Dodson, 454 U.S. 312 (1981); Monell v. New York City Dept. of Social Services, 436 U.S. 658, 694 (1978). It is not enough for a § 1983 plaintiff to show that the employees or agents of a municipality have violated or will violate the Constitution, for a municipality will not be held liable solely on a theory of *respondeat superior. See Monell, supra,* at 694.

The Court errs in suggesting that Lyons' prayer for injunctive relief in Count V of his first amended complaint concerns a policy that was not responsible for his injuries and that therefore could not support an award of damages. *Ante,* at n.7. Paragraph 8 of the complaint alleges that Lyons was choked "without provocation, legal justification or excuse." Paragraph 13 expressly alleges that "[t]he Defendant Officers were carrying out *the official policies, customs and practices* of the Los Angeles Police Department and the City of Los Angeles," and that "*by virtue thereof,* defendant City is liable for the actions" of the officers. (Emphasis added.) These allegations are incorporated in each of the Counts against the City, including Count V.

There is no basis for the Court's assertion that Lyons has failed to allege "that the City either orders or authorizes application of the chokeholds where there is no resistance or other provocations." *Ante,* at n.7. I am completely at a loss to understand how paragraphs 8 and 13 can be deemed insufficient to allege that the City's policy authorizes the use of chokeholds without provocation. The Court apparently finds Lyons' complaint wanting because, although it alleges that he was choked without provocation and that the officers acted pursuant to any official policy, it fails to allege *in haec verba* that the City's policy authorizes the choking of suspects without provocation. I am aware of no case decided since the abolition of the old common law forms of action, and the Court cites none, that in any way supports this crabbed construction of the complaint. A federal court is capable of concluding for itself that two plus two equals four.

The Court also errs in asserting that even if the complaint sufficiently alleges that the City's policy authorizes the use of chokeholds without provocation, such an allegation is in any event "belied by the record made on the application for preliminary injunction." *Ante,* at n.7. This conclusion flatly contradicts the District Court's express factual finding, which was left undisturbed by the Court of Appeals, that the officers applied a *"Department-authorized* chokehold which resulted in injuries to plaintiff." (Emphasis added.) The City does not contend that this factual finding is clearly erroneous.

In sum, it's absolutely clear that Lyons' requests for damages and for injunctive relief call into question the constitutionality of the City's policy concerning the use of chokeholds. If he does not show that that policy is unconstitutional, he will be no more entitled to damages than to an injunction.

III

Since Lyons' claim for damages plainly gives him standing, and since the success of that claim depends upon a demonstration that the City's chokehold policy is unconstitutional, it is beyond dispute that Lyons has properly invoked the District Court's authority to adjudicate the constitutionality of the City's chokehold policy. The dispute concerning the constitutionality of that policy plainly presents a "case or controversy" under Article III. The Court nevertheless holds that a federal court has no power under Article III to adjudicate Lyons' request, in the same lawsuit, for injunctive relief with respect to that very policy. This anomalous result is not supported either by precedent or by the fundamental concern underlying the standing requirement. Moreover, by fragmenting a single claim into multiple claims for particular types of relief and requiring a separate showing of standing for each form of relief, the decision today departs from this Court's traditional conception of standing and of the remedial powers of the federal courts.

A

It is simply disingenuous for the Court to assert that its decision requires "[n]o extension" of O'Shea v. Littleton, 414 U.S. 488 (1974), and Rizzo v. Goode, 423 U.S. 362 (1976). *Ante,* at 1666. In contrast to this case *O'Shea* and *Rizzo* involved disputes focusing solely on the threat of future injury which the plaintiffs in those cases alleged they faced. In *O'Shea* the plaintiffs did not allege past injury and did not seek compensatory relief. In *Rizzo,* the plaintiffs sought only declaratory and injunctive relief and alleged past instances of police misconduct only in an attempt to establish the substantiality of the threat of future injury. There was similarly no claim for damages based on past injuries in *Ashcroft v. Mattis,* 431 U.S. 171 (1977), or Golden v. Zwickler, 394 U.S. 103 (1969), on which the Court also relies.

These decisions do not support the Court's holding today. As the Court recognized in *O'Shea,* standing under Article III is established by an allegation of "threatened *or* actual injury." *Id.,* 414 U.S., at 493, quoting Linda R.S. v. Richard D., 410 U.S. 614, 617 (1973) (emphasis added). *See also* 414 U.S., at 493, n.2. Because the plaintiffs in *O'Shea, Rizzo, Mattis,* and *Zwickler* did not seek to redress past injury, their standing to sue depended entirely on the risk of future injury they faced. Apart from the desire to eliminate the possibility of future injury, the plaintiffs in those cases had no other personal stake in the outcome of the controversies.

By contrast, Lyons' request for prospective relief is coupled with his claim for damages based on past injury. In addition to the risk that he will be subjected to a chokehold in the future, Lyons has suffered past injury. Because he has a live claim for damages, he need not rely solely on the threat of future injury to establish his personal stake in the outcome of the controversy. In the cases relied on by the majority, the Court simply had no occasion to decide whether a plaintiff who has standing to litigate a dispute must clear a separate standing hurdle with respect to each form of relief sought.

B

The Court's decision likewise finds no support in the fundamental policy underlying the Article III standing requirement—the concern that a federal court not decide a legal issue if the plaintiff lacks a sufficient "personal stake in the outcome of the controversy as to assure that concrete adverseness which sharpens the presentation of issues upon which the court so largely depends for illumination of difficult . . . questions." Baker v. Carr, 369 U.S. 186, 204 (1962). As this Court stated in Flast v. Cohen, 392 U.S. 83, 101 (1968), "the question of standing is related only to whether the dispute sought to be adjudicated will be presented in an adversary context and in a form historically viewed as capable of judicial resolution." *See also* Valley Forge Christian College v. Americans United For Separation of Church and State, 454 U.S. 464, 472 (standing requirement ensures that "the legal questions presented to the court will be resolved, not in the rarified atmosphere of a debating society, but in a concrete factual context conducive to a realistic appreciation of the consequences of judicial action").

Because Lyons has a claim for damages against the City, and because he cannot prevail on that claim unless he demonstrates that the City's chokehold policy violates the Constitution, his personal stake in the outcome of the controversy adequately assures an adversary presentation of his challenge to the constitutionality of the policy. Moreover, the resolution of this challenge will be largely dispositive of his requests for declaratory and injunctive relief. No doubt the requests for injunctive relief may raise additional questions. But these questions involve familiar issues relating to the appropriateness of particular forms of relief, and have never been thought to implicate a litigant's standing to sue. The denial of standing separately to seek injunctive relief therefore cannot be justified by the basic concern underlying the Article III standing requirement.

C

By fragmenting the standing inquiry and imposing a separate standing hurdle with respect to each form of relief sought, the decision today departs significantly from this Court's traditional conception of the standing requirement and of the remedial powers of the federal courts. . . .

1

Our cases uniformly state that the touchstone of the Article III standing requirement is the plaintiff's personal stake in the underlying dispute, not in the particular types of relief sought. Once a plaintiff establishes a personal stake in a dispute, he has done all that is necessary to "invok[e] the court's authority . . . to challenge the action sought to be adjudicated." Valley Forge Christian College v. Americans United For Separation of Church and State, 454 U.S. 464, 471–472 (1982). *See, e.g., Flast v. Cohen,* 392 U.S., at 101 (stake in "the dispute to be adjudicated in the lawsuit"); Eisenstadt v. Baird, 405 U.S. 438, 443 (1972) (plaintiff must have "sufficient interest in challenging the statute's validity").

The personal stake of a litigant depends, in turn, on whether he has alleged a legally redressable injury. In determining whether a plaintiff has a sufficient personal stake in the outcome of a controversy, this Court has asked whether he "personally has suffered some actual *or* threatened injury," Gladstone Realtors v. Village of Bellwood, 441 U.S. 91, 99 (1979) (emphasis added), whether the injury "fairly can be traced to the challenged action." Simon v. Eastern Kentucky Welfare Rights Org., 426 U.S. 26, 41 (1976), and whether plaintiff's injury "is likely to be redressed by a favorable decision." *Simon, supra,* 426 U.S., at 38. *See also* Duke Power Co. v. Carolina Env. Study Group, 438 U.S. 59, at 74 (1978); Warth v. Seldin, 422 U.S. 490, 508 (1975). These well-accepted criteria for determining whether a plaintiff has established the requisite personal stake do not fragment the standing inquiry into a series of discrete questions about the plaintiff's stake in each of the particular types of relief sought. Quite the contrary, they ask simply whether the plaintiff has a sufficient stake in seeking a judicial resolution of the controversy.

Lyons has alleged past injury and a risk of future injury and has linked both to the City's chokehold policy. Under established principles, the only additional question in determining standing under Article III is whether the injuries he has alleged can be remedied or prevented by *some* form of judicial relief. Satisfaction of this requirement ensures that the lawsuit does not entail the issuance of an advisory opinion without the possibility of any judicial relief, and that the exercise of a court's remedial powers will actually redress the alleged injury. Therefore Lyons needs to demonstrate only that, should he prevail on the merits, "the exercise of the Court's remedial powers would redress the claimed injuries." *Duke Power Co., ibid* (emphasis added). *See also Warth v. Seldin,* 422 U.S., at 508; *Simon, supra,* 426 U.S., at 38. Lyons has easily made this showing here, for monetary relief would plainly provide redress for his past injury, and prospective relief would reduce the likelihood of any future injury. Nothing more has ever been required to establish standing.

The Court's decision turns these well accepted principles on their heads by requiring a separate standing inquiry with respect to each request for relief. Until now, questions concerning remedy were relevant to the threshold issue of standing only in the limited sense that some relief must be possible. The approach adopted today drastically alters the inquiry into remedy that must be made to determine standing.

IV

Apart from the question of standing, the only remaining question presented in the petition for certiorari is whether the preliminary injunction issued by the District Court must be set aside because it "constitute[s] a substantial interference in the operation of a municipal police department." Petition for Certiorari i. In my view it does not.

In the portion of its brief concerning this second question, the City argues that the District Court ignored the principles of federalism set forth in Rizzo v. Goode, 423 U.S. 362 (1976). Brief for the City of Los Angeles 40–47. The City's reliance on *Rizzo* is misplaced. That case involved an injunction which "significantly revised the internal procedures of the Philadelphia police department." *Id.*, at 379. The injunction required the police department to adopt "a comprehensive program for dealing adequately with civilian complaints" to be formulated in accordance with extensive "guidelines" established by the district court. *Id.*, at 369–370 quoting 357 F.Supp. 1289, 1321 (1973). Those guidelines specified detailed revisions of police manuals and rules of procedure, as well as the adoption of specific procedures for processing, screening, investigating and adjudicating citizen complaints. In addition, the district court supervised the implementation of the comprehensive program, issuing detailed orders concerning the posting and distribution of the revised police procedures and the drawing up of a "Citizen's Complaint Report" in a format designated by the court. The district court also reserved jurisdiction to review the progress of the police department. 423 U.S., at 364, n.2. This Court concluded that the sweeping nature of the injunctive relief was inconsistent with "the principles of federalism." 423 U.S., at 380.

The principles of federalism simply do not preclude the limited preliminary injunction issued in this case. Unlike the permanent injunction at issue in *Rizzo*, the preliminary injunction involved here entails no federal supervision of the LAPD's activities. The preliminary injunction merely forbids the use of chokeholds absent the threat of deadly force, permitting their continued use where such a threat does exist. This limited ban takes the form of a preventive injunction, which has traditionally been regarded as the least intrusive form of equitable relief. Moreover, the City can remove the ban by obtaining approval of a training plan. Although the preliminary injunction also requires the City to provide records of the uses of chokeholds to respondent and to allow the court access to such records, this requirement is hardly onerous, since the LAPD already maintains records concerning the use of chokeholds.

A district court should be mindful that "federal-court intervention in the daily operation of a large city's police department, . . . is undesirable and to be avoided if at all possible." *Rizzo, supra,* at 381 (BLACKMUN, J., dissenting).[23] The modest interlocutory relief granted in this case differs markedly, however, from the intrusive injunction involved in *Rizzo,* and simply does not implicate the federalism concerns that arise when a federal court undertakes to "supervise the functioning of the police department." 423 U.S., at 380.

V

Apparently because it is unwilling to rely solely on its unprecedented rule of standing, the Court goes on to conclude that, even if Lyons has standing, "[t]he equitable remedy is unavailable." *Ante,* at 1670. The Court's reliance on this alternative ground is puzzling for two reasons.

If, as the Court says, Lyons lacks standing under Article III, the federal courts have no power to decide his entitlement to equitable relief on the merits. Under the Court's own view of Article III, the Court's discussion in Part V is purely an advisory opinion. . . .

Even if the issue had been properly raised, I could not agree with the Court's disposition of it. With the single exception of *Rizzo v. Goode, supra,* all of the cases relied on by the Court concerned injunctions against state criminal proceedings. The rule of Younger v. Harris, 401 U.S. 37 (1971), that such injunctions can be issued only in extraordinary circumstances in which the threat of injury is "great and immediate," *id.,* at 44, reflects the venerable rule that equity will not enjoin a criminal prosecution, the fact that constitutional defenses can be raised in such a state prosecution, and an appreciation of the friction that injunctions against state judicial proceedings may produce. *See id.,* at 44; Steffel v. Thompson, 415 U.S. 452, 462 (1974); 28 U.S.C. § 2283.

Our prior decisions have repeatedly emphasized that where an injunction is not directed against a state criminal or quasi-criminal proceeding, "the relevant principles of equity, comity, and federalism" that underlie the *Younger* doctrine "have little force." *Steffel v. Thompson, supra,* at 462citing Lake Carrier's Assn. v. MacMullan, 406 U.S. 498, 509 (1972). Outside the special context in which the *Younger* doctrine applies, we have held that the appropriateness of injunctive

---

[23] Of course, municipalities may be enjoined under § 1983, *Monell, supra,* and this Court has approved of the issuance of injunctions by federal courts against state or municipal police departments where necessary to prevent the continued enforcement of unconstitutional official policies. *See, e.g.,* Allee v. Medrano, 416 U.S. 802 (1974); Hague v. CIO, 307 U.S. 496 (1939); Lankford v. Gelston, 364 F.2d 197 (CA4 1966) (en banc), cited with approval in *Allee, supra,* 416 U.S., at 816. Although federalism concerns are relevant in fashioning an appropriate relief, we have stated repeatedly that a federal court retains the power to order any available remedy necessary to afford full relief for the invasion of legal rights. *See, e.g.,* Swann v. Charlotte-Mecklenburg Board of Education, 402 U.S. 1, 14 (1971); Bell v. Hood, 327 U.S. 678, 684 (1946).

relief is governed by traditional equitable considerations. See Doran v. Salem Inn, Inc., 422 U.S. 922, 930 (1975). Whatever the precise scope of the *Younger* doctrine may be, the concerns of comity and federalism that counsel restraint when a federal court is asked to enjoin a state criminal proceeding simply do not apply to an injunction directed solely at a police department.

If the preliminary injunction granted by the District Court is analyzed under general equitable principles, rather than the more stringent standards of *Younger v. Harris,* it becomes apparent that there is no rule of law that precludes equitable relief and requires that the preliminary injunction be set aside. "In reviewing such interlocutory relief, this Court may only consider whether issuance of the injunction constituted an abuse of discretion." Brown v. Chote, 411 U.S. 452 (1973). . . .

VI

The Court's decision removes an entire class of constitutional violations from the equitable powers of a federal court. It immunizes from prospective equitable relief any policy that authorizes persistent deprivations of constitutional rights as long as no individual can establish with substantial certainty that he will be injured, or injured again, in the future. THE CHIEF JUSTICE asked in Bivens v. Six Unknown Fed. Narcotics Agents, 403 U.S. 388, 419 (1971) (dissenting opinion), "what would be the judicial response to a police order authorizing 'shoot to kill' with respect to every fugitive?" His answer was that it would be "easy to predict our collective wrath and outrage." *Ibid.* We now learn that wrath and outrage cannot be translated into an order to cease the unconstitutional practice, but only an award of damages to those who are victimized by the practice and live to sue and to the survivors of those who are not so fortunate. Under the view expressed by the majority today, if the police adopt a policy of "shoot to kill," or a policy of shooting one out of ten suspects, the federal courts will be powerless to enjoin its continuation. Compare Linda R.S. v. Richard D., 410 U.S. 614, 621 (1973) (WHITE, J., dissenting). The federal judicial power is now limited to levying a toll for such a systematic constitutional violation.

Floyd v. City of New York

283 F.R.D. 153 (S.D.N.Y. 2012)

■ SHIRA A. SCHEINDLIN, DISTRICT JUDGE:

I. INTRODUCTION

Police officers are permitted to briefly stop any individual, but only upon reasonable suspicion that he is committing a crime. The source of that limitation is the Fourth Amendment to the United States Constitution, which guarantees that "the right of the people to be secure in their persons, houses, papers, and effects, against unreasonable searches and seizures, shall not be violated." The Supreme Court has explained that this "inestimable right of personal security belongs as much to the citizen on the streets of our cities as to the homeowner closeted in his study to dispose of his secret affairs."

The right to physical liberty has long been at the core of our nation's commitment to respecting the autonomy and dignity of each person: "No right is held more sacred, or is more carefully guarded, by the common law, than the right of every individual to the possession and control of his own person, free from all restraint or interference of others, unless by clear and unquestionable authority of law." Safeguarding this right is quintessentially the role of the judicial branch.

No less central to the courts' role is ensuring that the administration of law comports with the Fourteenth Amendment, which "undoubtedly intended not only that there should be no arbitrary deprivation of life or liberty, or arbitrary spoliation of property, but that equal protection and security should be given to all under like circumstances in the enjoyment of their personal and civil rights."[4]

On over 2.8 million occasions between 2004 and 2009, New York City police officers stopped residents and visitors, restraining their freedom, even if only briefly.[5] Over fifty percent of those stops were of Black people and thirty percent were of Latinos, while only ten percent were of Whites.[6] The question presented by this lawsuit is whether the New York City Police Department ("NYPD") has complied with the laws and Constitutions of the United States and the State of New York. Specifically, the four named plaintiffs allege, on behalf of themselves and a putative class, that defendants have engaged in a policy and/or practice of unlawfully stopping and frisking people in violation of their Fourth Amendment right to be free from unlawful searches and seizures and their Fourteenth Amendment right to freedom from discrimination on the basis of race.

Plaintiffs David Floyd, Lalit Clarkson, Deon Dennis, and David Ourlicht are Black men who seek to represent a class of similarly situated people in this lawsuit against the City of New York, Police Commissioner Raymond Kelly, Mayor Michael Bloomberg, and named and unnamed police officers. On behalf of the putative class, plaintiffs seek equitable relief in the form of (1) a declaration that defendants' policies, practices, and/or customs violate the Fourth and Fourteenth Amendments, and (2)

---

[4] *Yick Wo v. Hopkins,* 118 U.S. 356, 367 (1886) (citation and quotation omitted). "Though the law itself be fair on its face and impartial in appearance, yet, if it is applied and administered by public authority with an evil eye and an unequal hand, so as practically to make unjust and illegal discriminations between persons in similar circumstances, material to their rights, the denial of equal justice is still within the prohibition of the Constitution." *Id.* at 373–74.

[5] As the Supreme Court has explained, being stopped and frisked "must surely be an annoying, frightening, and perhaps humiliating experience." *Terry,* 392 U.S. at 25.

[6] The parties use the terms Hispanic/Latino interchangeably.

a class-wide injunction mandating significant changes in those policies, practices, and/or customs.

This case presents an issue of great public concern: the disproportionate number of Blacks and Latinos, as compared to Whites, who become entangled in the criminal justice system. The specific claims raised in this case are narrower but they are raised in the context of the extensively documented racial disparities in the rates of stops, arrests, convictions, and sentences that continue through the present day. Five nonprofit organizations have filed an *amicus* brief with this Court arguing that the NYPD's stop and frisk practices are harmful, degrading, and demoralizing for too many young people in New York and twenty-seven of the fifty-one members of the New York City Council have filed a second *amicus* brief arguing that the practices are a citywide problem that "reinforce[ ] negative racial stereotypes" and have created "a growing distrust of the NYPD on the part of Black and Latino residents."

The NYPD's stop and frisk program was first presented to this Court over thirteen years ago, in a class action entitled *Daniels v. City of New York*. That case was resolved in 2003 through a settlement that required the City to adopt several remedial measures intended to reduce racial disparities in stops and frisks. Under the terms of that settlement, the NYPD enacted a Racial Profiling Policy; revised the form that police fill out when they conduct a stop so that the encounters would be more accurately documented; and instituted regular audits of the forms, among other measures.

In 2008, after the *Daniels* settlement expired, plaintiffs brought this action, alleging that defendants had failed to reform their policies and practices. In 2011, after examining the parties' voluminous submissions, I denied defendants' motion for summary judgment. In April of this year, upon another voluminous record, I granted in part and denied in part defendants' motion to exclude the testimony of Jeffrey Fagan, plaintiffs' statistics and criminology expert. Plaintiffs now move for certification of the following class:

> All persons who since January 31, 2005 have been, or in the future will be, subjected to the New York Police Department's policies and/or widespread customs or practices of stopping, or stopping and frisking, persons in the absence of a reasonable, articulable suspicion that criminal activity has taken, is taking, or is about to take place in violation of the Fourth Amendment, including persons stopped or stopped and frisked on the basis of being Black or Latino in violation of the Equal Protection Clause of the Fourteenth Amendment.

Because plaintiffs satisfy the legal standard for class certification, their motion is granted. . . .

IV. DISCUSSION

A. Plaintiffs Have Standing to Seek Injunctive Relief

Article III of the Constitution requires that a federal court entertain a lawsuit only if the plaintiff has standing to pursue the relief that she seeks. Concrete injury is a prerequisite to standing and a "plaintiff seeking injunctive or declaratory relief cannot rely on past injury to satisfy the injury requirement but must show a likelihood that he or she will be injured in the future."[92]

The Supreme Court emphasized this requirement in *City of Los Angeles v. Lyons,* when it held that Lyons, who had been subjected to a dangerous chokehold by a Los Angeles police officer, did not have standing to pursue an injunction against the police department's practice of using chokeholds because his past injury "does nothing to establish a real and immediate threat that he would again be stopped for a traffic violation, or for any other offense, by an officer or officers who would illegally choke him into unconsciousness without any provocation or resistance on his part."

Defendants argue that plaintiffs Clarkson, Dennis, and Floyd lack standing to seek injunctive relief. Clarkson and Dennis allege that they were each stopped improperly only once between 2004 and 2009 and Dennis and Floyd no longer live in New York (although Dennis regularly visits his friends and family here and intends to move back in the future and Floyd intends to move back to the City after he finishes medical school). Accordingly, defendants argue, "[plaintiffs'] assertion that they will again be stopped and deprived of their constitutional rights is wholly speculative."

The simplest way to address defendants' concern is by noting that David Ourlicht, the fourth plaintiff, indisputably does have standing and that "the presence of one party with standing is sufficient to satisfy Article Ill's case-or-controversy requirement."[97] *First,* unlike Lyons, who alleged only one past instance of unconstitutional police behavior, Ourlicht was stopped by NYPD officers three times in 2008 and once again in 2010, after this lawsuit was filed.[98] "The possibility of recurring injury ceases to be speculative when actual repeated incidents are documented."[99] *Second,* unlike the plaintiffs in *Lyons* Ourllicht's risk of future injury does not depend on his being arrested for unlawful conduct

---

[92] Deshawn v. Safir, 156 F.3d 340, 344 (2d Cir.1998) (citing City of Los Angeles v. Lyons, 461 U.S. 95, 105–06 (1983)).

[97] Rumsfeld v. Forum for Academic and Institutional Rights, Inc., 547 U.S. 47, 53 n.2 (2006).

[98] *See* Affidavit of David Ourlicht, Ex. 5 to Charney Decl., ¶¶ 6–18.

[99] Nicacio v. United States Immigration & Naturalization Serv., 768 F.2d 1133, 1136 (9th Cir.1985). *Accord* Aguilar v. Immigration & Customs Enforcement Div. of the United States Dep't of Homeland Sec., 811 F.Supp.2d 803, 828 (S.D.N.Y.2011) (finding standing in a case where one set of plaintiffs had allegedly been subject to two unlawful searches and other plaintiffs feared repeat injury because the searches were part of defendants' "condoned, widespread, and ongoing" practice).

and so he cannot avoid that injury by following the law. The risk of injury is not based on a string of unlikely contingencies: according to his sworn affidavit, Ourlicht was stopped and frisked while going about his daily life—walking down the sidewalk, sitting on a bench, getting into a car.[101]

Finally, as I explained in the *Daniels* litigation, the frequency of alleged injuries inflicted by the practices at issue here creates a likelihood of future injury sufficient to address any standing concerns. In *Lyons,* the police department's challenged policies were responsible for ten deaths; here, the police department has conducted over 2.8 million stops over six years and its paperwork indicates that, *at the very least,* 60,000 of the stops were unconstitutional (because they were based on nothing more than a person's "furtive movement"). Every day, the NYPD conducted 1200 stops; every day, the NYPD conducted nearly thirty facially unlawful stops based on nothing more than "subjective, promiscuous appeals to an ineffable intuition."[103] In the face of these widespread practices, Ourlicht's risk of future injury is " 'real and immediate,' not 'conjectural' or 'hypothetical,' " and he satisfies Article III's standing requirements. Because Ourlicht has standing, I need not consider the standing of the other plaintiffs.[105] I nevertheless note that Dennis and Floyd have each been stopped by the NYPD more than once (although two of Dennis' three stops occurred many years ago). Even Clarkson's single stop, in light of the tens of thousands of facially unlawful stops, would likely confer standing.[106] . . . .

42 U.S.C. § 14141 Cause of Action

(a) Unlawful conduct

It shall be unlawful for any governmental authority, or any agent thereof, or any person acting on behalf of a governmental authority, to engage in a pattern or practice of conduct by law enforcement officers or by officials or employees of any governmental agency with responsibility for the administration of juvenile justice or the incarceration of juveniles that deprives persons of rights, privileges, or immunities secured or protected by the Constitution or laws of the United States.

---

[101] *See* Hodgers-Durgin v. De La Vina, 199 F.3d 1037, 1041–42 (9th Cir.1999) (en banc) (stating that the Supreme Court in Spencer v. Kemna, 523 U.S. 1, 15 (1998) "characterized the denial of Article III standing in *Lyons* as having been based on the plaintiff's ability to avoid engaging in illegal conduct").

[103] United States v. Broomfield, 417 F.3d 654, 655 (7th Cir.2005) (Posner, *J.*) (criticizing the use of the vague term "furtive" and opining that "[w]hether you stand still or move, drive above, below, or at the speed limit, you will be described by the police as acting suspiciously should they wish to stop or arrest you. Such subjective, promiscuous appeals to an ineffable intuition should not be credited.").

[105] *See Forum for Academic and Institutional Rights, Inc.,* 547 U.S. at 53 n.2.

[106] "[T]here is no per se rule requiring more than one past act, or any prior act, for that matter, as a basis for finding a likelihood of future injury." Roe v. City of New York, 151 F.Supp.2d 495, 503 (S.D.N.Y.2001).

(b) Civil action by Attorney General

Whenever the Attorney General has reasonable cause to believe that a violation of paragraph (1) has occurred, the Attorney General, for or in the name of the United States, may in a civil action obtain appropriate equitable and declaratory relief to eliminate the pattern or practice.

United States v. City of Detroit, Michigan, and Detroit Police Department

U.S. District Court for the Eastern District of Michigan,
Case no. 03-72258, filed June 12, 2003

Complaint

The United States brings this action under 42 U.S.C. § 14141 to remedy a pattern or practice of conduct by law enforcement officers of the Detroit Police Department that deprives persons of rights, privileges, and immunities secured or protected by the Constitution or laws of the United States. The defendants, through their acts and omissions, are engaging in a pattern or practice of conduct by Detroit Police Department officers of subjecting individuals to uses of excessive force, false arrests, illegal detentions, and unconstitutional conditions of confinement. The defendants have failed to adequately train, supervise, and monitor police officers; to investigate, review and evaluate use of force incidents; to investigate alleged misconduct, and discipline officers who are guilty of misconduct; to review and evaluate the basis of seizures and warrantless arrests and secure timely judicial review of such arrests; to protect detainees from undue risks of harm; and to implement effective systems to ensure that management controls adopted by the Detroit Police Department are properly carried out. Accordingly, the United States seeks a judgment granting injunctive and declaratory relief for the defendants' violations of law.

The United States of America alleges:

DEFENDANTS

1. The Defendant City of Detroit ("City") is a chartered municipal corporation in the State of Michigan.

2. The Defendant Detroit Police Department ("DPD") is a law enforcement agency operated by the City.

JURISDICTION AND VENUE

3. This Court has jurisdiction of this action under 28 U.S.C. §§ 1331 and 1345.

4. The United States is authorized to initiate this action pursuant to 42 U.S.C. § 14141.

5. Venue is proper in the Eastern District of Michigan pursuant to 28 U.S.C. § 1391, as the defendants reside in and the claims arose in the Eastern District of Michigan.

FACTUAL ALLEGATIONS

6.   The defendants, through their acts or omissions, have engaged in and continue to engage in a pattern or practice of conduct by DPD officers of using excessive force against persons in Detroit.

7.   The defendants, through their acts or omissions, have engaged in and continue to engage in a pattern or practice of conduct by DPD officers of falsely arresting persons and improperly seizing persons in Detroit.

8.   The defendants, through their acts or omissions, have engaged in and continue to engage in a pattern or practice of conduct by DPD officers of failing to secure timely judicial review of warrantless arrests of persons in Detroit.

9.   The defendants, through their acts or omissions, have engaged in and continue to engage in a pattern or practice of conduct by DPD officers of failing to protect detainees in DPD holding cells from undue risks of harm by, inter alia, failing to ensure fire safety, failing to provide adequate medical and mental health care, failing to provide adequate supervision, and failing to ensure adequate environmental health and safety conditions.

10. The defendants are, through their acts or omissions, engaging in a pattern or practice of systemic deficiencies that has resulted in the pattern or practice by DPD officers that deprives persons of rights, privileges, and immunities secured or protected by the Constitution or laws of the United States described in paragraphs 6–9 above. These systemic deficiencies include, but are not limited to:

failing to implement policies, procedures, and practices regarding use of force that appropriately guide and monitor the actions of individual DPD officers;

failing to train DPD officers adequately to prevent the occurrence of misconduct;

failing to supervise DPD officers adequately to prevent the occurrence of misconduct;

failing to monitor adequately DPD officers who engage in or may be likely to engage in misconduct;

failing to implement policies and procedures whereby complaints and other allegations of DPD officer misconduct are adequately received and investigated;

failing to investigate adequately incidents in which a DPD officer uses force;

failing to fairly and adequately adjudicate or review citizen complaints, and incidents in which a DPD officer uses force;

failing to discipline adequately DPD officers who engage in misconduct;

failing to review adequately the basis for arrests and seizures by DPD officers;

failing to develop a mechanism to ensure timely judicial review of warrantless arrests;

failing to develop an adequate fire safety program for DPD holding cells;

failing to conduct adequate medical and mental health screening and failing to provide adequate care for serious medical needs of detainees in DPD holding cells;

failing to ensure DPD officers adequately supervise detainees in DPD holding cells; and

failing to maintain DPD holding cells in a sanitary manner.

CAUSE OF ACTION

11. Through the actions described in paragraphs 6–10 above, the defendants have engaged in and continue to engage in a pattern or practice of conduct by DPD officers that deprives persons of rights, privileges, or immunities secured or protected by the Constitution (including the Fourth and Fourteenth Amendments) or the laws of the United States, in violation of 42 U.S.C. § 14141.

PRAYER FOR RELIEF

12. The Attorney General is authorized under 42 U.S.C. § 14141 to seek declaratory and equitable relief to eliminate a pattern or practice of law enforcement officer conduct that deprives persons of rights, privileges, or immunities secured or protected by the Constitution or laws of the United States.

WHEREFORE, the United States prays that the Court:

a.   declare that defendants have engaged in a pattern or practice of conduct by DPD officers that deprives persons of rights, privileges, or immunities secured or protected by the Constitution or laws of the United States, as described in paragraphs 6–10 above;

b.   order the defendants, their officers, agents, and employees to refrain from engaging in any of the predicate acts forming the basis of the pattern or practice of conduct as described in paragraphs 6–10 above;

c.   order the defendants, their officers, agents, and employees to adopt and implement policies and procedures to remedy the pattern or practice of conduct described in paragraphs 6–10 above, and to prevent DPD officers from depriving persons of rights, privileges, or immunities secured or protected by the Constitution or laws of the United States; and

d.   order such other appropriate relief as the interests of justice may require.

Respectfully submitted,

JEFFREY G. COLLINS MI Bar # P37260 United States Attorney Eastern District of Michigan

PAMELA J. THOMPSON MI Bar # P26056 Executive Assistant United States Attorney Eastern District of Michigan

JUDITH E. LEVY MI Bar # P55882 Assistant United States Attorney Eastern District of Michigan 211 West Fort Street Suite 2001 Detroit, MI 48226 Telephone: (313) 226-9501 Facsimile: (313) 226-4609

JOHN ASHCROFT Attorney General

RALPH F. BOYD, JR. Assistant Attorney General Civil Rights Division

SHANETTA Y. BROWN CUTLAR Acting Chief Special Litigation Section Civil Rights Division

MAURA K. LEE JOHN A. HENDERSON Trial Attorneys Special Litigation Section Civil Rights Division

U.S. Department of Justice Patrick Henry Building 950 Pennsylvania Avenue NW Washington, DC 20530 Telephone: (202) 514-6255 Facsimile: (202) 514-4883

Filed: June 12, 2003

United States v. City of Detroit, Michigan, and Detroit Police Department

United States District Court for the Eastern District of Michigan, Case No. 03-72258,
Consent Judgment Entered June 12, 2003 [Excerpt]

III. USE OF FORCE POLICY

A.   General Use of Force Policies

14. The DPD shall revise its use of force policies to define force as that term is defined in this Agreement.

15. The use of force policy shall incorporate a use of force continuum that:

a.   identifies when and in what manner the use of lethal and less than lethal force are permitted;

b.   relates the force options available to officers to the types of conduct by individuals that would justify the use of such force; and

c.   states that de-escalation, disengagement, area containment, surveillance, waiting out a subject, summoning reinforcements or calling in specialized units are often the appropriate response to a situation.

16. The use of force policy shall reinforce that individuals should be provided an opportunity to submit to arrest before force is used and provide that force may be used only when verbal commands and other techniques that do not require the use of force would be ineffective or present a danger to the officer or others.

17. The use of force policy shall prohibit the use of choke holds and similar carotid holds except where deadly force is authorized.

18. The DPD shall develop a revised use of force policy within three months of the effective date of this Agreement. The policy shall be submitted for review and approval of the DOJ. The DPD shall implement the revised use of force policy within three months of the review and approval of the DOJ.

19. The use of force policy shall provide that a strike to the head with an instrument constitutes a use of deadly force.

B.   Use of Firearms Policy

20. The DPD shall revise its use of firearms policies to provide that officers must successfully qualify with their department-issued firearm and any other firearm they are authorized to use or carry on-duty on a bi-annual basis, as described in paragraph 113.

21. Officers who fail to re-qualify shall be relieved of police powers and relinquish immediately all department-issued firearms. Those officers who fail to re-qualify after remedial training within a reasonable time shall be subject to disciplinary action, up to and including a recommendation for termination of employment.

22. The firearm policy shall prohibit firing at or from a moving vehicle. The policy shall also prohibit officers from intentionally placing themselves in the path of a moving vehicle.

23. The DPD shall identify a limited selection of authorized ammunition and prohibit officers from possessing or using unauthorized firearms or ammunition. The DPD shall specify the number of rounds DPD officers shall carry.

C.   Intermediate Force Device Policy

24. The DPD shall select an intermediate force device, which is between chemical spray and firearms on the force continuum, that can be carried by officers at all times while on-duty. The DPD shall develop a policy regarding the intermediate force device, incorporate the intermediate force device into the force continuum and train all officers in its use on an annual basis.

D.   Chemical Spray Policy

25. The DPD shall revise its chemical spray policy to require officers to:

a.   provide a verbal warning and time to allow the subject to comply prior to the use of chemical spray, unless such warnings would present a danger to the officer or others;

b.   provide an opportunity for decontamination to a sprayed subject within twenty minutes of the application of the spray or apprehension of the subject;

c.   obtain appropriate medical assistance for sprayed subjects when they complain of continued effects after having been de-contaminated or they indicate that they have a pre-existing medical condition (e.g., asthma, emphysema, bronchitis or heart ailment) that may be aggravated by chemical spray and if such signs are observed the subject shall be immediately conveyed to a local hospital for professional medical treatment; and

d.   obtain the approval of a supervisor any time chemical spray is used against a crowd.

26. The DPD shall prohibit officers from using chemical spray on a handcuffed individual in a police vehicle. The DPD shall also prohibit officers from keeping any sprayed subject in a face down position, in order to avoid positional asphyxia.

INCIDENT DOCUMENTATION, INVESTIGATION, AND REVIEW

General Investigations of Police Action

27. The DPD and the City shall revise their policies regarding the conduct of all investigations to ensure full, thorough and complete investigations. All investigations shall, to the extent reasonably possible, determine whether the officer's conduct was justified and the DPD and the City shall prohibit the closing of an investigation being conducted by the DPD and/or the City simply because a subject or complainant is unavailable, unwilling or unable to cooperate, including a refusal to provide medical records or proof of injury.

28. The DPD and the City shall ensure that investigations are conducted by a supervisor who did not authorize, witness or participate in the incident and that all investigations contain:

a.   documentation of the name and badge number of all officers involved in or on the scene during the incident and a canvass of the scene to identify civilian witnesses;

b.   thorough and complete interviews of all witnesses, subject to paragraph 31 below and an effort to resolve material inconsistencies between witness statements;

c.   photographs of the subject's(s') and officer's(s') injuries or alleged injuries; and

d.   documentation of any medical care provided.

29. The DPD and the City shall revise their procedures for all investigatory interviews to require:

a.   officers who witness or are involved in an incident to provide a timely statement regarding the incident (subject to paragraph 31 below);

b.   whenever practicable and appropriate, interviews of complainants and witnesses be conducted at sites and times convenient for them, including at their residences or places of business; and

c.   that all IAD, OCI and Critical Firearm Discharge Investigations shall also include in-person video or audio tape-recorded interviews of all complainants, witnesses, and involved DPD officers and prohibit group interviews. In cases where complainants/witnesses refuse in-person video or audio tape recorded interviews, written statements shall be taken and signed by the complainant/witness along with a signed refusal statement by the complainant/witness.

30. The DPD and the City procedures for all investigatory interviews shall prohibit:

a. the use of leading questions that improperly suggest legal justifications for the officer's(s') actions when such questions are contrary to appropriate law enforcement techniques; and

b. the use of interviews via written questions when it is contrary to appropriate law enforcement techniques.

31. The DPD and the City shall develop a protocol for when statements should (and should not) be compelled pursuant to Garrity v. New Jersey, 385 U.S. 493 (1967).

32. The DPD shall revise its policies regarding all investigatory reports and evaluations to require:

a. a precise description of the facts and circumstances of the incident, including a detailed account of the subject's(s') or complainant's(s')and officer's(s') actions and an evaluation of the initial stop or seizure;

b. a review of all relevant evidence, including circumstantial, direct and physical evidence;

c. that the fact that a subject or complainant pled guilty or was found guilty of an offense shall not be considered as evidence of whether a DPD officer engaged in misconduct, nor shall it justify discontinuing the investigation;

d. reasonable credibility determinations, with no automatic preference given to an officer's statement over a non-officer's statement or discounting of a witness's statement merely because the witness has some connection to the subject or complainant;

e. an evaluation of whether an officer complied with DPD policy;

f. an evaluation of all uses of force, including the officer's tactics, and any allegations or evidence of misconduct uncovered during the course of the investigation;

g. all administrative investigations to be evaluated based on a preponderance of the evidence standard;

h. written documentation of the basis for extending the deadline of a report and evaluation and provide that the circumstances justifying an extension do not include an investigator's vacation or furlough and that problems with investigator vacations or workload should result in the matter being reassigned; and

i. any recommended non-disciplinary corrective action or disciplinary action be documented in writing.

33. The DPD shall revise its policies regarding the review of all investigations to require:

a.   investigations to be reviewed by the chain of command above the investigator;

b.   the reviewing supervisors to identify any deficiencies in those investigations and require the investigator to correct any deficiencies within seven days of the submission of the report and evaluation to the reviewing supervisor;

c.   the reviewing supervisors to recommend and the final reviewing authority to refer any incident with training, policy or procedural implications to the appropriate DPD unit;

d.   appropriate non-disciplinary corrective action and/or disciplinary action when an investigator fails to conduct or reviewing supervisor fails to evaluate an investigation appropriately; and

e.   a written explanation by any supervisor, including the Chief of Police, who disagrees with a finding or departs from a recommended non-disciplinary corrective action or disciplinary action, including the basis for the departure.

B.   Use of Force and Prisoner Injury Investigations

34. The DPD shall revise its reporting policies to require officers to document on a single auditable form any prisoner injury, use of force, allegation of use of force, and instance in which an officer draws a firearm and acquires a target.

35. The DPD shall revise its policies regarding use of force and prisoner injury notifications to require:

a.   officers to notify their supervisors following any use of force or prisoner injury;

b.   that upon such notice, a supervisor shall respond to the scene of all uses of force that involve a firearm discharge, a visible injury or a complaint of injury. A supervisor shall respond to all other uses of force on a priority basis. Upon arrival at the scene, the supervisor shall interview the subject(s), examine the subject(s) for injury, and ensure that the subject(s) receive needed medical attention;

c.   the supervisor responding to the scene to notify IAD of all serious uses of force, uses of force that result in visible injury, uses of force that a reasonable officer should have known were likely to result in injury, uses of force where there is evidence of possible criminal misconduct by an officer or prisoner injury; and

d.   IAD to respond to the scene of, and investigate, all incidents where there is evidence of possible criminal misconduct by an officer, a prisoner dies, suffers serious bodily injury or requires hospital admission, or involves a serious use of force, and to permit IAD to delegate all other use of force or prisoner injury investigations to the supervisor for a command investigation.

36. The DPD shall revise its use of force and prisoner injury investigation policies to require:

a. command use of force preliminary investigations to be completed within 10 days of the incident. These investigations shall include a synopsis of the incident, photographs of any injuries, witness statements, a canvas of the area, a profile of the officer's prior uses of force and allegations of misconduct, and a first-line supervisory evaluation. The final command use of force investigation shall be completed within 30 days of the incident;

b. IAD investigations to be completed within 60 days of the incident; and

c. copies of all reports and command investigations to be sent to IAD within 7 days of completion of the investigation.

C. Review of Critical Firearm Discharges and In-Custody Deaths

37. The DPD has created a Shooting Team, composed of officers from the Homicide Section and IAD. The Shooting Team shall respond to the scene and investigate all critical firearms discharges and in-custody deaths.

38. The DPD shall develop a protocol for conducting investigations of critical firearm discharges that, in addition to the requirements of paragraphs 27–36, requires:

a. the investigation to account for all shots fired, all shell casings, and the locations of all officers at the time the officer discharged the firearm;

b. the investigator to conduct and preserve in the investigative file all appropriate ballistic or crime scene analyses, including gunshot residue or bullet trajectory tests; and

c. the investigation to be completed within 30 days of the incident. If a Garrity statement is necessary, then that portion of the investigation may be deferred until 30 days from the declination or conclusion of the criminal prosecution.

39. The DPD shall require a command level force review team to evaluate all critical firearm discharges and in-custody deaths. The team shall be chaired by the Deputy Chief who directly supervises IAD. The DPD shall establish criteria for selecting the other members of the team.

40. The DPD policy that defines the command level force review team's role shall require the team to:

a. complete its review of critical firearm discharges that result in injury and in-custody deaths within 90 days of the resolution of any criminal review and/or proceedings and all other critical firearm discharges within 60 days and require the Chief of Police to complete his or her review of the team's report within 14 days;

b.   comply with the revised review of investigations policies and procedures;

c.   interview the principal investigators; and

d.   prepare a report to the Chief of Police in compliance with the revised investigatory report and evaluation protocol.

41. The Chair of the command level force review team shall annually review critical firearm discharges and in-custody deaths in aggregate to detect patterns and/or problems and report his or her findings and recommendations, including additional investigative protocols and standards for all critical firearm discharge and in-custody death investigations, to the Chief of Police.

V.   ARREST AND DETENTION POLICIES AND PRACTICES

A.   Arrest Policies

42. The DPD shall revise its arrest policies to define arrest and probable cause as those terms are defined in this Agreement and prohibit the arrest of an individual with less than probable cause.

43. The DPD shall review all arrests for probable cause at the time the arrestee is presented at the precinct or specialized unit. This review shall be memorialized in writing within 12 hours of the arrest. For any arrest unsupported by probable cause or in which an arraignment warrant was not sought, the DPD shall document the circumstances of the arrest and/or the reasons the arraignment warrant was not sought on an auditable form within 12 hours of the event.

B.   Investigatory Stop Policies

44. The DPD shall revise its investigatory stop and frisk policies to define investigatory stop and reasonable suspicion as those terms are defined in this Agreement. The policy shall specify that a frisk is authorized only when the officer has reasonable suspicion to fear for his or her safety and that the scope of the frisk must be narrowly tailored to those specific reasons.

45. The DPD shall require written documentation of all investigatory stops and frisks by the end of the shift in which the police action occurred. The DPD shall review all investigatory stops and frisks and document on an auditable form those unsupported by reasonable suspicion within 24 hours of receiving the officer's report.

C.   Witness Identification and Questioning Policies

46. The DPD shall revise its witness identification and questioning policies to comply with the revised arrest and investigatory stop policies. The DPD shall prohibit the seizure of an individual without reasonable suspicion, probable cause or consent of the individual and require that the scope and duration of any seizure be narrowly tailored to the reasons supporting the police action. The DPD shall prohibit the conveyance of

any individual to another location without reasonable suspicion, probable cause or consent of the individual.

47. The DPD shall develop the revised witness identification and questioning policies within three months of the effective date of this Agreement. The revised policies shall be submitted for review and approval of the DOJ. The DPD shall implement the revised witness identification and questioning policies within three months of the review and approval of the DOJ.

48. The DPD shall document the content and circumstances of all interviews, interrogations and conveyances during the shift in which the police action occurred. The DPD shall review in writing all interviews, interrogations and conveyances and document on an auditable form those in violation of DPD policy within 12 hours of the interview, interrogation or conveyance.

D.   Prompt Judicial Review Policies

49. The DPD shall revise its policies to require prompt judicial review, as defined in this Agreement, for every person arrested by the DPD. The DPD shall develop a timely and systematic process for all arrestees to be presented for prompt judicial review or to be released.

50. The DPD shall require that, for each arrestee, a warrant request for arraignment on the charges underlying the arrest is submitted to the prosecutor's office within 24 hours of the arrest.

51. The DPD shall document on an auditable form all instances in which the request for an arraignment warrant is submitted more than 24 hours after the arrest. The DPD shall also document on an auditable form all instances in which it is not in compliance with the prompt judicial review policy and in which extraordinary circumstances delayed the arraignment. The documentation shall occur by the end of the shift in which there was 1) a failure to request an arraignment warrant within 24 hours, 2) a failure to comply with the prompt judicial review policy, or 3) an arraignment delayed because of extraordinary circumstances.

E.   Hold Policies

52. The DPD shall revise its hold policies to define a hold as that term is defined in this Agreement and require that all holds be documented. The policy shall establish a timely and systematic process for persons in DPD custody who have holds issued by a City of Detroit court to have those holds cleared by presenting the arrestee to the court from which the warrant was issued or the setting and posting of bond where applicable. The fact that an arrestee has not been arraigned or charged on the current arrest shall not delay this process.

53. The DPD shall document all holds, including the time each hold was identified and the time each hold was cleared. The DPD shall document on an auditable form each instance in which a hold is not processed within twenty-four hours on a daily basis.

F.   Restriction Policies

54. The DPD shall develop a policy regarding restricting detainee's access to telephone calls and visitors that permits individuals in DPD custody access to attorneys and reasonable access to telephone calls and visitors.

55. The DPD shall require that such restrictions be documented and reviewed at the time the restriction is issued and reevaluated each day in which the restriction remains in effect. The DPD shall document on an auditable form any violation of the restriction policy by the end of the shift in which the violation occurred.

G.   Material Witness Policies

56. The DPD shall revise its material witness policies to define material witness as that term is defined in this Agreement and remove the term "police witness" from DPD policies and procedures.

57. The DPD shall obtain a court order prior to taking a material witness into DPD custody. The DPD shall document on an auditable form the detention of each material witness and attach a copy of the court order authorizing the detention.

H.   Documentation of Custodial Detention

58. The DPD shall revise its arrest and detention documentation to require, for all arrests, a record or file to contain accurate and auditable documentation of:

a.   the individual's personal information;

b.   the crime(s) charged;

c.   the time and date of arrest and release;

d.   the time and date the arraignment warrant was submitted;

e.   the name and badge number of the officer who submitted the arraignment warrant;

f.   the time and date of arraignment;

g.   the time and date each warrant was lodged and cleared, if applicable; and

h.   the individual's custodial status, e.g., new arrest, material witness or extradition.

I.   Command Notification

59. The DPD shall require the commander of the precinct and, if applicable, of the specialized unit to review in writing all reported violations of DPD arrest, investigatory stop and frisk, witness identification and questioning policies and all reports of arrests in which an arraignment warrant was not sought. The commander's review shall be completed within 7 days of receiving the document reporting the event. The commander's review shall include an evaluation of the actions

taken to correct the violation and whether any corrective or non-disciplinary action was taken.

60. The DPD shall require the commander of the precinct and, if applicable, of the specialized unit to review in writing all violations of DPD prompt judicial review, holds, restrictions and material witness policies on a daily basis. The commander's review shall include an evaluation of the actions taken to correct the violation and whether any corrective or non-disciplinary action was taken.

8. EMPIRICAL NOTE: STUDYING INSTITUTIONAL REFORM INJUNCTIONS

Do institutional reform injunctions work? At what cost? Scholars have studied the reform process in multiple jurisdictions. *See* Michael D. White et al., *Federal Civil Litigation as an Instrument of Police Reform: A Natural Experiment Exploring the Effects of the* Floyd *Ruling on Stop-and-Frisk in New York City,* 14 Oh. St. J. Crim. L. 9 (2016); Stephen Rushin & Griffin Edwards, *De-Policing,* 102 Cornell L. Rev. 721(2017); Joshua Chanin, *Evaluating Section 14141: An Empirical Review of Pattern or Practice Police Misconduct Reform,* 14 Oh. St. J. Crim. L. 67 (2016); Stephen Rushin, *Competing Case Studies of Structural Reform Litigation in American Police Departments,* 14 Oh. St. J. Crim. L. 113 (2016).

In general the research thus far shows that (1) During the period of judicial oversight, police compliance with constitutional standards (measured by data including reports of *Terry* and traffic stops, number of citizen complaints, and tort damages paid) improves; (2) crime may increase (or decrease less quickly) as a result of the agreement; but (3) crime increases are not dramatic and disappear over time; while (4) long-term improvements in police compliance with legal requirements occur in some departments, but others revert to prior practices after judicial oversight ends.

A recent study by Paul Cassell and Richard Fowles reports a dramatic result at odds with the findings of prior research. *See* Paul G. Cassell & Richard Fowles, *What Caused the 2016 Chicago Homicide Spike? An Examination of the "ACLU Effect" and the Role of Stops and Frisks in Preventing Gun Violence,* 2018 U. Ill. L. Rev. 1581. The authors find that following a civil settlement with the ACLU, Chicago police curtailed aggressive street patrol. The following year, Chicago homicides rose from 480 to 754. Cassell & Fowles attribute 245 of these additional homicides to the decreased use of stop-and-frisk.

Some skepticism may be in order, because (1) other jurisdictions subject to consent decrees experienced nothing like such a dramatic increase in violent crime; and (2) because Chicago's homicide rate has declined to nearly where it stood in 2015. *See* Ray Sanchez & Omar Jimenez, *Chicago Lauds Homicide Decline as Other U.S. Cities Combat*

Murders, at https://www.cnn.com/2020/01/02/us/chicago-us-cities-gun-violence/index.html (Jan. 2, 2020) ("the nation's third-most populous city recorded 492 murder in 2019, according to Chicago police—about 13% lower than 2018's total of 564.") The decline of course *might* have been even steeper without the ACLU lawsuit.

However the empirical research ultimately shakes out, we should distinguish the question of whether reform injunctions encourage compliance with constitutional requirements from the question of whether those constitutional standards are too restrictive or too permissive. Reform injunctions, like the one in Detroit, *supra,* impose substantive rules (like 12 hour probable cause review by the police), record-keeping requirements (like documenting stops-and-frisks, including the race of the suspect), and accountability procedures (like prompt investigations of citizen complaints). If these measures increase crime solely by reducing the amount of unconstitutional policing, it is the constitutional law, not the means by which that law comes to be observed, that deserves the blame. If by contrast reform injunctions prevent some unconstitutional policing but also prevent much constitutional policing along the way, the costs of whatever increased crime the research shows may more properly be attributed to the remedial, rather than the substantive, law.

CHAPTER 6

Self-Incrimination Clause Limits on Police Investigations

1. Origins of the Fifth Amendment

Lilburne's Case
Star Chamber, 1637

[Source: John Rushworth, 'Historical Collections: 1637 (3 of 5)', Historical Collections of Private Passages of State: Volume 2: 1629–38 (1721), pp. 461–481. URL: http://www.british-history.ac.uk/report.aspx?compid=74 904&strquery=johnlilburne Date accessed: 05 March 2009].

Feb. 13. Star-Chamber.

Information was preferred in Star-Chamber by the King's Attorney-General, against John Lilburne and John Warton, for the unlawful Printing and Publishing of Libellous and Seditious Books, Entituled News from Ipswich, &c. they were brought up to the Office, and there refused to take an Oath to answer Interrogatories, saying it was the Oath ex Officio, and that no free-born English man ought to take it, not being bound by the Law to accuse himself, (whence ever after he was called Free-born John) his offence was aggravated, in that he printed these Libellous and Seditious Books, contrary to a Decree in Star-Chamber, prohibiting printing without License: which Decree was made this Year in the Month of July, and was to this effect.

July 1637. A Decree of Star-Chamber against Printing without License.

That none shall presume to Print any Book or Pamphlet whatsoever, unless the same be first Licensed with all the Titles, Epistles, and Prefaces therewith imprinted, by the Lord Arch-bishop of Canterbury, or the Bishop of London for the time being, or by their appointment; and within the Limits of either University, by the Chancellor or Vice-Chancellor thereof, upon pain that every Printer so offending shall for ever thereafter be disabled to exercise the Art of Printing, and shall suffer such further punishment, as by this Court, or the High-Commission, shall be thought fitting; that before any Books imported from Forreign Parts shall be exposed to sale, a true Catalogue thereof shall be presented to the Arch-bishop of Canterbury, or the Bishop of London: And that no Officers of the Custom shall deliver any Forreign Books out of their Hands and Custody, before those Bishops shall have appointed one of their Chaplains, or some other Learned Man, with the Master and

Wardens of the Company of Stationers, or one of them, to be present at the opening of the Pack and Fardels, and to view the same. And those that disobey this Injunction, are to be Censured in this or the High-Commission Court, as the several Causes shall require. And if in this Search there happen to be found any schismatical or offensive Books, they shall be brought to the aforesaid Bishops, or the High-Commission Office, that the Offenders may be punished. That no Person whatsoever shall imprint in the Parts beyond the Sea, or Import from thence, any English Books, or whereof the greater part is English, whether formerly Printed or not. And that no Books whatsoever shall be re-printed, though formerly Licensed, without a new License first obtained, upon pain of like Censure and Punishment. And that if any Person whatsoever that is not an allowed Printer shall presume to set up a Press for Printing, or work at any such Press, or Set and Compose Letters for the same, he shall be set in the Pillory, and whipt through the City of London.

The 13th of February the said Lilburne and Warton were brought to the Bar at the Court of Star-Chamber, and the Court proceeded to Sentence, which you have here in the very words, as they were entred in the Registers Book, written out by Mr. Arthur himself, the Deputy Register, who was an able and friendly Man in his Place.

But before they proceeded to Sentence this ensuing Order was read.

In Camera Stellata coram Concilio ibidem 9. die Febr. Anno 13 Car' Regis.

John Lilburne and Warton brought to the Bar.

'Upon Information this day to this Honourable Court, by Sir John Banks Knight, His Majesties Attorney-General, That John Lilburne and John Warton, who are now at the Bar of this Court, were the 24th of January last ordered to be examined upon Interrogatories touching their unlawful Printing, publishing, and dispersing of Libellous and Seditious Books, contrary to the Decree of this Court, which was verified by Affidavit; and being brought up to the Office to appear and be examined accordingly, the said Lilburne refused to appear, and both of them denied to take an Oath to make answer to Interrogatories, as appears by Certificate of Mr. Goad: It was humbly pray'd that their Appearance may be Recorded, they being now present in Court, and that they may now have their Oaths tendred unto them; which if they shall refuse to take, that then this Court will proceed to a Censure against them for their high Contempt therein, as hath been used in like Cases; which the Court held fit. And hath therefore ordered, That their Appearance shall be Recorded, as is desired. And for that the said Delinquents do now again most contemptuously refuse to take their Oaths now tendred to them in open Court. Their Lordships have further ordered, That the said Lilburne and Warton shall be remanded to the Prison of the Fleet, there to remain close Prisoners until they conform themselves in obedience to take their Oaths, and be examined; and that unless they do take their Oaths, and yield to be examined by Monday-night next, their Lordships will, on the last sitting of this Term, proceed to Censure against them for their contempts therein, as is desired.

Hereupon the Court proceeded to Sentence.

In Camera Stellata coram Concilio ibidem 13 die Febr' Anno decimo tertio Car' Regis.

The Decree and Sentence in Star-Chamber against Jo. Lilburne, as it is on Record.

'Whereas, upon Information to this Court the ninth of this instant February, by Sir John Banks Knight, His Majesties Attorney-General, That John Lilburne and John Warton (then present at the Bar) were the 24th of January last ordered to be examined upon Interrogatories touching their unlawful printing, importing, publishing, and dispersing of Libellous and Seditious Books, contrary to the Decree of this Court, which was verified by Affidavit; and being brought up to the Office to appear and be examined, the said Lilburne refused to appear, and both of them denied to take an Oath to make some answer to Interrogatories, as appeared by the Certificate of Mr. Goad, Deputy Clark of this Court: The Court did on that day order, That their Appearances should be Recorded, they being present in Court as aforesaid; And that in respect the said Delinquents did then again contemptuously refuse to take their Oaths tendred to them in open Court, they should be remanded to the Prison of the Fleet, there to remain close Prisoners, until they conformed themselves in obedience to take their Oaths, and be examined; and that unless they did take their Oaths, and yield to be examined by Monday-night then next following, and now last past, their Lordships would on this sitting-day proceed to a Censure against them for their contempts therein. Now this day the said Lilburne and Warton being again brought to the Bar, His Majesties said Attorney informed this Honourable Court, that they still continued in their former obstinacy, and contemptuously refused to take their Oaths, to make true answer to the Interrogatories, although they had been sent for, and their Oaths assented to be given unto them by Mr. Goad Deputy-Clark of this Court, who now certified the same in Court: And therefore His Majesties said Attorney humbly pleaded on His Majesties behalf, That their Lordships would now proceed to Censure against the said Delinquents, for their great contempts and disobedience therein. Whereupon their Lordships endeavoured, by fair perswasions, to draw them to conformity and obedience, and withal offered, that if they yet would submit and take their Oaths, their Lordships would accept thereof, and not proceed to Censure against them. But such was the insufferable disobedience and contempt of the said Delinquents, that they still persisted in their former obstinacy, and wilfully refused to take their Oaths. In respect whereof the whole Court did, with an unanimous consent, declare and adjudge the said Lilburne and Warton guilty of a very high contempt and offence of dangerous consequence and evil example, and worthy to undergo very sharp, severe, and exemplary Censure, which might deter others from the like presumptuous boldness in refusing to take a legal Oath; without which many great and exorbitant offences, to the prejudice and danger of His Majesty, His Kingdoms, and Loving Subjects, might go away undiscovered, and unpunished. And therefore their Lordships have now ordered, adjudged and decreed, That the said Lilburne and Warton shall be remanded to the Fleet, there to remain until they conform themselves in obedience to the Orders of this Court, and that they shall pay Five Hundred Pounds a-piece for their several Fines to his Majesties use; and before their enlargements out of the Fleet, become bound with good Sureties for their good behaviour. And to the end that others may be the more deterred from daring to offend in the like kind hereafter, the Court hath further ordered and decreed, That the said John Lilburne shall be whipt through the Streets, from the Prison of the Fleet unto the Pillory, to be erected at such time, and in such (fn. 1) place as this Court shall hold fit and direct; and that both he and the said Warton shall be both of them set in the said Pillory, and from thence be returned to the Fleet, there to remain according to this Decree.

And the following Year in Easter-Term, falling on the 18th of April, was this Sentence executed with the utmost rigour on Lilburne, who was smartly whipt from the Fleet to Westminster.

Whilst he was whipt at the Cart, and stood in the Pillory, he uttered many bold Speeches against the Tyranny of Bishops, &c. and when his Head was in the hole of the Pillory, he scattered sundry Copies of Pamphlets, (said to be seditious) and tossed them among the People, taking them out of his Pocket; whereupon the Court of Star-Chamber (then sitting being informed) immediately ordered Lilburne to be gagged during the residue of the time he was to stand in the Pillory, which was done accordingly; and when he could not speak, he stamped with his Feet, thereby intimating to the Beholders, he would still speak were his Mouth at liberty; and the Court of Star-Chamber that day made also this following Order.

April 8. 1638. John Lilburne uttered scandalous Speeches in the Pillory.

'Whereas John Lilburne, Prisoner in the Fleet, by Sentence in Star-Chamber, did this day suffer condign Punishment for his several offences, by whipping at a Cart, and standing in the Pillory, and (as their Lordships were this day informed) during the time that his Body was under the said Execution, audaciously and wickedly, not only uttered sundry scandalous and seditious Speeches, but likewise scattered sundry Copies of Seditious Books amongst the People that beheld the said Execution, for which very thing, amongst other offences of like nature, he had been Censured in the said Court by the aforesaid Sentence. It was thereupon ordered by their Lordships, That the said Lilburne should be laid alone with Irons on his Hands and Legs in the Wards of the Fleet, where the basest and meanest efort of Prisoners are used to be put, and that the Warden of the Fleet take special care to hinder the resort of any Person whatsoever unto him, and particularly that he be not supplied with any Hand, and that he take special notice of all Letters, Writings, and Books brought unto him, and seize and deliver the same unto their Lordships; And take notice from time to time who they be that resort to the said Prison to visit the said Lilburne, or to speak with him, and inform the Board. And it was lastly ordered, That hereafter all Persons that shall be produced to receive Corporal Punishment according to Sentence of that Court, or by order of the Board, shall have their Garments searched before they be brought forth, and neither Writing nor other thing suffered to be about them, and their Hands likewise to be bound during the time they are under Punishment, whereof (together with the other Premisses) the said Warden of the Fleet is hereby required to take notice, and to have special care, that this their Lordships Order be accordingly observed.

And on the said 18th of April it was further ordered by the said Court of Star-Chamber,

John Lilburne to be examined touching his Speeches in the Pillory, and dispersing Libellous Books.

'That His Majesties Attorney and Sollicitor-General should be hereby prayed and required, to take strict examination of John Lilburne Prisoner in the Fleet, touching the demeanour and Speeches of him the said Lilburne during the time of his whipping and standing in the Pillory this day, according to sentence of His Majesties Court of Star-Chamber, particularly, whether the said Lilburne did at that time utter any Speeches tending to Sedition or to the dishonour of the said Court of Star-Chamber, or any Member of the said Court? and whether he did throw about and disperse at the same time any Seditious Pamphlets and Books, either of that sort for which he was formerly Censured, or any other of like nature? What the Speeches were, and who heard them? what the said Books were, and whence and of whom the said Lilburne had them? and what other material Circumstances they shall think fit to examine, either the said Lilburne upon, or any other Person by whom they shall think good to inform themselves for the better finding out the truth: And thereupon to make Certificate to the Board what they find, together with their opinions.

Lilburne having for some time endured close Imprisonment, lying with double Irons on his Feet and Hands in the Inner-Wards of the Prison, there happened a Fire in the Prison of the Fleet, near to the place where he was a Prisoner, which gave a jealousie that Lilburne, in his fury and anguish of pain, was desperate, and had set the Fleet-Prison on fire, not regarding himself to be burnt with it; whereupon the Inhabitants without the Fleet, (the Street then being not five or six yards over from the Prison-door) and the Prisoners within all cryed, Release Lilburne, or we shall all be burnt; and thereupon they run head-long, and made the Warden remove him out of his Hold, and the Fire was quenched, and he remained a Prisoner in a place where he had some more Air. He continued in Prison till November the third 1640. when the first long Parliament begun, and then he was released.

We beg of the Reader further pardon for a little digression. This very John Lilburne, after he had served the Parliament in the War many years, was imprisoned by them for speaking and publishing things against them, as Usurpers, and Enemies to Magna Charta, &c. which offended those times; whereupon he was banished the Kingdom on pain of death if he did return: but return he did, in defiance of those then in Power, and was thereupon sent to Newgate, and Arraigned at the Sessions-House in the Old-Bayly for his Life, and was there publickly acquitted by a Jury of Life and Death, notwithstanding the Law made to banish him; which for Joy occasioned a great Acclamation of the People then present. He writ many Books against those then in Power and Authority, and some particular Members thereof; insomuch as it was said by Henry Martin in favour of him, That if there were none living but himself, John would be against Lilburne, and Lilburne against John. At last he dyed a Quaker, and was buried in the Church-yard near Bedlam, 4000 Citizens and others accompanying his Corps to the Grave.

Pardon digression a little more to what followeth.

When the Impeachment of the House of Commons on John Lilburne's behalf went up to the House of Peers against those his Judges in Star-Chamber, it was thus urged by those that managed the same.

That Imprisonment is a Man buried alive, is made Corpus immobile Legis, the immoveable Subject of the Law. There is an end when Life is taken away, but in this no end. Nondum tibi cedit in gratiam, to put a Man out of his pain was accounted a Favour by the Romans.

Close Imprisonment was never used to the Primitive Christians by any Tyrant; for then that heavy Charge in Scripture, I was in Prison, and ye visited me not, might be answered; but a Close Imprisonment may presume a Famishment, and so Death. The Romans had four Punishments, Lapidatio, Combustio, Decollatio, and Strangulatio, but never famishing to death. This Man might have been so, as it was sworn.

Three years Imprisonment till the Parliament released him, and might otherwise have been for ever.

Whipping was painful and shameful, Flagellation for Slaves. In the Eleventh of Elizabeth, one Cartwright brought a Slave from Russia, and would scourge him, for which he was questioned; and it was resolved, That England was too pure an Air for Slaves to breath in. And indeed it was often resolved, even in Star-Chamber, That no Gentleman was to be whipt for any offence whatsoever; and his whipping was too severe. The Manager further saith,

That John Lilburne was a Free Citizen of London, descended from an ancient Family in the North, a Town in Northumberland, still bearing the Name of Lilburne, or rather Le-Isle-borne, by reason of the Water (fn.

2) that runs about it. The Arms belonging to the Family are three Water-budgets, an ancient bearing of Arms.

Now as to his whipping, observe the distance, from the Fleet to Westminster is about a Mile, that he had 500 Blows (one swears a great many more) with a terrible Corded-whip with knots upon it.

Among the Romans no Malefactor had above 40 Stripes, and with three Thongs; and St. Paul received but 39 Stripes, which was but 13 Blows. And it is worth the observation, that not long since, at Orleans in France, a Priest was sentenced to be whipt for Fornication with a poor Maid, telling her that St. Francis would come and lye with her such a night, at which time he feigned himself to be St. Francis, and was taken in Bed with her. The King's Advocates pressed the Judges, that he might receive 14 Blows with a three Corded-whip; but the Judges would not Sentence him to more than 13 Blows, because Ampliandi sunt favores; but if our Arithmetick be right, (not to sport with his pain) Lilburne had by this Numeration, three times Five Hundred Stripes in 500 Blows. The Manager further urged.

That this Punishment of the Pillory was first invented for Mountebanks and Cheats, that having gotten upon Banks and Fourms to abuse the People, were exalted in the same kind to be set upon the Pillory, an open shame to the Multitude.

Now Gagging is barbarous, and beastly; for Man differs from Beasts both Ratione and Oratione.

So that to sum up his Sufferings, by Imprisonment he was made a dead Trunk; by whipping, a Rogue; by Pillory, a Cheat; and by Gagging, a Beast. They had better have hanged him outright, &c.

Here followeth an Order of the House of Peers made upon John Lilburne's Appeal to them Anno 1640. against his Censure in Star-Chamber, and his Imprisonment, &c. which the Reader is desired to take in good part, although it be a digression in point of time.

John Lilburne.

Whereas the Cause of John Lilburne Gent. came this day to a Hearing at the Bar, by His Councel, being transmitted from the House of Commons, concerning a Sentence pronounced against him in the Star-Chamber, Feb. 17. Anno 13 Car. Regis, and after an Examination of the whole Proceedings, and a due consideration of the said Sentence, it is this day adjudged, ordered, and determined by the Lords in Parliament Assembled, That the said Sentence, and all Proceedings thereupon, shall forthwith be for ever totally vacuated, obliterated, and taken off the file in all Courts where they are yet remaining, as illegal, and most unjust, against the liberty of the Subject, and the Law of Land, and Magna Charta, and unfit to continue upon Record; and that the said Lilburne shall be for ever absolutely freed, and totally discharged from the said Sentence, and all Proceedings thereupon as fully and amply, as though never any such thing had been. And that all Estreats and Process in the

Court of Exchequer for levying of any Fine, (if any such be) shall be wholly cancelled and made void, any thing to the contrary in any wise notwithstanding.

Act for Regulating the Privy Council and for taking away the Court commonly called the Star Chamber

July 5, 1641

WHEREAS by the great charter many times confirmed in parliament, it is enacted, That no freeman shall be taken or imprisoned, or disseised of his freehold or liberties, or free customs, or be outlawed or exiled or otherwise destroyed, and that the King will not pass upon him, or condemn him; but by lawful judgment of his peers, or by the law of the land: (2) and by another statute made in the fifth year of the reign of King Edward the Third, it is enacted, That no man shall be attached by any accusation, nor forejudged of life or limb, nor his lands, tenements, goods nor chattels seized into the King's hands, against the form of the great charter and the law of the land: (3) and by another statute made in the five and twentieth year of the reign of the same King Edward the Third, it is accorded, assented and established, That none shall be taken by petition or suggestion made to the King, or to his council, unless it be by indictment or presentment of good and lawful people of the same neighbourhood where such deeds be done, in due manner, or by process made by writ original at the common law, and that none be put out of his franchise or freehold, unless he be duly brought in to answer, and forejudged of the same by the course of the law, and if any thing be done against the same, it shall be redressed and holden for none: (4) and by another statute made in the eight and twentieth year of the reign of the same King Edward the Third, it is amongst other things enacted, That no man of what estate or condition soever he be, shall be put out of his lands or tenements, nor taken, nor imprisoned, nor disinherited, without being brought in to answer by due process of law: (5) and by another statute made in the two and fortieth year of the reign of the said King Edward the Third, it is enacted, That no man be put to answer, without presentment before justices, or matter of record, or by due process and writ original, according to the old law of the land, and if any thing be done to the contrary, it shall be void in law, and holden for error: (6) and by another statute made in the six and thirtieth year of the same King Edward the Third, it is amongst other things enacted, That all pleas which shall be pleaded in any courts before any the King's justices, or in his other places, or before any of his other ministers, or in the courts and places of any other lords within the realm, shall be entred and enrolled in latin: (7) and whereas by the statutes made in the third year of King Henry the Seventh, power is given to the chancellor, the lord treasurer of England for the time being, and the keeper of the King's privy seal, or two of them, calling unto them a bishop and a temporal lord of the King's most honourable council, and the two chief justices of the King's bench and common pleas for the time being, or other two justices in their absence, to proceed as in that act is expressed, for the punishment of some particular offences therein mentioned: (8) and by the statute made in the one and twentieth year of King Henry the Eighth, the president of the council is associated to join with the lord chancellor and other judges in the said statute of the Third of Henry the Seventh mentioned; (9) but the said judges have not kept themselves to the points limited by the said statute, but have undertaken to punish where no law doth warrant, and to make decrees for things having no such authority, and to inflict heavier punishments than by any law is warranted:

II. And forasmuch as all matters examinable or determinable before the said judges, or in the court commonly called the star-chamber, may have their proper remedy and redress, and their due punishment and correction, by the common law of the land, and in the ordinary course of justice elsewhere; (2) and forasmuch as the reasons and motives inducing the erection and continuance of that court do now cease: (3) and the proceedings, censures and decrees of that court, have by experience been found to be an intolerable burthen to the subjects, and the means to introduce an arbitrary power and government; (4) and forasmuch as the council-table hath of late times assumed unto it self a power to intermeddle in civil causes and matters only of private interest between party and party, and have adventured to determine of the estates and liberties of the subject, contrary to the law of the land and the rights and privileges of the subject, by which great and manifold mischief and inconveniencies have arisen and happened, and much incertainty by means of such-proceedings hath been conceived concerning mens rights and estates; for settling whereof, and preventing the like in time to come,

III. Be it ordained and enacted by the authority of this present parliament, That the said court commonly called the star-chamber, and all jurisdiction, power and authority belonging unto, or exercised in the same court, or by any the judges, officers, or ministers thereof, be from the first day of August in the year of our Lord God one thousand six hundred forty and one, clearly and absolutely dissolved, taken away and determined; (2) and that from the said first day of August neither the lord chancellor, or keeper of the great seal of England, the lord treasurer of England, the keeper of the King's privy seal, or president of the council, nor any bishop, temporal lord, privy counsellor or judge, or justice whatsoever, shall have any power or authority to hear, examine or determine any matter or thing whatsoever, in the said court commonly called the star-chamber, or to make, pronounce or deliver any judgment, sentence, order or decree, or to do any judicial or ministerial act in the said court: (3) and that all and every act and acts of parliament, and all and every article, clause and sentence in them, and every of them, by which any jurisdiction, power or authority is given, limited or appointed unto the said court commonly called the star-chamber, or unto all or any the judges, officers or ministers thereof, or for any proceedings to be had or made in the said court, or for any matter or thing to be drawn into question, examined or determined there, shall for so much as concerneth the said court of star-chamber, and the power and authority thereby given unto it, be from the said first day of August repealed and absolutely revoked and made void. . . .

William Blackstone, IV Commentaries on the Laws and Customs of England

*294 (1765–1769)

WHEN a delinquent is arrested by any of the means mentioned in the preceding chapter, he ought regularly to be carried before a justice of the peace. And how he is there to be treated, I shall next shew, under the second head, of commitment and bail.

THE justice, before whom such prisoner is brought, is bound immediately to examine the circumstances of the crime alleged: and to this end by statute 2 & 3 Ph. & M. c. 10. he is to take in writing the examination of such prisoner, and the information of those who bring him: which, Mr Lambard observes, was the first warrant given for the examination of a felon in the English law. For, at the common law, nemo tenebatur prodere seipsum; and his fault was not to be wrung out of himself, but rather to be discovered by other means, and other men.

James Joiner's Case

Court of Oyer & Terminer, The Old Bailey, London, February 25, 1789

[source: http://www.oldbaileyonline.org/browse.jsp?id=t17890225-5-off20 &div=t17890225-5#highlight]

JAMES JOINER was indicted, for feloniously assaulting John Ray, on the King's Highway, on the 12th of February, putting him in fear and feloniously taking from his person, and against his will, a silver watch, value 5 l. 5 s. a hair chain, value 1 d. a steel key, value 1 d. a stone seal set in silver, value 3 s. and one guinea and 15 s. his property.

JOHN WRAY sworn.

I am a gentleman's servant out of place; on the 12th of February last, coming from Ealing, this said person met me; he stopped me about half after four in the afternoon; he put a pistol to my breast, and said your money, if you do not deliver it, I will shoot you; I delivered my money to him, which was a guinea, and fifteen shillings in silver; then he demanded my watch, which was a silver one, and I gave it to him; there was a hair chain, and a silver seal with a cornelian stone, and my name, J. W. on it; after I delivered him my property, I said I was a servant out of place, and he had taken all I had got; then says he, here is half a crown for you, and he gave me half a crown back; then he said now you walk behind me, and he made me walk behind him a hundred yards or more;

after that, he said now you may go about your business; and just as we were parting, he said if you will call at the angel in Hammersmith in about three weeks, I will leave the value of the watch and what money I have taken from you, I said very well, I will call.

Court. Were you content he should go away with your property in this manner?—No; I was obliged to be content; I was not satisfied with it. I called at the angel the next day, and they did not know any thing of him; I was sent for to the public office, and saw the prisoner there. From the time the prisoner stopt me, till we parted, took up five minutes; I was much frightened; it was day-light; I am positive as to his person; I looked at him very often as we were walking together: directly I saw him at Bow-street; I was very positive as to the person; the constable of Brentford produced the watch. He stopt me about two hundred yards from Gunnersbury-house.

WILLIAM WHEELER sworn.

I keep the Coach and Horses in Sion-lane; I apprehended the prisoner about half past six, on the thirteenth of February, in consequence of something that passed between me and a Mr. Hull; he was passing my door, returning towards Brentford; I took him on the pavement; he was walking, and Mr. Hull following him; I sent for a constable, after I had had him in custody about a quarter of an hour, to search him; he took him to the Watch-house; and then we put him in a chaise, and brought him to the Public-office; he was there searched; on him was found some duplicates, a string and a seal, and a pistol-key; the watch was found at the Watch-house door of Isleworth, where he was taken to first.

THOMAS FIELD sworn.

I am a constable of Isleworth; I was sent for on the thirteenth of February, to take the prisoner into custody; I took him to the cage; I found a pistol on him at Mr. Wheeler's house, which I took out of his pocket; when I got him to the cage, I was going to search him, and he pulled a watch out of his pocket, and held it in his hand; I laid hold of his hand, and desired him to give it to me; he refused to give it to me; he said he had not robbed any body; and by force, I pulled it from him, and some part of the chain, which we broke in our struggling; I have had it in my custody ever since, and the watch.

(Watch and the piece of chain produced; and the watch deposed to by the prosecutor, who knew it by the maker's name, and No. 332.)

Prosecutor. This is the watch, but not the chain I had to it.

JOHN SHALLARD sworn.

I am an officer belonging to Bow-street; when the prisoner was brought there, I searched him, and found this watch-chain in his pocket, and a pistol-key, and a quantity of gunpowder, a guinea and eighteen pence; I took him to the Watch-house; the prosecutor had given information at the office the night before; I believe he was brought to the office, about two hours after Wray gave the information, which was the night after he was robbed.

Wray. I was robbed on Thursday, the twelfth; I gave information the day after, which was Friday.

Shallard. It was on Saturday morning that the prisoner was examined.

(The watch-string and seal J. W. and bed-book, produced and deposed to by the prosecutor, which were found in the prisoner's pocket.)
JOHN HULL sworn.

I live at Twickenham; on the thirteenth of February, I saw the prisoner between the turnpike and Isleworth-town; between six and seven in the evening; it was on the foot-path, about a hundred yards beyond the turnpike.

Court. Then in consequence of something that passed between him and you, you apprehended him?—Yes.

How soon?—Directly; he went towards the turnpike, and I followed him; I called out, stop him! and he was stopped just before I got to him; just as he got through the turnpike, he was taken by two or three gardening men; it was before seven; then they took him to Mr. Wheler's, and from thence he was taken to the Round-house; I saw a canvas bag, sixteen bullets, and a mould, taken out of his pocket, and a pistol; that is all I know.

Field. I took the pistol out of his pocket myself (produced); this is the pistol I took out of his pocket; it was not loaded; it appeared to have been lately let off. I saw Shallard take the key out of his pocket, after I took him to Bow-street.

Shallard. The key fits the pistol.

(The pistol-key produced, which fitted the pistol.)
PRISONER's DEFENCE.

I bought the watch of a travelling Jew; I gave two guineas for it, the same day I was taken. There was an old gentleman coming from Isleworth; I passed him, and asked him what o'clock it was; he had me taken up for a robbery: I am intirely innocent of the whole of it.
GUILTY, Death.*

Tried by the first Middlesex Jury before Mr. Justice GROSE.

---

* Editor's Note: Joiner was pardoned 9th September 1789 on condition of being transported for life. *See* Proceedings of the Old Bailey, 9th September 1789, page 197, available online at http://www.oldbaileyonline.org/images.jsp?doc=178909090197.

SECTION 2

PHILOSOPHICAL NOTE: WHAT (IF ANYTHING) JUSTIFIES THE
PRIVILEGE AGAINST SELF-INCRIMINATION?

811

Virginia Declaration of Rights

1776

Art. VIII: . . . nor [in all capital or criminal prosecutions] can he be compelled to give evidence against himself . . .

Massachusetts Constitution

1780

Art. I, § 12:—no subject shall be held to answer for any crime or offence, until the same is fully and plainly, substantially and formally, described to him; or be compelled to accuse, or furnish evidence against himself.

Constitution of the United States, am. V

No person shall . . . be compelled in any criminal case to be a witness against himself . . . .

Judiciary Act, 1789, § 33

SEC. 33. *And be it further enacted*, That for any crime or offence against the United States, the offender may, by any justice or judge of the United States, or by any justice of the peace, or other magistrate of any of the United States where he may be found agreeably to the usual mode of process against offenders in such state, and at the expense of the United States, be arrested, and imprisoned or bailed, as the case may be, for trial before such court of the United States as by this act has cognizance of the offence. And copies of the process shall be returned as speedily as may be into the clerk's office of such court, together with the recognizances of the witnesses for their appearance to testify in the case; which recognizances the magistrate before whom the examination shall be, may require on pain of imprisonment.

2. PHILOSOPHICAL NOTE: WHAT (IF ANYTHING) JUSTIFIES THE PRIVILEGE AGAINST SELF-INCRIMINATION?

Murphy v. Waterfront Commission of New York Harbor

378 U.S. 52 (1964)

Policies of the Privilege

The privilege against self-incrimination 'registers an important advance in the development of our liberty—'one of the great landmarks in man's struggle to make himself civilized.' ' Ullmann v. United States,

350 U.S. 422, 426.[4] It reflects many of our fundamental values and most noble aspirations: our unwillingness to subject those suspected of crime to the cruel trilemma of self-accusation, perjury or contempt; our preference for an accusatorial rather than an inquisitorial system of criminal justice; our fear that self-incriminating statements will be elicited by inhumane treatment and abuses; our sense of fair play which dictates 'a fair state-individual balance by requiring the government to leave the individual alone until good cause is shown for disturbing him and by requiring the government in its contest with the individual to shoulder the entire load,' 8 Wigmore, Evidence (McNaughton rev., 1961), 317; our respect for the inviolability of the human personality and of the right of each individual 'to a private enclave where he may lead a private life,' United States v. Grunewald, 2 Cir., 233 F.2d 556, 581–582 (Frank J., dissenting), rev'd 353 U.S. 391; our distrust of self-deprecatory statements; and our realization that the privilege, while sometimes 'a shelter to the guilty,' is often 'a protection to the innocent.' Quinn v. United States, 349 U.S. 155, 162.

Jeremy Bentham, Rationale of Judicial Evidence, in VII Works of Jeremy Bentham

721 (John Bowring ed. 1843)

Pretences For The Exclusion [the privilege against self-incrimination].

1.   At the head of everything which, with or without the name of a reason, has been advanced, or is capable of being advanced, in the view of securing the attachment of the people to the exclusionary rule, let us place the old sophism, the well-worn artifice, sometimes called *petitio principii*, and which consists in the assumption of the propriety of the rule, as a proposition too plainly true to admit of dispute. . . . By assuming it as true, you hold up to their eyes the view of that universal assent, or assent equivalent to universal (dissenters being left out of the account,) which, from your assumption, they take for granted has been given to it: you represent all men, or (what comes to the same thing) all men whose opinions are worth regarding, as joining in the opinion: and by this means, besides the argument you present to the intellectual part of their frame, you present to its neighbour the volitional part another sort of argument, constituted by the fear of incurring the indignation or contempt of all reasonable men, by presuming to disbelieve or doubt what all such reasonable men are assured of. . . .

2.   The old woman's reason. The essence of this reason is contained in the word hard: 'tis hard upon a man to be obliged to criminate himself. Hard it is upon a man, it must be confessed, to be obliged to do anything that he does not like. That he should not much like to do what is meant by his criminating himself, is natural enough; for what it leads to, is, his being punished. What is no less hard upon him, is, that he should be

---

[4]   The quotation is from Griswold, The Fifth Amendment Today (1955), 7.

SECTION 2

PHILOSOPHICAL NOTE: WHAT (IF ANYTHING) JUSTIFIES THE
PRIVILEGE AGAINST SELF-INCRIMINATION?

813

punished: but did it ever yet occur to a man to propose a general abolition of all punishment, with this hardship for a reason for it? Whatever hardship there is in a man's being punished, that, and no more, is there in his thus being made to criminate himself: with this difference, that when he is punished,—punished he is by the very supposition; whereas, when he is thus made to criminate himself, although punishment may ensue, and probably enough will ensue, yet it may also happen that it does not. What, then, is the hardship of a man's being thus made to criminate himself? The same as that of his being punished: the same in kind, but inferior in degree: inferior, in as far as in the chance of an evil there is less hardship than in the certainty of it. Suppose, in both cases, conviction to be the result: does it matter to a man, would he give a pin to choose, whether it is out of his own mouth that the evidence is to come, or out of another's? . . . From his own mouth you will not receive the evidence of the culprit against him; but in his own hand, or from the mouth of another, you receive it without scruple: so that at bottom, all this sentimentality resolves itself into neither more nor less than a predilection—a confirmed and most extensive predilection, for bad evidence: for evidence, the badness of which you yourselves proclaim, and ground arguments and exclusions upon in a thousand cases. What every man knows, and what even yourselves, in spite of all your science, cannot be ignorant of, is,—that, of all men, the man himself is the last man who would willingly speak falsely to his own prejudice; and that, therefore, against every man, his own is the safest, the most satisfactory, of all evidence: and it is of this best and most trustworthy of all possible evidence, that your pretended tenderness scruples not to deprive the interests of truth and justice! . . . [T]he consequence will be, that, upon the aggregate number of offenders who for the offence in question will have suffered within a given length of time, the aggregate quantity of suffering undergone will be less than it would have been had the course pursued been the opposite. But, of any such rule as that here in question, the necessary effect (in so far as it has any) is, not to lessen that aggregate quantity of suffering, but to increase it. By whatsoever cause the ratio of the number of known, but yet unpunished, to the whole number of known, offenders, is increased,—in that same ratio, the known and apparent probability of punishment (in the eyes of a person having it in contemplation to engage in the commission of an offence of that sort) is diminished. But, on the mind of any given person, to produce, by means of punishment, an impression of any given degree of strength and efficiency, in proportion as the probability is diminished, the magnitude must be increased. . . . [I]it is because your law is so full of quibbles, exclusionary rules, and other points of practice, by which impunity is given, and seen to be given, to known delinquents, that (the probability of punishment being subjected to constant diminution) delinquency receives proportionable increase: and, for combating it, the only other resource remaining, and the only resource that a quibble-loving lawyer will endure to hear of, is an increase of the magnitude of the punishment.

To make sure, and do at once all that can be done, the punishment which on every such occasion he runs to in preference, is the punishment of death: death, simple death, as being, though not the highest and most impressive which human nature is capable of being subjected to (since afflictive death—death accompanied by torture, might, to an indefinite degree, be made higher,) the highest, however, which, in this age and country, men in general would endure the mention of. . . . But, by the increase given to the application of the punishment of death, increase is at the same time given to the propensity and the pretence for the application of other quibbles, and other impunity-giving rules. Under this system, that which consistency would require (not that, with such humanity, any sort or degree of consistency is compatible,) is, that for offences of all sorts there should never be any other than one sort of punishment, and that one sort death: for, so long as quibbles are in honour, and applied to delinquency in every shape,—delinquency, till the punishment be raised to this its maximum, will go on increasing. . . Such is the genesis of lawyercraft: death begets quibbles, and quibbles beget death . . . What cannot but be admitted is, that, by the effect of this impunity-giving rule, undue suffering has probably in some instances been prevented. Prevented? but to what extent? To the extent of that part of the field of penal law which is occupied by bad laws: by laws which prohibit that which ought not to have been prohibited, or command that which ought not to have been commanded. But, in the character of a remedy against the mischief of which such bad laws are productive, observe the nature and effect of this rule. Applying with equal force and efficiency to all penal laws without distinction—to the worst as well as to the best, it at the same time diminishes the efficiency of such as are good: while it is only by accident, and to an amount altogether precarious and unascertainable, that it does away the mischief with which such as are bad are pregnant. . . . . . By the principle of nullification, or the rule which excludes self-criminative evidence, not only are the guilty served, but it is they alone that are served: they alone, and without any mixture of the innocent. For when, though unfortunate enough to have become the object of suspicion, a man is really innocent, does he fly to any of these subterfuges? Not he, indeed, if character be of any value in his eyes: for, by recourse to any of them, what is no secret to anybody is, that so sure as punishment is escaped, character is sacrificed.

3.   The fox-hunter's reason. This consists in introducing upon the carpet of legal procedure the idea of fairness, in the sense in which the word is used by sportsmen. The fox is to have a fair chance for his life: he must have (so close is the analogy) what is called *law*,—leave to run a certain length of way for the express purpose of giving him a chance for escape. While under pursuit, he must not be shot: it would be as unfair as convicting him of burglary on a hen-roost, in five minutes' time, in a court of conscience. In the sporting code, these laws are rational, being obviously conducive to the professed end. Amusement is that end: a certain quantity of delay is essential to it: dispatch, a degree of dispatch

SECTION 2

PHILOSOPHICAL NOTE: WHAT (IF ANYTHING) JUSTIFIES THE
PRIVILEGE AGAINST SELF-INCRIMINATION?

815

reducing the quantity of delay below the allowed minimum, would be fatal to it. In the case of the fox, there is frequently an additional reason for fair play. By foul play, the source of the amusement might be exhausted: the breed of that useful animal might be destroyed, or reduced too low: the outlawry, so long ago fatal to wolves, might extend itself to foxes. In the mouth of the lawyer, this reason, were the nature of it seen to be what it is, would be consistent and in character. Every villain let loose one term, that he may bring custom the next, is a sort of a bag-fox, nursed by the common hunt at Westminster. The policy so dear to sportsmen, so dear to rat-catchers, cannot be supposed entirely unknown to lawyers. To different persons, both a fox and a criminal have their use: the use of a fox is to be hunted; the use of a criminal is to be tried. But inasmuch as, in the mouth of the lawyer, it would be telling tales out of school,—from such lips this reason must not be let out without disguise. If let out at all, it must be let drop in the form of a loose hint, so rough and obscure, that some country gentleman or other, who has a sympathy for foxes, may catch it up, and, taking it for his own, fight it up with that zeal with which genius naturally bestirs itself in support of its own inventions.

4.   Confounding interrogation with torture; with the application of physical suffering, till some act is done; in the present instance, till testimony is given to a particular effect required. On this occasion it is necessary to observe, that the act of putting a question to a person whose station is that of defendant in a cause, is no more an act of torture than the putting the same question to him would be, if, instead of being a defendant, he were an extraneous witness. Whatever he chooses to say, he is at full liberty to say; only under this condition, properly but not essentially subjoined, viz. (as in the case of an extraneous witness) that, if anything he says should be mendacious, he is liable to be punished for it, as an extraneous witness would be punished. This condition, essential in the case of an extraneous witness, is not equally so in the case of a party in the cause; since a party, by being such, stands exposed to a sort of punishment intrinsic to the cause,—viz. the loss of the cause: as where a defendant, in consideration of false responsion, evasive responsion, or obstinate silence, is concluded to be guilty: a punishment, of which an extraneous witness, not having any interest at stake in the cause, is not, on that occasion at least, susceptible. . . .

5.   Reference to unpopular institutions. Whatever Titius did was wrong: but this is among the things that Titius did; therefore this is wrong: such is the logic from which this sophism is deduced. In the apartment in which the court called the Court of Star-chamber sat, the roof had stars in it for ornaments; or else certain deeds to which Jews were parties, and by them called shetars or shtars, used to be kept there; or, possibly, there being no natural incompatibility, both these facts were true. Whether it was owing to the gilt stars, or to the Jew parchments, the judges of this court conducted themselves very badly: therefore judges should not sit in

a room that has had stars in the roof, or in a room in which Jew parchments have been kept. Had the conclusion been in this strain, the logic would not have been very convincing, but neither would the mischief have been very great. . . . The Inquisition (meaning the true inquisition, of the Spanish sort,) that used to work with such success in the extirpation or conversion of heretics, was a court in which it was the way of the judge to inquire into the business that came before him: to put questions to such persons as, in his conception, were likely to be more or less acquainted with the matter: and this, whether extraneous witnesses or parties. Now this it is, that was and is a most wicked and popish practice. Judges ought not to put questions: be the business what it may that comes before them, it ought to be the care of judges never so much as to attempt to see to the bottom of it. Here, then, we see the true source of all the odium; *viz.* not merely of that which has attached itself to this abominable court, but of that which attached itself to those other abominable courts. It was not by sitting in a room with stars or parchments in it; it was not by acting under a commission too high in itself, or that lay on too high a shelf; it was not by either of these causes that the two English courts, held in such just abborrence by all true Englishmen, were rendered so bad as they were,—but by their abominable practice of asking questions, by the abominable attempt to penetrate to the bottom of a cause. . . . This, at least, is among those things which they ought not to do: for no sooner do they make any such attempt, than they become inquisitors; popish, Spanish inquisitors, or worse: and those who, had the truth come out against them by other means, would have been convicts, become innocent and persecuted men; victims, or intended victims, of persecution, tyranny, and so forth. Of the Court of Star-chamber and the High Commission Court taken together (for to the present purpose they are not worth distinguishing,) the characteristic feature is, that, by taking upon them to execute the will of the king alone, as made known by proclamations, or not as yet known so much as by proclamations, they went to supersede the use of parliaments, substituting an absolute monarchy to a limited one. In the case of the High Commission Court, the mischief was aggravated by the use made of this arbitrary power in forcing men's consciences on the subject of religion. In the common-law courts, these enormities could not be committed, because (except in a few extraordinary cases) convictions having never, in the practice of these courts, been made to take place without the intervention of a jury, and the bulk of the people being understood to be adverse to these innovations, the attempt to get the official judges to carry prosecutions of the description in question into effect, presented itself as hopeless. In a state of things like this, what could be more natural than that, by a people infants as yet in reason, giants in passion, every distinguishable feature of a system of procedure directed to such ends should be condemned in the lump, should be involved in one undistinguishing mass of odium and abhorrence; more especially any particular instrument or feature, from which the system was seen to operate with a particular degree of efficiency towards such abominable ends? If, then, in the ordinary courts of law, the practice with respect to the admission of this source of information was wavering, or the opinion of the profession hesitating, nothing could be more natural than that the observation of the enormous mass of mischief and oppression to which it was continually made subservient, should turn the scale. Of this instrument in the hand of justice, or of persons in the place of justice, what was the characteristic property? Its sharpness. But at that particular conjuncture, employed as it was employed, its usefulness, great and pure as it would have been in other times, was converted entirely into mischief: its virtue was spent in the giving energy and efficiency to a system of operations hostile to the security and happiness of the body of the people. In those days, the supreme power of the state was de facto in the hands of the king alone: for as to that of parliament, it had never been anything better than a contingency; and in those days it was a contingency which it was intended, by those on whom it seemed to depend, should never happen: the improbability of its happening, must in those days, in the view of everybody, have been extreme. The king's power, then, was de facto absolute: being employed and directed against property, liberty, conscience, every blessing on which human nature sets a value,—every chance of safety depended upon the enfeeblement of it; every instrument on which the strength of that government in those days depended—every instrument which in happier times would to the people be a bond of safety, was an instrument of mischief, an object of terror and odium, which, could it have confined itself to the particular application then made of the instrument, and not have extended to the instrument itself, would have been no other than just, and reasonable, and well grounded. As to the ecclesiastical tribunal called the Inquisition, a circumstance that seems not generally understood, is, that the procedure was little or nothing more than the ordinary procedure employed in the same countries in the higher classes of criminal cases. Bad as the practice was, what there was peculiar to it belonged, therefore, not to the adjective system, but only to the substantive laws (the laws against heresy) to the execution of which it was applied. . . . [T]the close imprisonment and the practice of torture, . . . was common to both . . . If the ends pursued are mischievous, the means employed in the pursuit of them cannot, in so far as they are fit for the purpose, but be likewise mischievous. But upon which of the two objects, in this case, is the mischief to be charged? Not upon the means, surely, but upon the ends. Of the means, nothing more can rationally be required, than that they shall be such as shall not be productive of any mischief, other than that which results from their subserviency to the ends. . . . The perfection of a sword is in its sharpness: the sharper it is, if employed against friends, the more mischief it would do, would this be a reason for discarding the use of sharp swords, and using none but what had been blunted? No! the dictate of reason is,—let your sword be sharp, the sharper the better; but take care not to wound a friend with it. . . . [A]re they good laws? then why put it out of your power to execute them? Are they bad laws? then why are they suffered to subsist?

James Fitzjames Stephen, I History of the Criminal Law of England

441–442 (1883)

[The privilege] is one of the most characteristic features of English criminal procedure, and it presents a marked contrast to that which common to, I believe, all continental countries. It is, I think, highly advantageous to the guilty. It contributes greatly to the dignity and apparent humanity of a criminal trial. It effectually avoids the appearance of harshness, not say cruelty, which often shocks an English spectator in a French court of justice, and I think that the fact that the prisoner cannot be questioned stimulates the search for independent evidence.[2] The evidence in an English trial is, I think, usually much fuller and more satisfactory than the evidence in such French trials as I have been able to study.

On the other hand, I am convinced by much experience that questioning, or the power of giving evidence, is a positive assistance, and a highly important one, to innocent men, and I do not see why in the case of the guilty there need be any hardship about it. . . .

3. GENERAL FIFTH AMENDMENT DOCTRINE: COMPULSION, TESTIMONIAL EVIDENCE, INCRIMINATION

Vogt v. City of Hays, Kansas

844 F.3d 1235 (10th Cir. 2017), *cert. granted* Sept. 28, 2017, *writ of certiorari dismissed as improvidently granted,* 584 U.S. ___, 138 S.Ct. 1683 (2018)

■ Before HARTZ, BACHARACH, and MCHUGH, CIRCUIT JUDGES.

Opinion

■ BACHARACH, CIRCUIT JUDGE.

Mr. Matthew Vogt alleges a violation of the Fifth Amendment through the compulsion to incriminate himself and the use of his compelled statements in a criminal case. Based on the alleged Fifth Amendment violation, Mr. Vogt invokes 42 U.S.C. § 1983, suing (1) the City of Hays, Kansas; (2) the City of Haysville, Kansas; and (3) four police

---

[2] During the discussions which took place on the Indian Code of Criminal Procedure in 1872 some observations were made on the reasons which occasionally led native police officers to apply torture to prisoners. An experienced civil officer observed: "There is a great deal of laziness in it. It is far pleasanter to sit comfortably in the shade rubbing red pepper into a poor devil's eyes than to go about in the sun hunting up evidence." This was a new view to me, but I have no doubt of its truth.

officers. The district court dismissed the complaint for failure to state a claim, reasoning that

- the right against self-incrimination is only a trial right

and

- Mr. Vogt's statements were used in pretrial proceedings, but not in a trial.

We draw four conclusions:

1. The Fifth Amendment is violated when criminal defendants are compelled to incriminate themselves and the incriminating statement is used in a probable cause hearing.

2. The individual officers are entitled to qualified immunity.

3. The City of Haysville did not compel Mr. Vogt to incriminate himself.

4. Mr. Vogt has stated a plausible claim for relief against the City of Hays.

Accordingly, we (1) affirm the dismissal of the claims against the four police officers and Haysville and (2) reverse the dismissal of the claim against the City of Hays.

I.   Mr. Vogt alleges that his compelled statements were used in a criminal case.

Because this appeal is based on a dismissal for failure to state a valid claim, we credit the factual allegations in the complaint. Brown v. Montoya, 662 F.3d 1152, 1162 (10th Cir. 2011).

Mr. Vogt was employed as a police officer with the City of Hays. In late 2013, Mr. Vogt applied for a position with the City of Haysville's police department. During Haysville's hiring process, Mr. Vogt disclosed that he had kept a knife obtained in the course of his work as a Hays police officer.

Notwithstanding this disclosure, Haysville offered the job to Mr. Vogt. But his disclosure about the knife led Haysville to make the offer conditional: Mr. Vogt could obtain the job only if he reported his acquisition of the knife and returned it to the Hays police department. Two Haysville police officers said that they would follow up with Hays to ensure that Mr. Vogt complied with the condition.

Mr. Vogt satisfied the condition, reporting to the Hays police department that he had kept the knife. The Hays police chief reacted by ordering Mr. Vogt to submit a written report concerning his possession of the knife. Mr. Vogt complied, submitting a vague one-sentence report. He then provided Hays with a two-week notice of resignation, intending to accept the new job with Haysville.

In the meantime, the Hays police chief began an internal investigation into Mr. Vogt's possession of the knife. In addition, a Hays police officer required Mr. Vogt to give a more detailed statement in order to keep his job with the Hays police department. Mr. Vogt complied, and the Hays police used the additional statement to locate additional evidence.

Based on Mr. Vogt's statements and the additional evidence, the Hays police chief asked the Kansas Bureau of Investigation to start a criminal investigation. In light of this request, the Hays police department supplied Mr. Vogt's statements and additional evidence to the Kansas Bureau of Investigation. The criminal investigation led the Haysville police department to withdraw its job offer.

Mr. Vogt was ultimately charged in Kansas state court with two felony counts related to his possession of the knife. Following a probable cause hearing, the state district court determined that probable cause was lacking and dismissed the charges.

This suit followed, with Mr. Vogt alleging use of his statements (1) to start an investigation leading to the discovery of additional evidence concerning the knife, (2) to initiate a criminal investigation, (3) to bring criminal charges, and (4) to support the prosecution during the probable cause hearing. Mr. Vogt argues that these uses of his compelled statements violated his right against self-incrimination.

II. Standard of Review

We engage in *de novo* review of the district court's dismissal. Mocek v. City of Albuquerque, 813 F.3d 912, 921 (10th Cir. 2015). To survive the motion to dismiss, Mr. Vogt had to plead enough facts to create a facially plausible claim. Khalik v. United Air Lines, 671 F.3d 1188, 1190 (10th Cir. 2012). The claim is facially plausible if Mr. Vogt pleaded enough factual content to allow "the court to draw the reasonable inference that the defendant is liable for the misconduct alleged." Ashcroft v. Iqbal, 556 U.S. 662, 678 (2009).

III. The Meaning of a "Criminal Case" Under the Fifth Amendment

The Fifth Amendment[1] protects individuals against compulsion to incriminate themselves "in any criminal case." U.S. Const. amend. V. This amendment prohibits compulsion of law enforcement officers to make self-incriminating statements in the course of employment. Garrity v. New Jersey, 385 U.S. 493, 500 (1967). As a law enforcement officer, Mr. Vogt enjoyed protection under the Fifth Amendment against use of his compelled statements in a criminal case.

The district court held that Mr. Vogt had not stated a valid claim under the Fifth Amendment because the incriminating statements were never used at trial. We disagree, concluding that the phrase "criminal case" includes probable cause hearings.

---

[1] The Fifth Amendment applies to the states through incorporation of the Fourteenth Amendment. Malloy v. Hogan, 378 U.S. 1, 6 (1964).

A. Our precedents provide conflicting signals on whether the term "criminal case" includes pretrial proceedings as well as the trial.

The U.S. Supreme Court has not conclusively defined the scope of a "criminal case" under the Fifth Amendment. In dicta, the Supreme Court suggested in a 1990 opinion, *United States v. Verdugo-Urquidez*, that the right against self-incrimination is only a trial right. 494 U.S. 259, 264 (1990).

But the Supreme Court later appeared to retreat from that dicta. In *Mitchell v. United States*, for instance, the Court held that the right against self-incrimination extends to sentencing hearings. 526 U.S. 314, 320–21 (1999). The Court reasoned that "[t]o maintain that sentencing proceedings are not part of 'any criminal case' is contrary to the law and to common sense." *Id.* at 327.

Even more recently, the Court again addressed the scope of the Fifth Amendment in Chavez v. Martinez, 538 U.S. 760 (2003). In *Chavez*, the plaintiff sued a police officer under § 1983, alleging coercion of self-incriminating statements in violation of the Fifth Amendment. 538 U.S. at 764–65. Writing for himself and two other justices, Justice Thomas concluded that (1) the plaintiff had failed to state a valid claim because he had not been charged with a crime and (2) the plaintiff's statements had not been used in a criminal case. *Id.* at 766.

Though the Court did not produce a majority opinion on the Fifth Amendment issue, Justice Thomas's plurality opinion explained that "mere coercion does not violate the text of the Self-Incrimination Clause absent use of the compelled statements in a criminal case against the witness." *Id.* at 769. Justice Thomas added that "[a] 'criminal case' at the very least requires the initiation of legal proceedings." *Id.* at 766. Two other justices agreed with the outcome, reasoning that the Fifth Amendment's text "focuses on *courtroom use* of a criminal defendant's compelled, self-incriminating testimony." *Id.* at 777 (Souter, J., concurring in the judgment) (emphasis added).

The *Chavez* Court did not decide "the precise moment when a 'criminal case' commences." *Id.* at 766–67. Justice Thomas cited *Verdugo-Urquidez*, but apparently did not read it to limit the Fifth Amendment to use at trial. *See id.* at 767.

Three other justices stated that a violation of the Self-Incrimination Clause is complete the moment a confession is compelled. *Id.* at 795 (Kennedy, J., concurring in part and dissenting in part). Thus, even in light of *Verdugo-Urquidez*, these three justices concluded that the Fifth Amendment extended beyond use of a compelled statement at trial. *Id.* at 792.

Following *Chavez*, a circuit split developed over the definition of a "criminal case" under the Fifth Amendment. The Third, Fourth, and

Fifth Circuits have stated that the Fifth Amendment is only a trial right.[2] *See* Renda v. King, 347 F.3d 550, 552 (3d Cir. 2003) ("[A] plaintiff may not base a § 1983 claim on the mere fact that the police questioned her in custody without providing *Miranda* warnings when there is no claim that the plaintiff's answers were used against her at trial."); Burrell v. Virginia, 395 F.3d 508, 514 (4th Cir. 2005) ("[The plaintiff] does not allege any *trial* action that violated his Fifth Amendment rights; thus, *ipso facto*, his claim fails on the [*Chavez*] plurality's reasoning."); Murray v. Earle, 405 F.3d 278, 285 (5th Cir. 2005) ("The Fifth Amendment privilege against self-incrimination is a fundamental trial right which can be violated only *at* trial, even though pre-trial conduct by law enforcement officials may ultimately impair that right.").

In contrast, the Second, Seventh, and Ninth Circuits have held that certain pretrial uses of compelled statements violate the Fifth Amendment. For example, the Second Circuit has applied *Chavez* to hold that a bail hearing is part of a criminal case under the Fifth Amendment. Higazy v. Templeton, 505 F.3d 161, 171, 173 (2d Cir. 2007). The Seventh Circuit has similarly held that a criminal case under the Fifth Amendment includes not only bail hearings but also suppression hearings, arraignments, and probable cause hearings. Best v. City of Portland, 554 F.3d 698, 702–03 (7th Cir. 2009) (suppression hearing); Sornberger v. City of Knoxville, 434 F.3d 1006, 1027 (7th Cir. 2006) (bail hearings, arraignments, and probable cause hearings). And the Ninth Circuit has concluded that a Fifth Amendment violation occurs when "[a] coerced statement . . . has been relied upon to file formal charges against the declarant, to determine judicially that the prosecution may proceed, and to determine pretrial custody status." *See* Stoot v. City of Everett, 582 F.3d 910, 925 (9th Cir. 2009).

Different approaches have emerged because the *Chavez* Court declined to pinpoint when a "criminal case" begins. *See* Koch v. City of Del City, 660 F.3d 1228, 1245 (10th Cir. 2011) (noting that "the plurality in *Chavez* explicitly declined to decide 'the precise moment when a "criminal case" commences' "). Like the Supreme Court, we have not yet defined the starting point for a "criminal case." *See id.* at 1246 (avoiding this issue by holding that at the time of the plaintiff's arrest, "it was not clearly established that an individual has a Fifth Amendment right to refuse to answer an officer's questions during a *Terry* stop"); Eidson v. Owens, 515 F.3d 1139, 1149 (10th Cir. 2008) (declining to define the scope of the right against self-incrimination because the plaintiff "never incriminated herself during a custodial interrogation").

---

[2]   The defendants contend that the Sixth Circuit Court of Appeals has also held that the Fifth Amendment is only a trial right. Appellees' Br. at 20–21. But the court did so only in an unpublished opinion. Smith v. Patterson, 430 Fed.Appx. 438, 441 (6th Cir. 2011). The court's unpublished opinions do not constitute binding precedent even in the Sixth Circuit. Graiser v. Visionworks of America, Inc., 819 F.3d 277, 283 (6th Cir. 2016).

The defendants argue that we have consistently held that the Fifth Amendment right is only a trial right. We disagree.

In support of their argument, the defendants cite our opinions in Bennett v. Passic, 545 F.2d 1260 (10th Cir. 1976), and Pearson v. Weischedel, 349 Fed.Appx. 343 (10th Cir. 2009) (unpublished). These opinions do not help in answering our question. In *Bennett*, we held that civil liability may not arise from (1) failure to give *Miranda* warnings or (2) testimony about compelled statements. 545 F.2d at 1263–64. These scenarios are not involved here. And in our unpublished opinion in *Pearson*, we rejected a Fifth Amendment claim, stating that the plaintiff had pleaded guilty and had never gone to trial. *Pearson*, 349 Fed.Appx. at 348. Our analysis was brief and omitted discussion of *Chavez*. Thus, *Pearson* does not aid our inquiry.

In addition, the defendants read In re Grand Jury Subpoenas Dated Dec. 7 & 8 (Stover), 40 F.3d 1096 (10th Cir. 1994), to suggest that a violation of the right against self-incrimination occurs only at trial. This suggestion is based on a questionable interpretation of the opinion. In *Stover*, the parties agreed that a Fifth Amendment violation occurs when a grand jury returns an indictment based on a compelled statement. 40 F.3d at 1100–01. Notwithstanding the parties' agreement on this issue, we quoted language from an earlier opinion describing the Fifth Amendment as a trial right. *See id.* at 1103 ("The time for protection [of the right against self-incrimination] will come when, if ever, the government attempts to use [allegedly incriminating] information against the defendant at trial." (quoting United States v. Peister, 631 F.2d 658, 662 (10th Cir. 1980))).

Though we quoted this restrictive language, we also suggested in dicta that the parties had correctly assumed that the Fifth Amendment is triggered when a compelled statement is used during grand jury proceedings. *See id.* at 1103 ("If an officer, whose compelled statement has been considered by the grand jury, ultimately is indicted, that officer will be able to challenge the indictment and the government will be required to prove that its evidence derives entirely from legitimate sources or that the grand jury's exposure to the officer's statement was harmless."). Thus, *Stover* arguably suggests that the right against self-incrimination is not simply a trial right.

* * *

These precedents supply conflicting signals on whether the term "criminal case" extends beyond the trial itself. The dicta in *Verdugo-Urquidez* suggests that the term "criminal case" refers only to the trial. This dicta would ordinarily guide us, for Supreme Court dicta is almost as influential as a Supreme Court holding. Indep. Inst. v. Williams, 812 F.3d 787, 798 n.13 (10th Cir. 2016). But after deciding *Verdugo-Urquidez*, the Supreme Court interpreted the term "criminal case" in *Mitchell* to include sentencing proceedings. And even later, the Supreme Court declined in *Chavez* to define when a "criminal case" begins.

Like the Supreme Court, we have declined until now to unequivocally state whether the term "criminal case" covers pretrial proceedings as well as the trial. Precedents like *Stover* provide conflicting signals without squarely deciding the issue. Nonetheless, today's case requires us to decide whether the term "criminal case" covers at least one pretrial proceeding: a hearing to determine probable cause.

B. The right against self-incrimination applies to use in a probable cause hearing as well as at trial.

To decide this issue, we join the Second, Seventh, and Ninth Circuits, concluding that the right against self-incrimination is more than a trial right. In reaching this conclusion, we rely on

- the text of the Fifth Amendment, which we interpret in light of the common understanding of the phrase "criminal case," and

- the Framers' understanding of the right against self-incrimination.

The Fifth Amendment provides that no person shall be "compelled in any *criminal case* to be a witness against himself." U.S. Const. amend. V (emphasis added). The text of the Fifth Amendment does not contain

- the term "trial," which appears in the next two amendments, or

- the term "criminal prosecution," which is used in the next amendment.

See U.S. Const. amend. VI ("In all criminal prosecutions, the accused shall enjoy the right to a speedy and public trial. . . ."); *id.* amend. VII ("In suits at common law . . . the right of trial by jury shall be preserved. . . .").

The Supreme Court discussed the distinction between the language of the Fifth and Sixth Amendments in Counselman v. Hitchcock, 142 U.S. 547 (1892), *overruled in part on other grounds by* Kastigar v. United States, 406 U.S. 441 (1972). In *Counselman*, the government argued that a witness could not invoke the Fifth Amendment in a grand jury proceeding because a "criminal case" did not exist. 142 U.S. at 562–63. The Supreme Court rejected this argument. After analyzing the Fifth Amendment's text and underlying purpose, the Court held that the witness could plead the Fifth Amendment during a grand jury proceeding. *Id.* In the course of its analysis, the Court reasoned that the language "criminal case" is broader than the Sixth Amendment's phrase "criminal prosecution." *Id.*

We agree with the *Counselman* Court that the term "criminal case" is broader than the term "criminal prosecution." Indeed, on its face, the term "criminal case" appears to encompass all of the proceedings involved in a "criminal prosecution."

"The Constitution was written to be understood by the voters; its words and phrases were used in their normal and ordinary as distinguished from technical meaning. . . ." United States v. Sprague, 282 U.S. 716, 731 (1931). To determine the commonly understood meaning of the phrase "criminal case" at the time of ratification (1791), we examine dictionary definitions from the Founding era. *See* Gregory E. Maggs, *A Concise Guide to Using Dictionaries from the Founding Era to Determine the Original Meaning of the Constitution*, 82 Geo. Wash. L. Rev. 358, 365 (2014); *see also* William M. Carter, Jr., *Race, Rights, and the Thirteenth Amendment: Defining the Badges and Incidents of Slavery*, 40 U.C. Davis L. Rev. 1311, 1338 n.99 (2007) (stating that contemporaneous dictionaries "obviously . . . provide some guidance to the commonly understood meaning of a particular word at the time that word was used in the constitutional text").

The most authoritative dictionary of that era was Noah Webster's 1828 dictionary, An American Dictionary of the English Language. *See* John A. Sterling, *Above the Law: Evolution of Executive Orders (Part One)*, 31 UWLA L. Rev. 99, 107 (2000) (stating that most historians use Noah Webster's 1828 dictionary when trying to determine the meaning of words during adoption of the Constitution); *see also* Charles Wood, *Losing Control of America's Future—The Census, Birthright Citizenship, and Illegal Aliens*, 22 Harv. J.L. & Pub. Pol'y 465, 478 (1999) (stating that Noah Webster's 1828 dictionary was "the first and for many years the authoritative American dictionary"); Steven G. Calabresi & Andrea Matthews, *Originalism and* Loving v. Virginia, 2012 B.Y.U. L. Rev. 1393, 1425 (2012) (describing Noah Webster's 1828 dictionary as "an incredible achievement" and as a "dominant" source since its publication); Gregory E. Maggs, *A Concise Guide to Using Dictionaries from the Founding Era to Determine the Original Meaning of the Constitution,* 82 Geo. Wash. L. Rev. 358, 389–90 (2014) (stating that the Supreme Court often cites Noah Webster's 1828 dictionary as evidence of the original meaning of the Constitution, perhaps based on a belief "that the dictionary may reflect better the ways in which Americans used and understood the words in the Constitution"). Webster's 1828 dictionary defines "case" as "[a] cause or suit in court," stating that the term "is nearly synonymous with *cause*." Noah Webster, *Case, An American Dictionary of the English Language* (1st ed. 1828). And the dictionary defines the "nearly synonymous" term "cause" as "[a] suit or action in court." *Id., Cause.* Similarly, N. Bailey's 1789 dictionary broadly defines "case" as a "thing, matter, question." N. Bailey, The Universal Etymological English Dictionary, Case (26th ed. 1789).[3]

---

[3] The Founders recognized that a word's meaning often changes over time. *See* Caleb Nelson, *Originalism and Interpretive Conventions*, 70 U. Chi. L. Rev. 519, 534 (2003) ("Americans of the founding generation tended to agree with [Samuel Johnson, the 18th

The Founders' understanding of the term "case" suggests that the Fifth Amendment encompasses more than the trial itself. *See* Donald Dripps, *Akhil Amar on Criminal Procedure and Constitutional Law: "Here I Go Down that Wrong Road Again,"* 74 N.C. L. Rev. 1559, 1627 (1996).[4] "If the Framers had meant to restrict the right to 'trial,' they could have said so." Thomas Y. Davies, *Farther and Farther from the Original Fifth Amendment: The Recharacterization of the Right Against Self-Incrimination as a "Trial Right" in* Chavez v. Martinez, 70 Tenn. L. Rev. 987, 1014 (2003).

This interpretation is supported by the Supreme Court's opinion in Blyew v. United States, 80 U.S. (13 Wall.) 581 (1871). In *Blyew*, the Supreme Court addressed the meaning of the word "cases" in Article III's reference, "all cases affecting ambassadors, other public ministers, and consuls." 80 U.S. at 594. The *Blyew* Court explained that "[t]he words 'case' and 'cause' are constantly used as synonyms in statutes and judicial decisions, each meaning a proceeding in court, a suit, or action." *Id.* at 595. Like the dictionary definitions from 1828 to now, *Blyew* defines "case" broadly, suggesting that a "criminal case" is not limited to the criminal trial.

We are aided not only by Founding-era dictionary definitions and *Blyew* but also by the Framers' understanding of the phrase "in any criminal case." We have few contemporaneous clues of that understanding, for "references to the privilege [against self-incrimination] are scarce in the literature and debates surrounding the ratification of the Constitution and the Bill of Rights." Michael Edmund O'Neill, *The Fifth Amendment in Congress: Revisiting the Privilege Against Compelled Self-Incrimination*, 90 Geo. L.J. 2445, 2486 (2002). But the few existing clues suggest that the Framers viewed the Fifth Amendment as a right in pretrial proceedings as well as at trial.

---

century's leading lexicographer] that language change was inevitable."). But modern legal dictionaries define "case" much as our Founders did. *See* Black's Law Dict. 258 (Bryan A. Garner ed., 10th ed. 2014) (defining "case" as "[a] civil or criminal proceeding, action, suit, or controversy at law or in equity"); A Handbook of Criminal Law Terms 84 (Bryan A. Garner ed., 2000) (defining "case" as "[a] proceeding, action, suit, or controversy at law or in equity"); Dict. of Legal Terms 70 (Steven H. Gifis, 4th ed. 2008) (defining "case" as "an action, cause, suit, or controversy, at law or in equity"); *see also* Martin H. Redish & Adrianna D. Kastanek, *Settlement Class Actions, the Case-or-Controversy Requirement, and the Nature of the Adjudicatory Process,* 73 U. Chi. L. Rev. 545, 565 (2006) ("[C]urrent-day legal dictionaries define 'case' as a justiciable 'action or suit,' or an 'argument.'" (footnotes omitted)).

4   Professor Dripps stated:

A "case" in any event is not necessarily identical to a "prosecution." The Sixth Amendment uses the latter term, in dealing with the criminal trial. The Fifth Amendment, by contrast, contains a miscellany of rights, some against criminal and some against civil liabilities. We speak routinely of police investigators working on a case before they have a suspect. If we think of a "case" as a potential "prosecution" we can square the text of the Fifth Amendment with its history.

Donald Dripps, *Akhil Amar on Criminal Procedure and Constitutional Law: "Here I Go Down that Wrong Road Again,"* 74 N.C. L. Rev. 1559, 1627 (1996) (footnotes omitted).

One clue involves the changes in the Fifth Amendment from drafting to ratification. The amendment had been drafted by James Madison, who omitted the phrase "criminal case":

> No person shall be subject, except in cases of impeachment, to more than one punishment or one trial for the same offence; *nor shall be compelled to be a witness against himself*; nor be deprived of life, liberty, or property, without due process of law; nor be obliged to relinquish his property, where it may be necessary for public use, without just compensation.

James Madison, Remarks in Debate in the House of Representatives (June 8, 1789) (emphasis added), *reprinted in* 1 Debates and Proceedings in the Congress of the United States 448, 451–52 (Joseph Gales ed., 1834); United States Congress, Debates and Proceedings in the Congress of the United States 451–52 (Washington, D.C. 1834). This language "applied to civil as well as criminal proceedings and in principle to any stage of a legal inquiry, from the moment of arrest in a criminal case, to the swearing of a deposition in a civil one." Leonard W. Levy, Origins of the Fifth Amendment 423 (1968).

In the floor debate on whether to adopt the Bill of Rights, Representative Laurance expressed concern that Madison's wording would conflict with "laws passed." Statement of Representative John Laurance (Aug. 17, 1789), *reprinted in* 1 Debates and Proceedings in the Congress of the United States 782, 782. To avoid this conflict, Representative Laurance proposed to add the phrase "in any criminal case." *Id.* Representative Laurance's language was accepted in the House and Senate. Leonard W. Levy, Origins of the Fifth Amendment 424–26 (1968).

It is unclear which "laws" Representative Laurance was talking about. One possibility was the proposed Judiciary Act, which would allow the judiciary to compel production of documents in civil cases.[5] *See* United States v. Hubbell, 530 U.S. 27, 53–54 n.3 (2000) (Thomas, J., concurring). Another possibility was the Collections Act, which allowed officials to require oaths in customs declarations. Act of July 31, 1789, ch. 5 section 13, 1 Stat. 29, 39–40; *see* Thomas Y. Davies, *Recovering the Original Fourth Amendment*, 98 Mich. L. Rev. 547, 705 n.450 (1999). But whichever law was at risk, Representative Laurance was apparently trying to distinguish between potential criminal liability and civil liability. *See* Thomas Y. Davies, *Farther and Farther from the Original Fifth Amendment: The Recharacterization of the Right Against Self-Incrimination as a "Trial Right" in* Chavez v. Martinez, 70 Tenn. L. Rev. 987, 1017 (2003) ("[R]egardless of which provision Laurance referred to, it is still the case that his concern was not to limit the right to criminal

---

[5]   When Representative Laurance proposed to add the phrase "in any criminal case," the Judiciary Act of 1789 had passed in the Senate and remained pending in the House of Representatives. Michael Edmund O'Neill, *The Fifth Amendment in Congress: Revisiting the Privilege Against Compelled Self-Incrimination*, 90 Geo. L.J. 2445, 2484 (2002).

trials as such but only to preserve the distinction that the right applied only to potential criminal liability rather than civil liability.").

When Representative Laurance proposed to confine the Fifth Amendment to a "criminal case," there was a consensus that the right against self-incrimination was not limited to a suspect's own trial. To the contrary, "the historical sources show that the right against self-accusation was understood to arise primarily in pretrial or pre-prosecution settings rather than in the context of a person's own criminal trial." *Id.* at 1017–18. If this right were limited to one's own trial, the right would have served little purpose, for criminal defendants were then unable to testify in their own criminal cases. *See* Ferguson v. Georgia, 365 U.S. 570, 574 (1961) (stating that when the United States was formed, "criminal defendants were deemed incompetent as witnesses").

The most natural place for concern about compelled testimony would have been in proceedings outside of criminal trials, such as grand jury proceedings. *See* David Rossman, *Conditional Rules in Criminal Procedure: Alice in Wonderland Meets the Constitution*, 26 Ga. St. U.L. Rev. 417, 488 (2010).

After adopting Representative Laurance's language, the Senate reorganized the cluster of rights that ultimately went into the Fifth and Sixth Amendments. "In what was to be the Sixth Amendment the Senate clustered together the procedural rights of the criminally accused after indictment." Leonard W. Levy, Origins of the Fifth Amendment 427 (1968); *see also* Thomas Y. Davies, *Farther and Farther from the Original Fifth Amendment: The Recharacterization of the Right Against Self-Incrimination as a "Trial Right" in* Chavez v. Martinez, 70 Tenn. L. Rev. 987, 1013 (2003) ("[T]he Sixth Amendment plainly deals with rights that protect 'the accused' during the court phase of prosecutions, including trials."). This grouping of Sixth Amendment rights omitted the right against self-incrimination, which was put into the Fifth Amendment with other rights that unambiguously extended to pretrial proceedings as well as the trial:

> That the self-incrimination clause did not fall into the Sixth Amendment indicated that the Senate, like the House, did not intend to follow the implication of [Section 8 of the 1776 Virginia Declaration of Rights] . . . that the right not to give evidence against oneself applied merely to the defendant on trial. The Sixth Amendment, referring explicitly to the accused, protected him alone. Indeed the Sixth Amendment, with the right of counsel added, was the equivalent of Virginia's Section 8 and included all of its rights except that against self-incrimination. Thus, the location of the self-incrimination clause in the Fifth Amendment rather than the Sixth proves that the Senate, like the House, did not intend to restrict that clause to the criminal defendant only nor only to his trial. The Fifth Amendment, even with the self-incrimination clause restricted to criminal cases,

still puts its principles broadly enough to apply to witnesses and to any phase of the proceedings.

Leonard W. Levy, Origins of the Fifth Amendment 427 (1968); *see also* Thomas Y. Davies, *Farther and Farther from the Original Fifth Amendment: The Recharacterization of the Right Against Self-Incrimination as a "Trial Right" in* Chavez v. Martinez, 70 Tenn. L. Rev. 987, 1009–13 (2003) ("[T]he right against compelled self-accusation is in the wrong amendment to be a 'trial right.' "); Michael J. Zydney Mannheimer, *Ripeness of Self-Incrimination Clause Disputes*, 95 J. Crim. L. & Criminology 1261, 1322 (2005) ("It appears that the placement of the Self-Incrimination Clause in the Fifth Amendment rather than the Sixth signifies that a 'criminal case' can exist before a 'criminal prosecution[ ]' commences." (alteration in original)).

In sum, there is nothing to suggest that the Framers were seeking to confine the right against self-incrimination to trial. The Founders apparently viewed the right more broadly, envisioning it to apply beyond the trial itself.

The defendants argue that this interpretation of the Fifth Amendment is impractical because pretrial proceedings are often used to determine whether evidence is admissible at trial. We disagree.

For this argument, the defendants contend that courts have held in other contexts that evidence may be used in pretrial proceedings even if the evidence would be inadmissible at trial.[6] The defendants attempt to import this practice into the Fifth Amendment context. This attempt avoids the question by assuming that the use of compelled statements in pretrial proceedings is not rendered inadmissible by the Fifth Amendment. If the Fifth Amendment applies to pretrial proceedings, the evidence would be considered inadmissible in pretrial proceedings as well as at trial. As a result, the defendants' argument does not help us decide whether the Fifth Amendment precludes use of compelled statements in pretrial proceedings.

* * *

Mr. Vogt alleged that his compelled statements had been used in a probable cause hearing. As a result, we conclude that Mr. Vogt has adequately pleaded a Fifth Amendment violation consisting of the use of his statements in a criminal case.[7]

---

[6] The defendants also observe that the Fifth Amendment does not apply to physical evidence. Appellees' Br. at 25. But the defendants do not tie this observation to their argument for limiting the Fifth Amendment to a trial right.

[7] The defendants argue that Mr. Vogt

is not entitled to rely upon an inference that his alleged admissions were "admitted into evidence through witness testimony." Aplt. Brief, p. 31. No facts have been pled regarding the admission of any self-incriminatory statements into evidence or any witness testimony based thereon, and such facts cannot be reasonably inferred, because they are flatly inconsistent with the fact that the charges against Vogt were dismissed. The only reasonable inference to be drawn from the fact of dismissal is that

IV. We affirm the dismissal of the claims against the individual police officers and the City of Haysville.

Though we conclude that Mr. Vogt has adequately pleaded the use of his compelled statements in a criminal case, we affirm the dismissal of the (1) claims against the four police officers based on qualified immunity and (2) claims against the City of Haysville based on its lack of compulsion in Mr. Vogt's making of a self-incriminating statement.

A.   The four police officers are entitled to qualified immunity.

We conclude that the four police officers are protected by qualified immunity. . . .

Because it was not clearly established in 2013 or 2014 that the pretrial use of Mr. Vogt's statements would violate the Fifth Amendment, the four police officers are entitled to qualified immunity.

B.   Mr. Vogt did not adequately allege that Haysville had compelled the making of a self-incriminating statement.

As noted, Haysville conditioned its job offer to Mr. Vogt: he would get the job only if he told the Hays police department that he had taken the knife. According to Mr. Vogt, this condition compelled him to make self-incriminating statements to the City of Hays; Haysville responds that the condition on the job offer was not coercive. We agree with Haysville, concluding that the condition on the job offer did not compel Mr. Vogt to make a self-incriminating statement. Thus, we affirm the dismissal of the claim against Haysville.

The issue stems from the Supreme Court's opinion in Garrity v. New Jersey, 385 U.S. 493 (1967). There the Court held that public employers cannot require their employees to waive the right against self-incrimination as a condition of continued employment. 385 U.S. at 497–98, 500. In that case, police officers under investigation faced discharge if they refused to answer incriminating questions without immunity from criminal prosecution. *Id.* at 494, 497. In the Court's view, the officers faced a Hobson's choice amounting to compulsion: they had to decide between avoiding self-incrimination and losing their jobs. *Id.* at 497–98. Because the incriminating answers had been compelled, they could not be used against the officers in a subsequent criminal proceeding. *Id.*

Garrity has been applied outside of the conventional employment relationship. *See, e.g.*, Lefkowitz v. Turley, 414 U.S. 70, 82–83 (1973) (extending *Garrity* to public contractors); Spevack v. Klein, 385 U.S. 511, 514, 516 (1967) (applying the Fifth Amendment to potential disbarment). Thus, the Fifth Amendment may be triggered even by the threatened loss of an unsalaried position. For example, in *Lefkowitz v. Cunningham*, the

---

Vogt's admissions (if any) were not admitted into evidence by the court. Appellees' Br. at 37.

We disagree. Mr. Vogt's complaint states that the "compelled statements and fruits thereof were used against him in a criminal case." Appellant's App. at 15. At this stage, we can reasonably infer that these statements were used to support probable cause.

Supreme Court invalidated a state law requiring officers of political parties to either waive their right against self-incrimination or suffer automatic termination from office and a five-year disqualification from public office. 431 U.S. 801, 802–04 (1977). Though the political officers were unpaid, the Court held that the law had presented "grave consequences" because "party offices carry substantial prestige and political influence." *Id.* at 807. The Court also noted the law's potential economic consequences, for the claimant would suffer from the loss of professional standing and the possibility of holding future public offices. *Id.* In addition, the Court pointed out that the law was coercive because it impinged on an individual's right to participate in private, voluntary political associations—a key facet of the freedom guaranteed by the First Amendment. *Id.* at 807–08.

In each of these cases, individuals were threatened with the loss of some benefit or the infringement of an important right that they already enjoyed. These individuals already had a job, government contract, or right that was being threatened upon exercise of the right against self-incrimination. Our circumstances are different. Mr. Vogt was never an employee of Haysville, and his conditional job offer did not threaten the loss of livelihood or an existing job.

If Mr. Vogt had not wanted to incriminate himself, he could have declined the job offer and continued working for Hays. With that alternative freely available, Mr. Vogt was under no compulsion to comply with Haysville's condition to its job offer.

Mr. Vogt argues that Haysville threatened his ongoing employment relationship with Hays by promising to verify his future disclosure to Hays. According to Mr. Vogt, this threat created an additional measure of compulsion. But the complaint does not suggest that Haysville would contact the City of Hays even if Mr. Vogt had declined the employment offer. In fact, the complaint alleges that the City of Haysville promised to "follow-up with Hays to ensure that [Mr. Vogt] had complied with this *condition of employment*." Appellant's App. at 14 (emphasis added).

Because the complaint characterizes the disclosure requirement as a condition of the job offer, the only reasonable inference is that Haysville would not verify anything if Mr. Vogt were to decline the job offer. Thus, Haysville's promise to follow up with Hays did not compel Mr. Vogt to make a self-incriminating statement.

* * *

We conclude that the conditional job offer was not coercive. On this basis, we affirm the dismissal of the claim against Haysville.

V. Mr. Vogt has stated a valid claim against the City of Hays.

Hays urges three additional grounds for dismissal: (1) Mr. Vogt has not adequately pleaded causation; (2) Hays cannot incur liability because no one with final policymaking authority violated the Constitution; and

(3) violation of the Fifth Amendment cannot serve as the basis for a § 1983 claim.[11] We reject these arguments.

A. Mr. Vogt has adequately pleaded causation.

Hays argues that it did not cause a violation of the Fifth Amendment. Rather, Hays submits that it merely gave Mr. Vogt's compelled statements to the Kansas Bureau of Investigation, pointing out that Hays did not make the decision to pursue criminal charges or to use the statements in pretrial proceedings.

Section 1983 imposes liability on a state actor who "causes to be subjected . . . any citizen . . . to the deprivation of any rights." 42 U.S.C. § 1983. This language must be read against the backdrop of tort law, which makes individuals responsible for the natural consequence of their actions. Martinez v. Carson, 697 F.3d 1252, 1255 (10th Cir. 2012). Thus, causation exists if Hays initiated actions that it knew or reasonably should have known would cause others to deprive Mr. Vogt of his right against self-incrimination. *Id.* Accordingly, Hays could incur liability even if it had been someone else who used the compelled statements in a criminal case.

Mr. Vogt alleges in the complaint that Hays compelled self-incriminating statements, then initiated a criminal investigation that ended with use of the incriminating statements in a probable cause hearing. The complaint states that

- Mr. Vogt reported information to Hays concerning the knife,

- the Hays police chief conditioned Mr. Vogt's continued employment as a Hays police officer on his documenting the facts related to possession of the knife,

- Mr. Vogt wrote a vague one-sentence report, and

- a Hays police officer elicited further details about Mr. Vogt's possession of the knife.

The complaint adds that the Hays police chief then requested a criminal investigation of Mr. Vogt and furnished incriminating statements to investigators, which led to use of the incriminating statements in a probable cause hearing.

Taking these allegations as true, we conclude that Mr. Vogt adequately pleaded that Hays had started a chain of events that resulted in violation of the Fifth Amendment. *See* Stoot v. Everett, 582 F.3d 910, 926–27 (9th Cir. 2009) (concluding that a police officer, who allegedly

---

[11] Hays also argues that (1) witnesses in criminal proceedings enjoy absolute immunity from civil liability arising out of their testimony and (2) individuals testifying at trial do not act under color of law. But Mr. Vogt does not allege that the defendants acted unlawfully by testifying during the probable cause hearing. Rather, Mr. Vogt alleges that Hays unconstitutionally compelled him to incriminate himself. Though the use of those statements in the probable cause hearing would complete the alleged Fifth Amendment violation, the act of testifying does not serve as the basis of Mr. Vogt's claims.

coerced statements, may incur liability under § 1983 for violation of the Fifth Amendment when a prosecutor used those statements in a criminal case); McKinley v. Mansfield, 404 F.3d 418, 436–39 (6th Cir. 2005) (holding that police officers can incur § 983 liability for allegedly coercing a suspect to make self-incriminating statements even though it was another person, the prosecutor, who used the statements in a criminal case).

B. Mr. Vogt adequately pleaded that the Fifth Amendment violation had been committed by someone with final policymaking authority for the City of Hays.

Hays argues that it cannot incur liability for actions by the Hays police chief because he was not a final policymaker for the city. We disagree.

Cities cannot incur liability under § 1983 on a *respondeat superior* theory, but can be liable if a final policymaker takes unconstitutional action. *See* Monell v. Dep't of Soc. Servs. of City of New York, 436 U.S. 658, 691 (1978); Dill v. City of Edmond, 155 F.3d 1193, 1211 (10th Cir. 1998). "Whether an individual is a final policymaker for purposes of § 1983 liability 'is a legal issue to be determined by the court based on state and local law.'" *Dill*, 155 F.3d at 1210 (quoting Randle v. City of Aurora, 69 F.3d 441, 447 (10th Cir. 1995)). Mr. Vogt pleaded facts indicating that the Hays police chief was a final policymaker on the requirements for police employees.

This inquiry turns on whether the Hays police chief had authority to establish official policy on discipline of employees within the police department. *See id.* at 1211 (stating that whether the municipal police chief at the time of the alleged violation was "a final policymaker turns on whether he had the authority to establish official city policy on employee transfers and discipline within the police department"). To make this determination, we consider whether the police chief's decisions were constrained by general policies enacted by others, whether the decisions were reviewable by others, and whether the decisions were within the police chief's authority. *Randle*, 69 F.3d at 448.

The complaint alleges that the Hays police chief had final policymaking authority for the police department. There is nothing in the complaint to suggest that his decisions were subject to further review up the chain-of-command.

Hays argues that final policymaking authority rested with the City Manager and City Commission rather than the Police Chief. For this argument, Hays points to municipal ordinances stating that the city commission must hire a city manager, who appoints the police chief and administers city business. But the city ordinances do not specify who bears ultimate responsibility for discipline of police officers like Mr. Vogt.

We addressed a similar situation in Dill v. City of Edmond, 155 F.3d 1193 (10th Cir. 1998). That case involved a due process violation from a change in a police officer's position from detective to patrol officer. 155 F.3d at 1210. There the municipal charter designated the city manager as the municipality's administrative head, who had authority to appoint and remove the police chief and to hire and fire employees. *Id.* at 1211. Notwithstanding the city manager's powers, we concluded that the police chief was a final policymaker for disciplinary transfers of police officers. We had four reasons for this conclusion:

1.   The city ordinances had not directly stated who was authorized to determine the policy on transfers and discipline.

2.   Trial testimony had indicated that the transfer was based on a policy adopted by the police chief.

3.   The city manager had testified that he did not involve himself with transfers.

4.   The decision to transfer the plaintiff had fallen within the authority of the police chief.

Id.

We took a similar approach in Flanagan v. Munger, 890 F.2d 1557 (10th Cir. 1989). There too the issue was whether the municipal police chief had final policymaking authority for disciplinary decisions within the police department. 890 F.2d at 1568. In that case, the municipality admitted that the police chief had final authority to issue reprimands for its officers—an admission that we described as effectively disposing of the municipal liability issue. *Id.* Notwithstanding this admission, we analyzed the municipality's argument that the police chief lacked final policymaking authority under the municipal code. The municipality pointed out that

•   the city manager had to manage and supervise all matters related to the police department, its officers, and employees,

•   the city manager could set aside any action taken by the police chief and "supersede any department head in the functions of his position," and

•   "[t]he rules of the Civil Service Commission . . . govern[ed] disciplinary matters relative to uniformed personnel [e.g., review by City Council] except as otherwise provided by charter or ordinance."

Id. (quoting the city's municipal code) (alterations in original).

We acknowledged that the police chief's decisions were subject to review by the city manager and city council. *Id.* Nonetheless, we held that the police chief had final policymaking authority for disciplinary decisions within the police department. *Id.* at 1568–69.

We had two reasons. First, the municipal code empowered the police chief to directly manage and supervise the force and made him "responsible for the discipline, good order and proper conduct of the

Department, [and] the enforcement of all laws, ordinances and regulations pertaining thereto." *Id.* (quoting the city's municipal code) (alteration in original). Second, the municipal code did not create a mandatory or formal review of the police chief's action. *Id.* at 1569. Thus, we concluded that "for all intents and purposes the [police chief's] discipline decisions [were] final" and that "any meaningful administrative review [was] illusory." *Id.* at 1569. This conclusion led us to hold that the police chief had final policymaking authority even under the municipal code. *Id.*

Under *Dill* and *Flanagan*, we conclude that Mr. Vogt has adequately pleaded final policymaking authority on the part of the Hays police chief. As in *Dill* and *Flanagan*, the city has pointed to general supervisory responsibilities of the city manager. But there is nothing in the municipal ordinances suggesting that the city manager plays a meaningful role in disciplinary decisions within the police department. The absence of such provisions is fatal at this stage, where we must view all of the allegations and draw all reasonable inferences in favor of Mr. Vogt. *See* Dias v. City and Cty. of Denver, 567 F.3d 1169, 1178 (10th Cir. 2009). As a result, we conclude that Mr. Vogt has adequately pleaded final policymaking authority on the part of the Hays police chief.

C. Violation of the Fifth Amendment can serve as the basis for liability under § 1983.

In a single sentence, Hays contends that "*Chavez* held there is no claim for civil liability under the Fifth Amendment and that claims related to securing compelled/coerced statements required egregious government action under a substantive due process analysis." Appellees' Br. at 20. Hays does not explain or support this sentence, and it is incorrect. *Chavez* did not make such a holding. Thus, Hays's single sentence does not support the dismissal.

VI. Disposition

We affirm the dismissal of the claims against the City of Haysville and the four police officers. We reverse the dismissal of the claim against the City of Hays and remand for further proceedings consistent with this opinion.

■ HARTZ, CIRCUIT JUDGE, concurring:

I join Judge Bacharach's opinion for the panel. I write separately to emphasize the limits of what we are saying. We have addressed only issues raised by the parties. Some of the questions we have not answered are: (1) Even though the Fifth Amendment privilege against self-incrimination can be violated by use of the defendant's statements at a probable-cause hearing, can there be a violation when such use does not cause a criminal sanction to be imposed on the defendant (such as when, as here, the court does not find probable cause)? (2) When a person voluntarily discloses information to a government agency, does he or she thereby waive any Fifth Amendment objection to disclosing that same information to another government agency? (3) Under what circumstances can an employee who has given notice of resignation claim that a request for incriminatory information was coercive? And, most significantly, (4) In light of post-*Garrity* developments in Fifth Amendment doctrine, if a public employee believes that he or she is being coerced by the employer into making self-incriminatory statements, must the employee invoke the privilege against self-incrimination by refusing to provide information, or can the employee still, as in *Garrity*, provide the information and then demand immunity from use of the information? *See* Peter Westen, *Answer Self-Incriminating Questions or Be Fired,* 37 Am. J. Crim. L. 97 (2010).

United States v. Ponds
454 F.3d 313 (D.C. Cir. 2006)

■ Before: ROGERS, TATEL and BROWN, CIRCUIT JUDGES.

■ Opinion for the Court filed by CIRCUIT JUDGE ROGERS.

This appeal challenges the government's use of documents produced by Navron Ponds pursuant to a grant of immunity under 18 U.S.C. § 6002. Ponds' appeal of his convictions for tax evasion and fraud requires the court to address the breadth of that immunity for an act of production that, in its testimonial character, falls somewhere between the response to a fishing expedition addressed in United States v. Hubbell, 530 U.S. 27 (2000), and the production of documents whose existence was a "foregone conclusion" in Fisher v. United States, 425 U.S. 391 (1976). Because the government has failed to show with reasonable particularity that it knew of the existence and location of most of the subpoenaed documents, we hold that Ponds' act of production was sufficiently testimonial to implicate his right against self-incrimination under the Fifth Amendment to the Constitution. Although the government, to some extent, violated its immunity agreement with Ponds by impermissibly using his self-incriminating testimony and its derivative evidence, questions remain regarding the precise nature of its use and whether the constitutional error was harmless beyond a reasonable doubt. Accordingly, we reverse the judgment of conviction and remand the case to the district court to determine the extent of the government's impermissible use and whether that use was harmless beyond a reasonable doubt.

I.

In 1996, Navron Ponds, a criminal defense lawyer, agreed to represent a drug dealer named Jerome Harris. *See, e.g.,* United States v. Harris, 176 F.3d 476 (4th Cir.1999). As a retainer, Harris's mother agreed to give Ponds a white 1991 Mercedes Benz 500SL, which Ponds registered in his sister's name. Harris pled guilty. At his sentencing, the district court asked Harris about the whereabouts of the Mercedes for forfeiture purposes. Ponds failed to inform the court that he had the car.

In 2000, when the United States Attorney's Office for the District of Maryland learned this from Harris, it began a grand jury investigation of Ponds' acquisition of the Mercedes and his failure to reveal his possession of the car to the court, focusing on potential charges of contempt of court, obstruction of justice, and money laundering. *See* United States v. Ponds, 290 F.Supp.2d 71, 74 (D.D.C.2003).

Maryland Assistant United States Attorney ("MD-AUSA") Sandra Wilkinson executed a search warrant for Harris's jail cell to obtain the retainer agreement discussing the Mercedes. Federal Drug Enforcement Administration agents went to Ponds' apartment complex, Albemarle House, looking for the car. Parked outside were the Mercedes, and in another parking space rented by Ponds, a Porsche with the vanity license plate "I OBJECT." According to apartment personnel, Ponds drove the Mercedes and his sister, Laura Ponds Pelzer, drove the Porsche. MD-AUSA Wilkinson issued a subpoena duces tecum ordering Ponds to produce seven categories of documents and the Mercedes. When Ponds expressed his intent to invoke his Fifth Amendment privilege against self-incrimination, Wilkinson revised the subpoena to omit requests that Ponds actually produce the car and that he produce financial and tax records, and filed a motion pursuant to 18 U.S.C. § 6003 for a judicial order authorizing act-of-production immunity under 18 U.S.C. § 6002. The subpoena made six demands of Ponds to produce "any and all documents" from 1996 forward:

> 1. Referencing use, ownership, possession, custody and/or control of a white Mercedes Benz . . .;
>
> 2. That refer or relate to payment of legal fees by or on behalf of Jerome Harris whether by cash, currency, or some other form of payment;
>
> 3. That refer or relate to any vehicles in the custody or control of Jerome Harris if access to that vehicle was provided to you by any means, direct or indirect; and,
>
> 4. That refer or relate to Sloan Solomon, Christine Privott [Harris's mother] or Laura P. Pelzer [Ponds' sister];
>
> 5. Any and all correspondence between the Law Offices of Navron Ponds [and courts and prosecutors] in the matter of U.S. v. Jerome Harris, PJM 96-0269;
>
> 6. Records of employees of the law Office of Navron Ponds in the time frame of 1996 to the present.

The district court granted the immunity request and ordered Ponds to produce the subpoenaed documents.

Armed with act-of-production immunity, Ponds appeared before the grand jury and produced approximately 300 pages of documents. The documents included records showing that: (1) the Mercedes and Porsche were registered in the name of Ponds' sister; (2) Ponds had financial accounts with his sister; (3) Ponds and his sister sold a Georgia property they had jointly owned; (4) Ponds possessed money order receipts used to pay for various services, mostly involving the Mercedes; and (5) Ponds had a health insurance document indicating he had purchased insurance for himself and Magdalene Alexander. Ponds also testified before the grand jury, responding to the prosecutors' questions about the document production, including affirming that the health insurance document was responsive to the subpoena request for documents regarding his employees. Magdalene "Maggie" Alexander, Ponds' employee, was then called before the grand jury, where she testified about many of the produced documents and in detail about the process by which she helped Ponds produce them.

Soon after Ponds responded to the subpoena duces tecum, the Maryland United States Attorney's Office filed an ex parte application it had prepared before the subpoena response with the Maryland federal district court to authorize the Internal Revenue Service ("IRS") to disclose Ponds' 1996 and 1997 tax returns. The application was granted, and the IRS reported that Ponds had not filed tax returns in those years. Because Ponds was a resident of the District of Columbia, the Maryland prosecutors contacted the United States Attorney's Office for the District of Columbia about conducting a tax investigation of Ponds. These contacts involved several meetings and the transfer of documents produced by Ponds and of Maryland grand jury transcripts to DC-AUSA Mark Dubester and IRS Special Agent Nancy Becker.

The investigation continued, and in 2001, DC-AUSA Dubester applied for search warrants on the basis of an affidavit provided by Agent Becker that included information first learned in the Maryland grand jury. Based on those applications, the D.C. United States Attorney's Office secured warrants to search Ponds' home and office, where Agent Becker seized six boxes of documents. The documents revealed that Ponds had used a tax preparer, and the preparer's records were subpoenaed, uncovering further details about Ponds' financial affairs. With these materials and others subpoenaed from financial institutions, Ponds was indicted in the District of Columbia on five counts of tax evasion under 26 U.S.C. § 7201, one count of wire fraud under 18 U.S.C. § 1343, and one count of fraud in the first degree under 22 D.C.Code §§ 3821(a), 3822(a)(1).

Ponds filed a pretrial motion for a hearing pursuant to Kastigar v. United States, 406 U.S. 441 (1972), that would force the government to "demonstrate that the charges in this matter and the evidence it proposes to use . . . at trial do not derive directly or indirectly from Mr. Ponds's immunized testimony and production of documents." The district court conducted an evidentiary hearing at which it heard testimony from Agent Becker and MD-AUSA Wilkinson, and accepted proffered testimony from DC-AUSA Dubester. *See Ponds,* 290 F.Supp.2d at 73. The district court denied Ponds' motion to dismiss the indictment. *Id.* The jury convicted

Ponds on all counts,[1] and the district court, upon denying Ponds' motion for reconsideration of the *Kastigar* ruling or for a new trial, sentenced Ponds to twenty months imprisonment and restitution to the federal and District governments. Ponds appeals.

II.

18 U.S.C. § 6002 provides that:

> no testimony or other information compelled under [an immunity] order (or any information directly or indirectly derived from such testimony or other information) may be used against the witness in any criminal case, except a prosecution for perjury, giving a false statement, or otherwise failing to comply with the order.

This federal witness immunity statute has a constitutional dimension, as the Supreme Court in Kastigar, 406 U.S. 441, held that § 6002 "immunity from use and derivative use is coextensive with the scope of the [Fifth Amendment] privilege against self-incrimination" in that "[i]t prohibits the prosecutorial authorities from using the compelled testimony in any respect." *Id.* at 453. Thus, at issue in document production cases in which a witness with § 6002 immunity is subsequently prosecuted are two basic questions: (1) Was the defendant's act of producing the documents sufficiently testimonial that the Fifth Amendment privilege is implicated? (2) If so, did the government violate the defendant's Fifth Amendment rights (and the court order granting him immunity) by using sources of information derived from the immunized testimony in the prosecution? *See Hubbell*, 530 U.S. at 29–30.

The Fifth Amendment declares that "[n]o person . . . shall be compelled in any criminal case to be a witness against himself." U.S. CONST. amend. V. At one point in our history, this declaration was taken to mean that the government could not compel the production of private papers. *See* Boyd v. United States, 116 U.S. 616, 634–35 (1886). In 1976, the Supreme Court changed course, and it is now a "settled proposition that a person may be required to produce specific documents even though they contain incriminating assertions of fact or belief because the creation of those documents was not 'compelled' within the meaning of the privilege." *Hubbell*, 530 U.S. at 35–36 (summarizing *Fisher*, 425 U.S. 391). "[T]he act of producing documents in response to a subpoena," however, "may have a compelled testimonial aspect" in that the act "may implicitly communicate 'statements of fact,'" such as the witness's admission "that the papers existed, were in his possession or control, and were authentic." *Id.* at 36 & n. 19 (quoting United States v. Doe, 465 U.S. 605, 613 & n.11 (1984)). Whether the act of producing evidence in response to a subpoena is sufficiently testimonial that the Fifth

---

[1] In addition to the counts on which Ponds was indicted, Ponds was convicted of five "failure-to-file" counts which were charged by information. *See* 26 U.S.C. § 7203. The district court vacated those convictions without prejudice to a government motion to reinstate them if the convictions at issue here are vacated on appeal.

Amendment applies "depend [s] on the facts and circumstances of particular cases." *Fisher,* 425 U.S. at 410.

Two Supreme Court cases provide the framework for our analysis of the facts and circumstances of this case. In *Fisher,* 425 U.S. 391, the Court considered two cases in which IRS agents visited and interviewed taxpayers under investigation for tax violations. *See id.* at 393–94. After the interviews, the taxpayers obtained from their accountants documents used in preparing their tax returns and gave the documents to their lawyers. *See id.* at 394. Once the government discovered that the lawyers had the documents, it sought to subpoena the records. In one case, its subpoena demanded the accountant's workpapers pertaining to the taxpayer's books for three years, the retained copies of the taxpayer's returns for those years, and the retained copies of reports and other correspondence between the accountant and the taxpayer during those years. *Id.* After disavowing any Fifth Amendment protection for the contents of the documents themselves, the Court nevertheless recognized the testimonial aspect of the act of production because "[c]ompliance with the subpoena tacitly concedes the existence of the papers demanded and their possession or control by the taxpayer," as well as "the taxpayer's belief that the papers are those described in the subpoena." *Id.* at 410. Under the circumstances of that case, however, the Court concluded it was "doubtful that implicitly admitting the existence and possession of the papers rises to the level of testimony within the protection of the Fifth Amendment" because "[t]he existence and location of the papers are a foregone conclusion and the taxpayer adds little or nothing to the sum total of the Government's information by conceding that he in fact has the papers." *Id.* at 411. Because the subpoena was more a question of "surrender" than of "testimony," the Court held that "no constitutional rights are touched." *Id.* (quoting In re Harris, 221 U.S. 274, 279 (1911)).

Hubbell provides the counterpoint to *Fisher.* In *Hubbell,* the Supreme Court held that Hubbell's act of producing over 13,000 documents in response to a broad subpoena was sufficiently testimonial to implicate the Fifth Amendment because "the prosecutor needed [Hubbell]'s assistance both to identify potential sources of information and to produce those sources." 530 U.S. at 41. Some of the broadest demands of that subpoena asked for all documents referring to "any direct or indirect sources of money or other things of value received by or provided to Webster Hubbell" and "Webster Hubbell's schedule of activities." *Id.* at 46–47. The Court held that "the collection and production of the materials demanded was tantamount to answering a series of interrogatories asking a witness to disclose the existence and location of particular documents fitting certain broad descriptions," *id.* at 41, in which it was "unquestionably necessary for [Hubbell] to make extensive use of 'the contents of his own mind' in identifying the hundreds of documents responsive to the requests in the subpoena," *id.* at 43. The government claimed that it was a "foregone conclusion" that

Hubbell would possess the subpoenaed documents because "a businessman such as [Hubbell] will always possess general business and tax records that fall within the broad categories described in this subpoena," but the Court rejected that argument as "overbroad." *Id.* at 45.

The Supreme Court distinguished the circumstances in *Hubbell* from those in *Fisher:* "While in *Fisher* the Government already knew that the documents were in the attorneys' possession and could independently confirm their existence and authenticity through the accountants who created them, here the Government has not shown that it had any prior knowledge of either the existence or the whereabouts" of the produced documents. *Id.* at 44–45. Whether an act of production is sufficiently testimonial to implicate the Fifth Amendment, therefore, depends on the government's knowledge regarding the documents before they are produced. In *Fisher*, the government knew of the existence of a set of documents relating to defined topics that were in the hands of the taxpayers' attorneys; in *Hubbell*, the government could not show its prior awareness of the existence or location of the produced documents. When Hubbell was heard in this court, we described the inquiry this way:

> [T]he government must establish its knowledge of the existence, possession, and authenticity of the subpoenaed documents with 'reasonable particularity' before the communication inherent in the act of production can be considered a foregone conclusion. In making this assessment, though, the focus must remain upon the degree to which a subpoena "invades the dignity of the human mind," and on the quantum of information as to the existence, possession, or authenticity of the documents conveyed via the act of production.

United States v. Hubbell, 167 F.3d 552, 579–80 (D.C.Cir.1999) (citations omitted). Although the Supreme Court did not adopt the "reasonable particularity" standard in affirming our decision, it emphasized that the applicability of the Fifth Amendment turns on the level of the government's prior knowledge of the existence and location of the produced documents. *See Hubbell*, 530 U.S. at 44–45. Post-*Hubbell*, another circuit has applied the reasonable particularity standard to determine whether an act of production is sufficiently testimonial to implicate the Fifth Amendment. *See* In re Grand Jury Subpoena Dated April 18, 2003, 383 F.3d 905, 910 (9th Cir.2004). Because that standard conceptualizes the Supreme Court's focus in a useful way, so do we.

Once it is clear that an act of production is sufficiently testimonial to be protected by the Fifth Amendment's privilege against self-incrimination, the question remains how the government may use the compelled testimony and information derived therefrom in a later prosecution of the witness. In *Kastigar,* 406 U.S. 441, the Supreme Court held that § 6002 "immunity from use and derivative use is coextensive with the scope of the privilege against self-incrimination" in that "[i]t prohibits the prosecutorial authorities from using the compelled testimony in any respect." *Id.* at 453. Therefore, when a person accorded § 6002 immunity is subsequently prosecuted, the government bears "the affirmative duty to prove that the evidence it proposes to use is derived from a legitimate source wholly independent of the compelled testimony." *Id.* at 460.

With oral testimony, the bar on derivative use is easy to imagine. For example, if a murder suspect who has been granted immunity is called before a grand jury and asked whether he committed a murder and where the murder weapon is, his testimony may not be used against him in a criminal trial. In addition, the government may not use his testimony to retrieve the weapon for use against the witness at trial. Even if the government introduced the weapon without indicating that it learned of its location from the defendant's immunized grand jury testimony, only using fingerprints or DNA testing to link the weapon to the defendant, the weapon would still be barred because it was "directly or indirectly derived from" compelled testimony. If the police simply happened upon the weapon through an ongoing investigation, however, the weapon could be used against the witness because it was "derived from a legitimate source wholly independent of the compelled testimony." Kastigar, 406 U.S. at 460; *see Hubbell*, 167 F.3d at 583–84.

With act-of-production immunity, the key question is whether, despite the compelled testimony implicit in the production, the government remains free to use the contents of the (non-testimonial) produced documents. In *Hubbell,* the Supreme Court rejected the "manna from heaven" theory[2] by holding the use of the contents of produced documents to be a barred derivative use of the compelled testimonial act of production. The Court did so by stating that it "cannot accept the Government's submission that [Hubbell's] immunity did not preclude its derivative use of the produced documents" as it "was only through [Hubbell]'s truthful reply to the subpoena that the Government received the incriminating documents of which it made 'substantial use . . . in the investigation that led to the indictment.'" *Hubbell,* 530 U.S. at 42–43 (emphasis added). In context, these statements indicate that the Supreme Court understands the contents of the documents to be off-limits because they are a derivative use of the compelled testimony regarding the existence, location, and possession of the documents. As stated by this court in *Hubbell*: "If the government did not have a reasonably particular knowledge of subpoenaed documents' actual existence, let alone their possession by the subpoenaed party, and cannot prove knowledge of their existence through any independent means, Kastigar forbids the derivative use of the information contained therein against the immunized party." *Hubbell*, 167 F.3d at 585 (emphasis

---

[2] This theory states that "the act of production shields the witness from the use of any information (resulting from his subpoena response) beyond what the prosecution would receive if the documents appeared in the grand jury room or in his office unsolicited and unmarked, like manna from heaven." Hubbell, 167 F.3d at 602 (Williams, J., dissenting).

added). Or explained another way, the contents of the documents cannot be used against the witness because they are not "derived from a legitimate source wholly independent of the compelled testimony." *Kastigar,* 406 U.S. at 460. This approach treats documents revealed in an immunized act of production just like the weapon revealed pursuant to immunized testimony. If the existence or location of the item was revealed through compelled testimony, the item is derivative of the testimony and may not be used by the government against the witness-defendant.

After determining what may not be used against the witness-defendant, the further question remains how that information may not be used. The direct introduction of immunized information as evidence at trial would be a prohibited "use." *See Hubbell,* 530 U.S. at 41. But § 6002 goes further, "provid[ing] a sweeping proscription of any uses, direct or indirect, of the compelled testimony and any information derived therefrom," functioning as "a comprehensive safeguard, barring the use of compelled testimony as an 'investigatory lead,' and also barring the use of any evidence obtained by focusing investigation on a witness as a result of his compelled disclosures." *Kastigar,* 406 U.S. at 460 (footnotes omitted). In United States v. North, 910 F.2d 843 (D.C.Cir.1990), this court noted that "*Kastigar* does not prohibit simply 'a whole lot of use,' or 'excessive use,' or 'primary use' of compelled testimony. It prohibits 'any use,' direct or indirect." *Id.* at 861. Accordingly, this court held that the government's use of immunized testimony to refresh the recollection of a grand jury witness constituted a "use" of the compelled testimony. *See id.*

Taken together, the bar on the use of information derived from a testimonial act of production by a witness with § 6002 immunity and the breadth of that bar create real risks for prosecutors planning on prosecuting those whom they subpoena. "The decision to seek use immunity necessarily involves a balancing of the Government's interest in obtaining information against the risk that immunity will frustrate the Government's attempts to prosecute the subject of the investigation." *Doe,* 465 U.S. at 616. That risk was manifested in the government's prosecution of Ponds.

III.

The central question on appeal is whether the district court's reliance on "a sharp distinction" between the testimonial aspect of producing documents and the contents of the documents, *see Ponds,* 290 F.Supp.2d at 79, is contrary to an essential holding of the Supreme Court in *Hubbell* that the use of the contents of documents may be a barred derivative use of the testimony inherent in the immunized act of producing those documents. Throughout its opinion, the district court emphasizes its understanding that § 6002 immunity is limited to the act of production and does not extend to the contents of documents. *See id.* at 80–81, 83, 84, 85, 86, 88, 91. Ponds contends that the district court has returned to the repudiated manna-from-heaven rationale by seeming to think that nothing is amiss if the prosecution uses the contents of the documents without reference to the testimony inherent in the act of production.

A.

It is true that in *Hubbell* the Supreme Court drew a distinction between protected testimony as to the existence, location, and authenticity of documents inherent in the act of production and the unprotected contents of the documents themselves. *See Hubbell*, 530 U.S. at 37. This distinction, however, is only relevant in the context of determining whether an act of production implicates the Fifth Amendment. In that context, the contents of the documents are irrelevant for constitutional purposes because their preparation was not "compelled." *See Fisher*, 425 U.S. at 409–10; *Doe,* 465 U.S. at 610–11. Therefore, to determine whether an act of production implicates the Fifth Amendment, the court looks only to the communicative aspects of the act of production itself and to whether those tacit averments as to the existence and location of the documents add anything significant "to the sum total of the Government's information." *Fisher*, 425 U.S. at 411.

The "sharp distinction" upon which the district court relied becomes less relevant, however, when a court proceeds to "the conceptually separate and temporally subsequent *Kastigar* inquiry." *Hubbell*, 167 F.3d at 580. This is because § 6002, coextensive with the protections of the Fifth Amendment, s*ee Kastigar,* 406 U.S. at 453, provides that a witness compelled by the district court to testify over an assertion of the Fifth Amendment privilege is not only protected from having that testimony used against him, but is also protected from having "any information directly or indirectly derived from such testimony" used against him. When the government does not have reasonably particular knowledge of the existence or location of a document, and the existence or location of the document is communicated through immunized testimony, the contents of the document are derived from that immunized testimony, and therefore are off-limits to the government.

The government concedes that the contents of subpoenaed documents can sometimes be off-limits, describing the subpoena response in *Hubbell* as "sufficiently testimonial (as to the documents' existence and location) to be privileged, and to taint the contents of the documents themselves." Appellee's Br. at 25. The government attempts to minimize the distinction that the district court drew between contents and act of production. It contends that the district court understood that the act of production could taint the contents of produced documents, but found that Ponds' act of production did not taint the contents of the produced materials because his act of production did not make the extensive testimonial representations that Hubbell did. The government reads the district court as understanding that act-of-production immunity could reach the contents of documents, but that in this case, immunity did not reach the documents' contents.

The district court distinguished Ponds' case from *Hubbell* in finding "the degree of interpretation, locating, cataloging and assembling of documents so important in *Hubbell* . . . simply not demanded by the narrow subpoena at issue here." *Ponds,* 290 F.Supp.2d at 82. If the district court was correct that Ponds' act of production was insufficiently testimonial to implicate the Fifth Amendment, then it would be proper to deny protection to the contents of the produced documents. The district court opinion does not explicitly connect the discussion of the testimonial character of Ponds' act of production to its conclusion that the contents of the documents were unprivileged, however, which leads Ponds to contend that the district court had the errant understanding that § 6002 immunity only categorically reaches "testimony inherent in the act of production" and "plainly not the contents of the documents produced." *Ponds,* 290 F.Supp.2d at 81; *see, e.g., id.* at 84. Such an understanding would revive the rejected manna-from-heaven rationale whereby the government could use documents against an immunized party when it could do so without reference to how the documents were produced. That understanding would conflate the Fifth Amendment question—is the act of production sufficiently testimonial to warrant Fifth Amendment protection?—with the immunity question—has the government used compelled testimony or the information directly or indirectly derived therefrom in prosecuting the witness? *See Hubbell,* 167 F.3d at 580. Although the contents of the documents are irrelevant to determining whether the act of production was testimonial, the government's use of the contents of the documents is critical in determining whether there was a derivative use of the compelled testimony that violates § 6002.

B.

Applying the lessons of *Fisher* and *Hubbell* to determine whether Ponds' act of production is better characterized as "testimony" or "surrender," we begin by addressing the threshold question of whether the government has "establish[ed] its [pre-subpoena] knowledge of the existence, possession, and authenticity of the subpoenaed documents with 'reasonable particularity' " such that "the communication inherent in the act of production can be considered a foregone conclusion." *Hubbell,* 167 F.3d at 579. Ponds contends that his act of production was sufficiently testimonial to trigger Fifth Amendment protection because he used the contents of his mind to interpret the subpoena's directions and to identify the documents in his possession that he believed were responsive. He maintains that the government was not focused on any tax offenses or any documents relevant to such offenses, citing MD-AUSA Wilkinson's statement that she was "surprised" by some of the documents produced as evidence of the government's lack of previous awareness of the existence and location of some of the documents. The government relies on the district court's finding that the subpoena was "narrow and specific, and reflected that the government already knew of the existence of the types of documents sought and their possession by defendant." *Ponds,* 290 F.Supp.2d at 82.

As the critical inquiry is whether the government can show it had such "prior knowledge of either the existence or the whereabouts," *Hubbell,* 530 U.S. at 45, of the produced documents that their existence and location was a "foregone conclusion," *Fisher,* 425 U.S. at 411, the parties approach this inquiry by comparing and contrasting Ponds' subpoena to those in *Fisher* and *Hubbell.* By any measure, this subpoena falls somewhere in between the two: Unlike *Fisher,* the prosecutors here did not ask for "retained copies" of workpapers, tax returns, and correspondence about which they were sure of both the existence and location. Compare *Fisher,* 425 U.S. at 394, with *Ponds,* 290 F.Supp.2d at 74. Unlike *Hubbell,* the set of topics for which the Maryland prosecutors sought "any and all documents" "refer[ring] or relat[ing]" to is somewhat defined. Compare *Hubbell,* 530 U.S. at 46–49, with *Ponds,* 290 F.Supp.2d at 74. For most of the subpoena categories, however, the government has failed to establish its previous knowledge of the existence or location of the documents.

The existence and location of some subpoenaed documents were a foregone conclusion: For instance, the government must have known of the existence of the documents in Subpoena Demand No. 5, "[a]ny and all correspondence between the Law Offices of Navron Ponds [and courts and prosecutors] in the matter of U.S. v. Jerome Harris," because it was a party to that correspondence. And the government knew of the existence of documents referring to "payment of legal fees by or on behalf of Jerome Harris" (Subpoena Demand No. 2) because it had already seized a copy of Harris's retainer agreement from his prison cell. The failure of the government to identify each produced document specifically is of no moment. To be consistent with *Fisher,* in which there is no indication that the government knew of each document within the set of documents of which it was aware, the "reasonable particularity" standard cannot demand that the subpoena name every scrap of paper that is produced. Because the government already had sufficient knowledge about the Harris documents, Ponds was simply surrendering them, not testifying, by complying with those demands in the subpoena.

The government's prior knowledge of the existence or location of other subpoenaed documents has not been established. First, the government has not shown any prior knowledge that documents regarding the "use, ownership, possession, custody and/or control of a white Mercedes Benz" (Subpoena Demand No. 1) were in existence or in Ponds' possession. Before the subpoena, the government knew that the Mercedes was normally parked at Ponds' apartment and was registered to his sister. *See Ponds,* 290 F.Supp.2d at 83. But it had no idea that Ponds possessed some of the documents he produced—a registration card, auto insurance information, sales contracts, and the title—and has not shown it was even aware of the existence of the large range of correspondence and receipts that he produced regarding repairs and improvements to the Mercedes. In fact, MD-AUSA Wilkinson testified that "at the time that [she] sought Act of Production Immunity," she was Seeking to determine "whether or not there were other documents that proved the longevity of [Ponds'] ownership of this car." This statement confirms that the government did not know "whether or not" documents relating to the car existed or were in Ponds' possession. Ponds' act of producing the car-related documents testified to their existence and his possession, which effectively communicated that he had long been the beneficial owner of the car. The government's prior knowledge that Ponds had possession of a Mercedes registered to his sister might render harmless the government's improper use of the subpoenaed documents relating to the car, because the documents mostly confirmed what the government already suspected, but the government's prior knowledge that he possessed the Mercedes is not enough to establish with reasonable particularity its prior knowledge regarding the documents related to the Mercedes. As in *Hubbell*, where the Supreme Court rejected the government's claim of knowledge based on the "overbroad" claim that Hubbell was a businessman and therefore would have business-related documents, 530 U.S. at 45, the government cannot show knowledge by means of broad assumptions about car ownership, much less mere possession. *Cf. Hubbell*, 167 F.3d at 578.

Similarly, the government has not shown prior knowledge of the existence or location of documents relating to Ponds' sister, Laura Pelzer, (Subpoena Demand No. 4) a subpoena request that turned up documents regarding shared bank accounts and sales of shared real property. While in common parlance it might be a "foregone conclusion" that a person with a sibling will have documents relating or referring to the sibling— even if only a Christmas card or a parent's will—the reasonable particularity standard demands more. This court explained in *Hubbell* that "the government cannot simply subpoena business records and then claim the requisite knowledge for purposes of the Fifth Amendment by pointing to the existence of a business." *Hubbell*, 167 F.3d at 578. The court stated that "the [government]'s assertion that its knowledge of Hubbell's status as a consultant and a taxpayer carried with it a concomitant awareness of the existence and possession of his consulting and tax records similarly falls short." *Id.* at 579. Likewise, the government's knowledge of Ponds' status as a brother does not carry with it an awareness of the existence and possession of records about his sister. The government's prior knowledge that Ponds had a Mercedes and a sister cannot suffice to establish its prior knowledge of the existence and location of the documents relating or referring to those topics that Ponds, with immunity, produced in response to the subpoena.

In addition, the government has not shown that it had any prior knowledge of the existence or location of "[r]ecords of employees of the law Office of Navron Ponds in the time frame of 1996 to the present" (Subpoena Demand No. 6). The district court's determination that the existence and location of these documents was a foregone conclusion was based on pure inference: "[T]he Court concludes that it was a foregone conclusion in this day and age in the Washington area that a sole practitioner would have some staff, even if part-time or temporary, to assist him in his legal practice. Moreover, it was also a foregone conclusion that certain administrative documents, including health care forms, would exist with respect to such staff, and would be in defendant's possession." *Ponds,* 290 F.Supp.2d at 85. This reasoning is reminiscent of "the overbroad argument that a businessman . . . will always possess general business and tax records," *Hubbell,* 530 U.S. at 45, an argument the Supreme Court found could not "cure [the] deficiency" of the government's failure to demonstrate its "prior knowledge of either the existence or the whereabouts" of the produced documents in *Hubbell, id.*

The request for documents relating to any employees—when the government did not know whether Ponds had employees, much less whether he had specific documents relating to them—"was tantamount to answering a series of interrogatories," *id.* at 41, asking Ponds if he had employees, and if so, what their names were. This is made clear by the fact that Ponds was asked in the Maryland grand jury whether the "insurance record" "serve[s] to provide information called for in the subpoena with respect to information about the employees of your law office," an inquiry to which Ponds answered "yes." It is further clarified by the fact that the subpoena asks for records regarding "employees" in the plural, indicating that the government did not really know about Ponds' employment practices. MD-AUSA Wilkinson's infirm belief that she had at one time spoken with a secretary in Ponds' office—she testified that "it's possible I did, possible I didn't"—does not demonstrate the requisite knowledge of the existence and location of documents relating to Ponds' employees.

The face of the subpoena also displays the government's lack of knowledge when it asks for documents that "refer or relate to any vehicles in the custody or control of Jerome Harris if access to that vehicle was provided to you by any means" (Subpoena Demand No. 3). The "if" in that request demonstrates that the government did not know whether Harris had given Ponds access to any vehicles besides the Mercedes, much less whether there existed any documents that would prove such access. If Ponds had been directly asked when he appeared before the grand jury whether he had employees or whether Harris had given him access to any vehicles, the Fifth Amendment privilege would allow Ponds to refuse to answer. *See* Lefkowitz v. Cunningham, 431 U.S. 801, 804–05 (1977). The government cannot make an end-run around the Fifth Amendment by fishing for a document that will answer a question for which it could not demand an answer in oral examination.

In sum, the government has failed to show with reasonable particularity that it had prior knowledge of the existence and location of many of the subpoenaed documents necessary to render their existence and location a "foregone conclusion." The Supreme Court has not defined the precise amount of cognition on the part of an immunized party necessary to render a subpoena response "testimonial," but it is clear here that, as in *Hubbell*, the government "needed [Ponds'] assistance both to identify potential sources of information and to produce those sources," *Hubbell*, 530 U.S. at 41, and "it is undeniable that providing a catalog of existing documents," *id.* at 42, rendered this subpoena response "testimony" rather than mere "surrender." So much is evident in the government's admission that it was "surprised" by some of the documents produced.

C.

Having determined that portions of Ponds' act of production were testimonial, the next question is whether the government violated its immunity agreement with Ponds by using that "testimony or other information compelled under the order (or any information directly or indirectly derived from such testimony or other information)." 18 U.S.C. § 6002. "When the government proceeds to prosecute a previously immunized witness, it has 'the heavy burden of proving that all of the evidence it proposes to use [or has used] was derived from legitimate independent sources.'" *North*, 910 F.2d at 854 (quoting *Kastigar*, 406 U.S. at 461–62). As the primary evidence used to secure Ponds' indictment was the records seized during the searches of his home and office (and other information turned up from leads in those records), the inquiry under § 6002 must focus on the period before those searches to determine whether the subpoenaed documents derived from Ponds' act of production were used to either focus the investigation before the searches or to craft the search warrant affidavit, or if wholly independent evidence supported those actions. *See* United States v. Kurzer, 534 F.2d 511, 515 (2d Cir.1976).

Ponds contends that the government violated his Fifth Amendment privilege by using the produced documents at two points: in establishing its evasion theory of the case and in crafting the search warrant application. Of course, § 6002 is "a comprehensive safeguard, barring the use of compelled testimony as an 'investigatory lead,' and also barring the use of any evidence obtained by focusing investigation on a witness as a result of his compelled disclosures." *Kastigar*, 406 U.S. at 460 (footnotes omitted). Section 6002's "sweeping proscription," *id.*, of any use of compelled testimony without doubt bars the use of immunized information in an affidavit in support of a search warrant that turns up evidence used against the witness in a subsequent prosecution. *See* United States v. Nanni, 59 F.3d 1425, 1443 (2d Cir.1995).

The district court noted the "government conce[ssion] that, to a limited extent, the IRS made use of some documents the defendant had produced to the grand jury to support the search warrant affidavits." *Ponds,* 290 F.Supp.2d at 75. Furthermore, the district court found that "the record is clear (and the government acknowledges) that Maggie Alexander was identified and then made certain statements to the grand jury based on documents that the defendant [Ponds] produced" and that "[s]ome of those statements were included in the search warrant affidavit," *id.* at 87, but found this unproblematic because Ponds "cannot point to any testimonial aspect of [his] act of production—as opposed to the contents of the documents themselves—that was used by the government to obtain the search warrants," *id.* at 88. As discussed, this finding is legally erroneous because it fails to recognize that non-testimonial evidence derived from this testimonial act of production may not be used under § 6002.

Nevertheless, although the district court's findings regarding the use of immunized documents make clear that some impermissible derivative use occurred, the degree of the *Kastigar* violation is less apparent. The government is free to use a piece of information that appears in an immunized document if it can accomplish its "affirmative duty" of proving that the information was "derived from a legitimate source wholly independent of the compelled testimony." *Kastigar,* 406 U.S. at 460. As this court has emphasized that such an "inquiry must proceed witness-by-witness; if necessary, it will proceed line-by-line and item-by-item," *North,* 910 F.2d at 872, the district court is better positioned to make such a determination in the first instance.

Determining the precise manner in which Ponds' rights were violated is essential because the finding of a Kastigar violation does not resolve Ponds' challenge to his convictions. "Dismissal of the indictment or vacation of the conviction is not necessary where the use is found to be harmless beyond a reasonable doubt," *North,* 910 F.2d at 854 (citations omitted), because "the error complained of did not contribute to the [outcome] obtained," Chapman v. California, 386 U.S. 18, 24 (1967). Where, as here, the immunized evidence emerges early in the investigation, the court must determine whether the government "would have taken the same steps entirely apart from the motivating effect of the immunized testimony." *Nanni,* 59 F.3d at 1433. As to the use of Ponds' documents and Maggie Alexander's testimony in the search warrant affidavits, "[t]he question thus becomes whether that use was harmless beyond a reasonable doubt in the sense that the immunized testimony was so inconsequential that it could not have influenced either the government's decision to request search warrants or the issuing magistrate's decision to grant them." *Id.* at 1443. In this determination, "[t]he government cannot escape its error simply by showing the availability of 'wholly independent' evidence from which it might have procured indictment or conviction had it not used the immunized testimony," United States v. Pelletier, 898 F.2d 297, 303 (2d Cir.1990) (emphasis added), but must demonstrate beyond a reasonable doubt that the tax evasion case would have been vigorously pursued, and the search warrant sought and obtained, had the government not relied on the documents revealed by Ponds' act of production. Unless the government's use of *Kastigar* evidence, in light of evidence from independent sources, was " 'so unimportant and insignificant' and ha[s] so 'little, if any, likelihood of having changed the result of the proceeding' that [it] 'may be deemed harmless,' " United States v. Gallo, 859 F.2d 1078, 1082 (2d Cir.1988) (quoting *Chapman,* 386 U.S. at 22) (alterations omitted), the violation of Ponds' right not to be a witness against himself cannot be excused as harmless beyond a reasonable doubt.

The government has not shown that it had reasonably particular knowledge of the existence and location of some of the documents it subpoenaed from Ponds. It has conceded that, to some extent, it used those documents to prepare its prosecution of Ponds. Accordingly, we reverse the judgment of conviction and we remand the case to the district court to consider the degree of the government's impermissible use and to determine whether that use was harmless beyond a reasonable doubt.

4. *MIRANDA* DOCTRINE: BASIC PRINCIPLES

Miranda v. Arizona

384 U.S. 436 (1966)

■ MR. CHIEF JUSTICE WARREN delivered the opinion of the Court.

The cases before us raise questions which go to the roots of our concepts of American criminal jurisprudence: the restraints society must observe consistent with the Federal Constitution in prosecuting individuals for crime. More specifically, we deal with the admissibility of statements obtained from an individual who is subjected to custodial police interrogation and the necessity for procedures which assure that the individual is accorded his privilege under the Fifth Amendment to the Constitution not to be compelled to incriminate himself.

We dealt with certain phases of this problem recently in Escobedo v. State of Illinois, 378 U.S. 478 (1964). . . . This case has been the subject of judicial interpretation and spirited legal debate since it was decided two years ago. Both state and federal courts, in assessing its implications, have arrived at varying conclusions. A wealth of scholarly material has been written tracing its ramifications and underpinnings. Police and prosecutor have speculated on its range and desirability. We granted certiorari in these cases, 382 U.S. 924, 925, 937, in order further to explore some facets of the problems, thus exposed, of applying the privilege against self-incrimination to in-custody interrogation, and to give concrete constitutional guidelines for law enforcement agencies and courts to follow.

We start here, as we did in *Escobedo*, with the premise that our holding is not an innovation in our jurisprudence, but is an application of principles long recognized and applied in other settings. We have undertaken a thorough re-examination of the *Escobedo* decision and the principles it announced, and we reaffirm it. That case was but an explication of basic rights that are enshrined in our Constitution—that 'No person * * * shall be compelled in any criminal case to be a witness against himself,' and that 'the accused shall * * * have the Assistance of Counsel'—rights which were put in jeopardy in that case through official overbearing. These precious rights were fixed in our Constitution only after centuries of persecution and struggle. And in the words of Chief Justice Marshall, they were secured 'for ages to come, and * * * designed to approach immortality as nearly as human institutions can approach it,' Cohens v. Commonwealth of Virginia, 6 Wheat. 264, 387 (1821).

Our holding will be spelled out with some specificity in the pages which follow but briefly stated it is this: the prosecution may not use statements, whether exculpatory or inculpatory, stemming from custodial interrogation of the defendant unless it demonstrates the use of procedural safeguards effective to secure the privilege against self-incrimination. By custodial interrogation, we mean questioning initiated by law enforcement officers after a person has been taken into custody or otherwise deprived of his freedom of action in any significant way.[4] As for the procedural safeguards to be employed, unless other fully effective means are devised to inform accused persons of their right of silence and to assure a continuous opportunity to exercise it, the following measures are required. Prior to any questioning, the person must be warned that he has a right to remain silent, that any statement he does make may be used as evidence against him, and that he has a right to the presence of an attorney, either retained or appointed. The defendant may waive effectuation of these rights, provided the waiver is made voluntarily, knowingly and intelligently. If, however, he indicates in any manner and at any stage of the process that he wishes to consult with an attorney before speaking there can be no questioning. Likewise, if the individual is alone and indicates in any manner that he does not wish to be interrogated, the police may not question him. The mere fact that he may have answered some questions or volunteered some statements on his own does not deprive him of the right to refrain from answering any further inquiries until he has consulted with an attorney and thereafter consents to be questioned.

The constitutional issue we decide in each of these cases is the admissibility of statements obtained from a defendant questioned while in custody or otherwise deprived of his freedom of action in any significant way. In each, the defendant was questioned by police officers, detectives, or a prosecuting attorney in a room in which he was cut off from the outside world. In none of these cases was the defendant given a full and effective warning of his rights at the outset of the interrogation

---

[4]   This is what we meant in *Escobedo* when we spoke of an investigation which had focused on an accused.

process. In all the cases, the questioning elicited oral admissions, and in three of them, signed statements as well which were admitted at their trials. They all thus share salient features—incommunicado interrogation of individuals in a police-dominated atmosphere, resulting in self-incriminating statements without full warnings of constitutional rights.

An understanding of the nature and setting of this in-custody interrogation is essential to our decisions today. The difficulty in depicting what transpires at such interrogations stems from the fact that in this country they have largely taken place incommunicado. From extensive factual studies undertaken in the early 1930's, including the famous Wickersham Report to Congress by a Presidential Commission, it is clear that police violence and the 'third degree' flourished at that time. In a series of cases decided by this Court long after these studies, the police resorted to physical brutality—beatings, hanging, whipping— and to sustained and protracted questioning incommunicado in order to extort confessions.

The examples given above are undoubtedly the exception now, but they are sufficiently widespread to be the object of concern. Unless a proper limitation upon custodial interrogation is achieved—such as these decisions will advance—there can be no assurance that practices of this nature will be eradicated in the foreseeable future. The conclusion of the Wickersham Commission Report, made over 30 years ago, is still pertinent:

> 'To the contention that the third degree is necessary to get the facts, the reporters aptly reply in the language of the present Lord Chancellor of England (Lord Sankey): 'It is not admissible to do a great right by doing a little wrong. * * * It is not sufficient to do justice by obtaining a proper result by irregular or improper means.' Not only does the use of the third degree involve a flagrant violation of law by the officers of the law, but it involves also the dangers of false confessions, and it tends to make police and prosecutors less zealous in the search for objective evidence. As the New York prosecutor quoted in the report said, 'It is a short cut and makes the police lazy and unenterprising.' Or, as another official quoted remarked: 'If you use your fists, you are not so likely to use your wits.' We agree with the conclusion expressed in the report, that 'The third degree brutalizes the police, hardens the prisoner against society, and lowers the esteem in which the administration of justice is held by the public.' '

IV National Commission on Law Observance and Enforcement, Report on Lawlessness in Law Enforcement 5 (1931).

Again we stress that the modern practice of in-custody interrogation is psychologically rather than physically oriented. As we have stated before, 'Since Chambers v. State of Florida, 309 U.S. 227, this Court has recognized that coercion can be mental as well as physical, and that the blood of the accused is not the only hallmark of an unconstitutional inquisition.' Blackburn v. State of Alabama, 361 U.S. 199, 206 (1960). Interrogation still takes place in privacy. Privacy results in secrecy and this in turn results in a gap in our knowledge as to what in fact goes on in the interrogation rooms. A valuable source of information about present police practices, however, may be found in various police manuals and texts which document procedures employed with success in the past, and which recommend various other effective tactics.[8] These texts are used by law enforcement agencies themselves as guides.[9] It should be noted that these texts professedly present the most enlightened and effective means presently used to obtain statements through custodial interrogation. By considering these texts and other data, it is possible to describe procedures observed and noted around the country.

The officers are told by the manuals that the 'principal psychological factor contributing to a successful interrogation is privacy—being alone with the person under interrogation.' The efficacy of this tactic has been explained as follows:

> 'If at all practicable, the interrogation should take place in the investigator's office or at least in a room of his own choice. The subject should be deprived of every psychological advantage. In his own home he may be confident, indignant, or recalcitrant. He is more keenly aware of his rights and more reluctant to tell of his indiscretions of criminal behavior within the walls of his home. Moreover his family and other friends are nearby, their presence lending moral support. In his office, the investigator possesses all the advantages. The atmosphere suggests the invincibility of the forces of the law.'

To highlight the isolation and unfamiliar surroundings, the manuals instruct the police to display an air of confidence in the suspect's guilt and from outward appearance to maintain only an interest in confirming

---

[8]   The manuals quoted in the text following are the most recent and representative of the texts currently available. Material of the same nature appeals in Kidd, Police Interrogation (1940); Mulbar, Interrogation (1951); Dienstein, Technics for the Crime Investigator 97–115 (1952). Studies concerning the observed practices of the police appear in LaFave, Arrest: The Decision To Take a Suspect Into Custody 244–437, 490–521 (1965); LaFave, Detention for Investigation by the Police: An Analysis of Current Practices, 1962 Wash.U.L.Q. 331; Barrett, Police Practices and the Law-From Arrest to Release or Charge, 50 Calif.L.Rev. 11 (1962); Sterling, *supra*, n. 7, at 47–65.

[9]   The methods described in Inbau & Reid Criminal Interrogation and Confessions (1962), are a revision and enlargement of material presented in three prior editions of a predecessor text, Lie Detection and Criminal Interrogation (3d ed. 1953). The authors and their associates are officers of the Chicago Police Scientific Crime Detection Laboratory and have had extensive experience in writing, lecturing and speaking to law enforcement authorities over a 20-year period. They say that the techniques portrayed in their manuals reflect their experiences and are the most effective psychological stratagems to employ during interrogations. Similarly, the techniques described in O'Hara, Fundamentals of Criminal Investigation (1956), were gleaned from long service as observer, lecturer in police science, and work as a federal criminal investigator. All these texts have had rather extensive use among law enforcement agencies and among students of police science, with total sales and circulation of over 44,000.

certain details. The guilt of the subject is to be posited as a fact. The interrogator should direct his comments toward the reasons why the subject committed the act, rather than court failure by asking the subject whether he did it. Like other men, perhaps the subject has had a bad family life, had an unhappy childhood, had too much to drink, had an unrequited desire for women. The officers are instructed to minimize the moral seriousness of the offense, to cast blame on the victim or on society. These tactics are designed to put the subject in a psychological state where his story is but an elaboration of what the police purport to know already—that he is guilty. Explanations to the contrary are dismissed and discouraged.

The texts thus stress that the major qualities an interrogator should possess are patience and perseverance. One writer describes the efficacy of these characteristics in this manner:

'In the preceding paragraphs emphasis has been placed on kindness and stratagems. The investigator will, however, encounter many situations where the sheer weight of his personality will be the deciding factor. Where emotional appeals and tricks are employed to no avail, he must rely on an oppressive atmosphere of dogged persistence. He must interrogate steadily and without relent, leaving the subject no prospect of surcease. He must dominate his subject and overwhelm him with his inexorable will to obtain the truth. He should interrogate for a spell of several hours pausing only for the subject's necessities in acknowledgment of the need to avoid a charge of duress that can be technically substantiated. In a serious case, the interrogation may continue for days, with the required intervals for food and sleep, but with no respite from the atmosphere of domination. It is possible in this way to induce the subject to talk without resorting to duress or coercion. The method should be used only when the guilt of the subject appears highly probable.'

The manuals suggest that the suspect be offered legal excuses for his actions in order to obtain an initial admission of guilt. Where there is a suspected revenge-killing, for example, the interrogator may say:

'Joe, you probably didn't go out looking for this fellow with the purpose of shooting him. My guess is, however, that you expected something from him and that's why you carried a gun—for your own protection. You knew him for what he was, no good. Then when you met him he probably started using foul, abusive language and he gave some indication that he was about to pull a gun on you, and that's when you had to act to save your own life. That's about it, isn't it, Joe?'

Having then obtained the admission of shooting, the interrogator is advised to refer to circumstantial evidence which negates the self-defense explanation. This should enable him to secure the entire story. One text notes that 'Even if he fails to do so, the inconsistency between the subject's original denial of the shooting and his present admission of at least doing the shooting will serve to deprive him of a self-defense 'out' at the time of trial.'

When the techniques described above prove unavailing, the texts recommend they be alternated with a show of some hostility. One ploy often used has been termed the 'friendly-unfriendly' or the 'Mutt and Jeff' act:

> '* * * In this technique, two agents are employed. Mutt, the relentless investigator, who knows the subject is guilty and is not going to waste any time. He's sent a dozen men away for this crime and he's going to send the subject away for the full term. Jeff, on the other hand, is obviously a kindhearted man. He has a family himself. He has a brother who was involved in a little scrape like this. He disapproves of Mutt and his tactics and will arrange to get him off the case if the subject will cooperate. He can't hold Mutt off for very long. The subject would be wise to make a quick decision. The technique is applied by having both investigators present while Mutt acts out his role. Jeff may stand by quietly and demur at some of Mutt's tactics. When Jeff makes his plea for cooperation, Mutt is not present in the room.'

The interrogators sometimes are instructed to induce a confession out of trickery. The technique here is quite effective in crimes which require identification or which run in series. In the identification situation, the interrogator may take a break in his questioning to place the subject among a group of men in a line-up. 'The witness or complainant (previously coached, if necessary) studies the line-up and confidently points out the subject as the guilty party.' Then the questioning resumes 'as though there were now no doubt about the guilt of the subject.' A variation on this technique is called the 'reverse line-up':

> 'The accused is placed in a line-up, but this time he is identified by several fictitious witnesses or victims who associated him with diferent offenses. It is expected that the subject will become desperate and confess to the offense under investigation in order to escape from the false accusations.'

The manuals also contain instructions for police on how to handle the individual who refuses to discuss the matter entirely, or who asks for an attorney or relatives. The examiner is to concede him the right to remain silent. 'This usually has a very undermining effect. First of all, he is disappointed in his expectation of an unfavorable reaction on the part of the interrogator. Secondly, a concession of this right to remain silent impresses the subject with the apparent fairness of his interrogator.' After this psychological conditioning, however, the officer is told to point out the incriminating significance of the suspect's refusal to talk:

'Joe, you have a right to remain silent. That's your privilege and I'm the last person in the world who'll try to take it away from you. If that's the way you want to leave this, O.K. But let me ask you this. Suppose you were in my shoes and I were in yours and you called me in to ask me about this and I told you, 'I don't want to answer any of your questions.' You'd think I had something to hide, and you'd probably be right in thinking that. That's exactly what I'll have to think about you, and so will everybody else. So let's sit here and talk this whole thing over.'

Few will persist in their initial refusal to talk, it is said, if this monologue is employed correctly. In the event that the subject wishes to speak to a relative or an attorney, the following advice is tendered:

'(T)he interrogator should respond by suggesting that the subject first tell the truth to the interrogator himself rather than get anyone else involved in the matter. If the request is for an attorney, the interrogator may suggest that the subject save himself or his family the expense of any such professional service, particularly if he is innocent of the offense under investigation. The interrogator may also add, 'Joe, I'm only looking for the truth, and if you're telling the truth, that's it. You can handle this by yourself.' '

From these representative samples of interrogation techniques, the setting prescribed by the manuals and observed in practice becomes clear. In essence, it is this: To be alone with the subject is essential to prevent distraction and to deprive him of any outside support. The aura of confidence in his guilt undermines his will to resist. He merely confirms the preconceived story the police Seek to have him describe. Patience and persistence, at times relentless questioning, are employed. To obtain a confession, the interrogator must 'patiently maneuver himself or his quarry into a position from which the desired objective may be attained.' When normal procedures fail to produce the needed result, the police may resort to deceptive stratagems such as giving false legal advice. It is important to keep the subject off balance, for example, by trading on his insecurity about himself or his surroundings. The police then persuade, trick, or cajole him out of exercising his constitutional rights.

Even without employing brutality, the 'third degree' or the specific stratagems described above, the very fact of custodial interrogation exacts a heavy toll on individual liberty and trades on the weakness of individuals.[24] . . .

---

[24] Interrogation procedures may even give rise to a false confession. The most recent conspicuous example occurred in New York, in 1964, when a Negro of limited intelligence confessed to two brutal murders and a rape which he had not committed. When this was discovered, the prosecutor was reported as saying: 'Call it what you want-brain-washing, hypnosis, fright. They made him give an untrue confession. The only thing I don't believe is that Whitmore was beaten.' N.Y. Times, Jan. 28, 1965, p. 1, col. 5. In two other instances, similar

In the cases before us today, given this backgound, we concern ourselves primarily with this interrogation atmosphere and the evils it can bring. In No. 759, *Miranda v. Arizona*, the police arrested the defendant and took him to a special interrogation room where they secured a confession. In No. 760, *Vignera v. New York,* the defendant made oral admissions to the police after interrogation in the afternoon, and then signed an inculpatory statement upon being questioned by an assistant district attorney later the same evening. In No. 761, *Westover v. United States,* the defendant was handed over to the Federal Bureau of Investigation by local authorities after they had detained and interrogated him for a lengthy period, both at night and the following morning. After some two hours of questioning, the federal officers had obtained signed statements from the defendant. Lastly, in No. 584, *California v. Stewart*, the local police held the defendant five days in the station and interrogated him on nine separate occasions before they secured his inculpatory statement.

In these cases, we might not find the defendants' statements to have been involuntary in traditional terms. Our concern for adequate safeguards to protect precious Fifth Amendment rights is, of course, not lessened in the slightest. In each of the cases, the defendant was thrust into an unfamiliar atmosphere and run through menacing police interrogation procedures. The potentiality for compulsion is forcefully apparent, for example, in *Miranda*, where the indigent Mexican defendant was a seriously disturbed individual with pronounced sexual fantasies, and in *Stewart,* in which the defendant was an indigent Los Angeles Negro who had dropped out of school in the sixth grade. To be sure, the records do not evince overt physical coercion or patent psychological ploys. The fact remains that in none of these cases did the officers undertake to afford appropriate safeguards at the outset of the interrogation to insure that the statements were truly the product of free choice.

It is obvious that such an interrogation environment is created for no purpose other than to subjugate the individual to the will of his examiner. This atmosphere carries its own badge of intimidation. To be sure, this is not physical intimidation, but it is equally destructive of human dignity. The current practice of incommunicado interrogation is at odds with one of our Nation's most cherished principles—that the individual may not be compelled to incriminate himself. Unless adequate protective devices are employed to dispel the compulsion inherent in custodial surroundings, no statement obtained from the defendant can truly be the product of his free choice.

From the foregoing, we can readily perceive an intimate connection between the privilege against self-incrimination and police custodial

---

events had occurred. N.Y. Times, Oct. 20, 1964, p. 22, col. 1; N.Y. Times, Aug. 25, 1965, p. 1, col. 1. In general, see Borchard, Convicting the Innocent (1932); Frank & Frank, Not Guilty (1957).

questioning. It is fitting to turn to history and precedent underlying the Self-Incrimination Clause to determine its applicability in this situation.

II.

We sometimes forget how long it has taken to establish the privilege against self-incrimination, the sources from which it came and the fervor with which it was defended. Its roots go back into ancient times. Perhaps the critical historical event shedding light on its origins and evolution was the trial of one John Lilburn, a vocal anti-Stuart Leveller, who was made to take the Star Chamber Oath in 1637. The oath would have bound him to answer to all questions posed to him on any subject. He resisted the oath and declaimed the proceedings . . .

On account of the Lilburn Trial, Parliament abolished the inquisitorial Court of Star Chamber and went further in giving him generous reparation. The lofty principles to which Lilburn had appealed during his trial gained popular acceptance in England. These sentiments worked their way over to the Colonies and were implanted after great struggle into the Bill of Rights. Those who framed our Constitution and the Bill of Rights were ever aware of subtle encroachments on individual liberty. They knew that 'illegitimate and unconstitutional practices get their first footing * * * by silent approaches and slight deviations from legal modes of procedure.' Boyd v. United States, 116 U.S. 616, 635 (1886). The privilege was elevated to constitutional status and has always been 'as broad ad the mischief against which it seeks to guard.' Counselman v. Hitchcock, 142 U.S. 547, 562 (1892). We cannot depart from this noble heritage.

Thus we may view the historical development of the privilege as one which groped for the proper scope of governmental power over the citizen. As a 'noble principle often transcends its origins,' the privilege has come right-fully to be recognized in part as an individual's substantive right, a 'right to a private enclave where he may lead a private life. That right is the hallmark of our democracy.' United States v. Grunewald, 233 F.2d 556, 579, 581–582 (Frank, J., dissenting), rev'd, 353 U.S. 391 (1957). We have recently noted that the privilege against self-incrimination—the essential mainstay of our adversary system—is founded on a complex of values, Murphy v. Waterfront Comm. of New York Harbor, 378 U.S. 52, 55–57, n.5 (1964); Tehan v. United States ex rel. Shott, 382 U.S. 406, 414–415, n.12 (1966). All these policies point to one overriding thought: the constitutional foundation underlying the privilege is the respect a government—state or federal—must accord to the dignity and integrity of its citizens. To maintain a 'fair state-individual balance,' to require the government 'to shoulder the entire load,' 8 Wigmore, Evidence 317 (McNaughton rev. 1961), to respect the inviolability of the human personality, our accusatory system of criminal justice demands that the government seeking to punish an individual produce the evidence against him by its own independent labors, rather than by the cruel, simple expedient of compelling it from his own mouth. Chambers v. State of Florida, 309 U.S. 227, 235–238 (1940). In sum, the privilege is fulfilled only when the person is guaranteed the right 'to remain silent unless he chooses to speak in the unfettered exercise of his own will.' Malloy v. Hogan, 378 U.S. 1, 8 (1964).

The question in these cases is whether the privilege is fully applicable during a period of custodial interrogation. In this Court, the privilege has consistently been accorded a liberal construction. We are satisfied that all the principles embodied in the privilege apply to informal compulsion exerted by law-enforcement officers during in-custody questioning. An individual swept from familiar surroundings into police custody, surrounded by antagonistic forces, and subjected to the techniques of persuasion described above cannot be otherwise than under compulsion to speak. As a practical matter, the compulsion to speak in the isolated setting of the police station may well be greater than in courts or other official investigations, where there are often impartial observers to guard against intimidation or trickery.

This question, in fact, could have been taken as settled in federal courts almost 70 years ago, when, in Bram v. United States, 168 U.S. 532, 542 (1897), this Court held:

> 'In criminal trials, in the courts of the United States, wherever a question arises whether a confession is incompetent because not voluntary, the issue is controlled by that portion of the fifth amendment * * * commanding that no person 'shall be compelled in any criminal case to be a witness against himself.' '

In *Bram,* the Court reviewed the British and American history and case law and set down the Fifth Amendment standard for compulsion which we implement today:

> 'Much of the confusion which has resulted from the effort to deduce from the adjudged cases what would be a sufficient quantum of proof to show that a confession was or was not voluntary has arisen from a misconception of the subject to which the proof must address itself. The rule is not that, in order to render a statement admissible, the proof must be adequate to establish that the particular communications contained in a statement were voluntarily made, but it must be sufficient to establish that the making of the statement was voluntary; that is to say, that, from the causes which the law treats as legally sufficient to engender in the mind of the accused hope or fear in respect to the crime charged, the accused was not involuntarily impelled to make a statement when but for the improper influences he would have remained silent. * * *' 168 U.S., at 549. And see, id., at 542.

The Court has adhered to this reasoning. In 1924, Mr. Justice Brandeis wrote for a unanimous Court in reversing a conviction resting on a compelled confession, Ziang Sung Wan v. United States, 266 U.S. 1. He stated:

> 'In the federal courts, the requisite of voluntariness is not satisfied by establishing merely that the confession was not induced by a promise or a threat. A confession is voluntary in law if, and only if, it was, in fact, voluntarily made. A confession may have been given voluntarily, although it was made to police officers, while in custody, and in answer to an examination conducted by them. But a confession obtained by compulsion must be excluded whatever may have been the character of the compulsion, and whether the compulsion was applied in a judicial proceeding or otherwise. Bram v. United States, 168 U.S. 532.' 266 U.S., at 14–15.

Because of the adoption by Congress of Rule 5(a) of the Federal Rules of Criminal Procedure, and the Court's effectuation of that Rule in McNabb v. United States, 318 U.S. 332 (1943), and Mallory v. United States, 354 U.S. 449 (1957), we have had little occasion in the past quarter century to reach the constitutional issues in dealing with federal interrogations. These supervisory rules, requiring production of an arrested person before a commissioner 'without unnecessary delay' and excluding evidence obtained in default of that statutory obligation, were nonetheless responsive to the same considerations of Fifth Amendment policy that unavoidably face us now as to the States. In *McNabb,* 318 U.S., at 343–344, and in *Mallory,* 354 U.S., at 455–456, we recognized both the dangers of interrogation and the appropriateness of prophylaxis stemming from the very fact of interrogation itself.

Our decision in Malloy v. Hogan, 378 U.S. 1 (1964), necessitates an examination of the scope of the privilege in state cases as well. In *Malloy,* we squarely held the privilege applicable to the States, and held that the substantive standards underlying the privilege applied with full force to state court proceedings. There, as in Murphy v. Waterfront Comm. of New York Harbor, 378 U.S. 52 (1964), and Griffin v. State of California, 380 U.S. 609 (1965), we applied the existing Fifth Amendment standards to the case before us. Aside from the holding itself, the reasoning in *Malloy* made clear what had already become apparent—that the substantive and procedural safeguards surrounding admissibility of confessions in state cases had become exceedingly exacting, reflecting all the policies embedded in the privilege, 378 U.S., at 7–8.[33] The

---

[33] The decisions of this Court have guaranteed the same procedural protection for the defendant whether his confession was used in a federal or state court. It is now axiomatic that the defendant's constitutional rights have been violated if his conviction is based, in whole or in part, on an involuntary confession, regardless of its truth or falsity. Rogers v. Richmond, 365 U.S. 534, 544 (1961); Siang Sung Wan v. United States, 266 U.S. 1 (1924). This is so even if there is ample evidence aside from the confession to support the conviction, *e.g.,* Malinski v. People of State of New York, 324 U.S. 401, 404 (1945); Bram v. United States, 168 U.S. 532, 540–542 (1897). Both state and federal courts now adhere to trial procedures which seek to assure a reliable and clear-cut determination of the voluntariness of the confession offered at trial, Jackson v. Denno, 378 U.S. 368 (1964); United States v. Carignan, 342 U.S. 36, 38 (1951);

voluntariness doctrine in the state cases, as *Malloy* indicates, encompasses all interrogation practices which are likely to exert such pressure upon an individual as to disable him from making a free and rational choice. The implications of this proposition were elaborated in our decision in Escobedo v. State of Illinois, 378 U.S. 478, decided one week after *Malloy* applied the privilege to the States.

Our holding there stressed the fact that the police had not advised the defendant of his constitutional privilege to remain silent at the outset of the interrogation, and we drew attention to that fact at several points in the decision, 378 U.S., at 483, 485, 491. This was no isolated factor, but an essential ingredient in our decision. The entire thrust of police interrogation there, as in all the cases today, was to put the defendant in such an emotional state as to impair his capacity for rational judgment. The abdication of the constitutional privilege—the choice on his part to speak to the police—was not made knowingly or competently because of the failure to apprise him of his rights; the compelling atmosphere of the in-custody interrogation, and not an independent decision on his part, caused the defendant to speak.

A different phase of the *Escobedo* decision was significant in its attention to the absence of counsel during the questioning. There, as in the cases today, we sought a protective device to dispel the compelling atmosphere of the interrogation. In *Escobedo,* however, the police did not relieve the defendant of the anxieties which they had created in the interrogation rooms. Rather, they denied his request for the assistance of counsel, 378 U.S., at 481, 488, 491.[35] This heightened his dilemma, and made his later statements the product of this compulsion. *Cf.* Haynes v. State of Washington, 373 U.S. 503, 514 (1963). The denial of the defendant's request for his attorney thus undermined his ability to exercise the privilege—to remain silent if he chose or to speak without any intimidation, blatant or subtle. The presence of counsel, in all the cases before us today, would be the adequate protective device necessary to make the process of police interrogation conform to the dictates of the privilege. His presence would insure that statements made in the government-established atmosphere are not the product of compulsion.

It was in this manner that *Escobedo* explicated another facet of the pre-trial privilege, noted in many of the Court's prior decisions: the protection of rights at trial. That counsel is present when statements are taken from an individual during interrogation obviously enhances the integrity of the fact-finding processes in court. The presence of an attorney, and the warnings delivered to the individual, enable the

---

See also Wilson v. United States, 162 U.S. 613, 624 (1896). Appellate review is exacting, *see* Haynes v. State of Washington, 373 U.S. 503 (1963); Blackburn v. State of Alabama, 361 U.S. 199 (1960).

    [35] The police also prevented the attorney from consulting with his client. Independent of any other constitutional proscription, this action constitutes a violation of the Sixth Amendment right to the assistance of counsel and excludes any statement obtained in its wake. *See* People v. Donovan, 13 N.Y.2d 148, 243 N.Y.S.2d 841, 193 N.E.2d 628 (1963) (Fuld, J.).

defendant under otherwise compelling circumstances to tell his story without fear, effectively, and in a way that eliminates the evils in the interrogation process. Without the protections flowing from adequate warning and the rights of counsel, 'all the careful safeguards erected around the giving of testimony, whether by an accused or any other witness, would become empty formalities in a procedure where the most compelling possible evidence of guilt, a confession, would have already been obtained at the unsupervised pleasure of the police.' Mapp v. Ohio, 367 U.S. 643, 685 (1961) (Harlan, J., dissenting). *Cf.* Pointer v. State of Texas, 380 U.S. 400 (1965).

III

. . . Today, then, there can be no doubt that the Fifth Amendment privilege is available outside of criminal court proceedings and serves to protect persons in all settings in which their freedom of action is curtailed in any significant way from being compelled to incriminate themselves. We have concluded that without proper safeguards the process of in-custody interrogation of persons suspected or accused of crime contains inherently compelling pressures which work to undermine the individual's will to resist and to compel him to speak where he would not otherwise do so freely. In order to combat these pressures and to permit a full opportunity to exercise the privilege against self-incrimination, the accused must be adequately and effectively apprised of his rights and the exercise of those rights must be fully honored.

It is impossible for us to foresee the potential alternatives for protecting the privilege which might be devised by Congress or the States in the exercise of their creative rule-making capacities. Therefore we cannot say that the Constitution necessarily requires adherence to any particular solution for the inherent compulsions of the interrogation process as it is presently conducted. Our decision in no way creates a constitutional straitjacket which will handicap sound efforts at reform, nor is it intended to have this effect. We encourage Congress and the States to continue their laudable search for increasingly effective ways of protecting the rights of the individual while promoting efficient enforcement of our criminal laws. However, unless we are shown other procedures which are at least as effective in apprising accused persons of their right of silence and in assuring a continuous opportunity to exercise it, the following safeguards must be observed.

At the outset, if a person in custody is to be subjected to interrogation, he must first be informed in clear and unequivocal terms that he has the right to remain silent. For those unaware of the privilege, the warning is needed simply to make them aware of it—the threshold requirement for an intelligent decision as to its exercise. More important, such a warning is an absolute prerequisite in overcoming the inherent pressures of the interrogation atmosphere. It is not just the subnormal or woefully ignorant who succumb to an interrogator's imprecations, whether implied or expressly stated, that the interrogation will continue until a confession is obtained or that silence in the face of accusation is itself damning and will bode ill when presented to a jury. Further, the warning will show the individual that his interrogators are prepared to recognize his privilege should he choose to exercise it.

The Fifth Amendment privilege is so fundamental to our system of constitutional rule and the expedient of giving an adequate warning as to the availability of the privilege so simple, we will not pause to inquire in individual cases whether the defendant was aware of his rights without a warning being given.[38] Assessments of the knowledge the defendant possessed, based on information as to his age, education, intelligence, or prior contact with authorities, can never be more than speculation; a warning is a clearcut fact. More important, whatever the background of the person interrogated, a warning at the time of the interrogation is indispensable to overcome its pressures and to insure that the individual knows he is free to exercise the privilege at that point in time.

The warning of the right to remain silent must be accompanied by the explanation that anything said can and will be used against the individual in court. This warning is needed in order to make him aware not only of the privilege, but also of the consequences of forgoing it. It is only through an awareness of these consequences that there can be any assurance of real understanding and intelligent exercise of the privilege. Moreover, this warning may serve to make the individual more acutely aware that he is faced with a phase of the adversary system—that he is not in the presence of persons acting solely in his interest.

The circumstances surrounding in-custody interrogation can operate very quickly to overbear the will of one merely made aware of his privilege by his interrogators. Therefore, the right to have counsel present at the interrogation is indispensable to the protection of the Fifth Amendment privilege under the system we delineate today. Our aim is to assure that the individual's right to choose between silence and speech remains unfettered throughout the interrogation process. A once-stated warning, delivered by those who will conduct the interrogation, cannot itself suffice to that end among those who most require knowledge of their rights. A mere warning given by the interrogators is not alone sufficient to accomplish that end. Prosecutors themselves claim that the admonishment of the right to remain silent without more 'will benefit only the recidivist and the professional.' Even preliminary advice given to the accused by his own attorney can be swiftly overcome by the secret interrogation process. *Cf. Escobedo v. State of Illinois,* 378 U.S. 478, 485, n.5. Thus, the need for counsel to protect the Fifth Amendment privilege comprehends not merely a right to consult with counsel prior to

---

[38] *Cf.* Betts v. Brady, 316 U.S. 455 (1942), and the recurrent inquiry into special circumstances it necessitated. *See generally,* Kamisar, Betts v. Brady *Twenty Years Later: The Right to Counsel and Due Process Values,* 61 Mich.L.Rev. 219 (1962).

questioning, but also to have counsel present during any questioning if the defendant so desires.

The presence of counsel at the interrogation may serve several significant subsidiary functions as well. If the accused decides to talk to his interrogators, the assistance of counsel can mitigate the dangers of untrustworthiness. With a lawyer present the likelihood that the police will practice coercion is reduced, and if coercion is nevertheless exercised the lawyer can testify to it in court. The presence of a lawyer can also help to guarantee that the accused gives a fully accurate statement to the police and that the statement is rightly reported by the prosecution at trial.

An individual need not make a pre-interrogation request for a lawyer. While such request affirmatively secures his right to have one, his failure to ask for a lawyer does not constitute a waiver. No effective waiver of the right to counsel during interrogation can be recognized unless specifically made after the warnings we here delineate have been given. The accused who does not know his rights and therefore does not make a request may be the person who most needs counsel. . . .

In Carnley v. Cochran, 369 U.S. 506, 513 (1962), we stated: '(I)t is settled that where the assistance of counsel is a constitutional requisite, the right to be furnished counsel does not depend on a request.' This proposition applies with equal force in the context of providing counsel to protect an accused's Fifth Amendment privilege in the face of interrogation. Although the role of counsel at trial differs from the role during interrogation, the differences are not relevant to the question whether a request is a prerequisite.

Accordingly we hold that an individual held for interrogation must be clearly informed that he has the right to consult with a lawyer and to have the lawyer with him during interrogation under the system for protecting the privilege we delineate today. As with the warnings of the right to remain silent and that anything stated can be used in evidence against him, this warning is an absolute prerequisite to interrogation. No amount of circumstantial evidence that the person may have been aware of this right will suffice to stand in its stead. Only through such a warning is there ascertainable assurance that the accused was aware of this right.

If an individual indicates that he wishes the assistance of counsel before any interrogation occurs, the authorities cannot rationally ignore or deny his request on the basis that the individual does not have or cannot afford a retained attorney. The financial ability of the individual has no relationship to the scope of the rights involved here. The privilege against self-incrimination secured by the Constitution applies to all individuals. The need for counsel in order to protect the privilege exists for the indigent as well as the affluent. In fact, were we to limit these constitutional rights to those who can retain an attorney, our decisions today would be of little significance. The cases before us as well as the vast majority of confession cases with which we have dealt in the past involve those unable to retain counsel. While authorities are not required to relieve the accused of his poverty, they have the obligation not to take advantage of indigence in the administration of justice. Denial of counsel to the indigent at the time of interrogation while allowing an attorney to those who can afford one would be no more supportable by reason or logic than the similar situation at trial and on appeal struck down in Gideon v. Wainwright, 372 U.S. 335 (1963), and Douglas v. People of State of California, 372 U.S. 353 (1963).

In order fully to apprise a person interrogated of the extent of his rights under this system then, it is necessary to warn him not only that he has the right to consult with an attorney, but also that if he is indigent a lawyer will be appointed to represent him. Without this additional warning, the admonition of the right to consult with counsel would often be understood as meaning only that he can consult with a lawyer if he has one or has the funds to obtain one. The warning of a right to counsel would be hollow if not couched in terms that would convey to the indigent—the person most often subjected to interrogation—the knowledge that he too has a right to have counsel present. As with the warnings of the right to remain silent and of the general right to counsel, only by effective and express explanation to the indigent of this right can there be assurance that he was truly in a position to exercise it.[43]

Once warnings have been given, the subsequent procedure is clear. If the individual indicates in any manner, at any time prior to or during questioning, that he wishes to remain silent, the interrogation must cease.[44] At this point he has shown that he intends to exercise his Fifth Amendment privilege; any statement taken after the person invokes his privilege cannot be other than the product of compulsion, subtle or otherwise. Without the right to cut off questioning, the setting of in-custody interrogation operates on the individual to overcome free choice in producing a statement after the privilege has been once invoked. If the individual states that he wants an attorney, the interrogation must cease until an attorney is present. At that time, the individual must have an opportunity to confer with the attorney and to have him present during any subsequent questioning. If the individual cannot obtain an attorney and he indicates that he wants one before speaking to police, they must respect his decision to remain silent.

This does not mean, as some have suggested, that each police station must have a 'station house lawyer' present at all times to advise

---

[43] While a warning that the indigent may have counsel appointed need not be given to the person who is known to have an attorney or is known to have ample funds to secure one, the expedient of giving a warning is too simple and the rights involved too important to engage in ex post facto inquiries into financial ability when there is any doubt at all on that score.

[44] If an individual indicates his desire to remain silent, but has an attorney present, there may be some circumstances in which further questioning would be permissible. In the absence of evidence of overbearing, statements them made in the presence of counsel might be free of the compelling influence of the interrogation process and might fairly be construed as a waiver of the privilege for purposes of these statements.

prisoners. It does mean, however, that if police propose to interrogate a person they must make known to him that he is entitled to a lawyer and that if he cannot afford one, a lawyer will be provided for him prior to any interrogation. If authorities conclude that they will not provide counsel during a reasonable period of time in which investigation in the field is carried out, they may refrain from doing so without violating the person's Fifth Amendment privilege so long as they do not question him during that time.

If the interrogation continues without the presence of an attorney and a statement is taken, a heavy burden rests on the government to demonstrate that the defendant knowingly and intelligently waived his privilege against self-incrimination and his right to retained or appointed counsel. *Escobedo v. State of Illinois,* 378 U.S. 478, 490, n.14. This Court has always set high standards of proof for the waiver of constitutional rights, Johnson v. Zerbst, 304 U.S. 458 (1938), and we reassert these standards as applied to in custody interrogation. Since the State is responsible for establishing the isolated circumstances under which the interrogation takes place and has the only means of making available corroborated evidence of warnings given during incommunicado interrogation, the burden is rightly on its shoulders.

An express statement that the individual is willing to make a statement and does not want an attorney followed closely by a statement could constitute a waiver. But a valid waiver will not be presumed simply from the silence of the accused after warnings are given or simply from the fact that a confession was in fact eventually obtained. A statement we made in Carnley v. Cochran, 369 U.S. 506, 516 (1962), is applicable here:

> 'Presuming waiver from a silent record is impermissible. The record must show, or there must be an allegation and evidence which show, that an accused was offered counsel but intelligently and understandingly rejected the offer. Anything less is not waiver.'

Whatever the testimony of the authorities as to waiver of rights by an accused, the fact of lengthy interrogation or incommunicado incarceration before a statement is made is strong evidence that the accused did not validly waive his rights. In these circumstances the fact that the individual eventually made a statement is consistent with the conclusion that the compelling influence of the interrogation finally forced him to do so. It is inconsistent with any notion of a voluntary relinquishment of the privilege. Moreover, any evidence that the accused was threatened, tricked, or cajoled into a waiver will, of course, show that the defendant did not voluntarily waive his privilege. The requirement of warnings and waiver of rights is a fundamental with respect to the Fifth Amendment privilege and not simply a preliminary ritual to existing methods of interrogation.

The warnings required and the waiver necessary in accordance with our opinion today are, in the absence of a fully effective equivalent, prerequisites to the admissibility of any statement made by a defendant. No distinction can be drawn between statements which are direct confessions and statements which amount to 'admissions' of part or all of an offense. The privilege against self-incrimination protects the individual from being compelled to incriminate himself in any manner; it does not distinguish degrees of incrimination. Similarly, for precisely the same reason, no distinction may be drawn between inculpatory statements and statements alleged to be merely 'exculpatory.' If a statement made were in fact truly exculpatory it would, of course, never be used by the prosecution. In fact, statements merely intended to be exculpatory by the defendant are often used to impeach his testimony at trial or to demonstrate untruths in the statement given under interrogation and thus to prove guilt by implication. These statements are incriminating in any meaningful sense of the word and may not be used without the full warnings and effective waiver required for any other statement. In *Escobedo* itself, the defendant fully intended his accusation of another as the slayer to be exculpatory as to himself.

The principles announced today deal with the protection which must be given to the privilege against self-incrimination when the individual is first subjected to police interrogation while in custody at the station or otherwise deprived of his freedom of action in any significant way. It is at this point that our adversary system of criminal proceedings commences, distinguishing itself at the outset from the inquisitorial system recognized in some countries. Under the system of warnings we delineate today or under any other system which may be devised and found effective, the safeguards to be erected about the privilege must come into play at this point.

Our decision is not intended to hamper the traditional function of police officers in investigating crime. *See Escobedo v. State of Illinois*, 378 U.S. 478, 492. When an individual is in custody on probable cause, the police may, of course, seek out evidence in the field to be used at trial against him. Such investigation may include inquiry of persons not under restraint. General on-the-scene questioning as to facts surrounding a crime or other general questioning of citizens in the fact-finding process is not affected by our holding. It is an act of responsible citizenship for individuals to give whatever information they may have to aid in law enforcement. In such situations the compelling atmosphere inherent in the process of in-custody interrogation is not necessarily present.

In dealing with statements obtained through interrogation, we do not purport to find all confessions inadmissible. Confessions remain a proper element in law enforcement. Any statement given freely and voluntarily without any compelling influences is, of course, admissible in evidence. The fundamental import of the privilege while an individual is in custody is not whether he is allowed to talk to the police without the benefit of warnings and counsel, but whether he can be interrogated. There is no requirement that police stop a person who enters a police station and states that he wishes to confess to a crime, or a person who calls the police to offer a confession or any other statement he desires to make. Volunteered statements of any kind are not barred by the Fifth Amendment and their admissibility is not affected by our holding today.

To summarize, we hold that when an individual is taken into custody or otherwise deprived of his freedom by the authorities in any significant way and is subjected to questioning, the privilege against self-incrimination is jeopardized. Procedural safeguards must be employed to protect the privilege and unless other fully effective means are adopted to notify the person of his right of silence and to assure that the exercise of the right will be scrupulously honored, the following measures are required. He must be warned prior to any questioning that he has the right to remain silent, that anything he says can be used against him in a court of law, that he has the right to the presence of an attorney, and that if he cannot afford an attorney one will be appointed for him prior to any questioning if he so desires. Opportunity to exercise these rights must be afforded to him throughout the interrogation. After such warnings have been given, and such opportunity afforded him, the individual may knowingly and intelligently waive these rights and agree to answer questions or make a statement. But unless and until such warnings and waiver are demonstrated by the prosecution at trial, no evidence obtained as a result of interrogation can be used against him.[48]

IV.

A recurrent argument made in these cases is that society's need for interrogation outweighs the privilege. This argument is not unfamiliar to this Court. . . . The whole thrust of our foregoing discussion demonstrates that the Constitution has prescribed the rights of the individual when confronted with the power of government when it provided in the Fifth Amendment that an individual cannot be compelled to be a witness against himself. That right cannot be abridged. [The Court quotes from the dissent of Justice Brandeis in *Olmstead*.] . . . If the individual desires to exercise his privilege, he has the right to do so. This is not for the authorities to decide. An attorney may advise his client not to talk to police until he has had an opportunity to investigate the case, or he may wish to be present with his client during any police questioning. In doing so an attorney is merely exercising the good professional judgment he has been taught. This is not cause for considering the attorney a menace to law enforcement. He is merely carrying out what he is sworn to do under his oath—to protect to the extent of his ability the rights of his client. In fulfilling this responsibility

---

[48] In accordance with our holdings today and in *Escobedo v. State of Illinois*, 378 U.S. 478, 492; Crooker v. State of California, 357 U.S. 433 (1958) and Cicenia v. La Gay, 357 U.S. 504 (1958) are not to be followed

the attorney plays a vital role in the administration of criminal justice under our Constitution.

In announcing these principles, we are not unmindful of the burdens which law enforcement officials must bear, often under trying circumstances. We also fully recognize the obligation of all citizens to aid in enforcing the criminal laws. This Court, while protecting individual rights, has always given ample latitude to law enforcement agencies in the legitimate exercise of their duties. The limits we have placed on the interrogation process should not constitute an undue interference with a proper system of law enforcement. As we have noted, our decision does not in any way preclude police from carrying out their traditional investigatory functions. Although confessions may play an important role in some convictions, the cases before us present graphic examples of the overstatement of the 'need' for confessions. In each case authorities conducted interrogations ranging up to five days in duration despite the presence, through standard investigating practices, of considerable evidence against each defendant.[51] Further examples are chronicled in our prior cases.

It is also urged that an unfettered right to detention for interrogation should be allowed because it will often redound to the benefit of the person questioned. When police inquiry determines that there is no reason to believe that the person has committed any crime, it is said, he will be released without need for further formal procedures. The person who has committed no offense, however, will be better able to clear himself after warnings with counsel present than without. It can be assumed that in such circumstances a lawyer would advise his client to talk freely to police in order to clear himself.

Custodial interrogation, by contrast, does not necessarily afford the innocent an opportunity to clear themselves. A serious consequence of the present practice of the interrogation alleged to be beneficial for the innocent is that many arrests 'for investigation' subject large numbers of innocent persons to detention and interrogation. In one of the cases before us, No. 584, California v. Stewart, police held four persons, who were in the defendant's house at the time of the arrest, in jail for five days until defendant confessed. At that time they were finally released. Police stated that there was 'no evidence to connect them with any crime.' Available statistics on the extent of this practice where it is condoned indicate that these four are far from alone in being subjected to arrest, prolonged detention, and interrogation without the requisite probable cause.[53]

---

[51] Miranda, Vignera, and Westover were identified by eyewitnesses. Marked bills from the bank robbed were found in Westover's car. Articles stolen from the victim as well as from several other robbery victims were found in Stewart's home at the outset of the investigation.

[53] See, e.g., Report and Recommendations of the (District of Columbia) Commissioners' Committee on Police Arrests for Investigation (1962); American Civil Liberties Union, Secret Detention by the Chicago Police (1959). An extreme example of this practice occurred in the District of Columbia in 1958. Seeking three 'stocky' young Negroes who had robbed a restaurant,

Over the years the Federal Bureau of Investigation has compiled an exemplary record of effective law enforcement while advising any suspect or arrested person, at the outset of an interview, that he is not required to make a statement, that any statement may be used against him in court, that the individual may obtain the services of an attorney of his own choice and, more recently, that he has a right to free counsel if he is unable to pay.[54] A letter received from the Solicitor General in response to a question from the Bench makes it clear that the present pattern of warnings and respect for the rights of the individual followed as a practice by the FBI is consistent with the procedure which we delineate today. . . .

The practice of the FBI can readily be emulated by state and local enforcement agencies. The argument that the FBI deals with different crimes than are dealt with by state authorities does not mitigate the significance of the FBI experience.

The experience in some other countries also suggests that the danger to law enforcement in curbs on interrogation is overplayed. . . .

It is also urged upon us that we withhold decision on this issue until state legislative bodies and advisory groups have had an opportunity to deal with these problems by rule making. We have already pointed out that the Constitution does not require any specific code of procedures for protecting the privilege against self-incrimination during custodial interrogation. Congress and the States are free to develop their own safeguards for the privilege, so long as they are fully as effective as those described above in informing accused persons of their right of silence and in affording a continuous opportunity to exercise it. In any event, however, the issues presented are of constitutional dimensions and must be determined by the courts. The admissibility of a statement in the face of a claim that it was obtained in violation of the defendant's constitutional rights is an issue the resolution of which has long since been undertaken by this Court. Judicial solutions to problems of constitutional dimension have evolved decade by decade. As courts have

---

police rounded up 90 persons of that general description. Sixty-three were held overnight before being released for lack of evidence. A man not among the 90 arrested was ultimately charged with the crime. Washington Daily News, January 21, 1958, p. 5, col. 1; Hearings before a Subcommittee of the Senate Judiciary Committee on H.R. 11477, S. 2970, S. 3325, and S. 3355, 85th Cong., 2d Sess. (July 1958), pp. 40, 78.

[54] In 1952, J. Edgar Hoover, Director of the Federal Bureau of Investigation, stated: 'Law enforcement, however, in defeating the criminal, must maintain inviolate the historic liberties of the individual. To turn back the criminal, yet, by so doing, destroy the dignity of the individual, would be a hollow victory. 'We can have the Constitution, the best laws in the land, and the most honest reviews by courts—but unless the law enforcement profession is steeped in the democratic tradition, maintains the highest in ethics, and makes its work a career of honor, civil liberties will continually—and without end be violated. * * * The best protection of civil liberties is an alert, intelligent and honest law enforcement agency. There can be no alternative.,* * * Special Agents are taught that any suspect or arrested person, at the outset of an interview, must be advised that he is not required to make a statement and that any statement given can be used against him in court. Moreover, the individual must be informed that, if he desires, he may obtain the services of an attorney of his own choice.' Hoover, Civil Liberties and Law Enforcement: The Role of the FBI, 37 Iowa L.Rev. 175, 177–182 (1952).

been presented with the need to enforce constitutional rights, they have found means of doing so. That was our responsibility when *Escobedo* was before us and it is our responsibility today. Where rights secured by the Constitution are involved, there can be no rule making or legislation which would abrogate them.

V.

Because of the nature of the problem and because of its recurrent significance in numerous cases, we have to this point discussed the relationship of the Fifth Amendment privilege to police interrogation without specific concentration on the facts of the cases before us. We turn now to these facts to consider the application to these cases of the constitutional principles discussed above. In each instance, we have concluded that statements were obtained from the defendant under circumstances that did not meet constitutional standards for protection of the privilege.

No. 759. *Miranda v. Arizona.*

On March 13, 1963, petitioner, Ernesto Miranda, was arrested at his home and taken in custody to a Phoenix police station. He was there identified by the complaining witness. The police then took him to 'Interrogation Room No. 2' of the detective bureau. There he was questioned by two police officers. The officers admitted at trial that Miranda was not advised that he had a right to have an attorney present.[66] Two hours later, the officers emerged from the interrogation room with a written confession signed by Miranda. At the top of the statement was a typed paragraph stating that the confession was made voluntarily, without threats or promises of immunity and 'with full knowledge of my legal rights, understanding any statement I make may be used against me.'[67]

At his trial before a jury, the written confession was admitted into evidence over the objection of defense counsel, and the officers testified to the prior oral confession made by Miranda during the interrogation. Miranda was found guilty of kidnapping and rape. He was sentenced to 20 to 30 years' imprisonment on each count, the sentences to run concurrently. On appeal, the Supreme Court of Arizona held that Miranda's constitutional rights were not violated in obtaining the confession and affirmed the conviction. 98 Ariz. 18, 401 P.2d 721. In reaching its decision, the court emphasized heavily the fact that Miranda did not specifically request counsel.

---

[66] Miranda was also convicted in a separate trial on an unrelated robbery charge not presented here for review. A statement introduced at that trial was obtained from Miranda during the same interrogation which resulted in the confession involved here. At the robbery trial, one officer testified that during the interrogation he did not tell Miranda that anything he said would be held against him or that he could consult with an attorney. The other officer stated that they had both told Miranda that anything he said would be used against him and that he was not required by law to tell them anything.

[67] One of the officers testified that he read this paragraph to Miranda. Apparently, however, he did not do so until after Miranda had confessed orally.

We reverse. From the testimony of the officers and by the admission of respondent, it is clear that Miranda was not in any way apprised of his right to consult with an attorney and to have one present during the interrogation, nor was his right not to be compelled to incriminate himself effectively protected in any other manner. Without these warnings the statements were inadmissible. The mere fact that he signed a statement which contained a typed-in clause stating that he had 'full knowledge' of his 'legal rights' does not approach the knowing and intelligent waiver required to relinquish constitutional rights.

No. 760. *Vignera v. New York.*

Petitioner, Michael Vignera, was picked up by New York police on October 14, 1960, in connection with the robbery three days earlier of a Brooklyn dress shop. They took him to the 17th Detective Squad headquarters in Manhattan. Sometime thereafter he was taken to the 66th Detective Squad. There a detective questioned Vignera with respect to the robbery. Vignera orally admitted the robbery to the detective. The detective was asked on cross-examination at trial by defense counsel whether Vignera was warned of his right to counsel before being interrogated. The prosecution objected to the question and the trial judge sustained the objection. Thus, the defense was precluded from making any showing that warnings had not been given. While at the 66th Detective Squad, Vignera was identified by the store owner and a saleslady as the man who robbed the dress shop. At about 3 p.m. he was formally arrested. The police then transported him to still another station, the 70th Precinct in Brooklyn, 'for detention.' At 11 p.m. Vignera was questioned by an assistant district attorney in the presence of a hearing reporter who transcribed the questions and Vignera's answers. This verbatim account of these proceedings contains no statement of any warnings given by the assistant district attorney. At Vignera's trial on a charge of first degree robbery, the detective testified as to the oral confession. The transcription of the statement taken was also introduced in evidence. At the conclusion of the testimony, the trial judge charged the jury in part as follows:

> 'The law doesn't say that the confession is void or invalidated because the police officer didn't advise the defendant as to his rights. Did you hear what I said? I am telling you what the law of the State of New York is.'

Vignera was found guilty of first degree robbery. He was subsequently adjudged a third-felony offender and sentenced to 30 to 60 years' imprisonment. The conviction was affirmed without opinion by the Appellate Division, Second Department, 21 A.D.2d 752, 252 N.Y.S.2d 19, and by the Court of Appeals, also without opinion, 15 N.Y.2d 970, 259 N.Y.S.2d 857, 207 N.E.2d 527, remittitur amended, 16 N.Y.2d 614, 261 N.Y.S.2d 65, 209 N.E.2d 110. In argument to the Court of Appeals, the State contended that Vignera had no constitutional right to be advised of his right to counsel or his privilege against self-incrimination.

We reverse. The foregoing indicates that Vignera was not warned of any of his rights before the questioning by the detective and by the assistant district attorney. No other steps were taken to protect these rights. Thus he was not effectively apprised of his Fifth Amendment privilege or of his right to have counsel present and his statements are inadmissible.

No. 761. *Westover v. United States.*

At approximately 9:45 p.m. on March 20, 1963, petitioner, Carl Calvin Westover, was arrested by local police in Kansas City as a suspect in two Kansas City robberies. A report was also received from the FBI that he was wanted on a felony charge in California. The local authorities took him to a police station and placed him in a line-up on the local charges, and at about 11:45 p.m. he was booked. Kansas City police interrogated Westoveron the night of his arrest. He denied any knowledge of criminal activities. The next day local officers interrogated him again throughout the morning. Shortly before noon they informed the FBI that they were through interrogating Westover and that the FBI could proceed to interrogate him. There is nothing in the record to indicate that Westover was ever given any warning as to his rights by local police. At noon, three special agents of the FBI continued the interrogation in a private interview room of the Kansas City Police Department, this time with respect to the robbery of a savings and loan association and a bank in Sacramento, California. After two or two and one-half hours, Westover signed separate confessions to each of these two robberies which had been prepared by one of the agents during the interrogation. At trial one of the agents testified, and a paragraph on each of the statements states, that the agents advised Westover that he did not have to make a statement, that any statement he made could be used against him, and that he had the right to see an attorney.

Westover was tried by a jury in federal court and convicted of the California robberies. His statements were introduced at trial. He was sentenced to 15 years' imprisonment on each count, the sentences to run consecutively. On appeal, the conviction was affirmed by the Court of Appeals for the Ninth Circuit. 342 F.2d 684.

We reverse. On the facts of this case we cannot find that Westover knowingly and intelligently waived his right to remain silent and his right to consult with counsel prior to the time he made the statement.[69] At the time the FBI agents began questioning Westover, he had been in custody for over 14 hours and had been interrogated at length during that period. The FBI interrogation began immediately upon the conclusion of the interrogation by Kansas City police and was conducted

---

[69] The failure of defense counsel to object to the introduction of the confession at trial, noted by the Court of Appeals and emphasized by the Solicitor General, does not preclude our consideration of the issue. Since the trial was held prior to our decision in *Escobedo* and, of course, prior to our decision today making the objection available, the failure to object at trial does not constitute a waiver of the claim.

in local police headquarters. Although the two law enforcement authorities are legally distinct and the crimes for which they interrogated Westover were different, the impact on him was that of a continuous period of questioning. There is no evidence of any warning given prior to the FBI interrogation nor is there any evidence of an articulated waiver of rights after the FBI commenced its interrogation. The record simply shows that the defendant did in fact confess a short time after being turned over to the FBI following interrogation by local police. Despite the fact that the FBI agents gave warnings at the outset of their interview, from Westover's point of view the warnings came at the end of the interrogation process. In these circumstances an intelligent waiver of constitutional rights cannot be assumed.

We do not suggest that law enforcement authorities are precluded from questioning any individual who has been held for a period of time by other authorities and interrogated by them without appropriate warnings. A different case would be presented if an accused were taken into custody by the second authority, removed both in time and place from his original surroundings, and then adequately advised of his rights and given an opportunity to exercise them. But here the FBI interrogation was conducted immediately following the state interrogation in the same police station—in the same compelling surroundings. Thus, in obtaining a confession from Westover the federal authorities were the beneficiaries of the pressure applied by the local in-custody interrogation. In these circumstances the giving of warnings alone was not sufficient to protect the privilege.

No. 584. *California v. Stewart.*

In the course of investigating a series of purse-snatch robberies in which one of the victims had died of injuries inflicted by her assailant, respondent, Roy Allen Stewart, was pointed out to Los Angeles police as the endorser of dividend checks taken in one of the robberies. At about 7:15 p.m., January 31, 1963, police officers went to Stewart's house and arrested him. One of the officers asked Stewart if they could search the house, to which he replied, 'Go ahead.' The search turned up various items taken from the five robbery victims. At the time of Stewart's arrest, police also arrested Stewart's wife and three other persons who were visiting him. These four were jailed along with Stewart and were interrogated. Stewart was taken to the University Station of the Los Angeles Police Department where he was placed in a cell. During the next five days, police interrogated Stewart on nine different occasions. Except during the first interrogation session, when he was confronted with an accusing witness, Stewart was isolated with his interrogators.

During the ninth interrogation session, Stewart admitted that he had robbed the deceased and stated that he had not meant to hurt her. Police then brought Stewart before a magistrate for the first time. Since there was no evidence to connect them with any crime, the police then released the other four persons arrested with him.

Nothing in the record specifically indicates whether Stewart was or was not advised of his right to remain silent or his right to counsel. In a number of instances, however, the interrogating officers were asked to recount everything that was said during the interrogations. None indicated that Stewart was ever advised of his rights.

Stewart was charged with kidnapping to commit robbery, rape, and murder. At his trial, transcripts of the first interrogation and the confession at the last interrogation were introduced in evidence. The jury found Stewart guilty of robbery and first degree murder and fixed the penalty as death. On appeal, the Supreme Court of California reversed. 62 Cal.2d 571, 43 Cal.Rptr. 201, 400 P.2d 97. It held that under this Court's decision in *Escobedo*, Stewart should have been advised of his right to remain silent and of his right to counsel and that it would not presume in the face of a silent record that the police advised Stewart of his rights.[70]

We affirm. In dealing with custodial interrogation, we will not presume that a defendant has been effectively apprised of his rights and that his privilege against self-incrimination has been adequately safeguarded on a record that does not show that any warnings have been given or that any effective alternative has been employed. Nor can a knowing and intelligent waiver of these rights be assumed on a silent record. Furthermore, Stewart's steadfast denial of the alleged offenses through eight of the nine interrogations over a period of five days is subject to no other construction than that he was compelled by persistent interrogation to forgo his Fifth Amendment privilege.

■ MR. JUSTICE WHITE, with whom MR. JUSTICE HARLAN and MR. JUSTICE STEWART join, dissenting.

I.

The proposition that the privilege against self-incrimination forbids in-custody interrogation without the warnings specified in the majority opinion and without a clear waiver of counsel has no significant support in the history of the privilege or in the language of the Fifth Amendment. As for the English authorities and the common-law history, the privilege, firmly established in the second half of the seventeenth century, was never applied except to prohibit compelled judicial interrogations. The rule excluding coerced confessions matured about 100 years later, '(b)ut there is nothing in the reports to suggest that the theory has its roots in the privilege against self-incrimination. And so far as the cases reveal, the privilege, as such, seems to have been given effect only in judicial proceedings, including the preliminary examinations by authorized

---

[70] Because of this disposition of the case, the California Supreme Court did not reach the claims that the confession was coerced by police threats to hold his ailing wife in custody until he confessed, that there was no hearing as required by Jackson v. Denno, 378 U.S. 368 (1964), and that the trial judge gave an instruction condemned by the California Supreme Court's decision in People v. Morse, 60 Cal.2d 631, 36 Cal.Rptr. 201, 388 P.2d 33 (1964).

magistrates.' Morgan, *The Privilege Against Self-Incrimination,* 34 Minn.L.Rev. 1, 18 (1949).

Our own constitutional provision provides that no person 'shall be compelled in any criminal case to be a witness against himself.' These words, when '(c)onsidered in the light to be shed by grammar and the dictionary * * * appear to signify simply that nobody shall be compelled to give oral testimony against himself in a criminal proceeding underway in which he is defendant.' Corwin, *The Supreme Court's Construction of the Self-Incrimination Clause,* 29 Mich.L.Rev. 1, 2. And there is very little in the surrounding circumstances of the adoption of the Fifth Amendment or in the provisions of the then existing state constitutions or in state practice which would give the constitutional provision any broader meaning. . . .

II.

That the Court's holding today is neither compelled nor even strongly suggested by the language of the Fifth Amendment, is at odds with American and English legal history, and involves a departure from a long line of precedent does not prove either that the Court has exceeded its powers or that the Court is wrong or unwise in its present reinterpretation of the Fifth Amendment. It does, however, underscore the obvious—that the Court has not discovered or found the law in making today's decision, nor has it derived it from some irrefutable sources; what it has done is to make new law and new public policy in much the same way that it has in the course of interpreting other great clauses of the Constitution.[1] This is what the Court historically has done. Indeed, it is what it must do and will continue to do until and unless there is some fundamental change in the constitutional distribution of governmental powers.

But if the Court is here and now to announce new and fundamental policy to govern certain aspects of our affairs, it is wholly legitimate to examine the mode of this or any other constitutional decision in this Court and to inquire into the advisability of its end product in terms of the long-range interest of the country. At the very least, the Court's text and reasoning should withstand analysis and be a fair exposition of the constitutional provision which its opinion interprets. Decisions like these cannot rest alone on syllogism, metaphysics or some ill-defined notions of natural justice, although each will perhaps play its part. In proceeding to such constructions as it now announces, the Court should also duly consider all the factors and interests bearing upon the cases, at least insofar as the relevant materials are available; and if the necessary considerations are not treated in the record or obtainable from some

---

[1] Of course the Court does not deny that it is departing from prior precedent; it expressly overrules *Crooker* and *Cicenia, ante,* at 1630, n. 48, and it acknowledges that in the instant 'cases we might not find the defendants' statements to have been involuntary in traditional terms,' *ante,* at 1618.

other reliable source, the Court should not proceed to formulate fundamental policies based on speculation alone.

III.

First, we may inquire what are the textual and factual bases of this new fundamental rule. To reach the result announced on the grounds it does, the Court must stay within the confines of the Fifth Amendment, which forbids self-incrimination only if compelled. Hence the core of the Court's opinion is that because of the 'compulsion inherent in custodial surroundings, no statement obtained from (a) defendant (in custody) can truly be the product of his free choice,' *ante,* at 1619, absent the use of adequate protective devices as described by the Court. However, the Court does not point to any sudden inrush of new knowledge requiring the rejection of 70 years' experience. Nor does it assert that its novel conclusion reflects a changing consensus among state courts, *See* Mapp v. Ohio, 367 U.S. 643, or that a succession of cases had steadily eroded the old rule and proved it unworkable, *see* Gideon v. Wainwright, 372 U.S. 335. Rather than asserting new knowledge, the Court concedes that it cannot truly know what occurs during custodial questioning, because of the innate secrecy of such proceedings. It extrapolates a picture of what it conceives to be the norm from police investigatorial manuals, published in 1959 and 1962 or earlier, without any attempt to allow for adjustments in police practices that may have occurred in the wake of more recent decisions of state appellate tribunals or this Court. But even if the relentless application of the described procedures could lead to involuntary confessions, it most assuredly does not follow that each and every case will disclose this kind of interrogation or this kind of consequence.[2] Insofar as appears from the Court's opinion, it has not examined a single transcript of any police interrogation, let alone the interrogation that took place in any one of these cases which it decides today. Judged by any of the standards for empirical investigation utilized in the social sciences the factual basis for the Court's premise is patently inadequate.

Although in the Court's view in-custody interrogation is inherently coercive, the Court says that the spontaneous product of the coercion of arrest and detention is still to be deemed voluntary. An accused, arrested on probable cause, may blurt out a confession which will be admissible despite the fact that he is alone and in custody, without any showing that he had any notion of his right to remain silent or of the consequences of his admission. Yet, under the Court's rule, if the police ask him a single

---

[2] In fact, the type of sustained interrogation described by the Court appears to be the exception rather than the rule. A survey of 399 cases in one city found that in almost half of the cases the interrogation lasted less than 30 minutes. Barrett, *Police Practices and the Law— From Arrest to Release or Charge,* 50 Calif.L.Rev. 11, 41–45 (1962). Questioning tends to be confused and sporadic and is usually concentrated on confrontations with witnesses or new items of evidence, as these are obtained by officers conducting the investigation. *See generally* LaFave, Arrest: The Decision to Take a Suspect into Custody 386 (1965); ALI, A Model Code of Pre-Arraignment Procedure, Commentary § 5.01, at 170, n.4 (Tent.Draft No. 1, 1966).

question such as 'Do you have anything to say?' or 'Did you kill your wife?' his response, if there is one, has somehow been compelled, even if the accused has been clearly warned of his right to remain silent. Common sense informs us to the contrary. While one may say that the response was 'involuntary' in the sense the question provoked or was the occasion for the response and thus the defendant was induced to speak out when he might have remained silent if not arrested and not questioned, it is patently unsound to say the response is compelled. . . .

On the other hand, even if one assumed that there was an adequate factual basis for the conclusion that all confessions obtained during in-custody interrogation are the product of compulsion, the rule propounded by the Court will still be irrational, for, apparently, it is only if the accused is also warned of his right to counsel and waives both that right and the right against self-incrimination that the inherent compulsiveness of interrogation disappears. But if the defendant may not answer without a warning a question such as 'Where were you last night?' without having his answer be a compelled one, how can the Court ever accept his negative answer to the question of whether he wants to consult his retained counsel or counsel whom the court will appoint? And why if counsel is present and the accused nevertheless confesses, or counsel tells the accused to tell the truth, and that is what the accused does, is the situation any less coercive insofar as the accused is concerned? The Court apparently realizes its dilemma of foreclosing questioning without the necessary warnings but at the same time permitting the accused, sitting in the same chair in front of the same policemen, to waive his right to consult an attorney. It expects, however, that the accused will not often waive the right; and if it is claimed that he has, the State faces a severe, if not impossible burden of proof.

All of this makes very little sense in terms of the compulsion which the Fifth Amendment proscribes. That amendment deals with compelling the accused himself. It is his free will that is involved. Confessions and incriminating admissions, as such, are not forbidden evidence; only those which are compelled are banned. I doubt that the Court observes these distinctions today. By considering any answers to any interrogation to be compelled regardless of the content and course of examination and by escalating the requirements to prove waiver, the Court not only prevents the use of compelled confessions but for all practical purposes forbids interrogation except in the presence of counsel. That is, instead of confining itself to protection of the right against compelled self-incrimination the Court has created a limited Fifth Amendment right to counsel—or, as the Court expresses it, a 'need for counsel to protect the Fifth Amendment privilege * * *.' *Ante,* at 1625. The focus then is not on the will of the accused but on the will of counsel and how much influence he can have on the accused. Obviously there is no warrant in the Fifth Amendment for thus installing counsel as the arbiter of the privilege.

In sum, for all the Court's expounding on the menacing atmosphere of police interrogation procedures, it has failed to supply any foundation for the conclusions it draws or the measures it adopts. . . .

In some unknown number of cases the Court's rule will return a killer, a rapist or other criminal to the streets and to the environment which produced him, to repeat his crime whenever it pleases him. As a consequence, there will not be a gain, but a loss, in human dignity.

[The separate dissenting opinions of Justices Harlan and Clark are omitted.]

Dickerson v. United States

530 U.S. 428 (2000)

■ CHIEF JUSTICE REHNQUIST delivered the opinion of the Court.

In Miranda v. Arizona, 384 U.S. 436 (1966), we held that certain warnings must be given before a suspect's statement made during custodial interrogation could be admitted in evidence. In the wake of that decision, Congress enacted 18 U.S.C. § 3501, which in essence laid down a rule that the admissibility of such statements should turn only on whether or not they were voluntarily made. We hold that *Miranda,* being a constitutional decision of this Court, may not be in effect overruled by an Act of Congress, and we decline to overrule *Miranda* ourselves. We therefore hold that *Miranda* and its progeny in this Court govern the admissibility of statements made during custodial interrogation in both state and federal courts.

Petitioner Dickerson was indicted for bank robbery, conspiracy to commit bank robbery, and using a firearm in the course of committing a crime of violence, all in violation of the applicable provisions of Title 18 of the United States Code. Before trial, Dickerson moved to suppress a statement he had made at a Federal Bureau of Investigation field office, on the grounds that he had not received "*Miranda* warnings" before being interrogated. The District Court granted his motion to suppress, and the Government took an interlocutory appeal to the United States Court of Appeals for the Fourth Circuit. That court, by a divided vote, reversed the District Court's suppression order. It agreed with the District Court's conclusion that petitioner had not received *Miranda* warnings before making his statement. But it went on to hold that § 3501, which in effect makes the admissibility of statements such as Dickerson's turn solely on whether they were made voluntarily, was satisfied in this case. It then concluded that our decision in *Miranda* was not a constitutional holding, and that, therefore, Congress could by statute have the final say on the question of admissibility. 166 F.3d 667 (1999).

Because of the importance of the questions raised by the Court of Appeals' decision, we granted certiorari, 528 U.S. 1045 (1999), and now reverse.

In *Miranda,* we noted that the advent of modern custodial police interrogation brought with it an increased concern about confessions obtained by coercion. 384 U.S., at 445–458. Because custodial police interrogation, by its very nature, isolates and pressures the individual, we stated that "[e]ven without employing brutality, the 'third degree' or [other] specific stratagems, . . . custodial interrogation exacts a heavy toll on individual liberty and trades on the weakness of individuals." *Id.,* at 455. We concluded that the coercion inherent in custodial interrogation blurs the line between voluntary and involuntary statements, and thus heightens the risk that an individual will not be "accorded his privilege under the Fifth Amendment . . . not to be compelled to incriminate himself." *Id.,* at 439. Accordingly, we laid down "concrete constitutional guidelines for law enforcement agencies and courts to follow." *Id.,* at 442. Those guidelines established that the admissibility in evidence of any statement given during custodial interrogation of a suspect would depend on whether the police provided the suspect with four warnings. These warnings (which have come to be known colloquially as "*Miranda* rights") are: a suspect "has the right to remain silent, that anything he says can be used against him in a court of law, that he has the right to the presence of an attorney, and that if he cannot afford an attorney one will be appointed for him prior to any questioning if he so desires." *Id.,* at 479.

Two years after *Miranda* was decided, Congress enacted § 3501. That section provides, in relevant part:

"(a) In any criminal prosecution brought by the United States or by the District of Columbia, a confession . . . shall be admissible in evidence if it is voluntarily given. Before such confession is received in evidence, the trial judge shall, out of the presence of the jury, determine any issue as to voluntariness. If the trial judge determines that the confession was voluntarily made it shall be admitted in evidence and the trial judge shall permit the jury to hear relevant evidence on the issue of voluntariness and shall instruct the jury to give such weight to the confession as the jury feels it deserves under all the circumstances.

"(b) The trial judge in determining the issue of voluntariness shall take into consideration all the circumstances surrounding the giving of the confession, including (1) the time elapsing between arrest and arraignment of the defendant making the confession, if it was made after arrest and before arraignment, (2) whether such defendant knew the nature of the offense with which he was charged or of which he was suspected at the time of making the confession, (3) whether or not such defendant was advised or knew that he was not required to make any statement and that any such statement could be used against him, (4) whether or not such defendant had been advised prior to questioning of his right to the assistance of counsel; and (5) whether or not such defendant was without the assistance of counsel when questioned and when giving such confession.

"The presence or absence of any of the above—mentioned factors to be taken into consideration by the judge need not be conclusive on the issue of voluntariness of the confession."

Given § 3501's express designation of voluntariness as the touchstone of admissibility, its omission of any warning requirement, and the instruction for trial courts to consider a nonexclusive list of factors relevant to the circumstances of a confession, we agree with the Court of Appeals that Congress intended by its enactment to overrule *Miranda. See also* Davis v. United States, 512 U.S. 452, 464 (1994) (SCALIA, J., concurring) (stating that, prior to *Miranda,* "voluntariness *vel non* was the touchstone of admissibility of confessions"). Because of the obvious conflict between our decision in *Miranda* and § 3501, we must address whether Congress has constitutional authority to thus supersede *Miranda.* If Congress has such authority, § 3501's totality-of-the-circumstances approach must prevail over *Miranda's* requirement of warnings; if not, that section must yield to *Miranda's* more specific requirements.

The law in this area is clear. This Court has supervisory authority over the federal courts, and we may use that authority to prescribe rules of evidence and procedure that are binding in those tribunals. Carlisle v. United States, 517 U.S. 416, 426 (1996). However, the power to judicially create and enforce nonconstitutional "rules of procedure and evidence for the federal courts exists only in the absence of a relevant Act of Congress." Palermo v. United States, 360 U.S. 343, 353, n.11 (1959) (citing Funk v. United States, 290 U.S. 371, 382 (1933), and Gordon v. United States, 344 U.S. 414, 418 (1953)). Congress retains the ultimate authority to modify or set aside any judicially created rules of evidence and procedure that are not required by the Constitution. *Palermo, supra,* at 345–348; *Carlisle, supra,* at 426; Vance v. Terrazas, 444 U.S. 252, 265 (1980).

But Congress may not legislatively supersede our decisions interpreting and applying the Constitution. *See, e.g.,* City of Boerne v. Flores, 521 U.S. 507, 517–521 (1997). This case therefore turns on whether the *Miranda* Court announced a constitutional rule or merely exercised its supervisory authority to regulate evidence in the absence of congressional direction. Recognizing this point, the Court of Appeals surveyed *Miranda* and its progeny to determine the constitutional status of the *Miranda* decision. 166 F.3d, at 687–692. Relying on the fact that we have created several exceptions to *Miranda's* warnings requirement and that we have repeatedly referred to the *Miranda* warnings as "prophylactic," New York v. Quarles, 467 U.S. 649, 653, (1984), and "not themselves rights protected by the Constitution," Michigan v. Tucker,

417 U.S. 433, 444 (1974), the Court of Appeals concluded that the protections announced in *Miranda* are not constitutionally required.

We disagree with the Court of Appeals' conclusion, although we concede that there is language in some of our opinions that supports the view taken by that court. But first and foremost of the factors on the other side—that *Miranda* is a constitutional decision—is that both *Miranda* and two of its companion cases applied the rule to proceedings in state courts—to wit, Arizona, California, and New York. *See* 384 U.S., at 491–494, 497–499. Since that time, we have consistently applied *Miranda's* rule to prosecutions arising in state courts. *See, e.g.,* Stansbury v. California, 511 U.S. 318 (1994) *(per curiam)*; Minnick v. Mississippi, 498 U.S. 146489 (1990); Arizona v. Roberson, 486 U.S. 675 (1988); Edwards v. Arizona, 451 U.S. 477, 481–482 (1981). It is beyond dispute that we do not hold a supervisory power over the courts of the several States. Smith v. Phillips, 455 U.S. 209, 221 (1982) ("Federal courts hold no supervisory authority over state judicial proceedings and may intervene only to correct wrongs of constitutional dimension"); Cicenia v. La Gay, 357 U.S. 504, 508–509 (1958). With respect to proceedings in state courts, our "authority is limited to enforcing the commands of the United States Constitution." Mu'Min v. Virginia, 500 U.S. 415, 422 (1991). *See also* Harris v. Rivera, 454 U.S. 339, 344–345 (1981) *(per curiam)* (stating that "[f]ederal judges . . . may not require the observance of any special procedures" in state courts "except when necessary to assure compliance with the dictates of the Federal Constitution").[3]

The *Miranda* opinion itself begins by stating that the Court granted certiorari "to explore some facets of the problems . . . of applying the privilege against self-incrimination to in-custody interrogation, *and to give concrete constitutional guidelines for law enforcement agencies and courts to follow.*" 384 U.S., at 441–442 (emphasis added). In fact, the majority opinion is replete with statements indicating that the majority thought it was announcing a constitutional rule. Indeed, the Court's ultimate conclusion was that the unwarned confessions obtained in the four cases before the Court in *Miranda* "were obtained from the defendant under circumstances that did not meet constitutional standards for protection of the privilege."[5]

---

[3] Our conclusion regarding *Miranda's* constitutional basis is further buttressed by the fact that we have allowed prisoners to bring alleged *Miranda* violations before the federal courts in habeas corpus proceedings. *See* Thompson v. Keohane, 516 U.S. 99 (1995); *Withrow, supra,* at 690–695. Habeas corpus proceedings are available only for claims that a person "is in custody in violation of the Constitution or laws or treaties of the United States." 28 U.S.C. § 2254(a). Since the *Miranda* rule is clearly not based on federal laws or treaties, our decision allowing habeas review for *Miranda* claims obviously assumes that *Miranda* is of constitutional origin.

[5] Many of our subsequent cases have also referred to *Miranda's* constitutional underpinnings. *See, e.g., Withrow, supra,* at 691 (" 'Prophylactic' though it may be, in protecting a defendant's Fifth Amendment privilege against self-incrimination, *Miranda* safeguards a 'fundamental trial right' "); Illinois v. Perkins, 496 U.S. 292, 296 (1990) (describing *Miranda's* warning requirement as resting on "the Fifth Amendment privilege against self-incrimination"); Butler v. McKellar, 494 U.S. 407, 411 (1990) ("[T]he Fifth Amendment bars police-initiated interrogation following a suspect's request for counsel in the context of a separate

Additional support for our conclusion that *Miranda* is constitutionally based is found in the *Miranda* Court's invitation for legislative action to protect the constitutional right against coerced self-incrimination. After discussing the "compelling pressures" inherent in custodial police interrogation, the *Miranda* Court concluded that, "[i]n order to combat these pressures and to permit a full opportunity to exercise the privilege against self-incrimination, the accused must be adequately and effectively apprised of his rights and the exercise of those rights must be fully honored." *Id.,* at 467. However, the Court emphasized that it could not foresee "the potential alternatives for protecting the privilege which might be devised by Congress or the States," and it accordingly opined that the Constitution would not preclude legislative solutions that differed from the prescribed *Miranda* warnings but which were "at least as effective in apprising accused persons of their right of silence and in assuring a continuous opportunity to exercise it."[6] *Ibid.*

The Court of Appeals also relied on the fact that we have, after our *Miranda* decision, made exceptions from its rule in cases such as New York v. Quarles, 467 U.S. 649 (1984), and Harris v. New York, 401 U.S. 222 (1971). *See* 166 F.3d, at 672, 689–691. But we have also broadened the application of the *Miranda* doctrine in cases such as Doyle v. Ohio, 426 U.S. 610, (1976), and Arizona v. Roberson, 486 U.S. 675 (1988). These decisions illustrate the principle—not that *Miranda* is not a constitutional rule—but that no constitutional rule is immutable. No court laying down a general rule can possibly foresee the various circumstances in which counsel will seek to apply it, and the sort of modifications represented by these cases are as much a normal part of constitutional law as the original decision.

The Court of Appeals also noted that in Oregon v. Elstad, 470 U.S. 298 (1985), we stated that " '[t]he *Miranda* exclusionary rule . . . serves the Fifth Amendment and sweeps more broadly than the Fifth Amendment itself.' " 166 F.3d, at 690 (quoting *Elstad, supra,* at 306). Our decision in that case—refusing to apply the traditional "fruits" doctrine developed in Fourth Amendment cases—does not prove that *Miranda* is a nonconstitutional decision, but simply recognizes the fact that unreasonable searches under the Fourth Amendment are different from unwarned interrogation under the Fifth Amendment.

---

investigation"); Michigan v. Jackson, 475 U.S. 625, 629 (1986) ("The Fifth Amendment protection against compelled self-incrimination provides the right to counsel at custodial interrogations"); Moran v. Burbine, 475 U.S. 412, 427 (1986) (referring to *Miranda* as "our interpretation of the Federal Constitution"); *Edwards, supra,* at 481–482.

   [6]   The Court of Appeals relied in part on our statement that the *Miranda* decision in no way "creates a 'constitutional straightjacket.' " *See* 166 F.3d 667, 672 (C.A.4 1999) (quoting *Miranda,* 384 U.S., at 467). However, a review of our opinion in *Miranda* clarifies that this disclaimer was intended to indicate that the Constitution does not require police to administer the particular *Miranda* warnings, not that the Constitution does not require a procedure that is effective in securing Fifth Amendment rights.

As an alternative argument for sustaining the Court of Appeals' decision, the court-invited *amicus curiae*[7] contends that the section complies with the requirement that a legislative alternative to *Miranda* be equally as effective in preventing coerced confessions. *See* Brief for Paul G. Cassell as *Amicus Curiae* 28–39. We agree with the amicus "contention that there are more remedies available for abusive police conduct" than there were at the time *Miranda* was decided, *see*, e.g., Wilkins v. May, 872 F.2d 190, 194 (C.A.7 1989) (applying Bivens v. Six Unknown Fed. Narcotics Agents, 403 U.S. 388 (1971), to hold that a suspect may bring a federal cause of action under the Due Process Clause for police misconduct during custodial interrogation). But we do not agree that these additional measures supplement § 3501's protections sufficiently to meet the constitutional minimum. *Miranda* requires procedures that will warn a suspect in custody of his right to remain silent and which will assure the suspect that the exercise of that right will be honored. *See*, e.g., 384 U.S., at 467. As discussed above, § 3501 explicitly eschews a requirement of preinterrogation warnings in favor of an approach that looks to the administration of such warnings as only one factor in determining the voluntariness of a suspect's confession. The additional remedies cited by amicus do not, in our view, render them, together with § 3501, an adequate substitute for the warnings required by *Miranda*.

The dissent argues that it is judicial overreaching for this Court to hold § 3501 unconstitutional unless we hold that the *Miranda* warnings are required by the Constitution, in the sense that nothing else will suffice to satisfy constitutional requirements. *Post*, at 2341–2342, 2347–2348 (opinion of SCALIA, J.). But we need not go further than *Miranda* to decide this case. In *Miranda*, the Court noted that reliance on the traditional totality-of-the-circumstances test raised a risk of overlooking an involuntary custodial confession, 384 U.S., at 457, a risk that the Court found unacceptably great when the confession is offered in the case in chief to prove guilt. The Court therefore concluded that something more than the totality test was necessary. *See ibid.; see also id.*, at 467, 490–491. As discussed above, § 3501 reinstates the totality test as sufficient. Section 3501 therefore cannot be sustained if *Miranda* is to remain the law.

Whether or not we would agree with *Miranda's* reasoning and its resulting rule, were we addressing the issue in the first instance, the principles of *stare decisis* weigh heavily against overruling it now. *See*, e.g., Rhode Island v. Innis, 446 U.S. 291, 304 (1980) (Burger, C. J., concurring in judgment) ("The meaning of *Miranda* has become reasonably clear and law enforcement practices have adjusted to its strictures; I would neither overrule *Miranda*, disparage it, nor extend it

---

[7] Because no party to the underlying litigation argued in favor of § 3501's constitutionality in this Court, we invited Professor Paul Cassell to assist our deliberations by arguing in support of the judgment below.

at this late date"). While " '*stare decisis* is not an inexorable command,' " State Oil Co. v. Khan, 522 U.S. 3, 20 (1997) (quoting Payne v. Tennessee, 501 U.S. 808, 828 (1991)), particularly when we are interpreting the Constitution, Agostini v. Felton, 521 U.S. 203, 235 (1997), "even in constitutional cases, the doctrine carries such persuasive force that we have always required a departure from precedent to be supported by some 'special justification.' "

We do not think there is such justification for overruling *Miranda*. *Miranda* has become embedded in routine police practice to the point where the warnings have become part of our national culture. *See* Mitchell v. United States, 526 U.S. 314, 331–332 (1999) (SCALIA, J., dissenting) (stating that the fact that a rule has found " 'wide acceptance in the legal culture' " is "adequate reason not to overrule" it). While we have overruled our precedents when subsequent cases have undermined their doctrinal underpinnings, *see, e.g.*, Patterson v. McLean Credit Union, 491 U.S. 164, 173 (1989), we do not believe that this has happened to the *Miranda* decision. If anything, our subsequent cases have reduced the impact of the *Miranda* rule on legitimate law enforcement while reaffirming the decision's core ruling that unwarned statements may not be used as evidence in the prosecution's case in chief.

The disadvantage of the *Miranda* rule is that statements which may be by no means involuntary, made by a defendant who is aware of his "rights," may nonetheless be excluded and a guilty defendant go free as a result. But experience suggests that the totality-of-the-circumstances test which § 3501 seeks to revive is more difficult than *Miranda* for law enforcement officers to conform to, and for courts to apply in a consistent manner. *See, e.g.*, Haynes v. Washington, 373 U.S., at 515 ("The line between proper and permissible police conduct and techniques and methods offensive to due process is, at best, a difficult one to draw"). The requirement that *Miranda* warnings be given does not, of course, dispense with the voluntariness inquiry. But as we said in Berkemer v. McCarty, 468 U.S. 420 (1984), "[c]ases in which a defendant can make a colorable argument that a self-incriminating statement was 'compelled' despite the fact that the law enforcement authorities adhered to the dictates of *Miranda* are rare." *Id.*, at 433, n.20.

In sum, we conclude that *Miranda* announced a constitutional rule that Congress may not supersede legislatively. Following the rule of *stare decisis,* we decline to overrule *Miranda* ourselves. The judgment of the Court of Appeals is therefore

Reversed.

■ JUSTICE SCALIA, with whom JUSTICE THOMAS joins, dissenting.

Those to whom judicial decisions are an unconnected series of judgments that produce either favored or disfavored results will doubtless greet today's decision as a paragon of moderation, since it declines to overrule Miranda v. Arizona, 384 U.S. 436 (1966). Those who understand the judicial process will appreciate that today's decision is not a reaffirmation of *Miranda,* but a radical revision of the most significant element of *Miranda* (as of all cases): the rationale that gives it a permanent place in our jurisprudence.

Marbury v. Madison, 1 Cranch 137 (1803), held that an Act of Congress will not be enforced by the courts if what it prescribes violates the Constitution of the United States. That was the basis on which *Miranda* was decided. One will search today's opinion in vain, however, for a statement (surely simple enough to make) that what 18 U.S.C. § 3501 prescribes—the use at trial of a voluntary confession, even when a *Miranda* warning or its equivalent has failed to be given—violates the Constitution. The reason the statement does not appear is not only (and perhaps not so much) that it would be absurd, inasmuch as § 3501 excludes from trial precisely what the Constitution excludes from trial, viz., compelled confessions; but also that Justices whose votes are needed to compose today's majority are on record as believing that a violation of *Miranda* is *not* a violation of the Constitution. *See* Davis v. United States, 512 U.S. 452, 457–458 (1994) (opinion of the Court, in which KENNEDY, J., joined); Duckworth v. Eagan, 492 U.S. 195, 203 (1989) (opinion of the Court, in which KENNEDY, J., joined); Oregon v. Elstad, 470 U.S. 298 (1985) (opinion of the Court by O'CONNOR, J.); New York v. Quarles, 467 U.S. 649 (1984) (opinion of the Court by REHNQUIST, J.). And so, to justify today's agreed-upon result, the Court must adopt a significant *new,* if not entirely comprehensible, principle of constitutional law. As the Court chooses to describe that principle, statutes of Congress can be disregarded, not only when what they prescribe violates the Constitution, but when what they prescribe contradicts a decision of this Court that "announced a constitutional rule," *ante,* at 2333. As I shall discuss in some detail, the only thing that can possibly mean in the context of this case is that this Court has the power, not merely to apply the Constitution but to expand it, imposing what it regards as useful "prophylactic" restrictions upon Congress and the States. That is an immense and frightening antidemocratic power, and it does not exist.

It takes only a small step to bring today's opinion out of the realm of power-judging and into the mainstream of legal reasoning: The Court need only go beyond its carefully couched iterations that "*Miranda* is a constitutional decision," *ante,* at 2333, that "*Miranda* is constitutionally based," *ante,* at 2334, that *Miranda* has "constitutional underpinnings," *ante,* at 2334, n.5, and come out and say quite clearly: "We reaffirm today that custodial interrogation that is not preceded by *Miranda* warnings or their equivalent violates the Constitution of the United States." It cannot say that, because a majority of the Court does not believe it. The Court therefore acts in plain violation of the Constitution when it denies effect to this Act of Congress. . . .

It was once possible to characterize the so-called *Miranda* rule as resting (however implausibly) upon the proposition that what the statute here before us permits—the admission at trial of un-*Mirandized* confessions—violates the Constitution . . . .

So understood, *Miranda* was objectionable for innumerable reasons, not least the fact that cases spanning more than 70 years had rejected its core premise that, absent the warnings and an effective waiver of the right to remain silent and of the (thitherto unknown) right to have an attorney present, a statement obtained pursuant to custodial interrogation was necessarily the product of compulsion. Moreover, history and precedent aside, the decision in *Miranda,* if read as an explication of what the Constitution *requires,* is preposterous. There is, for example, simply no basis in reason for concluding that a response to the very first question asked, by a suspect who already *knows* all of the rights described in the *Miranda* warning, is anything other than a volitional act. *See Miranda, supra,* at 533–534 (White, J., dissenting). And even if one assumes that the elimination of compulsion absolutely requires informing even the most knowledgeable suspect of his right to remain silent, it cannot conceivably require the right to have *counsel* present. There is a world of difference, which the Court recognized under the traditional voluntariness test but ignored in *Miranda,* between compelling a suspect to incriminate himself and preventing him from foolishly doing so of his own accord. Only the latter (which is *not* required by the Constitution) could explain the Court's inclusion of a right to counsel and the requirement that it, too, be knowingly and intelligently waived. Counsel's presence is not required to tell the suspect that he *need* not speak; the interrogators can do that. The only good reason for having counsel there is that he can be counted on to advise the suspect that he *should* not speak. *See* Watts v. Indiana, 338 U.S. 49, 59 (1949) (Jackson, J., concurring in result in part and dissenting in part) ("[A]ny lawyer worth his salt will tell the suspect in no uncertain terms to make no statement to police under any circumstances").

Preventing foolish (rather than compelled) confessions is likewise the only conceivable basis for the rules (suggested in *Miranda, see* 384 U.S., at 444–445, 473–474), that courts must exclude any confession elicited by questioning conducted, without interruption, after the suspect has indicated a desire to stand on his right to remain silent, *see* Michigan v. Mosley, 423 U.S. 96, 105–106 (1975), or initiated by police after the suspect has expressed a desire to have counsel present, *see* Edwards v. Arizona, 451 U.S. 477, 484–485 (1981). Nonthreatening attempts to persuade the suspect to reconsider that initial decision are not, without more, enough to render a change of heart the product of anything other than the suspect's free will. Thus, what is most remarkable about the *Miranda* decision—and what made it unacceptable as a matter of straightforward constitutional interpretation in the *Marbury* tradition— is its palpable hostility toward the act of confession *per se,* rather than toward what the Constitution abhors, *compelled* confession.

For these reasons, and others more than adequately developed in the *Miranda* dissents and in the subsequent works of the decision's many critics, any conclusion that a violation of the *Miranda* rules *necessarily* amounts to a violation of the privilege against compelled self-incrimination can claim no support in history, precedent, or common sense, and as a result would at least presumptively be worth reconsidering even at this late date. But that is unnecessary, since the Court has (thankfully) long since abandoned the notion that failure to comply with *Miranda's* rules is itself a violation of the Constitution.

II

As the Court today acknowledges, since *Miranda* we have explicitly, and repeatedly, interpreted that decision as having announced, not the circumstances in which custodial interrogation runs afoul of the Fifth or Fourteenth Amendment, but rather only "prophylactic" rules that go beyond the right against compelled self-incrimination. Of course the seeds of this "prophylactic" interpretation of *Miranda* were present in the decision itself. *See Miranda,* 384 U.S., at 439 (discussing the "necessity for procedures which assure that the [suspect] is accorded his privilege"); *id.,* at 447 ("[u]nless a proper limitation upon custodial interrogation is achieved—such as these decisions will advance—there can be no assurance that practices of this nature will be eradicated"); *id.,* at 457 ("[i]n these cases, we might not find the defendants' statements to have been involuntary in traditional terms"); *ibid.* (noting "concern for adequate safeguards to protect precious Fifth Amendment rights" and the "potentiality for compulsion" in Ernesto *Miranda's* interrogation). In subsequent cases, the seeds have sprouted and borne fruit: The Court has squarely concluded that it is possible—indeed not uncommon—for the police to violate *Miranda* without also violating the Constitution.

Michigan v. Tucker, 417 U.S. 433 (1974), an opinion for the Court written by then-Justice REHNQUIST, rejected the true-to-*Marbury,* failure-to-warn-as-constitutional-violation interpretation of *Miranda.* It held that exclusion of the "fruits" of a *Miranda* violation—the statement of a witness whose identity the defendant had revealed while in custody—was not required. The opinion explained that the question whether the "police conduct complained of directly infringed upon respondent's right against compulsory self-incrimination" was a "separate question" from "whether it instead violated only the prophylactic rules developed to protect that right." 417 U.S., at 439. The "procedural safeguards" adopted in *Miranda,* the Court said, "were not themselves rights protected by the Constitution but were instead measures to insure that the right against compulsory self-incrimination was protected," and to "provide practical reinforcement for the right," 417 U.S., at 444. Comparing the particular facts of the custodial interrogation with the "historical circumstances underlying the privilege," *ibid.,* the Court concluded, unequivocally, that the defendant's statement could not be termed "involuntary as that term has been defined in the decisions of this Court," *id.,* at 445, and thus that there had been no constitutional violation, notwithstanding the clear violation of the "procedural rules later established in *Miranda,*" *ibid.* Lest there be any confusion on the point, the Court reiterated that the "police conduct at issue here did not abridge respondent's constitutional privilege against compulsory self-incrimination, but departed only from the prophylactic standards later laid down by this Court in *Miranda* to safeguard that privilege." *Id.,* at 446. It is clear from our cases, of course, that if the statement in *Tucker had* been obtained in violation of the Fifth Amendment, the statement and its fruits would have been excluded. *See* Nix v. Williams, 467 U.S. 431, 442 (1984).

The next year, in Oregon v. Hass, 420 U.S. 714 (1975), the Court held that a defendant's statement taken in violation of *Miranda* that was nonetheless *voluntary* could be used at trial for impeachment purposes. This holding turned upon the recognition that violation of *Miranda* is not unconstitutional compulsion, since statements obtained in actual violation of the privilege against compelled self-incrimination, "as opposed to . . . taken in violation of *Miranda,*" quite simply "may not be put to any testimonial use whatever against [the defendant] in a criminal trial," including as impeachment evidence. New Jersey v. Portash, 440 U.S. 450, 459 (1979). *See also* Mincey v. Arizona, 437 U.S. 385, 397–398 (1978) (holding that while statements obtained in violation of *Miranda* may be used for impeachment if otherwise trustworthy, the Constitution prohibits "*any* criminal trial use against a defendant of his *involuntary* statement").

Nearly a decade later, in New York v. Quarles, 467 U.S. 649 (1984), the Court relied upon the fact that "[t]he prophylactic *Miranda* warnings . . . are 'not themselves rights protected by the Constitution,' " *id.,* at 654 (quoting *Tucker, supra,* at 444), to create a "public safety" exception. In that case, police apprehended, after a chase in a grocery store, a rape suspect known to be carrying a gun. After handcuffing and searching him (and finding no gun)—but before reading him his *Miranda* warnings— the police demanded to know where the gun was. The defendant nodded in the direction of some empty cartons and responded that "the gun is over there." The Court held that both the unwarned statement—"the gun is over there"—and the recovered weapon were admissible in the prosecution's case in chief under a "public safety exception" to the "prophylactic rules enunciated in *Miranda.*" 467 U.S., at 653. It explicitly acknowledged that if the *Miranda* warnings were an imperative of the Fifth Amendment itself, such an exigency exception would be impossible, since the Fifth Amendment's bar on compelled self-incrimination is absolute, and its " 'strictures, unlike the Fourth's are not removed by showing reasonableness,' " 467 U.S., at 653, n.3. (For the latter reason, the Court found it necessary to note that respondent did not "claim that [his] statements were actually compelled by police conduct which overcame his will to resist," *id.,* at 654.)

The next year, the Court again declined to apply the "fruit of the poisonous tree" doctrine to a *Miranda* violation, this time allowing the admission of a suspect's properly warned statement even though it had been preceded (and, arguably, induced) by an earlier inculpatory statement taken in violation of *Miranda*. Oregon v. Elstad, 470 U.S. 298 (1985). As in *Tucker,* the Court distinguished the case from those holding that a confession obtained as a result of an unconstitutional search is inadmissible, on the ground that the violation of *Miranda* does not involve an "actual infringement of the suspect's constitutional rights," 470 U.S., at 308. *Miranda,* the Court explained, "sweeps more broadly than the Fifth Amendment itself," and "*Miranda*'s preventive medicine provides a remedy even to the defendant who has suffered no identifiable constitutional harm." 470 U.S., at 306–307. "[E]rrors [that] are made by law enforcement officers in administering the prophylactic *Miranda* procedures . . . should not breed the same irremediable consequences as police infringement of the Fifth Amendment itself." *Id.,* at 308–309.

In light of these cases, and our statements to the same effect in others, it is simply no longer possible for the Court to conclude, even if it wanted to, that a violation of *Miranda's* rules is a violation of the Constitution. But as I explained at the outset, that is what is required before the Court may disregard a law of Congress governing the admissibility of evidence in federal court. The Court today insists that the *decision* in *Miranda* is a "constitutional" one; that it has "constitutional underpinnings;" a "constitutional basis" and a "constitutional origin;" that it was "constitutionally based," and that it announced a "constitutional rule." It is fine to play these word games; but what makes a decision "constitutional" in the only sense relevant here— in the sense that renders it impervious to supersession by congressional legislation such as § 3501—is the determination that the Constitution *requires* the result that the decision announces and the statute ignores. By disregarding congressional action that concededly does not violate the Constitution, the Court flagrantly offends fundamental principles of separation of powers, and arrogates to itself prerogatives reserved to the representatives of the people.

The Court seeks to avoid this conclusion in two ways: First, by misdescribing these post-*Miranda* cases as mere dicta. The Court concedes only "that there is language in some of our opinions that supports the view" that *Miranda's* protections are not "constitutionally required." *Ante,* at 2333. It is not a matter of *language;* it is a matter of *holdings.* The proposition that failure to comply with *Miranda's* rules does not establish a constitutional violation was central to the *holdings* of *Tucker, Hass, Quarles,* and *Elstad.*

The second way the Court seeks to avoid the impact of these cases is simply to disclaim responsibility for reasoned decisionmaking. It says:

> "These decisions illustrate the principle—not that *Miranda* is not a constitutional rule—but that no constitutional rule is

immutable. No court laying down a general rule can possibly foresee the various circumstances in which counsel will seek to apply it, and the sort of modifications represented by these cases are as much a normal part of constitutional law as the original decision."

The issue, however, is not whether court rules are "mutable"; they assuredly are. It is not whether, in the light of "various circumstances," they can be "modifi[ed]"; they assuredly can. The issue is whether, *as mutated and modified,* they must *make sense.* The requirement that they do so is the only thing that prevents this Court from being some sort of nine-headed Caesar, giving thumbs-up or thumbs-down to whatever outcome, case by case, suits or offends its collective fancy. And if confessions procured in violation of *Miranda* are confessions "compelled" in violation of the Constitution, the post-*Miranda* decisions I have discussed do not make sense. The only reasoned basis for their outcome was that a violation of *Miranda* is *not* a violation of the Constitution. . . .

Finally, the Court asserts that *Miranda* must be a "constitutional decision" announcing a "constitutional rule," and thus immune to congressional modification, because we have since its inception applied it to the States. If this argument is meant as an invocation of *stare decisis,* it fails because, though it is true that our cases applying *Miranda* against the States must be reconsidered if *Miranda* is not required by the Constitution, it is likewise true that our cases (discussed above) based on the principle that *Miranda* is *not* required by the Constitution will have to be reconsidered if it *is.* So the *stare decisis* argument is a wash. If, on the other hand, the argument is meant as an appeal to logic rather than *stare decisis,* it is a classic example of begging the question: Congress's attempt to set aside *Miranda,* since it represents an assertion that violation of *Miranda* is not a violation of the Constitution, *also* represents an assertion that the Court has no power to impose *Miranda* on the States. To answer this assertion—not by showing why violation of *Miranda is* a violation of the Constitution—but by asserting that *Miranda does* apply against the States, is to assume precisely the point at issue. In my view, our continued application of the *Miranda* code to the States despite our consistent statements that running afoul of its dictates does not necessarily—or even usually—result in an actual constitutional violation, represents not the source of *Miranda's* salvation but rather evidence of its ultimate illegitimacy. *See generally* J. Grano, Confessions, Truth, and the Law 173–198 (1993); Grano, *Prophylactic Rules in Criminal Procedure: A Question of Article III Legitimacy,* 80 Nw. U.L.Rev. 100 (1985). As Justice STEVENS has elsewhere explained: "This Court's power to require state courts to exclude probative self-incriminatory statements rests entirely on the premise that the use of such evidence violates the Federal Constitution. . . . If the Court does not accept that premise, it must regard the holding in the *Miranda* case itself, as well as all of the federal jurisprudence that has evolved from that decision, as nothing more than an illegitimate exercise of raw judicial power." *Elstad,* 470 U.S., at 370285 (dissenting opinion). Quite so.

IV

Thus, while I agree with the Court that § 3501 cannot be upheld without also concluding that *Miranda* represents an illegitimate exercise of our authority to review state-court judgments, I do not share the Court's hesitation in reaching that conclusion. For while the Court is also correct that the doctrine of *stare decisis* demands some "special justification" for a departure from longstanding precedent—even precedent of the constitutional variety—that criterion is more than met here. To repeat Justice STEVENS' cogent observation, it is "[o]bviou[s]" that "the Court's power to reverse *Miranda*'s conviction rested *entirely* on the determination that a violation of the Federal Constitution had occurred." *Elstad,* 470 U.S., at 367, n.9, (dissenting opinion) (emphasis added). Despite the Court's Orwellian assertion to the contrary, it is undeniable that later cases (discussed above) have "undermined [*Miranda's*] doctrinal underpinnings," denying constitutional violation and thus stripping the holding of its only constitutionally legitimate support. *Miranda's* critics and supporters alike have long made this point.

The Court cites Patterson v. McLean Credit Union, 491 U.S. 164, 173 (1989), as accurately reflecting our standard for overruling, *See ante,* at 2336—which I am pleased to accept, even though *Patterson* was speaking of overruling statutory cases and the standard for constitutional decisions is somewhat more lenient. What is set forth there reads as though it was written precisely with the current status of *Miranda* in mind:

> "In cases where statutory precedents have been overruled, the primary reason for the Court's shift in position has been the intervening development of the law, through either the growth of judicial doctrine or further action taken by Congress. Where such changes have removed or weakened the conceptual underpinnings from the prior decision, . . . or where the later law has rendered the decision irreconcilable with competing legal doctrines or policies, . . . the Court has not hesitated to overrule an earlier decision."

491 U.S., at 173.

Neither am I persuaded by the argument for retaining *Miranda* that touts its supposed workability as compared with the totality-of-the-circumstances test it purported to replace. *Miranda's* proponents cite *ad nauseam* the fact that the Court was called upon to make difficult and subtle distinctions in applying the "voluntariness" test in some 30-odd due process "coerced confessions" cases in the 30 years between *Brown v. Mississippi,* 297 U.S. 278 (1936), and *Miranda.* It is not immediately apparent, however, that the judicial burden has been eased by the "bright-line" rules adopted in *Miranda*. In fact, in the 34 years since *Miranda* was decided, this Court has been called upon to decide nearly *60* cases involving a host of *Miranda* issues, most of them predicted with remarkable prescience by Justice White in his *Miranda* dissent. 384 U.S., at 545.

Moreover, it is not clear why the Court thinks that the "totality-of-the-circumstances test . . . is more difficult than *Miranda* for law enforcement officers to conform to, and for courts to apply in a consistent manner.". Indeed, I find myself persuaded by Justice O'CONNOR's rejection of this same argument in her opinion in *Williams,* 507 U.S., at 711–712 (O'CONNOR, J., joined by REHNQUIST, C. J., concurring in part and dissenting in part):

> "*Miranda,* for all its alleged brightness, is not without its difficulties; and voluntariness is not without its strengths. . . .

> ". . . *Miranda* creates as many close questions as it resolves. The task of determining whether a defendant is in 'custody' has proved to be 'a slippery one.' And the supposedly 'bright' lines that separate interrogation from spontaneous declaration, the exercise of a right from waiver, and the adequate warning from the inadequate, likewise have turned out to be rather dim and ill defined. . . .

> "The totality-of-the-circumstances approach, on the other hand, permits each fact to be taken into account without resort to formal and dispositive labels. By dispensing with the difficulty of producing a yes-or-no answer to questions that are often better answered in shades and degrees, *the voluntariness inquiry often can make judicial decisionmaking easier rather than more onerous.*"

(Emphasis added; citations omitted.)

But even were I to agree that the old totality-of-the-circumstances test was more cumbersome, it is simply not true that *Miranda* has banished it from the law and replaced it with a new test. Under the current regime, which the Court today retains in its entirety, courts are frequently called upon to undertake *both* inquiries. That is because, as explained earlier, voluntariness remains the *constitutional* standard, and as such continues to govern the admissibility for impeachment purposes of statements taken in violation of *Miranda,* the admissibility of the "fruits" of such statements, and the admissibility of statements challenged as unconstitutionally obtained *despite* the interrogator's compliance with *Miranda, see, e.g., Colorado v. Connelly,* 479 U.S. 157 (1986).

Finally, I am not convinced by petitioner's argument that *Miranda* should be preserved because the decision occupies a special place in the "public's consciousness." Brief for Petitioner 44. As far as I am aware, the public is not under the illusion that we are infallible. I see little harm in admitting that we made a mistake in taking away from the people the ability to decide for themselves what protections (beyond those required by the Constitution) are reasonably affordable in the criminal investigatory process. And I see much to be gained by reaffirming for the people the wonderful reality that they govern themselves—which means that "[t]he powers not delegated to the United States by the Constitution" that the people adopted, "nor prohibited . . . to the States" by that Constitution, "are reserved to the States respectively, or to the people," U.S. Const., Amdt. 10.

Today's judgment converts *Miranda* from a milestone of judicial overreaching into the very Cheops' Pyramid (or perhaps the Sphinx would be a better analogue) of judicial arrogance. In imposing its Court-made code upon the States, the original opinion at least *asserted* that it was demanded by the Constitution. Today's decision does not pretend that it is—and yet *still* asserts the right to impose it against the will of the people's representatives in Congress. Far from believing that *stare decisis* compels this result, I believe we cannot allow to remain on the books even a celebrated decision—*especially* a celebrated decision—that has come to stand for the proposition that the Supreme Court has power to impose extraconstitutional constraints upon Congress and the States. This is not the system that was established by the Framers, or that would be established by any sane supporter of government by the people.

I dissent from today's decision, and, until § 3501 is repealed, will continue to apply it in all cases where there has been a sustainable finding that the defendant's confession was voluntary.

5. *MIRANDA* DOCTRINE, FIRST LEVEL: "CUSTODY" AND "INTERROGATION"

a. "CUSTODY"

Howes v. Fields
565 U.S. 499 (2012)

■ JUSTICE ALITO delivered the opinion of the Court.

The United States Court of Appeals for the Sixth Circuit held that our precedents clearly establish that a prisoner is in custody within the meaning of Miranda v. Arizona, 384 U.S. 436, (1966), if the prisoner is taken aside and questioned about events that occurred outside the prison walls. Our decisions, however, do not clearly establish such a rule, and therefore the Court of Appeals erred in holding that this rule provides a permissible basis for federal habeas relief under the relevant provision of the Antiterrorism and Effective Death Penalty Act of 1996 (AEDPA), 28 U.S.C. § 2254(d)(1). Indeed, the rule applied by the court below does not represent a correct interpretation of our *Miranda* case law. We therefore reverse.

I

While serving a sentence in a Michigan jail, Randall Fields was escorted by a corrections officer to a conference room where two sheriff's deputies questioned him about allegations that, before he came to prison, he had engaged in sexual conduct with a 12-year-old boy. In order to get to the conference room, Fields had to go down one floor and pass through a locked door that separated two sections of the facility. Fields arrived at the conference room between 7 p.m. and 9 p.m.[1] and was questioned for between five and seven hours.[2]

At the beginning of the interview, Fields was told that he was free to leave and return to his cell. Later, he was again told that he could leave whenever he wanted. The two interviewing deputies were armed during the interview, but Fields remained free of handcuffs and other restraints. The door to the conference room was sometimes open and sometimes shut.

About halfway through the interview, after Fields had been confronted with the allegations of abuse, he became agitated and began to yell. Fields testified that one of the deputies, using an expletive, told him to sit down and said that "if [he] didn't want to cooperate, [he] could leave." Fields eventually confessed to engaging in sex acts with the boy. According to Fields' testimony at a suppression hearing, he said several times during the interview that he no longer wanted to talk to the deputies, but he did not ask to go back to his cell prior to the end of the interview.

When he was eventually ready to leave, he had to wait an additional 20 minutes or so because a corrections officer had to be summoned to escort him back to his cell, and he did not return to his cell until well after the hour when he generally retired.[3] At no time was Fields given *Miranda* warnings or advised that he did not have to speak with the deputies.

The State of Michigan charged Fields with criminal sexual conduct. Relying on *Miranda*, Fields moved to suppress his confession, but the trial court denied his motion. Over the renewed objection of defense counsel, one of the interviewing deputies testified at trial about Fields' admissions. The jury convicted Fields of two counts of third-degree

---

[1]   Fields testified that he left his cell around 8 p.m. and that the interview began around 8:30 p.m. App. to Pet. for Cert. 77a. Both the Michigan Court of Appeals and the Sixth Circuit stated that the interview began between 7 p.m. and 9 p.m.

[2]   The Court of Appeals stated that the interview lasted for approximately seven hours, a figure that appears to be based on the testimony of one of the interviewing deputies. Fields put the number of hours between five and five and a half, saying the interview began around 8:30 p.m. and continued until 1:30 a.m. or 2 a.m. The Michigan Court of Appeals stated that the interview ended around midnight, which would put the length of the interview at between three and five hours.

[3]   Fields testified that his normal bedtime was 10:30 p.m. or 11 p.m.

criminal sexual conduct, and the judge sentenced him to a term of 10 to 15 years of imprisonment. On direct appeal, the Michigan Court of Appeals affirmed, rejecting Fields' contention that his statements should have been suppressed because he was subjected to custodial interrogation without a *Miranda* warning. The court ruled that Fields had not been in custody for purposes of *Miranda* during the interview, so no *Miranda* warnings were required. The court emphasized that Fields was told that he was free to leave and return to his cell but that he never asked to do so. The Michigan Supreme Court denied discretionary review.

Fields then filed a petition for a writ of habeas corpus in Federal District Court, and the court granted relief. The Sixth Circuit affirmed, holding that the interview in the conference room was a "custodial interrogation" within the meaning of *Miranda* because isolation from the general prison population combined with questioning about conduct occurring outside the prison makes any such interrogation custodial per se. The Court of Appeals reasoned that this Court clearly established in Mathis v. United States, 391 U.S. 1 (1968), that "*Miranda* warnings must be administered when law enforcement officers remove an inmate from the general prison population and interrogate him regarding criminal conduct that took place outside the jail or prison." 617 F.3d 813, 820 (C.A.6 2010); *see also id.*, at 818 ("The central holding of *Mathis* is that a *Miranda* warning is required whenever an incarcerated individual is isolated from the general prison population and interrogated, i.e. [,] questioned in a manner likely to lead to self-incrimination, about conduct occurring outside of the prison"). Because Fields was isolated from the general prison population and interrogated about conduct occurring in the outside world, the Court of Appeals found that the state court's decision was contrary to clearly established federal law as determined by this Court in Mathis. 617 F.3d, at 823.

We granted certiorari.

II

Under AEDPA, a federal court may grant a state prisoner's application for a writ of habeas corpus if the state-court adjudication pursuant to which the prisoner is held "resulted in a decision that was contrary to, or involved an unreasonable application of, clearly established Federal law, as determined by the Supreme Court of the United States." 28 U.S.C. § 2254(d)(1). In this context, "clearly established law" signifies "the holdings, as opposed to the dicta, of this Court's decisions." Williams v. Taylor, 529 U.S. 362, 412 (2000).

In this case, it is abundantly clear that our precedents do not clearly establish the categorical rule on which the Court of Appeals relied, *i.e.*, that the questioning of a prisoner is always custodial when the prisoner is removed from the general prison population and questioned about events that occurred outside the prison. On the contrary, we have repeatedly declined to adopt any categorical rule with respect to whether the questioning of a prison inmate is custodial.

In Illinois v. Perkins, 496 U.S. 292 (1990), where we upheld the admission of un-Mirandized statements elicited from an inmate by an undercover officer masquerading as another inmate, we noted that "[t]he bare fact of custody may not in every instance require a warning even when the suspect is aware that he is speaking to an official, but we do not have occasion to explore that issue here." *Id.*, at 299 (emphasis added). Instead, we simply "reject[ed] the argument that *Miranda* warnings are required whenever a suspect is in custody in a technical sense and converses with someone who happens to be a government agent." *Id.*, at 297.

Most recently, in Maryland v. Shatzer, 559 U.S. 98 (2010), we expressly declined to adopt a bright-line rule for determining the applicability of *Miranda* in prisons. *Shatzer* considered whether a break in custody ends the presumption of involuntariness established in Edwards v. Arizona, 451 U.S. 477 (1981), and, if so, whether a prisoner's return to the general prison population after a custodial interrogation constitutes a break in *Miranda* custody. *See* 559 U.S., at ___. In considering the latter question, we noted first that "[w]e have never decided whether incarceration constitutes custody for *Miranda* purposes, and have indeed explicitly declined to address the issue." *Id.* (citing *Perkins, supra*, at 299; emphasis added). The answer to this question, we noted, would "depen[d] upon whether [incarceration] exerts the coercive pressure that *Miranda* was designed to guard against—the 'danger of coercion [that] results from the interaction of custody and official interrogation.' " (quoting *Perkins, supra*, at 297).

In concluding that our precedents establish a categorical rule, the Court of Appeals placed great weight on the decision in *Mathis*, but the Court of Appeals misread the holding in that case. In *Mathis*, an inmate in a state prison was questioned by an Internal Revenue agent and was subsequently convicted for federal offenses. The Court of Appeals held that *Miranda* did not apply to this interview for two reasons: A criminal investigation had not been commenced at the time of the interview, and the prisoner was incarcerated for an "unconnected offense." Mathis v. United States, 376 F.2d 595, 597 (C.A.5 1967). This Court rejected both of those grounds for distinguishing *Miranda*, 391 U.S., at 4, and thus the holding in *Mathis* is simply that a prisoner who otherwise meets the requirements for *Miranda* custody is not taken outside the scope of *Miranda* by either of the two factors on which the Court of Appeals had relied. Mathis did not hold that imprisonment, in and of itself, is enough to constitute *Miranda* custody.[4] Nor, contrary to respondent's submission, *See* Brief for Respondent 14, did Oregon v. Mathiason, 429

---

[4]   Indeed, it is impossible to tell from either the opinion of this Court or that of the court below whether the prisoner's interview was routine or whether there were special features that may have created an especially coercive atmosphere.

U.S. 492, 494 (1977) (per curiam), which simply restated in dictum the holding in *Mathis*.

The Court of Appeals purported to find support for its per se rule in *Shatzer*, relying on our statement that "[n]o one questions that Shatzer was in custody for *Miranda* purposes" when he was interviewed. 559 U.S., at ___. But this statement means only that the issue of custody was not contested before us. It strains credulity to read the statement as constituting an "unambiguous conclusion" or "finding" by this Court that Shatzer was in custody. 617 F.3d, at 822.

Finally, contrary to respondent's suggestion, *Miranda* itself did not clearly establish the rule applied by the Court of Appeals. *Miranda* adopted a "set of prophylactic measures" designed to ward off the " 'inherently compelling pressures' of custodial interrogation," *Shatzer, supra*, at ___ (quoting *Miranda*, 384 U.S., at 467), but *Miranda* did not hold that such pressures are always present when a prisoner is taken aside and questioned about events outside the prison walls. Indeed, *Miranda* did not even establish that police questioning of a suspect at the station house is always custodial. *See* Mathiason, *supra*, at 495 (declining to find that *Miranda* warnings are required "simply because the questioning takes place in the station house, or because the questioned person is one whom the police suspect").

In sum, our decisions do not clearly establish that a prisoner is always in custody for purposes of *Miranda* whenever a prisoner is isolated from the general prison population and questioned about conduct outside the prison.[5]

III

Not only does the categorical rule applied below go well beyond anything that is clearly established in our prior decisions, it is simply wrong. The three elements of that rule—(1) imprisonment, (2) questioning in private, and (3) questioning about events in the outside world—are not necessarily enough to create a custodial situation for *Miranda* purposes.

---

[5]   The state-court decision applied the traditional context-specific analysis to determine whether the circumstances of respondent's interrogation gave rise to "the coercive pressure that *Miranda* was designed to guard against." *Shatzer*, 559 U.S., at ___. The court first observed: "That a defendant is in prison for an unrelated offense when being questioned does not, without more, mean that he was in custody for the purpose of determining whether Miranda warnings were required." App. to Pet. for Cert. 56a (internal quotation marks omitted and emphasis added). In this case, the court noted, the "defendant was unquestionably in custody, but on a matter unrelated to the interrogation." *Ibid*. The Sixth Circuit concluded that the state court thereby limited *Miranda* in a way rejected by Mathis v. United States, 391 U.S. 1 (1968), and "curtail[ed]" the warnings to be given persons under interrogation by officers based on the reason why the person is in custody." *Id.*, at 4–5. We think the better reading is that the state court merely meant to draw a distinction between incarceration and *Miranda* custody. This reading is supported by the state court's subsequent consideration of whether the facts of the case were likely to create an atmosphere of coercion. App. to Pet. for Cert. 56a.

A

As used in our *Miranda* case law, "custody" is a term of art that specifies circumstances that are thought generally to present a serious danger of coercion. In determining whether a person is in custody in this sense, the initial step is to ascertain whether, in light of "the objective circumstances of the interrogation," Stansbury v. California, 511 U.S. 318, 322–323, 325 (1994) (per curiam), a "reasonable person [would] have felt he or she was not at liberty to terminate the interrogation and leave." Thompson v. Keohane, 516 U.S. 99, 112 (1995). And in order to determine how a suspect would have "gauge[d]" his "freedom of movement," courts must examine "all of the circumstances surrounding the interrogation." Stansbury, *supra*, at 322, 325 (internal quotation marks omitted). Relevant factors include the location of the questioning, *See Shatzer*, *supra*, at ___–___, its duration, *see* Berkemer v. McCarty, 468 U.S. 420, 437–438 (1984), statements made during the interview, *see* Mathiason, *supra*, at 495; Yarborough v. Alvarado, 541 U.S. 652 (2004); *Stansbury*, *supra*, at 325, the presence or absence of physical restraints during the questioning, *see* New York v. Quarles, 467 U.S. 649, 655 (1984), and the release of the interviewee at the end of the questioning, *see* California v. Beheler, 463 U.S. 1121, 1122–1123 (1983) (per curiam).

Determining whether an individual's freedom of movement was curtailed, however, is simply the first step in the analysis, not the last. Not all restraints on freedom of movement amount to custody for purposes of *Miranda*. We have "decline[d] to accord talismanic power" to the freedom-of-movement inquiry, *Berkemer*, *supra*, at 437, and have instead asked the additional question whether the relevant environment presents the same inherently coercive pressures as the type of station house questioning at issue in *Miranda*. "Our cases make clear . . . that the freedom-of-movement test identifies only a necessary and not a sufficient condition for *Miranda* custody." *Shatzer*, 559 U.S., at ___.

This important point is illustrated by our decision in *Berkemer v. McCarty*, *supra*. In that case, we held that the roadside questioning of a motorist who was pulled over in a routine traffic stop did not constitute custodial interrogation. *Id.*, at 423, 441–442. We acknowledged that "a traffic stop significantly curtails the 'freedom of action' of the driver and the passengers," and that it is generally "a crime either to ignore a policeman's signal to stop one's car or, once having stopped, to drive away without permission." *Id.*, at 436. "[F]ew motorists," we noted, "would feel free either to disobey a directive to pull over or to leave the scene of a traffic stop without being told they might do so." *Ibid.* Nevertheless, we held that a person detained as a result of a traffic stop is not in *Miranda* custody because such detention does not "sufficiently impair [the detained person's] free exercise of his privilege against self-incrimination to require that he be warned of his constitutional rights." 468 U.S., at 437. As we later put it, the "temporary and relatively nonthreatening detention involved in a traffic stop or *Terry* stop does not constitute

Miranda custody," *Shatzer, supra,* at ___ (citation omitted). *See* Terry v. Ohio, 392 U.S. 1 (1968).

It may be thought that the situation in *Berkemer*—the questioning of a motorist subjected to a brief traffic stop—is worlds away from those present when an inmate is questioned in a prison, but the same cannot be said of *Shatzer*, where we again distinguished between restraints on freedom of movement and *Miranda* custody. *Shatzer*, as noted, concerned the *Edwards* prophylactic rule, which limits the ability of the police to initiate further questioning of a suspect in *Miranda* custody once the suspect invokes the right to counsel. We held in *Shatzer* that this rule does not apply when there is a sufficient break in custody between the suspect's invocation of the right to counsel and the initiation of subsequent questioning. *See* 559 U.S., at ___. And, what is significant for present purposes, we further held that a break in custody may occur while a suspect is serving a term in prison. If a break in custody can occur while a prisoner is serving an uninterrupted term of imprisonment, it must follow that imprisonment alone is not enough to create a custodial situation within the meaning of *Miranda*.

There are at least three strong grounds for this conclusion. First, questioning a person who is already serving a prison term does not generally involve the shock that very often accompanies arrest. In the paradigmatic *Miranda* situation—a person is arrested in his home or on the street and whisked to a police station for questioning—detention represents a sharp and ominous change, and the shock may give rise to coercive pressures. A person who is "cut off from his normal life and companions," *Shatzer, supra,* at ___, and abruptly transported from the street into a "police-dominated atmosphere," *Miranda*, 384 U.S., at 456, may feel coerced into answering questions.

By contrast, when a person who is already serving a term of imprisonment is questioned, there is usually no such change. "Interrogated suspects who have previously been convicted of crime live in prison." *Shatzer,* 559 U.S., at ___. For a person serving a term of incarceration, we reasoned in *Shatzer*, the ordinary restrictions of prison life, while no doubt unpleasant, are expected and familiar and thus do not involve the same "inherently compelling pressures" that are often present when a suspect is yanked from familiar surroundings in the outside world and subjected to interrogation in a police station. *Id.*, at ___.

Second, a prisoner, unlike a person who has not been sentenced to a term of incarceration, is unlikely to be lured into speaking by a longing for prompt release. When a person is arrested and taken to a station house for interrogation, the person who is questioned may be pressured to speak by the hope that, after doing so, he will be allowed to leave and go home. On the other hand, when a prisoner is questioned, he knows that when the questioning ceases, he will remain under confinement. *Id.*, at ___, n.8.

Third, a prisoner, unlike a person who has not been convicted and sentenced, knows that the law enforcement officers who question him probably lack the authority to affect the duration of his sentence. *Id.*, at ___–___. And "where the possibility of parole exists," the interrogating officers probably also lack the power to bring about an early release. *Ibid.* "When the suspect has no reason to think that the listeners have official power over him, it should not be assumed that his words are motivated by the reaction he expects from his listeners." *Perkins,* 496 U.S., at 297. Under such circumstances, there is little "basis for the assumption that a suspect . . . will feel compelled to speak by the fear of reprisal for remaining silent or in the hope of [a] more lenient treatment should he confess." *Id.*, at 296–297.

In short, standard conditions of confinement and associated restrictions on freedom will not necessarily implicate the same interests that the Court sought to protect when it afforded special safeguards to persons subjected to custodial interrogation. Thus, service of a term of imprisonment, without more, is not enough to constitute *Miranda* custody.

B

The two other elements included in the Court of Appeals' rule—questioning in private and questioning about events that took place outside the prison—are likewise insufficient.

Taking a prisoner aside for questioning—as opposed to questioning the prisoner in the presence of fellow inmates—does not necessarily convert a "noncustodial situation . . . to one in which *Miranda* applies." *Mathiason,* 429 U.S., at 495. When a person who is not serving a prison term is questioned, isolation may contribute to a coercive atmosphere by preventing family members, friends, and others who may be sympathetic from providing either advice or emotional support. And without any such assistance, the person who is questioned may feel overwhelming pressure to speak and to refrain from asking that the interview be terminated.

By contrast, questioning a prisoner in private does not generally remove the prisoner from a supportive atmosphere. Fellow inmates are by no means necessarily friends. On the contrary, they may be hostile and, for a variety of reasons, may react negatively to what the questioning reveals. In the present case, for example, would respondent have felt more at ease if he had been questioned in the presence of other inmates about the sexual abuse of an adolescent boy? Isolation from the general prison population is often in the best interest of the interviewee and, in any event, does not suggest on its own the atmosphere of coercion that concerned the Court in *Miranda.*

It is true that taking a prisoner aside for questioning may necessitate some additional limitations on his freedom of movement. A prisoner may, for example, be removed from an exercise yard and taken, under close guard, to the room where the interview is to be held. But such procedures are an ordinary and familiar attribute of life behind bars. Escorts and special security precautions may be standard procedures regardless of the purpose for which an inmate is removed from his regular routine and taken to a special location. For example, ordinary prison procedure may require such measures when a prisoner is led to a meeting with an attorney.

Finally, we fail to see why questioning about criminal activity outside the prison should be regarded as having a significantly greater potential for coercion than questioning under otherwise identical circumstances about criminal activity within the prison walls. In both instances, there is the potential for additional criminal liability and punishment. If anything, the distinction would seem to cut the other way, as an inmate who confesses to misconduct that occurred within the prison may also incur administrative penalties, but even this is not enough to tip the scale in the direction of custody. "The threat to a citizen's Fifth Amendment rights that *Miranda* was designed to neutralize" is neither mitigated nor magnified by the location of the conduct about which questions are asked. *Berkemer*, 468 U.S., at 435, n.22.

For these reasons, the Court of Appeals' categorical rule is unsound.

IV

A

When a prisoner is questioned, the determination of custody should focus on all of the features of the interrogation. These include the language that is used in summoning the prisoner to the interview and the manner in which the interrogation is conducted. *See Yarborough,* 541 U.S., at 665. An inmate who is removed from the general prison population for questioning and is "thereafter . . . subjected to treatment" in connection with the interrogation "that renders him 'in custody' for practical purposes . . . will be entitled to the full panoply of protections prescribed by *Miranda*." *Berkemer*, 468 U.S., at 440.

"Fidelity to the doctrine announced in *Miranda* requires that it be enforced strictly, but only in those types of situations in which the concerns that powered the decision are implicated." *id.,* at 437; *see Shatzer,* 559 U.S., at ___; *Mathiason, supra*, at 495. Confessions voluntarily made by prisoners in other situations should not be suppressed. "Voluntary confessions are not merely a proper element in law enforcement, they are an unmitigated good, essential to society's compelling interest in finding, convicting, and punishing those who violate the law." *Shatzer, supra*, at ___ (internal quotation marks and citations omitted).

B

The record in this case reveals that respondent was not taken into custody for purposes of *Miranda*. To be sure, respondent did not invite the interview or consent to it in advance, and he was not advised that he was free to decline to speak with the deputies. The following facts also lend some support to respondent's argument that *Miranda*'s custody requirement was met: The interview lasted for between five and seven hours in the evening and continued well past the hour when respondent generally went to bed; the deputies who questioned respondent were armed; and one of the deputies, according to respondent, "[u]sed a very sharp tone,", and, on one occasion, profanity.

These circumstances, however, were offset by others. Most important, respondent was told at the outset of the interrogation, and was reminded again thereafter, that he could leave and go back to his cell whenever he wanted. *See id.*, at 89a–90a ("I was told I could get up and leave whenever I wanted"); *id.*, at 70a–71a. Moreover, respondent was not physically restrained or threatened and was interviewed in a well-lit, average-sized conference room, where he was "not uncomfortable." *Id.*, at 90a; *see id.*, at 71a, 88a–89a. He was offered food and water, and the door to the conference room was sometimes left open. *See id.*, at 70a, 74a. "All of these objective facts are consistent with an interrogation environment in which a reasonable person would have felt free to terminate the interview and leave." *Yarborough, supra*, at 664–665.

Because he was in prison, respondent was not free to leave the conference room by himself and to make his own way through the facility to his cell. Instead, he was escorted to the conference room and, when he ultimately decided to end the interview, he had to wait about 20 minutes for a corrections officer to arrive and escort him to his cell. But he would have been subject to this same restraint even if he had been taken to the conference room for some reason other than police questioning; under no circumstances could he have reasonably expected to be able to roam free. And while respondent testified that he "was told . . . if I did not want to cooperate, I needed to go back to my cell," these words did not coerce cooperation by threatening harsher conditions. App. to Pet. for Cert. 71a; *see id.*, at 89a ("I was told, if I didn't want to cooperate, I could leave"). Returning to his cell would merely have returned him to his usual environment. *See Shatzer, supra*, at ___ ("Interrogated suspects who have previously been convicted of crime live in prison. When they are released back into the general prison population, they return to their accustomed surroundings and daily routine—they regain the degree of control they had over their lives prior to the interrogation").

Taking into account all of the circumstances of the questioning—including especially the undisputed fact that respondent was told that he was free to end the questioning and to return to his cell—we hold that respondent was not in custody within the meaning of *Miranda*.

* * *

The judgment of the Court of Appeals is

Reversed.

■ JUSTICE GINSBURG, with whom JUSTICE BREYER and JUSTICE SOTOMAYOR join, concurring in part and dissenting in part.

Given this Court's controlling decisions on what counts as "custody" for *Miranda* purposes, I agree that the law is not "clearly established" in respondent Fields's favor. See, e.g., Maryland v. Shatzer, 559 U.S. ___, ___ (2010); Thompson v. Keohane, 516 U.S. 99, 112 (1995). But I disagree with the Court's further determination that Fields was not in custody under *Miranda*. Were the case here on direct review, I would vote to hold that *Miranda* precludes the State's introduction of Fields's confession as evidence against him.

Miranda v. Arizona, 384 U.S. 436 (1966), reacted to police interrogation tactics that eroded the Fifth Amendment's ban on compulsory self-incrimination. The opinion did so by requiring interrogators to convey to suspects the now-familiar warnings: The suspect is to be informed, prior to interrogation, that he "has a right to remain silent, that any statement he does make may be used as evidence against him, and that he has a right to the presence of an attorney, either retained or appointed." *Id.*, at 444.

Under what circumstances are *Miranda* warnings required? *Miranda* tells us "in all settings in which [a person's] freedom of action is curtailed in any significant way." *Id.*, at 467. Given the reality that police interrogators "trad[e] on the weakness of individuals," *i.e.*, their "insecurity about [themselves] or [their] surroundings," *id.*, at 455, the Court found the preinterrogation warnings set out in the opinion "indispensable," *id.*, at 469. Those warnings, the Court elaborated, are "an absolute prerequisite in overcoming the inherent pressures of the interrogation atmosphere," *id.*, at 468; they "insure" that the suspect is timely told of his Fifth Amendment privilege, and his freedom to exercise it, *id.*, at 469.

Fields, serving time for disorderly conduct, was, of course, "i[n] custody," but not "for purposes of *Miranda*," the Court concludes. I would not train, as the Court does, on the question whether there can be custody within custody. Instead, I would ask, as *Miranda* put it, whether Fields was subjected to "incommunicado interrogation . . . in a police-dominated atmosphere," 384 U.S., at 445, whether he was placed, against his will, in an inherently stressful situation, *see id.*, at 468, and whether his "freedom of action [was] curtailed in any significant way," *id.*, at 467. Those should be the key questions, and to each I would answer "Yes."

As the Court acknowledges, Fields did not invite or consent to the interview. He was removed from his cell in the evening, taken to a conference room in the sheriff's quarters, and questioned by two armed deputies long into the night and early morning. *Ibid.* He was not told at the outset that he had the right to decline to speak with the deputies. *Ibid.* Shut in with the armed officers, Fields felt "trapped." App. to Pet. for Cert. 71a. Although told he could return to his cell if he did not want to cooperate, *id.*, at 71a–72a, Fields believed the deputies "would not have allowed [him] to leave the room," *id.*, at 72a. And with good reason. More than once, "he told the officers . . . he did not want to speak with them anymore." 617 F.3d 813, 815 (C.A.6 2010). He was given water, App. to Pet. for Cert. 74a, but not his evening medications, *id.*, at 79a.* Yet the Court concludes that Fields was in "an interrogation environment in which a reasonable person would have felt free to terminate the interview and leave." *Ante,* at 1193 (quoting Yarborough v. Alvarado, 541 U.S. 652, 665 (2004)).

Critical to the Court's judgment is "the undisputed fact that [Fields] was told that he was free to end the questioning and to return to his cell." Never mind the facts suggesting that Fields's submission to the overnight interview was anything but voluntary. Was Fields "held for interrogation"? *See Miranda,* 384 U.S., at 471. Brought to, and left alone with, the gun-bearing deputies, he surely was in my judgment.

Miranda instructed that such a person "must be clearly informed that he has the right to consult with a lawyer and to have the lawyer with him during interrogation." *Ibid.* Those warnings, along with "warnings of the right to remain silent and that anything stated can be used in evidence against [the speaker]," *Miranda* explained, are necessary "prerequisite[s] to [an] interrogation" compatible with the Fifth Amendment. *Ibid.* Today, for people already in prison, the Court finds it adequate for the police to say: "You are free to terminate this interrogation and return to your cell." Such a statement is no substitute for one ensuring that an individual is aware of his rights.

For the reasons stated, I would hold that the "incommunicado interrogation [of Fields] in a police-dominated atmosphere," *id.*, at 445, without informing him of his rights, dishonored the Fifth Amendment privilege *Miranda* was designed to safeguard.

b. "INTERROGATION"

United States v. Woods

711 F.3d 737 (6th Cir. 2013)

OPINION

■ RONALD LEE GILMAN, CIRCUIT JUDGE.

Jermaine Byron Woods entered a conditional guilty plea to the charges of possessing crack cocaine with the intent to distribute, in violation of 21 U.S.C. § 841(a)(1) and (b)(1)(B)(iii), and of possessing a firearm in furtherance of a drug-trafficking crime, in violation of 18 U.S.C. § 924(c)(1)(A). He was sentenced to 108 months in prison.

Woods contends on appeal that his initial incriminating statement, as well as the discovery of a gun and drugs in his car, were the products of a custodial interrogation conducted in violation of his Fifth Amendment rights as articulated in Miranda v. Arizona, 384 U.S. 436

---

* Each night, Fields took an antidepressant and, due to his kidney transplant surgery, two antirejection medications. App. to Pet. for Cert. 79a.

(1966). His conditional guilty plea preserved the right to appeal the district court's denial of his motion to suppress the statement and the physical evidence. We conclude that the arresting officer was not required to give Woods the *Miranda* warnings before asking "What is in your pocket?" upon encountering a hard lump in Woods's clothing during the course of a lawful patdown incident to the arrest. We therefore AFFIRM the judgment of the district court.

I.   BACKGROUND

Woods's conviction arose from circumstances surrounding a traffic stop on June 15, 2010. On that day, Officer Luke Mardigian saw a red Pontiac speeding along West Edgewood Boulevard in Lansing, Michigan. The officer did not catch up to the Pontiac in time to pull it over, but pursued the car to a nearby residential parking lot where it had just been parked. As the occupant (later identified as Woods) began exiting the car, Officer Mardigian turned on his cruiser's overhead light and ordered Woods to re-enter the Pontiac and place his hands on the steering wheel. Woods did not immediately comply; he would neither put his feet back into the car nor place his hands on the steering wheel, and he repeatedly reached down toward the passenger side of the car. Concerned that Woods might have a weapon inside, Officer Mardigian eventually drew his gun, which caused Woods to finally comply with the officer's demands. Officer Mardigian then lowered his weapon, approached the car, advised Woods that he had been caught speeding, and asked Woods for identification. Woods provided a false name and said that he did not have any identification. Officer Mardigian decided at that point to arrest Woods for the offense of driving without a license. But in light of Woods's noncompliant behavior, Officer Mardigian waited for backup before making the arrest.

Officer Brian Rasdale soon arrived on the scene to provide backup, and the two officers approached the driver's side of the car to arrest Woods. Woods reacted by taking his right hand off the steering wheel and again reached toward the passenger side of the car. At that point the officers grabbed Woods by the wrists and pulled him out of the vehicle. They ordered him to get on his knees and then on his abdomen, and when he lay face down on the ground they handcuffed him behind his back. Officer Mardigian began to pat Woods down once the officers returned him to a standing position. In the course of the patdown, Officer Mardigian felt a hard lump in one of Woods's pockets and asked him "What is in your pocket?". Woods responded that he was "bogue," which is a street term meaning "in possession of something illegal," as in weapons or narcotics. Officer Mardigian then sought to confirm that he had correctly heard the response, and Woods repeated "I'm bogue." At that point, Officer Mardigian, who was concerned that Woods might be carrying a gun, asked him whether the contraband was drugs or a gun. Woods responded that it was a gun. Officer Mardigian next asked whether the gun was on Woods's person or in his car, to which Woods responded that it was in the car. (The object in Woods's pocket turned out to be his keys.)

Woods was then subjected to a thorough in-custody search and placed in the back of Officer Mardigian's cruiser. After securing Woods in the cruiser, Officer Mardigian approached the Pontiac. Looking in through the passenger's side window, the officer observed what looked like a handgun lying on the floorboard. Officer Mardigian then searched the car and recovered the gun, as well as a plastic bag containing crack cocaine. At no point during the entire episode were the *Miranda* warnings administered.

Based on the evidence uncovered during the search, the government indicted Woods in November 2010 on three counts of drugs and firearm charges. Woods moved to suppress his incriminating "bogue" statement, the drugs, and the gun. At the conclusion of a hearing held in January 2011, the district court denied the motion from the bench. Woods pleaded guilty to the charges shortly thereafter, preserving his right to appeal the denial of his motion to suppress. He has now exercised that right.

II. ANALYSIS

In adjudicating an appeal from the denial of a motion to suppress, we review the district court's factual findings under the clear-error standard and its legal conclusions de novo. United States v. Rodriguez-Suazo, 346 F.3d 637, 643 (6th Cir.2003). We consider the evidence in the light most favorable to the government. *Id.*

Woods contends on appeal, as he did below, that his statement that he was "bogue" was the product of an unwarned custodial interrogation and therefore inadmissible under *Miranda*. He argues that the gun and the cocaine are also inadmissible because they were discovered pursuant to his inadmissible incriminating statement and are therefore "the fruits of a poisonous tree." Woods does not dispute the legality of his arrest or of the search incident to the arrest.

The district court rested its denial of Woods's motion to suppress on the twin rationales that the statement was obtained lawfully under Terry v. Ohio, 392 U.S. 1 (1968), and that the physical evidence was admissible under the plain-view doctrine. These rulings, however, conflate the applicable Fifth Amendment analysis with inapposite Fourth Amendment doctrine, and the government accordingly makes no effort to defend the district court's rationales on appeal. Instead, the government bases its contention that suppression was not warranted on four alternative grounds. They are, in order of analytical priority, that: (1) the officer's question "What is in your pocket?" did not amount to an "interrogation" at all, so the requirement of reciting the *Miranda* warnings was not triggered; (2) even if there was a custodial interrogation and *Miranda* was triggered, the failure to recite the *Miranda* warnings was justified due to a concern for the officer's safety; (3) even if *Miranda* was violated, the physical evidence should not be suppressed because the Fifth Amendment does not require the suppression of the physical, nontestimonial fruits of a *Miranda* violation; and (4) even if *Miranda* was violated, the physical evidence should not be suppressed because it would have been inevitably discovered even without the violation. Because we can resolve this case on the basis of the first issue, there is no occasion to address the other three.

The threshold issue is whether Woods was subjected to a custodial interrogation. In the absence of a custodial interrogation, the requirement to recite the *Miranda* warnings is not triggered and the analysis is at an end. See, e.g., *Miranda*, 384 U.S. at 444; Berkemer v. McCarty, 468 U.S. 420 (1984). The government concedes that Woods was in custody at the time Officer Mardigian asked him "What is in your pocket?". So the only remaining issue is whether that question amounted to an "interrogation" within the meaning of *Miranda* jurisprudence.

The Supreme Court has held that "the term 'interrogation' under *Miranda* refers not only to express questioning, but also to any words or actions on the part of the police (other than those normally attendant to arrest and custody) that the police should know are reasonably likely to elicit an incriminating response from the suspect." Rhode Island v. Innis, 446 U.S. 291, 301 (1980). We conclude that Officer Mardigian's question in the present case does not meet this definition because it was an inquiry "normally attendant to arrest and custody."

The question "What is in your pocket?" was not an investigatory question or otherwise calculated to elicit an incriminating response, but rather a natural and automatic response to the unfolding events during the normal course of an arrest. Officer Mardigian was lawfully patting down Woods and, while doing so, came across a hard object in Woods's pocket that he could not identify. He then asked Woods what the object was. To ask "What's that?" or "What is in your pocket?" in such a situation is essentially an automatic, reflexive question directed at ascertaining the identity of an object that is legitimately within the officer's power to examine as part of a search incident to an arrest, and as such is "normally attendant" to an arrest. It had nothing to do with an interrogation as that term is commonly understood.

The answer to Officer Mardigian's question could have been either innocuous or incriminating. If the answer were innocuous ("It's my keys."), then the probable effect of the question would have been to spare both Officer Mardigian and Woods the trouble of a physical search to verify the object's identity ("Oh, okay, that's what it feels like, so I'll ask you to remove the keys from your pocket."). And that is the likely response in the run of cases, which means that prohibiting the question would create an incentive for a more intrusive physical search. If, on the other hand, the response had revealed that the object was contraband, it would have revealed nothing more than what Officer Mardigian would have found anyway as a result of his undisputed right to search Woods incident to the arrest. To say that Officer Mardigian had the right to physically go through Woods's pockets but could not simply ask him "What is in your pocket?" would be illogical.

To be sure, there will be the unusual case, like this one, where the police ask "What is in your pocket?" and the suspect responds by divulging incriminating information that has nothing to do with the question asked. But such a response is not "reasonably likely." Woods was asked a simple, nontrick question about what turned out to be keys in his pocket. That he would respond by volunteering that he had a weapon in his car is no more reasonably likely than that he would reveal that he was a drug dealer or a convicted felon. The unexpected and unresponsive reply cannot retroactively turn a non-interrogation inquiry into an interrogation. *See Innis*, 446 U.S. at 301–02 ("[T]he police surely cannot be held accountable for the unforeseeable results of their words or actions. . . ."); *Miranda*, 384 U.S. at 478 ("Volunteered statements of any kind are not barred by the Fifth Amendment and their admissibility is not affected by our holding today."); *see also* Tolliver v. Sheets, 594 F.3d 900, 917–18 (6th Cir.2010) (holding that express questioning following up on volunteered information was not an interrogation even though the response turned out to be incriminating); United States v. Lawrence, 952 F.2d 1034, 1036 (8th Cir.1992) (holding that where the police officer "did not even mention a gun" and "merely asked a few routine identification questions necessary for booking purposes," but the arrestee "volunteered . . . that he had thrown away a gun while fleeing," the "statement about the gun did not come in response to interrogation" and was therefore admissible).

The fact that Officer Mardigian's question was not reasonably likely to elicit an incriminating response beyond what he was already entitled to know (i.e., what was the object in Woods's pocket) is also important because it clarifies that the question was not intended to obtain incriminating information. Under *Innis,* the officer's intent is not dispositive in determining whether certain conduct amounts to custodial interrogation. *See* 446 U.S. at 301. But "[t]his is not to say that the intent of the police is irrelevant, for it may well have a bearing on whether the police should have known that their words or actions were reasonably likely to evoke an incriminating response." *Id.* at 301 n.7. Indeed, the Supreme Court has found that certain conduct did not amount to interrogation partly on the basis that it was not designed or intended to elicit incriminating information. *See id.* at 303 n.9 (noting that "[t]he record in no way suggests that the officers' remarks were designed to elicit a response" (emphasis in original) and finding that "[i]t is significant that the trial judge, after hearing the officers' testimony, concluded that [the officers' remark] was 'entirely understandable.' "); Arizona v. Mauro, 481 U.S. 520, 528 (1987) (holding that the police department's allowing the suspect to speak to his wife in the presence of a police officer with a tape recorder did not amount to an interrogation, in part because "[t]here is no evidence that the officers sent Mrs. Mauro in to see her husband for the purpose of eliciting incriminating statements"). In the present case, the fact that the question "What is in your pocket?" was not intended to elicit incriminating information strengthens the inference that the question was normally attendant to Woods's arrest and therefore did not constitute custodial interrogation.

We believe that our analysis is also consistent with common sense. If we were to hold that the question "What is in your pocket?" amounted to an interrogation such as to require *Miranda* warnings, we would be saying, in effect, that the police were acting lawfully when they drew a gun on Woods, dragged him out of his car by the wrists, ordered him to the ground, cuffed his hands behind his back, and patted him down; but the moment that they asked "What is in your pocket?", they went beyond the bounds of constitutionally permissible action. The Fifth Amendment does not require such an impractical regime of stilted logic.

Woods, however, resists the conclusion that Officer Mardigian's question did not amount to an interrogation, insisting that the Supreme Court's definition of interrogation is any "questioning initiated by law enforcement officers." *Miranda*, 384 U.S. at 444. According to Woods's Brief,

> [t]he recognized exception [to the definition of interrogation] for statements or conduct that are "normally attendant to arrest and custody" [quoting Innis, 446 U.S. at 301] applies not to express questioning as occurred here, but only to the expanded category of the 'functional equivalent of express questioning.' . . . We have found no case, and the government cites none, in which that language is used to exempt express questions.

To the contrary, we have found several post-Innis Supreme Court decisions holding that, under the circumstances, law enforcement's express questioning of a person in custody did not amount to an interrogation. One such case is South Dakota v. Neville, 459 U.S. 553 (1983), where the Supreme Court held:

> In the context of an arrest for driving while intoxicated, a police inquiry of whether the suspect will take a blood-alcohol test is not an interrogation within the meaning of *Miranda*. As we stated in Rhode Island v. Innis, 446 U.S. 291, 301 (1980), police words or actions "normally attendant to arrest and custody" do not constitute interrogation.

Id. at 564 n. 15.

Likewise, in Illinois v. Perkins, 496 U.S. 292 (1990), the Court held that an undercover police officer's questioning of a prison inmate did not constitute an interrogation:

> The state court here mistakenly assumed that because the suspect was in custody, no undercover questioning could take place. When the suspect has no reason to think that the listeners have official power over him, it should not be assumed that his

words are motivated by the reaction he expects from his listeners. When the agent carries neither badge nor gun and wears not police blue, but the same prison gray as the suspect, there is no interplay between police interrogation and police custody.

Id. at 297 (emphasis in original) (brackets and internal quotation marks omitted).

Finally, in Pennsylvania v. Muniz, 496 U.S. 582 (1990), the Court held that the defendant's incriminating statements in response to the police officer's question as to whether the defendant understood the instructions for certain sobriety tests was not the product of custodial interrogation:

The dialogue also contained limited and carefully worded inquiries as to whether Muniz understood those instructions, but these focused inquiries were necessarily "attendant to" [quoting *Innis,* 446 U.S. at 301] the police procedure held by the court to be legitimate. Hence, Muniz's incriminating utterances during this phase of the videotaped proceedings were "voluntary" in the sense that they were not elicited in response to custodial interrogation.

Id. at 603–04. The *Muniz* Court also concluded that the defendant's responses to the officer's question as to whether he understood the nature of a breathalyzer test and its legal consequences, and whether he was willing to submit to the test, "were not prompted by an interrogation within the meaning of *Miranda.*" *Id.* at 604–05.

In each of the above cases, the Supreme Court held that the express questioning of a suspect in custody did not amount to an interrogation. And in *Neville* and *Muniz,* the Court specifically relied on *Innis*'s definitional exclusion of conduct "normally attendant to arrest and custody." Woods's argument that any express questioning of a suspect in custody amounts to an interrogation, and that the "normally attendant" exclusion does not apply to express questions, is therefore conclusively refuted by the Court's caselaw.

Nor is there any reason to believe that the exclusion of certain express questions from the definition of interrogation is limited to the particular factual circumstances of *Neville, Perkins,* and *Muniz.* Suppose, for example, that an officer sees that the handcuffed suspect is grimacing in pain and asks "Are you okay?", to which the suspect responds "I killed her." Such a response—which, just like the response in the present case, would be an unexpected and unresponsive answer to the question posed—would not be the product of custodial interrogation and would therefore be admissible. *Cf.* Harryman v. Estelle, 616 F.2d 870, 879 (5th Cir.1980) (en banc) (Hill, J., concurring) ("Thus, if an officer responds to a loud noise by saying 'What's that?', I suggest that an answer such as 'I dropped my pistol' would be admissible in a prosecution for unlawful possession of a firearm."); *id.* at 880 (Reavley, J., concurring) (suggesting that questions such as "Can you hear me?", "What is the matter?", or "Where are your glasses?" do not amount to custodial interrogation).

Indeed, Woods's fixation on whether Officer Mardigian's statement was an express question is misdirected because it elevates form over substance in precisely the way that the Supreme Court cautioned against in *Innis.* In holding that a custodial interrogation may result from statements or conduct other than express questioning, the Court reasoned that "[t]o limit the ambit of *Miranda* to express questioning would place a premium on the ingenuity of the police to devise methods of indirect interrogation, rather than to implement the plain mandate of *Miranda." Innis,* 446 U.S. at 299 n.3. So the test is not whether the alleged interrogation is phrased in the form of a question or a declarative sentence, but whether the conduct implicates the concerns with police "compulsion" and "coercion" that animated the *Miranda* decision. *Id.* at 299–301. The proper implementation of *Innis, Mauro, Neville, Perkins,* and *Muniz* thus requires us to determine whether the words or actions on the part of the police are those normally attendant to arrest and custody, and whether they give rise to the concerns about police coercion that animated the *Miranda* decision. It does not require us to attach talismanic importance to whether the words are punctuated by a question mark.

In short, we hold that, under the circumstances of the present case, the question "What is in your pocket?" did not amount to a custodial interrogation. Officer Mardigian was therefore not required to recite the *Miranda* warnings prior to posing that question. And because we hold that Officer Mardigian's initial question did not constitute a custodial interrogation and that Woods's response that he was "bogue" was admissible, we need not decide whether the officer's subsequent questions—as to whether the contraband was drugs or a gun and whether it was on Woods's person or in his car—constituted a custodial interrogation. Those subsequent questions do not affect the outcome of this case because, following Woods's volunteered statement that he was in possession of contraband, the car would have inevitably been searched and the evidence would have come to light even in the absence of any further questioning. *See, e.g.,* United States v. Alexander, 540 F.3d 494, 504 (6th Cir.2008) (holding that the evidence in question was admissible despite the failure to provide *Miranda* warnings because it would have been inevitably discovered even in the absence of the defendant's confession).

III. CONCLUSION

For all of the reasons set forth above, we AFFIRM the judgment of the district court.

■ CLAY, CIRCUIT JUDGE, concurring.

The majority rejects Defendant's *Miranda* argument because it finds that the question asked by the police officer, "What is in your pocket?" constituted a proper inquiry incident to an arrest, and did not constitute custodial interrogation for *Miranda* purposes. Although I agree with the majority's reasoning, I believe that the court below could have upheld the lawfulness of the search based upon either the majority's rationale, or because the officer's inquiry was appropriate based upon the need to insure the officer's safety.

"[W]hen officers ask questions 'necessary to secure their own safety or the safety of the public' as opposed to 'questions designed solely to elicit testimonial evidence from a suspect,' they do not need to provide the warnings required by *Miranda*." United States v. Williams, 483 F.3d 425, 428 (6th Cir.2007) (quoting New York v. Quarles, 467 U.S. 649, 659 (1984)). This Court and seven of our sister circuits have already found that similar questions, in anticipation of a pat down, are permissible under the public-safety exception where the officer has a reasonable belief that there may be a weapon on the defendant's person. *See* United States v. Reyes, 353 F.3d 148, 152–53 (2d Cir.2003) (collecting cases); *see also, e.g.,* United States v. Mohammed, No. 10–4145, 501 Fed.Appx. 431, 443–44, 2012 WL 4465626, at *12 (6th Cir. Sept. 28, 2012) (unpublished) (applying exception where the handcuffed defendant was asked whether he had any weapons, drugs, or sharp objects on him); United States v. Lackey, 334 F.3d 1224, 1227–28 (10th Cir.2003) (applying exception where the handcuffed defendant was asked, "Do you have any guns or sharp objects on you?"). Similarly, the officer's question in this case was proper because the question is excepted from *Miranda*'s requirements due to public safety concerns. *See Quarles*, 467 U.S. at 659.

Both the non-coercive nature of the question asked, incident to the arrest, and the need for officer safety, support the conclusion that suppression based on *Miranda* was not warranted in this case.

6. *MIRANDA* DOCTRINE, SECOND LEVEL: "WAIVER," "INVOCATION," "COUNSEL," "SILENCE," AND "INITIATION"

Berghuis v. Thompkins
560 U.S. 370 (2010)

■ JUSTICE KENNEDY delivered the opinion of the Court.

The United States Court of Appeals for the Sixth Circuit, in a habeas corpus proceeding challenging a Michigan conviction for first-degree murder and certain other offenses, ruled that there had been two separate constitutional errors in the trial that led to the jury's guilty verdict. First, the Court of Appeals determined that a statement by the accused, relied on at trial by the prosecution, had been elicited in violation of Miranda v. Arizona, 384 U.S. 436 (1966). Second, it found that failure to ask for an instruction relating to testimony from an accomplice was ineffective assistance by defense counsel. *See* Strickland v. Washington, 466 U.S. 668 (1984). Both of these contentions had been rejected in Michigan courts and in the habeas corpus proceedings before the United States District Court. Certiorari was granted to review the decision by the Court of Appeals on both points. The warden of a Michigan correctional facility is the petitioner here, and Van Chester Thompkins, who was convicted, is the respondent.

I

A

On January 10, 2000, a shooting occurred outside a mall in Southfield, Michigan. Among the victims was Samuel Morris, who died from multiple gunshot wounds. The other victim, Frederick France, recovered from his injuries and later testified. Thompkins, who was a suspect, fled. About one year later he was found in Ohio and arrested there.

Two Southfield police officers traveled to Ohio to interrogate Thompkins, then awaiting transfer to Michigan. The interrogation began around 1:30 p.m. and lasted about three hours. The interrogation was conducted in a room that was 8 by 10 feet, and Thompkins sat in a chair that resembled a school desk (it had an arm on it that swings around to provide a surface to write on). App. 144a–145a. At the beginning of the interrogation, one of the officers, Detective Helgert, presented Thompkins with a form derived from the *Miranda* rule. It stated:

"NOTIFICATION OF CONSTITUTIONAL RIGHTS AND STATEMENT

"1. You have the right to remain silent.

"2. Anything you say can and will be used against you in a court of law.

"3. You have a right to talk to a lawyer before answering any questions and you have the right to have a lawyer present with you while you are answering any questions.

"4. If you cannot afford to hire a lawyer, one will be appointed to represent you before any questioning, if you wish one.

"5. You have the right to decide at any time before or during questioning to use your right to remain silent and your right to talk with a lawyer while you are being questioned." Brief for Petitioner 60 (some capitalization omitted).

Helgert asked Thompkins to read the fifth warning out loud. App. 8a. Thompkins complied. Helgert later said this was to ensure that Thompkins could read, and Helgert concluded that Thompkins understood English. *Id.*, at 9a. Helgert then read the other four *Miranda* warnings out loud and asked Thompkins to sign the form to demonstrate that he understood his rights. App. 8a–9a. Thompkins declined to sign the form. The record contains conflicting evidence about whether Thompkins then verbally confirmed that he understood the rights listed on the form. Compare *id.*, at 9a (at a suppression hearing, Helgert testified that Thompkins verbally confirmed that he understood his rights), with *id.*, at 148a (at trial, Helgert stated, "I don't know that I orally asked him" whether Thompkins understood his rights).

Officers began an interrogation. At no point during the interrogation did Thompkins say that he wanted to remain silent, that he did not want to talk with the police, or that he wanted an attorney. *Id.*, at 10a. Thompkins was "[l]argely" silent during the interrogation, which lasted about three hours. *Id.*, at 19a. He did give a few limited verbal responses, however, such as "yeah," "no," or "I don't know." And on occasion he communicated by nodding his head. *Id.*, at 23a. Thompkins also said that he "didn't want a peppermint" that was offered to him by the police and that the chair he was "sitting in was hard." *Id.*, at 152a.

About 2 hours and 45 minutes into the interrogation, Helgert asked Thompkins, "Do you believe in God?" *Id.*, at 11a, 153a. Thompkins made eye contact with Helgert and said "Yes," as his eyes "well[ed] up with tears." *Id.*, at 11a. Helgert asked, "Do you pray to God?" Thompkins said "Yes." *Id.*, at 11a, 153a. Helgert asked, "Do you pray to God to forgive you for shooting that boy down?" *Id.*, at 153a. Thompkins answered "Yes" and looked away. *Ibid.* Thompkins refused to make a written confession, and the interrogation ended about 15 minutes later. *Id.*, at 11a.

Thompkins was charged with first-degree murder, assault with intent to commit murder, and certain firearms-related offenses. He moved to suppress the statements made during the interrogation. He argued that he had invoked his Fifth Amendment right to remain silent, requiring police to end the interrogation at once, *See* Michigan v. Mosley, 423 U.S. 96, 103 (1975) (citing *Miranda*, 384 U.S., at 474), that he had not waived his right to remain silent, and that his inculpatory statements were involuntary. The trial court denied the motion.

At trial, the prosecution's theory was that Thompkins shot the victims from the passenger seat of a van driven by Eric Purifoy. Purifoy testified that he had been driving the van and that Thompkins was in the passenger seat while another man, one Myzell Woodward, was in the back. The defense strategy was to pin the blame on Purifoy. Purifoy testified he did not see who fired the weapon because the van was stopped and he was bending over near the floor when shots were fired. Purifoy explained that, just after the shooting, Thompkins, holding a pistol, told Purifoy, "What the hell you doing? Pull off." Purifoy then drove away from the scene. App. 170a.

So that the Thompkins jury could assess Purifoy's credibility and knowledge, the prosecution elicited testimony from Purifoy that he had been tried earlier for the shooting under an aiding-and-abetting theory. Purifoy and Detective Helgert testified that a jury acquitted him of the murder and assault charges, convicted him of carrying a concealed weapon in a motor vehicle, and hung on two other firearms offenses to which he later pleaded guilty. At Purifoy's trial, the prosecution had argued that Purifoy was the driver and Thompkins was the shooter. This was consistent with the prosecution's argument at Thompkins's trial.

After Purifoy's trial had ended—but before Thompkins's trial began—Purifoy sent Thompkins some letters. The letters expressed Purifoy's disappointment that Thompkins's family thought Purifoy was a "snitch" and a "rat." *Id.*, at 179a–180a. In one letter Purifoy offered to send a copy of his trial transcript to Thompkins as proof that Purifoy did not place the blame on Thompkins for the shooting. *Id.*, at 180a. The letters also contained statements by Purifoy that claimed they were both innocent. *Id.*, at 178a–179a. At Thompkins's trial, the prosecution suggested that one of Purifoy's letters appeared to give Thompkins a trial strategy. It was, the prosecution suggested, that Woodward shot the victims, allowing Purifoy and Thompkins to say they dropped to the floor when the shooting started. *Id.*, at 187a–189a.

During closing arguments, the prosecution suggested that Purifoy lied when he testified that he did not see Thompkins shoot the victims:

> "Did Eric Purifoy's Jury make the right decision? I'm not here to judge that. You are not bound by what his Jury found. Take his testimony for what it was, [a] twisted attempt to help not just an acquaintance but his tight buddy." *Id.*, at 202a.

Defense counsel did not object. Defense counsel also did not ask for an instruction informing the jury that it could consider evidence of the outcome of Purifoy's trial only to assess Purifoy's credibility, not to establish Thompkins's guilt.

The jury found Thompkins guilty on all counts. He was sentenced to life in prison without parole.

B

The trial court denied a motion for new trial filed by Thompkins's appellate counsel. The trial court rejected the claim of ineffective assistance of trial counsel for failure to ask for a limiting instruction regarding the outcome of Purifoy's trial, reasoning that this did not prejudice Thompkins. *Id.*, at 236a.

Thompkins appealed this ruling, along with the trial court's refusal to suppress his pretrial statements under *Miranda*. The Michigan Court of Appeals rejected the *Miranda* claim, ruling that Thompkins had not invoked his right to remain silent and had waived it. It also rejected the ineffective-assistance-of-counsel claim, finding that Thompkins failed to show that evidence of Purifoy's conviction for firearms offenses resulted in prejudice. App. to Pet. for Cert. 74a–82a. The Michigan Supreme Court denied discretionary review. 471 Mich. 866, 683 N.W.2d 676 (2004) (table).

Thompkins filed a petition for a writ of habeas corpus in the United States District Court for the Eastern District of Michigan. The District Court rejected Thompkins's *Miranda* and ineffective-assistance claims. App. to Pet. for Cert. 39a–72a. It noted that, under the Antiterrorism and Effective Death Penalty Act of 1996 (AEDPA), a federal court cannot grant a petition for a writ of habeas corpus unless the state court's adjudication of the merits was "contrary to, or involved an unreasonable application of, clearly established Federal law." 28 U.S.C. § 2254(d)(1). The District Court reasoned that Thompkins did not invoke his right to remain silent and was not coerced into making statements during the interrogation. It held further that the Michigan Court of Appeals was not unreasonable in determining that Thompkins had waived his right to remain silent.

The United States Court of Appeals for the Sixth Circuit reversed, ruling for Thompkins on both his *Miranda* and ineffective-assistance-of-counsel claims. 547 F.3d 572 (2008). The Court of Appeals ruled that the state court, in rejecting Thompkins's *Miranda* claim, unreasonably applied clearly established federal law and based its decision on an unreasonable determination of the facts. *See* 28 U.S.C. § 2254(d). The Court of Appeals acknowledged that a waiver of the right to remain silent need not be express, as it can be " 'inferred from the actions and words of the person interrogated.' " 547 F.3d, at 582 (quoting North Carolina v. Butler, 441 U.S. 369, 373 (1979)). The panel held, nevertheless, that the state court was unreasonable in finding an implied waiver in the circumstances here. The Court of Appeals found that the state court unreasonably determined the facts because "the evidence demonstrates that Thompkins was silent for two hours and forty-five minutes." 547 F.3d, at 586. According to the Court of Appeals, Thompkins's "persistent silence for nearly three hours in response to questioning and repeated invitations to tell his side of the story offered a clear and unequivocal message to the officers: Thompkins did not wish to waive his rights." *Id.*, at 588.

The Court of Appeals next determined that the state court unreasonably applied clearly established federal law by rejecting Thompkins's ineffective-assistance-of-counsel claim based on counsel's failure to ask for a limiting instruction regarding Purifoy's acquittal. The Court of Appeals asserted that because Thompkins's central strategy was to pin the blame on Purifoy, there was a reasonable probability that the result of Thompkins's trial would have been different if there had been a limiting instruction regarding Purifoy's acquittal.

We granted certiorari.

II

Under AEDPA, a federal court may not grant a habeas corpus application "with respect to any claim that was adjudicated on the merits in State court proceedings," 28 U.S.C. § 2254(d), unless the state court's decision "was contrary to, or involved an unreasonable application of,

clearly established Federal law, as determined by the Supreme Court of
the United States," § 2254(d)(1), or "was based on an unreasonable
determination of the facts in light of the evidence presented in the State
court proceeding," § 2254(d)(2). *See* Knowles v. Mirzayance, 556 U.S. 111
(2009). The relevant state-court decision here is the Michigan Court of
Appeals' decision affirming Thompkins's conviction and rejecting his
Miranda and ineffective-assistance-of-counsel claims on the merits.

III

The *Miranda* Court formulated a warning that must be given to
suspects before they can be subjected to custodial interrogation. The
substance of the warning still must be given to suspects today. A suspect
in custody must be advised as follows:

> "He must be warned prior to any questioning that he has the
> right to remain silent, that anything he says can be used against
> him in a court of law, that he has the right to the presence of an
> attorney, and that if he cannot afford an attorney one will be
> appointed for him prior to any questioning if he so desires." 384
> U.S., at 479.

All concede that the warning given in this case was in full compliance
with these requirements.

The dispute centers on the response—or nonresponse—from the
suspect.

A

Thompkins makes various arguments that his answers to questions
from the detectives were inadmissible. He first contends that he
"invoke[d] his privilege" to remain silent by not saying anything for a
sufficient period of time, so the interrogation should have "cease[d]"
before he made his inculpatory statements. *Id.*, at 474; *see Mosley,* 423
U.S., at 103 (police must " 'scrupulously hono[r]' " this "critical
safeguard" when the accused invokes his or her " 'right to cut off
questioning' " (quoting *Miranda, supra,* at 474, 479)).

This argument is unpersuasive. In the context of invoking the
Miranda right to counsel, the Court in Davis v. United States, 512 U.S.
452, 459 (1994), held that a suspect must do so "unambiguously." If an
accused makes a statement concerning the right to counsel "that is
ambiguous or equivocal" or makes no statement, the police are not
required to end the interrogation, *ibid.*, or ask questions to clarify
whether the accused wants to invoke his or her *Miranda* rights, 512 U.S.,
at 461–462.

The Court has not yet stated whether an invocation of the right to
remain silent can be ambiguous or equivocal, but there is no principled
reason to adopt different standards for determining when an accused has
invoked the *Miranda* right to remain silent and the *Miranda* right to
counsel at issue in *Davis. See, e.g.,* Solem v. Stumes, 465 U.S. 638, 648

(1984) ("[M]uch of the logic and language of [*Mosley*]," which discussed the *Miranda* right to remain silent, "could be applied to the invocation of the [*Miranda* right to counsel]"). Both protect the privilege against compulsory self-incrimination, *Miranda, supra,* at 467–473 by requiring an interrogation to cease when either right is invoked, *Mosley, supra,* at 103 (citing *Miranda, supra,* at 474,); Fare v. Michael C., 442 U.S. 707, 719 (1979).

There is good reason to require an accused who wants to invoke his or her right to remain silent to do so unambiguously. A requirement of an unambiguous invocation of *Miranda* rights results in an objective inquiry that "avoid[s] difficulties of proof and . . . provide[s] guidance to officers" on how to proceed in the face of ambiguity. *Davis,* 512 U.S., at 458–459. If an ambiguous act, omission, or statement could require police to end the interrogation, police would be required to make difficult decisions about an accused's unclear intent and face the consequence of suppression "if they guess wrong." *Id.,* at 461. Suppression of a voluntary confession in these circumstances would place a significant burden on society's interest in prosecuting criminal activity. *See id.,* at 459–461; Moran v. Burbine, 475 U.S. 412, 427 (1986). Treating an ambiguous or equivocal act, omission, or statement as an invocation of *Miranda* rights "might add marginally to *Miranda's* goal of dispelling the compulsion inherent in custodial interrogation." *Burbine,* 475 U.S., at 425. But "as *Miranda* holds, full comprehension of the rights to remain silent and request an attorney are sufficient to dispel whatever coercion is inherent in the interrogation process." *Id.,* at 427; *see Davis, supra,* at 460.

Thompkins did not say that he wanted to remain silent or that he did not want to talk with the police. Had he made either of these simple, unambiguous statements, he would have invoked his " 'right to cut off questioning.' " *Mosley, supra,* at 103 (quoting *Miranda, supra,* at 474). Here he did neither, so he did not invoke his right to remain silent.

B

We next consider whether Thompkins waived his right to remain silent. Even absent the accused's invocation of the right to remain silent, the accused's statement during a custodial interrogation is inadmissible at trial unless the prosecution can establish that the accused "in fact knowingly and voluntarily waived [*Miranda*] rights" when making the statement. *Butler,* 441 U.S., at 373. The waiver inquiry "has two distinct dimensions": waiver must be "voluntary in the sense that it was the product of a free and deliberate choice rather than intimidation, coercion, or deception," and "made with a full awareness of both the nature of the right being abandoned and the consequences of the decision to abandon it." Burbine, *supra,* at 421.

Some language in *Miranda* could be read to indicate that waivers are difficult to establish absent an explicit written waiver or a formal, express oral statement. *Miranda* said "a valid waiver will not be presumed simply from the silence of the accused after warnings are given or simply from the fact that a confession was in fact eventually obtained." 384 U.S., at 475; *see id.*, at 470 ("No effective waiver . . . can be recognized unless specifically made after the [*Miranda*] warnings . . . have been given"). In addition, the *Miranda* Court stated that "a heavy burden rests on the government to demonstrate that the defendant knowingly and intelligently waived his privilege against self-incrimination and his right to retained or appointed counsel." *Id.*, at.

The course of decisions since *Miranda*, informed by the application of *Miranda* warnings in the whole course of law enforcement, demonstrates that waivers can be established even absent formal or express statements of waiver that would be expected in, say, a judicial hearing to determine if a guilty plea has been properly entered. *Cf.* Fed. Rule Crim. Proc. 11. The main purpose of *Miranda* is to ensure that an accused is advised of and understands the right to remain silent and the right to counsel. *See Davis, supra*, at 460; *Burbine, supra*, at 427. Thus, "[i]f anything, our subsequent cases have reduced the impact of the *Miranda* rule on legitimate law enforcement while reaffirming the decision's core ruling that unwarned statements may not be used as evidence in the prosecution's case in chief." Dickerson v. United States, 530 U.S. 428, 443–444 (2000).

One of the first cases to decide the meaning and import of *Miranda* with respect to the question of waiver was *North Carolina v. Butler*. The *Butler* Court, after discussing some of the problems created by the language in *Miranda*, established certain important propositions. *Butler* interpreted the *Miranda* language concerning the "heavy burden" to show waiver, 384 U.S., at 475, in accord with usual principles of determining waiver, which can include waiver implied from all the circumstances. *See Butler, supra*, at 373. And in a later case, the Court stated that this "heavy burden" is not more than the burden to establish waiver by a preponderance of the evidence. Colorado v. Connelly, 479 U.S. 157, 168 (1986).

The prosecution therefore does not need to show that a waiver of *Miranda* rights was express. An "implicit waiver" of the "right to remain silent" is sufficient to admit a suspect's statement into evidence. *Butler, supra*, at 376. *Butler* made clear that a waiver of *Miranda* rights may be implied through "the defendant's silence, coupled with an understanding of his rights and a course of conduct indicating waiver." 441 U.S., at 373. The Court in *Butler* therefore "retreated" from the "language and tenor of the *Miranda* opinion," which "suggested that the Court would require that a waiver . . . be 'specifically made.' " Connecticut v. Barrett, 479 U.S. 523, 531–532 (1987) (Brennan, J., concurring in judgment).

If the State establishes that a *Miranda* warning was given and the accused made an uncoerced statement, this showing, standing alone, is insufficient to demonstrate "a valid waiver" of *Miranda* rights. *Miranda, supra*, at 475. The prosecution must make the additional showing that the accused understood these rights. *See* Colorado v. Spring, 479 U.S.

564, 573–575 (1987); *Barrett, supra*, at 530; *Burbine, supra*, at 421–422. *Cf.* Tague v. Louisiana, 444 U.S. 469, 469, 471 (1980) (per curiam) (no evidence that accused understood his *Miranda* rights); Carnley v. Cochran, 369 U.S. 506, 516 (1962) (government could not show that accused "understandingly" waived his right to counsel in light of "silent record"). Where the prosecution shows that a *Miranda* warning was given and that it was understood by the accused, an accused's uncoerced statement establishes an implied waiver of the right to remain silent.

Although *Miranda* imposes on the police a rule that is both formalistic and practical when it prevents them from interrogating suspects without first providing them with a *Miranda* warning, *see Burbine*, 475 U.S., at 427, it does not impose a formalistic waiver procedure that a suspect must follow to relinquish those rights. As a general proposition, the law can presume that an individual who, with a full understanding of his or her rights, acts in a manner inconsistent with their exercise has made a deliberate choice to relinquish the protection those rights afford. *See, e.g., Butler, supra*, at 372–376; *Connelly, supra*, at 169–170 ("There is obviously no reason to require more in the way of a 'voluntariness' inquiry in the *Miranda* waiver context than in the [due process] confession context"). The Court's cases have recognized that a waiver of *Miranda* rights need only meet the standard of Johnson v. Zerbst, 304 U.S. 458, 464 (1938). *See Butler, supra*, at 374–375; *Miranda, supra*, at 475–476 (applying *Zerbst* standard of intentional relinquishment of a known right). As *Butler* recognized, 441 U.S., at 375–376, *Miranda* rights can therefore be waived through means less formal than a typical waiver on the record in a courtroom, cf. Fed. Rule Crim. Proc. 11, given the practical constraints and necessities of interrogation and the fact that *Miranda*'s main protection lies in advising defendants of their rights, *see Davis*, 512 U.S., at 460; *Burbine*, 475 U.S., at 427.

The record in this case shows that Thompkins waived his right to remain silent. There is no basis in this case to conclude that he did not understand his rights; and on these facts it follows that he chose not to invoke or rely on those rights when he did speak. First, there is no contention that Thompkins did not understand his rights; and from this it follows that he knew what he gave up when he spoke. *See id.*, at 421. There was more than enough evidence in the record to conclude that Thompkins understood his *Miranda* rights. Thompkins received a written copy of the *Miranda* warnings; Detective Helgert determined that Thompkins could read and understand English; and Thompkins was given time to read the warnings. Thompkins, furthermore, read aloud the fifth warning, which stated that "you have the right to decide at any time before or during questioning to use your right to remain silent and your right to talk with a lawyer while you are being questioned." Brief for Petitioner 60 (capitalization omitted). He was thus aware that his right to remain silent would not dissipate after a certain amount of time and that police would have to honor his right to be silent and his right to counsel during the whole course of interrogation. Those rights, the warning made clear, could be asserted at any time. Helgert, moreover, read the warnings aloud.

Second, Thompkins's answer to Detective Helgert's question about whether Thompkins prayed to God for forgiveness for shooting the victim is a "course of conduct indicating waiver" of the right to remain silent. *Butler, supra,* at 373. If Thompkins wanted to remain silent, he could have said nothing in response to Helgert's questions, or he could have unambiguously invoked his *Miranda* rights and ended the interrogation. The fact that Thompkins made a statement about three hours after receiving a *Miranda* warning does not overcome the fact that he engaged in a course of conduct indicating waiver. Police are not required to rewarn suspects from time to time. Thompkins's answer to Helgert's question about praying to God for forgiveness for shooting the victim was sufficient to show a course of conduct indicating waiver. This is confirmed by the fact that before then Thompkins had given sporadic answers to questions throughout the interrogation.

Third, there is no evidence that Thompkins's statement was coerced. *See Burbine, supra,* at 421. Thompkins does not claim that police threatened or injured him during the interrogation or that he was in any way fearful. The interrogation was conducted in a standard-sized room in the middle of the afternoon. It is true that apparently he was in a straight-backed chair for three hours, but there is no authority for the proposition that an interrogation of this length is inherently coercive. Indeed, even where interrogations of greater duration were held to be improper, they were accompanied, as this one was not, by other facts indicating coercion, such as an incapacitated and sedated suspect, sleep and food deprivation, and threats. Cf. *Connelly,* 479 U.S., at 163–164, n.1. The fact that Helgert's question referred to Thompkins's religious beliefs also did not render Thompkins's statement involuntary. "[T]he Fifth Amendment privilege is not concerned 'with moral and psychological pressures to confess emanating from sources other than official coercion.'" *Id.,* at 170 (quoting Oregon v. Elstad, 470 U.S. 298, 305 (1985)). In these circumstances, Thompkins knowingly and voluntarily made a statement to police, so he waived his right to remain silent.

C

Thompkins next argues that, even if his answer to Detective Helgert could constitute a waiver of his right to remain silent, the police were not allowed to question him until they obtained a waiver first. *Butler* forecloses this argument. The *Butler* Court held that courts can infer a waiver of *Miranda* rights "from the actions and words of the person interrogated." 441 U.S., at 373. This principle would be inconsistent with a rule that requires a waiver at the outset. The *Butler* Court thus rejected the rule proposed by the *Butler* dissent, which would have "requir[ed] the police to obtain an express waiver of [*Miranda* rights] before proceeding with interrogation." *Id.*, at 379 (Brennan, J., dissenting). This holding also makes sense given that "the primary protection afforded suspects subject[ed] to custodial interrogation is the *Miranda* warnings themselves." *Davis*, 512 U.S., at 460. The *Miranda* rule and its requirements are met if a suspect receives adequate *Miranda* warnings, understands them, and has an opportunity to invoke the rights before giving any answers or admissions. Any waiver, express or implied, may be contradicted by an invocation at any time. If the right to counsel or the right to remain silent is invoked at any point during questioning, further interrogation must cease.

Interrogation provides the suspect with additional information that can put his or her decision to waive, or not to invoke, into perspective. As questioning commences and then continues, the suspect has the opportunity to consider the choices he or she faces and to make a more informed decision, either to insist on silence or to cooperate. When the suspect knows that *Miranda* rights can be invoked at any time, he or she has the opportunity to reassess his or her immediate and long-term interests. Cooperation with the police may result in more favorable treatment for the suspect; the apprehension of accomplices; the prevention of continuing injury and fear; beginning steps towards relief or solace for the victims; and the beginning of the suspect's own return to the law and the social order it seeks to protect.

In order for an accused's statement to be admissible at trial, police must have given the accused a *Miranda* warning. *See Miranda*, 384 U.S., at 471. If that condition is established, the court can proceed to consider whether there has been an express or implied waiver of *Miranda* rights. *Id.*, at 476. In making its ruling on the admissibility of a statement made during custodial questioning, the trial court, of course, considers whether there is evidence to support the conclusion that, from the whole course of questioning, an express or implied waiver has been established. Thus, after giving a *Miranda* warning, police may interrogate a suspect who has neither invoked nor waived his or her *Miranda* rights. On these premises, it follows the police were not required to obtain a waiver of Thompkins's *Miranda* rights before commencing the interrogation.

D

In sum, a suspect who has received and understood the *Miranda* warnings, and has not invoked his *Miranda* rights, waives the right to remain silent by making an uncoerced statement to the police. Thompkins did not invoke his right to remain silent and stop the questioning. Understanding his rights in full, he waived his right to remain silent by making a voluntary statement to the police. The police, moreover, were not required to obtain a waiver of Thompkins's right to remain silent before interrogating him. The state court's decision rejecting Thompkins's *Miranda* claim was thus correct under de novo review and therefore necessarily reasonable under the more deferential AEDPA standard of review, 28 U.S.C. § 2254(d). *See Knowles*, 556 U.S., at ___ (state court's decision was correct under de novo review and not unreasonable under AEDPA).

IV

[The Court rejects Thompkins's claim of ineffective assistance of counsel.]

* * *

The judgment of the Court of Appeals is reversed, and the case is remanded with instructions to deny the petition.

It is so ordered.

■ JUSTICE SOTOMAYOR, with whom JUSTICE STEVENS, JUSTICE GINSBURG, and JUSTICE BREYER join, dissenting.

The Court concludes today that a criminal suspect waives his right to remain silent if, after sitting tacit and uncommunicative through nearly three hours of police interrogation, he utters a few one-word responses. The Court also concludes that a suspect who wishes to guard his right to remain silent against such a finding of "waiver" must, counterintuitively, speak—and must do so with sufficient precision to satisfy a clear-statement rule that construes ambiguity in favor of the police. Both propositions mark a substantial retreat from the protection against compelled self-incrimination that Miranda v. Arizona, 384 U.S. 436 (1966), has long provided during custodial interrogation. The broad rules the Court announces today are also troubling because they are unnecessary to decide this case, which is governed by the deferential standard of review set forth in the Antiterrorism and Effective Death Penalty Act of 1996 (AEDPA), 28 U.S.C. § 2254(d). Because I believe Thompkins is entitled to relief under AEDPA on the ground that his statements were admitted at trial without the prosecution having carried its burden to show that he waived his right to remain silent; because longstanding principles of judicial restraint counsel leaving for another day the questions of law the Court reaches out to decide; and because the Court's answers to those questions do not result from a faithful application of our prior decisions, I respectfully dissent.

I

We granted certiorari to review the judgment of the Court of Appeals for the Sixth Circuit, which held that Thompkins was entitled to habeas relief under both *Miranda* and Strickland v. Washington, 466 U.S. 668 (1984). 547 F.3d 572 (2008). As to the *Miranda* claims, Thompkins argues first that through his conduct during the 3-hour custodial interrogation he effectively invoked his right to remain silent, requiring police to cut off questioning in accordance with *Miranda* and Michigan v. Mosley, 423 U.S. 96 (1975). Thompkins also contends his statements were in any case inadmissible because the prosecution failed to meet its heavy burden under *Miranda* of proving that he knowingly and intelligently waived his right to remain silent. The Sixth Circuit agreed with Thompkins as to waiver and declined to reach the question of invocation. 547 F.3d, at 583–584, n 4. In my view, even if Thompkins cannot prevail on his invocation claim under AEDPA, he is entitled to relief as to waiver. Because I would affirm the judgment of the Sixth Circuit on that ground, I would not reach Thompkins' claim that he received constitutionally ineffective assistance of counsel.

The strength of Thompkins' *Miranda* claims depends in large part on the circumstances of the 3-hour interrogation, at the end of which he made inculpatory statements later introduced at trial. The Court's opinion downplays record evidence that Thompkins remained almost completely silent and unresponsive throughout that session. One of the interrogating officers, Detective Helgert, testified that although Thompkins was administered *Miranda* warnings, the last of which he read aloud, Thompkins expressly declined to sign a written acknowledgment that he had been advised of and understood his rights. There is conflicting evidence in the record about whether Thompkins ever verbally confirmed understanding his rights.[1] The record contains no indication that the officers sought or obtained an express waiver.

As to the interrogation itself, Helgert candidly characterized it as "very, very one-sided" and "nearly a monologue." App. 10a, 17a. Thompkins was "[p]eculiar," "[s]ullen," and "[g]enerally quiet." *Id.*, at 149a. Helgert and his partner "did most of the talking," as Thompkins was "not verbally communicative" and "[l]argely" remained silent. *Id.*, at 149a, 17a, 19a. To the extent Thompkins gave any response, his answers consisted of "a word or two. A 'yeah,' or a 'no,' or 'I don't know.' . . . And sometimes . . . he simply sat down . . . with [his] head in [his] hands looking down. Sometimes . . . he would look up and make eye-contact would be the only response." *Id.*, at 23a–24a. After proceeding in this fashion for approximately 2 hours and 45 minutes, Helgert asked Thompkins three questions relating to his faith in God. The prosecution relied at trial on Thompkins' one-word answers of "yes." *See id.*, at 10a–11a.

Thompkins' nonresponsiveness is particularly striking in the context of the officers' interview strategy, later explained as conveying to Thompkins that "this was his opportunity to explain his side [of the story]" because "[e]verybody else, including [his] co-[d]efendants, had given their version," and asking him "[w]ho is going to speak up for you if you don't speak up for yourself?" *Id.*, at 10a, 21a. Yet, Helgert confirmed that the "only thing [Thompkins said] relative to his involvement [in the

---

[1]   At the suppression hearing, Detective Helgert testified that after reading Thompkins the warnings, "I believe I asked him if he understood the Rights, and I think I got a verbal answer to that as a 'yes.'" App. 9a. In denying the motion to suppress, the trial court relied on that factual premise. *Id.*, at 26a. In his later testimony at trial, Helgert remembered the encounter differently. Asked whether Thompkins "indicate[d] that he understood [the warnings]" after they had been read, Helgert stated "I don't know that I orally asked him that question." *Id.*, at 148a. Nevertheless, the Michigan Court of Appeals stated that Thompkins verbally acknowledged understanding his rights. App. to Pet. for Cert. 75a.

shooting]" occurred near the end of the interview—i.e., in response to the questions about God. *Id.*, at 10a–11a (emphasis added). The only other responses Helgert could remember Thompkins giving were that " '[h]e didn't want a peppermint' " and " 'the chair that he was sitting in was hard.' " *Id.*, at 152a. Nevertheless, the Michigan court concluded on this record that Thompkins had not invoked his right to remain silent because "he continued to talk with the officer, albeit sporadically," and that he voluntarily waived that right. App. to Pet. for Cert. 75a.

Thompkins' federal habeas petition is governed by AEDPA, under which a federal court may not grant the writ unless the state court's adjudication of the merits of the claim at issue "was contrary to, or involved an unreasonable application of, clearly established Federal law, as determined by the Supreme Court of the United States," or "was based on an unreasonable determination of the facts in light of the evidence presented in the State court proceeding." §§ 2254(d)(1), (2).

The relevant clearly established federal law for purposes of § 2254(d)(1) begins with our landmark *Miranda* decision, which "g[a]ve force to the Constitution's protection against compelled self-incrimination" by establishing " 'certain procedural safeguards that require police to advise criminal suspects of their rights under the Fifth and Fourteenth Amendments before commencing custodial interrogation,' " Florida v. Powell, 559 U.S. 50, ___–___ (2010) (quoting Duckworth v. Eagan, 492 U.S. 195, 201 (1989)). *Miranda* prescribed the now-familiar warnings that police must administer prior to questioning. *See* 384 U.S., at 479. *Miranda* and our subsequent cases also require police to "respect the accused's decision to exercise the rights outlined in the warnings." Moran v. Burbine, 475 U.S. 412, 420 (1986). "If [an] individual indicates in any manner, at any time prior to or during questioning, that he wishes to remain silent" or if he "states that he wants an attorney," the interrogation "must cease." 384 U.S., at 473–474.

Even when warnings have been administered and a suspect has not affirmatively invoked his rights, statements made in custodial interrogation may not be admitted as part of the prosecution's case in chief "unless and until" the prosecution demonstrates that an individual "knowingly and intelligently waive[d][his] rights." *Id.*, at 479; accord, *ante,* at 2260–2261. "[A] heavy burden rests on the government to demonstrate that the defendant knowingly and intelligently waived his privilege against self-incrimination and his right to retained or appointed counsel." *Miranda*, 384 U.S., at 475. The government must satisfy the "high standar[d] of proof for the waiver of constitutional rights [set forth in] Johnson v. Zerbst, 304 U.S. 458 (1938)." *Ibid.*

The question whether a suspect has validly waived his right is "entirely distinct" as a matter of law from whether he invoked that right. Smith v. Illinois, 469 U.S. 91, 98 (1984) (per curiam). The questions are related, however, in terms of the practical effect on the exercise of a suspect's rights. A suspect may at any time revoke his prior waiver of rights—or, closer to the facts of this case, guard against the possibility of a future finding that he implicitly waived his rights—by invoking the rights and thereby requiring the police to cease questioning. Accord, *ante,* at 2263–2264.

II

A

Like the Sixth Circuit, I begin with the question whether Thompkins waived his right to remain silent. Even if Thompkins did not invoke that right, he is entitled to relief because Michigan did not satisfy its burden of establishing waiver.

Miranda's discussion of the prosecution's burden in proving waiver speaks with particular clarity to the facts of this case and therefore merits reproducing at length:

> "If [an] interrogation continues without the presence of an attorney and a statement is taken, a heavy burden rests on the government to demonstrate that the defendant knowingly and intelligently waived his privilege against self-incrimination and his right to retained or appointed counsel . . . . Since the State is responsible for establishing the isolated circumstances under which [an] interrogation takes place and has the only means of making available corroborated evidence of warnings given during incommunicado interrogation, the burden is rightly on its shoulders.

> "An express statement that the individual is willing to make a statement and does not want an attorney followed closely by a statement could constitute a waiver. But a valid waiver will not be presumed simply from the silence of the accused after warnings are given or simply from the fact that a confession was in fact eventually obtained."

384 U.S., at 475.

Miranda went further in describing the facts likely to satisfy the prosecution's burden of establishing the admissibility of statements obtained after a lengthy interrogation: "Whatever the testimony of the authorities as to waiver of rights by an accused, the fact of lengthy interrogation or incommunicado incarceration before a statement is made is strong evidence that the accused did not validly waive his rights. In these circumstances the fact that the individual eventually made a statement is consistent with the conclusion that the compelling influence of the interrogation finally forced him to do so. It is inconsistent with any notion of a voluntary relinquishment of the privilege." *Id.,* at 476.

This Court's decisions subsequent to *Miranda* have emphasized the prosecution's "heavy burden" in proving waiver. *See, e.g.,* Tague v. Louisiana, 444 U.S. 469, 470–471 (1980) (per curiam); Fare v. Michael C., 442 U.S. 707, 724 (1979). We have also reaffirmed that a court may not presume waiver from a suspect's silence or from the mere fact that a confession was eventually obtained. *See* North Carolina v. Butler, 441 U.S. 369, 373 (1979).

Even in concluding that *Miranda* does not invariably require an express waiver of the right to silence or the right to counsel, this Court in *Butler* made clear that the prosecution bears a substantial burden in establishing an implied waiver. The Federal Bureau of Investigation had obtained statements after advising *Butler* of his rights and confirming that he understood them. When presented with a written waiver-of-rights form, Butler told the agents, " 'I will talk to you but I am not signing any form.' " 441 U.S., at 371. He then made inculpatory statements, which he later sought to suppress on the ground that he had not expressly waived his right to counsel.

Although this Court reversed the state-court judgment concluding that the statements were inadmissible, we quoted at length portions of the *Miranda* opinion reproduced above. We cautioned that even an "express written or oral statement of waiver of the right to remain silent or of the right to counsel" is not "inevitably . . . sufficient to establish waiver," emphasizing that "[t]he question is . . . whether the defendant in fact knowingly and voluntarily waived the rights delineated in the *Miranda* case." 441 U.S., at 373. *Miranda*, we observed, "unequivocally said . . . mere silence is not enough." 441 U.S., at 373. While we stopped short in *Butler* of announcing a per se rule that "the defendant's silence, coupled with an understanding of his rights and a course of conduct indicating waiver, may never support a conclusion that a defendant has waived his rights," we reiterated that "courts must presume that a defendant did not waive his rights; the prosecution's burden is great." *Ibid.*[2]

Rarely do this Court's precedents provide clearly established law so closely on point with the facts of a particular case. Together, *Miranda* and *Butler* establish that a court "must presume that a defendant did not waive his right[s]"; the prosecution bears a "heavy burden" in attempting to demonstrate waiver; the fact of a "lengthy interrogation" prior to obtaining statements is "strong evidence" against a finding of valid waiver; "mere silence" in response to questioning is "not enough"; and waiver may not be presumed "simply from the fact that a confession was in fact eventually obtained." *Miranda, supra*, at 475–476; *Butler, supra*, at 372–373.[3]

---

[2] The Court cites Colorado v. Connelly, 479 U.S. 157, 168 (1986), for the proposition that the prosecution's " 'heavy burden' " under *Miranda* "is not more than the burden to establish waiver by a preponderance of the evidence." *Ante*, at 2261. *Connelly* did reject a clear and convincing evidence standard of proof in favor of a preponderance burden. But nothing in *Connelly* displaced the core presumption against finding a waiver of rights, and we have subsequently relied on *Miranda*'s characterization of the prosecution's burden as "heavy." *See* Arizona v. Roberson, 486 U.S. 675, 680 (1988).

[3] Likely reflecting the great weight of the prosecution's burden in proving implied waiver, many contemporary police training resources instruct officers to obtain a waiver of rights prior to proceeding at all with an interrogation. See, *e.g.*, F. Inbau, J. Reid, J. Buckley, & B. Jayne,

It is undisputed here that Thompkins never expressly waived his right to remain silent. His refusal to sign even an acknowledgment that he understood his *Miranda* rights evinces, if anything, an intent not to waive those rights. *Cf.* United States v. Plugh, 576 F.3d 135, 142 (C.A.2 2009) (suspect's refusal to sign waiver-of-rights form "constituted an unequivocally negative answer to the question . . . whether he was willing to waive his rights"). That Thompkins did not make the inculpatory statements at issue until after approximately 2 hours and 45 minutes of interrogation serves as "strong evidence" against waiver. *Miranda* and *Butler* expressly preclude the possibility that the inculpatory statements themselves are sufficient to establish waiver.

In these circumstances, Thompkins' "actions and words" preceding the inculpatory statements simply do not evidence a "course of conduct indicating waiver" sufficient to carry the prosecution's burden. *See Butler, supra,* at 373.4 Although the Michigan court stated that Thompkins "sporadically" participated in the interview, App. to Pet. for Cert. 75a, that court's opinion and the record before us are silent as to the subject matter or context of even a single question to which Thompkins purportedly responded, other than the exchange about God and the statements respecting the peppermint and the chair. Unlike in *Butler,* Thompkins made no initial declaration akin to "I will talk to you." *See also* 547 F.3d, at 586–587 (case below) (noting that the case might be different if the record showed Thompkins had responded affirmatively to an invitation to tell his side of the story or described any particular question that Thompkins answered). Indeed, Michigan and the United States concede that no waiver occurred in this case until Thompkins responded "yes" to the questions about God. *See* Tr. of Oral Arg. 7, 30. I believe it is objectively unreasonable under our clearly established precedents to conclude the prosecution met its "heavy burden" of proof on a record consisting of three one-word answers, following 2 hours and 45 minutes of silence punctuated by a few largely nonverbal responses to unidentified questions.

B

Perhaps because our prior *Miranda* precedents so clearly favor Thompkins, the Court today goes beyond AEDPA's deferential standard of review and announces a new general principle of law. Any new rule, it must be emphasized, is unnecessary to the disposition of this case. If, in the Court's view, the Michigan court did not unreasonably apply our *Miranda* precedents in denying Thompkins relief, it should simply say so and reverse the Sixth Circuit's judgment on that ground. "It is a fundamental rule of judicial restraint . . . that this Court will not reach

Criminal Interrogation and Confessions 491 (4th ed.2004) (hereinafter Inbau) ("Once [a] waiver is given, the police may proceed with the interrogation"); D. Zulawski & D. Wicklander, Practical Aspects of Interview and Interrogation 55 (2d ed. 2002) ("Only upon the waiver of th[e] [*Miranda*] rights by the suspect can an interrogation occur"); *See also* Brief for National Association of Criminal Defense Lawyers et al. as Amici Curiae 11–12 (hereinafter NACDL brief) (collecting authorities).

constitutional questions in advance of the necessity of deciding them." Three Affiliated Tribes of Fort Berthold Reservation v. Wold Engineering, P. C., 467 U.S. 138, 157 (1984). Consistent with that rule, we have frequently declined to address questions beyond what is necessary to resolve a case under AEDPA. *See, e.g.,* Tyler v. Cain, 533 U.S. 656, 667–668 (2001) (declining to address question where any statement by this Court would be "dictum" in light of AEDPA's statutory constraints on habeas review); *cf.* Wiggins v. Smith, 539 U.S. 510, 522 (2003) (noting that Williams v. Taylor, 529 U.S. 362 (2000), "made no new law" because the "case was before us on habeas review"). No necessity exists to justify the Court's broad announcement today.

The Court concludes that when *Miranda* warnings have been given and understood, "an accused's uncoerced statement establishes an implied waiver of the right to remain silent." *Ante,* at 2262. More broadly still, the Court states that, "[a]s a general proposition, the law can presume that an individual who, with a full understanding of his or her rights, acts in a manner inconsistent with their exercise has made a deliberate choice to relinquish the protection those rights afford." *Ante,* at 2262.

These principles flatly contradict our longstanding views that "a valid waiver will not be presumed ... simply from the fact that a confession was in fact eventually obtained," *Miranda,* 384 U.S., at 475, and that "[t]he courts must presume that a defendant did not waive his rights," *Butler,* 441 U.S., at 373. Indeed, we have in the past summarily reversed a state-court decision that inverted *Miranda*'s antiwaiver presumption, characterizing the error as "readily apparent." *Tague,* 444 U.S., at 470–471. At best, the Court today creates an unworkable and conflicting set of presumptions that will undermine *Miranda*'s goal of providing "concrete constitutional guidelines for law enforcement agencies and courts to follow," 384 U.S., at 442. At worst, it overrules *sub silentio* an essential aspect of the protections *Miranda* has long provided for the constitutional guarantee against self-incrimination.

The Court's conclusion that Thompkins' inculpatory statements were sufficient to establish an implied waiver, ante, at 2263, finds no support in *Butler. Butler* itself distinguished between a sufficient "course of conduct" and inculpatory statements, reiterating *Miranda*'s admonition that " 'a valid waiver will not be presumed simply from ... the fact that a confession was in fact eventually obtained.' " *Butler, supra,* at 373 (quoting *Miranda, supra,* at 475). Michigan suggests Butler's silence " 'when advised of his right to the assistance of a lawyer,' " combined with our remand for the state court to apply the implied-waiver standard, shows that silence followed by statements can be a " 'course of conduct.' " Brief for Petitioner 26 (quoting *Butler, supra,* at 371). But the evidence of implied waiver in *Butler* was worlds apart from the evidence in this case, because Butler unequivocally said "I will talk to you" after having been read *Miranda* warnings. Thompkins, of course, made no such statement.

The Court also relies heavily on *Burbine* in characterizing the scope of the prosecution's burden in proving waiver. Consistent with *Burbine,* the Court observes, the prosecution must prove that waiver was " 'voluntary in the sense that it was the product of a free and deliberate choice rather than intimidation' " and " 'made with a full awareness of both the nature of the right being abandoned and the consequences of the decision to abandon it.' " *Ante,* at 2260 (quoting 475 U.S., at 421). I agree with the Court's statement, so far as it goes. What it omits, however, is that the prosecution also bears an antecedent burden of showing there was, in fact, either an express waiver or a "course of conduct" sufficiently clear to support a finding of implied waiver. Nothing in *Burbine* even hints at removing that obligation. The question in that case, rather, was whether a suspect's multiple express waivers of his rights were invalid because police "misinformed an inquiring attorney about their plans concerning the suspect or because they failed to inform the suspect of the attorney's efforts to reach him." *Id.,* at 420; *see also* Colorado v. Spring, 479 U.S. 564, 573 (1987). The Court's analysis in *Burbine* was predicated on the existence of waiver-in-fact.

Today's dilution of the prosecution's burden of proof to the bare fact that a suspect made inculpatory statements after *Miranda* warnings were given and understood takes an unprecedented step away from the "high standards of proof for the waiver of constitutional rights" this Court has long demanded. *Miranda, supra,* at 475; *cf.* Brewer v. Williams, 430 U.S. 387, 404 (1977) ("[C]ourts indulge in every reasonable presumption against waiver"); *Zerbst,* 304 U.S., at 464. When waiver is to be inferred during a custodial interrogation, there are sound reasons to require evidence beyond inculpatory statements themselves. *Miranda* and our subsequent cases are premised on the idea that custodial interrogation is inherently coercive. *See* 384 U.S., at 455 ("Even without employing brutality, the 'third degree' or [other] specific strategems . . . the very fact of custodial interrogation exacts a heavy toll on individual liberty and trades on the weakness of individuals"); Dickerson v. United States, 530 U.S. 428, 435 (2000). Requiring proof of a course of conduct beyond the inculpatory statements themselves is critical to ensuring that those statements are voluntary admissions and not the dubious product of an overborne will.

Today's decision thus ignores the important interests *Miranda* safeguards. The underlying constitutional guarantee against self-incrimination reflects "many of our fundamental values and most noble aspirations," our society's "preference for an accusatorial rather than an inquisitorial system of criminal justice"; a "fear that self-incriminating statements will be elicited by inhumane treatment and abuses" and a resulting "distrust of self-deprecatory statements"; and a realization that while the privilege is "sometimes a shelter to the guilty, [it] is often a protection to the innocent." Withrow v. Williams, 507 U.S. 680, 692 (1993) (internal quotation marks omitted). For these reasons, we have observed, a criminal law system "which comes to depend on the 'confession' will, in the long run, be less reliable and more subject to abuses than a system relying on independent investigation." *Ibid.* (some internal quotation marks omitted). "By bracing against 'the possibility of unreliable statements in every instance of in-custody interrogation,'" *Miranda*'s prophylactic rules serve to "'protect the fairness of the trial itself.'" 507 U.S., at 692 (quoting Johnson v. New Jersey, 384 U.S. 719, 730 (1966); Schneckloth v. Bustamonte, 412 U.S. 218, 240 (1973)). Today's decision bodes poorly for the fundamental principles that *Miranda* protects.

III

Thompkins separately argues that his conduct during the interrogation invoked his right to remain silent, requiring police to terminate questioning. Like the Sixth Circuit, I would not reach this question because Thompkins is in any case entitled to relief as to waiver. But even if Thompkins would not prevail on his invocation claim under AEDPA's deferential standard of review, I cannot agree with the Court's much broader ruling that a suspect must clearly invoke his right to silence by speaking. Taken together with the Court's reformulation of the prosecution's burden of proof as to waiver, today's novel clear-statement rule for invocation invites police to question a suspect at length—notwithstanding his persistent refusal to answer questions—in the hope of eventually obtaining a single inculpatory response which will suffice to prove waiver of rights. Such a result bears little semblance to the "fully effective" prophylaxis, 384 U.S., at 444, that *Miranda* requires. . . .

I disagree with [the majority's] novel application of *Davis*. Neither the rationale nor holding of that case compels today's result. *Davis* involved the right to counsel, not the right to silence. The Court in *Davis* reasoned that extending *Edwards* "'rigid' prophylactic rule to ambiguous requests for a lawyer would transform *Miranda* into a "'wholly irrational obstacl[e] to legitimate police investigative activity'" by "needlessly prevent[ing] the police from questioning a suspect in the absence of counsel even if [he] did not wish to have a lawyer present." *Davis, supra*, at 460. But *Miranda* itself "distinguished between the procedural safeguards triggered by a request to remain silent and a request for an attorney." *Mosley, supra*, at 104, n.10; accord, *Edwards, supra*, at 485. *Mosley* upheld the admission of statements when police immediately stopped interrogating a suspect who invoked his right to silence, but reapproached him after a 2-hour delay and obtained inculpatory responses relating to a different crime after administering fresh *Miranda* warnings. The different effects of invoking the rights are consistent with distinct standards for invocation. To the extent *Mosley* contemplates a more flexible form of prophylaxis than *Edwards*—and, in particular, does not categorically bar police from reapproaching a suspect who has invoked his right to remain silent—*Davis'* concern about " 'wholly irrational obstacles' " to police investigation applies with less force.

In addition, the suspect's equivocal reference to a lawyer in *Davis* occurred only after he had given express oral and written waivers of his rights. *Davis'* holding is explicitly predicated on that fact. *See* 512 U.S., at 461 ("We therefore hold that, after a knowing and voluntary waiver of the *Miranda* rights, law enforcement officers may continue questioning until and unless the suspect clearly requests an attorney"). The Court ignores this aspect of *Davis*, as well as the decisions of numerous federal and state courts declining to apply a clear-statement rule when a suspect has not previously given an express waiver of rights.[7]

In my mind, a more appropriate standard for addressing a suspect's ambiguous invocation of the right to remain silent is the constraint *Mosley* places on questioning a suspect who has invoked that right: The suspect's " 'right to cut off questioning' " must be " 'scrupulously honored.' " *See* 423 U.S., at 104. Such a standard is necessarily precautionary and fact specific. The rule would acknowledge that some statements or conduct are so equivocal that police may scrupulously honor a suspect's rights without terminating questioning—for instance, if a suspect's actions are reasonably understood to indicate a willingness to listen before deciding whether to respond. But other statements or actions—in particular, when a suspect sits silent throughout prolonged interrogation, long past the point when he could be deciding whether to respond—cannot reasonably be understood other than as an invocation of the right to remain silent. Under such circumstances, "scrupulous" respect for the suspect's rights will require police to terminate questioning under *Mosley*.[8]

To be sure, such a standard does not provide police with a bright-line rule. *Cf. ante,* at 2259–2260. But, as we have previously recognized, *Mosley* itself does not offer clear guidance to police about when and how interrogation may continue after a suspect invokes his rights. *See* Solem v. Stumes, 465 U.S. 638, 648 (1984); *see also Shatzer,* 559 U.S., at ___ (THOMAS, J., concurring in part and concurring in judgment). Given that police have for nearly 35 years applied *Mosley*'s fact-specific standard in questioning suspects who have invoked their right to remain

---

[7] See, *e.g.,* United States v. Plugh, 576 F.3d 135, 143 (C.A.2 2009) ("*Davis* only provides guidance . . . [when] a defendant makes a claim that he subsequently invoked previously waived Fifth Amendment rights"); United States v. Rodriguez, 518 F.3d 1072, 1074 (C.A.9 2008) (*Davis* ' " 'clear statement' " rule "applies only after the police have already obtained an unambiguous and unequivocal waiver of *Miranda* rights"); State v. Tuttle, 2002 SD 94, ¶ 14, 650 N.W.2d 20, 28; State v. Holloway, 2000 ME 172, ¶ 12, 760 A.2d 223, 228; State v. Leyva, 951 P.2d 738, 743 (Utah 1997).

[8] Indeed, this rule appears to reflect widespread contemporary police practice. Thompkins' amici collect a range of training materials that instruct police not to engage in prolonged interrogation after a suspect has failed to respond to initial questioning. *See* NACDL Brief 32–34. One widely used police manual, for example, teaches that a suspect who "indicates," "even by silence itself," his unwillingness to answer questions "has obviously exercised his constitutional privilege against self-incrimination." Inbau 498.

silent; that our cases did not during that time resolve what statements or actions suffice to invoke that right; and that neither Michigan nor the Solicitor General have provided evidence in this case that the status quo has proved unworkable, I see little reason to believe today's clear-statement rule is necessary to ensure effective law enforcement.

Davis' clear-statement rule is also a poor fit for the right to silence. Advising a suspect that he has a "right to remain silent" is unlikely to convey that he must speak (and must do so in some particular fashion) to ensure the right will be protected. *Cf.* Soffar v. Cockrell, 300 F.3d 588, 603 (C.A.5 2002) (en banc) (DeMoss, J., dissenting) ("What in the world must an individual do to exercise his constitutional right to remain silent beyond actually, in fact, remaining silent?"). By contrast, telling a suspect "he has the right to the presence of an attorney, and that if he cannot afford an attorney one will be appointed for him prior to any questioning if he so desires," *Miranda,* 384 U.S., at 479, implies the need for speech to exercise that right. *Davis'* requirement that a suspect must "clearly reques[t] an attorney" to terminate questioning thus aligns with a suspect's likely understanding of the *Miranda* warnings in a way today's rule does not. The Court suggests Thompkins could have employed the "simple, unambiguous" means of saying "he wanted to remain silent" or "did not want to talk with the police." *Ante,* at 2260. But the *Miranda* warnings give no hint that a suspect should use those magic words, and there is little reason to believe police—who have ample incentives to avoid invocation—will provide such guidance.

Conversely, the Court's concern that police will face "difficult decisions about an accused's unclear intent" and suffer the consequences of " 'guess[ing] wrong,' " ante, at 2260 (quoting *Davis,* 512 U.S., at 461), is misplaced. If a suspect makes an ambiguous statement or engages in conduct that creates uncertainty about his intent to invoke his right, police can simply ask for clarification. *See id.,* at 467 (Souter, J., concurring in judgment). It is hardly an unreasonable burden for police to ask a suspect, for instance, "Do you want to talk to us?" The majority in *Davis* itself approved of this approach as protecting suspects' rights while "minimiz[ing] the chance of a confession [later] being suppressed." *Id.,* at 461. Given this straightforward mechanism by which police can "scrupulously hono[r]" a suspect's right to silence, today's clear-statement rule can only be seen as accepting "as tolerable the certainty that some poorly expressed requests [to remain silent] will be disregarded," *id.,* at 471 (opinion of Souter, J.), without any countervailing benefit. Police may well prefer not to seek clarification of an ambiguous statement out of fear that a suspect will invoke his rights. But "our system of justice is not founded on a fear that a suspect will exercise his rights. 'If the exercise of constitutional rights will thwart the effectiveness of a system of law enforcement, then there is something very wrong with that system.' " *Burbine,* 475 U.S., at 458 (STEVENS, J., dissenting) (quoting Escobedo v. Illinois, 378 U.S. 478, 490 (1964)).

The Court asserts in passing that treating ambiguous statements or acts as an invocation of the right to silence will only " 'marginally' " serve *Miranda*'s goals. *Ante,* at 2260. Experience suggests the contrary. In the 16 years since *Davis* was decided, ample evidence has accrued that criminal suspects often use equivocal or colloquial language in attempting to invoke their right to silence. A number of lower courts that have (erroneously, in my view) imposed a clear-statement requirement for invocation of the right to silence have rejected as ambiguous an array of statements whose meaning might otherwise be thought plain.[9] At a minimum, these decisions suggest that differentiating "clear" from "ambiguous" statements is often a subjective inquiry. Even if some of the cited decisions are themselves in tension with *Davis*' admonition that a suspect need not " 'speak with the discrimination of an Oxford don' " to invoke his rights, 512 U.S., at 459 (quoting *id.*, at 476 (opinion of Souter, J.)), they demonstrate that today's decision will significantly burden the exercise of the right to silence. Notably, when a suspect "understands his (expressed) wishes to have been ignored . . . in contravention of the 'rights' just read to him by his interrogator, he may well see further objection as futile and confession (true or not) as the only way to end his interrogation." *Id.*, at 472–473.

For these reasons, I believe a precautionary requirement that police "scrupulously hono[r]" a suspect's right to cut off questioning is a more faithful application of our precedents than the Court's awkward and needless extension of *Davis*.

* * *

Today's decision turns *Miranda* upside down. Criminal suspects must now unambiguously invoke their right to remain silent—which, counterintuitively, requires them to speak. At the same time, suspects will be legally presumed to have waived their rights even if they have given no clear expression of their intent to do so. Those results, in my view, find no basis in *Miranda* or our subsequent cases and are inconsistent with the fair-trial principles on which those precedents are grounded. Today's broad new rules are all the more unfortunate because they are unnecessary to the disposition of the case before us. I respectfully dissent.

---

[9]   *See* United States v. Sherrod, 445 F.3d 980, 982 (C.A.7 2006) (suspect's statement " 'I'm not going to talk about nothin' ' " was ambiguous, "as much a taunt—even a provocation—as it [was] an invocation of the right to remain silent" . . . .

United States v. Hutchins

72 M.J. 294 (Ct. App. Mil. J. 2013)

■ ERDMANN, J., delivered the opinion of the court, in which STUCKY, J., and EFFRON, S.J., joined. RYAN, J., filed a separate opinion concurring in the result. BAKER, C.J., filed a separate dissenting opinion.

■ JUDGE ERDMANN delivered the opinion of the court.

Contrary to his pleas, Sergeant Lawrence G. Hutchins III was convicted by members at a general court-martial of making a false official statement, unpremeditated murder, larceny, and conspiracy to commit larceny, false official statements, murder, and obstruction of justice in violation of Articles 107, 118, 121, and 81, Uniform Code of Military Justice (UCMJ), 10 U.S.C. §§ 907, 918, 921, 881 (2006). The members sentenced Hutchins to reduction to E–1, confinement for fifteen years, dishonorable discharge, and a reprimand. The convening authority approved a sentence of reduction to E–1, confinement for eleven years, and a dishonorable discharge. . . .

We granted review to determine whether Hutchins's post-trial rights were influenced by unlawful command influence and whether the military judge erred when he denied the defense motion to suppress Hutchins's statement made to the Naval Criminal Investigative Service (NCIS) after having invoked his right to counsel. We hold that the NCIS request to Hutchins for his consent to search his belongings reinitiated communication with Hutchins in violation of his Fifth Amendment rights as interpreted by the Supreme Court in Edwards v. Arizona, 451 U.S. 477 (1981), and Oregon v. Bradshaw, 462 U.S. 1039 (1983). We therefore reverse the decision of the CCA, set aside the findings and the sentence, and return the case to the Judge Advocate General of the Navy.

Factual Background

The charges against Hutchins arose from an incident that occurred in April 2006 while Hutchins was a squad leader in Iraq and his unit was conducting counterinsurgency operations. The CCA summarized the facts of the offenses as follows:

> The appellant was assigned as squad leader for 1st Squad, 2nd Platoon, Kilo Company, 3rd Battalion, 5th Marines, assigned to Task Force Chromite, conducting counter-insurgency operations in the Hamdaniyah area of Iraq in April 2006. In the evening hours of 25 April 2006, the appellant led a combat patrol to conduct a deliberate ambush aimed at interdicting insurgent emplacement of improvised explosive devices (IEDs). The court-martial received testimony from several members of the squad that indicated the intended ambush mission morphed into a conspiracy to deliberately capture and kill a high value individual (HVI), believed to be a leader of the insurgency. The witnesses gave varying testimony as to the depth of their

understanding of alternative targets, such as family members of the HVI or another random military-aged Iraqi male.

Considerable effort and preparation went into the execution of this conspiracy. Tasks were accomplished by various Marines and their corpsman, including the theft of a shovel and AK-47 from an Iraqi dwelling to be used as props to manufacture a scene where it appeared that an armed insurgent was digging to emplace an IED. Some squad members advanced to the ambush site while others captured an unknown Iraqi man, bound and gagged him, and brought him to the would-be IED emplacement.

The stage set, the squad informed higher headquarters by radio that they had come upon an insurgent planting an IED and received approval to engage. The squad opened fire, mortally wounding the man. The appellant approached the victim and fired multiple rifle rounds into the man's face at point blank range.

The scene was then manipulated to appear consistent with the insurgent/IED story. The squad removed the bindings from the victim's hands and feet and positioned the victim's body with the shovel and AK-47 rifle they had stolen from local Iraqis. To simulate that the victim fired on the squad, the Marines fired the AK-47 rifle into the air and collected the discharged casings. When questioned about the action, the appellant, like other members of the squad, made false official statements, describing the situation as a legitimate ambush and a "good shoot." The death was brought to the appellant's battalion commander's attention by a local sheikh and the ensuing investigation led to the case before us.

2012 CCA LEXIS 93, at *4–*6, 2012 WL 933067 at *2 (paragraph formatting added).

On May 11, 2006, NCIS initiated an interrogation of Hutchins after advising him of his rights in accordance with Miranda v. Arizona, 384 U.S. 436 (1966), and Article 31(b), UCMJ, 10 U.S.C. § 831(b) (2006). Following Hutchins's invocation of his right to an attorney, NCIS properly terminated the interrogation. At that point Hutchins was confined to a trailer under guard where he was held essentially in solitary confinement and was not allowed to use a phone or to otherwise contact an attorney. The Government conceded that these conditions were restriction tantamount to confinement. However, despite the requirements of Military Rule of Evidence (M.R.E.) 305(d)(2) and Rule for Courts-Martial (R.C.M.) 305(f), the Government made no effort to secure an attorney for Hutchins during this period.

After a week of confinement under these conditions, on May 18, 2006, the same NCIS investigator who had interrogated Hutchins on

May 11 entered his trailer in the late evening and asked for permission to search his personal belongings. The investigator provided Hutchins with a Permissive Authorization for Search and Seizure form which reminded him that he was still under investigation for conspiracy, murder, assault, and kidnapping. While reading this form, Hutchins asked if the door was still open to give his side of the story. Hutchins consented to the search and signed the form.

The investigator informed Hutchins that he could talk to them but not that night.[4] The next morning Hutchins was taken to NCIS where he was readvised of his Article 31 rights. Hutchins waived his rights, was interrogated, and subsequently provided a detailed written confession.

Discussion

Introduction:

The Government argues that this case is governed by the holding in United States v. Frazier, 34 M.J. 135, 137 (C.M.A.1992), that "[a] request for consent to search does not infringe upon Article 31 or Fifth Amendment safeguards against self-incrimination because such requests are not interrogations and the consent given is ordinarily not a statement." We do not take issue with that basic principle and agree that the NCIS request to search Hutchins's personal belongings on May 18 was not an interrogation. The principle set forth in *Frazier*, however, does not end our inquiry. Once Hutchins requested an attorney, under *Edwards* he could not be further interrogated unless: (1) counsel had been made available; or, (2) Hutchins reinitiated further "communication, exchanges, or conversations." *Edwards*, 451 U.S. at 484–85. As no attorney was made available to Hutchins, the Edwards inquiry in this case centers on whether, under the circumstances of this case, it was the Government or Hutchins that reinitiated further communication under Edwards and Bradshaw.

Edwards and *Bradshaw*—Reinitiation of the Communication:

Since the Supreme Court's decision in *Edwards* in 1981, it has been clear that:

> [A]n accused . . . having expressed his desire to deal with the police only through counsel, is not subject to further interrogation by the authorities until counsel has been made available to him, unless the accused himself initiates further communication, exchanges, or conversations with the police.

Edwards, 451 U.S. at 484–85 (emphasis added).

There is no disagreement between the parties that *Edwards* applies to the circumstances of this case. However, the parties differ as to whether NCIS or Hutchins initiated further "communication, exchanges, or conversations." Hutchins argues that the request for consent to search

---

[4]   The investigator testified that he was exhausted after a long day and wanted to be fresh the next morning.

was an initiation of further communication by NCIS in violation of *Edwards* because it was directly related to the criminal investigation and was not merely incidental to the custodial relationship, citing *Bradshaw,* 462 U.S. at 1044. The Government responds that, under *Frazier,* the request for consent to search is not an interrogation and therefore such a request did not initiate further "interrogation" as proscribed by *Edwards.*

The fundamental purpose of the judicially crafted rule in *Edwards* is to "[p]reserv[e] the integrity of an accused's choice to communicate with police only through counsel." Patterson v. Illinois, 487 U.S. 285, 291 (1988). The need for such a rule is to provide added protection against the coercive pressures of continuous custody after an individual has invoked his right to counsel, because he is "cut off from his normal life and companions, thrust into and isolated in an unfamiliar, police-dominated atmosphere, where his captors appear to control his fate."[5] Maryland v. Shatzer, 559 U.S. 98, 106 (2010) (citations omitted) (internal quotation marks and brackets omitted).

"Fidelity to the doctrine announced in *Miranda* requires that it be enforced strictly, but only in those types of situations in which the concerns that powered the decision are implicated." Berkemer v. McCarty, 468 U.S. 420, 437 (1984). It is hard to imagine a situation where this would be more of a concern than in the present case, *i.e.,* while deployed to a foreign country in a combat environment Hutchins was held in essentially solitary confinement in a trailer for seven days after invoking his right to counsel; despite his request for counsel, no attorney was provided during this period and no explanation was provided to Hutchins as to why; he was held incommunicado (other than a chance conversation with a chaplain for three or four minutes); and he was not allowed to use a phone, the mail system, or other means of communication to contact an attorney, family, friends, or anyone else.

The Court in *Oregon v. Bradshaw* stated:

[The test in Edwards] was in effect a prophylactic rule, designed to protect an accused in police custody from being badgered by police officers . . . [and we] restated the requirement in Wyrick v. Fields, 459 U.S. 42, 46 (1982) (per curiam), to be that before a suspect in custody can be subjected to further interrogation

---

[5] "Fidelity to the doctrine announced in *Miranda* requires that it be enforced strictly, but only in those types of situations in which the concerns that powered the decision are implicated." *Berkemer v. McCarty,* 468 U.S. 420, 437, 104 S.Ct. 3138, 82 L.Ed.2d 317 (1984). It is hard to imagine a situation where this would be more of a concern than in the present case, i.e., while deployed to a foreign country in a combat environment Hutchins was held in essentially solitary confinement in a trailer for seven days after invoking his right to counsel; despite his request for counsel, no attorney was provided during this period and no explanation was provided to Hutchins as to why; he was held incommunicado (other than a chance conversation with a chaplain for three or four minutes); and he was not allowed to use a phone, the mail system, or other means of communication to contact an attorney, family, friends, or anyone else.

after he requests an attorney there must be a showing that the "suspect himself initiates dialogue with the authorities."

Bradshaw, 462 U.S. at 1044.

Not all communications initiated by an accused or law enforcement will trigger the protections under *Edwards*.[6] The Court in *Bradshaw* went on to distinguish between inquiries or statements by either a police officer or a defendant that represented a desire to open a more "generalized discussion relating directly or indirectly to the investigation" and those "inquiries or statements, by either an accused or a police officer, relating to routine incidents of the custodial relationship." *Id.* at 1045. The former circumstance constitutes a reinitiation of communication while the latter circumstance does not. The *Edwards* rule does not merely prohibit further interrogation without the benefit of counsel, it prohibits further "communication, exchanges, or conversations" that may (and in this case, did) lead to further interrogation. 451 U.S. at 485. Under *Bradshaw,* the issue before this court is whether the NCIS agent opened a more "generalized discussion relating directly or indirectly to the investigation" or whether his inquiry related to "routine incidents of the custodial relationship." 462 U.S. at 1045.

The NCIS investigator was forthright in his testimony that he initiated contact with Hutchins on May 18 to further the investigation.[7] The investigator testified that he requested permission to search Hutchins's personal belongings that he had brought from Abu Ghraib to look for any media that could contain photographs. In connection with this request Hutchins was provided a permissive search authorization to sign. Importantly, the search authorization again reminded Hutchins that he was under investigation for conspiracy, murder, assault, and kidnapping. Its purpose was to seek Hutchins's cooperation in the ongoing investigation by providing his consent to a search of his belongings. The investigator testified that it was while Hutchins was reading that form that he asked if there was still an opportunity to talk to NCIS and give his side of the story. This request for consent to search by the NCIS initiated a generalized discussion which related directly to the ongoing investigation as contrasted to a bare inquiry about routine incidents of Hutchins's custody.[8]

---

[6]   *See Bradshaw,* 462 U.S. at 1045 ("While we doubt that it would be desirable to build a superstructure of legal refinements around the word 'initiate' in this context, there are undoubtedly situations where a bare inquiry by either a defendant or by a police officer should not be held to 'initiate' any conversation or dialogue.").

[7]   [Defense Counsel]: Now, getting to your purpose for coming back to Sergeant Hutchins, you went back to Sergeant Hutchins to further your investigation, didn't you?
[Investigator]: Yes

[8]   *See Bradshaw,* 462 U.S. at 1045 ("There are some inquiries, such as a request for a drink of water or a request to use a telephone . . . relating to routine incidents of the custodial relationship, [that] will not generally 'initiate' a conversation in the sense in which that word was used in *Edwards*."); *see also* United States v. Applewhite, 23 M.J. 196, 199 (C.M.A.1987)

Frazier—A Request to Search is Not an Interrogation:

The Government's reliance on the holding in *Frazier* is misplaced in this situation. *Frazier* stands for the proposition that a request for consent to search does not "infringe upon Article 31 or Fifth Amendment safeguards against self-incrimination because such requests are not interrogations and the consent given is ordinarily not a statement." *Frazier,* 34 M.J. at 137. *Frazier,* however, did not involve or address the reinitiation of communications by law enforcement after an accused has invoked his right to counsel and cannot be held to modify or nullify the protections established by *Edwards* and *Bradshaw*.[9]

Conclusion:

Hutchins's subsequent May 19 statement was a direct result of the reinitiation of communication by NCIS.[10] Accordingly, under the circumstances of this case, it was error for the military judge to admit the statement made by Hutchins on May 19, 2006.[11] For an error in admitting the statement to be harmless beyond a reasonable doubt, this court must be convinced that there was no reasonable likelihood that its erroneous admission contributed to the verdict. *See* United States v. Mitchell, 51 M.J. 234, 240 (C.A.A.F.1999). The Government made use of Hutchins's detailed statement in its opening statement, closing argument, and rebuttal argument and as evidence to corroborate other evidence and to attack the opinion of the defense expert witness. Therefore, notwithstanding the other evidence of Hutchins's guilt, there is a reasonable likelihood that the statement contributed to the verdict.

Decision

The request by NCIS to Hutchins for his consent to search his belongings reinitiated communication with Hutchins in violation of his

---

(request to take a polygraph examination initiated by investigator after an invocation of right to counsel was "in blatant disregard of *Miranda* and *Edwards*").

[9] As noted, generally a request for consent to search does not itself implicate the Fifth Amendment. 34 M.J. at 135. This is because a request for consent to search is not considered "interrogation." *Id.*; *See also* M.R.E. 305(b)(2) (defining "interrogation" as including "any formal or informal questioning in which an incriminating response either is sought or is a reasonable consequence of such questioning"); Rhode Island v. Innis, 446 U.S. 291, 301 (1980) (" '[I]nterrogation' under Miranda refers not only to express questioning, but also to any words or actions on the part of police (other than those normally attendant to arrest and custody) that the police should know are reasonably likely to elicit an incriminating response."). To be clear, our decision in this case does not affect this basic proposition. However, the issue we address today is not whether the request for consent to search was an "interrogation," but rather was it a reinitiation of "further communication" prohibited by *Edwards* and *Bradshaw*.

[10] Although a request for consent to search is not in itself an interrogation under *Frazier,* we do not agree with the dissent's suggestion that such a request has no bearing on the separate legal question as to whether, under all the surrounding circumstances, the Government reinitiated a communication under *Edwards* and *Bradshaw*. United States v. Hutchins, 72 M.J. 294, 305–07 (C.A.A.F.2013) (Baker, C.J., dissenting). In this case, for example, the communication was more than a simple request for consent to search, but instead included an implicit accusatory statement.

[11] Because the Government reinitiated communication with Hutchins concerning the criminal investigation, it is unnecessary to resolve whether Hutchins knowingly and intelligently waived the prior invocation of his right to counsel before the interrogation that resulted in his statement on May 19, 2006. *See Edwards,* 451 U.S. at 482.

Fifth Amendment rights as interpreted by the Supreme Court in Edwards v. Arizona, 451 U.S. 477 (1981), and Oregon v. Bradshaw, 462 U.S. 1039 (1983). Accordingly, the decision of the United States Navy-Marine Corps Court of Criminal Appeals is reversed. The findings and the sentence are set aside. The record is returned to the Judge Advocate General of the Navy for referral to an appropriate convening authority who may authorize a rehearing.

■ RYAN, JUDGE (concurring in the result):

This case presents the very close question whether, under the circumstances, the Naval Criminal Investigative Service's (NCIS) request for consent to search Appellant's personal belongings constituted a reinitiation of interrogation under Edwards v. Arizona, 451 U.S. 477 (1981), and, therefore, a violation of Appellant's Fifth Amendment right to not incriminate himself. It is clear that a mere request for a permissive search authorization is not itself an interrogation, *see* United States v. Frazier, 34 M.J. 135, 137 (C.M.A.1992) ("A request for a consent to search does not infringe upon Article 31 or Fifth Amendment safeguards against self-incrimination because such requests are not interrogations and the consent given is ordinarily not a statement."), and I do not read the majority to suggest that it is.

Recognizing, however, that a mere request for a search authorization is not an interrogation does not answer the distinct question whether, under the unique circumstances of this case, the reinitiation of contact by NCIS for an otherwise permissible purpose was "reasonably likely to elicit an incriminating response from the suspect," and thus an interrogation nonetheless. Rhode Island v. Innis, 446 U.S. 291, 301 (1980) (footnote omitted). In my view, the admissibility of Appellant's confession turns on that question, and no cases with like facts clearly dictate the answer.

In *Edwards v. Arizona*, the Supreme Court held that "when an accused has invoked his right to have counsel present during custodial interrogation, a valid waiver of that right cannot be established by showing only that he responded to further police-initiated custodial interrogation even if he has been advised of his rights." 451 U.S. at 484. The Court further held that when an accused invokes his right to counsel, he is "not subject to further interrogation . . . until counsel has been made available to him, unless the accused himself initiates further communication, exchanges, or conversations with the police." *Id.* at 484–85. Statements made after a suspect invokes his right to counsel and in response to further custodial interrogation "d[o] not amount to a valid waiver and hence [are] inadmissible." *Id.* at 487.

This bright-line rule serves as a "second layer of prophylaxis" safeguarding "a suspect's right to have counsel present at a subsequent interrogation if he had previously requested counsel," Maryland v. Shatzer, 559 U.S. 98, ___ (2010) (citation and internal quotation marks omitted), and is separate and distinct from the question whether a suspect's waiver was otherwise "knowing, intelligent, and voluntary under the 'high standar[d] of proof . . . [set forth in] Johnson v. Zerbst, 304 U.S. 458 (1938),' " *Shatzer,* 130 S.Ct. at 1219 (alterations in original) (quoting Miranda v. Arizona, 384 U.S. 436, 475 (1966)); *see also* Oregon v. Bradshaw, 462 U.S. 1039, 1044–45 (1983) (plurality opinion); *id.* at 1053 (Marshall, J., with whom Brennan, J., Blackmun, J., and Stevens, J., joined, dissenting) (agreeing with the majority on this point of law). My agreement with Chief Judge Baker, then, that Appellant's waiver was not involuntary under "Zerbst's traditional standard of waiver," *Shatzer,* does not end the inquiry.

Edwards does not protect against all reinitiations of contact with a suspect held in continuous custody who has invoked his right to counsel—only those that the government should reasonably expect to result in an incriminating statement. *See Innis,* 446 U.S. at 301. We view the latter class of reinitiations with a jaundiced eye and compare it to the psychological ploys that necessitated the protections first instituted in *Miranda. See Miranda,* 384 U.S. at 448–57. Whether NCIS' reinitiation of contact with Appellant should be deemed a reinitiation of interrogation in contravention of *Edwards* turns on whether NCIS should have known that its actions were "reasonably likely to elicit an incriminating response." *Innis,* 446 U.S. at 301; *see also* United States v. Brabant, 29 M.J. 259, 262–63 (C.M.A.1989).

In making this determination, we must consider, among other things, that: (1) after Appellant invoked his right to counsel during his initial interrogation, he was held in sequestration in a war zone for seven days; (2) during this period of solitary confinement, Appellant was neither provided an attorney nor permitted to contact one; (3) Appellant was not permitted to speak with anyone other than the chaplain, use any facilities other than the head and shower, or have access to phones, computers, or other methods of communication; (4) the Government's explanation as to why it did not provide Appellant with an attorney or the ability to even contact one during this seven-day period of sequestration was that "[it] is not required," Audio recording of oral argument at 29:18, United States v. Hutchins, 72 M.J. 294 (C.A.A.F.2012) http://www.armfor.uscourts.gov/newcaaf/calendar/2012–11.htm # 13; (5) after Appellant was held in sequestration for seven days, the NCIS agent who had conducted Appellant's initial interrogation reinitiated contact with him to obtain a permissive search authorization; and (6) Appellant did not make a statement until the day following NCIS' request for consent to search and after cleansing warnings were provided.

While (6) is strong evidence that Appellant's confession was not involuntary under *Zerbst,* it does not answer the altogether different question whether, under the circumstances, NCIS should have known that its reinitiation of contact with Appellant, made for any purpose, was reasonably likely to elicit an incriminating statement in violation of

Edwards. The military judge did not consider this question, which is different from whether law enforcement was engaged in intentional subterfuge.

After considering the facts outlined above, and that the prosecution has the burden to "demonstrate by a preponderance of the evidence that [Appellant] initiated the communication leading to the waiver," Military Rule of Evidence 305(g)(2)(B)(i), I resolve this close question in Appellant's favor.

Moreover, while I agree with much of Chief Judge Baker's analysis of whether the Secretary of the Navy's (the Secretary) comments resulted in unlawful command influence, I disagree with two aspects of his discussion.

First, in my view, Chief Judge Baker blurs the distinction between the doctrines of actual and apparent unlawful command influence by suggesting that the Secretary of the Navy's comments did not constitute unlawful command influence either because (1) the Secretary did not intend to influence the outcome of Appellant's proceedings, or (2) his comments did not actually affect any judicial or reviewing authority. *See Hutchins,* 72 M.J. at 313, 314–15, 317–18 (Baker, C.J., dissenting). Of course, if a speaker intends to influence a judicial or reviewing authority and that speaker actually influences that authority, the speaker will have likely committed actual unlawful command influence. *See* United States v. Lewis, 63 M.J. 405, 414 (C.A.A.F.2006) (finding actual unlawful command influence where the Government's "orchestrated effort to unseat [the military judge] exceeded any legitimate exercise of [its] right" to challenge her). In my view, apparent unlawful command influence may be shown even without proof that the speaker intended to influence a particular authority or that any authority was actually influenced. The focus of apparent unlawful command influence is whether a reasonable, disinterested member of the public, fully informed of all the facts, would perceive the military justice system as fair. *Id.* at 415.

Second, Article 37, Uniform Code of Military Justice (UCMJ), 10 U.S.C. § 837 (2006), which prohibits unlawful command influence, has been in existence since the UCMJ was established in 1950, *see* Act of May 5, 1950, Pub.L. No. 81–506, ch. 169, 64 Stat. 107, 120 (Article 37), and there has been no showing whatsoever that its prohibition against unlawful command influence trammels upon the statutory or constitutional duties of senior civilian leaders such as the Secretary, or that the two are incompatible in any way. I thus disagree that there is any justification for the civilian head of the Department of the Navy's inflammatory comments on a case where neither appellate review nor the clemency process are complete. *But see Hutchins,* 72 M.J. at 313–14 (Baker, C.J., dissenting) ("Senior officials dealing with national security questions that also implicate military justice concerns must contemplate . . . the impact on foreign relations and national security of not commenting at all."). . . .

■ BAKER, CHIEF JUDGE (dissenting):

INTRODUCTION

I respectfully dissent for two reasons. First, I do not agree with the majority's conclusion that the Naval Criminal Investigation Service (NCIS) agent's request for a permissive search authorization constitutes reinitiation of communication in violation of Appellant's Fifth Amendment rights. Appellant initiated communication with the NCIS agents, and his statement was both voluntary and the result of a knowing waiver of his right to counsel. Therefore, the military judge did not abuse his discretion in denying the motion to suppress the statement, and the statement was properly admitted into evidence.

Second, by failing to address the allegations of unlawful command influence, the majority avoids a systemically important question and central aspect of the case, which warrants inquiry and consideration by this Court. This case raises matters of first impression involving the scope of Article 37, Uniform Code of Military Justice (UCMJ), 10 U.S.C. § 837 (2006), and the nature of a service secretary's clemency process, as well as the general question of whether the prohibition against unlawful command influence bars policymakers from addressing matters of national and foreign policy importance where they also involve issues of military justice and executive clemency. While I would ultimately find that Appellant has not met his burden of raising "some evidence" of unlawful command influence, these matters deserve full and fair consideration.

ADMISSIBILITY OF APPELLANT'S STATEMENT

Background

On May 10, 2006, Appellant and the members of his squad were transferred to Fallujah for questioning as "suspects in a homicide." Upon arrival, all members of his squad had their weapons confiscated and were not permitted to communicate with each other. Appellant and the other members were billeted in trailers referred to as "cans." "The doors of the trailer rooms were locked, and the locks had to be opened with a key from both sides." When outside the "cans," an escort remained with them at all times.

On May 11, 2006, NCIS agents questioned Appellant at Camp Fallujah. The agents informed Appellant that he was suspected of the offenses for which he was subsequently charged. He was also properly advised of his rights. Appellant waived his rights and stated that the shooting was part of an ambush. When the agents confronted him with evidence indicative of a homicide, Appellant invoked his right to counsel. The agents terminated the interrogation and returned Appellant to custody.

For the next seven days, Appellant remained in the "can." While Appellant spoke with the chaplain, he was not permitted to use morale, welfare, and recreation facilities, to have access to phones, computers, or mail, or to communicate with other members of the squad. Appellant was allowed to use the latrine and shower facilities. The military judge found that, during this time period, the Government "made no direct or indirect attempts to contact him . . . or to persuade him to reopen discussion." Nor did the Government provide Appellant with counsel, as requested.

On May 18, 2006, NCIS agents approached Appellant to obtain permissive authorization to search his belongings, which he granted. The military judge made findings, based on his assessment of the witnesses' testimony, that "the agents strictly restricted their contact with the accused to the request for permissive authorization for a search of his belongings" and "the government did not seek to discuss the case with the accused further." As they searched, Appellant asked if "the door was still open to discuss his side of the story." An agent reminded Appellant that he had exercised his right to counsel, and told Appellant that they did not have time to talk that night, which the military judge found "directly contradicts any allegation that this visit to his can was a subterfuge to reinitiate contact." The agent told Appellant that he was not sure what time the following day Appellant would be sent back to the United States, but said that they would speak with him if there was time.

The next day, May 19, the NCIS agents again informed Appellant of his rights. Appellant "expressly waived those rights and indicated a continued desire to reinitiate contact with the government without the benefit of counsel." Appellant gave a lengthy, detailed statement.

Discussion

This Court reviews a military judge's denial of a motion to suppress a confession for an abuse of discretion. A military judge's findings of fact are reviewed for clear error. United States v. Chatfield, 67 M.J. 432, 437 (C.A.A.F.2009) (citing United States v. Pipkin, 58 M.J. 358, 360 (C.A.A.F.2003); United States v. Leedy, 65 M.J. 208, 213 (C.A.A.F.2007)). However, voluntariness of a confession is a question of law that this Court reviews de novo. Chatfield, 67 M.J. at 437 (citing Arizona v. Fulminante, 499 U.S. 279, 287 (1991); United States v. Bubonics, 45 M.J. 93, 94–95 (C.A.A.F.1996)).

Appellant argues that the subsequent inculpatory statement on May 19 was involuntary and thus erroneously admitted into evidence. First, Appellant contends, and the majority incorrectly holds, that under Edwards v. Arizona, 451 U.S. 477 (1981), it was the agents, not Appellant, who reinitiated interrogation. Second, in the custodial context presented in Iraq, Appellant argues that the statement was not a product of voluntary choice, but that his will was overborne by seven days of custodial isolation in the "can."

Reinitiation of Communication

The majority's assertion that a request for a permissive search authorization constitutes reinitiation of communication in violation of Appellant's Fifth Amendment rights both misapprehends the *Edwards* doctrine and directly contradicts the jurisprudence of this Court and every federal court of appeals to have addressed this issue.

Under *Edwards,* when an accused invokes his right to counsel during custodial interrogation, he "is not subject to further interrogation by the authorities until counsel has been made available to him, unless the accused himself initiates further communication, exchanges, or conversations with the police." *Edwards,* 451 U.S. at 484–85.[1] On one side of the equation, the authorities are barred from interrogation, which has been broadly interpreted to include "express questioning or its functional equivalent" of "any words or actions . . . that the police should know are reasonably likely to elicit an incriminating response." Rhode Island v. Innis, 446 U.S. 291, 300–01 (1980). This Court has defined "reinitiation of interrogation" in violation of *Edwards* to include a confrontation having "the natural tendency to induce the making of a statement by" Appellant. United States v. Brabant, 29 M.J. 259, 262–63 (C.M.A.1989) (internal quotation marks omitted). On the other side, the accused may initiate further communication, exchanges, or conversations by making inquiries or statements that can "be fairly said to represent a desire on the part of an accused to open up a more generalized discussion relating directly or indirectly to the investigation." Oregon v. Bradshaw, 462 U.S. 1039, 1045 (1983).

In summary, while the authorities must halt the interrogation after invocation of the right to counsel, "[i]f a defendant makes a statement in response to words or actions by the police that do not constitute interrogation or if the defendant himself initiates further communications, the police are not prohibited from 'merely listening' to his voluntary statement." United States v. Jones, 600 F.3d 847, 855 (7th Cir.2010); *see also* Alvarez v. McNeil, 346 Fed.Appx. 562 (11th Cir.2009); Clayton v. Gibson, 199 F.3d 1162 (10th Cir.1999); United States v. Gonzalez, No. 97–4541, 1998 U.S.App. LEXIS 14891, 1998 WL 377901 (4th Cir. July 1, 1998) (unpublished table decision); United States v. Colon, 835 F.2d 27 (2d Cir.1987). "Volunteered statements of any kind are not barred by the Fifth Amendment." Miranda v. Arizona, 384 U.S. 436, 478 (1966).[2] As the majority acknowledges, this Court has already

---

[1] In military practice, Military Rule of Evidence (M.R.E.) 305(e)(1) incorporates the *Edwards* rule, stating:

> Absent a valid waiver of counsel under subdivision (g)(2)(B), when an accused or person suspected of an offense is subjected to custodial interrogation . . . and the accused or suspect requests counsel, counsel must be present before any subsequent custodial interrogation may proceed.

Subsection (g)(2)(B)(i) describes a waiver as valid, if by a preponderance of evidence the government demonstrates "the accused or suspect initiated the communication leading to the waiver."

[2] The majority conflates the two doctrines and interprets *Edwards* and *Bradshaw* as barring the authorities from initiating not only any words or actions that are reasonably likely to elicit an incriminating response, but any communication which has the result of leading directly or indirectly to discussion of the investigation. Moreover, in this case, the military judge found that the communication in question was no more than a request to search, a well-established exception to the *Edwards* rule. *See* infra pp. 297–99. The majority fails to cite any authority to support such an expansion of the *Edwards* and *Bradshaw* doctrines, in direct

determined that, "[a] request for a consent to search does not infringe upon Article 31 or Fifth Amendment safeguards against self-incrimination because such requests are not interrogations and the consent given is ordinarily not a statement." United States v. Frazier, 34 M.J. 135, 137 (C.M.A.1992).[3] Moreover, the military judge found that "the agents strictly restricted their contact with the accused to the request for permissive authorization for a search of his belongings" and "the government did not seek to discuss the case with the accused further." In other words, it was not a circumstance where the agents baited their words to encourage or elicit a response, which is further evidenced by the fact that the agents did not follow-up Appellant's question by taking an immediate statement, but waiting until the next day. As the military judge found, this "directly contradicts any allegation that this visit to his can was a subterfuge to reinitiate contact."

Federal courts of appeals that have considered this issue "unanimously agree that consenting to a search is not an incriminating statement under the Fifth Amendment because the consent is not evidence of a testimonial or communicative nature," United States v. Cooney, 26 Fed.Appx. 513, 523 (6th Cir.2002), and Fifth Amendment protections only apply to incriminating evidence of a testimonial or communicative nature. Schmerber v. California, 384 U.S. 757, 760–61 (1966).[4]

---

opposition to the case law of this Court and the federal courts of appeals. While the Supreme Court has not directly addressed this issue, Justices Brennan and Marshall, who dissented in *Bradshaw* in favor of a broader interpretation of *Edwards* protections, were clear that the doctrine only barred the authorities from words and acts amounting to interrogation. *See* James v. Arizona, 469 U.S. 990, 993 (1984) (order denying certiorari) (Brennan, J., with whom Marshall, J., joined, dissenting) ("Under the strict rule of *Edwards* and *Bradshaw* once an accused has invoked the right to counsel no further interrogation is permitted until the accused initiates a new dialogue with the authorities. Sergeant Midkiff's query '[i]s he going to show us where the body is,' though directed at Officer Davis, indisputably triggered James' statement 'I'll show you where the body is.' That James made the statement in response to Midkiff's inquiry is not, however, determinative of the 'initiation' question. If Midkiff's inquiry is not viewed as interrogation for Fifth Amendment purposes, then James' response might be a voluntary initiation of dialogue. Some official statements made within earshot of an accused in custody are not 'interrogation' even if they prompt a response.").

  [3] The majority's reference to United States v. Applewhite, 23 M.J. 196 (C.M.A.1987), is misplaced. Unlike consent to search, a polygraph examination involves evidence of a testimonial or communicative nature, which is why this Court held that it constituted further interrogation. *Id.* at 198 ("Rather than immediately ceasing all interrogation as the law requires, however, Agent Bernardi asked appellant to submit to further interrogation in the form of a polygraph examination.").

  [4] See, *e.g.*, United States v. Lewis, 921 F.2d 1294, 1303 (D.C.Cir.1990) ("[I]f the judge meant to suggest that an officer must issue a Miranda warning before asking permission to search an individual, 'every federal circuit court that has addressed the question has reached the opposite conclusion.' "); United States v. Faruolo, 506 F.2d 490, 495 (2d Cir.1974) (citation omitted) ("The argument that Miranda warnings are a prerequisite to an effective consent to search is not at all persuasive. . . . There is no possible violation of fifth amendment rights since the consent to search is not 'evidence of a testimonial or communicative nature.' "); Smith v. Wainwright, 581 F.2d 1149, 1152 (5th Cir.1978) ("[C]onsent to search is not a self-incriminating statement; '[i]t is not in itself evidence of a testimonial or communicative nature.' ") (second set of brackets in original) (citation omitted); United States v. Glenna, 878 F.2d 967, 971 (7th Cir.1989) ("[A]lthough the district court believed that the officers' request for consent to retrieve the registration papers was 'reasonably likely to evoke an incriminating response' and therefore ran afoul of Miranda, every federal circuit court that has addressed the question has reached

The majority fails to address, however, this Court's prior holdings that, since a request for consent to search does not constitute an interrogation, *Edwards* does not bar police authorities from requesting the suspect's consent to a search before he or she has consulted with counsel. United States v. Burns, 33 M.J. 316 (C.M.A.1991); United States v. Roa, 24 M.J. 297 (C.M.A.1987). In *Burns,* this Court rejected the appellant's claim that his Fifth Amendment and Article 31, UCMJ, 10 U.S.C. § 831 (2000), rights were violated by a request for consent to search after he invoked his right to counsel, holding that the argument was "plagued by a faulty premise, for it seems to ignore the significant distinctions outlined by us in *Roa.*" 33 M.J. at 320.

The Court explained:

[I]nterrogation is for the purpose of eliciting from a suspect communications about the matter under investigation. However, a consent to search does not of itself communicate any information about the investigated crime; and it is not a statement regarding an offense. Therefore, requesting consent to search property in which a suspect has an interest is not prohibited by his prior request for counsel, because Edwards provides protection only as to interrogation.

Id. (quoting *Roa,* 24 M.J. at 301 (Everett, C.J., concurring in the result)). Since consent "is not a statement" and a request for consent is not an "interrogation," consent to search is "a neutral fact which has no tendency to show that the suspect is guilty of any crime" and is not in itself incriminating. *Id.* (citations omitted) (internal quotation marks omitted). Therefore, the *Edwards* doctrine does not prevent authorities from making a search request after a suspect invokes the right to counsel. *Id.*

The other federal courts also agree that a defendant's consent to search is not an incriminating response, and therefore a request for consent is not "interrogation" and does not violate *Edwards. See* United States v. Knope, 655 F.3d 647, 654 (7th Cir.2011) ("Knope's argument [that his consent to search was invalid under Edwards because he signed after invoking his right to counsel] is foreclosed, however, by this court's holding that 'a consent to search is not an interrogation within the meaning of *Miranda.*' "); United States v. Bustamante, 493 F.3d 879, 892 (7th Cir.2007) ("Though all interrogation must cease once a defendant in custody has invoked his right to counsel, a request to search a vehicle or home is not likely to elicit an incriminating response and is therefore not interrogation."); United States v. Taylor, No. 99–4373, 2000 U.S.App. LEXIS 106 at *4, 2000 WL 6146 at *2 (4th Cir. Jan. 6, 2000) (unpublished

---

the opposite conclusion."); Cody v. Solem, 755 F.2d 1323, 1330 (8th Cir.1985) ("a consent to search is not an incriminating statement"); United States v. Lemon, 550 F.2d 467, 472 (9th Cir.1977) ("[C]onsent to a search is not the type of incriminating statement toward which the fifth amendment is directed."); United States v. Rodriguez-Garcia, 983 F.2d 1563, 1568 (10th Cir.1993); United States v. Hidalgo, 7 F.3d 1566, 1568 (11th Cir.1993).

table decision) ("There was no *Miranda* violation when, after Taylor informed investigators that he was not responding to any more questions, investigators asked him to consent to a search of his financial records. Asking for and receiving consent was not part of the interrogation because giving consent is not a self-incriminating statement."); United States v. Gonzalez, 1998 U.S.App. LEXIS 14891, at *3–*4, 1998 WL 377901, at *1 ("Gonzalez' consent to search, however, is not an interrogation that triggers his previously invoked right to counsel [under *Edwards*]."); United States v. Shlater, 85 F.3d 1251, 1256 (7th Cir.1996) ("Even though Shlater stated that he wished to have counsel present for any interrogation regarding the specific events of the evening, the law provides that request for counsel during the interrogation does not apply to the subsequent request for a consent to search."); Tukes v. Dugger, 911 F.2d 508 (11th Cir.1990) (denying habeas corpus claim based on consent to search obtained after defendant had invoked right to counsel); Dunn v. Pliler, 2008 U.S. Dist. LEXIS 32633, at *35–*39, 2008 WL 1701904, at *13–*15 (N.D.Cal.2008) (consent to search was voluntary after defendant had invoked right to counsel); State v. Crannell, 170 Vt. 387, 750 A.2d 1002, 1009 (2000), overruled in part on other grounds by State v. Brillon, 2008 VT 35 ¶ 41, 183 Vt. 475, 497, 955 A.2d 1108, 1123 ("The federal courts of appeal agree that a defendant's consent to search is not an incriminating response and therefore a request for consent is not "interrogation" subject to limitation by *Edwards*."). In *United States v. Harmon,* for example, the defendant invoked her right to counsel, but then made statements about what was in her work area after an officer requested her consent to search the area. 2006 U.S. Dist. LEXIS 390, at *18, 2006 WL 42083, at *6 (D.Kan.2006). The court found that since a request to search does not amount to interrogation, the defendant voluntarily initiated the statements and they should not be suppressed. *Id.*

In the present case, when Appellant invoked his right to counsel, the NCIS agents properly terminated the interrogation. Thus, when the agents requested Appellant's consent to search and provided him with a permissive search authorization, Appellant was not subject to interrogation in the form of "express questioning or its functional equivalent." *Innis,* 446 U.S. at 300–01. As this Court and every federal court of appeals that has considered the issue have found, a request for consent to search does not constitute an interrogation. A defendant's consent to search is neither of a testimonial or communicative nature, nor an incriminating response, and therefore a request for consent is not "interrogation" subject to limitation by Edwards. Furthermore, a request for consent to search, even if accompanied by a reminder on a form that the accused is under investigation, is not "for the purpose of eliciting from a suspect communications about the matter under investigation." *Burns,* 33 M.J. at 320 (internal quotation marks and citation omitted). Therefore, even under the standard proposed by the majority, the request cannot be said to "open up a more generalized discussion relating directly or indirectly to the investigation." *Bradshaw,* 462 U.S. at 1045.

Rather, in asking whether "the door was still open to discuss his side of the story," Appellant himself initiated "further communication, exchanges, or conversations with the police." *Edwards,* 451 U.S. at 484–85. The military judge's finding on this point, based on his assessment of the witnesses' testimony, is not clearly erroneous. Further, as a matter of law, Appellant's inquiry "evinced a willingness and a desire for a generalized discussion about the investigation; it was not merely a necessary inquiry arising out of the incidents of the custodial relationship." *Bradshaw,* 462 U.S. at 1045–46. That the agents understood the question in this manner is apparent from the fact that they immediately reminded the accused that he had exercised his right to counsel, and did not continue questioning until the following day after Appellant had expressly waived his rights. *See id.* at 1046.

Waiver

Absent an *Edwards* violation, the question becomes:

whether a valid waiver of the right to counsel and the right to silence had occurred, that is, whether the purported waiver was knowing and intelligent and found to be so under the totality of the circumstances, including the necessary fact that the accused, not the police, reopened the dialogue with the authorities.

Id. (quoting *Edwards,* 451 U.S. at 486 n.9); *see also* M.R.E. 305(g)(1) ("The waiver must be made freely, knowingly, and intelligently."). Such assessment is based on the totality of the circumstances, including: "the condition of the accused, his health, age, education, and intelligence; the character of the detention, including the conditions of the questioning and rights warning; and the manner of the interrogation, including the length of the interrogation and the use of force, threats, promises, or deceptions." United States v. Ellis, 57 M.J. 375, 379 (C.A.A.F.2002).[5]

The record reflects that Appellant first invoked his right to counsel, immediately terminating the interrogation. Appellant spent seven days in confinement, and then reinitiated conversation. The agents did not bait him into doing so with threats, promises, or inducements, but merely asked Appellant for a permissive search authorization. Appellant then had a further night to consider his waiver. The next day, Appellant received a cleansing warning and waived his rights.

Appellant does not contest that, after communicating with the agents during the search process on the evening of May 18, he was again orally advised of his right to counsel and that reinterrogation did not commence until the following day. He further does not contest that at

---

[5]   These factors go to the separate consideration of whether a valid waiver of the right to counsel and the right to silence occurred; they are not part of the *Edwards* determination.

that time and prior to questioning he received a cleansing warning orally and in writing. Ordinarily such circumstances are persuasive indication that a statement is voluntary. However, Appellant argues that the circumstances of his custodial detention in a combat zone should alter the analysis.

I would conclude that Appellant's detention conditions and lack of access to counsel for seven days did not vitiate what was otherwise his knowing and voluntary waiver. This conclusion is based on three factors. First, civilian courts have consistently found that solitary confinement, which also creates an inherent incentive to seek release by making a statement, alone does not render a waiver of rights involuntary. Appellant has not cited contrary authority. Custodial detention in the "can" no doubt creates its own pressure and incentive to obtain release, but Appellant has not made the case that as a matter of law his detention should be treated differently for Edwards purposes than solitary confinement, where there is a subsequent knowing and voluntary waiver of rights. *See, e.g.,* United States v. Webb, 311 Fed.Appx. 582, 584 (4th Cir.2009) (Webb initiated contact and knowingly and voluntarily waived his rights after being held in isolation for four days without access to counsel); United States v. Odeh (In re Terrorist Bombings of U.S. Embassies in E. Afr.), 552 F.3d 177, 214 (2d Cir.2008) ("Taking into account the totality of the circumstances, as we must, we cannot conclude that, because Al-'Owhali was detained incommunicado for fourteen days, the statements he made after waiving his *Miranda* rights were involuntary."); Clark v. Solem, 693 F.2d 59, 61–62 (8th Cir.1982) (sixty days of solitary confinement did not render plea involuntary); United States v. Kiendra, 663 F.2d 349, 351 (1st Cir.1981) (Nineteen year-old's solitary confinement for thirty days "cannot be presumed to have weakened his will to such an extent that he was incompetent to exercise his rights."); Brown v. United States, 356 F.2d 230, 232 (10th Cir.1966) (placement in disciplinary segregation for several days did not render confession involuntary).

Second, while the combat context in the present case may have added to the pressure Appellant may have felt in isolation, Appellant was also aware the he was returning to the United States on an imminent basis—in fact, the same day that Appellant made the statement. In other words, Appellant was not facing the prospect of an unknown and indeterminate period of custodial detention in the "can," the escape from which he might have concluded might only come from waiving his right to counsel and making a statement.

Finally, Appellant did not waive his rights immediately after reinitiating communication with the agents. Nor was he tricked, lured, or baited into doing so. Having opened the door to making a statement, Appellant was given the opportunity to reflect upon his decision overnight. This was not a snap decision or the product of a personality overborne.

Certainly, seven days in the "can" without access to counsel is anything but a model in light of *Edwards*. Generally, this Court expects "assignment of counsel for representational purposes at the earliest possible moment in the process of military justice." United States v. Jackson, 5 M.J. 223, 226 (C.M.A.1978). *But see Miranda*, 384 U.S. at 474 ("If authorities conclude that they will not provide counsel during a reasonable period of time in which investigation in the field is carried out, they may refrain from doing so without violating the person's Fifth Amendment privilege so long as they do not question him during that time."). At the same time, we are not charged in this case with determining best practice, but rather with determining whether Appellant's constitutional rights as described by *Edwards* were violated. In the absence of a *per se* rule that a delay in providing counsel invalidates an otherwise knowing and voluntary waiver, I would conclude that Appellant's rights were not violated. Appellant's waiver occurred following his reinitiating communication. A substantial delay occurred before the subsequent interrogation, in which Appellant could contemplate and consider his options. And, a cleansing warning was provided in both oral and written form. Thus, for the purpose of *Edwards* and M.R.E. 305, Appellant's statements were voluntary and the result of a knowing waiver under the totality of the circumstances. Therefore, I would hold that the military judge did not abuse his discretion in denying the motion to suppress the statement, and the statement was properly admitted into evidence.

UNLAWFUL COMMAND INFLUENCE

. . . .

In November 2009, while Appellant's case was pending before the CCA on direct appeal, the Secretary of the Navy (SECNAV) issued a press release and gave interviews discussing the case.[8] For example, of Appellant and his squad, the Secretary of the Navy stated:

> None of their actions lived up to the core values of the Marine Corps and the Navy. . . . This was not a "fog of war" case occurring in the heat of battle. This was carefully planned and executed, as was the cover-up. The plan was carried out exactly as it had been conceived.

[citation omitted] The Secretary of the Navy noted that the sentence was "commensurate" with the offense, and that Appellant had already received sufficient clemency. The Secretary of the Navy also publicly expressed "surprise" that members of the squad had been permitted to

---

[8] On September 12, 2011, the CCA granted Hutchins's motion to attach certain documents to the record which reported the Secretary of the Navy's comments. The CCA determined that "[t]he comments were publicly made and their content and timing are not in dispute." 2012 CCA LEXIS 93, at *6, 2012 WL 933067 at *2. The CCA summarized the Secretary's comments as expressing "surprise and disappointment with the sentences and the prospect of continuing service for the personnel involved in this case." 2012 CCA LEXIS 93, at *6 n. 1, 2012 WL 933067 at *2 n. 1.

remain on active duty. In addition, the Secretary announced his decision to direct their separation from the service. . . .

Discussion

In deciding this case based on the admission of Appellant's statement, the majority avoids a systemically important question involving unlawful command influence. This is a mistake. First, the issue of unlawful command influence was litigated throughout these proceedings. It is a central aspect of the case. As a result, Appellant's and the public's confidence in the ultimate outcome in the handling of this case rests in part on how this issue is addressed, or not addressed.

Second, this Court has referred to unlawful command influence as "the mortal enemy of military justice." United States v. Douglas, 68 M.J. 349, 355 (C.A.A.F.2010) (internal quotation marks and citation omitted). If that is the case, then the issue should warrant inquiry and consideration by the military justice system's highest, and only, civilian court. Moreover, this case raises matters of first impression involving the scope of Article 37, UCMJ, as well as the nature of a service secretary's clemency process. To what extent, if at all, does the prohibition against unlawful command influence bar policymakers from addressing matters of national and foreign policy importance where they also involve matters of military justice and executive clemency? . . . .

7. THE *MIRANDA* EXCLUSIONARY RULE

United States v. Nichols

438 F.3d 437 (4th Cir. 2006)

■ WILLIAM W. WILKINS, CHIEF JUDGE.

The United States appeals James David Nichols' sentence for bank robbery, *see* 18 U.S.C.A. § 2113(a) (West 2000), arguing that the district court improperly refused to consider at sentencing a statement obtained from Nichols in violation of Miranda v. Arizona, 384 U.S. 436, (1966), and Edwards v. Arizona, 451 U.S. 477(1981). Because the Fifth Amendment does not prohibit the district court from considering this statement at sentencing, we vacate Nichols' sentence and remand for resentencing.[1]

I.

On March 13, 2003, Nichols entered a branch of First Citizens Bank in Charlotte, North Carolina, and handed a bank teller a note stating, "This is A Robbery Give up the money or I shoot." J.A. 355. The teller gave Nichols approximately $5,000. Shortly after the bank robbery,

---

[1] On cross-appeal, Nichols argues that the district court violated the Sixth Amendment by applying a sentencing enhancement based on judge-found facts and by treating the sentencing guidelines as mandatory. *See* United States v. Booker, 543 U.S. 220 (2005). Because we are remanding for resentencing on other grounds, we need not consider Nichols' Booker claims; on remand, the district court should resentence Nichols in accordance with *Booker*. *See* United States v. Hughes, 401 F.3d 540, 546–47 (4th Cir.2005).

Nichols' father telephoned authorities to report that his son may have committed the robbery. A few days later, Detective James Michael Sanders of the Charlotte-Mecklenburg Police Department telephoned Nichols, who was then with his father, to arrange for Nichols to surrender to police. According to Nichols and his father, during this conversation Nichols informed Detective Sanders that he wanted an attorney, and Sanders assured Nichols he would receive one. Nichols and his father then met Detective Sanders at an agreed-upon location, and Nichols voluntarily returned what was left of the money obtained in the bank robbery. According to Nichols and his father, Nichols again informed Detective Sanders that he wanted an attorney, and Sanders again responded that Nichols would receive one.

Nichols was then taken into custody and transported to the police station. Although Nichols did not initiate further contact with police, Detective Sanders took Nichols to an interview room and reviewed with him an "Adult Waiver of Rights" form, *id.* at 94, which Nichols initialed in several places and signed at the bottom. In particular, Nichols initialed statements acknowledging that he had the rights to consult with an attorney, to have an attorney present during questioning, and to stop answering questions until he spoke with an attorney. Nichols also circled, initialed, and signed a portion of the form indicating that he voluntarily agreed to answer questions without an attorney present. Detective Sanders then interviewed Nichols, who confessed to robbing the bank and to carrying a .45-caliber pistol in his pants pocket during the robbery.

Nichols was indicted by a federal grand jury on charges of bank robbery, *see* 18 U.S.C.A. § 2113(a); armed bank robbery, *see* 18 U.S.C.A. § 2113(d) (West 2000); and using or carrying a firearm during and in relation to a crime of violence, *see* 18 U.S.C.A. § 924(c)(1)(A) (West Supp.2005). Nichols moved to suppress his confession-specifically, his admission to carrying a firearm during the robbery. He claimed that before he made any statements to police, he had requested an attorney and had been assured-despite his signing of the "Adult Waiver of Rights" form-that counsel would be made available to him. Thus, Nichols argued that the statements he gave in response to police questioning after he requested counsel were inadmissible. *See Edwards,* 451 U.S. at 484–85; *Miranda,* 384 U.S. at 474–76.

A magistrate judge conducted a hearing on Nichols' suppression motion. Nichols and his father testified (as described above) that Nichols twice requested counsel before his confession. Detective Sanders, however, testified that Nichols never requested an attorney prior to questioning. Noting that the resolution of Nichols' motion "comes down to a single factual question: namely, whether [Nichols] asked for an attorney before he was interrogated," J.A. 76, the magistrate judge found that the testimony of Nichols and his father "credibly establishes that an attorney was requested not once but twice," *id.* at 80. Because Nichols did not initiate the further communications with police after requesting an attorney, the magistrate judge recommended that Nichols' confession be suppressed.

The Government filed objections to the magistrate judge's recommended decision, arguing primarily that Nichols had not, in fact, requested counsel before police questioned him. Following a hearing, the district court adopted the findings and conclusions of the magistrate judge, including the finding that Nichols twice requested an attorney. The district court therefore granted Nichols' motion to suppress. Due to the suppression of Nichols' statement that he carried a firearm during the robbery-the only direct evidence that a firearm was present-the Government dismissed the armed bank robbery and firearm charges.

Nichols pleaded guilty to the bank robbery charge. In the presentence report (PSR), the probation officer did not recommend an enhancement for possession of a firearm during the robbery, *see* U.S. Sentencing Guidelines Manual § 2B3.1(b)(2)(C) (2004). The Government objected to this omission, arguing that Nichols had admitted to possessing a firearm during the robbery and that this statement, though suppressed for purposes of conviction, could be considered at sentencing. The probation officer rejected the Government's argument, stating that because "one of [Nichols'] fundamental rights under the United States Constitution was violated in securing this statement," enhancing Nichols' sentence based on that statement "would only compound the violation." J.A. 375. At sentencing, the district court adopted the probation officer's recommendation not to apply a firearm enhancement. The district court sentenced Nichols to 46 months imprisonment.

II.

The Government contends that the district court erroneously excluded from consideration at sentencing Nichols' statement that he possessed a firearm during the robbery. The Government argues that although this statement is inadmissible for purposes of conviction, there is no constitutional impediment to considering the statement in determining Nichols' sentence. We review this legal issue de novo. *See* United States v. Acosta, 303 F.3d 78, 84 (1st Cir.2002).

District courts traditionally have been "given wide latitude as to the information they may consider in passing sentence after a conviction." United States v. Howard-Arias, 679 F.2d 363, 367 (4th Cir.1982); *see* United States v. Tucker, 404 U.S. 443, 446 (1972) ("[B]efore making [the sentencing] determination, a judge may appropriately conduct an inquiry broad in scope, largely unlimited either as to the kind of information he may consider, or the source from which it may come."); Williams v. New York, 337 U.S. 241, 246 (1949) (explaining that courts have traditionally "exercise[d] a wide discretion in the sources and types of evidence used to assist [them] in determining the kind and extent of punishment to be imposed within limits fixed by law"); *see also* Nichols v. United States, 511 U.S. 738, 747 (1994) (noting that "the sentencing process . . . [is] less exacting than the process of establishing guilt"). That is because it is "[h]ighly relevant-if not essential-to [the] selection of an appropriate sentence" for the sentencing court to "possess [ ] . . . the fullest information possible concerning the defendant's life and characteristics." *Williams*, 337 U.S. at 247.

This broad discretion has been preserved under the sentencing guidelines. In resolving any dispute concerning a factor pertinent to the sentencing decision, "the court may consider relevant information without regard to its admissibility under the rules of evidence applicable at trial, provided that the information has sufficient indicia of reliability to support its probable accuracy." U.S.S.G. § 6A1.3(a), p.s. And, in selecting a particular sentence within the guideline range (or deciding whether to depart from that range), a district court "may consider, without limitation, any information concerning the background, character and conduct of the defendant, unless otherwise prohibited by law." *Id.* § 1B1.4; *see* 18 U.S.C.A. § 3661 (West 2000) ("No limitation shall be placed on the information concerning the background, character, and conduct of a person convicted of an offense which a court of the United States may receive and consider for the purpose of imposing an appropriate sentence.").

Nevertheless, we have recognized that "[t]here are . . . constitutional limitations" on the generally broad scope of information a court may consider at sentencing. United States v. Lee, 540 F.2d 1205, 1210 (4th Cir.1976). In particular, we have construed various Supreme Court decisions as "recogniz[ing] a due process right to be sentenced only on information which is accurate." *Id.* at 1211. For example, in *Tucker*, the Supreme Court held that it was improper for a sentencing court to consider a defendant's prior felony convictions that had been obtained without affording the defendant the right to counsel. *See Tucker*, 404 U.S. at 447–49. The Court emphasized that the sentence was "founded at least in part upon misinformation of constitutional magnitude," in that the defendant "was sentenced on the basis of assumptions concerning his criminal record which were materially untrue." *Id.* at 447 (internal quotation marks omitted); *see* Lee, 540 F.2d at 1211 ("[A]s the Court explained [in Tucker], the absence of counsel impugns the integrity of the fact-finding process so that a conviction obtained in the absence of counsel is unreliable.").

In *Lee,* however, we held that "reliable but illegally obtained evidence may generally be considered" at sentencing. *Lee,* 540 F.2d at 1207. There, the defendant (Lee) was convicted of illegally possessing a firearm. *See id.* In determining Lee's sentence, the district court considered a prior state court conviction for narcotics possession; that conviction, however, had been reversed on appeal because law enforcement officers had lacked probable cause to arrest Lee, rendering the subsequent search that yielded the narcotics invalid. *See id.* at 1210. In rejecting Lee's argument that the district court should not have considered the conviction, we recognized that "[m]ost illegally-obtained evidence . . . is not inherently unreliable; it is excluded at trial on the theory that exclusion will deter the making of illegal searches." *Id.* at 1211. We therefore explained that to determine whether illegally obtained evidence must be excluded at sentencing, the court must "evaluate the degree of deterrence which might be promoted by exclusion of such evidence . . . and weigh that degree of deterrence against the concomitant limitation of the right of the sentencing judge to impose sentence in the light of all relevant facts." *Id.* (citing United States v. Calandra, 414 U.S. 338, 349 (1974)). We noted that in most cases the additional deterrent effect of excluding from sentencing illegally obtained evidence already inadmissible for purposes of conviction "would be so minimal as to be insignificant." *Id.*

We thus concluded in *Lee* that "the disadvantages of applying the exclusionary rule at sentencing are large, the benefits small or non-existent, and . . . the rule should therefore not be extended." *Id.* at 1212. We noted, however, that we might reach the opposite conclusion if "it appeared that the government had illegally seized additional evidence with a view toward enhancing the defendant's sentence; for there, as long as the exclusionary rule persists, its rationale can be served only by excluding illegally-seized evidence from consideration at sentencing." *Id.*

Although *Lee* was a pre-guidelines decision, every other circuit has concluded that courts imposing sentences under the guidelines may generally consider evidence obtained in violation of the Fourth Amendment. *See Acosta*, 303 F.3d at 84–86 (collecting cases and reaching same conclusion).[3] These courts have relied largely on the same reasoning we articulated in *Lee*-namely, that "the deterrent effect of the exclusionary rule does not outweigh the detrimental effects of excluding reliable evidence on the court's ability to meet its goal of proper sentencing." *Acosta,* 303 F.3d at 85. These courts have further "recognized that the sentencing court needs to have the fullest information available to fashion an appropriate remedy and that the Sentencing Guidelines allow the sentencing court to consider" a broad range of information concerning the defendant. *Id.*

Here, the Government argues that we should extend the reasoning of *Lee* to permit consideration at sentencing of a statement obtained in violation of *Miranda* and *Edwards*. In *Miranda*, the Supreme Court held that to protect the Fifth Amendment privilege against compelled self-incrimination, a criminal suspect must be advised before custodial interrogation that, inter alia, he has the right to the presence of an attorney during questioning. *See Miranda*, 384 U.S. at 478–79. If the suspect requests counsel, "the interrogation must cease until an attorney is present." *Id.* at 474. In *Edwards*, the Supreme Court "re-confirm[ed]"

---

[3]   As in *Lee,* most of these courts have suggested that illegally seized evidence might be excluded from consideration at sentencing "if there is an indication that the police violated the defendant's Fourth Amendment rights with the intent to secure an increased sentence." Acosta, 303 F.3d at 85 (citing cases).

the *Miranda* principles regarding the right to counsel during custodial interrogation and held that once a suspect invokes that right, police may not interrogate the suspect further "until counsel has been made available to him, unless the accused himself initiates further communication, exchanges, or conversations with the police." *Edwards*, 451 U.S. at 484–85. Any statements obtained by police in violation of *Miranda* and *Edwards*—including statements that would otherwise be considered voluntary—are presumed involuntary and are inadmissible in the government's case-in-chief at trial. *See* Oregon v. Elstad, 470 U.S. 298, 307 (1985); *see also* McNeil v. Wisconsin, 501 U.S. 171, 177 (1991).

Only one federal appellate court, the Seventh Circuit, has specifically addressed whether statements obtained by police in violation of *Miranda* are admissible at sentencing. *See* Del Vecchio v. Ill. Dep't of Corr., 31 F.3d 1363, 1388 (7th Cir.1994) (en banc). In *Del Vecchio*, a state habeas petitioner challenged the admission, at the sentencing phase of his capital murder trial, of a 14-year-old confession to an earlier murder that he claimed was obtained in violation of *Miranda*. *See id*. The Seventh Circuit rejected this argument, holding that even if a *Miranda* violation were established, "that violation would not require exclusion of the confession during the sentencing proceedings" because "[t]he exclusionary rule is generally inapplicable during sentencing." *Id*. (citing Fourth Amendment cases); *see also id*. (explaining that "evidence which might be inadmissible at the guilt phase of a trial can be admitted at the sentencing phase, as long as the evidence is reliable"). The court further observed that "there was really no deterrent effect in applying the [exclusionary] rule; any police misconduct would have occurred fourteen years before the confession was introduced." *Id*.

We agree with the Seventh Circuit that statements obtained in violation of *Miranda*, if they are otherwise voluntary, may generally be considered at sentencing. The Supreme Court has repeatedly held that although statements obtained in violation of *Miranda* are inadmissible in the government's case-in-chief at trial, such statements, if reliable, may be used for other purposes and in other ways. *See, e.g.,* Elstad, 470 U.S. at 307 ("[T]he *Miranda* presumption, though irrebuttable for purposes of the prosecution's case in chief, does not require that the statements and their fruits be discarded as inherently tainted."). For example, the Court has held that in the absence of actual coercion, statements obtained without warning a defendant of his right to counsel under *Miranda* may be used to impeach the defendant's testimony at trial. *See* Harris v. New York, 401 U.S. 222, 224–26 (1971). The Court has similarly upheld the introduction, for impeachment purposes, of otherwise voluntary statements obtained after a suspect had invoked his *Miranda* right to counsel but before counsel was provided. *See* Oregon v. Hass, 420 U.S. 714, 722–24 (1975). Further, the Court has held that the Fifth Amendment does not bar the admission at trial of the testimony of witnesses discovered through a defendant's unwarned but otherwise voluntary statements, *see* Michigan v. Tucker, 417 U.S. 433, 446–52 (1974), nor does it bar the introduction of physical evidence discovered as a result of such statements, *see* United States v. Patane, 542 U.S. 630 (2004) (plurality opinion); *id.* at 2631 (Kennedy, J., concurring in the judgment). Moreover, the Court has held that when a defendant makes unwarned but otherwise voluntary statements, the Fifth Amendment normally does not require suppression of subsequent statements made after *Miranda* warnings are given. *See* Elstad, 470 U.S. at 318.

These decisions have relied on the same rationale as cases permitting the consideration of illegally seized evidence at sentencing-namely, a balancing of the deterrent effect expected to be achieved by extending the *Miranda* exclusionary rule against the harm resulting from the exclusion of reliable evidence from the truth-finding process. *See id.* at 308 ("[T]he absence of any coercion or improper tactics undercuts the twin rationales-trustworthiness and deterrence-for a broader rule."); *Hass*, 420 U.S. at 722 (explaining that voluntary statements to be used for impeachment "would provide valuable aid to the jury in assessing the defendant's credibility" and that "there is sufficient deterrence when the evidence in question is made unavailable to the prosecution in its case in chief"); *Harris*, 401 U.S. at 225 (similar); *Tucker,* 417 U.S. at 447–50 (holding that neither deterrence nor trustworthiness rationales of Fifth Amendment exclusionary rule supported exclusion of evidence at issue; emphasizing the need to "weigh the strong interest under any system of justice of making available to the trier of fact all concededly relevant and trustworthy evidence"); *see also* Missouri v. Seibert, 542 U.S. 600 (2004) (Kennedy, J., concurring in the judgment) ("Evidence [obtained in violation of *Miranda*] is admissible when the central concerns of *Miranda* are not likely to be implicated and when other objectives of the criminal justice system are best served by its introduction."); United States v. Havens, 446 U.S. 620, 627 (1980) (indicating that similar policies underlie Fourth and Fifth Amendment exclusionary rules).

Applying these principles here, we conclude that the policies underlying the *Miranda* exclusionary rule normally will not justify the exclusion of illegally obtained but reliable evidence from a sentencing proceeding. We believe that in most cases, the exclusion of evidence obtained in violation of *Miranda* from the government's case-in-chief at trial will provide ample deterrence against police misconduct. *See Hass,* 420 U.S. at 722; *Harris*, 401 U.S. at 225; cf. *Lee,* 540 F.2d at 1211. For example, as a result of the *Miranda-Edwards* violations here, the Government was required to dismiss two of the three charges against Nichols-including a firearm charge that carried a mandatory minimum sentence of five years imprisonment, required to be served consecutively to any other sentence, *see* 18 U.S.C.A. § 924(c)(1)(A)(i), (D)(ii) (West 2000). As we recognized in *Lee,* and as other circuits have noted, the additional deterrent effect of excluding illegally obtained evidence from sentencing usually would be minimal. *See Lee,* 540 F.2d at 1211; *Acosta,*

303 F.3d at 85; *cf. Hass*, 420 U.S. at 723 (characterizing as "speculative" the possibility that police may continue to question a suspect despite his request for counsel in order to obtain evidence for impeachment).[5]

In addition, absent coercive tactics by police, there is nothing inherently unreliable about otherwise voluntary statements obtained in violation of *Miranda* and *Edwards. See, e.g., Hass*, 420 U.S. at 722–23 (finding, in case in which police failed to honor defendant's request for counsel, no indication that defendant's subsequent statements were involuntary or coerced); *see also* Dickerson v. United States, 530 U.S. 428, 433–34 (2000) (discussing traditional standards for determining whether a confession was involuntary). Here, for instance, there is no claim that Nichols' confession-though obtained improperly after he requested counsel-was coerced or otherwise involuntary, nor could the record support such a claim. Nichols described his questioning, which lasted approximately four hours, as being conversational. During the interview, Nichols was not handcuffed or otherwise physically restrained. The door to Nichols' interview room was open, and he was allowed to smoke. Further, Nichols testified that he spoke with police because he believed it would benefit him to cooperate. During the telephone conversation with Nichols before his surrender, Detective Sanders indicated that if Nichols turned himself in, it would benefit him in connection with other state charges. At no time, however, did Detective Sanders make any specific promises or inducements in exchange for Nichols answering questions. *See* United States v. Mashburn, 406 F.3d 303, 309–10 (4th Cir.2005).

By contrast, the exclusion of reliable evidence hampers the ability of sentencing courts to consider all relevant information about the defendant in selecting an appropriate sentence. *See Lee,* 540 F.2d at 1211–12; Acosta, 303 F.3d at 85. Here, for example, the exclusion of Nichols' confession at sentencing prevented the district court from taking into account a significant aggravating factor in the bank robbery-Nichols' possession of a firearm.

In sum, we conclude that in cases such as this one-where there is no evidence that an illegally obtained statement was actually coerced or otherwise involuntary-the substantial burden on the sentencing process resulting from exclusion of that statement outweighs any countervailing concerns about police deterrence or unreliable evidence. As with evidence obtained in violation of the Fourth Amendment, "the disadvantages of applying the [*Miranda*] exclusionary rule at sentencing are large, [and] the benefits small or non-existent." *Lee,* 540 F.2d at 1212. We therefore conclude that in most cases, including this one, a district court may

---

[5]   As in *Lee,* however, we note that illegally obtained evidence might be subject to exclusion if there were some indication that the government obtained that evidence for the purpose of enhancing the defendant's sentence. *See Lee,* 540 F.2d at 1212. There is no such indication here.

consider at sentencing statements obtained in violation of *Miranda* and *Edwards*.[6]

Nor does our decision in *Mashburn* compel a different result. Although *Mashburn* involved a defendant's claim that the consideration at sentencing of certain statements he made in response to police questioning violated his *Miranda* rights, *see Mashburn,* 406 F.3d at 305, we were not called upon there to decide whether the *Miranda* exclusionary rule applied to sentencing proceedings, as neither party contested that issue, *see id.* at 306 (noting that "the parties agree that [Mashburn's] initial [unwarned] statements are irrebuttably presumed involuntary," and proceeding to consider whether subsequent warned statements should also be presumed involuntary).

III.

For the reasons set forth above, we conclude that the district court erroneously excluded from consideration at sentencing Nichols' statement that he carried a firearm during the robbery. We thus vacate Nichols' sentence and remand for resentencing consistent with this opinion.

VACATED AND REMANDED.

---

[6]   Nichols relies on Estelle v. Smith, 451 U.S. 454 (1981), in which the Supreme Court held that the admission, during the penalty phase of a capital murder trial, of statements obtained from the defendant in a court-ordered psychiatric examination violated the Fifth Amendment because the defendant was not warned, prior to the examination, that he had the right to remain silent and that any statements could be used against him at sentencing. *See Estelle,* 451 U.S. at 467–69. However, the Supreme Court has limited *Estelle's* Fifth Amendment holding to the "distinct circumstances" of that capital case and has "never extended [that] holding beyond its particular facts." Penry v. Johnson, 532 U.S. 782, 795 (2001) (internal quotation marks omitted). We recognize that in Mitchell v. United States, 526 U.S. 314 (1999)—also cited by Nichols—the Supreme Court relied on certain language from *Estelle* in holding that the privilege against self-incrimination applies during sentencing proceedings, even in non-capital cases. *See Mitchell,* 526 U.S. at 325–27. But, while *Mitchell* recognized the core principle that a defendant cannot be compelled to incriminate himself at sentencing, that case did not address whether the Miranda-Edwards exclusionary rule should be extended to preclude the introduction at sentencing of voluntary (though illegally obtained) prior statements. *See Patane,* 124 S.Ct. at 2627 (plurality opinion) (emphasizing that "any further extension" of *Miranda* and other rules protecting the privilege against self-incrimination "must be justified by its necessity for the protection of the actual right against compelled self-incrimination").

CHAPTER 7

THE SIXTH AMENDMENT COUNSEL CLAUSE AS A LIMIT ON POLICE INVESTIGATIONS

1. ORIGIN AND EVOLUTION OF THE SIXTH AMENDMENT COUNSEL CLAUSE

William Blackstone, IV Commentaries
*349–350

But it is a settled rule at common law, that no counsel shall be allowed a prisoner upon his trial, upon the general issue, in any capital crime, unless some point of law shall arise proper to be debated. A rule, which (however it may be palliated under cover of that noble declaration of the law, when rightly understood, that the judge shall be counsel for the prisoner; that is, shall fee that the proceedings against him are legal and strictly regular[t]) seems to be not at all of a piece with the rest of the humane treatment of prisoners by the English law. For upon what face of reason can that assistance be denied to save the life of a man, which yet is allowed him in prosecutions for every petty trespass? Nor indeed is it strictly speaking a part of out ancient law: for the mirrour, having observed the necessity of counsel in civil suits, "who know how to forward and defend "the cause, by the rules of law and customs of the realm," immediately afterwards subjoins; "and more necessary are they for defence upon indictments and appeals of felony, than upon other venial causes." And, to say the truth, the judges themselves are so sensible of this defect in our modern practice, that they seldom scruple to allow a prisoner counsel to stand by him at the bar, and instruct him what questions to ask, or even to ask questions for him, with respect to matters of fact: for as to matters of law, arising on the trial, they are intitled to the assistance of counsel. But still this is a matter of too much importance to be left to the good pleasure of any judge, and is worthy the interposition of the legislature; which has shewn it's inclination to indulge prisoners with this reasonable assistance, by enacting in statute 7 W. III. c. 3. that persons indicted for such high treason, as works a corruption of the blood, or misprision thereof, may make their full defence by counfel, not exceeding two, to be named by the prisoner and assigned

---

[t] Sir Edward Coke (3 Inst. 137.) gives another additional reason for this refusal, "because the evidence to convict a prisoner should be so manifest, as it could not be contradicted." It was therefore thought too dangerous an experiment, to let an advocate try, whether it could be contradicted or no.

by the court or judge: and this indulgence, by statute 20 Geo. II. c. 30. is extended to parliamentary impeachments for high treason, which were excepted in the former act.

Massachusetts Constitution
1780

Part I, art. XII: . . . every subject shall have a right to produce all proofs that may be favorable to him; to meet the witnesses against him face to face, and to be fully heard in his defence by himself, or his counsel at his election.

Constitution of the United States, am. VI

In all criminal prosecutions, the accused shall enjoy the right to a speedy and public trial, by an impartial jury of the State and district wherein the crime shall have been committed, which district shall have been previously ascertained by law, and to be informed of the nature and cause of the accusation; to be confronted with the witnesses against him; to have compulsory process for obtaining witnesses in his favor, and to have the Assistance of Counsel for his defence.

Judiciary Act of 1789
Ist. Cong., 1st sess., 1 Stat. 73

SEC. 35. *And be it further enacted,* That in all courts of the United States, the parties may plead and manage their own causes personally or by assistance of such counsel or attorneys at law as by the rules of the said courts respectively shall be permitted to manage and conduct causes therein. And there shall be appointed in each district a meet person learned in the law to act as attorney for the United States in such district, who shall be sworn or affirmed to the faithful execution of his office, whose duty it shall be to prosecute in such district all delinquents for crimes and offences, cognizable under the authority of the United States, and all civil actions in which the United States shall be concerned, except before the supreme court in the district in which that court shall be holden. And he shall receive as compensation for his services such fees as shall be taxed therefor in the respective courts before which the suits or prosecutions shall be. And there shall also be appointed a meet person, learned in the law, to act as attorney-general for the United States, who shall be sworn or affirmed to a faithful execution of his office; whose duty it shall be to prosecute and conduct all suits in the Supreme Court in which the United States shall be concerned, and to give his advice and opinion upon questions of law when required by the President of the United States, or when requested by the heads of any of the departments, touching any matters that may concern their departments, and shall receive such compensation for his services as shall by law be provided.

An Act for the Punishment of Certain Crimes Against the United States 1790

1st Cong., 2d sess., 1 Stat. 112

Sec. 29. *And be if [further] enacted,* That any person who shall be accused and indicted of treason, shall have a copy of the indictment, and a list of the jury and witnesses, to be produced on the trial for proving the said indictment, mentioning the names and places of abode of such witnesses and jurors, delivered unto him at least three entire days before he shall be tried for the same; and in other capital offences, shall have such copy of the indictment and list of the jury two entire days at least before the trial: And that every person so accused and indicted for any of the crimes aforesaid, shall also be allowed and admitted to make his full defence by counsel learned in the law; and the court before whom such person shall be tried, or some judge thereof, shall, and they are hereby authorized and required immediately upon his request to assign to such person such counsel, not exceeding two, as such person shall desire, to whom such counsel hall have free access at all seasonable hours; and every such person or persons accused or indicted of the crimes aforesaid, shall be allowed and admitted in his said defense to make any proof that he or they can produce, by lawful witness or witnesses, and shall have the like process of the court where or they shall be tried, to compel his or their witnesses to appear at his or their trial, as is usually granted to compel witnesses to appear on the prosecution against them.

United States v. Bollman

24 Fed. Cas. 1189 (C.C.D.C. 1807)

Mr. Jones, the attorney of the United States for the district of Columbia, moved the court to issue a bench-warrant upon a charge of treason against Erick Bollman and Samuel Swartwout, who had been brought, by a military force, from New Orleans, and detained here under a military guard. This motion was founded upon the affidavit of General Wilkinson, made in New Orleans, and a printed copy of the president's message to congress of the 22d of January, 1807. . . .

On the 27th of January, THE COURT (CRANCH, Chief Judge, contra) was of opinion that a bench-warrant should be issued to arrest Erick Bollman and Samuel Swartwout, on the charge of treason.

■ CRANCH, CHIEF JUDGE, said:

'I differ from the majority of the court in that opinion, because I do not think that the facts before us, supported by oath, show probable cause to believe that either Dr. Bollman or Mr. Swartwout has levied war against the United States.'

On the 29th of January, Mr. Jones moved that the prisoners, who were now brought in upon the bench-warrant, should be committed for trial upon the charge of treason.

Mr. Rodney, the attorney-general of the United States, objected to the prisoners being heard by counsel, to show cause why they ought not to be committed. He said he objected to it upon principles of humanity, because it would excite a public prejudice against them, if they should be committed after being heard by counsel. The 4th and 8th articles of the amendments of the constitution guaranteed to them an impartial trial. It would be a usurpation, by the court, of the province of the jury. It would be an innovation upon the common practice of the country. This preliminary proceeding is always ex parte. The prisoners might with as much propriety insist on being heard before the grand jury. Respublica v. Shaffer, 1 Dall. [1 U. S.] 236.

C. Lee, *contra*. To deny a man to be heard by counsel is to deny him a hearing. By the eighth article of the amendments of the constitution of the United States, in all criminal prosecutions, the accused has a right to the assistance of counsel for his defence. [Editor's Note: In the Bill of Rights proposed by Madison, the Sixth Amendment was listed eighth.] It is a serious injury to an innocent man to be committed to prison on a charge of treason. He ought to be permitted to show that, in law, the facts proved do not amount to treason; and that the offence is bailable. In Hamilton's Case, 3 Dall. [3 U. S.] 17, upon habeas corpus, it appeared that he was the only one of the insurgents who had been committed without a hearing, and the attorney-general endeavored to excuse it by the state of the country, and the urgency of the occasion. It would indeed be a great innovation if the prisoners should not be permitted to be heard by counsel. If their counsel can be heard they will contend that the prisoners ought not to be committed at all; and that if they are guilty of any offence, it is bailable. . . .

THE COURT permitted the prisoners to be heard by counsel, although FITZHUGH, Circuit Judge, and DUCKETT, Circuit Judge, doubted, as the general practice was to commit in the absence of counsel; but as this was an important case, and a new question, (at least no authority had been cited where an accused person had been denied this privilege,) they inclined to the side of lenity.

■ CRANCH, CHIEF JUDGE, had no doubt upon the question.[2]

---

[2] The following note appears in Judge Fitzhugh's note-book: 'The grounds of doubt of N. F. and A. B. D., were, that the inquiry for the purpose of committing is different from that to convict. A probable cause to believe that the party is guilty, if supported by oath or affirmation, will justify commitment. This inquiry is to be before a court, and not a jury. This is, therefore, not the stage when the constitution gives him the privilege of counsel as a matter of right, and this may be inferred from comparing the 7th and 8th articles of amendments to the constitution. By the 7th article, 'No person shall be held to answer for a capital or otherwise infamous crime, unless on a presentment or indictment of a grand jury, except in cases arising in the land or naval forces, or in the militia when in actual service, in time of war or public danger,' &c. By article 8th, 'in all criminal prosecutions the accused shall enjoy the right to a speedy and public trial, by an impartial jury, &c., and to have the assistance of counsel for his defence.' These two articles, evidently, cannot apply to the stages of prosecution previous to the impanelling a grand jury, and consequently the personal rights secured by them can extend only to the cases embraced by those articles. The counsel for the prisoners have not contended that the court should now call in the aid of a grand or petit jury, to ascertain their guilt or innocence; and yet

[The court issued a bench warrant to arrest the prisoners for treason and ordered them held without bail. Upon habeas corpus issued by the Supreme Court of the United States, at February term, 1807, the prisoners were discharged.]

Gideon v. Wainwright

372 U.S. 335 (1963)

■ MR. JUSTICE BLACK delivered the opinion of the Court.

Petitioner was charged in a Florida state court with having broken and entered a poolroom with intent to commit a misdemeanor. This offense is a felony under Florida law. Appearing in court without funds and without a lawyer, petitioner asked the court to appoint counsel for him, whereupon the following colloquy took place:

"The Court: Mr. Gideon, I am sorry, but I cannot appoint Counsel to represent you in this case. Under the laws of the State of Florida, the only time the Court can appoint Counsel to represent a Defendant is when that person is charged with a capital offense. I am sorry, but I will have to deny your request to appoint Counsel to defend you in this case.

"The Defendant: The United States Supreme Court says I am entitled to be represented by Counsel."

Put to trial before a jury, Gideon conducted his defense about as well as could be expected from a layman. He made an opening statement to the jury, cross-examined the State's witnesses, presented witnesses in his own defense, declined to testify himself, and made a short argument "emphasizing his innocence to the charge contained in the Information filed in this case." The jury returned a verdict of guilty, and petitioner was sentenced to serve five years in the state prison. Later, petitioner filed in the Florida Supreme Court this habeas corpus petition attacking his conviction and sentence on the ground that the trial court's refusal to

---

the crime with which they are charged is capital and highly infamous. If the constitution does not apply, it is a case unprovided for and is left as it stands by the state laws and practice, and the laws and practice in England. As far as a deduction can be drawn from practice, it is directly opposed to the present application; and no statutory provision on the subject is recollected; nor have the counsel mentioned any. The parties are not now on their trial, nor (in the language of the article cited) are they called upon to answer; but the object of the inquiry is, whether their conduct has been such as would justify the impanelling a grand jury. But if this dilatory mode of proceeding was to prevail, public inconvenience might arise. An accused person would evade even an arrest, by employing counsel to protract the time of a justice, or of the court in attempting to prove that they have no right to issue a warrant; or after arrest there would be frequent opportunities to escape if several days might be consumed in discussing the propriety of discharging, admitting to bail, or committing, and this too in offences of the blackest dye and where bail is not allowable. In this case the court have issued a bench-warrant to arrest the accused, grounded on an affidavit, in preference to vivâ voce testimony; and no doubt was intimated by the bench or the bar; and yet, if the 8th article of the constitution applies, they should have been confronted with the witnesses against them. From all which we infer that the persons accused are not entitled to those privileges to which they are in a more advanced stage of the trial, when innocence or guilt is to be decided by a jury. However, if it is the wish of Dr. Bollman and M. Swartwout to be heard by counsel, we have no strong objections, as it will be the most orderly and decent way of conducting the inquiry.

appoint counsel for him denied him rights "guaranteed by the Constitution and the Bill of Rights by the United States Government." Treating the petition for habeas corpus as properly before it, the State Supreme Court, "upon consideration thereof" but without an opinion, denied all relief. Since 1942, when Betts v. Brady, 316 U.S. 455, was decided by a divided Court, the problem of a defendant's federal constitutional right to counsel in a state court has been a continuing source of controversy and litigation in both state and federal courts. To give this problem another review here, we granted certiorari. Since Gideon was proceeding *in forma pauperis,* we appointed counsel to represent him and requested both sides to discuss in their briefs and oral arguments the following: "Should this Court's holding in Betts v. Brady, 316 U.S. 455, be reconsidered?" . . .

Treating due process as "a concept less rigid and more fluid than those envisaged in other specific and particular provisions of the Bill of Rights," the Court held that refusal to appoint counsel under the particular facts and circumstances in the *Betts* case was not so "offensive to the common and fundamental ideas of fairness" as to amount to a denial of due process. Since the facts and circumstances of the two cases are so nearly indistinguishable, we think the *Betts v. Brady* holding if left standing would require us to reject Gideon's claim that the Constitution guarantees him the assistance of counsel. Upon full reconsideration we conclude that *Betts v. Brady* should be overruled. . . .

We accept *Betts v. Brady's* assumption, based as it was on our prior cases, that a provision of the Bill of Rights which is "fundamental and essential to a fair trial" is made obligatory upon the States by the Fourteenth Amendment. We think the Court in *Betts* was wrong, however, in concluding that the Sixth Amendment's guarantee of counsel is not one of these fundamental rights. Ten years before *Betts v. Brady,* this Court, after full consideration of all the historical data examined in *Betts,* had unequivocally declared that "the right to the aid of counsel is of this fundamental character." Powell v. Alabama, 287 U.S. 45, 68 (1932). While the Court at the close of its *Powell* opinion did by its language, as this Court frequently does, limit its holding to the particular facts and circumstances of that case, its conclusions about the fundamental nature of the right to counsel are unmistakable. . . .

Not only these precedents but also reason and reflection require us to recognize that in our adversary system of criminal justice, any person haled into court, who is too poor to hire a lawyer, cannot be assured a fair trial unless counsel is provided for him. This seems to us to be an obvious truth. Governments, both state and federal, quite properly spend vast sums of money to establish machinery to try defendants accused of crime. Lawyers to prosecute are everywhere deemed essential to protect the public's interest in an orderly society. Similarly, there are few defendants charged with crime, few indeed, who fail to hire the best lawyers they can get to prepare and present their defenses. That government hires lawyers to prosecute and defendants who have the money hire lawyers to defend are the strongest indications of the widespread belief that lawyers in criminal courts are necessities, not luxuries. The right of one charged with crime to counsel may not be deemed fundamental and essential to fair trials in some countries, but it is in ours. From the very beginning, our state and national constitutions and laws have laid great emphasis on procedural and substantive safeguards designed to assure fair trials before impartial tribunals in which every defendant stands equal before the law. This noble ideal cannot be realized if the poor man charged with crime has to face his accusers without a lawyer to assist him. A defendant's need for a lawyer is nowhere better stated than in the moving words of Mr. Justice Sutherland in

Powell v. Alabama:

> "The right to be heard would be, in many cases, of little avail if it did not comprehend the right to be heard by counsel. Even the intelligent and educated layman has small and sometimes no skill in the science of law. If charged with crime, he is incapable, generally, of determining for himself whether the indictment is good or bad. He is unfamiliar with the rules of evidence. Left without the aid of counsel he may be put on trial without a proper charge, and convicted upon incompetent evidence, or evidence irrelevant to the issue or otherwise inadmissible. He lacks both the skill and knowledge adequately to prepare his defense, even though he have a perfect one. He requires the guiding hand of counsel at every step in the proceedings against him. Without it, though he be not guilty, he faces the danger of conviction because he does not know how to establish his innocence."

287 U.S., at 68–69.

The Court in *Betts v. Brady* departed from the sound wisdom upon which the Court's holding in *Powell v. Alabama* rested. Florida, supported by two other States, has asked that *Betts v. Brady* be left intact. Twenty-two States, as friends of the Court, argue that *Betts* was "an anachronism when handed down" and that it should now be overruled. We agree.

The judgment is reversed and the cause is remanded to the Supreme Court of Florida for further action not inconsistent with this opinion.

Reversed.

Mr. Justice Douglas. . . . My brother Harlan is of the view that a guarantee of the Bill of Rights that is made applicable to the States by reason of the Fourteenth Amendment is a lesser version of that same guarantee as applied to the Federal Government. Mr. Justice Jackson shared that view. But that view has not prevailed and rights protected against state invasion by the Due Process Clause of the Fourteenth

Amendment are not watered-down versions of what the Bill of Rights guarantees.

[The separate opinions of Justice Clark and Justice Harlan are omitted]

Escobedo v. Illinois
378 U.S. 478 (1964)

■ MR. JUSTICE GOLDBERG delivered the opinion of the Court.

The critical question in this case is whether, under the circumstances, the refusal by the police to honor petitioner's request to consult with his lawyer during the course of an interrogation constitutes a denial of 'the Assistance of Counsel' in violation of the Sixth Amendment to the Constitution as 'made obligatory upon the States by the Fourteenth Amendment,' Gideon v. Wainwright, 372 U.S. 335, 342, and thereby renders inadmissible in a state criminal trial any incriminating statement elicited by the police during the interrogation.

On the night of January 19, 1960, petitioner's brother-in-law was fatally shot. In the early hours of the next morning, at 2:30 a.m., petitioner was arrested without a warrant and interrogated. Petitioner made no statement to the police and was released at 5 that afternoon pursuant to a state court writ of habeas corpus obtained by Mr. Warren Wolfson, a lawyer who had been retained by petitioner.

On January 30, Benedict DiGerlando, who was then in police custody and who was later indicted for the murder along with petitioner, told the police that petitioner had fired the fatal shots. Between 8 and 9 that evening, petitioner and his sister, the widow of the deceased, were arrested and taken to police headquarters. En route to the police station, the police 'had handcuffed the defendant behind his back,' and 'one of the arresting officers told defendant that DiGerlando had named him as the one who shot' the deceased. Petitioner testified, without contradiction, that the 'detective said they had us pretty well, up pretty tight, and we might as well admit to this crime,' and that he replied, 'I am sorry but I would like to have advice from my lawyer.' A police officer testified that although petitioner was not formally charged 'he was in custody' and 'couldn't walk out the door.'

Shortly after petitioner reached police headquarters, his retained lawyer arrived. The lawyer described the ensuing events in the following terms:

'On that day I received a phone call (from 'the mother of another defendant') and pursuant to that phone call I went to the Detective Bureau at 11th and State. The first person I talked to was the Sergeant on duty at the Bureau Desk, Sergeant Pidgeon. I asked Sergeant Pidgeon for permission to speak to my client, Danny Escobedo. * * * Sergeant Pidgeon made a call to the Bureau lockup and informed me that the boy had been taken from the lockup to the Homicide Bureau. This was between 9:30 and 10:00 in the evening. Before I went anywhere, he called the Homicide Bureau and told them there was an attorney waiting to see Escobedo. He told me I could not see him. Then I went upstairs to the Homicide Bureau. There were several Homicide Detectives around and I talked to them. I identified myself as Escobedo's attorney and asked permission to see him. They said I could not. * * * The police officer told me to see Chief Flynn who was on duty. I identified myself to Chief Flynn and asked permission to see my client. He said I could not. * * * I think it was approximately 11:00 o'clock. He said I couldn't see him because they hadn't completed questioning. * * * (F)or a second or two I spotted him in an office in the Homicide Bureau. The door was open and I could see through the office. * * * I waved to him and he waved back and then the door was closed, by one of the officers at Homicide.[1] There were four or five officers milling around the Homicide Detail that night. As to whether I talked to Captain Flynn any later that day, I waited around for another hour or two and went back again and renewed by (sic) request to see my client. He again told me I could not. * * * I filed an official complaint with Commissioner Phelan of the Chicago Police Department. I had a conversation with every police officer I could find. I was told at Homicide that I couldn't see him and I would have to get a writ of habeas corpus. I left the Homicide Bureau and from the Detective Bureau at 11th and State at approximately 1:00 A.M. (Sunday morning) I had no opportunity to talk to my client that night. I quoted to Captain Flynn the Section of the Criminal Code which allows an attorney the right to see his client.'[2]

Petitioner testified that during the course of the interrogation he repeatedly asked to speak to his lawyer and that the police said that his lawyer 'didn't want to see' him. The testimony of the police officers confirmed these accounts in substantial detail.

Notwithstanding repeated requests by each, petitioner and his retained lawyer were afforded no opportunity to consult during the course of the entire interrogation. At one point, as previously noted, petitioner and his attorney came into each other's view for a few moments but the attorney was quickly ushered away. Petitioner testified 'that he heard a detective telling the attorney the latter would not be allowed to talk to (him) 'until they were done'" and that he heard the attorney being

---

[1] Petitioner testified that this ambiguous gesture 'could have meant most anything,' but that he 'took it upon (his) own to think that (the lawyer was telling him) not to say anything,' and that the lawyer 'wanted to talk' to him.

[2] The statute then in effect provided in pertinent part that: 'All public officers * * * having the custody of any person * * * restrained of his liberty for any alleged cause whatever, shall, except in cases of imminent danger of escape, admit any practicing attorney * * * whom such person * * * may desire to see or consult * * *.' Ill.Rev.Stat. (1959), c. 38, s 477. Repealed as of Jan. 1, 1964, by Act approved Aug. 14, 1963, H.B. No. 851.

refused permission to remain in the adjoining room. A police officer testified that he had told the lawyer that he could not see petitioner until 'we were through interrogating' him.

There is testimony by the police that during the interrogation, petitioner, a 22-year-old of Mexican extraction with no record of previous experience with the police, 'was handcuffed'[3] in a standing position and that he 'was nervous, he had circles under his eyes and he was upset' and was 'agitated' because 'he had not slept well in over a week.'

It is undisputed that during the course of the interrogation Officer Montejano, who 'grew up' in petitioner's neighborhood, who knew his family, and who uses 'Spanish language in (his) police work,' conferred alone with petitioner 'for about a quarter of an hour * * *.' Petitioner testified that the officer said to him 'in Spanish that my sister and I could go home if I pinned it on Benedict DiGerlando,' that 'he would see to it that we would go home and be held only as witnesses, if anything, if we had made a statement against DiGerlando * * *, that we would be able to go home that night.' Petitioner testified that he made the statement in issue because of this assurance. Officer Montejano denied offering any such assurance.

A police officer testified that during the interrogation the following occurred:

> 'I informed him of what DiGerlando told me and when I did, he told me that DiGerlando was (lying) and I said, 'Would you care to tell DiGerlando that?' and he said, 'Yes, I will.' So, I brought * * * Escobedo in and he confronted DiGerlando and he told him that he was lying and said, 'I didn't shoot Manuel, you did it.' '

In this way, petitioner, for the first time admitted to some knowledge of the crime. After that he made additional statements further implicating himself in the murder plot. At this point an Assistant State's Attorney, Theodore J. Cooper, was summoned 'to take' a statement. Mr. Cooper, an experienced lawyer who was assigned to the Homicide Division to take 'statements from some defendants and some prisoners that they had in custody,' 'took' petitioner's statement by asking carefully framed questions apparently designed to assure the admissibility into evidence of the resulting answers. Mr. Cooper testified that he did not advise petitioner of his constitutional rights, and it is undisputed that no one during the course of the interrogation so advised him.

Petitioner moved both before and during trial to suppress the incriminating statement, but the motions were denied. Petitioner was convicted of murder and he appealed the conviction. . . .

In Massiah v. United States, 377 U.S. 201, this Court observed that 'a Constitution which guarantees a defendant the aid of counsel at * * * trial could surely vouchsafe no less to an indicted defendant under

---

[3] The trial judge justified the handcuffing on the ground that it 'is ordinary police procedure.'

interrogation by the police in a completely extrajudicial proceeding. Anything less * * * might deny a defendant 'effective representation by counsel at the only stage when legal aid and advice would help him.'' *Id.*, 377 U.S., at 204, quoting DOUGLAS, J., concurring in Spano v. New York, 360 U.S. 315, 326.

The interrogation here was conducted before petitioner was formally indicted. But in the context of this case, that fact should make no difference. When petitioner requested, and was denied, an opportunity to consult with his lawyer, the investigation had ceased to be a general investigation of 'an unsolved crime.' Spano v. New York, 360 U.S. 315, 327 (STEWART, J., concurring). Petitioner had become the accused, and the purpose of the interrogation was to 'get him' to confess his guilt despite his constitutional right not to do so. At the time of his arrest and throughout the course of the interrogation, the police told petitioner that they had convincing evidence that he had fired the fatal shots. Without informing him of his absolute right to remain silent in the face of this accusation, the police urged him to make a statement. . . .

Petitioner, a layman, was undoubtedly unaware that under Illinois law an admission of 'mere' complicity in the murder plot was legally as damaging as an admission of firing of the fatal shots. Illinois v. Escobedo, 28 Ill.2d 41, 190 N.E.2d 825. The 'guiding hand of counsel' was essential to advise petitioner of his rights in this delicate situation. Powell v. Alabama, 287 U.S. 45, 69. This was the 'stage when legal aid and advice' were most critical to petitioner. *Massiah v. United States, supra*, 377 U.S., at 204. It was a stage surely as critical as was the arraignment in Hamilton v. Alabama, 368 U.S. 52, and the preliminary hearing in White v. Maryland, 373 U.S. 59. What happened at this interrogation could certainly 'affect the whole trial,' *Hamilton v. Alabama, supra*, 368 U.S. at 54, since rights 'may be as irretrievably lost, if not then and there asserted, as they are when an accused represented by counsel waives a right for strategic purposes.' *Ibid.* It would exalt form over substance to make the right to counsel, under these circumstances, depend on whether at the time of the interrogation, the authorities had secured a formal indictment. Petitioner had, for all practical purposes, already been charged with murder. . . .

In *Gideon v. Wainwright,* 372 U.S. 335, we held that every person accused of a crime, whether state or federal, is entitled to a lawyer at trial.[8] The rule sought by the State here, however, would make the trial no more than an appeal from the interrogation; and the 'right to use counsel at the formal trial (would be) a very hollow thing (if), for all practical purposes, the conviction is already assured by pretrial examination.' In re Groban, 352 U.S. 330, 344 (BLACK, J., dissenting).[9]

---

[8]   Twenty-two States, including Illinois, urged us so to hold.

[9]   The Soviet criminal code does not permit a lawyer to be present during the investigation. The Soviet Trial has thus been aptly described as 'an appeal from the pretrial investigation.' Feifer, Justice in Moscow (1964), 86.

'One can imagine a cynical prosecutor saying: "Let them have the most illustrious counsel, now. They can't escape the noose. There is nothing that counsel can do for them at the trial." Ex parte Sullivan, D.C., 107 F.Supp. 514, 517–518.

It is argued that if the right to counsel is afforded prior to indictment, the number of confessions obtained by the police will diminish significantly, because most confessions are obtained during the period between arrest and indictment, and 'any lawyer worth his salt will tell the suspect in no uncertain terms to make no statement to police under any circumstances.' Watts v. Indiana, 338 U.S. 49, 59 (Jackson, J., concurring in part and dissenting in part). This argument, of course, cuts two ways. The fact that many confessions are obtained during this period points up its critical nature as a 'stage when legal aid and advice' are surely needed. *Massiah v. United States, supra,* 377 U.S. at 204; *Hamilton v. Alabama, supra; White v. Maryland, supra.* The right to counsel would indeed be hollow if it began at a period when few confessions were obtained. There is necessarily a direct relationship between the importance of a stage to the police in their quest for a confession and the criticalness of that stage to the accused in his need for legal advice. Our Constitution, unlike some others, strikes the balance in favor of the right of the accused to be advised by his lawyer of his privilege against self-incrimination.

We have learned the lesson of history, ancient and modern, that a system of criminal law enforcement. which comes to depend on the 'confession' will, in the long run, be less reliable and more subject to abuses than a system which depends on extrinsic evidence independently secured through skillful investigation. As Dean Wigmore so wisely said:

> '(A)ny system of administration which permits the prosecution to trust habitually to compulsory self-disclosure as a source of proof must itself suffer morally thereby. The inclination develops to rely mainly upon such evidence, and to be satisfied with an incomplete investigation of the other sources. The exercise of the power to extract answers begets a forgetfulness of the just limitations of that power. The simple and peaceful process of questioning breeds a readiness to resort to bullying and to physical force and torture. If there is a right to an answer, there soon seems to be a right to the expected answer,—that is, to a confession of guilt. Thus the legitimate use grows into the unjust abuse; ultimately, the innocent are jeopardized by the encroachments of a bad system. Such seems to have been the course of experience in those legal systems where the privilege was not recognized.'

8 Wigmore, Evidence (3d ed. 1940), 309. (Emphasis in original.) . . .

We have also learned the companion lesson of history that no system of criminal justice can, or should, survive if it comes to depend for its continued effectiveness on the citizens' abdication through unawareness of their constitutional rights. No system worth preserving should have to fear that if an accused is permitted to consult with a lawyer, he will become aware of, and exercise, these rights. If the exercise of constitutional rights will thwart the effectiveness of a system of law enforcement, then there is something very wrong with that system.[14]

We hold, therefore, that where, as here, the investigation is no longer a general inquiry into an unsolved crime but has begun to focus on a particular suspect, the suspect has been taken into police custody, the police carry out a process of interrogations that lends itself to eliciting incriminating statements, the suspect has requested and been denied an opportunity to consult with his lawyer, and the police have not effectively warned him of his absolute constitutional right to remain silent, the accused has been denied 'The Assistance of Counsel' in violation of the Sixth Amendment to the Constitution as 'made obligatory upon the States by the Fourteenth Amendment,' Gideon v. Wainwright, 372 U.S., at 342, and that no statement elicited by the police during the interrogation may be used against him at a criminal trial. . . .

Crooker v. California, 357 U.S. 433, does not compel a contrary result. In that case the Court merely rejected the absolute rule sought by petitioner, that 'every state denial of a request to contact counsel (is) an infringement of the constitutional right without regard to the circumstances of the case.' Id., 357 U.S., at 440. (Emphasis in original.) In its place, the following rule was announced:

> '(S)tate refusal of a request to engage counsel violates due process not only if the accused is deprived of counsel at trial on the merits, * * * but also if he is deprived of counsel for any part of the pretrial proceedings, provided that he is so prejudiced thereby as to infact his subsequent trial with an absence of 'that fundamental fairness essential to the very concept of justice.' * * * The latter determination necessarily depends upon all the circumstances of the case.'

357 U.S., at 439–440. (Emphasis added.)

The Court, applying 'these principles' to 'the sum total of the circumstances (there) during the time petitioner was without counsel,' id., 357 U.S., at 440, concluded that he had not been fundamentally prejudiced by the denial of his request for counsel. Among the critical circumstances which distinguish that case from this one are that the petitioner there, but not here, was explicitly advised by the police of his constitutional right to remain silent and not to 'say anything' in response to the questions, id., 357 U.S., at 437, and that petitioner there, but not here, was a well-educated man who had studied criminal law while attending law school for a year. The Court's opinion in Cicenia v. La Gay,

---

[14] The accused may, of course, intelligently and knowingly waive his privilege against self-incrimination and his right to counsel either at a pretrial stage or at the trial. See Johnson v. Zerbst, 304 U.S. 458. But no knowing and intelligent waiver of any constitutional right can be said to have occurred under the circumstances of this case.

357 U.S. 504, decided the same day, merely said that the 'contention that petitioner had a constitutional right to confer with counsel is disposed of by *Crooker v. California * * *.*' That case adds nothing, therefore, to *Crooker*. In any event, to the extent that *Cicenia* or *Crooker* may be inconsistent with the principles announced today, they are not to be regarded as controlling.

Nothing we have said today affects the powers of the police to investigate 'an unsolved crime,' Spano v. New York, 360 U.S. 315, 327 (STEWART, J., concurring), by gathering information from witnesses and by other 'proper investigative efforts.' Haynes v. Washington, 373 U.S. 503, 519. We hold only that when the process shifts from investigatory to accusatory—when its focus is on the accused and its purpose is to elicit a confession—our adversary system begins to operate, and, under the circumstances here, the accused must be permitted to consult with his lawyer.

The judgment of the Illinois Supreme Court is reversed and the case remanded for proceedings not inconsistent with this opinion.

Reversed and remanded.

■ MR. JUSTICE HARLAN, dissenting.

I would affirm the judgment of the Supreme Court of Illinois on the basis of Cicenia v. La Gay, 357 U.S. 504, decided by this Court only six years ago. Like my Brother White, *post*, p. 1767, I think the rule announced today is most ill-conceived and that it seriously and unjustifiably fetters perfectly legitimate methods of criminal law enforcement.

■ MR. JUSTICE STEWART, dissenting.

I think this case is directly controlled by Cicenia v. La Gay, 357 U.S. 504, and I would therefore affirm the judgment.

Massiah v. United States, 377 U.S. 201, is not in point here. In that case a federal grand jury had indicted Massiah. He had retained a lawyer and entered a formal plea of not guilty. Under our system of federal justice an indictment and arraignment are followed by a trial, at which the Sixth Amendment guarantees the defendant the assistance of counsel. But Massiah was released on bail, and thereafter agents of the Federal Government deliberately elicited incriminating statements from him in the absence of his lawyer. We held that the use of these statements against him at his trial denied him the basic protections of the Sixth Amendment guarantee. Putting to one side the fact that the case now before us is not a federal case, the vital fact remains that this case does not involve the deliberate interrogation of a defendant after the initiation of judicial proceedings against him. The Court disregards this basic difference between the present case and Massiah's, with the bland assertion that 'that fact should make no difference.'

It is 'that fact,' I submit, which makes all the difference. Under our system of criminal justice the institution of formal, meaningful judicial proceedings, by way of indictment, information, or arraignment, marks the point at which a criminal investigation has ended and adversary proceedings have commenced. It is at this point that the constitutional guarantees attach which pertain to a criminal trial. Among those guarantees are the right to a speedy trial, the right of confrontation, and the right to trial by jury. Another is the guarantee of the assistance of counsel. Gideon v. Wainwright, 372 U.S. 335; Hamilton v. Alabama, 368 U.S. 52; White v. Maryland, 373 U.S. 59.

The confession which the Court today holds inadmissible was a voluntary one. It was given during the course of a perfectly legitimate police investigation of an unsolved murder. The Court says that what happened during this investigation 'affected' the trial. I had always supposed that the whole purpose of a police investigation of a murder was to 'affect' the trial of the murderer, and that it would be only an incompetent, unsuccessful, or corrupt investigation which would not do so. The Court further says that the Illinois police officers did not advise the petitioner of his 'constitutional rights' before he confessed to the murder. This Court has never held that the Constitution requires the police to give any 'advice' under circumstances such as these.

Supported by no stronger authority than its own rhetoric, the Court today converts a routine police investigation of an unsolved murder into a distorted analogue of a judicial trial. It imports into this investigation constitutional concepts historically applicable only after the onset of formal prosecutorial proceedings. By doing so, I think the Court perverts those precious constitutional guarantees, and frustrates the vital interests of society in preserving the legitimate and proper function of honest and purposeful police investigation.

Like my Brother CLARK, I cannot escape the logic of my Brother WHITE'S conclusions as to the extraordinary implications which emanate from the Court's opinion in this case, and I share their views as to the untold and highly unfortunate impact today's decision may have upon the fair administration of criminal justice. I can only hope we have completely misunderstood what the Court has said.

■ MR. JUSTICE WHITE, with whom MR. JUSTICE CLARK and MR. JUSTICE STEWART join, dissenting.

. . . The Court may be concerned with a narrower matter: the unknowing defendant who responds to police questioning because he mistakenly believes that he must and that his admissions will not be used against him. But this worry hardly calls for the broadside the Court has now fired. The failure to inform an accused that he need not answer and that his answers may be used against him is very relevant indeed to whether the disclosures are compelled. Cases in this Court, to say the least, have never placed a premium on ignorance of constitutional rights. If an accused is told he must answer and does not know better, it would be very doubtful that the resulting admissions could be used against him. When the accused has not been informed of his rights at all the Court characteristically and properly looks very closely at the surrounding circumstances. *See* Ward v. Texas, 316 U.S. 547; Haley v. Ohio, 332 U.S. 596; Payne v. Arkansas, 356 U.S. 560. I would continue to do so. But, in this case Danny Escobedo knew full well that he did not have to answer and knew full well that his lawyer had advised him not to answer.

I do not suggest for a moment that law enforcement will be destroyed by the rule announced today. The need for peace and order is too insistent for that. But it will be crippled and its task made a great deal more difficult, all in my opinion, for unsound, unstated reasons, which can find no home in any of the provisions of the Constitution.

Kirby v. Illinois
406 U.S. 682 (1972)

■ MR. JUSTICE STEWART announced the judgment of the Court and an opinion in which THE CHIEF JUSTICE, MR. JUSTICE BLACKMUN, and MR. JUSTICE REHNQUIST join.

In United States v. Wade, 388 U.S. 218and Gilbert v. California, 388 U.S. 263 this Court held 'that a post-indictment pretrial lineup at which the accused is exhibited to identifying witnesses is a critical stage of the criminal prosecution; that police conduct of such a lineup without notice to and in the absence of his counsel denies the accused his Sixth (and Fourteenth) Amendment right to counsel and calls in question the admissibility at trial of the in-court identifications of the accused by witnesses who attended the lineup.' *Gilbert v. California, supra*, at 272,. Those cases further held that no 'in-court identifications' are admissible in evidence if their 'source' is a lineup conducted in violation of this constitutional standard. 'Only a per se exclusionary rule as to such testimony can be an effective sanction,' the Court said, 'to assure that law enforcement authorities will respect the accused's constitutional right to the presence of his counsel at the critical lineup.' *Id.*, at 273. In the present case we are asked to extend the *Wade-Gilbert* per se exclusionary rule to identification testimony based upon a police station showup that took place before the defendant had been indicted or otherwise formally charged with any criminal offense.

On February 21, 1968, a man named Willie Shard reported to the Chicago police that the previous day two men had robbed him on a Chicago street of a wallet containing, among other things, traveler's checks and a Social Security card. On February 22, two police officers stopped the petitioner and a companion, Ralph Bean, on West Madison Street in Chicago.[1] When asked for identification, the petitioner produced

---

[1] The officers stopped the petitioner and his companion because they thought the petitioner was a man named Hampton, who was 'wanted' in connection with an unrelated criminal offense. The legitimacy of this stop and the subsequent arrest is not before us.

a wallet that contained three traveler's checks and a Social Security card, all bearing the name of Willie Shard. Papers with Shard's name on them were also found in Bean's possession. When asked to explain his possession of Shard's property, the petitioner first said that the traveler's checks were 'play money,' and then told the officers that he had won them in a crap game. The officers then arrested the petitioner and Bean and took them to a police station.

Only after arriving at the police station, and checking the records there, did the arresting officers learn of the Shard robbery. A police car was then dispatched to Shard's place of employment, where it picked up Shard and brought him to the police station. Immediately upon entering the room in the police station where the petitioner and Bean were seated at a table, Shard positively identified them as the men who had robbed him two days earlier. No lawyer was present in the room, and neither the petitioner nor Bean had asked for legal assistance, or been advised of any right to the presence of counsel.

More than six weeks later, the petitioner and Bean were indicted for the robbery of Willie Shard. Upon arraignment, counsel was appointed to represent them, and they pleaded not guilty. A pretrial motion to suppress Shard's identification testimony was denied, and at the trial Shard testified as a witness for the prosecution. In his testimony he described his identification of the two men at the police station on February 22, and identified them again in the courtroom as the men who had robbed him on February 20. He was cross-examined at length regarding the circumstances of his identification of the two defendants. The jury found both defendants guilty, and the petitioner's conviction was affirmed on appeal. People v. Kirby, 121 Ill.App.2d 323, 257 N.E.2d 589.[4] The Illinois appellate court held that the admission of Shard's testimony was not error, relying upon an earlier decision of the Illinois Supreme Court, People v. Palmer, 41 Ill.2d 571, 244 N.E.2d 173, holding that the *Wade-Gilbert* per se exclusionary rule is not applicable to preindictment confrontations. We granted certiorari, limited to this question. 402 U.S. 995.[5]

I

We note at the outset that the constitutional privilege against compulsory self-incrimination is in no way implicated here. The Court

---

[4] Bean's conviction was reversed. People v. Bean, 121 Ill.App.2d 332, 257 N.E.2d 562.

[5] The issue of the applicability of Wade and Gilbert to pre-indictment confrontation has severely divided the courts. Compare State v. Fields, 104 Ariz. 486, 455 P.2d 964; Perkins v. State, 228 So.2d 382 (Fla.); Buchanan v. Commonwealth, 210 Va. 664, 173 S.E.2d 792; State v. Walters, 457 S.W.2d 817 (Mo.), with United States v. Greene, 139 U.S.App.D.C. 9, 429 F.2d 193; Rivers v. United States, 400 F.2d 935 (CA5); United States v. Phillips, 427 F.2d 1035 (CA9); Commonwealth v. Guillory, 356 Mass. 591, 254 N.E.2d 427; People v. Fowler, 1 Cal.3d 335, 82 Cal.Rptr. 363, 461 P.2d 643; Palmer v. State, 5 Md.App. 691, 249 A.2d 482; People v. Hutton, 21 Mich.App. 312, 175 N.W.2d 860; Commonwealth v. Whiting, 439 Pa. 205, 266 A.2d 738; In re Holley, 107 R.I. 615, 268 A.2d 723; Hayes v. State, 46 Wis.2d 93, 175 N.W.2d 625.

emphatically rejected the claimed applicability of that constitutional guarantee in *Wade* itself:

> 'Neither the lineup itself nor anything shown by this record that Wade was required to do in the lineup violated his privilege against self-incrimination. We have only recently reaffirmed that the privilege 'protects an accused only from being compelled to testify against himself, or otherwise provide the State with evidence of a testimonial or communicative nature . . .' Schmerber v. State of California, 384 U.S. 757, 761.

388 U.S., at 221.

> 'We have no doubt that compelling the accused merely to exhibit his person for observation by a prosecution witness prior to trial involves no compulsion of the accused to give evidence having testimonial significance. It is compulsion of the accused to exhibit his physical characteristics, not compulsion to disclose to any knowledge he might have. . . .' *Id.*, at 222.

It follows that the doctrine of Miranda v. Arizona, 384 U.S. 436, has no applicability whatever to the issue before us; for the *Miranda* decision was based exclusively upon the Fifth and Fourteenth Amendment privilege against compulsory self-incrimination, upon the theory that custodial interrogation is inherently coercive.

The *Wade-Gilbert* exclusionary rule, by contrast, stems from a quite different constitutional guarantee—the guarantee of the right to counsel contained in the Sixth and Fourteenth Amendments. Unless all semblance of principled constitutional adjudication is to be abandoned, therefore, it is to the decisions construing that guarantee that we must look in determining the present controversy.

In a line of constitutional cases in this Court stemming back to the Court's landmark opinion in Powell v. Alabama, 287 U.S. 45, it has been firmly established that a person's Sixth and Fourteenth Amendment right to counsel attaches only at or after the time that adversary judicial proceedings have been initiated against him. *See Powell v. Alabama, supra*; Johnson v. Zerbst, 304 U.S. 458; Hamilton v. Alabama, 368 U.S. 52; Gideon v. Wainwright, 372 U.S. 335; White v. Maryland, 373 U.S. 59; Massiah v. United States, 377 U.S. 201; United States v. Wade, 388 U.S. 218; Gilbert v. California, 388 U.S. 263; Coleman v. Alabama, 399 U.S. 1.

This is not to say that a defendant in a criminal case has a constitutional right to counsel only at the trial itself. The *Powell* case makes clear that the right attaches at the time of arraignment, and the Court has recently held that it exists also at the time of a preliminary hearing. *Coleman v. Alabama, supra*. But the point is that, while members of the Court have differed as to existence of the right to counsel in the contexts of some of the above cases, all of those cases have involved points of time at or after the initiation of adversary judicial criminal proceedings—whether by way of formal charge, preliminary hearing, indictment, information, or arraignment.

The only seeming deviation from this long line of constitutional decisions was Escobedo v. Illinois, 378 U.S. 478. But *Escobedo* is not apposite here for two distinct reasons. First, the Court in retrospect perceived that the 'prime purpose' of *Escobedo* was not to vindicate the constitutional right to counsel as such, but, like *Miranda*, 'to guarantee full effectuation of the privilege against self-incrimination . . .' Johnson v. New Jersey, 384 U.S. 719, 729. Secondly, and perhaps even more important for purely practical purposes, the Court has limited the holding of *Escobedo* to its own facts, Johnson v. New Jersey, *supra*, at 733–734, and those facts are not remotely akin to the facts of the case before us.

The initiation of judicial criminal proceedings is far from a mere formalism. It is the starting point of our whole system of adversary criminal justice. For it is only then that the government has committed itself to prosecute, and only then that the adverse positions of government and defendant have solidified. It is then that a defendant finds himself faced with the prosecutorial forces of organized society, and immersed in the intricacies of substantive and procedural criminal law. It is this point, therefore, that marks the commencement of the 'criminal prosecutions' to which alone the explicit guarantees of the Sixth Amendment are applicable. *See Powell v. Alabama*, 287 U.S., at 66–71; Massiah v. United States, 377 U.S. 201; Spano v. New York, 360 U.S. 315, 324 (Douglas, J., concurring).

In this case we are asked to import into a routine police investigation an absolute constitutional guarantee historically and rationally applicable only after the onset of formal prosecutorial proceedings. We decline to do so. Less than a year after *Wade* and *Gilbert* were decided, the Court explained the rule of those decisions as follows: 'The rationale of those cases was that an accused is entitled to counsel at any 'critical stage of the prosecution,' and that a post-indictment lineup is such a 'critical stage." (Emphasis supplied.) Simmons v. United States, 390 U.S. 377, 382–383. We decline to depart from that rationale today by imposing a per se exclusionary rule upon testimony concerning an identification that took place long before the commencement of any prosecution whatever.

II

What has been said is not to suggest that there may not be occasions during the course of a criminal investigation when the police do abuse identification procedures. Such abuses are not beyond the reach of the Constitution. As the Court pointed out in *Wade* itself, it is always necessary to 'scrutinize any pretrial confrontation . . .' 388 U.S., at 227. The Due Process Clause of the Fifth and Fourteenth Amendments forbids a lineup that is unnecessarily suggestive and conducive to irreparable mistaken identification. Stovall v. Denno, 388 U.S. 293; Foster v.

California, 394 U.S. 440.[8] When a person has not been formally charged with a criminal offense, Stovall strikes the appropriate constitutional balance between the right of a suspect to be protected from prejudicial procedures and the interest of society in the prompt and purposeful investigation of an unsolved crime.

The judgment is affirmed.

■ MR. JUSTICE BRENNAN, with whom MR. JUSTICE DOUGLAS and MR. JUSTICE MARSHALL join, dissenting.

After petitioner and Ralph Bean were arrested, police officers brought Willie Shard, the robbery victim, to a room in a police station where petitioner and Bean were seated at a table with two other police officers. Shard testified at trial that the officers who brought him to the room asked him if petitioner and Bean were the robbers and that he indicated they were. The prosecutor asked him, 'And you positively identified them at the police station, is that correct?' Shard answered, 'Yes.' Consequently, the question in this case is whether, under Gilbert v. California, 388 U.S. 263 (1967), it was constitutional error to admit Shard's testimony that he identified petitioner at the pretrial station-house showup when that showup was conducted by the police without advising petitioner that he might have counsel present. Gilbert held, in the context of a post-indictment lineup, that '(o)nly a per se exclusionary rule as to such testimony can be an effective sanction to assure that law enforcement authorities will respect the accused's constitutional right to the presence of his counsel at the critical lineup.' Id., at 273. I would apply Gilbert and the principles of its companion case, United States v. Wade, 388 U.S. 218 (1967), and reverse.

In Wade, after concluding that the lineup conducted in that case did not violate the accused's right against self-incrimination, id., at 221–223, the Court addressed the argument 'that the assistance of counsel at the lineup was indispensable to protect Wade's most basis right as a criminal defendant—his right to a fair trial at which the witnesses against him might be meaningfully cross-examined,' id., at 223–224. The Court began by emphasizing that the Sixth Amendment guarantee 'encompasses counsel's assistance whenever necessary to assure a meaningful 'defence." Id., at 225. After reviewing Powell v. Alabama, 287 U.S. 45 (1932); Hamilton v. Alabama, 368 U.S. 52 (1961); and Massiah v. United States, 377 U.S. 201 (1964), the Court, 388 U.S., at 225, focused upon two cases that involved the right against self-incrimination:

'In Escobedo v. State of Illinois, 378 U.S. 478, we drew upon the rationale of Hamilton and Massiah in holding that the right to counsel was guaranteed at the point where the accused, prior to arraignment, was subjected to secret interrogation despite

---

[8] In view of our limited grant of certiorari, we do not consider whether there might have been a deprivation of due process in the particularized circumstances of this case. That question remains open for inquiry in a federal habeas corpus proceeding.

repeated requests to see his lawyer. We again noted the necessity of counsel's presence if the accused was to have fair opportunity to present a defense at the trial itself . . . .' United States v. Wade, 388 U.S., at 225–226.[3]

'(I)n Miranda v. State of Arizona, 384, U.S. 436, 86 S.Ct. 1602, 16 L.Ed.2d 694, the rules established for custodial interrogation included the right to the presence of counsel. The result was rested on our finding that this and the other rules were necessary to safeguard the privilege against self-incrimination from being jeopardized by such interrogation.'

Id., at 226.

The Court then pointed out that 'nothing decided or said in the opinions in (*Escobedo* and *Miranda*) links the right to counsel only to protection of Fifth Amendment rights.' *Ibid.* To the contrary, the Court said, those decisions simply reflected the constitutional

'principle that in addition to counsel's presence at trial, the accused is guaranteed that he need not stand alone against the State at any stage of the prosecution, formal or informal, in court or out, where counsel's absence might derogate from the accused's right to a fair trial. The security of that right is as much the aim of the right to counsel as it is of the other guarantees of the Sixth Amendment . . . .'

Id., at 226–227.

This analysis led to the Court's formulation of the controlling principle for pretrial confrontations:

'In sum, the principle of *Powell v. Alabama* and succeeding cases requires that we scrutinize any pre trial confrontation of the accused to determine whether the presence of his counsel is necessary to preserve the defendant's basic right to a fair trial as affected by his right meaningfully to cross-examine the witnesses against him and to have effective assistance of counsel at the trial itself. It calls upon us to analyze whether potential substantial prejudice to defendant's rights inheres in the particular confrontation and the ability of counsel to help avoid that prejudice.'

Id., at 2272 (emphasis in original).

---

[3] The plurality asserts that '*Escobedo* is not apposite here.' *Ante,* at 1882. It was, of course, 'apposite' in *Wade.* Hence, to say that Johnson v. New Jersey, 384 U.S. 719, 733–734 (1966), a case decided before *Wade,* 'limited the holding of *Escobedo* to its own facts,' *ante,* at 1882, even if true, is to say nothing at all that is relevant to the present case. The plurality also utilizes *Johnson* for the proposition 'that the 'prime purpose' of *Escobedo* was not to vindicate the constitutional right to counsel as such, but, like Miranda, 'to guarantee full effectuation of the privilege against self-incrimination . . ." *Ibid.* In view of *Wade*'s specific reliance upon *Escobedo* and *Miranda,* that, obviously, is no distinction either. Moreover, it implies that the purpose of *Wade* was 'to vindicate the constitutional right to counsel as such.' That was not the purpose of *Wade,* as my extended summary of the opinion demonstrates.

It was that constitutional principle that the Court applied in *Wade* to pretrial confrontations for identification purposes. The Court first met the Government's contention that a confrontation for identification is 'a mere preparatory step in the gathering of the prosecution's evidence,' much like the scientific examination of fingerprints and blood samples. The Court responded that in the latter instances 'the accused has the opportunity for a meaningful confrontation of the Government's case at trial through the ordinary processes of cross-examination of the Government's expert witnesses and the presentation of the evidence of his own experts.' The accused thus has no right to have counsel present at such examinations: 'they are not critical stages since there is minimal risk that his counsel's absence at such stages might derogate from his right to a fair trial.' *Id.*, at 227–228.

In contrast, the Court said, 'the confrontation compelled by the State between the accused and the victim or witnesses to a crime to elicit identification evidence is peculiarly riddled with innumerable dangers and variable factors which might seriously, even crucially, derogate from a fair trial.' *Id.*, at 228. Most importantly, 'the accused's inability effectively to reconstruct at trial any unfairness that occurred at the lineup may deprive him of his only opportunity meaningfully to attack the credibility of the witness' courtroom identification.' *Id.*, at 231–232.

... *Wade* did not require the presence of counsel at pretrial confrontations for identification purposes simply on the basis of an abstract consideration of the words 'criminal prosecutions' in the Sixth Amendment. Counsel is required at those confrontations because 'the dangers inherent in eyewitness identification and the suggestibility inherent in the context of the pretrial identification,' *Id.*, at 235, mean that protection must be afforded to the 'most basic right (of) a criminal defendant—his right to a fair trial at which the witnesses against him might be meaningfully cross-examined,' *id.*, at 224. Indeed, the Court expressly stated that '(L)egislative or other regulations, such as those of local police departments, which eliminate the risks of abuse and unintentional suggestion at lineup proceedings and the impediments to meaningful confrontation at trial may also remove the basis for regarding the stage as 'critical." *Id.*, at 239; *see id.*, at 239 n.30; *Gilbert v. California*, 388 U.S., at 273. Hence, 'the initiation of adversary judicial criminal proceedings,', is completely irrelevant to whether counsel is necessary at a pretrial confrontation for identification in order to safeguard the accused's constitutional rights to confrontation and the effective assistance of counsel at his trial.

■ MR. JUSTICE WHITE, dissenting.

United States v. Wade, 388 U.S. 218 (1967), and Gilbert v. California, 388 U.S. 263 (1967), govern this case and compel reversal of the judgment below.

2. "ATTACHMENT"

Rothgery v. Gillespie County

554 U.S. 191 (2008)

■ SOUTER, J., delivered the opinion of the Court, in which ROBERTS, C.J., and STEVENS, SCALIA, KENNEDY, GINSBURG, BREYER, and ALITO, JJ., joined. ROBERTS, C.J., filed a concurring opinion, in which SCALIA, J., joined. ALITO, J., filed a concurring opinion, in which ROBERTS, C.J., and SCALIA, J., joined. THOMAS, J., filed a dissenting opinion.

■ JUSTICE SOUTER delivered the opinion of the Court.

This Court has held that the right to counsel guaranteed by the Sixth Amendment applies at the first appearance before a judicial officer at which a defendant is told of the formal accusation against him and restrictions are imposed on his liberty. *See* Brewer v. Williams, 430 U.S. 387, 398–399 (1977); Michigan v. Jackson, 475 U.S. 625, 629, n.3 (1986). The question here is whether attachment of the right also requires that a public prosecutor (as distinct from a police officer) be aware of that initial proceeding or involved in its conduct. We hold that it does not.

I

A

Although petitioner Walter Rothgery has never been convicted of a felony,[1] a criminal background check disclosed an erroneous record that he had been, and on July 15, 2002, Texas police officers relied on this record to arrest him as a felon in possession of a firearm. The officers lacked a warrant, and so promptly brought Rothgery before a magistrate judge, as required by Tex.Crim. Proc.Code Ann., Art. 14.06(a) (West Supp.2007).[2] Texas law has no formal label for this initial appearance before a magistrate, see 41 G. Dix & R. Dawson, Texas Practice Series: Criminal Practice and Procedure § 15.01 (2d ed.2001), which is sometimes called the "article 15.17 hearing," *See, e.g.,* Kirk v. State, 199 S.W.3d 467, 476–477 (Tex.App.2006); it combines the Fourth Amendment's required probable-cause determination[3] with the setting of

---

[1] "[F]elony charges . . . had been dismissed after Rothgery completed a diversionary program, and both sides agree that [he] did not have a felony conviction." 491 F.3d 293, 294 (C.A.5 2007) (case below).

[2] A separate article of the Texas Code of Criminal Procedure requires prompt presentment in the case of arrests under warrant as well. *See* Art. 15.17(a) (West Supp.2007). Whether the arrest is under warrant or warrantless, article 15.17 details the procedures a magistrate judge must follow upon presentment. *See* Art. 14.06(a) (in cases of warrantless arrest, "[t]he magistrate shall immediately perform the duties described in Article 15.17 of this Code").

[3] *See* Gerstein v. Pugh, 420 U.S. 103, 113–114 (1975) ("[A] policeman's on-the-scene assessment of probable cause provides legal justification for arresting a person suspected of crime, and for a brief period of detention to take the administrative steps incident to arrest[,] . . . . [but] the Fourth Amendment requires a judicial determination of probable cause as a prerequisite to extended restraint of liberty following arrest").

bail, and is the point at which the arrestee is formally apprised of the accusation against him, *see* Tex.Crim. Proc.Code Ann., Art. 15.17(a).

Rothgery's article 15.17 hearing followed routine. The arresting officer submitted a sworn "Affidavit Of Probable Cause" that described the facts supporting the arrest and "charge[d] that . . . Rothgery . . . commit[ted] the offense of unlawful possession of a firearm by a felon— 3rd degree felony [Tex. Penal Code Ann. § 46.04]," App. to Pet. for Cert. 33a. After reviewing the affidavit, the magistrate judge "determined that probable cause existed for the arrest." *Id.*, at 34a. The magistrate judge informed Rothgery of the accusation, set his bail at $5,000, and committed him to jail, from which he was released after posting a surety bond. The bond, which the Gillespie County deputy sheriff signed, stated that "Rothgery stands charged by complaint duly filed . . . with the offense of a . . . felony, to wit: Unlawful Possession of a Firearm by a Felon." *Id.*, at 39a. The release was conditioned on the defendant's personal appearance in trial court "for any and all subsequent proceedings that may be had relative to the said charge in the course of the criminal action based on said charge." *Ibid.*

Rothgery had no money for a lawyer and made several oral and written requests for appointed counsel,[4] which went unheeded.[5] The following January, he was indicted by a Texas grand jury for unlawful possession of a firearm by a felon, resulting in rearrest the next day, and an order increasing bail to $15,000. When he could not post it, he was put in jail and remained there for three weeks.

On January 23, 2003, six months after the article 15.17 hearing, Rothgery was finally assigned a lawyer, who promptly obtained a bail reduction (so Rothgery could get out of jail), and assembled the paperwork confirming that Rothgery had never been convicted of a felony. Counsel relayed this information to the district attorney, who in turn filed a motion to dismiss the indictment, which was granted.

B

Rothgery then brought this 42 U.S.C. § 1983 action against respondent Gillespie County, claiming that if the County had provided a lawyer within a reasonable time after the article 15.17 hearing, he would not have been indicted, rearrested, or jailed for three weeks. The County's failure is said to be owing to its unwritten policy of denying appointed counsel to indigent defendants out on bond until at least the

---

[4] Because respondent Gillespie County obtained summary judgment in the current case, we accept as true that Rothgery made multiple requests.

[5] Rothgery also requested counsel at the article 15.17 hearing itself, but the magistrate judge informed him that the appointment of counsel would delay setting bail (and hence his release from jail). Given the choice of proceeding without counsel or remaining in custody, Rothgery waived the right to have appointed counsel present at the hearing. *See* 491 F.3d, at 295, n.2

entry of an information or indictment.[6] Rothgery sees this policy as violating his Sixth Amendment right to counsel.[7]

The District Court granted summary judgment to the County, *see* 413 F.Supp.2d 806, 807 (W.D.Tex.2006), and the Court of Appeals affirmed, *see* 491 F.3d 293, 294 (C.A.5 2007). The Court of Appeals felt itself bound by Circuit precedent, *see id.*, at 296–297 (citing Lomax v. Alabama, 629 F.2d 413 (C.A.5 1980), and McGee v. Estelle, 625 F.2d 1206 (C.A.5 1980)), to the effect that the Sixth Amendment right to counsel did not attach at the article 15.17 hearing, because "the relevant prosecutors were not aware of or involved in Rothgery's arrest or appearance before the magistrate on July 16, 2002," and "[t]here is also no indication that the officer who filed the probable cause affidavit at Rothgery's appearance had any power to commit the state to prosecute without the knowledge or involvement of a prosecutor," 491 F.3d, at 297.

We granted certiorari, and now vacate and remand.

II

The Sixth Amendment right of the "accused" to assistance of counsel in "all criminal prosecutions" is limited by its terms: "it does not attach until a prosecution is commenced." McNeil v. Wisconsin, 501 U.S. 171, 175 (1991); *see also* Moran v. Burbine, 475 U.S. 412, 430 (1986). We have, for purposes of the right to counsel, pegged commencement to " 'the initiation of adversary judicial criminal proceedings—whether by way of formal charge, preliminary hearing, indictment, information, or arraignment,' " United States v. Gouveia, 467 U.S. 180, 188 (1984) (quoting Kirby v. Illinois, 406 U.S. 682, 689 (1972) (plurality opinion)). The rule is not "mere formalism," but a recognition of the point at which "the government has committed itself to prosecute," "the adverse positions of government and defendant have solidified," and the accused "finds himself faced with the prosecutorial forces of organized society, and immersed in the intricacies of substantive and procedural criminal law." *Kirby, supra,* at 689. The issue is whether Texas's article 15.17 hearing marks that point, with the consequent state obligation to appoint counsel within a reasonable time once a request for assistance is made.

A

When the Court of Appeals said no, because no prosecutor was aware of Rothgery's article 15.17 hearing or involved in it, the court effectively focused not on the start of adversarial judicial proceedings, but on the

---

[6] Rothgery does not challenge the County's written policy for appointment of counsel, but argues that the County was not following that policy in practice. *See* 413 F.Supp.2d 806, 809–810 (W.D.Tex.2006).

[7] Such a policy, if proven, arguably would also be in violation of Texas state law, which appears to require appointment of counsel for indigent defendants released from custody, at the latest, when the "first court appearance" is made. *See* Tex.Crim. Proc.Code Ann., Art. 1.051(j). *See also* Brief for Texas Association of Counties et al. as Amici Curiae 13 (asserting that Rothgery "was statutorily entitled to the appointment of counsel within three days after having requested it").

activities and knowledge of a particular state official who was presumably otherwise occupied. This was error.

As the Court of Appeals recognized, *see* 491 F.3d, at 298, we have twice held that the right to counsel attaches at the initial appearance before a judicial officer, *see Jackson,* 475 U.S., at 629, n.3; *Brewer,* 430 U.S., at 399. This first time before a court, also known as the " 'preliminary arraignment' " or " 'arraignment on the complaint,' " *See*1 W. LaFave, J. Israel, N. King, & O. Kerr, Criminal Procedure § 1.4(g), p. 135 (3d ed.2007), is generally the hearing at which "the magistrate informs the defendant of the charge in the complaint, and of various rights in further proceedings," and "determine[s] the conditions for pretrial release," *ibid.* Texas's article 15.17 hearing is an initial appearance: Rothgery was taken before a magistrate judge, informed of the formal accusation against him, and sent to jail until he posted bail. *See supra*, at 2581–2582.[9] *Brewer* and *Jackson* control.

The *Brewer* defendant surrendered to the police after a warrant was out for his arrest on a charge of abduction. He was then "arraigned before a judge . . . on the outstanding arrest warrant," and at the arraignment, "[t]he judge advised him of his *Miranda* [v. Arizona, 384 U.S. 436 (1966)] rights and committed him to jail." *Brewer,* 430 U.S., at 391. After this preliminary arraignment, and before an indictment on the abduction charge had been handed up, police elicited incriminating admissions that ultimately led to an indictment for first-degree murder. Because neither of the defendant's lawyers had been present when the statements were obtained, the Court found it "clear" that the defendant "was deprived of . . . the right to the assistance of counsel." *Id.*, at 397–398. In plain terms, the Court said that "[t]here can be no doubt in the present case that judicial proceedings had been initiated" before the defendant made the incriminating statements. *Id.*, at 399. Although it noted that the State had conceded the issue, the Court nevertheless held that the defendant's right had clearly attached for the reason that "[a] warrant had been issued for his arrest, he had been arraigned on that warrant before a judge in a . . . courtroom, and he had been committed by the court to confinement in jail." *Ibid.*[10]

---

[9]   The Court of Appeals did not resolve whether the arresting officer's formal accusation would count as a "formal complaint" under Texas state law. *See* 491 F.3d, at 298–300 (noting the confusion in the Texas state courts). But it rightly acknowledged (albeit in considering the separate question whether the complaint was a "formal charge") that the constitutional significance of judicial proceedings cannot be allowed to founder on the vagaries of state criminal law, lest the attachment rule be rendered utterly "vague and unpredictable." Virginia v. Moore, 553 U.S. ___, ___ (2008). *See* 491 F.3d, at 300 ("[W]e are reluctant to rely on the formalistic question of whether the affidavit here would be considered a 'complaint' or its functional equivalent under Texas case law and Article 15.04 of the Texas Code of Criminal Procedures— a question to which the answer is itself uncertain. Instead, we must look to the specific circumstances of this case and the nature of the affidavit filed at Rothgery's appearance before the magistrate" (footnote omitted)). What counts is that the complaint filed with the magistrate judge accused Rothgery of committing a particular crime and prompted the judicial officer to take legal action in response (here, to set the terms of bail and order the defendant locked up).

[10]   The dissent says that "Brewer's attachment holding is indisputably no longer good law" because "we have subsequently held that the Sixth Amendment right to counsel is " 'offense

In *Jackson,* the Court was asked to revisit the question whether the right to counsel attaches at the initial appearance, and we had no more trouble answering it the second time around. Jackson was actually two consolidated cases, and although the State conceded that respondent Jackson's arraignment "represented the initiation of formal legal proceedings," 475 U.S., at 629, n.3, it argued that the same was not true for respondent Bladel. In briefing us, the State explained that "[i]n Michigan, any person charged with a felony, after arrest, must be brought before a Magistrate or District Court Judge without unnecessary delay for his initial arraignment." Brief for Petitioner in Michigan v. Bladel, O. & T. 1985, No. 84-1539, p. 24. The State noted that "[w]hile [Bladel] had been arraigned . . ., there is also a second arraignment in Michigan procedure . . ., at which time defendant has his first opportunity to enter a plea in a court with jurisdiction to render a final decision in a felony case." *Id.,* at 25. The State contended that only the latter proceeding, the "arraignment on the information or indictment," Y. Kamisar, W. LaFave, J. Israel, & N. King, Modern Criminal Procedure 28 (9th ed.1999) (emphasis deleted), should trigger the Sixth Amendment right. "The defendant's rights," the State insisted, "are fully protected in the context of custodial interrogation between initial arraignment and preliminary examination by the Fifth Amendment right to counsel" and by the preliminary examination itself.[12] *See* Bladel Brief, *supra,* at 26.

We flatly rejected the distinction between initial arraignment and arraignment on the indictment, the State's argument being "untenable" in light of the "clear language in our decisions about the significance of arraignment." *Jackson, supra,* at 629, n.3. The conclusion was driven by the same considerations the Court had endorsed in *Brewer*: by the time a defendant is brought before a judicial officer, is informed of a formally lodged accusation, and has restrictions imposed on his liberty in aid of the prosecution, the State's relationship with the defendant has become solidly adversarial. And that is just as true when the proceeding comes before the indictment (in the case of the initial arraignment on a formal complaint) as when it comes after it (at an arraignment on an

---

specific," '" *post,* at 2602 (opinion of THOMAS, J.) (quoting Texas v. Cobb, 532 U.S. 162, 164 (2001)), *i.e.,* that it does not "exten[d] to crimes that are 'factually related' to those that have actually been charged," *Cobb, supra,* at 167. It is true that *Brewer* appears to have assumed that attachment of the right with respect to the abduction charge should prompt attachment for the murder charge as well. But the accuracy of the dissent's assertion ends there, for nothing in *Cobb*'s conclusion that the right is offense specific casts doubt on *Brewer*'s separate, emphatic holding that the initial appearance marks the point at which the right attaches. Nor does *Cobb* reflect, as the dissent suggests, see *post,* at 2602, a more general disapproval of our opinion in *Brewer*. While Brewer failed even to acknowledge the issue of offense specificity, it spoke clearly and forcefully about attachment. *Cobb* merely declined to follow *Brewer*'s unmentioned assumption, and thus it lends no support to the dissent's claim that we should ignore what *Brewer* explicitly said.

   [12] The preliminary examination is a preindictment stage at which the defendant is allowed to test the prosecution's evidence against him, and to try to dissuade the prosecutor from seeking an indictment. *See* Coleman v. Alabama, 399 U.S. 1 (1970). In Texas, the defendant is notified of his right to a preliminary hearing, which in Texas is called an "examining trial," at the article 15.17 hearing. *See* Tex.Crim. Proc.Code Ann., Art. 15.17(a). The examining trial in Texas is optional only, and the defendant must affirmatively request it. *See* Reply Brief for Petitioner 25.

indictment). *See* Coleman v. Alabama, 399 U.S. 1, 8 (1970) (plurality opinion) (right to counsel applies at preindictment preliminary hearing at which the "sole purposes . . . are to determine whether there is sufficient evidence against the accused to warrant presenting his case to the grand jury, and, if so, to fix bail if the offense is bailable"); cf. Owen v. State, 596 So.2d 985, 989, n.7 (Fla.1992) ("The term 'arraign' simply means to be called before a court officer and charged with a crime").

B

Our latest look at the significance of the initial appearance was *McNeil,* 501 U.S. 171, which is no help to the County. In *McNeil* the State had conceded that the right to counsel attached at the first appearance before a county court commissioner, who set bail and scheduled a preliminary examination. *See id.,* at 173; *see also id.,* at 175 ("It is undisputed, and we accept for purposes of the present case, that at the time petitioner provided the incriminating statements at issue, his Sixth Amendment right had attached . . ."). But we did more than just accept the concession; we went on to reaffirm that "[t]he Sixth Amendment right to counsel attaches at the first formal proceeding against an accused," and observed that "in most States, at least with respect to serious offenses, free counsel is made available at that time . . . ." *Id.,* at 180–181.

That was 17 years ago, the same is true today, and the overwhelming consensus practice conforms to the rule that the first formal proceeding is the point of attachment. We are advised without contradiction that not only the Federal Government, including the District of Columbia, but 43 States take the first step toward appointing counsel "before, at, or just after initial appearance." App. to Brief for National Association of Criminal Defense Lawyers as Amicus Curiae 1a; *see id.,* at 1a–7a (listing jurisdictions); *see also* Brief for American Bar Association as Amicus Curiae 5–8 (describing the ABA's position for the past 40 years that counsel should be appointed "certainly no later than the accused's initial appearance before a judicial officer"). And even in the remaining 7 States (Alabama, Colorado, Kansas, Oklahoma, South Carolina, Texas, and Virginia) the practice is not free of ambiguity. *See* App. to Brief for National Association of Criminal Defense Lawyers as Amicus Curiae 5a–7a (suggesting that the practice in Alabama, Kansas, South Carolina, and Virginia might actually be consistent with the majority approach); *see also* n.7, *supra.* In any event, to the extent these States have been denying appointed counsel on the heels of the first appearance, they are a distinct minority.

C

The only question is whether there may be some arguable justification for the minority practice. Neither the Court of Appeals in its opinion, nor the County in its briefing to us, has offered an acceptable one.

1

The Court of Appeals thought *Brewer* and *Jackson* could be distinguished on the ground that "neither case addressed the issue of prosecutorial involvement," and the cases were thus "neutral on the point," 491 F.3d, at 298. With *Brewer* and *Jackson* distinguished, the court then found itself bound by Circuit precedent that " 'an adversary criminal proceeding has not begun in a case where the prosecution officers are unaware of either the charges or the arrest.' " *See* 491 F.3d, at 297 (quoting McGee v. Estelle, 625 F.2d 1206, 1208 (CA5 1980)). Under this standard of prosecutorial awareness, attachment depends not on whether a first appearance has begun adversary judicial proceedings, but on whether the prosecutor had a hand in starting it. That standard is wrong.

Neither *Brewer* nor *Jackson* said a word about the prosecutor's involvement as a relevant fact, much less a controlling one. Those cases left no room for the factual enquiry the Court of Appeals would require, and with good reason: an attachment rule that turned on determining the moment of a prosecutor's first involvement would be "wholly unworkable and impossible to administer," Escobedo v. Illinois, 378 U.S. 478, 496 (1964) (White, J., dissenting), guaranteed to bog the courts down in prying enquiries into the communication between police (who are routinely present at defendants' first appearances) and the State's attorneys (who are not), *see* Brief for Petitioner 39–41. And it would have the practical effect of resting attachment on such absurd distinctions as the day of the month an arrest is made, *see* Brief for Brennan Center of Justice et al. as Amici Curiae 10 (explaining that "jails may be required to report their arrestees to county prosecutor offices on particular days" (citing Tex.Crim. Proc.Code Ann., Art. 2.19)); or "the sophistication, or lack thereof, of a jurisdiction's computer intake system," Brief for Brennan Center, *supra*, at 11; s*ee also id.*, at 10–12 (noting that only "[s]ome Texas counties . . . have computer systems that provide arrest and detention information simultaneously to prosecutors, law enforcement officers, jail personnel, and clerks. Prosecutors in these jurisdictions use the systems to prescreen cases early in the process before an initial appearance" (citing D. Carmichael, M. Gilbert, & M. Voloudakis, Texas A & M U., Public Policy Research Inst., Evaluating the Impact of Direct Electronic Filing in Criminal Cases: Closing the Paper Trap 2–3 (2006), online at http://www.courts.state.tx.us/tfid/pdf/FinalReport7-12-06wackn.pdf (as visited June 19, 2008, and available in Clerk of Court's case file))).

It is not that the Court of Appeals believed that any such regime would be desirable, but it thought originally that its rule was implied by this Court's statement that the right attaches when the government has "committed itself to prosecute." *Kirby,* 406 U.S., at 689. The Court of Appeals reasoned that because "the decision not to prosecute is the quintessential function of a prosecutor" under Texas law, 491 F.3d, at

297 (internal quotation marks omitted), the State could not commit itself to prosecution until the prosecutor signaled that it had.

But what counts as a commitment to prosecute is an issue of federal law unaffected by allocations of power among state officials under a State's law, *cf. Moran,* 475 U.S., at 429, n.3 ("[T]he type of circumstances that would give rise to the right would certainly have a federal definition"), and under the federal standard, an accusation filed with a judicial officer is sufficiently formal, and the government's commitment to prosecute it sufficiently concrete, when the accusation prompts arraignment and restrictions on the accused's liberty to facilitate the prosecution, *see Jackson,* 475 U.S., at 629, n.3; *Brewer,* 430 U.S., at 399; *Kirby, supra,* at 689; *see also* n.9, *supra,* at 2584. From that point on, the defendant is "faced with the prosecutorial forces of organized society, and immersed in the intricacies of substantive and procedural criminal law" that define his capacity and control his actual ability to defend himself against a formal accusation that he is a criminal. *Kirby, supra,* at 689. By that point, it is too late to wonder whether he is "accused" within the meaning of the Sixth Amendment, and it makes no practical sense to deny it. *See* Grano, Rhode Island v. Innis: *A Need to Reconsider the Constitutional Premises Underlying the Law of Confessions,* 17 Am.Crim. L.Rev. 1, 31 (1979) ("[I]t would defy common sense to say that a criminal prosecution has not commenced against a defendant who, perhaps incarcerated and unable to afford judicially imposed bail, awaits preliminary examination on the authority of a charging document filed by the prosecutor, less typically by the police, and approved by a court of law" (internal quotation marks omitted)). All of this is equally true whether the machinery of prosecution was turned on by the local police or the state attorney general. In this case, for example, Rothgery alleges that after the initial appearance, he was "unable to find any employment for wages" because "all of the potential employers he contacted knew or learned of the criminal charge pending against him." Original Complaint in No. 1:04-CV-00456-LY (WD Tex., July 15, 2004), p. 5. One may assume that those potential employers would still have declined to make job offers if advised that the county prosecutor had not filed the complaint.

2

The County resists this logic with the argument that in considering the significance of the initial appearance, we must ignore prejudice to a defendant's pretrial liberty, reasoning that it is the concern, not of the right to counsel, but of the speedy-trial right and the Fourth Amendment. *See* Brief for Respondent 47–51. And it cites *Gouveia,* 467 U.S. 180, in support of its contention. *See* Brief for Respondent 49; *see also* Brief for Texas et al. as Amici Curiae 8–9. We think the County's reliance on *Gouveia* is misplaced, and its argument mistaken.

The defendants in *Gouveia* were prison inmates, suspected of murder, who had been placed in an administrative detention unit and denied counsel up until an indictment was filed. Although no formal judicial proceedings had taken place prior to the indictment, see 467 U.S., at 185, the defendants argued that their administrative detention should be treated as an accusation for purposes of the right to counsel because the government was actively investigating the crimes. We recognized that "because an inmate suspected of a crime is already in prison, the prosecution may have little incentive promptly to bring formal charges against him, and that the resulting preindictment delay may be particularly prejudicial to the inmate," id., at 192, but we noted that statutes of limitation and protections of the Fifth Amendment guarded against delay, and that there was no basis for "depart[ing] from our traditional interpretation of the Sixth Amendment right to counsel in order to provide additional protections for [the inmates]," ibid.

Gouveia's holding that the Sixth Amendment right to counsel had not attached has no application here. For one thing, Gouveia does not affect the conclusion we reaffirmed two years later in Jackson, that bringing a defendant before a court for initial appearance signals a sufficient commitment to prosecute and marks the start of adversary judicial proceedings. (Indeed, Jackson refutes the County's argument that Fifth Amendment protections at the early stage obviate attachment of the Sixth Amendment right at initial appearance. See supra, at 2585–2586.) And since we are not asked to extend the right to counsel to a point earlier than formal judicial proceedings (as in Gouveia), but to defer it to those proceedings in which a prosecutor is involved, Gouveia does not speak to the question before us.

The County also tries to downplay the significance of the initial appearance by saying that an attachment rule unqualified by prosecutorial involvement would lead to the conclusion "that the State has statutorily committed to prosecute every suspect arrested by the police," given that "state law requires [an article 15.17 hearing] for every arrestee." Brief for Respondent 24 (emphasis in original). The answer, though, is that the State has done just that, subject to the option to change its official mind later. The State may rethink its commitment at any point: it may choose not to seek indictment in a felony case, say, or the prosecutor may enter nolle prosequi after the case gets to the jury room. But without a change of position, a defendant subject to accusation after initial appearance is headed for trial and needs to get a lawyer working, whether to attempt to avoid that trial or to be ready with a defense when the trial date arrives.

3

A third tack on the County's part, slightly different from the one taken by the Fifth Circuit, gets it no further. The County stipulates that "the properly formulated test is not . . . merely whether prosecutors have had any involvement in the case whatsoever, but instead whether the State has objectively committed itself to prosecute." Id., at 31. It then informs us that "[p]rosecutorial involvement is merely one form of evidence of such commitment." Ibid. Other sufficient evidentiary indications are variously described: first (expansively) as "the filing of formal charges . . . by information, indictment or formal complaint, or the holding of an adversarial preliminary hearing to determine probable cause to file such charges," ibid. (citing *Kirby*, 406 U.S., at 689); then (restrictively) as a court appearance following "arrest . . . on an indictment or information," Brief for Respondent 32. Either version, in any event, runs up against *Brewer* and *Jackson*: an initial appearance following a charge signifies a sufficient commitment to prosecute regardless of a prosecutor's participation, indictment, information, or what the County calls a "formal" complaint.

So the County is reduced to taking aim at those cases. *Brewer* and *Jackson,* we are told, are "vague" and thus of "limited, if any, precedential value." Brief for Respondent 33, 35; *see also id.*, at 32, n.13 (asserting that *Brewer* and *Jackson* "neither provide nor apply an analytical framework for determining attachment"). And, according to the County, our cases (*Brewer* and *Jackson* aside) actually establish a "general rule that the right to counsel attaches at the point that [what the County calls] formal charges are filed," Brief for Respondent 19, with exceptions allowed only in the case of "a very limited set of specific preindictment situations," *id.*, at 23. The County suggests that the latter category should be limited to those appearances at which the aid of counsel is urgent and " 'the dangers to the accused of proceeding without counsel' " are great. *Id.*, at 28 (quoting Patterson v. Illinois, 487 U.S. 285, 298 (1988)). Texas's article 15.17 hearing should not count as one of those situations, the County says, because it is not of critical significance, since it "allows no presentation of witness testimony and provides no opportunity to expose weaknesses in the government's evidence, create a basis for later impeachment, or even engage in basic discovery." Brief for Respondent 29.

We think the County is wrong both about the clarity of our cases and the substance that we find clear. Certainly it is true that the Court in *Brewer* and *Jackson* saw no need for lengthy disquisitions on the significance of the initial appearance, but that was because it found the attachment issue an easy one. The Court's conclusions were not vague; *Brewer* expressed "no doubt" that the right to counsel attached at the initial appearance, 430 U.S., at 399, and *Jackson* said that the opposite result would be "untenable," 475 U.S., at 629, n.3.

If, indeed, the County had simply taken the cases at face value, it would have avoided the mistake of merging the attachment question (whether formal judicial proceedings have begun) with the distinct "critical stage" question (whether counsel must be present at a postattachment proceeding unless the right to assistance is validly waived). Attachment occurs when the government has used the judicial machinery to signal a commitment to prosecute as spelled out in *Brewer* and *Jackson*. Once attachment occurs, the accused at least[15] is entitled to the presence of appointed counsel during any "critical stage" of the postattachment proceedings; what makes a stage critical is what shows the need for counsel's presence.[16] Thus, counsel must be appointed within a reasonable time after attachment to allow for adequate representation at any critical stage before trial, as well as at trial itself.

The County thus makes an analytical mistake in its assumption that attachment necessarily requires the occurrence or imminence of a critical stage. *See* Brief for Respondent 28–30. On the contrary, it is irrelevant to attachment that the presence of counsel at an article 15.17 hearing, say, may not be critical, just as it is irrelevant that counsel's presence may not be critical when a prosecutor walks over to the trial court to file an information. As we said in *Jackson*, "[t]he question whether arraignment signals the initiation of adversary judicial proceedings . . . is distinct from the question whether the arraignment itself is a critical stage requiring the presence of counsel." 475 U.S., at 630, n.3. Texas's article 15.17 hearing plainly signals attachment, even if it is not itself a critical stage.[17]

III

Our holding is narrow. We do not decide whether the 6-month delay in appointment of counsel resulted in prejudice to Rothgery's Sixth Amendment rights, and have no occasion to consider what standards should apply in deciding this. We merely reaffirm what we have held before and what an overwhelming majority of American jurisdictions understand in practice: a criminal defendant's initial appearance before a judicial officer, where he learns the charge against him and his liberty is subject to restriction, marks the start of adversary judicial proceedings that trigger attachment of the Sixth Amendment right to counsel. Because the Fifth Circuit came to a different conclusion on this threshold issue, its judgment is vacated, and the case is remanded for further proceedings consistent with this opinion.

It is so ordered.

■ CHIEF JUSTICE ROBERTS, with whom JUSTICE SCALIA joins, concurring.

Justice THOMAS's analysis of the present issue is compelling, but I believe the result here is controlled by Brewer v. Williams, 430 U.S. 387

---

[15] We do not here purport to set out the scope of an individual's postattachment right to the presence of counsel. It is enough for present purposes to highlight that the enquiry into that right is a different one from the attachment analysis.

[16] The cases have defined critical stages as proceedings between an individual and agents of the State (whether "formal or informal, in court or out," see United States v. Wade, 388 U.S. 218, 226 (1967)) that amount to "trial-like confrontations," at which counsel would help the accused "in coping with legal problems or . . . meeting his adversary," United States v. Ash, 413 U.S. 300, 312–313 (1973); *See also* Massiah v. United States, 377 U.S. 201 (1964).

[17] The dissent likewise anticipates an issue distinct from attachment when it claims Rothgery has suffered no harm the Sixth Amendment recognizes. *Post*, at 2604. Whether the right has been violated and whether Rothgery has suffered cognizable harm are separate questions from when the right attaches, the sole question before us.

(1977), and Michigan v. Jackson, 475 U.S. 625 (1986). A sufficient case
has not been made for revisiting those precedents, and accordingly I join
the Court's opinion.

I also join Justice ALITO's concurrence, which correctly
distinguishes between the time the right to counsel attaches and the
circumstances under which counsel must be provided.

■ JUSTICE ALITO, with whom THE CHIEF JUSTICE and JUSTICE SCALIA
join, concurring.

I join the Court's opinion because I do not understand it to hold that
a defendant is entitled to the assistance of appointed counsel as soon as
his Sixth Amendment right attaches. As I interpret our precedents, the
term "attachment" signifies nothing more than the beginning of the
defendant's prosecution. It does not mark the beginning of a substantive
entitlement to the assistance of counsel. I write separately to elaborate
on my understanding of the term "attachment" and its relationship to the
Amendment's substantive guarantee of "the Assistance of Counsel for
[the] defence."

The Sixth Amendment provides in pertinent part that "[i]n all
criminal prosecutions, the accused shall enjoy the right . . . to have the
Assistance of Counsel for his defence." The Amendment thus defines the
scope of the right to counsel in three ways: It provides who may assert
the right ("the accused"); when the right may be asserted ("[i]n all
criminal prosecutions"); and what the right guarantees ("the right . . . to
have the Assistance of Counsel for his defence"). It is in the context of
interpreting the Amendment's answer to the second of these questions—
when the right may be asserted—that we have spoken of the right
"attaching." In Kirby v. Illinois, 406 U.S. 682, 688 (1972), a plurality of
the Court explained that "a person's Sixth and Fourteenth Amendment
right to counsel attaches only at or after the time that adversary judicial
proceedings have been initiated against him." A majority of the Court
elaborated on that explanation in Moore v. Illinois, 434 U.S. 220 (1977):

> "In *Kirby v. Illinois*, the plurality opinion made clear that the
> right to counsel announced in *Wade* and *Gilbert* attaches only to
> corporeal identifications conducted at or after the initiation of
> adversary judicial criminal proceedings—whether by way of
> formal charge, preliminary hearing, indictment, information, or
> arraignment. This is so because the initiation of such
> proceedings marks the commencement of the 'criminal
> prosecutions' to which alone the explicit guarantees of the Sixth
> Amendment are applicable. Thus, in *Kirby* the plurality held
> that the prosecution's evidence of a robbery victim's one-on-one
> stationhouse identification of an uncounseled suspect shortly
> after the suspect's arrest was admissible because adversary
> judicial criminal proceedings had not yet been initiated."

Id., at 226–227 (internal quotation marks and citations omitted).

When we wrote in *Kirby* and *Moore* that the Sixth Amendment right had "attached," we evidently meant nothing more than that a "criminal prosecutio[n]" had begun. Our cases have generally used the term in that narrow fashion. *See* Texas v. Cobb, 532 U.S. 162, 167 (2001) (internal quotation marks omitted); McNeil v. Wisconsin, 501 U.S. 171, 175 (1991); Michigan v. Harvey, 494 U.S. 344, 353 (1990); Satterwhite v. Texas, 486 U.S. 249, 254–255 (1988); Michigan v. Jackson, 475 U.S. 625, 629, and n.3 (1986); Moran v. Burbine, 475 U.S. 412, 428 (1986); United States v. Gouveia, 467 U.S. 180, 188 (1984); Edwards v. Arizona, 451 U.S. 477, 480, n.7 (1981); Doggett v. United States, 505 U.S. 647, 663, n.2 (1992) (THOMAS, J., dissenting); Patterson v. Illinois, 487 U.S. 285, 303–304 (1988) (STEVENS, J., dissenting); United States v. Ash, 413 U.S. 300, 322 (1973) (Stewart, J., concurring in judgment). *But see* Estelle v. Smith, 451 U.S. 454, 469 (1981) ("[W]e have held that the right to counsel granted by the Sixth Amendment means that a person is entitled to the help of a lawyer at or after the time that adversary judicial proceedings have been initiated against him . . ." (internal quotation marks omitted)); Brewer v. Williams, 430 U.S. 387, 398 (1977) ("[T]he right to counsel granted by the Sixth and Fourteenth Amendments means at least that a person is entitled to the help of a lawyer at or after the time that judicial proceedings have been initiated against him . . ."). Because pretrial criminal procedures vary substantially from jurisdiction to jurisdiction, there is room for disagreement about when a "prosecution" begins for Sixth Amendment purposes. As the Court, notes, however, we have previously held that "arraignments" that were functionally indistinguishable from the Texas magistration marked the point at which the Sixth Amendment right to counsel "attached." *See ante,* at 2584 (discussing *Jackson, supra,* and *Brewer, supra*).

It does not follow, however, and I do not understand the Court to hold, that the county had an obligation to appoint an attorney to represent petitioner within some specified period after his magistration. To so hold, the Court would need to do more than conclude that petitioner's criminal prosecution had begun. It would also need to conclude that the assistance of counsel in the wake of a Texas magistration is part of the substantive guarantee of the Sixth Amendment. That question lies beyond our reach, petitioner having never sought our review of it. *See* Pet. for Cert. i (inviting us to decide whether the Fifth Circuit erred in concluding "that adversary judicial proceedings . . . had not commenced, and petitioner's Sixth Amendment rights had not attached"). To recall the framework laid out earlier, we have been asked to address only the when question, not the what question. Whereas the temporal scope of the right is defined by the words "[i]n all criminal prosecutions," the right's substantive guarantee flows from a different textual font: the words "Assistance of Counsel for his defence."

In interpreting this latter phrase, we have held that "defence" means defense at trial, not defense in relation to other objectives that may be important to the accused. *See Gouveia, supra*, at 190 ("[T]he right to counsel exists to protect the accused during trial-type confrontations with the prosecutor . . ."); *Ash, supra*, at 309 ("[T]he core purpose of the counsel guarantee was to assure 'Assistance' at trial . . ."). We have thus rejected the argument that the Sixth Amendment entitles the criminal defendant to the assistance of appointed counsel at a probable cause hearing. *See* Gerstein v. Pugh, 420 U.S. 103, 122–123 (1975) (observing that the Fourth Amendment hearing "is addressed only to pretrial custody" and has an insubstantial effect on the defendant's trial rights). More generally, we have rejected the notion that the right to counsel entitles the defendant to a "preindictment private investigator." *Gouveia, supra*, at 191.

At the same time, we have recognized that certain pretrial events may so prejudice the outcome of the defendant's prosecution that, as a practical matter, the defendant must be represented at those events in order to enjoy genuinely effective assistance at trial. *See, e.g., Ash, supra*, at 309–310; United States v. Wade, 388 U.S. 218, 226 (1967). Thus, we have held that an indigent defendant is entitled to the assistance of appointed counsel at a preliminary hearing if "substantial prejudice . . . inheres in the . . . confrontation" and "counsel [may] help avoid that prejudice." Coleman v. Alabama, 399 U.S. 1, 9 (1970) (plurality opinion) (internal quotation marks omitted); *see also* White v. Maryland, 373 U.S. 59, 60 (1963) (per curiam). We have also held that the assistance of counsel is guaranteed at a pretrial lineup, since "the confrontation compelled by the State between the accused and the victim or witnesses to a crime to elicit identification evidence is peculiarly riddled with innumerable dangers and variable factors which might seriously, even crucially, derogate from a fair trial." *Wade, supra*, at 228. Other "critical stages" of the prosecution include pretrial interrogation, a pretrial psychiatric exam, and certain kinds of arraignments. *See Harvey*, 494 U.S., at 358, n.4; *Estelle, supra*, at 470–471; *Coleman, supra*, at 7–8 (plurality opinion).

Weaving together these strands of authority, I interpret the Sixth Amendment to require the appointment of counsel only after the defendant's prosecution has begun, and then only as necessary to guarantee the defendant effective assistance at trial. *Cf. McNeil*, 501 U.S., at 177–178 ("The purpose of the Sixth Amendment counsel guarantee—and hence the purpose of invoking it—is to protec[t] the unaided layman at critical confrontations with his expert adversary, the government, after the adverse positions of government and defendant have solidified with respect to a particular alleged crime" (emphasis and alteration in original; internal quotation marks omitted)). It follows that defendants in Texas will not necessarily be entitled to the assistance of counsel within some specified period after their magistrations. *See ante,* at 2591 (opinion of the Court) (pointing out the "analytical mistake" of assuming "that attachment necessarily requires the occurrence or imminence of a critical stage"). Texas counties need only appoint counsel as far in advance of trial, and as far in advance of any pretrial "critical stage," as necessary to guarantee effective assistance at trial. *Cf. ibid.* ("[C]ounsel must be appointed within a reasonable time after attachment to allow for adequate representation at any critical stage before trial, as well as at trial itself" (emphasis added)).

The Court expresses no opinion on whether Gillespie County satisfied that obligation in this case. Petitioner has asked us to decide only the limited question whether his magistration marked the beginning of his "criminal prosecutio[n]" within the meaning of the Sixth Amendment. Because I agree with the Court's resolution of that limited question, I join its opinion in full.

■ JUSTICE THOMAS, dissenting.

The Court holds today—for the first time after plenary consideration of the question—that a criminal prosecution begins, and that the Sixth Amendment right to counsel therefore attaches, when an individual who has been placed under arrest makes an initial appearance before a magistrate for a probable-cause determination and the setting of bail. Because the Court's holding is not supported by the original meaning of the Sixth Amendment or any reasonable interpretation of our precedents, I respectfully dissent.

I

The Sixth Amendment provides that "[i]n all criminal prosecutions, the accused shall enjoy the right . . . to have the Assistance of Counsel for his defence." The text of the Sixth Amendment thus makes clear that the right to counsel arises only upon initiation of a "criminal prosecutio[n]." For that reason, the Court has repeatedly stressed that the Sixth Amendment right to counsel "does not attach until a prosecution is commenced." McNeil v. Wisconsin, 501 U.S. 171, 175 (1991); *see also* United States v. Gouveia, 467 U.S. 180, 188 (1984) ("[T]he literal language of the Amendment . . . requires the existence of both a 'criminal prosecutio[n]' and an 'accused' "). Echoing this refrain, the Court today reiterates that "[t]he Sixth Amendment right of the 'accused' to assistance of counsel in 'all criminal prosecutions' is limited by its terms." *Ante,* at 2583 (footnote omitted).

Given the Court's repeated insistence that the right to counsel is textually limited to "criminal prosecutions," one would expect the Court's jurisprudence in this area to be grounded in an understanding of what those words meant when the Sixth Amendment was adopted. Inexplicably, however, neither today's decision nor any of the other numerous decisions in which the Court has construed the right to counsel has attempted to discern the original meaning of "criminal prosecutio[n]." I think it appropriate to examine what a "criminal prosecutio[n]" would have been understood to entail by those who adopted the Sixth Amendment.

A

There is no better place to begin than with Blackstone, "whose works constituted the preeminent authority on English law for the founding generation." *Alden v. Maine*, 527 U.S. 706, 715 (1999). Blackstone devoted more than 100 pages of his Commentaries on the Laws of England to a discussion of the "regular and ordinary method of proceeding in the courts of criminal jurisdiction." 4 W. Blackstone, Commentaries (hereinafter Blackstone).

At the outset of his discussion, Blackstone organized the various stages of a criminal proceeding "under twelve general heads, following each other in a progressive order." *Ibid.* The first six relate to pretrial events: "1. Arrest; 2. Commitment and bail; 3. Prosecution; 4. Process; 5. Arraignment, and it's incidents; 6. Plea, and issue." *Ibid.* (emphasis added). Thus, the first significant fact is that Blackstone did not describe the entire criminal process as a "prosecution," but rather listed prosecution as the third step in a list of successive stages. For a more complete understanding of what Blackstone meant by "prosecution," however, we must turn to chapter 23, entitled "Of the Several Modes of Prosecution." *Id.*, at *301. There, Blackstone explained that—after arrest and examination by a justice of the peace to determine whether a suspect should be discharged, committed to prison, or admitted to bail, *id.*, at *296—the "next step towards the punishment of offenders is their prosecution, or the manner of their formal accusation," *id.*, at *301 (emphasis added).

Blackstone thus provides a definition of "prosecution": the manner of an offender's "formal accusation." The modifier "formal" is significant because it distinguishes "prosecution" from earlier stages of the process involving a different kind of accusation: the allegation of criminal conduct necessary to justify arrest and detention. Blackstone's discussion of arrest, commitment, and bail makes clear that a person could not be arrested and detained without a "charge" or "accusation," i.e., an allegation, supported by probable cause, that the person had committed a crime. *See id.*, at *289–*300. But the accusation justifying arrest and detention was clearly preliminary to the "formal accusation" that Blackstone identified with "prosecution." *See id.*, at *290, *318.

By "formal accusation," Blackstone meant, in most cases, "indictment, the most usual and effectual means of prosecution." *Id.*, at *302. Blackstone defined an "indictment" as "a written accusation of one or more persons of a crime or misdemeanor, preferred to, and presented upon oath by, a grand jury." *Ibid.* (emphasis deleted). If the grand jury was "satisfied of the truth of the accusation," it endorsed the indictment, *id.*, at *305–*306, which was then "publicly delivered into court," *id.*, at *306, "afterwards to be tried and determined," *id.*, at *303, "before an officer having power to punish the [charged] offence," 2 T. Cunningham, A New and Complete Law Dictionary (2d ed. 1771).

In addition to indictment, Blackstone identified two other "methods of prosecution at the suit of the king." 4 Blackstone *312. The first was presentment, which, like an indictment, was a grand jury's formal accusation "of an offence, inquirable in the Court where it [was] presented." 5 G. Jacob, The Law-Dictionary 278–279 (1811). The principal difference was that the accusation arose from "the notice taken by a grand jury of any offence from their own knowledge or observation" rather than from a "bill of indictment laid before them." 4 Blackstone *301. The second was information, "the only species of proceeding at the suit of the king, without a previous indictment or presentment by a grand jury." *Id.*, at *308. After an information was filed, it was "tried," *id.*, at *309, in the same way as an indictment: "The same notice was given, the same process was issued, the same pleas were allowed, the same trial by jury was had, the same judgment was given by the same judges, as if the prosecution had originally been by indictment," *id.*, at *310.

From the foregoing, the basic elements of a criminal "prosecution" emerge with reasonable clarity. "Prosecution," as Blackstone used the term, referred to "instituting a criminal suit," *id.*, at *309, by filing a formal charging document—an indictment, presentment, or information—upon which the defendant was to be tried in a court with power to punish the alleged offense. And, significantly, Blackstone's usage appears to have accorded with the ordinary meaning of the term. *See* 2 N. Webster, An American Dictionary of the English Language (1828) (defining "prosecution" as "[t]he institution or commencement and continuance of a criminal suit; the process of exhibiting formal charges against an offender before a legal tribunal, and pursuing them to final judgment," and noting that "[p]rosecutions may be by presentment, information or indictment").

B

With Blackstone as our guide, it is significant that the Framers used the words "criminal prosecutions" in the Sixth Amendment rather than some other formulation such as "criminal proceedings" or "criminal cases." Indeed, elsewhere in the Bill of Rights we find just such an alternative formulation: In contrast to the Sixth Amendment, the Fifth Amendment refers to "criminal case[s]." U.S. Const., Amdt. 5 ("No person . . . shall be compelled in any criminal case to be a witness against himself").

In Counselman v. Hitchcock, 142 U.S. 547 (1892), the Court indicated that the difference in phraseology was not accidental. There the Court held that the Fifth Amendment right not to be compelled to be a witness against oneself "in any criminal case" could be invoked by a witness testifying before a grand jury. The Court rejected the argument that there could be no "criminal case" prior to indictment, reasoning that a "criminal case" under the Fifth Amendment is much broader than a "criminal prosecutio[n]" under the Sixth Amendment. *Id.*, at 563.

The following Term, the Court construed the phrase "criminal prosecution" in a statutory context, and this time the Court squarely held that a "prosecution" does not encompass preindictment stages of the criminal process. In Virginia v. Paul, 148 U.S. 107 (1893), the Court considered Revised Statute § 643, which authorized removal to federal court of any " 'criminal prosecution' " " 'commenced in any court of a State' " against a federal officer. *Id.*, at 115. The respondent, a deputy marshal, had been arrested by Virginia authorities on a warrant for murder and was held in county jail awaiting his appearance before a justice of the peace "with a view to a commitment to await the action of the grand jury." *Id.*, at 118. He filed a petition for removal of " 'said cause' " to federal court. *Ibid.* The question before the Court was whether a " 'criminal prosecution' " had " 'commenced' " within the meaning of the statute at the time the respondent filed his removal petition.

The Court held that a criminal prosecution had not commenced, and that removal was therefore not authorized by the terms of the statute. The Court noted that under Virginia law murder could be prosecuted only "by indictment found in the county court," and that "a justice of the peace, upon a previous complaint, [could] do no more than to examine whether there [was] good cause for believing that the accused [was] guilty, and to commit him for trial before the court having jurisdiction of the offence." *Ibid.* Accordingly, where "no indictment was found, or other action taken, in the county court," there was as yet no " 'criminal prosecution.' " *Id.*, at 119. The appearance before the justice of the peace did not qualify as a "prosecution":

"Proceedings before a magistrate to commit a person to jail, or to hold him to bail, in order to secure his appearance to answer for a crime or offence which the magistrate has no jurisdiction himself to try, before the court in which he may be prosecuted and tried, are but preliminary to the prosecution, and are no more a commencement of the prosecution, than is an arrest by an officer without a warrant for a felony committed in his presence." *Ibid.*

C

The foregoing historical summary is strong evidence that the term "criminal prosecutio[n]" in the Sixth Amendment refers to the commencement of a criminal suit by filing formal charges in a court with jurisdiction to try and punish the defendant. And on this understanding of the Sixth Amendment, it is clear that petitioner's initial appearance before the magistrate did not commence a "criminal prosecutio[n]." No formal charges had been filed. The only document submitted to the magistrate was the arresting officer's affidavit of probable cause. The officer stated that he "ha[d] good reason to believe" that petitioner was a felon and had been "walking around [an] RV park with a gun belt on, carrying a pistol, handcuffs, mace spray, extra bullets and a knife." App.

to Pet. for Cert. 33a. The officer therefore "charge[d]" that petitioner had "commit[ted] the offense of unlawful possession of a firearm by a felon—3rd degree felony." *Ibid.* The magistrate certified that he had examined the affidavit and "determined that probable cause existed for the arrest of the individual accused therein." *Id.*, at 34a. Later that day, petitioner was released on bail, and did not hear from the State again until he was indicted six months later.

The affidavit of probable cause clearly was not the type of formal accusation Blackstone identified with the commencement of a criminal "prosecution." Rather, it was the preliminary accusation necessary to justify arrest and detention—stages of the criminal process that Blackstone placed before prosecution. The affidavit was not a pleading that instituted a criminal prosecution, such as an indictment, presentment, or information; and the magistrate to whom it was presented had no jurisdiction to try and convict petitioner for the felony offense charged therein. *See* Teal v. State, 230 S.W.3d 172, 174 (Tex.Crim.App.2007) ("The Texas Constitution requires that, unless waived by the defendant, the State must obtain a grand jury indictment in a felony case"); Tex.Crim. Proc.Code Ann., Arts. 4.05, 4.11(a) (West 2005). That is most assuredly why the magistrate informed petitioner that charges "will be filed" in district court. App. to Pet. for Cert. 35a (emphasis added).

The original meaning of the Sixth Amendment, then, cuts decisively against the Court's conclusion that petitioner's right to counsel attached at his initial appearance before the magistrate. But we are not writing on a blank slate: This Court has a substantial body of more recent precedent construing the Sixth Amendment right to counsel. . . .

. . . . Even assuming, however, that the arraignment in *Brewer* was functionally identical to the initial appearance here, *Brewer* offered no reasoning for its conclusion that the right to counsel attached at such a proceeding. One is left with the distinct impression that the Court simply saw the word "arraignment" in *Kirby*'s attachment test and concluded that the right must have attached because the defendant had been "arraigned." There is no indication that *Brewer* considered the difference between an arraignment on a warrant and an arraignment at which the defendant pleads to the indictment.

The Court finds it significant that Brewer expressed " 'no doubt' " that the right had attached. *Ante,* at 2591 (quoting 430 U.S., at 399). There was no need for a "lengthy disquisitio[n]," the Court says, because *Brewer* purportedly "found the attachment issue an easy one." *Ante,* at 2591. What the Court neglects to mention is that Brewer's attachment holding is indisputably no longer good law. That is because we have subsequently held that the Sixth Amendment right to counsel is "offense specific," meaning that it attaches only to those offenses for which the defendant has been formally charged, and not to "other offenses 'closely related factually' to the charged offense." Texas v. Cobb, 532 U.S. 162,

164 (2001). Because the defendant in *Brewer* had been arraigned only on the abduction warrant, there is no doubt that, under *Cobb*, his right to counsel had not yet attached with respect to the murder charges that were subsequently brought. *See* 532 U.S., at 184 (BREYER, J., dissenting) (noting that under the majority's rule, "[the defendant's] murder conviction should have remained undisturbed"). But the Court in *Cobb* did not consider itself bound by *Brewer*'s implicit holding on the attachment question. *See* 532 U.S., at 169 ("Constitutional rights are not defined by inferences from opinions which did not address the question at issue"). And here, as in *Cobb*, *Brewer* did not address the fact that the arraignment on the warrant was not the same type of arraignment at which the right to counsel had previously been held to attach, and the parties did not argue the question. *Brewer* is thus entitled to no more precedential weight here than it was in *Cobb*.

Nor does *Jackson* control. In *Jackson,* as in *Brewer,* the attachment issue was secondary. The question presented was "not whether respondents had a right to counsel at their postarraignment, custodial interrogations," 475 U.S., at 629, but "whether respondents validly waived their right to counsel," *id.*, at 630. And, as in *Brewer*, the Court's waiver holding was vigorously disputed. *See* 475 U.S., at 637–642 (Rehnquist, J., dissenting); *see also Cobb, supra*, at 174–177 (KENNEDY, J., concurring) (questioning *Jackson*'s vitality). Unlike in *Brewer*, however, the attachment question was at least contested in *Jackson*— but barely. With respect to respondent Jackson, the State conceded the issue. *Jackson, supra*, at 629, n.3. And with respect to respondent Bladel, the State had conceded the issue below, *see* People v. Bladel, 421 Mich. 39, 77, 365 N.W.2d 56, 74 (1984) (Boyle, J., dissenting), and raised it for the first time before this Court, devoting only three pages of its brief to the question, *see* Brief for Petitioner in Michigan v. Bladel, O.T. 1985, No. 84-1539, pp. 24–26.

The Court disposed of the issue in a footnote. *See Jackson, supra*, at 629–630, n.3. As in *Brewer*, the Court did not describe the nature of the proceeding. It stated only that the respondents were "arraigned." 475 U.S., at 627–628. The Court phrased the question presented in terms of "arraignment," *id.*, at 626 ("The question presented by these two cases is whether the same rule applies to a defendant who has been formally charged with a crime and who has requested appointment of counsel at his arraignment"), and repeated the words "arraignment" or "postarraignment" no fewer than 35 times in the course of its opinion.

There is no way to know from the Court's opinion in *Jackson* whether the arraignment at issue there was the same type of arraignment at which the right to counsel had been held to attach in *Powell* and *Hamilton*. Only upon examination of the parties' briefs does it become clear that the proceeding was in fact an initial appearance. But *Jackson* did not even acknowledge, much less "flatly rejec[t] the distinction between initial arraignment and arraignment on the indictment." *Ante,* at 2586. Instead, it offered one sentence of analysis—"In view of the clear language in our decisions about the significance of arraignment, the State's argument is untenable"—followed by a string citation to four cases, each of which quoted *Kirby*. 475 U.S., at 629–630, n.3. For emphasis, the Court italicized the words "or arraignment" in *Kirby*'s attachment test. 475 U.S., at 629, n.3 (internal quotation marks omitted).

The only rule that can be derived from the face of the opinion in *Jackson* is that if a proceeding is called an "arraignment," the right to counsel attaches. That rule would not govern this case because petitioner's initial appearance was not called an "arraignment" (the parties refer to it as a "magistration"). And that would, in any case, be a silly rule. The Sixth Amendment consequences of a proceeding should turn on the substance of what happens there, not on what the State chooses to call it. But the Court in *Jackson* did not focus on the substantive distinction between an initial arraignment and an arraignment on the indictment. Instead, the Court simply cited *Kirby* and left it at that. In these circumstances, I would recognize *Jackson* for what it was—a cursory treatment of an issue that was not the primary focus of the Court's opinion. Surely Jackson's footnote must yield to our reasoned precedents.

Moreover, even looking behind the opinion, *Jackson* does not support the result the Court reaches today. Respondent Bladel entered a "not guilty" plea at his arraignment, *see* Brief for Petitioner in Michigan v. Bladel, O.T. 1985, No. 84-1539, p. 4, and both Hamilton v. Alabama, 368 U.S. 52 (1961), and White v. Maryland, 373 U.S. 59 (1963) (per curiam), had already held that a defendant has a right to counsel when he enters a plea. The Court suggests that this fact is irrelevant because the magistrate in Bladel's case "had no jurisdiction to accept a plea of guilty to a felony charge." *Ante,* at 2586, n.13. But that distinction does not appear in either *Hamilton* or *White. See Hamilton, supra,* at 55 ("Only the presence of counsel could have enabled this accused to know all the defenses available to him and to plead intelligently"); White, *supra,* at 60 ("[P]etitioner entered a plea before the magistrate and that plea was taken at a time when he had no counsel"). Thus, the most that *Jackson* can possibly be made to stand for is that the right to counsel attaches at an initial appearance where the defendant enters a plea. And that rule would not govern this case because petitioner did not enter a plea at his initial appearance.

And our reasoned precedents provide no support for the conclusion that the right to counsel attaches at an initial appearance before a magistrate. *Kirby* explained why the right attaches "after the initiation of adversary judicial criminal proceedings":

"The initiation of judicial criminal proceedings is far from a mere formalism. It is the starting point of our whole system of adversary criminal justice. For it is only then that the government has committed itself to prosecute, and only then that the adverse positions of government and defendant have solidified. It is then that a defendant finds himself faced with the prosecutorial forces of organized society, and immersed in the intricacies of substantive and procedural criminal law. It is this point, therefore, that marks the commencement of the 'criminal prosecutions' to which alone the explicit guarantees of the Sixth Amendment are applicable."

406 U.S., at 689–690 (plurality opinion).

None of these defining characteristics of a "criminal prosecution" applies to petitioner's initial appearance before the magistrate. The initial appearance was not an "adversary" proceeding, and petitioner was not "faced with the prosecutorial forces of organized society." Instead, he stood in front of a "little glass window," filled out various forms, and was read his *Miranda* rights. Brief for Respondent 5. The State had not committed itself to prosecute—only a prosecutor may file felony charges in Texas, *see* Tex.Code Ann., Crim. Proc. Arts. 2.01, 2.02 (West 2005), and there is no evidence that any prosecutor was even aware of petitioner's arrest or appearance. The adverse positions of government and defendant had not yet solidified—the State's prosecutorial officers had not yet decided whether to press charges and, if so, which charges to press. And petitioner was not immersed in the intricacies of substantive and procedural criminal law—shortly after the proceeding he was free on bail, and no further proceedings occurred until six months later when he was indicted.

Moreover, the Court's holding that the right to counsel attaches at an initial appearance is untethered from any interest that we have heretofore associated with the right to counsel. The Court has repeatedly emphasized that "[t]he purpose of the constitutional guaranty of a right to counsel is to protect an accused from conviction resulting from his own ignorance of his legal and constitutional rights." *Johnson,* 304 U.S., at 465. The "core purpose" of the right, the Court has said, is to "assure 'Assistance' at trial, when the accused [is] confronted with both the intricacies of the law and the advocacy of the public prosecutor." United States v. Ash, 413 U.S. 300, 309 (1973). The Court has extended the right to counsel to pretrial events only when the absence of counsel would derogate from the defendant's right to a fair trial. *See, e.g., Wade,* 388 U.S., at 227.

Neither petitioner nor the Court identifies any way in which petitioner's ability to receive a fair trial was undermined by the absence of counsel during the period between his initial appearance and his indictment. Nothing during that period exposed petitioner to the risk that he would be convicted as the result of ignorance of his rights. Instead, the gravamen of petitioner's complaint is that if counsel had been appointed earlier, he would have been able to stave off indictment by convincing the prosecutor that petitioner was not guilty of the crime alleged. But the Sixth Amendment protects against the risk of erroneous conviction, not the risk of unwarranted prosecution. *See Gouveia,* 467 U.S., at 191 (rejecting the notion that the "purpose of the right to counsel is to provide a defendant with a preindictment private investigator").

Petitioner argues that the right to counsel is implicated here because restrictions were imposed on his liberty when he was required to post bail. But we have never suggested that the accused's right to the assistance of counsel "for his defence" entails a right to use counsel as a sword to contest pretrial detention. To the contrary, we have flatly rejected that notion, reasoning that a defendant's liberty interests are protected by other constitutional guarantees. *See id.,* at 190 ("While the right to counsel exists to protect the accused during trial-type confrontations with the prosecutor, the speedy trial right exists primarily to protect an individual's liberty interest," including the interest in reducing the " 'impairment of liberty imposed on an accused while released on bail' ").

IV

In sum, neither the original meaning of the Sixth Amendment right to counsel nor our precedents interpreting the scope of that right supports the Court's holding that the right attaches at an initial appearance before a magistrate. Because I would affirm the judgment below, I respectfully dissent.

3. "CRITICAL STAGES"

Alexander v. Smith

311 Fed. Appx. 875 (6th Cir. 2009)

■ Before: BOGGS, CHIEF JUDGE; KETHLEDGE, CIRCUIT JUDGE; and THAPAR, DISTRICT JUDGE.

■ PER CURIAM.

Gregory Alexander was convicted of first-degree murder and sentenced to life imprisonment without the possibility of parole. He appeals the federal district court's dismissal of his petition for a writ of habeas corpus, which he filed pursuant to 28 U.S.C. § 2254. Because we find that all of the claims now before us were procedurally defaulted and that the petitioner has failed to demonstrate cause and prejudice or a miscarriage of justice, we affirm the district court's dismissal.

I

On July 2, 1998, a circuit court jury in Calhoun County, Michigan convicted the petitioner of first-degree murder, stemming from the shooting of Termain Watson on May 2, 1996, in Battle Creek, Michigan. On direct review before the Michigan Court of Appeals, he raised six claims, each arguing that the proceedings had violated his rights. In particular, he argued that (1) the prosecution improperly infringed on his right under the Fifth and Fourteenth Amendments not to testify, (2) the trial court erred in allowing the prosecution to endorse Antonio Postell, an incarcerated fellow prisoner, as a witness after several days of trial, (3) the trial court abused its discretion when it allowed Postell to testify, (4) the prosecution improperly made a "community protection" argument during his closing argument, (5) the trial court improperly ordered restitution, and (6) his trial counsel was ineffective for failing to challenge defendant's financial ability to make restitution. The Michigan Court of Appeals denied all of his claims and affirmed his conviction. People v. Alexander, No. 213899, 2000 WL 33534581 (Mich.Ct.App. Feb.8, 2000). The Michigan Supreme Court in turn declined his request for leave to appeal, stating that it did not believe the questions presented should be reviewed. People v. Alexander, 463 Mich. 860, 617 N.W.2d 334 (2000).

On collateral review in state and federal court, the petitioner raised thirteen separate claims. Three of these claims were previously raised on direct review, and ten additional claims were raised for the first time in collateral proceedings. . . .

Claim IV: The use of Postell's testimony at the petitioner's trial violated his Sixth Amendment right to counsel.

1.   Sixth Amendment Claim (Claim IV)

The petitioner contends that his counsel's failure to object to testimony by Antonio Postell, a fellow inmate who elicited incriminating comments from him in the absence of counsel, constitutes ineffective assistance of counsel. Postell met with detectives, in the midst of Alexander's trial, on June 26, 1998. And three days later on June 29, 2008, he met with prosecutors, and agreed to testify. If Postell had an agreement with prosecutors to elicit, or if they encouraged him to elicit, the statements, admission of his testimony violated Alexander's Sixth Amendment right to counsel. At the petitioner's original trial, Postell said no such relationship existed. Postell later recanted this testimony in the federal habeas proceeding, professing that a quid pro quo did exist whereby he would elicit incriminating statements from Alexander. As the petitioner notes, "Postell's testimony at the hearing before this Court [the federal district court], if believed, clearly would establish an agency relationship and entitlement to relief." Br. Appellant at 29. However, the district court explicitly found Postell's testimony at the evidentiary hearing was not credible. To the extent Postell recanted the claims he made at Alexander's trial, the magistrate judge found Postell's testimony to be "illogical," "internally inconsistent," uncorroborated by other evidence, inspired by the risk of retribution, and less plausible than both a video taped statement made prior to Alexander's criminal trial and his testimony at that trial.

Following the evidentiary hearing, a magistrate judge made a number of factual findings, adopted by the district court, that are diametrically opposed to the conclusions the petitioner proposes we adopt in these proceedings. The most critical of these findings were that no agreement existed between Postell and the State and that no government employee asked, suggested, or even encouraged Postell to elicit incriminating statements from Alexander. The district court also found that Postell had never before been a "proactive informant" and had never before received a deal in return for information or his testimony. Rather, Postell "acted solely on his own initiative in communicating with Gregory Alexander at the Calhoun County Jail," and that the police and prosecutors had no way of knowing that Postell "could or would engage Alexander in uncounselled communications relating to the murder of Tremain (sic) Watson." Communication between the two prisoners was not inevitable or foreseeable, as evidenced by the facts that Postell and Alexander were housed in separate cells on different levels of the Calhoun County Jail and that they communicated through the ventilation system. There is no good reason to find fault, let alone clear error, in the magistrate judge's findings, which were adopted by the district court. Given these factual findings, we proceed to consider whether Alexander's constitutional rights were violated by admission of Postell's testimony, and consequently, whether his counsel's assistance can be deemed ineffective in failing to object.

The Sixth Amendment provides that, "the accused shall enjoy the right . . . to have Assistance of Counsel for his defence." U.S. Const. amend VI. This right is triggered " 'at or after the time that judicial proceedings have been initiated . . . whether by way of formal charge, preliminary hearing, indictment, information, or arraignment.' " Fellers v. United States, 540 U.S. 519, 523 (2004) (quoting Brewer v. Williams, 430 U.S. 387, 398 (1977)). Once the Sixth Amendment has attached, the government may not "deliberately elicit" incriminating statements from the defendant without the presence of his attorney. *See* United States v. Henry, 447 U.S. 264, 270 (1980) (outlining the deliberate-elicitation standard). Unlike a defendant's Fifth Amendment rights, the Sixth Amendment is implicated even when an undercover officer or unidentified informant acting at the behest of the state questions the defendant. Massiah v. United States, 377 U.S. 201, 206 (1964). In other words, admission of statements made even when the defendant does not know he is being interrogated can violate the Sixth Amendment. *Ibid.*

The Supreme Court has cautioned, "the Sixth Amendment is not violated whenever—by luck or happenstance—the State obtains incriminating statements from the accused after the right to counsel has attached." Maine v. Moulton, 474 U.S. 159, 176 (1985). Rather, the Constitution is implicated when the police suggest an informant record conversations and help an informant record conversations with the defendant. *Ibid.* A defendant's Sixth Amendment right is also likely to be violated when an informant has an arrangement already in place with the state at the time of the conversation, and perhaps is compensated on a contingent basis. *Henry,* 447 U.S. at 270. In perhaps its broadest characterization of the rights protected by the Sixth Amendment, the

Supreme Court has stated that, "[b]y intentionally creating a situation likely to induce Henry to make incriminating statements without the assistance of counsel, the Government violated Henry's Sixth Amendment right to counsel." *Id.* at 274.

There is no dispute that Alexander's Sixth Amendment right to counsel had attached at the time of his statements to Postell. The issue before us is whether Alexander's counsel was ineffective for not arguing that admission of Postell's testimony in fact violated the Sixth Amendment even though he was not acting as an agent of state. Because Massiah and Sixth Circuit precedent simply do not give rise to a doctrine of implied state agency or allow for a finding that state agency existed as a matter of law under these circumstances, we hold counsel was not ineffective in failing to raise this claim. It is simply not clear under these circumstances that Alexander's constitutional rights were violated. Few decisions recognize a doctrine of implied state agency, absent express encouragement or agreement by the police, and what law does exist suggests it would not apply under the circumstances presented in this case.

The petitioner relies upon a Ninth Circuit case, Randolph v. California, 380 F.3d 1133 (9th Cir.2004), in contending his counsel was ineffective in not raising the Sixth Amendment issue at trial and on appeal. *Randolph* does suggest state agency may be implied by the totality of the circumstances. But this case was decided six years after Alexander's original trial and it reflects an extension, not an application, of *Massiah*. Our jurisprudence would not necessarily follow the Ninth Circuit. The Supreme Court has never held that an informant was acting on behalf of the state resulting in a *Massiah* violation merely because detectives or prosecutors "should have known" a particular informant "believed that he would receive leniency if he elicited incriminating statements" from the defendant. *Id.* at 1147. In reaching this conclusion, the Ninth Circuit creates an affirmative duty on the part of detectives or prosecutors to ensure informants understand whether or not they will receive a deal in exchange for eliciting statements. Even if such a rule is justified, it would be inapplicable here, where the informant has never before testified pursuant to a deal with prosecutors and did not share a cell with the petitioner such that conversation could be reasonably anticipated between the two parties. That communication between Postell and Alexander took place through the ventilation system bolsters the notion their communication was unforeseeable.

Failure of his trial and appellate counsel to present a novel legal argument when the caselaw is ambiguous does not constitute ineffective assistance. The Supreme Court has held, "the Constitution guarantees criminal defendants only a fair trial and a competent attorney. It does not insure that defense counsel will recognize and raise every conceivable constitutional claim." Engle v. Isaac, 456 U.S. 107, 134 (1982). Perhaps Alexander's Sixth Amendment claim is stronger than other claims raised in his first appeal as a matter of right, but failing to raise a claim that does not follow logically or entail an inevitable extension of preexisting Sixth Amendment jurisprudence does not render his appellate or trial counsel ineffective. The petitioner can cite no cases at the time of his original trial recognizing the doctrine he now says his counsel had a duty to raise. Even if the doctrine had been accepted by the court, its application to the facts at bar would remain highly questionable. These facts demonstrate that the petitioner cannot come close to satisfying the constitutional standard of ineffectiveness. Consequently, we must let the state's denial of habeas with respect to this claim stand. . . .

United States v. Kon Yu-Leung

910 F.2d 33 (2d Cir. 1990)

■ MAHONEY, CIRCUIT JUDGE:

The government appeals, pursuant to 18 U.S.C. § 3731 (1988), from an order of the United States District Court for the Eastern District of New York, Thomas C. Platt, Jr., Chief Judge, granting defendant-appellee John Ruotolo's motion to suppress physical evidence seized from his home during a consent search. The district court granted Ruotolo's motion because Ruotolo was not informed, at the time he consented to the search, that he had been indicted. The district court determined that a postindictment consent to a search is a critical stage of a criminal litigation to which the sixth amendment right to counsel accordingly attaches, and that Ruotolo could neither knowingly and intelligently decide whether to proceed without counsel nor validly consent to the search without being informed that he was under indictment.

We reverse and remand for a determination whether Ruotolo's consent was voluntarily given. We conclude that a consent to a search is not a critical stage of a criminal litigation. Accordingly, the sixth amendment right to counsel is inapplicable, and a fourth amendment analysis as to voluntariness is appropriate.

Background

On March 13, 1988, John Ruotolo was arrested at his home in Montclair, New Jersey pursuant to an arrest warrant which had been issued December 21, 1987. The consent search of his home that ensued shortly after his arrest is the subject of this appeal.

On December 21, 1987, the same day the arrest warrant was issued, a grand jury in the Eastern District of New York returned a sealed, fourteen-count indictment that charged Ruotolo and nine other defendants with, inter alia, conspiring to import substantial quantities of heroin into the United States from southeast Asia between January, 1984 and December, 1987. The Drug Enforcement Administration ("DEA") planned to arrest the indictees the evening of March 13, 1988. The scenario called for the initial arrest of the leader of the organization,

Kon Yu-Leung, followed in quick succession by the arrest of the other defendants worldwide.

Accordingly, between 8:00 and 9:00 p.m. on the evening of March 13, 1988, six DEA agents went to the vicinity of Ruotolo's home with the warrant for his arrest, and awaited word of Kon Yu-Leung's arrest. The agents wore civilian clothes and did not have their badges displayed. Upon being advised that Kon Yu-Leung had been arrested, the agents proceeded with Ruotolo's arrest at approximately 11:00 p.m. Agent Michael Pasterchick, who led the Ruotolo arrest, went to the side door of the house with four other agents, and the remaining agent went to the back of the house. Pasterchick, with his gun hidden but drawn, knocked on the door, which was answered by Ruotolo's thirteen-year-old daughter. Without identifying himself as a police officer, Pasterchick inquired as to Ruotolo's whereabouts. The daughter responded that her father was in the kitchen. She led Pasterchick to the kitchen, where he identified himself as a federal agent and arrested Ruotolo, placing him in handcuffs.

Pasterchick had been advised that Ruotolo, who had been a police officer in New York City for approximately twenty years, would most likely have numerous weapons in the house. Upon inquiry, Ruotolo confirmed the presence of guns. Ruotolo also told Pasterchick that his wife and two other children were in the house. Mrs. Ruotolo and the other children were summoned to the kitchen. Subsequently, Mrs. Ruotolo and the children were taken to a "library-type room" by a female agent.

Pasterchick and four other agents conducted a security sweep of the house, accompanied by Ruotolo. The agents found a loaded gun on top of the armoire in Ruotolo's bedroom. Ruotolo told them about a second gun in one of his sports jackets, and that weapon was also seized. The agents unloaded both guns and finished the sweep in approximately ten minutes. During the security sweep, the sixth agent remained with Mrs. Ruotolo and the children downstairs. At the conclusion of the sweep, which was conducted with weapons drawn, all agents holstered their guns.

The agents and Ruotolo returned to the kitchen, where Pasterchick read Ruotolo, from a printed card, the warnings prescribed by Miranda v. Arizona, 384 U.S. 436 (1966), and asked him whether he wished to answer any questions and would consent to a search of the house. Ruotolo responded, "I am not sure that I should answer any questions or if I should let you do a search of my home before talking to my lawyer. I don't have anything to hide, but I am not sure." Pasterchick responded, "Fine," but told Ruotolo that because of the ongoing investigation and arrests, he would not be allowed to make any telephone calls and therefore could not contact his attorney. Pasterchick then telephoned fellow agents to advise them that Ruotolo was under arrest and had declined to allow a search of his home, and to request that they proceed to obtain a search warrant. Pasterchick testified that he was aware that affidavits had been prepared in advance to obtain a search warrant for Ruotolo's home, should that prove necessary.

After making the call, Pasterchick returned to the kitchen and told the Ruotolos that arrangements were being made to obtain a warrant. He stated that the agents would remain in the house until he was advised whether a search warrant would be obtained. Ruotolo then initiated a conversation with Pasterchick regarding a consent search. Ruotolo asked Pasterchick whether his consent to a search would expedite matters, and, if so, whether Mrs. Ruotolo and he would be allowed to accompany the agents during the search. Although Pasterchick stated that a warrant was being obtained and he was accordingly indifferent to Ruotolo's consent to a search, Pasterchick also agreed that the agents would leave upon the conclusion of the search, and that the Ruotolos would be permitted to accompany the DEA agents during the search. Some time during the course of this dialogue, the agents cuffed Ruotolo's hands in front of, rather than behind, him to permit him to smoke cigarettes.

Ruotolo discussed the situation with his wife, and then consented to a search. Pasterchick then went to his car to obtain a consent form that he filled out and read aloud to Mr. and Mrs. Ruotolo, who both signed the form. The consent form was signed at 12:05 a.m. on the morning of March 14, 1988. Aside from the title and signatures, it read as follows:

> I, John Ruotolo and Gail Ruotolo, having been requested to consent to a search of my residence located at 1 Stonebridge, Montclair, NJ and having been duly advised of my constitutional rights to (1) refuse such consent, (2) to require that a search warrant be obtained prior to any search, (3) that if I do consent to a search, any evidence found as a result of such search, can and will be used against me in any civil or criminal proceedings, (4) that I may consult with an attorney of my choosing before or during the search and (5) that I may withdraw my consent to search at any time prior to its conclusion.
>
> After having been advised of my constitutional rights, I hereby knowingly, intelligently and voluntarily waive my above rights and consent to a search and authorize S/A Michael Pasterchick and other Special Agents of the Drug Enforcement Administration, United States Department of Justice, to conduct a complete search of the above described residence.

Two teams of agents, each accompanied by one of the Ruotolos, conducted the search of the house, which lasted about two hours. Upon its completion, Ruotolo was strip searched and then taken to a local jail. Before leaving, Ruotolo gave his wife a card containing an attorney's name and number, and told her to contact the attorney as soon as she could. Also prior to his departure, his handcuffs were removed to permit him to say good night to his daughters, who by then had gone to bed.

The search produced nineteen handguns, passports, sets of gold coins, various documents, and other items. Before the agents left the Ruotolo home, the items seized were inventoried by Pasterchick in the kitchen in the presence of Mrs. Ruotolo. Preparation of the inventory list took approximately two hours. The agents did not leave the Ruotolo home until approximately 5:00 a.m. on March 14, 1988.

The district court held hearings on December 9 and 12, 1988 on Ruotolo's motion to suppress the physical evidence seized during the search. Ruotolo contended, inter alia, that this evidence should be suppressed because his consent was obtained in violation of his sixth amendment right to counsel.

As indicated hereinabove, the district court ruled that a postindictment consent to a search is a critical stage of a criminal litigation to which the sixth amendment right to counsel attaches. The court also stated, in a lengthy footnote that reviewed the pertinent testimony at the suppression hearing, that "the consent in this case appears to have been voluntarily made and fairly bargained for." The court nonetheless concluded, in its central ruling:

> Ruotolo was not informed that he was under indictment at the time he gave his consent. Under the case of [sic] law of the Second Circuit, as it presently stands, this information was necessary before Ruotolo could knowingly and intelligently decide whether to proceed without counsel and consent to the search. The evidence seized from his home pursuant to his consent must therefore be suppressed.

The court excepted from its suppression ruling one gun that was seized in plain view during the security sweep, ruling that neither consent nor a search warrant was required for its seizure. The government appealed this ruling pursuant to 18 U.S.C. § 3731 (1988), providing the certification required by section 3731 "that the appeal is not taken for purpose of delay and that the [suppressed] evidence is a substantial proof of a fact material in the proceeding."

Discussion

We note at the outset that the central factual premise of the district court's ruling, that "Ruotolo was not informed that he was under indictment at the time he gave his consent" to the search, is not abundantly clear from the record presented to us. The warrant that authorized the DEA agents to arrest Ruotolo commanded them to "bring him . . . forthwith to the nearest magistrate to answer a(n) Indictment . . . charging him . . . with Conspiracy to import heroin into the United States . . ., [and] Importation of heroin into the United States . . ., in violation of Title 21 United States Code, Section(s) 952, 960, 963." Surely, then, if the arrest warrant had been served upon Ruotolo and he had read it, he would have been aware that he was under indictment. In the course of the suppression hearing, however, Pasterchick was never explicitly asked whether he served the arrest warrant upon Ruotolo. The nearest approach to this critical issue occurred during Pasterchick's cross-examination, as follows:

Q   But you are sure you had an arrest warrant?

A   I'm positive I saw the arrest warrant that night.

Q   I didn't ask you if you saw it. I asked you if you had it personally?

A   Yes.

Q   You had a copy on your person?

A   Yes.

Q   In your pocket?

A   It was in my briefcase, initially.

Q   When did you take it out of your briefcase?

A   We probably went to the car to get that.

Q   So when you approached the door, you didn't have the briefcase with you, did you?

A   No, I did not.

Q   So, you didn't have the arrest warrant with you when you approached the door of the Routollo's [sic] residence?

A   No.

Q   And it wasn't until after you had already concluded the arrest and done your security sweep that you went back out to the car to get your briefcase, correct?

A   Yes, that's probably correct.

Q   So, the earliest possible moment that you could have displayed this arrest warrant would have been after the arrest and the security sweep, correct?

A   It would have been after the arrest and the security sweep, yes.

As is apparent, this testimony leaves open the possibility that Ruotolo was shown the arrest warrant, and thus apprised that he had been indicted, after the arrest and the security sweep, but prior to his consent to the search of his home. The district court categorically stated, however, that "Ruotolo was not informed that he was under indictment at the time he gave his consent." Furthermore, the government has conceded in its appellate brief that this is the case, and presumably would not have done so if it could present a factual argument to the contrary. We therefore address the issue as framed by the district court.

It is settled constitutional law that "[a] person comes under the protection of the sixth . . . amendment right to counsel from the moment judicial proceedings are initiated against him, 'whether by way of formal charge, preliminary hearing, indictment, information, or arraignment.' " Carvey v. LeFevre, 611 F.2d 19, 21 (2d Cir.1979) (quoting Kirby v. Illinois, 406 U.S. 682, 689 (1972)). Once the right has attached, the defendant is entitled to the representation of counsel, if desired, at any "critical stage" of the criminal proceedings against him. *See* Michigan v. Jackson, 475 U.S. 625, 632 n.5 (1986); Coleman v. Alabama, 399 U.S. 1, 7–10 (1970); United States v. Wade, 388 U.S. 218, 236–37 (1967); *see also* United States v. Jackson, 886 F.2d 838, 843 (7th Cir.1989) ("Although the right [to counsel] attaches upon the commencement of adversarial proceedings, it only applies to 'critical stages' of those proceedings where absence of defense counsel or lack of advice might derogate from the accused's right to a fair trial."); Meadows v. Kuhlmann, 812 F.2d 72, 76 (2d Cir.) ("The Sixth Amendment right to counsel applies only to 'critical stages' of a criminal prosecution.").

Defining a "critical stage," the Supreme Court stated in *Wade*:

> [I]n addition to counsel's presence at trial, the accused is guaranteed that he need not stand alone against the State at any stage of the prosecution, formal or informal, in court or out, where counsel's absence might derogate from the accused's right to a fair trial. . . . The presence of counsel at such critical confrontations, as at the trial itself, operates to assure that the accused's interests will be protected consistently with our adversary theory of criminal prosecution.

388 U.S. at 226–27 (footnotes omitted).

Relinquishment of the sixth amendment right to counsel is closely circumscribed. "To preserve the fairness of the trial process the Court established an appropriately heavy burden on the Government before waiver could be found-'an intentional relinquishment or abandonment of a known right or privilege.' " Schneckloth v. Bustamonte, 412 U.S. 218, 236–37 (1973) (quoting Johnson v. Zerbst, 304 U.S. 458, 464 (1938)); *see also* Patterson v. Illinois, 487 U.S. 285, 292 (1988). Thus, in addition to establishing that a waiver is voluntary, *see Patterson,* 487 U.S. at 292 & n.4, the government must show that the defendant "has been sufficiently apprised of the nature of his Sixth Amendment rights, and of the consequences of abandoning those rights." *Patterson,* 487 U.S. at 296; *see also* Moran v. Burbine, 475 U.S. 412, 421 (1986) (waiver of *Miranda* rights); Adams v. United States ex rel. McCann, 317 U.S. 269, 279 (1942); *Johnson v. Zerbst,* 304 U.S. at 464.

Ruotolo contends that the application of these principles in the instant case requires suppression of the evidence seized from his home. Ruotolo concededly had been indicted at the time of his consent to the search which resulted in that seizure. Thus, the sixth amendment right to counsel had attached, and he was entitled to the advice of counsel at any critical stage of the proceedings against him. Accordingly, the pivotal threshold question is whether a consent to a search is a critical stage of a criminal proceeding.

In answering this question in the affirmative, the district court in this case relied upon three prior opinions of the United States District Court for the Eastern District of New York: United States v. Londono, 659 F.Supp. 758, 770 (E.D.N.Y.1987), aff'd on other grounds sub nom. United States v. Carmona, 858 F.2d 66 (2d Cir.1988) (per curiam); United States v. David, 565 F.Supp. 901, 904 (E.D.N.Y.), aff'd mem., 742 F.2d 1441 (2d Cir.1983); and United States v. Praetorius, 457 F.Supp. 329, 334 (E.D.N.Y.1978). We do not find these cases persuasive.

Praetorius required a "knowing, informed and intelligent waiver of counsel," 457 F.Supp. at 333, because "even if the defendant's statements were 'voluntary' for purposes of the Fifth Amendment," *id.*, they did not meet " 'the higher standard with respect to waiver of the right to counsel that applies when the Sixth Amendment has attached.' " *Id.* (quoting United States v. Satterfield, 558 F.2d 655, 657 (2d Cir.1976)). This seems clearly at odds with the later ruling in *Patterson* that "whatever warnings suffice for *Miranda*'s purposes will also be sufficient in the context of postindictment questioning." 487 U.S. at 298. *David* relied explicitly, *see* 565 F.Supp. at 904, upon the ruling in United States v. Mohabir, 624 F.2d 1140, 1153 (2d Cir.1980), that "a valid waiver of the Sixth Amendment right to have counsel present during post-indictment interrogation must be preceded by a federal judicial officer's explanation of the content and significance of this right." This ruling in *Mohabir* has been squarely rejected by the Supreme Court. *See Patterson,* 487 U.S. at 296 n.8. *Londono* followed both *Praetorius* and *David. See Londono,* 659 F.Supp. at 770.

In the absence of other cases addressing the issue whether a postindictment consent to a search is a "critical stage" for sixth amendment purposes, we look to the view courts have taken concerning analogous postindictment situations. The considerations animating this examination were expressed by the Supreme Court in *Wade,* 388 U.S. at 227, as follows:

> [T]he principle of Powell v. Alabama [, 287 U.S. 45 (1932),] and succeeding cases requires that we scrutinize any pretrial confrontation of the accused to determine whether the presence of his counsel is necessary to preserve the defendant's basic right to a fair trial as affected by his right meaningfully to cross-examine the witnesses against him and to have effective assistance of counsel at the trial itself. It calls upon us to analyze whether potential substantial prejudice to defendant's rights inheres in the particular confrontation and the ability of counsel to help avoid that prejudice.

A pretrial lineup was held to be a critical stage in *Wade. See id.* at 236–37. The Court pointed to the fact that a lineup is a trial-like confrontation, as well as to the potential for suggestiveness and overreaching by the prosecution. 388 U.S. at 227–39; *see also Meadows v. Kuhlmann,* 812 F.2d at 75–76. Similarly, postindictment interrogation was ruled a critical stage in *Michigan v. Jackson,* 475 U.S. at 630. On the other hand, a pretrial photo display identification has been held not to be a critical stage, *see* United States v. Ash, 413 U.S. 300, 321 (1973); nor is the taking of handwriting exemplars, *see* Gilbert v. California, 388 U.S. 263, 267 (1967); United States v. Jacobowitz, 877 F.2d 162, 169 (2d Cir, or of fingerprints or samples of blood, hair, or clothing, *see* Wade, 388 U.S. at 227.

The sixth amendment protects a defendant's right to a fair trial. Accordingly, "the 'trial' guarantees that have been applied to the 'pretrial' stage of the criminal process are similarly designed to protect the fairness of the trial itself." *Schneckloth,* 412 U.S. at 238–39; *see also* United States v. Gouveia, 467 U.S. 180, 189 (1984). It is therefore important to evaluate "whether confrontation with counsel at trial can serve as a substitute for counsel at the pretrial confrontation." Ash, 413 U.S. at 316. Thus, the taking of fingerprints, or of samples of blood, hair or clothing, is not deemed a critical stage because "the accused has the opportunity for a meaningful confrontation of the Government's case at trial through the ordinary processes of cross-examination of the Government's expert witnesses and the presentation of the evidence of his own experts." *Wade,* 388 U.S. at 227–28; *see also Ash,* 413 U.S. at 316.

These considerations weigh against a conclusion that a "critical stage" of the criminal proceeding against Ruotolo occurred at the time of his consent to the search of his home. No confrontation occurred, as in the case of a lineup, which would result in adverse consequences difficult to remedy at trial. No evidence was generated, as in the case of incriminating testimony, that was not already in existence and virtually certain to be available to the government in due course. In this connection, there is no contention that the government would not ultimately have obtained a warrant to search Ruotolo's home if his consent had not been forthcoming. In sum, it is difficult to ascertain what benefit would have accrued to Ruotolo, or what detriment he might have avoided, if counsel had been available to him at that juncture. We conclude that, at least on the facts presented in this case, Ruotolo's consent to the search of his residence was not a critical stage of the criminal proceeding against him.

The district court reached a contrary conclusion. The court noted that the Supreme Court, in *Patterson,* had attacked "the holding and the underlying reasoning of *Mohabir*" by ruling that *Miranda* warnings suffice to inform an indictee of his sixth amendment right to counsel, *see Patterson,* 487 U.S. at 296–97, and by explicitly rejecting *Mohabir*'s requirement that a sixth amendment waiver can properly be made only before a neutral judicial officer, *see id.* at 296 n.8. The district court also noted, however, that *Patterson,* which dealt with a defendant who had concededly been advised of his indictment, therefore did

> not address the question of whether or not an accused must be
> told that he has been indicted before a postindictment Sixth

Amendment waiver will be valid. Nor do we even pass on the desirability of so informing the accused-a matter that can be reasonably debated.

Patterson, 487 U.S. at 296 n.8.

The district court concluded that *Mohabir* "remains good law in this Circuit" as to the requirement that an accused be "told that he has been indicted before a postindictment Sixth Amendment waiver will be valid." The district court addressed the "critical stage" requirement (in addition to relying upon prior Eastern District cases discussed hereinabove) as follows:

Although *Patterson* involved postindictment statements as opposed to a consent to search, its analysis would appear to apply with equal force to both situations: in both, the value of counsel is limited to simple advice, i.e., whether to give consent or not, whether to answer a question or not.

As indicated earlier, we disagree with this analysis of the "critical stage" issue, at least on the facts presented here, and therefore do not reach the question whether an indictee must be explicitly advised that he has been indicted in order to render effective a waiver of sixth amendment rights. Finding the sixth amendment inapplicable, we conclude that Ruotolo's consent to the search of his home must be judged by fourth amendment standards, the question to which we now turn.

As indicated earlier, the district court considered the voluntariness of Ruotolo's consent in a lengthy footnote to its opinion, concluding that "the consent in this case appears to have been voluntarily made and fairly bargained for." As the government concedes in its brief, however, this statement did not constitute an ultimate finding as to voluntariness. Accordingly, we will not undertake this determination in the first instance, but rather set forth the general considerations pertinent to the ruling that must be made upon remand. . . .

Ruotolo contends that the refusal of the DEA agents to allow him to contact his attorney, the lateness of the hour, the presence of six DEA agents in his home, and the assurance that they would remain there indefinitely pending the availability of a search warrant combine to require a finding that his consent was not voluntarily given. At the suppression hearing, furthermore, Ruotolo's counsel stressed that the consent form signed by Ruotolo and his wife recited "that I may consult with an attorney of my choosing before or during the search," although it is uncontested that this was not the case. We note also that Ruotolo was handcuffed most of the time from his arrest until his departure from his residence. After the initial security sweep, however, he was cuffed with his hands in front of his body to allow him to smoke cigarettes, and the handcuffs were removed to allow him to take leave of his family prior to his departure.

In its review of this issue, the district court discounted much of the testimony of Ruotolo's wife and daughter in support of Ruotolo's contention that "the agents terrorized his family, forcing him to consent to search in order to get the agents out of the house as quickly as possible." The court noted that neither the coercion inherent in the fact of arrest, *See* United States v. Valencia, 645 F.2d 1158, 1165 (2d Cir.1980) (citing United States v. Watson, 423 U.S. 411, 424 (1976)), nor a representation that a warrant will be obtained if consent is withheld, s *see Calvente,* 722 F.2d at 1023 (citing United States v. Faruolo, 506 F.2d 490, 495 (2d Cir.1974); United States v. Lace, 669 F.2d 46, 52 (2d Cir. 1982), suffices to establish coercion. Nor does a finding of coercion follow from the fact that Ruotolo was handcuffed. *See* United States v. Crespo, 834 F.2d 267, 271 (2d Cir.1987). Ruotolo's relative sophistication, as a twenty-year police veteran and private investigator who had attended college, is a factor tending against a finding of involuntariness, *see id.* at 272; United States v. Price, 599 F.2d 494, 503 (2d Cir.1979), as is the fact that he was given *Miranda* warnings, *see* United States v. Jones, 475 F.2d 723, 730 (5th Cir. 1973).

In any event, the totality of the circumstances must be weighed and considered in light of established fourth amendment principles governing the issue of voluntariness. Cf. 3 W. LaFave, Search and Seizure § 8.2(b), at 181 (1987) ("While it is unlikely that a single coercive element will, standing alone, be enough to invalidate a consent, several of them in combination certainly will."). We remand for this determination by the district court.

Conclusion

The order of the district court granting defendant-appellee's motion to suppress physical evidence obtained during the consent search of his home is reversed, and the case is remanded for further proceedings not inconsistent with this opinion.

4. WAIVER

Montejo v. Louisiana

556 U.S. 778 (2009)

■ JUSTICE SCALIA delivered the opinion of the Court.

We consider in this case the scope and continued viability of the rule announced by this Court in Michigan v. Jackson, 475 U.S. 625 (1986), forbidding police to initiate interrogation of a criminal defendant once he has requested counsel at an arraignment or similar proceeding.

I

Petitioner Jesse Montejo was arrested on September 6, 2002, in connection with the robbery and murder of Lewis Ferrari, who had been found dead in his own home one day earlier. Suspicion quickly focused on

Jerry Moore, a disgruntled former employee of Ferrari's dry cleaning business. Police sought to question Montejo, who was a known associate of Moore.

Montejo waived his rights under Miranda v. Arizona, 384 U.S. 436 (1966), and was interrogated at the sheriff's office by police detectives through the late afternoon and evening of September 6 and the early morning of September 7. During the interrogation, Montejo repeatedly changed his account of the crime, at first claiming that he had only driven Moore to the victim's home, and ultimately admitting that he had shot and killed Ferrari in the course of a botched burglary. These police interrogations were videotaped.

On September 10, Montejo was brought before a judge for what is known in Louisiana as a "72-hour hearing"—a preliminary hearing required under state law.[1] Although the proceedings were not transcribed, the minute record indicates what transpired: "The defendant being charged with First Degree Murder, Court ordered N[o] Bond set in this matter. Further, Court ordered the Office of Indigent Defender be appointed to represent the defendant." App. to Pet. for Cert. 63a.

Later that same day, two police detectives visited Montejo back at the prison and requested that he accompany them on an excursion to locate the murder weapon (which Montejo had earlier indicated he had thrown into a lake). After some back-and-forth, the substance of which remains in dispute, Montejo was again read his *Miranda* rights and agreed to go along; during the excursion, he wrote an inculpatory letter of apology to the victim's widow. Only upon their return did Montejo finally meet his court-appointed attorney, who was quite upset that the detectives had interrogated his client in his absence.

At trial, the letter of apology was admitted over defense objection. The jury convicted Montejo of first-degree murder, and he was sentenced to death.

The Louisiana Supreme Court affirmed the conviction and sentence. 06–1807 (1/16/08), 974 So.2d 1238 (2008). As relevant here, the court rejected Montejo's argument that under the rule of *Jackson, supra*, the letter should have been suppressed. 974 So.2d, at 1261. *Jackson* held that "if police initiate interrogation after a defendant's assertion, at an arraignment or similar proceeding, of his right to counsel, any waiver of the defendant's right to counsel for that police-initiated interrogation is invalid." 475 U.S., at 636.

Citing a decision of the United States Court of Appeals for the Fifth Circuit, Montoya v. Collins, 955 F.2d 279 (1992), the Louisiana Supreme

---

[1]   "The sheriff or law enforcement officer having custody of an arrested person shall bring him promptly, and in any case within seventy-two hours from the time of the arrest, before a judge for the purpose of appointment of counsel." La.Code Crim. Proc. Ann., Art. 230.1(A) (West Supp.2009).

Court reasoned that the prophylactic protection of *Jackson* is not triggered unless and until the defendant has actually requested a lawyer or has otherwise asserted his Sixth Amendment right to counsel. 974 So.2d, at 1260–1261, and n.68. Because Montejo simply stood mute at his 72-hour hearing while the judge ordered the appointment of counsel, he had made no such request or assertion. So the proper inquiry, the court ruled, was only whether he had knowingly, intelligently, and voluntarily waived his right to have counsel present during the interaction with the police. *Id.*, at 1261. And because Montejo had been read his *Miranda* rights and agreed to waive them, the Court answered that question in the affirmative, 974 So.2d, at 1262, and upheld the conviction.

We granted certiorari.

II

Montejo and his amici raise a number of pragmatic objections to the Louisiana Supreme Court's interpretation of Jackson. We agree that the approach taken below would lead either to an unworkable standard, or to arbitrary and anomalous distinctions between defendants in different States. Neither would be acceptable.

Under the rule adopted by the Louisiana Supreme Court, a criminal defendant must request counsel, or otherwise "assert" his Sixth Amendment right at the preliminary hearing, before the *Jackson* protections are triggered. If he does so, the police may not initiate further interrogation in the absence of counsel. But if the court on its own appoints counsel, with the defendant taking no affirmative action to invoke his right to counsel, then police are free to initiate further interrogations provided that they first obtain an otherwise valid waiver by the defendant of his right to have counsel present.

This rule would apply well enough in States that require the indigent defendant formally to request counsel before any appointment is made, which usually occurs after the court has informed him that he will receive counsel if he asks for it. That is how the system works in Michigan, for example, Mich. Ct. Rule 6.005(A) (2009), whose scheme produced the factual background for this Court's decision in *Michigan v. Jackson*. Jackson, like all other represented indigent defendants in the State, had requested counsel in accordance with the applicable state law.

But many States follow other practices. In some two dozen, the appointment of counsel is automatic upon a finding of indigency, *e.g.,* Kan. Stat. Ann. § 22–4503(c) (2007); and in a number of others, appointment can be made either upon the defendant's request or sua sponte by the court, *e.g.,* Del.Code Ann., Tit. 29, § 4602(a) (2003). *See* App. to Brief for National Legal Aid & Defender Assn. et al. as Amici Curiae 1a–21a. Nothing in our *Jackson* opinion indicates whether we were then aware that not all States require that a defendant affirmatively request counsel before one is appointed; and of course we had no occasion there to decide how the rule we announced would apply to these other States.

The Louisiana Supreme Court's answer to that unresolved question is troublesome. The central distinction it draws—between defendants who "assert" their right to counsel and those who do not—is exceedingly hazy when applied to States that appoint counsel absent request from the defendant. How to categorize a defendant who merely asks, prior to appointment, whether he will be appointed counsel? Or who inquires, after the fact, whether he has been? What treatment for one who thanks the court after the appointment is made? And if the court asks a defendant whether he would object to appointment, will a quick shake of his head count as an assertion of his right?

To the extent that the Louisiana Supreme Court's rule also permits a defendant to trigger *Jackson* through the "acceptance" of counsel, that notion is even more mysterious: How does one affirmatively accept counsel appointed by court order? An indigent defendant has no right to choose his counsel, United States v. Gonzalez-Lopez, 548 U.S. 140, 151 (2006), so it is hard to imagine what his "acceptance" would look like, beyond the passive silence that Montejo exhibited.

In practice, judicial application of the Louisiana rule in States that do not require a defendant to make a request for counsel could take either of two paths. Courts might ask on a case-by-case basis whether a defendant has somehow invoked his right to counsel, looking to his conduct at the preliminary hearing—his statements and gestures—and the totality of the circumstances. Or, courts might simply determine as a categorical matter that defendants in these States—over half of those in the Union—simply have no opportunity to assert their right to counsel at the hearing and are therefore out of luck.

Neither approach is desirable. The former would be particularly impractical in light of the fact that, as amici describe, preliminary hearings are often rushed, and are frequently not recorded or transcribed. Brief for National Legal Aid & Defender Assn. et al. 25–30. The sheer volume of indigent defendants, *see id.*, at 29, would render the monitoring of each particular defendant's reaction to the appointment of counsel almost impossible. And sometimes the defendant is not even present. *E.g.,* La.Code Crim. Proc. Ann., Art. 230.1(A) (West Supp.2009) (allowing court to appoint counsel if defendant is "unable to appear"). Police who did not attend the hearing would have no way to know whether they could approach a particular defendant; and for a court to adjudicate that question ex post would be a fact-intensive and burdensome task, even if monitoring were possible and transcription available. Because "clarity of . . . command" and "certainty of . . . application" are crucial in rules that govern law enforcement, Minnick v. Mississippi, 498 U.S. 146, 151 (1990), this would be an unfortunate way to proceed. *See also* Moran v. Burbine, 475 U.S. 412, 425–426 (1986).

The second possible course fares no better, for it would achieve clarity and certainty only at the expense of introducing arbitrary distinctions: Defendants in States that automatically appoint counsel would have no opportunity to invoke their rights and trigger *Jackson*, while those in other States, effectively instructed by the court to request counsel, would be lucky winners. That sort of hollow formalism is out of place in a doctrine that purports to serve as a practical safeguard for defendants' rights.

III

But if the Louisiana Supreme Court's application of Jackson is unsound as a practical matter, then Montejo's solution is untenable as a theoretical and doctrinal matter. Under his approach, once a defendant is represented by counsel, police may not initiate any further interrogation. Such a rule would be entirely untethered from the original rationale of *Jackson*.

A

It is worth emphasizing first what is not in dispute or at stake here. Under our precedents, once the adversary judicial process has been initiated, the Sixth Amendment guarantees a defendant the right to have counsel present at all "critical" stages of the criminal proceedings. United States v. Wade, 388 U.S. 218, 227–228 (1967); Powell v. Alabama, 287 U.S. 45, 57 (1932). Interrogation by the State is such a stage. Massiah v. United States, 377 U.S. 201, 204–205 (1964); *See also* United States v. Henry, 447 U.S. 264, 274 (1980).

Our precedents also place beyond doubt that the Sixth Amendment right to counsel may be waived by a defendant, so long as relinquishment of the right is voluntary, knowing, and intelligent. Patterson v. Illinois, 487 U.S. 285, 292, n.4 (1988); Brewer v. Williams, 430 U.S. 387, 404 (1977); Johnson v. Zerbst, 304 U.S. 458, 464 (1938). The defendant may waive the right whether or not he is already represented by counsel; the decision to waive need not itself be counseled. Michigan v. Harvey, 494 U.S. 344, 352–353 (1990). And when a defendant is read his *Miranda* rights (which include the right to have counsel present during interrogation) and agrees to waive those rights, that typically does the trick, even though the *Miranda* rights purportedly have their source in the Fifth Amendment:

> "As a general matter . . . an accused who is admonished with the warnings prescribed by this Court in *Miranda* . . . has been sufficiently apprised of the nature of his Sixth Amendment rights, and of the consequences of abandoning those rights, so that his waiver on this basis will be considered a knowing and intelligent one."

Patterson, supra, at 296.

The only question raised by this case, and the only one addressed by the *Jackson* rule, is whether courts must presume that such a waiver is invalid under certain circumstances. 475 U.S., at 630. We created such a presumption in *Jackson* by analogy to a similar prophylactic rule established to protect the Fifth Amendment based *Miranda* right to have counsel present at any custodial interrogation. *Edwards v. Arizona,* 451 U.S. 477 (1981), decided that once "an accused has invoked his right to have counsel present during custodial interrogation . . . [he] is not subject to further interrogation by the authorities until counsel has been made available," unless he initiates the contact. *Id.,* at 484–485.

The *Edwards* rule is "designed to prevent police from badgering a defendant into waiving his previously asserted *Miranda* rights," *Harvey, supra,* at 350. It does this by presuming his postassertion statements to be involuntary, "even where the suspect executes a waiver and his statements would be considered voluntary under traditional standards." McNeil v. Wisconsin, 501 U.S. 171, 177 (1991). This prophylactic rule thus "protect[s] a suspect's voluntary choice not to speak outside his lawyer's presence." Texas v. Cobb, 532 U.S. 162, 175 (2001) (KENNEDY, J., concurring).

Jackson represented a "wholesale importation of the *Edwards* rule into the Sixth Amendment." *Cobb, supra,* at 175. The *Jackson* Court decided that a request for counsel at an arraignment should be treated as an invocation of the Sixth Amendment right to counsel "at every critical stage of the prosecution," 475 U.S., at 633, despite doubt that defendants "actually inten[d] their request for counsel to encompass representation during any further questioning," *id.,* at 632–633, because doubts must be "resolved in favor of protecting the constitutional claim," *id.,* at 633. Citing *Edwards,* the Court held that any subsequent waiver would thus be "insufficient to justify police-initiated interrogation." 475 U.S., at 635. In other words, we presume such waivers involuntary "based on the supposition that suspects who assert their right to counsel are unlikely to waive that right voluntarily" in subsequent interactions with police. *Harvey, supra,* at 350.

The dissent presents us with a revisionist view of *Jackson.* The defendants' request for counsel, it contends, was important only because it proved that counsel had been appointed. Such a non sequitur (nowhere alluded to in the case) hardly needs rebuttal. Proceeding from this fanciful premise, the dissent claims that the decision actually established "a rule designed to safeguard a defendant's right to rely on the assistance of counsel," *post,* at 2096–2097 (opinion of STEVENS, J.), not one "designed to prevent police badgering," *post,* at 2097. To safeguard the right to assistance of counsel from what? From a knowing and voluntary waiver by the defendant himself? Unless the dissent seeks to prevent a defendant altogether from waiving his Sixth Amendment rights, i.e., to "imprison a man in his privileges and call it the Constitution," Adams v. United States ex rel. McCann, 317 U.S. 269, 280 (1942)—a view with zero support in reason, history or case law—the answer must be: from police pressure, i.e., badgering. The antibadgering rationale is the only way to make sense of Jackson's repeated citations of *Edwards,* and the only way to reconcile the opinion with our waiver jurisprudence.[2]

B

With this understanding of what *Jackson* stands for and whence it came, it should be clear that Montejo's interpretation of that decision—that no represented defendant can ever be approached by the State and asked to consent to interrogation—is off the mark. When a court appoints counsel for an indigent defendant in the absence of any request on his part, there is no basis for a presumption that any subsequent waiver of the right to counsel will be involuntary. There is no "initial election" to exercise the right, *Patterson,* 487 U.S., at 291, that must be preserved through a prophylactic rule against later waivers. No reason exists to assume that a defendant like Montejo, who has done nothing at all to express his intentions with respect to his Sixth Amendment rights, would not be perfectly amenable to speaking with the police without having counsel present. And no reason exists to prohibit the police from inquiring. *Edwards* and *Jackson* are meant to prevent police from badgering defendants into changing their minds about their rights, but a defendant who never asked for counsel has not yet made up his mind in the first instance.

The dissent's argument to the contrary rests on a flawed a fortiori: "If a defendant is entitled to protection from police-initiated interrogation under the Sixth Amendment when he merely requests a lawyer, he is even more obviously entitled to such protection when he has secured a lawyer." *Post,* at 2095. The question in *Jackson,* however, was not whether respondents were entitled to counsel (they unquestionably were), but "whether respondents validly waived their right to counsel," 475 U.S., at 630; and even if it is reasonable to presume from a defendant's request for counsel that any subsequent waiver of the right was coerced, no such presumption can seriously be entertained when a lawyer was merely "secured" on the defendant's behalf, by the State itself, as a matter of course. Of course, reading the dissent's analysis, one would have no idea that Montejo executed any waiver at all.

In practice, Montejo's rule would prevent police-initiated interrogation entirely once the Sixth Amendment right attaches, at least in those States that appoint counsel promptly without request from the defendant. As the dissent in *Jackson* pointed out, with no expressed disagreement from the majority, the opinion "most assuredly [did] not hold that the *Edwards* per se rule prohibiting all police-initiated interrogations applies from the moment the defendant's Sixth

---

[2] The dissent responds that *Jackson* also ensures that the defendant's counsel receives notice of any interrogation, *post,* at 2096–2097, n.2. But notice to what end? Surely not in order to protect some constitutional right to receive counsel's advice regarding waiver of the right to have counsel present. Contrary to the dissent's intimations, neither the advice nor the presence of counsel is needed in order to effectuate a knowing waiver of the Sixth Amendment right. Our cases make clear that the *Miranda* waivers typically suffice; indeed, even an unrepresented defendant can waive his right to counsel. *See supra,* at 2085.

Amendment right to counsel attaches, with or without a request for counsel by the defendant." 475 U.S., at 640 (opinion of Rehnquist, J.). That would have constituted a "shockingly dramatic restructuring of the balance this Court has traditionally struck between the rights of the defendant and those of the larger society." *Ibid.*

Montejo's rule appears to have its theoretical roots in codes of legal ethics, not the Sixth Amendment. The American Bar Association's Model Rules of Professional Conduct (which nearly all States have adopted into law in whole or in part) mandate that "a lawyer shall not communicate about the subject of [a] representation with a party the lawyer knows to be represented by another lawyer in the matter, unless the lawyer has the consent of the other lawyer or is authorized to do so by law or a court order." Model Rule 4.2 (2008). But the Constitution does not codify the ABA's Model Rules, and does not make investigating police officers lawyers. Montejo's proposed rule is both broader and narrower than the Model Rule. Broader, because Montejo would apply it to all agents of the State, including the detectives who interrogated him, while the ethical rule governs only lawyers. And narrower, because he agrees that if a defendant initiates contact with the police, they may talk freely— whereas a lawyer could be sanctioned for interviewing a represented party even if that party "initiates" the communication and consents to the interview. Model Rule 4.2, Comment 3.

Montejo contends that our decisions support his interpretation of the *Jackson* rule. We think not. Many of the cases he cites concern the substantive scope of the Sixth Amendment—*e.g.,* whether a particular interaction with the State constitutes a "critical" stage at which counsel is entitled to be present—not the validity of a Sixth Amendment waiver. *See* Maine v. Moulton, 474 U.S. 159 (1985); *Henry,* 447 U.S. 264; *Massiah,* 377 U.S. 201; *see also Moran,* 475 U.S. 412. Since everyone agrees that absent a valid waiver, Montejo was entitled to a lawyer during the interrogation, those cases do not advance his argument.

Montejo also points to descriptions of the *Jackson* holding in two later cases. In one, we noted that "analysis of the waiver issue changes" once a defendant "obtains or even requests counsel." *Harvey,* 494 U.S., at 352. But elsewhere in the same opinion, we explained that *Jackson* applies "after a defendant requests assistance of counsel," 494 U.S., at 349; "when a suspect charged with a crime requests counsel outside the context of interrogation," *id.,* at 350; and to "suspects who assert their right to counsel," *ibid.* The accuracy of the "obtains" language is thus questionable. Anyway, since *Harvey* held that evidence obtained in violation of the *Jackson* rule could be admitted to impeach the defendant's trial testimony, 494 U.S., at 346, the Court's varying descriptions of when the rule was violated were dicta. The dictum from the other decision, *Patterson, supra,* at 290, n.3, is no more probative.[3]

---

[3]   In the cited passage, the Court noted that "[o]nce an accused has a lawyer, a distinct set of constitutional safeguards aimed at preserving the sanctity of attorney-client relationship

The upshot is that even on Jackson's own terms, it would be completely unjustified to presume that a defendant's consent to police-initiated interrogation was involuntary or coerced simply because he had previously been appointed a lawyer.

IV

So on the one hand, requiring an initial "invocation" of the right to counsel in order to trigger the *Jackson* presumption is consistent with the theory of that decision, but (as Montejo and his amici argue, *see* Part II, *supra*) would be unworkable in more than half the States of the Union. On the other hand, eliminating the invocation requirement would render the rule easy to apply but depart fundamentally from the Jackson rationale.

We do not think that stare decisis requires us to expand significantly the holding of a prior decision—fundamentally revising its theoretical basis in the process—in order to cure its practical deficiencies. To the contrary, the fact that a decision has proved "unworkable" is a traditional ground for overruling it. Payne v. Tennessee, 501 U.S. 808, 827 (1991). Accordingly, we called for supplemental briefing addressed to the question whether *Michigan v. Jackson* should be overruled.

Beyond workability, the relevant factors in deciding whether to adhere to the principle of stare decisis include the antiquity of the precedent, the reliance interests at stake, and of course whether the decision was well reasoned. Pearson v. Callahan, 555 U.S. 223 (2009). The first two cut in favor of abandoning *Jackson*: the opinion is only two decades old, and eliminating it would not upset expectations. Any criminal defendant learned enough to order his affairs based on the rule announced in *Jackson* would also be perfectly capable of interacting with the police on his own. Of course it is likely true that police and prosecutors have been trained to comply with *Jackson, see generally* Supplemental Brief for Larry D. Thompson et al. as Amici Curiae, but that is hardly a basis for retaining it as a constitutional requirement. If a State wishes to abstain from requesting interviews with represented defendants when counsel is not present, it obviously may continue to do so.[4]

---

takes effect." *Patterson,* 487 U.S., at 290, n.3. To support that proposition, the Court cited Maine v. Moulton, 474 U.S. 159 (1985), which was not a case about waiver. The passage went on to observe that "the analysis changes markedly once an accused even requests the assistance of counsel," 487 U.S., at 290, n.3 (emphasis in original), this time citing *Jackson*. Montejo infers from the "even requests" that having counsel is more conclusive of the invalidity of uncounseled waiver than the mere requesting of counsel. But the *Patterson* footnote did not suggest that the analysis "changes" in both these scenarios (having a lawyer, versus requesting one) with specific reference to the validity of waivers under the Sixth Amendment. The citation of *Moulton* (a nonwaiver case) for the first scenario suggests just the opposite.

[4] The dissent posits a different reliance interest: "the public's interest in knowing that counsel, once secured, may be reasonably relied upon as a medium between the accused and the power of the State," *post,* at 2098. We suspect the public would be surprised to learn that a criminal can freely sign away his right to a lawyer, confess his crimes, and then ask the courts to assume that the confession was coerced—on the ground that he had, at some earlier point in time, made a pro forma statement requesting that counsel be appointed on his behalf.

Which brings us to the strength of *Jackson*'s reasoning. When this Court creates a prophylactic rule in order to protect a constitutional right, the relevant "reasoning" is the weighing of the rule's benefits against its costs. "The value of any prophylactic rule . . . must be assessed not only on the basis of what is gained, but also on the basis of what is lost." *Minnick,* 498 U.S., at 161 (SCALIA, J., dissenting). We think that the marginal benefits of *Jackson* (viz., the number of confessions obtained coercively that are suppressed by its bright-line rule and would otherwise have been admitted) are dwarfed by its substantial costs (viz., hindering "society's compelling interest in finding, convicting, and punishing those who violate the law," *Moran, supra,* at 426).

What does the *Jackson* rule actually achieve by way of preventing unconstitutional conduct? Recall that the purpose of the rule is to preclude the State from badgering defendants into waiving their previously asserted rights. *See Harvey, supra,* at 350; *see also McNeil,* 501 U.S., at 177. The effect of this badgering might be to coerce a waiver, which would render the subsequent interrogation a violation of the Sixth Amendment. *See Massiah, supra,* at 204. Even though involuntary waivers are invalid even apart from *Jackson, see Patterson,* 487 U.S., at 292, n.4, mistakes are of course possible when courts conduct case-by-case voluntariness review. A bright-line rule like that adopted in *Jackson* ensures that no fruits of interrogations made possible by badgering-induced involuntary waivers are ever erroneously admitted at trial.

But without *Jackson,* how many would be? The answer is few if any. The principal reason is that the Court has already taken substantial other, overlapping measures toward the same end. Under *Miranda*'s prophylactic protection of the right against compelled self-incrimination, any suspect subject to custodial interrogation has the right to have a lawyer present if he so requests, and to be advised of that right. 384 U.S., at 474. Under *Edwards*' prophylactic protection of the *Miranda* right, once such a defendant "has invoked his right to have counsel present," interrogation must stop. 451 U.S., at 484. And under *Minnick*'s prophylactic protection of the *Edwards* right, no subsequent interrogation may take place until counsel is present, "whether or not the accused has consulted with his attorney." 498 U.S., at 153.

These three layers of prophylaxis are sufficient. Under the *Miranda-Edwards-Minnick* line of cases (which is not in doubt), a defendant who does not want to speak to the police without counsel present need only say as much when he is first approached and given the *Miranda* warnings. At that point, not only must the immediate contact end, but "badgering" by later requests is prohibited. If that regime suffices to protect the integrity of "a suspect's voluntary choice not to speak outside his lawyer's presence" before his arraignment, *Cobb,* 532 U.S., at 175 (KENNEDY, J., concurring), it is hard to see why it would not also suffice to protect that same choice after arraignment, when Sixth Amendment rights have attached. And if so, then *Jackson* is simply superfluous.

It is true, as Montejo points out in his supplemental brief, that the doctrine established by *Miranda* and *Edwards* is designed to protect Fifth Amendment, not Sixth Amendment, rights. But that is irrelevant. What matters is that these cases, like *Jackson*, protect the right to have counsel during custodial interrogation—which right happens to be guaranteed (once the adversary judicial process has begun) by two sources of law. Since the right under both sources is waived using the same procedure, *Patterson, supra,* at 296, doctrines ensuring voluntariness of the Fifth Amendment waiver simultaneously ensure the voluntariness of the Sixth Amendment waiver.

Montejo also correctly observes that the *Miranda-Edwards* regime is narrower than *Jackson* in one respect: The former applies only in the context of custodial interrogation. If the defendant is not in custody then those decisions do not apply; nor do they govern other, noninterrogative types of interactions between the defendant and the State (like pretrial lineups). However, those uncovered situations are the least likely to pose a risk of coerced waivers. When a defendant is not in custody, he is in control, and need only shut his door or walk away to avoid police badgering. And noninterrogative interactions with the State do not involve the "inherently compelling pressures," *Miranda, supra,* at 467, that one might reasonably fear could lead to involuntary waivers.

Jackson was policy driven, and if that policy is being adequately served through other means, there is no reason to retain its rule. *Miranda* and the cases that elaborate upon it already guarantee not simply noncoercion in the traditional sense, but what Justice Harlan referred to as "voluntariness with a vengeance," 384 U.S., at 505 (dissenting opinion). There is no need to take *Jackson*'s further step of requiring voluntariness on stilts.

On the other side of the equation are the costs of adding the bright-line *Jackson* rule on top of *Edwards* and other extant protections. The principal cost of applying any exclusionary rule "is, of course, letting guilty and possibly dangerous criminals go free . . . ." Herring v. United States, 555 U.S. 135, ___ (2009). *Jackson* not only "operates to invalidate a confession given by the free choice of suspects who have received proper advice of their *Miranda* rights but waived them nonetheless," *Cobb, supra,* at 174–175 (KENNEDY, J., concurring), but also deters law enforcement officers from even trying to obtain voluntary confessions. The "ready ability to obtain uncoerced confessions is not an evil but an unmitigated good." *McNeil,* 501 U.S., at 181. Without these confessions, crimes go unsolved and criminals unpunished. These are not negligible costs, and in our view the *Jackson* Court gave them too short shrift.[5]

---

[5] The dissent claims that, in fact, few confessions have been suppressed by federal courts applying *Jackson. Post,* at 2097–2098. If so, that is because, as the dissent boasts, "generations of police officers have been trained to refrain from approaching represented defendants," *post,* at 2098, n.4. Anyway, if the rule truly does not hinder law enforcement or make much practical difference, see *post,* at 2097–2098, and nn.3–4, then there is no reason to be particularly exercised about its demise.

Notwithstanding this calculus, Montejo and his amici urge the retention of *Jackson*. Their principal objection to its elimination is that the *Edwards* regime which remains will not provide an administrable rule. But this Court has praised *Edwards* precisely because it provides " 'clear and unequivocal' guidelines to the law enforcement profession," Arizona v. Roberson, 486 U.S. 675, 682 (1988). Our cases make clear which sorts of statements trigger its protections, *See* Davis v. United States, 512 U.S. 452, 459 (1994), and once triggered, the rule operates as a bright line. Montejo expresses concern that courts will have to determine whether statements made at preliminary hearings constitute *Edwards* invocations—thus implicating all the practical problems of the Louisiana rule we discussed above, *see* Part II, *supra*. That concern is misguided. "We have in fact never held that a person can invoke his *Miranda* rights anticipatorily, in a context other than 'custodial interrogation'. . . ." *McNeil, supra,* at 182, n.3. What matters for *Miranda* and *Edwards* is what happens when the defendant is approached for interrogation, and (if he consents) what happens during the interrogation—not what happened at any preliminary hearing.

In sum, when the marginal benefits of the *Jackson* rule are weighed against its substantial costs to the truth-seeking process and the criminal justice system, we readily conclude that the rule does not "pay its way," United States v. Leon, 468 U.S. 897, 907–908, n.6 (1984). *Michigan v. Jackson* should be and now is overruled.

V

Although our holding means that the Louisiana Supreme Court correctly rejected Montejo's claim under *Jackson*, we think that Montejo should be given an opportunity to contend that his letter of apology should still have been suppressed under the rule of *Edwards*. If Montejo made a clear assertion of the right to counsel when the officers approached him about accompanying them on the excursion for the murder weapon, then no interrogation should have taken place unless Montejo initiated it. *Davis, supra,* at 459. Even if Montejo subsequently agreed to waive his rights, that waiver would have been invalid had it followed an "unequivocal election of the right," *Cobb,* 532 U.S., at 176 (KENNEDY, J., concurring).

Montejo understandably did not pursue an *Edwards* objection, because *Jackson* served as the Sixth Amendment analogy to *Edwards* and offered broader protections. Our decision today, overruling *Jackson*, changes the legal landscape and does so in part based on the protections already provided by *Edwards*. Thus we think that a remand is appropriate so that Montejo can pursue this alternative avenue for relief. Montejo may also seek on remand to press any claim he might have that his Sixth Amendment waiver was not knowing and voluntary, *e.g.*, his argument that the waiver was invalid because it was based on misrepresentations by police as to whether he had been appointed a lawyer, *cf. Moran,* 475 U.S., at 428–429. These matters have heightened importance in light of our opinion today.

We do not venture to resolve these issues ourselves, not only because we are a court of final review, "not of first view," Cutter v. Wilkinson, 544 U.S. 709, 718, n.7 (2005), but also because the relevant facts remain unclear. Montejo and the police gave inconsistent testimony about exactly what took place on the afternoon of September 10, 2002, and the Louisiana Supreme Court did not make an explicit credibility determination. Moreover, Montejo's testimony came not at the suppression hearing, but rather only at trial, and we are unsure whether under state law that testimony came too late to affect the propriety of the admission of the evidence. These matters are best left for resolution on remand.

We do reject, however, the dissent's revisionist legal analysis of the "knowing and voluntary" issue. *Post,* at 2098–2101. In determining whether a Sixth Amendment waiver was knowing and voluntary, there is no reason categorically to distinguish an unrepresented defendant from a represented one. It is equally true for each that, as we held in Patterson, the *Miranda* warnings adequately inform him "of his right to have counsel present during the questioning," and make him "aware of the consequences of a decision by him to waive his Sixth Amendment rights," 487 U.S., at 293. Somewhat surprisingly for an opinion that extols the virtues of stare decisis, the dissent complains that our "treatment of the waiver question rests entirely on the dubious decision in *Patterson,"post,* at 2100. The Court in *Patterson* did not consider the result dubious, nor does the Court today.

* * *

This case is an exemplar of Justice Jackson's oft quoted warning that this Court "is forever adding new stories to the temples of constitutional law, and the temples have a way of collapsing when one story too many is added." Douglas v. City of Jeannette, 319 U.S. 157, 181 (1943) (opinion concurring in result). We today remove *Michigan v. Jackson*'s fourth story of prophylaxis.

The judgment of the Louisiana Supreme Court is vacated, and the case is remanded for further proceedings not inconsistent with this opinion.

It is so ordered.

■ JUSTICE ALITO, with whom JUSTICE KENNEDY joins, concurring.

Earlier this Term, in Arizona v. Gant, 556 U.S. 332 (2009), the Court overruled New York v. Belton, 453 U.S. 454 (1981), even though that case had been on the books for 28 years, had not been undermined by subsequent decisions, had been recently reaffirmed and extended, had proven to be eminently workable (indeed, had been adopted for precisely that reason), and had engendered substantial law enforcement reliance.

See Gant, supra (ALITO, J., dissenting). The Court took this step even though we were not asked to overrule *Belton* and this new rule is almost certain to lead to a host of problems. . . .

Justice SCALIA, who cast the deciding vote to overrule *Belton*, dismissed stare decisis concerns with the following observation: "[I]t seems to me ample reason that the precedent was badly reasoned and produces erroneous . . . results." *Gant, supra*, at 353 (concurring opinion). This narrow view of stare decisis provides the only principle on which the decision in Gant can be justified.

In light of *Gant*, the discussion of stare decisis in today's dissent* is surprising. The dissent in the case at hand criticizes the Court for "[a]cting on its own" in reconsidering Michigan v. Jackson, 475 U.S. 625 (1986). *Post*, at 2095–2096 (opinion of STEVENS, J.). But the same was true in *Gant*, and in this case, the Court gave the parties and interested amici the opportunity to submit supplemental briefs on the issue, a step not taken in Gant.

The dissent faults the Court for "cast[ing] aside the reliance interests of law enforcement," *post*, at 2097–2098, but in *Gant*, there were real and important law enforcement interests at stake. *See* 556 U.S., at 358–361 (ALITO, J., dissenting). Even the Court conceded that the *Belton* rule had "been widely taught in police academies and that law enforcement officers ha[d] relied on the rule in conducting vehicle searches during the past 28 years." 556 U.S., at 359. And whatever else might be said about *Belton*, it surely provided a bright-line rule.

A month ago, none of this counted for much, but today the dissent writes:

> "Jackson's bright-line rule has provided law enforcement officers with clear guidance, allowed prosecutors to quickly and easily assess whether confessions will be admissible in court, and assisted judges in determining whether a defendant's Sixth Amendment rights have been violated by police interrogation."

Post, at 2097–2098.

The dissent, finally, invokes *Jackson*'s antiquity, stating that "the 23-year existence of a simple bright-line rule" should weigh in favor of its retention. *Post*, at 2098. But in *Gant*, the Court had no compunction about casting aside a 28-year-old bright-line rule. I can only assume that the dissent thinks that our constitutional precedents are like certain wines, which are most treasured when they are neither too young nor too old, and that Jackson, at 23, is in its prime, whereas Belton, at 28, had turned brownish and vinegary.

---

* One of the dissenters in the present case, Justice BREYER, also dissented in *Gant* and would have followed *Belton* on stare decisis grounds. *See* 556 U.S., at 353–356. Thus, he would not overrule either *Belton* or Michigan v. Jackson, 475 U.S. 625 (1986).

I agree with the dissent that stare decisis should promote " 'the evenhanded . . . development of legal principles,' " *post,* at 2097 (quoting Payne v. Tennessee, 501 U.S. 808, 827–828 (1991)). The treatment of stare decisis in *Gant* fully supports the decision in the present case.

■ JUSTICE STEVENS, with whom JUSTICE SOUTER and JUSTICE GINSBURG join, and with whom JUSTICE BREYER joins, except for footnote 5, dissenting.

Today the Court properly concludes that the Louisiana Supreme Court's parsimonious reading of our decision in Michigan v. Jackson, 475 U.S. 625 (1986), is indefensible. Yet the Court does not reverse. Rather, on its own initiative and without any evidence that the longstanding Sixth Amendment protections established in *Jackson* have caused any harm to the workings of the criminal justice system, the Court rejects *Jackson* outright on the ground that it is "untenable as a theoretical and doctrinal matter." *Ante*, at 2085. That conclusion rests on a misinterpretation of *Jackson*'s rationale and a gross undervaluation of the rule of stare decisis. The police interrogation in this case clearly violated petitioner's Sixth Amendment right to counsel.

I

The Sixth Amendment provides that "[i]n all criminal prosecutions, the accused shall enjoy the right . . . to have the Assistance of Counsel for his defence." The right to counsel attaches during "the initiation of adversary judicial criminal proceedings," Rothgery v. Gillespie County, 554 U.S. 191, ___ (2008) (internal quotation marks omitted), and it guarantees the assistance of counsel not only during in-court proceedings but during all critical stages, including postarraignment interviews with law enforcement officers, *see* Patterson v. Illinois, 487 U.S. 285, 290 (1988).

In *Jackson,* this Court considered whether the Sixth Amendment bars police from interrogating defendants who have requested the appointment of counsel at arraignment. Applying the presumption that such a request constitutes an invocation of the right to counsel "at every critical stage of the prosecution," 475 U.S., at 633, we held that "a defendant who has been formally charged with a crime and who has requested appointment of counsel at his arraignment" cannot be subject to uncounseled interrogation unless he initiates "exchanges or conversations with the police," *id.*, at 626.

In this case, petitioner Jesse Montejo contends that police violated his Sixth Amendment right to counsel by interrogating him following his "72-hour hearing" outside the presence of, and without prior notice to, his lawyer. The Louisiana Supreme Court rejected Montejo's claim. Relying on the fact that the defendants in *Jackson* had "requested" counsel at arraignment, the state court held that *Jackson*'s protections did not apply to Montejo because his counsel was appointed automatically; Montejo had not explicitly requested counsel or affirmatively accepted the counsel appointed to represent him before he submitted to police interrogation. 06–1807, pp. 28–29 (1/16/08), 974 So.2d 1238, 1261.

I agree with the majority's conclusion that the Louisiana Supreme Court's decision, if allowed to stand, "would lead either to an unworkable standard, or to arbitrary and anomalous distinctions between defendants in different States," *ante,* at 2083. Neither option is tolerable, and neither is compelled by *Jackson* itself.

Our decision in *Jackson* involved two consolidated cases, both arising in the State of Michigan. Under Michigan law in effect at that time, when a defendant appeared for arraignment the court was required to inform him that counsel would be provided if he was financially needy and he requested representation. Mich. Gen. Ct. Rule 785.4(1) (1976). It was undisputed that the Jackson defendants made such a "request" at their arraignment: one by completing an affidavit of indigency, and the other by responding affirmatively to a question posed to him by the court. *See* App. in Michigan v. Jackson, O.T.1984, No. 84–1531, p. 168; App. in Michigan v. Bladel, O.T.1984, No. 84–1539, pp. 3a–4a. In neither case, however, was it clear that counsel had actually been appointed at the arraignment. Thus, the defendants' requests for counsel were significant as a matter of state law because they served as evidence that the appointment of counsel had been effectuated even in the absence of proof that defense counsel had actual notice of the appointments.

Unlike Michigan, Louisiana does not require a defendant to make a request in order to receive court-appointed counsel. Consequently, there is no reason to place constitutional significance on the fact that Montejo neither voiced a request for counsel nor affirmatively embraced that appointment post hoc. Certainly our decision in *Jackson* did not mandate such an odd rule. *See ante,* at 2083–2084 (acknowledging that we had no occasion to decide in Jackson how its rule would apply in States that do not make appointment of counsel contingent on affirmative request). If a defendant is entitled to protection from police-initiated interrogation under the Sixth Amendment when he merely requests a lawyer, he is even more obviously entitled to such protection when he has secured a lawyer. Indeed, we have already recognized as much. *See* Michigan v. Harvey, 494 U.S. 344, 352 (1990) (acknowledging that "once a defendant obtains or even requests counsel," *Jackson* alters the waiver analysis); *Patterson,* 487 U.S., at 290, n.3 (noting "as a matter of some significance" to the constitutional analysis that defendant had "not retained, or accepted by appointment, a lawyer to represent him at the time he was questioned by authorities" (emphasis added)). Once an attorney-client relationship has been established through the appointment or retention of counsel, as a matter of federal law the method by which the relationship was created is irrelevant: The existence of a valid attorney-client relationship provides a defendant with the full constitutional protection afforded by the Sixth Amendment.

II

Today the Court correctly concludes that the Louisiana Supreme Court's holding is "troublesome," *ante,* at 2084, "impractical," *ante,* at 2084, and "unsound," *ante,* at 2085. Instead of reversing the decision of the state court by simply answering the question on which we granted certiorari in a unanimous opinion, however, the majority has decided to change the law. Acting on its own initiative, the majority overrules *Jackson* to correct a "theoretical and doctrinal" problem of its own imagining, *see* ante, at 2085. A more careful reading of *Jackson* and the Sixth Amendment cases upon which it relied reveals that the rule announced in *Jackson* protects a fundamental right that the Court now dishonors.

The majority's decision to overrule *Jackson* rests on its assumption that *Jackson*'s protective rule was intended to "prevent police from badgering defendants into changing their minds about their rights," ante, at 2087; *see also* ante, at 2088–2089, just as the rule adopted in Edwards v. Arizona, 451 U.S. 477 (1981), was designed to prevent police from coercing unindicted suspects into revoking their requests for counsel at interrogation. Operating on that limited understanding of the purpose behind *Jackson*'s protective rule, the Court concludes that *Jackson* provides no safeguard not already secured by this Court's Fifth Amendment jurisprudence. *See* Miranda v. Arizona, 384 U.S. 436 (1966) (requiring defendants to be admonished of their right to counsel prior to custodial interrogation); *Edwards,* 451 U.S. 477 (prohibiting police-initiated interrogation following defendant's invocation of the right to counsel).

The majority's analysis flagrantly misrepresents *Jackson*'s underlying rationale and the constitutional interests the decision sought to protect. While it is true that the rule adopted in *Jackson* was patterned after the rule in *Edwards,* 451 U.S., at 484–485, the *Jackson* opinion does not even mention the anti-badgering considerations that provide the basis for the Court's decision today. Instead, *Jackson* relied primarily on cases discussing the broad protections guaranteed by the Sixth Amendment right to counsel—not its Fifth Amendment counterpart. *Jackson* emphasized that the purpose of the Sixth Amendment is to " 'protec[t] the unaided layman at critical confrontations with his adversary,' " 475 U.S., at 631 (quoting United States v. Gouveia, 467 U.S. 180 (1984)), by giving him " 'the right to rely on counsel as a "medium" between him[self] and the State,' " 475 U.S., at 632 (quoting Maine v. Moulton, 474 U.S. 159, 176 (1985)). Underscoring that the commencement of criminal proceedings is a decisive event that transforms a suspect into an accused within the meaning of the Sixth Amendment, we concluded that arraigned defendants are entitled to "at least as much protection" during interrogation as the Fifth Amendment affords unindicted suspects. *See, e.g.,* 475 U.S., at 632 ("[T]he difference between the legal basis for the rule applied in *Edwards* and the Sixth

Amendment claim asserted in these cases actually provides additional support for the application of the rule in these circumstances" (emphasis added)). Thus, although the rules adopted in *Edwards* and *Jackson* are similar, *Jackson* did not rely on the reasoning of *Edwards* but remained firmly rooted in the unique protections afforded to the attorney-client relationship by the Sixth Amendment.[2]

Once *Jackson* is placed in its proper Sixth Amendment context, the majority's justifications for overruling the decision crumble. Ordinarily, this Court is hesitant to disturb past precedent and will do so only when a rule has proven "outdated, ill-founded, unworkable, or otherwise legitimately vulnerable to serious reconsideration." Vasquez v. Hillery, 474 U.S. 254, 266 (1986). While stare decisis is not "an inexorable command," we adhere to it as "the preferred course because it promotes the evenhanded, predictable, and consistent development of legal principles, fosters reliance on judicial decisions, and contributes to the actual and perceived integrity of the judicial process." Payne v. Tennessee, 501 U.S. 808, 827–828 (1991).

Paying lip service to the rule of stare decisis, the majority acknowledges that the Court must consider many factors before taking the dramatic step of overruling a past decision. *See* ante, at 2088. Specifically, the majority focuses on four considerations: the reasoning of the decision, the workability of the rule, the reliance interests at stake, and the antiquity of the precedent. The Court exaggerates the considerations favoring reversal, however, and gives short shrift to the valid considerations favoring retention of the *Jackson* rule.

First, and most central to the Court's decision to overrule *Jackson*, is its assertion that *Jackson*'s " 'reasoning' "—which the Court defines as "the weighing of the [protective] rule's benefits against its costs," ante, at 2089—does not justify continued application of the rule it created. The balancing test the Court performs, however, depends entirely on its misunderstanding of *Jackson* as a rule designed to prevent police badgering, rather than a rule designed to safeguard a defendant's right to rely on the assistance of counsel.

Even accepting the majority's improper framing of *Jackson*'s foundation, the Court fails to show that the costs of the rule are more

---

[2] The majority insists that protection from police badgering is the only purpose the *Jackson* rule can plausibly serve. After all, it asks, from what other evil would the rule guard? *See ante*, at 2086. There are two obvious answers. First, most narrowly, it protects the defendant from any police-initiated interrogation without notice to his counsel, not just from "badgering" which is not necessarily a part of police questioning. Second, and of prime importance, it assures that any waiver of counsel will be valid. The assistance offered by counsel protects a defendant from surrendering his rights with an insufficient appreciation of what those rights are and how the decision to respond to interrogation might advance or compromise his exercise of those rights throughout the course of criminal proceedings. A lawyer can provide her client with advice regarding the legal and practical options available to him; the potential consequences, both good and bad, of choosing to discuss his case with police; the likely effect of such a conversation on the resolution of the charges against him; and an informed assessment of the best course of action under the circumstances. Such assistance goes far beyond mere protection against police badgering.

than negligible or differ from any other protection afforded by the right to counsel. The majority assumes, without citing any empirical or even anecdotal support, that any marginal benefits of the *Jackson* rule are "dwarfed by its substantial costs," which it describes as harm to " 'society's compelling interest in finding, convicting, and punishing those who violate the law.' " *Ante,* at 2089 (quoting Moran v. Burbine, 475 U.S. 412, 426 (1986)). That assumption is highly dubious, particularly in light of the fact that several amici with interest in law enforcement have conceded that the application of *Jackson*'s protective rule rarely impedes prosecution. *See* Supplemental Brief for Larry D. Thompson et al. as Amici Curiae 6 (hereinafter Thompson Supplemental Brief); Brief for United States as Amicus Curiae 12 (hereinafter United States Brief).

Next, in order to reach the conclusion that the *Jackson* rule is unworkable, the Court reframes the relevant inquiry, asking not whether the *Jackson* rule as applied for the past quarter century has proved easily administrable, but instead whether the Louisiana Supreme Court's cramped interpretation of that rule is practically workable. The answer to that question, of course, is no. When framed more broadly, however, the evidence is overwhelming that *Jackson*'s simple, bright-line rule has done more to advance effective law enforcement than to undermine it.

In a supplemental brief submitted by lawyers and judges with extensive experience in law enforcement and prosecution, amici Larry D. Thompson et al. argue persuasively that *Jackson*'s bright-line rule has provided law enforcement officers with clear guidance, allowed prosecutors to quickly and easily assess whether confessions will be admissible in court, and assisted judges in determining whether a defendant's Sixth Amendment rights have been violated by police interrogation. *See generally* Thompson Supplemental Brief 6. While amici acknowledge that "Jackson reduces opportunities to interrogate defendants" and "may require exclusion of evidence that could support a criminal conviction," they maintain that "it is a rare case where this rule lets a guilty defendant go free." *Ibid.* Notably, these representations are not contradicted by the State of Louisiana or other amici, including the United States. *See* United States Brief 12 (conceding that the *Jackson* rule has not "resulted in the suppression of significant numbers of statements in federal prosecutions in the past").[4] In short, there is

---

[4]   Further supporting the workability of the *Jackson* rule is the fact that it aligns with the professional standards and norms that already govern the behavior of police and prosecutors. Rules of Professional Conduct endorsed by the American Bar Association (ABA) and by every State Bar Association in the country prohibit prosecutors from making direct contact with represented defendants in all but the most limited of circumstances, see App. to Supplemental Brief for Public Defender Service for the District of Columbia et al. as Amici Curiae 1a–15a (setting forth state rules governing contact with represented persons); ABA Model Rule of Professional Conduct 4.2 (2008); 28 U.S.C. § 530B(a) (making state rules of professional conduct applicable to federal attorneys), and generations of police officers have been trained to refrain from approaching represented defendants, both because *Jackson* requires it and because, absent direction from prosecutors, officers are reticent to interrogate represented defendants. *See* United States Brief 11–12; *see also* Thompson Supplemental Brief 13 (citing Federal Bureau of Investigation, Legal Handbook for Special Agents § 7–4.1(7) (2003)). Indeed, the United States concedes that a decision to overrule the case "likely w[ill] not significantly alter the manner in

substantial evidence suggesting that *Jackson*'s rule is not only workable, but also desirable from the perspective of law enforcement.

Turning to the reliance interests at stake in the case, the Court rejects the interests of criminal defendants with the flippant observation that any who are knowledgeable enough to rely on *Jackson* are too savvy to need its protections, and casts aside the reliance interests of law enforcement on the ground that police and prosecutors remain free to employ the *Jackson* rule if it suits them. *See ante,* at 2088. Again as a result of its mistaken understanding of the purpose behind Jackson's protective rule, the Court fails to identify the real reliance interest at issue in this case: the public's interest in knowing that counsel, once secured, may be reasonably relied upon as a medium between the accused and the power of the State. That interest lies at the heart of the Sixth Amendment's guarantee, and is surely worthy of greater consideration than it is given by today's decision.

Finally, although the Court acknowledges that "antiquity" is a factor that counsels in favor of retaining precedent, it concludes that the fact *Jackson* is "only two decades old" cuts "in favor of abandoning" the rule it established. *Ante,* at 2089. I would have thought that the 23-year existence of a simple bright-line rule would be a factor that cuts in the other direction.

Despite the fact that the rule established in *Jackson* remains relevant, well grounded in constitutional precedent, and easily administrable, the Court today rejects it sua sponte. Such a decision can only diminish the public's confidence in the reliability and fairness of our system of justice.[5]

III

Even if *Jackson* had never been decided, it would be clear that Montejo's Sixth Amendment rights were violated. Today's decision eliminates the rule that "any waiver of Sixth Amendment rights given in a discussion initiated by police is presumed invalid" once a defendant has invoked his right to counsel. *Harvey*, 494 U.S., at 349 (citing *Jackson*, 475 U.S., at 636). Nevertheless, under the undisputed facts of this case, there is no sound basis for concluding that Montejo made a knowing and valid waiver of his Sixth Amendment right to counsel before acquiescing in

---

which federal law enforcement agents investigate indicted defendants." United States Brief 11–12.

[5] In his concurrence, Justice ALITO assumes that my consideration of the rule of stare decisis in this case is at odds with the Court's recent rejection of his reliance on that doctrine in his dissent in Arizona v. Gant, 556 U.S. 332 (2009). While I agree that the reasoning in his dissent supports my position in this case, I do not agree with his characterization of our opinion in *Gant*. Contrary to his representation, the Court did not overrule our precedent in New York v. Belton, 453 U.S. 454 (1981). Rather, we affirmed the narrow interpretation of *Belton*'s holding adopted by the Arizona Supreme Court, rejecting the broader interpretation adopted by other lower courts that had been roundly criticized by judges and scholars alike. By contrast, in this case the Court flatly overrules *Jackson*—a rule that has drawn virtually no criticism—on its own initiative. The two cases are hardly comparable. If they were, and if Justice ALITO meant what he said in *Gant*, I would expect him to join this opinion.

police interrogation following his 72-hour hearing. Because police questioned Montejo without notice to, and outside the presence of, his lawyer, the interrogation violated Montejo's right to counsel even under pre-*Jackson* precedent.

Our pre-*Jackson* case law makes clear that "the Sixth Amendment is violated when the State obtains incriminating statements by knowingly circumventing the accused's right to have counsel present in a confrontation between the accused and a state agent." *Moulton,* 474 U.S., at 176. The Sixth Amendment entitles indicted defendants to have counsel notified of and present during critical confrontations with the state throughout the pretrial process. Given the realities of modern criminal prosecution, the critical proceedings at which counsel's assistance is required more and more often occur outside the courtroom in pretrial proceedings "where the results might well settle the accused's fate and reduce the trial itself to a mere formality." United States v. Wade, 388 U.S. 218, 224 (1967).

In *Wade,* for instance, we held that because a post-indictment lineup conducted for identification purposes is a critical stage of the criminal proceedings, a defendant and his counsel are constitutionally entitled to notice of the impending lineup. Accordingly, counsel's presence is a "requisite to conduct of the lineup, absent an intelligent waiver." *Id.,* at 237 (internal quotation marks omitted). The same reasoning applies to police decisions to interrogate represented defendants. For if the Sixth Amendment entitles an accused to such robust protection during a lineup, surely it entitles him to such protection during a custodial interrogation, when the stakes are as high or higher. *Cf.* Spano v. New York, 360 U.S. 315, 326 (1959) (Douglas, J., concurring) ("[W]hat use is a defendant's right to effective counsel at every stage of a criminal case if, while he is held awaiting trial, he can be questioned in the absence of counsel until he confesses?").

The Court avoids confronting the serious Sixth Amendment concerns raised by the police interrogation in this case by assuming that Montejo validly waived his Sixth Amendment rights before submitting to interrogation.[6] It does so by summarily concluding that "doctrines ensuring voluntariness of the Fifth Amendment waiver simultaneously ensure the voluntariness of the Sixth Amendment waiver," *ante,* at 2089–2090; thus, because Montejo was given *Miranda* warnings prior to interrogation, his waiver was presumptively valid. Ironically, while the Court faults *Jackson* for blurring the line between this Court's Fifth and Sixth Amendment jurisprudence, it commits the same error by assuming

---

[6] The majority leaves open the possibility that, on remand, Montejo may argue that his waiver was invalid because police falsely told him he had not been appointed counsel. *See ante,* at 2091–2092. While such police deception would obviously invalidate any otherwise valid waiver of Montejo's Sixth Amendment rights, Montejo has a strong argument that, given his status as a represented criminal defendant, the *Miranda* warnings given to him by police were insufficient to permit him to make a knowing waiver of his Sixth Amendment rights even absent police deception.

that the *Miranda* warnings given in this case, designed purely to safeguard the Fifth Amendment right against self-incrimination, were somehow adequate to protect Montejo's more robust Sixth Amendment right to counsel.

The majority's cursory treatment of the waiver question rests entirely on the dubious decision in *Patterson,* in which we addressed whether, by providing *Miranda* warnings, police had adequately advised an indicted but unrepresented defendant of his Sixth Amendment right to counsel. The majority held that "[a]s a general matter . . . an accused who is admonished with the warnings prescribed . . . in *Miranda,* . . . has been sufficiently apprised of the nature of his Sixth Amendment rights, and of the consequences of abandoning those rights." 487 U.S., at 296. The Court recognized, however, that "because the Sixth Amendment's protection of the attorney-client relationship . . . extends beyond *Miranda*'s protection of the Fifth Amendment right to counsel, . . . there will be cases where a waiver which would be valid under *Miranda* will not suffice for Sixth Amendment purposes." *Id.,* at 297, n.9. This is such a case.

As I observed in *Patterson,* the conclusion that *Miranda* warnings ordinarily provide a sufficient basis for a knowing waiver of the right to counsel rests on the questionable assumption that those warnings make clear to defendants the assistance a lawyer can render during post-indictment interrogation. *See* 487 U.S., at 307 (dissenting opinion). Because *Miranda* warnings do not hint at the ways in which a lawyer might assist her client during conversations with the police, I remain convinced that the warnings prescribed in *Miranda*, while sufficient to apprise a defendant of his Fifth Amendment right to remain silent, are inadequate to inform an unrepresented, indicted defendant of his Sixth Amendment right to have a lawyer present at all critical stages of a criminal prosecution. The inadequacy of those warnings is even more obvious in the case of a represented defendant. While it can be argued that informing an indicted but unrepresented defendant of his right to counsel at least alerts him to the fact that he is entitled to obtain something he does not already possess, providing that same warning to a defendant who has already secured counsel is more likely to confound than enlighten.[8] By glibly assuming that the *Miranda* warnings given in this case were sufficient to ensure Montejo's waiver was both knowing and voluntary, the Court conveniently avoids any comment on the actual

---

[8] With respect to vulnerable defendants, such as juveniles and those with mental impairments of various kinds, amici National Association of Criminal Defense Lawyers et al. assert that "[o]verruling *Jackson* would be particularly detrimental . . . because of the confusing instructions regarding counsel that they would receive. At the initial hearing, they would likely learn that an attorney was being appointed for them, In a later custodial interrogation, however, they would be informed in the traditional manner of 'their right to counsel' and right to have counsel 'appointed' if they are indigent, notwithstanding that counsel had already been appointed in open court. These conflicting statements would be confusing to anyone, but would be especially baffling to defendants with mental disabilities or other impairments." Supplemental Brief for National Association of Criminal Defense Lawyers et al. as Amici Curiae 7–8.

advice Montejo received, which did not adequately inform him of his relevant Sixth Amendment rights or alert him to the possible consequences of waiving those rights.

A defendant's decision to forgo counsel's assistance and speak openly with police is a momentous one. Given the high stakes of making such a choice and the potential value of counsel's advice and mediation at that critical stage of the criminal proceedings, it is imperative that a defendant possess "a full awareness of both the nature of the right being abandoned and the consequences of the decision to abandon it," Moran v. Burbine, 475 U.S. 412, 421 (1986), before his waiver is deemed valid. *See* Iowa v. Tovar, 541 U.S. 77, 81 (2004); Johnson v. Zerbst, 304 U.S. 458, 464 (1938). Because the administration of *Miranda* warnings was insufficient to ensure Montejo understood the Sixth Amendment right he was being asked to surrender, the record in this case provides no basis for concluding that Montejo validly waived his right to counsel, even in the absence of *Jackson*'s enhanced protections.

IV

The Court's decision to overrule *Jackson* is unwarranted. Not only does it rest on a flawed doctrinal premise, but the dubious benefits it hopes to achieve are far outweighed by the damage it does to the rule of law and the integrity of the Sixth Amendment right to counsel. Moreover, even apart from the protections afforded by *Jackson*, the police interrogation in this case violated Jesse Montejo's Sixth Amendment right to counsel.

I respectfully dissent.

■ JUSTICE BREYER, dissenting.

I join Justice STEVENS' dissent except for footnote 5. Although the principles of stare decisis are not inflexible, I believe they bind the Court here. I reached a similar conclusion in Arizona v. Gant, 556 U.S. 332 (2009) (BREYER, J., dissenting), and in several other recent cases. . . .

5. THE SIXTH AMENDMENT EXCLUSIONARY RULE

Kansas v. Ventris

556 U.S. 586 (2009)

■ SCALIA, J., delivered the opinion of the Court, in which ROBERTS, C.J., and KENNEDY, SOUTER, THOMAS, BREYER, and ALITO, JJ., joined. STEVENS, J., filed a dissenting opinion, in which GINSBURG, J., joined.

■ JUSTICE SCALIA delivered the opinion of the Court.

We address in this case the question whether a defendant's incriminating statement to a jailhouse informant, concededly elicited in violation of Sixth Amendment strictures, is admissible at trial to impeach the defendant's conflicting statement.

I

In the early hours of January 7, 2004, after two days of no sleep and some drug use, Rhonda Theel and respondent Donnie Ray Ventris reached an ill-conceived agreement to confront Ernest Hicks in his home. The couple testified that the aim of the visit was simply to investigate rumors that Hicks abused children, but the couple may have been inspired by the potential for financial gain: Theel had recently learned that Hicks carried large amounts of cash.

The encounter did not end well. One or both of the pair shot and killed Hicks with shots from a .38-caliber revolver, and the companions drove off in Hicks's truck with approximately $300 of his money and his cell phone. On receiving a tip from two friends of the couple who had helped transport them to Hicks's home, officers arrested Ventris and Theel and charged them with various crimes, chief among them murder and aggravated robbery. The State dropped the murder charge against Theel in exchange for her guilty plea to the robbery charge and her testimony identifying Ventris as the shooter.

Prior to trial, officers planted an informant in Ventris's holding cell, instructing him to "keep [his] ear open and listen" for incriminating statements. App. 146. According to the informant, in response to his statement that Ventris appeared to have "something more serious weighing in on his mind," Ventris divulged that "[h]e'd shot this man in his head and in his chest" and taken "his keys, his wallet, about $350.00, and . . . a vehicle." *Id.*, at 154, 150.

At trial, Ventris took the stand and blamed the robbery and shooting entirely on Theel. The government sought to call the informant, to testify to Ventris's prior contradictory statement; Ventris objected. The State conceded that there was "probably a violation" of Ventris's Sixth Amendment right to counsel but nonetheless argued that the statement was admissible for impeachment purposes because the violation "doesn't give the Defendant . . . a license to just get on the stand and lie." *Id.*, at 143. The trial court agreed and allowed the informant's testimony, but instructed the jury to "consider with caution" all testimony given in exchange for benefits from the State. *Id.*, at 30. The jury ultimately acquitted Ventris of felony murder and misdemeanor theft but returned a guilty verdict on the aggravated burglary and aggravated robbery counts.

The Kansas Supreme Court reversed the conviction, holding that "[o]nce a criminal prosecution has commenced, the defendant's statements made to an undercover informant surreptitiously acting as an agent for the State are not admissible at trial for any reason, including the impeachment of the defendant's testimony." 285 Kan. 595, 606, 176 P.3d 920, 928 (2008). Chief Justice McFarland dissented, *id.*, at 611, 176 P.3d, at 930. We granted the State's petition for certiorari.

II

The Sixth Amendment, applied to the States through the Fourteenth Amendment, guarantees that "[i]n all criminal prosecutions, the accused shall . . . have the Assistance of Counsel for his defence." The core of this right has historically been, and remains today, "the opportunity for a defendant to consult with an attorney and to have him investigate the case and prepare a defense for trial." Michigan v. Harvey, 494 U.S. 344, 348 (1990). We have held, however, that the right extends to having counsel present at various pretrial "critical" interactions between the defendant and the State, United States v. Wade, 388 U.S. 218, 224 (1967), including the deliberate elicitation by law enforcement officers (and their agents) of statements pertaining to the charge, Massiah v. United States, 377 U.S. 201, 206 (1964). The State has conceded throughout these proceedings that Ventris's confession was taken in violation of *Massiah*'s dictates and was therefore not admissible in the prosecution's case in chief. Without affirming that this concession was necessary, *see* Kuhlmann v. Wilson, 477 U.S. 436, 459–460 (1986), we accept it as the law of the case. The only question we answer today is whether the State must bear the additional consequence of inability to counter Ventris's contradictory testimony by placing the informant on the stand.

A

Whether otherwise excluded evidence can be admitted for purposes of impeachment depends upon the nature of the constitutional guarantee that is violated. Sometimes that explicitly mandates exclusion from trial, and sometimes it does not. The Fifth Amendment guarantees that no person shall be compelled to give evidence against himself, and so is violated whenever a truly coerced confession is introduced at trial, whether by way of impeachment or otherwise. New Jersey v. Portash, 440 U.S. 450, 458–459 (1979). The Fourth Amendment, on the other hand, guarantees that no person shall be subjected to unreasonable searches or seizures, and says nothing about excluding their fruits from evidence; exclusion comes by way of deterrent sanction rather than to avoid violation of the substantive guarantee. Inadmissibility has not been automatic, therefore, but we have instead applied an exclusionary-rule balancing test. *See* Walder v. United States, 347 U.S. 62, 65 (1954). The same is true for violations of the Fifth and Sixth Amendment prophylactic rules forbidding certain pretrial police conduct. *See* Harris v. New York, 401 U.S. 222, 225–226 (1971); *Harvey, supra*, at 348–350.

Respondent argues that the Sixth Amendment's right to counsel is a "right an accused is to enjoy a[t] trial." Brief for Respondent 11. The core of the right to counsel is indeed a trial right, ensuring that the prosecution's case is subjected to "the crucible of meaningful adversarial testing." United States v. Cronic, 466 U.S. 648, 656 (1984). *See also* Powell v. Alabama, 287 U.S. 45, 57–58 (1932). But our opinions under the Sixth Amendment, as under the Fifth, have held that the right covers pretrial interrogations to ensure that police manipulation does not render counsel entirely impotent—depriving the defendant of " 'effective representation by counsel at the only stage when legal aid and advice would help him.' " *Massiah, supra,* at 204 (quoting Spano v. New York, 360 U.S. 315, 326 (1959) (Douglas, J., concurring)). *See also* Miranda v. Arizona, 384 U.S. 436, 468–469 (1966).

Our opinion in *Massiah*, to be sure, was equivocal on what precisely constituted the violation. It quoted various authorities indicating that the violation occurred at the moment of the postindictment interrogation because such questioning " 'contravenes the basic dictates of fairness in the conduct of criminal causes.' " 377 U.S., at 205 (quoting People v. Waterman, 9 N.Y.2d 561, 565 (1961)). But the opinion later suggested that the violation occurred only when the improperly obtained evidence was "used against [the defendant] at his trial." 377 U.S., at 206–207. That question was irrelevant to the decision in *Massiah* in any event. Now that we are confronted with the question, we conclude that the *Massiah* right is a right to be free of uncounseled interrogation, and is infringed at the time of the interrogation. That, we think, is when the "Assistance of Counsel" is denied.

It is illogical to say that the right is not violated until trial counsel's task of opposing conviction has been undermined by the statement's admission into evidence. A defendant is not denied counsel merely because the prosecution has been permitted to introduce evidence of guilt—even evidence so overwhelming that the attorney's job of gaining an acquittal is rendered impossible. In such circumstances the accused continues to enjoy the assistance of counsel; the assistance is simply not worth much. The assistance of counsel has been denied, however, at the prior critical stage which produced the inculpatory evidence. Our cases acknowledge that reality in holding that the stringency of the warnings necessary for a waiver of the assistance of counsel varies according to "the usefulness of counsel to the accused at the particular [pretrial] proceeding." Patterson v. Illinois, 487 U.S. 285, 298 (1988). It is that deprivation which demands a remedy.

The United States insists that "post-charge deliberate elicitation of statements without the defendant's counsel or a valid waiver of counsel is not intrinsically unlawful." Brief for United States as Amicus Curiae 17, n.4. That is true when the questioning is unrelated to charged crimes—the Sixth Amendment right is "offense specific," McNeil v. Wisconsin, 501 U.S. 171, 175 (1991). We have never said, however, that officers may badger counseled defendants about charged crimes so long as they do not use information they gain. The constitutional violation occurs when the uncounseled interrogation is conducted.

B

This case does not involve, therefore, the prevention of a constitutional violation, but rather the scope of the remedy for a violation that has already occurred. Our precedents make clear that the game of excluding tainted evidence for impeachment purposes is not worth the candle. The interests safeguarded by such exclusion are "outweighed by the need to prevent perjury and to assure the integrity of the trial process." Stone v. Powell, 428 U.S. 465, 488 (1976). "It is one thing to say that the Government cannot make an affirmative use of evidence unlawfully obtained. It is quite another to say that the defendant can . . . provide himself with a shield against contradiction of his untruths." *Walder, supra*, at 65. Once the defendant testifies in a way that contradicts prior statements, denying the prosecution use of "the traditional truth-testing devices of the adversary process," *Harris, supra*, at 225, is a high price to pay for vindication of the right to counsel at the prior stage.

On the other side of the scale, preventing impeachment use of statements taken in violation of *Massiah* would add little appreciable deterrence. Officers have significant incentive to ensure that they and their informants comply with the Constitution's demands, since statements lawfully obtained can be used for all purposes rather than simply for impeachment. And the ex ante probability that evidence gained in violation of *Massiah* would be of use for impeachment is exceedingly small. An investigator would have to anticipate both that the defendant would choose to testify at trial (an unusual occurrence to begin with) and that he would testify inconsistently despite the admissibility of his prior statement for impeachment. Not likely to happen—or at least not likely enough to risk squandering the opportunity of using a properly obtained statement for the prosecution's case in chief.

In any event, even if "the officer may be said to have little to lose and perhaps something to gain by way of possibly uncovering impeachment material," we have multiple times rejected the argument that this "speculative possibility" can trump the costs of allowing perjurious statements to go unchallenged. Oregon v. Hass, 420 U.S. 714, 723 (1975). We have held in every other context that tainted evidence—evidence whose very introduction does not constitute the constitutional violation, but whose obtaining was constitutionally invalid—is admissible for impeachment. *See ibid.; Walder,* 347 U.S., at 65; *Harris,* 401 U.S., at 226; *Harvey,* 494 U.S., at 348. We see no distinction that would alter the balance here.*

* * *

---

*   Respondent's amicus insists that jailhouse snitches are so inherently unreliable that this Court should craft a broader exclusionary rule for uncorroborated statements obtained by that means. Brief for National Association of Criminal Defense Lawyers 25–26. Our legal system, however, is built on the premise that it is the province of the jury to weigh the credibility of competing witnesses, and we have long purported to avoid "establish[ing] this Court as a rule-making organ for the promulgation of state rules of criminal procedure." Spencer v. Texas, 385 U.S. 554, 564 (1967). It would be especially inappropriate to fabricate such a rule in this case, where it appears the jury took to heart the trial judge's cautionary instruction on the unreliability of rewarded informant testimony by acquitting Ventris of felony murder.

We hold that the informant's testimony, concededly elicited in violation of the Sixth Amendment, was admissible to challenge Ventris's inconsistent testimony at trial. The judgment of the Kansas Supreme Court is reversed, and the case is remanded for further proceedings not inconsistent with this opinion.

It is so ordered.

■ JUSTICE STEVENS, with whom JUSTICE GINSBURG joins, dissenting.

In Michigan v. Harvey, 494 U.S. 344 (1990), the Court held that a statement obtained from a defendant in violation of the Sixth Amendment could be used to impeach his testimony at trial. As I explained in a dissent joined by three other Members of the Court, that holding eroded the principle that "those who are entrusted with the power of government have the same duty to respect and obey the law as the ordinary citizen." *Id.*, at 369. It was my view then, as it is now, that "the Sixth Amendment is violated when the fruits of the State's impermissible encounter with the represented defendant are used for impeachment just as it is when the fruits are used in the prosecutor's case in chief." *Id.*, at 355.

In this case, the State has conceded that it violated the Sixth Amendment as interpreted in Massiah v. United States, 377 U.S. 201, 206 (1964), when it used a jailhouse informant to elicit a statement from the defendant. No *Miranda* warnings were given to the defendant, nor was he otherwise alerted to the fact that he was speaking to a state agent. Even though the jury apparently did not credit the informant's testimony, the Kansas Supreme Court correctly concluded that the prosecution should not be allowed to exploit its pretrial constitutional violation during the trial itself. The Kansas Court's judgment should be affirmed.

This Court's contrary holding relies on the view that a defendant's pretrial right to counsel is merely "prophylactic" in nature. *See ante*, at 1845. The majority argues that any violation of this prophylactic right occurs solely at the time the State subjects a counseled defendant to an uncounseled interrogation, not when the fruits of the encounter are used against the defendant at trial. *Ante*, at 1846. This reasoning is deeply flawed.

The pretrial right to counsel is not ancillary to, or of lesser importance than, the right to rely on counsel at trial. The Sixth Amendment grants the right to counsel "[i]n all criminal prosecutions," and we have long recognized that the right applies in periods before trial commences, *See* United States v. Wade, 388 U.S. 218, 224 (1967). We have never endorsed the notion that the pretrial right to counsel stands at the periphery of the Sixth Amendment. To the contrary, we have explained that the pretrial period is "perhaps the most critical period of the proceedings" during which a defendant "requires the guiding hand of counsel." Powell v. Alabama, 287 U.S. 45, 57, 69 (1932); *see* Maine v.

Moulton, 474 U.S. 159, 176 (1985) (recognizing the defendant's "right to rely on counsel as a 'medium' between him and the State" in all critical stages of prosecution). Placing the prophylactic label on a core Sixth Amendment right mischaracterizes the sweep of the constitutional guarantee.

Treating the State's actions in this case as a violation of a prophylactic right, the Court concludes that introducing the illegally obtained evidence at trial does not itself violate the Constitution. I strongly disagree. While the constitutional breach began at the time of interrogation, the State's use of that evidence at trial compounded the violation. The logic that compels the exclusion of the evidence during the State's case in chief extends to any attempt by the State to rely on the evidence, even for impeachment. The use of ill-gotten evidence during any phase of criminal prosecution does damage to the adversarial process—the fairness of which the Sixth Amendment was designed to protect. *See* Strickland v. Washington, 466 U.S. 668, 685 (1984); *see also* Adams v. United States ex rel. McCann, 317 U.S. 269, 276 (1942) ("[The] procedural devices rooted in experience were written into the Bill of Rights not as abstract rubrics in an elegant code but in order to assure fairness and justice before any person could be deprived of 'life, liberty, or property' ").

When counsel is excluded from a critical pretrial interaction between the defendant and the State, she may be unable to effectively counter the potentially devastating, and potentially false,[2] evidence subsequently introduced at trial. Inexplicably, today's Court refuses to recognize that this is a constitutional harm.[3] Yet in *Massiah*, the Court forcefully explained that a defendant is "denied the basic protections of the [Sixth Amendment] guarantee when there [is] used against him at his trial evidence of his own incriminating words" that were "deliberately elicited from him after he had been indicted and in the absence of counsel." 377 U.S., at 206. Sadly, the majority has retreated from this robust understanding of the right to counsel.

Today's decision is lamentable not only because of its flawed underpinnings, but also because it is another occasion in which the Court has privileged the prosecution at the expense of the Constitution. Permitting the State to cut corners in criminal proceedings taxes the

---

[2] The likelihood that evidence gathered by self-interested jailhouse informants may be false cannot be ignored. *See* generally Brief for National Association of Criminal Defense Lawyers as Amicus Curiae. Indeed, by deciding to acquit respondent of felony murder, the jury seems to have dismissed the informant's trial testimony as unreliable.

[3] In the majority's telling, "simply" having counsel whose help is "not worth much" is not a Sixth Amendment concern. *Ante,* at 1846. Of course, the Court points to no precedent for this stingy view of the Counsel Clause, for we have never held that the Sixth Amendment only protects a defendant from actual denials of counsel. Indeed our venerable ineffective-assistance-of-counsel jurisprudence is built on a more realistic understanding of what the Constitution guarantees. *See* Strickland v. Washington, 466 U.S. 668 (1984); McMann v. Richardson, 397 U.S. 759, 771, n.14 (1970) ("[T]he right to counsel is the right to the effective assistance of counsel").

legitimacy of the entire criminal process. "The State's interest in truthseeking is congruent with the defendant's interest in representation by counsel, for it is an elementary premise of our system of criminal justice 'that partisan advocacy on both sides of a case will best promote the ultimate objective that the guilty be convicted and the innocent go free.'" *Harvey,* 494 U.S., at 3576 (STEVENS, J., dissenting) (quoting United States v. Cronic, 466 U.S. 648, 655 (1984)). Although the Court may not be concerned with the use of ill-gotten evidence in derogation of the right to counsel, I remain convinced that such shabby tactics are intolerable in all cases. I respectfully dissent.

United States v. Coker
433 F.3d 39 (1st Cir. 2005)

■ TORRUELLA, CIRCUIT JUDGE.

Defendant-appellant Edward Coker was convicted by a jury of one count of attempted arson in violation of 18 U.S.C. § 844(i). He now appeals, arguing that the district court erred in denying his motion to suppress a confession he made to federal agents because the agents violated his Sixth Amendment right to counsel. We affirm.

I. Background

In the early morning hours of July 28, 2002, a fire broke out inside an apartment building located at 43 High Rock Street in Lynn, Massachusetts. Police officers and firefighters arriving at the scene found that a glass panel on the front door of the apartment building had been shattered. After firefighters extinguished the fire, the officers determined that three small fires had been set inside the building. They also found what appeared to be a Molotov cocktail in the hallway of the third floor of the building. The officers interviewed residents of the building, two of whom stated that they had seen a black male, who had been driving a Nissan sports car with a T-roof, standing on the sidewalk outside the building yelling up at an apartment on the third floor. This man entered and exited the building just before the residents noticed the smell of smoke. One of the witnesses saw a straw hat in the man's car, while the other observed the man carrying a baseball bat.

Based on these statements, police issued a "be-on-the-lookout" ("BOLO") call for a man fitting the witnesses' description. Shortly thereafter, two officers responding to an unrelated noise disturbance complaint a short distance from High Rock Street saw Coker sitting in a Nissan sports car that matched the description in the BOLO. The officers approached the car and saw a straw hat and silver baseball bat in the front seat.[3] The officers later found a pair of rubber gloves and a butane lighter in the center console.

---

[3] The baseball bat had pieces of glass embedded in it. These pieces of glass were later matched to the glass from the shattered door panel at 43 High Rock Street.

The officers detained Coker and arranged for a "show-up" identification, meaning that they arranged for the two witnesses to be brought to Coker's location and tell the police whether he was the man they had seen. Both witnesses identified Coker as the man they had seen yelling and entering the building just before the fire started. Coker was then placed under arrest.

Coker was booked at the Lynn Police Department and charged with burning or aiding in the burning of a dwelling house, in violation of Mass. Gen. Laws ch. 266, § 1, and malicious or wanton injuries to personal property, in violation of Mass. Gen. Laws ch. 266, § 127. On July 31, 2002, Coker was arraigned in state district court, had an attorney appointed, and was released on personal recognizance.

Between July 28 and July 31, the Lynn Fire Department notified the Bureau of Alcohol, Tobacco, and Firearms ("BATF") of the incident because it had found what appeared to be a Molotov cocktail in the apartment building.[4] BATF Agent Konstantinos Balos ("Agent Balos") began an investigation to determine if the incident involved a federal crime. *See* 18 U.S.C. § 844. Agent Balos interviewed a number of witnesses to the alleged arson. Several Lynn police officers were present at these interviews. On August 8, 2002, Agent Balos and another BATF agent went to Coker's house and asked him to consent to an interview. At this time, Agent Balos knew that Coker was represented by counsel in the state case. Coker agreed to the interview and, driving his own car, followed the agents to the Lynn Fire Department, where the BATF maintains a satellite office. The agents brought Coker into a room, gave him a seat nearest an unlocked door, told him that he was not under arrest and was free to leave at any time, but nevertheless read Coker his *Miranda* rights, and gave him a copy of those rights. During the interview, which lasted around ninety minutes, Coker confessed to setting fire to the High Rock Street apartment building.[5] Towards the end of the interview, Coker became emotional, stating that he regretted setting the fire and felt like killing himself. Coker told the agents that he wanted to end the interview and left the station.

In April 2003, a federal grand jury indicted Coker, charging him with one count of attempted arson in violation of 18 U.S.C. § 844(i). Coker filed a motion to suppress the confession, arguing that the federal agents had violated his Sixth Amendment right to counsel. The district court denied the motion to suppress. On May 9, 2004, following a three-day jury trial, Coker was convicted. He was sentenced to 60 months' imprisonment. He

---

[4]   The device was submitted to a federal forensics laboratory and eventually determined to be a fake

[5]   Evidently, Coker had offered a resident of the building, Edith Drame, $40 for a bag of marijuana. Drame said she could get him the marijuana, took the money, and entered her apartment with no intention of coming back out. It was Drame's apartment that Coker was yelling at when the two witnesses saw him.

now appeals, arguing that the district court erred in denying his motion to suppress.

II. Discussion

A. Sixth Amendment Right to Counsel

We use a bifurcated standard in reviewing a district court's ruling on a motion to suppress, reviewing factual rulings for clear error and legal rulings de novo. United States v. Pardue, 385 F.3d 101, 104 (1st Cir.2004).

Under the Sixth Amendment, "[i]n all criminal prosecutions, the accused shall enjoy the right . . . to have the Assistance of Counsel for his defence." U.S. Const. amend. VI. This right to counsel "does not attach until a prosecution is commenced, that is, at or after the initiation of adversary judicial criminal proceedings—whether by way of formal charge, preliminary hearing, indictment, information, or arraignment." McNeil v. Wisconsin, 501 U.S. 171, 175 (1991) (internal quotation marks and citation omitted). The Supreme Court has held that "if police initiate interrogation after a defendant's assertion, at an arraignment or similar proceeding, of his right to counsel, any waiver of the defendant's right to counsel for that police-initiated interrogation is invalid." Michigan v. Jackson, 475 U.S. 625, 636 (1986).

In the instant case, we agree with the district court that "there is no dispute[ ] that Coker's Sixth Amendment right to counsel had attached as to the state charges at least by July 31, 2002, the date of his arraignment in state court, and that he did not validly waive that right before" his confession to the BATF agents. United States v. Coker, 298 F.Supp.2d 184, 189 (D.Mass.2003). Thus, there is no dispute that Coker's confession would not have been admissible in the state prosecution.

The Supreme Court has stated that "[t]he Sixth Amendment right [to counsel] . . . is offense specific. It cannot be invoked once for all future prosecutions." McNeil, 501 U.S. at 175. The issue currently before us is whether the uncharged federal arson offense was the same offense as the state arson offense for Sixth Amendment purposes when Coker confessed to the BATF agents. As Coker notes, both offenses involved the same essential elements of proof. If the two offenses were the same, then Coker's Sixth Amendment right to counsel had attached to the federal offense and was violated when the federal agents interviewed him.

Our resolution of this issue turns on our interpretation of Texas v. Cobb, 532 U.S. 162 (2001), in which the Supreme Court clarified the meaning of "offense" in the Sixth Amendment context. In *Cobb*, the defendant confessed to a home burglary but denied knowledge of the simultaneous disappearances of a woman and child from the burglarized home. *Id.* at 165. He was indicted for the burglary, had an attorney appointed, and was released on bond. *Id.* Over a year later, while the burglary charges were still pending, the defendant confessed to his father that he had killed the woman and her child. *Id.* His father informed the police, who arrested the defendant and advised him of his *Miranda* rights. *Id.* The defendant waived these rights, confessed to the murders, and was eventually convicted of capital murder. *Id.* at 165–66. The Texas Court of Criminal Appeals reversed the conviction, finding that "the Sixth Amendment's right to counsel had attached on the capital murder charge even though [the defendant] had not yet been charged with that offense" because the murder charge was "factually interwoven with the burglary." *Id.* at 166 (internal quotation marks omitted).[6] The court found that the defendant had asserted his Sixth Amendment right to counsel by accepting appointment of counsel in the burglary case, and therefore deemed the confession inadmissible. *Id.*

The Supreme Court reversed, rejecting the "factually related" exception to the offense-specific rule. *Id.* at 172–73. The Court re-emphasized that the Sixth Amendment is offense-specific and looked to its Fifth Amendment double jeopardy jurisprudence to define the term "offense" in the Sixth Amendment context. *Id.* The Court applied a test it had articulated in the double jeopardy context in Blockburger v. United States, 284 U.S. 299, 304 (1932): "where the same act or transaction constitutes a violation of two distinct statutory provisions, the test to be applied to determine whether there are two offenses or only one, is whether each provision requires proof of a fact which the other does not." *Cobb,* 532 U.S. at 173 (internal quotation marks and citation omitted). The burglary and murder charges were separate offenses under the *Blockburger* test. The Court thus found that the defendant's Sixth Amendment right to counsel had not attached to the murder charge. *Id.*

In the instant case, the state and federal arson charges contained the same essential elements. Thus, one might conclude that, under *Cobb* and *Blockburger,* Coker's federal and state offenses were the same for Sixth Amendment right to counsel purposes. However, of significant importance to the present case is the fact that the Court in *Cobb* stated that "[w]e see no constitutional difference between the meaning of the term 'offense' in the contexts of double jeopardy and of the right to counsel." *Id.* In its double jeopardy jurisprudence, the Court has held that a defendant's conduct in violation of two separate sovereigns ("the dual sovereignty doctrine") constitutes two distinct offenses. *See, e.g.,* Heath v. Alabama, 474 U.S. 82, 87–93 (1985). Thus, under the dual sovereignty doctrine, Coker's federal offense would be considered separate from his state offense for double jeopardy purposes.

The question thus becomes whether the Court in *Cobb* incorporated all of its double jeopardy jurisprudence (including the dual sovereignty doctrine) or merely the *Blockburger* test into its Sixth Amendment right to counsel jurisprudence. The Second Circuit has held that the Court incorporated only the *Blockburger* test into its Sixth Amendment jurisprudence and that the dual sovereignty doctrine does not apply in

---

[6] Following *McNeil,* some courts "read into *McNeil*'s offense-specific definition an exception for crimes that are 'factually related' to a charged offense." Cobb, 532 U.S. at 168.

the Sixth Amendment context. *See* United States v. Mills, 412 F.3d 325 (2d Cir.2005). In *Mills*, an information issued charging the defendant with multiple state firearms violations. *Id.* at 327. After the information had issued, local police officers interviewed the defendant without counsel present. *Id.* The parties did not dispute that this interview violated the defendant's Sixth Amendment right to counsel as to any subsequent state prosecution. *Id.* at 328. However, the federal government attempted to use Mills's statements to the local police in a subsequent federal prosecution for an offense with same elements as the state offense. *Id.* The Second Circuit held that, because the two offenses were the same under the *Blockburger* test, *Mills*'s statements were inadmissible in the federal prosecution. *Id.* at 330. The court rejected the government's argument that, under *Cobb*, the doctrine of dual sovereignty applied in the Sixth Amendment context. *Id.* ("The fact that *Cobb* appropriates the *Blockburger* test, applied initially in the double jeopardy context, does not demonstrate that *Cobb* incorporates the dual sovereignty doctrine."). Coker argues that we should follow the Second Circuit's rationale.

The Fifth Circuit, along with the district court in the instant case, has taken the position that the dual sovereignty doctrine should be applied in the Sixth Amendment context. *See* United States v. Avants, 278 F.3d 510 (5th Cir.2002). In *Avants,* the defendant was indicted in 1967 on Mississippi state murder charges related to the killing of African-American sharecropper named Ben White. *Id.* at 513. He was provided with counsel and released on bond. *Id.* While out on bond, the defendant was interviewed without counsel by FBI agents who were investigating a separate murder. *Id.* During the interview, the defendant confessed to killing White. *Id.* The FBI agents did not follow up on the confession because they were not investigating White's murder. *Id.* at 513–14. The defendant was later acquitted of the state murder charges. *Id.* at 514. In June 2000, the defendant was indicted for the murder by a federal grand jury and moved to suppress the confession he had made to the FBI agents. *Id.* The Fifth Circuit held that "the Supreme Court [in *Cobb*] has incorporated double jeopardy analysis, including the dual sovereignty doctrine, into its Sixth Amendment jurisprudence." *Id.* at 517. It therefore found that the defendant's uncounseled confession to federal agents was admissible in the federal trial. *Id.* at 522. The government argues that we should follow the Fifth Circuit's rationale.

After carefully examining *Cobb,* we conclude that the dual sovereignty doctrine applies for the purposes of defining what constitutes the same offense in the Sixth Amendment right to counsel context. In doing so, we reject the reasoning of the Second Circuit in *Mills* and adopt the reasoning of the Fifth Circuit in *Avants*. The court in *Mills* stated that "[n]owhere in *Cobb*, either explicitly or by imputation, is there support for a dual sovereignty exception" in the Sixth Amendment right to counsel context. *Mills,* 412 F.3d at 330. This statement, in our view, does not give adequate consideration to the Court's statement that it saw "no constitutional difference between the meaning of the term 'offense' in the contexts of double jeopardy and of the right to counsel." *Cobb,* 532 U.S. at 173. If the Court intended to incorporate only the *Blockburger* test into its Sixth Amendment jurisprudence, then its statement in *Cobb* would make no sense, as there would be a difference in the meaning of the term "offense" in the contexts of double jeopardy and of the right to counsel.[8]

This conclusion is bolstered by a footnote in *Cobb,* in which the Court stated that "we could just as easily describe the Sixth Amendment as 'prosecution specific,' insofar as it prevents discussion of charged offenses as well as offenses that, under *Blockburger,* could not be the subject of a later prosecution." *Id.* at 173 n.3. While the Court referenced only *Blockburger,* the statement indicates that the Court was referring to *Blockburger* in the context of its general double jeopardy jurisprudence. In other words, we understand the Court to have meant that if the government could not prosecute a defendant for an offense due to double jeopardy principles, then it could not question the defendant about that offense without implicating his Sixth Amendment right to counsel, even if the defendant had not yet been charged with the offense. In this case, double jeopardy principles would not have prevented the federal government from prosecuting Coker because of the dual sovereignty doctrine.[9] Therefore, because Coker was properly subject to a later federal prosecution, it follows from the Court's statement that the Sixth Amendment did not prevent discussion of the uncharged federal offense.

Coker argues that applying the dual sovereignty doctrine to cases such as his will permit law enforcement to perform an end run around a defendant's Sixth Amendment right to counsel. As the government notes, a similar argument was raised in Cobb and rejected by a majority of the Supreme Court. The defendant in *Cobb* had argued that applying the offense-specific rule in the Sixth Amendment right to counsel context "will prove disastrous to suspects' constitutional rights and will permit law enforcement officers almost complete and total license to conduct unwanted and uncounseled interrogations." *Cobb,* 532 U.S. at 171 (internal quotation marks omitted). In rejecting this argument, the Court emphasized that it failed adequately to appreciate two considerations:

> First, there can be no doubt that a suspect must be apprised of his rights against compulsory self-incrimination and to consult with an attorney before authorities may conduct custodial interrogation ... Second, it is critical to recognize that the

---

[8]   The difference, of course, would be that offenses with the same essential elements under the laws of two separate sovereigns would not constitute the "same offense" for double jeopardy purposes, while they would constitute the "same offense" for right to counsel purposes.

[9]   In this sense, the dual sovereignty doctrine serves as an exception to the *Blockburger* test. Given the Court's statement in *Cobb* that it saw no difference between the term "offense" in the double jeopardy and right to counsel contexts, we see no reason why the dual sovereignty doctrine would not serve as an exception to the Blockburger test in the right to counsel context.

Constitution does not negate society's interest in the ability of police to talk to witnesses and suspects, even those who have been charged with other offenses.

Id. at 171–72.

These considerations apply with equal force to the instant case, especially given the fact that Coker was given and waived his *Miranda* rights. *See id.* at 172 n.2 ("Even though the Sixth Amendment right to counsel has not attached to uncharged offenses, defendants retain the ability under *Miranda* to refuse any police questioning. . . ."). Further, any concerns we may have about potential "end runs" around the Sixth Amendment's protections are mitigated by an exception to the dual sovereignty doctrine first recognized by this court in United States v. Guzmán, 85 F.3d 823 (1st Cir.1996). In *Guzmán,* we interpreted certain language of the Supreme Court in Bartkus v. Illinois, 359 U.S. 121 (1959), to mean that an exception to the dual sovereignty doctrine (the "*Bartkus* exception") exists where "one sovereign so thoroughly dominates or manipulates the prosecutorial machinery of another that the latter retains little or no volition in its own proceedings." *Id.* at 827. This exception applies with equal force in the Sixth Amendment context. Thus, if it appears that one sovereign is controlling the prosecution of another merely to circumvent the defendant's Sixth Amendment right to counsel, under the *Bartkus* exception the dual sovereignty doctrine will not apply. We believe that this exception will help prevent law enforcement officials from making an end run around the right to counsel.

Coker next argues that, in the event we find that the dual sovereignty doctrine applies in the Sixth Amendment right to counsel context, we should apply the *Bartkus* exception to his case because the federal and state investigations were inextricably intertwined and because the federal agents were aware of the state charges and that Coker had a lawyer for those charges when they interviewed him.

In *Guzmán,* we stated that a defendant arguing for the exception to the dual sovereignty doctrine "must proffer evidence sufficient to establish a prima facie case that the two prosecutions were for the same offense." *Id.* In other words, Coker "must produce some evidence tending to prove that . . . one sovereign was a pawn of the other, with the result that the notion of two supposedly independent prosecutions is merely a sham." *Id.* Coker has failed to carry this entry-level burden.

The district court found that

[t]he state authorities began an investigation and interviewed witnesses on the day of the incident. Within a day or two, they notified the BATF of the possibility of a federal crime, and for a time the two sovereigns continued the investigation in parallel. Shortly after the BATF became involved, however, the state effectively ended its investigation. The federal investigation

continued, Coker was indicted by a federal grand jury, and the state charges against him were dropped.

Coker, 298 F.Supp.2d at 192. We find no clear error in these factual determinations made by the district court, nor do we believe that Coker has pointed to any evidence tending to show that one of the prosecutions was a sham. Rather, the "facts show nothing more than the rendering of routine intergovernmental assistance. Cooperative law enforcement efforts between independent sovereigns are commendable, and, without more, such efforts will not furnish a legally adequate basis for invoking the . . . exception to the dual sovereign rule." *Guzmán,* 85 F.3d at 828.

Coker relies heavily on the Eighth Circuit's decision in United States v. Red Bird, 287 F.3d 709 (8th Cir.2002). In *Red Bird,* the defendant was alleged to have committed a rape on a Native American reservation. *Id.* at 711. He was arraigned in a tribal court and had an attorney appointed to assist in his representation. *Id.* The FBI was informed of the charge, and a tribal investigator assisted an FBI agent in locating and interviewing the defendant without counsel's presence. *Id.* The defendant was later prosecuted on federal rape charges. *Id.* at 712. The Eighth Circuit rejected the government's dual sovereignty argument and found that evidence obtained from the interview was inadmissible. *Id.* at 714–15.

The basis for the court's decision in *Red Bird* is not entirely clear. On the one hand, the court looked to *Cobb* and, using the *Blockburger* test, determined that the tribal and federal offenses were the same for Sixth Amendment purposes because they contained the same essential elements. *Id.* at 715. In so doing, the court rejected the government's argument that the dual sovereignty doctrine applied in the Sixth Amendment context. On the other hand, the court repeatedly emphasized the interconnectedness of the tribal and federal investigations as a reason for finding that the dual sovereignty doctrine did not apply. For example, the court noted that tribal governments and federal authorities commonly worked together in investigating and prosecuting crimes committed on reservations and that "tribal sovereignty is unique and limited." *Id.* at 713, 715 (internal quotation marks and citation omitted).

Coker argues that *Red Bird* represents an exception to the dual sovereignty doctrine. While we think that *Red Bird* is not as clear as Coker believes, to the extent that *Red Bird* represents such an exception, Coker's case is distinguishable. As the government points out, the relationship between the state and federal investigations in Coker's case is different from the relationship between the tribal and federal investigations in *Red Bird.* In *Red Bird,* there was evidence that tribal and federal authorities commonly cooperated in investigations. In Coker's case, although there was a certain amount of routine intergovernmental assistance, there was no evidence that the two sovereigns consistently worked together in investigations. Further, there was no evidence here to suggest that one of the prosecutions was a sham or that one of the sovereigns was the pawn of the other, while in *Red Bird*, the limited and unique nature of tribal sovereignty caused the court's concern. We therefore find that the exception to the dual sovereignty doctrine does not apply to Coker's case.

In sum, we hold that, as a result of the Supreme Court's decision in *Cobb*, the dual sovereignty doctrine applies in the Sixth Amendment right to counsel context. The state and federal offenses in Coker's case were thus different offenses for Sixth Amendment purposes and Coker's right to counsel had not attached to the uncharged federal offense when he was interviewed by the federal agents. The district court did not err in denying Coker's motion to suppress.

B. Harmless Error

Even if we were to find that the district court erred in denying Coker's motion to suppress, any error would be harmless at best. Since the issue in this case is constitutional in nature, the government would have the burden of proving harmless error beyond a reasonable doubt. *See* United States v. Ventura-Cruel, 356 F.3d 55, 64 n. 12 (1st Cir.2003). In other words, the government would have to prove beyond a reasonable doubt that Coker would have been convicted even if his confession had not been admitted into evidence.

Coker correctly notes that we have stated that "[c]onfessions are by nature highly probative and likely to be at the center of the jury's attention." *Id.* at 64 (quoting United States v. León-Delfis, 203 F.3d 103, 112 (1st Cir.2000)). However, having reviewed the record, we are convinced that, even in the absence of the confession, the evidence against Coker was so overwhelming that he would have been convicted. . . .

III. Conclusion

For the foregoing reasons, Coker's conviction is affirmed.

■ CYR, SENIOR CIRCUIT JUDGE (Concurring).

The admission into evidence of the Coker confession violated the Sixth Amendment right to have counsel present during the post-indictment interview. I would affirm on the ground that the violation was harmless beyond a reasonable doubt. I write separately, since I am unable to agree with the panel decision that no Sixth Amendment violation occurred, and I am concerned that its alternate holding may invite serious precedential consequences. *See* California v. United States, 438 U.S. 645, 689 n.10 (1978) (stating that court's alternate holdings are not obiter dicta, but have full precedential effect); Natural Res. Def. Council, Inc. v. Nuclear Regulatory Comm'n, 216 F.3d 1180, 1189 (D.C.Cir.2000) (same).

Prior to *Cobb*, there was no question but that the "separate sovereign" doctrine, pursuant to which federal and state prosecutions for

The Sixth Amendment Counsel Clause as a Limit on
Police Investigations
1060
Chapter 7

the same offense were not deemed offensive to the Fifth Amendment double jeopardy clause, had no application outside the double jeopardy context. For instance, the separate sovereign doctrine neither applies to the Fourth Amendment protection from unreasonable searches and seizures, *see* Elkins v. United States, 364 U.S. 206, 208 (1960) ("[A]rticles obtained as a result of an unreasonable search and seizure by state officers, without involvement of federal officers," cannot "be introduced in evidence against a defendant over his timely objection in a federal criminal trial"), nor to the Fifth Amendment privilege against self-incrimination, *see* Murphy v. Waterfront Comm'n of N.Y. Harbor, 378 U.S. 52, 55 (1964) (stating that the policy reasons underlying the self-incrimination prohibition are "defeated when a witness can be whipsawed into incriminating himself under both state and federal law even though the constitutional privilege against self-incrimination is applicable to each"). *Elkins* and *Murphy* wisely recognized that allowing the separate sovereign doctrine to operate in the context of these important constitutional protections would encourage collusion between the federal and state sovereigns, one sovereign obtaining evidence in violation of defendants' constitutional rights, then passing the evidence on a "silver platter" to the other sovereign, which would then be free to utilize the tainted evidence in its own prosecution with no risk of suppression. *Elkins,* 364 U.S. at 208. Obviously, no comparable policy concerns regarding evidence-gathering are presented in the double jeopardy context.

Read properly, *Cobb* does not compel the anomaly which the majority now countenances, viz., permitting federal and state authorities to violate a defendant's Sixth Amendment right to counsel where they are prohibited from undertaking similar collusive actions with respect to Fourth Amendment and Fifth Amendment rights. Indeed, the Sixth Amendment right to counsel has been long recognized as among the constitutional protections most critical to ensuring the conduct of fair criminal trials. *See* Massiah v. United States, 377 U.S. 201, 205 (1964); Gideon v. Wainwright, 372 U.S. 335, 343–44 (1963); Johnson v. Zerbst, 304 U.S. 458, 462–63 (1938). In *Cobb,* the federal government was not involved. Rather, the State indicted *Cobb* for burglary, later interrogated him, without the aid of counsel, concerning a murder committed during that burglary, and used his incriminating statements during that post-indictment interview to indict him for that murder. On appeal, the question was whether the burglary and murder were the same "offense." Although some courts had devised a test which considered two crimes the same if they were factually related (*e.g.,* committed on the same day), the Court imported the *Blockburger* test from the double jeopardy definition of "offense," and held that two offenses are not the same for Sixth Amendment purposes if each requires proof of a fact that the other does not. *Cobb,* 532 U.S. at 173. It was in this straitened context that the Court stated that "[w]e see no constitutional difference between the meaning of the term 'offense' in the contexts of double jeopardy and of the right to counsel." *Id.*

Here, there is no question but that Coker was questioned after his indictment regarding the "same offense," and under *Cobb* and the *Blockburger* test, his Sixth Amendment right to counsel had attached. In order to find otherwise, one must assume that the Court held that, the particular facts of the case before it notwithstanding, it meant to decide that henceforth there would be no conceivable differences between the term "offense" in the double jeopardy and Sixth Amendment contexts. The Court in *Cobb* did not even consider the policy issues raised in *Elkins* and *Murphy,* for a simple reason: the case before it did not involve separate sovereigns.

> 'If there is one doctrine more deeply rooted than any other in the process of constitutional adjudication, it is that we ought not to pass on questions of constitutionality ... unless such adjudication is unavoidable.' ... It has long been the Court's 'considered practice not to decide abstract, hypothetical or contingent questions ... or to decide any constitutional question in advance of the necessity for its decision ... or to formulate a rule of constitutional law broader than is required by the precise facts to which it is to be applied ... or to decide any constitutional question except with reference to the particular facts to which it is to be applied.'

Clinton v. Jones, 520 U.S. 681, 690 n.11 (1997) (citations omitted). Especially in light of *Elkins* and *Murphy,* and their focus upon the important policy of preventing collusive end-runs around constitutional safeguards, there remains considerable doubt whether the Court, if and when confronted with a separate sovereign case, would hold that the Sixth Amendment right to counsel should be treated less cordially than the Fourth and Fifth Amendment rights, absent some compelling reason for doing so. *See* United States v. Mills, 412 F.3d 325, 329–30 (2d Cir.2005) (holding that *Cobb* did not intend to import separate sovereign doctrine into Sixth Amendment context); *cf.* United States v. Red Bird, 287 F.3d 709, 715 (8th Cir.2002) (refusing to apply separate sovereign doctrine to Sixth Amendment right to counsel in joint federal-tribal crime investigation). . . .

■ HOWARD, CIRCUIT JUDGE (Concurring).

I agree with Judge Torruella that the government did not violate defendant Edward Coker's Sixth Amendment right to counsel, and that Texas v. Cobb, 532 U.S. 162 (2001), is instructive as to why. Coker argues that the interests protected by the prohibition against government contact with an accused after the right to counsel has attached would be undermined if federal authorities, investigating whether an incident that already has given rise to state charges also should be charged as a parallel federal offense, were permitted to question the accused without first approaching his lawyer in the state proceeding. The argument is a classic one for substance over form: the substance of the right to counsel would be unduly compromised if, under these circumstances, the court were to accord dispositive significance to the fact that the federal crime being investigated, while containing the same elements as the charged state crime, is formally distinct because it is a crime against a separate sovereign.

The problem with Coker's argument is that, sometimes, a formalist approach itself serves substantive interests. In this case, the formalist approach urged by the government will serve an interest in permitting investigating authorities to talk with witnesses and suspects who have been charged with formally distinct offenses—even those arising from the same incident under investigation. And it will do so by means of a bright-line rule that eliminates the need for judgment calls about where constitutional boundaries might lie. As Judge Torruella explains, a majority of the Supreme Court—albeit a slim one—has in no less compelling circumstances favored the investigative interest over the admittedly substantial interests invoked by Coker. *See* Cobb, 532 U.S. at 171–72. Having constructed and justified the formalist approach, the Court should be the source of any change in legal direction.[13]

State v. Hunton

120 Wash.App. 1025 (2004) (unpublished)

■ SWEENEY, J.

Suppression of a lineup for identification does not rule out an in-court identification. But the in-court identification must be based on information independent of the suppressed lineup. State v. Redmond, 75 Wn.2d 62, 64–66, 448 P.2d 938 (1968). Here, the trial judge found that the bank employees' in-court identifications of Luke McDonald Hunton were sufficiently removed from the identifications made at a previous lineup the judge had suppressed. That finding is amply supported by this record. We also conclude there is ample evidence to support the elements of robbery. We reject the remainder of Mr. Hunton's assignments of error and affirm his conviction.

FACTS

Mr. Hunton robbed a Wells Fargo Bank and then the same branch of a Washington Trust Bank twice. He wore sunglasses and a baseball cap and calmly demanded 'hundreds, 50s and 20s.' Report of Proceedings (RP) at 1020, 1354, 1507–08. At trial an employee from each bank identified Mr. Hunton as the robber. And bank employees saw Mr. Hunton with a car that other witnesses connected to him in the first and last robberies. Another witness gave Mr. Hunton the New York Yankees baseball cap that he wore when he robbed Washington Trust. She also

---

[13] I acknowledge the merit of our concurring colleague's well articulated prudential concerns, but I cannot join his analysis of whether there has been a Sixth Amendment violation, because the analysis is in my view argumentum ad consequentiam.

recognized the shirt the robber was wearing in security photographs as one she had seen Mr. Hunton wear.

Three Washington Trust employees identified a plaid jacket in court that was seized from Mr. Hunton's sister's house. The robber wore the same or similar jacket. These same employees testified that the person who robbed the branch the first time was the same person who robbed it the second.

An acquaintance of Mr. Hunton's drove him to the bank on the day of the second robbery at Washington Trust. He asked to borrow her sunglasses before going in. Mr. Hunton returned $20 he had borrowed from her earlier when he got back to the car after he robbed the bank. She and another occupant of the car later reported to the 'Secret Witness' program. Mr. Hunton tried to rent an apartment on the day of this robbery. He flashed a number of $50 bills. Others saw him with a large number of $20 bills. He said he needed the apartment for only two weeks 'until he got out of town.' The landlord refused to rent to him. At trial, Mr. Hunton represented himself at his own insistence.

DISCUSSION

In-Court Identification

Mr. Hunton challenges the witnesses' identifications of him in court. He argues that bank employees Tara Brandt, Mary Kaplan, Jessica Niederkleine, and Desirae Beeler were not able to identify him in a photomontage, and yet 'many' of these witnesses were allowed to make an in-court identification. Appellant's Br. at 16–17.

First, neither Ms. Brandt (who was called as a defense witness) nor Ms. Beeler made in-court identifications. They were not even asked to do so. This argument does not then apply to them. Second, Ms. Niederkleine made an in-court identification only when Mr. Hunton asked if she thought he was the bank robber. Mr. Hunton cannot now object to a witness's direct answer to a question that he asked. Third, Ms. Kaplan testified at the evidentiary hearing that she did identify Mr. Hunton from a photomontage. Mr. Hunton's claim is then unsupported by this record.

Mr. Hunton next argues that the in-court identification was unduly suggestive. The issue is whether his in-court presence can be construed as an 'impermissibly suggestive' procedure, which created a substantial likelihood of irreparable misidentification that would call into question the reliability of the in-court identification. *See* State v. Hilliard, 89 Wn.2d 430, 438, 573 P.2d 22 (1977); State v. Shea, 85 Wn.App. 56, 59–60, 930 P.2d 1232 (1997); State v. McDonald, 40 Wn.App. 743, 746, 700 P.2d 327 (1985). An in-court identification is not inherently suggestive when a witness has previously identified the defendant, and the witness making that identification is subject to cross-examination and observation by the jury.[2] Finally, Mr. Hunton did not object to the court's ruling on this question at trial.

Mr. Hunton next argues that the in-court identifications were tainted by a lineup, the results of which the court suppressed. Pretrial Mr. Hunton moved to prohibit the three witnesses who identified him in the suppressed lineup from identifying him in court. The three witnesses identified at the hearing were Kathy Anderson, Toni Flagler, and Mary Kaplan. Because there is nothing in the record to show that Ms. Anderson identified Mr. Hunton in a physical lineup or even participated in one, we need not address his objection to her identification.

A post-indictment lineup is a critical stage in prosecution at which the accused must be given the opportunity to be represented by counsel.[3] The denial of a suspect's constitutional right to counsel at a pretrial lineup requires suppression of the identification in the State's case in chief against the defendant. Gilbert v. California, 388 U.S. 263, 272–73 (1967). But an in-court identification which stems from an independent source—one other than the pretrial lineup conducted in violation of the suspect's Sixth Amendment rights—will not be excluded. *Hilliard*, 89 Wn.2d at 439–40. As such, the witness may make an in-court identification if the prosecution shows by clear and convincing evidence that the in-court identification has a basis independent of the pretrial procedure. State v. Redmond, 75 Wn.2d 62, 65, 448 P.2d 938 (1968). That way the evidence is examined "by means sufficiently distinguishable to be purged of the primary taint" rather than a product of exploitation of the original illegality. *Id.* (quoting oral decision of trial court). An in-court identification has an independent source when the court finds that the witness can identify the defendant in court by remembering the events of the crime itself without relying upon the tainted pretrial event. *See* State v. Coburn, 10 Wn.App. 298, 306–07, 518 P.2d 747 (1973).

Several factors are relevant in determining whether the testimony had an independent source, including:

{1} the witness's prior opportunity to observe the suspect, {2} the existence of any discrepancy between any preconfrontation description and the defendant's actual description, {3} any prior identification of another person, {4} any prior identification of the defendant by photograph, {5} failure to identify the defendant on a prior occasion, {6} the lapse of time between the

---

[2] United States v. Bush, 749 F.2d 1227, 1232 (7th Cir.1984) (where the mere fact that the defendant is seated at the defense table while an in-court identification is made is '{t}he only suggestive circumstance identified by defendant,' then this 'circumstance alone is not enough to establish a violation of due process'); *see* State v. Kinard, 39 Wn.App. 871, 874, 696 P.2d 603 (1985) ('Where an in-court identification is challenged and there is no issue of impermissibly suggestive procedures, the question of reliability goes only to the weight of the testimony and not its admissibility.').

[3] Stovall v. Denno, 388 U.S. 293 (1967); United States v. Wade, 388 U.S. 218 (1967); *See also* State v. Martz, 8 Wn.App. 192, 195, 504 P.2d 1174 (1973) (declining to promulgate a state rule with respect to lineup procedures).

alleged act and the identification, and {7} whether the witness previously knew the defendant.

State v. Smith, 36 Wn.App. 133, 138, 672 P.2d 759 (1983) (citing Wade, 388 U.S. at 241).

The State argues that the factors for reliability are not significant to this analysis. The trial judge recited on the record that he had considered the appropriate factors. RP at 969 (citing State v. Traweek, 43 Wn.App. 99, 104, 715 P.2d 1148 (1986) (reliability factors); *Shea,* 85 Wn.App. at 59 (analysis for suggestibility)). And here, the trial judge reviewed the testimony of each witness at the pretrial hearing and identified an independent basis for the in-court identification. RP at 969. That is a decision then based on substantial evidence. *See Redmond,* 75 Wn.2d at 66.

[The court finds the defendant's other claims of error without merit and affirmed the convictions.]

CHAPTER 8

Due Process Limits on Police Investigations

1. Origins of the Fifth Amendment Due Process Clause

Edward S. McKechnie, Magna Carta: A Commentary on the Great Charter of King John
(1915)

CHAPTER THIRTY-NINE.

NULLUS liber homo capiatur vel imprisonetur, aut disseisiatur, aut utlagetur, aut exuletur, aut aliquo modo destruatur, nec super eum ibimus, nec super eum mittemus, nisi per legale judicium parium suorum vel per legem terre.

No freeman shall be taken or [and] imprisoned or disseised or exiled or in any way destroyed, nor will we go upon him nor send upon him, except by the lawful judgment of his peers or [and] by the law of the land.

This chapter occupies a prominent place in law-books, and is of considerable importance, although its value has sometimes been exaggerated.

I. Its Main Object. It has been usual to read it as a guarantee of trial by jury to all Englishmen; as absolutely prohibiting arbitrary commitment; and as solemnly undertaking to dispense to all and sundry an equal justice, full, free, and speedy. The traditional interpretation has thus made it, in the widest terms, a promise of law and liberty and good government to every one. A careful analysis of the clause, read in connection with its historical genesis, suggests the need for modification of this view. It was in accord with the practical genius of the Charter that it should here direct its energies, not to the enunciation of vague platitudes, but to the reform of a specific abuse. Its object was to prohibit John from resorting to what is sometimes whimsically known in Scotland as "Jeddart justice."[4] It forbade him for the future to place execution before judgment. . . . . .

---

[4] The same grim tradition applied to Lidford as to Jedburgh:
> "I oft have heard of Lydford law,'
> How in the morn they hang and draw,
> And sit in judgment after."

See Neilson, *Trial by Combat,* 131, and authorities cited there.

. . . In some cases John proceeded, or threatened to proceed, by force of arms against recalcitrants as though assured of their guilt, without waiting for legal procedure. Complaint was made of arrests and imprisonments suffered "without judgment" (absque judicio); and these are the very words of the "unknown charter"—"Concedit Rex Johannes quod non capiet homines absque judicio." The Articles of the Barons and Magna Carta expand this phrase. Absque judicio becomes nisi per legate judicium parium suorum vel per legem terrae, thus guarding, not merely against execution without judgment, but also against John's subtler device for attacking his enemies by a travesty of judicial process. The Charter asks not only for a "judgment," but for a "judgment of peers" and "according to the law of the land."

Edward Coke, II Institute on Magna Carta
50 (1640)

For the true sense and exposition of these words, see the statute of 37 Edw. 3, c. 8, where the words, 'by the law of the land' are rendered, 'without due process of law'; for there it is said, 'though it be contained in the great charter, that no man be taken, imprisoned or put out of his freehold, without process of the law'; that is, by indictment or presentment of good and lawful men, where such acts be done in due manner, or by writ original of the common law.

Virginia Declaration of Rights
1776

VIII That in all capital or criminal prosecutions a man hath a right to demand the cause and nature of his accusation to be confronted with the accusers and witnesses, to call for evidence in his favor, and to a speedy trial by an impartial jury of his vicinage, without whose unanimous consent he cannot be found guilty, nor can he be compelled to give evidence against himself; that no man be deprived of his liberty except by the law of the land or the judgement of his peers.

Ratification of the Constitution by the State of New York
July 26, 1788

WE the Delegates of the People of the State of New York, duly elected and Met in Convention, having maturely considered the Constitution for the United States of America, agreed to on the seventeenth day of September, in the year One thousand Seven hundred and Eighty seven, by the Convention then assembled at Philadelphia in the Common-wealth of Pennsylvania (a Copy whereof precedes these presents) and having also seriously and deliberately considered the present situation of the United States, Do declare and make known. . . .

That no Person ought to be taken imprisoned or disseised of his freehold, or be exiled or deprived of his Privileges, Franchises, Life, Liberty or Property but by due process of Law. . . . Under these impressions and declaring that the rights aforesaid cannot be abridged or violated, and that the Explanations aforesaid are consistent with the said Constitution, And in confidence that the Amendments which shall have been proposed to the said Constitution will receive an early and mature Consideration: We the said Delegates, in the Name and in the behalf of the People of the State of New York Do by these presents Assent to and Ratify the said Constitution. . . .

Constitution of the United States, am. V

No person shall be held to answer for a capital, or otherwise infamous crime, unless on a presentment or indictment of a Grand Jury, except in cases arising in the land or naval forces, or in the Militia, when in actual service in time of War or public danger; nor shall any person be subject for the same offence to be twice put in jeopardy of life or limb; nor shall be compelled in any criminal case to be a witness against himself, nor be deprived of life, liberty, or property, without due process of law; nor shall private property be taken for public use, without just compensation.

Constitution of the United States, am. IV, Section 1

All persons born or naturalized in the United States, and subject to the jurisdiction thereof, are citizens of the United States and of the state wherein they reside. No state shall make or enforce any law which shall abridge the privileges or immunities of citizens of the United States; nor shall any state deprive any person of life, liberty, or property, without due process of law; nor deny to any person within its jurisdiction the equal protection of the laws.

2. HISTORICAL NOTE: DUE PROCESS, RACE, AND THE SUPREME COURT 1919–1939

Brief of Black Cops Against Police Brutality as Amicus Curiae in Support of Respondents

2009 WL 3004475 (U.S.) (Appellate Brief) in Pottawattamie
County v. McGhee, *cert. dismissed,* 558 U.S. 1103 (2010)

In *Powell v. Alabama,* 287 U.S. 45 (1932)—the infamous case of the "Scottsboro boys"—the Court reversed the convictions of nine black youths accused of raping two white women. The judgment of history is that the accusation was false. *See* Michael J. Klarman, *The Racial Origins of Modern Criminal Procedure,* 99 Mich. L. Rev. 48, 79 (2000).

In other cases from this period, however, the conduct of the "investigations" and "trials" was so wholly unconcerned with truth that it is difficult to say whether the authorities framed the innocent or chose, by chance, targets who happened to be guilty. In *Moore v. Dempsey,* 261 U.S. 86 (1923), the Court, per Justice Holmes, granted federal habeas petitions brought by black prisoners sentenced to death for murders allegedly committed during the Elaine, Arkansas race riot of October 1919. *See generally* Jeanie M. Whayne, *Low Villains and Wickedness in High Places: Race and Class in the Elaine Riots,* 58 Ark. Hist. Q. 285 (1999); Grif Stockier, Blood in Their Eyes: The Elaine Race Massacres of 1919 (2001). In *Brown v. Mississippi,* 297 U.S. 278 (1936), a unanimous Court, per Chief Justice Hughes, reversed the murder convictions of blacks accused of murdering a white farmer. *See generally* Richard C. Cortner, A "Scottsboro" Case in Mississippi: The Supreme Court and *Brown v. Mississippi* (1986). Confessions obtained by physical torture provided the only evidence against them at trial. *See Brown,* 297 U.S. at 281–84.

These landmark cases had much in common. In each, blacks were accused of heinous crimes against white victims. In *Moore,* the supposed murders took place during an outbreak of mass violence by whites against blacks. White citizens suspected black members of a farmers' union to be planning an insurrection. On September 30, 1919, A.W. Adkins, a white railroad detective, and Charles Pratt, a white deputy sheriff, confronted members of the union outside a meeting held at a local church. The identity of the man firing the first shot is not known, but shots were fired. Adkins was killed and Pratt was wounded. *See* Whayne, *supra,* at 286–87. The killings provoked massive retaliatory violence. Twenty-five blacks and five whites are thought to have died in the bloodshed. *Id.*

Once the military restored order (after, by some accounts, participating in the race riot), hundreds of blacks were arrested and 79 indicted, twelve for murder. No whites were charged. The trials, conducted in a mob atmosphere, were show trials at which witnesses, coerced by threats including torture, gave implausible testimony that counsel for the defense accepted quiescently. *See Moore,* 261 U.S. at 89–90; Stockley, *supra,* at 106–37; Randall Kennedy, Race, Crime, and the Law 96–97 (1997).

In the Scottsboro case, white and black teens got into a fracas while hopping an open gravel car on a freight train. *See* James E. Goodman, Stories of Scottsboro 3–5 (1994) (summarizing the facts). The white kids lost the fight and were thrown off the train by the black kids. Two white women, Victoria Price and Ruby Bates, remained on the train with the blacks. The white youths reported the incident to a railroad agent who telegraphed to law enforcement officers down the line. These officers arrested the black youths on assault charges at the Paint Rock, Arkansas station. When deputies saw Price and Bates get off the train, the women accused the blacks of rape.

Again a hostile mob surrounded the courthouse. The trial court appointed counsel only on the day of trial. Trial was again perfunctory, the all-white jury hanging in only one of the cases. On account of one defendant's youth (thirteen), one juror held out for life imprisonment rather than the death penalty. The Supreme Court reversed the convictions. Although the Court centered attention on the denial of counsel, the decision rested on the Due Process Clause, and the overall unfairness of the proceedings figured prominently in the Court's reasoning.

Brown arose from the murder of a white planter named Raymond Stewart. Officers led by Deputy Cliff Dial, acting without probable cause, seized a black man named Arthur Ellington from his home, strung him up from a tree and whipped him. Ellington refused to confess. The next day, the officers rearrested Ellington, and also took into custody Henry Shields and Ed Brown, both also black, for the murder. The prisoners were flogged with a leather strap having a metal buckle. "[A]s the whippings progressed and were repeated, [the prisoners] changed or adjusted their confession in all particulars of detail so as to conform to the demands of their torturers." 297 U.S. at 282.

Before the indictment, the trial court conducted a preliminary examination of the suspects. The prisoners repeated their confessions in open court and disclaimed any improper pressures. The trial judge ruled the confessions admissible, although Ellington's neck still showed the mark of the rope. 297 U.S. at 281, 283. Indictment and trial followed immediately, owing to fears of mob action. The trial was again conducted amid tense fears of mob violence; machine guns were thought necessary to secure the courthouse. *See* Cortner, *supra,* at 10. The defendants took the stand and disavowed their confessions as coerced by torture, and the state called the deputies in rebuttal. The deputies freely admitted whipping the defendants. 297 U.S. at 284–85. The jury nonetheless convicted. The state Supreme Court rejected the motion for a new trial, reasoning that the defense had failed to renew the objection to the confessions after the trial evidence showed coercion. *See Brown v. Mississippi,* 158 So. 339, 342 (Miss. 1935). The Supreme Court, per Chief Justice Hughes, unanimously reversed on due process grounds. 297 U.S. at 287.

The state proceedings in *Moore, Powell* and *Brown* were trials in form but lynchings in function. *See* Klarman, *supra,* at 57 ("the state-imposed death penalty in these cases was little more than a formalization of the lynching process"). In all these cases, the public prosecutor had the choice to proceed or not. The choice was less easy than hindsight might make it, because honest legal proceedings might have driven the mob to a bloody frenzy. Nonetheless, the prosecutors might have cooperated in some plan to delay and remove the proceedings, or, if necessary to avoid complicity, resign their posts. Each, instead, chose to proceed in violation of the Constitution.

In the Elaine cases, John Elvis Miller served as prosecuting attorney for the First Judicial Circuit of Arkansas. *See* John Elvis Miller Papers (Miller Papers), *available online at* http://libinfo.uark.edu/Special Collections/findingaids/jemilleraid.html (last visited Sept. 10, 2009). After obtaining capital convictions against impoverished blacks, based on coerced evidence, at "trials" dominated by a hostile mob, Miller went on to serve, first as judge, then as United States Senator. *See* Miller Papers, *supra.*

Jackson County Solicitor H.G. Bailey conducted the prosecution of the Scottsboro defendants. *See* Robert F. Martin, *The Scottsboro Cases,* in Historic U.S. Court Cases: An Encyclopedia 637, 638–39 (John W. Johnson ed., 2d ed. 2001). Bailey, so far as we can tell, vanished from the view of history after the Scottsboro cases.

District Attorney John C. Stennis prosecuted Ellington, Brown, and Shields. *See* Cortner, *supra,* at 15. Stennis, like everyone else in the court who saw the rope marks on the neck of Ellington and heard the deputies testify to the flogging, was clearly aware of both the torture and the absence of any other evidence against the defendants. Like Miller, however, having won death sentences based on torture, Stennis left the prosecutor's job to become a judge. *See* Biographical Sketch of John C. Stennis, *available online at* http://library.msstate.edu/cprc/stennis/bio.asp (last visited Sept. 9, 2009). Like Miller, he was eventually made a Senator. *See* Kennedy, *supra,* at 106 note † ("John Stennis . . . paid no professional or political price for his part in the wrongful prosecutions of the defendants in *Brown*") (citations omitted). The United States Navy gave Stennis the honor of namesake for a *Nimitz* class carrier.

3. DUE PROCESS AS "FUNDAMENTAL FAIRNESS"

Brown v. Mississippi
297 U.S. 278 (1936)

■ MR. CHIEF JUSTICE HUGHES delivered the opinion of the Court.

The question in this case is whether convictions, which rest solely upon confessions shown to have been extorted by officers of the state by brutality and violence, are consistent with the due process of law required by the Fourteenth Amendment of the Constitution of the United States.

Petitioners were indicted for the murder of one Raymond Stewart, whose death occurred on March 30, 1934. They were indicted on April 4, 1934, and were then arraigned and pleaded not guilty. Counsel were appointed by the court to defend them. Trial was begun the next morning and was concluded on the following day, when they were found guilty and sentenced to death.

Aside from the confessions, there was no evidence sufficient to warrant the submission of the case to the jury. After a preliminary inquiry, testimony as to the confessions was received over the objection of defendants' counsel. Defendants then testified that the confessions were false and had been procured by physical torture. The case went to the jury with instructions, upon the request of defendants' counsel, that if the jury had reasonable doubt as to the confessions having resulted from coercion, and that they were not they were not to be considered as evidence. On their appeal to the Supreme Court of the State, defendants assigned as error the inadmissibility of the confessions. The judgment was affirmed. 158 So. 339.

Defendants then moved in the Supreme Court of the State to arrest the judgment and for a new trial on the ground that all the evidence against them was obtained by coercion and brutality known to the court and to the district attorney, and that defendants had been denied the benefit of counsel or opportunity to confer with counsel in a reasonable manner. The motion was supported by affidavits. At about the same time, defendants filed in the Supreme Court a 'suggestion of error' explicitly challenging the proceedings of the trial, in the use of the confessions and with respect to the alleged denial of representation by counsel, as violating the due process clause of the Fourteenth Amendment of the Constitution of the United States. The state court entertained the suggestion of error, considered the federal question, and decided it against defendants' contentions. 161 So. 465. Two judges dissented. 161 So. 470. We granted a writ of certiorari.

The grounds of the decision were (1) that immunity from self-incrimination is not essential to due process of law; and (2) that the failure of the trial court to exclude the confessions after the introduction of evidence showing their incompetency, in the absence of a request for such exclusion, did not deprive the defendants of life or liberty without due process of law; and that even if the trial court had erroneously overruled a motion to exclude the confessions, the ruling would have been mere error reversible on appeal, but not a violation of constitution right. 161 So. 465, at page 468.

The opinion of the state court did not set forth the evidence as to the circumstances in which the confessions were procured. That the evidence established that they were procured by coercion was not questioned. The state court said: 'After the state closed its case on the merits, the appellants, for the first time, introduced evidence from which it appears that the confessions were not made voluntarily but were coerced.' 161 So. 465, at page 466. There is no dispute as to the facts upon this point, and as they are clearly and adequately stated in the dissenting opinion of Judge Griffith (with whom Judge Anderson concurred), showing both the extreme brutality of the measures to extort the confessions and the participation of the state authorities, we quote this part of his opinion in full, as follows (161 So. 465, at pages 470, 471):

'The crime with which these defendants, all ignorant negroes, are charged, was discovered about 1 o'clock p.m. on Friday, March 30, 1934. On that night one Dial, a deputy sheriff, accompanied by others, came to the home of Ellington, one of the defendants, and requested him to accompany them to the house of the deceased, and there a number of white men were gathered, who began to accuse the defendant of the crime. Upon his denial they seized him, and with the participation of the deputy they hanged him by a rope to the limb of a tree, and, having let him down, they hung him again, and when he was let down the second time, and he still protested his innocence, he was tied to a tree and whipped, and, still declining to accede to the demands that he confess, he was finally released, and he returned with some difficulty to his home, suffering intense pain and agony. The record of the testimony shows that the signs of the rope on his neck were plainly visible during the so-called trial. A day or two thereafter the said deputy, accompanied by another, returned to the home of the said defendant and arrested him, and departed with the prisoner towards the jail in an adjoining county, but went by a route which led into the state of Alabama; and while on the way, in that state, the deputy stopped and again severely whipped the defendant, declaring that he would continue the whipping until he confessed, and the defendant then agreed to confess to such a statement as the deputy would dictate, and he did so, after which he was delivered to jail.

'The other two defendants, Ed Brown and Henry Shields, were also arrested and taken to the same jail. On Sunday night, April 1, 1934, the same deputy, accompanied by a number of white men, one of whom was also an officer, and by the jailer, came to the jail, and the two last named defendants were made to strip and they were laid over chairs and their backs were cut to pieces with a leather strap with buckles on it, and they were likewise made by the said deputy definitely to understand that the whipping would be continued unless and until they confessed, and not only confessed, but confessed in every matter of detail as demanded by those present; and in this manner the defendants confessed the crime, and, as the whippings progressed and were repeated, they changed or adjusted their confession in all particulars of detail so as to conform to the demands of their torturers. When the confessions had been obtained in the exact form and contents as desired by the mob, they left with the parting admonition and warning that, if the defendants changed their story at any time in any respect from that last stated, the perpetrators of the outrage would administer the same or equally effective treatment.

'Further details of the brutal treatment to which these helpless prisoners were subjected need not be pursued. It is sufficient to say that in pertinent respects the transcript reads more like pages torn from some medieval account than a record made within the confines of a modern civilization which aspires to an enlightened constitutional government.

'All this having been accomplished, on the next day, that is, on Monday, April 2, when the defendants had been given time to recuperate somewhat from the tortures to which they had been subjected, the two sheriffs, one of the county where the crime was committed, and the other of the county of the jail in which the prisoners were confined, came to the jail, accompanied by eight other persons, some of them deputies, there to hear the free and voluntary confession of these miserable and abject defendants. The sheriff of the county of the crime admitted that he had heard of the whipping, but averred that he had no personal knowledge of it. He admitted that one of the defendants, when brought before him to confess, was limping and did not sit down, and that this particular defendant then and there stated that he had been strapped so severely that he could not sit down, and, as already stated, the signs of the rope on the neck of another of the defendants were plainly visible to all. Nevertheless the solemn farce of hearing the free and voluntary confessions was gone through with, and these two sheriffs and one other person then present were the three witnesses used in court to establish the so-called confessions, which were received by the court and admitted in evidence over the objections of the defendants duly entered of record as each of the said three witnesses delivered their alleged testimony. There was thus enough before the court when these confessions were first offered to make known to the court that they were not, beyond all reasonable doubt, free and voluntary; and the failure of the court then to exclude the confessions is sufficient to reverse the judgment, under every rule of procedure that has heretofore been prescribed, and hence it was not necessary subsequently to renew the objections by motion or otherwise.

'The spurious confessions having been obtained—and the farce last mentioned having been gone through with on Monday, April 2d—the court, then in session, on the following day, Tuesday, April 3, 1934, ordered the grand jury to reassemble on the succeeding day, April 4, 1934, at 9 o'clock, and on the morning of the day last mentioned the grand jury returned an indictment against the defendants for murder. Late that afternoon the defendants were brought from the jail in the adjoining county and arraigned, when one or more of them offered to plead guilty, which the court declined to accept, and, upon inquiry whether they had or desired counsel, they stated that they had none, and did not suppose that counsel could be of any assistance to them. The court thereupon appointed counsel, and set the case for trial for the following morning at 9 o'clock, and the defendants were returned to the jail in the adjoining county about thirty miles away.

'The defendants were brought to the courthouse of the county on the following morning, April 5th, and the so-called trial was opened, and was concluded on the next day, April 6, 1934, and resulted in a pretended conviction with death sentences. The evidence upon which the conviction was obtained was the so-called confessions. Without this evidence, a peremptory instruction to find for the defendants would have been inescapable. The defendants were put on the stand, and by their testimony the facts and the details thereof as to the manner by which the confessions were extorted from them were fully developed, and it is further disclosed by the record that the same deputy, Dial, under whose guiding hand and active participation the tortures to coerce the confessions were administered, was actively in the performance of the supposed duties of a court deputy in the courthouse and in the presence of the prisoners during what is denominated, in complimentary terms, the trial of these defendants. This deputy was put on the stand by the state in rebuttal, and admitted the whippings. It is interesting to note that in his testimony with reference to the whipping of the defendant Ellington, and in response to the inquiry as to how severely he was whipped, the deputy stated, 'Not too much for a negro; not as much as I would have done if it were left to me.' Two others who had participated in these whippings were introduced and admitted it—not a single witness was introduced who denied it. The facts are not only undisputed, they are admitted, and admitted to have been done by officers of the state, in conjunction with other participants, and all this was definitely well known to everybody connected with the trial, and during the trial, including the state's prosecuting attorney and the trial judge presiding.'

1.   The state stresses the statement in Twining v. New Jersey, 211 U.S. 78, 114, that 'exemption from compulsory self-incrimination in the courts of the states is not secured by any part of the Federal Constitution,' and the statement in Snyder v. Massachusetts, 291 U.S. 97, 105, that 'the privilege against self-incrimination may be withdrawn and the accused put upon the stand as a witness for the state.' But the question of the right of the state to withdraw the privilege against self-incrimination is not here involved. The compulsion to which the quoted

statements refer is that of the processes of justice by which the accused may be called as a witness and required to testify. Compulsion by torture to extort a confession is a different matter.

The state is free to regulate the procedure of its courts in accordance with its own conceptions of policy, unless in so doing it 'offends some principle of justice so rooted in the traditions and conscience of our people as to be ranked as fundamental.' *Snyder v. Massachusetts, supra*; Rogers v. Peck, 199 U.S. 425, 434. The state may abolish trial by jury. It may dispense with indictment by a grand jury and substitute complaint or information. Walker v. Sauvinet, 92 U.S. 90; Hurtado v. California, 110 U.S. 516; *Snyder v. Massachusetts, supra.* But the freedom of the state in establishing its policy is the freedom of constitutional government and is limited by the requirement of due process of law. Because a state may dispense with a jury trial, it does not follow that it may substitute trial by ordeal. The rack and torture chamber may not be substituted for the witness stand. The state may not permit an accused to be hurried to conviction under mob domination—where the whole proceeding is but a mask—without supplying corrective process. Moore v. Dempsey, 261 U.S. 86, 91. The state may not deny to the accused the aid of counsel. Powell v. Alabama, 287 U.S. 45. Nor may a state, through the action of its officers, contrive a conviction through the pretense of a trial which in truth is 'but used as a means of depriving a defendant of liberty through a deliberate deception of court and jury by the presentation of testimony known to be perjured.' Mooney v. Holohan, 294 U.S. 103, 112. And the trial equally is a mere pretense where the state authorities have contrived a conviction resting solely upon confessions obtained by violence. The due process clause requires 'that state action, whether through one agency or another, shall be consistent with the fundamental principles of liberty and justice which lie at the base of all our civil and political institutions.' Hebert v. Louisiana, 272 U.S. 312, 316. It would be difficult to conceive of methods more revolting to the sense of justice than those taken to procure the confessions of these petitioners, and the use of the confessions thus obtained as the basis for conviction and sentence was a clear denial of due process.

2.   It is in this view that the further contention of the State must be considered. That contention rests upon the failure of counsel for the accused, who had objected to the admissibility of the confessions, to move for their exclusion after they had been introduced and the fact of coercion had been proved. It is a contention which proceeds upon a misconception of the nature of petitioners' complaint. That complaint is not of the commission of mere error, but of a wrong so fundamental that it made the whole proceeding a mere pretense of a trial and rendered the conviction and sentence wholly void. *Moore v. Dempsey, supra.* We are not concerned with a mere question of state practice, or whether counsel assigned to petitioners were competent or mistakenly assumed that their first objections were sufficient. In an earlier case the Supreme Court of

the State had recognized the duty of the court to supply corrective process where due process of law had been denied. In Fisher v. State, 145 Miss. 116, 134, 110 So. 361, 365, the court said: 'Coercing the supposed state's criminals into confessions and using such confessions so coerced from them against them in trials has been the curse of all countries. It was the chief iniquity, the crowning infamy of the Star Chamber, and the Inquisition, and other similar institutions. The Constitution recognized the evils that lay behind these practices and prohibited them in this country. * * * The duty of maintaining constitutional rights of a person on trial for his life rises above mere rules of procedure, and wherever the court is clearly satisfied that such violations exist, it will refuse to sanction such violations and will apply the corrective.'

In the instant case, the trial court was fully advised by the undisputed evidence of the way in which the confessions had been procured. The trial court knew that there was no other evidence upon which conviction and sentence could be based. Yet it proceeded to permit conviction and to pronounce sentence. The conviction and sentence were void for want of the essential elements of due process, and the proceeding thus vitiated could be challenged in any appropriate manner. *Mooney v. Holohan, supra.* It was challenged before the Supreme Court of the State by the express invocation of the Fourteenth Amendment. That court entertained the challenge, considered the federal question thus presented, but declined to enforce petitioners' constitutional right. The court thus denied a federal right fully established and specially set up and claimed, and the judgment must be reversed.

It is so ordered.

Crooker v. California
357 U.S. 433 (1958)

■ MR. JUSTICE CLARK delivered the opinion of the Court.

Petitioner, under sentence of death for the murder of his paramour, claims that his conviction in a California court violates Fourteenth Amendment due process of law because (1) the confession admitted into evidence over his objection had been coerced from him by state authorities, and (2) even if his confession was voluntary it occurred while he was without counsel because of the previous denial of his request therefor. The Supreme Court of California affirmed the conviction. 47 Cal.2d 348, 303 P.2d 753. Certiorari was granted because of the serious due process implications that attend state denial of a request to employ an attorney. 354 U.S. 908.[1] We conclude, however, that no violation of constitutional right has occurred.

---

[1]   The grant of certiorari was limited to two questions:

'1. Was the defendant denied due process of law by the refusal of the investigation officers to allow him to consult with an attorney upon demand being made to do so while he was in custody?

The record here clearly reveals that prior to petitioner's confession he asked for and was denied opportunity to call his lawyer. We first consider that denial in connection with petitioner's contention that his subsequent confession was involuntary in nature.

It is well established that the Fourteenth Amendment prohibits use of coerced confessions in state prosecutions. *E.g.,* Brown v. State of Mississippi, 1936, 297 U.S. 278; Watts v. State of Indiana, 1949, 338 U.S. 49; Fikes v. State of Alabama, 1957, 352 U.S. 191. As in Thomas v. State of Arizona, 356 U.S. 390, and Payne v. State of Arkansas, 356 U.S. 560, we consider the undisputed facts in the record to ascertain whether the confession resulted from police coercion or the exercise of petitioner's own free will.

The victim's son discovered her body the morning of July 5, 1955, stabbed and strangled to death in the bedroom of her Los Angeles home. She was last known to be alive about 1 a.m. the same day, when she talked with a friend by telephone.

Petitioner was arrested in his apartment at 1:30 that afternoon and subsequently was charged with the murder. He was then 31 years of age, a college graduate who had attended the first year of law school. While going to law school he had been a house boy in the home of the victim. That position led to an illicit relationship with her, which she had attempted several times to terminate in the month preceding her death. The week of her death, after telling petitioner they had been found out, she had requested, and he had agreed, that he would never see her again.

Despite this understanding, he returned to her house late in the afternoon of July 4. Finding no one at home, he did nearby for the ostensible purpose of discovering who was 'threatening' her. From his hiding place he watched the victim return home with an escort around midnight. Shortly thereafter he saw the escort leave and watched the victim talk on the telephone. He claims that he then left the vicinity to return to his apartment, never having entered the house that evening.

At the time of his arrest, petitioner was questioned about scratches that were evident on his neck and hands. He attributed the former to shaving and the latter to a traffic mishap on his way to the beach on July 4. However he refused to reveal where the accident occurred. After his apartment was searched, petitioner was taken to the Los Angeles Police Station, where he was photographed and asked to take a lie detector test. He refused to submit to the test, and indicated that he wanted to call an attorney. At no time, however, does it appear that petitioner was offered the use of a telephone. Aside from sporadic questioning at his apartment, petitioner was interrogated for the first time from 8:30–9:30 p.m., the questioning being conducted by four officers and centering around his

---

'2. Was the defendant denied due process of law by the admission into evidence of a confession which was taken from him while in custody and after he had been in such custody for fourteen hours and had not been allowed to consult with his attorney?'

refusal of the lie detector test. During this time he asked for an opportunity to get a lawyer, naming a specific attorney whom he thought might represent him, but was told that 'after (the) investigation was concluded he could call an attorney.'

At 9:30 p.m. petitioner was transferred to the West Los Angeles Police Station, where five officers questioned him from 11 p.m. until shortly after midnight. He then was formally 'booked,' and given a physical examination by a police physician. The third and last questioning period was conducted by the same five men from approximately 1–2 a.m. July 6. For the next hour petitioner wrote and signed a detailed confession of the murder. Afterward, he was taken to the victim's home to re-enact the crime. At 5 a.m. he was put in jail and permitted to sleep.

That afternoon, a full day after his arrest, he was taken to the office of the Los Angeles County District Attorney to orally repeat the written confession. Petitioner balked at doing so and again asked that his attorney be called. Thereupon the District Attorney placed the call for him and listened to the conversation while petitioner talked on an extension phone with the attorney. Neither petitioner nor his attorney was aware that a tape recording was being made of everything that transpired in the office. The District Attorney interrupted at one point to deny that petitioner was forced to answer police questions, and later to advise that the most convenient time for the attorney to see petitioner would be at 7 p.m. back at the West Los Angeles Police Station. After the phone call, petitioner was returned to jail to meet his attorney that evening. From that time forward, through both arraignment and trial, he was represented by his own counsel.

In the 14 hours between his arrest and confession, petitioner was given coffee and allowed to smoke whenever he liked. He also was given milk and a sandwich a few hours after his arrest. Before being transferred to the West Los Angeles Police Station he was advised by a police lieutenant, 'You don't have to say anything that you don't want to,' and he in fact refused to answer many questions both before and after the transfer. At such times he simply stated he 'would rather not answer, or rather not make a statement about that.'

The bare fact of police 'detention and police examination in private of one in official state custody' does not render involuntary a confession by the one so detained. Brown v. Allen, 1953, 344 U.S. 443, 476. Neither does an admonition by the police to tell the truth, Sparf v. United States, 1895, 156 U.S. 51, 55–56, nor the failure of state authorities to comply with local statutes requiring that an accused promptly be brought before a magistrate.[2] Fikes v. State of Alabama, 1957, 352 U.S. 191.

---

[2] Section 849 of the California Penal Code provides that a person arrested without a warrant must be brought before the nearest or most accessible magistrate in the county of arrest 'without unnecessary delay.' Cal.Penal Code, 1956, s 849.

Petitioner's claim of coercion, then, depends almost entirely on denial of his request to contact counsel.[3] This Court has not previously had occasion to determine the character of a confession obtained after such a denial. But we have held that confessions made by indigent defendants prior to state appointment of counsel are not thereby rendered involuntary, even in prosecutions where conviction without counsel would violate due process under the Fourteenth Amendment. Borwn v. Allen, 1953, 344 U.S. 443, 474–476; Stroble v. State of California, 1952, 343 U.S. 181, 196–198; Gallegos v. State of Nebraska, 1951, 342 U.S. 55, 64–68. To be sure, coercion seems more likely to result from state denial of a specific request for opportunity to engage counsel than it does from state failure to appoint counsel immediately upon arrest. That greater possibility, however, is not decisive. It is negated here by petitioner's age, intelligence, and education. While in law school he had studied criminal law; indeed, when asked to take the lie detector test, he informed the operator that the results of such a test would not be admissible at trial absent a stipulation by the parties. Supplementing that background is the police statement to petitioner well before his confession that he did not have to answer questions. Moreover, the manner of his refusals to answer indicates full awareness of the right to be silent. On this record we are unable to say that petitioner's confession was anything other than voluntary.

We turn now to the contention that even if the confession be voluntary, its use violates due process because it was obtained after denial of petitioner's request to contact his attorney. Petitioner reaches this position by reasoning first that he has been denied a due process right to representation and advice from his attorney,[4] and secondly that the use of any confession obtained from him during the time of such a denial would itself be barred by the Due Process Clause, even though freely made. We think petitioner fails to sustain the first point, and therefore we do not reach the second.

The right of an accused to counsel for his defense, though not firmly fixed in our common-law heritage, is of significant importance to the preservation of liberty in this country. *See* 1 Cooley's Constitutional Limitations (8th ed. 1927) 696–700; 2 Story on the Constitution (4th ed. 1893) § 1794. That right, secured in state prosecutions by the Fourteenth Amendment guaranty of due process, includes not only the right to have

---

[3] Even if within the scope of the limited grant of certiorari, claims of physical violence— 'third degree' methods—were denied by witnesses for the State, and hence are not part of the undisputed portions of the record which we consider here. The ambiguous reply by one police officer, 'I don't think we hurt you,' in response to petitioner's assertion in the District Attorney's office that the officer struck him, cannot alter the contradicted state of the evidence when the same officer categorically denied the claim on cross-examination at the trial.

[4] At times petitioner appears to urge 'a rule' barring use of a voluntary confession obtained after state denial of a request to contact counsel regardless of whether any violation of a due process right to counsel occurred. That contention is simply an appeal to the supervisory power of this Court over the administration of justice in the federal courts. *See* McNabb v. United States, 1943, 318 U.S. 332, which, significantly enough, petitioner cites. The short answer to such a contention here is that this conviction was had in a state, not a federal, court.

an attorney appointed by the State in certain cases, but also the right of an accused to 'a fair opportunity to secure counsel of his own choice.' Powell v. State of Alabama, 1932, 287 U.S. 45, 53; Chandler v. Fretag, 1954, 348 U.S. 3.

Under these principles, state refusal of a request to engage counsel violates due process not only if the accused is deprived of counsel at trial on the merits, *Chandler v. Fretag, supra*, but also if he is deprived of counsel for any part of the pretrial proceedings, provided that he is so prejudiced thereby as to infect his subsequent trial with an absence of 'that fundamental fairness essential to the very concept of justice.' Lisenba v. People of State of California, 1941, 314 U.S. 912, 236. 166. *Cf.* Moore v. State of Michigan, 1957, 355 U.S. 155, 160. The latter determination necessarily depends upon all the circumstances of the case.

In House v. Mayo, 1945, 324 U.S. 42, an uneducated man in his twenties, a stranger to the area, was brought before a court to be sentenced on two convictions previously returned against him. He was there presented for the first time with a burglary information filed by the State, asked for and was denied opportunity to engage counsel, and finally pleaded guilty to the information, thereby obviating any necessity for trial of the charge on the merits. We held that a due process right to counsel was denied.

In contrast, the sum total of the circumstances here during the time petitioner was without counsel is a voluntary confession by a college-educated man with law school training who knew of his right to keep silent. Such facts, while perhaps a violation of California law,[5] do not approach the prejudicial impact in *House v. Mayo, supra*, and do not show petitioner to have been so 'taken advantage of,' Townsend v. Burke, 1948, 334 U.S. 736, 739, as to violate due process of law.

Petitioner, however, contends that a different rule should determine whether there has been a violation of right to counsel. He would have every state denial of a request to contact counsel be an infringement of the constitutional right without regard to the circumstances of the case. In the absence of any confession, plea or waiver—or other event prejudicial to the accused—such a doctrine would create a complete anomaly, since nothing would remain that could be corrected on new trial. Refusal by state authorities of the request to contact counsel necessarily would then be an absolute bar to conviction. On the other hand, where an event has occurred while the accused was without his counsel which fairly promises to adversely affect his chances, the doctrine suggested by petitioner would have a lesser but still devastating effect on enforcement of criminal law, for it would effectively preclude police

[5] Section 825 of the California Penal Code provides that after an arrest, an attorney 'may at the request of the prisoner or any relative of such prisoner, visit the person so arrested.' Any officer in charge of the prisoner who wilfully refuses to let the attorney see the prisoner is made guilty of a misdemeanor. Cal.Penal Code, 1956, § 825.

questioning—fair as well as unfair—until the accused was afforded opportunity to call his attorney. Due process, a concept 'less rigid and more fluid than those envisaged in other specific and particular provisions of the Bill of Rights,' Betts v. Brady, 1942, 316 U.S. 455, 462, demands no such rule.[6]

Affirmed.

■ MR. JUSTICE DOUGLAS, with whom THE CHIEF JUSTICE, MR. JUSTICE BLACK and MR. JUSTICE BRENNAN concur, dissenting.

When petitioner was first arrested, and before any real interrogation took place, he asked that his attorney be present. 'I had no objection to talking with them about whatever they had to talk about, but * * * I wanted counsel with me * * *. I wanted an attorney with me before I would talk with them.'

That was petitioner's testimony; and it is verified by the testimony of Sergeant Gotch of the police.

'A. I stated to him that after our investigation was concluded he could call an attorney, and if he didn't have funds to hire an attorney, when he went to Court's public defender would be assigned to handle his case.

'He then stated that he had a friend who had been an instructor at Pepperdine College that would probably handle the case for him. I asked him who the name was, and he said it was a man by the name of Simpson, who lived in Long Beach.

'Q. He asked you if he could call an attorney at that time, and you told him that he could call after your investigation was completed, is that right?

'A. I told him, after I was through with the investigation, he could make a call.'

This demand for an attorney was made over and again prior to the time a confession was extracted from the accused. Its denial was in my view a denial of that due process of law guaranteed the citizen by the Fourteenth Amendment.

The Court finds no prejudice from the denial of the right to consult counsel; and it bases that finding on the age, intelligence, and education of petitioner. But it was said in Glasser v. United States, 315 U.S. 60, 76, 'The right to have the assistance of counsel is too fundamental and absolute to allow courts to indulge in nice calculations as to the amount

---

[6] It is suggested that this decision extends the rule of Betts v. Brady, 1942, 316 U.S. 455, to a capital case, thereby overruling, I should suppose, Powell v. State of Alabama, 287 U.S. 45, and related cases. But those decisions involve another problem, trial and conviction of the accused without counsel after state refusal to appoint an attorney for him. What due process requires in one situation may not be required in another, and this, of course, because the least change of circumstances may provide or eliminate fundamental fairness. The ruling here that due process does not always require immediate honoring of a request to obtain one's own counsel in the hours after arrest, hardly means that the same concept of fundamental fairness does not require state appointment of counsel before an accused is put to trial, convicted and sentenced to death.

of prejudice arising from its denial.' That was a federal prosecution. But what is true of the need for counsel is federal case is equally true in a state case.

Betts v. Brady, 316 U.S. 455, held that in a state criminal trial the request of the accused for counsel can be denied and a judgment of conviction sustained as not in violation of due process, where the offense is not a capital one, *cf.* Williams v. Kaiser, 323 U.S. 471, and the Court on review determines there was no fundamental unfairness resulting from the denial of counsel. The rule of *Betts v. Brady,* which never applied to a capital case, *see* Powell v. State of Alabama, 287 U.S. 45, is now made to do so. Assuming that *Betts v. Brady* was properly decided, there is no basis in reason for extending it to the denial of a request for counsel when the accused is arrested on a capital charge.

The Court properly concedes that the right to counsel extends to pretrial proceedings as well as to the trial itself. The need is as great then as at any time. The right to have counsel at the pretrial stage is often necessary to give meaning and protection to the right to be heard at the trial itself. *See* Chandler v. Fretag, 348 U.S. 3, 10. It may also be necessary as a restraint on the coercive power of the police. The pattern of the third degree runs through our cases: a lone suspect unrepresented by counsel against whom the full coercive force of a secret inquisition is brought to bear. *See* Lisenba v. State of California, 314 U.S. 219; Ashcraft v. State of Tennessee, 322 U.S. 143; Haley v. State of Ohio, 332 U.S. 596; Watts v. State of Indiana, 338 U.S. 49; Leyra v. Denno, 347 U.S. 556. The third degree flourishes only in secrecy. One who feels the need of a lawyer and asks for one is asking for some protection which the law can give him against a coerced confession. No matter what care is taken innocent people are convicted of crimes they did not commit, *see* Borchard, Convicting the Innocent (1932); Frank and Frank, Not Guilty (1957). We should not lower the barriers and deny the accused any procedural safeguard against coercive police practices.[1] The trial of the issue of coercion is seldom helpful. Law officers usually testify one way, the accused another. The citizen who has been the victim of these secret inquisitions has little chance to prove coercion. The mischief and abuse of the third degree will continue as long as an accused can be denied the

---

[1] The use of techniques that make man admit crimes they did not commit and embrace ideas they oppose is told in Communist Interrogation, Indoctrination and Exploitation of American Military and Civilian Prisoners, S.Rep. No. 2832, 84th Cong., 2d Sess.

Prof. Sam Bass Warner wrote in How Can The Third Degree Be Eliminated? 1 Bill of Rights Rev. 24, 25 (1940) 'Everywhere the formula for successful detective work is that laid down by former Captain Fiaschetti of the New York City police: 'You get a bit of information, and then you grab the suspect and break him down. That is how detective work is done—a general formula."

See Report of Committee on Lawless Enforcement of Law, Am.Bar Assn., 1 Am.J. Police Sci. 575; The Third Degree, 4 Report to the National Commission on Law Observance and Enforcement (1931) 13; The Report of the President's Committee on Civil Rights (1947) 25 et seq.

right to counsel at this the most critical period of his ordeal.[2] For what takes place in the secret confines of the police station may be more critical than what takes place at the trial. . . .

Or as stated by a Committee headed by Prof. Zechariah Chafee, 'A person accused of crime needs a lawyer right after his arrest probably more than at any other time.'[3] . . .

The Court speaks of the education of this petitioner and his ability to take care of himself. In an opinion written by Mr. Justice Sutherland the Court said, 'Even the intelligent and educated layman has small and sometimes no skill in the science of law. * * * He requires the guiding hand of counsel at every step in the proceedings against him.' Powell State of Alabama, 287 U.S. 45, 69. Mr. Justice Sutherland spoke of the trial itself. But what is true of the trial is true of the preparation for trial and of the period commencing with the arrest of the accused. No matter how well educated, and how well trained in the law an accused may be, he is sorely in need of legal advice once he is arrested for an offense that may exact his life. The innocent as well as the guilty may be caught in a web of circumstantial evidence that is difficult to break. A man may be guilty of indiscretions but not of the crime. He may be implicated by ambiguous circumstances difficult to explain away. He desperately needs a lawyer to help extricate him if he's innocent. He has the right to receive the benefit of the advice of his own counsel at the trial, as we held in

---

[2] Dean Roscoe Pound wrote in 1934 as follows about this problem: 'In the United States the feeling of police and prosecutors that they ought to be able to interrogate suspected persons long ago led to a systematic development of extra-legal or downright illegal examinations by officials, with every external appearance of legality. These examinations have become so much a matter of course that we may read in every morning paper how police or prosecutor examined (the word usually chosen is 'grilled') so and so for anywhere from ten to forty-eight or more consecutive hours, going at him in relays to wear him out and break him down. They are now taken to be the established practice. Prosecutors often conduct them with a pretence of authority when those subjected to them are ignorant, unadvised as to their rights, insignificant, or without means of employing counsel. Indeed, so bold have those who resort to those practices become, that we now read in the newspapers how this man or that was held 'incommunicado' in a police station or jail while the grilling process was going on. * * *

'No amount of thundering against the third degree and its derivatives and analogues will achieve anything. The temper of the public will not permit of strengthening the constitutional safeguards of the accused. For some time to come the tendency is likely to be in the opposite direction. Indeed, a feeling that the public are with them is largely behind the boldness with which highhanded, secret, extra-legal interrogations of persons held incommunicado are constantly carried on.

'My proposition is that the remedy for the third degree and its derivatives is to satisfy the reasonable demands of the police and the prosecutors for an interrogation of suspected persons and thus do away with the excuse for extralegal questionings.

'I submit that there should be express provision for a legal examination of suspected or accused persons before a magistrate; that those to be examined should be allowed to have counsel present to safeguard their rights; that provision should be made for taking down the evidence so as to guarantee accuracy. As things are, it is not the least of the abuses of the system of extra-legal interrogation that there is a constant conflict of evidence as to what the accused said and as to the circumstances under which he said or was coerced into saying it.' 24 J.Crim.L. & C. 1014, 1016, 1017.

[3] *See* Chafee, Documents on Fundamental Human Rights, Pamphlets 1–3 (1951–1952), p. 541.

Chandler v. Fretag, 348 U.S. 3, 9. That same right should extend to the pretrial stage.

The need of a lawyer in the pretrial investigation, if the constitutional rights of the accused are to be preserved, was stated by Mr. Justice BLACK, dissenting, in In re Groban, 352 U.S. 330, 340–343:

> 'The witness has no effective way to challenge his interrogator's testimony as to what was said and done at the secret inquisition. The officer's version frequently may reflect an inaccurate understanding of an accused's statements or, on occasion, may be deliberately distorted or falsified. While the accused may protest against these misrepresentations, his protestations will normally be in vain. This is particularly true when the officer is accompanied by several of his assistants and they all vouch for his story. But when the public, or even the suspect's counsel, is present the hazards to the suspect from the officer's misunderstanding or twisting of his statements or conduct are greatly reduced.

> 'The presence of legal counsel or any person who is not an executive officer bent on enforcing the law provides still another protection to the witness. Behind closed doors he can be coerced, tricked or confused by officers into making statements which may be untrue or may hide the truth by creating misleading impressions. While the witness is in the custody of the interrogators, as a practical matter, he is subject to their uncontrolled will. * * * Nothing would be better calculated to prevent misuse of official power in dealing with a witness or suspect than the scrutiny of his lawyer or friends or even of disinterested bystanders.'

The demands of our civilization expressed in the Due Process Clause require that the accused who wants a counsel should have one at any time after the moment of arrest.

4. DUE PROCESS AS "INCORPORATION"

Adamson v. California
332 U.S. 46 (1947)

■ MR. JUSTICE REED delivered the opinion of the Court.

The appellant, Adamson, a citizen of the United States, was convicted, without recommendation for mercy, by a jury in a Superior Court of the State of California of murder in the first degree. After considering the same objections to the conviction that are pressed here, the sentence of death was affirmed by the Supreme Court of the state. The provisions of California law which were challenged in the state proceedings as invalid under the Fourteenth Amendment to the Federal

Constitution are those of the state constitution and penal code in the margin. They permit the failure of a defendant to explain or to deny evidence against him to be commented upon by court and by counsel and to be considered by court and jury. The defendant did not testify. As the trial court gave its instructions and the District Attorney argued the case in accordance with the constitutional and statutory provisions just referred to, we have for decision the question of their constitutionality in these circumstances under the limitations of § 1 of the Fourteenth Amendment.

The appellant was charged in the information with former convictions for burglary, larceny and robbery and pursuant to § 1025, California Penal Code, answered that he had suffered the previous convictions. This answer barred allusion to these charges of convictions on the trial. Under California's interpretation of § 1025 of the Penal Code and § 2051 of the Code of Civil Procedure, however, if the defendant, after answering affirmatively charges alleging prior convictions, takes the witness stand to deny or explain away other evidence that has been introduced 'the commission of these crimes could have been revealed to the jury on cross-examination to impeach his testimony.' This forces an accused who is a repeated offender to choose between the risk of having his prior offenses disclosed to the jury or of having it draw harmful inferences from uncontradicted evidence that can only be denied or explained by the defendant.

In the first place, appellant urges that the provision of the Fifth Amendment that no person 'shall be compelled in any criminal case to be a witness against himself' is a fundamental national privilege or immunity protected against state abridgment by the Fourteenth Amendment or a privilege or immunity secured, through the Fourteenth Amendment, against deprivation by state action because it is a personal right, enumerated in the federal Bill of Rights.

Secondly, appellant relies upon the due process of law clause of the Fourteenth Amendment to invalidate the provisions of the California law, and as applied (a) because comment on failure to testify is permitted, (b) because appellant was forced to forego testimony in person because of danger of disclosure of his past convictions through cross-examination and (c) because the presumption of innocence was infringed by the shifting of the burden of proof to appellant in permitting comment on his failure to testify.

We shall assume, but without any intention thereby of ruling upon the issue, that state permission by law to the court, counsel and jury to comment upon and consider the failure of defendant 'to explain or to deny by his testimony any evidence or facts in the case against him' would infringe defendant's privilege against self-incrimination under the Fifth Amendment if this were a trial in a court of the United States under a similar law.[6] Such an assumption does not determine appellant's rights under the Fourteenth Amendment. It is settled law that the clause of the Fifth Amendment, protecting a person against being compelled to be a witness against himself, is not made effective by the Fourteenth Amendment as a protection against state action on the ground that freedom from testimonial compulsion is a right of national citizenship, or because it is a personal privilege or immunity secured by the Federal Constitution as one of the rights of man that are listed in the Bill of Rights.

The reasoning that leads to those conclusions starts with the unquestioned premise that the Bill of Rights, when adopted, was for the protection of the individual against the federal government and its provisions were inapplicable to similar actions done by the states. Barron v. Baltimore, 7 Pet. 243; Feldman v. United States, 322 U.S. 487, 490. With the adoption of the Fourteenth Amendment, it was suggested that the dual citizenship recognized by its first sentence, secured for citizens federal protection for their elemental provileges and immunities of state citizenship. The Slaughter-House Cases decided, contrary to the suggestion, that these rights, as privileges and immunities of state citizenship, remained under the sole protection of the state governments. This Court, without the expression of a contrary view upon that phase of the issues before the Court, has approved this determination. The power to free defendants in state trials from self-incrimination was specifically determined to be beyond the scope of the privileges and immunities clause of the Fourteenth Amendment in Twining v. New Jersey, 211 U.S. 78, 91–98. 'The privilege against self-incrimination may be withdrawn and the accused put upon the stand as a witness for the state.' The *Twining* case likewise disposed of the contention that freedom from testimonial compulsion, being specifically granted by the Bill of Rights, is a federal privilege or immunity that is protected by the Fourteenth Amendment against state invasion. This Court held that the inclusion in the Bill of Rights of this protection against the power of the national government did not make the privilege a federal privilege or immunity secured to citizens by the Constitution against state action. *Twining v. New Jersey, supra; Palko v. Connecticut, supra.* After declaring that state and national citizenship co-exist in the same person, the Fourteenth Amendment forbids a state from abridging the privileges and immunities of citizens of the United States. As a matter of words, this leaves a state free to abridge, within the limits of the due process clause, the privileges

---

[6] The California law protects a defendant against compulsion to testify, though allowing comment upon his failure to meet evidence against him. The Fifth Amendment forbids compulsion on a defendant to testify. Boyd v. United States, 116 U.S. 616, 631; *cf.* Davis v. United States, 328 U.S. 582, 587, 593. A federal statute that grew out of the extension of permissible witnesses to include those charged with offenses negatives a presumption against an accused for failure to avail himself of the right to testify in his own defense. 28 U.S.C. § 632, 28 U.S.C.A. § 632; Bruno v. United States, 308 U.S. 287. It was this statute which is interpreted to protect the defendant against comment for his claim of privilege. Wilson v. United States, 149 U.S. 60, 66; Johnson v. United States, 318 U.S. 189, 199.

and immunities flowing from state citizenship. This reading of the Federal Constitution has heretofore found favor with the majority of this Court as a natural and logical interpretation. It accords with the constitutional doctrine of federalism by leaving to the states the responsibility of dealing with the privileges and immunities of their citizens except those inherent in national citizenship. It is the construction placed upon the amendment by justices whose own experience had given them contemporaneous knowledge of the purposes that led to the adoption of the Fourteenth Amendment. This construction has become embedded in our federal system as a functioning element in preserving the balance between national and state power. We reaffirm the conclusion of the *Twining* and *Palko* cases that protection against self-incrimination is not a privilege or immunity of national citizenship.

Appellant secondly contends that if the privilege against self-incrimination is not a right protected by the privileges and immunities clause of the Fourteenth Amendment against state action, this privilege, to its full scope under the Fifth Amendment, inheres in the right to a fair trial. A right to a fair trial is a right admittedly protected by the due process clause of the Fourteenth Amendment. Therefore, appellant argues, the due process clause of the Fourteenth Amendment protects his privilege against self-incrimination. The due process clause of the Fourteenth Amendment, however, does not draw all the rights of the federal Bill of Rights under its protection. That contention was made and rejected in *Palko v. Connecticut*. It was rejected with citation of the cases excluding several of the rights, protected by the Bill of Rights, against infringement by the National Government. Nothing has been called to our attention that either the framers of the Fourteenth Amendment or the states that adopted intended its due process clause to draw within its scope the earlier amendments to the Constitution. *Palko* held that such provisions of the Bill of Rights as were 'implicit in the concept of ordered liberty,' became secure from state interference by the clause. But it held nothing more.

Specifically, the due process clause does not protect, by virtue of its mere existence the accused's freedom from giving testimony by compulsion in state trials that is secured to him against federal interference by the Fifth Amendment. *Twining v. New Jersey; Palko v. Connecticut, supra.* For a state to require testimony from an accused is not necessarily a breach of a state's obligation to give a fair trial. Therefore, we must examine the effect of the California law applied in this trial to see whether the comment on failure to testify violates the protection against state action that the due process clause does grant to an accused. The due process clause forbids compulsion to testify by fear of hurt, torture or exhaustion. It forbids any other type of coercion that falls within the scope of due process. California follows Anglo-American legal tradition in excusing defendants in criminal prosecutions from compulsory testimony. That is a matter of legal policy and not because of the requirements of due process under the Fourteenth Amendment. So our inquiry is directed, not at the broad question of the constitutionality of compulsory testimony from the accused under the due process clause, but to the constitutionality of the provision of the California law that permits comment upon his failure to testify. It is, of course, logically possible that while an accused might be required, under appropriate penalties, to submit himself as a witness without a violation of due process, comment by judge or jury on inferences to be drawn from his failure to testify, in jurisdictions where an accused's privilege against self-incrimination is protected, might deny due process. For example, a statute might declare that a permitted refusal to testify would compel an acceptance of the truth of the prosecution's evidence. . . .

There is no basis in the California law for appellant's objection on due process or other grounds that the statutory authorization to comment on the failure to explain or deny adverse testimony shifts the burden of proof or the duty to go forward with the evidence. Failure of the accused to testify is not an admission of the truth of the adverse evidence. Instructions told the jury that the burden of proof remained upon the state and the presumption of innocence with the accused. Comment on failure to deny proven facts does not in California tend to supply any missing element of proof of guilt. It only directs attention to the strength of the evidence for the prosecution or to the weakness of that for the defense. The Supreme Court of California called attention to the fact that the prosecutor's argument approached the borderline in a statement that might have been construed as asserting 'that the jury should infer guilt solely from defendant's silence.' That court felt that it was improbable the jury was misled into such an understanding of their power. We shall not interfere with such a conclusion. . . .

We find no other error that gives ground for our intervention in California's administration of criminal justice.

Affirmed.

■ MR. JUSTICE FRANKFURTER (concurring).

The short answer to the suggestion that the provision of the Fourteenth Amendment, which ordains 'nor shall any State deprive any person of life, liberty, or property, without due process of law,' was a way of saying that every State must thereafter initiate prosecutions through indictment by a grand jury, must have a trial by a jury of 12 in criminal cases, and must have trial by such a jury in common law suits where the amount in controversy exceeds $20, is that it is a strange way of saying it. It would be extraordinarily strange for a Constitution to convey such specific commands in such a roundabout and inexplicit way. After all, an amendment to the Constitution should be read in a "sense most obvious to the common understanding at the time of its adoption.' * * * For it was for public adoption that it was proposed.' *See* Mr. Justice Holmes in Eisner v. Macomber, 252 U.S. 189, 220. Those reading the English language with the meaning which it ordinarily conveys, those conversant with the political and legal history of the concept of due process, those sensitive to the relations of the States to the central government as well as the relation of some of the provisions of the Bill of Rights to the process of justice, would hardly recognize the Fourteenth Amendment as a cover for the various explicit provisions of the first eight Amendments. Some of these are enduring reflections of experience with human nature, while some express the restricted views of Eighteenth-Century England regarding the best methods for the ascertainment of facts. The notion that the Fourteenth Amendment was a covert way of imposing upon the States all the rules which it seemed important to Eighteenth Century statesmen to write into the Federal Amendments, was rejected by judges who were themselves witnesses of the process by which the Fourteenth Amendment became part of the Constitution. Arguments that may now be adduced to prove that the first eight Amendments were concealed within the historic phrasing of the Fourteenth Amendment were not unknown at the time of its adoption. A surer estimate of their bearing was possible for judges at the time than distorting distance is likely to vouchsafe. Any evidence of design or purpose not contemporaneously known could hardly have influenced those who ratified the Amendment. Remarks of a particular proponent of the Amendment, no matter how influential, are not to be deemed part of the Amendment. What was submitted for ratification was his proposal, not his speech. Thus, at the time of the ratification of the Fourteenth Amendment the constitutions of nearly half of the ratifying States did not have the rigorous requirements of the Fifth Amendment for instituting criminal proceedings through a grand jury. It could hardly have occurred to these States that by ratifying the Amendment they uprooted their established methods for prosecuting crime and fastened upon themselves a new prosecutorial system. . . .

A construction which gives to due process no independent function but turns it into a summary of the specific provisions of the Bill of Rights would, as has been noted, tear up by the roots much of the fabric of law in the several States, and would deprive the States of opportunity for reforms in legal process designed for extending the area of freedom. It would assume that no other abuses would reveal themselves in the course of time than those which had become manifest in 1791. Such a view not only disregards the historic meaning of 'due process.' It leads inevitably to a warped construction of specific provisions of the Bill of Rights to bring within their scope conduct clearly condemned by due process but not easily fitting into the pigeon-holes of the specific provisions. It seems pretty late in the day to suggest that a phrase so laden with historic meaning should be given an improvised content consisting of some but not all of the provisions of the first eight Amendments, selected on an undefined basis, with improvisation of content for the provisions so selected.

And so, when, as in a case like the present, a conviction in a State court is here for review under a claim that a right protected by the Due Process Clause of the Fourteenth Amendment has been denied, the issue is not whether an infraction of one of the specific provisions of the first eight Amendments is disclosed by the record. The relevant question is whether the criminal proceedings which resulted in conviction deprived the accused of the due process of law to which the United States Constitution entitled him. Judicial review of that guaranty of the Fourteenth Amendment inescapably imposes upon this Court an exercise of judgment upon the whole course of the proceedings in order to ascertain whether they offend those canons of decency and fairness which express the notions of justice of English-speaking peoples even toward those charged with the most heinous offenses. These standards of justice are not authoritatively formulated anywhere as though they were prescriptions in a pharmacopoeia. But neither does the application of the Due Process Clause imply that judges are wholly at large. The judicial judgment in applying the Due Process Clause must move within the limits of accepted notions of justice and is not to be based upon the idiosyncrasies of a merely personal judgment. The fact that judges among themselves may differ whether in a particular case a trial offends accepted notions of justice is not disproof that general rather than idiosyncratic standards are applied. An important safeguard against such merely individual judgment is an alert deference to the judgment of the State court under review.

■ MR. JUSTICE MURPHY, with whom MR. JUSTICE RUTLEDGE concurs, dissenting.

While in substantial agreement with the views of MR. JUSTICE BLACK, I have one reservation and one addition to make.

I agree that the specific guarantees of the Bill of Rights should be carried over intact into the first section of the Fourteenth Amendment. But I am not prepared to say that the latter is entirely and necessarily limited by the Bill of Rights. Occasions may arise where a proceeding falls so far short of conforming to fundamental standards of procedure as to warrant constitutional condemnation in terms of a lack of due process despite the absence of a specific provision in the Bill of Rights.

That point, however, need not be pursued here inasmuch as the Fifth Amendment is explicit in its provision that no person shall be compelled in any criminal case to be a witness against himself. That provision, as Mr. Justice BLACK demonstrates, is a constitutent part of the Fourteenth Amendment.

Moreover, it is my belief that this guarantee against self-incrimination has been violated in this case. Under California law, the judge or prosecutor may comment on the failure of the defendant in a criminal trial to explain or deny any evidence or facts introduced against him. As interpreted and applied in this case, such a provision compels a defendant to be a witness against himself in one of two ways:

1. If he does not take the stand, his silence is used as the basis for drawing unfavorable inferences against him as to matters which he might reasonably be expected to explain. Thus he is compelled, through his silence, to testify against himself. And silence can be as effective in this situation as oral statements.

2. If he does take the stand, thereby opening himself to cross-examination, so as to overcome the effects of the provision in question, he is necessarily compelled to testify against himself. In that case, his testimony on cross-examination is the result of the coercive pressure of the provision rather than his own volition.

Much can be said pro and con as to the desirability of allowing comment on the failure of the accused to testify. But policy arguments are to no avail in the face of a clear constitutional command. This guarantee of freedom from self-incrimination is grounded on a deep respect for those who might prefer to remain silent before their accusers. To borrow language from Wilson v. United States, 149 U.S. 60, 66: 'It is not every one who can safely venture on the witness stand, though entirely innocent of the charge against him. Excessive timidity, nervousness when facing others and attempting to explain transactions of a suspicious character, and offenses charged against him, will often confuse and embarrass him to such a degree as to increase rather than remove prejudices against him. It is not every one, however honest, who would therefore willingly be placed on the witness stand.'

We are obliged to give effect to the principle of freedom from self-incrimination. That principle is as applicable where the compelled testimony is in the form of silence as where it is composed of oral statements. Accordingly, I would reverse the judgment below.

■ MR. JUSTICE BLACK, dissenting.

The appellant was tried for murder in a California state court. He did not take the stand as a witness in his own behalf. The prosecuting attorney, under purported authority of a California statute, Cal.Penal Code, s 1323 (Hillyer-Lake 1945), argued to the jury that an inference of guilt could be drawn because of appellant's failure to deny evidence offered against him. The appellant's contention in the state court and here has been that the statute denies him a right guaranteed by the Federal Constitution. The argument is that (1) permitting comment upon his failure to testify has the effect of compelling him to testify so as to violate that provision of the Bill of Rights contained in the Fifth Amendment that 'No person * * * shall be compelled in any criminal case to be a witness against himself'; and (2) although this provision of the Fifth Amendment originally applied only as a restraint upon federal courts, Barron v. Baltimore, 7 Pet. 243, the Fourteenth Amendment was intended to, and did make the prohibition against compelled testimony applicable to trials in state courts.

The Court refuses to meet and decide the appellant's first contention. But while the Court's opinion, as I read it, strongly implies that the Fifth Amendment does not, of itself, bar comment upon failure to testify in federal courts, the Court nevertheless assumes that it does in order to reach the second constitutional question involved in appellant's case. I must consider the case on the same assumption that the Court does. For the discussion of the second contention turns out to be a decision which reaches far beyond the relatively narrow issues on which this case might have turned.

This decision reasserts a constitutional theory spelled out in Twining v. New Jersey, 211 U.S. 78, that this Court is endowed by the Constitution with boundless power under 'natural law' periodically to expand and contract constitutional standards to conform to the Court's conception of what at a particular time constitutes 'civilized decency' and 'fundamental principles of liberty and justice.' Invoking this *Twining* rule, the Court concludes that although comment upon testimony in a federal court would violate the Fifth Amendment, identical comment in a state court does not violate today's fashion in civilized decency and fundamentals and is therefore not prohibited by the Federal Constitution as amended.

The *Twining* case was the first, as it is the only decision of this Court, which has squarely held that states were free, notwithstanding to Fifth and Fourteenth Amendments, to extort evidence from one accused of crime. I agree that if *Twining* be reaffirmed, the result reached might appropriately follow. But I would not reaffirm the *Twining* decision. I think that decision and the 'natural law' theory of the Constitution upon which it relies, degrade the constitutional safeguards of the Bill of Rights and simultaneously appropriate for this Court a broad power which we are not authorized by the Constitution to exercise. Furthermore, the *Twining* decision rested on previous cases and broad hypotheses which have been undercut by intervening decisions of this Court. My reasons for believing that the *Twining* decision should not be revitalized can best be understood by reference to the constitutional, judicial, and general history that preceded and followed the case. That reference must be abbreviated far more than is justified but for the necessary limitations of opinion-writing.

The first 10 amendments were proposed and adopted largely because of fear that Government might unduly interfere with prized individual liberties. The people wanted and demanded a Bill of Rights written into their Constitution. The amendments embodying the Bill of Rights were intended to curb all branches of the Federal Government in the fields touched by the amendments—Legislative, Executive, and Judicial. The Fifth, Sixth, and Eighth Amendments were pointedly aimed at confining exercise of power by courts and judges within precise boundaries, particularly in the procedure used for the trial of criminal cases. Past history provided strong reasons for the apprehensions which brought these procedural amendments into being and attest the wisdom of their adoption. For the fears of arbitrary court action sprang largely from the past use of courts in the imposition of criminal punishments to suppress speech, press, and religion. Hence the constitutional limitations of courts' powers were, in the view of the Founders, essential supplements to the First Amendment, which was itself designed to protect the widest scope for all people to believe and to express the most divergent political, religious, and other views.

But these limitations were not expressly imposed upon state court action. In 1833, *Barron v. Baltimore, supra,* was decided by this Court. It specifically held inapplicable to the states that provision of the Fifth Amendment which declares: 'nor shall private property be taken for public use, without just compensation.' In deciding the particular point raised, the Court there said that it could not hold that the first eight amendments applied to the states. This was the controlling constitutional rule when the Fourteenth Amendment was proposed in 1866. . .

My study of the historical events that culminated in the Fourteenth Amendment, and the expressions of those who sponsored and favored, as well as those who opposed its submission and passage, persuades me that one of the chief objects that the provisions of the Amendment's first section, separately, and as a whole, were intended to accomplish was to make the Bill of Rights, applicable to the states. With full knowledge of the import of the *Barron* decision, the framers and backers of the Fourteenth Amendment proclaimed its purpose to be to overturn the constitutional rule that case had announced. This historical purpose has never received full consideration or exposition in any opinion of this Court interpreting the Amendment.[5]

In construing other constitutional provisions, this Court has almost uniformly followed the precept of Ex parte Bain, 121 U.S. 1, 12, that 'It is never to be forgotten that in the construction of the language of the Constitution * * *, as indeed in all other instances where construction becomes necessary, we are to place ourselves as nearly as possible in the condition of the men who framed that instrument.'.

Investigation of the cases relied upon in *Twining v. New Jersey* to support the conclusion there reached that neither the Fifth Amendment's prohibition of compelled testimony, nor any of the Bill of Rights, applies

---

[5] Another prime purpose was to make colored people citizens entitled to full equal rights as citizens despite what this Court decided in the Dred Scott case. Scott v. Sandford, 19 How. 393. A comprehensive analysis of the historical origins of the Fourteenth Amendment, Flack, The Adoption of the Fourteenth Amendment (1908) 94, concludes that 'Congress, the House and the Senate, had the following objects, and motives in view for submitting the first section of the Fourteenth Amendment to the States for ratification:

'1. To make the Bill of Rights (the first eight amendments) binding upon or applicable to, the States.

'2. To give validity to the Civil Rights Bill.

'3. To declare who were citizens of the United States.'

to the States, reveals an unexplained departure from this salutary practice. Neither the briefs nor opinions in any of these cases, except Maxwell v. Dow, 176 U.S. 581, make reference to the legislative and contemporary history for the purpose of demonstrating that those who conceived, shaped, and brought about the adoption of the Fourteenth Amendment intended it to nullify this Court's decision in *Barron v. Baltimore, supra,* and thereby to make the Bill of Rights applicable to the States. In *Maxwell v. Dow, supra,* the issue turned on whether the Bill of Rights guarantee of a jury trial was, by the Fourteenth Amendment, extended to trials in state courts. In that case counsel for appellant did cite from the speech of Senator Howard, which so emphatically stated the understanding of the framers of the Amendment—the Committee on Reconstruction for which he spoke—that the Bill of Rights was to be made applicable to the states by the Amendment's first section. The Court's opinion in *Maxwell v. Dow, supra,* acknowledged that counsel had 'cited from the speech of one of the Senators,' but indicated that it was not advised what other speeches were made in the Senate or in the House. The Court considered, moreover, that 'What individual Senators or Representatives may have urged in debate, in regard to the meaning to be given to a proposed constitutional amendment, or bill, or resolution, does not furnish a firm ground for its proper construction, nor is it important as explanatory of the grounds upon which the members voted in adopting it.'

In the *Twining* case itself, the Court was cited to a then recent book, Guthrie, Fourteenth Amendment to the Constitution (1898). A few pages of that work recited some of the legislative background of the Amendment, emphasizing the speech of Senator Howard. But Guthrie did not emphasize the speeches of Congressman Bingham, nor the part he played in the framing and adoption of the first section of the Fourteenth Amendment. Yet Congressman Bingham may, without extravagance, be called the Madison of the first section of the Fourteenth Amendment. In the *Twining* opinion the Court explicitly declined to give weight to the historical demonstration that the first section of the Amendment was intended to apply to the states the several protections of the Bill of Rights. It held that that question was 'no longer open' because of previous decisions of this Court which, however, had not appraised the historical evidence on that subject. The Court admitted that its action had resulted in giving 'much less effect to the 14th Amendment than some of the public men active in framing it' had intended it to have. With particular reference to the guarantee against compelled testimony, the Court stated that 'Much might be said in favor of the view that the privilege was guaranteed against state impairment as a privilege and immunity of national citizenship, but, as has been shown, the decisions of this court have foreclosed that view.'. Thus the Court declined and again today declines, to appraise the relevant historical evidence of the intended scope of the first section of the Amendment. Instead it relied upon previous cases, none of which had analyzed the evidence showing that one purpose of those who framed, advocated, and adopted the Amendment had been to make the Bill of Rights applicable to the States. None of the cases relied upon by the Court today made such an analysis.

For this reason, I am attaching to this dissent, an appendix which contains a resume, by no means complete, of the Amendment's history. In my judgment that history conclusively demonstrates that the language of the first section of the Fourteenth Amendment, taken as a whole, was thought by those responsible for its submission to the people, and by those who opposed its submission, sufficiently explicit to guarantee that thereafter no state could deprive its citizens of the privileges and protections of the Bill of Rights. Whether this Court ever will, or whether it now should, in the light of past decisions, give full effect to what the Amendment was intended to accomplish is not necessarily essential to a decision here. However that may be, our prior decisions, including *Twining*, do not prevent our carrying out that purpose, at least to the extent of making applicable to the states, not a mere part, as the Court has, but the full protection of the Fifth Amendment's provision against compelling evidence from an accused to convict him of crime. And I further contend that the 'natural law' formula which the Court uses to reach its conclusion in this case should be abandoned as an incongruous excrescence on our Constitution. I believe that formula to be itself a violation of our Constitution, in that it subtly conveys to courts, at the expense of legislatures, ultimate power over public policies in fields where no specific provision of the Constitution limits legislative power. And my belief seems to be in accord with the views expressed by this Court, at least for the first two decades after the Fourteenth Amendment was adopted.

In 1872, four years after the Amendment was adopted, the *Slaughter-House* cases came to this Court. The Court was not presented in that case with the evidence which showed that the special sponsors of the Amendment in the House and Senate had expressly explained one of its principal purposes to be to change the Constitution as construed in *Barron v. Baltimore, supra,* and make the Bill of Rights applicable to the states. Nor was there reason to do so. For the state law under consideration in the *Slaughter-House* cases was only challenged as one which authorized a monopoly, and the brief for the challenger properly conceded that there was 'no direct constitutional provision against a monopoly.' The argument did not invoke any specific provision of the Bill of Rights, but urged that the state monopoly statute violated 'the natural right of a person' to do business and engage in his trade or vocation. On this basis, it was contended that 'bulwarks that have been erected around the investments of capital are impregnable against state legislation.' These natural law arguments, so suggestive of the premises on which the present due process formula rest, were flatly rejected by a majority of the Court in the *Slaughter-House* cases. What the Court did hold was that the privileges and immunities clause of the Fourteenth Amendment only protected from state invasion such rights as a person has because he is a citizen of the United States. The Court enumerated some, but refused to enumerate all of these national rights. The majority of the Court emphatically declined the invitation of counsel to hold that the Fourteenth Amendment subjected all state regulatory legislation to continuous censorship by this Court in order for it to determine whether it collided with this Court's opinion of 'natural' right and justice. In effect, the *Slaughter-House* cases rejected the very natural justice formula the Court today embraces. The Court did not meet the question of whether the safeguards of the Bill of Rights were protected against state invasion by the Fourteenth Amendment. And it specifically did not say as the Court now does, that particular provisions of the Bill of Rights could be breached by states in part, but not breached in other respects, according to this Court's notions of 'civilized standards,' 'canons of decency,' and 'fundamental justice.'

After the *Slaughter-House* decision, the Court also said that states could, despite the 'due process' clause of the Fourteenth Amendment, take private property without just compensation, Davidson v. New Orleans, 96 U.S. 97; Pumpelly v. Green Bay & Mississippi Canal Co., 13 Wall. 166, 176, 177; abridge the freedom of assembly guaranteed by the First Amendment, United States v. Cruikshank, 92 U.S. 542; *see also* Prudential Ins. Co. v. Cheek, 259 U.S. 530, 543; Patterson v. Colorado, 205 U.S. 454; *cf.* Gitlow v. New York, 268 U.S. 652, 666 (freedom of speech); prosecute for crime by information rather than indictment, Hurtado v. People of California, 110 U.S. 516; regulate the price for storage of grain in warehouses and elevators, Munn v. Illinois, 94 U.S. 113. But this Court also held in a number of cases that colored people must, because of the Fourteenth Amendment, be accorded equal protection of the laws. *See, e.g.,* Strauder v. West Virginia, 100 U.S. 303; *cf.* Virginia v. Rives, 100 U.S. 313; *see also* Yick Wo. v. Hopkins, 118 U.S. 356.

Thus, up to and for some years after 1873, when *Munn v. Illinois, supra*, was decided, this Court steadfastly declined to invalidate states' legislative regulation of property rights or business practices under the Fourteenth Amendment unless there were racial discrimination involved in the state law challenged. The first significant breach in this policy came in 1889, in Chicago, M. & St. P.R. Co. v. Minnesota, 134 U.S. 418. A state's railroad rate regulatory statute was there stricken as violative of the due process clause of the Fourteenth Amendment. This was accomplished by reference to a due process formula which did not necessarily operate so as to protect the Bill of Rights' personal liberty safeguards, but which gave a new and hitherto undiscovered scope for the Court's use of the due process clause to protect property rights under natural law concepts. And in 1896, in Chicago, B. & Q.R. Co. v. Chicago, 166 U.S. 226, this Court, in effect, overruled *Davidson v. New Orleans, supra*, by holding, under the new due process-natural law formula, that the Fourteenth Amendment forbade a state from taking private property for public use without payment of just compensation.

Following the pattern of the new doctrine formalized in the foregoing decisions, the Court in 1896 applied the due process clause to strike down a state statute which had forbidden certain types of contracts. . . . And in 1905, three years before the *Twining* case, Lochner v. New York, 198 U.S. 45, followed the argument used in *Allgeyer* to hold that the due process clause was violated by a state statute which limited the employment of bakery workers to 60 hours per week and 10 hours per day.

The foregoing constitutional doctrine, judicially created and adopted by expanding the previously accepted meaning of 'due process,' marked a complete departure from the Slaughter-House philosophy of judicial tolerance of state regulation of business activities. Conversely, the new formula contracted the effectiveness of the Fourteenth Amendment as a protection from state infringement of individual liberties enumerated in the Bill of Rights. Thus the Court's second-thought interpretation of the Amendment was an about face from the Slaughter-House interpretation and represented a failure to carry out the avowed purpose of the Amendment's sponsors. This reversal is dramatized by the fact that the Hurtado case, which had rejected the due process clause as an instrument for preserving Bill of Rights liberties and privileges, was cited as authority for expanding the scope of that clause so as to permit this Court to invalidate all state regulatory legislation it believed to be contrary to 'fundamental' principles.

The *Twining* decision, rejecting the compelled testimony clause of the Fifth Amendment, and indeed rejecting all the Bill of Rights, is the end product of one phase of this philosophy. At the same time, that decision consolidated the power of the Court assumed in past cases by laying broader foundations for the Court to invalidate state and even federal regulatory legislation. For the *Twining* decision, giving separate consideration to 'due process' and 'privileges or immunities,' went all the way to say that the 'privileges or immunities' clause of the Fourteenth Amendment 'did not forbid the states to abridge the personal rights enumerated in the first eight Amendments * * *.' *Twining v. New Jersey, supra,* 211 U.S. at page 99. And in order to be certain, so far as possible, to leave this Court wholly free to reject all the Bill of Rights as specific restraints upon state action, the decision declared that even if this Court should decide that the due process clause forbids the states to infringe personal liberties guaranteed by the Bill of Rights, it would do so, not 'because those rights are enumerated in the first eight Amendments, but because they are of such a nature that they are included in the conception of due process of law.' 211 U.S. 78.

At the same time that the *Twining* decision held that the states need not conform to the specific provisions of the Bill of Rights, it consolidated the power that the Court had assumed under the due process clause by laying even broader foundations for the Court to invalidate state and even federal regulatory legislation. For under the *Twining* formula, which includes nonregard for the first eight amendments, what are 'fundamental rights' and in accord with 'canons of decency,' as the Court said in *Twining*, and today reaffirms, is to be independently 'ascertained from time to time by judicial action * * *.' 211 U.S. at page 101; 'what is due process of law depends on circumstances.' Moyer v. Peabody, 212 U.S. 78, 84. Thus the power of legislatures became what this Court would declare it to be at a particular time independently of the specific guarantees of the Bill of Rights such as the right to freedom of speech, religion and assembly, the right to just compensation for property taken for a public purpose, the right to jury trial or the right to be secure against unreasonable searches and seizures. Neither the contraction of the Bill of Rights safeguards nor the invalidation of regulatory laws by this Court's appraisal of 'circumstances' would readily be classified as the most satisfactory contribution of this Court to the nation . . .

Later decisions of this Court have completely undermined the phase of the *Twining* doctrine which broadly precluded reliance on the Bill of Rights to determine what is and what is not a 'fundamental' right. . . .

The Court's opinion in *Twining*, and the dissent in that case, made it clear that the Court intended to leave the states wholly free to compel confessions, so far as the Federal Constitution is concerned. *Twining v. New Jersey, supra, see* particularly 211 U.S. at pages 111–114, 125, 126. Yet in a series of cases since *Twining* this Court has held that the Fourteenth Amendment does bar all American courts, state or federal, from convicting people of crime on coerced confessions. Chambers v. Florida, 309 U.S. 227; Ashcraft v. Tennessee, 322 U.S. 143, 154, 155, and cases cited. Federal courts cannot do so because of the Fifth Amendment. Bram v. United States, 168 U.S. 532, 542, 562, 563. And state courts cannot do so because the principles of the Fifth Amendment are made applicable to the States through the Fourteenth by one formula or another. And taking note of these cases, the Court is careful to point out in its decision today that coerced confessions violate the Federal Constitution if secured 'by fear of hurt, torture or exhaustion.' Nor can a state, according to today's decision, constitutionally compel an accused to testify against himself by 'any other type of coercion that falls within the scope of due process.' Thus the Court itself destroys or at least drastically curtails the very *Twining* decision it purports to reaffirm. It repudiates the foundation of that opinion, which presented much argument to show that compelling a man to testify against himself does not 'violate' a 'fundamental' right or privilege. . . .

Conceding the possibility that this Court is now wise enough to improve on the Bill of Rights by substituting natural law concepts for the Bill of Rights. I think the possibility is entirely too speculative to agree to take that course. I would therefore hold in this case that the full protection of the Fifth Amendment's proscription against compelled testimony must be afforded by California. This I would do because of reliance upon the original purpose of the Fourteenth Amendment.

It is an illusory apprehension that literal application of some or all of the provisions of the Bill of Rights to the States would unwisely increase the sum total of the powers of this Court to invalidate state legislation. The Federal Government has not been harmfully burdened by the requirement that enforcement of federal laws affecting civil liberty comform literally to the Bill of Rights. Who would advocate its repeal?

. . .

■ MR. JUSTICE DOUGLAS joins in this opinion.

APPENDIX.

. . . II. When, on February 26, the proposed amendment [Editor's Note: The amendment then before the House was somewhat different than the revised amendment proposed by the Joint Committee on Reconstruction and ultimately adopted.] came up for debate, Mr. Bingham stated that 'by order * * * of the committee * * * I propose adoption of this amendment.' In support of it he said:

"* * * The amendment proposed stands in the very words of the Constitution of the United States as it came to us from the hands of its illustrious framers. Every word of the proposed amendment is to-day in the Constitution of our country, save the words conferring the express grant of power upon the Congress of the United States. The residue of the resolution, as the House will see by a reference to the Constitution, is the language of the second section of the fourth article, and of a portion of the fifth amendment adopted by the First Congress in 1789, and made part of the Constitution of the country. * * *

'Sir, it has been the want of the Republic that there was not an express grant of power in the Constitution to enable the whole people of every State, by congressional enactment, to enforce obedience to these requirements of the Constitution. Nothing can be plainer to thoughtful men than that if the grant of power had been originally conferred upon the Congress of the nation and legislation had been upon your statute-books to enforce these requirements of the Constitution in every State, that rebellion, which has scarred and blasted the land, would have been an impossibility. * * *

* * *

'And, sir, it is equally clear by every construction of the Constitution, its contemporaneous construction, its continued construction, legislative, executive, and judicial, that these great provisions of the Constitution, this immortal bill of rights embodied in the Constitution, rested for its execution and enforcement hitherto upon the fidelity of the States. * * *' Cong.Globe, *supra*, 1033, 1034.

Opposition speakers emphasized that the Amendment would destroy state's rights and empower Congress to legislate on matters of purely local concern. Cong.Globe, *supra*, 1054, 1057, 1063–1065, 1083, 1085–1087. *See also id.* at 1082. Some took the position that the Amendment was unnecessary because the Bill of Rights were already secured against state violation. *Id.* at 1059, 1066, 1088. Mr. Bingham joined issue on this contention:

'The gentleman seemed to think that all persons could have remedies for all violations of their rights of 'life, liberty, and property' in the Federal courts.

'I ventured to ask him yesterday when any action of that sort was ever maintained in any of the Federal courts of the United States to redress the great wrong which has been practiced, and which is being practiced now in more States than one of the Union under the authority of State laws, denying to citizens therein equal protection or any protection in the rights of life, liberty, and property.

* * *

'* * * A gentleman on the other side interrupted me and wanted to know if I could cite a decision showing that the power of the Federal Government to enforce in the United States courts the bill of rights under the articles of amendment to the Constitution had been denied. I answered that I was prepared to introduce such decisions; and that is exactly what makes plain the necessity of adopting this amendment.

'Mr. Speaker, on this subject I refer the House and the country to a decision of the Supreme Court, to be found in 7 Pet., at page 247, 8 L.Ed. 672, in the case of Barron v. The Mayor and City Council of Baltimore, involving the question whether the provisions of the fifth article of the amendments to the Constitution are binding upon the State of Maryland and to be enforced in the Federal courts. The Chief Justice says:

"The people of the United States framed such a Government for the United States as they supposed best adapted to their situation and best calculated to promote their interests. The powers they conferred on this Government were to be exercised by itself; and the limitations of power, if expressed in general terms, are naturally, and we think necessarily, applicable to the Government created by the instrument. They are limitations of power granted in the instrument itself, not of distinct governments, framed by different persons and for different purposes.

"If these propositions be correct, the fifth amendment must be understood as restraining the power of the General Government, not as applicable to the States.'

'I read one further decision on this subject—the case of the Lessee of Livingston v. Moore and others, 7 Pet., 469, at page 551, 8 L.Ed. 751. The court, in delivering its opinion, says:

"As to the Amendments of the Constitution of the United States, they must be put out of the case, since it is now settled that those amendments do not extend to the States; and this observation disposes of the next exception, which relies on the seventh article of those amendments.'

* * *

'The question is simply whether you will give by this amendment to the people of the United States the power, by legislative enactment, to punish officials of States for violation of oaths enjoined upon them by their Constitution? * * * Is the Bill of Rights to stand in our Constitution hereafter, as in the past five years within eleven States, a mere dead letter? It is absolutely essential to the safety of the people that it should be enforced.

'Mr. Speaker, it appears to me that this very provision of the bill of rights brought in question this day, upon this trial before the House, more than any other provision of the Constitution, makes that unity of government which constitutes us one people, by which and through which American nationality came to be, and only by the enforcement of which can American nationality continue to be. . . .

On May 23, 1866, Senator Howard introduced the proposed amendment to the Senate in the absence of Senator Fessenden who was sick. [Editor's Note: At this point the text of the proposed amendment is identical to the amendment proposed to the country and ultimately ratified.] Senator Howard prefaced his remarks by stating:

'I * * * present to the Senate * * * the views and the motives (of the Reconstruction Committee). * * * One result of their investigation has been the joint resolution for the amendment of the Constitution of the United States now under consideration. * * *

'The first section of the amendment * * * submitted for the consideration of the two Houses, relates to the privileges and immunities of citizens of the several States, and to the rights and privileges of all persons, whether citizens or others, under the laws of the United States. * * *

'It will be observed that this is a general prohibition upon all the States, as such, from abridging the privileges and immunities of the citizens of the United States. That is its first clause, and I regard it as very important. It also prohibits each one of the States from depriving any person of life, liberty, or property without due process of law, or denying to any person within the jurisdiction of the State the equal protection of its laws.

* * *

'It would be a curious question to solve what are the privileges and immunities of citizens of each of the States in the several States. * * * I am not aware that the Supreme Court have ever undertaken to define either the nature or extent of the privileges and immunities thus guarantied. * * * But we may gather some intimation of what probably will be the opinion of the judiciary by referring to * * * Corfield v. Coryell

(Fed.Cas. No. 3230) 4 Washington Circuit Court Reports, page 380. (Here Senator Howard quoted at length from that opinion.)

'Such is the character of the privileges and immunities spoken of in the second section of the fourth article of the Constitution. To these privileges and immunities, whatever they may be—for they are not and cannot be fully defined in their entire extent and precise nature—to these should be added the personal rights guarantied and secured by the first eight amendments of the Constitution; such as the freedom of speech and of the press; the right of the people peaceably to assemble and petition the Government for a redress of grievances, a right appertaining to each and all the people; the right to keep and to bear arms; the right to be exempted from the quartering of soldiers in a house without the consent of the owner; the right to be exempt from unreasonable searches and seizures, and from any search or seizure except by virtue of a warrant issued upon a formal oath or affidavit; the right of an accused person to be informed of the nature of the accusation against him, and his right to be tried by an impartial jury of the vicinage; and also the right to be secure against excessive bail and against cruel and unusual punishments.

'Now, sir, here is a mass of privileges, immunities, and rights, some of them secured by the second section of the fourth article of the Constitution, which I have recited, some by the first eight amendments of the Constitution; and it is a fact well worthy of attention that the course of decision of our courts and the present settled doctrine is, that all these immunities, privileges, rights, thus guarantied by the Constitution, or recognized by it, are secured to the citizens solely as a citizen of the United States and as a party in their courts. They do not operate in the slightest degree as a restraint or a prohibition upon state legislation. States are not affected by them, and it has been repeatedly held that the restriction contained in the Constitution against the taking of private property for public use without just compensation is not a restriction upon State legislation, but applies only to the legislation of Congress.

'Now, sir, there is no power given in the Constitution to enforce and to carry out any of these guarantees. They are not powers granted by the Constitution to Congress, and of course do not come within the sweeping clause of the Constitution authorizing Congress to pass all laws necessary and proper for carrying out the foregoing or granted powers, but they stand simply as a bill of rights in the Constitution, without power on the part of Congress to give them full effect; while at the same time the States are not restrained from violating the principles embraced in them except by their own local constitutions, which may be altered from year to year. The great object of the first section of this amendment is, therefore, to restrain the power of the States any compel them at all times to respect these great fundamental guarantees.' Cong.Globe, *supra*, 2764.

5. THE DUE PROCESS VOLUNTARINESS DOCTRINE SINCE *MIRANDA*

Dye v. Commonwealth of Kentucky

2013 WL 3122823 (Ky. June 20, 2013)

■ Opinion of the Court by JUSTICE SCOTT.

Appellant, Garrett Thomas Dye, pled guilty to Murder, Resisting Arrest, and Tampering with Physical Evidence. For these crimes, the Todd Circuit Court sentenced him to a total of fifty years' imprisonment. He now appeals as a matter of right, Ky. Const. § 110(2)(b), arguing that (1) his confession was coerced, (2) he did not knowingly and intelligently waive his *Miranda* rights, and (3) he unequivocally invoked his right to counsel. Additionally, he argues that all evidence seized pursuant to information obtained from his confession must be suppressed as "fruit of the poisonous tree." Because we conclude that Appellant's confession was involuntary, we now reverse and remand for further proceedings.

I. BACKGROUND

On the evening of February 4, 2011, Appellant's nine-year-old sister went missing after spending that afternoon with Appellant shoveling gravel in their driveway. Appellant's parents notified the Todd County Sheriff's Department of her disappearance, and just after midnight on February 5, 2011, the girl's dead body was discovered in a thicket about 100 yards from Appellant's home.

Because there were signs of blunt force trauma to the girl's head and face, a search warrant was issued that morning at 5:28 a.m. for the recovery of items from the property and its buildings potentially related to her death, including potential weapons, clothes, and shoes. Pursuant to this search warrant, a number of items were recovered from Appellant's home and surrounding property, including two shovels, various clothes, tennis shoes, and a buccal swab DNA sample from Appellant.[1]

The same morning, Appellant and his parents were taken to the Trenton Police Station for questioning, but Appellant's father requested that Appellant, who was seventeen years old at the time, not be questioned until a lawyer could be retained on his behalf. Appellant was not questioned at that time.

The next day, law enforcement went to Appellant's home and arrested him for his sister's murder. Appellant was read his *Miranda* rights before being transported to the Logan County Courthouse where four officers (two at a time) took turns interrogating him for approximately two hours in the Court Designated Worker's (CDW)

---

[1] The evidence seized pursuant to this search warrant is not at issue in this appeal.

Office.[2] During the interrogation, Appellant confessed to murdering his sister. That evening, a second search warrant ("the February 6 search warrant") was issued based upon information contained in Appellant's confession, and additional incriminating items (similar to those seized pursuant to the first search warrant) were retrieved from his home.

At trial, Appellant moved to suppress his confession on the grounds that his *Miranda* waiver was involuntary, his right to counsel was invoked but denied, and his confession was coerced. The trial court denied the motion on all grounds. Thereafter, Appellant pled guilty to all counts but reserved his right to appeal. The trial court sentenced him to fifty years' imprisonment for murder, twelve months for resisting arrest, and three years for tampering, all to run concurrently for a total of fifty years.

II. ANALYSIS

On appellate review of a trial court's denial of a motion to suppress, we generally apply the two-step process set out in Ornelas v. United States, 517 U.S. 690 (1996), and adopted by Kentucky in Adcock v. Commonwealth, 967 S.W.2d 6 (Ky.1998). Under this standard we review the trial court's findings of fact for substantial evidence, *id.* at 8, and then conduct a de novo review of the trial court's application of the law to the established facts to determine whether its ruling was correct as a matter of law, Welch v. Commonwealth, 149 S.W.3d 407, 409 (Ky.2004).

However, a simple application of this standard of review is insufficient in the case at bar because the trial court's findings of fact, although supported by substantial evidence in the record, are incomplete. For example, the trial court's order states that the officers told Appellant "how difficult things will be in the penitentiary." What the order omits, however, is the officers' actual message, *i.e.,* that if Appellant did not confess he would be convicted, receive the death penalty, and be the subject of serious and repeated prison violence while awaiting execution. Thus, application of our normal standard of reviewing a ruling on a motion to suppress is inadequate here because it would require us to ignore facts relevant to the question of whether Appellant's substantial rights were violated.[3]

---

[2] The CDW was not present during the interrogation.

[3] We by no means suggest that a reviewing court must sua sponte comb the record to determine whether the trial court's findings of fact on a motion to suppress are "complete." The Ornelas-Adcock standard of reviewing a trial court's findings of fact for substantial evidence is time-tested and will be sufficient in the great majority of cases. However, an appellate court reviewing for substantial evidence is not required to turn a blind eye to evidence in the record that is not fairly accounted for in the trial court's order when that evidence tends to show that a defendant's substantial rights have been violated. RCr 9.24 provides, in relevant part:

> [N]o error or defect in any ruling or order, or in anything done or omitted by the court or by any of the parties, is ground for granting a new trial or for setting aside a verdict or for vacating, modifying or otherwise disturbing a judgment or order unless it appears to the court that the denial of such relief would be inconsistent with substantial justice. The court at every stage of the proceeding must disregard any error or defect in the proceeding that does not affect the substantial rights of the parties.

Moreover, as the U.S. Supreme Court noted in *Haynes v. Washington*:

> It is well settled that the duty of constitutional adjudication resting upon this Court requires that the question whether the Due Process Clause of the Fourteenth Amendment has been violated by admission into evidence of a coerced confession be the subject of an independent determination here, *see, e.g.,* Ashcraft v. Tennessee, 322 U.S. 143, 147–148, [(1944)]; 'we cannot escape the responsibility of making our own examination of the record,' Spano v. New York, 360 U.S. 315, 316 [(1959)]. While, for purposes of review in this Court, the determination of the trial judge or of the jury will ordinarily be taken to resolve evidentiary conflicts and may be entitled to some weight even with respect to the ultimate conclusion on the crucial issue of voluntariness, we cannot avoid our responsibilities by permitting ourselves to be 'completely bound by state court determination of any issue essential to decision of a claim of federal right, else federal law could be frustrated by distorted fact finding.' Stein v. New York, 346 U.S. 156, 181 [(1953)].

373 U.S. 503, 515–16 (1963). Although the U.S. Supreme Court is the final arbiter of federal constitutional issues, we have previously recognized that "absent a substantial factual dispute in the evidence, voluntariness of a confession may be properly decided by a reviewing court." Mills v. Commonwealth, 996 S.W.2d 473, 481 (Ky.1999) (citing Jackson v. Denno, 378 U.S. 368, 391–92 (1964)), overruled on other grounds by Padgett v. Commonwealth, 312 S.W.3d 336 (Ky.2010). Most of Appellant's interrogation was audiotaped (although some parts are muffled or inaudible), and the material facts are not in dispute; we therefore invoke our authority to decide whether Appellant's confession was voluntary.

A. Coerced Confessions

In *Bailey v. Commonwealth*, we recited the relevant law concerning involuntary confessions:

> The Due Process Clause of the Fourteenth Amendment prohibits the admission of involuntary confessions: "[if the defendant's] will has been overborne and his capacity for self-determination critically impaired, the use of [the] confession offends due process." Schneckloth v. Bustamonte, 412 U.S. 218, 225–26 (1973). "The voluntariness of a confession is assessed based on the totality of the circumstances surrounding the making of the confession." Mills v. Commonwealth, 996 S.W.2d 473, 481 (Ky.1999). However, the threshold question to a voluntariness analysis is the presence or absence of coercive

---

The negative inference of this rule is that a court need not disregard an error or defect that does affect the substantial rights of the parties or appears to be inconsistent with substantial justice.

police activity: "coercive police activity is a necessary predicate to the finding that a confession is not Voluntary' within the meaning of the Due Process Clause of the Fourteenth Amendment." Colorado v. Connelly, 479 U.S. 157, 167 (1986).

194 S.W.3d 296, 300 (Ky.2006). Additionally,

> [t]he U.S. Supreme Court has described the "ultimate test" of the voluntariness of a confession as follows: "Is the confession the product of an essentially free and unconstrained choice by its maker?" Schneckloth, 412 U.S. at 225, 93 S.Ct. at 2047, 36 L.Ed.2d at 862 (internal citations omitted). Accordingly, in assessing voluntariness, "both the characteristics of the accused and the details of the interrogation are considered." Schneckloth, 412 U.S. at 226. When examining the characteristics of the accused, reviewing courts consider such factors as age, education, intelligence, and linguistic ability. Allee v. Commonwealth, 454 S.W.2d 336, 341 (Ky.1970).

Bailey, 194 S.W.3d at 300.

In *Henson v. Commonwealth,* we summarized the relevant inquiry as follows: "The three criteria used to assess voluntariness are 1) whether the police activity was 'objectively coercive;' 2) whether the coercion overbore the will of the defendant; and 3) whether the defendant showed that the coercive police activity was the 'crucial motivating factor' behind the defendant's confession." 20 S.W.3d 466, 469 (Ky.1999) (citing Morgan v. Commonwealth, 809 S.W.2d 704, 707 (Ky.1991)). We conclude that the interrogation techniques employed in this case satisfy these criteria.

1. Objectively Coercive Police Activity

First, the officers incorrectly and repeatedly informed Appellant that, if convicted, he could receive the death penalty (i.e., that he was "death eligible"). However, in Roper v. Simmons, the U.S. Supreme Court held that the Eighth and Fourteenth Amendments to the U.S. Constitution impose a categorical bar to executing individuals who were under eighteen years old at the time of the crimes. 543 U.S. 551, 578 (2005). It is undisputed that all four interrogating officers knew Appellant was seventeen years old. At the suppression hearing, the officers admitted that they misinformed Appellant regarding his death-eligibility but maintained that, at the time, they believed he was death-eligible. The officers did not offer an explanation as to why they believed Appellant was death-eligible and we cannot begin to speculate—in addition to Appellant being ineligible due to his age, no aggravating circumstances were ever alleged to exist in this case. KRS 532.025(3) forbids the imposition of the death penalty unless a murder is accompanied by an aggravating circumstance. *See* Young v. Commonwealth, 50 S.W.3d 148, 162 (Ky.2001).

Each death penalty reference was immediately followed by an officer asserting that the only way for Appellant to avoid execution was to confess to the murder. Perhaps the most troubling exchange between Appellant and the officers regarding the death penalty occurred about an hour into the interrogation. To this point, Appellant had not made any incriminating statements and the officers had left the room to give Appellant a break. During the break Appellant began to cry. When the officers returned to the room, the following exchange occurred:

> Officer: Are you sure you don't want anything? Use the bathroom or anything? You hungry or anything?
>
> Appellant: I don't know what I am. I'm just scared.
>
> Officer: I know you're scared, man. I know you are.
>
> Appellant: Is it the death penalty?
>
> Officer: I'm sorry?
>
> Appellant: Are they gonna give me the death penalty?
>
> Officer: Oh yeah.
>
> Appellant: [inaudible]
>
> Officer: Now, you'll probably spend twenty or thirty years on death row in a room all by yourself. . . . That's why I was trying to tell you man, this is the only chance you got to avoid all that right now. Tonight, tonight will be your only chance.
>
> Not only did the officer erroneously convey that Appellant was death-eligible, but also that he was certain to receive a death sentence unless he confessed to his sister's murder.

After a similar exchange, an officer told Appellant: "I hate to see you at seventeen years old go to the pen[etentiary] for the rest of your life or spend the next fifteen or twenty years of your life on death row. This is the only way you're going to avoid that." A few minutes later, an officer told Appellant: "We've put people on death row and electrocuted them with a whole lot less evidence than we got on you. I mean a whole lot less."

We hold that repeatedly threatening a seventeen-year-old with the death penalty is "objectively coercive." *Henson*, 20 S.W.3d at 469. The interrogating officers knew, or should have known, that Appellant was not death-eligible (1) due to his status as a juvenile, *see Roper*, 543 U.S. at 578, and (2) because there was no evidence or allegation of aggravating circumstances that would have otherwise made this case death-eligible. *See* KRS 532.025(2). We therefore conclude that the interrogating officers' untruthful threats were improperly employed to overbear Appellant's will and critically impair his capacity for self-determination. *Schneckloth*, 412 U.S. at 225–26. Thus, it is "objectively coercive." *Henson*, 20 S.W.3d at 469.

Likewise, the officers made several inappropriate allusions to prison violence or rape throughout the interrogation. For example, about an hour into the interrogation one of the officers warned Appellant: "I can tell you right now, a seventeen-year-old or eighteen-year-old young buck straight into [the Kentucky State Prison (KSP) at] Eddyville, killing a nine-year-old—you can imagine what they're going to do to you on a daily basis." A second officer told Appellant that he "wouldn't want nobody to have to do that to my own son, but that's exactly what they're going to do to you."

Later in the interview, the officers again told Appellant that unless he confessed he would be tried as an adult and incarcerated at KSP where, according to the officers, the inmates treat child murderers the same way they treat individuals convicted of a sexual crime against a child:

> Officer 1: Your status—with killing a nine-year-old—you're gonna be down there with the scum of the earth.
>
> Officer 2: And they won't spare no mercy on your ass. Even the guards, they gonna be like, "You piece of shit." . . . [Murder] and sexual assault . . .
>
> Appellant: Sexual assault?
>
> Officer 1: Any violent crime against a small child. . . . Everybody's gonna forget about you until you get to Eddyville then they'll remind you what happened. Every day they'll remind you.

We will not feign ignorance to the fact that the officers were alluding to prison violence and/or rape and that is precisely how Appellant understood these comments. We hold that attempting to persuade a seventeen-year-old that a confession is the only way he will avoid daily prison assault—sexual or otherwise—is "objectively coercive." *Henson*, 20 S.W.3d at 469.

Finally, we find it troublesome that the officers continually dissuaded Appellant from invoking his right to counsel. Although we need not determine whether Appellant unequivocally and unambiguously invoked his right to counsel, or whether the alleged waiver of his *Miranda* rights was coerced, this conduct is nonetheless relevant to our "totality of the circumstances" review. *See Mills,* 996 S.W.2d at 481. One exchange—about eighty minutes into the interrogation, and just moments before Appellant began confessing—is particularly bothersome:

> Officer 1: You know what your options are now.
>
> Appellant: I just don't want to say anything until my lawyers get here, and they can't get here until Monday.
>
> Officer 1: Well like I said, man, nobody's gonna tell you you can't have a lawyer, the thing is you don't have to have a lawyer to tell the truth. Like I told you, every person in the penitentiary had a lawyer. You know what I mean? Lawyers don't make you tell the truth.

Officer 2: The only thing that can make you tell the truth is because that's what you want to do and because that's what's in your heart.

. . . .

Let me bottom line it for you: I'm the case officer. And I will talk to you until the moon turns blue. But people that I don't like talking to is, guess what? Attorneys. Okay? So I'm not saying you have to sit here and talk to me, but if you want to and if there's something you want to say I wish to God you'd say it now before this officer gets here to transport you.

. . .

If you want to maintain being a hard-ass and not wanting to talk and blah-blah this and blah-blah that, then when you're ready to talk—when your attorney says, "Hey, we need to sit down and talk to the police"—uh uh. No. Because you had your chance right now.

When considered in context of the entire conversation, we believe that the intended effect of this exchange (and similar exchanges) was to alert Appellant, a seventeen-year-old, that if he did invoke his right to an attorney his opportunity to confess—and thereby avoid the death penalty and prison violence—would be lost. We hold that this is "objectively coercive." *Henson,* 20 S.W.3d at 469.

2.   Overborne Will

Upon thorough review of the interrogation, we conclude that inducing Appellant to forfeit his right to counsel and provide an immediate confession by playing to his fears of death and assault overbore his will. This is most clear in the two exchanges recounted above. First, after an hour of interrogation involving substantial discussion of the death penalty and references to inter-inmate violence, the officers left the room to give Appellant a break. Predictably, he began crying and when the officers returned he immediately told them that he was scared and asked them if he was really going to receive the death penalty. About twenty minutes later, the interrogators gave Appellant an ultimatum: confess and avoid the death penalty and life on death row, or invoke his right to counsel and lose his opportunity to confess. Unsurprisingly, Appellant began confessing moments later. This is sufficient for us to conclude that the second Henson prong is satisfied.

3.   Crucial Motivating Factor

For the same reasons as the second, the third *Henson* prong is satisfied: "the coercive police activity was the 'crucial motivating factor' behind the defendant's confession." 20 S.W.3d at 469. While Appellant spent the hour before the break denying any involvement in his sister's murder, Appellant's attitude completely changed after the reality set in that he either confess or face death. When the officers returned to the interrogation room from the break, the first things Appellant said were "I'm scared" and "Are they going to give me the death penalty?" He was told repeatedly that (1) this was his last and only chance to confess, (2) if he did confess he could avoid the death penalty, (3) but if he did not confess he was going to be executed, and (4) he would be subject to assault while on death row. Additionally, he was told that if he invoked his right to counsel he would lose his opportunity to confess. This coercive police activity was not ancillary to the confession; it was the "crucial motivating factor." *Id.*

We hold that under the totality of the circumstances, Appellant's confession was not "the product of an essentially free and unconstrained choice by its maker," *Schneckloth*, 412 U.S. at 225, but rather the product of "coercive police activity," *Connelly*, 479 U.S. at 167. Accordingly, it must be suppressed. *See, e.g.,* Johnson v. New Jersey, 384 U.S. 719, 729 n.9 (1966) ("Coerced confessions are, of course, inadmissible regardless of their alleged truth or falsity.") (citing Rogers v. Richmond, 365 U.S. 534 (1961)). "[C]ertain interrogation techniques, either in isolation or as applied to the unique characteristics of a particular suspect, are so offensive to a civilized system of justice that they must be condemned under the Due Process Clause of the Fourteenth Amendment." Miller v. Fenton, 474 U.S. 104, 109 (1985) (citing Brown v. Mississippi, 297 U.S. 278 (1936)). As the U.S. Supreme Court explained in *Schneckloth*:

> '[V]oluntariness' has reflected an accommodation of the complex of values implicated in police questioning of a suspect. At one end of the spectrum is the acknowledged need for police questioning as a tool for the effective enforcement of criminal laws. *See* Culombe v. Connecticut, *supra*, [367 U.S. 568] at 578–580 (1961)]. Without such investigation, those who were innocent might be falsely accused, those who were guilty might wholly escape prosecution, and many crimes would go unsolved. In short, the security of all would be diminished. *Haynes v. Washington,* 373 U.S. 503, 515. At the other end of the spectrum is the set of values reflecting society's deeply felt belief that the criminal law cannot be used as an instrument of unfairness, and that the possibility of unfair and even brutal police tactics poses a real and serious threat to civilized notions of justice. '(I)n cases involving involuntary confessions, this Court enforces the strongly felt attitude of our society that important human values are sacrificed where an agency of the government, in the course of securing a conviction, wrings a confession out of an accused against his will.' Blackburn v. Alabama, 361 U.S. 199, 206–207 [(1960)].

412 U.S. at 224–25. Due process demands suppression.

B.   Exclusion of Evidence

Because we are remanding to the trial court for further proceedings, we must address Appellant's related claim: whether the evidence seized pursuant to the February 6 search warrant—which was issued upon information contained in his involuntary confession—must also be suppressed as "fruit of the poisonous tree." *See* Wong Sun v. United States, 371 U.S. 471 (1963). This is a question the U.S. Supreme Court has not yet answered and one that this Court has not directly addressed.[4] *See generally* 1 McCormick on Evidence § 159 (7th Ed.2013); *see also* Yale Kamisar, *On the "Fruits" of* Miranda *Violations, Coerced Confessions, and Compelled Testimony*, 93 Mich. L.Rev. 929 (1995). However, there is substantial support for a Fifth Amendment exclusionary rule similar (or identical) to the "fruits" doctrine. *See generally* 1 McCormick on Evidence at § 159; Kamisar, *supra*, at 940–954. As one leading academic treatise explains:

> [T]he [United States] Supreme Court has not had direct occasion to decide whether, in the police interrogation context, the exclusionary rule requires suppression of reliable fruits of a statement obtained in violation of the Fifth Amendment. There is little doubt that this is the rule, however. First, the Court held in *Counselman v. Hitchcock* that the Fifth Amendment privilege prevents the government from using compelled grand jury testimony to obtain knowledge of . . . sources of information which may supply other means of convicting a defendant.[5] As Professor Yale Kamisar has observed, "ever since the 110-year-old case of *Counselman* . . . was decided, it has been plain that the privilege prohibits the derivative use, as well as the direct use, of compelled utterances."[6] There is no reason to believe that

---

[4] We acknowledge that our predecessor court has addressed similar issues. *See* Baughman v. Commonwealth, 206 Ky. 441, 267 S.W. 231 (1924); McQueen v. Commonwealth, 196 Ky. 227, 244 S.W. 681 (1922). However, neither *Baughman* nor *McQueen* involved federal constitutional claims. Rather, the confessions were analyzed under the so-called "Anti-Sweating Act," see KRS 422.110; *Baughman* also involved an alleged violation of Section 11 of the Kentucky Constitution. Both cases involved involuntary confessions in which the defendant identified "extraneous facts" leading to the discovery of reliable evidence. And, in both cases, the old Court of Appeals held that although the confessions were inadmissible, the evidence obtained pursuant to the "extraneous facts" was admissible. *Baughman*, 267 S.W. at 234–35; *McQueen*, 244 S.W. at 685. *Baughman* and *McQueen* were decided at a time when the prevailing theory on the admissibility of evidence obtained under these circumstances turned on reliability. *See* Yale Kamisar, *On the "Fruits" of* Miranda *Violations, Coerced Confessions, and Compelled Testimony*, 93 Mich. L.Rev. 929, 937–39 (1995). "During the period roughly extending to the 1950s, physical evidence uncovered as a result of an involuntary confession was, unsurprisingly, admissible—because the derivative evidence, unlike the confession, was reliable. Indeed, it was generally held that if the extrinsic evidence corroborated the confession . . . even the confession could be admitted." *Id.* at 937–38 (footnotes, citations, and internal quotation marks omitted).

In contrast, the modern view is "that the due process exclusionary rule for confessions (in much the same way as the Fourth Amendment exclusionary rule for physical evidence) is also intended to deter improper police conduct." *Id.* at 938–43 (quoting 1 Wayne R. LaFave & Jerold H. Israel, Criminal Procedure § 6.2, at 443 (1984)). Accordingly, it is unlikely that *McQueen* and *Baughman* would pass muster under the modern federal constitutional analysis applicable to coerced confessions.

[5] 142 U.S. 547, 586 (1892).

[6] Yale Kamisar, *A Look Back on a Half-Century of Teaching, Writing and Speaking About Criminal Law and Criminal Procedure,* 2 Ohio St. J.Crim. L. 69, 83 (2004).

a different rule applies to statements compelled by the police, rather than the grand jury.

And, the Court has applied the poisonous-tree principle in a police interrogation context, albeit outside the Fifth Amendment [in Harrison v. United States, 392 U.S. 219 (1968)]. . . . Since the "poisonous tree" in *Harrison* was a non-constitutional supervisory-authority rule, it follows that a violation of the Constitution itself (the Fifth Amendment privilege) requires implementation of the poisonous-tree doctrine.

Finally, it is worth observing that a plurality of the Court—including its most conservative members—recently recognized a Fifth Amendment fruit-of-the-poisonous-tree doctrine in dictum. In *Chavez v. Martinez*,[7] Justice Thomas, writing for the Chief Justice and Justices O'Connor and Scalia, observed that "our cases provide that those subjected to coercive police interrogations have an automatic protection from the use of their involuntary statements (or evidence derived from their statements) in any subsequent criminal trial."[8] Of course, the Fifth Amendment version of the fruit-of-the-poisonous-tree doctrine is subject to the same limiting principles as its counterparts in the Fourth and Sixth Amendments—the independent-source, inevitable discovery, and dissipation-of-taint-doctrines.

Joshua Dressier & Alan C. Michaels, Understanding Criminal Procedure: Volume 1: Investigation § 23.05[B][3][b][ii], at 464–65 (4th Ed.2006). Thus, it is generally recognized that the "fruits" doctrine applies, on principles of due process and deterrence, to Appellant's situation. *See* Kamisar, *supra*, at 937–43.[9]

---

[7]   538 U.S. 760 (2003).

[8]   *Id.* at 769 (latter emphasis added). Not all commentators agree that the fruit-of-the-poisonous-tree doctrine should apply to tangible evidence. Amar and Lettow, for example, make the following textual argument: the Fifth Amendment prohibits a defendant from being a "witness" against herself; tangible evidence is not a "witness" (as it does not testify); therefore, "[p]hysical evidence . . . can be introduced at trial whatever its source—even if that source is a compelled pre-trial utterance." [Akhil Reed Amar & Renee B. Lettow, *Fifth Amendment First Principles: The Self-incrimination Clause*, 93 Mich. L.Rev. 857, 900 (1995)].

[9]   We acknowledge the U.S. Supreme Court's fractured decision in United States v. Patane, 542 U.S. 630 (2004), lends additional, but limited, guidance. In *Patane*, Justice Thomas's plurality opinion held that the failure to give a suspect Miranda warnings does not require suppression of physical fruits of the suspect's unwarned but voluntary statements. *Id.* at 634. *Patane* is distinguishable from the present case in that Appellant was read his *Miranda* rights but his confession was coerced, i.e., involuntary. This is significant insofar as Justice Thomas's opinion relied, in part, on the fact police do not violate the Constitution by merely failing to provide *Miranda* warnings, *id.* at 637, and the "fruits" doctrine is a constitutional exclusionary requirement. *See* Oregon v. Elstad, 470 U.S. 298, 305 (1985).

However, the Fourteenth Amendment's Due Process clause is violated by coercive police activity resulting in a confession. Miller v. Fenton, 474 U.S. at 108 ("This Court has long held that certain interrogation techniques, either in isolation or as applied to the unique characteristics of a particular suspect, are so offensive to a civilized system of justice that they must be condemned under the Due Process Clause of the Fourteenth Amendment.") (citing

For example, in *California v. Ditson*, the Supreme Court of California opined:

> It appears to us to follow that if it offends "the community's sense of fair play and decency" to convict a defendant by evidence extorted from him in the form of an involuntary confession, that sense of fair play and decency is no less offended when a defendant is convicted by real evidence which the police have discovered essentially by virtue of having extorted such a confession. If the one amounts to a denial of a fair trial and due process of law, so must the other. If the one is the inadmissible product of 'police procedure which violates the basic notions of our accusatorial mode of prosecuting crime' (Watts v. Indiana (1949), *supra*, 338 U.S. 49), so must the other be. It does not appear that we can draw a constitutionally valid distinction between the two.

57 Cal.2d 415, 439, 20 Cal.Rptr. 165, 369 P.2d 714 (1962). We are persuaded by this analysis and now adopt it as law in Kentucky.

Apparently conceding that evidence seized under these circumstances must otherwise be suppressed, the Commonwealth argues that the evidence recovered pursuant to the February 6 search warrant is admissible under the "inevitable discovery" doctrine. *See* Nix v. Williams, 467 U.S. 431 (1991). In *Nix*, the U.S. Supreme Court held that evidence unlawfully obtained by police is nevertheless admissible "[i]f the prosecution can establish by a preponderance of the evidence that the information ultimately or inevitably would have been discovered by lawful means. . . ." *Id.* at 444. This "doctrine has been applied to the fruits of illegal searches as well as to the fruits of illegally obtained confessions." Hughes v. Commonwealth, 87 S.W.3d 850, 853 (Ky.2002) (citing United States v. Scott, 270 F.3d 30, 42 (1st Cir.2001); United States v. Kimes, 246 F.3d 800, 803–04 (6th Cir.2001); United States v. Ford, 184 F.3d 566, 577 (6th Cir.1999)).

We believe that whether the evidence seized pursuant to the February 6 search warrant would inevitably have been discovered is a question that should initially be addressed by the trial court after an appropriate hearing on the matter.

III. CONCLUSION

We conclude that Appellant's confession was involuntary under the Due Process Clause of the Fourteenth Amendment to the U.S. Constitution. We therefore reverse the judgment and sentence of the

---

Brown v. Mississippi, 297 U.S. 278 (1936)). Accordingly, extending the "fruits" doctrine to the factual scenario presented by this case is not inconsistent with the plurality opinion in *Patane*. We also note Justice Thomas authored the previously discussed plurality opinion in *Chavez*, which appears to approve of applying the "fruits" doctrine to cases like the one at bar. *See* footnotes 7 & 8, *supra*, and accompanying text.

Todd Circuit Court and remand to that court for further proceedings consistent with this opinion.

All sitting. All concur.

6. DUE PROCESS AND EYEWITNESS IDENTIFICATIONS

Perry v. New Hampshire
565 U.S. 228 (2012)

■ JUSTICE GINSBURG delivered the opinion of the Court.

In our system of justice, fair trial for persons charged with criminal offenses is secured by the Sixth Amendment, which guarantees to defendants the right to counsel, compulsory process to obtain defense witnesses, and the opportunity to cross-examine witnesses for the prosecution. Those safeguards apart, admission of evidence in state trials is ordinarily governed by state law, and the reliability of relevant testimony typically falls within the province of the jury to determine. This Court has recognized, in addition, a due process check on the admission of eyewitness identification, applicable when the police have arranged suggestive circumstances leading the witness to identify a particular person as the perpetrator of a crime.

An identification infected by improper police influence, our case law holds, is not automatically excluded. Instead, the trial judge must screen the evidence for reliability pretrial. If there is "a very substantial likelihood of irreparable misidentification," *Simmons v. United States,* 390 U.S. 377, 384 (1968), the judge must disallow presentation of the evidence at trial. But if the indicia of reliability are strong enough to outweigh the corrupting effect of the police-arranged suggestive circumstances, the identification evidence ordinarily will be admitted, and the jury will ultimately determine its worth.

We have not extended pretrial screening for reliability to cases in which the suggestive circumstances were not arranged by law enforcement officers. Petitioner requests that we do so because of the grave risk that mistaken identification will yield a miscarriage of justice.[1] Our decisions, however, turn on the presence of state action and aim to deter police from rigging identification procedures, for example, at a lineup, showup, or photograph array. When no improper law enforcement activity is involved, we hold, it suffices to test reliability through the

---

[1] The dissent, too, appears to urge that all suggestive circumstances raise due process concerns warranting a pretrial ruling. Neither Perry nor the dissent, however, points to a single case in which we have required pretrial screening absent a police-arranged identification procedure. Understandably so, for there are no such cases. Instead, the dissent surveys our decisions, heedless of the police arrangement that underlies every one of them, and inventing a "longstanding rule," that never existed. Nor are we, as the dissent suggests, imposing a *mens rea* requirement, or otherwise altering our precedent in any way. As our case law makes clear, what triggers due process concerns is police use of an unnecessarily suggestive identification procedure, whether or not they intended the arranged procedure to be suggestive.

rights and opportunities generally designed for that purpose, notably, the presence of counsel at postindictment lineups, vigorous cross-examination, protective rules of evidence, and jury instructions on both the fallibility of eyewitness identification and the requirement that guilt be proved beyond a reasonable doubt.

I

A

Around 3 a.m. on August 15, 2008, Joffre Ullon called the Nashua, New Hampshire, Police Department and reported that an African-American male was trying to break into cars parked in the lot of Ullon's apartment building. Officer Nicole Clay responded to the call. Upon arriving at the parking lot, Clay heard what "sounded like a metal bat hitting the ground.". She then saw petitioner Barion Perry standing between two cars. Perry walked toward Clay, holding two car-stereo amplifiers in his hands. A metal bat lay on the ground behind him. Clay asked Perry where the amplifiers came from. "[I] found them on the ground," Perry responded.

Meanwhile, Ullon's wife, Nubia Blandon, woke her neighbor, Alex Clavijo, and told him she had just seen someone break into his car. Clavijo immediately went downstairs to the parking lot to inspect the car. He first observed that one of the rear windows had been shattered. On further inspection, he discovered that the speakers and amplifiers from his car stereo were missing, as were his bat and wrench. Clavijo then approached Clay and told her about Blandon's alert and his own subsequent observations.

By this time, another officer had arrived at the scene. Clay asked Perry to stay in the parking lot with that officer, while she and Clavijo went to talk to Blandon. Clay and Clavijo then entered the apartment building and took the stairs to the fourth floor, where Blandon's and Clavijo's apartments were located. They met Blandon in the hallway just outside the open door to her apartment.

Asked to describe what she had seen, Blandon stated that, around 2:30 a.m., she saw from her kitchen window a tall, African-American man roaming the parking lot and looking into cars. Eventually, the man circled Clavijo's car, opened the trunk, and removed a large box.[2]

Clay asked Blandon for a more specific description of the man. Blandon pointed to her kitchen window and said the person she saw breaking into Clavijo's car was standing in the parking lot, next to the police officer. Perry's arrest followed this identification.

About a month later, the police showed Blandon a photographic array that included a picture of Perry and asked her to point out the man who had broken into Clavijo's car. Blandon was unable to identify Perry.

---

[2] The box, which Clay found on the ground near where she first encountered Perry, contained car-stereo speakers.

B

Perry was charged in New Hampshire state court with one count of theft by unauthorized taking and one count of criminal mischief. Before trial, he moved to suppress Blandon's identification on the ground that admitting it at trial would violate due process. Blandon witnessed what amounted to a one-person showup in the parking lot, Perry asserted, which all but guaranteed that she would identify him as the culprit.

The New Hampshire Superior Court denied the motion. To determine whether due process prohibits the introduction of an out-of-court identification at trial, the Superior Court said, this Court's decisions instruct a two-step inquiry. First, the trial court must decide whether the police used an unnecessarily suggestive identification procedure. If they did, the court must next consider whether the improper identification procedure so tainted the resulting identification as to render it unreliable and therefore inadmissible. *Ibid.* (citing *Neil v. Biggers,* 409 U.S. 188 (1972), and *Manson v. Brathwaite,* 432 U.S. 98 (1977)).

Perry's challenge, the Superior Court concluded, failed at step one: Blandon's identification of Perry on the night of the crime did not result from an unnecessarily suggestive procedure "manufacture[d] . . . by the police." Blandon pointed to Perry "spontaneously," the court noted, "without any inducement from the police." Clay did not ask Blandon whether the man standing in the parking lot was the man Blandon had seen breaking into Clavijo's car. Nor did Clay ask Blandon to move to the window from which she had observed the break-in.

The Superior Court recognized that there were reasons to question the accuracy of Blandon's identification: the parking lot was dark in some locations; Perry was standing next to a police officer; Perry was the only African-American man in the vicinity; and Blandon was unable, later, to pick Perry out of a photographic array. But "[b]ecause the police procedures were not unnecessarily suggestive," the court ruled that the reliability of Blandon's testimony was for the jury to consider.

At the ensuing trial, Blandon and Clay testified to Blandon's out-of-court identification. The jury found Perry guilty of theft and not guilty of criminal mischief.

On appeal, Perry repeated his challenge to the admissibility of Blandon's out-of-court identification. The trial court erred, Perry contended, in requiring an initial showing that the police arranged the suggestive identification procedure. Suggestive circumstances alone, Perry argued, suffice to trigger the court's duty to evaluate the reliability of the resulting identification before allowing presentation of the evidence to the jury.

The New Hampshire Supreme Court rejected Perry's argument and affirmed his conviction. Only where the police employ suggestive identification techniques, that court held, does the Due Process Clause require a trial court to assess the reliability of identification evidence before permitting a jury to consider it.

We granted certiorari to resolve a division of opinion on the question whether the Due Process Clause requires a trial judge to conduct a preliminary assessment of the reliability of an eyewitness identification made under suggestive circumstances not arranged by the police. 563 U.S. ___ (2011).[4]

II

A

The Constitution, our decisions indicate, protects a defendant against a conviction based on evidence of questionable reliability, not by prohibiting introduction of the evidence, but by affording the defendant means to persuade the jury that the evidence should be discounted as unworthy of credit. Constitutional safeguards available to defendants to counter the State's evidence include the Sixth Amendment rights to counsel, *Gideon v. Wainwright,* 372 U.S. 335, 343–345 (1963); compulsory process, *Taylor v. Illinois,* 484 U.S. 400, 408–409 (1988); and confrontation plus cross-examination of witnesses, *Delaware v. Fensterer,* 474 U.S. 15, 18–20 (1985) *(per curiam).* Apart from these guarantees, we have recognized, state and federal statutes and rules ordinarily govern the admissibility of evidence, and juries are assigned the task of determining the reliability of the evidence presented at trial. See *Kansas v. Ventris,* 556 U.S. 586, 594, n. (2009) ("Our legal system . . . is built on the premise that it is the province of the jury to weigh the credibility of competing witnesses."). Only when evidence "is so extremely unfair that its admission violates fundamental conceptions of justice," *Dowling v. United States,* 493 U.S. 342, 352 (1990) (internal quotation marks omitted), have we imposed a constraint tied to the Due Process Clause. See, *e.g., Napue v. Illinois,* 360 U.S. 264, 269 (1959) (Due process prohibits the State's "knowin[g] use [of] false evidence," because such use violates "any concept of ordered liberty.").

Contending that the Due Process Clause is implicated here, Perry relies on a series of decisions involving police-arranged identification procedures. In *Stovall v. Denno,* 388 U.S. 293 (1967), first of those decisions, a witness identified the defendant as her assailant after police

---

4 Compare *United States v. Bouthot,* 878 F.2d 1506, 1516 (C.A.1 1989) (Due process requires federal courts to "scrutinize all suggestive identification procedures, not just those orchestrated by the police."); *Dunnigan v. Keane,* 137 F.3d 117, 128 (C.A.2 1998) (same); *Thigpen v. Cory,* 804 F.2d 893, 895 (C.A.6 1986) (same), with *United States v. Kimberlin,* 805 F.2d 210, 233 (C.A.7 1986) (Due process check is required only in cases involving improper state action.); *United States v. Zeiler,* 470 F.2d 717, 720 (C.A.3 1972) (same); *State v. Addison,* 160 N.H. 792, 801, 8 A.3d 118, 125 (2010) (same); *State v. Reid,* 91 S.W.3d 247, 272 (Tenn.2002) (same); *State v. Nordstrom,* 200 Ariz. 229, 241, 25 P.3d 717, 729 (2001) (same); *Semple v. State,* 271 Ga. 416, 417–418, 519 S.E.2d 912, 914–915 (1999) (same); *Harris v. State,* 619 N.E.2d 577, 581 (Ind.1993) (same); *State v. Pailon,* 590 A.2d 858, 862–863 (R.I.1991) (same); *Commonwealth v. Colon-Cruz,* 408 Mass. 533, 541–542, 562 N.E.2d 797, 805 (1990) (same); *State v. Brown,* 38 Ohio St.3d 305, 310–311, 528 N.E.2d 523, 533 (1988) (same); *Wilson v. Commonwealth,* 695 S.W.2d 854, 857 (Ky.1985) (same).

officers brought the defendant to the witness' hospital room. *Id.,* at 295. At the time the witness made the identification, the defendant—the only African-American in the room—was handcuffed and surrounded by police officers. *Ibid.* Although the police-arranged showup was undeniably suggestive, the Court held that no due process violation occurred. *Id.,* at 302. Crucial to the Court's decision was the procedure's necessity: The witness was the only person who could identify or exonerate the defendant; the witness could not leave her hospital room; and it was uncertain whether she would live to identify the defendant in more neutral circumstances. *Ibid.*

A year later, in *Simmons v. United States,* 390 U.S. 377 (1968), the Court addressed a due process challenge to police use of a photographic array. When a witness identifies the defendant in a police-organized photo lineup, the Court ruled, the identification should be suppressed only where "the photographic identification procedure was so [unnecessarily] suggestive as to give rise to a very substantial likelihood of irreparable misidentification." *Id.,* at 384–385. Satisfied that the photo array used by Federal Bureau of Investigation agents in *Simmons* was both necessary and unlikely to have led to a mistaken identification, the Court rejected the defendant's due process challenge to admission of the identification. *Id.,* at 385–386. In contrast, the Court held in *Foster v. California,* 394 U.S. 440 (1969), that due process required the exclusion of an eyewitness identification obtained through police-arranged procedures that "made it all but inevitable that [the witness] would identify [the defendant]." *Id.,* at 443.

Synthesizing previous decisions, we set forth in *Neil v. Biggers,* 409 U.S. 188, 93 S.Ct. 375 (1972), and reiterated in *Manson v. Brathwaite,* 432 U.S. 98 (1977), the approach appropriately used to determine whether the Due Process Clause requires suppression of an eyewitness identification tainted by police arrangement. The Court emphasized, first, that due process concerns arise only when law enforcement officers use an identification procedure that is both suggestive and unnecessary. *Id.,* at 107, 109; *Biggers,* 409 U.S., at 198. Even when the police use such a procedure, the Court next said, suppression of the resulting identification is not the inevitable consequence. *Brathwaite,* 432 U.S., at 112–113; *Biggers,* 409 U.S., at 198–199.

A rule requiring automatic exclusion, the Court reasoned, would "g[o] too far," for it would "kee[p] evidence from the jury that is reliable and relevant," and "may result, on occasion, in the guilty going free." *Brathwaite,* 432 U.S., at 112; see *id.,* at 113 (when an "identification is reliable despite an unnecessarily suggestive [police] identification procedure," automatic exclusion "is a Draconian sanction," one "that may frustrate rather than promote justice").

Instead of mandating a *per se* exclusionary rule, the Court held that the Due Process Clause requires courts to assess, on a case-by-case basis, whether improper police conduct created a "substantial likelihood of misidentification." *Biggers,* 409 U.S., at 201; see *Brathwaite,* 432 U.S., at 116. "[R]eliability [of the eyewitness identification] is the linchpin" of that evaluation, the Court stated in *Brathwaite. Id.,* at 114. Where the "indicators of [a witness'] ability to make an accurate identification" are "outweighed by the corrupting effect" of law enforcement suggestion, the identification should be suppressed. *Id.,* at 114, 116. Otherwise, the evidence (if admissible in all other respects) should be submitted to the jury.[5]

Applying this "totality of the circumstances" approach, *id.,* at 110, the Court held in *Biggers* that law enforcement's use of an unnecessarily suggestive showup did not require suppression of the victim's identification of her assailant. 409 U.S., at 199–200. Notwithstanding the improper procedure, the victim's identification was reliable: She saw her assailant for a considerable period of time under adequate light, provided police with a detailed description of her attacker long before the showup, and had "no doubt" that the defendant was the person she had seen. *Id.,* at 200 (internal quotation marks omitted). Similarly, the Court concluded in *Brathwaite* that police use of an unnecessarily suggestive photo array did not require exclusion of the resulting identification. 432 U.S., at 114–117. The witness, an undercover police officer, viewed the defendant in good light for several minutes, provided a thorough description of the suspect, and was certain of his identification. *Id.,* at 115. Hence, the "indicators of [the witness'] ability to make an accurate identification [were] hardly outweighed by the corrupting effect of the challenged identification." *Id.,* at 116.

B

Perry concedes that, in contrast to every case in the *Stovall* line, law enforcement officials did not arrange the suggestive circumstances surrounding Blandon's identification. He contends, however, that it was mere happenstance that each of the *Stovall* cases involved improper police action. The rationale underlying our decisions, Perry asserts, supports a rule requiring trial judges to prescreen eyewitness evidence for reliability any time an identification is made under suggestive circumstances. We disagree.

Perry's argument depends, in large part, on the Court's statement in *Brathwaite* that "reliability is the linchpin in determining the admissibility of identification testimony." 432 U.S., at 114. If reliability is the linchpin of admissibility under the Due Process Clause, Perry maintains, it should make no difference whether law enforcement was

---

[5] Among "factors to be considered" in evaluating a witness' "ability to make an accurate identification," the Court listed: "the opportunity of the witness to view the criminal at the time of the crime, the witness' degree of attention, the accuracy of his prior description of the criminal, the level of certainty demonstrated at the confrontation, and the time between the crime and the confrontation." *Manson v. Brathwaite,* 432 U.S. 98 (1977) (citing *Neil v. Biggers,* 409 U.S. 188, 199–200 (1972)).

responsible for creating the suggestive circumstances that marred the identification.

Perry has removed our statement in *Brathwaite* from its mooring, and thereby attributes to the statement a meaning a fair reading of our opinion does not bear. As just explained, the *Brathwaite* Court's reference to reliability appears in a portion of the opinion concerning the appropriate remedy *when the police use an unnecessarily suggestive identification procedure.* The Court adopted a judicial screen for reliability as a course preferable to a *per se* rule requiring exclusion of identification evidence whenever law enforcement officers employ an improper procedure. The due process check for reliability, *Brathwaite* made plain, comes into play only after the defendant establishes improper police conduct. The very purpose of the check, the Court noted, was to avoid depriving the jury of identification evidence that is reliable, *notwithstanding* improper police conduct. 432 U.S., at 112–113.

Perry's contention that improper police action was not essential to the reliability check *Brathwaite* required is echoed by the dissent. Both ignore a key premise of the *Brathwaite* decision: A primary aim of excluding identification evidence obtained under unnecessarily suggestive circumstances, the Court said, is to deter law enforcement use of improper lineups, showups, and photo arrays in the first place. See 432 U.S., at 112. Alerted to the prospect that identification evidence improperly obtained may be excluded, the Court reasoned, police officers will "guard against unnecessarily suggestive procedures." *Ibid.* This deterrence rationale is inapposite in cases, like Perry's, in which the police engaged in no improper conduct.

Coleman v. Alabama, 399 U.S. 1 (1970), another decision in the *Stovall* line, similarly shows that the Court has linked the due process check, not to suspicion of eyewitness testimony generally, but only to improper police arrangement of the circumstances surrounding an identification. The defendants in *Coleman* contended that a witness' in-court identifications violated due process, because a pretrial stationhouse lineup was "so unduly prejudicial and conducive to irreparable misidentification as fatally to taint [the later identifications]." 399 U.S., at 3 (plurality opinion). The Court rejected this argument. *Id.,* at 5–6 (plurality opinion), 13–14 (Black, J., concurring), 22, n. 2 (Burger, C. J., dissenting), 28, n. 2, (Stewart, J., dissenting). No due process violation occurred, the plurality explained, because nothing "the police said or did prompted [the witness'] virtually spontaneous identification of [the defendants]." *Id.,* at 6. True, Coleman was the only person in the lineup wearing a hat, the plurality noted, but "nothing in the record show[ed] that he was required to do so." *Ibid.* See also *Colorado v. Connelly,* 479 U.S. 157, 163, 167 (1986) (Where the "crucial element of police overreaching" is missing, the admissibility of an allegedly unreliable confession is "a matter to be governed by the evidentiary laws of the forum, . . . and not by the Due Process Clause.").

Perry and the dissent place significant weight on *United States v. Wade,* 388 U.S. 218 (1967), describing it as a decision not anchored to improper police conduct. In fact, the risk of police rigging was the very danger to which the Court responded in *Wade* when it recognized a defendant's right to counsel at postindictment, police-organized identification procedures. 388 U.S., at 233, 235–236. "[T]he confrontation *compelled by the State* between the accused and the victim or witnesses," the Court began, "is peculiarly riddled with innumerable dangers and variable factors which might seriously, even crucially, derogate from a fair trial." *Id.,* at 228 (emphasis added). "A major factor contributing to the high incidence of miscarriage of justice from mistaken identification," the Court continued, "has been the degree of suggestion inherent in the manner in which *the prosecution* presents the suspect to witnesses for pretrial identification." *Ibid.* (emphasis added). To illustrate the improper suggestion it was concerned about, the Court pointed to police-designed lineups where "all in the lineup but the suspect were known to the identifying witness, . . . the other participants in [the] lineup were grossly dissimilar in appearance to the suspect, . . . only the suspect was required to wear distinctive clothing which the culprit allegedly wore, . . . the witness is told by the police that they have caught the culprit after which the defendant is brought before the witness alone or is viewed in jail, . . . the suspect is pointed out before or during a lineup, . . . the participants in the lineup are asked to try on an article of clothing which fits only the suspect." *Id.,* at 233 (footnotes omitted). Beyond genuine debate, then, prevention of unfair police practices prompted the Court to extend a defendant's right to counsel to cover postindictment lineups and showups. *Id.,* at 235.

Perry's argument, reiterated by the dissent, thus lacks support in the case law he cites. Moreover, his position would open the door to judicial preview, under the banner of due process, of most, if not all, eyewitness identifications. External suggestion is hardly the only factor that casts doubt on the trustworthiness of an eyewitness' testimony. As one of Perry's *amici* points out, many other factors bear on "the likelihood of misidentification,"—for example, the passage of time between exposure to and identification of the defendant, whether the witness was under stress when he first encountered the suspect, how much time the witness had to observe the suspect, how far the witness was from the suspect, whether the suspect carried a weapon, and the race of the suspect and the witness. Brief for American Psychological Association as *Amicus Curiae* 9–12. There is no reason why an identification made by an eyewitness with poor vision, for example, or one who harbors a grudge against the defendant, should be regarded as inherently more reliable, less of a "threat to the fairness of trial," than the identification Blandon made in this case. To embrace Perry's view would thus entail a vast enlargement of the reach of due process as a constraint on the admission of evidence.

Perry maintains that the Court can limit the due process check he proposes to identifications made under "suggestive circumstances." Tr. of Oral Arg. 11–14. Even if we could rationally distinguish suggestiveness from other factors bearing on the reliability of eyewitness evidence, Perry's limitation would still involve trial courts, routinely, in preliminary examinations. Most eyewitness identifications involve some element of suggestion. Indeed, all in-court identifications do. Out-of-court identifications volunteered by witnesses are also likely to involve suggestive circumstances. For example, suppose a witness identifies the defendant to police officers after seeing a photograph of the defendant in the press captioned "theft suspect," or hearing a radio report implicating the defendant in the crime. Or suppose the witness knew that the defendant ran with the wrong crowd and saw him on the day and in the vicinity of the crime. Any of these circumstances might have "suggested" to the witness that the defendant was the person the witness observed committing the crime.

C

In urging a broadly applicable due process check on eyewitness identifications, Perry maintains that eyewitness identifications are a uniquely unreliable form of evidence. See Brief for Petitioner 17–22 (citing studies showing that eyewitness misidentifications are the leading cause of wrongful convictions); Brief for American Psychological Association as *Amicus Curiae* 14–17 (describing research indicating that as many as one in three eyewitness identifications is inaccurate). We do not doubt either the importance or the fallibility of eyewitness identifications. Indeed, in recognizing that defendants have a constitutional right to counsel at postindictment police lineups, we observed that "the annals of criminal law are rife with instances of mistaken identification." *Wade,* 388 U.S., at 228.

We have concluded in other contexts, however, that the potential unreliability of a type of evidence does not alone render its introduction at the defendant's trial fundamentally unfair. See, *e.g., Ventris,* 556 U.S., at 594, n. *(declining to "craft a broa[d] exclusionary rule for uncorroborated statements obtained [from jailhouse snitches]," even though "rewarded informant testimony" may be inherently untrustworthy); *Dowling,* 493 U.S., at 353 (rejecting argument that the introduction of evidence concerning acquitted conduct is fundamentally unfair because such evidence is "inherently unreliable"). We reach a similar conclusion here: The fallibility of eyewitness evidence does not, without the taint of improper state conduct, warrant a due process rule requiring a trial court to screen such evidence for reliability before allowing the jury to assess its creditworthiness.

Our unwillingness to enlarge the domain of due process as Perry and the dissent urge rests, in large part, on our recognition that the jury, not the judge, traditionally determines the reliability of evidence. We also take account of other safeguards built into our adversary system that caution juries against placing undue weight on eyewitness testimony of questionable reliability. These protections include the defendant's Sixth Amendment right to confront the eyewitness. See *Maryland v. Craig*, 497 U.S. 836, 845 (1990) ("The central concern of the Confrontation Clause is to ensure the reliability of the evidence against a criminal defendant."). Another is the defendant's right to the effective assistance of an attorney, who can expose the flaws in the eyewitness' testimony during cross-examination and focus the jury's attention on the fallibility of such testimony during opening and closing arguments. Eyewitness-specific jury instructions, which many federal and state courts have adopted, likewise warn the jury to take care in appraising identification evidence. See, *e.g.*, *United States v. Telfaire*, 469 F.2d 552, 558–559 (C.A.D.C.1972) *(per curiam)* (D.C. Circuit Model Jury Instructions) ("If the identification by the witness may have been influenced by the circumstances under which the defendant was presented to him for identification, you should scrutinize the identification with great care."). See also *Ventris*, 556 U.S., at 594, n. *(citing jury instructions that informed jurors about the unreliability of uncorroborated jailhouse-informant testimony as a reason to resist a ban on such testimony); *Dowling*, 493 U.S., at 352–353. The constitutional requirement that the government prove the defendant's guilt beyond a reasonable doubt also impedes convictions based on dubious identification evidence.

State and federal rules of evidence, moreover, permit trial judges to exclude relevant evidence if its probative value is substantially outweighed by its prejudicial impact or potential for misleading the jury. See, *e.g.*, Fed. Rule Evid. 403; N.H. Rule Evid. 403 (2011). See also Tr. of Oral Arg. 19–22 (inquiring whether the standard Perry seeks differs materially from the one set out in Rule 403). In appropriate cases, some States also permit defendants to present expert testimony on the hazards of eyewitness identification evidence. See, *e.g.*, *State v. Clopten*, 2009 UT 84, A33, 223 P.3d 1103, 1113 ("We expect . . . that in cases involving eyewitness identification of strangers or near-strangers, trial courts will routinely admit expert testimony [on the dangers of such evidence].").

Many of the safeguards just noted were at work at Perry's trial. During her opening statement, Perry's court-appointed attorney cautioned the jury about the vulnerability of Blandon's identification. App. 115a (Blandon, "the eyewitness that the State needs you to believe[,] can't pick [Perry] out of a photo array. How carefully did she really see what was going on? . . . How well could she really see him?"). While cross-examining Blandon and Officer Clay, Perry's attorney constantly brought up the weaknesses of Blandon's identification. She highlighted: (1) the significant distance between Blandon's window and the parking lot, *id.*, at 226a; (2) the lateness of the hour, *id.*, at 225a; (3) the van that partly obstructed Blandon's view, *id.*, at 226a; (4) Blandon's concession that she was "so scared [she] really didn't pay attention" to what Perry was wearing, *id.*, at 233a; (5) Blandon's inability to describe Perry's facial features or other identifying marks, *id.,* at 205a, 233a–235a; (6) Blandon's failure to pick Perry out of a photo array, *id.,* at 235a; and (7) Perry's position next to a uniformed, gun-bearing police officer at the moment Blandon made her identification, *id.,* at 202a–205a. Perry's counsel reminded the jury of these frailties during her summation. *Id.,* at 374a–375a (Blandon "wasn't able to tell you much about who she saw. . . . She couldn't pick [Perry] out of a lineup, out of a photo array. . . . [Blandon said] [t]hat guy that was with the police officer, that's who was circling. Again, think about the context with the guns, the uniforms. Powerful, powerful context clues.").

After closing arguments, the trial court read the jury a lengthy instruction on identification testimony and the factors the jury should consider when evaluating it. The court also instructed the jury that the defendant's guilt must be proved beyond a reasonable doubt, and specifically cautioned that "one of the things the State must prove [beyond a reasonable doubt] is the identification of the defendant as the person who committed the offense,".

Given the safeguards generally applicable in criminal trials, protections availed of by the defense in Perry's case, we hold that the introduction of Blandon's eyewitness testimony, without a preliminary judicial assessment of its reliability, did not render Perry's trial fundamentally unfair.

* * *

For the foregoing reasons, we agree with the New Hampshire courts' appraisal of our decisions. Finding no convincing reason to alter our precedent, we hold that the Due Process Clause does not require a preliminary judicial inquiry into the reliability of an eyewitness identification when the identification was not procured under unnecessarily suggestive circumstances arranged by law enforcement. Accordingly, the judgment of the New Hampshire Supreme Court is

Affirmed.

■ JUSTICE THOMAS, concurring.

The Court correctly concludes that its precedents establish a due process right to the pretrial exclusion of an unreliable eyewitness identification only if the identification results from police suggestion. I therefore join its opinion. I write separately because I would not extend *Stovall v. Denno,* 388 U.S. 293, (1967), and its progeny even if the reasoning of those opinions applied to this case. The *Stovall* line of cases is premised on a "substantive due process" right to "fundamental fairness." . . . In my view, those cases are wrongly decided because the Fourteenth Amendment's Due Process Clause is not a "secret repository of substantive guarantees against 'unfairness.' " *BMW of North America, Inc. v. Gore,* 517 U.S. 559, 598–599, 116 S.Ct. 1589, 134 L.Ed.2d 809 (1996) (SCALIA, J., joined by THOMAS, J., dissenting); see also *McDonald v. Chicago,* 561 U.S. ___, ___, 130 S.Ct. 3020, 3062, 177

L.Ed.2d 894 (2010) (THOMAS, J., concurring in part and concurring in judgment) ("The notion that a constitutional provision that guarantees only 'process' before a person is deprived of life, liberty, or property could define the substance of those rights strains credulity"). Accordingly, I would limit the Court's suggestive eyewitness identification cases to the precise circumstances that they involved.

■ JUSTICE SOTOMAYOR, dissenting.

This Court has long recognized that eyewitness identifications' unique confluence of features—their unreliability, susceptibility to suggestion, powerful impact on the jury, and resistance to the ordinary tests of the adversarial process—can undermine the fairness of a trial. Our cases thus establish a clear rule: The admission at trial of out-of-court eyewitness identifications derived from impermissibly suggestive circumstances that pose a very substantial likelihood of misidentification violates due process. The Court today announces that that rule does not even "com[e] into play" unless the suggestive circumstances are improperly "police-arranged."

Our due process concern, however, arises not from the act of suggestion, but rather from the corrosive effects of suggestion on the reliability of the resulting identification. By rendering protection contingent on improper police arrangement of the suggestive circumstances, the Court effectively grafts a *mens rea* inquiry onto our rule. The Court's holding enshrines a murky distinction—between suggestive confrontations intentionally orchestrated by the police and, as here, those inadvertently caused by police actions—that will sow confusion. It ignores our precedents' acute sensitivity to the hazards of intentional and unintentional suggestion alike and unmoors our rule from the very interest it protects, inviting arbitrary results. And it recasts the driving force of our decisions as an interest in police deterrence, rather than reliability. Because I see no warrant for declining to assess the circumstances of this case under our ordinary approach, I respectfully dissent.[1]

I

The "driving force" behind *United States v. Wade,* 388 U.S. 218 (1967), *Gilbert v. California,* 388 U.S. 263 (1967), and *Stovall v. Denno,* 388 U.S. 293 (1967), was "the Court's concern with the problems of eyewitness identification"—specifically, "the concern that the jury not hear eyewitness testimony unless that evidence has aspects of reliability." *Manson v. Brathwaite,* 432 U.S. 98, 111–112. We have pointed to the " 'formidable' " number of "miscarriage[s] of justice from mistaken identification" in the annals of criminal law. *Wade,* 388 U.S., at 228. We have warned of the "vagaries" and " 'proverbially untrustworthy' " nature of eyewitness identifications. *Ibid.* And we have

---

[1] Because the facts of this case involve police action, I do not reach the question whether due process is triggered in situations involving no police action whatsoever.

singled out a "major factor contributing" to that proverbial unreliability: "the suggestibility inherent in the context of the pretrial identification." *Id.*, at 228.

Our precedents make no distinction between intentional and unintentional suggestion. To the contrary, they explicitly state that "[s]uggestion can be created intentionally or unintentionally in many subtle ways." *Id.*, at 229. Rather than equate suggestive conduct with misconduct, we specifically have disavowed the assumption that suggestive influences may only be "the result of police procedures intentionally designed to prejudice an accused." *Id.*, at 235; see also *id.*, at 236 (noting "grave potential for prejudice, intentional or not, in the pretrial lineup"); *id.*, at 239 (describing lack of lineup regulations addressing "risks of abuse and unintentional suggestion"). "Persons who conduct the identification procedure may suggest, intentionally or unintentionally, that they expect the witness to identify the accused." *Moore v. Illinois,* 434 U.S. 220, 224 (1977). The implication is that even police acting with the best of intentions can inadvertently signal " 'that's the man.' " *Wade,* 388 U.S., at 236; see also *Kirby v. Illinois,* 406 U.S. 682, 690–691 (1972) ("[I]t is always necessary to 'scrutinize *any* pretrial confrontation . . .' ").[2]

In *Wade* itself, we noted that the "potential for improper influence [in pretrial confrontations] is illustrated by the circumstances . . . [i]n the present case." 388 U.S., at 233–234. We then highlighted not the lineup procedure, but rather a preprocedure encounter: The two witnesses who later identified Wade in the lineup had seen Wade outside while "await[ing] assembly of the lineup." *Id.*, at 234. Wade had been standing in the hallway, which happened to be "observable to the witnesses through an open door." *Ibid.* One witness saw Wade "within sight of an FBI agent"; the other saw him "in the custody of the agent." *Ibid.* In underscoring the hazards of these circumstances, we made no mention of whether the encounter had been arranged; indeed, the facts suggest that it was not.

More generally, our precedents focus not on the act of suggestion, but on suggestion's "corrupting effect" on reliability. *Brathwaite,* 432 U.S., at 114. Eyewitness evidence derived from suggestive circumstances, we have explained, is uniquely resistant to the ordinary tests of the adversary process. An eyewitness who has made an identification often becomes convinced of its accuracy. "*Regardless of how the initial misidentification comes about,* the witness thereafter is apt to

---

[2]   *Wade* held that the dangers of pretrial identification procedures necessitated a right to counsel; that same day, *Stovall* held that a defendant ineligible for the *Wade* rule was still entitled to challenge the confrontation as a due process violation. Because the two were companion cases advancing interrelated rules to avoid unfairness at trial resulting from suggestive pretrial confrontations, *Wade*'s exposition of the dangers of suggestiveness informs both contexts. See *Manson v. Brathwaite,* 432 U.S. 98, 112 (1977) ("*Wade* and its companion cases reflect the concern that the jury not hear eyewitness testimony unless that evidence has aspects of reliability").

retain in his memory the image of the photograph rather than of the person actually seen, reducing the trustworthiness of subsequent . . . courtroom identification." *Simmons v. United States,* 390 U.S. 377, 383–384 (1968) (emphasis added); see also *Wade,* 388 U.S., at 229 (witness is "not likely" to recant). Suggestion bolsters that confidence.

At trial, an eyewitness' artificially inflated confidence in an identification's accuracy complicates the jury's task of assessing witness credibility and reliability. It also impairs the defendant's ability to attack the eyewitness' credibility. *Stovall,* 388 U.S., at 298. That in turn jeopardizes the defendant's basic right to subject his accuser to meaningful cross-examination. See *Wade,* 388 U.S., at 235, 87 S.Ct. 1926 ("[C]ross-examination . . . cannot be viewed as an absolute assurance of accuracy and reliability . . . where so many variables and pitfalls exist"). The end result of suggestion, whether intentional or unintentional, is to fortify testimony bearing directly on guilt that juries find extremely convincing and are hesitant to discredit. See *id.,* at 224 ("[A]t pretrial proceedings . . . the results might well settle the accused's fate and reduce the trial itself to a mere formality"); *Gilbert,* 388 U.S., at 273 ("[T]he witness' testimony of his lineup identification will enhance the impact of his in-court identification on the jury").

Consistent with our focus on reliability, we have declined to adopt a *per se* rule excluding all suggestive identifications. Instead, "reliability is the linchpin" in deciding admissibility. *Brathwaite,* 432 U.S., at 114. We have explained that a suggestive identification procedure "does not in itself intrude upon a constitutionally protected interest." *Id.,* at 113, n. 13; see also *Neil v. Biggers,* 409 U.S. 188, 198–199 (1972) (rejecting the proposition that "unnecessary suggestiveness alone requires the exclusion of evidence"). "Suggestive confrontations are disapproved because they increase the likelihood of misidentification"—and "[i]t is the likelihood of misidentification which violates a defendant's right to due process." *Id.,* at 198; see also *United States ex rel. Kirby v. Sturges,* 510 F.2d 397, 406 (C.A.7 1975) (Stevens, J.) ("The due process clause applies only to proceedings which result in a deprivation of life, liberty or property. . . . [I]f a constitutional violation results from a showup, it occurs in the courtroom, not in the police station"). In short, " 'what the *Stovall* due process right protects is an evidentiary interest.' " *Brathwaite,* 432 U.S., at 113, n. 14.

To protect that evidentiary interest, we have applied a two-step inquiry: First, the defendant has the burden of showing that the eyewitness identification was derived through "impermissibly suggestive" means.[3] *Simmons,* 390 U.S. at 384. second, if the defendant

---

[3] Our precedents refer to "impermissibly," "unnecessarily," and "unduly" suggestive circumstances interchangeably. See, *e.g., Brathwaite,* 432 U.S., at 105, n. 8, 107–108, 110, 112–113 ("impermissibly" and "unnecessarily"); *Neil v. Biggers,* 409 U.S. 188, 196–199 (1972) ("impermissibly" and "unnecessarily"); *Coleman v. Alabama,* 399 U.S. 1, 3–5 (1970) ("unduly" and "impermissibly"); *Simmons v. United States,* 390 U.S. 377, 383–384 (1968) ("unduly" and "impermissibly"). The Circuits have followed suit. *E.g., Thigpen v. Cory,* 804 F.2d 893, 895 (C.A.6

meets that burden, courts consider whether the identification was reliable under the totality of the circumstances. That step entails considering the witness' opportunity to view the perpetrator, degree of attention, accuracy of description, level of certainty, and the time between the crime and pretrial confrontation, then weighing such factors against the "corrupting effect of the suggestive identification." *Brathwaite*, 432 U.S., at 108. Most identifications will be admissible. The standard of "fairness as required by the Due Process Clause," *id.*, at 113, however, demands that a subset of the most unreliable identifications—those carrying a " 'very substantial likelihood of . . . misidentification' "—will be excluded. *Biggers*, 409 U.S., at 198.

II

A

The majority today creates a novel and significant limitation on our longstanding rule: Eyewitness identifications so impermissibly suggestive that they pose a very substantial likelihood of an unreliable identification will be deemed inadmissible at trial *only* if the suggestive circumstances were "police-arranged.". Absent "improper police arrangement," "improper police conduct," or "rigging," the majority holds, our two-step inquiry does not even "com[e] into play." I cannot agree.

The majority does not simply hold that an eyewitness identification must be the product of police action to trigger our ordinary two-step inquiry. Rather, the majority maintains that the suggestive circumstances giving rise to the identification must be "police-arranged," "police rigg[ed]," "police-designed," or "police-organized." Those terms connote a degree of intentional orchestration or manipulation. See Brief for Respondent 19 (no indication that police "deliberately tried to manipulate any evidence"); Brief for United States as *Amicus Curiae* 18 ("[N]o one deliberately arranged the circumstances to obtain an identification"). The majority categorically exempts all eyewitness identifications derived from suggestive circumstances that were not police-manipulated—however suggestive, and however unreliable—from our due process check. The majority thus appears to graft a *mens rea* requirement onto our existing rule.[4]

As this case illustrates, police intent is now paramount. As the Court acknowledges, Perry alleges an "*accidental* showup." Brief for Petitioner

---

1986) ("unduly"); *Green v. Loggins,* 614 F.2d 219, 223 (C.A.9 1980) ("unnecessarily or impermissibly"). All reinforce our focus not on the act of suggestion, but on whether the suggestiveness rises to such a level that it undermines reliability. Police machinations can heighten the likelihood of misidentification, but they are no prerequisite to finding a confrontation "so impermissibly suggestive as to give rise to a very substantial likelihood of . . . misidentification." *Simmons,* 390 U.S., at 384.

   4   The majority denies that it has imposed a *mens rea* requirement, see *ante,* at n. 1, but by confining our due process concerns to police-arranged identification procedures, that is just what it has done. The majority acknowledges that "whether or not [the police] intended the arranged procedure to be suggestive" is irrelevant under our precedents, *ibid.,* but still places dispositive weight on whether or not the police intended the procedure itself.

34 (emphasis added). He was the only African-American at the scene of the crime standing next to a police officer. For the majority, the fact that the police did not intend that showup, even if they inadvertently caused it in the course of a police procedure, ends the inquiry. The police were questioning the eyewitness, Blandon, about the perpetrator's identity, and were intentionally detaining Perry in the parking lot—but had not intended for Blandon to identify the perpetrator from her window. Presumably, in the majority's view, had the police asked Blandon to move to the window to identify the perpetrator, that could have made all the difference.

I note, however, that the majority leaves what is required by its arrangement-focused inquiry less than clear. In parts, the opinion suggests that the police must arrange an identification "procedure," regardless of whether they "inten[d] the arranged procedure to be suggestive." Elsewhere, it indicates that the police must arrange the "suggestive circumstances" that lead the witness to identify the accused. Still elsewhere it refers to "improper" police conduct, connoting bad faith. Does police "arrangement" relate to the procedure, the suggestiveness, or both? If it relates to the procedure, do suggestive preprocedure encounters no longer raise the same concerns? If the police need not "inten[d] the arranged procedure to be suggestive," *ante,* at n. 1, what makes the police action "improper"? And does that mean that good-faith, unintentional police suggestiveness in a police-arranged lineup can be "impermissibly suggestive"? If no, the majority runs headlong into *Wade.* If yes, on what basis—if not deterrence—does it distinguish unintentional police suggestiveness in an accidental confrontation?

The arrangement-focused inquiry will sow needless confusion. If the police had called Perry and Blandon to the police station for interviews, and Blandon saw Perry being questioned, would that be sufficiently "improper police arrangement"? If Perry had voluntarily come to the police station, would that change the result? Today's opinion renders the applicability of our ordinary inquiry contingent on a murky line-drawing exercise. Whereas our two-step inquiry focuses on overall reliability— and could account for the spontaneity of the witness' identification and degree of police manipulation under the totality of the circumstances— today's opinion forecloses that assessment by establishing a new and inflexible step zero.

B

The majority regards its limitation on our two-step rule as compelled by precedent. Its chief rationale is that none of our prior cases involved situations where the police "did not arrange the suggestive circumstances." That is not necessarily true, given the seemingly unintentional encounter highlighted in *Wade.* But even if it were true, it is unsurprising. The vast majority of eyewitness identifications that the State uses in criminal prosecutions are obtained in lineup, showup, and photograph displays arranged by the police. Our precedents reflect that practical reality.

It is also beside the point. Our due process concerns were not predicated on the source of suggestiveness. Rather, "[i]t is the likelihood of misidentification which violates a defendant's right to due process," *Biggers,* 409 U.S., at 198, and we are concerned with suggestion insofar as it has "corrupting effect[s]" on the identification's reliability. *Brathwaite,* 432 U.S., at 114. Accordingly, whether the police have created the suggestive circumstances intentionally or inadvertently, the resulting identification raises the same due process concerns. It is no more or less likely to misidentify the perpetrator. It is no more or less powerful to the jury. And the defendant is no more or less equipped to challenge the identification through cross-examination or prejudiced at trial. The arrangement-focused inquiry thus untethers our doctrine from the very " 'evidentiary interest' " it was designed to protect, inviting arbitrary results. *Id.,* at 113, n. 14.

Indeed, it is the majority's approach that lies in tension with our precedents. Whereas we previously disclaimed the crabbed view of suggestiveness as "the result of police procedures intentionally designed to prejudice an accused," *Wade,* 388 U.S., at 235, the majority's focus on police rigging and improper conduct will revive it. Whereas our precedents were sensitive to intentional and unintentional suggestiveness alike, today's decision narrows our concern to intentionally orchestrated suggestive confrontations. We once described the "primary evil to be avoided" as the likelihood of misidentification. *Biggers,* 409 U.S., at 198. Today's decision, however, means that even if that primary evil is at its apex, we need not avoid it at all so long as the suggestive circumstances do not stem from improper police arrangement.

C

The majority gives several additional reasons for why applying our due process rule beyond improperly police-arranged circumstances is unwarranted. In my view, none withstands close inspection.

First, the majority insists that our precedents "aim to deter police from rigging identification procedures," so our rule should be limited to applications that advance that "primary aim" and "key premise." That mischaracterizes our cases. We discussed deterrence in *Brathwaite* because Brathwaite challenged our two-step inquiry as *lacking* deterrence value. Brathwaite argued that deterrence demanded a *per se* rule excluding all suggestive identifications. He said that our rule, which probes the reliability of suggestive identifications under the totality of the circumstances, "cannot be expected to have a significant deterrent impact." *Id.,* at 111.

We rebutted Brathwaite's criticism in language the majority now wrenches from context: Upon summarizing Brathwaite's argument, we acknowledged "several interests to be considered." *Ibid.* We then compared the two rules under each interest: First, we noted the "driving force" behind *Wade* and its companion cases—"the concern that the jury not hear eyewitness testimony unless that evidence has aspects of reliability"—and found both approaches "responsive to this concern," but the *per se* rule to go "too far" in suppressing reliable evidence. 432 U.S., at 111–112. We noted a "second factor"—deterrence—conceding that the *per se* rule had "more significant deterrent effect," but noting that our rule "also has an influence on police behavior." *Id.,* at 112. Finally, we noted a "third factor"—"the effect on the administration of justice"— describing the *per se* rule as having serious drawbacks on this front. *Ibid.* That was no list of "primary aim[s]." Nor was it a ringing endorsement of the primacy of deterrence. We simply underscored, in responding to Brathwaite, that our rule was not without deterrence benefits. To the contrary, we clarified that deterrence was a subsidiary concern to reliability, the "driving force" of our doctrine. It is a stretch to claim that our rule cannot apply wherever "[t]his deterrence rationale is inapposite."

Second, the majority states that *Coleman v. Alabama,* 399 U.S. 1 (1970), held that "[n]o due process violation occurred . . . because nothing 'the police said or did prompted' " the identification and shows that our rule is linked "only to improper police arrangement." That misreads the decision. In *Coleman,* the petitioners challenged a witness' in-court identification of them at trial on grounds that it had been tainted by a suggestive pretrial lineup. We held that no due process violation occurred because the in-court identification appeared to be "entirely based upon observations at the time of the assault and not at all induced by the conduct of the lineup," and thus could not be said to stem from an identification procedure " 'so impermissibly suggestive as to give rise to a very substantial likelihood of irreparable misidentification.' " 399 U.S., at 5–6 (plurality opinion). We then dismissed each of the asserted suggestive influences as having had no bearing on the identification at all: The petitioners claimed that the police intimated to the witness that his attackers were in the lineup; we found the record "devoid of evidence that anything the police said or did" induced the identification. *Id.,* at 6. The petitioners claimed that they alone were made to say certain words; we found that the witness identified petitioners before either said anything. One petitioner claimed he was singled out to wear a hat; we found that the witness' identification "d[id] not appear . . . based on the fact that he remembered that [the attacker] had worn a hat." *Ibid.* Thus, far from indicating that improper police conduct is a prerequisite, *Coleman* merely held that there had been no influence on the witness. In fact, in concluding that the lineup was not " 'so impermissibly suggestive as to give rise to a very substantial likelihood of irreparable misidentification,' " *Coleman* indicates that the two-step inquiry is not truncated at the threshold by the absence of police misconduct.

Third, the majority emphasizes that we should rely on the jury to determine the reliability of evidence. But our cases are rooted in the assumption that eyewitness identifications upend the ordinary expectation that it is "the province of the jury to weigh the credibility of competing witnesses." *Kansas v. Ventris,* 556 U.S. 586, 594, n. *8 (2009). As noted, jurors find eyewitness evidence unusually powerful and their ability to assess credibility is hindered by a witness' false confidence in the accuracy of his or her identification. That disability in no way depends on the intent behind the suggestive circumstances.

The majority's appeals to protecting the jury's domain, moreover, appeared in dissent after dissent from our decisions. See *Foster v. California,* 394 U.S. 440, 447 (1969) (Black, J., dissenting) ("[T]he jury is the sole tribunal to weigh and determine facts" and "must . . . be allowed to hear eyewitnesses and decide for itself whether it can recognize the truth"); *Simmons,* 390 U.S., at 395 (Black, J., concurring in part and dissenting in part) ("The weight of the evidence . . . is not a question for the Court but for the jury"). So too does the majority's assurance that other constitutional protections like the Sixth Amendment rights to compulsory process and confrontation can suffice to expose unreliable identifications. Compare *Foster,* 394 U.S., at 448–449 (Black, J., dissenting) ("The Constitution sets up its own standards of unfairness in criminal trials," including the Sixth Amendment "right to compulsory process" and "right to confront . . . witnesses"). So too does the majority's appeal to leave reliability to the rules of evidence. Compare *Foster,* 394 U.S., at 448 (Black, J., dissenting) (" 'Rules of evidence are designed in the interests of fair trials' "), and *Stovall,* 388 U.S., at 306 (Black, J., dissenting) ("[T]he result . . . is to put into a constitutional mould a rule of evidence"). Those arguments did not prevail then; they should not prevail here.

Fourth, the majority suggests that applying our rule beyond police-arranged suggestive circumstances would entail a heavy practical burden, requiring courts to engage in "preliminary judicial inquiry" into "most, if not all, eyewitness identifications." But that is inaccurate. The burden of showing "impermissibly suggestive" circumstances is the defendant's, so the objection falls to the defendant to raise. And as is implicit in the majority's reassurance that Perry may resort to the rules of evidence in lieu of our due process precedents, trial courts will be entertaining defendants' objections, pretrial or at trial, to unreliable eyewitness evidence in any event. The relevant question, then, is what the standard of admissibility governing such objections should be. I see no reason to water down the standard for an equally suggestive and unreliable identification simply because the suggestive confrontation was unplanned.

It bears reminding, moreover, that we set a high bar for suppression. The vast majority of eyewitnesses proceed to testify before a jury. To date, *Foster* is the only case in which we have found a due process violation.

394 U.S., at 443. There has been no flood of claims in the four Federal Circuits that, having seen no basis for an arrangement-based distinction in our precedents, have long indicated that due process scrutiny applies to all suggestive identification procedures. See *Dunnigan v. Keane,* 137 F.3d 117, 128 (C.A.2 1998); *United States v. Bouthot,* 878 F.2d 1506, 1516 (C.A.1 1989); *Thigpen v. Cory,* 804 F.2d 893, 895 (C.A.6 1986); see also *Green v. Loggins,* 614 F.2d 219, 223 (C.A.9 1980). Today's decision nonetheless precludes even the possibility that an unintended confrontation will meet that bar, mandating summary dismissal of every such claim at the threshold.

Finally, the majority questions how to "rationally distinguish suggestiveness from other factors bearing on the reliability of eyewitness evidence," such as "poor vision" or a prior "grudge," and more broadly, how to distinguish eyewitness evidence from other kinds of arguably unreliable evidence. Our precedents, however, did just that. We emphasized the " 'formidable number of instances in the records of English and American trials' " of "miscarriage[s] of justice from mistaken identification." *Wade,* 388 U.S., at 228. We then observed that " 'the influence of improper suggestion upon identifying witnesses probably accounts for more miscarriages of justice than any other single factor.' " *Id.,* at 229. Moreover, the majority points to no other type of evidence that shares the rare confluence of characteristics that makes eyewitness evidence a unique threat to the fairness of trial. Jailhouse informants, unreliable as they may be, are not similarly resistant to the traditional tools of the adversarial process and, if anything, are met with particular skepticism by juries.

It would be one thing if the passage of time had cast doubt on the empirical premises of our precedents. But just the opposite has happened. A vast body of scientific literature has reinforced every concern our precedents articulated nearly a half-century ago, though it merits barely a parenthetical mention in the majority opinion. Over the past three decades, more than two thousand studies related to eyewitness identification have been published. One state supreme court recently appointed a special master to conduct an exhaustive survey of the current state of the scientific evidence and concluded that "[t]he research . . . is not only extensive," but "it represents the 'gold standard in terms of the applicability of social science research to law.' " *State v. Henderson,* 208 N.J. 208, 283, 27 A.3d 872, 916 (2011). "Experimental methods and findings have been tested and retested, subjected to scientific scrutiny through peer-reviewed journals, evaluated through the lens of meta-analyses, and replicated at times in real-world settings." *Ibid.;* see also Schmechel, O'Toole, Easterly, & Loftus, *Beyond the Ken? Testing Jurors' Understanding of Eyewitness Reliability Evidence,* 46 Jurimetrics 177, 180 (2006) (noting "nearly unanimous consensus among researchers about the [eyewitness reliability] field's core findings").

The empirical evidence demonstrates that eyewitness misidentification is " 'the single greatest cause of wrongful convictions in this country.' "[5] Researchers have found that a staggering 76% of the first 250 convictions overturned due to DNA evidence since 1989 involved eyewitness misidentification.[6] Study after study demonstrates that eyewitness recollections are highly susceptible to distortion by postevent information or social cues;[7] that jurors routinely overestimate the accuracy of eyewitness identifications;[8] that jurors place the greatest weight on eyewitness confidence in assessing identifications[9] even though confidence is a poor gauge of accuracy;[10] and that suggestiveness can stem from sources beyond police-orchestrated procedures.[11] THE MAJORITY TODAY nevertheless adopts an artificially narrow conception of the dangers of suggestive identifications at a time when our concerns should have deepened.

III

There are many reasons why Perry's particular situation might not violate due process. The trial court found that the circumstances surrounding Blandon's identification did not rise to an impermissibly suggestive level. It is not at all clear, moreover, that there was a very substantial likelihood of misidentification, given Blandon's lack of equivocation on the scene, the short time between crime and

---

[5] *State v. Henderson,* 208 N.J. 208, 231, 27 A.3d 872, 885 (2011); see also, *e.g., Benn v. United States,* 978 A.2d 1257, 1266 (D.C.2009); *State v. Dubose,* 285 Wis.2d 143, 162, 699 N.W.2d 582, 592 (2005); Dept. of Justice, Office of Justice Programs, E. Connors, T. Lundregan, N. Miller, & T. McEwen, Convicted by Juries, Exonerated by Science: Case Studies in the Use of DNA Evidence to Establish Innocence After Trial 24 (1996); B. Cutler & S. Penrod, Mistaken Identification: The Eyewitness, Psychology, and the Law 8 (1995); Wells, "Good, You Identified the Suspect": Feedback to Eyewitnesses Distorts their Reports of the Witnessing Experience, 83 J. of Applied Psychology No. 3 360 (1998).

[6] B. Garrett, Convicting the Innocent: Where Criminal Prosecutions Go Wrong 9, 48, 279 (2011); see also, *e.g.,* Innocence Project, Facts on Post-Conviction DNA Exonerations (75% of postconviction DNA exoneration cases in the U.S. involved eyewitness misidentification), http://www.innocenceproject.org/Content/Facts_on_PostConviction_DNA_Exonerations.php (as visited Jan. 11, 2012, and available in Clerk of Court's case file); Dept. of Justice, National Institute of Justice, Eyewitness Evidence: A Guide for Law Enforcement iii (1999) (85% of 28 felony convictions overturned on DNA evidence involved eyewitness misidentification).

[7] See, *e.g.,* Gabbert, Memon, Allan, & Wright, Say it to My Face: Examining the Effects of Socially Encountered Misinformation, 9 Legal & Criminological Psychol. 215 (2004); Douglass & Steblay, Memory Distortion in Eyewitnesses: A Meta-Analysis of the Post-Identification Feedback Effect, 20 Applied Cognitive Psychol. 859, 864–865 (2006).

[8] See Brigham & Bothwell, The Ability of Prospective Jurors to Estimate the Accuracy of Eyewitness Identifications, 7 Law & Hum. Behav. 19, 22–24, 28 (1983) (nearly 84% of study respondents overestimated accuracy rates of identifications); see also, *e.g.,* Sigler & Couch, Eyewitness Testimony and the Jury Verdict, 4 N. Am. J. Psychol. 143, 146 (2002).

[9] See Cutler & Penrod, Mistaken Identification, at 181–209; Lindsay, Wells, & Rumpel, Can People Detect Eyewitness-Identification Accuracy Within and Across Situations? 66 J. Applied Psychol. 79, 83 (1981).

[10] See Brewer, Feast, & Rishworth, The Confidence-Accuracy Relationship in Eyewitness Identification, 8 J. Experimental Psychol. Applied 44, 44–45 (2002) ("average confidence-accuracy correlations generally estimated between little more than 0 and .29"); see also, *e.g.,* Sporer, Penrod, Read, & Cutler, Choosing, Confidence, and Accuracy: A Meta-Analysis of the Confidence-Accuracy Relation in Eyewitness Identification Studies, 118 Psychol. Bull. 315 (1995).

[11] See Brief for Wilton Dedge et al. as *Amici Curiae* 8, n. 13.

confrontation, and the "fairly well lit" parking lot. App. 56. The New Hampshire Supreme Court, however, never made findings on either point and, under the majority's decision today, never will.

* * *

The Court's opinion today renders the defendant's due process protection contingent on whether the suggestive circumstances giving rise to the eyewitness identification stem from improper police arrangement. That view lies in tension with our precedents' more holistic conception of the dangers of suggestion and is untethered from the evidentiary interest the due process right protects. In my view, the ordinary two-step inquiry should apply, whether the police created the suggestive circumstances intentionally or inadvertently. Because the New Hampshire Supreme Court truncated its inquiry at the threshold, I would vacate the judgment and remand for a proper analysis. I respectfully dissent.

United States v. Sanders

708 F.3d 976 (7th Cir. 2013)

■ KANNE, CIRCUIT JUDGE.

In January 2008, Lamar E. Sanders and an accomplice abducted Timicka Nobles's daughter, R.E. The reason: to induce Nobles to rob her own mother. Nobles attempted to comply—she left a bag of cash for Sanders's accomplice to pick up—but law enforcement authorities were already apprised of the plot. They quickly arrested Sanders's accomplice, and Sanders turned himself in shortly thereafter. Fortunately, no one was injured, and police recovered the money. After a five-day trial, a jury found Sanders guilty of kidnapping and extortion. He now appeals his conviction and sentence. First, Sanders argues that the district court denied him due process by admitting Nobles's three identifications of him. . . . Finding no error, we affirm both the conviction and sentence.

I. BACKGROUND

Portage, Indiana. Saturday, January 5, 2008. 8:00 a.m.: Timicka Nobles has a busy morning. She has to be at work in Chicago soon. Plus, along the way, she needs to stop by her mother's house to drop off R.E., her ten-year-old daughter. Putting on shoes in the apartment entryway, Nobles and R.E. prepare to depart. As Nobles opens the front door, two men force their way inside. Pushing R.E. and Nobles back into the apartment, the men begin their ill-fated kidnapping operation. The first man, Ralph Scott, holds R.E. hostage in the living room, while the second man, Lamar Sanders, points a gun at Nobles and orders her into the bedroom. There, Sanders has Nobles face the wall as he lays out his demands.

Nobles must drive to her workplace in Chicago—a currency exchange owned by her mother. She will park her car nearby and leave it unlocked. Nobles will then enter the exchange as if nothing is wrong, as if it were any other day. Today, however, Nobles must empty the safe into a black garbage bag. She will take that bag, place it on the front seat of her car, and walk away. If she follows these instructions exactly, "things won't get messed up." (Trial Tr. at 390.)

Nobles acquiesces. As Sanders leads her back into the living room, she finds R.E. alone; Scott had left for Chicago minutes earlier in Sanders's Dodge Magnum. Nobles gives her daughter a quick hug before Sanders orders R.E. to blindfold herself with her headband. Notably, it does not entirely cover R.E.'s eyes; she can still see above and below the band.

Our antagonists did not learn from tales of countless foiled criminals never to leave a hostage unattended. As Sanders drove R.E. to Chicago in Scott's Chevy Trailblazer (while remaining in frequent phone contact with Scott), he did not follow Nobles. Realizing as much, Nobles stopped at a gas station and went into the attached convenience store. Concerned by Nobles's apparent distress, the clerk allowed her to use the store's phone. Nobles made a frantic phone call to her mother and warned her of the plot. Her mother alerted the security officers at the exchange, who in turn notified the Chicago Police. Thus, when Nobles arrived at the exchange, the authorities were prepared.

Nobles did as Sanders ordered. She took the money from the safe, placed it in a garbage bag, and set the bag on the front seat of her car. After Nobles walked away, Scott, who had parked Sanders's Magnum near the scene, approached and removed the money bag. As he did, two exchange security officers and a Chicago Police sergeant ran towards him. Fleeing the scene, Scott ditched the bag in a bush. The officers quickly caught up, arrested Scott, and recovered the money.

Observing Scott's downfall from a block away, Sanders ordered R.E. out of the Trailblazer and sped away. When R.E. removed her headband, she recognized where she was and walked to the currency exchange, where she was reunited with her mother. Just minutes after Scott's arrest, Sanders called his mother. He then called his Arizona-based girlfriend, Carlena Williams. Sanders told Williams that his phone—the same phone on which he was making the call—had been stolen. Williams paid Sanders's phone bill, so she promptly called Verizon and had service suspended on his phone (but she would reinstate the service later that same day).

Back in Chicago, R.E. identified Scott as the man who had guarded her in the living room. The police also searched Scott's pockets, where they found a key fob. Taking the device in hand, an officer continuously pressed the unlock button while walking up and down nearby streets. When the fob activated Sanders's Magnum, evidence technicians searched the car. Inside, they found Sanders's driver's license and seven photographs from a recent birthday party. In five of the images, Sanders appeared with various combinations of family and friends.

An officer took these photographs back to the exchange and interrupted Nobles's interview with a detective. The officer showed Nobles one or two photos and asked her if she recognized anyone. Witnesses disagree about how many and which specific photos Nobles saw. She viewed at most two photographs. Of those, one depicted Sanders with two women, while the other depicted him with two other men: Scott and Sanders's brother. All agree, however, that Nobles identified Sanders in at least one photograph as the second man in her apartment that morning. At this time, Nobles also gave an inaccurate verbal description of Sanders's build that was off by about five inches and sixty pounds. This interview occurred within a couple hours of the kidnapping. R.E. was not shown the photographs found in the car.

Approximately two hours after Nobles's first interview with law enforcement, officers drove her and R.E. to the Chicago Police Department. There, Nobles was shown a formal photo array. The array placed photos of Sanders alongside those of five other men with similar height, weight, and facial features. The other individuals in the photos were chosen based upon similarities to Sanders's actual features, as opposed to the inaccurate verbal description that Nobles gave during her first interview. Nobles again identified Sanders. R.E. was independently shown a different array in another room. She also identified Sanders. Following these identifications, the government issued a criminal complaint, and Sanders turned himself in shortly thereafter.

As the case proceeded to trial, Sanders moved to suppress Nobles's identifications of him. Sanders had three theories behind this motion. First, he argued that showing Nobles the birthday party photographs was so unnecessarily suggestive as to violate the Due Process Clause. Second, he asserted that the photo array was impermissibly suggestive because only he appeared in both the photos on the scene and in the subsequent array. Finally, Sanders claimed that any in-court identification by Nobles could only be the product of these previous, allegedly tainted, identifications. The district court denied Sanders's motion on all three grounds. . . .

At a five-day jury trial, the government presented a strong case. Nobles identified Sanders as the second man in her apartment the morning of the kidnapping. So did R.E. The government also presented cell phone records showing that Sanders's phone was in frequent contact with Scott's phone throughout the morning of the crime. Expert witnesses traced the cell towers used during these calls to show that the phones traveled the approximate path of the kidnappers. Although the phone records could not directly verify that Sanders had his phone, other evidence spoke to that question. The morning of the kidnapping, Sanders called Carlena Williams and told her that his phone was stolen. Records showed a corresponding call from Sanders's phone to Williams's phone, made from the vicinity of the currency exchange, approximately ten minutes after Scott's arrest. The records also showed that this call was made from Sanders's own phone—the same one he was claiming was stolen. Just after that call, Williams had the service on Sanders's phone suspended, although she reinstated it later that evening.

Defense counsel criticized Nobles's identifications and tried to implicate Nobles herself. Nobles remained romantically involved with Vincent E., R.E.'s father, who was also a fellow gang member of Sanders and Scott. Scott, who signed a plea agreement with the government, testified that Vincent had planned the whole plot and that Nobles was complicit in the scheme. The jury, however, did not believe Sanders's defense. On January 24, 2011, he was found guilty of one count of kidnapping under 18 U.S.C. § 1201 and one count of extortion under 18 U.S.C. § 1951. . . .

II. ANALYSIS

. . .

A. Identification Testimony

Our Constitution protects against "conviction based on evidence of questionable reliability." Perry v. New Hampshire, 565 U.S. 228, ___ (2012). Despite the importance of this right, the admission of evidence rarely implicates due process. See id. Rather, courts typically rely on other means to ensure reliable evidence—state and federal rules, as well as different constitutional guarantees, such as the Sixth Amendment rights to counsel and confrontation. Id. Yet, "when evidence 'is so extremely unfair that its admission violates fundamental conceptions of justice,'" due process, like the sleeping giant, awakens. Id. (quoting Dowling v. United States, 493 U.S. 342, 352 (1990)). In those situations, other protections have proven insufficient, and courts must step in to prevent injustice.

Unduly suggestive identification procedures represent one example of those fundamentally unfair situations. A procedure becomes so flawed as to implicate due process when it creates a "very substantial likelihood of irreparable misidentification." Neil v. Biggers, 409 U.S. 188, 198 (1972) (quoting Simmons v. United States, 390 U.S. 377, 384 (1968)). In such cases, the identification must be suppressed. Perry, 565 U.S. at ___. To decide whether a situation has risen to that level, we follow a two-pronged approach. First, we consider whether the identification procedure used by law enforcement was "both suggestive and unnecessary." Id. at ___; accord United States v. Gallo-Moreno, 584 F.3d 751, 757 (7th Cir.2009). Second, we examine the "totality of the circumstances" to determine whether other indicia of reliability "outweigh[ ] . . . the corrupting effect of law enforcement suggestion." Perry, 565 U.S. at ___ (internal quotation marks omitted); accord Gallo-Moreno, 584 F.3d at 757.

As the Supreme Court recently reiterated, courts will only consider the second prong if a challenged procedure does not pass muster under the first. See Perry, 565 U.S. at ___. To fail the first prong, however, even a "suggestive" procedure must also be "unnecessary." *Id.* In other words, the situation must have involved "improper state conduct"—one in which the circumstances did not justify law enforcement's suggestive behavior. *Id.* As these descriptions show, both prongs are highly situation-dependent, which may seem to blend the two inquires. Yet, they are distinct. The first prong focuses on police conduct—its suggestiveness and necessity in the specific situation at hand. In contrast, the second prong focuses on the identifying witness and her knowledge of the suspect absent the suggestive procedure. Perhaps, for example, the witness saw the suspect for several minutes in broad daylight. *See* United States v. Kimbrough, 528 F.2d 1242, 1246–47 (7th Cir.1976). Such considerations could lead us to conclude that an unduly suggestive identification was nonetheless reliable, such that its admission would not violate the Due Process Clause. *See id.*

We will therefore begin by applying this dual-pronged standard to Nobles's first two identifications of Sanders. The first identification occurred shortly after the crime, when Chicago Police officers showed Nobles the birthday party photographs removed from Sanders's car. The second identification occurred a few hours later, when Nobles took part in a formal photo array. After addressing those instances, we can examine Nobles's third identification, made during trial. If either of the first two procedures was unnecessarily suggestive, then the in-court identification must demonstrate an independent basis of reliability to be admissible. *See* United States v. Rogers, 387 F.3d 925, 937–38 (7th Cir.2004); *see also* Cossel v. Miller, 229 F.3d 649, 655 (7th Cir.2000). As we consider each of these three questions, our review is de novo with "due deference to the trial court's findings of historical fact." United States v. Benabe, 654 F.3d 753, 774 (7th Cir.2011) (internal quotation marks omitted).

1. Identification in the Birthday Party Photographs

Under the first prong of our inquiry, we now analyze whether showing Nobles the photographs found in Sanders's car was "both suggestive and unnecessary." *Perry*, 565 U.S. at ___.

a. Suggestiveness

According to Sanders, the police conducted a "show up" when they asked Nobles about the birthday party photographs. In a show up, the police present only one suspect to the identifying witness. United States v. Funches, 84 F.3d 249, 254 (7th Cir.1996). Consequently, show ups are "inherently suggestive." United States v. Hawkins, 499 F.3d 703, 707 (7th Cir.2007). Yet, it remains unclear whether this identification procedure actually was a show up, as defined by our case law. We have most often used that term to describe situations in which law enforcement have apprehended a suspect and then physically shown that person to a witness. *See, e.g.,* United States v. Newman, 144 F.3d 531, 535 (7th Cir.1998); Abrams v. Barnett, 121 F.3d 1036, 1040–41 (7th Cir.1997); *Funches*, 84 F.3d at 254. Here, however, the police showed

Nobles one (or potentially two) photographs of Sanders. Our cases leave unsettled whether we also consider it a "show up" when a witness is presented only with the suspect's photograph. Compare *Cossel,* 229 F.3d at 655 (describing a photographic "show-up"), with *Hawkins,* 499 F.3d at 708 (describing photographic identification as "akin to a showup").

An added wrinkle stems from witnesses' disagreement over which photographs Nobles saw. Again, a show up involves presenting a witness with only one suspect. Here, however, one of the photos allegedly shown to Nobles would have given her the opportunity to identify another male of similar features to Sanders (his brother). That said, the police showed Nobles at most two photographs, and those photos presented, at most, one other possible suspect for identification. For that reason, the procedure was closer to a show up than other photographic identification techniques, such as a line up, in which several suspects are presented. *Cf.* United States v. Clark, 989 F.2d 1490, 1495 n.2 (7th Cir.1993) (showing a witness two arrested suspects was more analogous to a show up than a line up). Still, for the sake of consistency, we will not refer to the procedure as a "show up."

When Sanders argues that this procedure was suggestive, he ignores a key trend in our case law. In recent years, we have noted proliferating social science data on the reliability of eyewitness testimony. *See* United States v. Ford, 683 F.3d 761, 766 (7th Cir.2012) (collecting articles). Accordingly, we have held that scientific sources should generally accompany an argument that a particular procedure was unnecessarily suggestive. United States v. Acox, 595 F.3d 729, 730 (7th Cir.2010) ("Lawyers' assertions that the effects of a photo spread are 'clear' or 'obvious' are no substitute for evidence"); *see also* United States v. Williams, 522 F.3d 809, 812 (7th Cir.2008). Sanders has not properly presented us with such data here. Although his counsel submitted several sources after oral argument, in accordance with Federal Rule of Appellate Procedure 28(j), this attempt is too little, too late. These sources raise complicated points that Sanders should have addressed in his briefs. A Rule 28(j) letter is not the appropriate forum to make new, complex arguments. Spiegla v. Hull, 481 F.3d 961, 965 (7th Cir.2007).[1]

Yet, we have not made social science data a strict requirement for us to determine whether a procedure was unnecessarily suggestive; "[o]ften the right disposition will be evident with or without the aid of social science." *Williams,* 522 F.3d at 812. Such is the case here. As stated earlier, the procedure employed by law enforcement, with the paucity of

---

[1]   Even if we considered Sanders's new sources, some of them do not even support his position. One book chapter, for example, compares the reliability of physical show ups with photographic ones (the book uses the term "show-up" to include single-photograph identification techniques). Jennifer E. Dysart & R.C.L. Lindsay, Show-up Identifications: Suggestive Technique or Reliable Method?, in 2 The Handbook of Eyewitness Psychology: Memory for People 137, 142–43 (R.C.L. Lindsay et al. eds., 2007). In so doing, the authors explain that, "[w]hen the identification procedure is conducted with the use of photographs, there is no significant difference in correct identification rates between show-ups and line-ups." *Id.* at 143.

suspects presented to Nobles, was similar to a show up. We have previously found show ups "inherently suggestive." *Hawkins,* 499 F.3d at 707. Therefore, it seems likely that this procedure was also suggestive. But since we do not have data to help us resolve that question, we think it best to set it aside for now. Rather, we can simply assume, for current purposes, that it was suggestive, because the disposition is nevertheless clear: Sanders's claim falters because he cannot prove that the procedure, even if suggestive, was also unnecessary.

b.   Necessity

As discussed, a procedure that is suggestive—even when inherently so—may still be necessary. *Perry,* 565 U.S. at ___; accord United States v. Recendiz, 557 F.3d 511, 525 (7th Cir.2009). As in all aspects of life, context matters. Thus, the circumstances surrounding an investigation can justify even a show up. *Hawkins,* 499 F.3d at 707–08.

Citing *United States v. Funches,* Sanders argues that show ups are only acceptable to "allow identification before the suspect has altered his appearance" or to "permit the quick release of innocent persons" if witnesses cannot identify the apprehended individual. 84 F.3d at 254. Sanders then argues that the situation here does not present one of those exceptions, thus rendering evidence derived from the procedure impermissible. *Funches,* however, merely listed "example[s]" of acceptable reasons for a show up; it did not claim to be exhaustive. *Id.* Moreover, *Funches* involved a physical show up, not a single-photograph identification procedure. *Id.* at 251–52. Photographic identification techniques, while perhaps similar in some ways to physical show ups, are also different in important ways. When police conduct a physical show up, they already have the suspect in custody. Therefore, there is not the same exigency to catch a criminal on the loose, which, depending on the situation, could justify the suggestive procedure.

For that reason, *Simmons v. United States,* rather than physical show up cases, presents the key precedent. 390 U.S. 377. In that case, Simmons committed an armed robbery of a bank with an accomplice. *Id.* at 379–80. The next morning, police obtained a few photographs that depicted Simmons with the man they suspected of being his accomplice. *Id.* at 380. Later that day, officers showed the photographs to five bank employees. *Id.* Every witness identified Simmons as one of the robbers. *Id.* After being convicted, Simmons argued that the photographic identification procedure violated the Due Process Clause. *Id.* at 381–82. The Supreme Court, however, disagreed, writing:

> [a] serious felony had been committed. The perpetrators were still at large. The inconclusive clues which law enforcement officials possessed led to . . . Simmons. It was essential for the FBI agents swiftly to determine whether they were on the right track, so that they could properly deploy their forces . . . and, if necessary, alert officials in other cities.

Id. at 384–85. These circumstances, the Court held, justified the identification procedure used. *Id.* at 386.

This case presents clear parallels to *Simmons*. Here, a serious felony had also been committed: someone had kidnapped R.E. to induce Nobles to rob her own mother's currency exchange. The police also had clues pointing to a suspect: Sanders. Although law enforcement officers had arrested Scott, they knew a second man was involved, and their best clues were the photos found in the car Scott drove. Finally, with an armed felon still on the loose, the police needed to act quickly. Showing Nobles the photos was the best way to proceed. In fact, the situation in this case presented even greater necessity than in Simmons. Here, police showed Nobles the photographs within a couple hours of the crime. In Simmons, on the other hand, the Supreme Court upheld a procedure in which the police did not show the photos to witnesses until the next day. With the crime much closer at hand here, the rationale for upholding the procedure as necessary is even more pressing.

Sanders's attempts to distinguish *Simmons* do not persuade. First, he argues that Simmons only challenged the witnesses' in-court identifications. Sanders does not explain why that distinction matters, but, in any event, his assertion is incorrect; Simmons also challenged the pretrial identifications that resulted from the procedures described above, just as Sanders does here. *Simmons*, 390 U.S. at 381–82. Second, Sanders contends that the witnesses in *Simmons* were shown mostly group photographs, thereby making the identifications more reliable than the one here. But that argument does not negate any of our necessity analysis, and finding a suggestive procedure unnecessary is a prerequisite to considering other indicia of reliability. *See Perry*, 565 U.S. at ___. Thus, because Sanders has not effectively distinguished *Simmons*, we need not turn to such considerations under the second prong.

Our own cases involving unnecessarily suggestive photographic identifications are not to the contrary. For example, in *United States v. Kimbrough*, the police showed the witness a composite sketch of the suspect followed by photos of only the defendant. 528 F.2d at 1244. Yet, the authorities had no good reason for failing to use more images; they could have easily produced an array using other available photos. *Id.* at 1244–45. Similarly, in *Israel v. Odom,* the police showed a rape victim only an image of her suspected assailant. 521 F.2d 1370, 1372 (7th Cir.1975). Before doing so, the police had left the scene of the crime, gone back to the station, pulled up a stored image of the suspect, and returned to the victim's home. *Id.* Given that sequence of events, "[n]o appreciable time would have been lost" by pulling a few extra files at the station so the victim could have viewed more potential suspects. *Id.* at 1375.

Those cases are distinguishable. Here, the police obtained the photographs on the scene of the crime itself, while an out-of-town victim was still present, and her memory was at its freshest. It would have taken significantly more time for the police to leave the scene, go to the station house, locate photos similar to those found in the car, and return. A dangerous suspect could have used that extra time to facilitate his escape. Thus, unlike in *Kimbrough* and *Israel,* the police in this case could not have produced a significantly less suggestive procedure without sacrificing critical time. In this quickly developing situation, showing Nobles the photographs was the most responsible way to proceed with the early stages of investigation. Law enforcement's procedure may have been suggestive to some degree, but it was also necessary.

Because we find that the procedure was necessary, we need not address the reliability prong of the analysis. *See Perry*, 565 U.S. at ___. Rather, we can rely on our criminal procedure to ensure due process. After we are convinced that no constitutional violation occurred, "the jury, not the judge, . . . determines the reliability of evidence." *Id.* at 728.

c.   Harmless Error

Although we do not think there was any error in admitting Nobles's first identification of Sanders, even if there was, we could alternatively resolve the issue as harmless error. . . .

III. CONCLUSION

For the foregoing reasons, we find all of Sanders's arguments unavailing. We therefore AFFIRM both his conviction and sentence.

United States v. Delgado

364 Fed.Appx. 876 (5th Cir. 2010)

■ PER CURIAM:[*]

Juan Antonio Delgado appeals his jury conviction on two counts of transporting an undocumented alien by means of a motor vehicle within the United States for private financial gain, in violation of 8 U.S.C. § 1324(a)(1)(A)(ii), (a)(1)(B)(i), and 18 U.S.C. § 2. On appeal, Delgado challenges the district court's admission of identification testimony, arguing that the identification procedures (which included a one-man showup) were unduly suggestive. For the following reasons, we AFFIRM the judgment of the district court.

FACTUAL AND PROCEDURAL BACKGROUND

On the night of March 9, 2008, a tractor trailer driven by Delgado, a United States citizen, was stopped by United States Border Patrol agents at the Interstate 35 checkpoint near Laredo, Texas. During the initial inspection of the tractor trailer, a Border Patrol dog signaled the possibility of concealed persons or contraband inside the tractor trailer. After opening the trailer, agents discovered fifteen undocumented immigrants (aliens) lying under a blue tarp amongst automobile parts in

---

[*]   Pursuant to 5TH CIR. R. 47.5, the court has determined that this opinion should not be published and is not precedent except under the limited circumstances set forth in 5TH CIR. R. 47.5.4.

the trailer. The Border Patrol agents then detained Delgado and the fifteen aliens.

The Border Patrol agents interviewed Delgado, obtained biographical information from him, photographed him, and placed him in a holding cell. The biographical information indicates that Delgado is of average height, and the Border Patrol photograph shows that, on the night of his arrest, Delgado had a mustache and a beard and was wearing a cap. Delgado also provided a statement to the Border Patrol in which he claimed that he did not know that the trailer was loaded with aliens and that he had no reason to suspect as much.

The Border Patrol agents also interviewed the aliens and decided to detain two of them, sisters Eusebia and Luisa Aviles-Vences, as material witnesses. Both provided statements regarding how and when they had come to the United States. Eusebia and Luisa were also brought separately by the Border Patrol agents to view Delgado and asked whether they could identify him as the driver of the tractor trailer. Luisa identified Delgado and provided information about his appearance. Eusebia provided some information about the person who put her in the trailer,[1] but upon seeing Delgado, she was unable to say whether he was that person.[2]

The Government charged Delgado with two counts of violating 8 U.S.C. § 1324(a)(1)(A)(ii), (a)(1)(B)(i), and 18 U.S.C. § 2 in using a motor vehicle to transport Eusebia and Luisa, aliens, for commercial advantage or private financial gain, while knowing, or recklessly disregarding, that they had come to, entered, and remained in the United States illegally. Before trial, Delgado filed a motion to suppress Eusebia's and Luisa's out-of-court identification statements,[3] arguing that the out-of-court identification process was impermissibly suggestive and thus conducive to irreparable mistake such that any identification of him by either Eusebia or Luisa would violate his due process rights. The district court denied the motion, but the court stated that the parties could examine the method of identification at trial, at which time Delgado could re-urge his motion to suppress.

At trial, Eusebia and Luisa testified that their aunt had arranged to smuggle them and their brother into the United States and transport them to Austin, Texas, for $2500 per person. Both sisters also testified that they had crossed into the United States via boat near Laredo, Texas,

---

[1] The record indicates that on March 9 Eusebia was able to confirm that the man she had seen by the trailer was wearing a cap and had a mustache.

[2] The record is unclear regarding whether the sisters viewed Delgado before providing information about his appearance.

[3] Delgado apparently considered the Border Patrol's report, which stated that both sisters had provided information that Delgado was present when they were loaded into the trailer, to be out-of-court identification evidence.

on March 5, 2008, and that they then stayed at a house in or around Laredo until March 7, 2008.[5]

Both sisters further testified that on March 7, 2008, they were taken by truck to a parked trailer. The sisters testified that they and other aliens got into the trailer, which contained automobile parts, and covered themselves with a blue tarp. Eusebia also testified that she saw a man standing outside the trailer who was wearing a cap, had a mustache, and was "not so tall, not so short." Both sisters testified that, after some time, the tractor pulling the trailer experienced mechanical problems, and all of the aliens got out of the trailer to wait for a truck to transport them back to the house where they were staying. Eusebia and Luisa testified that while waiting for the truck, they sat in the tractor that had been pulling the trailer. Eusebia also testified that the same man that she had seen earlier-the one with a mustache and cap-was sitting in the driver's seat.

The sisters also testified that on the night of March 9, 2008, they and other aliens were transported back to the same parked trailer. Eusebia testified that as she was approaching the trailer, she again saw the same man, with a mustache and beard and wearing a cap, that she had seen on March 7. When asked if the man she had seen was present in the courtroom, Eusebia identified Delgado as the person she had seen. On cross-examination, when Delgado asked why Eusebia was unable to identify Delgado or provide more information regarding his appearance on March 9, Eusebia testified that she had been scared and confused that night but that, on further reflection, she realized that Delgado was the man she had seen on March 7 and 9.

Luisa also testified that, while being loaded into the trailer on March 9, she saw a man, with a mustache and beard who was wearing a cap. Luisa further testified that this man told her to remain quiet while she was in the trailer. When asked if the man she had seen was present in the courtroom, Luisa also identified Delgado as the person she had seen.

Both sisters testified that, after again lying down in the trailer and covering themselves with a blue tarp, they traveled for approximately 30 minutes before the tractor trailer stopped. After some time, immigration officials opened the trailer and uncovered them and the other aliens.

Delgado did not re-urge his motion to suppress the sisters' identification testimony at trial; however, he did extensively cross-examine both sisters regarding the information they provided to the Border Patrol. At the close of the sisters' testimony, Delgado moved for a judgment of acquittal on the grounds that the material witnesses, Eusebia and Luisa, were not credible. Specifically, Delgado argued that the sisters' motivation in testifying for the Government was to keep their family together, that the sisters had been coached in their testimony, and

---

[5]   In their statement given to the Border Patrol on March 9, 2008, the sisters each claimed to have entered the United States on March 8, 2008. However, at trial, the sisters recanted that statement, claiming that they had been confused by the Border Patrol's questions when they stated that they had entered the United States on March 8, 2008.

that the descriptions the sisters had given of Delgado were exceedingly generalized. The district court denied the motion, stating that Delgado's arguments raised credibility questions that were best left for the jury.

The case was then submitted to the jury, which returned a guilty verdict on both counts of the indictment. The district court sentenced Delgado to 30 months of imprisonment on each count, the sentences on both counts to run concurrently. Delgado now appeals.

DISCUSSION

On appeal, Delgado argues that the out-of-court identification procedure used was impermissibly suggestive and unconstitutional. Specifically, Delgado challenges the manner in which the sisters were shown Delgado and subsequently questioned about him. Delgado urges that the subsequent identification testimony should have been suppressed because it was not reliable in light of the totality of the circumstances. We disagree.

In reviewing a motion to suppress identification testimony, " 'we accept the district court's findings of fact unless they are clearly erroneous, but we review de novo the court's ultimate conclusion of the constitutionality of the law enforcement action.' " United States v. Moody, 564 F.3d 754, 762 (5th Cir.2009) (quoting United States v. Guidry, 406 F.3d 314, 319 (5th Cir.2005)). In undertaking this inquiry, we may "consider the evidence admitted at both the suppression hearing and the trial." United States v. Jones, 239 F.3d 716, 718 (5th Cir.2001). Whether an identification is constitutionally admissible is a mixed question of law and fact. Moody, 564 F.3d at 762.

"The Due Process Clause protects against the use of evidence obtained from impermissibly suggestive identification procedures." Id. (citation and internal quotation marks omitted). "The admissibility of identification evidence is governed by a two-step test. . . ." Id. (quoting Guidry, 406 F.3d at 319). First, we ask whether the identification procedure was impermissibly suggestive. Second, we ask whether the procedure used posed a "very substantial likelihood of irreparable misidentification." Id. (quoting Guidry, 406 F.3d at 319). Identification testimony is inadmissible only if both questions are answered in the affirmative. Id. The linchpin of the admissibility inquiry is whether the identification is reliable. Manson v. Brathwaite, 432 U.S. 98, 114 (1977).

"[T]he practice of showing suspects singly to persons for the purpose of identification, and not as part of a lineup, has been widely condemned." Allen v. Estelle, 568 F.2d 1108, 1112 (5th Cir.1978) (internal punctuation, quotation marks, and citations omitted). However, even if an out-of-court identification procedure was impermissibly suggestive in violation of a defendant's due process rights, the resulting identification testimony may still be admissible if it is reliable in light of the totality of the circumstances. Amador v. Quarterman, 458 F.3d 397, 414 (5th Cir.2006). An identification is reliable if the identification procedures did not pose a "substantial likelihood of irreparable misidentification[;]" i.e., it meets the second *Brathwaite* prong. *Id.* If we determine that an identification meets the second *Brathwaite* prong, we need not examine whether the identification procedures satisfied the first *Brathwaite* prong to determine that the resulting identification is admissible. *Moody,* 564 F.3d at 762 n.10 (citing Coleman v. Quarterman, 456 F.3d 537, 544 (5th Cir.2006)). In assessing whether identification procedures posed a substantial likelihood of irreparable misidentification, we consider several factors: "(1) the opportunity of the witness to view the criminal at the crime scene; (2) the witness's degree of attention; (3) the accuracy of the witness's prior description of the criminal; (4) the level of certainty demonstrated by the witness at the confrontation; and (5) the length of time between the crime and the confrontation." *See id.* at 762–63 (quoting *Coleman,* 456 F.3d at 544).

The out-of-court identification procedures here did not pose a substantial likelihood of irreparable misidentification. First, Eusebia and Luisa had multiple opportunities, before they were shown Delgado by the Border Patrol agents, to view Delgado: The sisters twice had the opportunity to view the individuals involved in their transport while being loaded into the trailer, and both sisters sat in the tractor on March 7, with Eusebia testifying that Delgado was also present. Factor one therefore weighs in favor of reliability. *Cf. Amador,* 458 F.3d at 415 (factor one weighed in favor of reliability where witness had an opportunity to view defendant when they rode together in a taxicab); *Coleman,* 456 F.3d at 544 (factor one weighed in favor of reliability when witness, who was sitting in a car, had the opportunity to see the defendant when the defendant fired upon the car).

Second, Eusebia and Luisa were not engaged in other activities during their transportation, and they could thus focus on the people aiding them. Factor two therefore weighs in favor of reliability. *See Moody,* 564 F.3d at 763 (factor two weighed in favor of reliability where witness was focused on the crime in question and that crime was the "primary activity taking place at the time" (emphasis omitted)).

Third, the record is unclear concerning whether Eusebia and Luisa provided descriptions of Delgado prior to viewing him. Assuming (contrary to the Government's argument) that the sisters did not provide descriptions of Delgado before the out-of-court identification, the third factor weighs neither for nor against reliability. *See Moody,* 564 F.3d at 763 (holding that a defendant cannot rely on the third factor when there is "no testimony" regarding the witness's description of the defendant before the out-of-court identification). As such, we assume arguendo that factor three weighs neither for nor against reliability here.

Fourth, upon being shown Delgado at the Border Patrol station, Luisa identified him, without reservation. And though Eusebia was unable to confirm that Delgado was the man she had seen, her initial inability to identify Delgado is not dispositive. *See Amador,* 458 F.3d at

415 (holding that subsequent identification testimony could still be reliable even where witness was initially "reluctant to identify anyone until she was confident in her identification"). Additionally, at trial, neither Luisa nor Eusebia hesitated in identifying Delgado in open court, and, even after extensive cross-examination, both sisters testified consistently about Delgado's appearance and the events in question. Given Luisa's confidence at the out-of-court identification, the sisters' confidence in identifying Delgado in court, and the consistency of the sisters' testimony, we conclude that factor four weighs in favor of reliability. *See Moody*, 564 F.3d at 763 (finding in favor of reliability where description of defendant throughout examination was consistent); *Amador*, 458 F.3d at 415 (unchanging description of suspect at trial found to weigh in favor of reliability).

Fifth, Eusebia and Luisa had the opportunity to identify Delgado within days of their initial opportunity (on March 7) to view him and within hours of their subsequent opportunity (on March 9). Factor five therefore weighs in favor of reliability. *See Moody*, 564 F.3d at 763 (concluding that an identification made only a day or two after the incident weighed in favor of reliability); *Coleman*, 456 F.3d at 544 (determining that nine day wait between incident and identification weighed in favor of reliability).

Ultimately, as in *Brathwaite*:

> we cannot say that under all the circumstances of this case there is a very substantial likelihood of irreparable misidentification. Short of that point, such evidence is for the jury to weigh. We are content to rely upon the good sense and good judgment of American juries, for evidence with some element of untrustworthiness is customary grist for the jury mill. Juries are not so susceptible that they cannot measure intelligently the weight of identification testimony that has some questionable feature.

Brathwaite, 432 U.S. at 116 (citation and internal quotation marks omitted). Accordingly, we conclude that the out-of-court identification procedures here did not lead to a very substantial likelihood of irreparable misidentification, and we answer the second Brathwaite inquiry in the negative. Thus, we need not examine the first *Brathwaite* inquiry-whether the out-of-court identification procedures were unduly suggestive-to conclude that the district court properly denied the motion to suppress the identification testimony and properly left the identification testimony for the jury to consider. *Amador*, 458 F.3d at 415; *Coleman*, 456 F.3d at 544.

CONCLUSION

For the foregoing reasons, we AFFIRM the judgment of the district court.

AFFIRMED.

INDEX

References are to Pages